STANDARD DEDUCTION

Filing Status	2001 Amount
Married individuals filing joint returns and surviving spouses	$7,600
Heads of households	6,650
Unmarried individuals (other than surviving spouses and heads of households)	4,550
Married individuals filing separate return	3,800
Additional standard deductions for the aged and the blind	
Individual who is married and surviving spouses	900*
Individual who is unmarried and not a surviving spouse	1,100*
Taxpayer claimed as dependent on another taxpayer's return	750

*These amounts are $1,800 and $2,200, respectively, for a taxpayer who is both aged and blind.

Personal Exemption: 2001 $2,900   *Reduction in personal and dependency exemptions:* The personal and dependency exemption deductions are reduced or eliminated for certain high-income taxpayers. When a taxpayer's AGI exceeds the "phaseout begins after" amount described below, the deduction is reduced by 2% for each $2,500 (or fraction thereof) by which AGI exceeds such amount. For married persons filing separately, the exemption deduction is reduced by 2% for each $1,250 (or fraction thereof) by which AGI exceeds the "phaseout begins after" amount. The personal exemption deduction amount cannot be reduced below zero. The phaseout ranges are:

Filing Status	Phaseout Begins After	Phaseout Completed After
Married individuals filing joint return and surviving spouses	$199,450	$321,950
Heads of households	166,200	288,700
Unmarried taxpayers (other than surviving spouses and heads of households)	132,950	255,450
Married individuals filing separate returns	99,725	160,975

Itemized Deductions

The itemized deductions that are otherwise deductible for the tax year are reduced by the lesser of (1) 3% of the excess of AGI over a threshold amount, or (2) 80% of the amount of itemized deductions otherwise deductible for the tax year excluding medical expenses, investment interest expense, casualty losses, and wagering losses to the extent of wagering gains. The threshold amount for the 2001 tax year is $132,950 (except for married individuals filing separate returns for which it is $66,475).

PRENTICE HALL'S
FEDERAL TAXATION
2002

Individuals

EDITORS

THOMAS R. POPE
University of Kentucky

KENNETH E. ANDERSON
University of Tennessee

JOHN L. KRAMER
University of Florida

CONTRIBUTING AUTHORS

D. DALE BANDY
University of Central Florida

N. ALLEN FORD
University of Kansas

ROBERT L. GARDNER
Brigham Young University

MICHAEL S. SCHADEWALD
University of Wisconsin–Milwaukee

ANNOTATIONS

EDMUND D. FENTON
Belmont University

Prentice Hall

Upper Saddle River, NJ 07458

Acquisitions Editor: Alana Bradley
Editor-in-Chief: PJ Boardman
Editorial Assistant: Jane Avery
Marketing Manager: Beth Toland
Marketing Assistant: Brian Rappelfeld
Managing Editor (Production): John Roberts
Production Editor: Renata Butera
Production Assistant: Keri Jean
Permissions Coordinator: Suzanne Grappi
Associate Director, Manufacturing: Vincent Scelta
Production Manager: Arnold Vila
Design Manager: Patricia Smythe
Interior Design: BB&K Design Inc.
Cover Design: Steven Frim
Cover Image: Susan LeVan through Artville
Composition: Black Dot Graphics
Printer/Binder: Courier

Credits and acknowledgments borrowed from other sources and reproduced, with permission, in this textbook appear on appropriate page within the text.

Copyright © 2002, 2001, 1999, 1998, 1997 by Pearson Education, Inc., Upper Saddle River, New Jersey, 07458. All rights reserved. Printed in the United States of America. This publication is protected by Copyright and permission should be obtained from the publisher prior to any prohibited reproduction, storage in a retrieval system, or transmission in any form or by any means, electronic, mechanical, photocopying, recording, or likewise. For information regarding permission(s), write to: Rights and Permissions Department.

Prentice Hall

10 9 8 7 6 5 4 3 2 1
ISBN 0-13-055073-6
ISBN 0-13-029245-1 (IE)
ISBN 0-13-028658-3 (Looseleaf)

Contents

PREFACE xiii

CHAPTER 1
▶ **AN INTRODUCTION TO TAXATION 1-1**

History of Taxation in the United States 1-2
  Early Periods 1-2
  Revenue Acts From 1913 to the Present 1-3
  Revenue Sources 1-3

Types of Tax Rate Structures 1-4
  The Structure of Individual Income Tax Rates 1-4
  The Structure of Corporate Tax Rates 1-5
  Marginal, Average, and Effective Tax Rates for Taxpayers 1-5
  Determination of Taxable Income and Tax Due 1-7

Other Types of Taxes 1-7
  State and Local Income and Franchise Taxes 1-7
  Wealth Transfer Taxes 1-8
  Other Types of Taxes 1-11

Criteria for a Tax Structure 1-12
  Equity 1-12
  Certainty 1-13
  Convenience 1-13
  Economy 1-13

Objectives of the Federal Income Tax Law 1-14
  Economic Objectives 1-14
  Encouragement of Certain Activities and Industries 1-14
  Social Objectives 1-15

Entities in the Federal Income Tax System 1-15
  Taxpaying Entities 1-15
  Flow-Through Entities 1-16

Tax Law Sources 1-18

Enactment of a Tax Law 1-18
  Steps in the Legislative Process 1-18

Administration of the Tax Law and Tax Practice Issues 1-20
  Organization of the Internal Revenue Service 1-20
  Enforcement Procedures 1-21
  Selection of Returns for Audit 1-21
  Statute of Limitations 1-22
  Interest 1-22
  Penalties 1-22
  Administrative Appeal Procedures 1-23

Components of a Tax Practice 1-23
  Tax Compliance and Procedure 1-23
  Tax Research 1-23
  Tax Planning and Consulting 1-24
  Financial Planning 1-24

Computer Applications in Tax Practice 1-25
  Tax Return Preparation 1-25
  Tax Planning Applications 1-25
  Tax Research Applications 1-25

Problem Materials 1-26
  Discussion Questions 1-26
  Problems 1-28
  Case Study Problem 1-29
  Research Problem 1-30

CHAPTER 2
▶ **DETERMINATION OF TAX 2-1**

Formula for Individual Income Tax 2-2
  Basic Formula 2-2
  Definitions 2-3
  Tax Formula Illustrated 2-6

Deductions from Adjusted Gross Income 2-7
  Itemized Deductions 2-7
  Standard Deduction 2-10
  Personal Exemptions 2-12
  Dependency Exemptions 2-12
  Child Credit 2-17

Determining The Amount of Tax 2-18
  Filing Status 2-19
  Joint Return 2-19
  Surviving Spouse 2-20
  Head of Household 2-20
  Single Taxpayer 2-21
  Married Filing a Separate Return 2-21
  Abandoned Spouse 2-22
  Dependents with Unearned Income 2-22

Corporate Tax Formula and Rates 2-24

Treatment of Capital Gains and Losses 2-26
  Definition of Capital Assets 2-26
  Tax Treatment of Gains and Losses 2-26

Tax Planning Considerations 2-27
  Shifting Income Between Family Members 2-27
  Splitting Income 2-27
  Maximizing Itemized Deductions 2-27
  Filing Joint or Separate Returns 2-28

Compliance and Procedural Considerations 2-29
  Who Must File 2-29
  Due Dates for Filing Return 2-30
  Use of Forms 1040, 1040EZ, and 1040A 2-30
  System for Reporting Income 2-30

Problem Materials 2-31
  Discussion Questions 2-31
  Issue Identification Questions 2-32
  Problems 2-32
  Tax Form/Return Preparation Problems 2-37
  Case Study Problems 2-37
  Tax Research Problems 2-38

CHAPTER 3
▶ GROSS INCOME: INCLUSIONS 3-1

Economic and Accounting Concepts of Income 3-2
    Economic Concept 3-2
    Accounting Concept 3-2

Tax Concept of Income 3-3
    Administrative Convenience 3-3
    Wherewithal to Pay 3-4
    Gross Income Defined 3-4

To Whom Is Income Taxable? 3-6
    Assignment of Income 3-6
    Allocating Income Between Married People 3-6
    Income of Minor Children 3-8

When Is Income Taxable? 3-8
    Cash Method 3-8
    Accrual Method 3-11
    Hybrid Method 3-11

Items of Gross Income: Sec. 61(a) 3-12
    Compensation 3-12
    Business Income 3-13
    Gains from Dealings in Property 3-13
    Interest 3-13
    Rents and Royalties 3-15
    Dividends 3-16
    Alimony and Separate Maintenance Payments 3-17
    Pensions and Annuities 3-19
    Income from Life Insurance and Endowment Contracts 3-21
    Income from Discharge of Indebtedness 3-21
    Income Passed Through to Taxpayer 3-22

Other Items of Gross Income 3-22
    Prizes, Awards, Gambling Winnings, and Treasure Finds 3-22
    Illegal Income 3-23
    Unemployment Compensation 3-23
    Social Security Benefits 3-23
    Insurance Proceeds and Court Awards 3-24
    Recovery of Previously Deducted Amounts 3-25
    Claim of Right 3-26

Tax Planning Considerations 3-27
    Shifting Income 3-27
    Alimony 3-27
    Prepaid Income 3-27
    Taxable, Tax-Exempt, or Tax-Deferred Bonds 3-28
    Reporting Savings Bond Interest 3-28
    Deferred Compensation Arrangements 3-29

Compliance and Procedural Considerations 3-29

Problem Materials 3-30
    Discussion Questions 3-30
    Issue Identification Questions 3-33
    Problems 3-34
    Comprehensive Problems 3-37
    Tax Form/Return Preparation Problems 3-37
    Case Study Problems 3-38
    Tax Research Problem 3-38

CHAPTER 4
▶ GROSS INCOME: EXCLUSIONS 4-1

Items That Are Not Income 4-2
    Unrealized Income 4-2
    Self-Help Income 4-3
    Rental Value of Personal-Use Property 4-3
    Selling Price of Property 4-3

Major Statutory Exclusions 4-4
    Gifts and Inheritances 4-4
    Life Insurance Proceeds 4-5
    Adoption Expenses 4-6
    Awards for Meritorious Achievement 4-7
    Scholarships and Fellowships 4-7
    Distributions from Qualified State Tuition Programs 4-7
    Payments for Injury and Sickness 4-8
    Employee Fringe Benefits 4-9
    Foreign-Earned Income Exclusion 4-17
    Income from the Discharge of a Debt 4-18
    Exclusion for Gain from Smallbusiness Stock 4-20
    Other Exclusions 4-20

Tax Planning Considerations 4-21
    Employee Fringe Benefits 4-21
    Self-Help and Use of Personally Owned Property 4-22

Compliance and Procedural Considerations 4-22

Problem Materials 4-23
    Discussion Questions 4-23
    Issue Identification Questions 4-24
    Problems 4-25
    Comprehensive Problem 4-28
    Tax Form/Return Preparation Problems 4-29
    Case Study Problems 4-29
    Tax Research Problems 4-30

CHAPTER 5
▶ PROPERTY TRANSACTIONS: CAPITAL GAINS AND LOSSES 5-1

Determination of Gain or Loss 5-2
    Realized Gain or Loss 5-2
    Recognized Gain or Loss 5-4

Basis Considerations 5-5
    Cost of Acquired Property 5-5
    Property Received as a Gift: Gifts After 1921 5-6
    Property Received from a Decedent 5-8
    Property Converted from Personal Use to Business Use 5-9
    Allocation of Basis 5-10

Definition of a Capital Asset 5-12
    Influence of the Courts 5-13
    Other IRC Provisions Relevant to Capital Gains and Losses 5-14

Tax Treatment for Capital Gains and Losses of Noncorporate Taxpayers 5-16
    Capital Gains 5-16
    Adjusted Net Capital Gains (ANCG) 5-17
    Capital Losses 5-18

Tax Treatment of Capital Gains and Losses: Corporate Taxpayers 5-20

Sale or Exchange 5-21
    Worthless Securities 5-22
    Retirement of Debt Instruments 5-22
    Options 5-24
    Patents 5-25
    Franchises, Trademarks, and Trade Names 5-26
    Lease Cancellation Payments 5-27

Holding Period 5-28
    Property Received as a Gift 5-28
    Property Received from a Decedent 5-29
    Nontaxable Exchanges 5-29
    Receipt of Nontaxable Stock Dividends and Stock Rights 5-29

Preferential Treatment for Net Capital Gains 5-30
    Mobility of Capital 5-30
    Mitigation of the Effects of Inflation and the Progressive Tax System 5-30
    Lower the Cost of Capital 5-31

Tax Planning Considerations 5-31
    Selection of Property to Transfer By Gift 5-31
    Selection of Property to Transfer at Time of Death 5-32

Compliance and Procedural Considerations 5-33
    Documentation of Basis 5-33
    Reporting of Capital Gains and Losses on Schedule D 5-33

Problem Materials 5-36
    Discussion Questions 5-36
    Issue Identification Questions 5-38
    Problems 5-38
    Tax Form/Return Preparation Problems 5-43
    Case Study Problems 5-43
    Tax Research Problems 5-44

CHAPTER 6
▶ **DEDUCTIONS AND LOSSES 6-1**

For Versus From Adjusted Gross Income (AGI) Classification 6-3

Criteria for Deducting Business and Investment Expenses 6-4
    Business or Investment Requirement 6-5
    Ordinary Expense 6-7
    Necessary Expense 6-8
    Reasonable Expense 6-8
    Expenses and Losses Must Be Incurred By the Taxpayer 6-9

General Restrictions on the Deductibility of Expenses 6-10
    Capitalization Versus Expense Deduction 6-10
    Expenses Related to Exempt Income 6-11
    Expenditures That Are Contrary to Public Policy 6-12
    Other Expenditures That Are Specifically Disallowed 6-14

Proper Substantiation Requirement 6-16

When an Expense Is Deductible 6-18
    Cash Method 6-18
    Accrual Method 6-20

Special Disallowance Rules 6-22
    Wash Sales 6-22
    Transactions Between Related Parties 6-25
    Hobby Losses 6-28
    Vacation Home 6-31
    Expenses of an Office in the Home 6-34

Tax Planning Considerations 6-35
    Hobby Losses 6-35
    Unreasonable Compensation 6-35
    Timing of Deductions 6-36

Compliance and Procedural Considerations 6-36
    Proper Classification of Deductions 6-36
    Proper Substantiation 6-36
    Business Versus Hobby 6-37

Problem Materials 6-37
    Discussion Questions 6-37
    Issue Identification Questions 6-39
    Problems 6-39
    Comprehensive Problem 6-44
    Tax Form/Return Preparation Problems 6-45
    Case Study Problems 6-46
    Tax Research Problem 6-47

CHAPTER 7
▶ **ITEMIZED DEDUCTIONS 7-1**

Medical Expenses 7-2
    Qualified Individuals 7-2
    Qualified Medical Expenses 7-3
    Amount and Timing of Deduction 7-6

Taxes 7-9
    Definition of a Tax 7-9
    Deductible Taxes 7-9
    Nondeductible Taxes 7-9
    State and Local Income Taxes 7-10
    Personal Property Taxes 7-10
    Real Estate Taxes 7-10
    General Sales Tax 7-11
    Self-Employment Tax 7-11

Interest 7-12
    Definition of Interest 7-12
    Classification of Interest Expense 7-12
    Timing of the Interest Deduction 7-19

Charitable Contributions 7-21
    Qualifying Organization 7-21
    Type of Property Contributed 7-22
    Deduction Limitations 7-24
    Application of Carryovers 7-25
    Special Rules for Charitable Contributions Made By Corporations 7-26
    Summary of Deduction Limitations 7-26

Casualty and Theft Losses 7-28

Miscellaneous Itemized Deductions 7-28
    Certain Employee Expenses 7-28
    Expenses to Produce Income 7-28
    Cost of Tax Advice 7-28

Reduction of Certain Itemized Deductions 7-29

Tax Planning Considerations 7-30
    Medical Expense Deduction 7-30
    Interest Expense Deduction 7-31
    Deduction for Charitable Contributions 7-32

vi Individuals ▼ Contents

Compliance and Procedural Considerations 7-33
Medical Expenses 7-33
Contribution of Property 7-33
Charitable Contributions 7-33
Taxes 7-36

Problem Materials 7-37
Discussion Questions 7-37
Issue Identification Questions 7-38
Problems 7-38
Tax Form/Return Preparation Problems 7-42
Case Study Problems 7-44
Tax Research Problem 7-44

CHAPTER 8
▶ LOSSES AND BAD DEBTS 8-1

Transactions That May Result in Losses 8-2
Sale or Exchange of Property 8-2
Expropriated, Seized, or Confiscated Property 8-3
Abandoned Property 8-3
Worthless Securities 8-3
Demolition of Property 8-4

Classifying the Loss on the Taxpayer's Tax Return 8-4
Ordinary Versus Capital Loss 8-5
Disallowance Possibilities 8-6

Passive Losses 8-7
Computation of Passive Losses and Credits 8-7
Carryovers 8-8
Definition of a Passive Activity 8-10
Taxpayers Subject to Passive Loss Rules 8-12
Publicly Traded Partnerships 8-13
Rental Real Estate Trade or Business 8-14
Other Rental Real Estate Activities 8-15

Casualty and Theft Losses 8-17
Casualty Defined 8-17
Theft Defined 8-19
Deductible Amount of Casualty Loss 8-19
Limitations on Personal-Use Property 8-20
Netting Casualty Gains and Losses on Personal-Use Property 8-21
Casualty Gains and Losses Attributable to Business and Investment Property 8-22
When Losses Are Deductible 8-22

Bad Debts 8-24
Bona Fide Debtor-Creditor Relationship 8-24
Taxpayerus Basis in the Debt 8-25
Debt Must Be Worthless 8-26
Nonbusiness Bad Debts 8-26
Business Bad Debts 8-28
Accounting for the Business Bad Debt 8-28
Recovery of Bad Debts 8-28
Deposits in Insolvent Financial Institutions 8-28

Net Operating Losses 8-29
Computing the Net Operating Loss 8-30
Carryback and Carryover Periods 8-33
Recomputation of Taxable Income in the Carryover Year 8-33

Tax Planning Considerations 8-34
Bad Debts 8-34
Casualties 8-34
Net Operating Losses 8-34

Compliance and Procedural Considerations 8-35
Casualty Losses 8-35
Net Operating Losses 8-35
Worthless Securities 8-36

Problem Materials 8-36
Discussion Questions 8-36
Issue Identification Questions 8-38
Problems 8-38
Tax Form/Return Preparation Problems 8-42
Case Study Problems 8-43
Tax Research Problem 8-44

CHAPTER 9
▶ EMPLOYEE EXPENSES AND DEFERRED COMPENSATION 9-1

Classification of Employee Expenses 9-2
Nature of the Employment Relationship 9-2
Limitations on Unreimbursed Employee Expenses 9-3

Travel Expenses 9-4
Deductibility of Travel Expenses 9-4
Definition of Travel Expenses 9-5
General Qualification Requirements 9-6
Business Versus Pleasure 9-7
Foreign Travel 9-8
Additional Limitations on Travel Expenses 9-8

Transportation Expenses 9-9
Definition and Classification 9-9
Treatment of Automobile Expenses 9-10
Reimbursement of Automobile Expenses 9-12

Entertainment Expenses 9-12
50% Disallowance for Meal and Entertainment Expenses 9-12
Classification of Expenses 9-13
Business Meals 9-14
Entertainment Facilities and Club Dues 9-15
Business Gifts 9-15
Limitations on Entertainment Tickets 9-16

Reimbursed Employee Business Expenses 9-16

Moving Expenses 9-18
Expense Classification 9-19
Definition of Moving Expenses 9-19
Treatment of Employer Reimbursements 9-20

Education Expenses 9-20
Classification of Education Expenses 9-21
General Requirements for a Deduction 9-21

Office in Home Expenses 9-23
General Requirements for a Deduction 9-23
Deduction and Limitations 9-25

Deferred Compensation 9-26
Qualified Pension and Profit-Sharing Plans 9-27
Qualification Requirements for a Qualified Plan 9-28
Tax Treatment to Employees and Employers 9-29
Nonqualified Plans 9-31
Employee Stock Options 9-32
Plans for Self-Employed Individuals 9-35

Individual Retirement Accounts (IRAs) 9-36
Traditional IRA 9-36
Roth IRA 9-38
Education IRA 9-40
Simplified Employee Pensions 9-41
Simple Retirement Plans 9-41

Tax Planning Considerations 9-41
Moving Expenses 9-41
Providing Nontaxable Compensation to Employees 9-42
Rollover of Traditional IRA to Roth IRA 9-42

Compliance and Procedural Considerations 9-43
Subtantiating Travel and Entertainment Expenses 9-43
Reporting Employee Business Expenses 9-43
Reporting Moving Expenses 9-44
Reporting Office in Home Expenses 9-47
Qualification of Pension and Profit-Sharing Plans 9-47

Problem Materials 9-47
Discussion Questions 9-47
Issue Identification Questions 9-50
Problems 9-51
Tax Form/Return Preparation Problems 9-57
Case Study Problems 9-58
Tax Research Problem 9-59

CHAPTER 10
▶ **DEPRECIATION, COST RECOVERY, AMORTIZATION, AND DEPLETION 10-1**

Depreciation and Cost Recovery 10-2
General Considerations 10-2
Depreciation Methods 10-4
Section 179 Expensing Election 10-9
MACRS Restrictions 10-10

Amortization 10-13
Sec. 197 Intangibles 10-13
Research and Experimental Expenditures 10-16

Depletion, Intangible Drilling, and Development Costs 10-17
Depletion Methods 10-17
Treatment of Intangibledrilling and Development Costs 10-19

Tax Planning Considerations 10-20
Alternative Depreciation System Under MACRS 10-20
IDCs: Capitalization Versus Expensing Election 10-20
Use of Units of Production Depreciation 10-21
Structuring a Business Combination 10-21

Compliance and Procedural Considerations 10-21
IDC Election Procedures 10-21
Reporting Cost Recovery, Depreciation, Depletion, and Amortization Deductions 10-22
Research and Experimental Expenditures 10-22

Problem Materials 10-22
Discussion Questions 10-22
Issue Identification Questions 10-28
Problems 10-29
Tax Form/Return Preparation Problems 10-32
Case Study Problems 10-33
Tax Research Problem 10-34

CHAPTER 11
▶ **ACCOUNTING PERIODS AND METHODS 11-1**

Accounting Periods 11-2
Required Payments and Fiscal Years 11-3
Changes in the Accounting Period 11-4
Returns for Periods of Less Than 12 Months 11-5

Overall Accounting Methods 11-7
Cash Receipts and Disbursements Method 11-7
Accrual Method 11-9
Hybrid Method 11-10

Inventories 11-11
Determination of Inventory Cost 11-11

Special Accounting Methods 11-15
Long-Term Contracts 11-15
Installment Sales Method 11-17
Deferred Payment Sales 11-21

Imputed Interest 11-22
Imputed Interest Computation 11-23
Accrual of Interest 11-23
Gift, Shareholder, and Other Loans 11-24

Change in Accounting Methods 11-26
Amount of Change 11-26
Reporting the Amount of the Change 11-27
Obtaining IRS Consent 11-27

Tax Planning Considerations 11-28
Accounting Periods 11-28
Accounting Methods 11-28
Installment Sales 11-28

Compliance and Procedural Considerations 11-30
Reporting Installment Sales on Form 6252 11-30
Procedures for Changing to LIFO 11-30

Problem Materials 11-30
Discussion Questions 11-30
Issue Identification Questions 11-31
Problems 11-32
Tax Form/Return Preparation Problem 11-35
Case Study Problems 11-35
Tax Research Problems 11-36

CHAPTER 12
▶ **PROPERTY TRANSACTIONS: NONTAXABLE EXCHANGES 12-1**

Like-Kind Exchanges 12-2
Like-Kind Property Defined 12-2
A Direct Exchange Must Occur 12-5
Three-Party Exchanges 12-5
Receipt of Boot 12-6
Basis of Property Received 12-7
Exchanges Between Related Parties 12-8
Transfer of Non–Like-Kind Property 12-9
Holding Period for Property Received 12-9

Involuntary Conversions 12-10
Involuntary Conversion Defined 12-11
Tax Treatment of Gain Due to Involuntary Conversion Into Boot 12-12
Tax Treatment of Gain Due to an Involuntary Conversion Directly Into Similar Property 12-13

Replacement Property 12-13
Obtaining Replacement Property 12-15
Time Requirements for Replacement 12-15

Sale of Principal Residence 12-16
Principal Residence Defined 12-18
Sale of More Than One Principal Residence Within a Two-Year Period 12-19
Involuntary Conversion of a Principal Residence 12-20

Tax Planning Considerations 12-21
Avoiding the Like-Kind Exchange Provisions 12-21
Sale of a Principal Residence 12-22

Compliance and Procedural Considerations 12-23
Reporting of Involuntary Conversions 12-23
Reporting of Sale or Exchange of a Principal Residence 12-24

Problem Materials 12-24
Discussion Questions 12-24
Issue Identification Questions 12-25
Problems 12-26
Comprehensive Problem 12-30
Tax Form/Return Preparation Problems 12-31
Case Study Problems 12-32
Tax Research Problems 12-32

CHAPTER 13
▶ **PROPERTY TRANSACTIONS: SECTION 1231 AND RECAPTURE 13-1**

History of Sec. 1231 13-2

Overview of Basic Tax Treatment for Sec. 1231 13-3
Net Gains 13-3
Net Losses 13-3
Tax Rate for Net Sec. 1231 Gain 13-4

Section 1231 Property 13-5
Section 1231 Property Defined 13-5
Real or Depreciable Property Used in Trade or Business 13-5

Involuntary Conversions 13-6
Condemnations 13-6
Other Involuntary Conversions 13-7

Procedure for Sec. 1231 Treatment 13-7

Recapture Provisions of Sec. 1245 13-8
Purpose of Sec. 1245 13-9

Recapture Provisions of Sec. 1250 13-11
Purpose of Sec. 1250 13-11
Section 1250 Property Defined 13-11
Unrecaptured Section 1250 Gain 13-12
Recapture Rules for Residential Rental Property 13-12
Residential Rental Property that is Recovery Property 13-13
Recapture Rules for Nonresidential Real Estate 13-14
Low-Income Housing 13-15

Additional Recapture for Corporations 13-16
Summary of Sec. 1231, 1245 and 1250 Gains 13-16

Recapture Provisions—Other Applications 13-17
Gifts of Property Subject to Recapture 13-17
Transfer of Property Subject to Recapture at Death 13-18

Charitable Contributions 13-18
Like-Kind Exchanges 13-19
Involuntary Conversions 13-19
Installment Sales 13-19
Section 179 Expensing Election 13-21
Conservation and Land Clearing Expenditures 13-21
Intangible Drilling Costs and Depletion 13-21
Gain on Sale of Depreciable Property Between Related Parties 13-22

Tax Planning Considerations 13-23
Avoiding the Recapture Provisions 13-23

Compliance and Procedural Considerations 13-25
Reporting Sec. 1231 Gains and Losses on Form 4797 13-25
Reporting Gains Recaptured as Ordinary Income on Form 4797 13-25
Reporting Casualty or Theft Gain or Loss on Form 4684 13-29

Problem Materials 13-29
Discussion Questions 13-29
Issue Identification Questions 13-30
Problems 13-31
Tax Form/Return Preparation Problems 13-36
Case Study Problems 13-37
Tax Research Problem 13-38

CHAPTER 14
▶ **SPECIAL TAX COMPUTATION METHODS, TAX CREDITS, AND PAYMENT OF TAX 14-1**

Alternative Minimum Tax 14-2
Computational Aspects 14-2
Tax Preference Items 14-3
AMT Adjustments 14-4
Summary Illustration of the AMT Computation 14-6

Self-Employment Tax 14-7
Computing the Tax 14-7
What Constitutes Self-Employment Income 14-8

Overview of Tax Credits 14-9
Use and Importance of Tax Credits 14-9
Value of a Credit Versus a Deduction 14-9
Classification of Credits 14-9

Personal Tax Credits 14-9
Child Tax Credit 14-10
Child and Dependent Care Credit 14-11
Tax Credit for the Elderly and Disabled 14-12
Adoption Credit 14-13
Hope Scholarship Credit 14-14
Lifetime Learning Credit 14-15
Limitation on Personal Credits 14-16

Miscellaneous Credits 14-16
Foreign Tax Credit 14-16

General Business Credits 14-17
Credit for Increasing Research Activities 14-18
Disabled Access Credit 14-18
Tax Credit for Rehabilitation Expenditures 14-19
Business Energy Credits 14-19
Work Opportunity Credit 14-20

  Welfare-to-Work Credit 14-20
  Empowerment Zone Employment Credit 14-21
  Limitation Based Upon Tax Liability 14-21
Refundable Credits 14-22
  Earned Income Credit 14-22
Payment of Taxes 14-24
  Withholding of Taxes 14-24
  Estimated Tax Payments 14-27
Tax Planning Considerations 14-29
  Avoiding the Alternative Minimum Tax 14-29
  Avoiding the Underpayment Penalty for Estimated Tax 14-29
  Cash-Flow Considerations 14-30
  Use of General Business Tax Credits 14-30
  Foreign Tax Credits and the Foreign Earned Income Exclusion 14-30
  Child and Dependent Care Credit 14-31
Compliance and Procedural Considerations 14-32
  Alternative Minimum Tax Filing Procedures 14-32
  Withholding and Estimated Tax 14-32
  General Business Tax Credits 14-32
  Personal Tax Credits 14-32
Problem Materials 14-33
  Discussion Questions 14-33
  Issue Identification Questions 14-35
  Problems 14-35
  Comprehensive Problem 14-40
  Tax Form/Return Preparation Problems 14-41
  Case Study Problems 14-41
  Tax Research Problem 14-42

CHAPTER 15
▶ **TAX RESEARCH 15-1**
Overview of Tax Research 15-2
Steps in the Tax Research Process 15-3
Importance of the Facts to the Tax Consequences 15-5
  Ability to Design a Factual Situation Favoring the Taxpayer 15-6
The Sources of Tax Law 15-7
  The Legislative Process 15-7
  The Internal Revenue Code 15-8
  Treasury Regulations 15-8
  Administrative Interpretations 15-11
  Judicial Decisions 15-14
  Tax Treaties 15-24
  Tax Periodicals 15-24
Tax Services 15-25
  United States Tax Reporter 15-25
  Standard Federal Tax Reporter 15-26
  Federal Tax Coordinator 2d 15-26
  Law of Federal Income Taxation (Mertens) 15-27
  Tax Management Portfolios 15-27
  CCH Federal Tax Service 15-28
Citators 15-28
  CCH Citator 15-28
  Research Institute of America Citator 2nd Series 15-31

Computers as a Research Tool 15-34
Statements on Standards for Tax Services 15-34
Sample Work Papers and Client Letter 15-38
Problem Materials 15-38
  Discussion Questions 15-38
  Problems 15-39
  Comprehensive Problem 15-42
  Case Study Problem 15-42
  Tax Research Problems 15-43

CHAPTER 16
▶ **CORPORATIONS 16-1**
Definition of a Corporation 16-2
Similarities and Differences Between Corporations and Individuals 16-3
  Similarities 16-3
  Differences 16-3
Specific Rules Applicable to Corporations 16-3
  Capital Gains and Losses 16-3
  Dividends-Received Deduction 16-5
  Net Operating Losses 16-6
  Charitable Contributions 16-6
  Compensation Deduction Limitation for Publicly Held Corporations 16-7
Computation of Tax 16-8
  Computation of Taxable Income 16-8
  Computation of Regular Tax 16-8
  Computation of the Corporate Alternative Minimum Tax (AMT) 16-10
  Penalty Taxes 16-13
  Computation of Tax for Controlled Groups 16-16
  Consolidated Returns 16-19
Transfers of Property to Controlled Corporations 16-20
  Section 351 Nonrecognition Requirements 16-20
  Basis Considerations 16-21
  Treatment of Liabilities 16-22
Capitalization of the Corporation 16-23
Earnings and Profits 16-25
  Calculation of Earnings and Profits 16-25
  Current Versus Accumulated E&P 16-26
Nonmoney Distributions 16-27
  Tax Consequences to the Shareholders 16-27
  Tax Consequences to the Distributing Corporation 16-27
Stock Redemptions 16-28
  Determining Whether a Redemption is a Dividend or Capital Gain 16-29
  Redemption Provisions for Special Situations 16-31
Corporate Distributions in Complete Liquidation 16-31
  Tax Consequences to the Liquidating Corporation 16-31
  Tax Consequences to the Shareholders 16-32
  Section 332: Liquidation of A Subsidiary Corporation 16-33
Tax Planning Considerations 16-33
  Capital Structure and Section 1244 16-33
  Dividend Policy 16-35
  Use of Losses 16-35

Charitable Contributions 16-35
Dividends-Received Deduction 16-35

Compliance and Procedural Considerations 16-36
Filing Requirements 16-36
Schedule M-1 and M-2 Reconciliations 16-36
Maintenance of Records for E&P 16-37

Problem Materials 16-38
Discussion Questions 16-38
Issue Identification Questions 16-40
Problems 16-40
Tax Form/Return Preparation Problems 16-46
Case Study Problems 16-48
Tax Research Problem 16-48

CHAPTER 17
▶ PARTNERSHIPS AND S CORPORATIONS 17-1

Types of Flow-Through Entities 17-2
Partnerships 17-2
S Corporations 17-3
Limited Liability Companies 17-3
Limited Liability Partnerships 17-4

Taxation of Partnerships 17-4
Formation of a Partnership 17-4
Partnership Operations 17-7
Special Allocations 17-9
Allocation of Partnership Income, Deductions, Losses, and Credits to Partners 17-9
Basis Adjustments for Operating Items 17-10
Limitations on Losses and Restoration of Basis 17-11
Transactions Between a Partner and the Partnership 17-12
Partnership Distributions 17-13
Sale of a Partnership Interest 17-14
Optional Basis Adjustments 17-15
Electing Large Partnerships 17-16

Partnership Elections 17-18
Tax Year Restrictions 17-18
Cash Method of Accounting Restrictions 17-19

Taxation of S Corporations 17-19
Qualification Requirements 17-19
Election Requirements 17-21
Termination Conditions 17-22
S Corporation Operations 17-23
Basis Adjustments to S Corporation Stock 17-25
S Corporation Losses and Limitations 17-26
Other S Corporation Considerations 17-28

Tax Planning Considerations 17-30
Use of Operating Losses 17-30
Income Shifting Among Family Members 17-31
Optional Basis Adjustment Election Under Sec. 754 17-32

Compliance and Procedural Considerations 17-32
Partnership Filing Requirements and Elections 17-32
Reporting Partnership Items on Form 1065 17-33
S Corporation Filing Requirements and Accounting Method Elections 17-33
Reporting S Corporation Items on Form 1120S 17-33
Comparison of Alternative Forms of Business Organizations 17-34

Problem Materials 17-36
Discussion Questions 17-36
Issue Identification Questions 17-38
Problems 17-39
Comprehensive Problem 17-44
Tax Form/Return Preparation Problems 17-44
Case Study Problems 17-45
Tax Research Problems 17-46

CHAPTER 18
▶ TAXES AND INVESTMENT PLANNING 18-1

Investment Models 18-2
The Current Model 18-2
The Deferred Model 18-5
The Exempt Model 18-10
The Pension Model 18-10
Multiperiod Strategies 18-14
Summary and Comparison of Basic Investment Models 18-14

Other Applications of Investment Models 18-15
Flow-Through Entity Versus C Corporation 18-15
Current Salary Versus Deferred Compensation 18-20

Implicit Taxes and Clienteles 18-26

Problem Materials 18-29
Discussion Questions 18-29
Problems 18-30

TABLES
2000 Tax Tables and Rate Schedules T-1

APPENDICES
▶ APPENDIX A
Tax Research Working Paper File A-1
▶ APPENDIX B
Tax Forms B-1
▶ APPENDIX C
MACRS and ACRS Tables C-1
▶ APPENDIX D
Glossary D-1
▶ APPENDIX E
Statements on Standards for Tax Services E-1
▶ APPENDIX F
Index of Code Sections F-1
▶ APPENDIX G
Index of Treasury Regulations G-1
▶ APPENDIX H
Index of Government Promulgations H-1
▶ APPENDIX I
Index of Court Cases I-1
▶ APPENDIX J
Subject Index J-1

About the Editors

Thomas R. Pope is an Associate Professor of Accounting and Director of the Master of Science in Accountancy Program at the University of Kentucky. He received a B.S. from the University of Louisville and an M.S. and D.B.A. in business administration from the University of Kentucky. He teaches partnership and S corporation taxation, tax research and policy, and introductory taxation and has won outstanding teaching awards at the University, College, and School of Accountancy levels. He has published articles in *The Accounting Review, The Tax Adviser, Taxes,* and a number of other journals. Professor Pope's extensive professional experience includes eight years with Big Five accounting firms. Five of those years were with Ernst & Whinney (now part of Ernst & Young), including two years with their National Tax Department in Washington, D.C. He subsequently held the position of Senior Manager in charge of the Tax Department in Lexington, Kentucky. Professor Pope has also been a leader and speaker at professional tax conferences all over the United States and is active as a tax consultant.

Kenneth E. Anderson is a Distinguished Professor of Accounting at the University of Tennessee. He earned a B.B.A. from the University of Wisconsin-Milwaukee and subsequently attained the level of tax manager with Arthur Young & Company (now part of Ernst & Young). He then earned a Ph.D. from Indiana University. He teaches introductory taxation, corporate taxation, partnership taxation, and tax policy and has twice won the Beta Alpha Psi Outstanding Educator Award (1994 and 1995). Professor Anderson has published articles in *The Accounting Review, The Journal of the American Taxation Association, The Journal of Accountancy,* and a number of other journals. In addition, he is on the editorial board of *Advances in Taxation.*

John L. Kramer is the Arthur Andersen Professor of Accounting and Director of the Fisher School of Accounting at the University of Florida. He is a recipient of a Teaching Improvement Program award given by the University of Florida in 1994. He holds a Ph.D. in Business Administration, an M.B.A. from the University of Michigan (Ann Arbor), and a B.B.A. from the University of Michigan (Dearborn). He is a past-president of the American Taxation Association and the Florida Association of Accounting Educators, as well as a past editor of *The Journal of the American Taxation Association.* Professor Kramer has taught for the American Institute of CPAs, American Tax Institute of Europe, and a number of national and regional accounting firms. He is a frequent speaker at academic and professional conferences, as well as having served as an expert witness in a number of court cases. He has published over 50 articles in *The Accounting Review, The Journal of the American Taxation Association, The Tax Adviser, The Journal of Taxation* and other academic and professional journals.

About the Authors

D. Dale Bandy is the C.G. Avery Professor of Accounting in the School of Accounting at the University of Central Florida. He received a B.S. from the University of Tulsa, an M.B.A. from the University of Arkansas, and a Ph.D. from the University of Texas at Austin. He helped to establish the Master of Science in Taxation programs at the University of Central Florida and California State University, Fullerton, where he previously taught. In 1985, he was selected by the California Society of Certified Public Accountants as the Accounting Educator of the year. Professor Bandy has published 8 books and more than 30 articles in accounting and taxation. His articles have appeared in *Journal of Taxation, Journal of Accountancy, Advances in Taxation, Tax Adviser, CPA Journal, Management Accounting* and a number of other journals.

N. ALLEN FORD

N. Allen Ford is the Larry D. Homer/KPMG Peat Marwick Distinguished Teaching Professor of Professional Accounting at the University of Kansas. He received an undergraduate degree from Centenary College in Shreveport, Louisiana, and both the M.B.A. and Ph.D. in Business from the University of Arkansas. He has published over 30 articles related to taxation, financial accounting, and accounting education in journals such as *The Accounting Review, The Journal of the American Taxation Association,* and *The Journal of Taxation*. He served as president of the American Taxation Association in 1979-80. Professor Ford has received numerous teaching awards, at the college and university levels. In 1993, he received the Byron T. Shutz Award for Distinguished Teaching in Economics and Business. In 1996 he received the Ray M. Sommerfeld Outstanding Tax Educator Award, which is jointly sponsored by the American Taxation Association and Ernst & Young.

ROBERT L. GARDNER

Robert L. Gardner is the Robert J. Smith Professor of Accounting and the Associate Director of the School of Accountancy and Information Systems at Brigham Young University. He received a B.S. and M.B.A. from the University of Utah and a Ph.D. from the University of Texas at Austin. He has authored or coauthored two books and over 25 articles, and has received several teaching awards. Professor Gardner has served on the Board of Trustees of the American Taxation Association and served as President of the ATA in 1999-2000. He actively consults with several national CPA firms in their continuing education programs.

MICHAEL S. SCHADEWALD

Michael S. Schadewald is an Associate Professor of Accounting and Director of the Deloitte & Touche Center for Multistate Taxation at the University of Wisconsin-Milwaukee. He holds a Ph.D. from the University of Minnesota, an M.S. from the University of Wisconsin-Milwaukee, and a B.B.A. from the University of Wisconsin-Whitewater. He has co-authored a book on international taxation and has published over 30 articles in a number of accounting and tax journals, including *The Journal of the American Taxation Association, The Accounting Review, Contemporary Accounting Research,* and *The Journal of Taxation*. He serves on the editorial board of The Journal of the American Taxation Association, International Tax Journal, Issues in Accounting Education, and Journal of Accounting Education. He has been awarded numerous research grants and fellowships by Big-Five accounting firms, and worked in the Milwaukee office of Arthur Young (now part of Ernst & Young) prior to entering academics.

PREFACE

OBJECTIVES AND USE

This text is designed for use in a first course in federal taxation for undergraduate accounting and business students. The text materials have been updated to reflect recent legislative, judicial, and administrative changes in the tax law through January 1, 2001.

A companion volume, *Prentice Hall's Federal Taxation, 2002: Corporations, Partnerships, Estates, and Trusts,* is published for use in the second course in federal taxation. A combined two-semester volume, *Prentice Hall's Federal Taxation, 2002: Comprehensive,* joins 14 chapters of the *Individuals* volume with 14 chapters of the *Corporations, Partnerships, Estates, and Trusts* volume. Either the *Individuals* text or the *Comprehensive* volume may be used with a one-term survey course for undergraduate or graduate students.

Our objective is to provide a readable format with a high level of technical content. We accomplish this through a process of continuous review, improvement, and clarification of the text, examples, and problem material. If you find what you believe is an error, please provide the item to one of the editors along with your comments. We maintain this level of content by focusing on primary topics and relegating minor exceptions to footnotes.

FEATURES

▶ The 2002 Edition of *Prentice Hall's Federal Taxation* continues to include an online Multistate Income Taxation chapter. This chapter provides tax instructors with a vehicle to introduce students to a topic of increasing importance among tax practitioners. It provides an overview of state and local tax systems, as well as a more in-depth discussion of state income tax issues such as nexus, corporate filing options, the definition of state taxable income, allocation and apportionment, and state taxation of S Corporations, partnerships and limited liability companies. A complete set of assignment material is available with the chapter in addition to links to related Internet resources. Instructors and students may download the chapter, free of charge, from the web site that accompanies the book *(www.prenhall.com/phtax).*

▶ Chapter 15: Tax Research. This chapter has been extensively updated to (1) provide more information on the steps in the research process and (2) explain the role of computers in tax research. A special supplement called *How To Do Tax Research* is available from the website at www.prenhall.com/phtax. This supplement further enhances coverage by explaining how to electronically research a problem based on an actual case.

▶ A careful choice of topics. Users have found favor with the choice of topics and the extent of detail presented throughout the text. They are particularly pleased with our balance between exhaustive detail and too little detail for topics such as tax research, passive activity losses, and the alternative minimum tax.

▶ Unique chapter organization. The *Individuals* volume differs from other texts on the market with its early coverage of property transactions, two chapters on the taxation of business entities, and a highly acclaimed chapter on tax planning using the Scholes and Wolfson approach.

▶ Clear examples. Users regularly praise the clarity and number of examples in this text.

▶ Margin notes. Students appreciate learning about more than just tax rules so we developed a series of comments in the margin to enrich their learning experience.

PEDAGOGY

Key Points emphasize areas where students require repetition and reinforcement.
Typical Misconceptions identify concepts that students are likely to misunderstand and help them correct their thinking before they take a wrong approach.
Real World Examples provide facts and anecdotes about actual companies and real-life strategies.
Additional Comments elaborate on material presented in the text.
Self-Study Questions provide an in-text study guide. Each question is accompanied by a full solution.

Historical Notes offer a comprehensive understanding of concepts by examining them in their historical context.

Ethical Points focus on ethical questions that confront the tax practitioner, and are designated with an ethics icon.

▶ Topic Reviews. Each chapter contains several topic reviews to help students organize their understanding of the material and aid in preparing for exams. Many of these reviews are in tabular form for easy reference.

▶ Tax Planning Considerations. For the forward-looking part of the tax profession, students need to learn how to offer tax-saving advice for their clients. Our Tax Planning Considerations offer this insight once the basics of the rules have been established.

▶ Compliance and Procedural Considerations. Forms, procedures, and timing are addressed in the Compliance and Procedural Consideration section at the end of each chapter.

▶ Footnotes. An important component of "learning to learn" is knowing where to turn for authoritative information. We collected important references to the tax authorities in the footnotes for students to use as sources.

▶ A full complement of assignment material. The typical format for each chapter includes: discussion questions, issue identification questions, problems, comprehensive problems, tax form/return preparation problems, case study problems, and tax research problems. Tax return problems that can be solved using TaxCut software are marked with an icon.

▶ Oral and written communications. More emphasis is being placed on oral and written communication skills by the various accounting professional organizations (e.g., the American Institute of CPAs and the Accounting Education Change Commission). The case study problems at the end of each chapter are designed to meet this need by requiring students to consider a number of alternatives and present a written or oral solution to the problem. None of these case studies require the student to research the tax law.

▶ Expanded coverage of ethics. Most chapters contain boxes labeled "What Would You Do in This Situation?" and a reprinting of the AICPA's Statements on Standards for Tax Services appears in an appendix expands our coverage of ethics. The boxes include many controversies that are as yet unresolved or currently being considered by the courts. They represent choices that may put the practitioner at odds with the client, and are grounded on ethical parameters discussed in various standards, codes of conduct, or Treasury Department circulars. Students are asked to indicate what they would do if they found themselves in the same situation as well as the ethical implications of their actions. The boxes and the Statements on Standards for Tax Services enhance the Ethical Point margin notes and the Case Studies already found in the text.

▶ Stop & Think feature. These "speedbumps" ask students to stop and think about a business application of tax, or an extension of the basic material, at various points in the chapter. These are not "boxes," which typically fall outside the running text and can be bypassed. They are part of the text, complete with solutions to show students "how to do it," and identified by the icon you see here in the margin.

▶ Issue identification questions. Part of the process of learning involves sorting out important information from unimportant details. In an area as detail-oriented as taxation, developing the ability to identify key issues is of paramount importance. We include questions at the end of each chapter that ask students to focus on the important questions that practitioners face on a daily basis.

SUPPLEMENTAL MATERIALS

The text includes a full complement of supplementary materials. Adopters are encouraged to use these materials to enhance their teaching effectiveness and the students' learning experience. The following aids are available for instructor and student use:

INSTRUCTOR AIDS

▶ Loose-leaf Edition—All text versions are available in a three-hole punched, shrink-wrapped format.

▶ Instructor's Guide—This specially crafted instructor's guide includes sample syllabi, instructor's outlines, a series of interesting court cases to teach, a summary of modifications, deletions, and additions to the end-of-chapter problems, and selected teaching assignments. The instructor's outlines are also available on diskettes and may be downloaded from the faculty resources link at *www.prenhall.com/phtax*. Faculty password and user i.d. may be obtained from your Prentice Hall Representative.

▶ Solutions Manual—This volume includes solutions to the discussion questions, problems, and comprehensive problems. The solutions to the tax form/tax return preparation problems, case studies, and the research problems are included in the instructor's guide. The solutions manual is also available on disk and new to this edition: the solutions manual may be downloaded from the faculty resource link at *www.prenhall.com/phtax*. Faculty password and user i.d. may be obtained from your Prentice Hall representative.

▶ Test Bank—An extensive array of true-false, multiple choice, essay questions, and calculative problems are included.

▶ Prentice Hall Test Manager by ESA, Inc.—This easy-to-use computerized testing program can create exams, evaluate, and track student results. PH Test Manager also provides online testing capabilities. Test items are drawn from the test item file. Call-in testing at 1-800-550-1701 is also available on this title Monday-Friday, 8:00 a.m.-8:00 p.m., EST.

▶ PowerPoint Transparencies—Approximately 300 full color electronic transparencies are available for each book to enrich the teaching experience. Instructors can make additions or modifications to the transparencies prior to using them in class. The PowerPoint transparencies may also be downloaded from the faculty resource link *www.prenhall.com/phtax* site. Faculty password and user i.d. may be obtained from your Prentice Hall representative.

▶ Web Site—Prentice Hall has created a unique Web site designed to meet the needs of students and faculty. This Web site *www.prenhall.com/phtax* contains free student resources, free faculty resources, and premium student resources. These resources are noted below:

1. *Free* Student Resources include:
   Current events
   Internet resources
   Student study tips
These tools are not password protected

2. *Free* Faculty Resources include downloadable files for:
   PowerPoint transparencies
   Instructor's outlines
   Instructor solutions manual
   Teaching tips
   Solutions for online tax practice problems

These tools are provided at no charge to adopting faculty members and **are** password protected. (Faculty password and user i.d. may be obtained from your Prentice Hall representative.)

3. *Premium* Student Resources:
   ▶ Online "Study Guide"—Students can check their understanding of chapter topics with a variety of multiple-choice and true/false questions, computational problems, case study problems, and tax return preparation problems. Each quiz includes "hints," immediate scoring, graphical results reporter, explanation of incorrect answers, and the ability to e-mail results to a faculty member or other designated individual.
   ▶ Online tax cases for *Individuals* and *Corporations*
      a) *"Life of Riley" tax cases* require the student to research specific questions in order to complete the tax return for a given individual. Forms are available in a downloadable format.
      b) *"Endorphin USA" tax cases* require the student to research specific questions in order to complete the entire tax return for Endorphin USA as a C corporation, S corporation, or partnership. Forms are available in a downloadable format.

Students wishing to purchase the premium student resources can purchase directly through the Web site by clicking the Study Guide or Tax Cases link, or they can order the passcode for online supplements through their bookstore.

▶ **TaxCut Software**—This software allows you to easily prepare your individual tax return by asking you questions just like a tax professional would and filling in the form for you. TaxCut audits you return before you file, allows you to print IRS-approved forms on your own printer and offers context sensitive IRS instructions. The software is free to professors adopting a Prentice Hall tax text and students can purchase copies for $14.95 directly from Block Financial Corp. by using the coupons found in the book.

▶ **Tax Analysts' OneDisc CD-ROM**—Provides all the tools used by tax professionals to do research—Code, regulations, revenue rulings and procedures, court decisions and more! The software is free to professors adopting a Prentice Hall tax text and students can purchase copies for $19.99 directly from Tax Analysts by using the coupon found in the book.

ACKNOWLEDGMENTS

Our policy is to provide annual editions and to prepare timely updated supplements when major tax revisions occur. We are most appreciative of the suggestions made by outside reviewers because these extensive review procedures have been valuable to the authors and editors during the revision process.

We are also grateful to the various graduate assistants, doctoral students, and colleagues who have reviewed the text and supplementary materials and checked solutions to maintain a high level of technical accuracy. In particular, we would like to acknowledge the following colleagues who assisted in the preparation of supplemental materials for this text:

Priscilla Kenney (Supplements Coordinator)	University of Florida
Sally Baker	DeVry Institute of Technology
Arthur D. Cassill	University of North Carolina at Greensboro
Ann Burstein Cohen	SUNY at Buffalo
Craig J. Langstraat	University of Memphis
Thomas Omer	University of Illinois—Chicago
Caroline Strobel	University of South Carolina
Don Trippeer	East Carolina University
Ellen Cook	University of Louisiana—LaFayette

In addition, we want to thank Myron S. Scholes, Mark A. Wolfson, Merle Erickson, Edward L. Maydew, Terry Shevlin for allowing us to use the model discussed in their text, *Taxes and Business Strategy: A Planning Approach*, as the basis for material in Chapter 18.

Thomas R. Pope
Kenneth E. Anderson
John L. Kramer

CHAPTER 1

AN INTRODUCTION TO TAXATION

LEARNING OBJECTIVES

After studying this chapter, you should be able to

1. Discuss the history of taxation in the United States
2. Differentiate between the three types of tax rate structures
3. Describe the various types of taxes
4. Discuss what constitutes a "good" tax structure and the objectives of the federal income tax law
5. Describe the tax entities in the federal income tax system
6. Identify the various tax law sources and understand their implications for tax practice
7. Describe the legislative process for the enactment of the tax law
8. Describe the administrative procedures under the tax law
9. Describe the components of a tax practice and understand the importance of computer applications in taxation

CHAPTER OUTLINE

History of Taxation in the United States...1-2
Types of Tax Rate Structures...1-4
Other Types of Taxes...1-7
Criteria for a Tax Structure...1-12
Objectives of the Federal Income Tax Law...1-14
Entities in the Federal Income Tax System...1-15
Tax Law Sources...1-18
Enactment of a Tax Law...1-18
Administration of the Tax Law and Tax Practice Issues...1-20
Components of a Tax Practice...1-23
Computer Applications in Tax Practice...1-25

KEY POINT

In many situations, the use of the tax laws to influence human behavior is deliberate. As will be seen later in this chapter, tax laws are often used to achieve social and economic objectives.

The federal tax system has a substantial effect on investor, business, and personal decisions in the United States. The following examples illustrate the impact of the tax law on various decisions in our society:

▶ A business decision about whether to invest in a new plant or equipment may depend, in part, on the existence of favorable tax provisions.

▶ An employee may decide to accept a new job because the prospective employer offers favorable tax-free fringe benefits or an attractive deferred compensation plan.

▶ An individual may decide to buy a principal residence rather than rent comparable property because of the availability of tax deductions for mortgage interest and real estate taxes.

▶ The terms of a property settlement agreement pursuant to a divorce decree may be structured to take into account the tax laws governing alimony and property settlements.

The purpose of this text is to provide an introduction to the study of federal income taxation as applicable to individuals. However, before discussing the specifics of the U.S. federal income tax law, it is helpful to have a broad conceptual understanding of the taxation process. This chapter provides an overview of the following topics:

▶ Historical developments of the federal tax system
▶ Types of taxes levied and structural considerations
▶ Objectives of the tax law
▶ Tax law sources and the legislative process
▶ Internal Revenue Service (IRS) collection, examination, and appeals processes
▶ The nature of tax practice, including computer applications and tax research

HISTORY OF TAXATION IN THE UNITED STATES

OBJECTIVE 1

Discuss the history of taxation in the United States

EARLY PERIODS

The federal income tax is the dominant form of taxation in the United States. In addition, most states and some cities and counties also impose an income tax. Both corporations and individuals are subject to such taxes.

Before 1913 (the date of enactment of the modern-day federal income tax), the federal government relied predominantly on customs duties and excise taxes to finance its operations. The first federal income tax on individuals was enacted in 1861 to finance the Civil War but was repealed after the war. The federal income tax was reinstated in 1894, however, that tax was challenged in the courts because the U.S. Constitution required that an income tax be apportioned among the states in proportion to their populations. This type of tax system, which would be both impractical and difficult to administer, would mean that different tax rates would apply to individual taxpayers depending on their states of residence.

HISTORICAL NOTE

The reinstatement of the income tax in 1894 was the subject of heated political controversy. In general, the representatives in Congress from the agricultural South and West favored the income tax in lieu of customs duties. Representatives from the industrial eastern states were against the income tax and favored protective tariff legislation.

In 1895, the Supreme Court ruled that the tax was in violation of the U.S. Constitution.[1] Therefore, it was necessary to amend the U.S. Constitution to permit the passage of a federal income tax law. This was accomplished by the Sixteenth Amendment, which was ratified in 1913. The Sixteenth Amendment, while being an extraordinarily important amendment, consists of one sentence.

---

[1] *Pollock v. Farmers' Loan & Trust Co.*, 3 AFTR 2602, (USSC, 1895). Note, however, that a federal income tax on corporations that was enacted in 1909 was held to be constitutional because it was treated as an excise tax. See *Flint v. Stone Tracy Co.*, 3 AFTR 2834, (USSC, 1911).

Sixteenth Amendment to the Constitution of the United States
The Congress shall have power to lay and collect taxes on incomes, from whatever source derived, without apportionment among the several States, and without regard to any census or enumeration.

REVENUE ACTS FROM 1913 TO THE PRESENT

HISTORICAL NOTE
The Revenue Act of 1913 contained sixteen pages.

The Revenue Act of 1913 imposed a flat 1% tax (with no exemptions) on a corporation's net income. The rate varied from 1% to 7% for individuals, depending on the individual's income level. However, very few individuals paid federal income taxes because a $3,000 personal exemption ($4,000 for married individuals) was permitted as an offset to taxable income. These amounts were greater than the incomes of most individuals in 1913.

HISTORICAL NOTE
Before 1939, the tax laws were contained in the current revenue act, a reenactment of a prior revenue act plus amendments. In 1939, a permanent tax code was established; it was revised in 1954 and 1986.

Various amendments to the original law were passed between 1913 and 1939 as separate revenue acts. For example, a deduction for dependency exemptions was provided in 1917. In 1939, the separate revenue acts were codified into the Internal Revenue Code of 1939. A similar codification was accomplished in 1954. The 1954 codification, which was known as the Internal Revenue Code of 1954, included the elimination of many "deadwood" provisions, a rearrangement and clarification of numerous code sections, and the addition of major tax law changes. Whenever changes to the Internal Revenue Code (IRC) are made, the old language is deleted and the new language added. Thus, the statutes are organized as a single document, and a tax advisor does not have to read through the applicable parts of all previous tax bills to find the most current law. In 1986, major changes were made to the tax law, and the basic tax law was redesignated as the Internal Revenue Code of 1986.

The federal income tax became a "mass tax" on individuals during the early 1940s. This change was deemed necessary to finance the revenue needs of the federal government during World War II. In 1939, less than 6% of the U.S. population was subject to the federal income tax; by 1945, 74% of the population was taxed.[2] To accommodate the broadened tax base and to avoid significant tax collection problems, Congress enacted pay-as-you-go withholding in 1943.

A major characteristic of the federal income tax since its inception to today is the manner in which the tax law is changed or modified. The federal income tax is changed on an **incremental** basis rather than a complete revision basis. Under so-called incrementalism, when a change in the tax law is deemed necessary by Congress, the entire law is not changed but specific provisions of the tax law are added, changed, or deleted on an incremental basis. Thus, the federal income tax has been referred to as a "quiltwork" of tax laws, referring to the patchwork nature of the law. Without question, one of the principal reasons for the complexity of the federal income tax today is the incremental nature of the tax.

ADDITIONAL COMMENT
In 1996, 119 million individual income tax returns were filed, and collections from individuals totaled $656 billion.

REVENUE SOURCES

As mentioned earlier, the largest source of federal revenues is individual income taxes. Other major revenue sources include social security (FICA) taxes and corporate income taxes (see Table I1-1). Two notable trends from Table I1-1 are 1) the gradual increase in social security taxes from 1965 to 1999, and 2) the gradual decrease in corporate income taxes for the same period. Individual income taxes have slowly increasd during the thirty-year period.

---

[2] Richard Goode, *The Individual Income Tax* (Washington, DC: The Brookings Institution, 1964), pp. 2–4.

TYPICAL MISCONCEPTION

It is often assumed that the tax revenue from corporation income taxes is the largest source of tax revenue. However, the revenue generated from this tax represents approximately 11% of total federal revenues.

▼ **TABLE I1-1**
Breakdown of Federal Revenues

	1965	1975	1988	1999
Individual income taxes	43%	45%	44%	50%
Social insurance taxes and contribution	20	32	37	32
Corporation income taxes	23	15	10	10
Other	14	8	9	8
Total	100%	100%	100%	100%

Source: Council of Economic Advisors, *Economic Indicators* (Washington, DC: U.S. Government Printing Office, 1967, 1977, 2000).

TYPES OF TAX RATE STRUCTURES

OBJECTIVE 2

Differentiate between the three types of tax rate structures

THE STRUCTURE OF INDIVIDUAL INCOME TAX RATES

Virtually all tax structures are comprised of two basic parts: the **tax base** and the **tax rate**. The tax base is the amount to which the tax rate is applied to determine the tax due. For example, an individual's tax base for the federal income tax is *taxable income*, as defined and determined by the income tax law. Similarly, the tax base for the property tax is generally the fair market value of property subject to the tax. The tax rate is merely the percentage rate applied to the tax base.

Tax rates either may be progressive, proportional, or regressive. A **progressive rate** structure is one where the rate of tax increases as the tax base increases. The most notable tax that incorporates a progressive rate structure is the federal income tax. Thus, as a taxpayer's taxable income increases, a progressively higher rate of tax is applied. Currently, for individuals, the federal income tax rates begin at 15% and increase to 28%, 31%, 36%, and 39.6% as a taxpayer's taxable income increases.[3] Examples I1-1 and I1-2 show how the progressive rate structure of the federal income tax operates.

ADDITIONAL COMMENT

In the 1950's, the top marginal tax rate for individual taxpayers reached 92%. This astonishingly high rate only applied to taxpayers with very high taxable incomes but is still an extremely confiscatory tax rate.

EXAMPLE I1-1 ▶ Alice, who is single, has $20,000 taxable income in 2001 pays $3,000 in federal income taxes because a 15% tax rate is applied to taxable income up to $27,050. (For tax rates, see the inside front cover) Allen, who is also single, has taxable income of $40,000. A 15% rate applies to Allen's taxable income up to $27,050 and a 28% rate applies to taxable income over this amount. Thus, Allen's total tax is $7,684 [(0.15 × $27,050) + (0.28 × $12,950)]. If Allen's taxable income is $80,000, a 31% rate applies to $14,450 of his taxable income ($80,000 − $65,550) because the 31% rate applies to taxable income above $65,550 for a single individual and his total tax for the year is $19,317. Thus, the tax rates are progressive because the rate of tax increases as a taxpayer's taxable income increases. ◀

EXAMPLE I1-2 ▶ Assume the same facts as in Example I1-1 except that Alice has taxable income of $150,000. Of Alice's taxable income, $13,250 ($150,000 − $136,750) is subject to the 36% rate. Alternatively, assume that Allen has taxable income of $310,000. Of Allen's taxable income, $160,550 ($297,300 − $136,750) is subject to the 36% rate and $12,700 ($310,000 − $297,300) is subject to a marginal rate of 39.6%. ◀

---

[3] See the inside front cover for the 2001 tax rates and Chapter I2 for a discussion of the computation procedures. 2000 rate schedules and tax tables are located immediately before Appendix A.

An Introduction to Taxation ▼ **Individuals 1-5**

A **proportional tax rate**, sometimes called a **flat tax**, is one where the rate of tax is the same for all taxpayers, regardless of the level of their tax base. This type of tax rate is generally used for real estate taxes, state and local sales taxes, personal property taxes, customs duties, and excise taxes. A flat tax has been the subject of considerable discussion in the last couple of years and promises to be a highly controversial topic as the debate on federal income tax reform continues into the future.

EXAMPLE I1-3 ▶ Assume the same facts as in Example I1-1, except that a 17% tax rate applies to all amounts of taxable income. Based on the assumed flat tax rate structure, Alice's federal income tax is $3,400 on $20,000 of taxable income; Allen's tax is $6,800 on $40,000 of taxable income and $13,600 on $80,000 of taxable income. The tax rate is proportional because the 17% rate applies to both taxpayers without regard to their income level. As you can see, a proportional tax rate results in lower taxes for higher income taxpayers.[4] ◀

SELF-STUDY QUESTION

Assume a tax system with a tax of $1,000 on taxable income of $10,000 and a $1,500 tax on taxable income of $20,000. Is the tax rate system progressive, proportional, or regressive?

ANSWER

This tax system is regressive. Even though the amount of tax has increased, the rate of taxation has decreased from 10% on the first $10,000 of taxable income to 5% on the second $10,000 of taxable income.

A **regressive tax** rate decreases with an increase in the tax base (e.g., income). Regressive taxes, while not consistent with the fairness of the income tax,[5] are found in the United States. The social security (FICA) tax is regressive because a fixed rate of tax of 7.65% for both the employer and employee is levied up to a ceiling amount of $80,400 for 2001 ($76,200 in 2000). The employer and employee's FICA tax rate is only 1.45% for wages earned in excess of the ceiling amount. The sales tax, which is levied by many states, is also regressive when measured against the income base.

THE STRUCTURE OF CORPORATE TAX RATES

Corporations are separate entities and are subject to income tax. The federal corporate income tax reflects a stair-step pattern of progression that tends to benefit small corporations. The corporate rates are as follows:[6]

Taxable Income[7]	Tax
First $50,000	15% of taxable income
Over $50,000 but not over $75,000	$7,500 + 25% of taxable income over $50,000
Over $75,000 but not over $100,000	$13,750 + 34% of taxable income over $75,000
Over $100,000 but not over $335,000	$22,250 + 39% of taxable income over $100,000
Over $335,000	34% of taxable income
Over $10,000,000 but not over $15,000,000	$3,400,000 + 35% of taxable income over $10,000,000
Over $15,000,000 but not over $18,333,333	$5,150,000 + 38% over $15,000,000
Over $18,333,333	35% of taxable income

MARGINAL, AVERAGE, AND EFFECTIVE TAX RATES FOR TAXPAYERS

A taxpayer's **marginal tax rate** is the tax rate applied to an incremental amount of taxable income that is added to the tax base. The marginal tax rate concept is useful for planning because it measures the tax effect of a proposed transaction.

---

[4] This example assumes the same tax base (taxable income) for the flat tax as with the current federal tax. Most flat tax proposals allow few, if any, deductions and, therefore, would generate higher taxes than in the example.
[5] See the discussion of equity and fairness later in this chapter.
[6] For C corporations with taxable income over $100,000, the lower rates of tax on the first $75,000 of income are gradually phased out by applying a 5-percentage-point surtax on taxable income from $100,000 to $335,000 so that benefits of the favorable rates are eliminated once a corporation's taxable income reaches $335,000. Once taxable income exceeds $335,000 the tax equals 34% of taxable income. A 35% tax rate applies to taxable income in excess of $10 million. For corporations with taxable income in excess of $15 million, a 3 percentage-point-surtax applies to taxable income from $15 million to $18,333,333 to eliminate the lower 34% rate that applies to the first $10 million of taxable income.
[7] See the inside back cover for the 2001 corporation income tax rates.

EXAMPLE I1-4

▶ Vania, who is single, is considering the purchase of a personal residence that will provide a $20,000 tax deduction for interest expense and real estate taxes. Vania's taxable income would be reduced from $90,000 to $70,000 if she purchases the residence. Because a 31% tax rate applies to taxable income from $70,000 to $90,000, Vania's marginal tax rate is 31%. Thus, Vania's tax savings from purchasing the personal residence would be $6,200 (0.31 × $20,000). ◀

ADDITIONAL COMMENT
One method of calculating economic income is to start with adjusted gross income (AGI), add back items of excludible income, such as tax-exempt bond interest, proceeds of life insurance policies, etc., and then deduct certain nondeductible business expenses, such as life insurance premiums, penalties and fines, etc.

While the marginal tax rate measures the tax rate applicable to the next $1 of income or deduction for a taxpayer, there are two other tax rates that are used primarily by tax policymakers: average tax rate and effective tax rate. The **average tax rate** is computed by dividing the total tax liability by the amount of taxable income. This represents the average rate of tax for each dollar of taxable income. For example, a single taxpayer with taxable income of $350,000 in 2001 would incur a total tax liability of $115,557. The taxpayer's marginal tax rate is 39.6%, but his average tax rate is 33% ($115,557/$350,000).

The **effective tax rate** is the total tax liability divided by total economic income. **Total economic income** includes all types of economic income that a taxpayer has for the year. Thus, economic income is much broader than taxable income and includes most types of excludible income, such as tax-exempt bond interest, and generally permits business deductions but not personal-type deductions. It should be pointed out that economic income is *not* statutorily defined and experts may disagree on a precise calculation. The basic purpose of calculating the effective tax rate is to provide a broad measure of taxpayers' ability to pay taxes. Accordingly, the effective tax rate mainly is used by tax policymakers to determine the fairness of the income tax system.

EXAMPLE I1-5

▶ Amelia, who is single, has adjusted gross income of $40,000 and economic income of $55,000 in 2001. The difference is attributable to $15,000 of tax-exempt bond interest. If Amelia's taxable income is $30,000, Amelia's total tax is $4,884 [(0.15 × $27,050) + (0.28 × $2,950)]. Her average tax rate is 16.28% ($4,884 ÷ $30,000). Amelia's effective tax rate is 8.89% ($4,884 ÷ $55,000). Amelia's effective tax rate is considerably lower than her average tax rate because of her substantial amount of tax-exempt income. ◀

STOP & THINK

Question: Gwen, a single taxpayer, has seen her income climb to $200,000 in the current year. She wants a tax planner to help her reduce her tax liability. In planning for tax clients, tax professionals almost exclusively use the marginal tax rate in their analysis rather than the average tax rate. Why is the marginal tax rate much more important in the tax planning process than the average tax rate?

Solution: Because tax planning is done at the margin. A single taxpayer who has taxable income of $200,000 has a marginal tax rate of 36% (at 2001 rates), but an average tax rate of 29.84%, computed as follows:

Taxable income		$200,000
Tax on first $136,750 of taxable income		$36,910
Remaining taxable income	$63,250	
Times: Marginal tax rate	× 0.36	22,770
Total tax liability		$59,680

$$\text{Average tax rate} = \frac{\text{Total tax}}{\text{Taxable income}} = \frac{\$59,680}{\$200,000} = 29.84\%$$

If a tax planner could reduce Gwen's taxable income by $10,000, Gwen's tax liability would decrease by $3,600 ($10,000 × 0.36). When the taxpayer wants to know how much she can save through tax planning, the appropriate marginal tax rate yields the answer.

DETERMINATION OF TAXABLE INCOME AND TAX DUE

As will be discussed in later chapters, the federal income taxes imposed on all taxpayers (individuals, corporations, estates, and trusts) are based on the determination of taxable income. In general, taxable income is computed as follows:

Total income (income from whatever source derived)	$xxx
Minus: Exclusions (specifically defined items, such as tax-exempt bond interest)	(xx)
Gross income	$xxx
Minus: Deductions (business expenses and itemized deductions)	(xx)
Exemptions (not applicable for corporations)	(xx)
Taxable income	$xxx
Times: Applicable tax rate	× .xx
Income tax before credits	$xxx
Minus: Tax credits	(xx)
Total tax liability	$xxx
Minus: Prepayments	(xx)
Balance due or refund	$xxx

ADDITIONAL COMMENT

In the determination of tax rates, one should consider the incidence of taxation that involves the issue of who really bears the burden of the tax. If a city raises the real property tax but landlords simply raise rents to pass on the higher taxes to their tenants, the tax burden is shifted. The concept has important implications in determining any kind of average or effective tax rate.

Each different type of taxpayer (individuals, corporations, etc.) computes taxable income in a slightly different manner, but all use the general framework above. Individual taxpayers (Chapter I2) and corporation taxpayers (Chapter I16) are examined in this *Individuals* book (Chapter C3 of the *Comprehensive* edition). Corporations (in more detail), estates, and trusts are examined in *Prentice Hall's Federal Taxation: Corporations, Partnerships, Estates, and Trusts*.

OTHER TYPES OF TAXES

STATE AND LOCAL INCOME AND FRANCHISE TAXES

OBJECTIVE 3

Describe the various types of taxes

In addition to federal income taxes, many states and local jurisdictions impose income taxes on individuals and businesses. These state and local taxes have gradually increased over the years and currently represent a significant source of revenue for state and local governments but also represent a significant tax burden on taxpayers.

State and local income taxes vary greatly in both form and rates.[8] Only seven states do not impose an individual income tax.[9] In most instances, state income tax rates are mildly progressive and are based on an individual's federal adjusted gross income (AGI), with minor adjustments.[10] For example, a typical adjustment to a state income tax return is interest income on federal government bonds, which is subject to tax on the federal return but is generally not subject to state income taxes. Some states also allow a deduction for federal income taxes in the computation of taxable income for state income tax purposes.

States imposing a state income tax generally require the withholding of state income taxes and have established mandatory estimated tax payment procedures. The due date for filing state income tax returns generally coincides with the due date for the federal income tax returns (e.g., the fifteenth day of the fourth month following the close of the tax year for individuals).

ADDITIONAL COMMENT

State income tax rates for individuals have increased significantly in the past twenty years. Thirty-three states now have marginal tax rates of 6% or higher.

---

[8] For a thorough discussion of state and local taxes, see the chapter entitled *Multistate Income Taxation* that accompanies this textbook in electronic form on the Prentice Hall Federal Taxation 2001 webpage at www.prenhall.com/phtax.

[9] These states are Alaska, Florida, Nevada, South Dakota, Texas, Washington, and Wyoming. New Hampshire has an income tax that is levied only on dividend and interest income and Tennessee's income tax applies only to income from stocks and bonds.

[10] See Chapter I2 for a discussion of the AGI computation.

Most states impose a corporate income tax, although in some instances the tax is called a **franchise tax**. Franchise taxes usually are based on a weighted-average formula consisting of net worth, income, and sales.

WEALTH TRANSFER TAXES

U.S. citizens are subject to taxation on certain transfers of property to another person. The tax law provides a unified transfer tax system that imposes a single tax on transfers of property taking place during an individual's lifetime (gifts) and at death (estates). (See the inside back cover of the text for the transfer tax rate schedules.) Formerly, the gift and estate tax laws were separate and distinct. The federal estate tax was initially enacted in 1916. The original gift tax law dates back to 1932. The gift tax was originally imposed to prevent widespread avoidance of the estate tax (e.g., taxpayers could make tax-free gifts of property before their death). Both the gift and estate taxes are wealth transfer taxes levied on the transfer of property and are based on the fair market value (FMV) of the transferred property on the date of the transfer. Below are brief descriptions of the gift tax and estate tax.

> **KEY POINT**
>
> The $10,000 annual exclusion is an important tax-planning tool for wealthy parents who want to transfer assets to their children and thereby minimize their gift and estate taxes. A husband and wife who have three children could transfer a maximum of $60,000 to their children each year without incurring any gift tax.

THE FEDERAL GIFT TAX. The **gift tax** is an excise tax that is imposed on the donor (not the donee) for transfers of property that are considered to be a taxable gift. A gift, generally speaking, is a transfer made gratuitously and with donative intent. However, the gift tax law has expanded the definition to include transfers that are not supported by full and adequate consideration.[11] To arrive at the amount of taxable gifts for the current year, a $10,000 annual exclusion is allowed per donee.[12] In addition, an unlimited marital deduction is allowed for transfers between spouses.[13] The formula for computing the gift tax is as follows:

FMV of all gifts made in the current year			$x,xxx
Minus: Annual donee exclusions ($10,000 per donee)	$xx		
Marital deduction for gifts to spouse	xx		
Charitable contribution deduction	xx		(xxx)
Plus: Taxable gifts for all prior years			xxx
Cumulative taxable gifts (tax base)			$x,xxx
Times: Unified transfer tax rates			× .xx
Tentative tax on gift tax base			$ xxx
Minus: Unified transfer taxes paid in prior years			(xx)
Unified credit			(xx)
Unified transfer tax (gift tax) due in the current year			$ xx

> **ADDITIONAL COMMENT**
>
> The gift tax was enacted to make the estate tax more effective. Without a gift tax, estate taxes could be easily avoided by large gifts made before death.

Note that the gift tax is cumulative over the taxpayer's lifetime (i.e., the tax calculation for the current year includes the taxable gifts made in prior years). The detailed tax rules relating to the gift tax are covered in Chapter C12 in both *Prentice Hall's Federal Taxation: Corporations, Partnerships, Estates, and Trusts* and the *Comprehensive* volume. The following general concepts and rules for the federal gift tax are presented as background material for other chapters of this text dealing with individual taxpayers:

▶ Gifts between spouses are exempted from the gift tax due to the operation of an unlimited marital deduction.

▶ The primary liability for payment of the gift tax is imposed on the **donor**. The donee is contingently liable for payment of the gift tax in the event of nonpayment by the donor.

▶ A donor is permitted a $10,000 annual exclusion for gifts of a present interest to each donee.[14]

---

[11] Sec. 2512(b).
[12] Sec. 2503(b).
[13] Sec. 2523(a).
[14] A gift of a present interest is an interest that is already in existence and the donee is currently entitled to receive the income from the property. A gift of a future interest comes into being at some future date (e.g., property is transferred by gift to a trust in which the donee is not entitled to the income from the property until the donor dies) and is not eligible for the $10,000 annual exclusion.

- Charitable contributions are effectively exempted from the gift tax because an unlimited deduction is allowed.
- The tax basis of the property to the donee is generally the donor's cost. It is the lesser of the donor's cost and the property's FMV on the date of the gift if the property is sold by the donee at a loss. (See Chapter I5 for a discussion of the gift tax basis rules.)
- A unified tax credit equivalent to a $675,000 deduction is available in 2000 and 2001 to offset any gift tax on taxable gifts that exceed the $10,000 annual exclusion.[15] The equivalent deduction increases to $700,000 in 2002 and 2003.

EXAMPLE I1-6

Antonio makes the following gifts in the current year:
- $25,000 cash gift to his wife
- $15,000 contribution to the United Way
- Gift of a personal automobile valued at $25,000 to his adult son
- Gift of a personal computer valued at $4,000 to a friend

The $25,000 gift to his wife is not taxed because of a $10,000 annual exclusion and a $15,000 tax exemption for transfers to spouses (i.e., the marital deduction). The $15,000 contribution to the United Way is also not taxed because of the $10,000 annual exclusion and the $5,000 deduction for charitable contributions. The $25,000 gift Antonio made to his son is reduced by the $10,000 annual exclusion to each donee, leaving a $15,000 taxable gift.[16] The $4,000 gift to the friend is not taxed because of the annual exclusion of up to $10,000 in gifts to a donee in a tax year. Thus, total taxable gifts for the current year subject to the unified transfer tax are $15,000.

STOP & THINK

Question: An important but frequently overlooked aspect of gift taxes is the interaction of gift taxes and income taxes. In many cases, gifts are made *primarily* for income tax purposes. Why would a gift be made for income tax purposes?

Solution: Gifts are frequently made to shift income from one family member to another family member who is in a lower marginal tax bracket. For example, assume Fran and Jan are married, have one 15-year-old son, earn $400,000 per year from their business, and generate $100,000 per year in dividends and interest from a substantial portfolio of stocks and bonds. With such a high level of income, Fran and Jan are in the 39.6% marginal tax bracket. If they make a gift of some of the stocks and bonds to their son, the dividends and interest attributable to the gift are taxed to the son at his marginal tax rate (maybe 15%). If the son's marginal tax rate is lower than 39.6%, the family unit reduces its overall income taxes.

THE FEDERAL ESTATE TAX. The **federal estate tax** is part of the unified transfer tax system that is based on the total property transfers an individual makes both during his or her lifetime and at death.

EXAMPLE I1-7

Amy dies during the current year. The formula for computing the estate tax on Amy's estate is as follows:

---

[15] Before 1998, the equivalent deduction was $600,000. However, the Taxpayer Relief Act of 1997 increased the deduction to $625,000 for 1998, $650,000 for 1999, and gradually increases the deduction to $1,000,000 by 2006. The $675,000 exemption is in the form of a $220,550 tax credit for 2000 and 2001 and the $700,000 exemption is equal to a $229,800 credit in 2002 and 2003 ($211,300 for 1999, $202,050 for 1998, and $192,800 for 1997). This credit also gradually increases until 2006.

[16] This example assumes that the automobile is a gift rather than an obligation of support under state law and also assumes that Antonio's wife does not join with Antonio in electing to treat the gift to the son as having been made by both spouses (a gift-splitting election). In such event, donee exclusions of $20,000 (2 × $10,000) would be available, resulting in a taxable gift of only $5,000.

1-10 Individuals ▼ Chapter 1

TYPICAL MISCONCEPTION

It is sometimes thought that the federal estate tax raises significant amounts of revenue, but it has not been a significant revenue producer since World War II. Only 86,000 estate tax returns were filed in 1996.

Gross estate (FMV of all property owned by the decedent at the date of death)	$xxx,xxx
Minus: Deductions for funeral and administration expenses, debts of the decedent, charitable contributions, and the marital deduction for property transferred to a spouse	(x,xxx)
Taxable estate	$x,xxx
Plus: Taxable gifts made after 1976	xx
Tax base	$x,xxx
Times: Unified transfer tax rate(s)	× .xx
Tentative tax on estate tax base	$ xxx
Minus: Tax credits (e.g., the unified tax credit of $220,550 for 2000)	(xx)
Gift taxes paid after 1976	(xx)
Unified transfer tax (estate tax) due	$xx ◄

ADDITIONAL COMMENT

The unified transfer tax rate schedule contains rates that range from 18% to 55%.

The estate tax rules are discussed in more detail in Chapter C13 in *Prentice Hall's Federal Taxation: Corporations, Partnerships, Estates, and Trusts* and in the *Comprehensive* volume. The following general rules are provided as background material for subsequent chapters of this text dealing with individual taxpayers:

▶ The decedent's property is valued at its FMV on the date of death unless the alternative valuation date (six months after the date of death) is elected. The alternative valuation date may be elected only if the aggregate value of the gross estate decreases during the six-month period following the date of death and the election results in a lower estate tax liability.

▶ The basis of the property received by the estate and by the decedent's heirs is the property's FMV on the date of death (or the alternate valuation date if it is elected).

▶ Property transferred to the decedent's spouse is exempt from the estate tax because of the estate tax marital deduction provision.

EXAMPLE I1-8 ▶ Barry died in 2001, leaving a $1,000,000 gross estate. One-half of the property is transferred to his wife, taxable gifts (after the $10,000 annual exclusion) made after 1976 were $150,000, administrative and funeral expenses are $30,000, and debts of the decedent amount to $170,000. The estate tax due is computed as follows:

Gross estate	$1,000,000
Minus: Marital deduction	(500,000)
Funeral and administrative expenses	(30,000)
Decedent's debts	(170,000)
Taxable estate	$ 300,000
Plus: Taxable gifts made after 1976	150,000
Tax base	$ 450,000
Tentative tax on estate tax base	$ 138,800[a]
Minus: Tax credits (unified tax credit)	(220,550)
Unified transfer tax due	$ —0— ◄

[a] $70,800 + (0.34 × $200,000)

Because of the generous credit and deduction provisions (e.g., the unified tax credit and the unlimited marital deduction), few estates are required to pay estate taxes. As can be seen above, the gross estate of the decedent was $1 million but no estate taxes were due primarily because of the large marital deduction and the unified credit. However, estate taxes rise quickly as is demonstrated below in Example I1-9.

EXAMPLE I1-9 ▶ Assume the same facts for Barry as in Example I1-8 except that Barry's gross estate is $3,000,000 rather than $1,000,000. The estate tax due is computed as follows:

Gross estate	$3,000,000
Minus: Marital deduction	(1,500,000)
Funeral and administrative expenses	(30,000)
Decedent's debts	(170,000)

Taxable estate		$1,300,000
Plus:	Taxable gifts made after 1976	150,000
Tax base		$1,450,000
Tentative tax on estate tax base		$ 534,300
Minus:	Tax credits (unified tax credit)	(220,550)
Unified transfer tax due		$ 313,750 ◀

OTHER TYPES OF TAXES

Although this text focuses primarily on the federal income tax, some mention should be made of the following other types of taxes levied by federal, state, and local governments.

> **ADDITIONAL COMMENT**
> Proposals to decrease reliance on the federal income tax have focused on a value added tax and selective energy taxes. A value added tax is a sales tax levied at each stage of production on the "value added."

▶ **Property taxes** are based on the value of a taxpayer's property, which may include both real estate and personal property. Real estate taxes are a major source of revenue for local governments. In addition, some state and local governments levy a personal property tax on intangibles such as securities and tangible personal property (e.g., the value of a personal automobile).

▶ **Federal excise taxes** and **customs duties** on imported goods have declined in relative importance over the years but remain significant sources of revenue. Federal excise taxes are imposed on alcohol, tobacco, gasoline, telephone usage, production of oil and gas, and many other types of goods. Many state and local governments impose similar excise taxes on goods and services.

> **ADDITIONAL COMMENT**
> Anheuser-Busch Company ran a television commercial in 1990 during the deliberations on the Revenue Reconciliation Act of 1990 that asked viewers to call a toll-free telephone number to register their criticism of an increase in the excise tax on beer. The commercial asked viewers to "can the beer tax."

▶ **Sales taxes** are a major source of revenue for state and local governments. Sales taxes are imposed on retail sales of tangible personal property (e.g., clothing and automobiles). Some states also impose a sales tax on personal services (e.g., accounting and legal fees). Certain items often are exempt from the sales tax levy (e.g., food items or medicines), and the rates vary widely between individual state and local governments. Sales taxes are not deductible for federal income tax purposes unless incurred in a trade or business.

▶ **Employment taxes** include social security (**FICA**) and federal and state unemployment compensation taxes. If an individual is classified as an employee, the FICA tax that is imposed on the employee is comprised of two parts, 6.2% for old-age, survivors, and disability insurance (OASDI) and 1.45% for hospital insurance (HI), for a total of 7.65%. The OASDI portion is imposed on the first $80,400 (2001) of wages, whereas the HI portion has no ceiling. Both of these taxes are imposed on both the employer and employee. If an individual is self-employed, a self-employment tax is imposed at a 15.3% rate (12.4% for OASDI and 2.9% for HI) on the individual's self-employment income, with a ceiling on the OASDI portion of $80,400 (in 2001).[17] Similar to employees, there is no ceiling on the HI portion for self-employed individuals.

> **ADDITIONAL COMMENT**
> Revenue from employment taxes are indeed significant. In 1996, $491 billion in employment taxes were collected representing 36% of all Internal Revenue Service collections.

▶ Employers are required to pay federal and state unemployment taxes to fund the payment of unemployment benefits to former employees. The federal rate is 6.2% on the first $7,000 of wages for each employee in 2001.[18] However, a credit is granted for up to 5.4% of wages for taxes paid to the state government so that the actual amount paid to the federal government may be as low as 0.8%.[19] The amount of tax paid to the state depends on the employer's prior experience with respect to the frequency and amount of unemployment claims. In Kentucky, for example, the highest rate of unemployment tax imposed is 3% and this rate is subsequently adjusted down if the employer has a small number of unemployment claims.

The types of taxes and structural considerations that were previously discussed are summarized in Topic Review I1-1.

---

[17] Self-employed individuals receive an income tax deduction equal to 50% of taxes paid on their self-employment income and this deduction is also allowed to compute the amount of self-employment income (see Secs. 164(f) and 1402(a)(12) and Chapter I14).

[18] Sec. 3301.

[19] Sec. 3302. State unemployment taxes in some states are levied on tax bases above $7,000. For example, the wage base ceiling in North Carolina is $12,500 in 2001.

Topic Review I1-1

Types of Taxes and Tax Structure

TYPE OF TAX	TAX STRUCTURE	TAX BASE
Individuals:		
Federal income tax	Progressive	Gross income from all sources unless specifically excluded by law reduced by deductions and exemptions
State income tax	Progressive	Generally based on AGI for federal income tax purposes with adjustments
Federal gift tax	Progressive	FMV of all taxable gifts made during the tax year
Federal estate tax	Progressive	FMV of property owned at death plus taxable gifts made after 1976
Corporations:		
Federal corporate income tax	Progressive	Gross income from all sources unless specifically excluded by law reduced by deductions
State corporate income tax	Proportional or progressive	Federal corporate taxable income with adjustments
State franchise tax	Proportional	Usually based on a weighted-average formula consisting of net worth, income, and sales
Other Types of Taxes:		
Property taxes	Proportional	FMV of personal or real property
Excise taxes	Proportional	Customs and duties on imported and domestic goods from alcohol to telephone usage
Sales taxes	Proportional	Retail sales of tangible personal property or personal services
FICA and self-employment taxes	Regressive	Based on wages or self-employment income
Unemployment taxes	Regressive	Usually first $7,000 of an employee's wages

CRITERIA FOR A TAX STRUCTURE

OBJECTIVE 4

Discuss what constitutes a "good" tax structure and the objectives of the federal income tax law

Establishing criteria for a "good" tax structure was first attempted in 1776 by economist Adam Smith.[20] Smith's four "canons of taxation"—equity, certainty, convenience, and economy—are still used today when tax policy issues are discussed. Below is a discussion of these criteria and how they relate to income taxes as well as other taxes.

EQUITY

A rather obvious criteria for a good tax is that the tax be equitable or fair to taxpayers. However, equity or fairness is elusive because of the subjectivity of the concept. What one person may conclude is fair in a particular situation may be considered totally unfair by another person. In other words, fairness is relative in nature and is extremely difficult to measure. For example, the deductibility of mortgage interest on a taxpayer's home certainly seems to be a fair provision for taxpayers. However, for taxpayers who do not own a home but live in a rental apartment, the deductibility of mortgage interest may not be considered as fair because the renter cannot deduct any portion of the rent paid. In other types of situations, the federal tax law includes various measures to ensure that taxpayers are treated fairly. For example, a foreign tax credit is available to minimize the double taxation that would otherwise occur when U.S. taxpayers earn income in a foreign coun-

ADDITIONAL COMMENT

The Revenue Reconciliation Act of 1993 followed through on President Clinton's campaign promise to increase taxes on high-income taxpayers to correct perceived inequities resulting from the lowering of the top tax rates in the Tax Reform Act of 1986.

---

[20] Adam Smith, *The Wealth of Nations* (New York: Random House, Modern Library, 1937), pp. 777–779.

try that is taxed by both the United States and the country in which it is earned. (See the glossary at the end of this volume for a definition of tax credits and Chapter I14 for a discussion of the foreign tax credit.) Two aspects of equity are commonly discussed in the tax policy literature, **horizontal equity** and **vertical equity**. Horizontal equity refers to the notion that similarly situated taxpayers should be treated equally. Thus, two taxpayers who each have income of $50,000 should both pay the same amount of tax. Vertical equity, on the other hand, implies that taxpayers who are not similarly situated should be treated differently. Thus, if Taxpayer A has income of $50,000 and Taxpayer B has income of $20,000, Taxpayers A and B should not pay the same amount of income tax. Vertical equity provides that the incidence of taxation should be borne by those who have the **ability to pay** the tax, based on income or wealth. The progressive rate structure is founded on the vertical equity premise.

CERTAINTY

> **KEY POINT**
>
> Using retroactive dates for changes in the tax law does not help to accomplish the objective of certainty. For example, the effective date of the increase in the top tax rate was made retroactive to January 1, 1993, in tax legislation signed by President Clinton on August 19, 1993. This retroactive tax increase was unpopular with high-income taxpayers.

A certain tax (1) ensures a stable source of government operating revenues, and (2) provides taxpayers with some degree of certainty concerning the amount of their annual tax liability. A tax that is simple to understand and administer provides certainty for taxpayers. For many years, our income tax laws have been criticized as being overly complex and difficult to administer. Consider the remarks of a noted tax authority at a conference on federal income tax simplification:

> Tax advisers—at least some tax advisers—are saying that the income tax system is not working. They are saying that they don't know what the law provides, that the IRS does not know what the law provides, that taxpayers are not abiding by the law they don't know.[21]

While the above statement is over 20 years old, it is certainly still viable today. This uncertainty in the tax law causes frequent disputes between taxpayers and the IRS and has resulted in extensive litigation.

> **ADDITIONAL COMMENT**
>
> Humorist Jim Boren has proposed a constitutional amendment that would require any retroactive tax increases to be followed by retroactive elections for president, vice president and all members of Congress.

The federal tax system has made some attempts to provide certainty for taxpayers. For example, the IRS issues advance rulings to taxpayers, which provides some assurance concerning the tax consequences of a proposed transaction for the taxpayer who requests the ruling. The taxpayer may rely on the ruling if the transaction is completed in accordance with the terms of the ruling request. For example, if a merger of two corporations is being considered, the transaction can be structured so that the shareholders and the corporations do not recognize gain or loss. If a favorable ruling is received and the transaction is completed as planned, the IRS cannot later assert that the merger does not qualify for tax-free treatment.

CONVENIENCE

A tax law should be easily assessed, collected, and administered. Taxpayers should not be overly burdened with the maintenance of records and compliance considerations (preparation of their tax returns, payment of their taxes, and so on). One of the reasons that the sales tax is such a popular form of tax for state and local governments is that it is convenient for taxpayers to pay and for the government to collect. The consumer need not complete a tax return or keep detailed records.

ECONOMY

> **ADDITIONAL COMMENT**
>
> For tax year 1991, 49.5% of all individual tax returns were prepared by paid tax-return preparers. For that same year, the IRS received 34,950,000 telephone inquiries.

An economical tax structure should require only minimal compliance and administrative costs. The IRS collection costs, amounting to less than 0.5% of revenues, are minimal relative to the total collections of revenues from the federal income tax. Estimates of taxpayer compliance costs are less certain. One indicator of total compliance costs for taxpayers is the demand for tax professionals. Tax practice has been and continues to be one of the fastest growing areas in public accounting firms. Most large corporations also

---

[21] Sidney L. Roberts, "The Viewpoint of the Tax Adviser: An Overview of Simplification," *Tax Adviser*, January 1979, p. 32.

maintain sizable tax departments that engage in tax research, compliance, and planning activities. In addition, many commercial tax return preparer services are available to assist taxpayers who have relatively uncomplicated tax returns.

Fortune 500 companies spend over $1 billion annually complying with the tax laws, according to a study commissioned by the IRS.[22] The survey found that about 55% of the cost of compliance goes to pay in-house staff and about 16% goes to outside firms. The federal income tax system accounts for about 70% of this cost. State and local income tax compliance accounts for the remaining 30%. The companies surveyed said that the largest share of their tax compliance costs was for filing tax returns.

A more difficult question is whether the tax structure is economical in terms of taxpayer compliance. The issues of tax avoidance and tax evasion are becoming increasingly more important. The General Accounting Office (GAO) reported that two-thirds of tax returns are out of compliance, resulting in net income being underreported by 25 percent.[23]

OBJECTIVES OF THE FEDERAL INCOME TAX LAW

The primary objective of the federal income tax law is to raise revenues for government operations. In recent years, the federal government has broadened its use of the tax laws to accomplish various economic and social policy objectives.

ECONOMIC OBJECTIVES

The federal income tax law is used as a fiscal policy tool to stimulate private investment, reduce unemployment, and mitigate the effects of inflation on the economy. Consider the following example: Tax credits for businesses operating in distressed urban and rural areas (empowerment zones) are allowed to provide economic revitalization of such areas. This is a clear example of using the federal income tax law to stimulate private investment in specific areas.

Many items in the tax law are adjusted for inflation by using the consumer price index, including the tax brackets, personal and dependency exemptions, and standard deduction amounts. These inflation adjustments provide relief for individual taxpayers who would otherwise be subject to increased taxes due to the effects of inflation. (See Chapter 12 for a discussion of the tax computation for individuals.)

ENCOURAGEMENT OF CERTAIN ACTIVITIES AND INDUSTRIES

ADDITIONAL COMMENT

Among the provisions in the tax law that are designed to enhance the level of health care are the deductibility of medical expenses, deductibility of charitable contributions to hospitals, and exclusion of fringe benefits provided by employers for medical insurance premiums and medical care.

The federal income tax law also attempts to stimulate and encourage certain activities, specialized industries, and small businesses. One such example is the encouragement of research activities by permitting an immediate write-off of expenses and a special tax credit for increasing research and experimental costs. Special incentives are also provided to the oil and gas industry through percentage depletion allowances and an election to deduct intangible drilling costs.

Certain favorable tax provisions are provided for small businesses, including reduced corporate tax rates of 15% on the first $50,000 of taxable income and 25% for the next $25,000 of taxable income. Favorable ordinary loss (instead of capital loss) deductions are granted to individual investors who sell their small business corporation stock at a loss, provided that certain requirements are met.[24] In addition, noncorporate investors may exclude up to 50% of the gain realized from the disposition of qualified small business stock issued after August 10, 1993 if the stock is held for more than five years.[25]

---

[22] Joel Slemrod and Marsha Blumenthal, "Measuring Taxpayer Burden and Attitudes for Large Corporations: Report to the Coordinated Examination Program of the IRS," *Tax Notes*, December 20, 1993, p. 1422.

[23] News Report. "Compliance Said to Be Poor Among Sole Proprietorships," *Tax Notes*, December 12, 1994, p. 1328.

[24] Sec. 1244.

[25] Sec. 1202.

ADDITIONAL COMMENT
Deductible contributions made by self-employed individuals to their retirement plan (Keogh plans) totaled $8.8 billion in 1996. Charitable deductions totaled over $84.2 billion that same year.

SOCIAL OBJECTIVES

The tax law attempts to encourage or discourage certain socially desirable or undersirable activities. For example:

▶ Special tax-favored pension and profit-sharing plans have been created for employees and self-employed individuals to supplement the social security retirement system.

▶ Charitable contributions are deductible to encourage individuals to contribute to charitable organizations.

▶ The claiming of a deduction for illegal bribes, fines, and penalties has been prohibited to discourage activities that are contrary to public policy.

EXAMPLE I1-10 ▶ Able Corporation establishes a qualified pension plan for its employees whereby it makes all of the annual contributions to the plan. Able's contributions to the pension trust are currently deductible and not includible in the employee's gross income until the pension payments are distributed during their retirement years. Earnings on the contributed funds also are nontaxable until such amounts are distributed to the employees. ◀

EXAMPLE I1-11 ▶ Anita contributes $10,000 annually to her church, which is a qualified charitable organization. Anita's marginal tax rate is 28%. Her after-tax cost of contributing to the church is only $7,200 [$10,000 − (0.28 × $10,000)]. ◀

EXAMPLE I1-12 ▶ Ace Trucking Company incurs $10,000 in fines imposed by local and state governments for overloading its trucks during the current tax year. The fines are not deductible because the activity is contrary to public policy. ◀

The tax law objectives previously discussed are highlighted in Topic Review I1-2.

ENTITIES IN THE FEDERAL INCOME TAX SYSTEM

The federal income tax law levies taxes on taxpayers. However, not all entities that file income tax returns pay income taxes. For example, a partnership is required to file a tax return but does not pay any income tax because the income (or loss) of the partnership is allocated to the partners and they report the income or loss on their tax returns. Therefore, the various entities in the federal income tax system may be classified into two general categories, *taxpaying entities* and *flow-through entities*.[26] Taxpaying entities generally are required to pay income taxes on their taxable income. Flow-through entities, on the other hand, generally do not directly pay income taxes but merely pass the income on to a taxpaying entity. The major entities in each category are as follows:

Taxpaying Entities	*Flow-through Entities*
Individuals	Sole proprietorship
C corporations (regular corporations)	Partnershipss
	S corporations
	Limited Liability Company (LLC) or
	Limited Liability Partnership (LLP)
	Trusts

TAXPAYING ENTITIES

INDIVIDUALS. Individual taxpayers are the principal taxpaying entities in the federal income tax system. Since the taxation of individuals is the focus of this textbook, we will not discuss individuals here.

---

[26] Some entities have characteristics of both categories of entities, including certain types of trusts and S corporations.

Topic Review I1-2

Objectives of the Tax Law

Objective	Example
Stimulate investment	Provide a tax credit for the purchase of business equipment
Prevent taxpayers from paying a higher percentage of their income in personal income taxes due to inflation (bracket creep)	Index the tax rates, standard deduction, and personal and dependency exemptions for inflation
Encourage research activities that will in turn strengthen the competitiveness of U.S. companies	Allow research expenditures to be written off in the year incurred and offer a tax credit for increasing research and experimental costs
Encourage venture capital for small businesses	Reduce corporate income tax rates on the first $75,000 of taxable income. Allow businesses to immediately expense $20,000 (2000) of certain depreciable business assets acquired each year.
Encourage social objectives	Provide a tax deduction for charitable contributions; provide favorable tax treatment for contributions to qualified pension plans

C CORPORATIONS. C corporations, many times referred to as regular corporations, are entities that are subject to so-called double taxation. Double taxation results from the corporation paying income tax on its taxable income and shareholders paying income tax on any dividends received from the corporation. Thus, the same corporate income is subjected to taxation twice—once at the corporate level and second at the shareholder level. For many years, much tax planning has been directed at trying to so arrange the tax affairs of a C coporation to avoid double taxation.

A C corporation is required to file annually a tax return using Form 1120. The corporation's taxable income is subject to taxation at graduated tax rates ranging from 15% to 35% (see the inside back cover for corporation income tax rates). Corporation's must report most of its income for income tax purposes but also are allowed to deduct virtually all ordinary and necessary expenses to arrive at taxable income.

EXAMPLE I1-13 ▶ During the current year, Crimson Corporation generated gross income of $1,500,000 and had ordinary and necessary deductions of $900,000, resulting in taxable income of $600,000. Crimson would be subject to corporation income taxes of $204,000 (see corporation tax rate schedule). Crimson also paid $200,000 of dividends to shareholders during the current year. The dividends are not deductible by Crimson and are taxable to the shareholders, possibly at the highest individual rate of 39.6%. The double taxation of the $600,000 is an onerous amount of tax. ◀

EXAMPLE I1-14 ▶ If, in Example I1-13, the shareholders are also employees of the Crimson Corporation, the double taxation could be avoided if the $200,000 was paid in the form of salaries rather than dividends. In this case, the $200,000 would be deductible by the corporation resulting in taxable income of $400,0000 and tax of $136,000. Crimson would realize $68,000 of tax savings. The $200,000 would still be taxable to the shareholders. Since this technique seemingly is so simple to save significant income taxes, the tax law contains a number of tax rules that may reclassify salaries to employee/shareholders as dividends. See Chapter I16 of this text or Chapters C2-6 of the *Comprehensive* volume. ◀

FLOW-THROUGH ENTITIES

SOLE PROPRIETORSHIP. A sole proprietorship is the simplest form of business entity as there are no formal requirements to form such an entity. The net income earned by the proprietor is reported on Schedule C of Form 1040. Thus, the income of the sole proprietorship merely flows to the proprietor's individual tax return. The net income of the sole proprietorship is subject to income tax only once (at the individual level) but is also subject to self-employment tax (Social security and Medicare taxes).

PARTNERSHIPS. A partnership is the classic flow-through entity in that the income or loss of the partnership is allocated to the partners who report the income and pay tax on their tax returns. The partnership is really just a reporting entity as no income tax is paid by the partnership. Thus, the partnership form of the organization is not subject to double taxation. Partnerships report the income and deductions on Form 1065. However, the fact that partnerships are subject to unlimited liability is a major drawback of the partnership form.

EXAMPLE I1-15 ▶ Billy and Bob form the Billy-Bob Partnership as equal partners. During the current year, Billy-Bob earns net income of $300,000. The partnership is not subject to income taxation on the $300,000. On Form 1065, the partnership allocates $150,000 each to Billy and Bob, who report this amount on their individual income tax returns. ◀

S CORPORATIONS. S corporations (often referred to as Subchapter S corporations) are actual corporations pursuant to state law. The corporation is classified as an S corporation under the tax law if an election is made to the Internal Revenue Service. Basically, an S corporation is treated like a partnership for federal income tax purposes. Thus, the income or loss of the S corporation is allocated to the shareholders and reported on their individual tax returns. The corporation itself is not subject to tax. S corporations must file Form 1120S. While S corporations and partnerships appear to be nearly identical for federal income tax purposes, there are some significant differences. These differences are discussed later in this textbook as well as the other Prentice Hall textbooks.

LLC/LLP. Limited liability companies (LLCs) are the newest type of entity and are extremely popular as a form of organization. Basically, an LLC is a legal entity under state law that provides limited liability to its owners. Owners of an LLC are referred to as members. The principal tax advantage of LLCs is that they generally are treated as partnerships for tax purposes. Thus, the popularity of LLC's can be attributed to the fact that the members have limited liability and are only subject to a single level of taxation. Limited liability partnerships (LLPs) are slightly different than LLCs in that limited liability is not provided to a partner who commits an act of negligence or misconduct. However, limited liability is provided to all the other partners. LLP's are frequently used by professional service partnerships, such as public accounting firms. If an LLC or LLP is classified as a partnership, it files a Form 1065.

TRUSTS. Trusts are somewhat of a hybrid entity in that they may either be a taxpaying entity or flow-through entity. Also, there are a number of different types of trusts, so the discussion here is very general in nature. Trusts typically are subject to income taxation on all of its net income that is *not* distributed to the beneficiaries. The portion of net income that is distributed to beneficiaries is taxed to the beneficiaries. One drawback to the use of trusts is that the income tax rates are extremely progressive, reaching the 39.6% bracket when the taxable income of the trust reaches $8,650 in 2000. Trusts use Form 1041 to file its tax information.

EXAMPLE I1-16 ▶ Ben establishes a trust for the benefit of his daughter. The principal amount of the trust is $500,000 and is projected to earn approximately 10% per year. In the current year, the trust earned $50,000 of investment income and had $5,000 of expenses. If the trust did not make any distributions during the year to the daughter, the entire $45,000 (less a small exemption) would be subject to income taxation to the trust. Much of the taxable income would be subject to taxation of the 39.6% rate. Alternatively, if the trust distributed the entire $45,000 to the daughter, she would report the $45,000 on her individual tax return. Assuming she does not have significant other income, she would most likely be in the 28% marginal tax bracket. The trust's taxable income would be zero and would have no income tax liability. ◀

TAX LAW SOURCES

OBJECTIVE 5

Identify the various tax law sources and understand their implications for tax practice

The solution to any tax question may only be resolved by reference to tax law sources (also referred to as tax law authority). Tax law sources are generated from all three branches of the federal government, i.e., legislative, executive, and judicial. The principal sources of tax law are as follows:

Branch	Tax Law Source
Legislative	Internal Revenue Code
	Congressional Committee Reports
Executive (Administrative)	Income Tax Regulations
	Revenue Rulings
	Revenue Procedures
	Letter Rulings
Judicial	Court Decisions

ADDITIONAL COMMENT

Knowledge of tax law sources could be considered the most important topic in this book. It is similar to the old Chinese proverb that states that if you give a person a fish you have fed him for one day, but if you teach a person how to fish you have fed him for the rest of his life. By analogy, if a person has a knowledge of the tax law sources, he or she should be able to locate the answers to tax questions throughout his or her career.

A thorough knowledge of the various sources above as well as the relative weights attached to each source is vital to tax professionals. Because of the vast volume of tax law sources, the ability to "find the answer" to a tax question is of fundamental importance. In addition, the evaluation of the weight (or importance) of different sources of authority is also crucial in arriving at a proper conclusion. For example, a decision of the U.S. Supreme Court on a tax matter would certainly carry more weight than a Revenue Ruling issued by the Internal Revenue Service.

Clearly, the most authoritative source of tax law is the Internal Revenue Code, which is the tax law passed by Congress. However, Congress is not capable of anticipating every type of transaction that taxpayers might engage, so most of the statutes in the Code contain very general language. Because of the general language contained in the Code, both administrative and judicial interpretations are necessary to apply the tax law to specific situations and transactions. Thus, the regulations and rulings of the IRS and the decisions of the courts are an integral part of the federal income tax law. For a detailed discussion of tax law sources, see Chapter I15 (Chapter C1 of the *Comprehensive* edition). Topic Review I1-3 provides an overview of the tax law sources.

ENACTMENT OF A TAX LAW

OBJECTIVE 6

Describe the legislative process for the enactment of the tax law

Under the U.S. Constitution, the House of Representatives is responsible for initiating new tax legislation. However, tax bills may also originate in the Senate as riders to nontax legislative proposals. Often, major tax proposals are initiated by the President and accompanied by a Treasury Department study or proposal, and then introduced into Congress by one or more representatives from the President's political party.

STEPS IN THE LEGISLATIVE PROCESS

ADDITIONAL COMMENT

In 2000, the chairman of the House Ways and Means Committee was Rep. William Archer of Texas, and the chairman of the Senate Finance Committee was Sen. William Roth of Delaware.

The specific steps in the legislative process are discussed below and are summarized in Table I1-2. These steps typically include:

1. A tax bill is introduced in the House of Representatives and is referred to the House Ways and Means Committee.
2. The proposal is considered by the House Ways and Means Committee, and public hearings are held. Testimony may be given by members of professional groups such as the American Institute of CPAs and the American Bar Association and from various special-interest groups.
3. The tax bill is voted on by the House Ways and Means Committee and, if approved, is forwarded to the House of Representatives for a vote. Amendments to the bill from individual members of the House of Representatives are generally not allowed.

Topic Review I1-3

Tax Law Sources

SOURCE	KEY POINTS	WEIGHT OF AUTHORITY
LEGISLATIVE Internal Revenue Code	Contains provisions governing income, estate and gift, employment, alcohol, tobacco, and excise taxes.	Serves as the highest legislative authority for tax research, planning, and compliance activities.
ADMINISTRATIVE Treasury Regulations	Represents interpretations of the tax code by the Secretary of the Treasury. Regulations may be initially issued in proposed, temporary, and final form and are interpretative or legislative.	Legislative regulations have a higher degree of authority than interpretative regulations. Proposed regulations do not have authoritative weight.
IRS Rulings	The IRS issues Revenue Rulings (letter rulings or published rulings), Revenue Procedures, Information Releases, and Technical Advice Memoranda.	These pronouncements reflect the IRS's interpretation of the law and do not have the same level of scope and authority as Treasury Regulations.
JUDICIAL Judicial doctrines	Judicial doctrines are concepts that have evolved from Supreme Court cases that are used by the courts to decide tax issues. Examples include substance over form, tax benefit rule, and constructive receipt.	Judicial doctrines that evolve from Supreme Court cases have substantial weight of authority because a finding authority because a finding the force and effect of law.
Judicial interpretations	Tax cases are initially considered by a trial court (i.e., the Tax Court, a Federal district court, or the U.S. Court of Federal Claims). Either the taxpayer or the IRS may appeal to an appeals court. A final appeal is to the U.S. Supreme Court.	A trial court must abide by the precedents set by the court of appeals of the same jurisdiction. An appeals court is not required to follow the decisions of another court of appeals. A Supreme Court decision must be followed by the IRS, taxpayers, and the lower courts.

▼ TABLE I1-2
Steps in the Legislative Process

1. Treasury studies prepared on needed tax reform
2. President makes proposals to Congress
3. House Ways and Means Committee prepares House bill
4. Approval of House bill by the House of Representatives
5. Senate Finance Committee prepares Senate bill
6. Approval of Senate bill by the Senate
7. Compromise bill approved by a Joint Conference Committee
8. Approval of Joint Conference Committee bill by both the House and Senate
9. Approval or veto of legislation by the President
10. New tax law and amendments incorporated into the Code

4. If passed by the House, the bill is forwarded to the Senate for consideration by the Senate Finance Committee, and public hearings are held.
5. The tax bill approved by the Senate Finance Committee may be substantially different from the House of Representatives' version.
6. The Senate Finance Committee reports the Senate bill to the Senate for consideration. The Senate generally permits amendments (e.g., new provisions) to be offered on the Senate floor.
7. If approved by the Senate, both the Senate and House bills are sent to a Joint Conference Committee consisting of an equal number of members from the Senate and the House of Representatives.
8. The Senate and House bills are reconciled in the Joint Conference Committee. This process of reconciliation generally involves substantial compromise if the provisions of both bills are different. A final bill is then resubmitted to the House and Senate for approval.
9. If the Joint Conference Committee bill is approved by the House and Senate, it is sent to the President for approval or veto.
10. A presidential veto may be overturned if a two-thirds majority vote is obtained in both the House and Senate.
11. Committee reports are prepared by the staffs of the House Ways and Means Committee, the Senate Finance Committee, and the Joint Conference Committee as the bill progresses through Congress. These reports help to explain the new law before the Treasury Department drafts regulations on the tax law changes as well as to explain the intent of Congress for passing the new law.

ADDITIONAL COMMENT

The corridors near Congress's tax-writing rooms are called "Gucci Gulch," so named for the designer clothing worn by many of the lobbyists who congregate there when a tax bill is being considered.

HISTORICAL NOTE

The only practicing CPA ever elected to the U.S. Congress is Joe Dio Guardi. He was elected in 1984 from Westchester County, New York.

ADMINISTRATION OF THE TAX LAW AND TAX PRACTICE ISSUES

ORGANIZATION OF THE INTERNAL REVENUE SERVICE

The IRS is the branch of the Treasury Department that is responsible for administering the federal tax law. It is organized on a national, regional, district, and service center basis. The responsibilities and functions of the various administrative branches include the following:

▶ The Commissioner of Internal Revenue, appointed by the President, is the chief officer of the IRS. This individual is supported by the Chief Counsel's office, which is responsible for preparing the government's case for litigation of tax disputes.

▶ The National Office includes a deputy commissioner, a series of assistants to the commissioner, a chief inspector, and a chief counsel. A significant responsibility of the National Office is to process ruling requests and to prepare revenue procedures that assist taxpayers with compliance matters.

▶ Regional commissioners in the four IRS regions are responsible for the settlement of administrative appeals for disputed tax deficiencies.

▶ District directors supervise the performance of IRS audits and collection of delinquent taxes in 33 districts.

▶ Ten service centers perform tax return processing work. They also select tax returns for audit.

In 1998, the IRS Restructuring and Reform Act of 1998 (Act) was enacted with a major objective of reforming the manner in which the IRS administers the tax system. The taxpaying public has been increasingly critical of the IRS, especially in the allegedly insensitive and strong-arm tactics used against taxpayers. Therefore, the Act places a greater emphasis on serving the public and meeting taxpayer needs. While the Act mandates substantial organizational and operational changes to the IRS, only time will tell if this legislation will be successful. Details of the Act are outside the scope of this textbook.

OBJECTIVE 7

Describe the administrative procedures under the tax law

ADDITIONAL COMMENT

A survey of members of the American Institute of CPAs found that more than half of the 1,036 members who responded had an unfavorable opinion of the IRS, unchanged from a survey of three years prior. However, the accountants gave the IRS good marks for courtesy and a willingness to solve problems.

ENFORCEMENT PROCEDURES

All tax returns are initially checked for mathematical accuracy and items that are clearly erroneous. The Form W-2 amounts (e.g., wages, and so on), Form 1099 information return amounts (e.g., relating to dividend and interest payments, and so on) and other forms filed with the IRS are checked against the amounts reported on the tax return. If differences are noted, the IRS Center merely sends the taxpayer a bill for the corrected amount of tax and a statement of the differences. In some instances, the difference is due to a classification error by the IRS, and the additional assessment can be resolved by written correspondence. A refund check may be sent to the taxpayer if an overpayment of tax has been made.

> **EXAMPLE I1-17**
>
> **ADDITIONAL COMMENT**
> Individuals may call 800-366-4484 to report misconduct of IRS employees.

Bart is an author of books and properly reports royalties on Schedule C (Profit or Loss from Business). The IRS computer matching of the Form 1099 information returns from the publishing companies incorrectly assumes that the royalties should be reported on Schedule E (Supplemental Income and Loss). If the IRS sends the taxpayer a statement of the difference and an adjusted tax bill, this matter (including the abatement of added tax, interest, and penalties) should be resolved by correspondence with the IRS.

SELECTION OF RETURNS FOR AUDIT

> **ADDITIONAL COMMENT**
> A special task force has recommended that the percentage of returns audited be increased to 2.5%. Many individuals feel that the probability of being audited is so low as to be disregarded.

The U.S. tax system is based on self-assessment and voluntary compliance. However, enforcement by the IRS is essential to maintain the integrity of the tax system. The IRS uses both computers and experienced personnel to select returns for examination. With respect to the use of the computer, a **Discriminant Function System (DIF)** is used to classify returns to be selected for audit. The DIF system generates a "score" for a return based on the potential for the return to generate additional tax revenue. After returns are scored under the DIF system, the returns are manually screened by experienced IRS personnel who decide which returns warrant further examination. In the aggregate, less than 1% of all individual returns are selected for examination each year. Some examples of situations where individuals are more likely to be audited include the following:

- Investments and trade or business expenses that produce significant tax losses
- Itemized deductions exceeding an average amount for the person's income level
- Filing of a refund claim by a taxpayer who has been previously audited, where substantial tax deficiencies have been assessed
- Individuals who are self-employed with substantial business income or income from a profession (e.g., a medical doctor)

> **ETHICAL POINT**
> A CPA should not recommend a position to a client that exploits the IRS audit selection process.

AUDIT PROCEDURES. Audits of most individuals are handled through an **office audit procedure** in an office of the IRS. In most cases, an individual is asked to substantiate a particular deduction, credit, or income item (e.g., charitable contributions that appear to be excessive). The office audit procedure does not involve a complete audit of all items on the return.

> **EXAMPLE I1-18**

Brad obtains a divorce during the current year and reports a $30,000 deduction for alimony. The IRS may conduct an office audit to ascertain whether the amount is properly deductible as alimony and does not represent a disguised property settlement to Brad's ex-wife. Brad may be asked to submit verification (e.g., a property settlement agreement between the spouses that designates the payments as alimony).

> **KEY POINT**
> A taxpayer may appear on his or her own behalf before the IRS during an audit. An attorney or CPA in good standing is authorized to practice before the IRS upon the filing of a written statement that he or she is currently so qualified and is authorized to represent the taxpayer.

A **field audit procedure** often is used for corporations and individuals engaged in a trade or business. A field audit generally is broader in scope than the office audit (e.g., several items on the tax return may be reviewed). A field audit usually is conducted at the taxpayer's place of business or the office of his or her tax advisor.

Most large corporations are subject to annual audits. The year under audit may be several years prior to the current year because the corporation often will waive the statute of limitations pending the resolution of disputed issues.

STATUTE OF LIMITATIONS

Most taxpayers feel a sense of relief after they have prepared their income tax return and have mailed it to the IRS. However, the filing of the tax return is not necessarily the end of the story for that particular taxable year. It is possible, of course, that the IRS may select their tax return for audit after the return has been initially processed or a taxpayer may have filed an amended return to correct an error or omission.

Both the IRS and taxpayers can make corrections to a return after it has been originally filed. Fortunately, both only have a limited time period in which to make such corrections. This time period is called the **statute of limitations** and prevents either the taxpayer or the IRS from changing a filed tax return after the time period has expired. The general rule for the statute of limitations is three years from the later of the date the tax return was actually filed or its due date.[27] However, a six-year statute of limitations applies if the taxpayer omits items of gross income that in total exceed 25% of the gross income reported on the return.[28] The statute of limitations remains open indefinitely if a fraudulent return is filed or if no return is filed.[29]

> **REAL-WORLD EXAMPLE**
> Based on an IRS audit, the Mustang Ranch, Nevada's most famous legal bordello, was assessed some $13 million in taxes. When the amount owed could not be paid, the IRS sold the property to recoup the taxes.

EXAMPLE I1-19 ▶ Betty, a calendar-year taxpayer, is audited by the IRS in February 2001 for the tax year 1998. During the course of the audit, the IRS proposes additional tax for 1998 because Betty failed to substantiate certain travel and entertainment expense deductions. During the course of the audit, the IRS discovers that Betty failed to file a tax return for 1996, and in 1997 an item of gross income amounting to $26,000 was not reported. Gross income reported on the 1997 return was $72,000. Assuming Betty's 1998 return was filed on or before its due date (April 15, 1999), the IRS may assess a deficiency for 1998 because the three-year statute of limitations will not expire until April 15, 2002. A deficiency also may be assessed for the 1997 return because a six-year statute of limitations applies since the omission is more than 25% of the gross income reported on the return. A deficiency also may be assessed for 1996 as there is no statute of limitations for fraud. ◀

INTEREST

Interest accrues on both assessments of additional tax due and on refunds that the taxpayer receives from the government.[30] No interest is paid on a tax refund if the amount is refunded by the IRS within 45 days of the day prescribed for filing the return (e.g., April 15) determined without regard to extensions.[31] If a return is filed after the filing date, no interest is paid if the refund is made within 45 days of the date the return was filed.

> **ADDITIONAL COMMENT**
> More than 150 penalties can be imposed on taxpayers. In fact, applying the penalties has become so complicated that the IRS is currently considering ways to consolidate and simplify them.

EXAMPLE I1-20 ▶ Beverly, a calendar-year taxpayer, files her 2000 tax return on February 1, 2001, and requests a $500 refund. No interest accrues on the refund amount if the IRS sends the refund check to Beverly within 45 days of the due date (i.e., April 15, 2001). ◀

PENALTIES

Various nondeductible penalties are imposed on the net tax due for failure to comply, including

▶ A penalty of 5% per month (or fraction thereof) subject to a maximum of 25% for failure to file a tax return[32]

▶ A penalty of 0.5% per month (or fraction thereof) up to a maximum of 25% for failure to pay the tax that is due[33]

> **ADDITIONAL COMMENT**
> In addition to the penalties listed on this page, the government also assesses penalties for civil fraud and criminal fraud. Criminal fraud carries a maximum penalty of $100,000, a prison sentence of up to five years, or both.

---

[27] Secs. 6501(a) and (b)(1). Similar rules apply to claims for a refund filed by the taxpayer. Section 6511(a) requires that a refund claim be filed within three years of the date the return was filed or within two years of the date the tax was paid, whichever is later.

[28] Sec. 6501(e). See also *Stephen G. Colestock*, 102 T.C. 380 (1994), where the Tax Court ruled that the extended six-year limitation period applied to a married couple's entire tax liability for the tax year at issue, not just to items that constituted substantial omissions of gross income. Thus, the IRS was able to assert an increased deficiency and additional penalties attributable to a disallowed depreciation deduction.

[29] Sec. 6501(c).

[30] Sec. 6621(a). The rate is adjusted four times a year by the Treasury Department based on the current interest rate for short-term federal obligations. The interest rate individual taxpayers must pay to the IRS on underpayments of tax is the federal short-term rate plus three percentage points. The interest rate paid to taxpayers on overpayments of tax is the federal short-term rate plus two percentage points. The penalty assessed may be very small in some instances even though the taxpayer owes a large tax bill for the year because penalties are imposed on the net tax due.

[31] Sec. 6611(e).

[32] Sec. 6651(a)(1). The percentages are increased to 15% per month (or fraction thereof) up to a maximum of 75% if the penalty is for fraudulent failure to file under Sec. 6651(f).

- An accuracy-related penalty of 20% of the underpayment for items such as negligence or disregard of rules or regulations, any substantial understatement of income tax, or any substantial misstatement of valuation.[34]
- A 75% penalty for fraud[35]
- A penalty based on the current interest rate for underpayment of estimated taxes[36]

ADMINISTRATIVE APPEAL PROCEDURES

> **ADDITIONAL COMMENT**
> Pete Rose, major league baseball's all-time hit leader, was sent to prison in 1990 for income tax evasion.

If an IRS agent issues a deficiency assessment, the taxpayer may make an appeal to the IRS Appeals Division. Some disputes involve a gray area (e.g., a situation where some courts have held for the IRS whereas other courts have held for the taxpayer on facts that are similar to the disputed issue). In such a case, the taxpayer may be able to negotiate a compromise settlement (e.g., a percentage of the disputed tax amount plus interest and penalties) with the Appeals Division based on the "hazards of litigation" (i.e., the probability of winning or losing the case if it is litigated).

COMPONENTS OF A TAX PRACTICE

> **OBJECTIVE 8**
> Describe the components of a tax practice and understand the basic tax research process and computer applications

Tax practice is a rapidly growing field that provides substantial opportunities for tax specialists in public accounting, law, and industry. The tasks performed by a tax professional may range from the preparation of a simple Form 1040 for an individual to the conduct of tax research and planning for highly complex business situations. Tax practice consists of the following activities:

- Tax compliance and procedure (i.e., tax return preparation and representation of a client in administrative proceedings before the IRS)
- Tax research
- Tax planning and consulting
- Financial planning

TAX COMPLIANCE AND PROCEDURE

> **TYPICAL MISCONCEPTION**
> Many people believe that a tax practitioner should serve in the capacity of a neutral, unbiased expert. They tend to forget that tax practitioners are being paid to represent their clients' interests. A tax practitioner may sometimes recommend a position that is defensible, but where the weight of authority is on the side of the IRS.

Preparation of tax returns is a significant component of tax practice. Tax practitioners often prepare federal, state, and local tax returns for individuals, corporations, estates, trusts, and so on. In larger corporations, the tax return preparation (i.e., compliance) function usually is performed by a company's internal tax department staff. In such a case, a CPA or other tax practitioner may assist the client with the tax research and planning aspects of their tax practice, and may even review their return before it is filed.

An important part of tax practice consists of assisting the client in negotiations with the IRS. If a client is audited, the practitioner acts as the client's representative in discussions with the IRS agent. If a tax deficiency is assessed, the practitioner assists the client if an administrative appeal is contemplated with the IRS's Appellate Division. In most instances, an attorney is retained if litigation is being considered.

TAX RESEARCH

Tax research is the search for the best possible defensibly correct solution to a problem involving either a completed transaction (e.g., a sale of property) or a proposed transaction (e.g., a proposed merger of two corporations). Research involves each of the following steps:

---

[33] Sec. 6651(a)(2). If the failure to file penalty (5%) and the failure to pay the tax penalty (0.5%) are both applicable, the failure to file penalty is reduced by the failure to pay penalty per Sec. 6651(c)(1). Further, the penalty is increased to 1% per month after the IRS notifies the taxpayer that it will levy on the taxpayer's assets.

[34] Sec. 6662.
[35] Sec. 6663.
[36] Sec. 6654.

SELF-STUDY QUESTION

Do large national CPA firms generally stress the importance of tax research in connection with tax-return preparation or tax planning?

ANSWER

The large CPA firms emphasize their skills in tax planning. Sometimes a slight alteration of a proposed transaction can save the client substantial tax dollars. This is high-value-added work and can be billed at premium rates.

▶ Determine the facts.
▶ Identify the issue(s).
▶ Identify and analyze the tax law sources (i.e., code provisions, Treasury Regulations, administrative rulings, and court cases).
▶ Evaluate nontax (e.g., business) implications.
▶ Solve the problem.
▶ Communicate the findings to the client.

Tax research may be conducted in connection with tax return preparation, tax planning, or procedural activities. A more thorough discussion of tax research is presented in Chapter I15.

TAX PLANNING AND CONSULTING

Tax planning involves the process of structuring one's affairs so as to minimize the amount of taxes *and* maximize the after-tax return. Thus, optimal tax planning is *not* to just pay the least amount of tax but to maximize after-tax cash flows. A text on tax research and planning has delineated the following tax planning principles:[37]

▶ Keep sufficient records.
▶ Forecast the effect of future events.
▶ Support the plan with a sound business purpose.
▶ Base the plan on sound legal authorities.
▶ Do not carry a good plan too far.
▶ Make the plan flexible.
▶ Integrate the tax plan with other factors in decision making.
▶ Conduct research to learn whether a similar plan has previously proved unsuccessful (e.g., a court case involving similar facts may have upheld the IRS's position).
▶ Consider the "maximum" risk exposure of the client (e.g., if the plan is subsequently challenged by the IRS and the tax treatment is disallowed, what is the economic impact upon the taxpayer?).
▶ Consider the effect of timing (e.g., whether it is more beneficial to take a deduction in one year versus another).
▶ Shape the plan to the client's needs and desires.

ADDITIONAL COMMENT

Several national accounting firms have divided their tax departments into two basic groups, consulting and compliance. The tax consultants work with clients in tax planning and consulting matters and do not prepare tax returns. Tax returns are prepared by the compliance staff.

CPAs and attorneys frequently are engaged by their clients to perform consulting services to optimize the client's tax situation. For example, a major corporation client is considering the acquisition of a major international corporation and wants to make sure that the tax implications of such an acquisition are properly managed. The CPA will be engaged to perform a thorough review of the transaction to ensure that the client is fully aware of the tax results of the acquisition, and possibly may request an advance ruling from the IRS.

Because of the importance of planning in tax practice, subsequent chapters in this text include a separate section on tax planning to discuss issues that are related to the topical coverage. These tax planning principles should be kept in mind when attempting to use the tax planning recommendations. Also, a systematic approach to tax planning developed by two noted tax academicians, Myron Scholes and Mark Wolfson, is discussed in Chapter I18.

FINANCIAL PLANNING

A relatively new field for tax professionals is that of financial planning for individual clients. Since taxes are an integral part of any financial plan and since a tax specialist regularly meets with his or her clients (filing returns and other tax matters), the area of finan-

---

[37] Fred W. Norwood et al., *Federal Taxation: Research, Planning, and Procedures*, 2nd ed. (Englewood Cliffs, NJ: Prentice Hall, 1979), pp. 215–216.

cial planning has become increasingly a part of tax practice. The typical steps in performing a financial planning engagement include the following steps:

- ▶ Determine the client's financial goals and objectives
- ▶ Review the client's insurance coverage for adequacy and appropriateness
- ▶ Recommend an investment strategy, including risk analysis and asset allocation
- ▶ Review tax returns to ensure that, through proper tax planning, the client is maximizing his or her after-tax cash flow
- ▶ Review the client's retirement plans to assure compliance with the law and possible new alternatives
- ▶ Review all documents related to estate and gift planning and work with the client's attorney to minimize all transfer taxes and fulfill the client's objectives.

COMPUTER APPLICATIONS IN TAX PRACTICE

TAX RETURN PREPARATION

> **KEY POINT**
> The use of computers has become very important in tax practice ranging from tax return preparation to tax research. It is essential that students having an interest in taxation develop advanced computer skills.

> **ADDITIONAL COMMENT**
> The Volunteer Income Tax Assistance (VITA) program sponsored by the IRS is aimed at taxpayers who need help with their federal return but cannot afford to pay for the assistance. Many college students put their textbook knowledge to work through VITA programs.

To prepare tax returns, most tax practitioners purchase tax preparation software from companies such as Commerce Clearing House or Intuit. This software allows the preparation of accurate and professional-looking tax returns. A word of caution, however, is in order. As with any computer software, the preparation of tax returns using the computer requires as much knowledge and expertise from the preparer as doing the returns by hand. A recent trend in tax return preparation is the **electronic filing** of tax returns, i.e., a "paperless" tax return. Taxpayers send their returns electronically to the IRS for processing, thereby saving enormous amounts of paper and, perhaps, reducing human error. Computerized tax return software, *Tax Cut,* is available for use with this textbook.

TAX PLANNING APPLICATIONS

Performing tax planning for clients involves the evaluation of alternative courses of action. This evaluation process can be very time-consuming because of the tax calculations necessary to arrive at an optimal solution. The computer has become an essential tool in this process because of the speed in which the tax calculations can be made. Many tax professionals now use sophisticated software to perform tax planning for their clients. A prime example of the use of the computer in tax planning has been in deciding whether a taxpayer should invest in a Roth Individual Retirement Account (Roth IRA) or a regular IRA (see Chapter I9 for more details on IRAs). There are many factors to consider, including current and projected tax rates, current and projected level of income, etc. With the computer, a tax professional can vary the assumptions and create a number of alternatives within a relatively short period of time. To perform this task by hand would require an enormous commitment of time. As with most aspects of life, the impact of the computer on tax planning has been highly significant and will only increase in the future.

TAX RESEARCH APPLICATIONS

> **ADDITIONAL COMMENT**
> When performing LEXIS research, the researcher need not be concerned with how an editor might have indexed a court case because the LEXIS research is performed independently. Every word of virtually every case is available in the LEXIS service.

Computerized information-retrieval systems are used in tax research and are rapidly replacing books as the principal source of tax-related information. There are three types of computerized information-retrieval systems: (1) electronic or "on-line" services, (2) CD-ROM services, and (3) Internet services. As to on-line services, the oldest and most well-known data base is LEXIS, which was developed by Mead Data Central. The database for these computerized systems contains in full text the same tax law sources (e.g., cases, rulings, committee reports, regulations, and commentary and analysis) that are included in a manual tax service. The system is entered by using a keyword or phrase or by entering a Code section number or case name. Researchers need to be imaginative in thinking of search requests; a computerized system will not locate an authority unless it contains the exact wording the researcher specifies, even though it contains synonymous terms.

1-26 Individuals ▼ Chapter 1

EXAMPLE I1-21 ▶ A researcher is interested in whether a certain expenditure for clothing is deductible under Sec. 162 as a uniform expense. The researcher might instruct the computer to retrieve all cases containing the words "uniform" and "Sec. 162" in close proximity to each other. This search will turn up only cases containing those words. Cases using the words "work clothing" will not be retrieved. A more comprehensive search will take place if the researcher instructs the computerized system to look for either "uniform" or "work clothing" within close proximity to "Sec. 162." ◀

ADDITIONAL COMMENT

Using LEXIS, a tax researcher even has the ability to find decisions in which a particular judge concurred or dissented.

A number of tax services, including CCH's *Federal Tax Service*, RIA's *Federal Tax Coordinator 2d (RIA On Point)*, CCH's *Standard Federal Tax Reporter (CCH Access)* and BNA's *Tax Management Portfolios* are available on CD-ROM (compact disc read-only memory). The materials are organized the same as in the paper services. The CD-ROMs generally are updated monthly. Information is retrieved from the CD-ROMs by typing key words into the computer. For example, one may locate the index on the disk, consult the index, and then refer to the portion of the disk that discusses the tax consequences of a related issue. The disks, of course, allow pages and pages of information to be stored in practically no space and avoid the need to file new pages. Extensive material is available on the CCH *"Access"* CD-ROM. For example, the CD-ROM product includes *Standard Federal Tax Reporter, State Tax Reports,* letter rulings and IRS positions, Revenue Rulings and Revenue Procedures, IRS publications, tax forms and instructions, and court cases dating back to 1913. Tax-oriented periodicals often provide reviews of computer-based or CD-ROM research products.[38]

Another source of tax materials that is destined to become even more useful and important are materials on the Internet.[39] The principal Internet services are RIA's *Checkpoint* and CCH's *Tax Internet Research Network*. These commercial Internet services contain a wide range of materials available to tax researchers who subscribe to the service. In addition, the IRS has a home page (www.irs.ustreas.gov) that taxpayers can access for forms, publications, and other related materials. All of the major accounting firms and many other tax organizations have home pages that allow users to access a myriad of tax information.

PROBLEM MATERIALS

DISCUSSION QUESTIONS

I1-1 The Supreme Court in 1895 ruled that the income tax was unconstitutional because the tax needed to be apportioned among the states in proportion to their populations. Why would the requirement of proportionality be so difficult to administer?

I1-2 Why was pay-as-you-go withholding needed in 1943?

I1-3 Congressman Patrick indicates that he is opposed to new tax legislative proposals that call for a flat tax rate that are currently being considered by Congress because the new taxing structure would not be in accord with our traditional practice of taxing those who have the ability to pay the tax. Discuss the position of the congressman, giving consideration to tax rate structures (e.g., progressive, proportional, and regressive) and the concept of equity.

I1-4 The Governor of your state stated in a recent political speech that he has never supported any income tax increases as the tax rates have remained at the same level during his entire term of office. Yet, you believe that you are paying more tax this year than in previous years even though your income has not increased. How can both you and the Governor be correct? In other words, is it possible for the government to raise taxes without raising tax rates?

---

[38] See Editorial Staff, "CD-ROM Research Products Reviewed by Practitioners," *The Journal of Taxation,* July 1994, pp. 28–38. Also, for a thorough discussion of computerized tax research, see William A. Raabe, Gerald E. Whittenburg, and John C. Bost, *West's Federal Tax Research,* 3rd ed. (Minneapolis/St. Paul, MN: West Publishing Co., 1994), Chapters 13 and 14.

[39] For an excellent summary of the best sources for tax information on the Internet, see Ronald Flinn, "The Best Online Tax Sites," *Journal of Accountancy,* August, 1997, pp. 32-37.

I1-5 Carmen indicates that her average tax rate is 18% and her marginal tax rate is 28% for the current year. She is considering whether to make a charitable contribution to her church before the end of the tax year. Which tax rate is of greater significance in measuring the tax effect for her decision? Explain.

I1-6 Why are the gift and estate taxes both called wealth transfer taxes? What is the tax base for computing each of these taxes?

I1-7 Cathy, who is single, makes two gifts of $15,000 each to her two children.
   a. Is Cathy or her children primarily liable for the gift tax on the two gifts?
   b. If Cathy has never made a taxable gift in prior years, is a gift tax due on the two gifts?

I1-8 Carlos inherits 100 shares of Allied Corporation stock from his father. The stock cost his father $8,000 and had a $10,000 FMV on the date of his father's death. The alternate valuation date was not elected. What is Carlos's tax basis for the Allied stock when it is received from the estate?

I1-9 Most estates are not subject to the federal estate tax.
   a. Why is this the case?
   b. Do you believe most estates should be subject to the federal estate tax?

I1-10 Indicate which of the following taxes are generally progressive, proportional, or regressive:
   a. State income taxes
   b. Federal estate tax
   c. Corporate state franchise tax
   d. Property taxes
   e. State sales taxes

I1-11 Carolyn operates a small business as a sole proprietor (unincorporated). Carolyn is considering operating the business as a corporation because of nontax advantages (e.g., limited liability and ability to raise outside capital). From the standpoint of paying Social Security taxes, would the total Social Security taxes increase or decrease if the business is incorporated? Why?

I1-12 The three different levels of government (federal, state, and local) must impose taxes to carry out their functions. For each of the types of taxes below, discuss which level of government primarily uses that type of tax.
   a. Property taxes
   b. Excise taxes
   c. Sales taxes
   d. Income taxes
   e. Employment taxes

I1-13 A "good" tax structure has four characteristics.
   a. Briefly discuss the four characteristics.
   b. Using the four characteristics, evaluate the following tax structures:
      1. Federal income tax
      2. State sales tax
      3. Local ad valorem property tax

I1-14 Two commonly-recognized measures of the fairness of an income tax structure are "horizontal equity" and "vertical equity."
   a. Discuss what is meant by horizontal equity and vertical equity as it pertains to the income tax.
   b. Why is it so difficult to design a "fair" tax structure?

I1-15 The primary objective of the federal income tax law is to raise revenue. What are its secondary objectives?

I1-16 If the objectives of the federal tax system are multifaceted and include raising revenues, providing investment incentives, encouraging certain industries, and meeting desired social objectives, is it possible to achieve a simplified tax system? Explain.

I1-17 Distinguish between *taxpaying entities* and *flow-through entities* from the standpoint of the federal income tax law.

I1-18 Discuss what is meant by the term "double taxation" of corporations. Develop an example of double taxation using a corporation and shareholder.

I1-19 Limited liability companies (LLCs) are very popular today as a form of organization. Assume a client asks you to explain what this new type of organization is all about. Prepare a brief description of the federal income tax aspects of LLCs.

I1-20 Why is a thorough knowledge of sources of tax law so important for a professional person who works in the tax area?

I1-21 The Internal Revenue Code is the most authoritative source of income tax law. In trying to resolve an income tax question, however, a tax researcher also consults administrative rulings (Income Tax Regulations, Revenue Rulings, etc.) and court decisions. Why wouldn't the tax researcher just consult the Code since it is the highest authority? Similarly, why is there a need for administrative rulings and court decisions?

I1-22 Congressional committee reports are an important source of information concerning the legislative enactment of tax law.
   a. Name the three Congressional committee reports that are issued in connection with a new tax bill.
   b. Of what importance are Congressional committee reports to tax practitioners?

I1-23 What is the primary service function provided by the National Office of the IRS?

I1-24 What types of taxpayers are more likely to be audited by the IRS?

I1-25 Anya is concerned that she will be audited by the IRS.
   a. Under what circumstances is it possible that the IRS will review each line item on her tax return?
   b. Is it likely that all items on Anya's return will be audited?

I1-26 a. What does the term "hazards of litigation" mean in the context of taxation?
b. Why would the IRS or a taxpayer settle or compromise a case based on the "hazards of litigation"?

I1-27 If a taxpayer receives a tax refund from the IRS, does this mean that the IRS feels that the return is correct and will not be subject to audit?

I1-28 State the statute of limitations for transactions involving:
a. Fraud (e.g., failure to file a tax return)
b. Disallowance of tax deduction items
c. The omission of rental income equal to 30% of the taxpayer's gross income

I1-29 In reference to tax research, what is meant by *the best possible defensibly correct solution*?

I1-30 The profession of tax practice involves four principal areas of activity. Discuss these four areas.

I1-31 Many tax professionals have moved into the field of financial planning for their clients.
a. How do taxes impact financial planning for a client?
b. Why do tax professionals have a perfect opportunity to perform financial planning for their clients?

I1-32 Is the principal goal of tax planning to absolutely minimize the amount of taxes that a taxpayer must pay?

I1-33 Explain how a computer can assist a tax practitioner in tax planning activities and making complex tax calculations.

PROBLEMS

I1-34 *Tax Rates.* Latesha, a single taxpayer, had the following income and deductions for the tax year 2001:

INCOME:	Salary	$ 60,000
	Business Income	25,000
	Dividends from stocks	10,000
	Tax-exempt bond interest	5,000
	TOTAL INCOME	100,000
DEDUCTIONS:	Business expenses	$ 9,900
	Itemized deductions	20,000
	Personal exemption	2,900
	TOTAL DEDUCTIONS	32,800

a. Compute Latesha's taxable income and federal tax liability for 2001.
b. Compute Latesha's marginal, average, and effective tax rates.
c. For tax planning purposes, which of the three rates in b. is the most important?

I1-35 *Marginal Tax Rate.* Jill and George are married and file a joint return. They expect to have $350,000 of taxable income in the next year and are considering whether to purchase a personal residence that would provide additional tax deductions of $80,000 for mortgage interest and real estate taxes.
a. What is their marginal tax rate for purposes of making this decision? (Ignore the effects of a phase-out of personal exemptions and itemized deductions (see Chapters I2 and I7, respectively).
b. What is the tax savings if the residence is acquired?

I1-36 *Gift Tax.* Chuck, a married taxpayer, makes the following gifts during the current year: $20,000 to his church, $30,000 to his daughter, and $25,000 to his wife.
a. What is the amount of Chuck's taxable gifts for the current year (assuming that he does not elect to split the gifts with his spouse)?
b. How would your answer to Part a change if a gift-splitting election were made?

I1-37 *Estate Tax.* Clay dies in the current year and has a gross estate valued at $800,000. Six months after his death, the gross assets are valued at $900,000. The estate incurs funeral and administration expenses of $125,000. It also has debts amounting to $75,000, and Clay bequeaths $350,000 of the property to his wife. During his life Clay made no taxable gifts.
a. What is the amount of Clay's taxable estate?
b. What is the tax base for computing Clay's estate tax?
c. What is the amount of estate tax owed if the tentative estate tax (before credits) is $70,800?

d. Alternatively, if, six months after his death, the gross assets in Clay's estate declined in value to $700,000, can the administrator of Clay's estate elect the alternate valuation date? What are the important factors that the administrator should consider as to whether the alternate valuation date should be elected?

I1-38 *Comparison of Tax Entities.*
a. Keith Thomas began a new consulting business in January 1, 2001. He organized the business as a C corporation, KT Inc. During 2001, the corporation was reasonably successful and generated revenues of $1,050,000. KT, Inc. had operating expenses of $800,000 before any payments to Keith. During 2001, KT, Inc. paid dividends to Keith in the amount of $250,000. Assume that Keith had other income (interest, dividends, etc.) of $30,000, itemized deductions of $40,000, is married (wife has no income) and has no children. Compute the total tax liability of KT, Inc. and Keith for 2001. Ignore any phaseouts of itemized deductions or personal exemptions.
b. Instead of organizing the consulting business as a C corporation, assume Keith organized the business as a limited liability company, KT, LLC. KT, LLC made a distribution of $250,000 to Keith during 2001. Compute the total tax liability of KT, LLC and Keith for 2001. Ignore any phaseouts of itemized deductions or personal exemptions.

I1-39 *Interest and Penalties.* In 2000, Paul, who is single, has a comfortable salary from his job as well as income from his investment portfolio. However, he is habitually late in filing his federal income tax return. He did not file his 2000 income tax return until November 30, 2001 (due date was April 15, 2001) and no extensions of time to file the return were filed. Below are amounts from his 2000 return:

Taxable income	$100,000
Total tax liability on taxable income	25,681
Total federal tax withheld from his salary	18,000

Paul sent a check with his return to the IRS for the balance due of $7,681. He is relieved that he has completed his filing requirement for 2000 *and* has met his financial obligation to the government for 2000.

Has Paul met *all* of his financial obligations to the IRS for 2000? If not, what additional amounts will Paul be liable to pay to the IRS?

I1-40 *IRS Audits.* Which of the following individuals is most likely to be audited:
a. Connie has a $20,000 net loss from her unincorporated business (a cattle ranch). She also received a $200,000 salary as an executive of a corporation.
b. Craig has AGI of $20,000 from wages and uses the standard deduction.
c. Dale fails to report $120 of dividends from a stock investment. His taxable income is $40,000 and he has no other unusually large itemized deductions or business expenses. A Form 1099 is reported to the IRS.

I1-41 *Statute of Limitations.* In April 2001, Dan is audited by the IRS for the year 1999. During the course of the audit, the agent discovers that Dan's deductions for business travel and entertainment are unsubstantiated and a $600 deficiency assessment is proposed for 1999. The agent also discovers that Dan failed to report $40,000 of gross business income on his 1997 return. Gross income of $60,000 was reported in 1997. The agent also discovers that Dan failed to file a tax return in 1996.

Will the statute of limitations prevent the IRS from issuing a deficiency assessment for 1999, 1997, or 1996? Explain.

CASE STUDY PROBLEM

I1-42 John Gemstone, a wealthy client, has recently been audited by the IRS. The agent has questioned the following deduction items on Mr. Gemstone's tax return for the year under review:

- A $10,000 loss deduction on the rental of his beach cottage.
- A $20,000 charitable contribution deduction for the donation of a painting to a local art museum. The agent has questioned whether the painting is overvalued.
- A $15,000 loss deduction from the operation of a cattle breeding ranch. The agent is concerned that the ranch is not a legitimate business (i.e., is a hobby).

Your supervisor has requested that you represent Mr. Gemstone in his discussions with the IRS.

a. What additional questions should you ask Mr. Gemstone in an attempt to substantiate the deductibility of the above items?
b. What tax research procedures might be applied to build the best possible case for your client?

RESEARCH PROBLEM

I1-43 Read the following two cases and explain why the Supreme Court reached different conclusions for cases involving similar facts and issues:
- *CIR v. Court Holding Co.*, 33 AFTR 593, 45-1 USTC ¶9215 (USSC, 1945)
- *U.S. v. Cumberland Public Service Co.*, 38 AFTR 978, 50-1 USTC ¶9129 (USSC, 1950)

CHAPTER 2

DETERMINATION OF TAX

LEARNING OBJECTIVES

After studying this chapter, you should be able to

1. Use the tax formula to compute an individual's taxable income
2. Determine the amount allowable for the standard deduction
3. Determine the amount and the correct number of personal and dependency exemptions
4. Determine the amount of child credit
5. Determine the filing status of individuals
6. Explain the tax formula for corporations
7. Explain the basic concepts of property transactions

CHAPTER OUTLINE

Formula for Individual Income Tax...2-2
Deductions from Adjusted Gross Income...2-7
Determining the Amount of Tax...2-18
Corporate Tax Formula and Rates...2-24
Treatment of Capital Gains and Losses...2-26

Each year, over 100 million individuals and married couples file tax forms on which they compute their federal income tax. The income tax is imposed "on the taxable income of every individual."[1] The amount of tax actually owed by an individual taxpayer is determined by applying a complex set of rules that together make up the income tax law. To understand the income tax, it is necessary to study the basic formula on which the income tax computation is based. Therefore, this chapter introduces the income tax formula and begins the development of its components. Because the income tax formula constitutes the basis of the income tax, most of the remainder of this book is an expansion of the formula. For that reason, it is essential that the reader understand the formula presented here before proceeding to subsequent chapters.

FORMULA FOR INDIVIDUAL INCOME TAX

OBJECTIVE 1

Use the tax formula to compute an individual's taxable income

BASIC FORMULA

Most individuals compute their income tax by using the formula illustrated in Table I2-1. The formula itself appears rather simple. However, the complexity of the income tax results from the intricate rules that must be applied in order to arrive at the amounts that enter into the formula.

The tax formula is incorporated into the income tax form. The tax formula illustrated in Table I2-1 can be compared with Form 1040, which is reproduced in Figure I2-1. Some differences exist between the tax formula below and the tax form itself. For example, taxpayers generally are not required to report exclusions (nontaxable income) on their tax returns. One exception does require taxpayers to disclose tax-exempt interest income. A number of separate schedules are used to report various types of income. For example, income from a sole proprietorship is reported on Schedule C where gross income from the business is reduced by related expenses which are deductions for AGI. Only the net income from the business actually appears on Form 1040. Also, Form 1040 is used to collect other taxes such as the self-employment tax. Hence, a line is provided for that tax on Form 1040. The main reason for differences between the formula and the form is administrative convenience. That is, there is no reason to require taxpayers to disclose income if the income is not subject to tax, it is simpler to report business income on a separate schedule, and it is convenient to collect other taxes on the same tax form.

ADDITIONAL COMMENT

"There is one difference between a tax collector and a taxidermist—the taxidermist leaves the hide." This is a quote from Mortimer Caplan, former Director of the Bureau of Internal Revenue, *Time*, Feb. 1, 1963.

ADDITIONAL COMMENT

The IRS estimates that the average taxpayer will spend 3 hours and 59 minutes for just preparing a Form 1040. When the estimated time for recordkeeping, learning about the law, and sending the form is added to the preparation time, the total time estimate jumps to 9 hours and 54 minutes. Each additional form and schedule adds even more time.

ADDITIONAL COMMENT

Comedian Jay Leno's explanation as to why the IRS calls it Form 1040 was, "For every $50 you earn, you get $10 and they get $40."

▼ **TABLE I2-1**
Tax Formula for Individuals

Income from whatever source derived		$xxx,xxx
Minus:	Exclusions	(xxx)
Gross income		$ xx,xxx
Minus:	Deductions for adjusted gross income	(xxx)
Adjusted gross income		$ x,xxx
Minus:	Deductions from adjusted gross income:	
	Greater of itemized deductions or the standard deduction	(xx)
	Personal and dependency exemptions	(xx)
Taxable income		$ x,xxx
Times:	Tax rate or rates (from tax table or schedule)	
Gross tax		$ xx
Minus:	Credits and prepayments	(x)
Net tax payable or refund due		$ xx

---

[1] Sec. 1.

Determination of Tax ▼ **Individuals 2-3**

Examination of the formula reveals terms such as *gross income, exclusions, adjusted gross income, exemptions, gross tax,* and *credits*. These terms and others that make up the formula are defined below.

DEFINITIONS

INCOME. The term **income** includes both taxable and nontaxable income. Although the term is not specifically defined in the tax law, it does include income from any source.[2] Its meaning is close to that of the term **revenue**. However, it does not include a "return of capital." Thus, in the case of the sale of property, only the gain, not the entire sales proceeds, is viewed as income. This view extends to the sale of inventory, where gross profit is viewed as income, as opposed to the sale price. Also, no income results from any receipts received from borrowed funds.

EXCLUSION. *[not on tax return]* Not all income is taxable. An **exclusion** is any item of income that the tax law says is not taxable. Congress, over the years, has specifically excluded certain types of income from taxation for various social, economic, and political reasons. Chapter I4 discusses specific exclusions and the reasons for their existence. Table I2-2 contains a sample of the major exclusions from gross income.

GROSS INCOME. **Gross income** is income reduced by exclusions. In other words, it is income from taxable sources and is reported on the return (excluded income need not be disclosed). Section 61(a) contains a partial list of items of gross income. The items listed in Sec. 61(a) are shown in Table I2-3. Note, however, that Sec. 61(a) states that unless otherwise provided, "gross income means all income from whatever source derived, including (but not limited to)" the listed items of income. Thus, even though an item is omitted from the list does not necessarily mean that the item is excluded. For example, illegal income, although omitted from the list, is taxable.[3]

ADDITIONAL COMMENT
The Revenue Reconciliation Act of 1993 contains a provision that increased the amount of the checkoff for the Presidential Election Campaign Fund from $1 to $3. The amount was increased because too few individuals were using the checkoff and a shortfall in the fund was projected for the 1996 election cycle. The checkoff can be found on Form 1040 below the address section.

TYPICAL MISCONCEPTION
It is easy to confuse an exclusion with a deduction. An exclusion is a source of income that is omitted from the tax base, whereas a deduction is an expense that is subtracted in arriving at taxable income. Both have the effect of reducing taxable income.

ADDITIONAL COMMENT
One common exclusion, interest on state and local government bonds, must be reported on the tax return in amount only. It is not added to the other income items. In 1996, this reported tax-exempt interest totaled $49 billion.

▼ **TABLE I2-2**
Major Exclusions

Gifts and inheritances
Life insurance proceeds
Welfare and certain other transfer payments
Certain scholarships and fellowships
Certain payments for injury and sickness
    Personal physical injury settlements
    Worker's compensation
    Medical expense reimbursements
Certain employee fringe benefits
    Health plan premiums
    Group term life insurance premiums (limited)
    Meals and lodging
    Employee discounts
    Dependent care
Certain foreign-earned income
Interest on state and local government bonds
Certain interest of Series EE bonds
Certain improvements by lessee to lessor's property
Child support payments
Property settlements pursuant to a divorce
Gain from the sale of a personal residence (limited)

---

[2] Sec. 61(a).

[3] *U.S. v. Manley S. Sullivan,* 6 AFTR 6753, 1 USTC ¶236 (USSC, 1927).

TABLE I2-3
Gross Income Items Listed in Sec. 61(a)

Compensation for services, including fees, commissions, fringe benefits, and similar items
Gross income derived from business
Gains derived from dealings in property
Interest
Rents
Royalties
Dividends
Alimony and separate maintenance payments
Annuities
Income from life insurance and endowment contracts
Pensions
Income from the discharge of indebtedness
Distributive share of partnership gross income
Income in respect of a decedent
Income from an interest in an estate or trust

DEDUCTIONS FOR ADJUSTED GROSS INCOME. In general, taxpayers may deduct expenses that are specifically allowed by the tax law. Allowable deductions include business-type expenses, investment expenses, or personal expenses that are specifically provided for in the IRC, such as charitable contributions. Purely personal expenses generally are not deductible.

Deductions fall into two categories for individual taxpayers: deductions *for* adjusted gross income and deductions *from* adjusted gross income. In general, **deductions for adjusted gross income** are expenses connected with a trade or business. For the most part, **deductions from adjusted gross income** are personal expenses that Congress has chosen to allow. This classification scheme, however, is not always followed. For example, alimony paid, which is not a business expense, is a deduction *for* adjusted gross income. Table I2-4 contains a partial list of deductions *for* adjusted gross income that is taken from Sec. 62. Deductions for adjusted gross income are discussed further in Chapter I6 of this textbook.

ADJUSTED GROSS INCOME. **Adjusted gross income (AGI)** is a measure of income that falls between gross income and taxable income. AGI is important because it is used in numerous other tax computations, especially to impose limitations. For example, AGI is used to establish floors for the medical deduction and casualty loss deduction and to establish a ceiling for the charitable contribution deduction.

DEDUCTIONS FROM ADJUSTED GROSS INCOME. Section 62 lists deductions *for* AGI (see Table I2-4). Thus, any allowable deduction not listed in Sec. 62 is a deduction *from* AGI. The two categories of deductions *from* adjusted gross income are (1) itemized deductions or the standard deduction and (2) personal and dependency exemptions.[4] Deductions from AGI are discussed further in Chapter I7 of this textbook.

ITEMIZED DEDUCTIONS AND THE STANDARD DEDUCTION. As mentioned above, taxpayers generally cannot deduct personal expenses.[5] Congress, however, allows taxpayers to deduct specified personal expenses such as charitable contributions and medical expenses. In addition, taxpayers are allowed to itemize expenses related to the production or collection of income, the management of property held for the production of income, and the determination, collection, or refund of any tax.[6]

ADDITIONAL COMMENT
In 1996, there were 42.6 million tax returns filed with AGI under $15,000, and 1.5 million returns filed with AGI over $200,000.

ADDITIONAL COMMENT
In 1996, total AGI on all individual tax returns filed was just over $4.5 trillion, an increase of 8.9% from the previous year.

ADDITIONAL COMMENT
Itemized deductions were claimed on 29.3% of all returns filed in 1996 and amounted to 56.8% of all standard and itemized deductions.

---

[4] Sec. 63.
[5] Sec. 262.
[6] Sec. 212.

Determination of Tax ▼ **Individuals 2-5**

▼ **TABLE I2-4**
Deductions for Adjusted Gross Income Listed in Sec. 62

Trade and business deductions
Reimbursed employee expenses and certain expenses of performing artists
Losses from the sale or exchange of property
Deductions attributable to rents and royalties
Certain deductions of life tenants and income beneficiaries of property
Contributions to retirement plans (Keoghs and IRAs) and certain distributions
Penalties forfeited because of premature withdrawal of funds from time savings accounts
*One-half of self-employment taxes paid
*Portion of health insurance costs incurred by a self-employed person
Alimony
Moving expenses
Certain required repayments of supplemental unemployment compensation
Jury duty pay remitted to an individual's employer
Certain environmental expenditures (reforestation and clean fuel)
Interest on education loans
Contribution to medical savings account

*Though not actually mentioned in Sec. 62, self-employment taxes and health insurance costs of self-employed persons are defind by Secs. 164(f) and 162(l) respectively as trade or business deductions thereby indirectly enabling taxpayers to deduct portions of these amounts for AGI.

HISTORICAL NOTE

In 1986, when parents were required merely to list the names of their children to claim them as a dependent, 77 million children were claimed. In 1987, when taxpayers were required to list children's Social Security numbers to prove that the exemptions were valid, the number of children claimed as dependents decreased to 70 million.

HISTORICAL NOTE

As recently as 1986, the highest marginal tax rate was 50%, and as recently as 1981, it was 70%.

SELF-STUDY QUESTION

If a taxpayer is in the 28% marginal tax bracket, would he or she prefer $100 of tax credits or $300 of tax deductions?

ANSWER

The taxpayer would prefer the $100 of tax credits. The $300 of deductions will result in a tax savings of $84 ($300 × .28), whereas the $100 of credits would result in a tax savings of $100.

Taxpayers have the choice of claiming either itemized deductions or the standard deduction. The amount of the standard deduction varies depending on the taxpayer's filing status, age, and vision. As a practical matter, for most taxpayers the standard deduction is greater than the total itemized deductions. Taxpayers with small amounts of deductible expenses do not itemize and, in fact, do not have to keep records of medical expenses and other itemized deductions. The relationship between itemized deductions and the standard deduction is discussed later in this chapter.

PERSONAL AND DEPENDENCY EXEMPTIONS. A **personal exemption** generally is allowed for each taxpayer and his or her spouse and an additional dependency exemption is permitted for each dependent. Both personal and dependency exemptions are equal to $2,800 in 2000 and $2,900 in 2001. The amount of an exemption is adjusted annually for increases in the cost of living.

TAXABLE INCOME. **Taxable income** is adjusted gross income reduced by deductions *from* AGI. It is the amount of income that is taxed.

TAX RATES AND GROSS TAX. Tax rates are the percentage rates, set by Congress, at which income is taxed. There are five individual income tax rates: 15%, 28%, 31%, 36%, and 39.6%. Taxpayers may compute their tax by multiplying the percentage rates found in the tax rate schedules times taxable income. However, most taxpayers simply look in a tax table to find their gross tax. These two alternatives are discussed in more detail later in this chapter. The **gross tax** is the amount of tax determined by this process.

CREDITS AND PREPAYMENTS. **Tax credits**, which include prepayments, are amounts that can be subtracted from the gross tax to arrive at the net tax due or refund due. Credits may be classified as either refundable or nonrefundable tax credits. **Refundable tax credits** are allowed to reduce a taxpayer's tax liability to zero and, if some credit still remains, are refundable (paid) by the government to the taxpayer. Prepayments of tax, which are amounts paid to the government during the year through means such as withholding from wages, and selected other items are classified as **refundable tax credits**. **Nonrefundable tax credits** are allowances that have been created by Congress for various social, economic, and political reasons such as the child and dependent care credit. Nonrefundable tax credits can

2-6 Individuals ▼ Chapter 2

▼ **TABLE I2-5**
Partial List of Tax Credits

Refundable

    Withholding from wages and back-up withholding
    Estimated tax payments
    Overpayment of prior year's tax
    Excess Social Security taxes paid
    Nonhighway-use gasoline tax
    Earned income credit
    Regulated investment company credit
    Payments made with extension request
    Child credit (in some cases)

Nonrefundable

    Adoption expense credit
    Credit for the elderly and disabled
    Foreign tax credit
    Child and dependent care credit
    Business energy credit
    Qualified electric vehicle credit
    Research and experimentation credit
    Low-income housing credit
    Building rehabilitation credit
    Hope and lifetime learning credits

be subtracted from the tax and may reduce the tax liability to zero. However, if the nonrefundable credits exceed the tax liability, none of the excess will be paid to the taxpayer. A partial list of refundable and nonrefundable tax credits can be found in Table I2-5.

TAX FORMULA ILLUSTRATED
The following example illustrates the tax formula and Form 1040.

EXAMPLE I2-1 ▶ The following facts relate to Larry S. and Jane V. Lane for 2000. Betty is their 9 year-old dependent daughter.

Salary	$75,000
Interest Income:	
Taxable	1,000
Exempt	500
Individual Retirement Account (IRA) contribution	2,000
Itemized deductions	12,300
Personal and dependency exemptions (3 × $2,800)	8,400
Federal income taxes withheld from salary	9,000

Their tax is computed as follows:

Income:		
Salary		$75,000
Taxable interest		1,000
Exempt interest		500
Total		$76,500
Minus:	Exclusion:	
	Exempt interest	(500)
Gross income		$76,000
Minus:	Deductions for AGI:	
	IRA contribution	(2,000)
Adjusted gross income		$74,000
Minus:	Deductions from AGI:	
	Itemized deductions	(12,300)
	Personal and dependency exemptions	(8,400)
Taxable income		$53,300

Gross tax (2000 tax table)		$9,231
Minus: Credits and prepayments		
Child credit	(500)	
Federal income tax withheld	(9,000)	(9,500)
Tax refund		$269

This tax is also computed on Form 1040 (see Figure I2-1). Note that certain additional information, such as the taxpayers' address and Social Security numbers, also is included on the return.

DEDUCTIONS FROM ADJUSTED GROSS INCOME

ITEMIZED DEDUCTIONS

Itemized deductions are claimed only if the total of such expenses exceeds the standard deduction. Here, consideration is given to which expenses may be itemized and the relationship between itemized deductions and the standard deduction.

ADDITIONAL COMMENT

Of the total itemized deductions reported in 1996, interest paid in the amount of $227.6 billion comprised the largest portion at 39.1%. Taxes paid came in second with 34.8% of total itemized deductions.

ADDITIONAL COMMENT

The phase-out of itemized deductions for taxpayers in the 36% tax bracket effectively raises their marginal tax rate by 1.08% which could be considered a hidden tax rate.

DEDUCTIBLE ITEMS. Congress allows taxpayers to itemize specified personal expenses. These specified expenses include medical expenses, taxes, investment and residential interest, charitable contributions, casualty and theft losses, and employee expenses. In addition, taxpayers are allowed to itemize expenses related to the production or collection of nonbusiness income, the management of property held for the production of income, and the determination, collection, or refund of any tax. A partial list of itemized deductions is found in Table I2-6.

ITEMIZED DEDUCTION FLOORS. There are four adjusted gross income floors associated with itemized deductions. AGI floors represent amounts in which the deduction is allowable only if it exceeds the floor amount. Three of the floors apply to specific categories of itemized deductions; the remaining floor applies to total itemized deductions. The floors based on AGI are as follows:

▶ Medical expenses: only medical expenses over 7.5% of AGI of are deductible.

▼ TABLE I2-6
Partial List of Itemized Deductions

Medical expenses (over 7.5% of adjusted gross income)
Certain taxes
   State, local, and foreign income and real property taxes
   State and local personal property taxes
Residential interest and investment interest (limited)
Charitable contributions (limited)
Casualty and theft losses (over 10% of adjusted gross income)
Miscellaneous deductions (over 2% of adjusted gross income)
   Employee expenses (e.g., professional and union dues, professional publications, travel, transportation, education, job hunting, office-in-home, special clothing, and 50% of entertainment expenses)
   Expenses for producing investment income (e.g., accounting and legal fees, safe deposit rental, fees paid to an IRA custodian)
   Tax advice and tax return preparation and related costs
Other miscellaneous deductions
   Federal estate tax attributable to income in respect of a decedent
   Gambling losses to the extent of winnings
   Amortization of bond premium
   Amounts restored under claim of right

Form 1040 U.S. Individual Income Tax Return 2000

Department of the Treasury—Internal Revenue Service
For the year Jan. 1–Dec. 31, 2000, or other tax year beginning , 2000, ending , 20
OMB No. 1545-0074

Label (See instructions on page 19.) Use the IRS label. Otherwise, please print or type.

Your first name and initial: Larry S.
Last name: Lane
Your social security number: 123 45 6789

If a joint return, spouse's first name and initial: Jane V.
Last name: Lane
Spouse's social security number: 987 65 4321

Home address (number and street): 116 E. Edwards
City, town or post office, state, and ZIP code: Lubbock, Texas

Important! You must enter your SSN(s) above.

Presidential Election Campaign (See page 19.)
Note. Checking "Yes" will not change your tax or reduce your refund.
Do you, or your spouse if filing a joint return, want $3 to go to this fund?
You: ☐ Yes ☒ No   Spouse: ☐ Yes ☒ No

Filing Status
Check only one box.

1. ☐ Single
2. ☒ Married filing joint return (even if only one had income)
3. ☐ Married filing separate return. Enter spouse's social security no. above and full name here. ▶
4. ☐ Head of household (with qualifying person). (See page 19.) If the qualifying person is a child but not your dependent, enter this child's name here. ▶
5. ☐ Qualifying widow(er) with dependent child (year spouse died ▶). (See page 19.)

Exemptions

- 6a ☒ **Yourself.** If your parent (or someone else) can claim you as a dependent on his or her tax return, **do not** check box 6a
- b ☒ Spouse
- c Dependents:

(1) First name	Last name	(2) Dependent's social security number	(3) Dependent's relationship to you	(4) ✓ if qualifying child for child tax credit (see page 20)
Betty	Lane	125 25 7774		✓
				☐
				☐
				☐
				☐
				☐

If more than six dependents, see page 20.

No. of boxes checked on 6a and 6b: **2**
No. of your children on 6c who:
• lived with you: **1**
• did not live with you due to divorce or separation (see page 20)
Dependents on 6c not entered above
Add numbers entered on lines above ▶ **3**

d Total number of exemptions claimed

Income

Attach Forms W-2 and W-2G here. Also attach Form(s) 1099-R if tax was withheld.

If you did not get a W-2, see page 21.

Enclose, but do not attach, any payment. Also, please use Form 1040-V.

7	Wages, salaries, tips, etc. Attach Form(s) W-2	**75,000**
8a	Taxable interest. Attach Schedule B if required	**1,000**
b	Tax-exempt interest. **Do not** include on line 8a 8b 500	
9	Ordinary dividends. Attach Schedule B if required	
10	Taxable refunds, credits, or offsets of state and local income taxes (see page 22)	
11	Alimony received	
12	Business income or (loss). Attach Schedule C or C-EZ	
13	Capital gain or (loss). Attach Schedule D if required. If not required, check here ▶ ☐	
14	Other gains or (losses). Attach Form 4797	
15a	Total IRA distributions 15a b Taxable amount (see page 23)	15b
16a	Total pensions and annuities 16a b Taxable amount (see page 23)	16b
17	Rental real estate, royalties, partnerships, S corporations, trusts, etc. Attach Schedule E	
18	Farm income or (loss). Attach Schedule F	
19	Unemployment compensation	
20a	Social security benefits 20a b Taxable amount (see page 25)	20b
21	Other income. List type and amount (see page 25)	
22	Add the amounts in the far right column for lines 7 through 21. This is your **total income** ▶	**76,000**

Adjusted Gross Income

23	IRA deduction (see page 27) 23 **2,000**	
24	Student loan interest deduction (see page 27) 24	
25	Medical savings account deduction. Attach Form 8853 25	
26	Moving expenses. Attach Form 3903 26	
27	One-half of self-employment tax. Attach Schedule SE 27	
28	Self-employed health insurance deduction (see page 29) 28	
29	Self-employed SEP, SIMPLE, and qualified plans 29	
30	Penalty on early withdrawal of savings 30	
31a	Alimony paid b Recipient's SSN ▶ 31a	
32	Add lines 23 through 31a	**2,000**
33	Subtract line 32 from line 22. This is your **adjusted gross income** ▶	**74,000**

For Disclosure, Privacy Act, and Paperwork Reduction Act Notice, see page 56.   Cat. No. 11320B   Form **1040** (2000)

FIGURE 12-1 ▶ FORM 1040

Form 1040 (2000) — Page 2

Tax and Credits

34 Amount from line 33 (adjusted gross income) — **34** 74,000

35a Check if: ☐ You were 65 or older, ☐ Blind; ☐ Spouse was 65 or older, ☐ Blind.
Add the number of boxes checked above and enter the total here ▶ **35a**

b If you are married filing separately and your spouse itemizes deductions, or you were a dual-status alien, see page 31 and check here ▶ **35b** ☐

Standard Deduction for Most People

Single: $4,400
Head of household: $6,450
Married filing jointly or Qualifying widow(er): $7,350
Married filing separately: $3,675

36 Enter your **itemized deductions** from Schedule A, line 28, **or standard deduction** shown on the left. **But** see page 31 to find your standard deduction if you checked any box on line 35a or 35b **or** if someone can claim you as a dependent — **36** 12,300

37 Subtract line 36 from line 34 — **37** 61,700

38 If line 34 is $96,700 or less, multiply $2,800 by the total number of exemptions claimed on line 6d. If line 34 is over $96,700, see the worksheet on page 32 for the amount to enter — **38** 8,400

39 **Taxable income.** Subtract line 38 from line 37. If line 38 is more than line 37, enter -0- — **39** 53,300

40 Tax (see page 32). Check if any tax is from **a** ☐ Form(s) 8814 **b** ☐ Form 4972 — **40** 9,231

41 Alternative minimum tax. Attach Form 6251 — **41**

42 Add lines 40 and 41 ▶ **42** 9,231

43 Foreign tax credit. Attach Form 1116 if required — **43**

44 Credit for child and dependent care expenses. Attach Form 2441 — **44**

45 Credit for the elderly or the disabled. Attach Schedule R — **45**

46 Education credits. Attach Form 8863 — **46**

47 Child tax credit (see page 36) — **47** 500

48 Adoption credit. Attach Form 8839 — **48**

49 Other. Check if from **a** ☐ Form 3800 **b** ☐ Form 8396 **c** ☐ Form 8801 **d** ☐ Form (specify) _____ — **49**

50 Add lines 43 through 49. These are your **total credits** — **50** 500

51 Subtract line 50 from line 42. If line 50 is more than line 42, enter -0- ▶ **51** 8,731

Other Taxes

52 Self-employment tax. Attach Schedule SE — **52**

53 Social security and Medicare tax on tip income not reported to employer. Attach Form 4137 — **53**

54 Tax on IRAs, other retirement plans, and MSAs. Attach Form 5329 if required — **54**

55 Advance earned income credit payments from Form(s) W-2 — **55**

56 Household employment taxes. Attach Schedule H — **56**

57 Add lines 51 through 56. This is your **total tax** ▶ **57** 8,731

Payments

If you have a qualifying child, attach Schedule EIC.

58 Federal income tax withheld from Forms W-2 and 1099 — **58** 9,000

59 2000 estimated tax payments and amount applied from 1999 return — **59**

60a Earned income credit (EIC) — **60a**

b Nontaxable earned income: amount ▶ _____ and type ▶ _____

61 Excess social security and RRTA tax withheld (see page 50) — **61**

62 Additional child tax credit. Attach Form 8812 — **62**

63 Amount paid with request for extension to file (see page 50) — **63**

64 Other payments. Check if from **a** ☐ Form 2439 **b** ☐ Form 4136 — **64**

65 Add lines 58, 59, 60a, and 61 through 64. These are your **total payments** ▶ **65** 9,000

Refund

Have it directly deposited! See page 50 and fill in 67b, 67c, and 67d.

66 If line 65 is more than line 57, subtract line 57 from line 65. This is the amount you **overpaid** — **66** 269

67a Amount of line 66 you want **refunded to you** ▶ **67a** 269

b Routing number _____ ▶ **c** Type: ☐ Checking ☐ Savings

d Account number _____

68 Amount of line 66 you want **applied to your 2001 estimated tax** ▶ **68**

Amount You Owe

69 If line 57 is more than line 65, subtract line 65 from line 57. This is the **amount you owe**. For details on how to pay, see page 51 ▶ **69**

70 Estimated tax penalty. Also include on line 69 — **70**

Sign Here

Joint return? See page 19.
Keep a copy for your records.

Under penalties of perjury, I declare that I have examined this return and accompanying schedules and statements, and to the best of my knowledge and belief, they are true, correct, and complete. Declaration of preparer (other than taxpayer) is based on all information of which preparer has any knowledge.

Your signature: *Larry S. Lane* | Date: 4-15-01 | Your occupation: Attorney | Daytime phone number: (555) 555-1212

Spouse's signature. If a joint return, **both** must sign: *Jane V. Lane* | Date: 4-15-01 | Spouse's occupation: Student | May the IRS discuss this return with the preparer shown below (see page 52)? ☐ Yes ☐ No

Paid Preparer's Use Only

Preparer's signature ▶ _____ | Date _____ | Check if self-employed ☐ | Preparer's SSN or PTIN _____

Firm's name (or yours if self-employed), address, and ZIP code ▶ _____ | EIN _____ | Phone no. ( ) _____

Form **1040** (2000)

FIGURE 12-1 ▶ FORM 1040 (CONTINUED)

- Casualty losses: only casualty losses in excess of 10% of AGI are deductible.
- Miscellaneous itemized deductions: only miscellaneous itemized deductions in excess of 2% of AGI are deductible.
- High income taxpayers: higher income taxpayers must reduce total itemized deductions by 3% of their AGI over $132,950 in 2001 ($128,950 in 2000).[7] The amount for married persons filing separate returns is $66,475 in 2001 ($64,475 in 2000).

These floors are discussed in more detail in Chapter I7.

EXAMPLE I2-2 ▶ John and Jane file a joint tax return and report AGI of $150,000. Their itemized deductions include $14,000 of medical expenses and home mortgage interest of $10,000. The AGI floor reduces the medical expense deduction to $2,750 [$14,000 − (0.075 × $150,000)]. Total itemized deductions before the overall reduction is $12,750 ($2,750 + $10,000). This amount must be reduced by $512 [($150,000 − $132,950) × 0.03] as a result of the overall floor for itemized deductions. Thus, the total itemized deductions allowed would be $12,238 ($12,750 − $512). ◀

OBJECTIVE 2

Determine the amount allowable for the standard deduction

STANDARD DEDUCTION

Itemized deductions are claimed only if the total amount of such deductions exceeds the standard deduction. The **standard deduction** is an amount set by Congress. It varies depending on the taxpayer's filing status, age, and vision.

KEY POINT
The dollar amount of the standard deduction generally increases each year because it is indexed to the rate of inflation.

Filing Status	Standard Deduction 2000	Standard Deduction 2001
Single individual other than heads of households	$4,400	$4,550
Married couples filing joint returns and surviving spouses	7,350	7,600
Married people filing separate returns	3,675	3,800
Heads of households	6,450	6,650

The differences between the 2000 and 2001 amounts represent adjustments for the increase in the cost of living.

In 2001, a married taxpayer's standard deduction is increased by $900 ($850 in 2000) if he or she is elderly or blind ($1,800 ($1,700 in 2000) if the taxpayer is elderly *and* blind) or has a spouse who is elderly or blind (for a maximum possible increase of $3,600 for a married couple). If an unmarried taxpayer is elderly or blind, his or her standard deduction is increased by $1,100 ($2,200 if the taxpayer is elderly *and* blind). Thus, in 2001, a single taxpayer, age 65 and not blind, is entitled to a $5,650 standard deduction. Two special rules relating to age and blindness are noted below.

- The increase in the standard deduction for elderly taxpayers is available if the taxpayer turns 65 during the tax year. It is interesting that a taxpayer is considered to be age 65 on the day before his or her sixty-fifth birthday. Thus, a taxpayer who reaches age 65 on January 1 of a year is deemed to have reached age 65 on December 31 of the preceding year. The adjustment is allowed on the final return of a deceased taxpayer only if he or she reached age 65 before death.
- The IRC defines blindness as corrected vision in the better eye of no better than 20/200 or a field of no greater than 20 degrees. Vision is determined as of the last day of the tax year or, in the case of a deceased taxpayer, as of the date of death.

The standard deduction simplifies the computation of taxable income. As previously noted, for most taxpayers the standard deduction is greater than total itemized deductions. Those taxpayers do not itemize and, in fact, do not even have to keep records of medical expenses and other itemized deductions.

Who actually itemizes and who does not? High-income taxpayers are more likely to itemize than low-income taxpayers simply because they incur more expenses that can be

---

[7] The reduction in the itemized deductions cannot exceed 80% of the total itemized deductions other than medical expenses, investment interest expenses, casualty losses, and wagering losses. (See Chapter I7 for a discussion of the 80% overall limitation.)

itemized. This is true even though the AGI floors (previously discussed) affect high-income taxpayers more than low-income taxpayers. Another characteristic of taxpayers who generally itemize their deductions are individuals who own their homes and incur home mortgage expenses and property taxes. These two expenses are deductible and alone usually exceed the standard deduction.

EXAMPLE I2-3 ▶ In 2001, Joan is single, and a homeowner who incurs property taxes on her home of $2,000, makes charitable contributions of $500, and pays mortgage interest of $4,000. Joan's adjusted gross income is $30,000. Her taxable income is computed as follows:

Adjusted gross income		$30,000
Minus: Itemized deductions:		
Charitable contributions	$ 500	
Property taxes	2,000	
Mortgage interest	4,000	(6,500)
Minus: Personal exemption		(2,900)
Taxable income		$20,600 ◀

Joan would itemize her deductions because they ($6,500) are greater than her standard deduction ($4,550).

EXAMPLE I2-4 ▶ Assume the same facts as in Example I2-3 except that Joan is not a homeowner. Thus, she has no property taxes or mortgage interest but does pay rent of $600 per month for an apartment. Her taxable income is computed as follows:

Adjusted gross income	$30,000
Minus: Standard deduction	(4,550)
Minus: Personal exemption	(2,900)
Taxable income	$22,550 ◀

Joan would use the standard deduction because it ($4,550) is greater than her itemized deduction ($500). Rent paid for a personal apartment is not deductible.

LOSS OF THE STANDARD DEDUCTION. Congress decided that a few taxpayers should not be permitted to use the standard deduction as they possibly would receive an unintended tax benefit.[8] The standard deduction is unavailable to three categories of taxpayers:

▶ An individual filing a return for a period less than twelve months because of a change in accounting period.
▶ A married taxpayer filing a separate return in instances where the other spouse itemizes.
▶ Nonresident aliens.

To illustrate why Congress does not permit certain taxpayers to claim the standard deduction, consider what could happen if a married couple files separate returns but only one spouse itemizes. On a separate return in 2001 when the standard deduction is $3,800, one spouse could claim all itemized deductions while the other uses the standard deduction.

EXAMPLE I2-5 ▶ Clay and Joy, a married couple, have incomes of $15,000 and $14,000, respectively. Their itemized deductions total $4,500. They would claim a $7,600 standard deduction on a joint return. If Clay filed a separate return and claimed all of the deductions, his itemized deductions of $4,500 would be greater than the $3,800 standard deduction. If Joy could claim the standard deduction on her return, their total deductions would equal $8,300 ($4,500 + $3,800). The law, however, requires that either they both itemize or they both use the standard deduction. ◀

Limitation on the Standard Deduction. A special rule applies to any individual for whom the dependency exemption is allowable to another taxpayer. In 2001, the standard deduction of the dependent is limited to the greater of 1) the dependent's earned income

---

[8] Sec. 63(c)(6).

plus $250, or 2) $750 ($700 in 2000). The purpose of this limitation is to prevent parents from shifting unearned income, such as interest and dividends, to their children and avoid paying tax on such income. Without this rule, children could use the standard deduction to offset income from interest and dividends.

EXAMPLE I2-6 ▶ Webb and Beth are married, in the 36% marginal tax rate bracket, and have one son, Vincent, age 15. Vincent has no income and is claimed as a dependent by his parents. Webb and Beth transfer stocks and bonds to Vincent that earn $3,000 in dividends and interest. Their goal is to shift the $3,000 of income to Vincent to utilize his standard deduction. However, since Vincent is claimed as a dependent by his parents on their return, Vincent's standard deduction is limited to $750, i.e., the *greater* of $750 or his earned income plus $250 ($0 + $250). ◀

EXAMPLE I2-7 ▶ Assume the same facts as in Example I2-6 except Vincent has a part-time job and earns $2,000 in wages. Vincent's standard deduction would be $2,250 ($2,000 + $250). Alternatively, if Vincent's wages were $5,000, his standard deduction would be $4,550 (the maximum for a single individual). ◀

OBJECTIVE 3

Determine the amount and the correct number of personal and dependency exemptions

PERSONAL EXEMPTIONS

In general, taxpayers cannot deduct personal expenses except for certain itemized deductions that are specifically authorized under the tax law. Congress has recognized the need to protect a small amount of income from tax in order to allow the taxpayer to meet personal expenses. Thus, almost every individual taxpayer is allowed a personal exemption of $2,800 in 2000 and $2,900 in 2001. Because there are two taxpayers on a joint return filed by a married couple, they are allowed two personal exemptions. In addition, if a married person files a separate return, the taxpayer can claim a personal exemption for his or her spouse if the spouse has no gross income during the year and the spouse is not the dependent of another taxpayer.[9]

Under current law, only one exemption is allowed for each person. Therefore, if an individual can be claimed as a dependent by another person, that individual is not entitled to a personal exemption on his or her own return. Despite the loss of the personal exemption, most dependents owe little or no tax. Since a person who may be claimed as a dependent typically has a very low amount of income, such person can usually offset his or her income by the standard deduction.

DEPENDENCY EXEMPTIONS

ADDITIONAL COMMENT

One should forsake any preconceived notions as to what constitutes a dependent before examining the dependency tests.

KEY POINT

For someone to be claimed as a dependent, *all* five dependency tests must be satisfied.

In addition to claiming one personal exemption, an individual also may claim an exemption for each dependent. An individual qualifies as a dependent only if he or she meets all five of the following tests:[10]

▶ Support: The taxpayer must provide over 50% of the dependent's support.

▶ Gross income: The dependent's gross income must be less than the amount of the exemption. However, a taxpayer's children who are either, (1) full-time students and under age 24 or (2) under the age of 19, are exempt from this requirement.

▶ Joint return: In general, a married dependent cannot file a joint return.

▶ Relationship: Dependents must either be related to the taxpayer or reside with the taxpayer.

▶ Citizenship: Dependents must be U.S. citizens, residents, or nationals or they must reside in Canada or Mexico.

The full exemption is available for dependents who are born or die during the year. No exemption is available for unborn or stillborn children. All dependents must have social security numbers, and the numbers must be correctly reported on the taxpayer's return.[11] The five tests are discussed below.

---

[9] Sec. 151(b).
[10] Sec. 152.
[11] Sec. 151(e). The IRS has the authority to disallow dependency exemptions for otherwise qualified dependents without social security numbers and with incorrectly reported social security numbers. A missing or incorrectly reported social security number may also bar an otherwise eligible individual from claiming head-of-household filing status.

Determination of Tax ▼ **Individuals 2-13**

SUPPORT TEST. The taxpayer normally must provide over one-half of the dependent's financial support during the year. Support includes amounts spent by the taxpayer, the dependent, and other individuals. Welfare[12] and Social Security benefits[13] spent on support count even if they are excluded from gross income.

EXAMPLE I2-8 ▶ Tarer provided $3,000 of support for his mother, Mary. Tarer's sister provided $1,000. Mary spent $4,500 of her savings for her own support. Because Mary provided at least one-half of her own support, she cannot be claimed as a dependent. ◀

EXAMPLE I2-9 ▶ George's father received Social Security benefits of $6,600, of which $1,800 were deposited into a savings account. He spent the remaining $4,800 on food, clothing, and lodging. George spent $5,600 to support his father. George meets the support test because the amount saved is not counted in the support test. ◀

ADDITIONAL COMMENT

A TV set bought by a parent for his 12-year-old child and set up in her bedroom was considered support. (Rev. Rul. 77-282, 1977-2 CB 52.) A power lawn mower, however, bought by a parent of a 13-year-old child was not considered support. The parent had assigned the child the job of mowing the lawn, and the power mower was intended to make the job more palatable. The lawn mower was considered a family item that benefits all members of the household. (Rev. Rul. 77-282, 1977-2 CB 52.)

Support includes amounts spent for food, clothing, shelter, medical and dental care, education, and the like.[14] Support is not limited to these items.[15] Support does not include the value of services rendered by the taxpayer to the dependent.[16] A scholarship received by a son or daughter[17] is not counted as support in deciding whether a parent provided over one half of the child's support.[18] Also, the IRS and the courts have excluded various other expenses from support.[19]

Generally, the amount of support equals the cost of the item, but in the case of support provided in a noncash form, such as lodging, the amount of support equals the fair market value or fair rental value. The cost of an item such as a television or an automobile is included in support if the item actually is support.[20]

EXAMPLE I2-10 ▶ Vicki's mother lives with her. Vicki purchased clothing for her mother costing $800, and provided her with a room that Vicki estimates she could have rented for $2,800. Vicki spent $2,500 for groceries she shared with her mother and $1,200 for utilities. In addition, Vicki purchased a television for $750 that she placed in the living room. Vicki and her mother both used the television. Vicki's support for her mother, at a minimum, includes:

Clothing	$ 800
Rental value of room	2,800
Food	1,250
Total	$4,850

Whether a portion of the utilities could be included in support would depend on whether the rental rate for the room included utilities. The fact that the mother used the television set probably would not be sufficient to cause its cost to be viewed as support. On the other hand, if the television set was a gift to the mother, was placed in her room, and was used exclusively by her, the cost probably would qualify as support. ◀

If a taxpayer contributes a lump sum for the support of two or more individuals, the amount is allocated between the individuals on a pro rata basis unless proof exists to the contrary.[21]

EXAMPLE I2-11 ▶ Jaime pays rent of $6,000 for an apartment occupied by his sisters Alice, Beth, and Cindy. Alice spends $3,000 toward her own support, Beth spends $1,000, and Cindy spends $1,000. Jaime is

---

[12] Rev. Rul. 71-468, 1971-2 C.B. 115.
[13] Rev. Ruls. 57-344, 1957-2 C.B. 112, and 58-419, 1958-2 C.B. 57.
[14] Reg. Sec. 1.152-1(a)(2)(i).
[15] Examples of other items that have been held to be support include church contributions (Rev. Rul. 58-67, 1958-1 C.B. 62), telephone (*William K. Price, III,* 1961 PH T.C. Memo ¶61,173, 20 TCM 886), medical insurance premiums (*James Edward Parker,* 1959 PH T.C. Memo ¶52,182, 18 TCM 800), child care (*Marvin D. Tucker,* 1957 PH T.C. Memo ¶57,118, 16 TCM 488), toys (*Loren S. Brumber,* 1952 PH T.C. Memo ¶52,087, 11 TCM 289), and vacations (*George R. Melat,* 1953 PH T.C. Memo ¶53,141, 12 TCM 443).
[16] *Frank Markarian v. CIR.,* 16 AFTR 2d 5785, 65-2 USTC ¶9699 (7th Cir., 1965).
[17] Including adopted children, stepchildren, and foster children (if the foster children live with the taxpayer for the entire year).
[18] Sec. 152(d).
[19] Examples of items that have been excluded are funeral expenses (Rev. Rul. 65-307, 1965-2 C.B. 40), taxes (Rev. Rul. 58-67, 1958-1 C.B. 62), a rifle, lawn mower, and boat insurance (*Harriet C. Flower v. U.S.,* 52 AFTR 1383, 57-1 USTC ¶9655 (D.C. Pa., 1957)), and life insurance premiums (*John F. Miller,* 1959 PH T.C. Memo ¶59,155, 18 TCM 673).
[20] Rev. Rul. 77-282, 1977-2 C.B. 52.
[21] Rev. Rul. 64-222, 1964-2 C.B. 47.

assumed to have provided $2,000 of support for each sister. Thus, assuming the other four tests are met, Jaime can claim exemptions for Beth and Cindy, but not for Alice.

SELF-STUDY QUESTION

A parent provides $4,000 of support for his 17-year-old son. The son earns $5,000 during the year but only spends $3,000 for his own support. Will the parent be considered to have provided over 50% of the son's support?

ANSWER

Yes; only the amount actually spent by the son is taken into account.

While a taxpayer normally must provide over one-half of a dependent's support, there are two exceptions to this general rule:

- A multiple support declaration permits one member of a group of taxpayers who collectively provide over 50% of an individual's support to claim the dependency exemption.
- Special rules determine which parent will receive dependency exemptions for children in the case of a divorce.

Often several people contribute to the support of a dependent. Under normal rules, no one would be able to claim a dependency exemption unless one member of the group provided over one-half of the total support. However, when the group provides over one-half of the support of an individual but no one member of the group provides over one-half of the support, eligible members of the group are allowed to designate one group member to claim the exemption. Each eligible member (other than the taxpayer receiving the exemption) must complete a Multiple Support Declaration (Form 2120) stating that he or she will not claim a dependency exemption under these rules. An eligible member is one who contributes more than 10% of the dependent's support and meet all requirements for claiming a dependency exemption except the support requirement.[22]

EXAMPLE I2-12 ▶ John T. Abel lives alone. His support comes from the following sources:

Andy (son)	$ 400
Gabe (son)	2,800
Mable (daughter)	2,000
Betty (friend)	2,800
Total	$8,000

Either Gabe or Mable can claim a dependency exemption if the other completes Form 2120. Andy cannot claim the exemption because he did not provide over 10% of John's support. Betty cannot claim a dependency exemption because she is not related and John does not live with her. For this reason, Andy and Betty need not complete Form 2120. A completed Form 2120 is illustrated in Figure I2-2. ◀

ADDITIONAL COMMENT

Form 8332 may be completed each year by the custodial parent to relinquish the dependency exemption for only that year, or it may be completed once relinquishing the exemption for all future years.

As noted, special rules determine which parent will receive dependency exemptions for children in the case of a divorce or separation.[23] These rules are intended to avoid disputes over which parent provided more than one-half of a child's support. Generally, the parent who has custody of a child for the greater part of the year is entitled to the dependency exemption even if he or she did not provide over one-half of the child's support.[24]

The noncustodial parent may claim the dependency exemption only if the custodial parent agrees in writing. The signed statement must be attached to the noncustodial parent's return each year in which the exemption is claimed. Form 8332 may be used for this purpose. In the case of a divorce or separation, the custodial spouse probably would be reluctant to relinquish the dependency exemption for a child. A noncustodial parent, however, might be able to negotiate the exemption in exchange for increased child support payments.

EXAMPLE I2-13 ▶ Hal and Pam obtain a divorce under the terms of which Pam receives custody of their son. Hal is ordered to pay $600 per month of child support. In absence of a written agreement to the contrary, Pam will receive the dependency exemption for the child. ◀

---

[22] Sec. 152(c).
[23] Including adopted children, stepchildren, and foster children (if the foster children live with the taxpayer for the entire year).
[24] This assumes that together the parents provided over one-half of the support, that no multiple support agreement is in effect, that together the parents had custody of the child for over one-half of the year, and that the parents were divorced, separated, or lived apart for the last half of the year (Sec. 152(e)).

Form **2120** (Rev. November 2000) Department of the Treasury Internal Revenue Service	**Multiple Support Declaration** ▶ Attach to Form 1040 or Form 1040A of person claiming the dependent.	OMB No. 1545-0071 Attachment Sequence No. **114**

Name of person claiming the dependent: **Gabe I. Abel**

Social security number: **123 45 6789**

During the calendar year _____, I paid over 10% of the support of:

John T. Abel
Name of person supported

I could have claimed this person as a dependent except that I did not pay over half of his or her support. I understand that this person is being claimed as a dependent on the Federal income tax return of:

Gabe I. Abel
Name of person claiming the dependent

111 W. Baker St. Lawrence, N.J. 08649
Address of person claiming the dependent

I agree not to claim this person as a dependent on my Federal income tax return for any tax year that began in the above calendar year.

Mabel B. Abel
Your signature

222 11 0001
Your social security number

402 N. Lable Lane
Address (number, street, apt. no.)

4-15-01
Date

Lawrence, N.J. 08649
City, state, and ZIP code

FIGURE 12-2 ▶ FORM 2120

EXAMPLE 12-14 ▶ Assume the same facts as in Example 12-13 except that Pam negotiates child support payments of $800 per month and agrees in writing to allow Hal to claim the dependency exemption for the child. The written agreement will enable Hal to claim the dependency exemption for the child. ◀

EXAMPLE 12-15 ▶ Andy and Beth obtain a divorce under the terms of which they share custody of their daughter. Whoever has custody for the greater part of the year receives the dependency exemption for the daughter unless they agree otherwise in writing. ◀

GROSS INCOME TEST. Generally, a dependent's gross income must be less than the amount of the dependency exemption ($2,900 in 2001). The statutory definition of gross income is used in applying this limitation. Therefore, nontaxable scholarships, tax-exempt bond interest, and nontaxable Social Security benefits are not considered, but salary, taxable interest, and rent are considered in deciding whether the person meets this test.

An important exception applies to the gross income test. The gross income test is waived for a child[25] of the taxpayer who is either under age 19, or if a full-time student, under age 24. A child is considered to be a student if he or she is in full-time attendance at a qualified educational institution during at least five months of the year. To be full-time, a student must carry the number of hours or courses the educational institution requires a student to take to be considered full-time. Note, however, that this is only an exception to the gross income test. Therefore, a self-supporting student cannot be claimed as a dependent by his or her parents. Such a student fails the support test.

EXAMPLE 12-16 ▶ Jim, age 22, is a college student and receives more than half of his support from his parents. Jim earned $6,000 from a summer job. Even though Jim earned more than the dependency exemption amount of $2,900 (2001), his parents may claim him as a dependent because the gross income test is waived and all of the other tests are met. Jim, of course, would not be able to claim himself on his own return.

---

[25] Including adopted children, stepchildren, and foster children (if the foster children live with the taxpayer for the entire year).

One of the important details of this test is that the dependent must be a *child* of the taxpayer. Thus, if Jim was supported by his aunt and uncle (rather than his parents), the aunt and uncle could not claim Jim because the gross income test is not met.

JOINT RETURN TEST. Generally, a taxpayer may not claim a dependency exemption for a married dependent who files a joint return. However, a taxpayer is entitled to the exemption if the dependent files a joint return solely to claim a refund of tax withheld (i.e., there is no tax on the joint return and there would have been no tax on two separate returns).[26] It is important for married dependents to weigh the taxes that would be saved by the family from an exemption against the taxes that would be saved by filing a joint return. Depending on the circumstances, either alternative may be more beneficial.

TYPICAL MISCONCEPTION

It is sometimes incorrectly believed that in order to claim someone as a dependent, the person must in all cases reside in the home of the taxpayer. They do not always realize that residency is a substitute for the relationship test.

RELATIONSHIP TEST. To be claimed as a dependent, a person either must be related to the taxpayer or reside with the taxpayer for the entire tax year.[27] Both immediate family and extended family relationships meet this test. Immediate family relationships include those based on blood, adoption, or marriage, and extended family relationships include only those based on blood or adoption.

Immediate family relationships include

- Parents (including adoptive parents, stepparents, mother-in-law, and father-in-law)
- Siblings (including adoptive siblings, stepbrothers, stepsisters, brothers-in-law, sisters-in-law, half brothers, and half sisters)
- Children (including adoptive children, stepchildren, sons-in-law, daughters-in-law, and foster children who live with the taxpayer for the entire year)

Extended family relationships include

- Grandparents and their ancestors
- Grandchildren and their descendants
- Aunts and uncles
- Nephews and nieces

EXAMPLE I2-17 ▶ Jesse supports three people: Tina, an unrelated child who lives with him; his cousin Judy, who lives in another state; and his mother Vicki, who lives in her own home. Jesse can claim two dependency exemptions: one for Tina, who lives with Jesse (a person who lives with the taxpayer need not be related) and one for his mother. Jesse cannot claim a dependency exemption for Judy (cousins do not meet the relationship test). ◀

On a joint return the dependent needs to be related to only one spouse.[28] Once established, an immediate family relationship is not terminated by death or divorce.

EXAMPLE I2-18 ▶ Ken and Lisa support Lisa's mother and claim her as a dependent on a joint return. Following Lisa's death, Ken continues to support Lisa's mother. Lisa's mother continues to be Ken's mother-in-law and can be claimed as a dependent by Ken. On the other hand, if Ken and Lisa had been supporting Lisa's niece, Ken would not be entitled to a dependency exemption. Although she would continue to be Ken's niece, she is not his niece by blood and cannot be claimed as a dependent unless she resides with Ken. ◀

CITIZENSHIP TEST. A dependent must be a U.S. citizen,[29] national,[30] or resident,[31] or be a resident of Canada or Mexico. The citizenship or residence test need only be met for part of the year.

---

[26] Rev. Ruls. 54-567, 1954-2 C.B. 108, and 65-34, 1965-1 C.B. 86. The theory is that the taxpayer is filing a claim for refund and not actually filing a tax return.
[27] The relationship between the taxpayer and the dependent cannot violate a local law (Sec. 152(b)(5)). The exemption has been disallowed where the relationship constituted "cohabitation" and was illegal in the state (*Cassius L. Peacock, III,*, 1978 PH T.C. Memo ¶78,030, 37 TCM 177).

[28] Reg. Sec. 1.152-2(d).
[29] U.S. citizens living in foreign countries can claim dependency exemptions for adopted children even if the children are not U.S. citizens.
[30] A U.S. national is an individual born in an outlying possession such as American Samoa.
[31] A resident is a person who is not a U.S. citizen and who is legally residing in the United States with intent to stay here permanently (see Sec. 7701(b)).

SELF-STUDY QUESTION

Beth's mother, who is a U.S. citizen, has moved to France to spend her retirement years. She has retained her U.S. citizenship, but she is now a resident of France. Is it possible for Beth to claim her mother as a dependent?

ANSWER

Yes, the mother need only be a U.S. citizen.

PHASE-OUT OF PERSONAL AND DEPENDENCY EXEMPTIONS. Both personal and dependency exemptions are phased out for high-income taxpayers. Exemptions are phased out at a rate of 2% for each $2,500 ($1,250 for married people filing separate returns), or fraction thereof, of adjusted gross income above thresholds shown below. Thus, the entire amount of a taxpayer's personal and dependency exemptions will phase-out when his adjusted gross income exceeds the threshold amount by $122,500 ($61,250 on separate returns). Below are the phase-out amounts for 2001:[32]

	Phase-Out Begins	Phase-Out Ends (More Than)
Single	$132,950	$255,450
Joint return	199,450	321,950
Head of household	166,200	288,700
Married, filing separately	99,725	160,975

EXAMPLE I2-19 ▶ In 2001, Lee, a single taxpayer with no dependents, reports AGI of $138,700. The usual amount of the personal exemption of $2,900 is reduced by 6% to $2,726 ($5,750 excess AGI ÷ $2,500 = 2.3 which is rounded to 3; 3 × 2% = 6%). ◀

Note that the phase-out begins when the taxpayer's adjusted gross income *exceeds* the threshold. Thus, a single taxpayer with AGI of exactly $132,950 is entitled to the full amount of his or her personal and dependency exemptions, whereas a single taxpayer with AGI of $132,950 is entitled to only 98% of his or her personal and dependency exemptions.

STOP & THINK

Question: Jack and Leslie, who have four dependent children, are in the process of getting a divorce. Leslie is a surgeon and earns a net income of $400,000 per year from her medical practice. Jack is a pilot and earns a salary of $140,000. The only other source of income is $20,000 of income from interest and dividends which is divided equally. One major stumbling block in structuring the divorce settlement is deciding which person will be allowed to claim the children as dependents. Either Jack or Leslie will qualify under the income tax rules to claim any or all of the children and both will qualify for head-of-household filing status. The attorneys have come to you for advice. From an income tax standpoint, which parent would benefit the most from being able to claim the children in 2001, or should they each claim two of the children?

Solution: Since Leslie's income is well above the 2001 phase-out limit for personal and dependency exemptions ($288,700), she would not receive any tax benefit from claiming any or all of the children for income tax purposes. Jack, on the other hand, will get a tax benefit from the dependency exemptions because the phase-out amounts for a taxpayer filing as head of household begin at $166,200 and his AGI is only $150,000 ($140,000 + $10,000). Therefore, for income tax purposes only, Jack should claim the four children since he will receive a tax benefit from the dependency exemptions, whereas Leslie would receive no tax benefit if she claimed the children because her AGI is so high that her deduction for personal and dependency exemptions would be zero.

The rules for deducting personal and dependency exemptions are summarized in Topic Review I2-1.

OBJECTIVE 4

Determine the amount of child credit

CHILD CREDIT

Under Sec. 24 of the IRC, individual taxpayers may claim a "child credit" of $500 for each qualifying child. The credit is reduced by $50 for each $1,000 (or fraction thereof) by which the taxpayer's modified adjusted gross income exceeds a threshold amount ($110,000 on joint returns, $75,000 for single taxpayers, and $55,000 for married per-

---

[32] Sec. 151(d). The thresholds are adjusted for inflation. In 2000, the phase-out began at $128,950 for single taxpayers, $193,400 for a joint return, $161,150 for a head of household, and $96,700 for a married individual filing a separate return.

Topic Review I2-1

Personal and Dependency Exemptions

EXEMPTIONS IN GENERAL

- One exemption is available for each taxpayer (except when the taxpayer is the dependent of another) and for each dependent.
- The amount of each exemption, which is adjusted annually for inflation, is $2,900 in 2001 and $2,800 in 2000.
- Exemptions are phased out for high-income taxpayers. For example, on a joint return the phase-out begins when the couple's adjusted gross income exceeds $199,450 and is completed when AGI reaches $321,950.

DEPENDENCY EXEMPTIONS

- One exemption is allowed for each dependent. As noted above, the exemptions are phased out for higher-income taxpayers.
- Five conditions must be met for each dependency exemption. The dependent must be supported by the taxpayer, must meet a gross income test, generally must not file a joint return, must be related to the taxpayer (or live with the taxpayer), and must meet a citizenship or residence test.

ADDITIONAL COMMENT

There are now two credits that have similar names: the child credit and the child and dependent care credit. They are quite different in how the credit amounts are computed and which dependents qualify.

sons filing separate returns). These thresholds are not indexed for inflation. Modified adjusted gross income is AGI plus any amounts excluded from gross income under Secs. 911, 931, and 933 which relate to certain foreign earned income and possession's income. To qualify for the credit, a child must be a U.S. citizen, national, or resident under the age of 17 who qualifies as the taxpayer's dependent, and who is the taxpayer's descendent, stepchild, or foster child. See Chapter I14 for more information regarding the child credit.

EXAMPLE I2-20 ▶ Jane and Bill have two eligible dependent children and a modified AGI of $120,300. They have excess AGI of $10,300 ($120,300 − $110,000) and are entitled to a credit of $450 [(2 × $500) − (11 × $50)]. ◀

DETERMINING THE AMOUNT OF TAX

Once taxable income has been computed, the next step is to determine the gross tax. Most individuals determine the amount of gross tax by looking in the tax table (See page T-2 after Chapter I18 in *Individuals* volume or after Chapter C15 in the *Comprehensive* volume.). This method allows the taxpayer to arrive at the gross tax without the need for multiplication and, therefore, simplifies the computation and reduces the number of errors. Individuals are required to use the tax table unless taxable income exceeds the maximum income in the table (currently $100,000), or if the taxpayer files a short period return on account of a change in the annual accounting period.

Taxpayers who cannot use the tax table instead use the tax rate schedule (located after Chapter I18 and on the inside cover of the text). Taxpayers using the tax rate schedule must actually compute the tax.

EXAMPLE I2-21 ▶ Liz is single and has taxable income of $48,210 in 2000. Liz's tax is determined by reference to the tax table for single taxpayers. (At the time of this writing, the 2000 tax table was the most recent available.) The tax from the table is $10,091. ◀

EXAMPLE I2-22 ▶ Jack and Pam are married, file a joint tax return, and have taxable income of $105,000 in 2001. They will use the tax rate schedule to compute their tax. The tax is computed as follows:

Tax on $45,200 at 0.15	$ 6,780
Tax on remaining $59,800 at 0.28	16,744
Gross tax	$23,524

This tax can also be computed by using the rate schedule (Schedule Y) as follows:

$$\$6{,}780 + [(\$105{,}000 - \$45{,}200) \times .28] = \underline{\$23{,}524}$$

OBJECTIVE 5

Determine the filing status of individuals

FILING STATUS

There are five tax brackets applicable to individual taxpayers: 15%, 28%, 31%, 36%, and 39.6%. These rates are progressive in that as a taxpayer's income increases, the taxpayer moves into higher tax brackets. The income level at which higher tax brackets begin depends on the taxpayer's filing status. There are five different filing statuses but only four rate schedules and/or tax tables because married couples filing jointly and certain surviving spouses use the same rate schedule or tax table. The five filing statuses are

- Married filing jointly
- Surviving spouse
- Head of household
- Single
- Married filing separately

KEY POINT

Currently the highest tax rates are those for married filing separately, and the lowest are those for married filing jointly.

SELF-STUDY QUESTION

If Congress were to adopt a truly proportional tax system, would it be necessary to have the four different tax rate schedules?

ANSWER

No, in a proportional tax system, there is no need for different rate schedules because all taxable income would be taxed at the same rate.

Before 1948, one rate schedule was used by all taxpayers. If a husband and wife both had income, each filed a return. This treatment was deemed to be unfair because various states allocated income between spouses differently. Some states used a community property law system while other states used a common law system. Today, only a few states continue to use the community property law system.[33]

In general, community property law allocates community income equally between a husband and wife, regardless of which spouse actually earns the income. In other states, income belongs to the spouse who produces the income. With a progressive tax system, placing income on one return instead of two can result in a much greater tax. For this reason, couples residing in noncommunity property states often paid more tax than their counterparts who resided in community property states. In 1948, Congress developed the joint-rate schedule to rectify this problem. Unmarried taxpayers who headed families felt they also should receive tax relief because they shared their incomes with their families. So, in 1957, Congress created a rate schedule for heads of households. Below is a discussion of who is covered by each filing status.

JOINT RETURN

A *joint return* can be filed by a man and woman if they meet certain tests.

- They must be legally married as of the last day of the tax year.[34] Whether a couple is married depends on the laws of the state of residence.[35] Couples in the process of a divorce are still considered married until the date the divorce becomes final. A couple need not be living together in order to file a joint return. A joint return can be filed if one spouse dies during the year as long as the survivor does not remarry before the year-end. The executor of the estate must agree to the filing of a joint return.
- They must have the same tax year-end (except in the case of death).
- Both the husband and wife must be U.S. citizens or residents. An exception allows a joint return if the nonresident alien spouse agrees to report all of his or her income on the return.[36]

STOP & THINK

Question: Some couples who get married may find their tax liabilities increase even if their combined incomes remain unchanged. Others find that their tax liabilities decrease. Explain why taxes increase for some couples, but decrease for others.

---

[33] Several states had either adopted or had begun to adopt community property laws in order to reduce the federal taxes paid by their residents. After the joint rate schedule was created, states without a tradition of community property law returned to common law. For a more detailed discussion of community property states, see page I3-6.

[34] Sec. 6013.

[35] Thus, common law marriages recognized by the state of residence are covered. On the other hand, an annulled marriage is viewed as never having been valid. Thus, such a couple cannot file a joint return.

[36] Nonresident aliens are taxed only on income earned in the United States. If a joint return is filed by a U.S. citizen and his or her foreign spouse, they would receive the benefit of the low rate schedule, even though only the U.S. citizen reported income on the return. Thus, to file a joint return, the couple must agree to report both incomes (Sec. 6013(g)).

2-20 Individuals ▼ Chapter 2

ADDITIONAL COMMENT
Since marital status for the entire year is determined on the last day of the year, some couples actually plan for their wedding to occur on December 31 or January 1. In general, if only one person has income, the wedding should take place on December 31. If both have income, a January 1 wedding is best (for tax purposes).

Solution: Couples who marry ordinarily move from two returns where incomes are taxed using the rate schedule for single individuals to one return where the combined incomes are taxed using the joint rate schedule. The less progressive joint rate schedule results in a lower tax if one spouse had most of the income because more of that spouse's income is taxed at lower rates. However, when the husband and wife had approximately equal incomes, their combined incomes are taxed at higher rates on one joint return. Even though the rate schedule for married couples is the least progressive of the individual rate schedules, the combined tax is higher because the second income is added to the first and taxed at higher rates. This increased tax is called the "marriage penalty."

SURVIVING SPOUSE

A widow or widower can file a joint return for the year his or her spouse dies if the widow or widower does not remarry. For the two years after the year of death, the widow or widower can file as a surviving spouse only if he or she meets specific conditions. The **surviving spouse** (sometimes called a qualifying widow or widower) must[37]

▶ Have not remarried as of the year end in which surviving spouse status is claimed.

▶ Be a U.S. citizen or resident.

▶ Have qualified to file a joint return in the year of death.

▶ Have at least one dependent child[38] living at home during the entire year and the taxpayer must pay over half of the expenses of the home.

KEY POINT
The surviving-spouse provision entitles the taxpayer to the lower joint return tax rate schedule and to the higher joint return standard deduction.

In the year of death, a joint return can be filed. On the joint return, the income of the deceased spouse (earned before death) and the survivor are both reported. Personal exemptions are allowed for both spouses. In the two years following death, surviving spouse status can be claimed only if the conditions outlined above are met. Only the surviving spouse's income is reported and, of course, no personal exemption is available for the deceased spouse. What the two situations have in common is that in both instances, the taxpayer can use the more favorable joint rate schedule and standard deduction amount.

EXAMPLE I2-23 ▶ Connie and Carl are married and have no dependent children. Carl dies in 2001. Connie can file a joint return, even though her husband died before the end of the year. Alternatively, Connie can file as a married individual filing a separate return. In 2002, however, Connie must file as a single taxpayer since she has no dependent children who would qualify her as a surviving spouse or a head of household. Alternatively, if Connie and Carl had dependent children, Connie could file as a surviving spouse for 2002 and 2003 and use the joint return rate schedules. ◀

STOP & THINK
Question: Most recently widowed individuals do not qualify for surviving spouse status. Why?

Solution: Most individuals are widowed late in life after their children are grown and have left home. As having a dependent child is a requirement for surviving spouse status, these individuals do not qualify for the special lower tax rate. Such individuals may ordinarily file a joint return in the year of the spouse's death.

ADDITIONAL COMMENT
Due in part by the high divorce rate in this country, the number of head-of-household returns has increased. In 1975, only 6% of all returns had the filing status of head-of-household. In 1996, that number was 14%, or 16.5 million returns.

HEAD OF HOUSEHOLD

A second rate schedule or tax table is available to a head of household. The head of household rates are higher than those applicable to married taxpayers filing jointly and surviving spouses, but lower than those applicable to other single taxpayers. To claim head-of-household status, a taxpayer must meet all of the following conditions:[39]

---

[37] Sec. 2(a).
[38] Includes an adopted child, a stepchild, or a foster child.
[39] Sec. 2(b).

- Be unmarried as of the last day of the tax year. Exceptions apply to individuals married to nonresident aliens[40] and to abandoned spouses.[41] An individual cannot claim head-of-household status in the year his or her spouse died. Such individuals must file a joint return or a separate return.
- Not be a surviving spouse.
- Be a U.S. citizen or resident.
- Pay over half of the costs of maintaining as his or her home a household in which a dependent relative lives for more than half of the tax year. The dependency exemption cannot be based on a multiple support agreement. There are two special rules. First, a taxpayer with a dependent parent qualifies even if the parent does not live with the taxpayer. Second, an unmarried descendant who lives with the taxpayer,[42] need not be the taxpayer's dependent.

The second exception often comes into play in cases of divorced parents. As noted earlier in the chapter, a written agreement can give the dependency exemption to the noncustodial parent. This exception may allow the custodial parent to still claim head-of-household status.

EXAMPLE I2-24 ▶ Brad and Ellen divorce. Ellen receives custody of their child, and Brad is ordered by the court to pay child support of $6,000 per year. Ellen agrees in writing to allow Brad to claim the dependency exemption for the child. If Ellen maintains the home in which she and her child live, she can claim head-of-household status even though the child is Brad's dependent. ◀

ADDITIONAL COMMENT
In 1996, approximately 20 married couples filed joint returns for every married couple that filed separately.

As noted, the taxpayer must pay over half of the costs of maintaining the household. These expenses include property taxes, mortgage interest, rent, utility charges, upkeep and repairs, property insurance, and food consumed on the premises. Such costs do not include clothing, education, medical treatment, vacations, life insurance, transportation, or the value of services provided by the taxpayer.[43]

SINGLE TAXPAYER

An unmarried individual who does not qualify as a surviving spouse or a head of household must file as a single taxpayer. The tax rates are higher than those that apply to other unmarried taxpayers.

EXAMPLE I2-25 ▶ Becky, a single taxpayer with no dependents, files her first tax return. She will file as a single taxpayer. ◀

KEY POINT
Several disadvantages are associated with the filing of separate returns by married individuals. For example, a taxpayer may lose all or part of the benefits of the deduction for individual retirement accounts, the child care credit, and the earned income credit.

MARRIED FILING A SEPARATE RETURN

Married individuals who choose to file separate returns must use the separate rate schedule. The rates on this schedule are higher than other individual rate schedules. The implications of joint returns versus separate returns are discussed later in this chapter.

EXAMPLE I2-26 ▶ On December 31, Rose marries Joe. Because they were married before the year ended, they may elect to file jointly. Alternatively, they may file separate returns with each using the rate schedule applicable to separate returns. ◀

The filing requirements for individuals are summarized in Topic Review I2-2.

---

[40] Specifically, this refers to an individual married to a nonresident alien if he or she meets the remaining head-of-household requirements.
[41] Abandoned spouse rules are discussed under a separate heading later in this chapter.
[42] Includes an adopted child, stepchild, and a descendant of a natural or adopted child.
[43] Reg. Sec. 1.2-2(d).

Topic Review I2-2

Filing Status and Requirements

FILING STATUS	MUST MAINTAIN HOUSEHOLD	MUST HAVE DEPENDENT	MARITAL STATUS	MUST BE CITIZEN	TAX RATES
Joint	No requirement	No	Married	Yes	Lowest rates, but two incomes are combined
Surviving spouse	Yes	Yes, son or daughter	Widowed in prior or second prior year	Yes	Uses same schedule as married couple filing joint return
Head of household	Yes	Generally, yes	Generally, single	Yes	Intermediate tax rates
Single	No requirement	No	Single	No	Highest tax rates for unmarried taxpayers
Separate	No requirement	No	Married	No	Highest tax rates

KEY POINT

When one thinks of a person who would qualify as an abandoned spouse, one thinks of a person in dire financial condition. If no relief were granted, this person would be required to use the married filing separately tax rate schedule, which contains the highest rates.

ABANDONED SPOUSE

The particular rate schedule a taxpayer uses can have a great impact on the amount of tax. Without any special rule, an abandoned spouse would be required to file using the rate schedules for a married person filing separately. Congress has provided relief for taxpayers in this situation if they can meet certain conditions. A married individual can claim head-of-household status if [44]

▶ The taxpayer lived apart from his or her spouse for the last six months of the year.

▶ The taxpayer pays over half of the cost of maintaining a household in which the taxpayer and a dependent son or daughter live for over half of the year.[45]

▶ The taxpayer is a U.S. citizen or resident.

The requirement that the taxpayer have a dependent child is met if a taxpayer who is otherwise qualified to claim the child as a dependent signs an agreement that allows the child's noncustodial parent to claim the dependency exemption for the child.[46]

EXAMPLE I2-27 ▶ In October, Bob and Gail decide to separate. Gail supports their children after the separation and pays the costs of maintaining their home. Gail cannot claim abandoned spouse status because Bob lived with her for over one-half of the year. If she had obtained a divorce before the end of the year, she could have filed as a head of household. In the absence of a divorce, Gail must file a separate return, unless both Bob and Gail agree to file a joint return. ◀

EXAMPLE I2-28 ▶ Assume the same facts as in Example I2-27 except that Gail continues to support her children and pay household expenses during the next year. She can file as a head of household even if she has not obtained a divorce. ◀

DEPENDENTS WITH UNEARNED INCOME

In the past, taxpayers in high tax brackets were able to reduce their tax liability by shifting income to children and other dependents. Under prior law, no tax was due if the income was less than the dependent's personal exemption and standard deduction. Even if the shifted income was greater than these amounts, there was a tax savings if the dependent was in a low tax bracket. Under current law, three rules apply that curtail the advantages of shifting income to dependents:

▶ Dependents do not receive a personal exemption on their own returns.

▶ A dependent's standard deduction is reduced to the greater of $750 or the dependent's earned income (such as salary) plus $250.

---

[44] Sec. 2(c).
[45] Includes adopted child, stepchild, and foster child.
[46] Sec. 152(e).

KEY POINT
Children under the age of 14 will not have their net unearned income tax at their parents' tax rate until the children's unearned income exceeds $1,500.

▶ The tax on the net unearned income (such as dividends and interest) of a child under age 14 is figured by reference to the parents' tax rate if it is higher than the child's.

The first two rules have been discussed previously in this chapter. The third rule is discussed below.

EXAMPLE I2-29 ▶ In 2001, Tim is a self-supporting 18-year-old who received $2,000 of dividends and $900 from a part-time summer job. He is entitled to the regular standard deduction and a personal exemption because his parents may not claim him as a dependent (does not meet the support test). Tim owes no tax as these deductions exceed his income. ◀

EXAMPLE I2-30 ▶ Assume the same facts as in Example I2-29 except that Tim is a dependent of his parents, and they are in the 28% tax bracket. Because Tim is a dependent, he is not entitled to a personal exemption. Tim's standard deduction is limited to the greater of $750 or his earned income plus $250 (but not more than $4,550). Because his earned income is $900, the standard deduction is $1,150 ($900 + $250). Therefore, Tim's taxable income is $1,750 ($2,900 AGI − $1,150 standard deduction). Since Tim is over age 13, he is not subject to the kiddie tax on his unearned income and his regular tax rate (15%) is used. The tax is $263 (0.15 × $1,750). ◀

Under the third rule, often called the kiddie tax, part of the **net unearned income** of a dependent child under age 14 is taxed at the child's rate, and part at the parents' marginal tax rate if that rate is higher than the child's. This tax can be computed following a three-step process:

1. Compute the child's taxable income in the normal fashion for dependents as discussed earlier in this chapter.

2. Compute the child's net unearned income:

Unearned income (described below)	$XXX
Less: Statutory deduction of $750	(XXX)
Less: Greater of	
a. $750 of standard deduction, or	
b. Itemized deductions directly connected with the production of the unearned income.	(XXX)
Equals: Net unearned income	$XXX

3. Compute the child's tax:

Net unearned income times parents' marginal tax rate	$XXX
Plus: Difference between taxable income and net unearned income times child's tax rate	XXX
Equals: Child's total tax	$XXX

WHAT WOULD YOU DO IN THIS SITUATION?

CHOICE OF RATE SCHEDULES

Jane Brown married Jim four years ago. Two years ago Jim lost his job. After looking for work for several months, Jim left town to look for work, and Jane has not heard from him. Jim's brother told Jane that he had heard that Jim lived in Texas, but a friend said he heard that Jim had been killed in an automobile accident. Jane went back to school and completed a program as an medical technician. She returned to work this year, and she earned $35,000. She has asked you to prepare her tax return this year. She has asked you whether she should file as a single taxpayer, married person filing separately, or as a married person filing jointly. Because she has had a low income until recently, she has taken no legal steps to resolve her status. What should she do?

Unearned income is the child's investment income including dividends, taxable interest, capital gains, rents, royalties and other income that is not earned income (such as salary).[47]

EXAMPLE I2-31 ▶ Assume the same facts as in Example I2-30 except that Tim is age 13. His standard deduction is still $1,150 and his taxable income is also $1,750. Since Tim is under age 14, a portion of his unearned income may be subject to tax at his parents' 28% rate. The computation of Tim's tax is as follows:

1. Compute Tim's taxable income:

Wages		$ 900
Dividends		2,000
Adjusted gross income		$2,900
Standard deduction	$1,150	
Personal exemption	0	1,150
Taxable income		$1,750

2. Compute Tim's net unearned income:

Unearned income: Dividends	$2,000
Statutory deduction	(750)
Portion of standard deduction	(750)
Net unearned income	$ 500

3. Compute Tim's tax

Tax on net unearned income: $500 × 28%	$ 140
Tax on taxable income minus net unearned income: ($1,750 − $500) × 15%	188
Total income tax	$ 328 ◀

In figuring the tax where the parents file separate returns, the tax rate of the parent with the greater taxable income is used. If the parents are divorced, the parent with custody is the relevant parent.

Parents of a child under age 14 may elect to include the child's dividend and interest income on their own return.[48] This rule eliminates the need to file a tax return for the child. To be eligible for the election, the child's gross income must come solely from dividends and interest, and such income must not exceed $7,500. Furthermore, there can be no withholding or estimated payment using the child's Social Security number.[49]

CORPORATE TAX FORMULA AND RATES

OBJECTIVE 6

Explain the tax formula for corporations

The corporate tax formula and rates are discussed here to provide basic information needed for subsequent chapters. Corporations are divided into two groups. First, **C corporations**, also called **regular corporations**, are treated as separate entities for tax purposes and pay income taxes on the corporation's taxable income. Shareholders are taxed on dividends they receive from C corporations but are not taxed on the corporation's undistributed income. The second group, **S corporations**, generally are not treated as separate entities for tax purposes but are referred to as flow-through entities. Thus, each S corporation shareholder is required to report a pro rata share of the S corporation's income on his or

---

[47] Sec. 1(g)(4).
[48] Sec. 1(g)(7).
[49] Parents may use Form 8814, Parents' Election to Report Child's Interest and Dividends. If the child's income from dividends and interest is between $750 and $1,500, the child's tax is 15% of the income over $750. If the income is over $1,500, the child's tax is computed by multiplying the parents' tax rate times the child's income over $1,500 and adding $112.50. For example, if the child's dividend income is $2,000 and the parents' tax bracket is 28%, the child's tax is $252.50 [0.28 × ($2,000 − $1,500) + $112.50].

ADDITIONAL COMMENT

In 1996, there were 4.8 million corporate tax returns filed.

KEY POINT

The tax formula for C corporations differs from the tax formula for individuals in several important respects. The corporate tax formula does not contain an adjusted gross income figure, personal and dependency exemptions, or the standard deduction.

her tax return even if the income is not distributed. The shareholders must elect to be covered by the S corporation rules. Corporations must also meet a series of conditions, such as having 75 or fewer shareholders, before they can elect S corporation status. The detailed rules for C corporations are covered in Chapter I16, S corporations are covered in Chapter I17 of the *Individuals* volume. Both C corporations and S corporations are covered more extensively in the *Corporations, Partnerships, Estates, and Trusts* volume and the *Comprehensive* volume.

The tax formula for C corporations is presented in Table I2-7. The major difference between the formulas for individual and corporate taxpayers is the fact that there is only one category of deductions for corporations. Personal expenses do not come into consideration. Therefore, there are no itemized deductions, standard deductions, or personal exemptions. The tax rates applicable to C corporations are as follows:[50]

Taxable Income	Tax
First $50,000	15% of taxable income
Over $50,000, but not over $75,000	$7,500 + 25% of taxable income over $50,000
Over $75,000, but not over $100,000	$13,750 + 34% of taxable income over $75,000
Over $100,000, but not over $335,000	$22,250 + 39% of taxable income over $100,000
Over $335,000, but not over $10,000,000	$113,900 + 34% of taxable income over $335,000
Over $10,000,000, but not over $15,000,000	$3,400,000 + 35% of taxable income over $10,000,000
Over $15,000,000, but not over $18,333,333	$5,150,000 + 38% of taxable income over $15,000,000
Over $18,333,333	$6,416,667 + 35% of taxable income over $18,333,333

Note that the corporate tax rates reflect a stair-step pattern of progression, with the two highest rates of 39% and 38% in the middle of the progression. The benefits of the two lowest tax rates of 15% and 25% are completely eliminated by the application of the 39% tax rate to taxable income between $100,000 and $335,000. Likewise, the benefit of the 34% tax rate on taxable income between $335,000 and $10,000,000 is eliminated by the application of a 38% tax rate on taxable income between $15,000,000 and $18,333,333.

▼ **TABLE I2-7**
Tax Formula for C Corporations

Income from whatever source derived	$xxx
Minus: Exclusions	(xxx)
Gross income	$xxx
Minus: Deductions	(xxx)
Taxable income	$xxx
Times: Tax rates	× .xx
Gross tax	$xxx
Minus: Credits and prepayments	(xxx)
Net tax payable or refund due	$xxx

---

[50] Income of certain personal service corporations is taxed at a flat rate of 35%.

In one sense, there is no formula to compute an S corporation's taxable income because the corporation normally does not pay a tax. S corporations do file returns, but the returns are more informational in nature, much like tax returns of a partnership. A residual income total, known as ordinary income, is computed on the return. Special items, such as capital gains and losses and charitable contributions, are kept separate from the ordinary income amount. This is because every item that would receive special treatment on a shareholder's return is passed through to the shareholder with its status intact. Each shareholder reports his or her share of the ordinary income and his or her share of each special item. Losses pass through and generally can be deducted by shareholders up to their respective bases in the corporation's stock. The deductibility of losses is also subject to other rules, such as the at-risk and passive activity loss rules, and are covered in Chapter I8.

TREATMENT OF CAPITAL GAINS AND LOSSES

OBJECTIVE 7

Explain the basic concepts of property transactions

Capital gains and losses have been accorded favored tax treatment since 1922. Favored tax treatment essentially means that capital gains are taxed at a lower rate than is ordinary income. A purpose of the special rules is to distinguish capital appreciation from gains attributable to ordinary business transactions and speculation. This goal is accomplished by defining capital assets to not include certain business property (e.g., inventory and trade receivables) and by requiring taxpayers to hold capital assets for minimum time periods in order to benefit from the lower rates that are available to capital gains.

The discussion below is intended as a brief introduction to capital gains and losses. A detailed discussion of this topic is contained in Chapter I5.

DEFINITION OF *CAPITAL ASSETS*

HISTORICAL NOTE

Net capital gains reported on individual income tax returns dropped from nearly $300 billion in 1986 to about $133 billion in 1987. The latter amount was more in line with 1984 and 1985. The large amount reported in 1986 was due to the fact that a 60% long-term capital gain deduction was available to individuals in 1986, but was repealed as of December 31, 1986. Many taxpayers sold capital assets to take advantage of the lower effective rates that existed in 1986.

A **capital gain** or **loss** is the gain or loss from the sale or exchange of a capital asset. Unfortunately, the tax law merely states what is not a capital asset. In other words, **capital assets** are assets other than those listed in Sec. 1221. A detailed discussion is found in Chapter I5. Here we simply note the categories of properties included on the list, which are thereby excluded from capital asset status are inventory, trade receivables, certain properties created by the efforts of the taxpayer (such as works of art), depreciable business property and business land, and certain government publications. All other assets are considered capital assets and include investment property (such as stocks and bonds) and personal use property (such as personal residence or automobile). As noted, a purpose of the rules applicable to capital gains and losses is to distinguish capital appreciation from gains derived from ordinary business operations. The profit from the sale of inventory and trade receivables is viewed as business profit as opposed to capital appreciation. Thus, a gain realized by an artist on the sale of one of his or her own works is ordinary income from personal services. However, gain from the sale of artwork held as an investment or for personal-use would be treated as a capital gain.

TAX TREATMENT OF GAINS AND LOSSES

ADDITIONAL COMMENT

The amount of net capital gains reported on 1996 tax returns totaled $245 billion, an increase of 50.5% from 1995.

Capital gains and losses are divided into long-term (associated with property held over one year) and short-term (associated with property held one year or less). Individual taxpayers pay a maximum 20% tax on a net long-term capital gain (a 10% tax in the case of individuals who are in the 15% tax bracket). A net short-term capital gain is taxed at the same rate as other income.

On the other hand, individuals who suffer net capital losses can deduct only up to $3,000 of the losses from other income. A net capital loss in excess of $3,000 can be carried over and offset against future capital gains or, subject to the $3,000 limitation, deducted from other income.

TAX PLANNING CONSIDERATIONS

SHIFTING INCOME BETWEEN FAMILY MEMBERS

Because of the progressive tax system, families often can reduce their taxes by **shifting income** to family members who are in lower tax brackets.

> **EXAMPLE I2-32** ▶ Mary, who is in the 36% tax bracket, shifted $5,000 of income to her 22-year-old son, Steve by making a gift of a 10%, $50,000 corporate bond. Steve had no income as he suffered a business loss. In absence of the shift, 36% of the income would have gone for taxes. There is no tax on Steve's return because the income is offset by his loss. ◀

> **EXAMPLE I2-33** ▶ Farouk, who is in the 36% tax bracket, shifted $2,000 of income to his 18-year-old daughter, Dana, who is in the 15% tax bracket. The tax savings from the shift is $420 [(0.36 × $2,000) − (0.15 × $2,000)]. ◀

ADDITIONAL COMMENT
All 50 states have enacted laws that simplify the procedures for making gifts to minors. This type of law, which in most states is called the Uniform Gifts to Minors Act, is especially important when making gifts of securities.

As noted earlier in this chapter, the net unearned income of children under the age of 14 is taxed at their parents' tax rate. Hence, a shifting of income to young children is often an ineffective method of minimizing tax.

Shifting income must be distinguished from assigning income. Earned income is taxed to the person who produces it. Income from property is taxed to the person who owns the property. Ordering income to be paid to another is an assignment of income that does not change who is taxed on the income. Normally, in the case of income from property, ownership of the property must be transferred in order to shift the income.

> **EXAMPLE I2-34** ▶ John owns stock in Valley Corporation. John orders the corporation to pay this year's dividends to his daughter. John will be taxed on the income even though he has assigned it to another person. ◀

> **EXAMPLE I2-35** ▶ Kay owns stock in Valley Corporation. Kay gives the stock to her 17-year-old son. Future dividends on Valley stock will be taxed to the son instead of to Kay. ◀

Individuals often are unwilling to give property away completely. As a result, personal preference may limit the amount of tax planning that is possible.

SPLITTING INCOME

Splitting income consists of creating additional taxable entities, especially corporations, in order to reduce an individual's effective tax rate.

> **EXAMPLE I2-36** ▶ Tom is a taxpayer in the 36% tax bracket and is involved in a variety of businesses. One business has been producing $20,000 of income per year for several years. Tom incorporates the business. The first $50,000 of a corporation's income is taxed at a 15% rate. Thus, the tax on the income is reduced by $4,200 [(0.36 × $20,000) − (0.15 × $20,000)]. ◀

The creation of a new corporate entity to split income is not always desirable because the corporation's income will be taxed to the shareholder as a dividend if it is distributed. In addition, if income is allowed to accumulate in a corporation indefinitely, it may be subject to the accumulated earnings tax.[51]

KEY POINT
The ability to maximize itemized deductions by the timing of expenditures is somewhat limited. The two most significant items that would lend themselves to such a strategy are property taxes and charitable contributions. Prepaid interest is not deductible until accrued.

MAXIMIZING ITEMIZED DEDUCTIONS

Timing expenditures properly often can increase deductions. In general, cash-basis taxpayers deduct expenses in the year paid. If itemized deductions are less than the standard deduction, the taxpayer will receive no tax benefit from the deductions. A taxpayer in that situation could defer some payments or accelerate others to maximize expenses in one year, thereby creating a sufficient amount of deductions in that year.

---

[51] Amounts accumulated in a corporation in excess of $250,000 may be subject to this tax. However, amounts accumulated for business purposes are exempt. This subject is discussed briefly in Chapter I16 and extensively in *Prentice Hall's Federal Taxation: Corporations, Partnerships, Estates and Trusts*.

EXAMPLE I2-37 ▶ Jean's property taxes are due on January 1 of each year. Jean is a single, cash-basis, calendar-year taxpayer. Itemized deductions other than property taxes total $2,000 in each year. Jean pays the 2001 property taxes of $1,600 on January 1, 2001 and the 2002 property taxes of $1,600 on December 31, 2001. In the absence of doubling up, Jean would not be able to itemize in either year. The itemized deductions of $3,600 ($2,000 + $1,600) would be less than the standard deduction of $4,550. By doubling up, Jean has itemized deductions of $5,200 ($2,000 + $1,600 + $1,600) in 2001. ◀

Medical expenses are deductible only to the extent they exceed 7.5% of a taxpayer's AGI. In situations where medical expenses are just under 7.5% of AGI, taxpayers may be able to create a deduction by doubling up.

EXAMPLE I2-38 ▶ Troy's AGI is $20,000. So far in 2001, Troy's medical expenses have totaled $1,300. Troy has received a bill from his dentist for $500 that is due January 15, 2002. By paying the bill in 2001, Troy will have a deduction for medical expenses of $300 [$1,300 + $500 − (0.075 × $20,000)]. This assumes that Troy's other itemized deductions exceed the standard deduction.[52] ◀

FILING JOINT OR SEPARATE RETURNS

FACTORS TO BE CONSIDERED. In general, married couples may file either joint or separate returns. As noted earlier, if one spouse has significantly more than half of their combined income, filing separately will increase the couple's total income tax. Because of the potential tax saving from a joint return and because it is simpler to prepare one return than two, most married couples file jointly.

It should be noted that the joint return is not always preferred. Separate returns may result in increased deductions. Because only one spouse's income is reported on a separate return, medical expenses are more likely to exceed the 7.5% of adjusted gross income floor if one spouse incurs most of the medical expenses. Similarly, casualty losses involving personal-use assets, which are allowable only to the extent that they exceed 10% of AGI, may be deductible on separate returns.

One significant impact of the joint return is the joint income tax liability. Both the husband and wife may be liable for taxes owed on a joint return. This could be a major problem if a couple separates or divorces after filing a return.

EXAMPLE I2-39 ▶ Jim and Pat file a joint return. They are both informed as to the relevant information pertaining to the return. The next year they separate, and Jim moves out of town without leaving a forwarding address. The IRS audits their joint return and disallows $400 of charitable contributions deducted on the original return. Pat may be held responsible for the additional taxes owed. The IRS does not have to attempt to locate Jim in order to collect the tax. ◀

ETHICAL POINT
Because innocent spouse rules are strict, it may sometimes be safer to file a separate return than run the risk of being held responsible for the acts of another.

INNOCENT SPOUSE PROVISION. When married couples file a joint return, each spouse generally is liable for the entire tax and any penalties imposed.[53] This is the case even if all of the income was earned by one spouse. This rule could prove unfair in some instances, especially where one spouse concealed information from the other. For that reason, the Code contains an **innocent spouse** provision. An innocent spouse is relieved of the liability for tax on unreported income if:

▶ The amount is attributable to erroneous items of the other spouse.

▶ The innocent spouse did not know and had no reason to know that there was such an understatement of tax.

▶ Under the circumstances, it would be inequitable to hold the innocent spouse liable for the understatement.

▶ The innocent spouse elects relief within two years after the IRS begins collection activities.[54]

---

[52] For a discussion of restrictions on the deductibility of prepaid medical expenses, see Chapter I7.

[53] Sec. 6013(d)(3).
[54] Sec. 6015(b).

EXAMPLE 12-40 ▶ Dan and Joy file a joint return. Dan traveled much of the time and Joy had little information as to his whereabouts or income. Joy worked and her own salary was the sole source of her support. Their return was audited by the IRS. The audit disclosed that Dan had not reported income from a job he had held for several months during the year. In this situation, Joy may be able to use the innocent spouse provision in order to avoid being held liable for the tax on the unreported income. ◀

The election is permitted when the innocent spouse was aware of the understatement, but did not know or have reason to know the extent of the understatement. Relief is limited to the related portion of the understatement attributable to the "unknown" amounts.

SEPARATE LIABILITY ELECTION. Couples who file joint returns and are subsequently divorced, widowed, or separated may make a separate liability election. An electing spouse is liable only for the portion of any understatement attributable to him or her.

EXAMPLE 12-41 ▶ Al and Ann divorce after filing a joint return. An IRS examination of the return reveals $20,000 of unreported income attributable to Al and $10,000 of unallowable deductions attributable to Ann. Together, these amounts result in an understatement of their tax by $9,000. If Ann can establish that she was unaware of Al's unreported income, she can make a separate liability election. She will be liable only for $3,000 of tax as she is responsible for only one third of the understatement. The allocation would not be different because only part of the deductions were disallowed because of an AGI floor. ◀

The election must be made within two years after the IRS begins collections efforts. The election may be made by both spouses. The election is invalid if the spouse responsible for the errors transfers assets to the "innocent" spouse in an effort to avoid payment.

ELECTING TO CHANGE TO A JOINT RETURN. In general, a husband and wife who file separate returns for a given year may elect to change to a joint return by filing an amended joint return. This change is permitted after the due date but must occur within three years of the due date including extensions. Taxpayers may not change from a joint return to separate returns after the due date.[55]

COMPLIANCE AND PROCEDURAL CONSIDERATIONS

WHO MUST FILE

Whether an individual must file a tax return is based on the amount of the individual's gross income.[56] The fact that the individual owes no tax does not mean that a return need not be filed. The gross income filing levels are as follows:[57]

	2000	2001
Single	$ 7,200	$ 7,450
Single (65 or over)	8,300	8,550
Married, filing jointly	12,950	13,400
Married, filing jointly (one spouse 65 or over)	13,800	14,300
Married, filing jointly (both 65 or over)	14,650	15,200
Surviving spouse	10,150	10,500
Surviving spouse (65 or over)	11,250	11,600
Married, filing separately	2,800	2,900
Married, living separately from spouse at year-end	2,800	2,900
Head of household	9,250	9,550
Head of household (65 or over)	10,350	10,650

ADDITIONAL COMMENT
The IRS is encouraging nonfilers (i.e., individuals and businesses who should have filed previous tax returns but did not) to come forward. The IRS estimates that there were 6 million nonfilers in 1990 alone.

ADDITIONAL COMMENT
A file-by-telephone system has been tested in some states in the last few years. The filers dial a toll-free telephone number and enter tax return data with a touch-tone telephone. While the taxpayer is still on the line, the IRS calculates any refund or tax due. The taxpayers then mail a signed Form 1040-TEL.

---

[55] Reg. Sec. 1.6013-1(a). However, a couple who filed a joint return whose marriage is later annulled must file amended returns as singles (Rev. Rul. 76-255, 1976-2 C.B. 40).
[56] *Gross income* has its usual meaning except that the gain excluded from the sale of a personal residence and excluded foreign earned income are included (Sec. 6012(c)).
[57] Sec. 6012(a)(1).

2-30 Individuals ▼ Chapter 2

ADDITIONAL COMMENT
The IRS is required to impound tax refunds to help other agencies collect overdue student loans, child support, etc. However, the IRS found that people whose refunds were offset in 1985 and 1986 were far more likely than others to file no returns in the next two years or to file returns without paying all they owed.

There are three situations where taxpayers must file even if the gross income is less than the amounts shown above:

▶ Taxpayers who receive advance payments of the earned income credit (see Chapter I14) must file regardless of their income levels.

▶ Taxpayers with net self-employment income of $400 or more must file regardless of their total gross income.

▶ Taxpayers who can be claimed as a dependent by another must file if they have either unearned income over $750 or total gross income over the standard deduction.

In general, taxpayers must file if their gross income equals or exceeds the sum of the personal exemption and the standard deduction (including the additional standard deduction due to age but not blindness). The blindness allowance and dependency exemptions are not considered. If the disallowance of the standard deduction rules apply, the standard deduction is ignored in determining whether taxpayers must file.

EXAMPLE I2-42 ▶ In 2001, Carol is a single, self-supporting taxpayer with no dependents. Carol must file if her gross income is $7,450 or greater ($4,550 + $2,900). ◀

KEY POINT
It is possible that a taxpayer may be required to file an income tax return but still have no tax liability.

DUE DATES FOR FILING RETURN

An individual taxpayer must file on or before the fifteenth day of the fourth month following the close of his or her tax year.[58] For calendar-year taxpayers, the due date is April 15. If the due date falls on a Saturday, Sunday, or a legal holiday, the due date is the next day that is not a Saturday, Sunday, or holiday.[59]

An automatic four-month extension of time to file is given to taxpayers who file Form 4868 by the due date for the return. This is an extension to file the return, not an extension of the time to pay the tax. The taxpayer must estimate the amount of tax due and pay it with Form 4868.[60] Taxpayers who are unable to file their returns within the four-month extension period may request an additional two month extension of time by timely filing Form 2688.

ADDITIONAL COMMENT
In 1996, 66 million returns were filed on Form 1040, 23 million on Form 1040A, and 21 million on Form 1040EZ.

USE OF FORMS 1040, 1040EZ, AND 1040A

The primary individual tax return is Form 1040. Complicated returns often involve many additional forms and schedules. Two shorter forms are available to taxpayers with less-complicated tax returns. Form 1040EZ is available to single taxpayers and married individuals who file a joint return. Such taxpayers must have taxable income of less than $50,000 and claim no dependents. To use Form 1040EZ, the taxpayer's income must consist of salary and wages plus no more than $400 of taxable interest income. No deductions (other than the standard deduction) or credits (other than withholding from salary and wages) can be taken on the return.

Form 1040A is available to taxpayers who have somewhat more involved returns. Form 1040A can be used by taxpayers claiming any number of exemptions or any filing status. Salary, wages, dividends, interest, pension and annuity income, and unemployment compensation can be reported on Form 1040A. Taxpayers may deduct IRA contributions. Taxpayers may also claim credits for withholding, child care, and earned income.

SELF-STUDY QUESTION
It is sometimes said that the hallmark of the U.S. federal income tax system is voluntary compliance. With so much information being reported to the IRS, how voluntary is the system?

ANSWER
The system is not very voluntary with respect to income subject to reporting. But some sources of income, such as income from self-employment, are not subject to reporting by a third party. Also, the IRS would have to audit a tax return to verify most of the deductions.

SYSTEM FOR REPORTING INCOME

There is a significant and expanding relationship between computers, tax returns, the taxpayer identification system, and information returns. The IRS keeps records based on taxpayer identification numbers. Individual taxpayers report information based on Social Security numbers, whereas employer identification numbers (EIN) are used by corporations, other taxpayers, and tax-exempt entities. Individuals who employ others have both a Social Security number and an employer identification number.

---

[58] Sec. 6072(a).
[59] Sec. 7503.

[60] Reg. Sec. 1.6081-4(a)(1)-(5)-(5).

Employers, banks, stockbrokers, savings and loans, and so on report payments they make to others along with the payee's identification number. Today, the IRS computers match much of the reported information with tax returns, using the taxpayer identification number as the cross-reference. The need for accurate information returns is obvious. Some major information returns are listed below:

Basic Form	Type of Payment	Required if Amount Equals or Exceeds
1099-R	Pensions and annuities	$600
W-2	Salary, wages, etc.	600
1099-DIV	Dividends	10
1099-INT	Interest	600[61]
1099-B	Sale of a security	All
1099-G	Unemployment compensation, tax refunds, etc.	10
1099-MISC	Rent, royalties, etc.	600
1099-R	Total lump-sum distributions from retirement plans	600[62]

This information-reporting system makes it more difficult for taxpayers to avoid IRS detection if they omit income from their returns.

PROBLEM MATERIALS

DISCUSSION QUESTIONS

I2-1 a. The tax law refers to gross income, yet the term gross income is not found on Form 1040. Explain.
b. Why is it important to understand the concept of gross income even though the term is not found on Form 1040?

I2-2 Explain the distinction between income and gross income.

I2-3 a. Explain the distinction between a deduction and a credit.
b. Which is worth more, a $10 deduction or a $10 credit?
c. Explain the difference between refundable and nonrefundable credits.

I2-4 List the five conditions that must be met in order to claim a dependency exemption. Briefly explain each one.

I2-5 a. Briefly explain the concept of support.
b. If a taxpayer provides 50% or less of another person's support, is it possible for the taxpayer to claim a dependency exemption? Explain.
c. Does support include the value of an automobile? Explain.

I2-6 Under what circumstances must a taxpayer use a rate schedule instead of a tax table?

I2-7 a. What determines who must file a tax return?
b. Is an individual required to file a tax return if he or she owes no tax?

I2-8 Many homeowners itemize deductions while many renters claim the standard deduction. Explain.

I2-9 Tax rules are often very precise. For example, a taxpayer must ordinarily provide "over 50%" of another person's support in order to claim a dependency exemption. Why is the threshold "over 50%" as opposed to "50% or more."

I2-10 What is the normal due date for the return of a calendar-year individual taxpayer? What happens to the due date if it falls on a Saturday, Sunday, or holiday?

I2-11 Why are there five filing statuses but only four rate schedules?

I2-12 Can tax-exempt income qualify as support? Explain.

I2-13 Can a scholarship qualify as support?

I2-14 Explain the purpose of the multiple support agreement.

I2-15 Summarize the rules that explain which parent receives the dependency exemption for children in cases of divorce.

I2-16 What conditions must be met by a married couple before they can file a joint return?

I2-17 Explain what is meant by the phrase *maintain a household*.

I2-18 Under what circumstances, if any, can a married person file as a head of household?

---

[61] For banks and corporations the amount is $10.

[62] Except that all IRA distributions must be reported.

I2-19   a. Explain the principal difference in the tax treatment of an S corporation and a C corporation.
         b. Why would a C corporation be used if an S corporation is generally exempt from tax?

I2-20   a. What assets are excluded from capital asset status?
         b. Are capital gains given favorable tax treatment?
         c. What is the significance of an asset being classified as a capital asset?

I2-21   Are capital losses deductible?

I2-22   Is there any tax advantage for an individual who has held an appreciated capital asset for eleven months to delay the sale of the asset? Explain.

I2-23   a. Explain the difference between income splitting and income shifting.
         b. Why are taxpayers interested in shifting income from one tax return to another within the same family or economic unit?
         c. Is there a relationship between the tax on unearned income of a minor and taxpayers who attempt to shift income?

I2-24   a. Who is liable for additional taxes on a joint return?
         b. Why is this so important?

I2-25   Can couples change from joint returns to separate returns? Separate to joint?

ISSUE IDENTIFICATION QUESTIONS

I2-26   This year, Yung Tseng, a U.S. citizen, supported his nephew who is attending school in the United States. Yung is a U.S. citizen, but his nephew is a citizen of Hong Kong. The nephew has a student visa, but he hopes to become a permanent U. S. resident. Other family members hope to come to the U.S. What issues must be considered by Yung?

I2-27   Joan's parents were killed in an automobile accident late last year, and she moved in with her sister Joy. Their brother, Ed, provides $300 per month to help with Joan's expenses. Joy provides Joan with a room and she also pays some of Joan's expenses such as clothing and meals. Joan has no source of support other than Joy and Ed. What issues should Joy and Ed consider?

I2-28   Carmen and Carlos, who have filed joint tax returns for several years, separated this year. Carlos works in construction and is often paid in cash. Carlos says he only worked a few weeks this year and made $11,000. In prior years he made approximately $35,000 per year, and Carmen is surprised that his income is so low this year. Carmen received a salary of $38,000 as a medical laboratory technician. They have no dependents and claim the standard deduction. What tax issues should Carmen and Carlos consider?

I2-29   Jane and Bill have lived in a home Bill inherited from his parents. Their son Jim lives with them. Bill and Jane obtain a divorce during the current year. Under the terms of the divorce, Jane receives possession of the home for a period of five years and custody of Jim. Bill is obligated to furnish over one-half of the cost of the maintenance, taxes, and insurance on the home and pay $6,000 of child support per year. Bill lives in an apartment. What tax issues should Jane and Bill consider?

PROBLEMS

I2-30   *Computation of Tax.* The following information relates to two married couples:

	Lanes	Waynes
Salary (earned by one spouse)	$20,000	$110,000
Interest income	1,000	5,000
IRA contribution	2,000	0
Itemized deductions	8,000	9,000
Exemptions	5,800	5,800
Withholding	850	22,000

Compute the 2001 tax due or refund due for each couple. Assume that the itemized deductions have been reduced by the applicable floors.

I2-31   *Dependency Exemptions.* Anna, age 65, who lives with her unmarried son, Mario, received $7,000, which was used for her support during the year. The sources of support were as follows:

Social Security benefits	$1,500
Mario	2,600
Caroline, an unrelated friend	800
Doug, Anna's son	500
Elaine, Anna's sister	1,600
Total	$7,000

(handwritten: more than 10% — Mult. Supp. Agreemt.)

a. Who might be able to claim Anna as a dependent?
b. What must be done before Mario can claim the exemption?
c. Can anyone claim head-of-household status based on Anna's dependency exemption? Explain. *(handwritten: no - not as result of mult. supp. agreement)*
d. Can Mario claim an old age allowance for his mother? Explain. *(handwritten: no - P12-16)*

I2-32 *Computation of Taxable Income.* The following information for 2001 relates to Tom, a single taxpayer, age 18:

Salary	$1,800
Interest income	1,600
Itemized deductions	600

a. Compute Tom's taxable income assuming he is self-supporting.
b. Compute Tom's taxable income assuming he is a dependent of his parents.

I2-33 *Joint Versus Separate Returns.* Carl and Carol have salaries of $14,000 and $22,000, respectively. Their itemized deductions total $5,000. They are married and both are under age 65.
a. Compute their taxable income assuming they file jointly.
b. Compute their taxable incomes assuming they file separate returns and that Carol claims all of the itemized deductions.

I2-34 *Joint Versus Separate Returns.* Hal attended school much of 2001, during which time he was supported by his parents. Hal married Ruth in December 2001. Hal graduated and commenced work in 2002. Ruth worked during 2001 and earned $18,000. Hal's only income was $800 of interest. Hal's parents are in the 28% tax bracket. Thus, claiming Hal as a dependent would save them $812 (0.28 × $2,900) of taxes.
a. Compute Hal and Ruth's gross tax if they file a joint return.
b. Compute Ruth's gross tax if she files a separate return in order to allow Hal's parents to claim him as a dependent.
c. Which alternative would be better for the family? In other words, will filing a joint return save Hal and Ruth more than $812?

I2-35 *Dependency Exemptions.* Wes and Tina are a married couple and provide financial assistance to several persons during the current year. For the situations below, determine whether the individuals qualify as dependency exemptions for Wes and Tina. In all of the situations below, assume that any dependency tests not mentioned have been met.
a. Brian is age 24 and Wes and Tina's son. He is a full-time student and lives in an apartment near campus. Wes and Tina provide over 50% of his support. Brian works as a waiter and earned $3,200 in the current year.
b. Same as a. except that Brian is a part-time student.
c. Sherry is age 22 and Wes and Tina's daughter. She is a full-time student and lives in the college dormitory. Wes and Tina provide over 50% of her support. Sherry works part-time as a bookkeeper and earned $3,000 in the current year.
d. Same as c. except that Sherry is a part-time student.
e. Granny, age 82, is Tina's grandmother and lives with Wes and Tina. During the current year, Granny's only sources of income were her Social Security of $4,800 and interest on U.S. bonds of $3,000. Granny uses her income to pay for 40% of her total support, Wes and Tina provide the remainder of Granny's support.
f. Wes and Tina provide 75% of the support for Charley, age 5, who lives with Tina's brother, Bob and his wife. Charley's parents were tragically killed in an accident two years ago and Bob and his wife are taking care of Charley in their home awaiting adoption proceedings. However, Bob does not have the financial resources to care for Charley on his own and Wes and Tina provide the above funds to help support Charley.

I2-36 *Dependency Exemption and Child Credit: Divorced Parents.* Joe and Joan divorce during the current year. Joan receives custody of their three children. Joe agrees to pay $2,000 of child support for each child.

a. Assuming no written agreement, who will receive the dependency exemption and child credit for the children? Explain.
b. Would it make any difference if Joe could prove that he provided over one-half of the support for each child?

I2-37 *Filing Status, Dependency Exemptions and Child Credit.* For the following taxpayers, indicate which tax form should be used, the applicable filing status, and the number of personal and dependency exemptions available, and the number of children who qualify for the child credit.
a. Arnie is a single college student who earned $7,700 working part-time. He had $200 of interest income and received $1,000 of support from his parents.
b. Buddy is a single college student who earned $7,700 working part-time. He had $600 of interest income and received $1,000 of support from his parents.
c. Cindy is divorced and received $6,000 of alimony from her former husband and earned $12,000 working as a secretary. She also received $1,800 of child support for her son who lives with her. According to a written agreement, her former husband is entitled to receive the dependency exemption.
d. Debbie is a widow, age 68, who receives a pension of $8,000, nontaxable social security benefits of $8,000, and interest of $4,000. She has no dependents.
e. Edith is married, but her husband left her two years ago and she has not seen him since. Edith supported herself and her daughter, age 6. She paid all household expenses. Her income of $16,000 consisted of a salary of $15,200 and interest of $800.

I2-38 *Marriage and Taxes.* Bill and Mary plan to marry in December 2001. Bill's salary is $32,000 and he owns his own residence. His itemized deductions total $9,000. Mary's salary is $36,000. Her itemized deductions total only $1,600 as she does not own her own residence. For purposes of this problem, assume 2002 tax rates, exemptions, and standard deductions are the same as 2001.
a. What will their tax be if they marry before year-end and file a joint return?
b. What will their combined taxes be for the year if they delay the marriage until 2002?
c. What factors contribute to the difference in taxes?

I2-39 *Dependency Exemptions and Child Credit.* How many dependency exemptions are the following taxpayers entitled to, assuming the people involved are U.S. citizens? Which dependents qualify for child credit?
a. Andrew supports his cousin Mary, who does not live with him. Mary has no income and is single.
b. Bob and his wife are filing a joint return. Bob provided over one-half of his father's support. The father received Social Security benefits of $6,000 and taxable interest income of $800. The father is single and does not live with them.
c. Clay provides 60% of his single daughter's support. She earned $3,000 while attending school during the year as a full-time student. She is 22 years old.
d. Dave provided 30% of his mother's support and she provided 55% of her own support. Dave's brother provided the remainder. The brother agreed to sign a multiple support agreement.

I2-40 *Amount of Personal Exemptions and Child Credit.* Juan and Maria are married and have two young children. Their adjusted gross income in 2001 is $280,000 and have itemized deductions of $38,000.
a. Assuming they can validly claim four personal and dependency exemptions, what is the amount of their personal and dependency exemptions that they will subtract in arriving at taxable income?
b. What is the amount of their child credit?

I2-41 *Filing Requirement.* Which of the following taxpayers must file a 2001 return?
a. Amy, age 19 and single, has $7,050 of wages, $300 of interest, and $350 of self-employment income.
b. Betty, age 67 and single, has a taxable pension of $4,100 and Social Security benefits of $6,200.
c. Chris, age 15 and single, is a dependent of his parents. Chris has earned income of $1,600 and interest of $400.
d. Dawn, age 15 and single, is a dependent of her parents. She has earned income of $400 and interest of $1,600.
e. Doug, age 25, and his wife are separated. He earned $3,000 while attending school during the year.

I2-42 *Head of Household.* In the following situations, indicate whether the taxpayer qualifies as a head of household.
  a. Allen is divorced from his wife. He maintains a household for himself and his dependent mother.
  b. Beth is divorced from her husband. She maintains a home for herself and supports an elderly aunt who lives in a retirement home.
  c. Cindy was widowed last year. She maintains a household for herself and her dependent daughter, who lived with her during the year.
  d. Dick is not divorced, but lived apart from his wife for the entire year. He maintains a household for himself and his dependent daughter. He does not receive any financial support from his wife.

I2-43 *Filing Status.* For the following independent situations, determine the optimum filing status for the years in question.
  a. Wayne and Celia had been married for 24 years when Wayne died in an accident in October, 1999. Celia and her son, Wally, age 21 in 1999, continued to live at home in 1999, 2000, 2001, and 2002. Wally worked part-time (earning $5,000 in each of the four years) and attended the University on a part-time basis. Celia provided more than 50% of Wally's support for all four years. What is Celia's filing status for 1999, 2000, 2001, and 2002?
  b. Juanita is a single parent who in 2001 maintained a household for her unmarried son Josh, age 19. Josh graduated from high school in 2000 and has not decided whether to attend college. Thus, in 2001, Josh worked full-time and earned $9,000. Juanita provided approximately 40% of Josh's support in 2001 but provided all the expenses of maintaining the household. What is Juanita's filing status for 2001?
  c. Gomer and Gertrude are married and have one dependent son in 2001. In April, 2001, Gomer left Gertrude a note informing her that he needed his freedom and he was leaving her. As of December 31, 2001, Gertrude had not seen nor heard a word from Gomer since April. Gertrude fully supported her son and completely maintained the household. What is Gertrude's filing status in 2001 assuming she was still legally married at December 31, 2001?

I2-44 *Computation of Taxable Income.* Jim and Pat are married and file jointly. In 2001, Jim earned a salary of $46,000. Pat is self-employed. Her gross business income was $49,000 and her business expenses totaled $24,000. Each contributed $2,000 to a deductible IRA. Their itemized deductions total $10,000. Compute Parts a, b, and c without regard to self-employment tax.
  a. Compute their gross income.
  b. Compute their adjusted gross income.
  c. Compute their taxable income assuming they have a dependent daughter.

I2-45 *Itemized or Standard Deduction.* Jan, a single taxpayer, has adjusted gross income of $250,000, home mortgage interest of $4,000, and charitable contributions of $3,000. Should she itemize her deductions or claim the standard deduction?

I2-46 *Kiddie Tax.* Debbie is 16 years old and a dependent of her parents. She earns $4,300 working part-time and receives $1,600 interest on savings. She saves both the salary and interest. What is her taxable income? Would her taxable income or tax be different if Debbie were 13 years old?

I2-47 *Personal and Dependency Exemptions.* Determine the number of personal and dependency exemptions in each of the following situations. Assume any condition for a dependency exemption not mentioned is met.
  a. Allen supports his older sister, who lives in her own apartment.
  b. Bob supports his aunt and her husband, who live in their own apartment.
  c. Charles and his two brothers support their mother. They agree to allow Charles to claim the exemption.
  d. Dan provides $3,000 of support for his sister, and she spent $2,900 of taxable interest income for her own support.

I2-48 *Computation of Tax, Standard Deduction, and Kiddie Tax.* Anthony and Latrisha are married and have two sons, James, age 16 and Jonas, age 13. Both sons are properly claimed as dependency exemptions. Anthony and Latrisha's taxable income is $130,000 in 2001 and they file a joint return. Both James and Jonas had part-time jobs as well as some unearned income. Below is a summary of their total income.

	James	Jonas
Wages	$2,800	$ 400
Dividends from stocks	1,800	2,000

Compute the taxable income and tax liability for James and Jonas.

I2-49 *Computation of Tax.* Compute the tax on $60,000 of taxable income assuming the taxpayer is the following:
a. A S corporation
b. A C corporation
c. A married couple filing a joint return
d. A single taxpayer

I2-50 *Child Credit.* In 2001, Harry a single taxpayer with AGI of $87,600 claims exemptions for four dependent children, all under age 17. What is the amount of his child credit?

I2-51 *Capital Gains.* Larry and Jane have $400,000 of taxable income. They plan to sell stock they have held for 11 months. Their gain will be $10,000. For purposes of this problem, ignore personal exemptions, itemized deductions or any other phaseouts.
a. What will be the additional tax they pay if they sell the stock now?
b. What will the tax be if they keep the stock for 2 more months? Assume the price does not change.

I2-52 *Timing of Deductions.* Virginia is a cash-basis, calendar-year taxpayer. Her salary is $20,000, and she is single. She plans to purchase a residence in 2002. She anticipates her property taxes and interest will total $7,000. Each year, Virginia contributes approximately $1,000 to charity. Her other itemized deductions total approximately $1,000. For purposes of this problem, assume 2002 tax rates, exemptions, and standard deductions are the same as 2001.
a. What will her gross tax be in 2001 and 2002 if she contributes $1,000 to charity in each year?
b. What will her gross tax be in 2001 and 2002 if she contributes $2,000 to charity in 2001 but makes no contribution in 2002?
c. What will her gross tax be in 2001 and 2002 if she makes no contribution in 2001 but contributes $2,000 in 2002?
d. Alternative c results in a lower tax than either a or b. Why?

I2-53 *Tax Forms and Filing Status.* Which tax form is used by the following individuals?
a. Anita is single, age 68, and has a salary of $22,000 and interest of $300.
b. Betty owns an apartment complex that produced rental income of $36,000. Expenses totaled $38,500.
c. Clay's wife died last year. He qualifies as a surviving spouse. His salary is $24,000.
d. Donna is a head of household. Her salary is $17,000 and she has $200 of interest income.

I2-54 *Computation of Tax.* Jose is a single taxpayer with a dependent daughter who lives with him. His salary is $44,000. Jose realized a long-term capital loss on the sale of stock of $45,000. He contributed $2,000 to a deductible IRA. His itemized deductions total $7,000.
a. Compute Jose's adjusted gross income.
b. Compute Jose's taxable income.
c. Compute Jose's gross tax.

I2-55 *Kiddie Tax.* Ralph and Tina (husband and wife) transferred taxable bonds worth $20,000 to Pam, their 12-year-old daughter. Pam received $1,800 of interest on the bonds in the current year. Ralph and Tina have a combined taxable income of $51,000.
a. Compute Ralph and Tina's gross tax. Assume they do not include Pam's income on their return.
b. Can Ralph and Tina claim a child credit for Pam?
c. Compute Pam's taxable income and gross tax.
d. What would be Pam's tax if she were age 16?

I2-56 *Progressive or Proportional Tax.* Assume Gail is a wealthy widow whose husband died last year. Her dependent daughter lives with her for the entire year. Gail has dividend and interest income totaling $370,000 and she pays property taxes and home mortgage interest totaling $20,000.
a. What filing status applies to Gail?

b. Compute her taxable income and gross tax.
c. Assume that Gail does not have a daughter. What is Gail's filing status?
d. Compute Gail's taxable income and gross tax assuming she does not have a daughter.

TAX FORM/RETURN PREPARATION PROBLEMS

I2-57 Aida Petosa (Soc. Sec. no. 123-45-6789) is the 12-year-old daughter of Alfredo Petosa (Soc. Sec. no. 987-65-4321). Her only income is $2,800 of interest on savings. Alfredo qualifies as a head of household, and his taxable income is $52,000. Compute her tax using Form 8615.

I2-58 James S. (Soc. Sec. no. 123-45-6789) and Lulu B. Watson (Soc. Sec. no. 987-65-4321) reside at 999 E. North Street, Richmond, Virginia 23174. They have one dependent child, Waldo, age 4 (Soc. Sec. no. 123-45-4321) and they are both under 65 years old. They do not wish to take advantage of the presidential election campaign check-off. Other relevant information includes

James's salary as a mechanic	$19,000
Lulu's salary as a teacher	24,000
Interest (First National Bank)	1,100
Withholding	4,000

Complete their Form 1040A.

I2-59 John R. Lane (Soc. Sec. no. 123-44-6666) lives at 1010 Ipsen Street, Yorba Linda, California 90102. John, a single taxpayer, age 66, provided 100% of his cousin's support. The cousin lives in Arizona. He wants to take advantage of the presidential election campaign check-off. John is an accountant. Other relevant information includes

Salary	$20,000
Taxable pension	30,000
Interest income	300
IRA deduction	2,000
Itemized deductions (from Schedule A)	6,000
Withholding	8,000

Assume that the supplemental Schedule A has already been completed. Complete Form 1040.

CASE STUDY PROBLEMS

I2-60 Bala and Ann purchased as investments three identical parcels of land over a several-year period. Two years ago they gave one parcel to their daughter, Kim, who is now age 12. They have an offer from an investor who is interested in acquiring all three parcels. The buyer is able to purchase only two of the parcels now, but wants to purchase the third parcel two or three years from now, when he expects to have available funds to acquire the property. Because they paid different prices for the parcels, the sales will result in different amounts of gains and losses. The sale of one parcel owned by Bala and Ann will result in a $20,000 gain and the sale of the other parcel will result in a $28,000 loss. The sale of the parcel owned by Kim will result in a $19,000 gain. Kim has no other income and does not expect any significant income for several years. Bala and Ann, however, are in the 31% tax bracket. They do not have any other capital gains this year. Which two properties would you recommend that they sell this year? Why?

I2-61 Larry and Sue separated at the end of the year. Larry has asked Sue to sign a joint income tax return for the year because he feels that the tax will be lower on a joint return. Larry and Sue both work. Sue received a salary of $25,000 and Larry's salary was $20,000. Larry works as a waiter at a local restaurant and received tips. The restaurant asked Larry to indicate the amount of tips he received so that they could report the information to the IRS. Larry reported to the employer that the tips amounted to $3,000, but Sue believes that the amount was probably $6,000 to $10,000. They do not have enough expenses to itemize. Sue has asked you what are the advantages and risks of filing a joint return.

TAX RESEARCH PROBLEMS

I2-62 Ed has supported his stepdaughter, her husband, and their child since his wife's death three years ago. Ed promised his late wife that he would support her daughter from a former marriage and her daughter's husband until they both finished college. They live in another state, and meet gross income filing requirements. Is Ed entitled to dependency exemptions for the three individuals?

A partial list of research sources is

- Sec. 152
- Reg. Sec. 1.152-2
- *Desio Barbetti*, 9 T.C. 1097 (1947)

I2-63 Bob and Sue were expecting a baby in January, but Sue was rushed to the hospital in December. She delivered the baby but it died the first night. Are Bob and Sue entitled to a dependency exemption for the baby?

Research sources include Rev. Rul. 73-156, 1973-1 C.B. 58.

I2-64 Larry has severe vision problems and, in the past, he has claimed the additional standard deduction available to blind taxpayers. This year Larry's doctor prescribed a new type of contact lens that greatly improved his vision. Naturally, Larry was elated, but unfortunately new problems developed. He suffered severe pain, infection, and ulcers from wearing the new lens. The doctor recommended that he remove the lens and after several weeks his eyes healed. The doctor told him that he could wear the contacts again, but only for brief time periods, or the problems would recur. Can Larry claim the additional standard deduction available to blind taxpayers?

Research sources include *Emanuel Hollman*, 38 T.C. 251 (1963).

CHAPTER 3

GROSS INCOME: INCLUSIONS

LEARNING OBJECTIVES
After studying this chapter, you should be able to

1. Explain the difference between the economic, accounting, and tax concepts of income
2. Explain the principles used to determine who is taxed on a particular item of income
3. Determine when a particular item of income is taxable under both the cash and accrual methods of reporting
4. Apply the rules of Sec. 61(a) to determine whether items such as compensation, dividends, alimony, and pensions are taxable

CHAPTER OUTLINE

Economic and Accounting Concepts of Income...3-2
Tax Concept of Income...3-3
To Whom Is Income Taxable?...3-6
When Is Income Taxable?...3-8
Items of Gross Income: Sec. 61(a)...3-12
Other Items of Gross Income...3-22

Computation of an individual's income tax liability begins with the determination of income. Although the meaning of the term *income* has long been debated by economists, accountants, tax specialists, and politicians, no universally operational definition has been accepted.

The Sixteenth Amendment to the Constitution gave Congress the power to tax "income from whatever source derived." To ensure the constitutionality of the income tax, this phrase is incorporated in Sec. 61(a), where **gross income** is defined as follows: "Except as otherwise provided . . . gross income means all income from whatever source derived."

This chapter examines the concept of income for the purpose of determining what items of income are taxable. Chapter I4 considers items of income that are excluded from gross income. As noted in Chapter I2, many provisions in the tax law are created by a process of political compromise. Thus, there is no single explanation of why certain items are taxable and others are not. For this reason, determining whether a particular item of income is taxable often proves difficult.

ECONOMIC AND ACCOUNTING CONCEPTS OF INCOME

OBJECTIVE 1

Explain the difference between the economic, accounting, and tax concepts of income

ECONOMIC CONCEPT

In economics, *income* is defined as the amount an individual could consume during a period and remain as well off at the end of the period as he or she was at the beginning of the period. To the economist, therefore, income includes both the wealth that flows to the individual and changes in the value of the individual's store of wealth. Or, more simply, income equals consumption plus the change in wealth.

EXAMPLE I3-1 ▶ Alice earned a salary of $40,000. She consumed $30,000 of food, clothing, housing, medical care, and other goods and services. Assets owned by Alice were worth $100,000 at the beginning of the year. Her assets, including $10,000 of salary that was saved, were worth $115,000 at the end of the year. Her liabilities did not change during the year. Alice's economic income is $45,000 [$30,000 + ($115,000 − $100,000)]. ◀

Under the economist's definition, unrealized gains, as well as gifts and inheritances, are income. Furthermore, the economist adjusts for inflation in measuring income. An individual has no income to the extent that an increase in the measured value of property is caused by a decrease in the value of the measuring unit. In other words, inflation does not increase wealth and, therefore, does not cause an individual to be better off.

ACCOUNTING CONCEPT

In accounting, income is measured by a transaction approach. Accountants usually measure income when it is *realized* in a transaction. Values measured by transactions are relatively objective as accountants recognize (i.e., report) income, expenses, gains, and losses that have been realized as a result of a completed transaction. Accountants believe that the economic concept of income is too subjective to be used as a basis for financial reporting and, therefore, have traditionally used historical costs in measuring income instead of using unconfirmed estimates of changes in market value. In accounting, the meaning of the term *realization* is critical to the income measurement process. *Realization* generally results upon the occurrence of two events, (1) a change in the form or substance of a taxpayer's property (or phrased another way, a severance of the economic interest in the property), and (2) a transaction with a second party. Thus, if a taxpayer sells some property for cash, a realization has clearly occurred, i.e., the property has been changed to cash and the transaction was with a second party. Conversely, the mere increase in value of property owned by a taxpayer will not result in the realization of income because there has been no change in the form of the property and no transaction with a second party.

EXAMPLE I3-2 ▶ Assume the same facts as in Example I3-1. The amount consumed by Alice, the increase in the value of the property owned by her, and inflation are all ignored by the accountant in measuring her income. Only when she sells or otherwise disposes of the assets that have increased in value will the accountant recognize the gain. Thus, Alice's accounting income is $40,000. ◀

TAX CONCEPT OF INCOME

The income tax law essentially has adopted the accountant's concept of income rather than the economist's. The reasons for this generally relate to matters of administrative convenience and the wherewithal-to-pay concept. However, as we will see later, there are many differences between income for tax purposes and accounting income.

In general, three conditions must be met for amounts to be taxable.

- There must be economic benefit. The economic benefit is not limited to cash payments. Employees who receive a company's stock, rather than cash, are receiving an economic benefit. Taxpayers benefit even if they direct that payments be made to other persons. As a result, employees cannot avoid being taxed on their earnings by ordering that their salaries be paid to creditors or family members.

- The income must be realized. In general, realization occurs when the earning process is complete and a transaction with another party takes place that permits an objective measure of the income. This objective measurement increases "administrative convenience" which is discussed below. Unlike financial accounting, there are many exceptions that result in income being reported when the taxpayer receives payment even if that is at a time other than when the earning process is complete. These exceptions result in taxes being owed when the taxpayer has the "wherewithal to pay" (see below). Taxpayers who use the "cash method" of reporting, discussed later in the chapter, are normally taxed when payment is received.

- The income must be recognized. Some items of income are not taxable because of special provisions in the tax law. For example, certain real estate exchanges and corporate reorganizations are not taxable because of statutory nonrecognition rules. In such cases, the taxpayer receives a lower basis in replacement property, and that often means the income is recognized when the replacement property is sold. The tax law also contains exclusions that exempt specific types of income such as scholarships, inheritances, and municipal bond interest. Within statutory limitations, taxpayers are never taxed on such items of income.

ADMINISTRATIVE CONVENIENCE

The economic concept of income is considered to be too subjective to be used as a basis for determining income taxes. The need for objectivity in taxation is evident. If taxpayers were required to report increases in value as income, some individuals would certainly understate values to reduce their tax liabilities. The IRS and even the most honest taxpayer often would disagree over values and, as a result, the tax system would be extremely difficult to administer. The disputes over valuation issues would be constant, and the courts would be burdened with added litigation. This problem is evidenced by the few situations where valuations are required in the determination of tax. For example, taxpayers who contribute property to charity usually can deduct the value of the property. The courts are continuously having to resolve disputes between taxpayers and the IRS over the value of such contributions. Furthermore, in the case of certain large contributions of property, taxpayers are required to attach to their returns appraisals of the contributed property. Recently, penalties were added to the law for persons who substantially overvalue contributions.

In some instances, objectivity is achieved at the price of equity. For example, a taxpayer who owns land that has substantially declined in value generally cannot recognize the decline in value until it is realized through a disposition of the land. Similarly, an increase in value, no matter how large, is not taxed until a sale or exchange of the property has occurred. A taxpayer with a modest salary may feel that it is unfair that he or she is taxed on the salary while another person is not taxed on unrealized gains amounting to millions of dollars. As noted above, however, it would be practically impossible to fairly and consistently administer an income tax law that was based on values.

WHEREWITHAL TO PAY

The wherewithal-to-pay concept holds that tax should be collected when the taxpayer is in the best position to pay the tax. A taxpayer who sells property and collects the cash is in a better position to pay the tax than a taxpayer who owns property that is merely increasing in value without a sale.

This concept is the rationale for several tax provisions. For example, the tax law allows a cash-basis taxpayer who sells property on the installment basis to report the gain as the installment payments are collected, rather than at the time of the sale. Losses, on the other hand, cannot be reported on the installment basis, as the wherewithal-to-pay is not an issue. The concept is also used to justify differences between the tax law and financial accounting principles. Prepaid income is not income from an accounting standpoint until it is earned. The tax law, however, takes the position that prepaid income is subject to taxation at the time it is collected, rather than as it is earned. At the time of collection, the taxpayer clearly has the cash available to pay the tax. If the tax were deferred until the income is earned, the taxpayer may no longer have the cash.

GROSS INCOME DEFINED

Section 61(a) provides the following general definition and listing of income items:

> General Definition.—Except as otherwise provided in this subtitle, gross income means all income from whatever source derived, including (but not limited to) the following items:
> 1. Compensation for services, including fees, commissions, fringe benefits, and similar items
> 2. Gross income derived from business
> 3. Gains derived from dealings in property
> 4. Interest
> 5. Rents
> 6. Royalties
> 7. Dividends
> 8. Alimony and separate maintenance payments
> 9. Annuities
> 10. Income from life insurance and endowment contracts
> 11. Pensions
> 12. Income from discharge of indebtedness
> 13. Distributive share of partnership gross income
> 14. Income in respect of a decedent
> 15. Income from an interest in an estate or trust

This definition certainly is not all-inclusive. For example, it does not indicate whether specific items of income such as insurance settlements, gambling winnings, or illegal income are taxable. One point is apparent: The phrase *[e]xcept as otherwise provided* means that all sources of income are presumed to be taxable unless there is a specific exclusion in the income tax law. The IRS does not have to prove that an item of income is taxable. Rather, the taxpayer must prove that the item of income is excluded. Thus, gambling winnings and illegal income are taxable simply because no specific provisions in the tax law exclude such amounts from taxation.

FORM OF RECEIPT. Gross income is not limited to amounts received in the form of cash. According to Reg. Sec. 1.61-1(a), income may be "realized in any form, whether in money, property, or services." The important question is whether the taxpayer receives an economic benefit. This rule covers barter transactions which are direct exchanges of property and services. Each party to the transaction is taxed on the value of the property or services received in the exchange. In general, the cost basis of property given up in a barter

---

KEY POINT

Section 446(a) states that taxable income shall be computed under the method of accounting on the basis of which the taxpayer regularly computes his or her income in keeping his or her books. This provision would seem to require that tax accounting rules would conform to financial accounting rules. However, as will be seen later in this and other chapters, there are many differences.

KEY POINT

Congress has not adopted any particular concept or theory of income for tax purposes. Except as specifically limited by statute, the definition of income is broad and general.

SELF-STUDY QUESTION

Why should taxpayers who are using the cash method of accounting be required to include in gross income the value of property or services received?

ANSWER

If taxpayers were not required to include the value of property or services received in gross income, many taxpayers would arrange their financial affairs so that they would receive property or services instead of cash.

transaction can be subtracted from the value of the property received in arriving at the taxable amount.

EXAMPLE I3-3 ▶ King Corporation transfers 1,000 shares of its stock to its president. The stock has no restrictions and is part of the president's compensation. The president must include the value of the stock in gross income. ◀

EXAMPLE I3-4 ▶ Ali, an attorney, performs legal services for Paul, a painter, in exchange for Paul's promise to paint Ali's residence. Each taxpayer realizes income equal to the value of services received when the services are performed. Thus, Ali must report income in an amount equal to the value of the painting services provided by Paul. Paul must report the value of Ali's legal services. These amounts, assuming an arms-length transaction, should be the same. ◀

EXAMPLE I3-5 ▶ USA Corporation distributes an automobile to Vicki, a shareholder, in lieu of a cash dividend. Vicki must report the value of the automobile as dividend income. ◀

EXAMPLE I3-6 ▶ Len has fallen behind on loan payments due to a bank. The bank obtains a court order requiring Len's employer to pay part of Len's wages directly to the bank. Len will be taxed on the full wages even though a portion goes directly to the bank. ◀

EXAMPLE I3-7 ▶ Wayne borrowed $3,000 from his employer. The employer awarded year-end bonuses to other employees but told Wayne that the debt was being forgiven in lieu of a bonus. Wayne must include the $3,000 in income. ◀

STOP & THINK *Question:* As noted, income is taxable even if it is paid in a form other than cash. What problem does this treatment produce for the IRS and taxpayers?

Solution: Two major problems are created: valuation and enforcement. First, it is necessary to determine the market value of property and services when income is received in a form other than cash. Determining values can be difficult. Second, enforcement by the IRS is made much more difficult because such income is not documented by canceled checks, credit card receipts, or other records. Thus, as demonstrated in Example I3-4 above, many of these so-called "traded services" are not reported as income. This evasion of income represents billions of lost tax revenues to the government.

INDIRECT ECONOMIC BENEFIT. As indicated earlier, the issue of taxability of income often depends on whether the taxpayer receives an economic benefit. In general, if a taxpayer benefits from an item, it is taxable. Frequently, however, an employer may make an expenditure in which its employees may incidentally or indirectly benefit. For example,

▶ Security guards patrol an employer's plant, protecting both the employer's property and the employees. The employees receive an indirect benefit for the protection provided by the security guards.
▶ An employer requires employees to undergo an annual checkup, the cost of which is paid by the employer.
▶ An employer provides protective clothing worn by employees while on the job.
▶ A shipping company provides sleeping accommodations to sailors while ships are at sea.
▶ A company requires certain employees to wear shoes manufactured by the company and provide regular reports on the quality of the shoes.

It is now well-established that taxpayers may exclude such indirect benefits from gross income. This judicially-developed rule holds that an expenditure is excludible if it is made in order to serve the business needs of the employer and any benefit to the employee is secondary and incidental.

Congress also has established rules dealing with situations where expenditures are made primarily to benefit employees. While expenditures made by employers that primarily benefit employees are generally taxable, there are instances whereby such expenditures are not taxable. These rules, which are discussed in Chapters I4 and I9, permit employees to exclude certain fringe benefits (such as employee discounts) from gross income.

TO WHOM IS INCOME TAXABLE?

OBJECTIVE 2

Explain the principles used to determine who is taxed on a particular item of income

Once it is established that income is taxable, it is necessary to determine to whom it is taxable. Although such determinations are usually easy, there are circumstances where income is not necessarily taxed to the person who receives it. If physical receipt of income was the only test, a family might reduce or eliminate its income tax by having income paid to children and other members who are in low tax brackets or have no tax liability.

ASSIGNMENT OF INCOME

In 1930, the Supreme Court held in a landmark case, *Lucas v. Earl*, that an individual is taxed on the earnings from his or her personal services.[1] Specifically, the Supreme Court held that a husband was taxed on the earnings from his law practice, even though he had signed a legally enforceable agreement with his wife that the earnings would be shared equally. An agreement to assign income does not permit a person to avoid being taxed on the income. The Court used the previously developed analogy that likens income to the fruit and capital to the tree.[2] Accordingly, the fruit (income) could not be attributed to a tree other than the one on which it grew.

In 1940, the Supreme Court, in *Helvering v. Horst*, extended the assignment of income doctrine to income from property.[3] In this case, the taxpayer detached interest coupons from bonds and gave the coupons to his son. The son collected the interest and reported it on his own return. The Supreme Court held that the taxpayer was taxed on the interest income because he owned the bonds. This holding leads to a basic rule that the income from property is taxed to the owner of the property. To transfer the income from property, the taxpayer must transfer ownership of the property itself.[4]

Although married couples may file joint returns today, this privilege did not become available until 1948. Assignment of income is an issue today when other individuals such as parents and children are involved, and it can still be an issue with married couples if they file separate returns.

KEY POINT

The law makes a clear distinction between an assignment of income and an assignment of income-producing property. The income is taxable to the assignor in the former case, but where there is a bona fide gift of property the income is taxable to the assignee.

ADDITIONAL COMMENT

The community property states are generally located in the western or southwestern United States. Generally these states were settled by immigrants from France and Spain, and their state laws reflect this fact. The common law is derived from English common law.

ADDITIONAL COMMENT

Community property laws are sometimes difficult to generalize. Depending on the specific law within a community property state, one-half of estimated taxes paid by one spouse may or may not be used by the other spouse on a separate return.

ALLOCATING INCOME BETWEEN MARRIED PEOPLE

For federal income tax purposes, income is allocated between a husband and wife depending on the state of residence. Forty-two states follow a common law property system, whereas eight states[5] use a community property system. Under common law, income is generally taxed to the individual who earns the income, either through labor or capital. Thus, in the case of a married couple, if the wife owns stock in her separate name and receives dividends from such stock, the income is taxed entirely to the wife. Generally, the only joint income in a common law state is income from jointly owned property.[6]

In community property states, income may be either separate or community. **Community income** is considered to belong equally to the spouses. In all community property states, the income from the personal efforts of either spouse is considered to belong

---

[1] *Lucas v. Earl*, 8 AFTR 10287, 2 USTC ¶496 (USSC, 1930).
[2] The analogy had been used some ten years earlier in *Eisner v. Myrtle H. Macomber*, 3 AFTR 3020, 1 USTC ¶32 (USSC, 1920). The court originally used the analogy in efforts to distinguish income from capital.
[3] *Helvering v. Horst*, 24 AFTR 1058, 40-2 USTC ¶9787 (USSC, 1940).
[4] A series of rather specific rules allocates income between the former and current owner when income-producing property is transferred. For example, in the case of bonds transferred by gift, the IRS has ruled that interest must be allocated based on the number of days the bonds were held by each owner during the interest period (Rev. Rul. 72-312, 1972-1 C.B. 22). A similar allocation must be made if bonds are sold (Rev. Rul. 72-224, 1972-1 C.B. 30).
[5] The states are Arizona, California, Idaho, Louisiana, Nevada, New Mexico, Texas, and Washington. Wisconsin's marital property law, though not providing for community property, is basically the same as community property.
[6] Historically, tenancy by the entirety, a form of joint ownership between spouses, allocated all income to the husband. Today, the laws of many states allocate income from property held in tenancy by the entirety equally between the spouses.

equally to the spouses. Furthermore, income from community property is considered to be community income. Thus, if a wife's salary is used to purchase stock, subsequent dividends are community income.

Couples can have separate property even in community property states. **Separate property** consists of all property owned before marriage and gifts and inheritances acquired after marriage. Whether income from separate property is community or separate depends on the state. In Idaho, Louisiana, and Texas, income from separate property is community income. In Arizona, California, Nevada, New Mexico, and Washington, such income is separate income.

EXAMPLE 13-8 ▶ A husband and wife file separate returns. The husband's salary is $40,000 and the wife's salary is $48,000. The wife received $1,000 of dividends on stock she had inherited from her parents. Interest of $1,200 was received on bonds that were purchased from the husband's salary. They received $2,600 in rent from farm land that they purchased jointly. The income would be allocated, depending on the state of residence, as follows:

California (Community Property State)	Husband	Wife
Salary	$44,000	$44,000
Dividends		1,000
Interest	600	600
Rent	1,300	1,300
Total	$45,900	$46,900

Texas (Community Property State)	Husband	Wife
Salary	$44,000	$44,000
Dividends	500	500
Interest	600	600
Rent	1,300	1,300
Total	$46,400	$46,400

Pennsylvania (Common Law State)	Husband	Wife
Salary	$40,000	$48,000
Dividends		1,000
Interest	1,200	
Rent	1,300	1,300
Total	$42,500	$50,300 ◀

These rules are important if couples file separate returns. The community income rules can prove to be a problem if one spouse conceals income from the other. Normally, each spouse is expected to report one-half of all community income. This treatment is inequitable if one spouse is not aware that the community income was earned. Special rules excuse an innocent spouse who fails to report community income on a separate return, provided that the spouse had no knowledge or reason to know of the item and, as a result, the inclusion of the community income would be inequitable.[7] A corresponding provision permits the IRS to include the entire amount in the income of the other spouse.[8]

STOP & THINK *Question:* The tax treatment of income earned in a common law state versus a community property state can be very inconsistent. As noted, the Supreme Court, in *Lucas v. Earl*, decided that a husband was taxed on all his income even though he agreed to share that income with his wife. Nevertheless, community income in a community property state is divided equally between husbands and wives even if one spouse earned all of the income. Why the tax distinction?

Solution: Lucas v. Earl dealt with a case in a common law state where the husband was legally entitled to the income, but decided to divide it with his wife. In community property states, couples are legally obligated to share their incomes. The federal income tax law respects the different property law systems of the states and taxes the income of per-

---

[7] Sec. 66(b).   [8] Sec. 66(c).

INCOME OF MINOR CHILDREN

As noted earlier, whether a husband or wife is taxed on income is determined by state law. However, earnings of a minor child are taxed to the child regardless of the state's property law system. Therefore, earnings of a child from either personal services (compensation) or from property (dividends, interest, rents, etc.) are taxed to the child, not the child's parents. As noted in Chapter I2, the unearned income of a child under age 14 may be taxed at the parents' tax rate if it is higher than the child's rate. Alternatively, the parents may elect to include the child's unearned income on their return. In the case of spouses, the spouse who has a legal right to such income determines who is taxed on it. In the case of children, however, the individual who earned the income determines who is taxed on it.

WHEN IS INCOME TAXABLE?

OBJECTIVE 3

Determine when a particular item of income is taxable under both the cash and accrual methods of reporting

The year in which income is taxed depends on the taxpayer's accounting method. The three primary overall accounting methods are the **cash receipts and disbursements method,** the **accrual method,** and the **hybrid method.** While taxpayers have the right to choose a method of accounting, the chosen method still must clearly reflect income as determined by the IRS. The IRS has the power to change the accounting method used by a taxpayer if, in the opinion of the IRS, the method being used does not clearly reflect income. Further, the Regulations require taxpayers to use the accrual method for determining purchases and sales when a taxpayer maintains an inventory.[9] However, the IRS recently ruled that taxpayers whose annual gross receipts for the three prior years averaged $1 million or less are exempt from the requirement and may use the cash method.[10] This exception means that small taxpayers do not have to account for inventories and may currently expense cash payments made for the purchase of inventory.

Section 448 requires C corporations (and partnerships with corporate partners), tax shelters, and certain trusts to use the accrual method of accounting. Qualified personal service corporations, certain types of farms, and entities with average gross receipts under $5 million are exempt from the requirement.

Once an accounting method has been adopted, it cannot be changed without permission of the IRS. See Chapter I11.

KEY POINT

Neither the IRC nor the Regulations define the terms *accounting* and *accounting method.*

CASH METHOD

The **cash receipts and disbursements method** of accounting is used by most individual taxpayers and most small businesses. (See Chapter I11 for a more complete discussion of who is permitted to use the cash method.) Under this method, income is reported in the year the taxpayer actually or constructively receives the income rather than in the year the income is earned. The income can be received by the taxpayer or the taxpayer's agent and be in the form of cash, other property, or services.[11] In the case of property or services, the amount included in income is the value of the property or services. An accounts receivable or other unsupported promise to pay is considered to have no value under the cash method and, as a result, no income is recognized until the receivable is collected. Topic Review I3-1 summarizes when various types of income are reported.

The fact that prepaid income is usually taxed when received, rather than when earned, often results in a mismatching of income and expenses.

ADDITIONAL COMMENT

Taxpayers engaged in more than one trade or business may use a different method of accounting for each separate trade or business.

ADDITIONAL COMMENT

The use of the cash receipts and disbursements method of accounting gives the taxpayer some control over the timing of the recognition of income and deductions. It also has the advantage of simplicity.

EXAMPLE I3-9 ▶ In December of the current year, Troy, who owns an apartment building, collects the first and last months' rent from the tenant. Troy must report two months' rent in the current year. The

---

[9] Reg. Sec. 1.446-1(c)(2)(i).
[10] Rev. Proc. 2000-22, I.R.B. 2000-02, 1008. This exception is referred to as the *small taxpayer exception.*

[11] An agent can be an employee, relative, or other person authorized to receive the income.

Topic Review I3-1

When Income Is Taxable

ITEM	CASH BASIS	ACCRUAL BASIS
Compensation	Year actually or constructively received.	Year earned or year received if prepaid.
Interest	Year actually or constructively received.	Year accrued or year received if prepaid.
Discount on Series E or EE Bonds	Choice of reporting interest as it accrues or at maturity.	Year accrued.
Dividends	Year actually or constructively received.	Year actually or constructively received.
Rent	Year actually or constructively received (does not apply to a deposit).	Year accrued or year received if prepaid (year accrued if services are associated, e.g., in a hotel or motel) (does not apply to a deposit).
Services (maintenance contracts, dance lessons, etc.)	Year actually or constructively received.	Year accrued or year received if prepaid except that a taxpayer may report the income as it accrues if all the services are to be performed by the end of the next tax year.
Sale of goods	The cash method cannot be used to report sale of goods if inventories are an income-producing factor.	Year of sale or year cash is received if prepaid except may elect to report in year of sale if goods are not on hand, amount received is less than cost of item, and same accounting method is used for financial accounting.
Subscriptions (newspapers, magazines, etc.)	Year actually or constructively received.	Year earned or year cash is received, if prepaid, except may elect to report income as newspaper, etc., is published.
Memberships (automobile clubs, etc.)	Year actually or constructively received.	Year earned or year received if prepaid (certain nonstock corporations may elect to report prepaid amounts over the membership period, if the period covers three years or less).
Sale of property (other than stock)	Year actually or constructively received.	Year transaction is completed (e.g., the close of escrow in case of sale of real estate).
Sale of stock	Year transaction is executed.	Year transaction is executed.

actual expenses associated with the last month's rental are not incurred until the last month. However, Troy must report two months' income this year, but may only deduct one month's expenses. ◀

Reporting prepaid income can have harsh results because it is not offset by related deductions. If the income is taxed before the expenses are incurred, the taxpayer may not have enough cash to pay the expenses when they are incurred.[12] This burden is mitigated, in part, by Treasury Regulations and Revenue Procedures discussed in this chapter (e.g., the treatment of prepaid income, page I3-11).

CONSTRUCTIVE RECEIPT. As noted, a cash-basis taxpayer must report income in the year in which it is actually or constructively received. Constructive receipt means that the income is made available to the taxpayer so that he may draw upon it at any time. However, income is not constructively received if the taxpayer's control of its receipt is subject to substantial limitations or restrictions. This rule prevents taxpayers from deferring income that is otherwise available by merely "turning their backs" on it. A taxpayer cannot defer income recognition by refusing to accept payment until a later taxable year.

Examples of constructive receipt where taxpayers are required to report taxable income even though no cash is actually received include:

ADDITIONAL COMMENT
There is no recognized doctrine of constructive payment.

REAL-WORLD EXAMPLE
Paul Hornung, a former football player with the Green Bay Packers, was awarded an automobile in 1961 for being the outstanding player in the NFL championship game, but he did not actually receive it until 1962. He attempted to invoke the constructive receipt doctrine and report the income in 1961. The court held that he could not claim constructive receipt because the car was not set aside in the year of the award. *Paul V. Hornung*, 47 T.C. 428 (1967).

---
[12] This mismatching of income and expenses affects both cash and accrual basis taxpayers.

- A check received after banking hours[13]
- Interest credited to a bank savings account[14]
- Bond interest coupons that have matured but have not been redeemed[15]
- Salary available to an employee who does not accept payment[16]

An amount is not considered to be constructively received if:

- It is subject to substantial limitations or restrictions.
- The payor does not have the funds necessary to make payment.
- The amount is unavailable to the taxpayer.

EXAMPLE I3-10 ▶ Beth owns an ordinary life insurance policy with a cash surrender value. She need not report any income as the cash surrender value increases because the requirement that she cancel the policy in order to collect the cash surrender value constitutes a substantial restriction. If she cancels the policy, she reports as income the difference between the cash surrender value collected and net premiums paid. ◀

EXAMPLE I3-11 ▶ Cathy has received a paycheck from her employer but has been told to hold the check until the employer has sufficient funds to cover the payroll. Cathy need not report the amount of the check as income until funds are deposited to the employer's account. ◀

EXAMPLE I3-12 ▶ On December 2, 2001, Dan sold land for $100,000, payable on February 2, 2002. During the negotiations, the buyer offered to pay cash. Because the parties did not agree to a cash transaction, there was no constructive receipt in 2001. Under the terms of the sale, funds were not available at the time of sale. Thus, Dan is permitted to defer the recognition of income under the contract since the contract is made before the income is earned. ◀

HISTORICAL NOTE
Series EE bonds, officially known as United States Energy Savings Bonds, have been offered for sale since January 1, 1980.

EXCEPTIONS. There are exceptions to the basic rule that cash-basis taxpayers report income when it is actually or constructively received.

- The interest on Series E and Series EE U.S. savings bonds need not be reported until the final maturity date, which varies but may be as long as forty years after the date of issue, and can be deferred even longer if the bonds are exchanged within one year of the final maturity date for Series HH U.S. savings bonds.[17] Many taxpayers purchase bonds with a maturity date that occurs after retirement when the taxpayers expect to be in a lower tax bracket.

EXAMPLE I3-13 ▶ Tenisha purchased a Series EE U.S. savings bond in the current year for $2,500 that matures in 10 years. The bond will not pay any interest until the bond matures; at maturity, the bond will be worth $5,000. Tenisha is not required to report any interest income for tax purposes until the bond matures. At maturity, when Tenisha receives the $5,000, she will report $2,500 of interest income. If she desires to defer the interest further, she could exchange her Series EE bond for a Series HH bond within one year. ◀

- Special rules also apply to farmers and ranchers. Farmers may report crop insurance proceeds in the year following receipt if the crop would have ordinarily been sold in the following year. Ranchers who sell livestock on account of a drought, flood, or other weather related condition may delay reporting income until the following year if they can establish that the livestock sale would otherwise have taken place in a later tax year.[18] These rules help taxpayers avoid a bunching of income into one year.

---

[13] *Charles F. Kahler*, 18 T.C. 31 (1952).
[14] Reg. Sec. 1.451-2(b).
[15] Ibid.
[16] *James J. Cooney*, 18 T.C. 883 (1952).
[17] Series E bonds were issued prior to 1980; Series EE bonds were issued after 1979. The interest on the Series HH bonds is taxable as received.

[18] Recognizing the volatile nature of farming and ranching, Congress established a special averaging technique for farmers and ranchers, effective in 1998. Electing farmers and ranchers compute their tax on the average income for the current and three preceding years. Sec. 1301.

Gross Income: Inclusions ▼ Individuals 3-11

ACCRUAL METHOD

Taxpayers using the accrual method of accounting generally report income in the year it is earned. Income is considered to have been earned when all the events have occurred that fix the right to receive the income and when the amount of income can be determined with reasonable accuracy.[19] In the case of a sale of property, income normally accrues when title passes to the buyer.[20] Income from services accrues as the services are performed.

> **REAL-WORLD EXAMPLE**
> The Ninth Circuit Court of Appeals has held that "markers" customers gave to a gambling casino to evidence their indebtedness to the casino required accrual even though the receivables were legally unenforceable under state law. The court found that there need only be a "reasonable expectancy" that payment would be made. *Flamingo Resort, Inc. v. U.S.*, 50 AFTR 2d 82-502, 82-1 USTC ¶9136 (9th Cir., 1982).

PREPAID INCOME. A major exception to the normal operation of the accrual method is the rules applicable to the receipt of prepaid income. Prepaid income is generally taxable in the year of receipt. For example, if a lender receives January interest in the preceding December, it is taxable in the year received, whether the lender uses the cash or accrual method. This treatment, of course, differs from financial accounting, where the interest would be reported as it accrues.

Two important exceptions to the general rule are worth noting. Accrual-basis taxpayers may defer recognizing income in the case of certain advance payments for *goods* and in the case of certain advance payments for *services* to be rendered. A taxpayer may defer advance payments for goods (inventory) if the taxpayer's method of accounting for the sale is the same for tax and financial accounting purposes.[21]

Under Rev. Proc. 71-21, a taxpayer may defer advance payments for services if the payments are for services to be performed before the end of the tax year following the year of receipt.[22] Such payments may be reported as the services are performed, e.g., the taxpayer may allocate the payment received over the current and succeeding years. The rule is not available if a payment covers a time period that extends beyond the end of the tax year following the year of receipt. The rule can be applied to a variety of services such as dance lessons, maintenance contracts (but not warranties included in the sales price of a product), and rent (if services are associated with the rent, as with a hotel or motel).

> **EXAMPLE I3-14**
> **REAL-WORLD EXAMPLE**
> A dance studio using the accrual method was required to include in taxable income all advance payments for lessons in the form of cash and negotiable notes, plus contract installments due but remaining unpaid at year end. *Mark E. Schlude v. CIR*, 11 AFTR 2d 751, 63-1 USTC ¶9284 (USSC, 1963).

Bear Corporation, an accrual-basis taxpayer that uses the calendar year as its tax year, sells computer courses under contracts ranging from three months to two years. The contracts covered by Rev. Proc. 71-21 vary depending on the month of sale. For example, contracts sold in July for a term of longer than 18 months are not covered by the rule, and all income must be reported for these contracts in the year of the sale. Assume Bear Corporation sold three contracts in July 2001: one for three months costing $90, one for one year costing $300, and one for two years costing $500. Income would be recognized as follows:

Length of Contract	2001	2002
3 months	$ 90	
12 months	150	$150
24 months	500	

HYBRID METHOD

The **hybrid method** of accounting is a combination of the cash and accrual methods. Under the hybrid method, some items of income or expense are reported under the cash basis and others are reported under the accrual method. The method is most often encountered in small businesses that maintain inventories and are required to use the accrual method of accounting for purchases and sales of goods. Such businesses often prefer to use the cash method of reporting for other items because the cash method is simpler and may provide greater flexibility for tax planning. A taxpayer using the hybrid method of accounting would use the accrual method with respect to purchases and sales of goods but would use the cash method in computing all other items of income and expenses.

---

[19] Reg. Sec. 1.451-1(a).
[20] Regulation Sec. 1.446-1(c)(1)(ii), however, does permit taxpayers the right to accrue income from the sale of inventory when the goods are shipped, when the product is delivered or accepted, or when title passes, as long as the method is consistently used.
[21] Reg. Sec. 1.451-5.
[22] 1971-2 C.B. 549.

STOP & THINK

Question: Taxpayers who are eligible to use the cash method often choose the cash method of reporting income over the accrual method. Why is the cash method generally more favorable for income tax purposes?

Solution: Taxpayers who have the option frequently choose the cash method over the accrual method because it is simpler, offers greater tax planning opportunity, and results in taxes being owed when income is received. The cash method is simpler because taxpayers are not required to make the complex accruals associated with the accrual method. Planning opportunities are greater because cash basis taxpayers can deduct expenses when paid thereby allowing taxpayers to control their tax liability. Under the accrual method, prepaid expenses are not deductible when paid, but must be deducted over the periods benefitted. Finally, cash basis taxpayers do not have to pay taxes until they receive the money. Under the accrual method, income is reported when it is earned even if it has not been received. As a result, accrual basis taxpayers sometimes have to pay the tax before they actually receive the income they have earned.

EXAMPLE I3-15 ▶ Jane begins a new retail business which has sales of $400,000 during the first year. She has no receivables as all sales are for cash. She purchases $240,000 of merchandise during the year. At year end she has not paid for $30,000 of the merchandise she purchased, and she has $50,000 of inventory on hand. Her other expenses for the year total $150,000. As her average gross receipts are less than $1 million she can use either the cash or accrual method. Her business income computed under both methods is as follows:

	Accrual		Cash
Sales		$400,000		$400,000
Purchases	$240,000		$210,000	
Inventory	50,000		–	
Cost of sales		190,000		210,000
Gross profit		210,000		190,000
Expenses		150,000		150,000
Net income		$ 60,000		$40,000

Note that under the accrual method, Jane deducts the cost of the merchandise she sells during the year, while under the cash method she deducts as cost of sales the amount she pays during the year for merchandise. This difference results in a reported income that is $20,000 less under the cash method.

Another difference between the two methods is that under the cash method revenues are not reported until they are collected. If Jane had credit customers, she would not include year end receivables in income. Instead they are reported in later taxable years when they are collected.

Finally, this example assumes that expenses are the same under the cash and accrual method. In many cases they are different. Accrual basis taxpayers deduct expenses as they are incurred while cash basis taxpayer deduct expenses as they are paid. Thus, an accrual basis taxpayer deducts expenses that are accrued but unpaid at year end, while a cash basis taxpayer generally can deduct prepaid expenses. ◀

ITEMS OF GROSS INCOME: SEC. 61(a)

OBJECTIVE 4

Apply the rules of Sec. 61(a) to determine whether items such as compensation, dividends, alimony, and pensions are taxable

Section 61(a), quoted earlier in this chapter, states that gross income includes, but is not limited to, fifteen specifically listed types of income. Several of these items are discussed below.

COMPENSATION

Compensation is payment for personal services. It includes salaries, wages, fees, commissions, tips, bonuses, and specialized forms of compensation such as director's fees, jury fees, and marriage fees received by clergymen. What the compensation is called, how it is computed, the form and frequency of payment, and whether the compensation is subject

ADDITIONAL COMMENT

Salaries and wages constituted 74.4% of total AGI reported in 1996.

to withholding is of little significance. Similarly, the fact that the services are part-time, one-time, seasonal, or temporary is immaterial.

There are exclusions, however, for a variety of employer-provided fringe benefits such as group term life insurance premiums, health and accident insurance premiums, employee discounts, contributions to retirement plans, and free parking. In addition, there is a limited exclusion applicable to foreign-earned income. Both fringe benefits and the foreign-earned income exclusion are discussed in Chapter I4.

BUSINESS INCOME

The term *gross income* usually refers to the total amount received from a particular source. In the case of businesses that provide services (e.g., accounting and law), the gross business income is the total amount received. In the case of manufacturing, merchandising, and mining, however, gross income is total sales less the cost of goods sold. Thus, gross income for tax purposes is comparable to gross profit for financial accounting purposes.

The cost of goods sold is, in effect, treated as a return of capital. Chapter I4 discusses a well-established tax concept that a return of capital is not income and, therefore, cannot be subject to the income tax. Chapter I11 discusses how inventories are valued.

SELF-STUDY QUESTION

A retail company had sales of $1,000,000 and the following costs: goods sold, $400,000, salaries, $200,000, and rent and other expenses, $100,000. What is the company's gross income?

ANSWER

The gross income is $600,000. The sales figure is reduced by the cost of goods sold.

GAINS FROM DEALINGS IN PROPERTY

Gains realized from property transactions are included in gross income unless a nonrecognition rule applies. As is true with business inventories, taxpayers may deduct the cost of property in order to arrive at the gain from a property transaction.[23] The tax law contains over 30 nonrecognition rules, which allow taxpayers to postpone the recognition of gains and losses from certain types of property transactions. In a few instances, these rules allow taxpayers to permanently exclude gains from gross income.[24]

Losses are not offset against gains in computing gross income. Rather, most losses are deductions *for* adjusted gross income. Furthermore, net capital losses for individuals are subject to provisions that limit the amount that can be deducted from other income to $3,000 per year. Losses from the sale or disposition of an asset held for personal use are not deductible.

TYPICAL MISCONCEPTION

It is sometimes mistakenly assumed that interest paid on federal obligations such as Treasury bonds, notes, and bills will also qualify for tax exemption.

INTEREST

Interest is compensation for the use of money. Taxable interest includes interest on bank deposits, corporate bonds, mortgages, life insurance policies, tax refunds, most U.S. government obligations,[25] and foreign government obligations.[26] Nontaxable interest is discussed below.

ADDITIONAL COMMENT

Many tax advisers consider the exclusion of interest on municipal bonds to be one of the few remaining tax shelters. As a result, municipal bond funds have flourished in recent years.

TAX-EXEMPT INTEREST. Since the inception of the federal income tax in 1913, interest on obligations of states, territories, and U.S. possessions and their political subdivisions has been tax exempt.[27] Bonds issued by school districts, port authorities, toll road commissions, counties, and fire districts have been held to be tax exempt. In addition, Sec. 501(c)(3) organizations may issue up to $150 million of tax-exempt bonds. Such organizations include private universities, hospitals, churches, and similar nonprofit organizations.

As noted above, this exclusion does not extend to interest paid on most U.S. government obligations or foreign government obligations, nor does the exclusion exempt from taxation gains from the sale of state or local government bonds or interest on tax refunds paid by state and municipal governments.

There has always been some uncertainty as to whether the federal government could tax interest on state and local government obligations. The basic question is whether tax-

---

[23] Note that *business income* and *gains from dealings in property* are overlapping terms. The gross profit from the sale of inventory is actually both business income and a gain from a property transaction. Typically, however, the phrase *gains from dealings in property* may be assumed to mean gains from dealings in property other than inventory, so as to avoid confusion.

[24] For example, Sec. 121 allows taxpayers to exclude a limited amount of gain from a sale of a personal residence.

[25] The interest on many federal obligations issued before March 1, 1942 is tax exempt.

[26] Reg. Sec. 1.61-7.

[27] Sec. 103(a)(1).

ADDITIONAL COMMENT

The doctrine of intergovernmental immunity also results in most states exempting from taxation income received from U.S. obligations.

KEY POINT

The exclusion is available only to an individual who purchased the bond after reaching age 24. The exclusion is not available to an individual who owns a bond that was purchased by another individual, other than a spouse. Therefore, the exclusion is not allowable if bonds are purchased by a parent and put in the name of a child.

SELF-STUDY QUESTION

Young parents, whose annual income is currently $45,000, begin a regular program of purchasing Series EE savings bonds for their 8-year-old daughter's college education. Is there any risk that when the bonds are redeemed the interest income will not be excludable?

ANSWER

Yes, the parents' income may increase over the years to such an extent that the interest exclusion will not be available.

ing these obligations would violate the doctrine of intergovernmental immunity in that the tax would reduce the ability of state and local governments to finance their operations because taxable bonds usually pay a higher rate of interest than tax-exempt bonds. The belief that taxing state and local government interest is unconstitutional is no longer widely held. While there have been efforts to tax interest on state and local bonds, the only changes have been to limit the use of bonds for private activities,[28] federally insured loans,[29] and arbitrage.[30]

SERIES EE SAVINGS BOND EXCLUSION. Taxpayers may purchase and eventually redeem Series EE bonds tax-free if they use the proceeds to pay certain college expenses for themselves, a spouse, or dependents.[31]

To qualify for the exclusion:

▶ The bonds must be purchased after 1989 by an individual who is age 24 or older at the time of the purchase.

▶ The bonds must be purchased by the owner and cannot be a gift to the owner.

▶ The receipts from the bond redemption must be used for tuition and fees, which are first reduced by tax-exempt scholarships, veterans benefits, Hope and Lifetime Learning credits, and other similar amounts.[32]

▶ Married couples living together must file a joint return to obtain the exclusion.

The full amount of interest is excluded only if the combined amount of principal and interest received during the year does not exceed the net qualified educational expenses (tuition and fees reduced by exempt scholarships, etc.), and the taxpayer's 2001 modified adjusted gross income is not over $55,750 ($83,650 for married individuals filing a joint return). The exclusion is fully phased-out for taxpayers whose 2001 modified AGI is more than $70,750 ($113,650 for married individuals filing a joint return).[33]

If the net qualified education expenses are less than the total principal and interest, a portion of the interest is excluded based on the ratio of the qualified educational expenses to the total principal and interest. The tentative exclusion is equal to

$$\text{Series EE interest} \times \frac{\text{Net qualified educational expenses}}{\text{Series EE interest} + \text{Principal}}$$

EXAMPLE I3-16

ADDITIONAL COMMENT

A child born today will require about $100,000 for a four-year college education. If interest rates are around 6%, one would have to save about $245 a month until the child entered school to be able to pay this amount.

▶ In 2001, Lois redeems Series EE bonds and receives $6,000, consisting of $1,875 of interest and $4,125 of principal. Assume that the net qualifying education expenses total $4,800. Lois's educational expenses equal 80% of the total amount received ($4,800 ÷ $6,000). Thus, her exclusion is limited to $1,500 (0.80 × $1,875). ◀

As noted, the amount of the exclusion is further reduced if modified adjusted gross income exceeds a $55,750 threshold ($83,650 for married individuals filing a joint return). Modified adjusted gross income includes the interest from education savings bonds and certain otherwise excludable foreign income.[34] The reduction is computed as follows:

$$\text{Otherwise excludable amount} \times \frac{\text{Excess modified AGI}}{\$15,000\ (\$30,000\ \text{for joint filers})}$$

---

[28] Interest from state and local bonds issued for private activities such as the construction of sports facilities, convention centers, and industrial park sites is taxable. A limited amount of tax-exempt bonds can be issued each year by a state for "qualified" private activities such as airport construction, redevelopment, and student loans. The limit is the greater of $150 million or $50 per resident (Sec. 146(d)). Though exempt from regular income tax, interest from these "qualified" private activity bonds is subject to the alternative minimum tax (see Chapter I14).

[29] Sec. 149(b).

[30] Sec. 148. Interest from state or local government bonds issued for the purpose of using the proceeds to buy higher-yield investments is taxable. Such bonds are called arbitrage bonds.

[31] Sec. 135(c).

[32] The exclusion is not permitted for amounts paid for sports, games, or hobbies unless they are part of a degree program (Sec. 135(c)(2)(B)).

[33] Each of these amounts is adjusted annually for inflation. In 2000, the phase-out started at $54,100 ($81,100 on joint returns) and ended at $69,100 ($111,100 on joint returns).

[34] Specifically, modified adjusted gross income includes amounts that qualify for the foreign earned income exclusion (Sec. 911), the exclusion for possession's income (Sec. 931), and the exclusion for income from Puerto Rico (Sec. 933). The limitation is determined after taking the partial exclusion for Social Security benefits and railroad retirement (Sec. 86), claiming the allowable deduction for retirement contributions (Sec. 219), and applying the passive loss limitation (Sec. 469).

EXAMPLE I3-17 ▶ Assume the same facts as in Example I3-16. Also assume that Lois is single and has other adjusted gross income of $58,875. Lois's otherwise available exclusion of $1,500 is reduced by $500 to $1,000. This reduction is computed by dividing the excess modified AGI of $5,000 ($58,875 + $1,875 − $55,750) by $15,000 and multiplying the result by $1,500. ◀

RENTS AND ROYALTIES

Amounts received as rents or royalties are included in gross income. As noted earlier, prepaid rent is taxable when received. Security deposits, which are refundable to tenants upon the expiration of a lease, are not included in gross income. The deposit is included in gross income only if it is not refunded upon the expiration of the lease.

EXAMPLE I3-18 ▶ In December 2001, Buddy rents an apartment to Gary. Buddy receives the first and last months' rent plus a security deposit of $500. Buddy must include in 2001 gross income both the first and last months' rent. Assume that Gary moves out of the apartment in 2003 and Buddy keeps $300 of the security deposit to cover repairs costing $200 and five days' unpaid rent, which amounts to $100. In 2003, Buddy would include the $300 in gross income and could deduct $200 for repairs. ◀

Royalties from copyrights, patents, and oil, gas, and mineral rights are all taxable as ordinary income. **Royalties** are proceeds paid to an owner by others who do business under some right belonging to the owner. Amounts received by a lessor to cancel, amend, or modify a lease also are taxable.

STOP & THINK

Question: Financial accounting contains extensive rules distinguishing "operating leases" from "capital leases." The IRC has no such rules. While the tax law does require the capitalization of leases that are in substance a purchase of the asset, most authority relating to the distinction comes from court cases. Why doesn't the tax law adopt specific rules relating to leased property?

Solution: The financial accounting rules that require businesses to capitalize some leases were established because of concern that long-term lease commitments represented unrecorded liabilities. The unrecorded liabilities distort a company's balance sheet, but may not distort reported income. Since the tax law is concerned with the reporting of income rather than the balance sheet, neither Congress nor the Treasury Department has seen the need to adopt leasing rules like those in financial accounting.

IMPROVEMENTS BY LESSEES. Improvements made by a lessee that increase the value of leased property are included in the lessor's income only if the improvements are made in lieu of paying rent or if rent is reduced because of the improvements. In such situations, the lessor must include the fair market value (FMV) of the improvement in gross income when it is made to the property.[35]

EXAMPLE I3-19 ▶ Rita rents an apartment to Anna. The apartment normally would rent for $500 per month, but Rita agrees to accept $200 per month for the first year if Anna builds a block wall around the property. Rita estimates that she would have to pay someone $3,000 to build the wall. Rita is accepting reduced rent and must report gross income of $3,000 when the wall is added to the property. The $3,000 could be added to Rita's basis in the property and should qualify as a depreciable asset. ◀

Improvements not made in lieu of rent are not income to the lessor. No adjustment is made to the lessor's basis in the property and, therefore, no depreciation is allowable. Gain or loss is recognized only when the property is disposed of.[36] Whether the improvements are in lieu of rent depends on the intent of the parties. This determination is based on the facts of the particular situation. The rental rate, the terms of the rental agreement, and whether the improvements have an estimated useful life exceeding the term of the lease may all be indications of intent.

---

[35] Reg. Sec. 1.109-1.   [36] Reg. Sec. 1.1019-1.

DIVIDENDS

Distributions to shareholders are taxable as dividends only to the extent they are made from either the corporation's current earnings and profits (a concept similar, although not identical, to current year's net income for financial accounting purposes) or accumulated earnings and profits (a concept similar, although not identical, to beginning of the year retained earnings).[37] Earnings and profits are discussed in Chapter I16 and in greater depth in *Prentice Hall's Federal Taxation: Corporations, Partnerships, Estates & Trusts* text and the *Comprehensive* volume. Distributions in excess of current and accumulated earnings and profits are treated as a nontaxable recovery of capital. Such distributions reduce the shareholder's basis in the stock. Distributions in excess of the basis of the stock are classified as capital gains.

> **ADDITIONAL COMMENT**
> Shareholders of closely held corporations generally do not want to receive dividends from their corporations. The reason? They are taxed as ordinary income and the corporation does not receive a tax deduction for the payments.

EXAMPLE I3-20 ▶ Liz is the sole shareholder in Atlantic Corporation and has owned the stock for five years. The basis of her stock is $50,000. Atlantic distributes $40,000 to Liz. Accumulated earnings and profits at the beginning of the year equal $25,000, and current earnings and profits equal $10,000. Liz will report $35,000 of taxable dividend income and a nontaxable return of capital equal to $5,000. In addition, Liz must reduce her basis in the stock by $5,000. Alternatively, if the distribution to Liz were $100,000, she would report $35,000 of taxable dividend income, $50,000 as a nontaxable return of capital, and a $15,000 long-term capital gain. ◀

STOCK DIVIDENDS. A **stock dividend** is a distribution by a corporation to its shareholders of the corporation's own stock. In 1920, the Supreme Court held that simple stock dividends could not be taxed because they were not income.[38] More precisely, income had not been realized because there was no real change in the taxpayer's interest or the risks faced by the taxpayer. Over the years, however, the exclusion for stock dividends has been narrowed. If a shareholder has the option of receiving either cash or stock, the shareholder is taxed even if he or she opts to receive stock. The option to receive cash constitutes constructive receipt of the cash. Today, many other features of a stock dividend may cause it to be taxed. For example, a distribution in which preferred stock is distributed to some common shareholders and common stock is distributed to others is taxable.[39] The recipient of a taxable stock dividend includes the value of the stock received in gross income, and that amount becomes the basis of the shares received.

A nontaxable stock dividend has no effect on a shareholder's income in the year received. The basis of the old shares is allocated between the old shares and the new shares. Furthermore, the holding period for the new shares starts on the same date as the holding period of the old.

> **ADDITIONAL COMMENT**
> Many mutual funds do not want their shareholders to have a large tax bill on the undistributed capital gains allocated among the shareholders. Some mutual funds will sell stocks in the portfolio that can be sold at a loss to offset gains incurred earlier in the year.

EXAMPLE I3-21 ▶ Carol purchases 100 shares of Mesa Corporation stock for $1,100 (or $11 per share). Carol receives 10 shares of Mesa stock as a nontaxable stock dividend. After the dividend, Carol owns 110 shares of stock with a total basis of $1,100 (or $10 per share). All of the stock is assumed to have been acquired at the time of the original purchase. ◀

CAPITAL GAIN DIVIDENDS. A **capital gain dividend** is a distribution by a regulated investment company (commonly called a *mutual fund*) of capital gains realized from the sale of investments in the fund. Such dividends also include any undistributed capital gains allocated to shareholders by such companies.[40] Capital gain dividends are long-term regardless of how long the shareholder has owned the stock of the regulated investment company.

> **REAL-WORLD EXAMPLE**
> In the 1989 trial of Leona Helmsley, the billionaire hotel queen, it was disclosed that she had billed her companies for millions of dollars in personal items. The items ranged from a $12.99 girdle to a $1 million limestone-and-marble pool enclosure at her estate. She was sentenced to four years in prison and fined $7.1 million. The amounts paid to her by her companies represented constructive dividends.

CONSTRUCTIVE DIVIDENDS. In many corporations, the same individuals are both shareholders and employees. A corporation may not deduct dividends paid to shareholders but is permitted to deduct reasonable compensation. Questions are often raised as to whether amounts reported as compensation are really disguised dividends. If an amount called compensation is unreasonably high, it will be disallowed and reclassified as a divi-

---

[37] Sec. 316(a). The federal income tax became effective on March 1, 1913. Thus, income accumulated before that date can still be distributed on a tax-exempt basis.

[38] *Eisner v. Myrtle H. Macomber*, 3 AFTR 3020, 1 USTC ¶32 (USSC, 1920).
[39] Reg. Sec. 1.305-4.
[40] Sec. 852(b).

dend.[41] Often the reasonableness of compensation is determined by comparing the compensation paid to the employee-shareholders with amounts paid to others performing similar services.

EXAMPLE I3-22 ▶ Carmen owns 100% of the stock in Florida Corporation and receives a $400,000 salary for serving as president. The corporation reports no taxable income and pays no dividends. Presidents of similar companies received salaries ranging from $75,000 to $160,000. The IRS probably would disallow a portion of Carmen's salary as unreasonable. The disallowed portion would be treated as a dividend. ◀

ADDITIONAL COMMENT
In one case, the taxpayer, who was also the president and principal shareholder, diverted cash from vending and pinball machines at his truck stops/restaurants to his personal use. The IRS's position was that these diverted cash amounts were a constructive dividend. *Hagaman v. Com.*, 69 AFTR 2d 92-906 (1992, CA6).

Constructive dividends are not limited to shareholder-employee compensation payments but may include situations where the shareholder also is a landlord (e.g., property is rented to the corporation at an amount greater than its fair rental value). A shareholder also may receive a constructive dividend because of a creditor or vendor relationship. It is not necessary that a dividend be formally declared or that distributions be in proportion to stock holdings. **Constructive dividends** are often distributions that are intended to result in a deduction to the corporation and taxable income (such as compensation) to the shareholder.[42] Other constructive dividends are intended to produce a nonreportable benefit to the shareholder,[43] or even result in a deduction to the corporation without income to the shareholder.[44]

ALIMONY AND SEPARATE MAINTENANCE PAYMENTS

Any payment pursuant to a divorce or legal separation must be classified as one of the following for tax purposes:

(1) Alimony;
(2) Child support; or
(3) Property settlement.

The treatment of a payment depends on its classification. Alimony is deductible by the payor spouse and taxable to the payee spouse. Neither child support payments nor property settlements have any tax ramifications, that is, they are not subject to tax to the payee spouse nor deductible by the payor spouse.

Example I3-23 demonstrates the significant difference in taxation that can occur when a payment is classified as either alimony or a property settlement.

EXAMPLE I3-23 ▶

ADDITIONAL COMMENT
Child-support payments are not treated as alimony and are neither deductible by the payor spouse nor includible in income of the payee spouse.

ADDITIONAL COMMENT
If any amount specified in the divorce instrument will be reduced due to the happening of a contingency relating to a child or reduced at a time that can clearly be associated with such contingency, the amount of the reduction is treated as child support.

Helen earned $500,000 and, as a result of her divorce, she was required to pay William $250,000. If the payment were viewed as a property settlement, Helen could not deduct any of the $250,000 payment and William would not be required to include the payment in his income. However, if the $250,000 were viewed as alimony, Helen could deduct the full amount in computing her adjusted gross income. William would report the $250,000 as alimony income. ◀

The tax law has rather specific rules that distinguish alimony, child support, and property settlements. Under current law, in order to be treated as **alimony**, payments must meet all of the following requirements:[45]

▶ Be made in cash (not property)
▶ Be made pursuant to a divorce, separation, or a written agreement between the spouses
▶ Terminate at the death of the payee

---

[41] Sec. 162(a)(1).
[42] Other examples include excessive royalties (*Peterson & Pegau Baking Co.*, 2 B.T.A. 637 (1925)) and rent (*Limericks, Inc. v. CIR*, 36 AFTR 649, 48-1 USTC ¶9146 (5th Cir., 1948)).
[43] Examples include bargain sales of corporate assets to shareholders (*J. E. Timberlake v. CIR*, 30 AFTR 583, 42-2 USTC ¶9822 (4th Cir., 1942)), redemptions of a shareholder's stock (Sec. 302), and loans to shareholders that are actually dividends (*George Blood Enterprises, Inc.*, 1976 PH T.C. Memo ¶76,102, 35 TCM 436).
[44] Examples include paying an employee's personal expenses (*The Lang Chevrolet Co.*, 1967 PH T.C. Memo ¶67,212, 26 TCM 1054) and purchasing assets for an employee's use (*Joseph Morgenstern*, 1955 PH T.C. Memo ¶55,086, 14 TCM 282).
[45] Before 1942, alimony was not deductible (*Gould v. Gould*, 3 AFTR 2958, 1 USTC ¶13 (USSC, 1917)). The original rules were revised in 1984 and again in 1986. Prior rules apply to earlier divorces unless both spouses elect to apply current rules.

ETHICAL POINT

Tax consultants who advise divorcing couples may face an ethical dilemma because advice that benefits one spouse may be detrimental to the other, and because of the need to maintain confidential client relationships.

▶ Not be designated as being other than alimony (e.g., child support)
▶ Be made between people who are living in separate households

These rules are summarized in Topic Review I3-2. Certain aspects of these rules will be discussed further.

A **property settlement** is a division of property pursuant to a divorce. In general, each spouse is entitled to the property brought into the marriage and a share of the property accumulated during marriage.[46] A division of property does not result in any income to either spouse, nor does either spouse receive a tax deduction. The basis of property received by either spouse as a result of the divorce or separation remains unchanged.

EXAMPLE I3-24 ▶ As a result of a divorce, Dawn receives stock that she had purchased with her former husband during their marriage. They had purchased the stock for $12,000. At the time of the divorce, the stock was worth $14,000. Neither Dawn nor her former husband reports income from the transfer of the stock because the stock was acquired as a property settlement. If Dawn subsequently sold the stock for $15,000, she would report a $3,000 gain. ◀

One unusual rule found in the current law that relates to alimony is the so-called **recapture provision**. This provision was established to prevent a large property settlement that might take place after a divorce from being treated as alimony so as to produce a deduction for the payor. In essence, the concept of recapture in connection with a divorce means that the payor of the alimony (who has taken a deduction for such amounts in prior years) must report the recapture amount in his or her income. The payee (who has reported the income in prior years) receives a deduction for the recaptured amount. This recapture occurs because the payments that originally were reported as alimony are being reclassified as property settlements.

Recapture occurs if payments decrease sharply in either the second or third year. Specifically, the amount of second-year alimony recaptured is equal to the second-year alimony reduced by the total of $15,000 plus the third-year alimony. The amount of first-

Topic Review I3-2

Tax Rules for Alimony

TREATMENT OF RECIPIENT

The recipient of alimony must include the amounts received in gross income. Property settlements and child support payments are not taxable.

TREATMENT OF PAYOR

The payor of alimony may deduct amounts paid *for* adjusted gross income. Property settlements and child support payments are not deductible.

APPLICABLE TO

Payments must be pursuant to a divorce, separation, or a written agreement between spouses.

REQUIREMENTS

Spouses must be living in separate households. Payments must be in the form of cash paid to (or for the benefit of) a spouse or former spouse. Payments must terminate at the death of the payee. Payments may not be designated as being other than alimony (such as child support or a property settlement).

RECAPTURE

If the amount of payments declines in the second or third year, a portion of the early payments may have to be recaptured as income by the payor. The payee may deduct the same recaptured amount.

---

[46] How the property accumulated during marriage is divided may be determined by an agreement of the parties, or if they are unable to agree, on a basis of state law.

year alimony recaptured is equal to the first-year alimony reduced by the total of $15,000 plus the average alimony paid in the second year (reduced by the recapture for that year) and the third year. The calculation of recapture for both the first and second years is shown below.

$$R_2 = A_2 - (\$15,000 + A_3)$$

$$R_1 = A_1 - [\$15,000 + (A_2 + A_3 - R_2)/2)]$$

A_i = Alimony paid in first (A_1), second (A_2), and third year (A_3) respectvely.

R_i = Recaptured alimony from the first (R_1) and second year (R_2) respectively.

Both first- and second-year amounts are recaptured by requiring the payor to report the excess as income (and allowing the payee to deduct the same amount) in the third year. Recapture is not required if payments cease because of the death of either spouse or remarriage of the recipient.

EXAMPLE I3-25 ▶ As a result of their divorce, Hal is ordered to pay to Rose $100,000 alimony in 2001 and $20,000 per year thereafter until her death or remarriage. Hal must recapture the amount of the decrease that exceeds $35,000, or $65,000 ($100,000 − $20,000 − $15,000). The $65,000 of alimony in 2001 must be reported by Hal as income during 2003. Also, Rose may deduct the $65,000 *for* AGI in 2003. ◀

EXAMPLE I3-26 ▶ As a result of their separation, Mary agrees to pay Tom $20,000 per year. The payments are to cease if Tom remarries. In the year after the agreement is reached, Tom remarries and Mary discontinues the payments. No recapture is required because the payments are contingent on the remarriage of the recipient and the payments have been discontinued because of the occurrence of this contingency. ◀

PENSIONS AND ANNUITIES

ADDITIONAL COMMENT

The three largest sources of non-wage income in 1996, in rank order, were net capital gains, pensions and annuities, and business and professional net income.

An **annuity** is a series of regular payments that will continue for a fixed period of time or until the death of the recipient. Taxpayers occasionally purchase annuities from insurance companies to provide a source of funds during retirement years. The insurance company may agree to make payments to the insured for the remainder of the insured's life. The retired individual is assured of a steady flow of funds for life. The price paid for the annuity represents its cost. The insured taxpayer is permitted to recover this cost tax-free.

Individuals receiving an annuity are permitted to exclude their cost, but are taxed on the remaining portion of the annuity. The following steps can be followed to determine the nontaxable portion of the annuity:

ADDITIONAL COMMENT

The expected return is limited to amounts receivable as an annuity. It does not include amounts that may be paid after death, nor does it include anticipated dividends.

▶ Determine the **expected return multiple**. This multiple is the number of years that the annuity is expected to continue and may be a stated term, say ten years, or it may be for the remainder of the taxpayer's life. In the latter situation, the expected return multiple (life expectancy) is determined by referring to a table (see Table I3-1) developed by the IRS.

▶ Determine the **expected return**. This return is computed by multiplying the amount of the annual payment by the expected return multiple.

▶ Determine the **exclusion ratio**. This ratio is computed by dividing the investment in the contract (its cost) by the expected return (from above).

▶ Determine the **current year's exclusion**. This exclusion is computed by multiplying the exclusion ratio (from above) times the amount received during the year.

EXAMPLE I3-27 ▶ David, age 65, purchases an annuity for $30,000. Under the terms of the annuity, David is to receive $300 per month ($3,600 per year) for the rest of his life.

▶ The expected return multiple is 20.0. The multiple is obtained from Table I3-1.
▶ The expected return is $72,000 (20.0 × $3,600).
▶ The exclusion ratio is 0.417 ($30,000 ÷ $72,000).
▶ The exclusion is $1,500 (0.417 × $3,600). ◀

▼ TABLE I3-1
Ordinary Life Annuities (One Life) Expected Return Multiple

Age	Multiple	Age	Multiple	Age	Multiple
5	76.6	42	40.6	79	10.0
6	75.6	43	39.6	80	9.5
7	74.7	44	38.7	81	8.9
8	73.7	45	37.7	82	8.4
9	72.7	46	36.8	83	7.9
10	71.7	47	35.9	84	7.4
11	70.7	48	34.9	85	6.9
12	69.7	49	34.0	86	6.5
13	68.8	50	33.1	87	6.1
14	67.8	51	32.2	88	5.7
15	66.8	52	31.3	89	5.3
16	65.8	53	30.4	90	5.0
17	64.8	54	29.5	91	4.7
18	63.9	55	28.6	92	4.4
19	62.9	56	27.7	93	4.1
20	61.9	57	26.8	94	3.9
21	60.9	58	25.9	95	3.7
22	59.9	59	25.0	96	3.4
23	59.0	60	24.2	97	3.2
24	58.0	61	23.3	98	3.0
25	57.0	62	22.5	99	2.8
26	56.0	63	21.6	100	2.7
27	55.1	64	20.8	101	2.5
28	54.1	65	20.0	102	2.3
29	53.1	66	19.2	103	2.1
30	52.2	67	18.4	104	1.9
31	51.2	68	17.6	105	1.8
32	50.2	69	16.8	106	1.6
33	49.3	70	16.0	107	1.4
34	48.3	71	15.3	108	1.3
35	47.3	72	14.6	109	1.1
36	46.4	73	13.9	110	1.0
37	45.4	74	13.2	111	.9
38	44.4	75	12.5	112	.8
39	43.5	76	11.9	113	.7
40	42.5	77	11.2	114	.6
41	41.5	78	10.6	115	.5

Source: Reg. Sec. 1.72-9 Table V.
Note: This table should be used if any or all investments were made on or after July 1, 1986. If all investments were made before July 1, 1986, use Reg. Sec. 1.72-9 Table I (not shown).

After the entire cost of an annuity has been recovered, the full amount of all future payments is taxable. On the other hand, if an individual dies before recovering the entire cost, the remaining unrecovered cost can be deducted as an itemized deduction on that individual's final return. Insurance companies and businesses with retirement plans compute the taxable portion of annuities and report the amounts to recipients on Form 1099.

KEY POINT
The simplified method is used only for annuity distributions from qualified retirement plans. All other annuity distributions are taxed in accordance with the general rules above.

SIMPLIFIED METHOD FOR QUALIFIED RETIREMENT PLAN ANNUITIES. Distributions from pensions and other qualified retirement plans are often paid in the form of an annuity. Both the employer and the employee often contribute funds to plans during the years of employment. When an employee retires, the amounts contributed and income accumulated thereon become available to the retired employee. In some cases, the retired employee has the option of receiving a lump-sum payment or an annuity. The employee's cost is limited to amounts contributed (usually through withholding) by the employee that were previously taxed to the employee. The employee may recover this cost tax-free. The employee's cost does not include employer contributions.

A simplified method is now used to determine the taxable portion of an annuity paid from a qualified retirement plan (such as a pension). Under the simplified method, the nontaxable portion of each annuity payment is equal to the employee's investment in the annuity divided by the number of anticipated payments as determined from the following table:

Age of Primary Annuitant on the Start Date	Number of Anticipated Payments
55 and under	360
56-60	310
61-65	260
66-70	210
71 and over	160

EXAMPLE I3-28 ▶ Jack, age 62, retires, and receives a $1,000 per month annuity from his employer's qualified pension plan. Jack contributed $65,000 to the plan prior to his retirement. Under the simplified method, Jack would exclude $250 per month as a return of capital. This is calculated by dividing $65,000 by 260 anticipated payments. ◀

If payments are paid other than monthly, the number of anticipated payments is adjusted accordingly. Thus, if payments are made quarterly, the number from the table is divided by four.

KEY POINT
Under current law, a taxpayer must generally pay tax on a portion of each withdrawal made before the normal starting date of the annuity.

ADVANCE PAYMENTS. Many pensions contain provisions that allow taxpayers to withdraw amounts before the normal starting date. Under current law, an amount withdrawn from a pension before the starting date is considered to be in part a recovery of the employee's contributions and part a recovery of the employer's contributions.[47] After all contributions have been withdrawn, additional withdrawals are fully taxable. In addition to being subject to the regular income tax, any amount withdrawn may also be subject to a 10% nondeductible penalty. The penalty is not applicable to certain taxpayers, such as one who is age 59½ or older. This early withdrawal penalty is discussed in more detail in Chapter I9.

EXAMPLE I3-29 ▶ Dick, age 45 and in good health, withdrew $2,000 from a pension plan during the current year. No exception exempts Dick from the 10% penalty. Dick had contributed $40,000 to the plan, and his employer had contributed $60,000. Dick must include $1,200 (0.60 × $2,000) in income. Because no exception applies, Dick must also pay an additional penalty of $120 (0.10 × $1,200). The penalty is not deductible by Dick. ◀

INCOME FROM LIFE INSURANCE AND ENDOWMENT CONTRACTS

The face amount of life insurance received because of the death of the insured is not taxable. If the proceeds are left with the insurance company and as a result earn interest, the interest payments are taxable. (See Chapter I4 for a detailed discussion of life insurance and endowment contracts.)

INCOME FROM DISCHARGE OF INDEBTEDNESS

In general, the forgiveness of debt is a taxable event. The person who owed the money must report the amount forgiven as income unless one of several exceptions found in the tax law applies. These exceptions are discussed in Chapter I4.

---

[47] Sec. 72(e).

INCOME PASSED THROUGH TO TAXPAYER

Generally, entities are subject to income tax based on the amount of taxable income. Corporations, as an example, are subject to income taxation. However, certain types of entities are not subject to income taxation as the taxable income is taxed directly to the owners of the entity rather than the entity itself. Such entities are referred to as "flow-through entities." Section 61 specifically lists three such instances: the distributive share of a partnership's income, income in respect of a decedent, and income from an interest in an estate or trust. Though not mentioned in Sec. 61, similar treatment is accorded S corporation income. In each case, the income that is produced by the entity merely flows through to the owner or beneficiary of such entity. The rules can be summarized as follows:

> **KEY POINT**
> The pass-through of income by a partnership can create a situation known as phantom income. In this situation, a partner is required to report income on his or her individual tax return, but the partner may not have received a cash distribution from the partnership.

- Each partner reports his or her share of the partnership's income. Each partner deducts his or her share of the partnership's expenses. The income and deductions are reported by the partners whether or not any amount is actually distributed by the partnership during the year.

- Income in respect of a decedent is income earned by an individual before death that is paid to another after the death. For example, salary earned by a husband who uses the cash method of accounting before his death in an automobile accident may be paid to his widow after the accident. The recipient, in this case the widow, is taxed on the income if it has not been taxed to the decedent before his death.

- Income earned by estates and trusts is subject to taxation.[48] However, distributions to beneficiaries are deductible by estates and trusts and are taxable to the beneficiaries. Thus, if a trust had a net income of $20,000 and distributed $15,000 to the beneficiary of the trust, the trust would be taxed on $5,000 and $15,000 would be taxed to the beneficiary. The income taxation of estates and trusts is covered more fully in *Prentice Hall's Federal Taxation: Corporations, Partnerships, Estates, and Trusts*.

- S corporations are taxed much like partnerships. Each shareholder in the corporation is taxed on his or her proportionate share of the corporation's income whether or not the income is actually distributed.

OTHER ITEMS OF GROSS INCOME

The preceding discussions considered items of gross income specifically listed in Sec. 61(a). However, the fact that an item of income is listed in Sec. 61(a) does not necessarily cause it to be taxable. Rather, the condition that causes an item of income to be taxable is that it is not specifically excluded. Some items of gross income not mentioned in Sec. 61(a) are discussed below.

PRIZES, AWARDS, GAMBLING WINNINGS, AND TREASURE FINDS

In general, prizes, awards, gambling winnings, and treasure finds are taxable.[49] Winnings in contests, competitions, and quiz shows as well as awards from an employer to an employee in recognition of some achievement in connection with his or her employment are taxable.[50] The amount to be included in gross income is the fair market value of the goods or services received. Total gambling winnings must be included in gross income.[51] This includes proceeds from lotteries, raffles, sweepstakes, and the like. Gambling losses

---

[48] Note the distinction between income in respect of a decedent and the income of an estate. Income in respect of a decedent is the income earned before death that was never taxed to the decedent. An example would be interest that was accrued but unpaid at death. Income of an estate is income earned after death that is paid to the estate. An example would be interest that accrues after the decedent's death.

[49] Exclusions for scholarships and fellowships and a limited exclusion for prizes awarded for scientific, charitable, or similar meritorious achievements are discussed in Chapter I4.
[50] Sec. 74 and Reg. Sec. 1.74-1.
[51] *U.S. v. Manley S. Sullivan*, 6 AFTR 6753, 1 USTC ¶236 (USSC, 1927).

(up to the amount of the current year's winnings) are allowable as an itemized deduction.[52] The Regulations state that a treasure find constitutes gross income to the extent of its value in the year in which it is reduced to undisputed possession.[53]

EXAMPLE I3-30 ▶ Several years ago, Colleen purchased a used piano at an auction for $15. In the current year, she finds $4,500 of currency hidden in the piano. Colleen must report the $4,500 as income in the current year.[54] ◀

REAL-WORLD EXAMPLE

An accountant collected from a client money that was to be used to pay the client's taxes. Then the accountant appropriated the money for his own use. The accountant was held to have received unreported income. *Richard A. Reeves,* 1977 PH T.C. Memo ¶ 77,114, 36 TCM 500.

ILLEGAL INCOME

Income from illegal activities is taxable.[55] Some people find this part of the tax law surprising, but this fact serves as the basis for many criminal convictions given that few criminals report their illegal income. For example, Al Capone was convicted of income tax evasion, not bootlegging or other crimes. It is not necessary to prove that an individual had illegal income, but merely that the individual had income that was not reported.

Individuals have used varied defenses against this rule. One taxpayer was successful in convincing the Supreme Court that he should not be taxed on embezzlement gains because he had an unconditional obligation to repay the amount embezzled,[56] but the Supreme Court reversed this position in a later case.[57] The court concluded that although an obligation to repay existed, the taxpayer had no "consensual recognition" (intent) to repay. In addition to embezzlement of funds, the courts have held that a kidnapper's ransom was taxable,[58] along with profits from bookmaking,[59] card playing,[60] forgery,[61] stealing,[62] bank robbery,[63] sale of narcotics,[64] illegal sale of liquor,[65] and bribes.[66] (See Chapter I6 for a discussion of related deductions.)

ADDITIONAL COMMENT

Welfare payments are not normally required to be included in gross income. However, if the welfare payments are fraudulently received under state or federal assistance programs, they must be included in the recipient's gross income.

UNEMPLOYMENT COMPENSATION

For many years, unemployment compensation was excluded from gross income. In 1978, Congress changed the law to tax unemployment compensation because these benefits are a substitute for taxable wages. Initially, unemployment compensation was taxable only if adjusted gross income exceeded certain base amounts. However, beginning in 1987, all unemployment compensation is now fully taxable for both government-financed programs and employer-financed benefits.

SOCIAL SECURITY BENEFITS

Social Security benefits were excluded from gross income until 1984. Between 1984 and 1993, up to 50% of Social Security benefits were taxable. Beginning in 1994, up to 85% of Social Security benefits may be taxable. Under Sec. 86, the portion of Social Security benefits that are taxable depends on the taxpayer's provisional income and filing status. *Provisional income* is computed using the following formula:

Adjusted gross income (excluding Social Security benefits)		$xx,xxx
Plus: Tax-exempt interest		x,xxx
Excluded foreign income		x,xxx
50% of Social Security benefits		x,xxx
Provisional income		$xx,xxx

---

[52] Sec. 165(d).
[53] Reg. Sec. 1.61-14(a).
[54] *Ermenegildo Cesarini v. U.S.,* 26 AFTR 2d 5107, 70-2 USTC ¶9509 (6th Cir., 1970).
[55] Reg. 1.61-14(a).
[56] *CIR v. Laird Wilcox,* 34 AFTR 811, 46-1 USTC ¶9188 (USSC, 1946).
[57] *Eugene C. James v. U.S.,* 7 AFTR 2d 1361, 61-1 USTC ¶9449 (USSC, 1961).
[58] *Murray Humphreys v. CIR,* 28 AFTR 1030, 42-1 USTC ¶9237 (7th Cir., 1942).

[59] *James P. McKenna,* 1 B.T.A. 326 (1925).
[60] *L. Weiner,* 10 B.T.A. 905 (1928).
[61] *Cass Sunstein,* 1966 PH T.C. Memo ¶66,043, 25 TCM 247.
[62] *Mathias Schira v. CIR,* 50 AFTR 1404, 57-1 USTC ¶9413 (6th Cir., 1957).
[63] *Gary Ayers,* 1978 PH T.C. Memo ¶78,341, 37 TCM 1415.
[64] *Antonino Farina v. McMahon,* 2 AFTR 2d 5918, 58-2 USTC ¶9938 (D.C. N.Y., 1958).
[65] *U.S. v. Manley S. Sullivan,* 6 AFTR 6753, 1 USTC ¶236 (USSC, 1927).
[66] *U.S. v. Patrick Commerford,* 12 AFTR 364, 1933 CCH ¶9255 (2nd Cir., 1933).

REAL-WORLD EXAMPLE

The requirement that tax-exempt income be included in determining the taxable portion of Social Security benefits has been challenged on the basis that such provision is unconstitutional. However, the court held that this provision placed only an indirect burden on the governmental unit that issued the tax-exempt bonds, which was not protected by the intergovernmental immunity doctrine. *H.J. Goldin v. Baker*, 59 AFTR 2d 87-444, 87-1 USTC ¶9128, (2nd Cir., 1987).

MARRIED FILING SEPARATELY. In the case of a married person filing separately, taxable Social Security benefits are equal to the lesser of

- 85% of Social Security benefits, or
- 85% of provisional income

MARRIED FILING JOINTLY. For married couples filing jointly, the computation of the taxable portion of Social Security benefits is as follows:

- If provisional income is $32,000 or less, no Social Security benefits are taxable.
- If provisional income is over $32,000 (but not over $44,000), taxable Social Security benefits equal the lesser of:
  50% of the Social Security benefits, or
  50% of the excess of provisional income over $32,000
- If provisional income is over $44,000, taxable Social Security benefits are equal to the lesser of:
  85% of the Social Security benefits, or
  85% of provisional income over $44,000, plus the lesser of (1) $6,000 or (2) 50% of Social Security benefits.

SINGLE TAXPAYERS. For single taxpayers, the computation of the taxable portion of Social Security benefits is as follows:

- If provisional income is $25,000 or less, no Social Security benefits are taxable.
- If provisional income is over $25,000 (but not over $34,000), taxable Social Security benefits are equal to the lesser of:
  50% of the Social Security benefits, or
  50% of the excess of provisional income over $25,000
- If provisional income is over $34,000, taxable Social Security benefits are equal to the lesser of:
  85% of the Social Security benefits, or
  85% of provisional income over $34,000, plus the lesser of (1) $4,500 or (2) 50% of Social Security benefits

▶ **EXAMPLE I3-31** ▶ Holly is a single taxpayer with a taxable pension of $22,000, tax-exempt interest of $10,000, and Social Security benefits of $8,000. Her provisional income is $36,000, determined as follows:

	Adjusted gross income	$22,000
Plus:	Tax-exempt interest	10,000
	50% of Social Security benefits	4,000
	Provisional income	$36,000

The taxable Social Security benefits are equal to $5,700, which is the lesser of $6,800 (0.85 × $8,000) or $5,700 ($1,700* + the lesser of $4,500 or $4,000**).

*($36,000 provisional income − $34,000 threshold) × 0.85.
**50% of the Social Security benefits.   ◀

The result of the computation excludes from gross income the Social Security benefits received by lower-income individuals but taxes a portion (up to 85%) of the benefits received by taxpayers with higher incomes.

The term **Social Security benefits** refers to basic monthly retirement and disability benefits paid under Social Security and also to tier-one railroad retirement benefits. It does not include supplementary Medicare benefits that cover the cost of doctors' services and other medical benefits.

ADDITIONAL COMMENT

For a 65-year-old taxpayer who retired in 1994, the maximum monthly individual Social Security benefit was $1,148.

INSURANCE PROCEEDS AND COURT AWARDS

In general, insurance proceeds and court awards are taxable. Two exceptions are accident and health insurance benefits and the face amount of life insurance. (See Chapter I4 for a discussion of these benefits.)

Insurance proceeds or court awards received because of the destruction of property are included in gross income only to the extent that the proceeds exceed the adjusted basis of the property. Involuntary conversion provisions permit taxpayers to avoid being taxed if they reinvest the proceeds in a qualified replacement property.[67] If the proceeds are less than the property's adjusted basis, they reduce the amount of any deductible loss. Proceeds of insurance guarding against loss of profits because of a casualty are taxable.[68] Similarly, if a taxpayer had to sue a customer to collect income owed to the taxpayer, the amount collected is taxable just as it would have been had the taxpayer collected the income without going to court.

EXAMPLE I3-32 ▶ Gulf Corporation's factory was destroyed by fire. Gulf Corporation collected insurance of $400,000, which equaled its basis in the building, and $250,000 for the profits lost during the time the company was rebuilding its factory. The $400,000 is not taxable because it constitutes a recovery of the basis of the factory. The $250,000 is taxable because it represents lost income. Recall that the income would have been taxable had it been earned by the company from regular operations. ◀

Although few exclusions are designed specifically for insurance proceeds or court awards, such amounts may be covered by other, more general exclusions. For example, Sec. 104(a)(2) excludes "damages (other than punitive damages) received . . . on account of personal physical injuries or sickness." Thus, amounts collected because of physical injury suffered in an automobile accident are excluded (See Chapter I4).

RECOVERY OF PREVIOUSLY DEDUCTED AMOUNTS

On occasion, a taxpayer may deduct an amount in one year but recover the amount in a subsequent year. In general, the amount recovered must be included in the gross income in the year it is recovered. Cash-basis taxpayers encounter this situation more often than accrual-basis taxpayers because their expenses are generally deductible in the year they are paid. If the amount was overpaid, the taxpayer can anticipate a refund.

EXAMPLE I3-33 ▶ During 2001, Cindy's employer withheld $1,000 from her wages for state income taxes. She claimed the $1,000 as an itemized deduction on her 2001 federal income tax return. Her itemized deductions totaled $12,000. On her 2001 state income tax return, her state income tax was only $800. As a result, Cindy received a $200 refund from the state in 2002. Because Cindy deducted the full $1,000 in 2001, she must report the $200 refund as income on her 2002 federal income tax return. ◀

Any recovery of a previously deducted amount may lead to income recognition. Recovery, however, is often associated with expenses such as state income taxes or bad debts deducted in one year but recovered in a later year, medical expenses deducted in one year but reimbursed by insurance in a later year, casualty losses deducted in one year but reimbursed by court award or insurance in a later year, and deductions for amounts paid by check where the payee never cashed the check.

Several related rules should be noted:

▶ If the refund or other recovery occurs in the same year, the refund or recovery reduces the deduction and is not reported as income.

▶ Interest on the amount refunded is taxable and is not subject to the tax benefit rule (discussed below).

▶ The character of the income reported in the year of repayment is dependent on the type of deduction previously reported. For instance, if the taxpayer deducted a short-term capital loss in one year, the subsequent recovery would be a short-term capital gain.[69]

---

[67] The involuntary conversion provisions are discussed in Chapter I12.
[68] *Oppenheim's Inc. v. Kavanagh*, 39 AFTR 468, 50-1 USTC ¶9249 (D.C.-Mich., 1950).
[69] *F. Donald Arrowsmith Exr. v. CIR*, 42 AFTR 649, 52-2 USTC ¶9527 (USSC, 1952).

TAX BENEFIT RULE. As noted above, a taxpayer who recovers an amount deducted in a previous year must report as gross income the amount recovered. The amount recovered need not be included in income, however, if the taxpayer received no tax benefit. A tax benefit occurs only if the deduction reduced the tax for the year.[70]

EXAMPLE I3-34 ▶ In 2001, Jack's employer withheld $1,200 from his wages for state income tax. Jack claimed the $1,200 as an itemized deduction on his 2001 federal income tax return. Because of a variety of losses incurred by Jack, he reported a negative taxable income of $32,000 during 2001. The state refunded the $1,200 during 2002. Jack will not have to report the $1,200 as gross income on his federal return. He would have owed no federal income tax in 2001 even without the deduction for state income taxes. Therefore, Jack received no tax benefit from the deduction. ◀

REAL-WORLD EXAMPLE
An attorney collected fees from clients of his employer. Because the attorney and his employer were engaged in a dispute over ownership of the money, he deposited the disputed amount in a trust account. The attorney was taxable on the amounts in the year received because he had control over the funds under the claim of right doctrine. *Edward J. Costello, Jr.,* 1985 PH T.C. Memo ¶85,571, 50 TCM 1463.

Tax benefit may be absent in other situations. For example, a taxpayer's total itemized deductions may have been less than the standard deduction, or the expense may have been less than the applicable floor. To illustrate, medical expenses can be deducted only to the extent that they exceed 7.5% of adjusted gross income. If a taxpayer does not deduct medical expenses because they are less than the floor, the taxpayer does not have to report a subsequent reimbursement of the expense as income. If only a portion of an expense produces a tax benefit, only that portion has to be reported as income.

EXAMPLE I3-35 ▶ In 2001, Chris, an unmarried individual, had $1,350 withheld from her wages for state income tax. Her itemized deductions consisted of state income taxes of $1,350 and charitable contributions of $3,350. Her itemized deductions exceed the standard deduction by $150 ($1,350 + $3,350 − $4,550). If Chris received a state income tax refund of $200 in 2002 she must report only $150 as gross income in 2002. She benefited only from $150 of the deduction and so that is all she has to report as income. ◀

CLAIM OF RIGHT

Sometimes taxpayers receive disputed amounts. For example, a contractor may receive payment on a job when the quality of the work is being questioned by the customer, a salesperson may receive commissions when there is a question as to whether the sales are final, or a litigant may receive a court award even though the case is on appeal. Under the claim of right doctrine, the recipient of a disputed amount must include the amount received in gross income as long as the use of the funds is unrestricted.

EXAMPLE I3-36 ▶ Jane wins a court case against a customer requiring the customer to pay her $10,000. The customer is unhappy with the result of the case and indicates that he plans to appeal, but pays the $10,000 to avoid interest on the amount in the event he loses the appeal. Jane must include the $10,000 in gross income even though she will have to repay the amount if she loses the appeal. ◀

EXAMPLE I3-37 ▶ Assume the same facts as in Example I3-36 except that the $10,000 is placed in escrow by the court awaiting the outcome of the appeal. Jane does not have to report the amount as she does not have use of the funds. ◀

Of course, taxpayers may be required to repay the disputed amount in a subsequent year. Such taxpayers may deduct the previously reported amount in the year of repayment. The taxes saved from such a deduction, however, may be considerably less than the original tax. If the repayment is over $3,000, taxpayers have the option of reducing the current tax by the tax paid in the prior year or years on the repaid amount.[71]

EXAMPLE I3-38 ▶ Assume the same facts as in Example I3-36, except that after reporting the disputed $10,000 Jane loses the appeal and must repay the $10,000 to her customer. If Jane was in the 28% tax bracket when she reported the disputed amount she would have paid a $2,800 (0.28 × $10,000) tax on the disputed amount. If she were in the 15% bracket when she made the

---

[70] Sec. 111.   [71] Sec. 1341.

repayment, she would recover only $1,500 by deducting the $10,000. Because the amount exceeds $3,000, Jane has the option of determining her current year's tax by deducting from the tax she would otherwise pay the $2,800 tax she paid in the earlier year. This credit is allowed in lieu of receiving a deduction of $10,000.

TAX PLANNING CONSIDERATIONS

SHIFTING INCOME — *Get legal adv. before not after*

KEY POINT
The advantage of shifting income to children has been increased since the revision of the tax rate schedules in 1993. The highest and lowest marginal tax rates in 1992 were 31% and 15%, respectively. In 1993 and in subsequent years, the highest and lowest marginal rates are 39.6% and 15%, respectively.

A family can reduce its taxes by shifting income from family members who are in high tax brackets (e.g., parents) to family members who are in low tax brackets (e.g., children). Assignment of income rules prevent shifting from being done by merely redirecting the payment. Thus, a father cannot avoid a tax on his salary by ordering his employer to pay the salary to his daughter. Nevertheless, income can be shifted by transferring ownership of the property. For example, children may own stock in the family business. Dividends on the stock are taxed to the children. In the case of a child under age 14, however, the parents' (as opposed to the child's) tax rate applies to unearned income in excess of $1,500. Series EE bonds may prove useful to avoid the kiddie tax because the interest is deferred until the bond is redeemed or matures. The maturity date, of course, may be after the child reaches age 14. Another shifting technique is for the child to work for the family business and be paid a reasonable salary. Such income is taxed at the child's tax rate, even if the child is under 14 years old, and can be offset by the child's own standard deduction.

Shifting of income is constrained by several factors. As noted, the assignment of income doctrine limits transfers. Reasonableness limitations constrain compensation and other payments. Furthermore, outright gifts of property are subject to gift taxes. Also, individuals are reluctant to transfer wealth to children for a variety of personal reasons. However, the tax saving potential of shifting income is often so great as to prompt many well-to-do families to use available shifting techniques.

ALIMONY

Whether payments made in connection with a divorce or separation are classified as alimony is of major tax significance. Such classification results in a deduction for the payor and income to the payee. Alimony is actually one way to shift income.

EXAMPLE I3-39 ▶ Tony, who has a 36% marginal tax rate, makes payments of $40,000 to his former wife. If it is deductible as alimony, Tony will save $14,400 (0.36 × $40,000) a year in federal income taxes. The amount of tax that the former wife must pay depends on how much other income she has and whether she has deductions that reduce the tax. Her tax might be even higher than her former husband's or as little as zero. ◀

ADDITIONAL COMMENT
In 1996, $5.4 billion of alimony paid was reported as a deduction, while only $4.6 billion was reported as taxable income.

Two points are clear. One is that both parties should understand the implication of having amounts treated as alimony. Second, the designation of the payments as alimony may be beneficial to both parties. The payor will, of course, benefit from a tax deduction. The payee may benefit because the payor may agree to make larger alimony payments since the payments are tax deductible.

PREPAID INCOME

As explained earlier in this chapter, prepaid income is generally taxable when received. This accelerated recognition of income may be a significant disadvantage to the taxpayer if the related expenses are incurred in a later tax year. Thus, tax planning for prepaid amounts is essential.

EXAMPLE I3-40 ▶ Phil owns an apartment complex and requires tenants to pay the first and last months' rent before they move in. Rita, on the other hand, owns an apartment complex and requires tenants to pay the first month's rent and a refundable deposit (which equals one month's rent).

Although the full amount received by Phil is taxable when it is received, only one-half of the amount received by Rita is taxable when it is received. Rita is required to refund the deposit, assuming the tenant vacates leaving the property in good condition and having paid all rent. Therefore, the deposit is not taxable. ◄

HISTORICAL NOTE

In 1954 Congress passed Sec. 452, allowing deferral of certain prepaid income, but in 1955 Congress retroactively repealed this section.

Taxpayers receiving advance payments in connection with services may be able to meet the requirements of Rev. Proc. 71-21 (discussed earlier in the chapter); taxpayers receiving advance payments associated with the sale of merchandise may be able to meet the requirements of Reg. Sec. 1.451-5 (also discussed in this chapter). Also, special rules exist for subscription income, membership fees, crop insurance proceeds, and drought sales of livestock, all of which allow taxpayers to defer recognizing income.

TAXABLE, TAX-EXEMPT, OR TAX-DEFERRED BONDS

Which should a taxpayer choose: taxable bonds, tax-exempt bonds, or tax-deferred bonds? The answer depends on the relative interest rates and the taxpayer's current and future tax brackets. **Taxable bonds** yield the highest return, but the interest is taxable. **Tax-exempt bonds** yield a lower return. **Tax-deferred bonds** generally yield a return somewhere close to that of taxable bonds. Interest on U.S. Series EE savings bonds is tax exempt if it is used for educational purposes and if other requirements of Sec. 135 are met (see the discussion earlier in this chapter). If these conditions are not met, the tax is deferred until the bonds are redeemed. The taxpayer may be in a lower bracket when the tax is eventually paid, and in the meantime, the interest that will eventually go to pay taxes is earning additional income.

The decision between taxable and exempt bonds is a rather easy one if the risk of the investments is assumed to be approximately equal. A taxpayer should invest in exempt bonds instead of taxable bonds if the interest on the exempt bonds is greater than the interest on the taxable bonds multiplied by 1 minus the taxpayer's marginal tax bracket (expressed as a decimal). Stated in a formula, this means invest in tax-exempt bonds if

$$\text{Return on the tax-exempt bonds} > \text{Return on the taxable bonds} \times (1 - \text{Marginal tax bracket})$$

EXAMPLE I3-41 ▶

SELF-STUDY QUESTION

The highest marginal tax rate is currently 39.6%, but it was 31% in 1992. Assume that interest rates on taxable bonds have remained constant at 10% since 1992. Considering only the effect of the tax rates, is the rate of interest on tax-exempt bonds likely to have fallen, risen, or remained the same?

ANSWER

Everything else being equal, one would expect the spread between taxable and nontaxable bonds to have widened. A taxpayer having a marginal tax rate of 31% would be indifferent between a taxable bond yielding 10% and a tax-exempt bond yielding 6.9%. However, if the marginal tax rate is 39.6%, the yield on the tax-exempt bond would have to decline to 6.04% for the taxpayer to remain indifferent.

Robert's marginal tax bracket is 28% and he is trying to decide between tax-exempt bonds, which pay 6% interest, and taxable bonds paying 8% interest. Robert should invest in the exempt bonds because 6% is greater than 5.76% [0.08 × (1 − 0.28)]. ◄

Comparison of taxable bonds or exempt bonds to tax-deferred bonds is more complicated. As noted, the advantages of the tax-deferred bonds are twofold. First, the taxpayer may be in a lower tax bracket when the tax is paid (e.g., taxpayers who plan to redeem the bonds after retirement). Second, the amount that will eventually go to pay the tax earns income until the tax must be paid. Although the computation is not covered here, it is noted that taxpayers who anticipate that they will be in lower tax brackets and who plan to leave funds invested for several years may benefit from choosing Series EE U.S. savings bonds over taxable bonds. See Chapter I18 in the *Individuals* text for a further discussion of taxable, tax exempt, and tax deferred investments.

REPORTING SAVINGS BOND INTEREST

It may be desirable to purchase Series EE bonds in the child's name despite the fact that such interest is subject to the kiddie tax (see Chapter I2). This is because there is no income tax as long as the child's annual income is less than $700. However, even if a child is not otherwise required to file a return, it is necessary to report interest on Series EE bonds annually by filing a tax return.[72] Taxpayers who have not been reporting savings bond interest annually may change to annual reporting, but are required to report both current and previously accrued interest in the year of the change.[73]

---

[72] *Philip Apkin*, 86 T.C. 692 (1986).

[73] Reg. Sec. 1.454-1(a)(4), Ex. (1).

Taxpayers who report savings bond interest annually are allowed to change to the deferral method without IRS approval.[74] This is particularly useful where the decision to report interest currently was made before the imposition of the kiddie tax. Taxpayers who make this election are bound by it for five years.

DEFERRED COMPENSATION ARRANGEMENTS

Deferred compensation plans can be used as a means of avoiding the constructive receipt of income. Although income is normally taxable when the funds become available to the taxpayer, an advance contractual agreement can produce different results. Corporate executives, professional athletes, and others often sign agreements providing for compensation to be paid at future dates. Such agreements can produce tax savings because the recipients expect to be in a lower tax bracket. Because the arrangements are advance contractual agreements, the deferral of income does not constitute taxpayers "turning their backs" on the income.

EXAMPLE I3-42 ▶ Alonzo, a 35-year-old professional basketball player, signs a contract specifying that he will be paid $400,000 per year for ten years even if he does not play. Because of his age, both Alonzo and the team recognize that he will probably play for one or two more years. If the agreement had specified that he was to receive a salary of $1,300,000 per year for two years, most of the income would have been taxed at the highest rates. By spreading the amount over a longer period, Alonzo pays tax at lower rates on much of the income. Alonzo is compensated for the delayed payment by receiving a larger total amount [i.e., $4 million ($400,000 × 10 years) versus $2.6 million ($1.3 million × 2 years)]. ◀

COMPLIANCE AND PROCEDURAL CONSIDERATIONS

ADDITIONAL COMMENT
The dollar amount of tax-exempt interest income is recorded on Form 1040, line 8b, but is not included in the tax base. The IRS requires the reporting of this type of income probably because it may affect the taxability of Social Security benefits.

Form 1040 lists various types of income. Some items of income (wages, tax refunds, alimony, pensions and annuities, unemployment compensation, Social Security benefits, and other income) are listed directly on Form 1040. Most expenses related to these items of income are deducted as miscellaneous itemized deductions on Schedule A.

Most other types of income (and related deductions) are reported on special schedules.

Topic Review I3-3 summarizes the procedures for reporting income, and related deductions.

EXAMPLE I3-43 ▶ John J. Alexander has several items of income and related deductions:

KEY POINT
The amount labeled "total income" on line 22 of Form 1040 is not gross income, adjusted gross income, or taxable income.

Salary	$40,000
Deductible alimony payments	6,000
Taxable interest	300
Dividends: Ford Motor Co.	150
Omaha Mutual Fund ($120 is a return of capital distribution and $50 is a capital gain dividend)	600
Rent income (depreciation, interest, repairs, and other related expenses total $8,000)	11,000

The reporting of these items of income is illustrated on page 1 of Form 1040 (Figure I3-1) and on Schedule B of Form 1040 (Figure I3-2). Salary and interest (because the interest is less than $400) are entered directly on Form 1040. Note that on Schedule B, the capital gain distribution and the nontaxable distribution are subtracted in arriving at reported dividends. Rental income would be entered on Schedule E (not illustrated), and the net income after deducting related expenses is transferred to Form 1040. Alimony received and alimony payments are reported on page 1 of Form 1040. ◀

---

[74] Rev. Proc. 89-46, 1989-2 C.B. 597.

Topic Review I3-3

Reporting of Income

Type of Income	Reported On	Related Deductions Are Claimed On
Wages, salaries, tips, etc.	Form 1040	Schedule A and various other forms: moving, Form 3903; travel, transportation, etc., Form 2106
Interest	Form 1040 (if less than $400), otherwise Schedule B	Schedule A (miscellaneous deductions if any, e.g., safe deposit box fees)
Dividends	Form 1040 (if less than $400), otherwise Schedule B	Schedule A (miscellaneous deductions if any, e.g., safe deposit box fees)
Refund of state or local income taxes	Form 1040 (instructions contain a worksheet)	Schedule A (miscellaneous deductions if any, e.g., fee paid for tax advice)
Alimony	Form 1040	Schedule A (miscellaneous deduction, if any, e.g., legal fee associated with alimony)
Business income	Schedule C or C-EZ (net income or loss is transferred to Form 1040)	Schedule C or C-EZ (e.g., depreciation, advertising, repairs)
Capital gains	Schedule D	Schedule D (capital losses) or Schedule A (investment expenses)
Supplemental gains	Form 4797	Form 4797 (e.g., ordinary losses)
Pensions and annuities	Form 1040 (instructions contain a worksheet)	Generally no related deductions
Rents, royalties, partnerships, S corporations, estates, trusts, etc.	Schedule E	Schedule E
Farm income	Schedule F	Schedule F
Unemployment compensation	Form 1040	Generally no related deductions
Social Security benefits	Form 1040 (instructions contain a worksheet)	Generally no related deductions
Other income	Form 1040	Schedule A (miscellaneous deductions, if any)

PROBLEM MATERIALS

DISCUSSION QUESTIONS

I3-1 What phrase is found in both the Sixteenth Amendment to the Constitution and Sec. 61(a)?

I3-2 Contrast the accounting and economic concepts of income.

I3-3 Why does the tax concept of income more closely resemble the accounting concept of income than the economic concept?

I3-4 Explain the meaning of the term *wherewithal to pay* as it applies to taxation.

I3-5 If a loan is repaid, the lender does not have to include the repayment in gross income. There is no exclusion in the tax law that permits taxpayers to omit such amounts from gross income. How can this be explained?

I3-6 A landlord who receives prepaid rent is required to report that amount as gross income when the payment is received. Why would Congress choose to do this? What problem does this create for the taxpayer?

I3-7 Office space is often rented without carpet, wall covering, or window covering. Furthermore, many rental agreements specify that these improvements cannot be removed by a tenant if removal causes any damage to the property. What issue does this raise?

I3-8 Does the fact that an item of income is paid in a form other than cash mean it is nontaxable? Explain.

I3-9 Explain the significance of *Lucas v. Earl* and *Helvering v. Horst*.

I3-10 Under present-day tax law, community property rules are followed in allocating income between husband and wife. Is this consistent with *Lucas v. Earl*? Explain.

I3-11 Ricardo owns a small unincorporated business. His 15-year-old daughter Jane works in the business on a part-time basis and was paid wages of $3,000 during the current year. Who is taxed on the child's earnings: Jane or her father? Explain.

Form 1040 — U.S. Individual Income Tax Return 2000

Department of the Treasury—Internal Revenue Service (99)   IRS Use Only—Do not write or staple in this space.

For the year Jan. 1–Dec. 31, 2000, or other tax year beginning _____, 2000, ending _____, 20 _____   OMB No. 1545-0074

Label (See instructions on page 19.)

Use the IRS label. Otherwise, please print or type.

- Your first name and initial: **John J.**
- Last name: **Alexander**
- Your social security number: **123 45 6789**
- If a joint return, spouse's first name and initial: _____
- Last name: _____
- Spouse's social security number: _____
- Home address (number and street). If you have a P.O. box, see page 19.: **41 Oak St.**
- Apt. no.: _____
- City, town or post office, state, and ZIP code. If you have a foreign address, see page 19.: **Orlando, Florida 32816**

Important! You must enter your SSN(s) above.

Presidential Election Campaign (See page 19.)

Note. Checking "Yes" will not change your tax or reduce your refund.
Do you, or your spouse if filing a joint return, want $3 to go to this fund?

- You: ☐ Yes ☒ No
- Spouse: ☐ Yes ☐ No

Filing Status

Check only one box.

1. ✓ Single
2. ☐ Married filing joint return (even if only one had income)
3. ☐ Married filing separate return. Enter spouse's social security no. above and full name here. ▶ _____
4. ☐ Head of household (with qualifying person). (See page 19.) If the qualifying person is a child but not your dependent, enter this child's name here. ▶ _____
5. ☐ Qualifying widow(er) with dependent child (year spouse died ▶ _____). (See page 19.)

Exemptions

- 6a ☐ **Yourself.** If your parent (or someone else) can claim you as a dependent on his or her tax return, **do not** check box 6a
- b ☐ **Spouse**
- c **Dependents:**

(1) First name Last name	(2) Dependent's social security number	(3) Dependent's relationship to you	(4) ✓ if qualifying child for child tax credit (see page 20)
			☐
			☐
			☐
			☐
			☐
			☐

If more than six dependents, see page 20.

- No. of boxes checked on 6a and 6b: **1**
- No. of your children on 6c who:
  - lived with you
  - did not live with you due to divorce or separation (see page 20)
- Dependents on 6c not entered above
- Add numbers entered on lines above ▶ **1**

d Total number of exemptions claimed

Income

Attach Forms W-2 and W-2G here. Also attach Form(s) 1099-R if tax was withheld.

If you did not get a W-2, see page 21.

Enclose, but do not attach, any payment. Also, please use Form 1040-V.

Line	Description	Amount
7	Wages, salaries, tips, etc. Attach Form(s) W-2	40,000
8a	Taxable interest. Attach Schedule B if required	300
8b	Tax-exempt interest. Do not include on line 8a	
9	Ordinary dividends. Attach Schedule B if required	580
10	Taxable refunds, credits, or offsets of state and local income taxes (see page 22)	
11	Alimony received	
12	Business income or (loss). Attach Schedule C or C-EZ	
13	Capital gain or (loss). Attach Schedule D if required. If not required, check here ▶ ☒	50
14	Other gains or (losses). Attach Form 4797	
15a	Total IRA distributions _____ b Taxable amount (see page 23)	
16a	Total pensions and annuities _____ b Taxable amount (see page 23)	
17	Rental real estate, royalties, partnerships, S corporations, trusts, etc. Attach Schedule E	3,000
18	Farm income or (loss). Attach Schedule F	
19	Unemployment compensation	
20a	Social security benefits _____ b Taxable amount (see page 25)	
21	Other income. List type and amount (see page 25)	
22	Add the amounts in the far right column for lines 7 through 21. This is your **total income** ▶	43,930

Adjusted Gross Income

Line	Description	Amount
23	IRA deduction (see page 27)	
24	Student loan interest deduction (see page 27)	
25	Medical savings account deduction. Attach Form 8853	
26	Moving expenses. Attach Form 3903	
27	One-half of self-employment tax. Attach Schedule SE	
28	Self-employed health insurance deduction (see page 29)	
29	Self-employed SEP, SIMPLE, and qualified plans	
30	Penalty on early withdrawal of savings	
31a	Alimony paid b Recipient's SSN ▶ 987 65 4321	6,000
32	Add lines 23 through 31a	6,000
33	Subtract line 32 from line 22. This is your **adjusted gross income** ▶	37,930

For Disclosure, Privacy Act, and Paperwork Reduction Act Notice, see page 56.   Cat. No. 11320B   Form **1040** (2000)

FIGURE 13-1 ▶ FORM 1040 (PAGE 1)

Schedules A&B (Form 1040) 2000 — OMB No. 1545-0074 — Page **2**

Name(s) shown on Form 1040. Do not enter name and social security number if shown on other side.

John J. Alexander

Your social security number: *123 45 6789*

Schedule B—Interest and Ordinary Dividends

Attachment Sequence No. **08**

Part I — Interest

(See page B-1 and the instructions for Form 1040, line 8a.)

Note. If you had over $400 in taxable interest, you must also complete Part III.

1. List name of payer. If any interest is from a seller-financed mortgage and the buyer used the property as a personal residence, see page E-1 and list this interest first. Also, show that buyer's social security number and address ▶

Note. If you received a Form 1099-INT, Form 1099-OID, or substitute statement from a brokerage firm, list the firm's name as the payer and enter the total interest shown on that form.

2. Add the amounts on line 1
3. Excludable interest on series EE and I U.S. savings bonds issued after 1989 from Form 8815, line 14. You **must** attach Form 8815
4. Subtract line 3 from line 2. Enter the result here and on Form 1040, line 8a ▶

Part II — Ordinary Dividends

(See page B-1 and the instructions for Form 1040, line 9.)

Note. If you had over $400 in ordinary dividends, you must also complete Part III.

5. List name of payer. Include only ordinary dividends. If you received any capital gain distributions, see the instructions for Form 1040, line 13 ▶

Payer	Amount
Ford Motor Company	150
Omaha Mutual Fund	430

Note. If you received a Form 1099-DIV or substitute statement from a brokerage firm, list the firm's name as the payer and enter the ordinary dividends shown on that form.

6. Add the amounts on line 5. Enter the total here and on Form 1040, line 9 ▶ **580**

Part III — Foreign Accounts and Trusts

(See page B-2.)

You must complete this part if you (a) had over $400 of interest or ordinary dividends; (b) had a foreign account; or (c) received a distribution from, or were a grantor of, or a transferor to, a foreign trust.

7a. At any time during 2000, did you have an interest in or a signature or other authority over a financial account in a foreign country, such as a bank account, securities account, or other financial account? See page B-2 for exceptions and filing requirements for Form TD F 90-22.1 — **No: X**

b. If "Yes," enter the name of the foreign country ▶

8. During 2000, did you receive a distribution from, or were you the grantor of, or transferor to, a foreign trust? If "Yes," you may have to file Form 3520. See page B-2 — **No: X**

For Paperwork Reduction Act Notice, see Form 1040 instructions. Schedule B (Form 1040) 2000

FIGURE 13-2 ▶ SCHEDULES A & B (PAGE 2)

I3-12 Define the term *constructive receipt*. Explain its importance.

I3-13 Explain three restrictions on the concept of constructive receipt.

I3-14 When is income considered to be earned by an accrual-basis taxpayer?

I3-15 a. Explain the difference between the treatment of prepaid income under the tax law and under financial accounting.
b. Why are the two treatments so different?
c. What problem does this treatment create for taxpayers?

I3-16 Under what conditions is an accrual-basis taxpayer allowed to defer reporting amounts received in the advance of the delivery of goods?

I3-17 Under what conditions is an accrual-basis taxpayer allowed to defer reporting advance payments received for services?

I3-18 a. Is the interest received from government obligations taxable? Explain.
b. What impact does the fact that some bond interest is tax exempt have on interest rates?
c. Is an investor always better off buying tax-exempt bonds? Explain.

I3-19 Are improvements made by a lessee to a lessor's property included in the income of the lessor?

I3-20 Explain the relationship between dividends and earnings and profits.

I3-21 On what basis did the Supreme Court in *Eisner v. Macomber* decide that stock dividends are nontaxable?

I3-22 What is the significance of a constructive dividend?

I3-23 Explain the importance of the distinction between alimony and a property settlement.

I3-24 a. Are items of income not listed in Sec. 61 taxable? Explain.
b. Because there is no specific exclusion for unrealized income, why is it not taxable?
c. Can income be realized even when a cash-method taxpayer does not receive cash?
d. Does a cash basis taxpayer realize income upon the receipt of a note?

I3-25 a. Briefly explain the tax benefit rule.
b. Is a taxpayer required to report the reimbursement of a medical expense by insurance as income if the reimbursement is received in the year following the year of the expenditure?

I3-26 What opportunities are available for a taxpayer to defer the recognition of certain types of prepaid income? That is, what advice could you give someone who wishes to defer the reporting of prepaid income?

I3-27 Taxpayers who deduct an expense one year but recover it the next year are required to include the recovered amount in gross income. The tax benefit rule provides relief if the original deduction did not result in any tax savings. Does this rule provide relief to taxpayers who are in a higher tax bracket in the year they recover the previously deducted expense?

I3-28 George, a wealthy investor, is uncertain whether he should invest in taxable or tax-exempt bonds. What tax and nontax factors should he consider?

I3-29 Do you agree or disagree with the following statement: A taxpayer should not have to report income when debt is forgiven because the taxpayer receives nothing. Explain.

I3-30 Jack and June are retired and receive $10,000 of social security benefits and taxable pensions totaling $25,000. They have been offered $20,000 for a automobile that they restored after they retired. They did most of the restoration work themselves and the sale will result in a gain of $12,000. What tax issues should Jack and June consider?

ISSUE IDENTIFICATION QUESTIONS

I3-31 State Construction Company is owned equally by Andy, Bill, and Charlie. Andy works in the corporation full-time, and Bill and Charlie work elsewhere. When Andy left his previous job to work for State, he signed a contract specifying that he would receive a salary of $50,000 per year. This year, Andy felt that the company could expand if it purchased more equipment, and he offered to delay receiving $20,000 of his salary so the funds could be used to purchase the equipment. Bill and Charlie agreed, and the equipment was purchased. It is expected that State will have enough cash to pay Andy by early March of next year. What tax issues should Andy consider?

I3-32 Lisa and her daughter Jane are equal shareholders is Lisa's Flooring, Inc. Lisa founded the corporation and was the sole owner for over twenty years. The company is very successful and Lisa has accumulated a fairly large estate. When Jane turned age twenty-five last year, Lisa gave her half of the corporation's stock. The gift was properly reported on Lisa's gift tax return. Both Lisa and Jane now work full-time for the corporation. Lisa received a salary of $55,000 per year before Jane started working for the company. After Jane started working, Lisa reduced her salary to $15,000 and started paying Jane a salary of $50,000. Lisa indicates that she still makes most major decisions in the company, but she hopes that Jane will play a more important role as she becomes more familiar with the company. What tax issues should Lisa and the corporation consider?

I3-33 Larry's Art Gallery sells oil paintings, lithographs, and bronzes to collectors and corporations. Customers often come to Larry looking for special pieces. In order to meet customer needs, Larry often accepts orders and then travels looking for the desired item, which he purchases and delivers to the customer. The pieces are expensive, and Larry requires customers to demonstrate their sincerity by providing deposits. If it turns out that the item costs more than expected, Larry contacts the buyer and asks for additional funds. If the item costs less than expected, Larry refunds the excess amount. Also, Larry sometimes returns amounts he received in advance because he is unable to find what the customer wants. What tax issues should Larry's Art Gallery consider?

PROBLEMS

I3-34 *Noncash Compensation.* For each of the following items indicate whether the individual taxpayer must include any amount in gross income:
a. York Corporation gave 100 shares of stock to each of its employees. York Corporation wanted to retain its cash for expansion, so the company transferred the stock, worth $12 per share, to its employees in lieu of a raise.
b. Yellow Corporation encourages its employees to take flu shots. The company does so to reduce time off due to sickness. The company pays for the shots, which cost $20 each.
c. Zip Corporation paid its directors $1,000 each. One director, who was working in a foreign country for the entire year, received the $1,000 fee, even though he did not attend any directors' meetings.

I3-35 *Constructive Receipt.* Which of the following constitutes constructive receipt?
a. A salary check received at 6:00 p.m. on December 31, after all the banks have closed.
b. A rent check, received on December 30 by the manager of an apartment complex. The manager normally collects the rent for the owner. The owner was out of town.
c. A paycheck received on December 29 that was not honored by the bank because the employer's account did not have sufficient funds.
d. A check received on December 30. The check was postdated January 2 of the following year.
e. A check received on January 2. The check had been mailed on December 30.

I3-36 *Cash and Accrual Methods.* Carmen opens a retail store. Her sales during the first year are $600,000 of which $30,000 have not been collected at year end. Her purchases are $400,000. She still owes $20,000 to her suppliers, and at year end she has $50,000 of inventory on hand. Expenses for the year equal $160,000.
a. Compute her net income from the business assuming she elects the accrual method.
b. Compute her net income from the business assuming she elects the cash method.
c. Would paying her suppliers the amount she owes before year end change her net income under accrual method of reporting? under the cash method?

I3-37 *Series EE Bond Interest.* In 1997, Harry and Mary purchased Series EE bonds, and in 2001 redeemed the bonds, receiving $500 of interest and $1,500 of principal. Their income from other sources totaled $30,000. They paid $2,200 in tuition and fees for their dependent daughter. Their daughter is a qualified student at State University.
a. How much of the Series EE bond interest is excludable?
b. Assuming that the daughter received a $1,000 scholarship, how much of the interest is excludable? Ignore any tax credits that might be available.
c. Assuming the daughter received the $1,000 scholarship and that the parents' income from other sources is $89,150, how much of the interest is excludable?

I3-38 *Alimony.* As a result of their divorce, Fred agrees to pay alimony to Tammy of $20,000 per year. The payments are to cease in the event of Fred's or Tammy's death or in the event of Tammy's remarriage. In addition, Tammy is to receive their residence, which cost them $100,000 but is worth $140,000.
a. Does the fact that Tammy receives the residence at the time of the divorce mean that there is a reduction in alimony, which will lead to Fred having to recapture an amount in the subsequent year?
b. How will the $20,000 payments be treated by Fred and Tammy?
c. Would recapture of the payments be necessary if payment ceased because of Tammy's remarriage?
d. What is Tammy's basis in the residence?

Gross Income: Inclusions ▼ Individuals 3-35

I3-39 *Constructive Dividend.* Brad owns a successful corporation that has substantial earnings and profits. During the year, the following payments were made by the corporation:
  a. Salary of $250,000 to Brad. Officers in other corporations performing similar services receive between $50,000 and $85,000.
  b. Rent of $25,000 to Brad. The rent is paid in connection with an office building owned by Brad and used by the corporation. Similar buildings rent for about the same amount.
  c. Salary of $5,000 to Brad's daughter, who worked for the company full-time during the summer and part-time during the rest of the year while she attended high school.
  d. Alimony of $40,000 to Brad's former wife. Although Brad was personally obligated to make the payments, he used corporation funds to make the payments.

Discuss the likelihood of these payments being treated as constructive dividends. If a payment is deemed to be a constructive dividend, indicate how such a payment will be treated.

I3-40 *Constructive Dividend.* Which of the following would likely be a constructive dividend?
  a. An unreasonable salary paid to a shareholder.
  b. An unreasonable salary paid to the daughter of a shareholder.
  c. A sale of a corporation's asset to a shareholder at fair market value.
  d. A payment by a corporation of a shareholder's debts.
  e. A payment by a corporation of a shareholder's personal expenses.

I3-41 *Prepaid Rent.* Stan rented an office building to Clay for $3,000 per month. On December 29, 2000, Stan received a deposit of $4,000 in addition to the first and last months' rent. Occupancy began on January 2, 2001. On July 15, 2001, Clay closed his business and filed for bankruptcy. Stan had collected rent for February, March, and April on the first of each month. Stan had received May rent on May 10, but collected no payments afterwards. Stan withheld $800 from the deposit because of damage to the property and $1,500 for unpaid rent. He refunded the balance of the deposit to Clay. What amount would Stan report as gross income for 2000? for 2001?

I3-42 *Rental Income.* Ed owns Oak Knoll Apartments. During the year, Fred, a tenant, moved to another state. Fred paid Ed $1,000 to cancel the two-year lease he had signed. Ed subsequently rented the unit to Wayne. Wayne paid the first and last months' rents of $800 each and a security deposit of $500. Ed also owns a building that is used as a health club. The club has signed a fifteen-year lease at an annual rental of $17,000. The owner of the club requested that Ed install a swimming pool on the property. Ed declined to do so. The owner of the club finally constructed the pool himself at a cost of $15,000. What amount must Ed include in gross income?

I3-43 *Gross Income.* Joy collected $800 interest on corporate bonds and a salary of $32,000 from her employer. Joy won $100 for having the lowest golf score in her country club's golf tournament. She also won $500 in the state lottery. The ticket cost $5. Joy also stole $50 from her mother's purse when she was not looking. Which amounts are taxable?

I3-44 *Interest Income.* Holly inherited $10,000 of City of Atlanta bonds in February. In March, she received interest of $500, and in April she sold the bonds at a $200 gain. Holly redeemed Series E U.S. savings bonds that she had purchased several years ago. The accumulated interest totaled $800. Holly received $300 of interest on bonds issued by the City of Quebec, Canada. What amount, if any, of gross income must Holly report?

I3-45 *Annuity Income.* Tim retired during the current year at age 58. He purchased an annuity from American National Life Company for $40,000. The annuity pays Tim $500 per month for life.
  a. Compute Tim's annual exclusion.
  b. How much income will Tim report each year after reaching age 84?

I3-46 *Pension Income.* Beth turns 65 and retires from her position as a garment worker. She immediately began receiving a monthly pension for the remainder of her life of $300 from a qualified retirement plan. Over the years she worked, Beth made $13,104 of nondeductible contributions to the pension fund through withholding. How much must Beth report as income from the pension during the current year?

I3-47 *Social Security Benefits.* Dan and Diana file a joint return. Dan earned $30,000 during the year before losing his job. He subsequently received unemployment compensation of $1,000. Diana received Social Security benefits of $5,000.
  a. Determine the taxable portion of the Social Security benefits.

b. What is the taxable portion of the Social Security benefits if Dan earned $45,000 before losing his job?

I3-48 *Social Security Benefits.* Lucia is a 69-year-old single individual who receives a taxable pension of $10,000 per year and Social Security benefits of $7,000. Lucia is considering the possibility of selling stock she has owned for years and using the funds to purchase a summer home. She will realize a gain of $20,000 when she sells the stock, which has been paying $1,000 of dividends each year. Lucia says her brother recommended that she sell half of the stock this year and half next year because selling all of the stock at once would affect the tax treatment of her Social Security benefits.
   a. Compute her AGI under the assumption she sells all of the stock now after receiving $1,000 dividends from the stock.
   b. Repeat the computation under the assumption she sells only half of the stock this year and also receives $1,000 dividends from the stock.

I3-49 *Social Security Benefits.* Gary and Gail file a joint return. Gary's salary is $42,000, and they received taxable interest of $1,000. Gail received $7,000 of Social Security benefits. What amount, if any, of the benefits are taxable?

I3-50 *Adjusted Gross Income.* Amir, who is single, retired from his job this year. He received a salary of $25,000 for the portion of the year that he worked, tax-exempt interest of $3,000, and dividends from domestic corporations of $2,700. On September 1, he began receiving monthly pension payments of $1,000 and Social Security payments of $600. Assume an exclusion ratio of 40% for the pension. Amir owns a duplex that he rents to others. He received rent of $12,000 and incurred $17,000 of expenses related to the duplex. He continued to actively manage the property after he retired from his job. Compute Amir's adjusted gross income.

I3-51 *Recovery of Previously Deducted Expense.* In 2002, Fred received a $1,000 refund of state income taxes withheld from his salary during 2001. For each of the following cases, indicate whether Fred must include any portion of the refund in his 2002 gross income.
   a. Fred did not itemize during 2001.
   b. Fred does not itemize during 2002.
   c. Fred uses the accrual method for determining his deduction for state income taxes.
   d. Fred suffered a net loss during 2001 of $20,000.
   e. Fred suffered a net loss during 2002 of $20,000.
   f. Fred's itemized deductions during 2002 exceeded the standard deduction by $400.

I3-52 *Recovery of Previously Deducted Expense.* As the result of unexpected surgery, Jan incurred $14,000 of medical expenses in 2001. At the end of 2001, her medical insurance had paid only $5,000. Jan anticipates that the company will eventually pay an additional $7,000 of the bill. Because her AGI is $30,000 and there is a 7.5% floor for medical deductions, Jan can deduct medical expenses over $2,250. Her other itemized deductions exceed the standard deduction.
   a. If Jan pays the balance of the $9,000 medical expenses before the end of the year, can she claim a deduction in 2001?
   b. If she is reimbursed $7,000 in 2002, how will the reimbursement be treated?

I3-53 *Court Awards and Insurance Settlements.* What amount, if any, must be included in gross income by the following taxpayers?
   a. Allen received $1,000 from his insurance company because his boat, which cost $2,000, was sunk during a storm.
   b. Collin owns Collins Construction Company. Len started Colins Construction Company and obtained a number of contracts with people who thought they were dealing with Collins Construction Company. Collin sued and collected $40,000, which was the profit he lost because of the contracts, and punitive damages of $80,000.
   c. Dick loaned his brother $2,000. Dick had to sue in order to recover the amount of the loan.
   d. Fran, an accountant, had to sue a client in order to collect her audit fee of $8,000. Would Fran's accounting method make any difference?

I3-54 *Claim of Right.* USA Corporation hired Jesse to install a computer system for the company and paid him $8,000 for the work. USA soon realized that there were problems with the system and asked Jesse to refund the payment. At the end of the year the dispute had not been resolved. Jesse is in the 28% tax bracket in the year he did the original work. During the next year, when he is in the 15% tax bracket, Jesse refunds the $8,000 to USA.

a. Is the original payment taxable to Jesse when he receives it?
b. What options are available to Jesse when he repays the $8,000?
c. What option would have been available to Jesse if he had been asked to repay only $2,000?

I3-55 *Tax Planning.* Bart and Kesha are in the 36% tax bracket. They are interested in reducing the taxes they pay each year. They are currently considering several alternatives. For each of the following alternatives, indicate how much tax, if any, they would save.
a. Make a gift of bonds valued at $5,000 that yield $400 per year interest to their 14-year-old daughter, who has no other income.
b. Sell the bonds from Part a rather than give them to their daughter, and buy tax-exempt bonds that pay 6%. Assume the bonds can be sold for $5,000.
c. Give $1,000 cash to a charity. Assume they itemize deductions.
d. Pay their daughter a salary of $10,000 for services rendered in their unincorporated business.

I3-56 *Series EE Bond Interest and Kiddie Tax.* In 2001, Ken and Lynn paid $5,000 to purchase Series EE bonds in the name of their 11-year-old son. The son has no other income, and they are in the 28% tax bracket. The taxable interest during the first year will be $400 if an election is made to accrue the interest on an annual basis.
a. Will the child owe any tax on the bond interest?
b. Does the son need to file a tax return?
c. What are the tax consequences in 2001 and subsequent years if annual gifts are made to their son?

COMPREHENSIVE PROBLEMS

I3-57 Matt and Sandy reside in a community property state. Matt left home in April 2001 because of disputes with his wife, Sandy. Subsequently, Matt earned $15,000. Before leaving home in April, Matt earned $3,000. Sandy was unaware of Matt's whereabouts or his earnings after he left home. The $3,000 earned by Matt before he left home was spent on food, housing, and other items shared by Matt and Sandy. Matt and Sandy have one child, who lived with Sandy after the husband left home.
a. Is any portion of Matt's earnings after he left home taxable to Sandy?
b. What filing status is applicable to Sandy if she filed a return?
c. How much income would Sandy be required to report if she filed?
d. Is Sandy required to file?

I3-58 Gary earned $57,000 as an executive. Gary, who is single, supported his half sister, who lives in a nursing home. Gary received the following interest: $400 on City of Los Angeles bonds, $200 on a money market account, and $2,100 on a loan to his brother.
Gary spent one week serving on a jury and received $50.
Gary received a refund of federal income taxes withheld during the prior year of $1,200 and a state income tax refund of $140. Gary had itemized deductions last year of $8,000.
Gary received dividends on Ace Corporation of $1,000 and on Tray Corporation of $1,400. Gary's itemized deductions equal $9,000, and withholding for federal income taxes is $10,000. Compute Gary's tax due or refund due.

TAX FORM/RETURN PREPARATION PROBLEMS

I3-59 Sally W. Emanual had the following dividends and interest during the current year:

Acorn Corporation bond interest		$ 700
City of Boston bonds interest		1,000
Camp Bank interest		250
Jet Corporation dividend		300
North Mutual fund		
Capital gain distribution	100	
Ordinary dividend	150	
Nontaxable distribution	200	450
Blue Corporation foreign dividend		250

Additional information pertaining to Sally Emanual includes

Salary	$32,000
Rent income	12,000
Expenses related to rent income	14,000
Pension benefits	8,000
Alimony paid to Sally	4,000

The taxable portion of the pension is $7,000. Sally actively participates in the rental activity. Other relevant information includes

Address: 430 Rumsey Place, West Falls, California 92699
Occupation: Credit manager
Social Security number: 123-45-4321
Marital status: Single

Complete Sally's Schedule B and page 1 of her Form 1040. Assume Schedule E has already been prepared.

CASE STUDY PROBLEMS

I3-60 Jim and Linda are your tax clients. They were divorced two years ago, and the divorce decree stated that Jim was to make monthly payments to Linda. The court designated $300 per month as alimony and $200 per month as child support, or a total of $6,000 per year. Jim has been unemployed for much of the year and paid Linda $2,000 that he said was for child support. In addition, Jim transferred the title to a three-year-old automobile with a $4,000 FMV and basis of $7,000 in exchange for her promise not to pursue any claim she has against him for the unpaid child support and alimony. Does Linda have to report any alimony and is Jim entitled to an alimony deduction? Draft a memo for the file that discusses the tax consequences for both Jim and Linda.

I3-61 John and Mary (your clients) have two small children and are looking for ways to help fund the children's college education. They have heard that Series EE bonds are a tax-favored way of saving and have requested your opinion on the tax consequences. They have asked your opinion regarding the relative advantages of purchasing Series EE bonds in their names versus the children's names. John and Mary have indicated that they expect to have a high level of income in the future and that their children may receive other income sources from future inheritances. Prepare a client memo making recommendations about the tax consequences of Series EE bond investments for John and Mary.

I3-62 Lee and Jane have been your firm's clients for most of the twenty years they have been married. Recently Lee came to you and said that he and Jane are obtaining a divorce, and he wants you to help him with some of the tax and financial issues that may come up during the divorce. The next day, Jane called asking you for the same assistance. What ethical issues do you see present? What possible conflicts may arise if you represent both Lee and Jane?

TAX RESEARCH PROBLEM

I3-63 William owns a building that is leased to Lester's Machine Shop. Lester requests that William rewire the building for new equipment Lester plans to purchase. The wiring would cost about $4,000, but would not increase the value of the building because its only use is in connection with the specialized equipment. Rather than lose Lester as a lessee, William agrees to forgo one month's rent of $1,000 if Lester will pay for the wiring. Because Lester does not want to move, he agrees. What amount, if any, must William include in gross income?

A partial list of research sources is
- Sec. 109
- Reg. Sec. 1.109-1
- *CIR v. Grace H. Cunningham*, 2 AFTR 2d 5511, 58-2 USTC ¶9771 (9th Cir., 1958)

CHAPTER 4

GROSS INCOME: EXCLUSIONS

LEARNING OBJECTIVES
After studying this chapter, you should be able to

1. Explain the conditions that must exist for an item to be excluded from gross income
2. Determine whether an item is income
3. Decide whether specific exclusions are available
4. Understand employment-related fringe benefit exclusion items

CHAPTER OUTLINE

Items That Are Not Income...4-2
Major Statutory Exclusions...4-4

KEY POINT

Given the sweeping definition of *income*, it is generally difficult to establish that an item is not income.

EXAMPLE I4-1 ▶

EXAMPLE I4-2 ▶

Chapter I3 discussed specific items that must be included in gross income. This chapter considers items that are excluded from gross income. Under Sec. 61(a), all items of income are taxable unless specifically excluded. Taxpayers who wish to avoid being taxed have two basic alternatives. One approach is to establish that the item is not income. If an item is not income (e.g., if it is a return of capital), it is not subject to the income tax. The second approach is to establish that a specific exclusion applies to the item of income.

Matt borrowed $10,000 from the bank. Although Matt received $10,000, it is not income because he is obligated to repay the amount borrowed. No specific statutory authority states that borrowed funds are excluded from taxation. Presumably, the fact that borrowed funds are not income is considered to be both fundamental and obvious. ◀

Sheila enrolled in State University. The university awarded her a $1,000 tuition scholarship because of her high admission test scores and grades. Section 117 excludes such scholarships from gross income. As a result, Sheila need not report the scholarship as income. ◀

OBJECTIVE 1

Explain the conditions that must exist for an item to be excluded from gross income

REAL-WORLD EXAMPLE

Grants made to Native Americans by the federal government under the Indian Financing Act of 1974 to expand Native American–owned economic enterprises are excludable from gross income. Rev. Rul. 77-77, 1977-1 C.B. 11.

The major source of exclusions are those specific items contained in the IRC. These exclusions have evolved over the years and were enacted by Congress for a variety of reasons, including social and economic objectives.

Another source of exclusions are referred to as *administrative exclusions*. Exclusions exist because specific provisions in the Internal Revenue Code allow them. While the IRS has no authority to create exclusions, the IRS does have the authority to interpret the meaning of the Code. A liberal interpretation of the statute by the IRS may result in a broad definition of what constitutes an exclusion, and such a broad definition may reasonably be termed an administrative exclusion. For example, Sec. 102 excludes gifts received from gross income. The IRS has followed the practice of excluding certain welfare benefits from gross income, presumably because such benefits may be viewed as gifts.[1] The IRS could take the position that welfare benefits are not gifts. That position would no doubt be challenged in the courts.

The term *judicial exclusions* should be considered in the same vein. Although the courts cannot create exclusions, they can interpret the statute and decide whether a particular item is covered by a statutory exclusion.

ITEMS THAT ARE NOT INCOME

OBJECTIVE 2

Determine whether an item is income

TYPICAL MISCONCEPTION

It is sometimes erroneously assumed that severance pay, embezzlement proceeds, gambling winnings, hobby income, prizes, rewards, and tips are not taxable.

As noted above, some items are not income and, therefore, are not subject to the income tax. In addition to amounts obtained by a loan (discussed above), four other items are not considered income:

▶ Unrealized income
▶ Self-help income
▶ Rental value of personal-use property
▶ Gross selling price of property (as opposed to the profit or gain earned on the sale)

UNREALIZED INCOME

Income that is not realized is not subject to income taxation. Thus, if a taxpayer owns stock in a company and the stock increases in value but the taxpayer does not sell the stock, no taxable income is realized.

This issue of the taxability of unrealized income was addressed over 80 years ago in *Eisner v. Macomber*, where the Supreme Court held that a stock dividend cannot be taxed

---

[1] For example, see Rev. Rul. 57-102, 1957-1 C.B. 26, which excludes from gross income public assistance payments to blind persons.

because the taxpayer had "received nothing that answers the definition of income within the meaning of the Sixteenth Amendment."[2] An ordinary stock dividend does not alter the existing proportionate ownership interest of any stockholder, nor does it increase the value of the individual's holdings. In effect, the court concluded that realization must occur before income is recognized. Although narrowed by subsequent legislation and litigation, ordinary stock dividends continue to be excluded from gross income even today. Perhaps more important, *Eisner v. Macomber* established realization as a criterion for the recognition of income.

SELF-HELP INCOME

Although self-help income is considered as income by economists, it is not recognized as income by the IRS or by the courts. Taxpayers commonly benefit from activities such as painting their own homes or repairing their own automobiles. If a taxpayer hires someone else to do the work, the taxpayer has to earn the income, pay tax on such income, and use the after-tax income to pay for the work. In either case, the taxpayer receives the same economic benefit, but the economic benefit derived from self-help is not included in the taxpayer's gross income.

This situation should be contrasted with taxable exchanges of services. A mechanic might agree to repair a painter's automobile in exchange for the painter's promise to paint the mechanic's home. In this instance, when the parties exchange services, each party realizes income equal to the value of the services received.

> **TYPICAL MISCONCEPTION**
> When a taxpayer purchases an older house and remodels the kitchen or makes other improvements, there is a tendency to assume correctly that the taxpayer has no income from this activity, but it is often incorrectly assumed that the basis of the house can be increased by the value of the taxpayer's labor.

> **STOP & THINK**
>
> *Question:* The discussion of self-help income refers to an exchange of services between two individuals, such as a painter and a mechanic. How can a taxable barter transaction be distinguished from an act of friendship which is repaid?
>
> *Solution:* When one person helps another without any promise of repayment, the act of kindness does not represent an exchange and is not taxable. Friends help one another from time to time without contractual reciprocity. As a result, such acts are not taxable. The distinction between a taxable barter exchange and acts of friendship is not always easy to make.

RENTAL VALUE OF PERSONAL-USE PROPERTY

Taxpayers are not taxed on the rental value of personally owned property. For example, taxpayers who own their own home receive the economic benefit of occupancy without being taxed on the rental value of the property. It would be very difficult to keep records and value benefits obtained from self-help and the personal use of property. For that reason, no significant effort has ever been made to tax such benefits.[3]

> **ADDITIONAL COMMENT**
> The tax situation of a homeowner is quite different than that of someone who lives in an apartment. The failure to include the rental value of the home as income in addition to the deduction of mortgage interest and property taxes favors homeowners.

SELLING PRICE OF PROPERTY

If property is sold at a gain, the gain and not the entire sales price is taxable. Because the basic principle is almost universally accepted, the Supreme Court has never had to rule directly on whether the entire sale proceeds could be taxed. The IRS and the courts seemed to accept the basic principle even before the rule became part of the statute.[4] The primary reason for this principle (often referred to as the "recovery of capital" principle) is that a portion of the selling price represents a return of capital to the seller.

---

[2] 3 AFTR 3020, 1 USTC ¶32 (USSC, 1920).
[3] In 1928, the government tried unsuccessfully to tax the value of produce grown and consumed by a farmer (*Homer P. Morris*, 9 B.T.A. 1273 (1928)). The court stated, "To include the value of such products [would be to] in effect include in income something which Congress did not intend should be so regarded." The court did not explain how or why it reached this conclusion. In 1957, the IRS successfully disallowed the deduction of expenses incurred in raising such produce (*Robert L. Nowland v. CIR*, 51 AFTR 423, 57-1 USTC ¶9684 (4th Cir., 1957)).

[4] Section 202(a) of the Revenue Act of 1924 is the predecessor of current Sec. 1001(a), which describes that only the gain portion of the sale proceeds is included in gross income. S. Rept. No. 398, 68th Cong., 1st Sess., p. 10 (1924) states that Sec. 202(a) sets forth general rules to be used in the computation of gain or loss. The Senate report further states that the provision "merely embodies in the law the present construction by the Department and the courts of the existing law."

MAJOR STATUTORY EXCLUSIONS

OBJECTIVE 3

Decide whether specific exclusions are available

While Congress has created statutory exclusions for a variety of reasons, most exclusions have been enacted for reasons of social policy or reasons of incentive. The concept of social policy, that is, a concept of social generosity or benevolence, has prompted the government to exclude items such as:

- Gifts and inheritances (Sec. 102)
- Life insurance proceeds (Sec. 101)
- Public assistance payments
- Qualified adoption expenses (Sec. 137)
- Payments for personal physical sickness and injury (Sec. 104)
- Discharge of indebtedness during bankruptcy or insolvency (Sec. 108)
- Gain on sale of personal residence (Sec. 121)
- Partial exclusions for Social Security benefits (Sec. 86)

Other exclusions may be explained in terms of economic incentive, that is, the government's desire to encourage or reward a particular type of behavior.

- Awards for meritorious achievement (Sec. 74(b))
- Various employee fringe benefits (Secs. 79, 105, 106, 124, 125, 129, 132)
- Partial exclusion for scholarships (Sec. 117)
- Foreign-earned income (Sec. 911)
- Interest on state and local government obligations (Sec. 103)

Other reasons may exist for some of the exclusions listed above. For example, one reason income from the discharge of indebtedness during bankruptcy is excluded from gross income is the fact that such taxpayers would be unlikely to have the resources needed to pay the tax. (See Chapter I3 for a discussion of tax-exempt interest and Social Security benefits, and Chapter I12 for the treatment of gain on the sale of a personal residence.)

ADDITIONAL COMMENT

Tax expenditure estimates measure the decreases in individual and corporate income tax liabilities that result from provisions in income tax laws and regulations that provide economic incentives or tax relief to particular kinds of taxpayers.

GIFTS AND INHERITANCES

Congress has excluded the value of gifts and inheritances received from gross income since the inception of the income tax in 1913. Section 102 excludes the value of property received during the life of the donor (*inter vivos* **gifts**) and transfers at death (**testamentary gifts**—bequests, devises, and inheritances).[5] The recipient of such property is taxed on the income produced by the property after the transfer.[6] It should be noted that a donor, under the assignment of income doctrine, cannot avoid the income tax by making a gift of income. To avoid paying tax on income, a donor must make a gift of the underlying property to the donee.

TYPICAL MISCONCEPTION

Some people still believe that gifts above the gift exclusion amount of $10,000 are taxable to the donees. They are not since the Code specifically exempts all gifts, regardless of the amount. The donor may, however, depending on the circumstances, pay a gift tax.

EXAMPLE I4-3 ▶ Stan owns stock in a corporation and orders the corporation to pay dividends on the stock to his daughter. Even though his daughter received the dividends, Stan must include the dividends in his gross income. Stan could avoid being taxed on future dividends by making a gift of the stock to his daughter. ◀

It is often difficult to distinguish gifts, which are not included in the recipient's gross income, from other transfers, which are taxable. Gifts sometimes closely resemble prizes and awards.[7]

EXAMPLE I4-4 ▶ Tina received a free automobile for being the ten millionth paying guest at an amusement park. The automobile is not considered a gift but a prize and is taxable to Tina. ◀

---

[5] Although excluded from gross income, such transfers may be subject to the gift tax or the estate tax which are imposed on the transferor.
[6] Reg. Sec. 1.102-1.

[7] Recall that under Sec. 74 (discussed in Chapter I3) most prizes and awards are taxable.

Also, some payments made to employees by employers may resemble gifts.

EXAMPLE I4-5 ▶ At Christmas, Red Corporation paid $500 to each employee who had been with the company for more than five years. These payments are not considered gifts for tax purposes and are taxable to the employees. ◀

REAL-WORLD EXAMPLE

Amounts received by a dealer from players in the operation of a gambling casino were not excludable as gifts even though impulsive generosity or superstition may be the dominant motive. The amounts were similar to tips, which are taxable. *Louis R. Tomburello*, 86 T.C. 540 (1986).

Whether a transfer is a gift depends on the intent of the donor. A donor is expected to be motivated by love, affection, kindness, sympathy, generosity, admiration, or similar emotions. In the two preceding examples, the transfers probably were made for business motives and not necessarily for donative reasons. Thus, the automobile is a taxable prize, and the amounts paid to employees represent taxable awards for services rendered, but see the discussion of Sec. 274 later in this chapter.

Transfers of money or property between family members frequently create problems of classification. For example, assume a father, who owns a business, hires his 10-year old son to work in the business. Is the payment to the son a salary (and, therefore, deductible by the business) or is it really just a gift from the father to the son? The answer depends on the true value of the services performed by the son. If the son truly performs services that are commensurate with the salary paid, the payment may properly be classified as a salary. On the other hand, if the son is paid an amount that exceeds the value of the services, the excess amount will be treated as a gift.

LIFE INSURANCE PROCEEDS

Life insurance proceeds paid to a beneficiary because of the insured person's death are not taxable.[8] The exclusion applies whether the proceeds are paid in a lump sum or in installments. Amounts received in excess of the face amount of the policy usually are taxable as interest.

EXAMPLE I4-6 ▶ Buddy is the beneficiary of a $100,000 insurance policy on his mother's life. Upon her death, he elects to receive $13,000 per year for ten years instead of the lump sum. He receives $10,000 per year tax-free ($100,000 ÷ 10), but the remaining $3,000 per year is taxable as interest. ◀

EXAMPLE I4-7 ▶ Assume the same facts as in Example I4-6, except that Buddy elects to receive the full $100,000 face amount upon his mother's death. None of the $100,000 is taxable. ◀

The exclusion exists because life insurance benefits closely resemble inheritances, which are not taxable.

There is one exception that may result in a portion of the face amount of a life insurance policy being included in gross income.[9] The life insurance exclusion generally is not available if the insurance policy is obtained by the beneficiary in exchange for valuable consideration from a person other than the insurance company. For example, an individual may purchase an existing life insurance policy for cash from another individual. In this situation, the exclusion for death benefits is limited to the consideration paid plus the premiums or other sums subsequently paid by the buyer.

EXAMPLE I4-8 ▶ Kwame is the owner and beneficiary of a $100,000 policy on the life of his father. Kwame sells the policy to his brother Anwar for $10,000. Anwar subsequently pays premiums of $12,000. Upon his father's death, Anwar must include $78,000 [$100,000 − ($10,000 + $12,000)] in gross income. However, if Kwame gave the policy to his brother, all of the proceeds would be excluded from gross income because the gift of the policy does not constitute valuable consideration. ◀

ADDITIONAL COMMENT

The proceeds of a life insurance policy payable to named beneficiaries can be excluded from the federal estate tax when the decedent does not possess any incidents of ownership. This provision and the exclusion from gross income of life insurance proceeds underscore the favored position of life insurance.

The proceeds are excludable under the general exclusion for life insurance proceeds if the beneficiary's basis is found by reference to the transferor's basis (as would be true in the case of a gift), or if the policy is transferred to the insured, the insured's partner, a partnership that includes the insured, or a corporation in which the insured is a shareholder or officer.

---

[8] Sec. 101(a).

[9] Sec. 101(a)(2).

SELF-STUDY QUESTION

A corporation acquires a life insurance policy on the president of the corporation, and the corporation is named as the beneficiary of the policy. Are the insurance premiums deductible?

ANSWER

No, the premiums are not deductible because any costs incurred to produce tax-exempt income are nondeductible.

SURRENDER OR SALE OF POLICY. The exclusion for life insurance is available for amounts payable by reason of the death of the insured. In general, if a life policy is sold or surrendered for a lump sum before the death of the insured, the amount received is taxable to the extent that it exceeds the net premiums paid.[10] On the other hand, no loss is recognized if a life insurance policy is surrendered before maturity and premiums paid exceed the cash surrender value.[11]

"Accelerated death benefits" may be excluded from gross income. Accelerated death benefits include payments made to a terminally ill person and periodic payments made to a chronically ill person. A person is terminally ill if a physician certifies that he is reasonably likely to die within 24 months. A person is chronically ill if he has a disability requiring long-term care (e.g., nursing home care). In general, the exclusion for periodic payments made to a chronically ill person is limited to the greater of $200 per day ($190 per day in 2000), or the actual cost of such care. The exclusion covers amounts received from the insurance provider or from a "viatical settlement provider" (i.e., person in the business of providing accelerated death benefits).

EXAMPLE I4-9 ▶ Harry has been diagnosed with AIDS and is expected to live less than a year. Harry is covered by a life insurance policy with a $100,000 face amount. The insurance company offers terminally ill individuals the option of receiving 75% of the policy face amount. If Harry accepts the settlement, the amount he receives is excludable from gross income because he is a terminally ill individual. ◀

EXAMPLE I4-10 ▶ Mary suffered a severe stroke and has been admitted to a nursing home where she is expected to remain for the rest of her life. She is certified by a licensed health care practitioner as being a "chronically ill individual." Her nursing home expenses amount to $130 per day. Mary has elected to receive $150 per day from a $200,000 face amount life insurance policy as accelerated death benefits. Because she is a chronically ill individual, Mary may exclude the full amount she receives as it is less than daily limitation of $200 established by law. ◀

DIVIDENDS ON LIFE INSURANCE AND ENDOWMENT POLICIES. Dividends on life insurance and endowment policies are normally not taxable because they are considered to be a partial return of premiums paid. The dividends are taxable to the extent that the total dividends received exceed the total premiums paid. Also, if dividends are left with the insurance company and earn interest, the interest is taxable.

ADOPTION EXPENSES

Congress provides tax benefits for qualified adoption expenses in the form of tax credits (see Chapter I14) or an exclusion for amounts paid pursuant to an adoption assistance plan created by an employer. An employee is allowed a $5,000 per child exclusion ($6,000 for a child with special needs) from gross income for qualified adoption expenses paid by an employer under an adoption assistance program.[12] The exclusion is phased-out ratably for taxpayers with modified adjusted gross income of $75,000 to $115,000.

Qualified adoption expenses include adoption fees, court costs, attorney fees, and other expenses related to an adoption. An adoption assistance program is a separate written plan of an employer, exclusively for the benefit of its employees, to provide adoption assistance.

EXAMPLE I4-11 ▶ Reggie and Rhonda are married, have AGI of $90,000, and adopt a child. Rhonda's employer maintains a written adoption assistance program. They spend $8,000 during the year in connection with the adoption, all of which is paid by Rhonda's employer pursuant to the plan. Reggie and Rhonda must include in their gross income an amount of $4,875, computed as follows:

---

[10] Sec. 72(e)(2). In some instances where distributions are made before the recipient reaches age 59½, a 10% penalty applies (see Sec. 72(q)).

[11] *London Shoe Co. v. CIR.*, 16 AFTR 1398, 35-2 USTC ¶9664 (2nd Cir., 1935).

[12] Sec. 137.

Total adoption expenses paid from the plan	$8,000
Maximum exclusion	5,000
Phase-out percentage [$15,000/($115,000 − $75,000)]	37.5%
Reduction in exclusion	1,875
Exclusion amount ($5,000 − $1,875)	3,125
Amount includible in gross income ($8,000 − $3,125)	4,875

AWARDS FOR MERITORIOUS ACHIEVEMENT

ADDITIONAL COMMENT
Notice that to exclude awards for meritorious achievement, the award must not come into the possession of the taxpayer.

As noted in Chapter I3, prizes and awards generally are taxable. An exception is applicable to awards and prizes made for religious, charitable, scientific, educational, artistic, literary, or civic achievement if the recipient:

▶ Was selected without action on his or her part to enter the contest or the proceeding,

▶ Does not have to perform substantial future services as a condition to receiving the prize or award, and

▶ Designates that the payor is to pay the amount of the award to either a government unit or a charitable organization.[13]

The recipient of such an award normally would owe no tax if he or she collected the proceeds and then contributed the proceeds to a charity because the gift would qualify as a deductible charitable contribution. However, the exclusion changes AGI and thereby affects other computations. Also, this rule is beneficial in situations where the taxpayer could not deduct the full amount of the award because of the limitation on the charitable contribution deduction (generally 50% of AGI; see Chapter I7) or in the case of a small award to a taxpayer who does not itemize.

SCHOLARSHIPS AND FELLOWSHIPS

ADDITIONAL COMMENT
Athletic scholarships for fees, books, and supplies awarded by a university to students who are expected, but not required, to participate in a particular sport can be excludable.

KEY POINT
The exclusion for scholarships does not include amounts received for room, board, and laundry.

Subject to certain limitations, scholarships are excluded from gross income.[14] A scholarship is an amount paid or allowed to a student, whether an undergraduate or graduate, to aid degree-seeking individuals.

The exclusion for scholarships is limited to the amount of the scholarship used for *qualified tuition and related expenses*. Qualified tuition and related expenses typically include tuition and fees, books, supplies, and equipment required for courses of instruction at an educational organization. The value of services and accommodations supplied such as room, board, and laundry are not excluded. The exclusion for scholarships does not extend to salary paid for services even if all candidates for a particular degree are required to perform the services.[15]

EXAMPLE I4-12 ▶ Becky is awarded a $5,000 per year scholarship by State University. Becky spends $3,000 of the scholarship for tuition, books, and supplies, and $2,000 is for room and board. In addition, Becky works part-time on campus and earns $4,000, which covers the rest of her room and board and other expenses. Becky is taxed on the $2,000 of the scholarship spent for room and board and $4,000 of salary earned from her part-time job. ◀

DISTRIBUTIONS FROM QUALIFIED STATE TUITION PROGRAMS

Several states have established tuition programs under which donors make contributions that entitle designated beneficiaries to waiver or payment of qualified higher education expenses. Such expenses include tuition, books, fees, supplies, room and board not covered by other tax favored benefits (e.g., scholarships, veterans' benefits, Education Savings Bonds exclusion, and Hope/Lifetime Learning credits). Sec. 259 states that income is recognized by a beneficiary only to the extent waivers or distributions made on

---

[13] Sec. 74.
[14] Sec. 117.
[15] Scholarships may need to be reviewed to determine whether the amount constitutes compensation. A "scholarship" awarded to the winner of a televised beauty pageant by a profit-making corporation was ruled to be compensation for performing subsequent services for the corporation (Rev. Rul. 68-20, 1968-1 C.B. 55). An employer-paid "scholarship" was held to be compensation in a situation where the employee was on leave and was required to return to work after finishing the degree (*Richard E. Johnson v. Bingler*, 23 AFTR 2d 69-1212, 69-1 USTC ¶9348 (USSC, 1969)). However, in Ltr. Rul. 9526020 (September 10, 1995) the IRS ruled that grants to law students are not taxable even if they are conditioned upon the students agreeing to practice upon graduation in public, nonprofit, or other low paying sectors.

the beneficiary's behalf exceed donor contributions. Donors recognize no income unless they receive refunds that exceed the amounts they contributed.

EXAMPLE I4-13 ▶ Jane's parents contributed $24,000 to a qualified state tuition program. Under the plan, her net qualified costs of $36,000 will be waived. Jane's parents recognize no income under the plan. She begins classes in the fall semester and her qualified expenses of $4,500 are waived. Jane can exclude $3,000 ($24,000 / $36,000 × $4,500) from gross income, and she must include the remaining $1,500 in gross income. ◀

PAYMENTS FOR INJURY AND SICKNESS

Sec. 104(a) excludes from gross income the "amount of any damages (other than punitive damages) . . . received . . . on account of personal physical injuries or physical sickness." Thus, for example, a taxpayer may exclude an insurance settlement for physical injury that resulted from an automobile accident. The exclusion does not cover amounts awarded for nonphysical injuries (such as a damaged reputation or libel) except that taxpayers may exclude reimbursements for medical expenses related to nonphysical injuries.

EXAMPLE I4-14 ▶ After she was denied a promotion, Jane sued her employer claiming sex discrimination. She was awarded $5,000 to cover the medical bills she incurred because of the related emotional distress, $20,000 to punish her employer for discrimination, and $10,000 to compensate her for lost wages. The $5,000 awarded to cover medical bills is excluded from gross income, but not the amounts awarded as punitive damages or lost wages. ◀

The exclusion under Sec 104(a) applies to damages received because of emotional distress in only two situations: (1) when the payments are for medical expenses related to the emotional distress, and (2) when the payments are for emotional distress *attributable* to a physical injury (including physical injury suffered by another person).

Sometimes, victims are awarded amounts that are intended to punish the guilty party. These so called "punitive damages" are taxable even when they are awarded for physical injuries.

EXAMPLE I4-15 ▶ Mary was injured in an automobile accident caused by another driver. Mary's daughter, Sarah, was in the automobile, but she was not physically injured. The other driver's insurance company was required by a court to pay Mary $10,000 to cover medical bills relating to her injuries, $5,000 to compensate her for emotional distress caused by the injuries and 15,000 of punitive damages. Sarah was paid $3,000 to compensate her for distress caused by her witnessing her mother's injuries. Only the $15,000 of punitive damages are taxable to Mary as the other amounts are compensatory damages related to her physical injuries. Sarah's damage award of $3,000 is also excludable. ◀

Sec. 104(a)(3) excludes from gross income amounts collected under an accident and health insurance policy purchased by the taxpayer, even if the benefits are a substitute for lost income. In addition, Sec. 101 specifies that benefits received under a qualified long term care insurance contract may be excluded from gross income, but limits the exclusion to the greater of $200 per day ($190 per day in 2000) or the actual cost of such care.[16] Such policies pay for nursing home and other types of long term care. If the benefits exceed the actual cost of such care, but are less than $200 per day, no portion of the benefits is taxable.

EXAMPLE I4-16 ▶ Chuck purchased a disability income policy from an insurance company. Chuck subsequently suffered a heart attack. Under the terms of the policy Chuck received $1,000 per month for the five months he was unable to work. The amounts received are not taxable, even though the payments are a substitute for the wages lost due to the illness. ◀

---

[16] Sec. 101.

Gross Income: Exclusions ▼ **Individuals 4-9**

This exclusion is not applicable if the accident and health benefits are provided by the taxpayer's employer.[17]

EXAMPLE I4-17 ▶ Assume the same facts as in Example I4-16 except that Chuck's employer paid the premiums on the policy. The amounts received by Chuck are taxable. ◀

EXAMPLE I4-18 ▶ Ruth suffered a serious stroke and was admitted to a nursing home. During the year, she was in a nursing home for 140 days. Nursing home charges, physician fees and other related expenses totaled $22,050.

Under Ruth's long-term care insurance contract, she received reimbursements of $24,000. The reimbursements are not includible in Ruth's gross income because the amounts are less than the allowed exclusion amount of $28,000 (140 days ×$200). This exclusion applies even though she was reimbursed more than her actual costs. Alternatively, if the reimbursements had been $29,000, she would be required to report $1,000 ($29,000 −$28,000) as gross income. ◀

If the cost of the coverage is shared by the employer and the taxpayer, a portion of the benefits is taxable. For example, if the employer paid one-half of the premiums, one-half of the benefits would be taxable. The principal reason for the different tax treatment is that employer-paid coverage represents a tax-free employee fringe benefit, whereas employee-paid premiums are from after-tax dollars.

In the case of an award intended to reimburse the taxpayer for medical expenses, it follows that the taxpayer cannot deduct the reimbursed medical expenses.[18] If the award exceeds the actual expense, it is not taxable except in the case of employer-financed accident and health insurance.[19]

State worker's compensation laws establish fixed amounts to be paid to employees suffering specific job-related injuries. Section 104(a)(1) specifically excludes worker's compensation from gross income, even though the payments are intended, in part, to reimburse injured workers for loss of future income and even if the injuries are nonphysical.

EMPLOYEE FRINGE BENEFITS

OBJECTIVE 4

Understand employment-related fringe benefit exclusion items

In general, employee compensation is taxable regardless of the form it takes. Nevertheless, the tax law encourages certain types of fringe benefits by allowing an employer to deduct the cost of the benefit, by permitting the employee to exclude the benefit from gross income, or by permitting both the employer deduction and an employee exclusion. Employee fringe benefits subject to special rules include employee insurance, Sec. 132 benefits, meals and lodging, dependent care, and cafeteria plans. These fringe benefits are discussed below.

ADDITIONAL COMMENT

Many companies provide health care benefits to retired employees. However, due to mounting medical insurance bills, a rising retiree population, and an FASB rule that requires firms to recognize the associated liability, a number of companies are requiring retired workers to pick up a larger portion of their medical costs.

EMPLOYER-PAID INSURANCE. Employers commonly provide group insurance coverage for employees. In general, employers may deduct the premiums paid for life, health, accident, and disability insurance. Normally an employee does not have to include in gross income premiums paid on his or her behalf for health, accident, and disability insurance. Special rules applicable to life insurance premiums are discussed below.

Benefits received from medical, health, and group term life insurance coverage generally are excluded from an employee's gross income. Benefits received from a disability policy are normally taxable, but may qualify for the credit for the elderly and disabled (see Chapter I14). The tax treatments of employer-financed and taxpayer-financed insurance coverage are compared in Topic Review I4-1.

In general, premiums paid by an employer on behalf of employees are deductible. However, medical premiums including long-term health insurance premiums paid by self-employed individuals are subject to special tax treatment. In 2001, a self-employed individual may deduct 60% of the *medical* premiums attributable to coverage as a business

---

[17] A limited credit is available to taxpayers who receive such benefits. See Chapter I14 for a discussion of the credit for the elderly and disabled.
[18] See Chapter I3 for a discussion of the reimbursement of an expense deducted in a preceding year.
[19] Sec. 105(a).

Topic Review I4-1

Treatment of Insurance

	PREMIUMS PAID BY	
	EMPLOYER	*EMPLOYEE*
Medical and health Premiums	Premiums not included in employee's gross income. Premiums deductible by employer.	Premiums deductible as medical expense subject to 7.5% of AGI limitation.
Benefits	Excluded from employee's gross income except when benefits exceed actual expenses.	Excluded from gross income.
Disability Premiums	Premiums not included in employee's gross income. Premiums deductible by employer.	Not deductible.
Benefits	Included in employee's gross income. May qualify for credit for elderly and disabled.	Excluded from gross income.
Life insurance Premiums	Included in employee's gross income (except for limited exclusion applicable to group term life insurance). Premiums deductible by employer (assuming employer is not the beneficiary).	Not deductible.
Benefits	Excluded from gross income.	Excluded from gross income.

ADDITIONAL COMMENT

The tax expenditure estimate associated with the exclusion of contributions by employers for medical insurance premiums and medical care for the period 1994–1998 is $213 billion.

KEY POINT

The nondiscrimination requirements for self-insured accident and health plans are designed to ensure that such plans do not discriminate against rank-and-file workers.

ADDITIONAL COMMENT

The Economic Strategy Institute estimates that domestic auto producers have to pay about $400 per car to cover their health care and pension costs.

expense.[20] These business expenses are allowed as a deduction for adjusted gross income (see Chapter I6 for a discussion of classification of deductions for individuals). The self-employed taxpayer may deduct the remaining medical premiums as a medical expense if his total medical expenses exceed 7.5% of the AGI reported on his individual return.

The rules relating to accident and health insurance are more generous than those for some other types of benefits. Under Sec. 106, employers can deduct insurance premiums and employees need not report the premiums as income. This is true even if the insurance is offered only to officers and other highly compensated employees.

Some employers provide self-insured accident and health plans to employees. Under such plans the employer pays employee medical expenses directly rather than paying insurance premiums. Such plans are subject to nondiscrimination requirements. *Discrimination* is defined in terms of an eligibility test (whether a sufficient number of non–highly compensated employees are covered) and benefits (whether non–highly compensated employees receive benefits comparable to highly compensated employees). Highly compensated employees include the five highest-paid officers, greater-than-10% shareholders, and highest-paid 25% of all other employees.[21] If a plan discriminates in favor of highly compensated employees, these employees must include in gross income any medical reimbursements they receive that are not available to other employees.

In general, life insurance premiums paid by an employer on an employee's behalf are deductible by the employer and are includable in the employee's gross income.[22] A limited exception is applicable to group term life insurance coverage. In general, premiums attributable to the first $50,000 of group term life insurance coverage may be excluded from an employee's gross income.[23] To qualify group term life insurance premiums for the exclusion, broad coverage of employees is required. Though somewhat different, the rules may

---

[20] Sec. 162(l). The deductible portion of such premiums is 60% in 1999, 2000, and 2001, 70% in 2002, and 100% thereafter. In addition, the amount of long-term care insurance premiums eligible to be deducted by self-employed persons are subject to the limitations in Sec. 213(d)(10).
[21] Sec. 105(h)(5).
[22] If the employer is the beneficiary of the policy, the employee receives no economic benefit and, as a result, need not include the premiums in gross income. Such premium payments would not be deductible by the employer. Subsequent benefits would not be included in the employer's gross income.
[23] Sec. 79(a).

be compared to those associated with self-insurance coverage.[24] The amount of coverage can vary between employees as long as the coverage bears a uniform relationship to each employee's compensation.

EXAMPLE I4-19 ▶ Data Corporation provides group term life insurance coverage for each full-time employee. The coverage is equal to one year's compensation. The arrangement constitutes a qualified group term life insurance plan. ◀

TYPICAL MISCONCEPTION
Many individuals erroneously believe that all life insurance coverage provided by employers is exempt from income.

The group term life insurance exclusion is available only for employees, whether active or retired. Thus, proprietors and partners are not employees and, therefore, the premiums paid on their behalf are not deductible.

In the case of coverage that exceeds $50,000, employees must include in gross income the amount established by the Regulations. (See Table I4-1)

EXAMPLE I4-20 ▶ USA Corporation provides Joy, age 61, with $150,000 of group term life insurance coverage. Joy must include in gross income $792, an amount determined by reference to Table I4-1 [($100,000/$1,000 × $.66) × 12 = $792]. ◀

The amount that must otherwise be included in an employee's gross income is reduced by any premiums paid by the employee.

If group term life insurance coverage discriminates in favor of key employees, each key employee must include in gross income the greater of the premiums paid on his or her behalf or the amount determined based on Table I4-1 without any exclusion for the first $50,000 of coverage.

STOP & THINK

Question: Does the fact that employers can provide health insurance and group term life insurance to employees on a tax-favored basis mean that such benefits should be provided to all employees? Explain.

Solution: No. Providing such benefits to all employees may be inefficient. Some employees have other health coverage (e.g., coverage through a spouse's employer). Employees with no dependents may not want life insurance coverage. As a result, employers who provide all employees with such benefits may be spending money on coverage that some employees neither want nor need. A cafeteria plan, discussed later in this chapter, is often a more efficient option. Such plans permit employees to choose either cash or from a menu of tax-favored benefits.

▼ TABLE I4-1
Uniform One-Month Group Term Premiums for $1,000 of Life Insurance Coverage

Employee's age	Premiums
Under 25	$0.05
25 to 29	.06
30 to 34	.08
35 to 39	.09
40 to 44	.10
45 to 49	.15
50 to 54	.23
55 to 59	.43
60 to 64	.66
65 to 69	1.27
70 and above	2.06

Source: Reg. Sec. 1.79-3(d)(2).

---

[24] For example, the rules refer to "key employees" as opposed to highly compensated employees. The term *key employee* is somewhat narrower in scope.

4-12 Individuals ▼ Chapter 4

HISTORICAL NOTE
A limited exclusion from income for unemployment compensation was repealed in the Tax Reform Act of 1986.

SECTION 132 FRINGE BENEFITS. It has become common for employers to provide employees with such diverse benefits as free parking, membership in professional organizations, and small discounts on products sold by the employer. Section 132 was added to the IRC in 1984 to clarify whether certain types of benefits are taxable. Section 132 lists six types of fringe benefits that may be excluded from an employee's gross income (see Topic Review I4-2). Any costs incurred by an employer to provide the specified benefits are deductible under Sec. 162 if they meet the "ordinary and necessary" test of that section.[25] Benefits covered by Sec. 132 include:

- No-additional-cost benefits (e.g., a hotel employee's use of a vacant hotel room)
- Qualified employee discounts (e.g., discounts on merchandise sold by the employer)
- Working condition benefits (e.g., membership fees in professional organizations paid by an employer)
- De minimis benefits (e.g., coffee provided by the employer)
- Qualified transportation and parking fringes (transportation benefits [e.g., transit passes, tokens, and vouchers] limited to $65 per month in 2000 and 2001 and parking, limited to $175 per month in 2000 and $180 per month in 2001)
- Athletic facilities (e.g., employer-owned tennis courts used by employees)

ADDITIONAL COMMENT
The nondiscrimination rules do not apply to working condition fringe benefits. For example, if a corporation makes bodyguards available only to key officers, the working condition fringe benefit exclusion would still apply.

No-additional-cost benefits are limited to services, as opposed to property. Common examples of no-additional-cost benefits include the use of vacant hotel rooms by hotel employees and standby air flights provided to airline employees. The employer may not incur substantial additional costs, including forgone revenue, in providing the services to the employee. Thus, a hotel may allow employees to stay in vacant hotel rooms even though the hotel incurs additional utility and laundry costs as a result of the stay. However, the hotel cannot allow the employees to stay in lieu of paying guests. No-additional-cost benefits are limited to services provided to employees, their spouses, dependent children, and to retired and disabled employees. The term employee includes partners who perform services for a partnership. In addition, the benefits may be extended, on a reciprocal basis, to employees of other companies in the same line of business.

Employers may permit employees to purchase goods and services at a discount from the price charged regular customers. In the case of services, the discount is limited to 20% of the price charged regular customers. In the case of property, the discount is limited to the company's gross profit percent. No discounts are permitted on real property or investment property (e.g., houses or stocks). Further, the discounts must be from the same line of business in which the employee works. The discounts may be provided to the same persons as no-additional-cost benefits except that the discounts may not be provided on a reciprocal basis to employees of companies in the same line of business.

Discrimination is prohibited with respect to certain benefits. The benefits must be made available to employees in general rather than to highly compensated employees only. (See Topic Review I4-2 for specific rules.)

SELF-STUDY QUESTION
Western Airlines and Central Airlines have a reciprocal agreement that permits employees of the other airline to travel for free on a standby basis. Stan, an employee of Western Airlines, takes a free flight on Central Airlines that would have cost $800. What is Stan's income?

ANSWER
None, reciprocal agreements with regard to no-additional-cost services are permitted.

EMPLOYEE AWARDS. As noted earlier, it is often difficult to distinguish between gifts and awards. The de minimis rule mentioned above permits employers to make small gifts such as a holiday turkey or a watch at retirement without the employee having to include the value of the gift in gross income. The employer is entitled to a deduction for the cost of such gifts.

Section 74 provides a similar rule for **employee achievement awards** and **qualified plan awards**.[26] Such awards must be in the form of tangible personal property other than cash and must be based on safety records or length of service. Employee achievement awards are limited to $400 for any one employee during the year. Furthermore, the awards must

---

[25] See Chapter I6 for a discussion of Sec. 162 and its requirements. Section 274 does provide one exception to the general rule. The costs of maintaining recreational facilities (such as swimming pools) are not deductible if the facilities are made available on a discriminatory basis (e.g., only officers may use the facilities).

[26] Sec. 74(c). The definitions and requirements for employee achievement awards and qualified plan awards are contained in Sec. 274(j).

Topic Review I4-2

Summary of Sec. 132 Fringe Benefits

Section	Benefit	May Be Made Available to	Comments
132(b)	No-additional-cost (e.g., telephone, unused hotel rooms for hotel employees, unused airline seats for airline employees)	Employees, spouses, dependents, and retirees	The services must be of the same types that are sold to customers and in the line of business in which the employee works. Discrimination is prohibited.
132(c)	Qualified employee discounts	Employees, spouses, dependents, and retirees	Discounts on services limited to 20%. Discounts on merchandise are limited to the employer's gross profit percentage. No discount is permitted on real estate, stock, or other investment type property. Discrimination is prohibited.
132(d)	Working condition (e.g., free magazines, outplacement, and memberships)	Employees	Discrimination is permitted. Special rules apply to tuition reductions for employees of educational institutions and to an auto salesperson's demonstrator.
132(e)	De minimis (e.g., free coffee, holiday turkeys, or use of company eating facilities)	Employees	Eating facilities must be made available on a nondiscriminatory basis.
132(f)	Qualified transportation fringes (e.g., transit passes, tokens, and parking)	Employees	Limited in 2001 to $180 per month for parking and $65 per month for other transportation fringes.
132(j)(4)	Recreation and athletic facilities (e.g., gyms, pools, saunas, tennis courts)	Employees, spouses, dependents, and retirees.	If discrimination is present, employer loses deduction.

be presented as part of a meaningful presentation and awarded under circumstances that do not create a significant likelihood of the payment being disguised compensation. Qualified plan awards must be granted under a written plan and may not discriminate in favor of highly compensated employees. The average cost of qualified plan awards is limited to $400, but individual awards can be as large as $1,600.

▶ An award for length of service cannot qualify under the IRC if it is received during the employee's first five years of employment or if the employee has received a length-of-service award during the year or any of the preceding four years.

▶ No more than 10% of an employer's eligible employees may receive an excludable safety achievement award during any year. Eligible employees are employees whose positions involve significant safety concerns.

EXAMPLE I4-21 ▶ Each year, USA Corporation presents length-of-service awards to employees who have been with the company five, ten, fifteen, or twenty years. The presentations are made at a luncheon sponsored by the company and include gifts such as desk clocks, briefcases, and watches, none of which cost more than $400. The awards, which qualify as employee achievement awards, are deductible by USA Corporation and are not taxable as income to USA's employees. ◀

Gifts to employees that do not qualify as employee achievement awards or qualified plan awards can be excluded by the employee only if the awards can be excluded as de minimis amounts under Sec. 132(e).

MEALS AND LODGING. Section 119 provides a limited exclusion for the value of meals and lodging that are provided to employees at either no cost or a reduced cost.

- Meals provided by an employer may be excluded from an employee's gross income if they are furnished on the employer's premises and for the convenience of the employer.
- Lodging provided by an employer may be excluded from an employee's gross income if it is furnished on the employer's premises and for the convenience of the employer, and the employee is required to accept the lodging as a condition of employment.

The requirement that meals and lodging be furnished on the premises of the employer refers to the employee's place of employment.[27] In one case, the Tax Court held that the business premises requirement was met in a situation where a hotel manager lived in a residence across the street from the hotel he managed.[28]

The convenience of the employer test considers whether a substantial noncompensatory business reason exists for providing the meals or lodging. Thus, the test is met if the owner of an apartment complex furnishes a unit to the manager of the complex because it is necessary to have the manager present on the premises even when he or she is off duty.

The value of lodging cannot be excluded from gross income unless the employee is required to accept the lodging as a condition of employment. This requirement is not met if the employee has a choice of accepting the lodging or receiving a cash allowance. Furthermore, meal allowances do not qualify for the exclusion because the employer does not actually provide the meal.[29] Section 132 (discussed earlier in this chapter) provides a de minimis exception. Some employers provide supper money to employees who must work overtime. If such benefits are occasionally provided to employees, the amount is excludable from the employees' gross income.

> **REAL-WORLD EXAMPLE**
> Many university presidents are furnished with personal residences, the value of which they can generally exclude from gross income.

> **REAL-WORLD EXAMPLE**
> A brewery provided houses on the business premises to officers. The value of the houses was excludable because it was important to have the officers available for around-the-clock operations of the business. *Adolph Coors Co.,* 1968 PH T.C. Memo ¶68, 256, 27 TCM 1351.

EXAMPLE I4-22 ▶ A hospital maintains a cafeteria that is used by employees, patients, and visitors. Employees are provided free meals while on duty in order to be available for emergency calls. Since the meals are provided on the employer's premises and for the convenience of the employer, the value of the meals are excluded from the employees' gross income. ◀

EXAMPLE I4-23 ▶ A state highway patrol organization provides its officers with a daily meal allowance to compensate them for meals eaten while they are on duty. Officers typically eat their meals at the restaurant of their choice. Because the officers receive cash instead of meals, the amount provided must be included in the officers' gross income. ◀

EXAMPLE I4-24 ▶ A large corporation requires five of its employees to work overtime two evenings each year when the company takes inventory. The corporation gives each of the employees a small amount to cover the cost of the dinner for the two evenings. The amounts constitute supper money and are excluded from the employees' gross income. ◀

Section 119 provides that if employees can exclude the value of meals from gross income, the employer can deduct the full cost of the meal. Further, if more than half of the employees who receive meals meet the "convenience of the employer" test, then all employees who receive meals can exclude the value from gross income.

MEALS AND ENTERTAINMENT. One obvious question is whether employees who are reimbursed by their employers when they entertain customers must include the reimbursement in gross income. If they must include the reimbursement in gross income, can they deduct the cost of the entertainment and meals? Assuming conditions for deductibil-

---

[27] Reg. Sec. 1.119-1(c)(1).
[28] *Jack B. Lindeman,* 60 T.C. 609 (1973).
[29] *CIR v. Robert J. Kowalski,* 40 AFTR 2d 77-6128, 77-2 USTC ¶9748 (USSC, 1977).

ity are met, the tax law clearly allows 50% of the cost of entertaining customers to be deducted (discussed in Chapter I9). Can the employee deduct the meals and entertainment that he personally consumes?

EXAMPLE I4-25 ▶ Joe is a sales representative for Zero Corporation. As a part of his regular duties, Joe buys lunch for Wayne, a Zero Corporation customer. Fifty percent of the cost of Wayne's meal is deductible either by Joe if he pays for the luncheon without being reimbursed by his employer, or by the Zero Corporation if it reimburses Joe for the cost. Can Joe deduct 50% of the cost of his own meal if he pays for it and is not reimbursed? If Zero pays for the meal, must Joe include in his gross income the cost of his own lunch? ◀

In the above question, Joe apparently can deduct the portion of the luncheon that applies to himself. While this issue is not clearcut, the IRS has indicated in Rev. Rul. 63-144 that it will not pursue the issue except where taxpayers claim deductions for substantial amounts of personal expenses.[30] In any case, it is an accepted practice today for taxpayers to deduct 50% of the total cost of a meal (taxpayer and customer) unless the practice is considered abusive.[31]

EMPLOYEE DEATH BENEFITS. Occasionally, an employer may make payments to the family or friends of an employee who dies. In some instances, the payments might be viewed as a gift made for reasons such as the financial need of the family, kindness, or charity. Alternatively, the amount might constitute a payment of compensation based on the past services of the deceased employee. Gifts are, of course, excluded from gross income, whereas compensation is taxable. The treatment of payments made to the family or other beneficiaries of the employee's estate is determined by the following rules:

▶ Payments for past services (such as bonuses, accrued wages, and unused vacation pay) are taxable as income to the family and are deductible by the employer. The important issue is whether the employee would have received this amount had he or she lived. If the employer was legally obligated to make the payment at the time of the employee's death, the payments are taxable to the recipient.

▶ Other amounts may be either taxable compensation or excludable gifts depending on the facts and circumstances. If the amount is a gift, it is not deductible by the employer. If the amount is taxable income to the deceased employee's family, it is deductible by the employer.

WHAT WOULD YOU DO IN THIS SITUATION?

FRINGE BENEFIT

National Boats manufactures pleasure boats sold to consumers. The boats range in price from $40,000 to $1,500,000. Jake is the president of National Boats. The company provides Jake with one of its more expensive boats. The company pays for fuel, insurance, and other costs, and deducts these expenses along with depreciation on the boat. The company states that Jake is responsible for testing and for demonstrating the boat to possible customers. Jake has had the same boat for two years, and the company plans to provide him with a new boat next month.

You asked Jake how often he uses the boat. He indicated that he uses it once or twice each month on weekends, except during the winter. You asked him who accompanies him, and what types of testing he conducts. He seemed reluctant to answer the question, but acknowledged that his family often accompanies him on the boat, and said that he tests it during ordinary operations to determine how it performs. He added that potential customers who have also accompanied him included neighbors and friends. What tax issues do you see?

---

[30] Rev. Rul. 63-144, 1963-2 C.B. 129.
[31] See, however, *Richard A. Sutter*, 21 T.C. 170 (1953), where the Tax Court ruled that business meals, entertainment, etc. for one's own self are inherently personal and nondeductible. *Sutter* has been cited and upheld some 50 times.

In determining whether the amount is taxable, the courts have considered such factors as whether the employer derived benefit from the payment, whether the employee had been fully compensated, and whether the payment was made to the family and not to the estate. The Supreme Court stated, "The most critical consideration [in determining whether a transfer is a gift] is the transferor's 'intention.'"[32] Although the case did not deal with death benefits, it did establish the importance of motive in determining whether a payment is a gift. Thus, the transfer should be made for reasons such as kindness, sympathy, generosity, affection, or admiration.

It should be noted that it is more difficult to establish that a payment is a gift in situations where the payments are made to persons owning stock in the corporation making the payment. Such payments may be construed as constructive dividends, which are not deductible by the corporation but are taxable income to the recipients.[33]

DEPENDENT CARE. **Dependent care assistance programs** are employer-financed programs that provide care for an employee's children or other dependents. An employee may exclude up to $5,000 of assistance each year ($2,500 for a married individual filing a separate return). The care must be of a type that, if paid by the employee, would qualify for the dependent care credit. Furthermore, the credit is scaled down if the employee receives benefits under the employer's plan. (See Chapter I14 for a discussion of the child and dependent care rules.) The program cannot discriminate in favor of highly compensated employees or their dependents.[34]

EDUCATIONAL ASSISTANCE. Under Sec. 127 educational assistance plans, employers pay employee educational costs. Employees may exclude from gross income annual payments of up to $5,250. However, Sec. 127 does not apply to expenses paid for graduate-level courses. This rule is scheduled to expire on December 31, 2001, and it is uncertain whether it will be extended.

CAFETERIA PLANS. **Cafeteria plans**, also called flexible spending accounts, are plans that offer employees the option of choosing cash or statutory nontaxable fringe benefits (such as group term life insurance, medical insurance, adoption expenses, child care, etc.). If the employee chooses cash, the cash is taxable. However, if the employee chooses a statutory nontaxable fringe benefit, the value of the benefit is excluded from gross income.[35] In other words, the fact that the employee could have chosen cash does not cause the fringe benefit to be taxed. The plan cannot discriminate in favor of highly compensated employees or their dependents or spouses.[36] Employer plans may specify what benefits are offered and may limit the amount of benefits individual employees may receive.

Some plans supplement wages; others are wage reduction plans. In supplemental wage plans, employer funds are used to pay fringe benefits. In the case of wage reduction plans, employees elect to receive reduced wages in exchange for the fringe benefits. In both cases, employees receive benefits without being taxed on them.

Employers often allow employees to use such funds to pay medical expenses. Typically, the plans supplement medical insurance, and funds are used to pay dental bills and other medical expenses not covered by regular insurance. In general, employees annually elect to set-aside funds to pay medical expenses, and the employer pays the expenses using the set aside funds. One problem with the agreements is that they are binding for one year. As a result, the employee loses the funds if the actual medical expenses are less than the amount set aside. Employers, on the other hand, are obligated to pay expenses up to the agreed amount even if the full amount has not yet been withheld from the employee's wages. Thus, the employer may lose money if an employee terminates employment after incurring the designated amount of medical expenses but before the full amount is withheld.

> **ADDITIONAL COMMENT**
> The $5,000 limit was placed on the exclusion for dependent care assistance programs because it was thought to be inequitable to provide an unlimited dependent care exclusion but a limited child care credit for people who pay their own child care expenses.

> **ADDITIONAL COMMENT**
> The classification of an employee as highly compensated is made on the basis of the facts and circumstances of each case. Any officers and shareholders owning more than 5% of the stock are classified as highly compensated employees.

> **ADDITIONAL COMMENT**
> About half of the large employers in the United States offer flexible spending accounts.

> **ADDITIONAL COMMENT**
> While the main benefit of a cafeteria plan is to offer tax-free choices to employees, the plan must also offer at least one taxable benefit.

---

[32] *CIR v. Mose Duberstein*, 5 AFTR 2d 1626, 60-2 USTC ¶9515 (USSC, 1960).
[33] *Ernest L. Poyner v. CIR*, 9 AFTR 2d 1151, 62-1 USTC ¶9387 (4th Cir., 1962).
[34] Sec. 129.
[35] Long-term care insurance (sometimes called nursing home insurance) can be offered to employees on a tax-favored basis, but that benefit cannot be offered as part of a flexible spending account.
[36] Sec. 125.

ADVANTAGE OF FRINGE BENEFITS. The major advantage of taking fringe benefits (such as those descibed above) in lieu of a cash payment is the fact that employees do not have to use after-tax income to obtain the product or service.

EXAMPLE I4-26 ▶ Dan, an employee of Central Corporation, has a $40,000 life insurance policy and pays the premiums out of his salary. Since his salary is taxable, the premiums are paid on an after-tax basis. Kay, an employee for Western Corporation, is covered by a $40,000 group term life insurance policy financed by Western Corporation. Western Corporation pays the premiums on the policy. Because the premiums are excludable, Kay does not have to report the premiums as income. ◀

EXAMPLE I4-27 ▶ John's employer establishes a cafeteria plan which allows each employee to set aside up to $5,000 for health insurance premiums and medical reimbursements. John, whose salary has been $30,000, agrees to a salary reduction of $4,000 of which $2,500 is to cover his health insurance premiums and $1,500 is available to reimburse his medical expenses. Under the arrangement, John's salary is reduced to $26,000 for tax purposes. Neither the health insurance coverage nor the medical expense reimbursement is taxable. During the year, John incurs $1,400 of medical expenses not covered by insurance. He receives a reimbursement for all of the expenses. His employer retains the remaining $100. Alternatively, if the medical expenses were $1,800, John would receive a reimbursement of $1,500 and he must pay the remaining $300 of expenses out of after-tax salary dollars. ◀

STOP & THINK

Question: Employers and employees both pay FICA taxes on salaries. Fringe benefits such as health insurance are exempt from both income taxes and FICA taxes. What is the tax effect of an employee's decision to elect health insurance coverage in exchange for a reduced salary?

Solution: The employee's income and FICA taxes are both lowered. The employer is permitted an income tax deduction for either the salary payment or the payment of the health insurance premium. The employer's FICA tax is reduced because the health insurance benefit also is exempt from that tax.

INTEREST-FREE LOANS. One benefit that was often used in the past was interest-free loans to employees. The advantage of this type of transaction was diminished by the Tax Reform Act of 1984. Under present law, interest must generally be imputed on interest-free loans. (See Chapter I11 for a detailed discussion of rules applicable to interest-free loans.)

ADDITIONAL COMMENT
Many U.S. embassies and consulates in foreign countries provide income tax assistance.

ADDITIONAL COMMENT
Foreign-earned income does not include amounts paid to an employee of the U.S. government or any U.S. government agency or instrumentality.

FOREIGN-EARNED INCOME EXCLUSION

In general, the income of U.S. citizens is subject to the U.S. income tax even if the income is derived from sources outside the United States. The foreign income of U.S. citizens also may be taxed by the host country possibly leading to a substantial double tax on the same income. The double tax is mitigated by a **foreign tax credit**. Subject to limitations, U.S. citizens may subtract from their U.S. income tax liability the income taxes they pay to foreign countries. (See Chapter I14 for a discussion of foreign tax credit.)

In the case of foreign-earned income, individuals have available the alternative option in 2001 of excluding the first $78,000 of foreign-earned income from gross income.[37] The *exclusion* is available in lieu of the foreign tax credit. If both a husband and wife have foreign-earned income, each may claim an exclusion. Community property rules are ignored in determining the amount of the exclusion. Thus, if only one spouse has foreign-earned income, only one exclusion is available. The principal reasons for the exclusion are to encourage U.S. businesses to operate in foreign countries and to hire U.S. citizens and resident aliens to manage the businesses. The hope is that such operations will improve the balance of payments. Taxpayers who elect the exclusion in one year may switch to the foreign tax credit in any subsequent year. Taxpayers who change from the exclusion to the

---

[37] Sec. 911(b)(2). The foreign earned income exclusion was, for many years, $70,000. It is scheduled to increase to $80,000 in increments of $2,000 each year, beginning in 1998. Beginning in 2008, the exclusion will be indexed for inflation.

credit may not reelect the exclusion before the sixth tax year after the tax year in which the change was made.[38] The IRS can waive the six-year limitation in special situations (such as an individual employee changing the location of his or her foreign employment).

Foreign-earned income includes an individual's earnings from personal services rendered in a foreign country. The place where the services are performed determines whether earned income is foreign or U.S. source income. If an individual is engaged in a trade or business in which both personal services and capital are material income-producing factors, no more than 30% of the net profits from the business may be excluded.[39] Furthermore, pensions, annuities, salary paid by the U.S. government, and deferred compensation do not qualify for the exclusion.[40]

To qualify for the foreign-earned income exclusion, the taxpayer must either be a bona fide resident of one or more foreign countries for an entire taxable year, or be present in one or more foreign countries for 330 days during a period of 12 consecutive months.[41] The exclusion limitation for a year must be prorated if the taxpayer is not present in, or a resident of, a foreign country or countries for the entire year.

> **TYPICAL MISCONCEPTION**
> A taxpayer must be present in one or more foreign countries for 330 days during a period of twelve consecutive months, rather than 330 days during a calendar year.

EXAMPLE I4-28 ▶ Sondra is given a temporary assignment to work in foreign country T. She arrives in T on October 19, 2001 and leaves on October 1, 2002. Although Sondra does not establish a permanent residence in T, she is present in T for at least 330 days out of a twelve-month period beginning on October 20, 2001. Thus, 73 days fall in 2001 and the rest in 2002. Sondra's exclusion for 2001 is limited to $15,600 [(73 ÷ 365) × $78,000]. She may exclude $15,600 or the income she earns in foreign country T during 2001, whichever is less. ◀

Deductions directly attributable to the excluded foreign-earned income are disallowed. Expenses attributable to foreign-earned income must be allocated if foreign-earned income exceeds the exclusion. The disallowed portion is determined by multiplying the total amount of such expenses by the ratio of excluded earned income over total foreign-earned income.

EXAMPLE I4-29 ▶ Connie earned $120,000 during 2001 while employed in a foreign country for the entire year. She is entitled to an exclusion of $78,000. Connie incurred $12,000 of travel, transportation, and other deductible expenses attributable to the foreign-earned income. She may deduct only $4,200 of such expenses because $7,800 [($78,000 ÷ $120,000) × $12,000] is allocated to the excluded income and, therefore, not deductible. The $4,200 is classified as a miscellaneous itemized deduction and subject to the 2% of AGI floor associated with such deductions. ◀

U.S. citizens working in foreign countries must often pay more for housing than they would pay in the United States. Therefore, an additional exclusion from gross income is available for housing costs that exceed 16% of the salary paid government employees in Step 1 of grade GS-14. This GS-14 grade is used to establish a standard for taxpayers in general.

EXAMPLE I4-30 ▶ Wayne is employed in Tokyo, Japan, and earns a salary of $120,000. His housing costs are $32,000 for the year and are reasonable considering the high cost of living in Tokyo. Assume that 16% of the GS-14 (Step 1) salary is $10,171. Wayne can exclude $99,829 from gross income [($78,000 + ($32,000 − $10,171)]. ◀

INCOME FROM THE DISCHARGE OF A DEBT

If debt of a taxpayer is cancelled or forgiven, the taxpayer may have to include the cancelled amount in gross income. It is important to distinguish a debt cancellation from a gift, a bequest, or a renegotiation of the purchase price.

EXAMPLE I4-31 ▶ Farouk loaned his daughter $4,000 to help her purchase an automobile. Several months after she purchased the automobile, but before she repaid the $4,000, Farouk's daughter married. Farouk told his daughter that he was "tearing up" the $4,000 note as a wedding present. In this instance, the amount forgiven would constitute an excludable gift and would not be taxable as income to the daughter. ◀

---

[38] Sec. 911(e)(2).
[39] Sec. 911(d)(2)(B).
[40] Sec. 911(b)(1)(B).
[41] Sec. 911(d).

Gross Income: Exclusions ▼ **Individuals 4-19**

EXAMPLE I4-32 ▶ Clay purchased a used automobile from a dealer for $6,000. He paid $2,000 down and agreed to pay the balance of $4,000 over three years. After Clay purchased the automobile, he determined that it was defective. Clay tried to return the automobile, but the automobile dealer refused. Clay threatened to sue the dealer. To resolve the problem, the dealer offered to reduce the balance due on the purchase-money debt from $4,000 to $2,500. Clay agreed. The transaction constitutes a reduction in the purchase price of the automobile. Clay will not recognize any income, but must reduce the basis in his automobile from $6,000 to $4,500. ◀

EXAMPLE I4-33 ▶ Blue Corporation issued bonds for $1,000 when interest rates were low. After a few years, interest rates increased and the bond price declined to $850. Blue Corporation purchased the bonds on the open market. Blue will recognize $150 of income from the discharge of indebtedness. ◀

EXAMPLE I4-34 ▶ Indy Coal Company has seen its business decline during the past two years. The Company has a significant amount of bank debt that was incurred over the years to fund its coal operations. In order to maintain its operations, Indy entered into an agreement with the bank whereby the bank agreed to cancel 50% of Indy's debt. Assuming Indy was solvent at the time of the cancellation, Indy must report the discharge of indebtedness as gross income. ◀

STOP & THINK

Question: In Example I4-34, the bank agreed to cancel 50% of Indy Coal Company's debt. Why would a lender agree to unilaterally cancel a borrower's debt?

Solution: A bank might cancel a portion of a borrower's debt in order to protect the remaining portion of the debt. If the debt forced the company into bankruptcy, the bank may be able to collect none or only a small percentage of the debt. If the cancellation would help stabilize Indy, the bank may be able to collect at least 50% of the debt. Further, if Indy becomes a viable company in the years ahead, the bank will have a good customer to earn profits in the future.

REAL-WORLD EXAMPLE

A taxpayer purchased and retired its own bonds. The purchase resulted in a gain because the bonds were payable in British pounds, which had been devalued. The gain was excludable. *Kentucky & Indiana Terminal Railroad Co. v. U.S.*, 13 AFTR 2d 1148, 64-1 USTC ¶9374 (6th Cir., 1964).

The enforceability of a debt under state law may also determine whether the forgiveness results in income. For example, one case held that the forgiveness of a gambling debt was not included in gross income where the debt was unenforceable under state law.[42]

DISCHARGE IN BANKRUPTCY AND INSOLVENCY. Section 61(a)(12) indicates that gross income includes income from the discharge of an indebtedness. Section 108, on the other hand, provides for the following exceptions where the discharge of an indebtedness is not taxable:

▶ The discharge occurs in bankruptcy.
▶ The discharge occurs when the taxpayer is insolvent.

These exceptions are intended to allow a "fresh start" for bankrupt and other financially troubled taxpayers. Since a taxpayer is not required to include the discharge in gross income, he is required to reduce certain tax attributes. For example, if the taxpayer has a net operating loss carryover, the NOL carryover must be reduced by the excluded discharge.

KEY POINT

A discharge of debt in bankruptcy does not generate income.

If a debt is reduced during bankruptcy proceedings, the taxpayer recognizes no income even if the reduction in debt exceeds the available tax attributes. In the case of an insolvent taxpayer, no income is recognized as long as the taxpayer is insolvent after the reduction in debt takes place. A taxpayer is insolvent if the debts owed by the taxpayer exceed the FMV of assets owned. Thus, an insolvent taxpayer reduces the tax attributes to the point of solvency. From that point on, any reduction in debt results in the recognition of income even if all tax attributes have not been offset.

ADDITIONAL COMMENT

Also excludable is the income from the cancellation of a student loan pursuant to a provision under which part of the debt is discharged due to working for a period of time in certain professions for a broad class of employers.

STUDENT LOAN FORGIVENESS. Under Sec. 108(f)(2), the discharge of certain student loans is excluded from gross income if the discharge is contingent on the individual's performing certain public services. The loans must have been made by governmental, edu-

---

[42] *David Zarin v. CIR*, 66 AFTR 2d 90-5679, 90-2 USTC ¶50,530 (3rd Cir., 1990).

cational, or charitable organizations, and the loan proceeds must have been used to pay the cost of attending an educational institution or used to refinance outstanding student loans. Further, the loan forgiveness must be contingent upon the individual's working for a specified time period in certain professions, and the services must normally be performed for someone other than the lender.

EXAMPLE I4-35 ▶ Lee borrowed $60,000 from the federal government to attend medical school. Under the terms of the loan, $20,000 of debt is forgiven for each year she practices medicine in designated low-income neighborhoods. Lee does not have to include the debt forgiveness in gross income. ◀

EXCLUSION FOR GAIN FROM SMALL BUSINESS STOCK

Noncorporate taxpayers may exclude up to 50% of the gain realized on the disposition of qualified small business stock issued after August 10, 1993, if the stock is held for more than five years.[43] The remaining gain is taxed at a rate not greater than 28% resulting in a maximum effective rate of 14%. For each issuer of qualified small business stock, there is a limit on the amount of gain a taxpayer may exclude. The amount of gain eligible for the exclusion may not exceed the greater of $10 million, reduced by amounts previously excluded for gains on the company's stock, or ten times the taxpayer's aggregate adjusted basis of the stock disposed of during the year.[44] When measuring the taxpayer's aggregate basis for the stock to determine the maximum amount of gain to exclude, the fair market value of the assets contributed to the corporation is used.

EXAMPLE I4-36 ▶ Dennis contributed property with a basis of $1,000,000 and an FMV of $4,000,000 to a qualified small business corporation for all of its common stock. If he sells one-half of the stock after five years for $14,000,000, he may exclude $6,750,000 of the $13,500,000 ($14,000,000 − $500,000) realized gain. The maximum gain eligible for the exclusion is the greater of $10,000,000 or $20,000,000 [10 times the $2,000,000 basis ($4,000,000 FMV × 0.50) of the stock sold]. Thus, none of the $13,500,000 realized gain is subject to the limitation. ◀

Moreover, taxpayers do not have to recognize any gain if they reinvest the proceeds from the sale of small business stock in other small business stock within 60 days of the sale. Gain is recognized only to the extent that the amount realized from the sale exceeds the cost of the replacement stock. The basis of the replacement stock is reduced by the amount of gain not recognized. To qualify for the replacement provision the original stock must have been held for over 6 months.

EXAMPLE I4-37 ▶ Assume the same facts as in Example I4-36, except that Dennis purchases $13,000,000 of small business investment stock within 60 days. Dennis taxed only on $1,000,000 ($14,000,000 − $13,000,000) of his $13,500,000 realized gain. Dennis' basis for the new stock, however, is $500,000 ($13,000,000 cost of the new stock − $12,500,000 portion of the gain that is not taxed). ◀

A corporation may issue qualified small business stock only if the corporation is a C corporation that is not an excluded corporation with an aggregate adjusted basis of not more than $50 million of gross assets, and at least 80% of the value of its assets must be used in the active conduct of one or more qualified trades or businesses.[45]

OTHER EXCLUSIONS

The tax law contains other exclusions that are either covered elsewhere in the text or are of limited application. Table I4-2 lists several such exclusions.

---

[43] Sec. 1202(a).
[44] Sec. 1202(b)(1).
[45] Secs. 1202(d) and (e). Excluded corporations are those engaged in providing professional services (e.g., law and health), financial services (e.g., banking and insurance), hospitality (e.g., hotels and restaurants), farming, and mining and oil and gas production.

▼ TABLE I4-2
Other Exclusions

Section	Applies to	Comments
121	Gain from sale of personal residence	Taxpayers may exclude up to $250,000 ($500,000 in the case of a married couple filing a joint return) of gain from the sale of a personal residence. (See Chapter I12 for a detailed discussion of this provision.)
101(h)	Annuities paid to survivors of public safety officers	Annuities paid to survivors of public safety officers, such as firefighters and police officers, killed in the line of duty are excluded.
104(a)	Military disability pay	Military personnel may exclude disability pay, combat pay (noncommissioned personnel only), and housing allowances.
112	Combat pay	
134	Military housing allowance	
107	Housing allowance for ministers	Ministers may exclude either the rental value of their homes or a rental allowance if provided in connection with their religious duties.
119	Campus housing	A limited exclusion is provided to employees of educational institutions when they are provided with on campus housing.
131	Foster care payments	Certain allowances received by foster care providers are excluded from gross income.
162(o)	Rural letter carrier's allowance	Rural letter carriers may exclude the "equipment maintenance allowance" they receive for the use of their personal automobiles in delivering the mail. They receive no deduction for the use of their automobiles.
408A(d)	Roth IRA distributions	Qualified distributions from Roth IRAs are excluded from gross income (see Chapter I9 for a detailed discussion of the provisions.)
530(d)	Education IRA distributions	Qualified distributions from Education IRAs are excluded from gross income (see Chapter I9 for a detailed discussion of this provision.)
988(e)	Personal foreign currency gains	Individuals are excused from recognizing gain on the disposition of foreign currency in any personal transaction, provided that the gain does not exceed $200.

TAX PLANNING CONSIDERATIONS

EMPLOYEE FRINGE BENEFITS

The tax law encourages certain forms of fringe benefits by allowing an employer to deduct the cost of the benefit while permitting the employee to exclude the benefit from gross income. This deduction does not represent an income tax advantage to the employer because compensation, whether in the form of cash or nontaxable fringe benefits, is deductible if reasonable in amount. While employees receive the greatest income tax benefit from the exclusion of fringe benefits from gross income, employers receive a small benefit from the fact that fringe benefits are not subject to Social Security and Medicare taxes.

ADDITIONAL COMMENT

A case can be made for the desirability of encouraging employers to provide health insurance and other fringe benefits. However, these provisions may contribute to increases in the cost of insurance and medical care.

EXAMPLE I4-38 ▶ USA Company has decided to offer $20,000 of group term life insurance coverage for each of its employees at an average annual premium cost of $100 per employee. Tim, an employee of USA Corporation, is in the 15% tax bracket. Because USA is offering a nontaxable fringe benefit, Tim will owe no additional income tax. If Tim had received a salary increase of $100, he would have had to pay an additional income tax of $15 (0.15 × $100). The remaining $85 of after-tax income would probably not have been sufficient to obtain the same amount of life insurance coverage. ◀

Excluding fringe benefits from gross income favors employees who are subject to higher tax rates.

EXAMPLE I4-39 ▶ Assume the same facts as in Example I4-38 except that Tim is in the 36% tax rate. Tim would save $36 (0.36 × $100) of taxes by receiving the group term life insurance coverage instead of the $100 salary increase. ◀

> **ADDITIONAL COMMENT**
> Fringe benefits offered by potential employers are important consideration factors when weighing total compensation packages.

It is not always desirable for employers to offer nontaxable fringe benefits. Some employees are not interested in certain benefits. For example, in the case of married couples where both spouses are employed, it is not necessary for both employers to provide medical insurance coverage for both spouses. Alternatively, single employees may not feel the need for group term life insurance and employees with no children are uninterested in employer-provided child care.

To avoid providing fringe benefits that are unneeded or unwanted, many employers have turned to cafeteria plans. Under cafeteria plans, employees may select from a list of nontaxable fringe benefits. On the other hand, employees who so choose may receive cash in lieu of some or all of the nontaxable benefits. Thus, each employee selects what he or she wants most. One common result is that high-tax-rate employees select the nontaxable fringe benefits, whereas other employees choose to receive cash.

SELF-HELP AND USE OF PERSONALLY OWNED PROPERTY

As noted earlier in this chapter, self-help income and income derived from the use of personal property are not taxable. Thus, self-help and personal ownership of property are favored by the tax system. Taxpayers who rent their personal residences cannot deduct rental payments, but taxpayers who own their residences do not pay rent and may deduct interest and real estate taxes as itemized deductions. Thus, the tax law encourages ownership of personal residences.

Effective tax planning necessitates weighing the tax incentives with other nontax factors. Taxpayers with little accumulated funds may find it difficult to purchase a residence despite the availability of tax incentives. Taxpayers who move frequently may find that transaction costs such as real estate commissions and other closing costs are greater than the tax benefits obtained from home ownership. Other factors such as the personal preference of the taxpayer and anticipated inflation rates must also be considered.

Self-help must be viewed in the same way. Taxpayers who are deciding whether to paint their own residences or hire someone else to do it must consider factors such as personal preference and the amount of income that could be produced if the time were spent working at an activity that produces taxable income.

COMPLIANCE AND PROCEDURAL CONSIDERATIONS

> **ADDITIONAL COMMENT**
> Taxpayers filing Form 1040 are asked to report any tax-exempt interest income on line 8b.

Taxpayers are usually not required to disclose excluded income on their tax returns. For example, a taxpayer who receives a tax-exempt scholarship need not disclose that income on his or her tax return. An exception is provided for tax-exempt interest and Social Security benefits, which must be disclosed on the tax return. If a taxpayer's only income is from tax-exempt sources, the taxpayer need not file a tax return. Whether an individual must file a return is based on the amount of the individual's gross income for the year (see Chapter I2).

This chapter considers the taxability of various fringe benefits. The rules regarding the need for an employer to withhold federal income taxes or to report a payment on an employee's Form W-2 (Statement of Income Tax Withheld on Wages) closely parallel the gross income rules. (See Chapter I14 for a discussion of these reporting requirements.) In general, if a fringe benefit is nontaxable, employers do not withhold from the benefit, nor do they report the benefit on the employee's W-2 at year-end. On the other hand, if the benefit is taxable, it is subject to withholding and is reported on the employee's W-2 at year-end. Thus, employers do not withhold for nontaxable meals and lodging provided to employees[46] or a moving expense reimbursement if the expenses are deductible.[47] Similarly, no withholding is required for the following fringe benefits if they are nontaxable: scholarships and fellowships covered by Sec. 117, dependent care covered by Sec. 129, and miscellaneous fringes covered by Sec. 132.

There are exceptions to this basic system. Certain fringe benefits are not subject to withholding even if the benefits are taxable. These include group-term life insurance coverage and medical expense reimbursements.

In general, fringe benefits which are exempt from the income tax are also exempt from Social Security and Medicare taxes. For example, medical insurance coverage and group term life coverage of up to $50,000 can be provided to employees without either the employer or the employee owing any Social Security or Medicare taxes on the premiums. This is true if the employee elects the benefits instead of cash salary under a cafeteria plan.

Employers who are obligated to withhold from employee wages are subject to penalty if they fail to withhold, fail to provide employees with correct W-2s, or fail to correctly report the compensation and withholding information to the IRS.[48] In general, the failure to report wages and withholding to either employees or the IRS is subject to penalty generally equal to $50 per failure. The failure to withhold can result in a penalty equal to 100% of the amount that should have been withheld. The penalty can be imposed on the employer and other people, such as officers or accountants, who are responsible for withholding.

Occasionally, employees do not want employers to withhold taxes from their wages. Officers or others who choose not to withhold from employee wages face an extremely burdensome penalty, particularly if a large number of employees are involved. Therefore, it is important that employers comply with withholding requirements. One closely related issue is whether an individual is an employee subject to withholding or an independent contractor, as only employee wages are subject to withholding (see Chapter I14).

PROBLEM MATERIALS

DISCUSSION QUESTIONS

I4-1 What is meant by the terms *administrative exclusion* and *judicial exclusion*?

I4-2 There is no specific statutory exclusion for welfare benefits. Nevertheless, the IRS has ruled that such benefits are not taxable. Is this within the authority of the IRS?

I4-3 What was the issue in the tax case *Eisner* v. *Macomber*? Why is the case important?

I4-4 Most exclusions exist for one of two reasons. What are those reasons? Give examples of exclusions that exist for each.

I4-5 a. If a gift of property is made, who is taxed on income produced by the property?
b. How can interfamily gifts reduce a family's total tax liability?

I4-6 a. What role does intent play in determining whether a transfer is a gift and therefore not subject to the income tax?
b. Are tips received by employees from customers excludable from gross income as gifts? Explain.

I4-7 What is the tax significance of the face amount of a life insurance policy?

I4-8 What conditions must be met for an award to qualify for an exclusion under Sec. 74?

I4-9 Which of the requirements for the Sec. 74 awards exclusion most severely limits its use? Does the exclusion benefit taxpayers more if they itemize their deductions or use the standard deduction?

I4-10 a. Define the term *scholarship* as it is used in Sec. 117.
b. If a scholarship covers room and board, is it excludable?
c. If an employer provides a scholarship to an employee who is on leave of absence, is that scholarship taxable?
d. Is the amount paid by a university to students for services excludable from the students' gross income?

I4-11 What special rules are applicable to non–degree candidates who receive scholarships?

---

[46] Reg. Sec. 31.3401(a)-1(b)(9).
[47] See Sec. 3401 for withholding requirements for numerous special situations.
[48] Secs. 6672, 6674, and 6721 respectively.

4-24 Individuals ▼ Chapter 4

I4-12 Is the personal injury exclusion found in Sec. 104 limited to physical injury? Explain.

I4-13 Answer the following questions relative to employer-financed medical and health, disability, and life insurance plans.
   a. May employers deduct premiums paid on employee insurance?
   b. Do employees have to include such premiums in gross income?
   c. Are benefits paid to the employee included in the employee's gross income?

I4-14 Special rules are applicable in situations where group term life insurance coverage exceeds $50,000. How are key employees treated?

I4-15
   a. What are the six major types of fringe benefits covered by Sec. 132?
   b. What tax advantage is offered relative to such benefits?
   c. Are such benefits available to employees only or may the benefits also be offered to spouses, dependents, and retirees?
   d. Is discrimination prohibited relative to Sec. 132 benefits?
   e. What is the tax impact on the employer and employees if an employer's plan is discriminatory?

I4-16 What conditions must be met if an employee is to exclude meals and lodging furnished by an employer?

I4-17 The president and vice president of USA Corporation receive benefits that are unavailable to other employees. These benefits include free parking, payment of monthly expenses in a local club, discounts on products sold by the corporation, and payment of premiums on a whole life insurance policy. Which of the benefits must be included in the gross income of the president and vice president?

I4-18 Are the same fringe benefits that are available to employees also available to self-employed individuals?

I4-19 If an employee takes a customer to lunch and discusses business, can the employee deduct 50% of the meal for both the customer and himself? Explain.

I4-20 Are distributions from a qualified state tuition program taxable?

I4-21 What types of income qualify for the foreign-earned income exclusion?

I4-22 Are taxpayers who claim the foreign-earned income exclusion entitled to deduct expenses incurred in producing that income? Explain.

I4-23
   a. Why is it important to distinguish debt cancellation from a gift, bequest, or renegotiation of a purchase price?
   b. What happens to the basis of an asset if the taxpayer renegotiates its purchase price?

I4-24
   a. Under what conditions is the discharge of indebtedness not taxable?
   b. If a father forgives a daughter's debt to him, is she required to include such amount in her gross income?

I4-25 Bankrupt and insolvent taxpayers do not recognize income if debt is discharged. They must, however, reduce specified tax attributes. What is involved?

I4-26 Are employee awards taxable? Explain.

I4-27 Why are cafeteria plans helpful in the design of an employee benefit plan that provides nontaxable fringe benefits?

I4-28 Both high-income and low-income employees are covered by cafeteria plans. Under such plans, all employees may select from a list of nontaxable fringe benefits or they may elect to receive cash in lieu of these benefits.
   a. Which group of employees is more likely to choose nontaxable fringe benefits in lieu of cash? Explain.
   b. Is this result desirable from a social or economic point of view? Explain.

ISSUE IDENTIFICATION QUESTIONS

I4-29 Luke, who retired this year, lives in a four-plex owned by Julie. Luke's income decreased when he retired, and he now has difficulty paying his rent. Julie offered to reduce Luke's rent if he would agree to mow the lawn, wash windows, and provide other maintenance services. Luke accepted, and Julie reduced the monthly rental from $650 to $300. What are the tax issues that should be considered by Luke and Julie?

I4-30 Mildred worked as a maid for 27 years in the home of Larry and Kay. When she retired, they presented her with a check for $25,000, indicating that it was a way of showing their appreciation for her years of loyal service. What tax issues should Mildred and her employer consider?

I4-31 Troy Department Stores offers employees discounts on merchandise carried in the store. Newly hired employees receive a 10% discount. The discount rate increases 1% each year until employees have 20 years of service when the discount rate is capped at 30%. What tax issues should Troy and the employees consider?

I4-32 Jerry works in the human resources department of Ajax Corporation. One of his responsibilities is to interview prospective employees. Two or three days each week, Jerry takes a prospective employee to lunch, and Ajax reimburses him for the cost of the meals. What tax issues should Jerry and Ajax Corporation consider?

PROBLEMS

I4-33 *Self-Help Income.* In which of the following situations would the taxpayer realize taxable income?
a. A mechanic performs work on his own automobile. The mechanic would have charged a customer $400 for doing the same work.
b. A mechanic repairs his neighbor's personal automobile. In exchange, the neighbor, an accountant, agrees to prepare the mechanic's tax return. The services performed are each worth $200.
c. A mechanic repairs his daughter's automobile without any charge.

I4-34 *Excludable Gifts.* Which of the following would constitute excludable gifts?
a. Alice appeared on a TV quiz show and received a prize of $500.
b. Bart received $500 from his employer because he developed an idea that reduced the employer's production costs.
c. Chuck borrowed $500 from his mother in order to finance his last year in college. Upon his graduation, Chuck's mother told him he did not have to repay the $500. She intended the $500 to be a graduation present.

I4-35 *Life Insurance Proceeds.* Dan is the beneficiary of a $50,000 insurance policy on the life of his mother. Upon her death, Dan has the choice of receiving either the face amount of the policy or five annual installments of $12,000 each.
a. How much income must Dan report if he elects to receive the face value of the policy?
b. How much income must Dan report if he elects to receive the installments?

I4-36 *Transfer of Life Insurance.* Ed is the beneficiary of a $20,000 insurance policy on the life of his mother. Because Ed needs funds, he sells the policy to his sister, Amy, for $6,000. Amy subsequently pays premiums of $8,000.
a. How much income must Amy report if she collects the face value of the policy upon the death of her mother?
b. Would Amy have to report any income if her brother had given her the policy? Assume the only payment she made was $8,000 for the premiums.

I4-37 *Settlement of Life Insurance Policy.* Sue is age 73 and has had a great deal of difficulty living independently as she suffers from severe rheumatoid arthritis. She is covered by a $400,000 life insurance policy, and her children are named as her beneficiaries. Because of her health, Sue decides to live in a nursing home, but she does not have enough income to pay her nursing home bills which are expected to total $42,000 per year. The insurance company offers disabled individuals the option of either a reduced settlement on their policies or an annuity. Given Sue's age and health she has the option of receiving $3,200 per month or a lump sum payment of $225,000. To date, Sue has paid $80,000 in premiums on the policy.
a. How much income must Sue report if she chooses the lump sum settlement?
b. How much income must Sue report if she elects the annuity?
c. How much income would Sue have to report if her nursing home bills amounted to only $36,000 per year?

I4-38 *Insurance Policy Dividends.* Hank carries a $100,000 insurance policy on his life. Premiums paid over the years total $8,000. Dividends on the policy have totaled $6,000. Hank has left the dividends on the policy with the insurance company. During the current year, the insurance company credited $600 of interest on the accumulated dividends to Hank's account.
a. How much income is Hank obligated to report in connection with the policy?
b. Would it make any difference if the accumulated dividends equaled $9,000 instead of $6,000?

I4-39 *Prizes and Awards.* For each of the following, indicate whether the amount awarded is taxable:
a. Irene won $100 playing bingo at her church.
b. Jack was awarded a $100 prize for a painting he entered in a community art show.
c. Kay was selected as coach of the year by the local school board. Kay received a $200 cash award, which was presented at the district's annual awards banquet. Awards were also presented to outstanding teachers, administrators, and students. The board selected the recipients based on its knowledge of each individual and his or her achievements.

I4-40 *Scholarships.* For each of the following, indicate the amount that must be included in the taxpayer's gross income:
a. Larry was given a $1,500 tuition scholarship to attend Eastern Law School. In addition, Eastern paid Larry $4,000 per year to work part-time in the campus bookstore.
b. Marty received a $10,000 football scholarship for attending Northern University. The scholarship covered tuition, room and board, laundry, and books. Four thousand dollars of the scholarship was designated for room and board and laundry. It was understood that Marty would participate in the school's intercollegiate football program, but Marty was not required to do so.
c. Western School of Nursing requires all third-year students to work twenty hours per week at an affiliated hospital. Each student is paid $6 per hour. Nancy, a third-year student, earned $6,000 during the year.

I4-41 *Research Grants.* Otto is a biology professor who teaches at Southern University. The University awarded Otto a $2,000 grant to study the surface of the flatworm. Otto was expected to spend three months during the summer conducting the study. In addition, Otto was awarded $1,500 for supplies and typing, travel, and other incidental costs. The actual expenses totaled $1,500. How much income must Otto report?

I4-42 *Payments for Personal Injury.* Determine which of the following may be excluded as payments for sickness and injury.
a. Pat was injured in an automobile accident. The other driver's insurance company paid him $2,000 to cover medical expenses and a compensatory amount of $4,000 for pain and suffering.
b. A newspaper article stated that Quincy had been convicted of tax evasion. Quincy, in fact, had never been accused of tax evasion. He sued and won a compensatory settlement of $4,000 from the newspaper.
c. Rob, who pays the cost of a commercial disability income policy, fell and injured his back. He was unable to work for six months. The insurance company paid him $1,800 per month during the time he was unable to work.
d. Steve fell and injured his knee. He was unable to work for four months. His employer-financed disability income policy paid Steve $1,600 per month during the time he was unable to work.
e. Ted suffered a stroke. He was unable to work for five months. His employer continued to pay Ted his salary of $1,700 per month during the time he was unable to work.

I4-43 *Employee Benefits.* Ursula is employed by USA Corporation. USA Corporation provides medical and health, disability, and group term life insurance coverage for its employees. Premiums attributable to Ursula were as follows:

Medical and health	$1,800
Disability	300
Group term life (face amount is $40,000)	200

During the year, Ursula suffered a heart attack and subsequently died. Before her death, Ursula collected $14,000 as a reimbursement for medical expenses and $5,000 of disability income. Upon her death, Ursula's husband collected the $40,000 face value of the life insurance policy.
a. What amount can USA Corporation deduct for premiums attributable to Ursula?
b. How much must Ursula include in income relative to the premiums paid?
c. How much must Ursula include in income relative to the insurance benefits?
d. How much must Ursula's widower include in income?

I4-44 *Group Term Life Insurance.* Data Corporation has four employees and provides group term life insurance coverage for all four employees. Coverage is nondiscriminatory and is as follows:

Employee	Age	Key Employee	Coverage	Actual Premiums
Andy	62	yes	$200,000	$4,000
Bob	52	yes	40,000	700
Cindy	33	no	80,000	600
Damitria	33	no	40,000	300

a. How much may Data Corporation deduct for group term life insurance premiums?
b. How much income must be reported by each employee?

I4-45 *Life Insurance Proceeds.* Joe is the beneficiary of a life insurance policy taken out by his father several years ago. Joe's father died this year and Joe has the option of receiving $100,000 cash or electing to receive $14,000 per year for the remainder of his life. Joe is now 65. Joe's father paid $32,000 in premiums over the years.
  a. How much must Joe include in gross income this year if he elects to accept the $100,000 face amount?
  b. How much must be included in Joe's gross income if he elects to receive installment payments?

I4-46 *Employee Benefits.* Al flies for AAA Airlines. AAA provides its employees with several fringe benefits. Al and his family are allowed to fly on a space-available basis on AAA Airline. Tickets used by Al and his family during the year are worth $2,000. AAA paid for a subscription to two magazines published for pilots. The subscriptions totaled $80. The airline paid for Al's meals and lodging while he was away from home overnight in connection with his job. Such meals and lodging cost AAA $10,000. Although Al could not eat while flying, he was allowed to drink coffee provided by the airline. The coffee was worth about $50. AAA provided Al with free parking, which is valued at $100 per month. The airline treated Al and his family to a one-week all-expenses-paid vacation at a resort near his home. This benefit was awarded because of Al's outstanding safety record. The value of the vacation was $2,300. Which of these benefits are taxable to Al?

I4-47 *Employee Benefits.* Jet Corporation is involved in the purchase and rental of several large apartment complexes. Questions have been raised about the treatment of several items pertaining to Jet Corporation and its employees. Jet Corporation employs a manager for each complex. The manager is required to occupy a unit in the complex in order to be available at all hours. The average rental value of the units is $7,800 per year. The corporation's president finds that it is beneficial to the corporation if he entertains bankers and others with whom Jet does business. He does such entertaining about once each month and the corporation pays the cost. Business is discussed at the meals. The cost for the year of such entertaining was $600, and about one-third of the cost was attributable to meals consumed by the president.

Each year as the company closes its books, the controller and certain other members of the accounting staff must work overtime. The company pays each employee supper money totaling $25 during this period.

The corporation's vice president is expected to travel on business-related matters to visit various properties owned by the corporation. Because of the distances involved, the vice president must stay away from home several nights. Total meals and lodging incurred on the trips total $3,000, most of which is attributable to the vice president himself.

Which amounts are deductible by the corporation? Which are taxable to the employee?

I4-48 *Death Benefits.* After an illness of several weeks, Phil died. Although there was no legal obligation to make any payment, Phil's former employer made a payment of $15,000 to his widow. The corporation sent the widow a letter with the check indicating that the amount was being awarded in recognition of Phil's many years of loyal service.
  a. Is the employer entitled to deduct the amount it paid to Phil's widow?
  b. Is any portion of the amount received by Phil's widow taxable? If yes, how much?

I4-49 *Foreign-Earned Income Exclusion.* For each of the following cases, indicate the amount of the foreign-earned income exclusion. (Disregard the effect of exemptions for certain allowances under Sec. 912.)
  a. Sam, a U.S. citizen, is an assistant to the ambassador to Spain. Sam lives and works in Spain. His salary of $40,000 is paid by the U.S. government.
  b. Jim, a U.S. citizen, owns an unincorporated oil drilling company that operates in Argentina, where he resides. The business is heavily dependent on equipment owned by Jim. His profit for the year totaled $100,000.
  c. Ken, a U.S. citizen, works for a large Japanese corporation. Ken is employed in the United States, but must travel to Japan several times each year. During the current year he spent sixty days in Japan. This is typical of most years. His salary is $45,000.

I4-50 *Foreign-Earned Income Exclusion.* On January 5, Rita left the United States for Germany, where she had accepted an appointment as vice president of foreign operations. Her employer, USA Corporation, told her the assignment would last about two years. Rita decided not to establish a permanent residence in Germany because her assignment was for only two years. Her salary for the year is $234,000. Rita incurred travel, transportation, and other related expenses totaling $6,000, none of which is reimbursed.

a. What is Rita's foreign-earned income exclusion?
b. How much may she deduct for travel and transportation?

I4-51 *Discharge of Debt.* During bankruptcy, USA Corporation debt was reduced from $780,000 to $400,000. USA Corporation's assets are valued at $500,000. USA's NOL carryover was $400,000.
a. Is USA Corporation required to report any income from the discharge of its debts?
b. Which tax attributes are reduced and by how much? Assume USA does not make any special elections when reducing its attributes.

I4-52 *Discharge of Debt.* Old Corporation has suffered losses for several years, and its debts total $500,000; Old's assets are valued at only $380,000. Old's creditors agree to reduce Old's debts by one-half in order to permit the corporation to continue to operate. Old's NOL carryover is $150,000.
a. What impact does the reduction in debt have on Old's NOL?
b. Is Old required to report any income?

I4-53 *Court and Insurance Awards.* Determine whether the following items represent taxable income.
a. As the result of an age discrimination suit, Pat received a cash settlement of $40,000. One-half of the settlement represented wages lost by Pat as a result of the discrimination and the balance represented an award based on personal injury.
b. Matt sued the local newspaper for a story that reported that he was affiliated with organized crime. The court awarded him $50,000 of libel damages.
c. Pam was injured in an automobile accident and received $10,000 from an employer-sponsored disability policy. In addition, her employer-financed medical insurance policy reimbursed her for $15,000 of medical expenses.

I4-54 *Cafeteria Plan.* Jangyoun is a married taxpayer with a dependent 4-year-old daughter. His employer offers a flexible spending account under which he can choose to receive cash or, alternatively, choose from certain fringe benefits. These benefits include health insurance that costs $2,500 and child care that costs $2,600. Assume Jangyoun is in the 28% tax bracket.
a. How much would Jangyoun save in income taxes if he chooses to participate in the employer's health insurance plan? Assume that he does not have sufficient medical expenses to itemize his deductions.
b. Would you recommend that Jangyoun participate in the employer's health insurance plan if his wife's employer already provides comparable health insurance coverage for the family?
c. Would you recommend that Jangyoun participate in the employer-provided child care option if he has the alternative option of claiming a child care credit of $480.

I4-55 *Exclusion of Gain from Small Business Stock.* Jose acquired 1,000 shares of Acorn Corporation common stock by transferring property with an adjusted basis of $1,000,000 and fair market value of $4,000,000 for 100% of the stock. Acorn is a qualified small business corporation. After six years, Jose sells all of the Acorn Corporation common stock for $16,000,000.
a. What is the amount of gain that may be excluded from Jose's gross income?
b. What would your answer be if the fair market value of the Acorn stock were only $1,000,000 upon its issue?
c. What would your answer be if the stock were sold after two years?
d. Can Jose avoid recognizing gain by purchasing replacement stock?

COMPREHENSIVE PROBLEM

I4-56 Pat was divorced from her husband in 1996. During the current year she received alimony of $18,000 and child support of $4,000 for her 11-year old son, who lives with her. Her former husband had asked her to sign an agreement giving him the dependency exemption for the child but she declined to do so. After the divorce she accepted a position as a teacher in the local school district. During the current year she received a salary of $22,000. The school district paid her medical insurance premiums of $1,900 and provided her with group term life insurance coverage of $40,000. The premiums attributable to her coverage equaled $160. During her marriage, Pat's parents loaned her $8,000 to help with the down payment on her home. Her parents told her this year that they understand her financial problems and that they were cancelling the balance on the loan, which was $5,000. They did so because they wanted to help their only daughter.

Pat received dividends from National Motor Company of $4,600 and interest on State of California bonds of $2,850.

Pat sold her personal automobile for $2,800 because she needed a larger car. The automobile had cost $8,000. She purchased a new auto for $11,000. Pat had itemized deductions of $8,600. Assume her withholding and estimated payments total $8,000. Compute her taxable income for the current year.

TAX FORM/RETURN PREPARATION PROBLEMS

I4-57 A. J. Paige, Social Security number 111-22-3333, is the vice president of marketing (Japan) for International Industries, Inc. (III). III is headquartered at 123 Main Street, Los Angeles, California 92601. A. J., who is single, accepted the position and became a resident of Japan on July 8 of last year. Her business address is 86 Sano, Tokyo, Japan. A. J.'s visa permits her to stay in Japan indefinitely. Her only trips to the United States in the current year were for vacations (August 2 to 16 and December 21 to 28). A. J.'s contract specifies that her appointment is to last indefinitely, but states that III is to pay her $4,000 per year to cover the cost of two vacation trips to the United States. Her salary is $140,000, out of which she pays rent on an apartment of $28,000 per year. A. J. has no family or residence in the United States. She paid an income tax in Japan of $23,500. Complete a Form 2555 for the current year.

I4-58 Alice Johnson, Social Security number 222-23-3334, is a single mother of two children, Jack and Jill, ages 15 and 17, respectively, and is employed as a secretary by State University of Florida. She has the following items pertaining to her income tax return for the current year:

- Received a $20,000 salary from her employer, who withheld $4,000 federal income tax.
- Received a gift of 1,000 shares of Ace Corporation stock with a $100,000 FMV from her mother. She also received $4,000 of cash dividends from the Ace Corporation.
- Received $1,000 of interest income on bonds issued by the City of Tampa.
- Received a stock dividend (qualifying under Sec. 305) of 50 shares of Ace Corporation stock with a $5,000 FMV.
- Alice's employer paid $2,000 of medical and health insurance premiums on her behalf.
- Maintains a household for herself and two children and provides more than 50% of their support. In the prior year, however, she entered into an agreement with her ex-husband that provided that he is entitled to the dependency exemptions for the children.
- Received $12,000 alimony and $6,000 child support from her ex-husband (Charlie Johnson).
- State University provided $60,000 of group term life insurance. Alice is 42 years old and is not a key employee. Assume the table in the text is applicable all year.
- Received a $1,000 cash award from her employer for being designated the Secretary of the Year.
- Total itemized deductions are $7,000.

Complete Form 1040 and accompanying schedules for Alice Johnson's federal income tax return for the current year.

CASE STUDY PROBLEMS

I4-59 Able Corporation is a closely held company engaged in the manufacture and retail sales of automotive parts. Able maintains a qualified pension plan for its employees but has not offered nontaxable fringe benefits.

You are a tax consultant for the company who has been asked to prepare suggestions for the adoption of an employee fringe benefit plan. Your discussions with the client's chief financial officer reveal the following:

- Employees currently pay their own premiums for medical and health insurance.
- No group term life insurance is provided.
- The company owns a vacant building that could easily be converted to a parking garage.
- Many of the employees purchase automobile parts from the company's retail outlets and pay retail price.

- The president of the corporation would like to provide a dependent care assistance program under Sec. 129 for its employees.

Required: Prepare a client memo that recommends the adoption of an employee fringe benefit program. Your recommendations should discuss the pros and cons of different types of nontaxable fringe benefits.

I4-60 Jay Corporation owns several automobile dealerships. This year, the corporation initiated a policy of giving the top salesperson at each dealership a free vacation trip to Florida. The president believes that this is an effective sales incentive. The cost of the vacations is deductible by the corporation as compensation paid to employees, and is taxable to the recipients. Nevertheless, the president objects to reporting the value of the vacations as income on the W-2s of the recipients and to withholding taxes from wages for the value of the trips. He feels that this undermines the effectiveness of the incentive. What are the implications of this behavior for the corporation and the president?

TAX RESEARCH PROBLEMS

I4-61 Ann is a graduate economics student at State University. State University awarded her a $1,000 scholarship. In addition, Ann works as a half-time teaching assistant in the Economics Department at State University. For her services she is paid $7,000 per year and her tuition is waived. Her tuition would be $8,000 were it not for the waiver. Ann paid $500 for her books and supplies and she incurred living expenses of $7,400. Determine how much gross income Ann must report.

A partial list of research sources is

- Sec. 117(d)
- Prop. Reg. 1.117-6(d)(5)

I4-62 Kim leased an office building to USA Corporation under a ten-year lease specifying that at the end of the lease USA had to return the building to its original condition if any modifications were made. USA changed the interior of the building, and at the end of the lease USA paid Kim $30,000 instead of making the required repairs. Does Kim have to include the payment in gross income?

A partial list of research sources is

- Sec. 109
- *Boston Fish Market Corp.*, 57 T.C. 884 (1972)
- *Sirbo Holdings Inc. v. CIR*, 31 AFTR 2d 73-1005, 73-1 USTC ¶9312 (2nd Cir., 1973)

I4-63 As a result of a fire damaging their residence, the Taylors must stay in a motel for five weeks while their home is being restored. They pay $2,000 for the room and $500 for meals. Their homeowner's policy pays $2,500 to reimburse them for the cost. They estimate that during the five-week period they would normally spend $300 for meals. Is the reimbursement taxable?

A partial list of research sources is

- Sec. 123
- Reg. Sec. 1.123-1

I4-64 Bold Corporation paid $25 to each full-time employee at year end in recognition of the holidays. Bold Corporation is interested in whether the amounts are taxable income to its employees, and whether the company can deduct the amounts.

A partial list of research sources is

- Sec. 74(c), 102, 132(c), and 274(b)
- Reg. Sec. 1.132-6(e)(1)
- *Hallmark Cards, Inc. v U.S.*, 9 AFTR2d 391, 62-1 USTC ¶9162 (DC-Mo, 1961).
- Rev. Rul. 59-58, 1959-1 CB 17.

CHAPTER 5

PROPERTY TRANSACTIONS: CAPITAL GAINS AND LOSSES

LEARNING OBJECTIVES

After studying this chapter, you should be able to

1. Determine the realized gain or loss from the sale or other disposition of property
2. Determine the amount realized from the sale or other disposition of property
3. Determine the basis of property
4. Distinguish between capital assets and other assets
5. Understand how capital gains and losses affect taxable income
6. Recognize when a sale or exchange has occurred
7. Determine the holding period for an asset when a sale or disposition occurs

CHAPTER OUTLINE

Determination of Gain or Loss...5-2
Basis Considerations...5-5
Definition of a Capital Asset...5-12
Tax Treatment for Capital Gains and Losses of Noncorporate Taxpayers...5-16
Tax Treatment of Capital Gains and Losses: Corporate Taxpayers...5-20
Sale or Exchange...5-21
Holding Period...5-28
Preferential Treatment for Net Capital Gains...5-30
Tax Planning Considerations...5-31
Compliance and Procedural Considerations...5-33

HISTORICAL NOTE

A preferential tax rate on capital gains was included in the tax law from 1921 to 1987. A modest preferential rate was reintroduced in 1991, with capital gains for noncorporate taxpayers being subject to a maximum 28% tax rate and ordinary income being subject to a maximum tax rate of 31%. The capital gains differential became more significant in 1993 when the highest marginal rate was increased to 39.6%.

Gross income includes "gains derived from dealings in property,"[1] and certain "losses from sale or exchange of property"[2] are allowed as deductions from gross income to determine adjusted gross income. All recognized gains and losses must eventually be classified as either *capital* or *ordinary*. Before 1987, long-term capital gains (LTCGs) generally were taxed at lower rates than ordinary gains or short-term capital gains (STCGs).[3] The Tax Reform Act of 1986 substantially eliminated the difference in tax treatment for capital gain income and ordinary income. However, as tax rates have increased since 1986, Congress has again created preferential treatment for capital gains for certain taxpayers.

For tax years beginning after 1990, the maximum tax rate imposed on net capital gains (the excess of the net long-term capital gain (NLTCG) over the net short-term capital loss (NSTCL)) recognized by noncorporate taxpayers is 28%. Because the maximum tax rate on ordinary income is currently 39.6%, noncorporate taxpayers could benefit by having a gain classified as LTCG. This benefit for net LTCG was increased with the passage of the Taxpayer Relief Act of 1997, which enacted major changes in the tax treatment of capital gains. Net capital gain (NCG) is still defined as the excess of NLTCG over NSTCL, but taxpayers must now compute adjusted net capital gain (ANCG) which might be taxed at rates of 8%, 10%, 18%, or 20% if recognized after May 6, 1997.

Capital losses must be offset against capital gains, and net capital losses are subjected to restrictions on their deductibility. Thus, most taxpayers prefer to have losses classified as ordinary instead of capital.

Most property transactions have tax consequences to the taxpayer. For example, when a sale, exchange, or abandonment occurs, the taxpayer must determine the realized gain or loss, the portion of the realized gain or loss that must be recognized (if any), and the character of the gain or loss. This chapter focuses on determining the realized gain or loss and the portion of the recognized gain or loss that is classified as capital or ordinary. When classifying a recognized gain or loss, (i.e., the gain or loss actually reported on the taxpayer's tax return) three important questions must be considered:

▶ What type of property has been sold or exchanged?
▶ When has a sale or exchange occurred?
▶ When did the holding period for the property commence?

In this chapter, these three questions are considered as well as difficulties associated with determining the basis of the property sold or exchanged and the amount of realized gains or losses.

DETERMINATION OF GAIN OR LOSS

OBJECTIVE 1

Determine the realized gain or loss from the sale or other disposition of property

REALIZED GAIN OR LOSS

To determine the **realized gain** or **loss**, the amount realized from the sale or exchange of property is compared with the adjusted basis of that property. A gain is realized when the amount realized is greater than the basis, and a loss is realized when the amount realized is less than the basis of the property.[4]

EXAMPLE I5-1 ▶ Jack sells an asset with an adjusted basis of $10,000 to Judy for $14,000. Because the amount realized is greater than the basis, Jack has a realized gain of $4,000 ($14,000 − $10,000). ◀

Despite the fact that most transfers of property involve a sale, gains and losses may also be realized on certain other types of dispositions of property, such as exchanges, condemnations, casualties, thefts, bond retirements, and corporate distributions. However, gains and losses are generally not realized when property is disposed of by gift or bequest.

---

[1] Sec. 61(a)(3).
[2] Sec. 62(a)(3).
[3] See page I5-27 and below for a discussion of the holding period for capital assets. A capital gain or loss is long-term or short-term depending on the length of time the asset has been held by the taxpayer.
[4] Sec. 1001(a).

EXAMPLE I5-2 ▶ Alice owns land that is held for investment and has a basis of $20,000. The land is taken by the city by right of eminent domain, and she receives a payment of $30,000 for the land. This condemnation is treated as a sale or disposition, and Alice's realized gain is $10,000 ($30,000 − $20,000). ◀

EXAMPLE I5-3 ▶ Two years ago, Bob purchased stock of a newly formed corporation for $10,000. During the current year, he receives a $12,000 distribution, constituting a return of capital, from the corporation. This distribution is treated as a sale. Therefore, Bob has a realized gain of $2,000 ($12,000 − $10,000). Bob's basis for the stock is now zero because his basis of $10,000 has been recovered. ◀

For a sale or other disposition to occur, there must be an identifiable event. Mere changes in the value of property are not normally recognized as a disposition for purposes of determining a realized gain or loss.

STUDY AID

Students should pay close attention to the technical terms used in tax law. For example, the similar sounding terms of "realized gain" and "recognized gain" are often different dollar amounts for the sale of an asset.

Many reasons exist for not taxing unrealized gains and losses that arise due to a mere change in value. The Treasury Regulations state that "A loss is not ordinarily sustained prior to the sale or other disposition of the property, for the reason that until such sale or other disposition occurs there remains the possibility that the taxpayer may recover or recoup the adjusted basis of the property."[5] Because of administrative difficulties associated with determining FMV, disputes with the Internal Revenue Service would be greatly increased if unrealized gains were taxed and unrealized losses were allowed as deductions. In addition, payment of tax on income is generally required only when a taxpayer has the wherewithal to pay the tax (e.g., the taxpayer has received cash from the sale or other disposition of property and can therefore pay the tax on the gain).

AMOUNT REALIZED. The amount realized from a sale or other disposition of property is the sum of any money received plus the FMV of all other property received.

EXAMPLE I5-4 ▶ Tony sells land to Rita for $15,000 in cash and a machine having a $3,000 FMV. The amount realized by Tony is $18,000 ($15,000 + $3,000). ◀

OBJECTIVE 2

Determine the amount realized from the sale or other disposition of property

From a practical standpoint, the determination of FMV is a question of fact and often creates considerable controversy between taxpayers and the IRS. **Fair market value (FMV)** is "the price at which property would change hands between a willing buyer and a willing seller, neither being under any compulsion to buy or sell."[6] In some cases, the FMV of the asset given in the exchange may be easier to determine than the FMV of the property received. In those cases, the FMV of the property given may be used to measure the amount realized. If a buyer assumes the seller's liability or takes the property subject to the debt, the courts have included the amount of the liability when determining the amount realized.[7]

EXAMPLE I5-5 ▶ Anna exchanges land subject to a liability of $20,000 for $35,000 of stock owned by Mario. Mario takes the property subject to the liability. The amount realized by Anna is $55,000 ($35,000 + $20,000 liability assumed by Mario). If Anna's adjusted basis for the land exchanged is $42,000, her realized gain is $13,000 ($55,000 amount realized − $42,000 adjusted basis). ◀

In the above example, Anna receives stock with a $35,000 FMV and is relieved of a $20,000 debt. Mario's taking the property subject to the debt is equivalent to providing Anna with cash of $20,000. Thus, the amount realized by Anna is $55,000.

Generally, selling expenses such as sales commissions and advertising incurred in order to sell or dispose of the property reduce the amount realized.

EXAMPLE I5-6 ▶ Doug sells stock of Laser Corporation, which has a cost basis of $10,000, for $17,000. Doug pays a sales commission of $300 to sell the stock. The amount realized by Doug is $16,700 ($17,000 − $300) and he has a realized gain of $6,700 ($16,700 − $10,000). ◀

---

[5] Reg. Sec. 1.1001-1(c)(1).
[6] CIR v. Homer H. Marshman, 5 AFTR 2d 1528, 60-2 USTC ¶9484 (6th Cir., 1960).
[7] Beulah B. Crane v. CIR, 35 AFTR 776, 47-1 USTC ¶9217 (USSC, 1947).

TYPICAL MISCONCEPTION
The difference between the assumption of a liability and the taking of the property subject to the debt is sometimes confusing. The latter means that the lender can satisfy the debt only by repossessing the property. In the former case, where the buyer assumes the debt, the lender can satisfy the debt by repossessing the property and by going after other assets of the buyer.

ADJUSTED BASIS. The initial adjusted basis of property depends on how the property is acquired (e.g., by purchase, gift, or inheritance). Most property is acquired by purchase and therefore its initial basis is the cost of the property. However, if property is acquired from a decedent, its basis to the estate or heir is its FMV either at the date of death or, if the alternate valuation date is elected, six months from the date of death. The rules for determining the adjusted basis are discussed in subsequent sections of this chapter. Once the initial basis is determined, it may be adjusted upward or downward. Capital additions (also called capital expenditures) are expenditures that add to the value or prolong the life of property or adapt the property to a new or different use. Capital additions increase the basis. Capital recoveries, such as the deductions for casualty losses, cost recovery, and depreciation, reduce the basis. A property's adjusted basis can be determined by the following equation:

Initial basis
+ Capital additions (e.g., new porch for a building)
− Capital recoveries (e.g., depreciation deduction)
= Adjusted basis

ETHICAL POINT
The taxpayer may have lost records relating to the basis of the assets acquired many years earlier. In that case, the CPA can accept estimates of the missing data made by the taxpayer.

Capital expenditures are distinguished from expenditures that are deductible as ordinary and necessary business expenses. For example, the cost of repairing a roof may be a deductible expense, whereas the cost of replacing a roof is a capital addition. It is sometimes difficult to determine whether an item is a capital expenditure or a business expense. Because of the preference for an immediate tax deduction, taxpayers normally prefer to classify expenditures as expenses rather than as capital expenditures.

EXAMPLE I5-7 ▶ Ellen pays $2,500 for a major overhaul of an automobile used in her trade or business. The $2,500 is capitalized as part of the automobile's cost rather than deducted as a repair expense. ◀

Capital recoveries reduce the adjusted basis. The most common form of capital recovery is the deduction for depreciation or cost recovery. As discussed in Chapter I10, the accelerated cost recovery system (ACRS) provides a deduction for cost recovery and applies to most property placed in service after December 31, 1980, and before 1987. A modified ACRS form of depreciation (MACRS) is mandatory for most tangible depreciable property placed in service after 1986.

EXAMPLE I5-8 ▶ Jeremy paid $100,000 for equipment two years ago and has claimed depreciation deductions of $37,000 for the two years. The cost of repairs during the same period was $6,000. At the end of the two-year period, the property's adjusted basis is $63,000 ($100,000 − $37,000). The amount spent for repairs does not affect the basis. ◀

ADDITIONAL COMMENT
In addition to depreciation, other capital recoveries that reduce the adjusted basis of property include depletion, amortization, corporate distributions that are a return of basis, compensation or awards for involuntary conversions, deductible casualty losses, insurance reimbursements, and cash rebates received by a purchaser.

RECOVERY OF BASIS DOCTRINE. The recovery of basis doctrine states that taxpayers are allowed to recover the basis of an asset without being taxed because such amounts are a return of capital that the taxpayer has invested in the property. If a taxpayer receives a $12,000 return of capital distribution from a corporation when the taxpayer's basis for its investment in the corporation's stock is $10,000, the first $10,000 received represents a recovery of basis and only the $2,000 excess amount is treated as a gain realized on a sale or exchange of the stock investment. In many cases, basis is recovered in the form of a deduction for depreciation, cost recovery, or a casualty loss.

TYPICAL MISCONCEPTION
It is sometimes incorrectly believed that all realized gains and losses are recognized for tax purposes. Although most realized gains are recognized, some realized losses are not. For example, losses on the sale or exchange of property held for personal use cannot be recognized.

RECOGNIZED GAIN OR LOSS
Realized gain or loss represents the difference between the amount realized and the adjusted basis when a sale or exchange occurs. The amount of gain or loss that is actually reported on the tax return is called the **recognized gain or loss**. In some instances, gain or loss is not recognized due to special provisions in the tax law (e.g., a gain or loss may be deferred or a loss may be disallowed).

Losses are generally deductible if they are incurred in carrying on a trade or business, incurred in an activity engaged in for profit, and casualty and theft losses. Realized losses

Property Transactions: Capital Gains and Losses ▼ Individuals 5-5

on the sale or exchange of assets held for personal use are not recognized for tax purposes. Therefore, a taxpayer who incurs a loss on the sale or exchange of a personal-use asset does not fully recover the basis. As explained in Chapter I8, realized losses on personal-use assets may be recognized to some extent if the property is disposed of by casualty or theft.

EXAMPLE I5-9 ▶ Ralph purchases a personal residence for $60,000. Deductions for depreciation are not allowed because the asset is not used in a trade or business or held for the production of income. If Ralph sells the house for $55,000, the realized loss of $5,000 is not deductible, and he recovers only $55,000 of his original $60,000 basis. ◀

BASIS CONSIDERATIONS

OBJECTIVE 3

Determine the basis of property

COST OF ACQUIRED PROPERTY

In most cases, the basis of property is its cost. Cost is the amount paid for the property in cash or the FMV of other property given in the exchange. Any costs of acquiring the property and preparing the property for use are included in the cost of the property.

EXAMPLE I5-10 ▶ Penny purchases equipment for $15,000 and pays delivery costs of $300. Installation costs of $250 are also incurred. The cost of the equipment is $15,550 ($15,000 + $300 + $250). ◀

Funds borrowed and used to pay for an asset are included in the cost. Obligations of the seller that are assumed by the buyer increase the asset's cost.

EXAMPLE I5-11 ▶ Peggy purchases an asset by paying cash of $40,000 and signs a note payable to the seller for $60,000. She also assumes a lien against the property in the amount of $2,000. Her basis for the asset is its cost of $102,000 ($40,000 + $60,000 + $2,000). ◀

UNIFORM CAPITALIZATION RULES. Before 1987, taxpayers often had a degree of flexibility with respect to capitalizing or expensing certain costs. The Tax Reform Act of 1986 created one set of capitalization rules applicable to all taxpayers and all types of activities. These uniform capitalization rules, which apply principally to inventory, are provided in Sec. 263A and discussed in Chapter I11.

ADDITIONAL COMMENT

The sales tax is a good example of a tax that would be paid in connection with the acquisition of property.

The uniform capitalization rules also affect property other than inventory if the property is used in a taxpayer's trade or business or in an activity engaged in for profit. Taxes paid or accrued in connection with the acquisition of property are included as part of the cost of the acquired property. Taxes paid or accrued in connection with the disposition of property reduce the amount realized on the disposition.[8]

EXAMPLE I5-12 ▶ The Compact Corporation owns and operates a funeral home. The corporation purchases a hearse for $30,000 and pays sales taxes of $1,500. The cost basis for the hearse is $31,500 ($30,000 + $1,500). ◀

CAPITALIZATION OF INTEREST. Interest on debt paid or incurred during the production period to finance production expenditures incurred to construct, build, install, manufacture, develop, or improve real or tangible personal property must be capitalized.[9] The real or tangible personal property must have "a long useful life, an estimated production period exceeding two years, or an estimated production period exceeding one year and a cost exceeding $1,000,000."[10] Property has a long useful life if it is real property or property with a class life of at least 20 years. The production period starts when "production of the property begins and ends when the property is ready to be placed in service or is ready to be held for sale."[11]

EXAMPLE I5-13 ▶ The Indiana Corporation started construction of a $3 million motel on July 1, 2000, and borrowed an amount equal to the motel's construction costs. The motel is completed and ready for

---

[8] Sec. 164(a).
[9] Sec. 263A(f).
[10] Sec. 263A(f)(1)(B).
[11] Sec. 263A(f)(4)(B).

service on October 1, 2001. Interest incurred for the construction loan for the period from July 1, 2000 through October 1, 2001, is included in the motel's cost. The capitalized interest cost is depreciated over the motel's recovery period (see Chapter I10). ◄

ADDITIONAL COMMENT

If a stockholder leaves his or her stock with a broker in street name, the stockholder can specifically identify the shares sold by simply informing the broker which shares he or she wishes to sell. The date basis of the shares sold should appear on the confirmation from the broker.

IDENTIFICATION PROBLEMS. In most cases, the adjusted basis of property is easily identified with the property that is sold. However, problems occur when property is homogenous in nature such as when an investor owns several blocks of common stock of the same corporation that are purchased on different dates at different prices. The Regulations require the taxpayer to adequately identify the particular stock that is sold or exchanged.[12] Many investors allow brokers to hold their stock in street name (i.e., the brokerage firm holds title to the stock certificates) and thus do not make a physical transfer of securities. Such investors need to be careful to provide specific instructions to the broker as to which securities should be sold. If the stock sold or exchanged is not adequately identified, the first-in, first-out (FIFO) method must be used to identify the stock.[13] With the FIFO method, the stock sold or exchanged is presumed to come from the first lot or lots acquired.

EXAMPLE I5-14 ▶

Tammy purchased 300 shares of the Acme Corporation stock last year:

Month Acquired	Size of Block	Basis
January	100 shares	$4,000
May	100	5,000
October	100	6,000

In March of the current year Tammy sells 120 shares of the stock for $5,160. If Tammy specifically identifies the stock sold as being all of the stock purchased in October and 20 shares purchased in May, her realized loss is $1,840 [$5,160 − ($6,000 + $1,000)]. ◄

If Tammy did not specifically identify the stock that is sold, the FIFO method is used, and her realized gain is $160 [$5,160 − ($4,000 + $1,000)].

PROPERTY RECEIVED AS A GIFT: GIFTS AFTER 1921

ADDITIONAL COMMENT

Upon receipt of property from a relative, one should inquire as to its basis at that time. It might be years later that the asset is sold and the information about the donor's basis may be lost or forgotten.

The basis of property received as a gift is generally the same as the donor's basis.[14] If the FMV of the property at time of the gift is less than the donor's basis, the donee may have to use one basis if the property is subsequently disposed of at a gain and another if the property is disposed of at a loss. As discussed later in this chapter, the basis may be increased by a portion or all of the gift tax paid because of the transfer.

Current rules for determining the donee's basis for property received as a gift are a function of the relationship between the FMV of the property at the time the gift is made and the donor's basis. If the FMV is equal to or greater than the donor's basis, the donee's basis is the same as the donor's basis for all purposes. However, if the FMV is less than the donor's basis, the donee has a dual basis for the property, that is, a basis for loss and a basis for gain. If the donee later transfers the property at a loss, the donee's basis is the property's FMV at the time of the gift (basis for loss). However, if the donee transfers the property at a gain, the donee's basis is the same as the donor's basis (basis for gain).

EXAMPLE I5-15 ▶

Kevin makes a gift of property with a basis of $350 to Janet when it has a $425 FMV. If Janet sells the property for $450, she has a realized gain of $100 ($450 − $350). If Janet sells the property for $330, she has a realized loss of $20 ($330 − $350). Because the FMV of the property at the time of the gift is more than the donor's basis, the donee's basis is $350 for determining both gain and loss. ◄

The following example illustrates the scenario when a taxpayer has a dual basis. The basis for determining a gain is different from the basis for determining a loss.

---

[12] Reg. Sec. 1.1012-1(c)(1).
[13] For mutual fund investors, the IRS has authorized the use of FIFO, specific identification, or two average cost basis methods if only a portion of the fund shares is redeemed or sold. (See Reg. Sec. 1.1012-1(e) and Chapter I17).
[14] Sec. 1015(a).

EXAMPLE I5-16 ▶

ADDITIONAL COMMENT
If Maggie in Example I5-16 sells the land for $750, she has a $150 gain. If she sells the land for $400, she has a $100 loss and there is no gain or loss if she sells the land for $560.

KEY POINT
Although unrealized losses cannot be shifted to another taxpayer, unrealized gains can be shifted.

KEY POINT
No gift tax can be added to the basis of the property if the donor's basis is greater than the FMV of the property.

Chuck makes a gift of property with a basis of $600 to Maggie when the property has a $500 FMV. Maggie's basis for the property is $600 if the property is sold at a gain (i.e., for more than $600), but the basis is $500 if the property is sold at a loss (i.e., for less than $500). If the property is sold for $500 or more but not more than $600, no gain or loss is recognized. ◀

The dual basis rules were designed to prevent tax-avoidance schemes. Taxpayers are prevented from shifting unrealized losses to another taxpayer by making gifts of such "loss" property. For example, a low-income taxpayer who owns property that has depreciated in value might transfer the property by gift to a high-income taxpayer who would receive greater tax benefit from the deduction of the loss upon the subsequent sale of the property. The loss basis rules prevent the donee from recognizing a loss on the sale of the property because the basis for loss is the lesser of the donor's basis or FMV on the date of the gift.

EFFECT OF GIFT TAX ON BASIS. If the donor pays a gift tax on the transfer of property, the donee's basis may be increased. This increase occurs only if the FMV of the property exceeds the donor's basis on the date of the gift. For taxable gifts after 1976,[15] the increase in the donee's basis is equal to a pro rata portion of the gift tax that is attributable to the unrealized appreciation in the property. The amount of the addition to the donee's basis is determined as follows:[16]

$$\text{Gift tax paid} \times \frac{\text{FMV at time of the gift} - \text{Donor's basis}}{\text{Amount of the gift}}$$

The amount of the gift is the FMV of the property less the amount of the annual exclusion.[17]

EXAMPLE I5-17 ▶

During the current year, Cindy makes one gift of property with a $20,000 basis to Jessie when the property has a $60,000 FMV. Cindy pays a gift tax of $20,500. The amount of the gift is $50,000 ($60,000 − $10,000). Jessie's basis for the property for determining both gain and loss is $36,400 [$20,000 + (0.80 × $20,500)]. Thus, 80% [($60,000 − $20,000)/$50,000] of the gift tax is added to Jessie's basis. ◀

EXAMPLE I5-18 ▶

During the current year, Sally makes a gift of property with a basis of $50,000 to Troy when the property has a $40,000 FMV. Sally pays a gift tax of $1,000. Troy's basis for the property is not affected by the gift tax paid by Sally because the FMV is less than the donor's basis at the time of the gift. Troy's basis for the property is $50,000 for purposes of determining gain and $40,000 for purposes of determining loss. ◀

? STOP & THINK

Question: Pete wants to make a gift of either ABC common stock (basis of $44,000 and FMV of $50,000) or XYZ common stock (basis of $73,000 and FMV of $50,000) to his nephew. Pete and his nephew have the same tax rate. Which stock should he give to his nephew?

Solution: Pete should give the ABC stock to his nephew because the nephew's basis for determining a gain or loss is $44,000 plus a portion of any gift tax Pete pays. The nephew's basis for XYZ common stock is $50,000 to determine a loss and $73,000 to determine a gain. If the nephew sells XYZ stock for less than $73,000, no loss is recognized and thus some of the basis is not used. Note that Pete would have a $23,000 loss if he sells the XYZ stock for $50,000. Furthermore, the nephew's basis for the XYZ stock is not increased if Pete has to pay a gift tax on the $40,000 taxable gift.

---

[15] For gifts after September 2, 1958 and before 1977, the entire amount of the gift tax paid is added to the donee's basis. However, the basis may not exceed the property's FMV on the date of the gift.
[16] Sec. 1015(d)(6).
[17] Sec. 1015(d)(2) and Sec. 2503(b). An annual exclusion of $10,000 per year is allowed for each donee. See Chapter I1 for a limited discussion of the annual exclusion and Chapter C12 of the *Corporations, Partnerships, Estates, and Trusts* and *Comprehensive* volumes for a more detailed discussion.

PROPERTY RECEIVED FROM A DECEDENT

The basis of property received from a decedent is generally the FMV of the property at the date of the decedent's death or an alternate valuation date.[18] This can result in either a step up (increase) or step down (decrease) in basis.

> **EXAMPLE I5-19** ▶ Patrick inherits property having an $80,000 FMV on the date of the decedent's death. The decedent's basis in the property is $47,000. The executor of the estate does not elect the alternate valuation date. Patrick's basis for the property is $80,000. ◀

> **EXAMPLE I5-20** ▶ Dianna inherits property having a $60,000 FMV at the date of the decedent's death. The decedent's basis in the property is $72,000. The alternate valuation date is not elected. Dianna's basis for the property is $60,000. ◀

REAL-WORLD EXAMPLE
The alternate valuation date was used in valuing the estates of many individuals owning large portfolios of common stocks who died shortly before the stock market crash in October 1987.

Instead of using the FMV on the date of death to determine the estate tax, the executor of the estate may elect to use the FMV on the alternate valuation date. The alternate valuation date is generally six months after the date of death. If the alternate valuation date is elected, the basis for all of the assets in the estate is their FMV on that date unless the property is distributed by the estate to the heirs or is sold before the alternate valuation date. If the alternate valuation date is used, property distributed or sold after the date of the decedent's death and before the alternate valuation date has a basis equal to its FMV on the date of distribution or the date it is disposed of.[19]

If the estate is small enough that an estate tax return is not required, the value of the property on the alternate valuation date may not be used.[20]

> **EXAMPLE I5-21** ▶ Marilyn inherits all of the property owned by an individual who dies in April, when the property has a $100,000 FMV. The value of the property six months later is $90,000. Because of the size of the estate, no estate tax is due. The alternate valuation date may not be used, and Marilyn's basis for the property is $100,000. Note that Marilyn does not want the alternate valuation date to be used because her basis would be $90,000 instead of $100,000. ◀

As noted above, the basis of the property to the estate and the heirs can be affected if the alternate valuation date is used to value the estate's assets. The alternate valuation date may be elected only if the value of the gross estate and the amount of estate tax after credits are reduced as a result of using the alternate valuation date.[21] This means that the aggregate value of the assets determined by using the alternate valuation date may be used only if the total value of the assets has decreased during the six-month period.

> **EXAMPLE I5-22** ▶ Helmut inherits all of the property owned by an individual who dies in March when the FMV of the property is $900,000. Six months after the date of death, the property has a $950,000 FMV. The property is distributed to Helmut in December. Use of the alternate valuation date is not permitted because the value of the gross estate has increased. Therefore, his basis in the property is $900,000, the FMV on the date of death. ◀

An executor may elect to use the alternate valuation date to reduce the estate taxes owed by the estate. However, the income tax basis of the property included in the estate is also reduced for the heirs who inherit the property.

> **EXAMPLE I5-23** ▶ Michelle inherits property with a $900,000 FMV at the date of the decedent's death. Because the FMV of the property on the alternate valuation date (six months after the date of the decedent's death) is $850,000, the executor of the estate elects to use $850,000 to value the property for estate tax purposes. Michelle's basis for the property is thus $850,000 instead of $900,000. ◀

---

[18] Sec. 1014(a).
[19] Sec. 2032(a).
[20] Rev. Rul. 56-60, 1956-1 C.B. 443. For a decedent dying after 1986, Sec. 6018(a) requires an estate tax return to be filed if the sum of the gross estate and the adjusted taxable gifts made by the decedent after December 31, 1976 exceeds $600,000. The $600,000 is being gradually increased to $1,000,000 by 2006. For 2001 and 2002, the amounts are $675,000 and $700,000 respectively.
[21] Credits available include the unified transfer tax credit and possibly credits for state death taxes, gift taxes, foreign death taxes, and the credit for taxes on prior transfers.

Property Transactions: Capital Gains and Losses ▼ Individuals 5-9

COMMUNITY PROPERTY. If the decedent and the decedent's spouse own property under community property laws,[22] one-half of the property is included in the decedent's estate and its basis to the surviving spouse is its FMV.[23] The Internal Revenue Code also provides that the surviving spouse's one-half share of the community property is adjusted to the FMV.[24] In effect, the surviving spouse's share of the community property is considered to have passed from the decedent.

EXAMPLE I5-24 ▶ Matt and Jane, a married couple, live in Texas, a community property state, and jointly own land as community property that cost $110,000. The land has an $800,000 FMV when Jane dies, leaving all of her property to Matt. His basis for the entire property is $800,000. ◀

In a common law state, only one-half of the jointly owned property is included in the decedent's estate and is adjusted to its FMV. The survivor's share of the jointly held property is not adjusted.

EXAMPLE I5-25 ▶ Barry and Maria, a married couple, live in Iowa, a common law state, and jointly own land that cost $200,000. The property has a $700,000 FMV when Barry dies, leaving all of his property to Maria. Her basis for the land is $450,000 [$100,000 + (0.50 × $700,000)]. ◀

PROPERTY CONVERTED FROM PERSONAL USE TO BUSINESS USE

ADDITIONAL COMMENT

It is important to estimate the FMV of property at the time the property is converted from personal use to business use.

Often, taxpayers who own personal-use assets convert these assets to an income-producing use or for use in a trade or business. When this conversion occurs, the property's basis must be determined. The basis for computing depreciation is the lower of the FMV or the adjusted basis of the property at the time the asset is transferred from personal use to an income-producing use or for use in a trade or business.[25] This rule prevents taxpayers from obtaining the benefits of depreciation to the extent that the property has declined in value during the period that it is held for personal use.

EXAMPLE I5-26
REAL-WORLD EXAMPLE

A taxpayer sold a personal residence to a purchaser, and the purchaser rented the property from the taxpayer until financing could be secured. The rental agreement was executed simultaneously with the sales agreement and was incidental to the sale. The taxpayer was not permitted to recognize any loss on the sale because the property was never converted to rental property. *Henry B. Dawson*, 1972 PH T.C. Memo 31 TCM 5.

▶ Olga owns a boat that cost $2,000 and is used for personal enjoyment. At a time when the boat has a $1,400 FMV, Olga transfers the boat to her business of operating a marina. The basis for depreciation is $1,400 because the FMV is less than Olga's adjusted basis at the time of conversion to business use. The $600 decline ($2,000 − $1,400) that occurred while Olga used the boat for personal use may not be deducted as depreciation. ◀

If the boat's FMV in Example I5-26 is more than $2,000, the basis for depreciation is $2,000 because the FMV is higher than its adjusted basis at the time the asset is transferred to business use.

If a personal-use asset is transferred to business use when its FMV is less than its adjusted basis, the basis for determining a loss on a subsequent sale or disposition of the property is its FMV on the date of the conversion to business use less any depreciation taken before the disposition.[26]

EXAMPLE I5-27 ▶ Susanna purchased a personal residence for $50,000 and subsequently converted the property to rental property. At the time of the conversion, the property had a $46,000 FMV. Assume depreciation of $20,700 has been deducted when the property is sold for $21,000. The basis of the property at the time of the sale is $25,300 ($46,000 − $20,700). Thus, her loss on the sale is $4,300 ($21,000 − $25,300). ◀

The rule for determining the basis, that is, lower of adjusted basis or FMV, applies only to the sale of converted property at a loss. The basis for determining gain is its adjusted basis at the time of conversion less any depreciation taken before the disposition.

---

[22] Community property states are Arizona, California, Idaho, Louisiana, New Mexico, Nevada, Texas, and Washington. Wisconsin has a marital property law that is basically the same as community property.
[23] Sec. 1014(a).
[24] Sec. 1014(b)(6).
[25] Reg. Sec. 1.167(g)-1.
[26] Reg. Sec. 1.165-9(b)(2).

EXAMPLE I5-28 ▶ Assume the same facts as in Example I5-27, except that the property is sold for $31,000 instead of $21,000. The basis of the property is $29,300 ($50,000 − $20,700) and her gain is $1,700 ($31,000 − $29,300). ◀

Without the rule for determining basis of personal-use property converted to business property, taxpayers would have an incentive to convert nonbusiness assets that have declined in value to business use before selling the asset to convert nondeductible losses into deductible losses.

EXAMPLE I5-29 ▶ Craig owns a personal-use asset with a basis of $80,000 and a $50,000 FMV. If he sells the asset for its FMV, the $30,000 loss ($50,000 − $80,000) is not deductible because losses on the sale of personal-use assets are not deductible. If Craig converts the asset to business use and then immediately sells the asset for $50,000, no loss is realized because the basis of the asset for purposes of determining loss is $50,000. ◀

ALLOCATION OF BASIS

REAL-WORLD EXAMPLE
A taxpayer purchased a group of lots and allocated the total cost evenly among the lots. The court, however, held that more cost should be allocated to the waterfront lots than to the interior lots. *Biscayne Bay Islands Co.*, 23 B.T.A. 731 (1931).

When property is obtained in one transaction and portions of the property are subsequently disposed of at different times, the basis of the property is allocated to the different portions of the property. Gain or loss is computed at the time of disposal for each portion. If one purchases a 20-acre tract of land and later sells the entire tract, an allocation of basis is not needed. However if the taxpayer divides the property into smaller tracts of land for resale, the cost of the 20-acre tract must be allocated among the smaller tracts of land.

BASKET PURCHASE. If more than one asset is acquired in a single purchase transaction (i.e., a basket purchase), the cost must be apportioned to the various assets acquired. The allocation is based on the relative FMVs of the assets.

EXAMPLE I5-30 ▶ Kelly purchases a duplex for $80,000 to use as a rental property. The land has a $15,000 FMV, and the building has a $65,000 FMV. Kelly's bases for the land and the building are $15,000 and $65,000, respectively. ◀

SELF-STUDY QUESTION
If Kelly in Example I5-30 paid $2,000 for the cost of a title search and other costs that must be capitalized, what is the basis of the land and building?

ANSWER
Land $15,375
Building $66,625

Because no depreciation deduction is allowed for land, taxpayers tend to favor a liberal allocation of the total purchase price to the building. Appraisals or other measures of FMV may be used to make the allocation.

COMMON COSTS. As in the case of financial accounting, common costs incurred to obtain or prepare an asset for service must be capitalized and allocated to the basis of the individual assets.

EXAMPLE I5-31 ▶ Priscilla acquires three machines for $60,000, which have FMVs of $30,000, $20,000, and $10,000, respectively. Costs of delivery amount to $2,000, and costs to install the three machines amount to $1,000. The total installation and delivery costs of $3,000 are allocated to each of the three machines based on their FMVs.

The allocation of the $3,000 of common costs occurs as follows:

$$\text{Machine No. 1:} \quad \frac{\$30,000 \text{ FMV}}{\$30,000 + \$20,000 + \$10,000} \times \$3,000 = \$1,500$$

$$\text{Machine No. 2:} \quad \frac{\$20,000 \text{ FMV}}{\$30,000 + \$20,000 + \$10,000} \times \$3,000 = \$1,000$$

$$\text{Machine No. 3:} \quad \frac{\$10,000 \text{ FMV}}{\$30,000 + \$20,000 + \$10,000} \times \$3,000 = \$500$$

The bases for each of the three machines are $31,500, $21,000, and $10,500, respectively. ◀

NONTAXABLE STOCK DIVIDENDS RECEIVED. If a nontaxable stock dividend is received, a portion of the basis of the stock on which the stock dividend is received is allocated to the new shares received from the stock dividend.[27] The cost basis of the previously acquired shares is then reduced by the amount of basis that is allocated to the stock dividend shares. If the stock received as a stock dividend is the same type as the stock owned before the dividend, the total basis of the stock owned before the dividend is allocated equally to all shares now owned.

EXAMPLE I5-32 ▶ Wayne owns 1,000 shares of Bell Corporation common stock with a $44,000 basis. Wayne receives a nontaxable 10% common stock dividend and now owns 1,100 shares of common stock. The basis for each share of common stock is now $40 ($44,000 ÷ 1,100). ◀

If the stock received as a stock dividend is not the same type as the stock owned before the dividend, the allocation is based on relative FMVs.

EXAMPLE I5-33 ▶ Stacey owns 500 shares of Montana Corporation common stock with a $60,000 basis. She receives a nontaxable stock dividend payable in 50 shares of preferred stock. At time of the distribution, the common stock has a $40,000 FMV ($80 × 500 shares), and the preferred stock has a $10,000 FMV ($200 × 50 shares). After the distribution, Stacey owns 50 shares of preferred stock with a basis of $12,000 [($10,000 ÷ $50,000) × $60,000]. Thus, $12,000 of the basis of the common stock is allocated to the preferred stock and the basis of the common stock is reduced from $60,000 to $48,000. ◀

KEY POINT
Corporations issue stock rights to shareholders so that the shareholders will be able to maintain their same proportional ownership in the corporation. This is called the preemptive right.

NONTAXABLE STOCK RIGHTS RECEIVED. Stock rights represent rights to acquire shares of a specified corporation's stock at a specific exercise price when certain conditions are met. The exercise price is usually less than the market price when the stock rights are issued. Stock rights may be distributed to employees as compensation, and they are often issued to shareholders to encourage them to purchase more stock, thereby providing more capital for the corporation.

If the FMV of nontaxable stock rights received is less than 15% of the FMV of the stock, the basis of the stock rights is zero unless the taxpayer elects to allocate the basis between the stock rights and the stock owned before distribution of the stock rights.[28]

EXAMPLE I5-34 ▶ Tina owns 100 shares of Bear Corporation common stock with a $27,000 basis and a $50,000 FMV. She receives 100 nontaxable stock rights with a total FMV of $4,000. Because the FMV of the stock rights is less than 15% of the FMV of the stock (0.15 × $50,000 = $7,500), the basis of the stock rights is zero unless Tina elects to make an allocation. ◀

REAL-WORLD EXAMPLE
In 1993, United States Cellular Corporation issued one right for each common share held. Each whole right entitled the holder to buy one common share for $33.

If in Example I5-34, Tina elects to allocate the basis of $27,000 between the stock rights and the stock, the basis of the rights is $2,000 ([$4,000 ÷ $54,000] × $27,000) and the basis of the stock is $25,000 ([$50,000 ÷ $54,000] × $27,000).

The decision to allocate the basis affects the gain or loss realized on the sale or disposition of the stock rights because the basis of the rights is zero unless an allocation is made. Furthermore, the basis of any stock acquired by exercising the rights is affected by whether or not a portion of the basis is allocated to the rights. The basis of stock acquired by exercising the stock rights is the amount paid plus the basis of the stock rights exercised.

EXAMPLE I5-35 ▶ George receives 10 stock rights as a nontaxable distribution, and no basis is allocated to the stock rights. With each stock right, George may acquire one share of stock for $20. If he exercises all 10 stock rights, the new stock acquired has a basis of $200 ($20 × 10 shares). If George sells all 10 stock rights for $135, he has a realized gain of $135 ($135 − 0). ◀

If the FMV of a nontaxable stock right received is equal to or greater than 15% of the FMV of the stock, the basis of the stock owned before the distribution must be allocated between the stock and the stock rights.

EXAMPLE I5-36 ▶ Helen owns 100 shares of NMO common stock with a $14,000 basis and a $30,000 FMV. She receives 100 stock rights with a total FMV of $5,000. Because the FMV of the stock rights is at least 15% of the FMV of the stock, the $14,000 basis must be allocated between the stock rights and the stock. The basis of the stock rights is $2,000 [($5,000 ÷ $35,000) × $14,000] and the basis of the stock is $12,000 [($30,000 ÷ $35,000) × $14,000]. ◀

---

[27] Sec. 307(a).　　　　　　　　　　　　　　　　[28] Sec. 307(b)(1).

A recipient of stock rights generally has three courses of action. The stock rights can be sold or exchanged, in which case the basis allocated to the stock rights, if any, is used to determine the gain or loss. The stock rights may be exercised, and any basis allocated to the rights is added to the purchase price of the acquired stock. The stock rights may be allowed to expire, in which case no loss is recognized, and any basis allocated to the rights is reallocated back to the stock. If the stock rights received in Example I5-36 expire without being exercised, Helen does not recognize a loss and the basis of her 100 shares of common stock is $14,000.

Property basis rules are highlighted in Topic Review I5-1.

DEFINITION OF A CAPITAL ASSET

OBJECTIVE 4

Distinguish between capital assets and other assets

Instead of defining capital assets, Sec. 1221 provides a list of properties that are **not** capital assets. Thus, a capital asset is any property owned by a taxpayer *other* than the types of property specified in the IRC. Property which is not a capital asset includes the following:

1. Inventory or property held primarily for sale to customers in the ordinary course of a trade or business.

Topic Review I5-1

Property Basis Rules

METHOD ACQUIRED	BASIS OF THE ACQUIRED PROPERTY
1. Acquired by direct purchase	1. Basis includes the amount paid for the property, costs of preparing the property for use, obligations of the seller that are assumed by the buyer, and liabilities to which the property is subject.
2. Acquired as a gift. (a) FMV on the date of the gift is equal to or greater than the donor's basis (b) FMV on the date of the gift is less than the donor's basis	2. (a) The donee's basis is the same as the donor's basis plus a pro rata portion of the gift tax attributable to the property's unrealized appreciation at the time of the gift. (b) The donee's gain basis is the donor's basis and the loss basis is FMV. No increase for any gift tax paid.
3. Received from a decedent (a) Alternative valuation date is not elected (b) Alternative valuation date is elected	3. (a) The basis is its FMV on the date of death. (b) The basis of nondistributed property is its FMV on the alternative valuation date. If the property is distributed or sold this date, its basis is FMV on the date of sale or distribution.
4. Converted from personal to business use	4. The basis for a loss (as well as for depreciation) is the lesser of its adjusted basis or FMV at the date of conversion. The basis for a gain is its adjusted basis at the date of conversion.
5. Nontaxable stock dividend	5. Basis of the stock dividend shares includes a pro rata portion of the adjusted basis of the underlying shares owned.
6. Nontaxable stock right	6. If the FMV of the rights is less than 15% of the stock's FMV, the basis of the rights is zero unless an election is made. Basis of the underlying stock is allocated to the rights based on the respective FMV's of the stock and the rights.

2. Property used in the trade or business and subject to the allowance for depreciation provided in Sec. 167 or real property used in a trade or business. (As explained in Chapter I13, these properties are referred to as *Sec. 1231 assets* if held by the taxpayer more than one year.)
3. Accounts or notes receivable acquired in the ordinary course of a trade or business for services rendered or from the sale of property described in item 1.
4. Other assets including
    a. A letter, memorandum, or similar property held by a taxpayer for whom such property was prepared or produced.
    b. A copyright; a literary, musical, or artistic composition; a letter or memorandum; or similar property held by a taxpayer whose personal efforts created such property or whose basis in the property for determining a gain is determined by reference to the basis of such property in the hands of one who created the property or one for whom such property was prepared or produced.
    c. A U.S. government publication held by a taxpayer who receives the publication by any means other than a purchase at the price the publication is offered for sale to the public.
    d. A U.S. government publication held by a taxpayer whose basis in the property for determining a gain is determined by reference to the basis of such property in the hands of a taxpayer in item 4c (e.g., certain property received by gift).

> **TYPICAL MISCONCEPTION**
> It is common in financial accounting classes to include property used in a trade or business in the definition of a capital asset. For example, factory buildings, machinery, trucks, and office buildings would be defined as capital assets. However, such items are not capital assets for tax purposes.

EXAMPLE I5-37 ▶ Maxine owns a building used in her business. Other business assets include equipment, inventory, and accounts receivable. None of the assets are classified as capital assets. ◀

Chapter I13 provides an in-depth discussion of business assets such as buildings, land, and equipment. Although these items are not capital assets, Sec. 1231 provides in many cases that the gain on the sale or exchange of such an asset is eventually taxed as a long-term capital gain.

EXAMPLE I5-38 ▶ Eric owns an automobile that is held for personal use and also owns a copyright for a book he has written. Because the copyright is held by the taxpayer whose personal efforts created the property, it is not a capital asset. The automobile held for personal use is a capital asset. ◀

> **SELF-STUDY QUESTION**
> Doug owns a personal residence, an automobile, 100 shares of Ford Motor Company, and a poem he wrote for his girlfriend. Which of these assets are capital assets?
>
> **ANSWER**
> All of the items are capital assets except the poem, which is a literary composition.
>
> **ADDITIONAL COMMENT**
> If an asset such as an automobile is used in part in a trade or business and in part for personal use, then the business part of the car is not a capital asset, but the other part is a capital asset.

By analyzing Examples I5-37 and I5-38, one can conclude that the classification of an asset is often determined by its use. An automobile used in a trade or business is not a capital asset but is considered a capital asset when it is held for personal use. Examples of assets that qualify as capital assets include a personal residence, land held for personal use, and investments in stocks and bonds. In addition, certain types of assets are specifically given capital asset status, such as patents, franchises, etc. These and other special assets are discussed later in this chapter.

INFLUENCE OF THE COURTS

In *Corn Products Refining Co.*, the Supreme Court rendered a landmark decision when it determined that the sale of futures contracts related to the purchase of raw materials resulted in ordinary rather than capital gains and losses.[29] The Corn Products Company, a manufacturer of products made from grain corn, purchased futures contracts for corn to ensure an adequate supply of raw materials. While delivery of the corn was accepted when needed for manufacturing operations, unneeded contracts were later sold. Corn Products contended that any gains or losses on the sale of the unneeded contracts should be capital gains and losses because futures contracts are customarily viewed as security investments, which qualify as capital assets. The Supreme Court held that these transactions represented an integral part of the business for the purpose of protecting the company's manufacturing operations and that the gains and losses should, therefore, be ordinary in nature.

---

[29] *Corn Products Refining Co. v. CIR*, 47 AFTR 1789, 55-2 USTC ¶9746 (USSC, 1955).

> **ETHICAL POINT**
>
> A CPA should not prepare or sign a tax return for a client unless the position or issue has (1) a realistic possibility of being sustained on its merits, or (2) is not frivolous and is adequately disclosed in the return.

Although the *Corn Products* doctrine has been interpreted as creating a nonstatutory exception to the definition of a capital asset when the asset is purchased for business purposes, the Supreme Court ruled in the 1988 *Arkansas Best Corporation* case that the motivation for acquiring assets is irrelevant to the question of whether assets are capital assets. Arkansas Best, a bank holding company, sold shares of a bank's stock that had been acquired for the purpose of protecting its business reputation. Relying on the *Corn Products* doctrine, the company deducted the loss as ordinary. The Supreme Court ruled that the loss was a capital loss because the stock is within the broad definition of the term *capital asset* in Sec. 1221 and is outside the classes of property that are excluded from capital-asset status.[30] *Arkansas Best* apparently limits the application of *Corn Products* to hedging transactions that are an integral part of a taxpayer's system of acquiring inventory.

OTHER IRC PROVISIONS RELEVANT TO CAPITAL GAINS AND LOSSES

A number of IRC sections provide special treatment for certain types of assets and transactions. For example, loss on the sale or exchange of certain small business stock that qualifies as Sec. 1244 stock is treated as an ordinary loss rather than a capital loss to the extent of $50,000 per year ($100,000 if the taxpayer is married and files a joint return).[31]

> **ADDITIONAL COMMENT**
>
> For purposes of Sec. 1236, a security is defined as any share of stock in any corporation, note, bond, debenture, or evidence of indebtedness, or any evidence of an interest in or right to subscribe to or purchase any of the above.

DEALERS IN SECURITIES. Normally, a security dealer's gain on the sale or exchange of securities is ordinary income. Section 1236 provides an exception for dealers in securities if the dealer clearly identifies that the property is held for investment. This act of identification must occur before the close of the day on which the security is acquired, and the security must not be held primarily for sale to customers in the ordinary course of the dealer's trade or business at any time after the close of the day of purchase.

EXAMPLE I5-39 ▶ Allyson, a dealer in securities, purchases Cook Corporation stock on April 8, and identifies the stock as being held for investment on that date. Four months later, Allyson sells the stock. Any gain or loss recognized due to the sale is capital gain or loss. ◀

Once a dealer clearly identifies a security as being held for investment, any loss on the sale or exchange of the security is treated as a capital loss.

EXAMPLE I5-40 ▶ Kris, a dealer in securities, purchases Boston Corporation stock and clearly identifies the stock as being held for investment on the date of purchase. Eight months later, the security is removed from the investment account and held as inventory. If the security is later sold at a gain, the gain is an ordinary gain. However, if the stock is sold at a loss, the loss is a capital loss. ◀

For tax years ending on or after December 31, 1993, securities dealers must use the mark-to-market method for their inventory of securities. Securities must be valued at FMV at the end of each taxable year. Dealers in securities recognize gain or loss each year as if the security is sold on the last day of the tax year. Gains and losses are generally treated as ordinary rather than capital. Gains or losses due to adjustments in subsequent years or resulting from the sale of the security must be adjusted to reflect gains and losses already taken into account when determining taxable income.[32]

EXAMPLE I5-41 ▶ Jim Spikes, a dealer in securities and calendar-year taxpayer, purchases a security for inventory on October 10, 2001, for $10,000 and sells the security for $18,000 on July 1, 2002. The security's FMV on December 31, 2001 is $15,000. Jim recognizes $5,000 of ordinary income in 2001 and $3,000 of ordinary income in 2002. ◀

---

[30] *Arkansas Best Corporation v. CIR*, 61 AFTR 2d 88-655, 88-1 USTC ¶9210 (USSC, 1988).
[31] Secs. 1244(a) and (b). (See Chapter I8 for additional discussion on small business corporation stock losses.)
[32] Sec. 475. The mark-to-market rule also applies to some securities that are not inventory, but does not apply to any security that is held for investment and certain other transactions (see Sec. 475(b)).

REAL PROPERTY SUBDIVIDED FOR SALE. A taxpayer who engages in regular sales of real estate is considered to be a dealer, and any gain or loss recognized is ordinary gain or loss rather than capital gain or loss. A special relief provision is provided in Sec. 1237 for nondealer, noncorporate taxpayers who subdivide a tract of real property into lots (two or more pieces of real property are considered to be a tract if they are contiguous). Part or all of the gain on the sale of the lots may be treated as a capital gain if the following provisions of Sec. 1237 are satisfied:

> **ADDITIONAL COMMENT**
> The conversion of an apartment building into condominiums does not qualify under Sec. 1237, even if the property has been held for five years and no substantial improvements have been made.

- During the year of sale, the noncorporate taxpayer must not hold any other real property primarily for sale in the ordinary course of business.
- Unless the property is acquired by inheritance or devise, the lots sold must be held by the taxpayer for a period of at least five years.
- No substantial improvement may be made by the taxpayer while holding the lots if the improvement substantially enhances the value of the lot.[33]
- The tract or any lot may not have been previously held primarily for sale to customers in the ordinary course of the taxpayer's trade or business unless such tract at that time was covered by Sec. 1237.

The primary advantage of Sec. 1237 is that potential controversy with the IRS is avoided as to whether a taxpayer who subdivides investment property is a dealer. Section 1237 does not apply to losses. Such losses are capital losses if the property is held for investment purposes, or ordinary losses if the taxpayer is a dealer.

If the Sec. 1237 requirements are satisfied, all gain on the sale of the first five lots may be capital gain. Starting in the tax year during which the sixth lot is sold, 5% of the selling price for all lots sold in that year and succeeding years is ordinary income.

EXAMPLE I5-42 ▶ Jean subdivides a tract of land held as an investment into seven lots, and all requirements of Sec. 1237 are satisfied. The lots have a fair market value of $10,000 each and have a basis of $4,000. Jean incurs no selling expenses and sells four lots in 2001 and three lots in 2002. In 2001, all of the $24,000 [4 lots × ($10,000 − $4,000)] gain is capital gain. In 2002, the year in which the sixth lot is sold, $1,500 of the gain is ordinary income [0.05 × ($10,000 × 3 lots)], and the remaining $16,500 {[3 lots × ($10,000 − $4,000)] − $1,500} gain is capital gain. ◀

EXAMPLE I5-43 ▶ Assume the same facts as in Example I5-42, except that all seven lots are sold in 2001. The amount of ordinary income recognized is $3,500 [0.05 × ($10,000 × 7 lots)], and the remaining $38,500 {[7 lots × ($10,000 − $4,000)] − $3,500} gain is capital gain. ◀

> **ADDITIONAL COMMENT**
> If a taxpayer sells any lots from a tract and does not sell any others for a period of five years, the remaining property is considered a new tract.

Based on Examples I5-42 and I5-43, the advantage of selling no more than five lots in the first year should be apparent. Expenditures incurred to sell or exchange the lots are also treated favorably because they are first applied against the portion of the gain treated as ordinary income. Because selling expenses (e.g., commissions) are often equal to or greater than 5% of the selling price, this offset against ordinary income may result in the elimination of the ordinary income portion of the gain. Selling expenses in excess of the gain taxed as ordinary income reduce the amount realized on the sale or exchange.

NONBUSINESS BAD DEBT. Although the topic of bad debts is discussed in Chapter I8, it is important to note that bad debt losses from nonbusiness debts are deductible only as short-term capital losses (STCLs).[34] This treatment applies regardless of when the debt occurred. A nonbusiness bad debt is deductible only in the year in which the debt becomes totally worthless.

EXAMPLE I5-44 ▶ Two years ago, Alice loaned $4,000 to a friend. During the current year, the friend declares bankruptcy and the debt is entirely worthless. Assuming that Alice has no other gains and losses from the sale or exchange of capital assets during the year, she deducts $3,000 in determining adjusted gross income (AGI) and has a STCL carry forward of $1,000. ◀

---

[33] Certain improvements are not treated as substantial under Sec. 1237(b)(3) if the lot is held for at least ten years.

[34] Sec. 166(d)(1)(B).

TAX TREATMENT FOR CAPITAL GAINS AND LOSSES OF NONCORPORATE TAXPAYERS

OBJECTIVE 5

Understand how capital gains and losses affect taxable income

To recognize capital gain or loss, it is necessary to have a sale or exchange of a capital asset. Once it is determined that a capital gain or loss has been realized and is to be recognized, it is necessary to classify the gains and losses as either short-term or long-term. If the asset is held for one year or less, the gain or loss is classified as a short-term capital gain (STCG) or a short-term capital loss (STCL). If the capital asset is held for more than one year, the gain or loss is classified as a long-term capital gain (LTCG) or long-term capital loss (LTCL).[35]

CAPITAL GAINS

ADDITIONAL COMMENT

1996 was a good year for taxpayers owning capital assets. Total net capital gains reported that year were $245.9 billion, up 50.5% from 1995. Net capital losses were $8.8 billion, down 8.0%.

Net capital gain (NCG), which may receive favorable tax treatment, is defined as the excess of net long-term capital gain over net short-term capital loss.[36] NCG may be taxed at 8%, 10%, 18%, 20%, 25% or 28%. Part or all of NCG may be adjusted net capital gain (ANCG). ANCG, which is explained later, is subject to the lower rates of 10% and 20% and rates as low as 8% or 18% for tax years beginning after December 31, 2000, if the holding period is more than five years.[37]

To compute net capital gain, first determine all STCGs, STCLs, LTCGs, LTCLs, and then net gains and losses as described below.

NET SHORT-TERM CAPITAL GAIN. If total STCGs for the tax year exceed total STCLs for that year, the excess is defined as net short-term capital gain (NSTCG). As discussed later, NSTCG may be offset by net long-term capital loss (NLTCL).

EXAMPLE I5-45 ▶ Hal has two transactions involving the sale of capital assets during the year. As a result of those transactions, he has a STCG of $4,000 and a STCL of $3,000. Hal's NSTCG is $1,000 ($4,000 − $3,000), and his AGI increases by $1,000. His gross income increases by $4,000, and he is entitled to a $3,000 deduction for AGI. ◀

NET LONG-TERM CAPITAL GAIN. If the total LTCGs for the tax year exceed the total LTCLs for that year, the excess is defined as net long-term capital gain (NLTCG). As indicated earlier, a NCG exists when NLTCG exceeds net short-term capital loss (NSTCL).

EXAMPLE I5-46 ▶ Clay has two transactions involving the sale of capital assets during the year. As a result of the transactions, he has a LTCG of $4,000 and a LTCL of $3,000. Clay has a NLTCG and a net capital gain of $1,000. His AGI increases by $1,000. ◀

EXAMPLE I5-47 ▶ Linda has four transactions involving the sale of capital assets during the year. As a result of the transactions, she has a STCG of $5,000, a STCL of $7,000, a LTCG of $10,000, and a LTCL of $2,000. After the initial netting of short-term and long-term gains and losses, Linda has a NSTCL of $2,000 ($7,000 − $5,000) and a NLTCG of $8,000 ($10,000 − $2,000). Because the NLTCG exceeds the NSTCL by $6,000 ($8,000 − $2,000), her NCG is $6,000. ◀

LOWER RATES FOR ADJUSTED NET CAPITAL GAIN (ANCG). The new rates of 20% and 10% apply to ANCG recognized for sales after May 6, 1997, and the rate to use depends upon the taxpayer's tax bracket. The maximum rate for ANCG recognized by

---

[35] While the Taxpayer Relief Act of 1997 reduced the rates for most LTCGs, it increased the required holding period to more than 18 months to be eligible for the lower rates of 10% and 20%. During the last few months of 1997, gain resulting from the sale of a capital asset might be taxed at many different rates depending on whether or not the holding period is one year or less, more than one year but not more than 18 months, or more than 18 months. These changes in the law dramatically increased the complexity associated with the taxation of capital gains. The 1998 Restructuring and Reform Act eliminated the more than 18-month holding period requirement for tax years ending after 1997 and returned to the more than one year requirement to be LTCG.

[36] Sec. 1222(11).

[37] Sec. 1(h).

noncorporate taxpayers (individuals, estates and trusts) is 20% unless the taxpayer's regular tax rate is 15%. Taxpayers whose rate is 15% are subject to a rate of only 10% on ANCG.[38]

EXAMPLE I5-48 ▶ Sandy is single with taxable income of $100,000 without considering the sale of a capital asset, Merck stock, in December 2001 for $15,000. The stock was purchased four years earlier for $3,000. Sandy has $12,000 of NLTCG which is ANCG taxed at 20%. ◀

EXAMPLE I5-49 ▶ Assume the same facts as in Example I5-48 except Sandy's taxable income without the capital gain is $11,400. The $12,000 ANCG is taxed at 10% because her taxable income is less than the $27,050 that is subject to the 15% rate.

Computation of the tax becomes more complicated if the ANCG causes taxable income to exceed the amount subject to the 15% tax rate, i.e., $27,050 for a single taxpayer. If a single taxpayer has taxable income of $30,000 that includes $9,000 of ANCG, the taxpayer's tax is determined as follows:

Tax on $21,000 (taxable income without the ANCG)	$3,150	($21,000 × 15%)
+ Tax on $6,050 ($27,050 − $21,000) of the ANCG at 10%	605	($6,050 × 10%)
+ Tax on $2,950 ($9,000 − $6,050) at 20% because the taxable income is greater than $27,050.	590	($2,950 × 20%)
Total tax	$4,345	

◀

SELF-STUDY QUESTION

Mary sells common stock for a gain of $10,000 on December 29, 2001. The settlement date, or date that Mary will receive the proceeds from the stockbroker, is January 2, 2002. Will Mary report the gain on her 2001 or 2002 tax return?

ANSWER

Mary is required to report the gain in the year of the sale (2001). Losses are also recognized in the year of sale.

ADJUSTED NET CAPITAL GAINS (ANCG)

ANCG is NCG without regard to:

1. 28-percent rate gain and
2. unrecaptured section 1250 gain.[39]

The term *28-percent rate gain* is the sum of collectibles gain and section 1202 gain over the sum of collectibles loss, NSTCL and LTCL carried forward from a preceding year.

For many taxpayers, NCG and ANCG will be the same amount. Collectibles gain is explained below. Section 1202 gain refers to the 50% exclusion of net capital gain discussed in Chapter I4 and below. Unrecaptured Sec. 1250 gain which is taxed at a maximum rate of 25% is explained in Chapter I13.

COLLECTIBLES GAIN. As a general rule, gains resulting from the sale of collectibles such as artwork, rugs, antiques, stamps and most coins are not taxed at the lower tax rates of 10% and 20% but may be taxed at a maximum rate of 28%. Recall that NCG is reduced by collectibles gains to determine ANCG.

EXAMPLE I5-50 ▶ Danny, whose tax rate is 36%, purchased Bowling common stock and antique chairs for investment on March 10, 1999. He sells the assets in April of 2001 and has a gain of $8,000 on the sale of the stock and $10,000 on the sale of the antique chairs. His NLTCG is $18,000, and his NCG is $18,000. His ANCG is $8,000 since $10,000 of the NCG is a collectibles gain. His tax on the capital gains is $4,400 [(20% × $8,000) + (28% × $10,000)]. ◀

SEC. 1202 GAIN. As explained in Chapter I4, Sec. 1202 provides that noncorporate taxpayers may exclude 50% of the gain resulting from the sale or exchange of qualified small business stock issued after August 10, 1993, if the stock is held for more than five years. A corporation may have qualified small business stock only if the corporation is a C corporation and at least 80% of the value of its assets must be used in the active conduct of one or more qualified trades or businesses.[40]

Normally, the excluded gain is 50% of any gain resulting from the sale or exchange of qualified small business stock held for more than five years and the remaining half of the gain is taxed at a maximum rate of 28%. However, the excluded gain may be less than 50% of the gain, because the amount of gain that may be excluded by a taxpayer for one corporation is 50% of the lesser of $10,000,000 or ten times the aggregate basis of the

---

[38] Sec. 1(h).
[39] Sec. 1(h)(4).
[40] Sec. 1202.

EXAMPLE I5-51 ▶ Raef purchased $200,000 of newly issued Monona common stock on October 1, 1996. On December 15, 2001, he sells the stock for $3.8 million. He excludes $1.9 million of the gain, and the remaining $1.9 million of gain is Sec. 1202 gain taxed at 28%. ◀

EXAMPLE I5-52 ▶ Matthew, whose tax rate is 31%, has the following capital gains this year:

STCG	$10,000
LTCG (artwork)	12,000
LTCG (stock of AT&T)	17,000
LTCG (qualified small business stock held more than five years)	45,000

ADDITIONAL COMMENT
If Raef's gain in Example 5-51 is $12 million, he excludes $5 million, $5 million of the gain is taxed at 28%, and $2 million is taxed at 20%.

Matthew may exclude $22,500 of the $45,000 Sec. 1202 gain. His NCG is $51,500 ($12,000 + $17,000 + $22,500). His ANCG is $17,000. The increase in his tax is $16,160. [31%($10,000) + 28%($12,000) + 20%($17,000) + 28%($22,500)] ◀

CAPITAL LOSSES

To have a capital loss, one must sell or exchange the capital asset for an amount less than its adjusted basis. As in the case of capital gains, the one-year period is used to determine whether the capital loss is short-term or long-term.

NET SHORT-TERM CAPITAL LOSS. If total STCLs for the tax year exceed total STCGs for that year, the excess is defined as a net short-term capital loss (NSTCL). As indicated above, the NSTCL is first offset against any NLTCG to determine the net capital gain.

If the NSTCL exceeds the NLTCG, the capital loss may be offset, in part, against other income. The NSTCL may be deducted in full (i.e., on a dollar-for-dollar basis) against a noncorporate taxpayer's ordinary income for amounts up to $3,000 in any one year.[41]

EXAMPLE I5-53 ▶ Bob has gross income of $60,000 before considering capital gains and losses. If Bob has a NLTCG of $10,000 and a NSTCL of $15,000, he has $5,000 of NSTCL in excess of NLTCG and may deduct $3,000 of the losses from gross income. Assuming no other deductions for AGI, Bob's AGI is $57,000 ($60,000 − $3,000). ◀

ADDITIONAL COMMENT
A husband and wife filing a joint return may use capital losses carried forward from years when they were single. Also, a divorced couple may use capital losses carried forward from a joint return year to their single returns.

In Example I5-53, $10,000 of the NSTCL is used to offset the $10,000 of NLTCG, and $3,000 of the NSTCL is used to reduce ordinary income. However, $2,000 of the loss is not used. This net capital loss is carried forward for an indefinite number of years.[42] The loss retains its original character and will be treated as a STCL occurring in the subsequent year. If a taxpayer dies with an unused capital loss carryover, it expires.

EXAMPLE I5-54 ▶ Last year, Milt had a NSTCL of $8,000 and a NLTCG of $2,600. The netting of short-term and long-term gains and losses resulted in a $5,400 excess of NSTCL over NLTCG, and $3,000 of this amount was offset against ordinary income. Milt's NSTCL carryforward is $2,400. During the current year he sells a capital asset and generates a STCG of $800. His NSTCL is $1,600 ($2,400 − $800), and the loss is offset against $1,600 of ordinary income. ◀

REAL-WORLD EXAMPLE
In 1975 an amendment was added to a tax bill in the House Ways and Means Committee that would have permitted individuals to take a three-year carryback for capital losses. When *The Wall Street Journal* disclosed that the provision would provide Ross Perot with a $15 million tax break, the amendment was defeated.

NET LONG-TERM CAPITAL LOSS. If total LTCLs for the tax year exceed total LTCGs for the year, the excess is defined as net long-term capital loss (NLTCL). If there is both a NSTCG and a NLTCL, the NLTCL is initially offset against the NSTCG on a dollar-for-dollar basis. If the NLTCL exceeds the NSTCG, the excess is offset against ordinary income on a dollar-for-dollar basis up to $3,000 per year.

EXAMPLE I5-55 ▶ In the current year, Gordon has a NLTCL of $9,000 and a NSTCG of $2,000. He must use $2,000 of the NLTCL to offset the $2,000 NSTCG, and then use $3,000 of the $7,000 ($9,000 − $2,000)

---

[41] Sec. 1211(b). A $1,500 limitation applies to a married individual filing a separate return.

[42] Sec. 1212(b) and Reg. Sec. 1.1212-1(b).

NLTCL to offset $3,000 of ordinary income. Gordon's carryforward of NLTCL is $4,000 [$9,000 − ($2,000 + $3,000)]. This amount is treated as a LTCL in subsequent years.

If an individual has both NSTCL and NLTCL, the NSTCL is offset against ordinary income first, regardless of when the transactions occur during the year.

EXAMPLE I5-56 ▶ In the current year, Beth has a NSTCL of $2,800 and a NLTCL of $2,000. The entire NSTCL is offset initially against $2,800 of ordinary income on a dollar-for-dollar basis. Because capital losses can be offset against only $3,000 of ordinary income, $200 of NLTCL is used to offset $200 ($3,000 − $2,800) of ordinary income. The NLTCL carryover to the next year is $1,800 ($2,000 − $200).

CAPITAL LOSSES APPLIED TO CAPITAL GAINS BY GROUPS. Taxpayers separate their LTCGs and LTCLs into three tax rate groups: (1) 28% group, (2) 25% group, and (3) the 20% group. The 28% group includes capital gains and losses when the capital asset is a collectible held more than one year and half of the gain from the sale of certain small business stock held for more than five years. The 25% group consists of unrecaptured Sec. 1250 gain discussed in Chapter I13, and there are no losses for this group. The 20% or 10% group, depending upon the taxpayer's tax rate, includes capital gains and losses when the holding period is more than one year and the capital asset is not a collectible or Sec. 1202 small business stock.

When a taxpayer has NSTCL and NLTCG, the NSTCL is first offset against NLTCG from the 28% group, then the 25% group and finally the 20% (or 10%) group. This treatment of NSTCL is favorable for taxpayers. Note that a taxpayer could have NLTCLs in one group, except the 25% group, and NLTCGs in another group. A net loss from the 28% group is first offset against gains in the 25% group then net gains in the 20% (or 10%) group. A net loss from the 20% group is first offset against net gains in the 28% group then gains in the 25% group.[43]

EXAMPLE I5-57 ▶ Leroy, whose tax rate is 36%, has NSTCL of $20,000, a $25,000 LTCG from the sale of a rare stamp held 16 months and an $18,000 LTCG from the sale of stock held for three years. The $20,000 NSTCL is offset against $20,000 of the collectibles gain in the 28% group. Leroy's tax liability increases by $5,000 [($5,000 × 28%) + ($18,000 × 20%)]. ◀

EXAMPLE I5-58 ▶ Elizabeth, whose tax rate is 36%, has NSTCG of $40,000, a $30,000 LTCG from the sale of a collectible, a $10,000 LTCG in the 25% group, and a $22,000 LTCL from the sale of stock held for four years. The $22,000 LTCL in the 20% group is first offset against $22,000 of the LTCG in the 28% group. Elizabeth's tax liability increases by $19,140 [($8,000 × 28%) + ($10,000 × 25%) + ($40,000 × 36%)]. ◀

STOP & THINK

Question: Srinija has a salary of $100,000. If she sells a non-personal use asset during the year and has a $40,000 loss, why is it important that the asset not be a capital asset?

Solution: Only $3,000 of a $40,000 capital loss is used as a deduction to reduce her gross income each year. Her AGI is $97,000 if the asset is a capital asset, and she has a $37,000 capital loss carryforward. All of the $40,000 loss is used to reduce her gross income if the asset is not a capital asset and her AGI is $60,000. It is possible that Srinija might not care whether or not the asset is a capital asset if she has capital gains that could be reduced by capital losses. If the asset is a personal-use asset, the loss is not deductible regardless of whether or not it is a capital asset.

TAX TREATMENT FOR NET CAPITAL GAIN. Congress eliminated preferential tax rates on NCG in 1986 but did provide some preferential treatment in 1990 when the maximum rate on NCG was reduced to 28%.[44] However, this tax reduction only bene-

---

[43] Notice 97-59, I.R.B. 1997-45
[44] For years prior to 1990, a myriad of rules have applied. Prior to 1987, noncorporate taxpayers received a deduction from gross income equal to 60% of the taxpayer's net capital gain. For years 1987-1990, net capital gains were subject to tax at ordinary income rates.

fited taxpayers whose tax rate exceeded 28%. The change in 1997 to rates as low as 10% benefits all noncorporate taxpayers if they hold the capital asset for more than one year. The new lower rates should make taxpayers more interested in having capital gain income instead of ordinary income. Investors are likely to have an increased preference for growth stocks as opposed to stocks with high dividends.

Taxpayers who own mutual funds must recognize their share of capital gains even if no distributions are received. Many mutual fund shareholders reinvest their distributions instead of withdrawing assets from the mutual fund. Mutual funds must classify the gains as short-term or long-term, and long-term gains will need to be separated by rate groups. When shareholders of a mutual fund recognize their share of capital gains when no distribution is actually received, the basis for their shares is increased.

EXAMPLE I5-59 ▶ Eunice, whose tax rate is 36%, is a shareholder of Canyon Mutual Fund. The basis for her shares is $23,000. At the end of the current year, she received a statement from Canyon indicating her share of the following: dividend income, $200; STCG, $300; 28-percent rate gain, $1,000; and ANCG of $1,500. The increase in her taxes as a result of her ownership of the mutual shares is $760 [($500 × 36%) + ($1,000 × 28%) + ($1,500 × 20%)]. The basis for her shares of Canyon Mutual Fund is $26,000. ◀

TAX TREATMENT OF CAPITAL GAINS AND LOSSES: CORPORATE TAXPAYERS

Most topics covered in this chapter concerning capital gains and losses, including the classification of an asset as a capital asset, rules for determining holding periods, and the procedure for offsetting capital losses against capital gains, apply to both corporate and noncorporate taxpayers. However, a major difference is that the lower tax rates of 10%, 20%, 25% and 28% on net capital gain for noncorporate taxpayers do not apply to corporations. A second significant difference relates to the treatment of capital losses: Unlike the noncorporate taxpayer, who may offset capital losses against ordinary income up to $3,000, corporations may offset capital losses only against capital gains. Corporate taxpayers may carry capital losses back to each of the three preceding tax years (the earliest of the three tax years first and then to the next two years) and forward for five years to offset capital gains in such years. When a corporate taxpayer carries a loss back to a preceding year or forward to a following year, the loss is treated as a STCL.[45]

EXAMPLE I5-60 ▶ The Peach Corporation has income from operations of $200,000, a NSTCG of $40,000, and a NLTCL of $56,000 during the current year. The $40,000 NSTCG is offset by $40,000 NLTCL. The remaining $16,000 of NSTCL may not be offset against the $200,000 of other income but may be carried back three years and then forward five years to offset capital gains arising in these years. If Peach has NLTCG and/or NSTCG in the previous three years, a refund of taxes paid during those years will be received during the current year. ◀

NEW MAXIMUM RATE ON NET CAPITAL GAIN FOR CORPORATIONS. While the House proposed a reduction in the corporate tax rate on net capital gain, the proposal was rejected although a maximum rate of 35% was created for net capital gain for tax years ending after 1997. Corporations apply a maximum rate of 35% to the corporation's net capital gain.[46] Given the present tax rates for corporations, the existence of the 35% alternative rate for net capital gain will have little benefit.

Topic Review I5-2 summarizes the principal differences in the tax treatment of capital gains and losses for corporate and noncorporate taxpayers.

---

[45] Sec. 1212(a).

[46] Sec. 1201.

Topic Review I5-2

Comparison of Corporate and Noncorporate Taxpayers: Capital Gains and Losses

	NONCORPORATE	CORPORATE
A statutory maximum tax rate applicable to net capital gain	Yes, 10%, 20%, 25% and 28%	Yes, but rate is 35%
Offset of net capital losses against ordinary income	Yes, up to $3,000	No
Carryback of capital losses	No	Yes, three years as STCLs
Carryforward of capital losses	Yes, indefinitely	Yes, five years as STCLs

STOP & THINK

Question: Most taxpayers believe that if they have a long-term capital gain, their income taxes will be less on the LTCG than on their other ordinary income. Explain why all taxpayers do not have a tax savings from a net capital gain.

Solution: Noncorporate taxpayers whose marginal tax rate is 28% or less will not have a reduction in taxes if the LTCG is gain from the sale of a collectible, or the recognized half of the gain from the sale of qualified small business stock under Sec. 1202. Also, corporations are not eligible for the lower rates available to noncorporate taxpayers and pay taxes on NLTCG at the same rate as ordinary income except the rate may not exceed 35% on the NLTCG.

SALE OR EXCHANGE

OBJECTIVE 6

Recognize when a sale or exchange has occurred

As previously indicated, capital gains and losses result from the sale or exchange of capital assets. Although Sec. 1222 does not define a sale or an exchange, a **sale** is generally considered to be a transaction where one receives cash or the equivalent of cash, including the assumption of one's debt. An **exchange** is a transaction where one receives a reciprocal transfer of property, as distinguished from a transaction where one receives only cash or a cash equivalent.[47]

EXAMPLE I5-61 ▶ Two years ago, Bart acquired 100 shares of Alaska Corporation common stock for $12,000 to hold as an investment. Bart sells 50 shares of the stock to Sandy for $10,000 and transfers the other 50 shares to Gail in exchange for land that has a $10,000 FMV. In each transaction, Bart realizes a $4,000 ($10,000 − $6,000) LTCG due to the sale or exchange of a capital asset. The transfer to Sandy qualifies as a sale, and the transfer to Gail qualifies as an exchange. ◀

TYPICAL MISCONCEPTION

Because the carryover for net operating losses is 20 years, it is sometimes erroneously assumed that the carryover for corporate capital losses is also 20 years instead of five years.

To qualify as a sale or exchange, the transaction must be bona fide. Transactions between related parties such as family members are closely scrutinized. For example, a sale of property on credit to a relative may be a disguised gift if there is no intention of collecting the debt. If this is the case, a subsequent bad debt deduction due to the debt's worthlessness is disallowed. In some instances, the Code specifically states that a particular transaction or event either qualifies or does not qualify for sale or exchange treatment. For example, the holder of an option who fails to exercise such an option treats the lapse of the option as a sale or exchange.[48] However, abandonment of property is generally not deemed to be a sale or exchange.[49]

---

[47] Reg. Sec. 1.1002-1(d).
[48] Sec. 1234(b) and Reg. Sec. 1.1234-1(b).
[49] Reg. Secs. 1.165-2 and 1.167(a)-8.

WORTHLESS SECURITIES

ADDITIONAL COMMENT
The worthlessness of a security is treated as a sale or exchange so that the taxpayer is not forced to arrange for someone to buy the security for a token amount.

If a security that is a capital asset becomes worthless during the year, Sec. 165(g)(1) specifies that any loss is treated as a loss from the sale or exchange of a capital asset on the last day of the tax year. The term includes stock, a stock option, and "a bond, debenture, note or certificate, or other evidence of indebtedness, issued by a corporation or by a government or political division thereof, with interest coupons or in registered form."[50] Whether a security has become worthless during the year is a question of fact, and the taxpayer has the burden of proof to show evidence of worthlessness.[51]

EXAMPLE I5-62 ▶ Charlotte purchased $40,000 of bonds issued by the Jet Corporation in March 2000. In February 2001, Jet is declared bankrupt, and its bonds are worthless. Charlotte has a LTCL of $40,000 because the bonds have become worthless and are deemed to have been sold on the last day of 2001. The more-than-one-year holding period requirement is satisfied by the last day of 2001. ◀

REAL-WORLD EXAMPLE
A corporation owned 76% of the stock of a Mexican company. The corporation later acquired the remaining 24% of the stock, allegedly for the purpose of avoiding interference by minority shareholders. Later the corporation claimed an ordinary loss on the worthless Mexican stock because it owned at least 80% of the stock. The Court treated the loss as a capital loss because the acquisition of the remaining stock was without a business purpose. *Hunter Mfg. Co.*, 21 T.C. 424 (1953).

SECURITIES IN AFFILIATED CORPORATIONS. If the security that becomes worthless is a security in a domestic affiliated corporation owned by a corporate taxpayer, the worthless security is not considered a capital asset. Thus, a corporate taxpayer's loss due to owning worthless securities in an affiliated corporation is treated as an ordinary loss. Because capital losses are of only limited benefit to corporate taxpayers, the classification of the loss as ordinary is preferable.

To qualify as an affiliated corporation, the parent corporation must own at least 80% of the voting power of all classes of stock and at least 80% of each class of nonvoting stock. The subsidiary corporation must be engaged in the active conduct of an operating business as opposed to being a passive investment company (i.e., more than 90% of its aggregate gross receipts must be from sources other than passive types of income such as royalties, dividends, and interest).[52]

EXAMPLE I5-63 ▶ Ace Corporation owns 80% of all classes of stock issued by the same Jet Corporation described in Example I5-62. Jet Corporation is actively engaged in an operating business and has no income from passive investments before being declared bankrupt. Ace's loss from its worthless stock investment is an ordinary loss instead of a capital loss because Jet is an affiliated corporation. Ace owns at least 80% of all classes of Jet's stock and more than 90% of Jet's gross receipts are from sources other than passive types of income. ◀

RETIREMENT OF DEBT INSTRUMENTS

Generally, the collection of a debt is not a sale or an exchange. However, if a debt instrument is retired, amounts received by the holder are treated as being received in an exchange.[53] Debt instruments include bonds, debentures, notes, certificates, and other evidences of indebtedness.

EXAMPLE I5-64 ▶ In 1996 the Rocket Corporation issued $50,000 of five-year, interest-bearing bonds that were purchased by Elaine as an investment for $49,800. Elaine receives $50,000 at maturity in 2001. Retirement of the debt instrument is an exchange, and the $200 gain is a LTCG.[54] ◀

Although Congress has provided that retirements of debt instruments are treated as exchanges, Congress is not willing to allow taxpayers to convert large amounts of potential ordinary interest income into capital gain by purchasing debt instruments at a substantial discount. As illustrated in Example I5-64, a small amount of bond discount is sometimes converted to capital gain. However, if the discount is large enough to be classified as original issue discount, the discount must be amortized and included in gross income for each day the debt instrument is held. Original issue discount (OID) is defined as "the excess (if any) of the stated redemption price at maturity over the issue price.[55]

---

[50] Sec. 165(g)(2).
[51] *Minnie K. Young v. CIR*, 28 AFTR 365, 41-2 USTC ¶9744 (2nd Cir., 1941).
[52] Sec. 165(g)(3).
[53] Sec. 1271(a).
[54] If Rocket Corporation issued the bonds with the intention of calling the bonds before maturity Sec. 1271(a)(2) treats the gain as ordinary income.
[55] Sec. 1273(a)(1).

EXAMPLE I5-65 ▶ On January 1, 2001, Connie purchases $100,000 of the City Corporation's newly issued bonds for $85,000. The bonds mature in 20 years. In 2001 and in subsequent years Connie must annually recognize as interest income a portion of the $15,000 of OID. ◀

The OID is considered to be zero if the amount of discount "is less than ¼ of 1% of the stated redemption price at maturity, multiplied by the number of complete years to maturity."[56] In Example I5-64, the $200 discount is not OID because it is less than $625 (0.0025 × $50,000 × 5 years). If Connie pays more than $95,000 for the bonds in Example I5-65, the OID is zero.

ADDITIONAL COMMENT
Two different types of bonds are sold at a discount: original issue discount (OID) bonds and market discount bonds. OID bonds are issued at a discount, whereas market discount bonds have market discount resulting from a rise in interest rates after the issuance of the bonds.

ORIGINAL ISSUE DISCOUNT. Instead of spreading the OID ratably over the life of the bond, amortization of the discount is based on an interest amortization method. This method is called the **constant interest rate method**. The total amount of interest income is determined by multiplying the interest yield to maturity by the adjusted issue price. With this method of amortizing the discount, the amount of OID amortized increases for each year the bond is held. In Example I5-65, Connie recognizes a larger amount of interest income in 2002 than in 2001 due to amortization of the OID.

The daily portion of the OID for any accrual period is "determined by allocating to each day in any accrual period its ratable portion to the increase during such accrual period in the adjusted issue price of the debt instrument."[57] The increase in the adjusted issue price for any accrual period is shown below.

REAL-WORLD EXAMPLE
Time Warner has issued zero coupon bonds, which are a type of OID bonds. These bonds mature in year 2013 and in late 2000 traded at 108.

$$\text{Increase in the adjusted issue price} = \left[\text{Adjusted issue price at the beginning of the accrual period} \times \text{Yield to maturity} \right] - \text{Interest payments during the accrual period}$$

EXAMPLE I5-66 ▶ On June 30, 2001, Fred purchases a 10%, $10,000 corporate bond for $9,264. The bond is issued on June 30, 2001, and matures in five years. Interest is paid semiannually, and the effective yield to maturity is 12% compounded semiannually. In 2001, Fred recognizes interest income of $556, as illustrated in Table I5-1. The adjusted issue price as of January 1, 2002 is $9,320. This is the sum of the issue price plus any amounts of OID includible in the income of any holder since the date of issue. ◀

KEY POINT
The owner of an OID bond is normally required to accrue interest income each year.

If a debt instrument is sold or exchanged before maturity, part of the original issue discount is included in the seller's income. The amount to be included depends on the number of days the debt instrument is owned by the seller within the accrual period.

EXAMPLE I5-67 ▶ Assume the same facts as in Example I5-66, except that Fred sells the corporate bond to Carolyn on February 24, 2003 (the 55th day in the accrual period). Fred must include $20 [(55 days ÷ 181 days in the accrual period) × $67] of accrued interest for the period of January 1, 2003 to February 24, 2003 in income for 2003. Fred's basis for the bond increases by $20. Thus, his basis for determining a gain or loss is $9,462 ($9,442 + $20). ◀

MARKET DISCOUNT BONDS PURCHASED AFTER APRIL 30, 1993. The sale or exchange of a market discount bond may result in part or all of the gain being classified as ordinary income. The Revenue Reconciliation Act of 1993 substantially increased the number of bonds subject to the market discount provisions.[58] A market discount bond is a bond that is acquired in the bond market at a discount. Market discount is the excess of the stated redemption price of the bond at maturity over the taxpayer's basis for such bond immediately after it is acquired.

---

[56] Sec. 1273(a)(3).
[57] Sec. 1272(a)(3).
[58] Ordinary income treatment for accrued market discount does not apply to owners of taxable market discount bonds issued on or before July 18, 1984 if the bonds were acquired before May 1, 1993. Owners of tax-exempt bonds are not required to accrue market discount if the bonds were acquired before May 1, 1993 (regardless of the issue date).

TABLE I5-1
Computation for Interest Income in Examples I5-66 and I5-67

	Interest Received (1)	Amortization of Original Issue Discount (2)	Interest Income (3) = (1) + (2)	Taxpayer's Basis for the Bond
6-30-01				$ 9,264
12-31-01	$ 500	$ 56[a]	$ 556	9,320[b]
6-30-02	500	59	559	9,379
12-31-02	500	63	563	9,442
6-30-03	500	67	567	9,509
12-31-03	500	71	571	9,580
6-30-04	500	75	575	9,655
12-31-04	500	79	579	9,734
6-30-05	500	84	584	9,818
12-31-05	500	89	589	9,907
6-30-06	500	93[c]	593	10,000
	$5,000	$736	$5,736	

[a] 6% × $9,264 − $500 = $56.
[b] $9,264 + $56 = $9,320.
[c] This figure is adjusted for rounding.

EXAMPLE I5-68 ▶ On January 1, Stephano purchased $100,000 of 8%, 20-year bonds for $82,000. The bonds were issued at par by the Solar Corporation two years ago on January 1. The bonds are market discount bonds. ◀

Similar to original issue discount, there is a de minimis rule for determining market discount. Market discount is zero if the discount is less than ¼ of 1% of the stated redemption price of the bond at maturity multiplied by the number of complete years to maturity.[59] If Stephano had paid $95,500 or more for the Solar Corporation bonds in Example I5-68, the bonds would not be market discount bonds.[60]

Gain realized on disposition of the market discount bond is ordinary income to the extent of the accrued market discount.[61] The ratable accrual method (straight line method computed on a daily basis) is used to determine the amount of the accrued market discount recognized as ordinary income.[62] The market discount is allocated on the basis of the number of days the taxpayer held the bond relative to the number of days between the acquisition date and maturity date.

EXAMPLE I5-69 ▶ Assume the same facts as in Example I5-68 except that Stephano sells the bonds to Kimberly three years later for $86,400. $3,000 (3/18 × $18,000) of the $4,400 ($86,400 − $82,000) gain is ordinary income and the remaining gain is LTCG. If Stephano sold the bond for more than $82,000 but less than $85,000, all of the gain is ordinary income. The entire $18,000 gain is ordinary income if the bond is held to maturity. ◀

ADDITIONAL COMMENT

An option is a contract in which the owner of property agrees with a potential buyer that the potential buyer has the right to buy the property at a fixed price within a certain period of time.

OPTIONS

The owner of an option to buy property may sell the option, exercise the option, or allow the option to expire. If the option is exercised, the amount paid for the option is added to the purchase price of the property acquired.[63]

---

[59] Sec. 1278(a)(2)(C).
[60] $100,000 × .25% × 18 years = $4,500.
[61] Sec. 1276(a)(1).
[62] Sec. 1276(b)(1). A taxpayer may elect to use the constant interest rate method (see Sec. 1276(b)(2)).
[63] Rev. Rul. 58-234, 1958-1 C.B. 279.

Property Transactions: Capital Gains and Losses ▼ Individuals 5-25

EXAMPLE I5-70 ▶ On August 5, 2001, Len pays $600 for an option to acquire 100 shares of Hill Corporation common stock for $80 per share at any time before December 20, 2001. Len exercises the option on November 15, 2001 and pays $8,000 for the stock. Len's basis for the 100 shares of Hill is $8,600 ($8,000 + $600), and the stock's holding period begins on November 15, 2001. ◀

ADDITIONAL COMMENT

The Wall Street Journal publishes daily a list of all call and put options traded on the Chicago Board, the American Stock Exchange, and other exchanges where these options are traded.

When an option is sold or allowed to expire, a sale or exchange has occurred and gain or loss is therefore recognized.[64] The character of the underlying property determines whether the gain or loss from the sale or expiration of the option is capital or ordinary in nature. If the optioned property is a capital asset, the option is treated as a capital asset and capital gain or loss is recognized on the sale or exchange.

EXAMPLE I5-71 ▶ On March 2, 2001, Holly pays $270 for an option to acquire 100 shares of Arkansas Corporation stock for $30 per share at any time before December 10, 2001. As a result of an increase in the market value of the Arkansas stock, the market price of the option increases and Holly sells the option for $600 on August 2, 2001. Because the Arkansas stock is a capital asset in the hands of Holly, the option is a capital asset and she must recognize a STCG of $330 ($600 − $270). ◀

EXAMPLE I5-72 ▶ On October 12, 2000, Mary paid $400 for an option to acquire 100 shares of Portland Corporation stock for $50 per share at any time before February 19, 2001. The price never exceeds $50 before February 19, 2001, and Mary does not exercise the option. Because the option expires, Mary recognizes a STCL of $400 in 2001. ◀

SELF-STUDY QUESTION

Marc writes a call option on stock owned by him and receives $800 on November 1, 2000. The value of the stock declines and the option is allowed to expire on February 15, 2001. When does Marc recognize the $800 gain?

ANSWER

Marc recognizes the gain in 2001 when the transaction is completed.

Transactions in which taxpayers purchase or write options to buy (calls) are quite common today. An investor who anticipates that the market value of a stock or security (e.g., common stock) will increase during the next few months may purchase a call option instead of actually buying the stock. As indicated above, the tax treatment for the option depends on whether the call is exercised, sold, or expires. Someone, however, must be willing to write a call on the stock. Typically an owner of the same stock will write a call option. The writer of the call receives a payment for granting the right to purchase the stock at a fixed price within a given period of time.

If the call is exercised, the writer of the call adds the amount received for the call to the sales price to determine the amount realized.[65] If the call is not exercised within the given time period and thus expires, the writer retains the amount received for the option and recognizes a STCG. The gain is short-term even if the option is written and held for more than a year.

EXAMPLE I5-73 ▶ Sam owns 100 shares of Madison Corporation common stock, which he purchased on May 1, 1994, for $4,000. On November 8, 2001, Sam writes a call that gives Joan, an investor, the option to purchase Sam's 100 shares of Madison stock at $60 per share any time before April 19, 2002. The current market price of Madison stock is $56 per share, and Sam receives $520 for writing the call. If the call is exercised, Sam has a LTCG of $2,520 [($6,000 + $520) − $4,000]. If the call is not exercised and expires on April 19, 2002, Sam must recognize a STCG of $520 in 2002. ◀

EXAMPLE I5-74 ▶ Assume the same facts as in Example I5-73, but consider instead the tax treatment for Joan, the holder of the call. If Joan exercises the call, the basis of the stock is $6,520 ($6,000 + $520). If she does not exercise the call, a STCL of $520 is recognized. If Joan sells the call, the amount received is compared with her basis in the call ($520) to compute Joan's gain or loss. ◀

KEY POINT

A copyright held by a taxpayer whose personal efforts created it is omitted from the definition of a capital asset. However, a patent can be considered a capital asset. In effect, the tax law could be said to favor individuals whose efforts lead to scientific or technological advancement.

PATENTS

To encourage technological progress and to clarify whether a transfer of rights to a patent is capital gain or ordinary income, Congress created Sec. 1235, which allows the holder of a patent to treat the gain resulting from the transfer of all substantial rights in a patent as LTCG. This tax treatment is more favorable than that accorded to producers of artistic, literary, and musical works, who receive ordinary rather than capital gain from the sale of their works.

---

[64] Sec. 1234(a).

[65] Rev. Rul. 58-234, 1958-1 C.B. 279.

REQUIREMENTS FOR CAPITAL GAIN TREATMENT. Section 1235 provides that the transfer of all substantial rights to a patent by the holder of the patent is treated as a sale or exchange of a capital asset that has been held long-term. Thus, long-term capital gain is recognized on the transfer of a patent regardless of its holding period or the character of the asset. Favorable long-term capital gain treatment applies even if the transferor of the patent receives periodic payments contingent on the productivity, use, or disposition of the property transferred.[66]

> **EXAMPLE I5-75** ▶ Clay invents a small utensil used to peel shrimp. He has a patent on the utensil and transfers all rights to the patent to a manufacturing company. Clay receives $100,000 plus 40 cents per utensil sold. Because Sec. 1235 applies, the total of the lump-sum payment and the royalty payments received less his cost basis for the patent is recognized as a LTCG. ◀

SUBSTANTIAL RIGHTS. The principal requirement in Sec. 1235 is that the holder must transfer all substantial rights to the patent. The Regulations state that the circumstances of the whole transaction should be considered in determining whether all substantial rights to a patent have been transferred.[67] All substantial rights have not been transferred if the patent rights of the purchaser are limited geographically within the country of issuance or the rights are for a period less than a patent's remaining life.

> **EXAMPLE I5-76** ▶ Bruce, an inventor, transfers one of his U.S. patents on a manufacturing process to a manufacturer located in Utah. The manufacturer's rights to use the patent are limited to the state of Utah. Because the use of the patent is limited to a geographical area, all substantial rights have not been transferred, and Sec. 1235 does not apply. Payments received for the use of the patent are royalties and taxed as ordinary income. ◀

DEFINITION OF A HOLDER. Long-term capital gain treatment applies only to a holder of the patent rights. For purposes of Sec. 1235, a holder is an individual whose efforts created the property or an individual who acquires the patent rights from the creator for valuable consideration before the property covered by the patent is placed in service or used. Furthermore, the acquiring individual may not be related to the creator or be the creator's employer.

Section 1235 may not be used by corporate taxpayers because corporations are not permitted to be classified as holders. Although a partnership is not permitted to be a holder, individual partners may qualify as holders to the extent of the partner's interest in the patent owned by the partnership.

> **EXAMPLE I5-77** ▶ Joy purchases a patent from Martin, whose efforts created the patent. The purchase occurs before the property is placed in service or used. Joy and Martin are unrelated individuals, and Joy is not Martin's employer. For purposes of Sec. 1235, both Joy and Martin qualify as holders. ◀

ADDITIONAL COMMENT
The scope of Sec. 1253 is very broad. A franchise "includes an agreement which gives one of the parties to the agreement the right to distribute, sell, or provide goods, services, or facilities within a specified area."

REAL-WORLD EXAMPLE
Shaquille O'Neal, the NBA star of the Orlando Magic, has obtained a trademark on his nickname, Shaq. The trademark covers nearly 200 products including athletic shoes, cake decorations, bathroom tissue, bathtub toys, and kites.

FRANCHISES, TRADEMARKS, AND TRADE NAMES

Before the enactment of Sec. 1253, significant uncertainty existed as to whether the transfer of a franchise, trademark, or trade name should be treated as a sale or exchange or as a licensing agreement. If the transfer is tantamount to a sale of the property, payments received should be treated by the transferor as a return of capital and capital gain, and the transferee should be required to capitalize and amortize such payments. However, if the transfer represents a licensing agreement, the transferor should recognize ordinary income and the transferee should receive an ordinary deduction for such payments.

Section 1253, which applies to the granting of a franchise, trademark, or trade name, as well as renewals and transfers to third parties, attempts to resolve the uncertainty by stating, "A transfer of a franchise, trademark, or trade name shall not be treated as a sale or exchange of a capital asset if the transferor retains any significant power, right, or continuing interest with respect to the subject matter of the franchise, trademark, or trade name."[68]

---

[66] Sec. 1235(a).
[67] Reg. Sec. 1.1235-2(b).
[68] Sec. 1253(a). Section 1253(e) prevents the basic Sec. 1253 rules from applying to the transfer of a professional sports franchise.

The IRC provides examples of some rights that are to be considered a "significant power, right, or continuing interest."[69] These rights include the right to

- Disapprove of any assignment.
- Terminate the agreement at will.
- Prescribe standards of quality for products, product services, and facilities.
- Require the exclusive selling or advertising of the transferor's products or services.
- Require the transferee to purchase substantially all of its supplies and equipment from the transferor.

If the transferor does not retain any significant power, right, or continuing interest in the property, the transferor treats the transfer as a sale of the franchise and has the benefits of capital gain treatment. However, any amounts received that are contingent on the productivity, use, or disposition of such property must be treated as ordinary income by the transferor.

EXAMPLE I5-78 ▶ Rose, who owns a franchise with a basis of $100,000, transfers the franchise to Ruth and retains no significant power, right, or continuing interest. Rose receives a $250,000 down payment when the agreement is signed and annual payments for five years equal to 10% of all sales in excess of $2,000,000. Rose has a capital gain of $150,000 with respect to the initial payment, but all of the payments received during the next five years will be ordinary income because they are contingent payments. ◀

Under Sec. 1253, the transferee may deduct payments that are contingent on the productivity, use, or disposition of such property as business expenses. Generally, other payments are capitalized and amortized over a period of 15 years.[70] In practice, payments received for the transfer of a franchise are generally treated as ordinary income to the transferor and are deductible by the transferee because in most franchise agreements the transferor desires to maintain significant powers, rights, or continuing interests in the franchise operation. Also, in many instances the payments are, in part, predicated on the success of the franchised business and are, therefore, established as contingent payments.

REAL-WORLD EXAMPLE
A taxpayer sold a building with the purchaser paying $500,000 and the lessee of the building paying $60,000 under a separate agreement to cancel the lease. The $60,000 was treated as ordinary income because no "sale or exchange" of the property occurred in return for the lessee's $60,000 payment. *Gary Gurvey v. U.S.*, 57 AFTR 2d. 86-1062, 86-1 USTC ¶9260 (D.C. Ill., 1986).

LEASE CANCELLATION PAYMENTS

A lease arrangement may be terminated before the lease period expires, and a lease cancellation payment may be made as consideration for the other party's agreement to terminate the lease. Either a lessor or a lessee may receive such a payment because the payment is normally made by the person who wants to cancel the lease. The tax treatment may differ significantly depending on which party is the recipient.

PAYMENTS RECEIVED BY LESSOR. The Supreme Court has ruled that lease cancellation payments received by a lessor are treated as ordinary income on the basis that the payments represent a substitute for rent.[71] Lease cancellation payments are included in the lessor's income in the year received, even if the lessor uses an accrual method.[72]

PAYMENTS RECEIVED BY LESSEE. Payments received by a lessee for canceling a lease are considered amounts received in exchange for the lease.[73] If the lease is a capital asset, any gain or loss is a capital gain or loss.

EXAMPLE I5-79 ▶ Jim has a three-year lease on a house used as his personal residence. The lessor has an opportunity to sell the house and has agreed to pay $1,000 to Jim to cancel the lease. Assuming that Jim has no basis in the lease, the gain of $1,000 is capital gain because the lease is a capital asset. ◀

---

[69] Sec. 1253(b)(2).
[70] Sec. 197(a).
[71] *Walter M. Hort v. CIR*, 25 AFTR 1207, 41-1 USTC ¶9354 (USSC, 1941).
[72] *Farrelly-Walsh, Inc.*, 13 B.T.A. 923 (1928).
[73] Sec. 1241.

Holding Period

OBJECTIVE 7

Determine the holding period for an asset when a sale or disposition occurs

The length of time an asset is held before it is disposed of (i.e., the *holding period*) is an important factor in determining whether any gain or loss resulting from the disposition of a capital asset is treated as long-term or short-term. To be classified as a long-term capital gain or loss, the capital asset must be held more than one year.[74] To determine the holding period, the day of acquisition is excluded and the disposal date is included.[75]

If the date of disposition is the same date as the date of acquisition, but a year later, the asset is considered to have been held for only one year. If the property is held for an additional day, the holding period is more than one year.

EXAMPLE I5-80 ▶ Arnie purchased a capital asset on April 20, 2000, and sells the asset at a gain on April 21, 2001. The gain is classified as a LTCG. If the asset is sold on or before April 20, 2001, the gain is a STCG. ◀

ADDITIONAL COMMENT

When determining the holding period for marketable securities, it is important to use the "trade" dates, not the "settlement" dates.

The fact that all months do not have the same number of days is not a factor in determining the one-year period. Acquisitions made on the last day of any month must be held until the first day of the thirteenth subsequent month in order to have been held for more than one year.

EXAMPLE I5-81 ▶ Alford sells stock held as an investment and recognizes a gain, and Sec. 1202 does not apply. If the capital asset was purchased on May 31, 2000, the gain is LTCG subject to the 20% or 10% rate if the asset is sold on or after June 1, 2001. If sold on or before May 31, 2001, the new 20% and 10% rates do not apply. ◀

ADDITIONAL COMMENT

One June 1, 1995, the Securities and Exchange Commission adopted a new set of rules that will require investors who purchase or sell securities to deliver the funds to pay for the securities or deliver the certificates to be sold within three days of when the order is placed. Formerly, investors had five days to deliver funds or certificates.

HOLDING PERIOD OF MORE THAN FIVE YEARS. Even lower rates may apply if the capital asset is sold after December 31, 2000, when the holding period is more than five years. The maximum rate is 18% instead of 20% for taxpayers whose tax rate exceeds 15%, and taxpayers whose tax rate is 15% have a rate of 8% instead of 10%.[76]

The beginning of the five-year holding period differs depending on the taxpayer's normal tax rate. If the taxpayer's tax rate is more than 15%, the lower 18% rate applies only if the asset is acquired after December 31, 2000, and the asset's holding period is more than five years. These taxpayers may elect to have property acquired before 2001 treated as acquired on January 1, 2001, if they elect to have a deemed sale of the asset. Any appreciation as of January 1, 2001, is recognized as a gain and taxes on the gain must be paid. Any loss from the deemed sale is not recognized.

EXAMPLE I5-82 ▶ Judd, whose tax rate is at least 28%, purchased a capital asset on June 22, 2000, for $10,000. On January 1, 2001, the asset's FMV is $12,000. If Judd sells the asset on July 13, 2006, for $50,000, the $40,000 gain is taxed at 20%. If Judd elects to recognize a $2,000 gain on January 1, 2001, his $38,000 gain in 2006 is taxed at 18%. ◀

If the taxpayer's tax rate is 15%, the capital asset may be purchased before January 1, 2001, and the holding period for the five-year requirement starts when the asset is purchased. If Judd's tax rate in the above example is 15%, the gain is taxed at 8% if the asset is sold on or after June 23, 2005.

PROPERTY RECEIVED AS A GIFT

If a person receives property as a gift and uses the donor's basis to determine the gain or loss from a sale or exchange, the donor's holding period is added to the donee's holding period.[77] In other words, the donee's holding period includes the donor's holding period. If, however, the donee's basis is the FMV of the property on the date of the gift, the donee's holding period starts on the date of the gift. This situation occurs when the FMV

---

[74] Sec. 1222. A six-month holding period was applied to property acquired after June 27, 1984 and before January 1, 1988.
[75] H. M. Hooper, 26 B.T.A. 758 (1932), and Rev. Rul. 70-598, 1970-2 C.B. 168.
[76] Sec. 1(h)(2).
[77] Sec. 1223(1) and Reg. Sec. 1.1223-1(b).

is less than the donor's basis on the date of the gift and the property is subsequently sold at a loss.

> **EXAMPLE I5-83** ▶ Cindy receives a capital asset as a gift from Marc on July 4, 2001, when the asset has a $4,000 FMV. Marc acquired the property on April 12, 2001, for $3,400. If Cindy sells the asset after April 12, 2002, any gain or loss is LTCG or LTCL. Cindy's basis is the donor's cost because the FMV of the property is higher than the donor's basis on the date of the gift. Because Cindy takes Marc's basis, Marc's holding period is tacked on. ◀

> **EXAMPLE I5-84** ▶ Roy receives a capital asset as a gift from Diane on September 12, 2001, when the asset has a $6,000 FMV. Diane acquired the asset on July 1, 2000, for $6,500. If the asset is sold at a gain (i.e., for more than $6,500), Roy's holding period starts on July 1, 2000, the date when Diane acquired the property, because the donor's basis of $6,500 is used by Roy to compute the gain. If the asset is sold at a loss (i.e., for less than $6,000), Roy's holding period does not start until the date of the gift—September 12, 2001—because Roy's basis is the $6,000 FMV. The FMV is used to compute the loss because it is less than the donor's basis on the date of the gift. ◀

ADDITIONAL COMMENT
The provision permitting the holding period of property received from a decedent to be deemed to be long-term is a rule of convenience. It is not necessary to try to determine when the decedent actually acquired the property.

PROPERTY RECEIVED FROM A DECEDENT

The holding period of property received from a decedent is always deemed to be long-term. If the person who receives the property from the decedent sells the property within one year after the decedent's death, the property is considered to be held for more than one year.[78]

> **EXAMPLE I5-85** ▶ The executor of Paul's estate sells certain securities for $41,000 on September 2, 2001, which are valued in the estate at their FMV of $40,000 on June 5, 2002, the date of Paul's death. The estate has a LTCG of $1,000 because the securities are considered to have been held long-term. The gain is taxed at 20% or 10%. ◀

NONTAXABLE EXCHANGES

ADDITIONAL COMMENT
The like-kind exchange rules under Sec. 1031 allow taxpayers to trade certain types of business and investment properties with no tax consequences arising from the exchange.

In a nontaxable exchange, the basis of the property received is determined by taking into account the basis of the property given in the exchange. If the properties are capital assets or Sec. 1231 assets, the holding period of the property received includes the holding period of the surrendered property.[79] In essence, the holding period of the property given up in a tax-free exchange is tacked on to the holding period of the property received in the exchange.

RECEIPT OF NONTAXABLE STOCK DIVIDENDS AND STOCK RIGHTS

If a shareholder receives nontaxable stock dividends or stock rights, the holding period of the stock received as a dividend or the stock rights received includes the holding period for the stock owned by the shareholder.[80] However, if the stock rights are exercised, the holding period for the stock purchased begins with the date of exercise.

> **EXAMPLE I5-86** ▶ As a result of owning Circle Corporation stock acquired three years ago, Paula receives nontaxable stock rights on June 5, 2001. Any gain or loss on the sale of the rights is long-term, regardless of whether any basis is allocated to the rights, because the holding period of the rights includes the holding period of the stock. ◀

> **EXAMPLE I5-87** ▶ Assume the same facts as in Example I5-86, except that the stock rights are exercised on August 20, 2001. The holding period for the newly acquired Circle stock begins on the date of exercise. ◀

STOP & THINK *Question:* Carter owns 500 shares of Okoboji, Inc. (current market price of $310) with a basis of $101,500 acquired three years ago. In May of the current year, she receives 500 stock rights and exercises those rights that entitle her to purchase 500 shares of Okoboji at $300 per share. The current market price of the stock right is $40 per right. She plans

---
[78] Sec. 1223(11).
[79] Sec. 1223(1).
[80] Sec. 1223(5) and Reg. Sec. 1.1223-1(e).

to sell the 500 shares obtained by exercising the stock rights in January when she expects the market price to be $350 per share. Why should she elect to allocate basis to the stock rights?

Solution: If she does not allocate basis, her STCG will be $25,000 ($175,000 − $150,000). If she allocates basis to the stock rights, the basis of the 500 shares obtained when she exercises the rights is $161,600 ($150,000 + $16,100), and her STCG will be $13,400 ($175,000 − $161,600). Note that Carter might benefit by waiting a few months before selling because the gain might then be LTCG. She could also sell the original 500 shares and have a LTCG of $73,500 or $85,100.

PREFERENTIAL TREATMENT FOR NET CAPITAL GAINS

HISTORICAL NOTE

In part the preferential treatment of net capital gains was repealed in the Tax Reform Act of 1986 because Congress believed that the reduction of individual tax rates on such forms of capital income as business profits, interest, dividends, and short-term capital gains eliminated the need for a reduced rate for net capital gains.

Preferential treatment for capital gains was first created by the Revenue Act of 1921, which became effective on January 1, 1922. Despite almost continuous controversy concerning the need for preferential treatment, some form of preferential treatment for capital gains has existed since 1922. The range of controversy concerning the need for preferential tax treatment for capital gains is wide. Some maintain that capital gains do not represent income and should not be taxed, whereas others maintain that capital gains are no different from any other type of income and should be taxed accordingly.[81] A few of the most common arguments are discussed below.

MOBILITY OF CAPITAL

Without some form of preferential treatment, taxpayers who own appreciated capital assets may be unwilling to sell or exchange the asset if high tax rates exist, despite the presence of more attractive investment opportunities. In essence, the taxpayer may be "locked in" to holding an appreciated capital asset instead of shifting resources to more profitable investments.

EXAMPLE I5-88 ▶ Carmen owns Missouri Corporation stock with a $4,000 basis and a $20,000 FMV. She anticipates that the future after-tax annual return will be 10% on the Missouri stock and 12% on Kansas Corporation stock that has a similar level of risk. Assume her marginal tax rate is 50% (without consideration of favorable capital gain rates or deductions). Without preferential treatment of capital gains, Carmen will have to pay a tax of $8,000 ($16,000 × 0.50) on the sale of the Missouri stock and will have only $12,000 ($20,000 − $8,000) to invest in the Kansas stock. With a 12% return, she will receive an investment return of only $1,440 ($12,000 × 0.12), as compared with $2,000 ($20,000 × 0.10) if she maintains the investment in the Missouri stock. ◀

The "locked-in" effect is reduced if tax rates are lowered. The justification for eliminating the special 60% deduction for long-term capital gains after 1986 was due to a significant reduction in the top marginal tax rate applicable to ordinary income.

MITIGATION OF THE EFFECTS OF INFLATION AND THE PROGRESSIVE TAX SYSTEM

Because the tax laws do not generally reflect the effect of changes in purchasing power due to inflation, the sale or exchange of a capital asset may produce inequitable results. In fact, taxes may have to be paid even where a transaction results in an inflation-adjusted loss.

EXAMPLE I5-89 ▶ Beverly purchased a capital asset nine years ago for $100,000. If the asset is sold today for $180,000 and the general price level has increased by 100% during the nine-year period, Beverly will have a taxable gain of $80,000, despite suffering an inflation-adjusted loss of $20,000 [$180,000 sale price − ($100,000 × 200%)]. ◀

---

[81] Walter J. Blum, "A Handy Summary of the Capital Gains Argument," *Taxes—The Tax Magazine*, 35 (April 1957), pp. 247–66.

ADDITIONAL COMMENT

The American Assembly at Columbia University, in its final report on *Reforming and Simplifying the Federal Tax System* issued in 1985, recommends that capital gains be taxed as ordinary income if they are adjusted for inflation.

With a progressive tax system, the failure to adjust for inflation creates an even greater distortion. However, it should be noted that this distortion applies to all assets, not just capital assets.

LOWER THE COST OF CAPITAL

By reducing the tax rate on capital gains, investors are more willing to provide businesses with capital and the cost of capital is reduced. A lower cost of capital encourages capital formation to create more jobs and improve our competitive position in the global economy. Reducing the cost of capital is particularly important for the formation and growth of small business.

TAX PLANNING CONSIDERATIONS

SELECTION OF PROPERTY TO TRANSFER BY GIFT

Many tax reasons exist for making gifts of property, although the donor may incur a gift tax liability if the gift is a taxable gift. For example, taxpayers may give income-producing property to a taxpayer subject to a lower tax rate, or property expected to appreciate in the future may be given away to reduce estate taxes. Individuals may annually give property of $10,000 or less to a donee without making a taxable gift.[82]

EXAMPLE I5-90 ▶ Maya, who is single, owns marketable securities with a $6,200 basis and $10,000 FMV. She makes gifts of the marketable securities to Phil and cash of $10,000 to Roy. Because of the $10,000 annual exclusion per donee, Maya's gifts are not taxable gifts. ◀

EXAMPLE I5-91 ▶ Harry, who is single, makes a gift of land with a $240,000 basis and a $930,000 FMV to Rita. Harry's taxable gift is $920,000 ($930,000 − $10,000), and he incurs a gift tax liability. Rita's basis is $240,000 + 75% of the gift tax paid by Harry [($930,000 − $240,000)/$920,000 = 75%]. ◀

Individuals often reduce future estate taxes by making gifts. By using the annual exclusion, an individual may reduce future estate taxes and avoid the gift tax.

EXAMPLE I5-92 ▶ Christine owns only one asset—cash of $900,000—and has no liabilities. In December of the current year, she gives $10,000 to each of her five grandchildren. Because of the $10,000 annual exclusion per donee, Christine's gifts are not taxable gifts. By making the gifts, she reduces her potential gross estate by $50,000 (5 × $10,000). ◀

ADDITIONAL COMMENT

A husband and wife can each make a $10,000 gift to their daughter, enabling her to receive a total of $20,000 annually without the parents incurring a gift tax.

The selection of which property to give is important if one is attempting to reduce future estate taxes. It is generally preferable to make gifts of properties that are expected to significantly increase in value during the postgift period before the donor's death. Any increases in value after the date of the gift are not included in the donor's gross estate.

EXAMPLE I5-93 ▶ In 1994, Hal owned Sun Corporation stock with a $100,000 FMV and Union Corporation stock with a $100,000 FMV. Hal expected the Sun stock to increase in value at a moderate rate and the Union stock to increase at a substantial rate. In 1994, Hal made a gift of the Union stock to Dana. Hal's taxable gift in 1994 was $90,000 ($100,000 − $10,000). Hal dies in the current year when the FMVs of the Sun and Union stocks are $180,000 and $425,000, respectively. The postgift appreciation of $325,000 ($425,000 − $100,000) is not included in Hal's gross estate. By giving the Union stock instead of the Sun stock in 1994, Hal reduces his gross estate by $245,000. ◀

Gifts are often made for income tax purposes to shift income to other family members who are in a lower income tax bracket than the donor.

---

[82] Sec. 2503(b).

EXAMPLE I5-94 ▶ In 2001, Anne has a marginal tax rate of 28% and owns Atlantic Corporation bonds, which have a $5,000 basis and $8,000 FMV. The bonds pay interest of $900 per year. If Anne gives the bonds to her dependent child, the interest income is shifted to the child. If the child has no other income, the child's taxable income is $150 ($900 − $750 standard deduction), and the child's marginal tax rate is 15%. The gift results in an annual income tax savings to the family unit of $229.50 [(0.28 × $900) − (0.15 × $150)]. The rate of tax that is imposed may be the parent's rate (see Chapter I2) if the child is less than 14 years old and has net unearned income in excess of $1,500.

In addition to shifting the interest income, Anne has also shifted a potential gain of $3,000. The child's basis for the bonds is $5,000 because the donee takes the donor's basis when the FMV of the property at the time of the gift is greater than the donor's basis. No gain is recognized by Anne when the gift is made, and a future sale of the property by the child may be taxed at a lower income tax rate. ◀

Although gifts of appreciated property may generate desirable income tax benefits, it is not usually advantageous to make a gift of property that has an FMV less than its basis because the donee's basis for determining a loss is the FMV. The excess of the donor's basis over the FMV at the time of the gift may never generate any tax benefit for the donor or the donee. Therefore, the donor should sell the asset and make a gift of the proceeds if the loss on the sale is deductible.

EXAMPLE I5-95 ▶ Bob owns Red Corporation stock with an $8,000 basis and $6,000 FMV, which is held as an investment. Bob wishes to make a graduation gift of the marketable securities to Angela, although he expects her to sell the stock and purchase a car. If Angela sells the stock for $6,000, no gain or loss is recognized because her loss basis for the stock is $6,000. In addition, no loss is recognized by Bob on the gift of the stock to Angela. Instead of giving the stock, Bob should sell it to recognize a $2,000 capital loss and then give the proceeds from the sale to Angela. ◀

SELF-STUDY QUESTION
Doug owns IBM Corporation shares, which have a $50,000 FMV and basis of $75,000. Doug makes a deathbed telephone call to his stockbroker and sells the IBM shares. Assuming that Doug is in the 31% bracket and had no other capital gains or losses, calculate the tax savings associated with the sale.

ANSWER
Doug saves $930 ($3,000 × 0.31). It should be noted that the loss is limited to $3,000; if Doug dies, the unused capital loss of $22,000 is lost.

The effect of gift taxes paid by the donor on the donee's basis for property received is another reason why it may be more advantageous to give appreciated property rather than property with an FMV less than its basis. A portion of the gift taxes paid as a result of giving appreciated property is added to the property's basis. However, payment of gift taxes due to the gift of property that has an FMV less than its basis does not result in an increase in the donee's basis.

SELECTION OF PROPERTY TO TRANSFER AT TIME OF DEATH

An integral part of gift and estate planning is the selection of property to be transferred to family members and others both during the taxpayer's lifetime and upon death. Usually, taxpayers find it advantageous to retain highly appreciated property in their estates and transfer such property at death to the taxpayer's heirs because the basis of the inherited property will be increased to its FMV at the date of death (or six months from the date of death if the alternate valuation date is elected). Of course, the impact of gift and estate taxes also play a major role in this planning process.

Investment and business assets that have declined in value (i.e., the FMV is less than the basis) should normally be sold before death to obtain an income tax deduction for the loss. If the property is not sold or otherwise disposed of before death, the basis of the inherited property is reduced to its FMV.

EXAMPLE I5-96 ▶ Paul owns two farms of similar size and quality. Each farm has a $500,000 FMV. Paul's basis for the first farm is $100,000, and his basis for the second farm is $430,000. Eventually, Paul plans for both farms to be owned by Roberta. However, he would like to transfer ownership of one farm now and retain the other farm until his death. Paul should make a gift of the second farm and transfer the first farm to Roberta upon his death because the second farm has appreciated less in value. When Paul dies and devises the first farm to Roberta, she will have a basis for the property equal to its FMV at the date of death even though Paul's basis is only $100,000. ◀

COMPLIANCE AND PROCEDURAL CONSIDERATIONS

DOCUMENTATION OF BASIS

KEY POINT

Many taxpayers do not maintain adequate records that can be used to document the basis of their most important asset, their personal residence. For example, taxpayers can increase the basis of their residence if they have the driveway paved or add a new room or porch.

The importance of being able to determine and document the basis of assets acquired by a taxpayer cannot be overemphasized. Accurate records of asset acquisitions, dispositions, and adjustments to basis are essential. When more than one asset is acquired at the same time, the amount paid must be allocated among the assets acquired based on their relative FMVs. Subsequent adjustments to basis, such as those due to capital improvements and depreciation deductions, must be documented.

Because the basis of property can be determined by reference to another person's basis for that asset (e.g., gifts), taxpayers should be particularly aware of obtaining documentation for that basis at the time of the transfer. In the case of a gift, the taxpayer's basis may be affected by any gift tax paid by the donor. A copy of the donor's gift tax return is useful in documenting the upward adjustment to the donor's basis in determining the donee's basis.

Taxpayers who inherit property may use the decedent's federal Estate Tax Return (Form 706) to determine the FMV at the time of the decedent's death or FMV as of the alternate valuation date. However, the appraised value used for estate tax purposes is only presumptively correct for basis purposes. Although the FMVs used to determine the estate tax are typically used to determine basis, neither the taxpayer nor the IRS is barred from using an FMV for basis purposes that differs from the values used for the estate tax return.[83]

REPORTING OF CAPITAL GAINS AND LOSSES ON SCHEDULE D

Capital gains and losses are reported by individuals on Schedule D, which is then attached to Form 1040. Part I is used to report short-term capital gains and losses, and Part II is used to report long-term capital gains and losses. In Part II, a separate column is provided for NCG that is taxed at 28%. Part III is a summary of Parts I and II, while computation of the tax liability is presented in Part IV. Because of the different rates that may apply to NCG, 35 lines are used to compute the tax. The total tax is then entered on line 40 of page 2 of Form 1040. Because of different rates that apply to NCG, Schedule D is now one of the most difficult forms for taxpayers to prepare.

Capital gains due to installment sales are first reported on a separate form before being included on Schedule D. The taxpayer's share of capital gains and losses from partnerships, S corporations, and fiduciaries is reported in Parts I and II on lines 5 and 12. The carryover of capital losses is also included in Parts I and II on lines 6 and 14.

A filled-in copy of Schedule D is shown in Figure I5-1. It includes the computations relating to the information in Example I5-97.

EXAMPLE I5-97 ▶ Virgil Brady uses the following information to prepare his Schedule D for 2000. He sold 200 shares of Tennis Corporation stock for $13,000 on June 20, 2000. The shares were purchased on October 2, 1999 for $8,700. He has an STCL carryforward from 1999 of $8,200. He sold a piano for $4,000 on May 30, 2000. The piano was purchased on April 12, 1991 for $2,500 and used by his two sons.

Virgil has an STCG of $4,300 that is offset by the $8,200 of STCL carryforward on line 6. His NSTCL of $3,900 ($8,200 − $4,300) is shown on line 7. His $1,500 LTCG as a result of the sale of the piano is on line 8. Because this is his only sale of a capital asset held more than one year, his NLTCG on line 16 is $1,500.

On line 17, the NSTCL of $3,900 and NLTCG of $1,500 are combined and shown on line 17 as $2,400. This net capital loss of $2,400 is recorded on line 18 and is deducted on line 13 of Form 1040. ◀

---

[83] Rev. Rul. 54-97, 1954-1 C.B. 113 and *Achille F. Ford v. U.S.*, 5 AFTR 2d 1157, 60-1 USTC ¶9375 (Ct. Cls., 1960).

SCHEDULE D
(Form 1040)
Department of the Treasury
Internal Revenue Service (99)

Capital Gains and Losses

▶ Attach to Form 1040. ▶ See Instructions for Schedule D (Form 1040).
▶ Use Schedule D-1 for more space to list transactions for lines 1 and 8.

OMB No. 1545-0074

2000

Attachment Sequence No. **12**

Name(s) shown on Form 1040: **Virgil Brady**

Your social security number: **444 44 4444**

Part I — Short-Term Capital Gains and Losses—Assets Held One Year or Less

(a) Description of property (Example: 100 sh. XYZ Co.)	(b) Date acquired (Mo., day, yr.)	(c) Date sold (Mo., day, yr.)	(d) Sales price (see page D-6)	(e) Cost or other basis (see page D-6)	(f) Gain or (loss) Subtract (e) from (d)
1 200 Tennis Corp.	10-2-99	6-20-00	13,000	8,700	4,300

2 Enter your short-term totals, if any, from Schedule D-1, line 2 . . . . **2**

3 **Total short-term sales price amounts.** Add column (d) of lines 1 and 2 . . . . . **3**

4 Short-term gain from Form 6252 and short-term gain or (loss) from Forms 4684, 6781, and 8824 . . . . **4**

5 Net short-term gain or (loss) from partnerships, S corporations, estates, and trusts from Schedule(s) K-1 . . . . **5**

6 Short-term capital loss carryover. Enter the amount, if any, from line 8 of your 1999 Capital Loss Carryover Worksheet **6** (8,200)

7 **Net short-term capital gain or (loss).** Combine column (f) of lines 1 through 6 ▶ **7** (3,900)

Part II — Long-Term Capital Gains and Losses—Assets Held More Than One Year

(a) Description of property (Example: 100 sh. XYZ Co.)	(b) Date acquired (Mo., day, yr.)	(c) Date sold (Mo., day, yr.)	(d) Sales price (see page D-6)	(e) Cost or other basis (see page D-6)	(f) Gain or (loss) Subtract (e) from (d)	(g) 28% rate gain or (loss) * (see instr. below)
8 Piano	4-12-91	5-30-00	4,000	2,500	1,500	

9 Enter your long-term totals, if any, from Schedule D-1, line 9 . . . . **9**

10 **Total long-term sales price amounts.** Add column (d) of lines 8 and 9 . . . . . **10**

11 Gain from Form 4797, Part I; long-term gain from Forms 2439 and 6252; and long-term gain or (loss) from Forms 4684, 6781, and 8824 . . . . **11**

12 Net long-term gain or (loss) from partnerships, S corporations, estates, and trusts from Schedule(s) K-1 . . . . **12**

13 Capital gain distributions. See page D-1 . . . . **13**

14 Long-term capital loss carryover. Enter in both columns (f) and (g) the amount, if any, from line 13 of your 1999 Capital Loss Carryover Worksheet . . . . . **14** ( ) ( )

15 Combine column (g) of lines 8 through 14 . . . . **15**

16 **Net long-term capital gain or (loss).** Combine column (f) of lines 8 through 14 ▶ **16** 1,500

Next: Go to Part III on the back.

* **28% rate gain or loss** includes **all** "collectibles gains and losses" (as defined on page D-6) and up to 50% of the eligible gain on qualified small business stock (see page D-4).

For Paperwork Reduction Act Notice, see Form 1040 instructions. Cat. No. 11338H Schedule D (Form 1040) 2000

FIGURE 15-1 ▶ PARTS I–II OF SCHEDULE D FOR EXAMPLE 15-97

5-34

Schedule D (Form 1040) 2000 — Page 2

Part III — Summary of Parts I and II

17 Combine lines 7 and 16. If a loss, go to line 18. If a gain, enter the gain on Form 1040, line 13 .... **17** (2,400)

Next: Complete Form 1040 through line 39. Then, go to **Part IV** to figure your tax if:
- Both lines 16 and 17 are gains **and**
- Form 1040, line 39, is more than zero.

Otherwise, **stop here.**

18 If line 17 is a loss, enter here and as a (loss) on Form 1040, line 13, the **smaller** of these losses:
- The loss on line 17 **or**
- ($3,000) or, if married filing separately, ($1,500) **18** (2,400)

Next: Skip **Part IV** below. Instead, complete Form 1040 through line 37. Then, complete the **Capital Loss Carryover Worksheet** on page D-6 if:
- The loss on line 17 exceeds the loss on line 18 **or**
- Form 1040, line 37, is a loss.

Part IV — Tax Computation Using Maximum Capital Gains Rates

19 Enter your taxable income from Form 1040, line 39 ....
20 Enter the **smaller** of line 16 or line 17 of Schedule D ....
21 If you are filing Form 4952, enter the amount from Form 4952, line 4e ....
22 Subtract line 21 from line 20. If zero or less, enter -0- ....
23 Combine lines 7 and 15. If zero or less, enter -0- ....
24 Enter the **smaller** of line 15 or line 23, but not less than zero ....
25 Enter your unrecaptured section 1250 gain, if any, from line 17 of the worksheet on page D-8 ....
26 Add lines 24 and 25 ....
27 Subtract line 26 from line 22. If zero or less, enter -0- ....
28 Subtract line 27 from line 19. If zero or less, enter -0- ....
29 Enter the **smaller** of:
- The amount on line 19 **or**
- $26,250 if single; $43,850 if married filing jointly or qualifying widow(er); $21,925 if married filing separately; or $35,150 if head of household

30 Enter the **smaller** of line 28 or line 29 ....
31 Subtract line 22 from line 19. If zero or less, enter -0- ....
32 Enter the **larger** of line 30 or line 31 ....
33 Figure the tax on the amount on line 32. Use the Tax Table or Tax Rate Schedules, whichever applies

Note. If the amounts on lines 29 and 30 are the same, skip lines 34 through 37 and go to line 38.

34 Enter the amount from line 29 ....
35 Enter the amount from line 30 ....
36 Subtract line 35 from line 34 ....
37 Multiply line 36 by 10% (.10) ....

Note. If the amounts on lines 19 and 29 are the same, skip lines 38 through 51 and go to line 52.

38 Enter the **smaller** of line 19 or line 27 ....
39 Enter the amount from line 36 ....
40 Subtract line 39 from line 38 ....
41 Multiply line 40 by 20% (.20) ....

Note. If line 26 is zero or blank, skip lines 42 through 51 and go to line 52.

42 Enter the **smaller** of line 22 or line 25 ....
43 Add lines 22 and 32 ....
44 Enter the amount from line 19 ....
45 Subtract line 44 from line 43. If zero or less, enter -0- ....
46 Subtract line 45 from line 42. If zero or less, enter -0- ....
47 Multiply line 46 by 25% (.25) ....

Note. If line 24 is zero or blank, skip lines 48 through 51 and go to line 52.

48 Enter the amount from line 19 ....
49 Add lines 32, 36, 40, and 46 ....
50 Subtract line 49 from line 48 ....
51 Multiply line 50 by 28% (.28) ....
52 Add lines 33, 37, 41, 47, and 51 ....
53 Figure the tax on the amount on line 19. Use the Tax Table or Tax Rate Schedules, whichever applies
54 **Tax on all taxable income (including capital gains).** Enter the **smaller** of line 52 or line 53 here and on Form 1040, line 40. ....

Schedule D (Form 1040) 2000

FIGURE I5-1 ▶ PARTS III–IV OF SCHEDULE D FOR EXAMPLE I5-90

PROBLEM MATERIALS

DISCUSSION QUESTIONS

I5-1 What problem may exist in determining the amount realized for an investor who exchanges common stock of a publicly traded corporation for a used building? How is the problem likely to be resolved?

I5-2 In 1992 Ellen purchased a house for $60,000 to use as her personal residence. She paid $12,000 and borrowed $48,000 from the local savings and loan company. In 1995 she paid $10,000 to add a room to the house. In 1997 she paid $625 to have the house painted and $800 for built-in bookshelves. As of January 1 of the current year, she has reduced the $48,000 mortgage to $44,300. What is her basis for the house?

I5-3 Vincent pays $20,000 for equipment to use in his trade or business. He pays sales tax of $800 as a result of the purchase. Must the $800 sales tax be capitalized as part of the purchase price?

I5-4 Sergio owns 200 shares of Palm Corporation common stock, purchased during the prior year: 100 shares on July 5, for $9,000; and 100 shares on October 15, for $12,000. When Sergio sells 50 shares for $8,000 on July 18 of the current year, he does not identify the particular shares sold. Determine the amount and character of the gain.

I5-5 On August 5 of the current year, David receives stock of Western Corporation as a gift from his grandfather, who acquired the stock on January 15, 1987. Under what conditions would David's holding period start on
a. August 5 of the current year?
b. January 15, 1987?

I5-6 Jim inherits property from his brother, who dies in March of the current year, when the property has a $980,000 FMV. This property is the only property included in his brother's gross estate and there is a taxable estate. The FMV of the property as of the alternate valuation date is $900,000.
a. Why might the executor of the brother's estate elect to use the alternate valuation date to value the property?
b. Why might Jim prefer the executor to use FMV at time of the death to value the property?
c. If the marginal estate tax rate is 37% and Jim's marginal income tax rate is 28%, which value should the executor use?

I5-7 Martha owns 500 shares of Columbus Corporation common stock at the beginning of the year with a basis of $82,500. During the year, Columbus declares and pays a 10% nontaxable stock dividend. What is her basis for each of the 50 shares received?

I5-8 Mario owns 2,000 shares of Nevada Corporation common stock at the beginning of the year. His basis for the stock is $38,880. During the year, Nevada declares and pays a stock dividend. After the dividend, Mario's basis for each share of stock owned is $18. What is the percentage dividend paid by Nevada?

I5-9 A corporate taxpayer plans to build a $6 million office building during the next 18 months. How must the corporation treat the interest on debt paid or incurred during the production period?

I5-10 Andy owns an appliance store where he has merchandise such as refrigerators for sale. Roger, a bachelor, owns a refrigerator, which he uses in his apartment for personal use. For which individual is the refrigerator a capital asset?

I5-11 Why did the Supreme Court rule in the *Corn Products* case that a gain due to the sale of futures contracts is ordinary income instead of capital gain?

I5-12 When is the gain on the sale or exchange of securities by a dealer in securities classified as capital gain?

I5-13 In 1982, Florence purchased 30 acres of land. She has not used the land for business purposes or made any substantial improvements to the property. During the current year, she subdivides the land into 15 lots and advertises the lots for sale. She sells four lots at a gain.
  a. What is the character of the gain on the sale of the four lots?
  b. Explain how the basis of each lot would be determined.

I5-14 Amy has LTCGs that are taxed at different tax rates, 20%, 25% and 28%. She also has NSTCLs that amount to less than her NLTCG. That procedure for offsetting the NSTCL against the LTCGs is favorable to her. Explain.

I5-15 Four years ago, Susan loaned $7,000 to her friend Joe. During the current year, the $7,000 loan is considered worthless. Explain how Susan should treat the worthless debt for tax purposes.

I5-16 Why did the Supreme Court rule in *Arkansas Best* that the stock of a corporation purchased by the taxpayer to protect the taxpayer's business reputation was a capital asset?

I5-17 The Top Corporation, a producer of lumber, acquires 25% of the stock of the First Corporation, which operates retail lumber yards. Top's primary reason for making the purchase is to obtain a potential customer. Explain how the *Corn Products* case could be used to argue that the stock of First owned by Top is not a capital asset. Explain how the *Arkansas Best* case could be used to argue that the stock of First owned by Top is a capital asset.

I5-18 The effective tax rate on gain of $1,000,000 resulting from the sale of qualified small business stock held more than five years is 14%. Do you agree or disagree? Explain.

I5-19 Nancy and the Minor Corporation own bonds of the East Corporation. Minor Corporation owns 80% of the stock of East Corporation. East Corporation has declared bankruptcy this year, and bondholders will receive only 26% of the face value of the debt. Explain why the loss is a capital loss for Nancy but an ordinary loss for the Minor Corporation.

I5-20 On January 1 of the current year, the Orange Corporation issues $500,000 of 11%, 20-year bonds for $480,000. Determine the amount of original issue discount, if any.

I5-21 Today, Juanita purchases a 15-year, 7% bond of the Sunflower Corporation issued four years ago at par. She purchases the bond as an investment at a discount from the par value. If she sells the bonds two years from now, explain why some or all of the gain may be ordinary income.

I5-22 Judy just obtained a patent on a new product she has developed. Bell Corporation wishes to market the product and will pay 12% of all future sales of the product to Judy. How can she be sure that the payments received will be treated as a long-term capital gain?

I5-23 When is the transferor of a franchise unable to treat the transfer as a sale or an exchange of a capital asset?

I5-24 How does a lessor treat payments received for canceling a lease?

I5-25 What is the first day that an individual could sell a capital asset purchased on March 31, 2001 and have a holding period of more than one year?

I5-26 Phil, a cash-basis taxpayer, sells the following marketable securities, which are capital assets during 2001. Determine whether the gains or losses are long-term or short-term. Also determine the net capital gain and adjusted net capital gain for 2001.

Capital Asset	Basis	Date Acquired	Trade Date in 2001	Sales Price
A	$40,000	Feb. 10, 2000	Aug. 12	$52,000
B	20,000	Dec. 5, 2000	May 2	17,000
C	30,000	Apr. 9, 1999	Dec. 10	37,400

I5-27 How might the current treatment of capital losses discourage an individual investor from purchasing stock of a high-risk, start-up company?

I5-28 An individual taxpayer has realized a $40,000 loss on the sale of an asset that had a holding period of eight months. Explain why the taxpayer may be indifferent as to whether the asset is a capital asset.

I5-29 If Pam transfers an asset to Fred and the asset is subject to a liability that is assumed by Fred, how does Fred's assumption of the liability affect the amount realized by Pam? How does Fred's assumption of the liability affect his basis for the property?

I5-30 Calvin, whose tax rate is 40% is considering two alternative investments on January 1, 19Y1. He can purchase $100,000 of 10% bonds due in five years or purchase $100,000 of Hobbes, Inc. common stock. The bonds are issued at par, pay interest annually on December 31, and mature at the end of five years. Interest received can be reinvested at 10%. Assume that he knows with relative certainty that the value of the stock will increase 8% each year (i.e., the value of the Hobbes stock will be $108,000 at the end of 19Y1) and the interest and principal for the bonds will be paid as scheduled. On December 31, 19Y5, he will sell the stock or receive the bond principal plus the last interest payment. Which alternative should Calvin select if he wants to have the greater amount of money as of January 1, 19Y6? Provide supporting information for your answer.

ISSUE IDENTIFICATION QUESTIONS

I5-31 Acorn Corporation, a company that purchases malt barley from farmers and sells it to brewers, is interested in determining whether a new variety of barley will grow successfully in the Pacific Northwest. The corporation has acquired the seed from Europe and will conduct the experiments with the cooperation of farmers in the area. If the experiments prove successful, Acorn will sell the remaining seed to the farmers. What tax issues should Acorn Corporation consider?

I5-32 Lisa and John are in the business of breeding beavers to produce fur for sale. They recently purchased a pair of breeding beavers for $30,000 from XUN, Inc. and agreed to pay interest at 10% each year for five years. After the five-year period, they could pay the debt by delivering seven beavers to XUN, Inc. provided that each beaver was at least nine months old. Identify the tax issues involved in this situation.

I5-33 Mike, a real estate broker in California, recently inherited a farm from his deceased uncle and plans to sell the farm to the first available buyer. His uncle purchased the property 12 years ago for $600,000. The FMV of the farm on the date of the uncle's death was $500,000. Mike sells the farm for $520,000 seven months after his uncle's death. What tax issues should Mike consider?

I5-34 Sylvia, a dentist with a marginal tax rate of 39.6% and excellent skills as a carpenter, started the construction of a house that she planned to give to her son as a surprise when he returned from Saudia Arabia, where he is serving in the military. She began construction on March 23, 2000, and finished the house on July 10, 2001, at a total cost of $70,000. Her son is expected to be home on September 1, 2001.

On July 30, 2001, Roscoe offered Sylvia $145,000 for the house and Sylvia considered the offer to be so attractive that she accepted it. She decided that she could purchase a suitable home for her son for about $100,000. What tax issues should Sylvia consider?

PROBLEMS

I5-35 *Amount Realized.* Tracy owns a nondepreciable capital asset held for investment. The asset was purchased for $150,000 six years earlier and is now subject to a $45,000 liability. During the current year, Tracy transfers the asset to Tim in exchange for $74,000 cash and a new automobile with a $40,000 FMV to be used by Tracy for personal use; Tim assumes the $45,000 liability. Determine the amount of Tracy's LTCG or LTCL.

I5-36 *Basis of Property Received as a Gift.* Doug receives a duplex as a gift from his uncle. The uncle's basis for the duplex and land is $90,000. At the time of the gift, the land and building have FMVs of $40,000 and $80,000, respectively. No gift tax is paid by Doug's uncle at the time of the gift.
a. To determine gain, what is Doug's basis for the land?
b. To determine gain, what is Doug's basis for the building?
c. Will the basis of the land and building be the same as in Parts a and b for purposes of determining a loss?

I5-37 *Sale of Property Received as a Gift.* During the current year, Stan sells a tract of land for $800,000. The property was received as a gift from Maxine on March 10, 1987, when the property had a $310,000 FMV. The taxable gift was $300,000. Maxine purchased the property on April 12, 1980, for $110,000. At the time of the gift, Maxine paid a gift tax of $12,000. In order to sell the property, Stan paid a sales commission of $16,000.
a. What is Stan's realized gain on the sale?
b. How would your answer to Part a change, if at all, if the FMV of the gift property was $85,000 as of the date of the gift?

I5-38 *Sale of Asset Received as a Gift.* Bud receives 200 shares of Georgia Corporation stock from his uncle on July 20, 2001, when the stock has a $45,000 FMV. The taxable gift is $45,000, since his uncle made another gift to Bud for $10,000 in January. The uncle pays a gift tax of $1,500. The uncle paid $30,000 for the stock on April 12, 1995.

Without considering the transactions below, Bud has AGI of $25,000 in 2001. No other transactions involving capital assets occur during the year. Analyze each transaction below, independent of the others, and determine Bud's AGI in each case.
a. He sells the stock on October 12, 2002, for $48,000.
b. He sells the stock on October 12, 2002, for $28,000.
c. He sells the stock on December 16, 2001, for $42,000.

I5-39 *Basis of Property Converted from Personal Use.* Irene owns a truck costing $15,000 and used for personal activities. The truck has a $9,600 FMV when it is transferred to her business, which is operated as a sole proprietorship.
a. What is the basis of the truck for determining depreciation?
b. What is Irene's realized gain or loss if the truck is sold for $5,000 after claiming depreciation of $4,000?

I5-40 *Stock Rights.* Cathy owns 100 shares of Atlanta Corporation common stock. She purchased the stock on July 25, 1986, for $4,000. On May 2 of the current year, she receives a nontaxable distribution of 100 stock rights. Each stock right has a $10 FMV, and the FMV of the Atlanta common stock is $70 per share. With each stock right, Cathy may acquire one share of Atlanta common for $68 per share. Assuming that Cathy elects to allocate basis to the stock rights, answer the following:
a. What is the basis allocated to the stock rights?
b. If she sells the stock rights on June 10 for $1,080, what are the amount and character of the recognized gain?
c. If she exercises the stock rights on May 14, what is the basis of the 100 shares purchased and when does the holding period start?
d. If she does not elect to allocate basis to the stock rights, what are the amount and character of the gain if she sells the stock rights on June 10 for $1,080?

I5-41 *Real Property Subdivided for Sale.* Beth acquired only one tract of land seven years ago as an investment. In order to sell the land at a higher price, she decides to subdivide it into 20 lots. She pays for improvements such as clearing and leveling, but the improvements are not considered to be substantial. Each lot has a basis of $2,000, and a selling price of $6,000. Selling expenses of $480 were incurred to sell two lots last year. This year, ten lots are sold, and selling expenses amount to $1,900. How much ordinary income and capital gain must be recognized in the prior and current year?

I5-42 *Marginal Tax Rates.* Mr. and Mrs Dunbar have taxable income of $80,000. Consider the following independent cases where capital gains are recognized and determine the marginal tax rate for the capital gain in each case. Ignore the effect of increasing AGI on deductions.
 CASE A - $10,000 gain from sale of Storm Lake common stock held for seven months.
 CASE B - $10,000 gain from sale of antique clock held for six years.
 CASE C - $10,000 gain from sale of Ames preferred stock held for three years.

I5-43 *Netting Gains and Losses* Trisha, whose tax rate is 36%, sells the following capital assets in 2001 with gains and losses as shown:

Asset	Gain or (Loss)	Holding Period
A	$15,000	15 months
B	7,000	20 months
C	(3,000)	14 months

a. Determine Trisha's increase in tax liability as a result of the three sales. All assets are stock held for investment. Ignore the effect of increasing AGI on deductions and phase-out amounts.
b. Determine her increase in tax liability if the holding period for asset B is 8 months.
c. Determine her increase in tax liability if the holding periods are the same as in (a) but asset B is an antique clock.

I5-44 *Computing the Tax.* Donna files as a head of household in 2001 and has taxable income of $90,000, including the sale of a stock held as an investment for two years at a gain of $20,000. Only one asset was sold during the year and Donna does not have any capital loss carryovers.
a. What is the amount of Donna's tax liability?
b. What is the amount of Donna's tax liability if the stock is held for 11 months?

I5-45 *Computing the Tax.* Wayne is single and has no dependents. Without considering his $11,000 adjusted net capital gain (ANCG) his taxable income in 2001 is as follows:

AGI		$132,950
Home mortgage interest	$22,250	
State and local income taxes	8,000	
Charitable contributions	7,000	
Personal exemption	2,900	40,150
Taxable income		$92,800

a. What is Wayne's tax liability without the ANCG?
b. What is Wayne's tax liability with the ANCG?

I5-46 *Computing the Sales Price.* An investor in a 23% tax bracket owns land that is a capital asset with a $70,000 basis and a holding period of three years. The investor wishes to sell the asset at a price high enough so that he will have $120,000 in cash after paying the taxes. What is the minimum price which the investor could accept?

I5-47 *Capital Gains and Losses.* Consider the four independent situations below for an unmarried individual, and analyze the effects of the capital gains and losses on the individual's AGI. For each case, determine AGI after considering the capital gains and losses.

	Situation 1	Situation 2	Situation 3	Situation 4
AGI (excluding property transactions)	$40,000	$50,000	$60,000	$70,000
STCG	6,000	2,000	5,000	6,000
STCL	2,000	5,000	4,000	15,000
LTCG	3,500	15,000	10,000	9,000
LTCL	2,500	4,000	12,000	4,000

I5-48 *Capital Losses.* To better understand the rules for offsetting capital losses and how to treat capital losses carried forward, analyze the following data for an unmarried individual for the period 1998 through 2001. No capital loss carryforwards are included in the figures. For each year, determine AGI and the capital losses to be carried forward to a later tax year.

	1998	1999	2000	2001
AGI (excluding property transactions)	$40,000	$50,000	$60,000	$70,000
STCG	4,000	5,000	7,000	10,000
STCL	9,000	3,000	5,000	12,000
LTCG	6,000	10,000	2,200	6,000
LTCL	5,000	21,000	1,000	9,500
AGI (including property transactions)	_____	_____	_____	_____
STCL to be carried forward	_____	_____	_____	_____
LTCL to be carried forward	_____	_____	_____	_____

I5-49 *Character of Loss.* The Michigan Corporation owns 20% of the Wolverine Corporation. The Wolverine stock was acquired eight years ago to ensure a steady supply of raw materials. Michigan also owns 30% of Spartan Corporation and 85% of Huron Corporation. Stock in both corporations was acquired more than ten years ago for investment purposes. During the current year, Wolverine, Spartan, and Huron are deemed bankrupt, and the stocks are considered worthless. Describe how Michigan should treat its losses.

I5-50 *Original Issue Discount.* On December 31, 2000, Phil purchased $20,000 of newly issued bonds of Texas Corporation for $16,568. The bonds are dated December 31, 2000. The bonds are 9%, 10-year bonds paying interest semiannually on June 30 and December 31. The bonds are priced to yield 12% compounded semiannually.
a. What is the amount of the original issue discount?
b. For the first semiannual period, what is the amount of the original issue discount Phil must recognize as ordinary income?
c. What is the total amount of interest income Phil must recognize in 2001?
d. What is Phil's basis for the bonds as of December 31, 2001?

I5-51 On January 1, 1999, Swen paid $184,000 for $200,000 of the 8%, 20-year bonds of Penn Corporation, issued on January 1, 1995, at par. The bonds are held as an investment. Determine the gain and the character of the gain if the bonds are sold on January 1, 2001 for
a. $191,000
b. $185,750
c. $183,000

I5-52 *Capital Gains and Losses.* During 2001, Gary receives a $50,000 salary and has no deductions for AGI. In 2000, Gary had a $5,000 STCL and no other capital losses or capital gains. Consider the following sales and determine Gary's AGI for 2001.

- An automobile purchased in 1996 for $10,800 and held for personal use is sold for $7,000.
- On April 10, 2001, stock held for investment is sold for $21,000. The stock was acquired on November 20, 2000, for $9,300.

I5-53 *Call Options.* On February 10, 2001, Gail purchases 20 calls on Red Corporation for $250 per call. Each call represents an option to buy 100 shares of Red stock at $42 per share any time before November 25, 2001. Compute the gain or loss recognized, and determine whether the gain or loss is long-term or short-term for Gail in the following situations:
a. The 20 calls are sold on May 15, 2001, for $310 per call.
b. The calls are not exercised but allowed to expire.
c. The calls are exercised on July 15, 2001 and the 2,000 shares of Red Corporation stock are sold on July 20, 2002, for $50 per share.

I5-54 *Call Writing.* Dan owns 500 shares of Rocket Corporation common stock. The stock was acquired two years ago for $30 per share. On October 2, 2001, Dan writes five calls on the stock, which represent options to buy the 500 shares of Rocket at $75 per share. For each call, Dan receives $210. The calls expire on June 22, 2002. Consider the following transactions and describe the tax treatment for Dan:
a. The five calls are exercised on December 4, 2001.
b. The calls are not exercised and allowed to expire.

I5-55 *Gains and Losses and Basis.* Betty incurs the following transactions during the current year. Without considering the transactions, her 2001 AGI is $40,000. Analyze the transactions and answer the questions below:

- On March 10, 2001, she sells a painting for $2,000. Betty is the artist, and she completed the painting in 1997. Her basis for the painting is $50.
- On June 18, 2001, she receives $28,500 from the sale of stock purchased by her uncle in 1992 for $10,000, which she inherits on February 20, 2001, as a result of her uncle's death. The stock's FMV on that date is $30,000.
- On July 30, 2001, she sells land for $25,000 that was received as a gift from her brother on April 8, 2001, when the land's FMV was $30,000. Her brother purchased the land for $43,000 on October 12, 1993. No gift tax was paid.

a. What is her NSTCL or NSTCG?
b. What is her NLTCL or NLTCG?
c. What is the effect of capital gains and losses on her AGI?
d. What is her capital loss carryforward to 2002?

I5-56 *Corporate Capital Gains and Losses.* Determine the taxable income for the Columbia Corporation for the following independent cases:

Case	Income from Operations	STCG (NSTCL)	NLTCG (NLTCL)
A	$110,000	$30,000	$44,000
B	100,000	(50,000)	65,000
C	80,000	(37,000)	30,000
D	90,000	(15,000)	(9,000)

I5-57 *Original Issue Discount.* On January 1, 2000, Sean purchased an 8%, $100,000 corporate bond for $92,277. The bond was issued on January 1, 2000 and matures on January 1, 2005. Interest is paid semiannually, and the effective yield to maturity is 10% compounded semiannually. On July 1, 2001, Sean sells the bond for $95,949. A schedule of interest amortization for the bond is shown in Table I5-2 on page 5-42.
a. How much interest income must Sean recognize in 2000?
b. How much interest income must Sean recognize in 2001?
c. How much gain must Sean recognize in 2001 on the sale of the bond?

I5-58 *Basis and Shifting Income.* Dale purchased Blue Corporation stock six years ago for $1,000 as an investment. He intends to hold the stock until funds are needed to help pay for his daughter's college education. Today the stock has a $6,500 FMV and Dale decides to sell the stock and give the proceeds, less any taxes paid on the sale, to Tammy, his 18-year-old daughter. Dale's marginal tax rate is 28% and Tammy's marginal tax rate is 15%. Tammy has no other gross income and receives more than half of her support from Dale.

▼ TABLE I5-2
Interest Amortization for Problem I5-57

	Interest Received (1)	Amortization of Discount (2)	Interest Income (3) = (1) + (2)
6-30-00	$4,000	$614	$4,614
12-31-00	4,000	645	4,645
6-30-01	4,000	677	4,677
12-31-01	4,000	711	4,711
6-30-02	4,000	747	4,747
12-31-02	4,000	783	4,783
6-30-03	4,000	823	4,823
12-31-03	4,000	864	4,864
6-30-04	4,000	907	4,907
12-31-04	4,000	952	4,952

a. After the sale and payment of taxes, how much cash will be given to Tammy?
b. If Dale gives the stock to Tammy and she sells the stock for $6,500, how much cash will Tammy have available for college?

I5-59 *Capital Gains and Losses.* Martha has $40,000 AGI without considering the following information. During the year, she incurs a LTCL of $10,000 and has a gain of $14,000 due to the sale of a capital asset held for more than a year.
a. If the $14,000 gain is not properly classified as a LTCG (i.e., is improperly treated as an ordinary gain), determine Martha's AGI.
b. If the $14,000 gain is properly classified as a LTCG, determine her AGI.
c. If Martha has a $2,500 STCL carryover from earlier years, how would the answers to Parts a and b be affected?

I5-60 *Capital Gains and Losses.* Without considering the following capital gains and losses, Charlene has taxable income of $140,000 and a marginal tax rate of 36%. During the year, she sold stock held for nine months at a gain of $10,000; stock held for three years at a gain of $15,000; and a collectible asset held for six years at a gain of $20,000. Ignore the effect of the gains on any threshold amounts and assume that her marginal tax rate of 36% does not change.
a. What is her taxable income after considering the three gains and the increase in her tax liability?
b. In addition to the above three sales, assume that she sells another asset and has a STCL of $14,000. What is her taxable income after considering the four transactions and the increase in her tax liability as a result of the four transactions?
c. In addition to the above three sales in a., assume that she sells another collectible asset held seven years as an investment and has a $27,000 capital loss. What is her taxable income after considering the four transactions and the increase in her tax liability?

I5-61 *Corporate Capital Gains and Losses.* In 1996, the City Corporation sold a capital asset and incurred a $40,000 LTCL that was carried forward to subsequent years. That sale was the only sale of a capital asset that City had made until 2001, when City sells a capital asset and recognizes a STCG of $53,000. Without considering the STCG from the sale, City's taxable income is $250,000.
a. Determine the corporation's NSTCG for 2001.
b. Determine the corporation's 2001 taxable income.
c. If the sale of the asset in 1996 had occurred in 1995, determine the corporation's 2001 taxable income.

TAX FORM/RETURN PREPARATION PROBLEMS

I5-62 Given the following information for Jane Cole, complete Schedule D of Form 1040 through Part III.

- Stock options, which she purchases on February 14 of the current year for $850, expire on October 1.
- On July 1, she sells for $1,500 her personal-use automobile acquired on March 31, 1990 for $8,000.
- On August 16, she sells for $3,100 her stock of York Corporation purchased as an investment on February 16, for $1,600.
- On March 15, she sells for $5,600 an antique brass bed, a gift from her grandmother on January 10, 1988, when its FMV was $1,600. The bed was purchased by her grandmother on April 2, 1979 for $1,800.
- She has a STCL carryover of $250 from last year.

I5-63 Spencer Duck (SSN 277-31-7264) is single and his eight-year-old son, Mitch, lives with him nine months of the year in a rented condominium at 321 Hickory Drive in Ames, Iowa. Mitch lives with his mother, Spencer's ex-wife, during the summer months. His mother provides more than half of Mitch's support and Spencer has agreed to allow her to claim Mitch as her dependent. Spencer has a salary of $34,000 and itemized deductions of $4,000. Taxes withheld during the year amount to $7,000. On July 14 of the current year, he sold the following assets:

- Land was sold for $35,000. The land was received as a property settlement on January 10, 1996, when the land's FMV amounted to $30,000. His ex-wife's basis for the land, purchased on January 10, 1985, was $18,600.
- A personal-use computer acquired on March 2 last year for $4,000 was sold for $2,480.
- A membership card for a prestigious country club was sold for $8,500. The card was acquired on October 10, 1993, for $6,000.
- Marketable securities held as an investment were sold for $20,000. The securities were inherited from his uncle, who died on March 10 of the current year when FMV of the securities was $21,000. The uncle purchased the securities on May 10, 1990, for $10,700.

In addition to the above sales, Spencer received a $100 refund of state income taxes paid last year. Spencer used the standard deduction last year to compute his tax liability. Prepare Form 1040 and Schedule D for the current year.

CASE STUDY PROBLEMS

I5-64 As a political consultant for an aspiring politician, you have been hired to evaluate the following statements that pertain to capital gains and losses. Evaluate the statement and provide at least a one-paragraph explanation of each statement. As you prepare your answer, consider the fact that the aspiring politician does not have much knowledge about taxation.
  a. The tax on capital gains is considered a voluntary tax.
  b. The tax treatment for capital gains and losses after 1986 and before 1991 made it disadvantageous for individuals to sell or exchange capital assets as opposed to selling or exchanging assets that are not capital assets.
  c. On October 22, 1986, the Tax Reform Act of 1986 was passed, which eliminated the 60% of net capital gain deduction (i.e., an individual taxpayer with $10,000 of net capital gain was entitled to a $6,000 deduction when computing AGI) before January 1, 1987. Many state governments enjoyed a substantial increase in 1986 tax revenue.
  d. High-income taxpayers receive the most benefit from preferential treatment for capital gains.

I5-65 Your client, Apex Corporation, entered into an agreement with an executive to purchase his personal residence at its current FMV in the event that his employment is terminated by the company during a five-year period. The executive's job was terminated before the end of the five-year period and Apex acquired the house for $500,000. Due to a downturn in the real estate market, a $200,000 loss was incurred by the company upon the resale of the house. The chief financial officer of Apex insists that the loss be characterized as ordinary, based on the *Corn Products* doctrine. Your research into this matter reveals that the weight of authority heavily favors capital loss treatment (i.e., case law based on facts identical to the above issue held that the loss was capital rather than ordinary). You therefore conclude that the client's position does not have a realistic possibility of being sustained administratively or judicially on its merits if challenged by the IRS. What responsibility do you have as a tax practitioner relative to preparing the client's tax return and rendering continuing tax consulting services to the client? (See the Section *Statements on Standards for Tax Services* in Chapter I1 for a discussion of these issues.)

TAX RESEARCH PROBLEMS

I5-66 Tom Williams is an equal partner in a partnership with the Kansas Corporation. Williams, an inventor, produced a new process while working for the partnership, which has been patented by the partnership. Before making any use of the patent, the partnership entered into a contract granting all rights to use the process for the life of the patent to the Mason Manufacturing Co.

The time between receiving the patent and entering into the contract with Mason amounted to eight months. Mason agreed to pay 0.3% of all sales revenue generated by products produced as a result of the process. If Mason fails to make payments on a timely basis, Mason's right to use the process is forfeited and the agreement between the partnership and Mason is canceled. Will any of the proceeds collected qualify as LTCG under Sec. 1235?

A partial list of research sources is
- Reg. Sec. 1.1235-2
- *George N. Soffron*, 35 T.C. 787 (1961)

I5-67 Lynette, a famous basketball player, is considering the possibility of transferring the sole right to use her name to promote basketball shoes produced and sold by the NIK Corporation. NIK will pay $2 million to obtain the right to use Lynette's name for the next 40 years. NIK may use the name on the shoes and as a part of any of the company's advertisements for basketball shoes. If Lynette signs the contract and receives the $2 million payment, will she have to recognize capital gain or ordinary income?

A partial list of research sources is
- Sec. 1221
- Rev. Rul. 65-261, 1965-2 C.B. 281

I5-68 Jack, a tenured university professor, has been a malcontent for many years at Rockport University. The university has recently offered to pay $200,000 to Jack if he will relinquish his tenure position and resign. Jack is of the opinion that tenure is an intangible capital asset and the $200,000 received for release of the tenure should be a long-term capital gain. Explain why you agree or disagree

A partial list of research sources is
- *Harry M. Flower*, 61 T.C. 140 (1973)
- *Estelle Goldman*, 1975 PH T.C. Memo ¶75,138, 34 TCM 639

I5-69 Web Baker was hired three years ago by the Berry Corporation to serve as CEO for the company. As part of his employment contract, the corporation had agreed to purchase his residence at FMV in the event the company decided to fire him. Last year, Berry, unsatisfied with Web's performance, fired him and purchased the residence for $350,000. Berry immediately listed the house with a real estate agency. Soon after the purchase, the real estate market in the area experienced a serious decline, especially in higher-priced homes. Berry sold the house this year for $270,000 and paid selling expenses of $12,000. How should the Berry Corporation treat the $92,000 loss?

A partial list of research sources is
- Sec. 1221
- Rev. Rul. 82-204, 1982-2 C.B. 192
- *Azar Nut Co. v. CIR*, 67 AFTR 2d 91-987, 91-1 USTC ¶50,257 (5th Cir., 1991)

CHAPTER 6

DEDUCTIONS AND LOSSES

LEARNING OBJECTIVES

After studying this chapter, you should be able to

1. Distinguish between deductions *for* and *from* AGI
2. Discuss the criteria for deducting business and investment expenses
3. List the substantiation requirements for deducting travel and entertainment expenses
4. Explain the timing of deductions under both the cash and accrual methods of accounting
5. Explain the tax consequences of wash sales
6. Explain the tax consequences of transactions between related parties
7. Discuss the criteria for determining whether an activity is a hobby or a trade or business
8. Determine the tax consequences of vacation homes

CHAPTER OUTLINE

For versus From Adjusted Gross Income (AGI) Classification...6-3

Criteria for Deducting Business and Investment Expenses...6-4

General Restrictions on the Deductibility of Expenses...6-10

Proper Substantiation Requirement...6-16

When an Expense is Deductible...6-18

Special Disallowance Rules...6-22

The next five chapters (I6–I10) deal with deductions. As you recall from Chapters I3 and I4, the principles governing the reporting of income are based on an "all inclusive" system of taxation, that is, gross income includes all items of income unless specifically excluded by statute. In contrast, deductions or losses are not allowed for tax purposes unless the statute specifically provides for the deduction. For example, a taxpayer who pays medical expenses during the year may deduct such expenses because the statute specifically allows for the deduction of medical expenses under Sec. 213 of the IRC. A taxpayer's ability to claim a deduction on his or her tax return is commonly referred to as being permitted as a matter of "legislative grace."

Chapter I6 discusses the general requirements for the deductibility of taxpayer expenditures and losses. Chapter I7 deals with itemized deductions of individual taxpayers, such as medical expenses, taxes, charitable contributions, interest expense and other miscellaneous deductions. Chapter I8 covers two major areas, the deductibility of losses and bad debts. Chapter I9 discusses employee compensation and expenses, and Chapter I10 discusses tax depreciation, amortization, and depletion.

As was mentioned above, expenditures are deductible only if specifically allowed by the IRC. However, it would be impossible for the IRC to specify *every* type of deductible expense that a taxpayer might incur. Therefore, the IRC has developed a framework for analyzing the nature of an expenditure. If the expenditure meets the criteria developed in the framework, the item is deductible. This framework has three general categories of deductions:

(1) Expenses incurred in connection with a **trade or business** (Sec. 162);
(2) Expenses incurred in connection with the **production of income** (Sec. 212);
(3) Other types of expenses that fall within specific provisions of the IRC, such as personal expenditures for medical expenses, taxes, certain types of interest expense, etc.

The first two categories of deductions above, trade or business and production of income expenses, are those incurred in connection with profit-motivated activities. The IRC does not attempt to specify every conceivable type of deductible expense under these two categories (Secs. 162 and 212). Rather, the IRC sets forth general guidelines for deductibility. Any expense incurred in connection with a trade or business or for the production of income is deductible if it falls within these general guidelines and is not specifically excluded from deductibility by the IRC. For example, although the IRC does not specifically provide for the deductibility of utilities or maintenance and repairs, these expenditures are deductible if incurred in a profit-motivated activity. These general guidelines are discussed later in this chapter.

A trade or business, as discussed below, is a business activity of the taxpayer. The term production of income includes expenses incurred for the following:

▶ Production or collection of income

▶ Management, conservation, or maintenance of property held for the production of income

▶ Determination, collection, or refund of any tax

As will be discussed later, the distinction between a trade or business and the production of income is important because it can affect both the amount and type of the deduction. Expenses incurred in both types of activities must meet additional standards of deductibility; that is, they must also be ordinary, necessary, and reasonable in the context of the activity in which they are incurred. Losses incurred in either type of activity are deductible.

Section 262 also provides, in general, that no deduction is allowed for any personal, living, or family expenses. However, the tax law does specifically provide for the deductibility of certain personal expenditures or losses. For example, casualty losses (subject to specific limitations) are allowed for personal-use property. Taxpayers may also deduct personal expenditures for certain types of interest, taxes, medical expenses, alimony, and retirement savings if the expenditures meet strict requirements. These deductions and losses for personal expenditures are discussed in Chapters I7 and I8.

FOR VERSUS FROM ADJUSTED GROSS INCOME (AGI) CLASSIFICATION

OBJECTIVE 1

Distinguish between deductions for and from AGI

As demonstrated in Chapter I2, the tax formula for individuals divides all allowable business, investment, and personal deductions into the following two categories:

- Deductions subtracted from gross income in order to calculate adjusted gross income (*for* AGI deductions)
- Deductions subtracted from AGI to arrive at the amount of taxable income (*from* AGI deductions)

Section 62 specifically identifies deductions *for* AGI. All other deductions for individuals are deductions *from* AGI. The more common *for* AGI deductions include the following, subject to certain limitations:

- All allowable expenses incurred in a taxpayer's trade or business, but not including an employee's unreimbursed business expenses
- Employee business expenses that are reimbursed by the employer
- Losses from the sale or exchange of trade, business, or investment property
- Expenses attributable to the production of rent or royalty income
- Moving expenses
- Contributions to certain pension, profit-sharing, or retirement plan arrangements
- Penalties paid to a bank or other savings institution because of the early withdrawal of funds from a certificate of deposit or time savings account
- Alimony
- Interest paid by certain individuals on qualified educational loans
- Contributions to qualified medical savings accounts
- One-half of the self-employment tax imposed on self-employed individuals and 60% of health insurance costs paid by such individuals (see Chapter I14).[1]

KEY POINT

Many *for* AGI deductions are either expenses incurred in a trade or business or investment expenses or losses. Most of the deductible personal expenses are deductible *from* AGI.

For individuals, the distinction between deductions *for* AGI and *from* AGI is critical for two reasons. First, as explained in Chapter I2, the tax formula allows individuals to deduct the greater of the standard deduction or the total of the *from* AGI (itemized) deductions in arriving at taxable income. A taxpayer does not receive any benefit for these deductions if their total for the year does not exceed the standard deduction. Furthermore, certain itemized deductions for taxpayers with adjusted gross income over certain levels are phased out and lost. (See Chapter I7 for a discussion of these limits.) *For* AGI deductions, on the other hand, reduce AGI (and consequently taxable income), even if the standard deduction is used in computing taxable income. The concept of AGI has no application to corporations, estates, or trusts.

EXAMPLE I6-1 ▶ Brad, a single individual with no dependents, incurs $1,500 of deductible expenses and earns $30,000 in gross income during 2001. If the expenses are all deductions *from* AGI, Brad's taxable income is $22,550 (i.e., Brad receives a $2,900 deduction for his personal exemption and a $4,550 standard deduction). Brad receives no direct tax benefit from the expenses because they do not exceed the standard deduction. However, if the $1,500 of expenses are all deductions *for* AGI, Brad's taxable income is $21,050. In this latter case, Brad receives a full tax benefit from the expenses.

---

[1] Sections 62, 162(l) and 164(f). This 60% increases to 70% in 2002 and 100% for 2003 and beyond. Other deductions *for* AGI include deductions for depreciation and depletion for life tenants and income beneficiaries of property, a portion of certain lump-sum distributions from qualified pension plans, reforestation expenses, required repayments of supplemental unemployment compensation benefits, certain expenses incurred for clean-fuel vehicles and refueling property, and jury duty pay that is remitted to an employer.

	Deductions from AGI	Deductions for AGI
Gross income	$30,000	$30,000
Minus: *For* AGI deductions	0	(1,500)
AGI	$30,000	$28,500
Minus: Standard deduction	(4,550)	(4,550)
Personal exemption	(2,900)	(2,900)
Taxable income	$22,550	$21,050

KEY POINT

For many individuals, the benefit of a *from* AGI deduction is lost because that particular deduction is less than its applicable limit or, the total of the itemized deductions is less than the standard deduction. Furthermore, certain itemized deductions of taxpayers with AGI over certain levels are phased out.

A second important reason for the proper classification of deductions is that AGI helps establish limits on certain deductions *from* AGI, such as medical expenses, casualty losses, charitable contributions, and miscellaneous itemized deductions. For example, an individual may deduct certain miscellaneous itemized deductions only to the extent that the sum of these deductions for the year exceeds 2% of the individual's AGI. These expenses include unreimbursed employee business expenses,[2] expenses incurred to produce investment income,[3] and the cost of tax advice and tax return preparation (see Chapter I7). Medical expenses are deductible only to the extent that their total exceeds 7.5% of the individual's AGI for the year. Casualty losses on personal-use property are first reduced by $100 per casualty event. After this reduction, they are deductible only to the extent that the sum exceeds 10% of the individual's AGI. The deduction for charitable contributions, on the other hand, may not exceed 50% of the taxpayer's AGI. (See Chapter I7 for a discussion of these deductions and their limits.)

Deductions for AGI are generally located in two places on the tax return. First, some deductions for AGI appear on the front page of Form 1040 (lines 23–31a). These deductions include such items as moving expenses, alimony paid, and student loan interest. Second, other deductions appear on separate schedules, such as Schedule C (Profit or Loss from Business), Schedule E (Supplemental Income or Loss), or Schedule F (Profit or Loss from Farming). The profit or loss from these schedules carry over to the front page of Form 1040 as part of gross income. Thus, the deductions on these schedules are deductions *for* AGI. Figure I2-1 (Chapter I2) contains the front page of Form 1040.

CRITERIA FOR DEDUCTING BUSINESS AND INVESTMENT EXPENSES

OBJECTIVE 2

Discuss the criteria for deducting business and investment expenses

Business and investment expenses are deductible only if they meet certain requirements. Thus, deductible business or investment expenses must be:

- Related to a profit-motivated activity of the taxpayer (i.e., a business or investment activity rather than a personal expenditure)
- Ordinary
- Necessary
- Reasonable in amount
- Properly documented (discussed later in the chapter under the heading Proper Substantiation Requirement), and
- An expense of the taxpayer (not someone else's expense)

Furthermore, as discussed later in this chapter under the heading General Restrictions on the Deductibility of Expenses, taxpayers may not deduct expenditures meeting certain criteria. Thus, an expenditure is not deductible if it is

---

[2] These expenses include unreimbursed expenditures for travel and transportation, supplies, special clothing or uniforms, union dues, and subscriptions to trade journals. Reimbursed employee expenses are deductible *for* AGI and thus, are deductible in full. See Chapter I9.

[3] These expenses include rental fees for safe deposit boxes used to hold investment property, subscriptions to investment journals, bank service charges on checking accounts used in an investment or income-producing activity, and fees paid for consulting advice. Expenses incurred in an investment or income-producing activity that generates either rental or royalty income are deductions *for* AGI.

- A capital expenditure
- Related to tax-exempt income
- Illegal or in violation of public policy, or
- Specifically disallowed by the tax law.

These criteria and related matters are discussed later.

BUSINESS OR INVESTMENT REQUIREMENT

Except for a few personal expenses, all deductible expenditures or losses must be incurred in a profit-motivated activity. For individuals, most of these expenses are deductible either under Sec. 162 as an expense incurred in a trade or business or under Sec. 212 as an expense incurred for the production of income or for the maintenance and conservation of income-producing property (an investment activity). Thus, the requirement of an activity being profit-motivated is really two-pronged: (1) a determination whether an expenditure is incurred in an activity engaged in for profit, and (2) a distinction between a trade or business and an investment activity.

ACTIVITY ENGAGED IN FOR PROFIT. This first part of the test classifies the expense as having been incurred in either a profit-motivated activity or a personal activity. Classifying expenses as either profit-motivated or personal can be quite difficult. For example, is the activity of coin collecting a hobby that is personal in nature, a profit-motivated business, or an investment activity? No single objective test is available. Rather, one must examine all the facts and circumstances surrounding the activity in which the expense is incurred. These factors, as well as other issues dealing with the determination of whether or not a particular activity is profit-motivated, are examined in more detail later in this chapter in the section entitled Hobby Losses.

REAL WORLD EXAMPLE

A taxpayer attempted to deduct treasure-hunting costs as a business expense, but the court concluded that there was no profit motive. The taxpayer kept no business records, the time spent was negligible and appeared to be recreational in nature, and no income was produced from the activity. *William J. Hezel,* 1985 PH T.C. Memo ¶85,010, 49 TCM 458.

TRADE OR BUSINESS VERSUS INVESTMENT CLASSIFICATION. The second part of the profit-motive test is the determination of whether a particular activity is a trade or business of the taxpayer or only an investment. This distinction is important for several reasons. First, a loss on the sale of the assets used in the activity may be an ordinary loss if the activity is a trade or business.[4] If it is an investment activity, however, the loss is classified as a capital loss which, as explained in Chapter I5, receives different treatment. Second, this distinction may control whether an expense of the activity is a deduction *for* AGI or a deduction *from* AGI. In general, expenses incurred in a trade or business are deductions *for* AGI whereas investment expenses other than those incurred to produce rents and royalties are deductions *from* AGI. Finally, each year taxpayers may currently deduct up to $24,000 in 2001 and 2002 ($20,000 in 2000 and increasing to $25,000 in 2003 and thereafter) of tangible personal property purchased during the year for use in a trade or business; the same expenditures must be capitalized and depreciated over several years if they are incurred in an investment activity. (See Chapter I10 for a discussion of the Sec. 179 current deduction for capital expenditures.)

EXAMPLE I6-2 ▶ Robin is a self-employed financial consultant. She meets daily with a variety of clients to discuss their investments. Because she must keep abreast of the latest market quotes and strategies, Robin subscribes to several trade publications, newsletters, and quote services. She also purchased a $4,000 computer to be used exclusively in her consulting business. The expenses incurred for these publications and services are deductions *for* AGI because Robin incurred them in her consulting business. Furthermore, she can currently deduct the $4,000 paid for the computer under the special rules of Sec. 179 because it is a business asset. ◀

On the other hand, expenses incurred in an investment activity, other than those incurred to produce rents and royalties, are miscellaneous itemized deductions *from* AGI and are deductible only to the extent that they exceed 2% of AGI (see Chapter I7).

---

[4] Under Sec. 1231, the exact treatment depends on the total gains and losses from such property for the year. See Chapter I13 for a discussion of Sec. 1231.

EXAMPLE I6-3 ▶ Steve is a wealthy attorney who invests in the stock market and keeps abreast of the latest market quotes and strategies by subscribing to several trade publications and newsletters. He also purchased a computer to use exclusively for tracking his investments. Steve generally spends a few hours each day studying this information and analyzing his portfolio. The subscription expenses are deductions *from* AGI because they are incurred in an investment (rather than a business) activity and do not relate to the production of rents and royalties. Furthermore, Steve cannot currently deduct the entire cost of the computer but must depreciate the cost over a period of five years. The deductibility of all of the above items depends on whether Steve's total miscellaneous itemized deductions exceed 2% of his AGI and whether Steve itemizes his deductions instead of using the standard deduction. ◀

> **ADDITIONAL COMMENT**
>
> A trade or business is an activity with a profit motive and some type of economic activity. An investment activity requires a profit motive but does not require economic activity.

Despite these important differences in treatment, the distinction between an investment activity and a trade or business is not always clear. A precise definition of what constitutes a trade or business is not found in the IRC or Treasury Regulations. Judicial law provides some guidelines. In one of the first cases dealing with the issue, the Supreme Court stated that the carrying on of a trade or business involves "holding one's self out to others as engaged in the selling of goods or services."[5]

Later, another Supreme Court case emphasized that one must examine all the surrounding facts and circumstances in order to determine the underlying nature of an activity.[6] In that case, the taxpayer owned a large portfolio of stocks, bonds, and real estate. The taxpayer's holdings were so large that he rented offices and hired employees to help him manage the properties. The Court, however, regarded these activities as investment activities despite the size of the holdings and the amount of work and effort involved because the taxpayer merely kept records and collected interest and dividends from his securities. Other cases, however, indicate that a taxpayer who invests in stocks and bonds may be considered to be in a business if he or she frequently buys and sells securities in order to make a short-term profit on the daily swings in the market.

LEGAL AND ACCOUNTING FEES. Legal and accounting fees are generally deductible if they are incurred in the regular conduct of a trade or business or for the production of income. Fees incurred for the determination, collection, or refund of any tax are also deductible. As mentioned previously, trade or business expenses and expenses incurred in producing rents and royalties are deductible *for* AGI. Likewise, fees paid for the determination, collection, or refund of any tax are deductible *for* AGI if they are allocable to the taxpayer's trade or business or to the production of rents and royalties. These expenses include fees paid to prepare a taxpayer's Schedule C (Profit or Loss from Business), Part I of Schedule E (Supplemental Income and Loss, which is used to report rental and royalty income), and Schedule F (farm income and expenses).[7] Other tax related fees are deductible *from* AGI as miscellaneous itemized deductions, subject to the 2% of AGI limitation.

Taxpayers may not deduct legal expenses incurred for personal purposes. Likewise, taxpayers may not deduct legal fees incurred in the acquisition of property. Instead, these expenses must be capitalized and added to the cost of the property.

EXAMPLE I6-4 ▶ During the current year, Lia pays legal and accounting fees for the following:

Services rendered with regard to a contract dispute in Lia's business	$ 8,000
Services rendered in resolving a federal tax deficiency relating to Lia's business	2,500
Tax return preparation fees:	
Allocable to preparation of Schedule C	1,600
Allocable to preparation of Schedules A and B and to the remainder of Form 1040	400
Legal fees incident to a divorce	1,200
Total	$13,700

---

[5] *Deputy v. Pierre S. DuPont*, 23 AFTR 808, 40-1 USTC ¶9161 (USSC, 1940).
[6] *Eugene Higgins v. CIR*, 25 AFTR 1160, 41-1 USTC ¶9233 (USSC, 1941). See also *Chang H. Liang*, 23 T.C. 1040 (1955), and *Ralph E. Purvis v. CIR*, 37 AFTR 2d 76-968, 76-1 USTC ¶9270 (9th Cir., 1976); and *Samuel B. Levin v. U.S.*, 43 AFTR 2d 79-612, 79-1 USTC ¶9331 (ct. Cls., 1979).
[7] Rev. Rul. 92-29, 1992-1 C.B. 20.

Lia may deduct $12,100 ($8,000 + $2,500 + $1,600) *for* AGI. The remaining $400 of tax preparation fees are deductible *from* AGI as a miscellaneous itemized deduction subject to the 2% of AGI limitation. The legal fees incident to the divorce are personal expenses and generally are not deductible. However, Lia could take a partial deduction *from* AGI as a miscellaneous itemized deduction to the extent that the legal fees relate to giving tax advice incident to the divorce. ◄

In certain cases, legal expenses incurred in defending one's reputation or in defending against criminal charges may be deductible. In these situations, however, the legal action must have a direct relationship to the taxpayer's business or income-producing activity. In criminal proceedings, the Supreme Court has held that as long as the expenses are business expenses, they are deductible, even if the taxpayer is convicted.[8]

EXAMPLE 16-5 ▶ Mario is engaged in the business of underwriting and selling securities to the public. In the current year, Mario is charged and convicted on criminal charges of securities fraud. The conviction is appealed, but the conviction is upheld. Mario incurs $80,000 in attorney's fees in the unsuccessful defense. In this case, the legal expenses are directly related to Mario's business. Additionally, they are ordinary and necessary. Despite Mario's conviction, the attorney's fees is deductible. ◄

KEY POINT

Whether an expense can be considered ordinary is sometimes very subjective. For example, Supreme Court Justice Cardozo in 1933 in *Thomas H. Welch v. Helvering*, 12 AFTR 1456, 3 USTC ¶1164 (USSC, 1933) stated that, "The standard set up by the statute is not a rule of law; it is a way of life. Life in all its fullness must supply the answer to the riddle."

ORDINARY EXPENSE

To be deductible, a business or investment expense must be **ordinary**. Although the IRC does not provide either a definition or an application of this requirement, the Treasury Regulations under Sec. 212 indicate that for an expense to be ordinary it must be reasonable in amount and it must bear a reasonable and proximate relationship to the income-producing activity or property. This means that there must be more than a remote connection between the expense and the anticipated income. It does not mean that the property must be producing income currently.

EXAMPLE 16-6 ▶ During the current year, Ahmed purchases a plot of land, on which there is an old vacant warehouse. Ahmed anticipates making a long-run profit from the investment because the value of the land is expected to appreciate eventually due to commercial development in the area. To help cover the costs of holding the property, Ahmed plans to rent storage space in the warehouse. During the current year, Ahmed incurs the following expenses, although he is unable to rent the warehouse:

ADDITIONAL COMMENT

A General Accounting Office report finds that tax cheating is widespread among self-employed taxpayers. These workers represent only 13% of all taxpayers, but account for approximately 40% of all underreported individual income. The report identified truckers as one of the least compliant groups.

Expenses	Amount
Property taxes	$1,000
Interest	4,000
Insurance	800
Utilities	200

All of these expenditures qualify as ordinary deductible expenses under Sec. 212 because they bear a reasonable and proximate relationship to the income Ahmed hopes to obtain, even though he generated no income from the property during the year. However, Ahmed might not be able to deduct them all in the current year because of the passive loss limitations explained in Chapter 18. ◄

The Supreme Court has ruled that for an expense to be ordinary it must be customary or usual in the context of a particular industry or business community.[9] Thus, an expenditure may be ordinary in the context of one type of business, but not in the context of another.

EXAMPLE 16-7 ▶ For many years, Hank has been an officer in Green Corporation, which is engaged in the grain business. Green Corporation purchases its grain from various suppliers. Last year, Green Corporation went bankrupt and was relieved from having to pay off its debts to its suppliers. In the current year, Hank enters into a contract to act as a commissioned agent to purchase grain for

---

[8] *CIR v. Walter F. Tellier*, 17 AFTR 2d 633, 66-1 USTC ¶9319 (USSC, 1966).
[9] *Thomas H. Welch v. Helvering*, 12 AFTR 1456, 3 USTC ¶1164 (USSC, 1933) and *Deputy v. Pierre S. DuPont*, 23 AFTR 808, 40-1 USTC ¶9161 (USSC, 1940).

Green Corporation. To reestablish a relationship with suppliers whom Hank knew previously, Hank decides to pay off as many of Green Corporation's debts as he can. Hank is under no legal obligation to do so. Hank's payments are not ordinary. Rather, they are extraordinary expenditures made for goodwill to establish Hank in a new trade or business, and they must be capitalized. ◄

An expense may be ordinary with respect to a taxpayer even though that taxpayer encounters it only once.

EXAMPLE I6-8 ▶ For several years, Donna has been engaged in the business of making and selling false teeth. Most of the advertisements, orders, and deliveries of the teeth are done through the mail. During the current year, the post office judged that some of the advertisements were false. As a result, a fraud order is issued under which the post office stamps "Fraudulent" on all letters addressed to Donna, and then returns them to the senders. In an unsuccessful suit to prevent the post office from continuing this practice, Donna expends $25,000 in lawyer's fees. These fees are ordinary business expenses because they are incurred in an action that normally or ordinarily would be taken under the circumstances. ◄

The Supreme Court has also indicated that the term *ordinary* as used in this context refers to an expenditure that is currently deductible rather than an expenditure that must be capitalized.[10]

> **REAL WORLD EXAMPLE**
> Payments made by a corporation to an individual who was a 50% shareholder were necessary in order to prevent him from interfering in the management of the business and damaging the corporation's reputation. *Fairmont Homes, Inc.*, 1983 PH T.C. Memo ¶83,209, 45 TCM 1340.

NECESSARY EXPENSE

In addition to being ordinary, a deductible investment or business expense must also be necessary. The Supreme Court has indicated that an expense is considered necessary if it is "appropriate and helpful" in the taxpayer's business.[11] To meet this appropriate or helpful standard, an expenditure need not be necessary in the sense that it is indispensable. Rather, the test seems to be whether a reasonable or prudent businessperson would incur the same expenditure under similar circumstances.

EXAMPLE I6-9 ▶ The expenditures in Example I6-7 (the payment of debts from a former business) and Example I6-8 (the payment of legal fees) are both necessary because they are appropriate and helpful in each case. However, the expenditure in Example I6-7 is not ordinary and, therefore, is not deductible. The expenditure in Example I6-8 is deductible because it meets both tests. ◄

REASONABLE EXPENSE

Section 162 and Treasury Regulations under Sec. 212 provide that in order to be deductible the expense must be reasonable. Problems with meeting this standard generally arise in the context of salaries being paid to an individual who is both a shareholder and an employee in a closely held business. In this type of situation, a controlling shareholder of a corporation receives a payment, characterized as salary, that the IRS asserts is too large for the services rendered.

EXAMPLE I6-10 ▶ Brian, the controlling shareholder and an employee of Central Corporation, receives an annual salary of $650,000 from the corporation. Based on several factors, such as the size of Central Corporation's total operations and a comparison of salary received by officers of comparably sized corporations, the IRS contends that Brian's salary should be no higher than $300,000. If Central successfully defends the $650,000 salary, the corporation is able to deduct the full amount as salary expense. If the defense is not successful, the excess $350,000 is considered a dividend to the extent of earnings and profits, and no deduction is available to Central Corporation for this amount. In either event, Brian must take the full $650,000 into income. (See the Tax Planning Considerations section in this chapter for a discussion of the use of a payback agreement in these situations.) ◄

In an attempt to link executive compensation to productivity and business performance and to discourage a common practice of increasing executive compensation despite

---

[10] *CIR v. S. B. Heininger*, 31 AFTR 783, 44-1 USTC ¶9109 (USSC, 1943). See also *CIR v. Walter F. Tellier*, 17 AFTR 2d 633, 66-1 USTC ¶9319 (USSC, 1966).

[11] *Thomas H. Welch v. Helvering*, 12 AFTR 1456, 3 USTC ¶1164 (USSC, 1933).

declines in business performance, Congress enacted Sec. 162(m) that disallows a deduction for certain employee compensation that exceeds a yearly amount of $1 million. This limit applies to compensation payable by a publicly held corporation to the corporation's chief executive officer and its four highest compensated officers for the taxable year. Compensation based on commissions or other performance goals is not subject to this limitation.

The tests for determining whether a business or investment expense is deductible are summarized in Topic Review I6-1.

> **KEY POINT**
> Since the Sec. 162(m) compensation deduction limit applies only to publicly-held corporations, privately-held corporations are faced with the general reasonableness standard which looks at the particular facts and circumstances.

EXPENSES AND LOSSES MUST BE INCURRED BY THE TAXPAYER

Generally, taxpayers may not take a deduction for a loss or expense of another person. Thus, a deduction is allowed only for the taxpayer's own losses and expenses. This requirement prevents taxpayers from engaging in manipulative schemes.

EXAMPLE I6-11 ▶ April and Bruce, the elderly parents of Carol, live in their own home. They have little income and Carol must help to support them. During the current year, the interest and property taxes due on April and Bruce's home total $2,000. April and Bruce file a joint return. They have no other expenses that qualify as itemized deductions. Thus, April and Bruce plan to use the standard deduction, and the benefit of the $2,000 expenditure for interest and taxes will be lost. In an attempt to take advantage of a deduction that otherwise would be lost, Carol pays the interest and taxes out of her business. Carol's business cannot deduct these payments because they are not a liability of the business. ◀

> **ADDITIONAL COMMENT**
> When one taxpayer pays the expenses of another, neither taxpayer is entitled to the deduction.

This general rule applies to all types of expenditures, whether incurred in a trade or business, an investment activity, or a personal activity for which deductions are allowed. There is one exception: under Sec. 213 taxpayers may take a deduction for medical expenses paid on behalf of a dependent. Medical expenses also qualify as a deduction if they are paid for a person who would qualify as a dependent except for the fact that the gross income test is not met (see Chapter I2).

EXAMPLE I6-12 ▶ During the current year, Dan incurs $3,400 in deductible medical expenses. Dan is not a full-time student and is not under age 19 but is otherwise supported by Tom, his father. Dan's gross income for the year is $15,000. If Tom pays Dan's medical expenses, Tom may deduct the expenses as an itemized deduction even though Tom may not take a dependency exemption for Dan. ◀

Topic Review I6-1

Tests for Deductibility as a Business or Investment Expense

TEST	APPLICATION
Ordinary	▶ Based on the facts and circumstances. ▶ Reasonable and proximate relationship to the activity. ▶ Customary or usual in context of the industry. ▶ Need not be encountered by the taxpayer more than once.
Necessary	▶ Based on the facts and circumstances. ▶ Appropriate and helpful. ▶ Need not be indispensable. ▶ Would a reasonable or prudent businessperson incur the same expense?
Reasonable	▶ Based on the facts and circumstances. ▶ Applies to all business and investment expenses. ▶ Compensation paid to an owner-employee of a small corporation is the most commonly contested area. ▶ Compensation in excess of $1 million payable by a publicly held corporation to its key executives may not be deductible.

General Restrictions on the Deductibility of Expenses

As mentioned earlier on page I6-4, certain types of expenditures are not deductible. These types of expenditures fall within certain categories which are discussed below.

CAPITALIZATION VERSUS EXPENSE DEDUCTION

GENERAL CAPITALIZATION REQUIREMENTS. Under Sec. 263, current deductions may not be taken for capital expenditures. Generally, expenses that add to the value of, substantially prolong the useful life of, or change the use of the property are considered capital expenditures and are not currently deductible. Thus, capital expenditures include the cost of acquiring or constructing buildings, machinery, equipment, furniture, and any similar property that has a useful life that extends substantially beyond the end of the tax year. Taxpayers must also capitalize the cost of goodwill purchased in connection with the acquisition of the assets of a going concern.[12] (See Chapter I10 for a discussion of the amortization of goodwill.)

Some assets, such as buildings, machinery, equipment, furniture and fixtures, purchased goodwill, and customer lists are depreciable or amortizable and may provide deductions that are spread over more than one tax year. Others, such as land, stock, and partnership interests, are neither depreciable nor amortizable and the taxpayer must wait until the asset is sold or disposed of to recover the cost. In some instances, it is difficult to ascertain whether an asset is eligible for depreciation or amortization. For example, the Tax Court has held that antique violin bows and an antique bass violin are depreciable property, overriding the IRS's arguments that they should not be depreciable because they were actually appreciating in value and it was impossible to determine their useful life.[13]

Maintenance and repair expenditures that only keep an asset in a normal operating condition are deductible if they do not increase the value or prolong the useful life of the asset. Distinguishing between a currently deductible expenditure and a capital expenditure can be difficult because expenditures for normal maintenance and repair can cost more than a capital improvement. Normal maintenance and repair may also increase the value of an asset. In one Tax Court case, the court held that expenditures incurred in replacing support beams and floor joists to shore up a sagging floor were deductible, whereas the court held that the cost of placing a new floor over an old one was a capital expenditure.[14] A tax advisor must examine all of the facts and circumstances to determine whether the expenditures constitute part of an overall plan of improvement or a change in use of the asset.

> **ADDITIONAL COMMENT**
>
> Some provisions permit taxpayers to depreciate or amortize capital expenditures over a relatively short period of time. For example, there is a rapid write-off available for pollution control facilities under Sec. 169 and for organization costs of corporations under Sec. 248.

ELECTION TO DEDUCT CURRENTLY. Taxpayers sometimes may elect a current deduction for certain capital expenditures. Taxpayers often prefer a current deduction over capitalizing and depreciating an asset because of the time value of money. Some expenditures that taxpayers may elect to deduct currently[15] include

- Cost of fertilizers incurred by farmers
- Cost of soil and water conservation incurred by farmers
- Intangible drilling costs incurred in drilling oil and gas wells
- Costs for tertiary injectants
- Costs for certain mining development projects

---

[12] Reg. Sec. 1.263(a)-2(h). See also *Indopco, Inc., v. CIR*, 69 AFTR 2d 92-694, 92-1 USTC ¶50,113 (USSC, 1992), where expenses incurred by a corporation that was the target of a "friendly" takeover were held to be nondeductible capital expenditures because they provided long-term benefits to the corporation. In this case, the Supreme Court held that these long-term benefits do not need to be associated with a specific identifiable asset.

[13] *Richard L. Simon*, 103 T.C. 247 (1994) and *Brian P. Liddle*, 76 AFTR 2d 95-6255, 95-2 USTC ¶50,488 (3rd Cir., 1959). The IRS has stated it will not follow these decisions. See AOD 96-9, 7/15/96.

[14] Reg. Sec. 1.162-4. See also *Standard Fruit Product Co.*, 1949 PH T.C. Memo ¶49,207, 8 TCM 733.

[15] See Secs. 180, 175, 263(c), 193, 616, 190, and 174.

> ► Costs incurred to remove architectural and transportation barriers to the handicapped and elderly
> ► Costs for certain qualified research and experimental expenditures

Taxpayers may also elect to deduct certain amounts each year for the purchase of qualified tangible personal property used in a trade or business instead of depreciating the property over its useful life. This deduction is limited to $24,000 in 2001 and 2002 and $25,000 in 2003 and thereafter. This election under Sec. 179 is examined in chapter I10.

CAPITALIZATION OF DEDUCTION ITEMS. The exceptions mentioned above provide a current deduction for expenditures that are normally capital in nature. Section 266 provides for the capitalization of certain expenses that normally are deductible. Section 266 is elective and applies to the following items:

> ► Annual property taxes, interest on a mortgage, and other carrying charges incurred on unimproved and unproductive real estate.
> ► Annual property taxes, interest, employment taxes, and other necessary expenses incurred for the development, improvement, or construction of real property, up to the time the development or construction is completed. For these expenses to be capitalized, the real property may be either improved or unimproved, productive or unproductive.
> ► Interest and employment taxes incurred in transporting and installing personalty (as opposed to realty) up to the time when the property is first put into use by the taxpayer.

A taxpayer may make a new election to capitalize the expenses on unimproved and unproductive real estate each year.

BOOK-TAX COMPARISON
Although for tax purposes a taxpayer may elect to deduct these capital expenditures, for book purposes capital expenditures must still be capitalized and depreciated or amortized. This difference in treatment gives rise to a book-tax adjustment.

REAL-WORLD EXAMPLE
The cost of maintenance and upkeep on unimproved and unproductive real estate does not qualify as carrying charges eligible for capitalization. Rev. Rul. 71-475, 1971-2 C.B. 304.

EXAMPLE I6-13 ► During 2001 and 2002, Nancy pays property taxes of $5,000 on a piece of land. During 2001, the land is vacant and unproductive. In 2002, Nancy uses the land as a parking lot, generating $7,000 in income. Nancy can elect to capitalize the taxes in 2001 because the property is both unimproved and unproductive. In 2002, however, the land is productive, and Nancy cannot elect to capitalize the taxes. Because the expenses relate to the production of rental income, they are deductible *for* AGI. If the land remains unproductive during 2002, Nancy can elect to capitalize the taxes paid in 2002. However, the election is optional and need not be made for 2002 merely because it is made in 2001. ◄

For the development or construction of real property, an election to capitalize the other expenses incurred during the development or construction period remains in effect for that year and for all subsequent years until the end of the construction period. However, a taxpayer may make the election on each new project separately.

EXAMPLE I6-14 ► During the current year, Paul begins construction of an office building and a hotel. Paul incurs $20,000 in property taxes during the construction of the office building and $12,000 for the hotel. The election to capitalize the taxes on the office building does not bind Paul to make the same election with respect to the taxes on the hotel. ◄

SELF-STUDY QUESTION
Chuck borrows $100,000 at a 10% rate of interest and invests the $100,000 in exempt bonds yielding 8%. Chuck is in the 28% tax bracket. Calculate what Chuck's cash flow on these transactions would be on an after-tax basis if expenses related to exempt income were deductible.

ANSWER
Chuck has $8,000 of exempt income and $10,000 of interest expense. However, if the interest expense were deductible, its after-tax cost would be $7,200 ($10,000 − 2,800). Chuck's cash flow would be $800 ($8,000 − $7,200) on an unsound economic investment.

If a taxpayer elects to capitalize this type of expense under Sec. 266, it is added to the basis of the property to which it pertains. If the property is depreciable, a deduction is allowed for the expenses as the property is depreciated. Taxpayers are motivated to make this election if they have large net operating loss (NOL) carryovers, or if they expect to be in a significantly higher tax rate in future years and thus feel that the benefit of the deduction is greater in the future.

Section 263A also requires certain taxpayers to capitalize certain costs into inventory instead of taking a current deduction. (See Chapter I11 for a discussion of inventories.)

EXPENSES RELATED TO EXEMPT INCOME

Under Sec. 265, taxpayers may not deduct any expense allocated or related to tax-exempt income. The purpose of this disallowance is to prevent a double tax benefit to the taxpayer.

BOOK-TAX COMPARISON

For book purposes, tax-exempt income and related expenses are included in the calculation of net income. For tax purposes, they are excluded from gross income.

Interest expense on debt the taxpayer incurs in order to purchase or carry tax-exempt securities is specifically disallowed. Thus, the disallowance depends on the taxpayer's intended use of the loan proceeds. Intent is generally determined by an examination of all the facts and circumstances surrounding the transaction. Intent to carry the tax-exempt securities can be shown if the tax-exempt securities are used as collateral in securing a loan.[16] If an individual who holds tax-exempt securities later incurs some debt, no disallowance will occur if the debt is incurred to finance personal items (e.g., a mortgage on a personal residence). However, if a taxpayer incurs the debt to finance an investment, a portion of the interest is generally disallowed. Even though the interest is not incurred to carry tax-exempt securities, it still may not be deductible. For example, if a taxpayer incurs interest on personal debt, it is not deductible. (See Chapter I7 for a discussion of limitations on the deductibility of personal interest.)

EXAMPLE I6-15 ▶ Sam, an individual, has invested $80,000 in Gold Corporation stock, $120,000 in real estate, and $50,000 in tax-exempt municipal bonds. During the current year, Sam borrows $70,000 for the purpose of investing in a limited partnership. For the year, he pays $6,000 interest on the loan. Under these circumstances, the IRS will presume that Sam has incurred a portion of the debt in order to carry the tax-exempt securities and will disallow a portion of the deduction. Sam may overcome that presumption if he can show that he could not have sold the tax-exempt securities. He cannot overcome this presumption if he can show only that the sale of the bonds would have resulted in a loss. If Sam instead borrowed the money to purchase a personal residence, the IRS probably would not attempt to disallow the deduction. (See Chapter I7 for a discussion of restrictions on the deductibility of interest for personal residences.) ◀

EXPENDITURES THAT ARE CONTRARY TO PUBLIC POLICY

REAL-WORLD EXAMPLE

A subcontractor involved with the construction of a new shopping mall made kickbacks to the supervisor of the primary contractor. The kickbacks were deductible because they were not illegal, and the kickbacks were also ordinary and necessary because the subcontractor would not have been able to continue to work if the kickbacks had not been made. *Raymond Bertolini Trucking Co. v. CIR* 54 AFTR 2d 84-5413, 1984-2 USTC ¶9591 (6th Cir., 1984).

Certain expenditures, even though incurred in a profit-motivated activity, may not be deductible if the payment itself is illegal or if the payment is a penalty or fine resulting from an illegal act. These nondeductible expenses generally fall within one of the following categories:

▶ Illegal payments to government officials or employees
▶ Other illegal payments
▶ Kickbacks, rebates, and bribes under Medicare and Medicaid
▶ Payments of fines and penalties
▶ Payment of treble damages under the federal antitrust laws

BRIBES AND KICKBACKS. Under Sec. 162(c)(1), any illegal bribe or kickback made to any official or employee of a government is not deductible. This applies to payments made to

▶ Federal officials and employees
▶ State, local, and foreign government officials and employees
▶ Officials and employees of an agency of a government

EXAMPLE I6-16 ▶ During February of the current year, Road Corporation enters into a contract with the State of Iowa to construct a five-mile stretch of a new highway. Under the terms of the contract, Road Corporation must complete the project by October 22 of the current year. If it is not completed and accepted by Iowa on or before that date, Iowa will fine Road Corporation $5,000 per day for every day after that date until the project is accepted. By October 20, the project foreman realizes that the company will not make the deadline if it complies with all the requirements imposed by the state inspector assigned to the project. To avoid the fine, the foreman arranges for the inspector to "look the other way" on several of the requirements in exchange for a payment of $8,000. Because this payment constitutes an illegal bribe to a government official, the payment is not deductible. ◀

---

[16] Rev. Proc. 72-18, 1972-1 C.B. 740. *See also Wisconsin Cheeseman, Inc. v. U.S.*, 21 AFTR 2d 383, 68-1 USTC ¶9145 (7th Cir., 1968).

Taxpayers may not deduct illegal payments to officials or employees of a foreign government if the payment is unlawful under the Foreign Corrupt Practices Act of 1977, unless such payments constitute a normal way of doing business in that country. In all cases, the burden rests on the government to prove the illegality of the payment.

Illegal bribes, kickbacks, and other illegal payments made to people other than a government official or employee are nondeductible if they are illegal under a federal law that subjects the payor to a criminal penalty or loss of the privilege of doing business. In addition, illegal payments under a state law imposing the same penalties are nondeductible if the state law is generally enforced. Here, the definition of a kickback includes a payment for referring a client, patient, or customer.

The courts and the IRS have made a distinction between an illegal nondeductible kickback and a rebate of the purchase price. If the rebate is made directly to the purchaser by the seller, it is considered an adjustment to the selling price and, as such, is an *exclusion* (rather than a deduction) from gross income.[17] The distinction between the two payments seems to be that the rebate is actually negotiated as part of the selling price.

Section 162(c)(3) specifically disallows a deduction for any kickback, rebate, or bribe under Medicare and Medicaid. Disallowed amounts include payments made by physicians or by suppliers and providers of goods and services who receive payment under the Social Security Act or a federally funded state plan. Unlike payments to foreign government or nongovernment employees and officials, these payments need not be illegal under federal or state law.

> **ETHICAL POINT**
> A CPA discovers that a client included fines and penalties in a miscellaneous expense section of a previously filed tax return. The CPA should recommend the filing of an amended return. However, the CPA is not obligated to inform the IRS, and the CPA may not do so without the client's permission, except where required by law.

STOP & THINK

Question: Queen, Inc. is engaged in the ship and boat repair business. Since the competition is very tough, Queen generally kicks back approximately 10% of any repair bill to any ship captain who brings his ship to Queen for repairs. Queen's customers include individual owners of large ocean-going yachts and fishing boats, as well as government vessels owned by state, federal, and foreign governments. During the current year, Queen expended $80,000 in kickbacks paid to the captains of privately-owned yachts and boats, $40,000 to the owners of privately-owned vessels, and $100,000 to the captains of state, federal, and foreign government vessels. The crews of these government vessels are government employees. What is the proper tax treatment of these payments?

Solution: The $40,000 in kickbacks paid directly to the owners of the privately-owned vessels are treated as merely a rebate in the price of the services and reduces Queen's gross income, unless the payments could result in the imposition of a criminal penalty or loss of the privilege of doing business. The kickbacks paid to the captains of the state and federal vessels are not deductible because they are paid to employees of state and federal governments. Likewise, the payments to the captains of the foreign vessels are not deductible if the payments are unlawful under the Foreign Corrupt Practices Act.

FINES AND PENALTIES. Section 162(f) of the IRC also disallows a deduction for the payment of any fine or penalty paid to a government because of the violation of a law. Furthermore, it disallows a deduction for two-thirds of any payment for damages made as a result of a conviction (or a guilty or no-contest plea) in an action regarding a criminal violation of the federal antitrust laws.[18]

EXAMPLE I6-17 ▶ During the current year, the United States files criminal and civil actions against Allen, the president of Able Corporation, and Betty, the president of Bell Corporation, for conspiring to fix and maintain prices of electrical transformers. Both Allen and Betty enter pleas of no contest, and the appropriate judgments are entered. Subsequent to this action, Circle Corporation sues both Able and Bell Corporations for treble damages of $300,000. In settlement, Able and Bell Corporations each pay Circle Corporation $75,000. The maximum that Able and Bell Corporations may each deduct is $25,000 ($75,000 ÷ 3). ◀

---

[17] Rev. Rul. 82-149, 1982-2 C.B. 56.   [18] Sec. 162(g).

EXPENSES RELATING TO AN ILLEGAL ACTIVITY. Interestingly, although the payment of an illegal bribe or kickback and the payment of a fine or penalty as the result of an illegal act are both nondeductible, expenses incurred in an illegal activity are generally deductible if they are ordinary, necessary, and reasonable and the income from the illegal activity is also reported.[19]

> **EXAMPLE I6-18** ▶ Fred owns and operates a small financial services business involved in the sale of securities and the lending of money. Fred often sells securities to customers in other states. However, because he did not register the business with the appropriate state or federal authorities, the operation of the business is illegal. During the current year, Fred incurs the following expenses:
>
> | | |
> |---|---:|
> | Interest | $ 20,000 |
> | Salaries | 140,000 |
> | Depreciation | 7,000 |
> | Printing | 5,000 |
> | Bribe to employee of state securities commission | 12,000 |
> | Total | $184,000 |
>
> If Fred reports the income from this activity, the deductible expenses for the year total $172,000. The illegal payment of $12,000 to the government employee is not deductible. ◀

One exception to this general rule exists. Section 280E disallows a deduction for expenses incurred in an illegal business of trafficking or dealing in drugs.

OTHER EXPENDITURES THAT ARE SPECIFICALLY DISALLOWED

The IRC also specifically disallows deductions for certain other expenses, even though they might meet all the requirements mentioned above. These include political contributions and lobbying expenses and, in certain situations, business start-up expenses.

POLITICAL CONTRIBUTIONS AND LOBBYING EXPENSES. Political contributions and lobbying expenses constitute one general category of disallowed expenses. Taxpayers may not deduct expenditures made in connection with the following:

- Influencing legislation
- Participating or intervening in any political campaign of any candidate for public office
- Attempting to influence the general public with respect to elections, legislative matters, or referendums
- Communicating directly with the President, Vice President, and certain other federal employees and officials

Sec. 162(e) also denies a deduction for contributions to tax-exempt organizations that carry on lobbying activities if a principal purpose of the contribution is to obtain a deduction for what otherwise would have been disallowed. The IRC also disallows payments made for advertising in a convention or any other program if any part of the proceeds of the publication will directly or indirectly benefit a specific political party or candidate.[20]

Taxpayers may deduct lobbying expenses incurred to influence legislation on a local level if the legislation is of direct interest to the taxpayer's business. Local legislation includes actions by a legislative body of any political subdivision of a state (e.g., city or county council), but does not include any state or federal action. These deductible expenditures include expenses of communicating with or dues paid to an organization of which the taxpayer is a member. For administrative convenience, the deduction disallowance does not apply to any in-house expenditure attributable to such activities as long as the total of such expenditures for the taxable year does not exceed $2,000. In-house expendi-

---

[19] *CIR v. Neil Sullivan, et al.*, 1 AFTR 2d 1158, 58-1 USTC ¶9368 (USSC, 1958).

[20] Sec. 276(a). Nondeductible political contributions also include payments for admission to a dinner or program where the proceeds will benefit a party or candidate, or admission to an inaugural ball, party, or concert if the activity is identified with a political party or candidate.

tures are expenses incurred directly by the taxpayer other than amounts paid to a professional lobbyist or dues that are allocable to lobbying. Additionally, the deduction disallowance does not apply to taxpayers engaged in the business of lobbying.

> **EXAMPLE I6-19** ▶ Kate is the senior partner of a large New York law firm. During the year, she flies to Washington, D.C., to testify before a Congressional subcommittee with regard to proposed changes in the Social Security taxes imposed on employers. Such changes directly affect her business because they affect the amount of taxes she must pay on behalf of her employees. Kate's ordinary and necessary expenses incurred with respect to the trip are not deductible because the expenses were incurred to influence federal rather than local legislation. ◀

If the legislation cannot reasonably be expected to directly affect the taxpayer's trade or business, the expenses are not deductible.

> **EXAMPLE I6-20** ▶ Kate is the owner of a real estate company in Chicago. The city of Chicago has proposed legislation to increase the hotel room tax. Kate spends time researching and traveling to speak to the Chicago City Council regarding this legislation. Kate's lobbying expenses are not deductible. While they are used to influence legislation on the local level, they are not of direct interest to her business. ◀

BUSINESS INVESTIGATION AND PREOPENING EXPENSES. Section 195 of the IRC also specifically disallows a current deduction for business start-up expenditures. Instead, these expenses are capitalized and are subject to amortization if an election is made to amortize the start-up costs over a period of not less than 60 months starting with the month in which the new business begins. Start-up expenditures specifically include three types of expenditures:

▶ *Business investigation expenses*. These expenses are costs a taxpayer incurs in reviewing and analyzing a prospective business before deciding whether to acquire or create it. The key here is that the expenses are incurred before the actual decision. These expenses include such items as analyses and surveys of markets, traffic patterns, products, labor supplies, and distribution facilities.

ADDITIONAL COMMENT
Costs incurred in connection with the issuance of stock or securities do not qualify as start-up costs. These costs are charged to Paid in Capital.

▶ *Preopening or start-up costs*. Preopening or start-up costs are expenses incurred after a taxpayer decides to acquire or create the business but before the business activity itself has started. These costs include expenditures for training employees; advertising; securing supplies, distributors, and potential customers; and expenditures for professional services in setting up the business's books and records. These costs must be incurred by a taxpayer who is not engaged in any existing business or is engaged in a business that is unrelated to the business being acquired or created.

▶ *Expenses incurred in connection with an investment activity*. These expenses are costs incurred in connection with an investment activity that the taxpayer anticipates will become an active trade or business.

As defined by Sec. 195, start-up expenditures do not include these same types of expenses when they are incurred by a taxpayer who is already engaged in a business similar to the new one being created or acquired. In such a case, the taxpayer may deduct these expenditures currently because they are incurred in the taxpayer's existing business. Figure I6-1 provides a flowchart to assist in properly classifying these types of expenditures.

STOP & THINK

Question: Shauna works in an automobile manufacturing plant in Detroit, Michigan. In January of the current year, she took a two-week vacation in order to fly to Orlando, Florida. While in Orlando, she spent some time investigating the possibility of opening a store in nearby Coco Beach. In total, she spent $800 on airfare, $1,500 on hotels and food, $300 on equipment rentals, and $300 on a car rental. In addition to spending time on the beach talking to people and checking out the rental equipment, she also spent some time talking to shop owners and real estate agents. After some analysis, however, Shauna has decided to keep her job in Detroit. What is the proper tax treatment for these expenditures?

6-16 Individuals ▼ Chapter 6

```
                    Start
                      │
                      ▼
              ┌───────────────┐
              │ Are expenses  │
              │ incurred by a │         ┌──────────────┐
              │   taxpayer    │  Yes    │   Expenses   │
              │   already     │────────▶│     are      │
              │ established   │         │  currently   │
              │ in a similar  │         │  deductible  │
              │   business?   │         │ (Sec. 195 does│
              └───────────────┘         │   not apply) │
                      │                 └──────────────┘
                      │ No
                      ▼
              ┌───────────────┐         ┌──────────────┐
              │     Does      │         │   Sec. 195   │
              │  the taxpayer │  Yes    │  allows the  │
              │  enter the new│────────▶│  taxpayer to │
              │   business?   │         │elect to amortize│
              │               │         │ costs over a │
              │               │         │   60 month   │
              │               │         │    period    │
              └───────────────┘         └──────────────┘
                      │
                      │ No
                      ▼
                ┌───────────┐
                │ Generally │
                │    not    │
                │deductibleª│
                └───────────┘
```

ª Rev. Rul. 57-418, 1957-2 C.B. 143 and Rev. Rul. 77-254, 1977-2 C.B. 63; *Morton Frank*, 20 T.C. 511 (1953).

FIGURE I6-1 ▶ DEDUCTIBILITY OF BUSINESS INVESTIGATION AND START-UP COSTS

Solution: In general, Sec. 162 of the IRC allows a deduction for expenses incurred in a business. Expenses incurred before the business starts are not incurred in a business and thus are not deductible under Sec. 162. However, under Sec. 195 certain expenditures such as business investigation expenses and start-up costs can be capitalized and amortized over a 60-month period, beginning with the month in which the new business begins. Unfortunately Shauna did not open the new business. Thus, she may not deduct or amortize any of these expenses.

Topic Review I6-2 summarizes the restrictions on the deductibility of these items.

PROPER SUBSTANTIATION REQUIREMENT

OBJECTIVE 3

List the substantiation requirements that must be met to deduct travel and entertainment expenses

Generally, the burden of proving the existence of a deduction or loss falls on the taxpayer. Thus, a taxpayer must properly substantiate all deductible expenses. Taxpayers should retain items such as receipts, cancelled checks, and paid bills documenting deductible expenditures in the event the IRS audits a return and requests proof. Occasionally, the courts will allow a deduction that is not properly substantiated by the taxpayer if it is evident that an expenditure has been made. In these cases, the amount of the deduction is estimated based on all the facts and circumstances. This procedure is known as the *Cohan* rule and derives its name from a court case in which the judge allowed a deduction for an estimated amount of certain expenses.[21] The most prudent course of action, of course, is to retain proper documentation rather than to rely upon the *Cohan* rule.

---

[21] *George M. Cohan v. CIR*, 8 AFTR 10552, 2 USTC ¶489 (2nd Cir., 1930). Interestingly, the *Cohan* case dealt with travel and entertainment expenses. Because of the subsequent enactment of Sec. 274(d), the *Cohan* rule may not be used in order to deduct entertainment expenses. It is still effective for other types of expenses.

Topic Review I6-2

Restrictions on the Deductibility of Expense Items

Item	Restrictions Imposed
1. Capital expenditures	The general rule is that the expenditure is not currently deductible if its life extends beyond the end of the year. Special elections are available to currently deduct certain capital expenditures (e.g., research and experimental costs under Sec. 174; and limited amounts per year for acquisitions of tangible personal property used in a trade or business under Sec. 179).
2. Carrying charges	An election may be made under Sec. 266 to capitalize certain expenses that are normally deductible such as property and employment taxes, interest, and carrying charges on unimproved unproductive real estate.
3. Expenses related to tax exempt income	Expenses such as interest incurred on debt used to purchase or carry tax-exempt securities are disallowed under Sec. 265.
4. Expenditures contrary to public policy	Such expenditures are generally not deductible. Examples include bribes and kickbacks, fines and penalties, and expenses of an illegal activity involved with trafficking or dealing in drugs.
5. Legal and accounting fees	Legal and accounting fees can be either *for* AGI deductible business expenses, nondeductible personal use expenditures, or *from* AGI fees incurred in the determination of any tax (e.g., tax return preparation fees).
6. Political contributions and lobby expenses	The general rule is that such items are not deductible (e.g., costs of influencing public opinion), but there are certain exceptions (e.g., costs of appearing before local legislative bodies on topics directly related to the taxpayer's business).
7. Business investigation and preopening expenses	The following rules apply: a. Currently deductible if the taxpayer is already engaged in a similar business. b. Not deductible if the taxpayer is not currently engaged in a similar business and does not enter the new business. c. Amortized over 60 months if the taxpayer enters the new business and makes an election. d. Deductible if expenditures constitute specific items such as legal expenses incurred in drafting purchase documents in an unsuccessful attempt to acquire a specific business. However, general investigation expenditures in search of a new business are not deductible.

EXAMPLE I6-21 ▶ In April of the current year, Terry took his tax records to a CPA to have his prior year's income tax return prepared. As part of the return, the CPA attached a supplemental schedule listing all of Terry's items of income and expense. After the return was prepared and filed, Terry's records were stolen. Upon audit two years later, the IRS disallowed Terry's deductions because there were no records to substantiate the expenses. When the case was litigated, the court allowed deductions for an estimated amount of expenses under the *Cohan* rule because of the list that was attached to Terry's return and because the court believed that Terry had testified honestly in his own behalf.[22] ◀

HISTORICAL NOTE

Justice Learned Hand, in permitting a deduction for unsubstantiated amounts in *George M. Cohan v. CIR*, 8 AFTR 10552, 2 USTC ¶489 (2nd Cir, 1930), wrote "absolute certainty in such matters is usually impossible and it is not necessary; the Board should make as close an approximation as it can, bearing heavily if it chooses on the taxpayer whose inexactitude is of his own making."

Additionally, Sections 274 and 280F provide specific and more stringent recordkeeping requirements for travel, entertainment, business gifts, computers, and vehicles used for transportation. In these cases no deduction may be taken unless the taxpayer substantiates the expenditure by either an adequate record or sufficient evidence that corroborates the taxpayer's statement. This substantiation may take the form of account books, diaries, logs, receipts and paid bills, trip sheets, expense reports, and statements of witnesses. The information that must be substantiated includes the following:

▶ Amount of the expense

▶ Time and place of the travel or entertainment

▶ Date and description of the gift

▶ Business purpose of the expenditure

---

[22] *Layard M. White*, 1980 PH T.C. Memo ¶80,582, 41 TCM 671.

- Business relationship to the taxpayer of the person entertained or of the person who received the gift

The *Cohan* rule may not be used for these types of expenses. (See Chapter I9 for a more complete discussion regarding the deductibility of these types of expenses.)

WHEN AN EXPENSE IS DEDUCTIBLE

OBJECTIVE 4

Explain when deductions may be taken under both the cash and accrual methods of accounting

Because taxable income is generally measured on an annual basis, the question of when a particular expense is deductible is critical. The answer to this question largely depends on which method of accounting is being used.[23] The most common methods include the following:

- Cash receipts and disbursements method (cash method)
- Accrual method
- Hybrid method (a combination of the cash and accrual methods where some items are accounted for on the cash method and other items are accounted for on the accrual method)

Taxpayers normally use the same method for computing taxable income that they use in keeping their regular financial accounting records. However, except for the use of the last-in, first-out (LIFO) method of accounting for inventory, the tax law does not generally require conformity. For example, many companies use the straight-line depreciation method for financial accounting purposes and the modified accelerated cost recovery system (MACRS) for tax purposes. This difference in depreciation methods, of course, results in a book-tax adjustment.

ADDITIONAL COMMENT

Section 446(b) provides that in cases where no method of accounting has been regularly used or if the method used does not clearly reflect income, then the computation of taxable income is to be made under a method that, in the opinion of the IRS, does clearly reflect income.

CASH METHOD

Under the cash method of accounting, expenses are deductible when they are actually paid. As long as it is subsequently honored, payment by check is considered a cash payment in the year the check is mailed or delivered even though it is delivered so late on the last day of the year that the payee could not have cashed it.[24] If a check is mailed near the end of the year it is important to have evidence that the check was mailed in the year in which the deduction is claimed. Furthermore, the use of a credit card to satisfy an obligation is considered a cash payment at the time of the charge rather than at the time the charge is paid.

A mere promise to pay, or the issuance of a note payable, does not constitute a payment under the cash method. Thus, a charge on an open account with a creditor is not deductible until cash is actually transferred in satisfaction of the charge.

ADDITIONAL COMMENT

If a taxpayer using the cash method pays an expense with borrowed funds, the expense is deductible when paid instead of when the loan is repaid.

EXAMPLE I6-22 ▶ Peter, a calendar-year taxpayer, is the sole owner of a plumbing repair business. The business uses the cash method of accounting. Under an arrangement with one of his suppliers, Peter and his employees can pick up supplies at any time during the month by merely signing for them. At the end of the month, the supplier sends Peter a bill for the charges. Peter always pays the bill in full during the following month. In December of the current year, Peter charges $1,500 for supplies. During the same month Peter purchases a plumbing fixture for $250 from another supplier. Peter uses his charge card at the time of purchase. Peter must deduct the $250 during the current year. However, the $1,500 charged on the open account is deductible when paid in the following year. ◀

---

[23] Methods of accounting as they relate to the reporting of income are discussed in Chapter I3. Methods of accounting as they relate to deductibility of expenses and losses are covered in this chapter. For an overall discussion of accounting methods, see Chapter I11.

[24] *CIR v. Estate of M. A. Bradley*, 10 AFTR 1405, 3 USTC ¶904 (6th Cir., 1932) and *Charles F. Kehler*, 18 T.C. 31 (1952).

PREPAID EXPENSES. In general, a capital expenditure or the prepayment of expenses by a cash method taxpayer does not result in a current deduction if the expenditure creates an asset having a useful life that extends substantially beyond the close of the tax year. This can occur when a taxpayer makes expenditures for prepaid rent, services, or interest. However, in the case of prepaid rent, a circuit court of appeals decision has held that a current deduction may be taken for the entire amount of an expenditure if the period covered by the prepayment does not exceed one year and the taxpayer is obligated to make the prepayment.[25]

▶ **EXAMPLE I6-23** ▶ On November 1 of the current year, Twyla enters into a lease arrangement with Rashad to rent Rashad's office space for the following 36 months. By prepaying the rent for the entire 36-month period, Twyla is able to obtain a favorable monthly lease payment of $800. This prepayment creates an asset (a leasehold) with a useful life that extends substantially beyond the end of the taxable year. Thus, only $1,600 ($800 × 2 months) of the total payment is deductible in the current year. The rest must be capitalized and amortized over the life of the lease. However, assume that under the terms of the lease, Twyla is obligated to make three annual payments of $9,600 each November 1 for the subsequent 12 months. On November 1 of the current year, Twyla pays Rashad $9,600 for the first 12-month period. Because Twyla is obligated to make the prepayment and the period covered by the prepayment does not exceed one year, the entire $9,600 is deductible in the current year using the reasoning of the previously cited circuit court decision. ◀

PREPAID INTEREST. The IRC requires that prepaid interest expense be deducted over the period of the loan to which the interest charge is allocated.[26] Receipt of a discounted loan does not represent prepaid interest expense. Instead, the interest is deemed to be paid as the loan is repaid.

▶ **EXAMPLE I6-24** ▶ During the current year, Richelle borrows $1,000 from the bank for use in her business. Richelle uses the cash method of accounting in her business. Under the terms of the loan, the bank discounts the loan by $80, paying Richelle $920. When the loan comes due in the following year, however, Richelle is to repay the full $1,000. Richelle cannot deduct the $80 of interest expense until she repays the loan in the following year. ◀

REAL-WORLD EXAMPLE

A taxpayer made an overpayment of the federal income tax in 1975. In 1979, the IRS offset the overpayment against interest the taxpayer owed to the IRS. It was held that the interest expense was deductible in 1979 rather than in 1975. *Saverio Eboli,* 93 T.C. 123 (1989).

Taxpayers often prepay interest in the form of points. A point is one percent of the loan amount. Thus, the payment of two points on a $100,000 loan amounts to $2,000. While points must generally be amortized over the life of the loan, points paid in connection with the purchase or improvement of a principal residence are deductible when paid. According to the IRS, points paid in connection with the purchase (but not the improvement) of a principal residence are automatically deductible in the year paid if the following four requirements are met:

- the closing agreement clearly designates the amounts as points
- the amount is computed as a percentage of the amount borrowed
- the charging of points is an established business practice in the geographic area, and
- the points are paid in connection with the purchase of the taxpayer's principal residence which is used to secure the loan.[27]

REAL LIFE EXAMPLE

The mortgage company will, at the end of the year, mail to the taxpayer a Form 1098 which shows the amount of interest and points paid.

Although points paid on loans incurred to *improve* the taxpayer's principal residence do not fall under this safe harbor rule, they still are currently deductible if the loan is secured by the residence, the payment of points is an established business practice in the geographic area in which it is incurred, and the amount of the prepayment does not exceed the amount generally charged.

---

[25] *Martin J. Zaninovich v. CIR,* 45 AFTR 2d 80-1442, 80-1 USTC ¶9342 (9th Cir., 1980) and *Bonaire Development Co. v. CIR,* 50 AFTR 2d 82-5167, 82-2 USTC ¶9428 (9th Cir., 1982). See also *Stephen A. Keller v. CIR,* 53 AFTR 2d 84-663, 84-1 USTC ¶9194 (8th Cir., 1984).

[26] Sec. 461(g).

[27] Rev. Proc. 94-27, I.R.B. 94-15, 17. As explained in Chapter I7, acquisition indebtedness incurred to acquire a personal residence is limited to $1,000,000. Hence, points that are allocated to the loan principal in excess of this limit are not deductible either.

A taxpayer may not currently deduct points paid to refinance a mortgage on a principal residence because the points are not paid in connection with the purchase or improvement of the taxpayer's residence.[28]

EXAMPLE I6-25 ▶ During the current year, Pam purchases a principal residence for $150,000, paying $50,000 down and financing the remainder with a 20-year mortgage secured by the property. Pam must make monthly payments on the mortgage. At the closing, Pam must pay three points as a loan origination fee. Because these points are paid in connection with the purchase of a principal residence, Pam may deduct $3,000 ($100,000 × 0.03) as interest expense during the current year. In addition, Pam may also deduct the interest portion of each monthly payment made during the year. On the other hand, assume that Pam takes out the $100,000 loan in order to refinance her home at a lower interest rate. The $3,000 prepaid interest is not currently deductible. Instead, Pam must deduct the interest ratably over the term of the loan. Thus, Pam may deduct an additional $12.50 ($3,000 ÷ 240 payments) interest expense for each payment that she makes during the year. ◀

If a home is sold and the refinanced mortgage is paid off, any unamortized portion of the points is deductible in the year of repayment. Points paid by the seller will be treated as incurred by the purchaser, and therefore are currently deductible by the purchaser if the other requirements are met and they are subtracted from the purchase price of the residence.[29]

The cash method of accounting provides some degree of flexibility to taxpayers since under this method, taxpayers generally can deduct expenses when paid rather than when accrued. Thus, subject to the limitations mentioned above with regard to prepaid expenses, taxpayers may to some degree accelerate or defer deductions from one year to another by merely accelerating or deferring payment. However, the IRC imposes limitations on the use of the cash method. For example, inventories must be accounted for under the accrual method.[30] Furthermore, under Sec. 448, most C corporations (corporations that have not elected Subchapter S status), partnerships that have a C corporation as a partner, and tax shelters may not use the cash method. However, there are exceptions to this general rule for personal service corporations, small businesses with average annual gross receipts of $5 million or less, and businesses involved in the farming and timber businesses. (See Chapter I11 for a complete discussion of the different accounting methods that may be used for computing taxable income.)

ACCRUAL METHOD

HISTORICAL NOTE
Although Congress began taxing income under the 16th Amendment in 1913, it was not until the Revenue Act of 1916 that the accrual method of accounting was recognized.

An **accrual method** taxpayer deducts expenses in the period in which they accrue. Generally items accrue when the transaction meets both an **all-events test** and an **economic performance test**.[31]

ALL-EVENTS TEST. The all-events test is met when both of the following occur:
▶ The existence of a liability is established.
▶ The amount of the liability is determined with reasonable accuracy.

EXAMPLE I6-26 ▶ During the current year, Phil provides services for Louis. Louis uses the accrual method of accounting. Phil claims that Louis owes $10,000 for the services. Louis admits owing Phil $6,000, but contests the remaining $4,000. Because the amount of the liability can be accurately established only with respect to $6,000, Louis can deduct only that amount. If Louis pays the full $10,000, he may deduct the full amount in the year of payment, even though the contested amount ($4,000) is not resolved until a subsequent taxable year.[32] If Phil loses the lawsuit and

---

[28] Rev. Rul. 87-22, 1987-1 C.B. 146, and Rev. Proc. 87-15, 1987-1 C.B. 624. However, the Eighth Circuit has allowed a current deduction for points paid upon the refinancing of a mortgage loan because the original loan was merely a "bridge" or temporary loan until permanent financing could be arranged. See *James R. Huntsman v. CIR*, 66 AFTR 2d 90-5020, 90-2 USTC ¶50,340 (8th Cir., 1990).
[29] Rev. Proc. 94-27, I.R.B. 94-15, 17.
[30] However taxpayers with average annual gross receipts of $1 million or less are not required to use the accrual method of accounting for inventories. See Rev. Proc. 2000-22, IRB 2000-22, 1008. Taxpayers who must use the accrual method for inventories may also use the hybrid method, which requires the accrual method for cost of goods sold but permits the cash method for all other expenses.
[31] Reg. Sec. 1.461-1(a)(2) and Sec. 461(h).
[32] Reg. Sec. 1.461-2(a)(1).

repays Louis the $4,000, Louis will include that amount in income under the tax benefit rule (see Chapter I11). ◄

Because of the all-events test, taxpayers may not deduct additions to reserves for estimated expenses such as warranty expenses. Instead, the taxpayer deducts the expenses in the year in which such work is actually performed.

EXAMPLE I6-27 ► Best Corporation uses the accrual method of accounting and is engaged in the business of painting and rustproofing automobiles. Best Corporation provides a 5-year warranty for new vehicles and a 2-year warranty for used vehicles. Best Corp. extends the warranty only to the person who owns the car at the time the car is painted. Furthermore, in order to keep the warranty in force, the customer must present the vehicle to Best Corporation for inspection each year. The warranty is void if the vehicle is involved in an accident. Even though for financial accounting purposes Best Corporation may provide a reserve for estimated warranty expenses and deduct a reasonable addition to the reserve on an annual basis, no income tax deduction is allowed until the warranty work is actually done. ◄

ECONOMIC PERFORMANCE TEST. To be currently deductible under the accrual method, an expense must also meet an economic performance test. Exactly when economic performance is deemed to have occurred depends on the type of transaction. Table I6-1 contains a listing of various types of transactions that may arise and identifies when economic performance is deemed to have occurred under Sec. 461(h).

EXAMPLE I6-28 ► On December 20 of the current year, Chris, an accrual method taxpayer, enters into a binding contract with Pat to have Pat clean and paint the exterior of Chris's business building. Under the terms of the contract, Pat is to do the work in March of the following year. The total cost of the job is $4,000. Chris pays 10% down at the time the contract is signed. Because the job is not to be done until the following year, economic performance has not occurred in the current year and Chris may not deduct any portion of the expense in the current year. ◄

HISTORICAL NOTE
The economic performance test was added by Congress in the Tax Reform Act of 1984. Congress was concerned that in some situations taxpayers could deduct expenses currently, but the actual cash expenditure might not be made for several years. Taking a current deduction in such situations overstated the real cost because the time value of money was ignored.

An exception to the economic performance test provides that taxpayers may take a current deduction for recurring liabilities if all of the following occur:
► The all-events test is met during the year.
► Economic performance of the item occurs within the shorter of 8½ months after the close of the tax year, or a reasonable period after the close of the tax year.
► The expense is recurring and the taxpayer consistently treats the item as incurred in the tax year.
► Either the item is not material or the accrual of the item in the tax year results in a more proper matching against income than accruing the item in the tax year in which economic performance occurs.

This exception for recurring liabilities is available for the first four types of transactions identified in Table I6-1, but may not be used for the last type of transaction in the table.

ADDITIONAL COMMENT
The economic performance test does not apply to accruals for estimated expenses that are specifically allowed by the IRC.

EXAMPLE I6-29 ► Dawn is a calendar-year, accrual method taxpayer. Every year at the end of October, Dawn enters into a contract with Sam to provide snow removal services for the parking lots at Dawn's business. This contract extends for five months through the end of March of the following year. Because the all-events test is met (the liability is fixed), the expense recurs every year, economic performance occurs within the requisite period of time, and the item is not material, Dawn may deduct the entire expense in the year in which the contract is signed. ◄

A special rule under Sec. 461(c) applies to real property taxes. Under this provision, a taxpayer may elect to accrue real property taxes ratably over the period to which the taxes relate. Once made, this election may not be changed without permission from the IRS.

EXAMPLE I6-30 ► Under the law of State X, the lien date for real property taxes for calendar year 2001 is January 1, 2001. The tax is payable in full on November 30, 2001. Alpha Corp. is an accrual method taxpayer that has a January 31 fiscal year-end. On January 1, 2001, real property taxes of $100,000 are assessed against a building Alpha Corp. owns. Alpha pays the taxes on November 30, 2001.

TABLE I6-1
When Economic Performance Is Deemed to Have Occurred

Event That Gives Rise to Liability	When Economic Performance Is Deemed to Have Occurred (i.e. when the accrual method taxpayer may take the deduction)
Another person provides the taxpayer with property or services	When the property or services are actually provided[a]
Taxpayer uses property	As the property is used[a]
Taxpayer must provide property or services to another person	As the taxpayer provides property or services to the other person[b]
Taxpayer must make payments to another, including payments for rebates and refunds, awards or prizes, insurance or service contracts, and taxes.	As payments to the other person are made
Taxpayer must make payments to another person because of a tort, breach of contract, violation of law, or injury claim under a worker's compensation act	As payments to the other person are made

[a] Economic performance may be deemed to have occurred at the earlier date of payment if the taxpayer reasonably expects the property or services to be provided within 3½ months after the payment is made. Reg. Sec. 1.461-4(d)(6)(ii).
[b] Economic performance may also occur as the taxpayer incurs costs in connection with the obligation to provide the property or services. Reg. Sec. 1.461-4(d)(4)(i).

If Alpha does not make the election to use the ratable accrual method, none of the payment is deductible in Alpha's fiscal year ending January 31, 2001 because the payment date is more than 8½ months after the January 31, 2001 year-end.

On the other hand, if Alpha makes the election, it may deduct $8,333 ($100,000 × 1/12) in its fiscal year that ends January 31, 2001 and $91,667 ($100,000 × 11/12) in its fiscal year that ends January 31, 2002.

If the taxes are due and paid on September 30, 2001, Alpha would be better off not making the ratable accrual election. In this case, the recurring item exception applies because the payment is made within 8½ months of Alpha's 2001 fiscal year-end. Thus, if Alpha does not make the election, all of the $100,000 is deductible in the fiscal year ending on January 31, 2001. ◀

The rules for determining when an expense is deductible are presented in Topic Review I6-3.

SPECIAL DISALLOWANCE RULES

OBJECTIVE 5

Explain the tax consequences of wash sales

In addition to the general rules of deductibility mentioned above, certain types of transactions are subject to further limitations and disallowances. These include transactions known as wash sales, transactions between related persons, gambling losses, losses associated with an activity determined to be a hobby, expenses of renting a vacation home, and expenses of an office in the taxpayer's home. These special disallowance rules are discussed below.

WASH SALES
Section 1091 disallows losses incurred on wash sales of stock or securities in the year of sale. For purposes of Sec. 1091, a **wash sale** occurs when

▶ A taxpayer realizes a loss on the sale of stock or securities, and

Topic Review I6-3

When an Expense Is Deductible

CASH METHOD: DEDUCTIBLE WHEN PAID

Payment Is Made When
- Cash or other property is transferred.
- A check is delivered or mailed.
- An item is charged on a credit card.
  Note: A mere promise to pay or delivery of a note payable is not considered payment.

Prepaid Expenses
- Generally are deductible over the period covered.
- Deductible when paid if the period covered does not exceed one year.
- Prepaid interest is generally deductible ratably over the period covered by the loan.
- Points are deductible when paid if:
  —The loan is used to purchase or improve the taxpayer's principal residence.
  —The loan is secured by the residence.
  —Points are established business practice in the geographical area.
  —The points do not exceed the amount generally charged.
  —For points paid to purchase a principal residence, the closing agreement clearly designates the amounts as points and the amount must be computed as a percentage of the amount borrowed.

ACCRUAL METHOD: DEDUCTIBLE WHEN ACCRUED

In General
- The accrual method must be used for inventories (except for taxpayers with average annual gross receipts of $1 million or less).
- Accrual occurs when both all-events test and economic performance have been met.

All-Events Test
- The existence of a liability is established and
- The amount of the liability is determined.

Economic Performance
- When economic performance is deemed to occur depends on the transaction involved (see Table I6-1).
- May be deemed to occur in the year the all-events test is met if all of the following tests are met:
  —Actual economic performance occurs within the shorter of:
    8½ months after taxable year or a reasonable period after the taxable year.
  —The expense is recurring and is treated consistently from year to year.
  —Either:
    The item is immaterial or
    Deducting the expense in the year the all-events test is met results in a more proper matching of income and deductions.

▶ The taxpayer acquires "substantially identical" stock or securities within a 61-day period of time that extends from 30 days before the date of sale to 30 days after the date of sale.[33]

Thus, the purpose of the wash sale rule is to prevent taxpayers from generating artificial tax losses in situations where taxpayers do not intend to reduce their holdings in the stock or securities that are sold.

EXAMPLE I6-31 ▶ Leslie realizes $10,000 in short-term capital gains (STCGs) through dealings in the stock market during the current year. Realizing that STCGs are fully includible in gross income unless they are offset against realized capital losses, Leslie analyzes her portfolio to determine whether she owns any stocks that have declined in value. She finds that the FMV of her Edison Corporation common stock is only $8,000, even though she originally purchased it for $16,000. Despite this

---

[33] Here the term *acquire* includes an acquisition of the stock either by purchase or in a taxable exchange. The term *stock or securities* includes contracts or options to acquire or sell stock or securities (see Sec. 1091(a)).

6-24 Individuals ▼ Chapter 6

paper loss on the stock, Leslie feels that Edison Corporation is still a good investment and wants to retain the stock. If Leslie attempts to take advantage of the paper loss on the Edison stock by selling the stock she owns and repurchasing a similar number of shares of Edison common stock within the 61-day period, the loss is disallowed.

SELF-STUDY QUESTION

During 1997, you bought 100 shares of X stock on each of three occasions. You paid $158 a share for the first block of 100 shares, $100 a share for the second block, and $95 a share for the third block. On December 23, 2001, you sold 300 shares of X stock for $125 a share. On January 6, 2002, you bought 250 shares of identical X stock. Can you deduct the loss realized on the first block of stock?

ANSWER

You cannot deduct the loss of $33 a share on the first block because within 30 days after the date of sale you bought 250 identical shares of X stock. In addition, you cannot reduce the gain realized on the sale of the second and third blocks of stock by this loss. Publication 550.

At times, taxpayers may attempt to circumvent the wash sale provisions through either a sham transaction or an indirect repurchase of the securities. If this is the case, the wash sale provisions still prevent the recognition of the loss. The Supreme Court has held that losses on sales of stock by a husband were disallowed when the stockbroker was instructed to purchase the same number of shares in his wife's name.[34]

In some instances a taxpayer may be tempted to circumvent the wash sale provisions by merely delaying the repurchase of the substantially identical stock. This tactic should work as long as a written agreement to repurchase the stock does not exist at the time of the sale or at any time within the 61-day period mandated by the Sec. 1091 wash sale provisions. If such an agreement is made, the courts will disallow the loss, even though the actual purchase does not occur within the 61-day period.[35]

In certain cases, taxpayers may still recognize losses on transactions that literally fall within the wash sale requirements. For example, a taxpayer may purchase stock and then sell a portion of those shares within 30 days where the intent is merely to reduce the stock holdings. Taken together, these two transactions meet the tests of Sec. 1091. However, because the purpose of the sale is to reduce the taxpayer's holdings rather than to generate an artificial tax loss, the loss on the sale is allowed.[36] Section 1091 also does not apply to losses realized in the ordinary course of business by a dealer in stock or securities.

If fewer shares of stock are acquired within the 61-day period than were disposed of, only a proportionate amount of the total loss is disallowed.

EXAMPLE I6-32 ▶

Several years ago, Henry purchased 100 shares of New Corporation common stock for $2,000 ($20 per share). On July 2 of the current year, Henry sells all 100 shares for $1,000. On July 30 of the current year, Henry purchases 75 shares (three-fourths of the original shares) of New Corporation common stock. As a result of the reacquisition, three-fourths of the total loss ($750) is disallowed. Henry recognizes the remaining $250 loss.

SUBSTANTIALLY IDENTICAL STOCK OR SECURITIES. Only the acquisition of substantially identical stock or securities will cause a disallowance of the loss. The IRC and the Treasury Regulations do not define the term *substantially identical*. Judicial and administrative rulings have held that bonds issued by the same corporation generally are not considered substantially identical if they differ in terms (e.g., interest rate and term to maturity). However, bonds of the same corporation that differ only in their maturity dates (e.g., the bonds do not come due for 16 years and mature within a few months of each other) have been held to be substantially identical. The preferred stock of a corporation generally is not considered substantially identical to the common stock of the same corporation.[37]

KEY POINT

The recognition of a loss on a wash sale is only being deferred because the investor can increase the basis of the acquired stock by the disallowed loss.

BASIS OF STOCK. If a loss is disallowed because of the wash sale provisions, the basis of the acquired stock that causes the nonrecognition is increased to reflect the disallowance. This increase means that the disallowed loss is merely postponed and will eventually be recognized either in the form of a reduced gain or an increased loss upon the subsequent sale or disposition of the stock that causes the loss disallowance. Because the amount of the increase in basis is equal to the postponed loss, the taxpayer eventually recovers the cost of the original shares of stock. If there has been more than one purchase of replacement stock and the amount of stock purchased within the 61-day period

---

[34] *John P. McWilliams v. CIR*, 35 AFTR 1184, 47-1 USTC ¶9289 (USSC, 1947).
[35] Rev. Rul. 72-225, 1972-1 C.B. 59, and *Frank Stein*, 1977 PH T.C. Memo ¶77,241, 36 TCM 992.
[36] Rev. Rul. 56-602, 1956-2 C.B. 527.
[37] *Marie Hanlin, Executrix v. CIR*, 39-2 USTC ¶9783 (3d Cir., 1939). However, the IRS held in Rev. Rul. 77-201, 1977-1 C.B. 250, that the convertible preferred stock of a corporation is substantially identical to its common stock if the preferred stock has the same voting rights and is subject to the same dividend restrictions as the common stock, is unrestricted as to its convertibility, and sells at relatively the same price (taking into consideration the conversion ratio).

exceeds the stock that is sold, the stock that is deemed to have caused the disallowance of the loss is accounted for chronologically. The holding period of the replacement stock includes the period of time the taxpayer held the stock that was sold.

EXAMPLE I6-33 ▶ Ingrid enters into the following transactions with regard to Pacific Corporation common stock:

Date	Transaction	Amount
January 4, 1993	Purchases 600 shares	$30,000
October 2, 2001	Purchases 400 shares	10,000
October 12, 2001	Sells original 600 shares	12,000
October 20, 2001	Purchases 200 shares	5,000
October 25, 2001	Purchases 300 shares	8,400

Because Ingrid purchases more than 600 shares within the 61-day period before and after the date of sale (the purchases made on October 2, 20, and 25), the entire loss of $18,000 ($30,000 − $12,000) is postponed. Four hundred shares (two-thirds of the number of shares sold) are purchased on October 2 and 200 shares (one-third) are purchased on October 20. Thus, the basis of the 400 shares of stock purchased on October 2 is $22,000 [$10,000 purchase price + ($18,000 disallowed loss × 0.667)]. The basis of the 200 shares of stock purchased on October 20 is $11,000 [$5,000 + ($18,000 disallowed loss × 0.333)]. Both of these blocks of stock have a holding period that starts on January 4, 1993.[38] The basis of the 300 shares of stock purchased on October 25 is its purchase price of $8,400. Its holding period begins on October 25. ◀

STOP & THINK

Question: With regard to his investments in the stock market, the current year has been like a roller coaster ride for Doug. He is now wanting to do some year-end tax planning. For the year to date, he has realized a net gain of $12,000 on his stock investments. Although some of his current stock holdings have unrealized losses, he feels that they are excellent investments that will provide excellent returns in the next year or two. His stock broker has suggested that he sell enough of his holdings to realize a $12,000 loss (to offset the $12,000 capital gain) and then simply repurchase some of the stock. What advice would you give Doug as he discusses this strategy with his broker?

Solution: By realizing $12,000 in capital losses this year, Doug may be able to offset the capital gains he has already recognized. In order to recognize these losses, however, he must make sure that the wash sale provisions do not apply. Thus, he must either 1) purchase stock of different corporations or 2) delay the repurchase of the same issue of stock for at least 31 days after the date of sale. Since Doug is happy with his current investments, perhaps the second strategy is the best. Of course, other non-tax issues must also be considered. For example, does Doug think that the prices will go up quickly within the next 30 days? If so, he may lose out on some significant gains while he is waiting to repurchase the stock. Additionally, the transaction costs (such as commissions) must also be considered.

TRANSACTIONS BETWEEN RELATED PARTIES

OBJECTIVE 6

Explain the tax consequences of transactions between related parties

Section 267 places transactions between certain related parties under special scrutiny because of the potential for tax abuse. For example, a taxpayer could sell a piece of property at a loss to a wholly owned corporation. Without any restrictions on the deductibility of the loss, the individual could recognize the loss while still retaining effective control of the property. Under Sec. 267, related taxpayers may not take current deductions on two specific types of transactions between them. These transactions are

▶ Losses on sales of property

▶ Accrued expenses that remain unpaid at the end of the tax year

---

[38] An asset's holding period is important in determining whether subsequent gain or loss on the asset is long-term or short-term gain or loss. This is explained further in Chapter I5.

6-26 Individuals ▼ Chapter 6

ADDITIONAL COMMENT
Section 267 does not define the word property, but the IRS and the courts have given it a broad meaning.

RELATED PARTIES DEFINED. Section 267 defines the following relationships as related parties:

- Individuals and their families. The term *family* includes an individual's spouse, brothers and sisters (including half-brothers and half-sisters), ancestors, and lineal descendants.
- An individual and a corporation in which the individual owns more than 50% of the value of the outstanding stock.
- Various relationships between grantors, beneficiaries, and fiduciaries of a trust or trusts, or between the fiduciary of a trust and a corporation if certain ownership requirements are met.
- A corporation and a partnership if the same persons own more than 50% in value of the stock of the corporation and more than 50% of the partnership.
- Two corporations if the same persons own more than 50% in value of the outstanding stock of both corporations and at least one of the corporations is an S corporation.
- Other complex relationships involving trusts, corporations and individuals.

TAX ADVISER TIP
The related party rules many times cause the tax consequences to be different than what was expected. Be sure that your clients provide all details to you ahead of time when relatives are involved in the transaction. You might be able to help structure the transaction in a way that meets your client's expectations.

Several of these relationships depend on an individual's ownership of a corporation. For example, if a taxpayer does not own more than 50% of a corporation's stock, the individual and the corporation are not related, and a loss on the sale of business or investment property between the two is deductible. Occasionally individuals might attempt to circumvent the related party rules by dispersing the ownership of a corporation (e.g., among close family members) while retaining economic control. To prevent these tactics, Sec. 267 contains constructive ownership rules whereby a taxpayer is deemed to own stock owned by certain other persons. These constructive ownership rules are as follows:

- Stock owned by an individual's family is treated as owned by the individual. Here the definition of *family* is the same as that of *related parties* (i.e. spouse, brothers and sisters, ancestors, and lineal descendants).
- Stock owned by a corporation, partnership, estate, or trust is treated as owned proportionately by the shareholders, partners, or beneficiaries.
- If an individual partner in a partnership owns (or is treated as owning) stock in a corporation, the individual is treated as owning any stock of that corporation owned by any other partner in the partnership. This does not occur, however, if the only stock the individual owns (or is considered to own) is what his or her family owns.[39]
- Stock ownership that is attributed to a shareholder or partner from an entity can be reattributed to another taxpayer under any of the constructive ownership rules. However, stock ownership attributed to a taxpayer under the family or partner rules cannot be reattributed.

These rules are illustrated by the following examples:

EXAMPLE I6-34 ▶ Alice and Beth are equal partners in the AB Partnership. Beth owns 60% of First Corporation's stock, and Craig, Alice's husband, owns the other 40%. The ownership of the partnership and the corporation is demonstrated in Figure I6-2. Under the constructive ownership rules, Alice is considered to own Craig's 40% of the First Corporation stock. Alice is not considered to own the First Corporation stock owned by her partner Beth, because the only First Corporation stock Alice owns (or is considered to own) is that owned by her husband. If Alice sells property at a loss to First Corporation, the loss is recognized because Alice does not directly or constructively own more than 50% of the First Corporation stock. ◀

EXAMPLE I6-35 ▶ Assume the same facts as in Example I6-34, except that the First Corporation stock is owned 50% by the AB Partnership and 25% each by Beth and Craig. The ownership of the partnership and the corporation is shown in Figure I6-3. In addition to Craig's 25%, Alice is considered to own 50% of the stock owned by the AB Partnership because of her 50% ownership in AB. The other half of AB's stock ownership is attributed to her partner, Beth. However, Alice is also

---
[39] Reg. Sec. 1.267(c)-1(b), Exs. (2) and (3).

FIGURE I6-2 ▶ ILLUSTRATION FOR EXAMPLE I6-34

treated as owning the First Corporation stock Beth owns both actually and constructively (50%). Thus, Alice is treated as owning 100% of the First Corporation stock. In this case, Alice will not be able to recognize a loss on the sale of property to First Corporation. ◀

DISALLOWED LOSSES. If a loss is disallowed under Sec. 267, the original seller of the property receives no tax deduction. The disallowed loss has no effect on the purchaser's basis. The cost basis to the purchaser is equal to the amount paid for the property. However, partial relief is provided because on a subsequent sale of the property, the related purchaser may reduce the recognized gain by the amount of the disallowed loss. This offsetting of a subsequent gain is available only to the related person who originally purchased the property. If the disallowed loss is larger than the subsequent gain, or if the purchaser sells the property at a loss, no deduction is allowed for the unused loss. This may result in a partial disallowance of an overall economic loss for the related parties because there is no upward basis adjustment for the previously disallowed loss (as is the case for a wash sale).

EXAMPLE I6-36 ▶ Assume three separate scenarios in which Sam sells a tract of land during the current year. In each case assume that Sam purchased the land from his father, Frank, for $10,000. Frank's basis at the time of the original sale was $15,000 in each case. Thus, Frank's $5,000 loss on each land sale was disallowed.

FIGURE I6-3 ▶ ILLUSTRATION FOR EXAMPLE I6-35

6-28 Individuals ▼ Chapter 6

KEY POINT

The loss disallowance rule for related parties is more severe compared to the loss disallowance rule on wash sales. In a related party transaction, it is possible to lose the tax benefit of all or a portion of the economic loss.

	Scenario 1	Scenario 2	Scenario 3
Selling price	$17,000	$12,000	$ 8,000
Minus: Sam's basis	(10,000)	(10,000)	(10,000)
Sam's realized gain (loss)	$ 7,000	$ 2,000	$(2,000)
Minus: Frank's disallowed loss (up to Sam's gain)	(5,000)	(2,000)	—0—
Sam's recognized gain (loss)	$2,000	—0—	($2,000)

In Scenario 1, Sam and Frank together have incurred an aggregate gain of $2,000 ($17,000 − $15,000). Thus, Frank's full disallowed loss reduces Sam's subsequent gain. In Scenario 2, the aggregate economic loss incurred by Sam and Frank is actually $3,000 ($12,000 − $15,000). However, the actual amount of the tax loss recognized for Sam and Frank is zero. In Scenario 3, the actual tax loss would have been $7,000 ($8,000 − $15,000) instead of $2,000 if Frank had held the land until its eventual sale. ◄

A similar rule found in Sec. 707(b)(1) disallows losses between a partner and a partnership in which the partner owns directly or indirectly over 50% of the partnership and between two partnerships in which the same people own directly or indirectly over 50% in each partnership. The constructive ownership rules of Sec. 267 apply here in determining ownership (see *Prentice Hall's Federal Taxation: Corporations, Partnerships, Estates, and Trusts* text or the *Comprehensive* volume).

KEY POINT

The effect of Sec. 267 with respect to unpaid expenses is to place an accrual method taxpayer on the cash method for amounts owed to a related cash method taxpayer.

UNPAID EXPENSES. Under Sec. 267, a related obligor of any unpaid expenses must defer the deduction for those expenses until the year in which the related payee recognizes the amount as income. In effect, this rule prevents an accrual-method taxpayer from taking a deduction for an unpaid expense in the earlier year of accrual while the related cash-method taxpayer recognizes the payment as income in the subsequent year.

For unpaid expenses, the definition of *related parties* in Sec. 267 is expanded to include a personal-service corporation and any employee-owner.[40] A personal-service corporation is one whose principal activity is the performance of personal services that are substantially performed by employee-owners. An employee-owner is an employee who owns any of the outstanding stock of the personal-service corporation.[41]

EXAMPLE 16-37 ▶

Michelle owns 100% of the outstanding stock of Hill Corporation. Michelle is a cash method taxpayer and Hill Corporation is an accrual method taxpayer. Both taxpayers are calendar-year taxpayers. In a bona fide transaction, Hill borrows some funds from Michelle. By the end of the current year, $8,000 interest had accrued on the loan. However, Hill Corporation does not pay the interest to Michelle until February of the following year. Because Michelle is a cash method taxpayer, she reports the interest income when she receives it in the following year. Although Hill is an accrual method taxpayer, it must defer the deduction for the interest expense until it pays the interest in February of the following year. The results are the same if Hill Corporation is a personal service corporation and Michelle is an employee and owns only 20% of the Hill stock. ◄

For purposes of these unpaid expenses, the definition of *related parties* is also expanded to include various relationships involving partnerships or S corporations and any person who owns (either actually or constructively) any interest in these entities.[42]

OBJECTIVE 7

Discuss the criteria used to determine whether an activity is a hobby or a trade or business

HOBBY LOSSES

Certain activities have both profit-motivated and personal attributes. In these cases all of the relevant factors must be examined to determine the tax status of the activity since, in general, expenses incurred in a profit-motivated activity such as a business or investment are deductible, whereas most expenses associated with personal activities such as hobbies are not. The factors the IRS uses to determine whether an activity is profit-motivated are found in Reg. Sec. 1.183-2(b) and include the following:

---

[40] Sec. 267(a)(2).
[41] Secs. 269A(b) and 441(i)(2). In determining the ownership of an employee-owner, the constructive ownership rules of Sec. 318 as modified by Sec. 441(i)(2) are used. These rules differ substantially from the constructive ownership rules of Sec. 267.
[42] Sec. 267(e). A discussion of these modifications is beyond the scope of this book.

- Whether the taxpayer conducts the activity in a businesslike manner
- The expertise of the taxpayer or the taxpayer's advisors
- The time and effort expended by the taxpayer in carrying on the activity
- Whether the assets used in the activity are expected to appreciate in value
- The taxpayer's success in carrying on other similar activities
- The taxpayer's history of income or losses with respect to the activity
- The amount of occasional profits, if any, that are earned
- The taxpayer's financial status
- Any elements of personal pleasure or recreation the activity might involve

ADDITIONAL COMMENT
Many of the court cases dealing with profit motive under Sec. 183 are ranch and farm cases. In fact, Sec. 183, now titled "Activities Not Engaged in for Profit" was originally titled "Farm Losses, etc." in the Tax Reform Act of 1969.

No one of these factors is determinative. In fact, the IRS also may consider other factors not listed. Furthermore, the IRS does not make a determination by merely counting the number of factors that are present. Instead, the decision depends on an examination of all the factors together. The IRS can, therefore, make the decision on a more subjective basis than the taxpayer might like. If the IRS asserts that an activity is a personal one (i.e., a hobby) rather than a business or investment, the burden of proof rests on the taxpayer to prove otherwise.

EXAMPLE I6-38 ▶ Paula, a successful attorney with an annual income of $200,000, also enjoys raising and training quarter horses. She generally spends 5 to 6 hours each week training, showing, or racing the horses. Over the last 4 years her winnings from shows and races have amounted to $16,000. Over that same period, she has generated an additional $8,000 of income from stud fees and the sale of colts. Often the horses are used to take Paula's family or friends riding. In addition, Paula often participates in equestrian clinics and demonstrations for 4-H Clubs and other similar groups. Paula employs a high school student to feed the horses each day and to clean the stalls weekly. And, Paula hires a professional horse trainer for 4 hours each week to help her train the horses.

In this case, several factors such as the level of earnings, the hiring of professional help, and the amount of time spent in the activity might indicate that Paula is engaged in a business. Other factors, such as the time spent riding with family and friends, the voluntary clinics and demonstrations, and the small amount of revenue generated as compared with Paula's other income, support the position that Paula merely has a hobby of raising horses. ◀

In cases where a clear profit motive cannot be shown under the factors mentioned above, the Code provides a test whereby an activity may be presumed to be one engaged in for profit. This test is met if the activity shows a profit for any three years during a consecutive five-year period. The five-year period consists of the year in question plus the previous four years.[43] This presumption is rebuttable (i.e., if the taxpayer meets the test, the burden of proof is shifted to the IRS to show that the activity *is not* profit motivated). Otherwise, the taxpayer would be required to prove that the activity *is* profit-motivated.

KEY POINT
Section 183(d) primarily serves to shift the burden of proof from the taxpayer to the IRS.

If the activity is determined to be a business, the taxpayer may deduct all qualified business expenses from the gross income, even if a net loss results.[44] However, if the activity is determined to be a hobby, the expenses are generally deductible as a miscellaneous itemized deduction but only to the extent of the gross income from the activity. A net loss may not be reported from the activity if it is a hobby.

EXAMPLE I6-39 ▶ Lorenzo, a stockbroker, enjoys raising pedigreed poodles. Although he mainly raises them for recreation and relaxation after work, Lorenzo periodically sells some of his poodles. Lorenzo reports $850 in income and $2,900 in expenses from the activity on his 2001 tax return. Upon auditing Lorenzo's 2001 return, the IRS disallowed the expenses in excess of the income, arguing that the activity is a hobby rather than a business or investment. If Lorenzo can prove that he realized a profit from the poodle-raising operation for any three years from 1997 through 2001 inclusive, the presumption will be made that the poodles are raised for a profit and not

---

[43] Sec. 183(d). If the major part of the activity involves breeding, training, showing, or racing horses, the five-year period is extended to a seven-year period, and a profit must be shown in only two, rather than three, of the years covered by that seven-year period.

[44] If the activity is a passive activity, the loss may be suspended. See Chapter 18 for a discussion of the passive loss rules.

for recreation. The IRS then has the burden of proof to show that the activity is really a hobby. If Lorenzo cannot show a profit for three years out of the five-year period, he would have to rely on the factors mentioned in the Treasury Regulations to convince the IRS and/or the courts that the activity is a business.

If Lorenzo's poodle-raising activity is determined to be a business, Lorenzo would report a net loss of $2,050 ($2,900 expenses − $850 income), assuming the loss is not incurred in a passive activity (see Chapter I8). If the activity is determined to be a hobby, however, Lorenzo may deduct only $850 of the expenses (up to the amount of the gross income) as an itemized deduction. As explained later, these expenses must be deducted in a certain order. The remaining expenses are not allowed as tax deductions. ◀

> **ADDITIONAL COMMENT**
> Gross income from an activity not engaged in for profit is defined to include the total gains from the sale, exchange, or other disposition of property, and all other gross receipts derived from such activity. Cost of goods sold can be deducted from gross receipts to calculate gross income.

DEDUCTIBLE EXPENSES. Some hobby activities generate gross income, even though profit is not a primary motive for the activity. In such situations, Sec. 183 allows the taxpayer to deduct the expenses related to the hobby, but only to the extent of the gross income from the hobby. Furthermore, a hobby-related expense is deductible only if it would have been deductible if incurred in a trade or business or an investment activity.

In essence, a taxpayer may deduct all the hobby-related expenses as long as there is enough gross income from the activity to cover the expenses. However, a hobby cannot generate a tax loss that is then used to offset a taxpayer's other types of income.

ORDER OF THE DEDUCTIONS. If the hobby expenses exceed the amount of gross income generated by the hobby, the expenses must be deducted against the gross income in the following order:

▶ **Tier 1:** Expenses that may be deducted even though they are not incurred in a trade or business (e.g., itemized deductions such as taxes, certain interest, and casualty losses)

▶ **Tier 2:** Other expenses of the hobby that could have been deducted if they had been incurred in a profit-motivated activity, but which do not reduce the tax basis of any of the assets used in the hobby (e.g., utilities and maintenance expenses)

▶ **Tier 3:** The expenses of the hobby that could have been deducted if incurred in a profit-motivated activity and that reduce the basis of the hobby's assets (e.g., depreciation on fixed assets used in the hobby)[45]

> **ADDITIONAL COMMENT**
> Hobby expenses are subject to the 2% of AGI limitation on miscellaneous itemized deductions. However, if the hobby expense is one that is deductible whether or not incurred in an income producing activity, such as real property taxes on a home, it is fully deductible.

To the extent that the expenses are taken as deductions against the gross income of the activity, they are deductions *from* AGI and are deductible only if the taxpayer has itemized deductions in excess of the standard deduction. The tier 1 expenses are reported in their respective sections on Schedule A of Form 1040. The tier 2 and tier 3 expenses allocated to the hobby are treated as miscellaneous itemized deductions and are, therefore, deductible only to the extent that they exceed 2% of AGI (see Chapter I7). Gross income from a hobby is reported as other income on Form 1040. If gross income is not sufficient to cover all of the tier 1 expenses, the excess tier 1 expenses may also be deducted as itemized deductions on Schedule A of Form 1040 because these expenses are allowed in any event. Any remaining expenses in the other two tiers are disallowed and may not be carried over to a subsequent year.

If depreciation expense is disallowed, it is not necessary to reduce the cost basis of the asset to the extent of the disallowance.

EXAMPLE I6-40 ▶ Lynn raises various plants and flowers in a small greenhouse constructed specifically for that purpose. During the current year, Lynn reports gross income from the greenhouse activities of $1,700. Lynn also incurs the following expenses:

Property taxes on the greenhouse	$1,150
Utilities	300
Depreciation (assuming the activity is considered a business.)	800

If the greenhouse activity is considered to be a hobby rather than a business, the deductions Lynn may take are computed as follows:

---

[45] Reg. Sec. 1.183-1(b).

REAL LIFE EXAMPLE

Good records are very important in establishing the existence of a business rather than a hobby. A taxpayer, who owned and operated an apple orchard, asserted that he maintained sufficient business records, consisting of bank deposit slips, check stubs, and tax forms. A separate bank account was also maintained. But the taxpayer did not present any production records for the apple orchard. In fact, at trial, the taxpayer was not even certain of the exact number of trees in the orchard. Thus, the court found that due to the limited records, the taxpayer's activity was considered to be a hobby rather than a business. *Zdun*, TC Memo 1998-296 (1998).

Income From greenhouse		$1,700
Tier 1 Expenses:		
Property taxes	$1,150	
Tier 2 Expenses:		
Utilities	300	
Tier 3 Expenses:		
Depreciation[a]	250	$1,700
Total		$0

[a]Limited to greenhouse income remaining after accounting for the Tier 1 and Tier 2 expenses.

VACATION HOME

Because owning a second home or dwelling unit may have both personal and profit-motivated attributes, deductions for expenses related to the rental of a vacation home that is also used as a residence by the taxpayer may be disallowed or limited by Sec. 280A.

OBJECTIVE 8

Determine the tax consequences of vacation homes

RESIDENCE DEFINED. For the restrictive rules of Sec. 280A to apply, the property must be a dwelling unit that qualifies as the taxpayer's residence. As used in this context, the term *dwelling unit* is quite expansive. Property such as boats and mobile homes may be considered dwelling units. The determining factor is whether the property provides shelter and accommodations for eating and sleeping.[46] Thus, a mini-motorhome that contains the appropriate accommodations has been held to be a dwelling unit subject to the rules and limitations of Sec. 280A. The fact that the unit is small and cramped is disregarded.

A dwelling unit is considered to be used by the taxpayer as a residence if the number of days during which the taxpayer uses the property for personal use throughout the year exceeds the greater of the following:

- ▶ 14 days, or
- ▶ 10% of the number of days during the year that the property is rented at a fair rental[47]

SELF-STUDY QUESTION

What is the maximum number of days during a year that a taxpayer may use a property for personal use and not have it considered to be used as a residence?

ANSWER

If a property was rented for 332 days it could be used by the taxpayer for 33 days and not be considered a residence.

EXAMPLE I6-41 ▶ Sarah owns a houseboat on Lake Powell that she personally uses for 21 days out of the year. During the year she also rented the boat for a total of 300 days. Even though Sarah's personal use exceeds 14 days during the year, the houseboat is not considered a residence under Sec. 280A because Sarah's personal use does not exceed 30 days during the year (10% of the 300 rental days for the year). ◀

For purposes of the residence test, a day of personal use includes any day that the property is used

- ▶ For personal purposes by the taxpayer or the taxpayer's family. *Family* is defined here as including a taxpayer's spouse, brothers and sisters, ancestors, and lineal descendants.[48]
- ▶ By any individual under a reciprocal-use arrangement.[49]
- ▶ By any individual who does not pay a fair rental for the use of the property.[50]

Despite the family-use rule, if a taxpayer rents property at a fair rental to a family member who uses the property as a principal residence, such use does not constitute personal use by the taxpayer.

---

[46] *Ronald L. Haberkorn*, 75 T.C. 259 (1980), and *John O. Loughlin v. U.S.*, 50 AFTR 2d 82-5827, 82-2 USTC ¶9543 (D.C. Minn., 1982).

[47] Sec. 280A(d)(1). In certain cases, this residence test might be met when a taxpayer uses a property as his or her principal residence for part of the year and rents the property for the rest of the year. This could occur, for example, when a taxpayer moves from his or her home and turns the old residence into a rental unit. In such a case, special rules prevent the home from being classified as a residence under Sec. 280A, thus preventing the application of the limitations.

[48] Under Sec. 280A(d)(2), a day during which the taxpayer spends substantially full time on repairs and maintenance does not count as a personal-use day.

[49] Sec. 280A(d)(2)(B). A reciprocal-use arrangement is one whereby another person uses the taxpayer's property in exchange for the taxpayer's use of the other person's property.

[50] Sec. 280A(d)(2)(C). Exactly what constitutes a fair rental must be determined by an examination of all the associated facts and circumstances.

6-32 Individuals ▼ Chapter 6

EXAMPLE I6-42 ▶ During the current year, Peggy purchases a small house as an investment and rents the property to Stan, her married son, who uses the property as his principal residence. Peggy's son pays her a fair rental for the property. Because Stan uses the property as his principal residence and pays Peggy a fair rental for the property, Stan's personal use of the property does not constitute personal use by Peggy. Thus, the rules of Sec. 280A do not apply to limit the expenses that Peggy may deduct. ◀

> **KEY POINT**
>
> A second home is going to be classified as either rental property, a residence, or some combination of the two. If it is classified as some combination of rental property and a residence, the expenses of the property must be allocated between the two categories.

ALLOCATION OF EXPENSES. Expenses related to the property must be allocated between personal use and rental use. Generally, no deduction is allowed for expenses that are allocable to personal use. However, qualified mortgage interest and real estate taxes are deductible even when allocated to personal use because such expenses are deductible on personal residences.[51] Expenses allocated to the rental use are deductible under Sec. 280A, but only to the extent of the gross income generated by the property. The property may not generate a loss which is used to reduce other income of the taxpayer. Expenses that are not deductible because they exceed the gross income from the property may be carried over to the subsequent year and taken as a deduction, limited to the gross income of that year.[52] Expenses that are allocated to the rental use of the property and deducted against the gross income must be taken in the same order (explained previously) that the expenses under the hobby loss rules of Sec. 183 are deducted. Example I6-40 illustrates these rules.

Allocation Formula. In allocating expenses between the personal use and the rental use of the property, the following formula is used:[53]

$$\text{Rental use expenses} = \frac{\text{Number of rental days}}{\text{Total number of days used}} \times \text{Total expenses for the year}$$

The denominator of the allocation fraction is the sum of the days the property is rented plus the days that the property is used for personal purposes. The days when the property is not used are not included in the formula.

Some courts have modified the allocation formula by allowing the use of the total number of days in the year as the denominator for qualified residential interest and taxes.[54] Use of this ratio allocates less interest and taxes to the rental use, allowing more of the other expenses to be deducted against the rental income. Subject to limitations, the interest and taxes not allocated to the rental use are still deductible as itemized deductions. Example I6-43 uses the allocation formula that has been sanctioned by the courts.

EXAMPLE I6-43 ▶ Joan owns a cabin near the local ski resort. During the year, Joan and Joan's family use the cabin a total of 25 days. The cabin is also rented to out-of-state skiers for a total of 50 days during the year, generating rental income of $10,000. Joan incurs the following expenses:

Expense	Amount
Property taxes	$1,500
Interest on mortgage	3,000
Utilities	2,000
Insurance	1,500
Security and snow removal	2,500

Joan would have been entitled to $12,000 depreciation if the property had been entirely rental property held for investment. However, because the property is also used for personal purposes, the amount of deductions (for AGI) Joan may take with respect to the property during the year is as follows:

---

[51] No deduction is allowed for interest incurred with respect to a personal residence if the debt on which the interest is paid is not secured by the property or the taxpayer has not chosen the property as a second residence for purposes of deducting the interest as qualified residential interest (see Chapter I7). For purposes of the discussion and examples used here, the assumption is made that the interest qualifies as qualified residential interest.

[52] Sec. 280A(c)(5)(B). The expenses that are carried over to the subsequent year are deductible to the extent of the property's gross income of that year, even though the property is not used by the taxpayer as a residence during that year.

[53] Sec. 280A(e)(1).

[54] *Dorance D. Bolton v. CIR*, 51 AFTR 2d 82-305, 82-2 USTC ¶9699 (9th Cir., 1982). See also *Edith G. McKinney v. CIR*, 52 AFTR 2d 83-6281, 83-2 USTC ¶9655 (10th Cir., 1983).

Deductions and Losses ▼ Individuals 6-33

SELF-STUDY QUESTION

Assume that a taxpayer rents his cabin to an individual who occupies it on a Saturday afternoon. Two weeks later the tenant leaves the cabin on a Saturday morning. Has the cabin been rented for more than 14 days?

ANSWER

No, although the tenant was on the premises for 15 calendar days, he is treated as having rented the property for only 14 days.

Item	Calculation	Amount
Rental income		$10,000
Interest and taxes	$4,500 × $\frac{50}{365}$	(616)[a]
All other expenses except depreciation	$6,000 × $\frac{50}{75}$	(4,000)
Depreciation	$12,000 × $\frac{50}{75}$	(5,384)[b]
Net income from property		$0

The income and these expenses are reported on Schedule E. Thus, the expenses allocated to the rental use are *for* AGI deductions. In addition to the deductions above, Joan may also deduct $3,884 ($4,500 − $616) interest and taxes as itemized deductions on Schedule A if the interest is qualified residence interest (see Chapter I7) and her total itemized deductions exceed her standard deduction.

[a] Under the approach favored by the IRS, $3,000 ($4,500 × 50/75) of interest and taxes would be used to offset the gross income and only $3,000 of depreciation would be deductible.
[b] $8,000 of the depreciation is allocated to the rental use (50/75 × $12,000). Since the deduction for depreciation is limited to $5,384, the additional $2,616 ($8,000 − $5,384) can be carried over and deducted in the next year if the gross income of that year is sufficient to cover all the expenses allocable to the rental use. If there had been sufficient gross income, Joan could have taken $8,000 depreciation. ◀

NOMINAL NUMBER OF RENTAL DAYS. If a property qualifies as a taxpayer's residence under Sec. 280A and it is rented for less than 15 days during the year, the law takes the approach that the property is completely personal in nature. As such, no rental income is included in gross income and no expenses may be deducted. However, expenses such as qualified residential interest and taxes may still be deducted as itemized deductions. (See Chapter I7 for a discussion of the limitations on interest.)

EXAMPLE I6-44 ▶ Assume the same facts as in Example I6-43, except that during the year Joan rents the cabin out for only 12 days and the amount of rental income is $2,400. The cabin qualifies as Joan's residence because her personal use exceeds 14 days. Because the cabin is rented for less than 15 days during the year, Joan may only take itemized deductions of $4,500 for the qualified residential interest and taxes. She may not deduct the other expenses. In addition, she does not include the $2,400 in gross income. ◀

KEY POINT

Assume that a taxpayer owns a beachfront condo. The taxpayer personally uses the condo for only 12 days during the year and rents the property for 35 days. Section 280A does not apply because the taxpayer has not used the property for over 14 days. However, if the taxpayer cannot demonstrate a profit motive, it may still be treated as a hobby. If so, the deductibility of the expenses allocated to the rental use is limited to the gross income generated by the property. Furthermore, the interest allocated to the personal use of the property is not deductible as qualified residential interest (see Chapter I7).

NOMINAL NUMBER OF PERSONAL USE DAYS. If a taxpayer does not have enough personal use days during the year to qualify the property as a residence (i.e., the personal use is not more than the greater of 14 days or 10% of the rental days), the Sec. 280A rules and limitations do not apply. If the owner demonstrates a profit motive, the property is treated as rental property. On the other hand, if the property does not qualify as either rental property or as the taxpayer's residence, the property is considered a hobby. Under these circumstances, the expenses must still be allocated between the rental use and the personal use. The taxpayer treats the taxes allocated to the personal use as itemized deductions. None of the interest allocated to the personal use is deductible because it is not qualified residential interest. (See Chapter I7 for a discussion of the deductibility of personal interest and qualified residential interest.) Tier 2 and 3 expenses allocated to the personal use are not deductible. The income from the property and all of the expenses allocated to the rental use are reported on Schedule E of Form 1040. As such, the expenses are *for* AGI deductions. Any net income or loss from the property is subject to the passive loss rules, which may limit the deductibility of any losses from the property (see Chapter I8). The rules of Sec. 280A regarding the rental of property are summarized in Figure I6-4.

EXAMPLE I6-45 ▶ Assume the same facts as in Example I6-43 except that Joan and her family use the cabin only 10 days during the year and rent it out for 65 days of the year. Joan may take the following deductions with respect to the property during the year:

6-34 Individuals ▼ Chapter 6

```
                                                                    (1) Income is reported on
                                                                        Schedule E.
                                                                    (2) Tier 1 expenses allocated
              Start                                                     to rental use are deducted
                                                                        on Schedule E.
                                                                    (3) Tier 1 expenses allocated
                                                                        to personal use are
                                                                        Schedule A itemized
                                                                        deductions.(b)
           Meets         Yes       Rented        Yes                (4) Tier 2 and 3 expenses allocated
         residence                over 14                               to rental use are deducted on
          test?(a)                 days?                                Schedule E to the extent of
                                                                        the remaining gross income
                                    No                                  from the rental.
                                                                    (5) Remaining tier 2 and 3 expenses
                           (1) Income is not reported.                  allocated to rental use are
                           (2) Tier 1 expenses are Schedule             carried over to following year.
             No                A itemized deductions.(b)            (6) Tier 2 and 3 expenses allocated
                           (3) Tier 2 and 3 expenses are                to personal use are nondeductible.
                               nondeductible.                       (7) The passive loss rules do not apply.


     (1) Income is reported on Schedule E.
     (2) Tier 1 expenses allocated to rental
         use are reported on Schedule E.
     (3) Tier 1 expenses allocated to
         personal use are Schedule A
         itemized deductions.(c)
     (4) Tier 2 and 3 expenses allocated
         to rental use are deducted on
         Schedule E.
     (5) The passive loss rules apply.
```

(a) Personal use is more than the larger of (1) 14 days or (2) 10% of rental days.
(b) In order for the interest to be deductible, it must be "qualified residence interest" (See Chapter 7).
(c) In order for the interest to be deductible as qualified residence, the property must not have been rented at all during the year (see Chapter 7).

FIGURE I6-4 ▶ SECTION 280A: LIMITATION OF DEDUCTIONS ON RENTAL OF RESIDENTIAL PROPERTY

	Calculation	Amount
Rental income		$10,000
Interest	$3,000 × $\frac{65}{365}$	(535)[a]
Taxes	$1,500 × $\frac{65}{365}$	(267)[a]
Other expenses	$6,000 × $\frac{65}{75}$	(5,200)
Depreciation	$12,000 × $\frac{65}{75}$	(3,998)[b]
	Total	$ 0

[a] Under the approach favored by the IRS, $3,900 ($4,500 × 65/75) of interest and taxes would have been allocated to the rental use. Joan would treat the remaining $1,233 in taxes ($1,500 − $267) as an itemized deduction. However, Joan may not deduct the remaining $2,465 ($3,000 − $535) interest because it does not qualify as deductible residential interest.
[b] A total of $10,400 depreciation is allocated to the rental use ($12,000 × 65/75). Since the deduction is limited to $3,998, the additional $6,402 ($10,400 − $3,998) can be carried over and deducted in the next year if the gross income of that year is sufficient to cover all the expenses allocable to the rental use.

EXPENSES OF AN OFFICE IN THE HOME

Unless the taxpayer meets certain strictly imposed requirements, Sec. 280A disallows any deduction for home office expenses. In general, for a taxpayer to deduct office-in-home expenses, the office must have been regularly and exclusively used as either of the following:

- The principal place of business for a trade or business of the taxpayer; or
- A place where the taxpayer meets or deals with clients in the normal course of business

For employees to take a deduction for home office expenses, the use must also have been for the convenience of the employer. In addition, a separate structure not attached to the taxpayer's house may qualify if regularly and exclusively used in connection with the taxpayer's business. (See Chapter I9 for a comprehensive discussion of these rules.)

TAX PLANNING CONSIDERATIONS

HOBBY LOSSES

Deductions for expenses incurred in a hobby activity are limited to the gross income generated by the hobby for the year. However, if the gross income exceeds the deductions from the activity in at least three out of five consecutive years, (two out of seven for activities involving the breeding, training, showing, or racing of horses) the activity is presumed to be a business, and the limits on the deductibility of expenses do not apply. Thus, if possible, taxpayers should use care in timing the realization of items of income and expense. For example, if an activity has shown a profit in only two out of the previous four years, a taxpayer may consider accelerating some of the income into the fifth year or deferring some of the expenses of the activity into the following year. Under the cash method of accounting, this can be done by delaying payment for some of the expenses or accelerating income-generating transactions. Note that meeting the three-out-of-five-year test does not automatically ensure the activity will be treated as a business. It merely compels the IRS to prove the activity is *not* a business. Under these circumstances, the IRS may be less inclined to challenge the deductions.

UNREASONABLE COMPENSATION

If the IRS feels that a salary payment to an officer of a corporation is excessive, it will often recharacterize the excess portion as a dividend. If that happens, the corporation cannot deduct the full amount of the salary payment. To prevent a potential future disallowance, the parties may enter into a payback or hedge agreement, which provides that the employee must return to the corporation any payment held to be excessive. A payback agreement must meet the following requirements to be effective:

ETHICAL POINT

In some cases it is difficult to ascertain whether an activity is a trade or business or a hobby. A CPA should not prepare or sign a tax return unless he or she in good faith believes that the return takes a position that has a realistic possibility of being sustained on its merits.

WHAT WOULD YOU DO IN THIS SITUATION?

SERIOUS WINE OR HOBBY LOSS?

Mr. Bouteilles Gerbeuses has been your longtime tax client. He has amassed an impressive portfolio of real estate, securities, and joint venture investments. His net worth is substantial.

Despite all his material well-being, Mr. Gerbeuses wants to take on a new challenge—that of producing fine wines. He has not had any formal wine training but he has decided to start his own winery, named *Cuvée de Prestige*. He will pattern it after the great wine houses of Europe.

He already owns several hundred acres of agriculturally zoned land in the wine producing region of the Noir Valley. It happens to adjoin his home in the Wemadeit Country Club and Retirement Resort subdivision. He anticipates a life of semi-retirement by engaging in the art of malolactic fermentation and blending of his *blanc de blancs* and *pinot noir* grapes into his own estate wine. He expects his start-up capital investment to be over $5 million and does not expect the first harvest to take place for at least seven years after the initial planting of grape vines. He expects to offset any losses by his other income.

Assuming Mr. Gerbeuses comes to you for tax advice on his new wine venture, what tax and ethical issues should be considered?

▶ It must be entered into before the payment is actually made.
▶ It must legally obligate the employee to repay the excess amount.[55]

The IRS may take the position that the existence of the payback agreement itself is evidence that the compensation is excessive. This situation may be avoided if the payback agreement is included in the general corporate bylaws rather than in a specific contract with a particular employee.[56]

TIMING OF DEDUCTIONS

Because of the time value of money, taxpayers generally prefer to deduct an expenditure as a current expense rather than capitalize it. If an expenditure is required to be capitalized, the deductions (e.g., for depreciation or amortization) are spread over several years. In addition, some capital expenditures (e.g., land) are not subject to depreciation or amortization. In some situations, however, the taxpayer may prefer to capitalize rather than expense a particular item. For example, if a taxpayer has net operating losses (NOLs) that are about to expire, a current deduction may prevent the use of these losses.[57]

In some cases it is difficult to determine whether an item should be treated as a capital expenditure or a deduction item (e.g., certain repairs may in the aggregate be treated as a capital expenditure). In addition, certain types of expenditures, such as for research and experimentation, may be either capitalized (subject to amortization) or expensed at the election of the taxpayer. Consideration should be given to the taxpayer's tax situation when this decision is made. In making this decision, taxpayers should consider NOL carryovers that might be expiring. They should also compare their current marginal tax rate with their anticipated future marginal tax rate.

COMPLIANCE AND PROCEDURAL CONSIDERATIONS

SELF-STUDY QUESTION

A professor in the Department of Accounting also teaches continuing education courses for the state CPA society as a sole proprietor. If she is a member of the state CPA society, are her dues deductible on Schedule C or as an itemized deduction?

ANSWER

Certainly, she would prefer to have the dues deductible on Schedule C so that they will not be subject to the 2% limit on miscellaneous itemized deductions. This question demonstrates the difficulty of classifying some deductions, and the answer probably depends on the primary reason for membership in the organization.

PROPER CLASSIFICATION OF DEDUCTIONS

Individuals report trade or business expenses on Schedule C (Profit or Loss from Business or Profession). It is similar to an income statement for business-related income and expenses. The net income computed on Schedule C is then included in gross income on Form 1040. Because business-related expenses are deducted in arriving at the taxable income from the business, these expenses are deductions *for* AGI. Similar treatment is given to expenses attributable to the production of rental and royalty income because they are reported on Schedule E, which is an income statement. The other deductions *for* AGI have specific lines on Form 1040 itself where they are deducted.[58] All of these deductions appear before line 33 (where AGI appears) of Form 1040.

Deductions *from* AGI are reported on Schedule A, where they are totaled and then transferred to Line 36 of Form 1040.

PROPER SUBSTANTIATION

The burden of proving the deductibility of any expense generally rests on the taxpayer. This has always been the case. However, in recent years Congress and the IRS have become increasingly concerned about the propriety of many deductions. In the case of

---

[55] *Vincent E. Oswald*, 49 T.C. 645 (1968); and *J. G. Pahl*, 67 T.C. 286 (1976). See also *Ernest H. Berger*, 37 T.C. 1026 (1962).
[56] *Charles Schneider and Co. v. CIR*, 34 AFTR 2d 74-5422, 74-2 USTC ¶9563 (8th Cir., 1974). See also *Plastics Universal Corp.*, 1979 PH T.C. Memo ¶79,355, 39 TCM 32. Additionally, some taxpayers have been successful in defending their current level of compensation where they proved that they had been undercompensated in prior years. See *Acme Construction Co., Inc.*, 1995 RIA T.C. Memo ¶95,600, 69 TCM 1596.
[57] A NOL arises when business expenses exceed business income for a year. This excess can be carried to another year (generally back two years and forward twenty years) and is deducted against the income of that year. If the years to which the NOL is carried do not have enough income, the NOL is lost when the carryover period expires. See Chapter I8 for a discussion of NOLs.
[58] Some of these expenses, such as employee business expenses (Form 2106) and moving expenses (Form 3903), are summarized on separate forms. These separate forms, however, are not net income statements in the same sense that Schedules C and E are.

travel and entertainment expenses, the Code states that no deduction may be taken for an expense that is not properly documented. This information must include the amount of the expense, the time and place of the travel or entertainment activity, the business purpose, and the business relationship of the people entertained.

BUSINESS VERSUS HOBBY

Self-employed individuals who claim a home office deduction on Schedule C must attach Form 8829, which is used to allocate direct and indirect expenses to the appropriate use. Form 8829 need not be filed by employees who claim home office expenses on Form 2106.

When an activity has both profit-making and personal attributes, the burden is normally on the taxpayer to prove that the activity is a business. However, if a taxpayer can show that the activity has generated a profit in at least three out of five consecutive years (two out of seven for activities involving the breeding, training, showing, and racing of horses), the burden of proof shifts to the IRS. Because the statute of limitations generally runs three years after the filing of a return for any particular year (i.e., for audit purposes the year is closed and the IRS cannot assess any tax deficiency for that year), a potential problem exists for taxpayers who want to rely on this presumption during the first year or two of an activity's life. In these cases, the taxpayer may elect to defer the determination of whether the presumption applies until the fifth (seventh) year of operation. The effect of this election is to keep the year in question open with respect to that activity until sufficient years have passed that the presumptive test may be applied. If the taxpayer subsequently does not meet the presumptive test, the IRS can still assess a deficiency for that activity for the prior year, because the year is still open. This election is made by filing Form 5213 (Election to Postpone Determination as to Whether the Presumption That an Activity Is Engaged In for Profit Applies) and must be filed within three years after the due date for the year in which the taxpayer first engages in the activity.

> **ADDITIONAL COMMENT**
>
> When the election is made to defer the determination of whether a particular activity is engaged in for profit, the statute of limitations is automatically extended for all years in the postponement period. However, the automatic extension applies only to items that might be disallowed under the hobby loss rules.

Problem Materials

DISCUSSION QUESTIONS

I6-1 Why is the distinction between deductions *for* AGI and deductions *from* AGI important for individuals?

I6-2 Sam owns a small house that he rents out to students attending the local university. Are the expenses associated with the rental unit deductions *for* or *from* AGI?

I6-3 During the year, Sara sold a capital asset at a loss of $2,000. She had held the asset as an investment. Is her deduction for this capital loss a deduction *for* or a deduction *from* AGI?

I6-4 Discuss the difference in tax treatment between reimbursed employee business expenses and unreimbursed employee business expenses.

I6-5 For the current year, Mario a single individual with no dependents, receives income of $55,000 and incurs deductible expenses of $9,000.
   a. What is Mario's taxable income assuming that the expenses are deductions *for* AGI.
   b. What is Mario's taxable income assuming that the expenses are miscellaneous itemized deductions *from* AGI.

I6-6 Deductible business or investment expenses must be related to a profit-motivated activity.
   a. What are the factors used in determining whether an activity is profit-motivated?
   b. Why are these factors so important in making this determination?

I6-7 If an activity does not generate a profit in three out of five consecutive years, is it automatically deemed to be a hobby? Why or why not?

I6-8 Because expenses incurred both in a business and for the production of investment income are deductible, why is it important to determine in which category a particular activity falls?

I6-9 In order for a business expense to be deductible it must be *ordinary*, *necessary*, and *reasonable*. Explain what these terms mean.

I6-10 What are the criteria for distinguishing between a deductible expense and a capital expenditure?

I6-11 Why are expenses related to tax-exempt income disallowed?

I6-12 Under what circumstances may a taxpayer deduct an illegal bribe or kickback?

I6-13 Michelle pays a CPA $400 for the preparation of her federal income tax return. Michelle's only sources of income are her salary from employment and interest and dividends from her investments.
   a. Is this a deductible expense? If so, is it a deduction *for* or *from* AGI?
   b. Assume the same facts as in Part a except that in addition to her salary and investment and dividend income, Michelle also owns a small business. Of the $400 fee paid to the CPA, $250 is for the preparation of her Schedule C (Profit or Loss from Business). How much, if any, of the $400 is a deductible expense? Identify it as either *for* or *from* AGI.

I6-14 Jennifer flies to her state capital to lobby the legislature to build a proposed highway that is planned to run through the area where her business is located.
   a. What part, if any, of her expenses are deductible?
   b. Would it make a difference if the proposed road were a city road rather than a state highway, and Jennifer lobbied her local government?
   c. Assume the same facts in Part a except that Jennifer's total expenses are $1,500. Are these expenses deductible?

I6-15 During November and December of last year, Tom incurred the following expenses in investigating the feasibility of opening a new restaurant in town:

Expenses to do a market survey	$3,000
Expenses to identify potential suppliers of goods	$2,000
Expenses to identify a proper location	$1,000

Explain the proper treatment of these expenses under the following scenarios:
   a. Tom already owns another restaurant in town and is wanting to expand. Tom opens the new restaurant in February of the current year.
   b. Tom is tiring of his current job as an outside salesperson and wants to go into business for himself. He opens the restaurant in February of the current year.
   c. Tom is tiring of his current job as an outside salesperson and wants to go into business for himself. However, after getting the results of the investigations back, he decides against opening a restaurant.

I6-16 What documentation is required in order for a travel or entertainment expense to be deductible?

I6-17 Under what circumstances can prepaid expenses be deducted in the year of payment by a taxpayer using the cash method of accounting?

I6-18 Under what circumstances would a taxpayer use both the cash method and the accrual method of accounting at the same time?

I6-19 Whether the economic performance test is satisfied depends on the type of transaction and whether the transaction is recurring.
   a. When does economic performance occur for a taxpayer who must provide property or services to another person?
   b. When does economic performance occur when another person provides the taxpayer with property or services?
   c. Explain the exception to the economic performance test for recurring liabilities.

I6-20 Why did Congress enact the wash sale provisions?

I6-21 The wash sale rules disallow a loss in the year of sale when substantially identical stock or securities are acquired by the taxpayer within a 61-day period. What types of stock or securities are considered substantially identical?

I6-22 Under Sec. 267, current deductions may not be taken on certain transactions between related parties.
   a. Who is considered a member of a taxpayer's family under the related party transaction rules of Sec. 267?
   b. Identify some of the other relationships that are considered related parties for purposes of Sec. 267. Why are these other relationships included in the definition?

I6-23 Under the related party rules of Sec. 267, why has Congress imposed the concept of constructive ownership?

I6-24 If property is sold at a loss to a related taxpayer, under what circumstances can at least partial benefit be derived from the disallowed loss?

I6-25 Assume that Jill is engaged in painting as a hobby. During the year, she earns $1,000 from sales of her paintings and incurs $2,500 expenses for supplies and lessons. Jill's salary for the year is $70,000. What is the tax treatment of the hobby income and expenses?

I6-26 Under Sec. 280A, what constitutes personal use of a vacation home by the taxpayer?

I6-27 Under Sec. 280A, how are expenses allocated to the rental use of a vacation home? In what order must the expenses be deducted against the gross income of the property?

I6-28 Under Sec. 280A, how will a taxpayer report the income and expenses of a vacation home if it is rented out for only 12 days during the year?

ISSUE IDENTIFICATION QUESTIONS

I6-29 David, a CPA for a large accounting firm, works 10- to 12-hour days. As a requirement for his position, he must attend social events to recruit new clients. He also has private clients in his unincorporated professional practice. David purchased exercise equipment for $3,000. He works out on the equipment to maintain his stamina and good health that enables him to carry such a heavy workload. What tax issues should David consider?

I6-30 Gus, a football player who was renegotiating his contract with the Denver Broncos, paid his ex-girlfriend $25,000 to drop a sexual assault complaint against him and keep the matter confidential. The Broncos stated that if criminal charges were filed and made public, they would terminate his employment. What tax issues should Gus consider?

I6-31 Kathleen pays $3,000 mortgage interest on the home that she and her husband live in. Kathleen and her husband live with Molly, Kathleen's mother. The title to the home is in Kathleen's name. However, the mortgage is Molly's obligation. Kathleen claims Molly as her dependent on her current tax return. What tax issues should Kathleen consider?

I6-32 Katie and Alan are avid boaters and water skiers. They also enjoy parasailing. This year, they started a new parasailing venture to give rides to patrons. Katie and Alan are both employed full-time in other pursuits, but they take patrons out during the summer months, on weekends and holidays. Alan has attended classes on boat operation and parasailing instruction. Katie and Alan have owned a boat for four years, but because of the heavy usage this summer, they replaced their old boat in July. They plan on replacing their boat with a new one every two years now. They use their boat in the parasailing activity and for recreational purposes. This year, Katie and Alan earned $5,400 from chartering activities and incurred $11,600 of expenses associated with their boating and parasailing. What tax issues should Katie and Alan consider?

PROBLEMS

I6-33 *For or From AGI Deductions.* Michele is an architect employed by a local architectural firm. During the year, Michele incurs the following unreimbursed expenses:

Item	Amount
Professional association fees	$400
Subscriptions to professional journals	225
Travel from the office to client's offices	350
Photocopying	75
Taking clients to dinner	500

a. Identify which of these expenses are deductible and indicate whether they are deductions *for* or *from* AGI.
b. Would the answer to Part a change if the architectural firm reimburses Michele for these expenses?
c. Assume all of the same facts as in Part a, except that Michele is self-employed. Identify which of the expenses are deductible, and indicate whether they are deductions *for* or *from* AGI.

I6-34 *From AGI Deductions.* During the current year, Brandon, an individual who is married with 2 minor children, incurred the following deductible expenses (before any limitations are applied):

Medical expenses	$12,000
Real estate taxes	4,000
Interest on a principal residence	6,300
Charitable contributions	2,500
Net personal casualty losses (already reduced by the $100 limit)	3,000
Miscellaneous itemized deductions	2,800

Brandon's AGI for the current year is $120,000. What is Brandon's taxable income?

I6-35 *For vs. From AGI.* During the current year, Kimberly, a single taxpayer, reports the following items of income and expense:

Income:
Salary $150,000
Dividends from Alta Corporation   800
Interest income from a savings account   1,500
Rental income from a small apartment she owns   8,000
Expenses:
Medical   6,000
Interest on a principal residence   7,000
Real property taxes on the principal residence   4,300
Charitable contributions   4,000
Casualty loss - personal   6,100
Miscellaneous itemized deductions   1,200
Loss from the sale of Delta Corporation stock
  (held for two years)   2,000
Expenses incurred on the rental apartment:
  Maintenance   500
  Property taxes   1,000
  Utilities   2,400
  Depreciation   1,700
  Insurance   800
Alimony payments   10,000

Assuming all of these items are deductible and that the amounts are before any limitations, what is Kimberly's taxable income for the year?

I6-36 *Capitalization Versus Expense.* Lavonne incurs the following expenditures on an apartment building she owns:

Item	Amount
Replace the roof	$25,000
Repaint the exterior	7,000
Install new locks	1,500
Replace broken windows	1,200
Replace crumbling sidewalks and stairs	7,000

Discuss the proper tax treatment for these expenditures.

I6-37 *Political Contributions and Lobbying Expenses.* Sam is a sole proprietor who owns several apartment complexes and office buildings. The leasing and managing of these buildings constitutes Sam's only business activity. During the current year Sam incurred the following:

- $900 in airfare and lodging incurred on a trip to Washington, D.C. The purpose of the trip was to protest proposed tax rate increases for individuals and corporations.
- $700 for renting space on billboards along the highway. The billboards express his concern regarding pending legislation that would significantly increase property taxes.
- $500 in airfare and hotel bills incurred on a trip to the state capital. The purpose of the trip was to meet with the legislative subcommittee on property taxation.
- $50 for a subscription to a political newsletter published by a national political party.
- $150 in making a presentation to the county council protesting a proposed increase in the property tax levy.

a. What is the total amount Sam may deduct because of these expenditures?
b. Assume all the same facts as in Part a except that the expenses for the trip to the state capital are only $300 instead of $500. What amount may Sam deduct because of these expenditures?

I6-38 *Legal and Accounting Expenses.* During the current year, Sam from Problem I6-37 incurs the following expenses. Which of these expenditures are deductible? Are they *for* or *from* AGI deductions?
a. $200 in attorney's fees for title searches on a new property Sam has acquired.
b. $450 in legal fees in an action brought to collect back rents.
c. $500 to his CPA for the preparation of his federal income tax return. $400 is for the preparation of Schedule C (Profit or Loss from Business).
d. $300 in attorney's fees for drafting a will.

e. $250 in attorney's fees in an unsuccessful attempt to prevent the city from rezoning the area of the city where several of his office buildings are located.

I6-39 **Illegal Payments.** Damian is engaged in the business of purchasing and importing carpets from Iran. Importing these carpets from Iran is illegal. Following is a list of income and expense items for the year:

Item	Amount
Sales	$750,000
Cost of goods sold	270,000
Salaries	75,000
Freight	22,500
Bribes to customs officials	30,000
Lease payments on warehouses	15,000
Interest expense	12,000

a. What is Damian's taxable income from the illegal business activity?
b. Assume the same facts as in Part a except that Damian's business consists of buying and selling marijuana and cocaine. What is Damian's taxable income from this illegal business activity?

I6-40 **Illegal Payments.** Indicate whether Glenda can deduct the $5,000 payment in each of the following independent situations.
a. Glenda is a supplier of medical supplies. In order to secure a large sales contract to the regional Veterans Administration Hospital, Glenda makes a gift of $5,000 to the hospital's purchasing agent. The payment is illegal under state law.
b. Assume the same facts as in Part a, except that the payment is made to the purchasing agent of a government-owned hospital in Brazil.
c. Assume the same facts in Part a, except that the payment is made to the purchasing agent of a privately owned hospital in Idaho.

I6-41 **Business Investigation Expenditures.** During January and February of the current year, Mario incurs $3,000 in travel, feasibility studies, and legal expenses to investigate the feasibility of opening a new entertainment gallery in one of the new suburban malls in town. Mario already owns two other entertainment galleries in other malls in town.
a. What is the proper tax treatment of these expenses if Mario decides not to open the new gallery?
b. What is the proper tax treatment of these expenses if Mario decides to open the new gallery?

I6-42 **Business Investigation Expenditures.** Assume the same facts as in Problem I6-41, except that Mario does *not* already own the other entertainment galleries.
a. What is the proper tax treatment of these expenses if Mario does not open the new gallery?
b. What is the proper tax treatment of these expenses if Mario decides to open the new gallery on May 1 of the current year?

I6-43 **Prepaid Expenses.** Pamela, an engineering consultant, is self-employed and uses the cash method of accounting. Compute the amount of Pamela's current year deductions for the following transactions:
a. On November 1 of the current year, she entered into a lease to rent some office space for five years. The lease agreement states that the lease payments are $12,000 per year, payable in advance each November 1 for the following 12-month period. Under the terms of the lease, Pamela is required to pay a $5,000 deposit, refundable upon the termination of the lease.
b. On December 1 of the current year, Pamela also renewed her malpractice insurance, paying $18,000 for the three-year contract.
c. On December 31 of the current year, Pamela mailed out a check for $5,000 for drafting services performed for her by an individual who lives in another city.
d. On December 31, she also picked up $700 worth of stationery and other office supplies. Pamela has an open charge account with the office supply company, which bills Pamela monthly for charges made during the year.
e. Finally, on December 31, Pamela picked up some work that a local printing company had done for her, which amounted to $1,000. She charged the $1,000 with her business credit card.

I6-44 *Prepaid Expenses.* During the current year, Richard and Alisha, a married couple who use the cash method of accounting, purchased a principal residence for $320,000. They paid $40,000 down and financed the remaining $280,000 of the purchase price with a 30-year mortgage. At the closing, they also paid $500 for an appraisal, $500 for a title search, and 1.5 points representing additional interest over the term of the loan. At the end of the year, Richard and Alisha received a statement from the mortgage company indicating that $12,000 of their total monthly payments made during the year represents interest and $1,000 is a reduction of the principal balance.
  a. What is the total amount Richard and Alisha may deduct in the current year arising from the purchase and ownership of their home?
  b. What is the treatment of the other items that are not deductible?

I6-45 *Wash Sales.* Boyd owns 500 shares of Atwood Corporation common stock. Boyd purchased the 500 shares on April 17, 1994 for $10,000. On December 8, 2000, Boyd sells all 500 shares for $5,000. On January 2, 2001, Boyd buys 250 shares of Atwood Corporation common stock for $2,500 and 50 shares of Atwood Corporation preferred stock for $1,000. The preferred stock is nonvoting, nonconvertible.
  a. What is Boyd's realized and recognized loss on the December 8 sale of stock?
  b. What is Boyd's basis and the holding periods of the stock?

I6-46 *Wash Sales.* Vicki owns 1,000 shares of Western Corporation common stock, which she purchased on March 8, 1994, for $12,000. On October 3, 2001, she purchases an additional 300 shares for $3,000. On October 12, 2001, she sells the original 1,000 shares for $8,500. On November 1, 2001, she purchases an additional 500 shares for $4,000.
  a. What is Vicki's recognized gain or loss as a result of the sale on October 12, 2001?
  b. What are the basis and the holding period of the stock Vicki continues to hold?
  c. How would your answers to Parts a and b change if the stock Vicki purchases during 2001 is Western nonvoting, nonconvertible, preferred stock instead of Western common stock?

I6-47 *Constructive Ownership.* During the current year, Bart sells a small tract of land to Apple Corporation. The selling price is $25,000. Bart purchased the land for $35,000 four years ago. The Apple Corporation stock is owned as follows:

Owner	Percentage Ownership
Bart	10%
Bart's wife	10
Bart's brother	10
Tony (Bart's friend)	25
Bart's uncle	10
Wallace Corporation	35

Wallace Corporation is owned equally by Bart, Bart's brother, and Bart's uncle.
  a. What is Bart's ownership (actual and constructive) of the Apple stock?
  b. What is the amount of loss Bart may recognize?
  c. How would your answers to Parts a and b change if Bart's brother-in-law owned 10% of Apple corporation's stock instead of Bart's brother?

I6-48 *Constructive Ownership.* PIB Partnership is owned 20% by Shore, 40% by Steve, and 40% by Thann. Burnham, Inc. is owned 70% by PIB Partnership, 10% by Ralph, 10% by Thann, and 10% by Shore. Ralph and Thann are brothers. All other individuals are unrelated. During the current year, Ralph sold a piece of land to Burnham, Inc. for $90,000. Ralph originally purchased the land as an investment a few years ago for $100,000.
  a. How much of the loss may Ralph recognize?
  b. Now assume all the same facts except that the sale occurred between Thann and Burnham, Inc. How much of the loss may Thann recognize?
  c. Now assume the same facts as in b. except that Burnham, Inc. is owned 60% by Shore and 40% by Ralph. Thann sells the land to Burnham, Inc. How much of the loss may Thann recognize?

I6-49 *Related Party Transactions.* Sally is an attorney who computes her taxable income using the cash method of accounting. Sage Corporation, owned 60% by Sally's brother and 40% by her cousin, uses the accrual method of accounting. Sally is a calendar-year taxpayer, whereas Sage Corporation's fiscal year ends on January 31. During 2001, Sally does some consulting work for Sage Corporation for a fee of $10,000. The work is completed on December 15. For each of the following assumptions, answer the following

questions: During which tax year must Sally report the income? During which tax year must Sage Corporation deduct the expense?
a. The payment to Sally is made on December 27, 2001.
b. The payment to Sally is made on January 12, 2002.
c. The payment to Sally is made on February 3, 2002.

I6-50 *Related Party Transactions.* During the current year, Delta Corporation sells a tract of land for $80,000. The sale is made to Shirley, Delta Corporation's sole shareholder. Delta Corporation originally purchased the land five years earlier for $95,000.
a. What is the amount of gain or loss that Delta Corporation will recognize on the sale during the current year?
b. Assume that in the following year, Shirley sells the land for $85,000. What is the amount of gain or loss Shirley will recognize? What are the tax consequences to Delta Corporation upon the subsequent sale by Shirley?
c. Assume that in the following year, Shirley sells the land for $70,000. What is the amount of gain or loss Shirley will recognize?
d. Assume that in the following year, Shirley sells the land for $105,000. What is the amount of gain or loss Shirley will recognize?

I6-51 *Hobby Loss Presumptive Rule.* Rachel Schutz is a high school English teacher. In her spare time, she likes to make her own body lotion, lip-gloss, and bath and shower gel. She uses the bath products herself and gives them to her friends and relatives as gifts. In 2000, Rachel started attending arts and crafts festivals to sell her products three or four times a year, and she hands out her business card so her customers can buy directly from her by phone or email. In 2000, Rachel reported a net loss of $375 from the activity. In 2001, she reported a loss of $460. Rachel is audited for the year 2001, and the agent disallows the $460 loss. Rachel is pretty sure she will make a profit on her sales in 2002, and she assumes she will continue to make a profit after 2002. Rachel is not sure that she can prove that her activity is not a hobby right now. What can she do to avoid proving that her loss is not a hobby loss?

I6-52 *Hobby Loss Presumptive Rule.* Ari is an investment banker who has been engaged in raising and breeding show horses for the past eight years. During those years Ari has reported the following net income or loss from the activity:

Year	Net Income (Loss)
1994	$(800)
1995	(200)
1996	(500)
1997	(800)
1998	300
1999	(900)
2000	(1,300)
2001	(800)

Ari is audited for the year 2001, and the agent disallows the $800 loss. Can Ari make an election for 2001 to keep the year open in anticipation of meeting the presumptive rule for the year? Why or why not?

I6-53 *Hobby Losses.* Chuck, a dentist, raises prize rabbits for breeding and showing purposes. Assume that the activity is determined to be a hobby. During the year the activity generates the following items of income and expense:

Item	Amount
Sale of rabbits for breeding stock	$800
Prizes and awards	300
Property taxes on rabbit hutches	300
Feed	600
Veterinary fees	500
Depreciation on rabbit hutches	300

a. What is the total amount of deductions Chuck may take during the year with respect to the rabbit raising activities?
b. Identify which expenses may be deducted and indicate whether they are deductions *for* or *from* AGI.
c. By what amount is the cost basis of the rabbit hutches to be reduced for the year?

I6-54 *Hobby Losses.* Assume the same facts as in Problem I6-53, except that the income from the sale of rabbits is $1,200.
   a. What is the total amount of deductions Chuck may take during the year with respect to the rabbit raising activities?
   b. Identify which expenses may be deducted and indicate whether they are deductions *for* or *from* AGI.
   c. By what amount is the cost basis of the rabbit hutches to be reduced for the year?

I6-55 *Rental of Vacation Home.* During the current year, Kim incurs the following expenses with respect to her beachfront condominium in Hawaii:

Item	Amount
Insurance	$ 500
Repairs and maintenance	700
Interest on mortgage	3,000
Property taxes	1,000
Utilities	800

In addition to the expenses listed above, Kim could have deducted a total of $8,000 depreciation if the property had been acquired only for investment purposes. During the year, Kim uses the condominium 20 days for vacation. She also rented it out for a total of 60 days during the year, generating a total gross income of $9,000.
   a. What is the total amount of deductions for and from AGI that Kim may take during the current year with respect to the condominium?
   b. What is the effect on the basis of the condominium?

I6-56 *Rental of Vacation Home.* Assume all of the same facts as in Problem I6-55, except that during the year Kim rents the condominium a total of 14 days. How does Kim report the income and deductions from the property?

COMPREHENSIVE PROBLEM

I6-57 Bryce, a bank official, is married and files a joint return. During the current year he engages in the following activities and transactions:
   a. Being an avid fisherman, Bryce develops an expertise in tying flies. At times during the year, he is asked to conduct fly-tying demonstrations, for which he is paid a small fee. He also periodically sells flies that he makes. Income generated from these activities during the year is $2,500. The expenses for the year associated with Bryce's fly-tying activity include $125 personal property taxes on a small trailer that he uses exclusively for this purpose, $2,900 in supplies, $270 in repairs on the trailer, and $200 in gasoline for traveling to the demonstrations.
   b. Bryce sells a small building lot to his brother for $40,000. Bryce purchased the lot four years ago for $47,000, hoping to make a profit.
   c. Bryce enters into the following stock transactions: (None of the stock qualifies as small business stock).

Date	Transaction
March 22	Purchases 100 shares of Silver Corporation common stock for $2,800
April 5	Sells 200 shares of Gold Corporation common stock for $8,000. The stock was originally purchased two years ago for $5,000.
April 15	Sells 200 shares of Silver Corporation common stock for $5,400. The stock was originally purchased three years ago for $9,400.
May 20	Sells 100 shares of United Corporation common stock for $12,000. The stock was originally purchased five years ago for $10,000.

   d. Bryce's salary for the year is $115,000. In addition to the items above, he also incurs $5,000 in other miscellaneous deductible itemized expenses.
Answer the following questions regarding Bryce's activities for the year.
1. Compute Bryce's taxable income for the year.
2. What is Bryce's basis in the Silver stock he continues to own?

TAX FORM/RETURN PREPARATION PROBLEMS

I6-58 Dave Stevens, age 34, is a self-employed physical therapist. His wife Sarah, age 31, teaches English as a Second Language at a local language school. Dave's social security number is 417-46-9403. Sarah's social security number is 528-95-6271. Sarah and Dave have three children—Andrew, age 8; Isaac, age 6; and Mira, age 3. The children's social security numbers are respectively 377-83-2836, 377-64-7283, and 377-17-1415. They live at 12637 Pheasant Run, West Bend, Oregon 74658. They paid $8,900 in qualified residence interest and $2,400 in property taxes on their home. They also had cash charitable contributions of $14,000. They had no other itemized deductions. Sarah and Dave earned interest on CDs of $3,200. Sarah's salary for the year is $32,000, from which $9,600 in federal income tax and $1,400 in state income tax were withheld. Dave's office is located at Suite 402, 942 Woodview Drive, Portland, Oregon 74624, and his employer ID number is 22-7584904. Dave has been practicing for 4 years, and he uses the cash method of accounting. During the current year, Dave recorded the following items of income:

Revenue from patient visits	$300,000
Interest earned on the office checking balance	225

The following expenses were recorded on the office books:

Property taxes on the office	$4,500
Mortgage interest on the office	12,000
Depreciation on the office	4,500
Malpractice insurance	37,500
Utilities	3,750
Office staff salaries	51,000
Rent payments on equipment	15,000
Office magazine subscriptions	150
Office supplies	24,000
Medical journals	330

Prepare Dave and Sarah's tax return (Form 1040, Schedules A, B, C, and SE) for the current year.

I6-59 Lyle and Kaye James are married, have two minor children, Jessica age 8 and Jerron age 4, and are filing a joint tax return in the current year. They are both employed. Lyle and Kaye, ages 38 and 37, respectively, have combined salaries of $240,000 from which $42,000 of federal income tax and $10,000 of state income tax are withheld. Lyle and Kaye own two homes. Their primary residence is located at 11620 N. Mount Ave., New Haven, Connecticut 22222, and their vacation home is on the beach in Fort Lauderdale, Florida. They often rent their vacation home to supplement their income. The following items are related to the James' ownership of the two homes:

Item	New Haven	Fort Lauderdale
Rental income	$ —	$15,000
Qualified residence interest	7,200	5,000
Property taxes	1,400	1,000
Utilities	1,000	1,300
Repairs	200	300
Depreciation	0	3,500
Advertising	0	200
Insurance	1,500	1,500

The James used their Fort Lauderdale home 20 days during the year. They rented the vacation home 60 days during the year. The James have no other income or expense items. Lyle and Kaye's Social Security numbers are 111-22-3333 and 444-55-6666, respectively. Jessica and Jerron's social security numbers are 123-45-6789 and 888-99-1010.

File the James' income tax return Form 1040, Schedules A and E using the currently available forms and rates.

6-46 Individuals ▼ Chapter 6

TAX CUT

I6-60 Chris, age 56, and Scarlet Lindsay, age 54, are married and are filing jointly in the current year. Their social security numbers are 123-45-6789 and 987-65-4321, respectively. Chris's salary for the year is $97,000, from which $19,000 of federal income tax and $4,000 of state income tax were withheld. Scarlet is the sole owner of Scarlet Used & Vintage Books, a proprietorship that supplements the couple's income. The store is located at 450 W. Center Street, Kaysville, Ohio 11111. Scarlet reports the following income and expenses related to her business operation:

Revenues	$50,000
Cost of goods sold	10,000
City business license	400
Yellow pages advertisement	40
Depreciation on store	3,500
Real estate tax on store	1,000
Supplies	500
Wages & salaries	15,000

Scarlet subscribes to the following journals:

Book Archivist Monthly	$50
Wall Street Journal	150
Money Magazine	45
Reader's Digest	60
U.S. News & World Report	55

Chris and Scarlet jointly purchase stock in various corporations and make the following transactions in the current year: (None of the stock qualifies as small business stock).

Date	Transaction	Price Paid/Sold
2/15	Bought 50 shares of Lake common stock (own no other Lake stock)	$1,000
5/14	Bought 100 shares of Bass common stock (own no other Bass stock)	3,000
5/24	Sold 25 shares of Lake common stock	500
5/27	Bought 50 shares of Lake common stock	900
	Sold 50 shares of Bass common stock	1,750
7/12	Bought 100 shares of Bass common stock	2,800

During the year, Chris and Scarlet receive dividend income of $600 from Biggs, Inc. and taxable interest income of $400 from American Bank, make political contributions of $300, and pay $50 for use of a safety deposit box to store certain documents Scarlet needs in her business.

Chris and Scarlet own only one home at 237 E. 100 N., Kaysville, Ohio 11111. Their deductible mortgage interest for the year is $9,000 and their real estate tax is $2,300. Chris and Scarlet filed their state income tax return for the prior year in April of this year and paid an additional $400 of state income tax. In April of the current year, they also paid $180 to a CPA for preparing their federal and state income tax returns for the prior year, $100 of which was for the preparation of Scarlet's Schedule C.

Chris and Scarlet have no other deductions.

Prepare Chris and Scarlet's tax return (Form 1040, Schedules A, C, D, and SE) for the current year.

CASE STUDY PROBLEMS

I6-61 John and Kathy Brown have just been audited and the IRS agent disallowed the business loss they claimed in 1999. The agent asserted that the activity was a hobby, not a business.

John and Kathy live in Rochester, New York, near Lake Ontario. Kathy is a CPA and John was formerly employed by an insurance firm. John's firm moved in 1994 and John resolved not to move to the firm's new location. Instead of seeking other employment John felt he could supplement his income by using his fishing expertise. He had been an avid fisherman for 15 years and he owned a large Chris-Craft fly-bridge which he chartered to paying parties.

In 1995 Kathy and John developed a business plan, established a bank account for the charter activities, developed a bookkeeping system, and acquired insurance to cover the boat and the passengers. John fulfilled all the requirements to receive a U.S. Coast Guard operating license, a New York sport trolling license, and a seller's permit. These licenses and permits were necessary to legally operate a charter boat. 1995 was the first year of their activity.

John advertised in local papers and regional sport fishing magazines. He usually had three or four half-day paying parties each week. John spent at least one day maintaining and repairing his boat. Kathy usually accompanied John on charters three or four times each year.

John's charter activity was unprofitable the first two years. In 1997, John and Kathy restructured the activity to improve profitability. The restructuring included increasing advertising, participating in outdoor shows, and negotiating small contracts with local businesses. After the restructuring, the activity provided a small profit in 1997 and 1998.

In 1999 John started working with another insurance company in the area on a full-time basis. Even though he returned to the insurance business, John normally took two paying parties and one nonpaying, promotional party each week throughout the fishing season. John's costs unexpectedly increased and he lost $8,000 in the activity during 1999. John and Kathy deducted the entire loss on Schedule C of their 1999 tax return.

Required: Prepare a memo to the Browns recommending what position they should take and why. Show the logic used in arriving at your recommendation.

I6-62 Peter Baumann, your client, wants to sell a printing press to Chamberlain Corporation for $50,000. Pete has used the press in his business for two years and its adjusted basis is $90,000. The Coxmann Partnership, Chloe International, Inc., Watts, Inc., and Raleigh Corporation own Chamberlain Corporation equally. Pete and Emily Cox each own 50% of the Coxmann Partnership. Emily owns 70% of Chloe International, Inc., and Pete's sister Susan owns the other 30%. Pete's brother, Brian, owns 100% of Watts, Inc. And, Wade and Catherine Chamberlain, friends of Pete, own Raleigh Corporation equally. Peter wants to know what the tax consequences will be if he sells the computer to Chamberlain Corporation. In a memo to Pete, explain any tax consequences of the proposed sale and any alternatives that would provide a better result.

TAX RESEARCH PROBLEM

I6-63 Richard Penn lives in Harrisburg, Pennsylvania. Richard is the president of an architectural firm. Richard has become known throughout the community for excellent work and honesty in his business dealings. Richard believes his reputation is an integral part of the success of the firm.

Oil was found recently in the area around Harrisburg and some geologists believed the reserves were large. A few well-respected businesspeople organized Oil Company to develop a few wells. Although some oil was being extracted, the oil corporation lacked capital to develop the oil fields to their expected potential. After reading the geologists' report, Richard felt that Oil Company was a good investment; therefore, he acquired 25% of the company. A short time after Richard's acquisition, the price of foreign oil decreased sharply. The drop in foreign oil prices caused Oil Company to be unprofitable due to its high production costs. Three months later Oil Company filed bankruptcy.

The bankruptcy proceedings were reported in the local newspaper. Many of Oil Company's creditors were real estate developers that engaged Richard's architectural firm to provide designs. After Oil Company declared bankruptcy the architectural firm's business noticeably decreased.

Richard felt the decline in business was related to the bankruptcy of Oil Company. Richard convinced his partner to use the accumulated earnings of the firm to repay all the creditors of Oil Company.

Richard has asked you whether his firm can deduct the expenses of repaying Oil Company's creditors. After completing your research explain to Richard why the expenses are or are not deductible.

A partial list of research sources is as follows:

- Sec. 162
- *Thomas H. Welch v. Helvering,* 12 AFTR 1456, 3 USTC ¶1164 (USSC, 1933)
- *William A. Thompson, Jr.,* 1983 PH T.C. Memo ¶83,487, 46 TCM 1109

CHAPTER 7

ITEMIZED DEDUCTIONS

LEARNING OBJECTIVES

After studying this chapter, you should be able to

1. Identify qualified medical expenses and compute the medical expense deduction
2. Determine the timing of a medical expense deduction and the effect of a reimbursement
3. Identify taxes that are deductible as itemized deductions
4. Identify different types of interest deductions
5. Compute the amount of investment interest deduction
6. Compute the deduction for qualified residence interest
7. Compute the amount of a charitable contribution deduction and identify limitations
8. Identify certain miscellaneous itemized deductions subject to the 2% of AGI limit
9. Compute total itemized deductions for a taxpayer who is subject to the itemized deduction phase-out.

CHAPTER OUTLINE

Medical Expenses...7-2
Taxes...7-9
Interest...7-12
Charitable Contributions...7-21
Casualty and Theft Losses...7-28
Miscellaneous Itemized Deductions...7-28
Reduction of Certain Itemized Deductions...7-29

As explained in Chapter I6, most deductible expenses for individuals fit into three general categories:

- Expenses incurred in a trade or business
- Expenses incurred for the production of income (an investment activity) or for tax advice
- Certain specified personal expenses

Once an expense is determined to be deductible based on the above categories, the expense must be classified as either *for* AGI or *from* AGI. The distinction between *for* and *from* AGI was discussed in Chapter I6. This chapter focuses on deductions *from* AGI, also referred to as **itemized deductions**, which include medical expenses, taxes, interest, and charitable contributions. Other itemized deductions such as unreimbursed employee business expenses are discussed in Chapter I9 and casualty losses on personal-use property are discussed in Chapter I8.

In arriving at taxable income, individuals may subtract from AGI the larger of the standard deduction or the sum of all itemized deductions. However, as explained later in this chapter, certain itemized deductions are reduced if a taxpayer's AGI exceeds certain limits.

MEDICAL EXPENSES

ADDITIONAL COMMENT

In 1998, the deduction for medical expenses represented only 4.8% of the total dollar amount of itemized deductions.

Medical expenses, which comprise one category of deductible personal expenditures, are deductible because Congress felt that excessive medical expenses might ultimately affect a taxpayer's ability to pay his or her federal income tax. However, under Sec. 213, taxpayers may deduct medical expenses only to the extent the expenses exceed 7.5% of the taxpayer's AGI. To qualify as a medical expense deduction, the expenditure must have been incurred for the medical care of a qualified individual. Taxpayers may not take a deduction for medical expenses to the extent the expenses are reimbursed (i.e., compensated for by insurance or otherwise).

QUALIFIED INDIVIDUALS

To deduct medical expenses, taxpayers must pay the expenses on behalf of themselves, their spouses, or their dependents.

TAXPAYER'S DEPENDENT. Deductible medical expenses include those paid on behalf of a taxpayer's dependent as well as on behalf of a person for whom the taxpayer could take a dependency exemption except for the failure to meet the gross income or joint return tests.[1]

EXAMPLE I7-1

KEY POINT

Medical expenses are deductible for a person who satisfies only the support, relationship, and citizenship dependency tests.

In March of the current year, Jean's son, Steve, is involved in an automobile accident. Steve is 25 years old at the time of the accident and has worked full-time for part of the year, earning a total of $10,000. Because Steve has no medical insurance and cannot pay the medical bills or support himself as a result of the accident, Jean pays Steve's medical expenses and supports him for the rest of the year. Because Jean provides over one-half of Steve's support for the year and Steve, except for the gross income test, otherwise qualifies as Jean's dependent, Jean may deduct the medical expenses she pays on his behalf. Jean may not claim a dependency exemption for Steve because the gross income test is not satisfied. ◀

CHILDREN OF DIVORCED PARENTS. As long as one divorced parent is entitled to the dependency exemption under Sec. 152(e), the parent who pays medical expenses on behalf of the children may deduct the expenses. The parent taking the medical expense deduction need not be the parent who is entitled to the dependency exemption.

---

[1] Sec. 152. See Chapter I2 for the tests that must be met to claim another individual as a dependent.

QUALIFIED MEDICAL EXPENSES

OBJECTIVE 1
Identify qualified medical expenses and compute the medical expense deduction

The **medical expense deduction** is available only for expenditures paid for medical care. Section 213 defines *medical care* as amounts paid for

- The diagnosis, cure, mitigation, treatment, or prevention of disease
- The purpose of affecting any structure or function of the body
- Transportation primarily for and essential to the first two items listed above
- Qualified long-term care services
- Insurance covering all of the items listed above

DIAGNOSIS, CURE, MITIGATION, TREATMENT, OR PREVENTION OF DISEASE. Although the term *medical expense* is not precisely defined, it is clear that medical expenses are deductible only if they are paid for procedures or treatments that are legal in the locality in which they are performed. For example, taxpayers may not deduct expenditures for controlled substances.[2] The definition of medical care covers preventive measures such as routine physical and dental examinations. However, other expenses should be "confined strictly to expenses incurred primarily for the prevention or alleviation of a physical or mental defect or illness." Thus, unless they are for routine physical or dental examinations, the expenditures must be for the purpose of curing a specific ailment rather than related to the general health of an individual. This determination is especially critical when the expenditures in question are for items such as vacations, weight loss programs, or stop smoking programs. Such expenses may or may not be incurred for a specific ailment.

ADDITIONAL COMMENT
One cannot deduct the cost of nonprescription medicine (except insulin), toothpaste, toiletries, maternity clothes, diaper service, or funeral expenses.

EXAMPLE 17-2 ▶ Helmut is nervous and irritable because of pressures at work and begins to suffer angina symptoms. In order to relax and get away from it all, he takes an ocean cruise around the world. Helmut's angina symptoms ease while he is on the cruise. However, the Tax Court held that a cruise is not a proven medical necessity because Helmut's physician did not specifically prescribe it. Although the cruise was beneficial to Helmut's general health, it was not deductible.[3] ◀

EXAMPLE 17-3 ▶ Dave enrolls in a weight reduction program on the advice of two doctors who prescribe the program as a means of relieving his obesity, hypertension, and certain hearing problems. In a private letter ruling, the IRS held that these expenses qualify as deductible medical expenditures because they are incurred for specific medical conditions.[4] ◀

Although receipt of a doctor's recommendation for incurring the cost appears to lend a great deal of weight to deductibility, it is not always sufficient. For example, a taxpayer could not deduct the cost of dancing lessons for an emotionally disturbed child, even though the lessons proved to be beneficial and were recommended by a physician. Likewise, a taxpayer suffering from arthritis could not deduct the cost of ballroom dance lessons, even though the lessons were recommended by a doctor. On the other hand, the IRS has ruled that the cost of a clarinet and clarinet lessons was deductible when recommended by an orthodontist to correct a malocclusion of a child's teeth.[5] Thus, determining the deductibility of certain expenditures can be difficult.

REAL-WORLD EXAMPLE
Navajo Indians were entitled to deduct amounts paid to Navajo medicine men for practices called "sings" that were incurred to treat their ill child. *Raymond H. Tso*, 1980 PH T.C. Memo ¶80,399, 40 TCM 1277.

Range of Deductible Medical Services. According to the Treasury Regulations, typical medical expenses include payments for a wide range of medical, dental, and other diagnostic and healing services. Thus, taxpayers may deduct payments to licensed or certified medical professionals such as general practitioners, obstetricians, surgeons, ophthalmologists, opticians, dentists, and orthodontists. Furthermore, deductible medical expenditures include payments for medical services rendered by individuals such as chiropractors, osteopaths, and psychotherapists who may or may not be required to be licensed or certi-

---

[2] Reg. Sec. 1.213-1(e)(1)(ii). See also Rev. Rul. 97-9, I.R.B. 1997-9.
[3] *Daniel E. Mizl*, 1980 PH T.C. Memo ¶80,227, 40 TCM 552. Even if the taxpayer's physician had prescribed the trip, it still may not have been deductible. See Reg. Sec. 1.213-1(e)(1)(ii).
[4] Ltr. Rul. 8004111 (October 31, 1979).
[5] *John J. Thoene*, 33 T.C. 62 (1959), *Rose C. France v. CIR*, 50 AFTR 2d 81-5504, 1982-1 USTC ¶9225 (6th Cir., 1982), and Rev. Rul. 62-210, 1962-2 C.B. 89.

fied.[6] Taxpayers may deduct payments to Christian Science practitioners as well as acupuncture treatment if the treatment is received for a specific medical purpose.[7] Qualified medical expenses also include payment for hospital services, nursing services, laboratory fees, X-rays, artificial teeth or limbs, ambulance hire, eyeglasses, and prescribed medicines and insulin. Nondeductible expenses include expenditures for nonprescription medicines, drugs, vitamins, and other types of health foods that improve the individual's general health.

In order to deduct costs incurred for schools and camps, the taxpayer must show that the facility is equipped with the appropriate medical equipment and is regularly engaged in providing medical services. For example, expenses a taxpayer incurred to send his mentally handicapped son to a school with a special curriculum for such children was held to be deductible. Similarly, a taxpayer was able to deduct the cost of sending a child with psychiatric problems to a school specializing in learning disorders. However, taxpayers generally may not deduct the cost of sending children with special medical problems to schools or camps that do not have the proper equipment, facilities, or curriculum for such problems.

> **TYPICAL MISCONCEPTION**
> There is a tendency to define qualifying medical expenses too narrowly. This may be caused, in part, by comparison with expense reimbursement limitation policies of health insurance companies.

MEDICAL PROCEDURES AFFECTING ANY FUNCTION OR STRUCTURE OF THE BODY. Deductible medical expenditures also include payments for services affecting any function or structure of the body, even though no specific illness or disease exists. Thus, qualifying medical expenses include expenditures for such items as physical therapy, obstetrical services, eyeglasses, dental examinations and cleaning, and hearing aids. Under Sec. 213, cosmetic surgery or any other similar procedure does not qualify as a medical expense unless such surgery is necessary to correct a deformity arising from a congenital abnormality, a personal injury resulting from an accident or trauma, or a disfiguring disease. Cosmetic surgery is defined as any procedure undertaken to improve a person's appearance that does not meaningfully promote the proper function of the body or prevent or treat an illness or disease.

TRANSPORTATION ESSENTIAL TO MEDICAL CARE. Taxpayers may deduct transportation expenses that are incurred primarily for and essential to qualified medical care. Thus, taxpayers may deduct actual out-of-pocket automobile expenditures, taxis, airfare, ambulance fees, and other forms of transportation if the travel is for medical reasons. However, no deduction is allowed if the travel is undertaken for recreational purposes or for the general improvement of the taxpayer's health.

> **REAL-WORLD EXAMPLE**
> The transportation costs of a trip to the Shrine in Lourdes, France, were not deductible because the trip was taken to obtain spiritual aid to supplement medical care and not on the suggestion of a physician. *Vincent P. Ring*, 23 T.C. 950 (1955).

In lieu of the actual cost of the use of an automobile, the IRS allows a deduction of 12 cents for each mile that the automobile is driven for medical reasons. In addition to the standard mileage rate, taxpayers may also deduct the cost of tolls and parking. Certain courts have held that the cost of meals and lodging while en route to a medical facility is part of deductible travel costs incurred for medical purposes. However, taxpayers may not deduct the cost of meals eaten on trips that are too short to warrant a stop for meals. Additionally, taxpayers may deduct only 50% of the cost of meals. (See Chapter 19 for a discussion of the 50% disallowance rule for meals and entertainment.) The IRC limits the potential deduction for the cost of lodging to $50 per night. Furthermore, lodging expenses qualify as medical expenditures only if the travel is primarily for and essential to medical care, the medical care is provided in a licensed hospital (or a facility that is related or equivalent to a licensed hospital), and there is no significant element of personal pleasure or recreation in the travel. The $50 limitation on lodging is imposed on a per-individual basis. Thus, if the patient is unable to travel alone, an additional $50 per night may be deducted for the lodging costs of a nurse, parent, or spouse.

---

[6] Reg. Sec. 1.213-1(e)(1) and Rev. Rul. 63-91, 1963-1 C.B. 54. See also Ltr. Rul. 8919009 (February 6, 1989) where a pregnant woman was entitled to a deduction for the cost of childbirth classes to the extent that they prepared her for the childbirth. However, the cost of the classes where she received instructions on the care of the unborn child represented a flat fee that allowed a coach to attend the class with the taxpayer. Thus, one-half of the fee was deemed attributable to the coach and was not allowed as a qualified medical expense.

[7] Rev. Rul. 72-593, 1972-2 C.B. 180 and IRS Special Ruling, February 2, 1943.

Qualified Long-Term Care. Taxpayers may also deduct expenditures for qualified long-term care as medical expenses subject to the 7.5% of AGI limitation. Long-term care is defined as medical services required by a chronically ill individual which are provided under a prescribed plan of care. Under Sec. 7702B, such items include expenditures for diagnostic, preventive, therapeutic, curing, treating, mitigating, rehabilitative, and personal care services. A chronically ill individual generally is someone who, for a period of at least 90 days, cannot perform at least two daily living tasks such as eating, toileting (including continence), bathing, or dressing.

Expenditures for long-term care insurance premiums also qualify as medical deductions, subject to an annual limit based upon the age of an individual.[8]

CAPITAL EXPENDITURES FOR MEDICAL CARE. Generally, taxpayers may not deduct capital expenditures for federal income tax purposes. For assets used in a trade or business or held for the production of income, taxpayers must recover such costs through depreciation, cost recovery, or amortization. Capital expenditures incurred for personal medical purposes are not depreciable or amortizable. However, a current deduction is available when the capital expenditure is made to acquire an asset primarily for the medical care of the taxpayer, the taxpayer's spouse, or the taxpayer's dependents. To qualify as a deduction, the expenditure must be incurred as a medical necessity for primary use by the individual in need of medical treatment, and the expenditure must be reasonable in amount. Deductible capital expenditures for medical care are classified into three categories:[9]

▶ Expenditures that relate only to the sick or handicapped person, not to the permanent improvement or betterment of the taxpayer's property (e.g., eyeglasses, dogs or other animals that assist the blind or the deaf, artificial teeth and limbs, wheelchairs, crutches, and portable air conditioners purchased for the sole use of a sick person)

▶ Expenditures that permanently improve or better the taxpayer's property as well as provide medical care (e.g., a swimming pool installed in the home of an individual suffering from arthritis)

▶ Expenditures to remove structural barriers in the home of a physically handicapped individual such as costs of constructing entrance ramps, widening doorways and halls, lowering kitchen cabinets, adding railings, etc.

> **REAL-WORLD EXAMPLE**
> The cost of installing an elevator in the home upon the recommendation of a physician to help a patient with a heart condition was deductible to the extent that it did not increase the value of the home. *James E. Berry v. Wiseman,* 2 AFTR 2d 6015, 58-2 USTC ¶9870 (D.C. Okla., 1958).

Capital expenditures that relate only to the sick person (the first category) are fully deductible in the year paid. Expenditures that improve the residence (the second category) are deductible only to the extent that the amount of the expenditure exceeds the increase in the fair market value (FMV) of the residence brought about by the capital expenditure. Expenditures to remove physical barriers in the home of a physically handicapped individual (the third category) are deductible in full (i.e., the increase in the home's value is deemed to be zero). In addition, any costs of operating or maintaining the assets in all three categories are deductible as long as the medical reason for the capital expenditure continues to exist.[10] The deductibility of all of the above expenditures are subject to the 7.5% floor.

EXAMPLE I7-4 ▶ During the current year, Rita is injured in an industrial accident. As a result, she sustains a chronic disabling leg injury, which requires her to spend much time in a wheelchair. Rita's physician recommends that a swimming pool be installed in her backyard and that she devote several hours each day to physical exercise. During the year, Rita makes the following expenditures:

Wheelchair	$ 2,500
Swimming pool	27,000
Operation and maintenance of the pool	1,800
Entrance ramp and door modification	5,000

---

[8] For 2001, if the individual is 40 years of age or less, the annual deductible limit for the premiums is $230. For individuals over 40 but less than 50 the limit is $430. For those over 50 but less than 60 the limit is $860; over 60 but less than 70 the limit is $2,290; and over 70 the limit is $2,860. See Rev. Proc. 2001-13, I.R.B. 2001-3, Sec. 3.10 for the inflation-adjusted numbers for 2001.

[9] Reg. Sec. 1.213-1(e)(1)(iii) and H. Rept. No. 99-841, 99th Cong., 2d Sess. p. II-22 (1986).

[10] Rev. Rul. 87-106, 1987-2 C.B. 67.

7-6 Individuals ▼ Chapter 7

REAL-WORLD EXAMPLE

Taxpayers made nonrefundable advance payments required as a condition for an institution's future acceptance of their handicapped child for lifetime care in the event that taxpayers could not care for child. The amounts paid were deductible as expenses for medical care in the year paid. Rev. Rul. 75-303, 1975-2 C.B. 87. This current deduction for prepaid amounts is only available for certain lifetime care expenditures incurred in situations described in this ruling. Rev. Rul. 93-72, I.R.B. 1993-34,7.

A qualified appraiser estimates that the swimming pool increases the value of Rita's home by only $20,000. Rita's medical expenses for the year include $2,500 for the wheelchair, $7,000 for the swimming pool (the excess of the cost of the pool over the increase in the FMV of the home), $1,800 for the operation and maintenance of the pool, and $5,000 for the ramp and door modification. ◀

COSTS OF LIVING IN INSTITUTIONS. The entire cost of in-patient hospital care, including meals and lodging, qualifies as a medical expense. However, if an individual is in an institution other than a hospital (e.g., a nursing home or a special school for the handicapped), the deductibility of the costs involved depends on the facts of the particular case. If the principal reason for the taxpayer's presence in an institution is the need for and availability of the medical care furnished by that institution, the entire costs of meals, lodging, and other services necessary for furnishing the medical care are qualified medical expenditures.

ADDITIONAL COMMENT

A taxpayer cannot deduct the 1.45% Medicare (hospital insurance benefits) tax that is withheld from wages as part of the Social Security tax.

MEDICAL INSURANCE PREMIUMS. Qualified medical expenses also include all premiums paid for medical insurance, including premiums paid for supplementary medical insurance for the aged under the Social Security Act and premiums paid for qualified long-term care insurance contracts. In many cases, taxpayers pay premiums for insurance coverage that extends beyond mere medical care. For example, in addition to the standard medical care coverage, an insurance policy may provide coverage for loss of income or loss of life, limb, or sight. In such cases, a deduction is allowed for the medical care portion of the premium only if the cost of each type of insurance is either separately stated in the contract or is furnished to the policyholder by the insurance company in a separate statement.[11]

EXAMPLE I7-5 ▶

Each month Malazia pays $300 for an insurance policy under which she is reimbursed for any doctor or hospital charges she incurs. In addition, the policy will pay two-thirds of her regular salary each month if she becomes disabled. Finally, the policy will pay her $10,000 for the loss of any limb. At the end of the year, her insurance company issues a statement that allocates two-thirds of the premiums to the medical insurance coverage. Malazia's medical care expenditure is $2,400 ($300 × 12 × 0.667). ◀

If a taxpayer pays the premiums attributable to an individual or group medical insurance plan, the payments are deductible as medical expenses which in most cases are itemized deductions. However, in 2001 self-employed individuals may deduct 60% of these amounts as deductions *for* AGI, and in 2002 they may deduct 70% for AGI. The remainder is deductible as an itemized deduction. Any amounts paid by the taxpayer's employer are excluded from the employee's gross income and are not includible in the taxpayer's medical expenses.[12]

AMOUNT AND TIMING OF DEDUCTION

OBJECTIVE 2

Determine the timing of a medical expense deduction and the effect of a reimbursement

The amount and timing of the allowable medical expense deduction depend on when the medical expenses are actually paid, the taxpayer's AGI, and whether any reimbursement is received for the medical expenses.

TIMING OF THE PAYMENT. In general, taxpayers may deduct medical expenses only in the year they actually pay the expenses. This rule applies regardless of the taxpayer's method of accounting or when the event that caused the expenditure occurs.[13] Thus, if medical care is received during the year but remains unpaid as of the end of the year, taxpayers must defer the deduction for that care until the year they pay for the medical care. If the obligation is charged on a credit card, payment is deemed to have been made on the

---

[11] Sec. 213(d). See also Rev. Ruls. 66-216, 1966-2 C.B. 100, and 79-175, 1979-1 C.B. 117.

[12] Sections 162 and 106. The amount self-employed individuals may deduct *for* AGI increases to 100% beginning in 2003 and thereafter.

[13] Reg. Sec. 1.213-1(a)(1). However, medical expenses paid within one year from the day following the taxpayer's death are treated as paid at the time they are incurred (see Sec. 213(c)).

date of the charge, not on the later date when the credit card balance is paid. Conversely, if medical care is prepaid, the deduction is deferred until the year the care is actually rendered unless there is a legal obligation to prepay or unless the prepayment is a requirement for the receipt of the medical care.[14]

LIMITATION ON AMOUNT DEDUCTIBLE. As previously noted, a medical expense deduction is allowed only for the years in which the taxpayer itemizes his or her deductions and the taxpayer's expenditures for medical care exceed 7.5% of AGI.

> **EXAMPLE 17-6**
>
> During the current year, Kelly incurs qualified medical expenditures of $3,000. Her AGI for the year is $30,000. After subtracting the floor, she has $750 ($3,000 − [0.075 × $30,000]) of deductible medical expenses. These medical expenses are added to Kelly's other itemized deductions to determine whether they exceed the standard deduction.

SELF-STUDY QUESTION

Why does the IRS not require that the taxpayer file an amended return when a reimbursement is received in a later year?

ANSWER

The administrative burden on the IRS of processing additional returns would be too great.

MEDICAL INSURANCE REIMBURSEMENTS. Taxpayers may only deduct unreimbursed medical expenditures. It does not matter whether the reimbursement is from an insurance plan purchased from an insurance company, a medical reimbursement plan of an employer, or a payment resulting from litigation.

If the taxpayer receives reimbursement in the same year the medical expenses are paid, the deduction is reduced by the amount of the reimbursement. If a taxpayer receives a reimbursement in a year subsequent to the year of payment, the taxpayer must include the reimbursement in gross income for the year the payment is received to the extent that the taxpayer derived a tax benefit from the deduction in the previous year. If the taxpayer did not take a deduction in the prior year, the taxpayer doesn't need to report the reimbursement as income. This may occur because the taxpayer's total itemized deductions do not exceed the standard deduction or because the taxpayer's total medical expenses do not exceed 7.5% of AGI. If a deduction was taken in the prior year, however, the taxpayer must report as income the lesser of the amount of the reimbursement or the amount by which the taxable income of the prior year was reduced because of medical expenses.

> **EXAMPLE 17-7**
>
> During 2001, Diane, a single taxpayer under age 65, reports the following items of income and expense:
>
> | | |
> |---|---:|
> | AGI | $35,000 |
> | Total qualified medical expenses | 3,500 |
> | Itemized deductions other than medical | 3,800 |
>
> Diane's taxable income for 2001 is calculated as follows:
>
> | | | | |
> |---|---:|---:|---:|
> | AGI | | | $35,000 |
> | Reduction: larger of itemized deductions or standard deduction | | | |
> | Medical expenses | $3,500 | | |
> | Minus: 7.5% of AGI | (2,625) | 875 | |
> | Other itemized deductions | | 3,800 | |
> | Total itemized deductions | | $4,675 | |
> | Standard deduction | | $4,550 | (4,675) |
> | Personal exemption | | | (2,900) |
> | Taxable income | | | $27,425 |
>
> If during 2002 Diane receives a reimbursement of $1,000 for medical expenses incurred the prior year, she must include $125 ($4,675 − $4,550) in gross income for 2002 (the amount of the tax benefit from the medical expense deduction for the prior year). This amount can be calculated by comparing the actual taxable income for 2001 with what would have been the 2001 taxable income if the reimbursement had been received that year.

---

[14] Rev. Rul. 78-39, 1978-1 C.B. 73 and *Robert M. Rose v. CIR*, 26 AFTR 2d 70-5653, 70-2 USTC ¶9646 (5th Cir., 1970). See also Rev. Ruls. 75-302, 1975-2 C.B. 86, and 75-303, 1975-2 C.B. 87.

AGI		$35,000
Reduction: larger of itemized deductions or standard deduction		
Medical expenses	$3,500	
Minus: Reimbursement	(1,000)	
7.5% of AGI	(2,625)	
Excess medical expenses	0	
Plus: Other itemized deductions	3,800	
Total itemized deductions	$3,800	
Standard deduction	$4,550	(4,550)
Personal exemption		(2,900)
Taxable income (assuming reimbursement was received in 2001)		$27,550
Minus: Actual 2001 taxable income		(27,425)
Tax benefit		$125 ◀

Topic Review I7-1 highlights the principal requirements for the medical expense deduction previously discussed.

STOP & THINK

Question: Vince and Diane are married and file a joint tax return. For the current year they estimate their AGI at $100,000. They also estimate their itemized deductions for taxes, interest, and charitable contributions total $9,000. Up to the current date they have incurred $7,000 in deductible medical expenses. For several months they have been considering laser surgery on Diane's eyes. The total expenditure for the operations will be $4,000 and is not covered by their medical insurance. Since they already have spent so much this year on medical expenses and they do not anticipate such large expenses next year they are considering delaying the eye operation until next year. They estimate next year's AGI to be approximately $110,000. Does this decision make sense from a tax point of view?

Solution: From a tax point of view, Diane should consider having and paying for the operation this year. If so, $4,000 is added to the prior $7,000 medical expenditures for a total of $11,000 for the year. After applying the 7.5% of AGI limitation, $3,500 [$11,000 − ($100,000 × 0.075)] of the medical expenses is deductible. If they wait until next year and if their estimates are correct, none of the medical expenses in either year are deductible because of the 7.5% of AGI limitation.

Topic Review I7-1

Medical Expense Deductions

ITEMS	DEDUCTION RULES AND LIMITATIONS
Qualifying expenditures	(a) Expenditures for the diagnosis, cure, mitigation, treatment, or prevention of disease and qualified long-term care. (b) Transportation at $0.12 per mile and lodging limited to $50 per-night, per-person, and 50% of meals. (c) Medical and qualified long-term care insurance premiums. (d) Capital expenditures (subject to specific limitations).
Qualifying individuals	Taxpayer, spouse, dependents, and children of divorced parents even if not dependent.
Amount and timing of the deduction	Deduct in the year paid unless prepayment is required or there is a legal obligation to pay. Medical expenses are subject to a 7.5% of AGI nondeductible limitation.
Treatment of insurance reimbursements	The deduction is reduced if the reimbursement is received in the year of payment. Reimbursements received in a subsequent year are included in gross income of the year received if tax benefit was received in the earlier year.

Itemized Deductions ▼ Individuals 7-9

TAXES

OBJECTIVE 3

Identify taxes that are deductible as itemized deductions

Section 164 provides taxpayers with a federal income tax deduction for specifically listed taxes that are paid or accrued during the taxable year. Generally, cash-method taxpayers are entitled to the deduction when the taxes are paid, whereas taxpayers using the accrual method deduct taxes in the year they accrue. Other taxes are specifically listed as nondeductible. To be deductible as a tax, the assessment in question must be a tax rather than a fee or charge imposed by a government for providing specific goods or services.

DEFINITION OF A TAX

ADDITIONAL COMMENT

In 1998, the deduction for taxes represented 36.1% of the total dollar amount of itemized deductions, making it the second largest itemized deduction.

A *tax* is a mandatory assessment levied under the authority of a political entity for the purpose of raising revenue to be used for public or governmental purposes. Thus, fees, assessments, or fines imposed for specific privileges or services are not deductible as taxes under Sec. 164. These nontax items include

- Vehicle registration and inspection fees
- Registration tags for pets
- Toll charges for highways and bridges
- Parking meter charges
- Charges for sewer, water, and other services
- Special assessments against real estate for items such as sidewalks, lighting, and streets

However, if taxpayers incur these nontax fees and charges in a business or income-producing activity, these items may be either capitalized or deducted as ordinary and necessary business expenses or ordinary and necessary expenses incurred for the production of income.

DEDUCTIBLE TAXES

The following taxes are specifically deductible under Sec. 164:

- State, local, and foreign real property taxes
- State and local personal property taxes if based on value
- State, local, and foreign income, war profits, and excess profits taxes
- Other state, local, and foreign taxes that are paid or incurred in either a trade or business or an income-producing activity

All of these taxes are imposed by a government body other than the federal government. Federal taxes other than the generation-skipping transfer tax are not deductible for federal income tax purposes.[15] However, federal customs and excise taxes incurred in the taxpayer's business or income-producing activity are deductible as ordinary and necessary expenses under Secs. 162 or 212. Likewise, the *employer's* portion of federal Social Security taxes and federal and state unemployment taxes are deductible by the employer as ordinary and necessary business expenses if the employee works in the employer's business or income-producing activity.

SELF-STUDY QUESTION

Would a taxpayer normally prefer to deduct foreign taxes or take a foreign tax credit?

ANSWER

Normally the foreign tax credit is better because a credit provides a direct dollar-for-dollar reduction of the tax liability rather than a reduction of taxable income.

NONDEDUCTIBLE TAXES

The following taxes are not deductible under Sec. 164:

- Federal income taxes
- Federal estate, inheritance, legacy, succession, and gift taxes
- Federal import or tariff duties and excise taxes unless incurred in the taxpayer's business or for the production of income
- Employee's portion of Social Security and other payroll taxes
- State and local sales taxes and state inheritance, legacy, succession, and gift taxes

---

[15] The generation-skipping transfer tax is imposed by the United States on certain distributions from a trust (see Sec. 2601). Furthermore, under Sec. 691(c) a taxpayer who includes income in respect of a decedent in taxable income may deduct estate tax attributable to that amount.

- Foreign income taxes if the taxpayer elects to take the taxes as a credit against his or her federal income tax liability
- Property taxes on real estate to the extent the taxes are treated as imposed on another taxpayer

STATE AND LOCAL INCOME TAXES

> **BOOK-TAX DIFFERENCE**
> For financial accounting purposes, all taxes are deducted in arriving at net income after taxes. However, for tax purposes, only certain taxes are deductible.

For individuals, state and local income taxes are normally an itemized (*from* AGI) deduction. Thus, a taxpayer does not receive any federal income tax benefit if these taxes, in addition to the other itemized deductions, do not exceed the standard deduction. Cash-method taxpayers deduct all state and local income taxes paid or withheld during the year even if the taxes are attributable to another tax year.

> **EXAMPLE I7-8**
>
> **ADDITIONAL COMMENT**
> Every state except Alaska, Florida, Nevada, South Dakota, Texas, Washington, and Wyoming has some type of income tax.

▶ During 2001, Rita had $1,500 in state income taxes withheld from her salary. On April 15, 2002, Rita pays an additional $400 when she files her 2001 state income tax return. On her 2001 federal income tax return, Rita may deduct the $1,500 in state income taxes withheld from her salary during 2001 as an itemized deduction. The $400 that Rita pays on April 15, 2002 is deductible on her 2002 federal income tax return, even though the liability relates to her 2001 state income tax return. ◀

If a taxpayer receives a refund of state income taxes deducted in a prior year, the taxpayer must include the refund as income in the year of the refund to the extent the taxpayer received a tax benefit from the prior deduction. This calculation is done in the same way the tax benefit from a medical expense reimbursement was calculated in Example I7-7.

PERSONAL PROPERTY TAXES

Many state and local governments impose personal property taxes. For individuals, the key issue is whether the levy is a deductible tax under Sec. 164 or a nondeductible fee. To qualify as a deductible personal property tax, the levy must meet two basic tests:

- The tax must be an ad valorem tax on personal property. In other words, the amount of the tax is determined by the property's value rather than some other measure such as a vehicle's weight or model year.
- The tax must be imposed on an annual basis, even if it is not collected annually.[16]

If a personal property tax is based partly on value and partly on some other basis, only the ad valorem portion is deductible.

> **EXAMPLE I7-9**
>
> **ADDITIONAL COMMENT**
> Several states impose a tax on the value of a taxpayer's investment portfolio. This is an example of a deductible intangible personal property tax.

▶ Banner County imposes on all passenger automobiles a property tax of 1% of value plus 20 cents per hundredweight. Clay's automobile has a value of $10,000 and weighs 1,500 pounds. Clay may deduct $100 ($10,000 × 0.01) under Sec. 164. Clay may not deduct the remaining $300 (1,500 × 0.20) under Sec. 164; however, he may deduct it as an ordinary business expense if the automobile is used in his business. ◀

For individuals, personal property taxes are *from* AGI (itemized) deductions unless they are incurred in an individual's trade or business or for the production of rental income.

REAL ESTATE TAXES

Apportionment of Taxes. When real estate is sold during the year, the federal income tax deduction for property taxes imposed on that real estate is allocated between the seller and the purchaser based on the amount of time each taxpayer owns the property during the real property tax year. The real property tax year may or may not coincide with the taxpayer's tax year. The apportionment, based on the number of days each party holds the property during the real property tax year of sale, assumes that the purchaser owns the property on the date of the sale. This apportionment is mandatory for all taxpayers even

---
[16] Reg. Sec. 1.164-3(c).

though one of the parties (i.e., the purchaser or seller) may have actually paid the entire property tax bill. The party who actually pays the taxes (either the buyer or the seller) deducts his or her share of the taxes in the year the taxes are paid unless an election is made under Sec. 461(c) to accrue the taxes. The tax consequences do not depend on who actually pays the real estate taxes or whether the real estate taxes are prorated under the agreement.

EXAMPLE I7-10 ▶ The real property tax year for Bannock County is the calendar year. Property taxes for a particular real property tax year become a lien against the property as of June 30 of that year, and the owner of the property on that date becomes liable for the tax. However, the taxes are not payable until February 28 of the subsequent year. On May 30 of the current year, Sandy, a cash-method taxpayer, sells a building to Roger, who is also a cash-method taxpayer. The real estate taxes on the property for the current year are $1,095. Although Roger is liable for the payment of the tax, Sandy is treated as having paid $447 ($1,095 × 149/365 [the numerator of 149 is the number of days from January 1 through May 29 and the denominator is the entire real property tax year]) on the date of the sale. Roger may deduct his share of the taxes, equaling $648 ($1,095 × 216/365), in the subsequent year (i.e., the year during which Roger actually pays the full amount of property tax due of $1,095). On the other hand, if the taxes become a lien against the property on April 1, Sandy is the owner of the building on that date and, since she is liable for the tax, she will be the one who actually pays the tax. Under these circumstances, the result is the same (i.e. Sandy deducts $447 and Roger deducts $648) except that Roger may take the $648 deduction in the year of sale rather than in the year of payment. ◀

ADDITIONAL COMMENT
Delinquent taxes of the seller that are paid by the buyer as part of the contract price are not deductible.

Generally, the sales agreement provides for the proper apportionment of property taxes between the buyer and seller. Thus, in the closing statement, the amount of the taxes apportioned to each party generally is stated separately from the selling price of the property.[17]

TYPICAL MISCONCEPTION
It is common to fail to differentiate between assessments for new construction and for repairs. For example, an assessment for street repairs is deductible, but an assessment for the construction of a new street is not deductible.

REAL PROPERTY ASSESSMENTS FOR LOCAL BENEFITS. Local governments often make assessments against real estate for the purpose of funding local improvements. These assessments may be for such items as street improvements, sidewalks, lighting, drainage, and sewer improvements. If the tax is assessed only against the property that benefits from the improvement, it is not deductible, even though the general public may also be incidentally benefited.[18] Such assessments are capitalized as part of the property's adjusted basis.

Real property taxes incurred on personal-use assets, such as a personal residence, are deductible *from* AGI. Real property taxes incurred on business property or property held for the production of rental income are deductions *for* AGI.

GENERAL SALES TAX
Before 1987, Sec. 164 allowed a deduction for sales taxes. However, that deduction was eliminated by the Tax Reform Act of 1986 for 1987 and subsequent years. Instead, the sales tax is treated as part of the purchase price of the property, increasing its basis.

SELF-EMPLOYMENT TAX
Self-employed individuals pay a tax on their self-employment income in lieu of the payment of a Social Security payroll tax on salary. The self-employment tax rate and total amount of tax are equal to the combined employee and employer Social Security tax (i.e., 12.4% with a ceiling of $80,400 in 2001; and no ceiling for the 2.9% additional Medicare hospital insurance premium for self-employed individuals). However, self-employed individuals may deduct one-half of the self-employment taxes paid as a *for* AGI deduction.[19]

---

[17] However, if the agreement does not provide for an apportionment of taxes, the seller's gain or loss on the sale (and the purchaser's basis in the property) must be adjusted either upward or downward, depending on which party actually pays the taxes.
[18] Reg. Sec. 1.164-4. However, if the assessment against the local benefits is made for maintenance, repair, or interest charges on the benefits, the assessment is deductible. The burden of proof to show how much of the assessment is deductible falls on the taxpayer (see Sec. 164(c)(1)).
[19] Sec. 164(f). (See Chapter I14 for a discussion of the self-employment tax.)

INTEREST

OBJECTIVE 4
Identify different types of interest deductions

In years past, taxpayers could deduct virtually all interest paid or accrued in the taxable year. Gradually, however, Congress has enacted numerous exceptions into the tax law rendering several types of interest nondeductible. For example, individuals may not deduct personal interest expense, such as interest paid on personal credit cards, automobile loans, etc. Interest incurred in connection with a trade or business is always deductible. Thus, to determine the amount of interest expense deduction, taxpayers must properly classify their interest expense for the year. The interest expense categories include the following:

- Active trade or business
- Passive activity
- Investment
- Personal
- Qualified residence
- Student loan

ADDITIONAL COMMENT
In 1998, the deduction for interest paid represented 39.8% of the total dollar amount of itemized deductions, making it the largest itemized deduction.

DEFINITION OF INTEREST

Interest is defined as "compensation for the use or forbearance of money."[20] Thus, finance charges, carrying charges, loan discounts, premiums, loan origination fees, and points are all considered interest if they represent a cost for the use of money.

CHARGE FOR SERVICES. In addition to interest, borrowers may incur other charges in connection with borrowing money. These service charges include fees for appraisals, title searches, bank service charges, and the annual service charge on credit cards. Unless incurred in a trade or business, these expenses are not deductible because they all represent nondeductible personal expenses. As explained in the section in this chapter entitled Personal Interest, although finance charges on credit cards represent interest rather than service costs, they likewise are not deductible unless incurred in a trade or business.

BANK SERVICE CHARGES AND FINANCE CHARGES. Bank service charges on checking accounts are nondeductible expenses for services rendered rather than interest. The annual service charge on credit cards is also a charge for services rather than interest. However, finance charges on credit cards are interest. Late payments charged by public utilities are interest expense because they are not incurred for any specific service.[21] Of course, if these expenses are incurred in a trade or business, they are deductible.

KEY POINT
The classification of interest expense depends on the use to which the borrowed money is put, not on the nature of the property used to secure the loan.

CLASSIFICATION OF INTEREST EXPENSE

The deductibility of interest generally depends on the purpose for which the indebtedness is incurred because interest incurred in certain activities is subject to limitation and disallowance. For example, interest expense incurred in the taxpayer's active business is deductible in full against the business income (a deduction *for* AGI, taken on Schedule C), whereas interest expense allocated to the purchase of the taxpayer's residence is subject to the limitations applicable to that type of interest and is an itemized deduction (a deduction *from* AGI). In general, other than certain interest on a personal residence, taxpayers may not deduct interest allocated to personal-use expenditures.

Pursuant to the Treasury Regulations, taxpayers must allocate interest expense to the different interest expense categories by identifying the use of the borrowed money. Property used as collateral in securing the debt normally has no bearing on the allocation of the interest expense.[22]

---

[20] *Deputy v. Pierre S. DuPont*, 23 AFTR 808, 40-1 USTC ¶9161 (USSC, 1940).
[21] Rev. Rul. 73-136, 1973-1 C.B. 68 and Rev. Rul. 74-187, 1974-1 C.B. 48. However, interest on a credit card or interest charged by a public utility is not deductible if it is personal interest.
[22] Temp. Reg. Sec. 1.163-8T. The major exception to this rule deals with home equity loans where the funds borrowed may be used for any purpose. Home equity loans are discussed later in this chapter.

EXAMPLE I7-11 ▶ Cathy pledges some stock and securities as collateral for a $30,000 loan. She then purchases an automobile with the proceeds of the loan. The automobile is used 100% of the time for personal use. Even though the collateral for the loan is investment property, the interest expense is allocated to a personal-use asset and is not deductible. ◀

If the taxpayer deposits borrowed funds in a bank rather than spend them immediately, the deposit is considered an investment, and the interest on the loan is investment interest until the funds are withdrawn and expended. Then the interest expense is allocated to the category for which the expenditure is made, regardless of when the interest expense for the debt is actually paid. This reallocation occurs as of the date the check is written on the account as long as the check is delivered or mailed within a reasonable period of time.[23]

EXAMPLE I7-12 ▶ On March 1 of the current year, José borrows $100,000 and immediately deposits the funds into an account that contains no other funds. José makes no additional deposits nor payments. On May 1 of the current year, he withdraws $40,000 from the account and purchases a sailboat to be used for personal purposes. On July 1, José withdraws an additional $50,000 and purchases a passive activity. For the current year, the interest expense on the loan is categorized as follows: from March 1 through April 30, all of the expense is investment interest expense. 40% ($40,000/$100,000) of the interest expense attributable to the period May 1 through June 30 is classified as personal interest and the remainder is investment interest. The interest expense attributable to the period from July 1 to the end of the year is classified as 40% personal interest, 50% passive activity interest, and 10% investment interest. ◀

If both borrowed and personal funds are mingled in the same account, expenditures from that account are treated as coming first from the borrowed funds.[24]

EXAMPLE I7-13 ▶ On April 1 of the current year, Diane borrows $30,000 and deposits it into a checking account that contains $10,000 of personal funds. On May 1 of the current year, Diane purchases a passive activity for $15,000, and on June 1 she purchases a personal automobile for $20,000. The $15,000 expended for the passive activity on May 1 is treated as coming from the borrowed funds. Thus, as of that date, one-half of the interest expense on the debt is reallocated from investment interest to passive activity interest. $15,000 of the funds expended for the personal automobile on June 1 is treated as coming from the borrowed funds, and the remaining $5,000 is treated as coming from the personal funds. Thus, as of June 1, the remaining interest expense on the debt is reallocated to personal interest. ◀

When a debt is repaid, the repayment is allocated to the expenditures made with that debt in the following order: (1) personal expenditures, (2) investment expenditures and passive activity expenditures other than rental real estate, (3) passive activity expenditures in rental real estate, and (4) trade or business expenditures.

ACTIVE TRADE OR BUSINESS. Generally, a taxpayer may deduct without limit any interest expense incurred in the taxpayer's active trade or business. As explained in Chapter I6, the determination of whether a particular activity constitutes a trade or business or an investment depends on an examination of all the relevant facts and circumstances. For individuals, estates, trusts, and certain corporations, however, it is not sufficient that the interest be incurred in the taxpayer's trade or business. In addition, the taxpayer must *materially participate* in the business. If not, the activity is considered passive, and losses from the activity (including the interest expense) are subject to the passive loss limitation rules (see Chapter I8 for a discussion of these rules). Interest incurred in an active trade or business is a deduction *for* AGI.

---

[23] Temp. Reg. Sec. 1.163-8T(c). If during any one month several expenditures are made from an account, the taxpayer may elect to treat all the expenditures as if made on the first day of the month. However, this election is made on each account separately and is available only for accounts where the borrowed funds are already in the account as of the first day of the month. If the funds are not in the account as of the first day of the month, the expenditures may be treated as made on the date that the borrowed funds are deposited in the account. See Temp. Reg. Sec. 1.163-8T(c)(4)(iv).

[24] Temp. Reg. Sec. 1.163-8T(c)(4)(ii). However, if an expenditure is made out of the mingled funds within 15 days of the deposit of the borrowed funds into the account, the taxpayer may designate the expenditure to which the borrowed funds are allocated.

PASSIVE ACTIVITY. Individuals, estates, trusts, and certain corporations that incur losses from passive activities are subject to the passive loss limitation rules explained in Chapter I8. These rules prevent taxpayers from offsetting passive activity losses against other types of income such as salary, interest, dividends, and income from an active business. Taxpayers must include interest expense attributable to the passive activity in computing the net income or loss generated from the activity, and thus may not be able to deduct the interest under these limitation rules (see Chapter I8 for a discussion of these rules).

OBJECTIVE 5
Compute the amount of investment interest deduction

INVESTMENT INTEREST. Individuals and other noncorporate taxpayers are limited on the deductibility of interest expense attributable to investments. Without any limitation, high-income taxpayers could realize significant tax savings by borrowing money to invest in assets that are appreciating in value but produce little or no current income. This would enable the taxpayer to offset current highly taxed income with a current interest deduction, while deferring the taxable income from the investment until it is sold at a later date. This technique also would enable taxpayers to increase their capital gain income and reduce their ordinary income. This procedure is favorable to taxpayers because the tax on capital gains is, in many cases, less than the tax on ordinary income.

Because of these concerns, Sec. 163(d) limits the current deduction for investment interest expense to the taxpayer's net investment income for the taxable year. Any investment interest expense disallowed as a current deduction is carried over and treated as investment interest expense incurred in the following year.

EXAMPLE I7-14 ▶ In the current year, Rita earns $27,000 in net investment income and incurs $40,000 of investment interest expense. Rita's interest expense deduction for the year is limited to $27,000, the amount of her net investment income.

The remaining investment interest expense of $13,000 ($40,000 − $27,000) may be carried over and deducted in a subsequent year. This carryover amount is treated as paid or accrued in the subsequent year and is subject to the disallowance rules that pertain to the subsequent year. ◀

Investment Interest. Investment interest is interest expense on indebtedness properly allocable to property held for investment. This includes property that generates portfolio types of income such as interest, dividends, annuities, and royalties. It does not include business interest, personal interest, qualified residence interest, or interest incurred in connection with any activity that is determined to be passive. Under Sec. 469, all rental activities are deemed to be passive (see Chapter I8 for a discussion of the passive loss limitation rules). Thus, interest incurred in owning and renting property is subject to the passive loss limitation rather than the investment interest limitation.

Investment interest also does not include interest expense incurred to purchase or carry tax-exempt securities. This interest is not deductible at all. Without this disallowance, a taxpayer could, in certain circumstances, actually borrow funds at a higher rate of interest than the rate at which they were reinvested, while still generating a positive net cash flow because the government would be subsidizing the transaction through the interest deduction on the borrowings.

ADDITIONAL COMMENT

Net capital gain is eliminated in the calculation of net investment income. Congress believed that it was inappropriate for a taxpayer to be taxed on net capital gain at a favorable rate and to also be able to use that gain to deduct otherwise nondeductible investment interest against ordinary income that might otherwise be taxed at a higher rate.

Net Investment Income. For purposes of the investment interest limitation, the term **net investment income** means the excess of the taxpayer's investment income over investment expenses. Investment income is gross income from property held for investment, including items such as dividends, interest, annuities, and royalties (if not earned in a trade or business). Investment income also includes net gain (all gains minus all losses) on the sale of investment property, but only to the extent that the net gain exceeds the net capital gain (net long-term capital gains in excess of net short-term capital losses). Stated another way, net short-term capital gains are included in the definition of net investment income.

As explained in Chapter I5, net capital gain is generally taxed at a 20% maximum rate. Including net capital gain in the definition of investment income would increase the amount of deductible investment interest expense, which might offset other income that is taxed at higher rates. Thus, generally, net capital gain attributable to the disposition of property held for investment is excluded from the definition of investment income.

However, net capital gain from the disposition of investment property is included in the definition to the extent that the taxpayer elects to subject the gain from the disposition of investment property to the regular tax rates.[25] Gains on business and personal-use property are not included in the calculation of investment income.

EXAMPLE I7-15 ▶ During the current year, Michael incurs $15,000 investment interest expense, earns $7,000 of dividends and $3,000 interest income. He also reports the following gains and losses from the sale of stocks and bonds during the year:

Short-term capital gains	$4,000
Short-term capital losses	(3,000)
Long-term capital gains	5,000
Long-term capital losses	(2,000)

Considering all of Michael's other income and deductions for the year, assume that he is subject to a 39.6% marginal tax rate. Michael's net capital gain is $3,000 (net long-term capital gain of $3,000 in excess of net short-term capital losses of $0). He also has a $1,000 ($4,000 − $3,000) net short-term capital gain. Thus, of his total capital gain of $4,000 ($9,000 of total gains − $5,000 of total losses), only $1,000 ($4,000 net gain − $3,000 net capital gain) is included in investment income. If Michael does not make an election, his investment income is $11,000 ($10,000 of dividends and interest plus $1,000 net short-term capital gain). He may deduct $11,000 of the investment interest expense in the current year. The excess investment interest for the current year of $4,000 ($15,000 − $11,000) is carried over to the next year. The $3,000 net capital gain is subject to the 20% ceiling tax rate on net capital gain. If Michael makes the election, his investment income is $14,000 (the $3,000 net capital gain is included), and he may deduct $14,000 of the investment interest expense. Thus, only $1,000 ($15,000 − $14,000) of investment interest expense is not currently deductible and is carried over to the next year. However, his $3,000 net capital gain is subject to the 39.6% ordinary income tax rate. ◀

ADDITIONAL COMMENT
Investment expenses are those which are deductible on the tax return, after the 2% limitation.

Investment expenses include all deductions (except interest) that are directly connected with the production of investment income. These expenses include rental fees for safe-deposit boxes, fees for investment counsel,[26] and subscriptions to investment and financial planning journals. As explained later in this chapter (see the section of this chapter titled Miscellaneous Itemized Deductions), these investment expenses are deductible only to the extent they exceed 2% of the taxpayer's AGI for the year. Only the investment expenses remaining after application of this limitation are used in computing the net investment income. Furthermore, in computing the amount of the disallowed investment expenses, the 2% of AGI limitation is applied to the noninvestment expenses first.[27] Any remaining 2% of AGI limitation is then used to reduce the noninterest investment expenses.

EXAMPLE I7-16 ▶ Kevin's AGI for the current year is $200,000. Included in his AGI is $175,000 salary and $25,000 of investment income. In earning the investment income, Kevin paid investment interest expense of $33,000. He also incurred the following expenditures subject to the 2% of AGI limitation:

Investment expenses:	
Subscriptions to investment journals	$ 700
Investment counseling	2,000
Safe-deposit box rental	300
Noninvestment expenses:	
Unreimbursed employee business expenses	1,500
Tax return preparation fees (non–business-related)	500

Kevin's investment interest expense deduction for the year is computed by first determining the deductible investment expenses (other than interest) and the net investment income.

---

[25] Secs. 1(h)(3) and 163(d)(4)(B).
[26] Sec. 163(d)(4)(C). Not included here are commissions for the sale or purchase of investment property. A commission paid on the purchase of property is added to the purchase price (and the basis) of the property. A commission paid on the sale of property reduces the amount realized.

[27] H. Rept. No. 99-841, 99th Cong., 2d Sess., pp. II-153 and 154 (1986). The noninvestment expenses subject to the 2% of AGI limitation include unreimbursed employee business expenses, hobby expenses up to the income from the hobby, and tax return preparation fees.

Investment expenses:		
Subscriptions	$ 700	
Investment counseling	2,000	
Safe-deposit box rental	300	$3,000
Disallowed by the 2% limitation:		
2% of AGI ($200,000 × 0.02)	$4,000	
Unreimbursed employee expenses	(1,500)	
Tax return preparation fees	(500)	
Investment expenses (remainder of 2% limit allocated to investment expenses)		(2,000)
Deductible investment expenses		$1,000
Net investment income ($25,000 − $1,000)		$24,000

The investment interest expense deduction is limited to $24,000. The remaining investment interest of $9,000 ($33,000 − $24,000) is carried over and deducted in a subsequent year (subject to the disallowance rules that pertain to the subsequent year). ◀

OBJECTIVE 6
Compute the deduction for qualified residence interest

PERSONAL INTEREST. In general, the tax law does not allow a deduction for interest expense on debt incurred for personal purposes. Thus, taxpayers may not deduct interest on credit cards, car loans, and consumer debt. However, if certain requirements are met, taxpayers may deduct interest on debt to acquire a personal residence as well as interest on certain student loans.

QUALIFIED RESIDENCE INTEREST. Subject to certain limitations discussed below, individuals may deduct **qualified residence interest.** To be qualified residence interest, the interest payment must be either acquisition indebtedness or home equity indebtedness with respect to a qualified residence of the taxpayer. In all cases the debt must be secured by the residence.[28] A qualified residence (discussed below) may consist of the taxpayer's principal residence and a second residence.

ADDITIONAL COMMENT
Banks and other financial institutions that have received mortgage interest from homeowners are required to report interest of $600 or more to the IRS and to the homeowners on Form 1098.

Acquisition Indebtedness. Acquisition indebtedness is any debt that is secured by the residence and is incurred in acquiring, constructing, or substantially improving the qualified residence. Debt may be treated as qualified acquisition indebtedness if the residence is acquired within 90 days before or after the date that the debt is incurred. In the case of the construction or substantial improvement of a residence, debt incurred before the completion of the construction or improvement can qualify as acquisition debt to the extent of construction expenditures that are made no more than 24 months before the date the debt is incurred. Furthermore, debt incurred after construction is complete and within 90 days of the completion date may qualify as acquisition indebtedness to the extent of any construction expenditures made within the 24-month period ending on the date the debt is incurred.[29] As payments of principal are made on the loan, the amount of acquisition debt is reduced and cannot be increased unless the residence is substantially improved. Acquisition indebtedness may be refinanced (and therefore treated as acquisition indebtedness) to the extent that the principal amount of the refinancing does not exceed the principal amount of the acquisition debt immediately before the refinancing.

EXAMPLE I7-17 ▶ Kay acquired a personal residence in 1989 for $100,000 and borrowed $85,000 on a mortgage that was secured by the property. In the current year the principal balance of the mortgage has been reduced to $60,000. Kay's acquisition indebtedness in the current year is only $60,000 and

---

[28] Sec. 163(h). If the loan is not secured by the residence, it does not qualify. In one instance the taxpayer agreed to purchase her ex-husband's interest in their residence. The terms of the sale were $10,000 down plus an unsecured $25,000 note. In a private ruling, the IRS ruled that because the note was not secured by the residence, the interest on the note was not qualified residence interest. (See Ltr. Rul. 8752010 September 18, 1987). However, if under any state or local homestead law the security interest is ineffective or unenforceable, the interest expense still qualifies as qualified residence interest. See Sec. 163(h)(4)(C). In another letter ruling the taxpayer borrowed money to purchase a residence securing the debt by pledging stock and bonds. Here also, the IRS denied the deduction because the loan was not secured by the residence. (See Ltr. Rul. 8906031 November 10, 1988).

[29] Notice 88-74, 1988-2 C.B. 385.

cannot be increased above $60,000 (except by indebtedness incurred to substantially improve the residence). If she refinances the existing mortgage in the current year and the refinanced debt is $70,000, only $60,000 (the principal balance of the existing acquisition indebtedness) qualifies as acquisition indebtedness. ◀

Qualified acquisition indebtedness is limited to $1,000,000 ($500,000 for a married individual filing a separate return). Qualified acquisition indebtedness incurred before October 13, 1987 (pre-October 13, 1987 indebtedness) is not subject to any limitation. However, the aggregate amount of pre-October 13, 1987 indebtedness reduces the $1,000,000 limitation on the indebtedness incurred after October 13, 1987.

> **ADDITIONAL COMMENT**
> Many banks, in attempting to generate new loan business, have heavily advertised the tax advantages of home equity indebtedness.

Home Equity Indebtedness. Taxpayers may also deduct interest incurred on home equity indebtedness (so-called home equity loans). Subject to certain limits, home equity indebtedness is any indebtedness (other than acquisition indebtedness) that is secured by a qualified residence of the taxpayer. The proceeds of the loan may be used for any purpose (including purchasing or improving a qualified residence), as long as the loan is secured by the taxpayer's qualified residence. However, home equity indebtedness is limited to the lesser of:

▶ The FMV of the qualified residence in excess of the acquisition indebtedness with respect to that residence, or

▶ $100,000 ($50,000 for a married individual filing a separate return)

The $1,000,000 limit on acquisition indebtedness and the $100,000 limit on home equity indebtedness are two separate limits. The maximum amount of indebtedness on which a taxpayer may deduct qualified residence interest is generally limited to $1,100,000 if an individual has $100,000 or more equity in the property.

EXAMPLE 17-18 ▶ On April 23 of the current year, Kesha borrows $125,000 to purchase a new sailboat. The loan is secured by her personal residence. On that date, the outstanding balance on the original debt Kesha incurred to purchase the residence is $400,000 and the FMV of the residence is $900,000. The original debt is also secured by Kesha's residence. Kesha may deduct the interest paid on the $400,000 of acquisition indebtedness, plus the interest paid on $100,000 of the home equity loan. The interest on $25,000 ($125,000 − $100,000) is treated as personal interest and is, therefore, not deductible. The home equity loan is limited to the lesser of $100,000 or the FMV of the residence in excess of the outstanding acquisition indebtedness (the lesser of $100,000 or ($900,000 − $400,000)). ◀

Points Paid as Qualified Residence Interest. Often taxpayers must pay **points** on real estate debt. A point is equal to 1% of the loan amount. Thus, two points paid on a $60,000 mortgage equal $1,200 ($60,000 × .02). Points often represent prepaid interest because the stated rate of interest for the loan is lower than the current rate of interest. Generally, prepaid interest paid in the form of points must be capitalized and amortized over the life of the loan. However, points paid on a loan incurred to purchase the taxpayer's principal residence (acquisition indebtedness) are automatically deductible when paid if certain requirements are met. The IRS has also indicated that points paid on Veteran Administration (VA) and Fedeal Home Administration (FHA) loans are also currently deductible as interest if they are clearly designated as points incurred in connection with the indebtedness.[30]

EXAMPLE 17-19 ▶ During the current year, Kevin and Donna purchase a new home for $300,000, putting $100,000 down and borrowing $200,000. At the closing, they are required to pay one and one-half points as a loan discount in connection with the loan, which is secured by a mortgage against the home. The practice of charging points is an established business practice where they live.

---

[30] These requirements, mentioned in Chapter 16, are as follows: The points must be paid in connection with the purchase (not the improvement) of the taxpayer's principal residence, the closing agreement must clearly designate the amounts as points paid in connection with the acquisition debt, the amount must be computed as a percentage of the amount borrowed, the points must conform with established business practices, and the loan must be secured by the residence. Rev. Proc. 94-27, I.R.B. 94-15, 17. See also Rev. Proc. 92-12A, 1992-1 C.B. 664.

These points represent prepaid interest on the purchase of a principal residence. Thus, in addition to the interest portion of every payment they make during the year, Kevin and Donna may also deduct $3,000 ($200,000 × 0.015) as interest paid during the year of purchase. ◀

Taxpayers must capitalize points paid on a loan to purchase property other than a principal residence or for refinancing a mortgage on a principal residence. If the property is business, investment, or a qualified residence (the taxpayer's principal residence and one other that the taxpayer chooses) the taxpayers may amortize the points over the life of the loan.[31]

In order for the points to be currently deductible, the purchaser of the principal residence (borrower) must have paid for them with unborrowed funds. However, amounts provided by the borrower as down payments, escrow deposits, earnest money, or other funds are treated as paid for the points. Furthermore, as long as the borrower provides sufficient funds in these other categories, he or she is treated as having paid the points even if the seller has paid for them on behalf of the borrower.[32]

Qualified Residence. For any tax year, a taxpayer may have two qualified residences:

▶ Taxpayer's principal residence
▶ One other residence selected by the taxpayer, with regard to which the taxpayer meets the residence test of Sec. 280A(d)(1).

In order to meet this residence test, the taxpayer must have personally used the property more than the greater of 14 days or 10% of any rental days during the year.[33]

EXAMPLE I7-20

Fred owns a lakeside cabin that he uses for vacations. He also rents the cabin out to others when he is not using it. During the year Fred rents the cabin out at a fair rental for 90 days. Fred personally uses the cabin for a total of 22 days. Because Fred's personal use for the year (22 days) exceeds 14 days [the greater of 14 days or 9 days (10% of the rental days)], the cabin qualifies as his residence for purposes of deducting qualified residence interest for the year. ◀

ADDITIONAL COMMENT

Whether property is a residence for tax purposes is determined based on all the facts and circumstances, including the good faith of the taxpayer. A residence generally includes a house, condominium, mobile home, boat, or house trailer, that contains sleeping space and toilet and cooking facilities. Treas. Reg. § 1.163-10T(p)(3)(ii).

Despite the residence test, the taxpayer may select a property that has not been rented by the taxpayer at any time during the year as the second residence on which qualified residence interest may be deducted.

STOP & THINK

Question: Jana is about to purchase a new sport utility vehicle for $35,000. If she pays $5,000 down, the dealer is prepared to offer her a loan for the remaining $30,000 at 8% interest. In investigating other possible sources of funds, she found out that her brokerage firm would lend her the $30,000 at 9% interest if she pledged her stock as collateral. At her local credit union, she found that she could borrow the $30,000 at 10% interest if she took out a home equity loan by using her home as security. Jana is confused about which loan she should take.

Solution: The best way to analyze this problem is by comparing the after-tax interest rates of the loans. Jana may not deduct the interest paid to the car dealer because it is personal interest. Thus, its after-tax interest rate remains at 8%. Furthermore, even though Jana uses her stock holdings as collateral, the interest on the loan from the brokerage firm is non-deductible personal interest because the proceeds of the loan are used to purchase personal property rather than investment property. Its after-tax interest rate remains at 9%. Only the interest on the home equity loan from the credit union is potentially

---

[31] Rev. Rul. 87-22, 1987-1 C.B. 146, and Rev. Proc. 87-15, 1987-1 C.B. 624. The 8th Circuit Court of Appeals has held in one case that points paid on refinancing a "bridge" or temporary loan are currently deductible. *James R. Huntsman v. CIR,* 66 AFTR 2d 90-5020, 90-2 USTC ¶ 50,340 (8th Cir., 1990) rev'g 91 TC 57 (1988). However, the IRS has announced that it will not follow *Huntsman* in circuits other than the circuit in which the case was decided (IRS Action on Decision CC-1991-02, Feb. 11, 1991).

[32] Reg. Sec. 1.6050H-1(f)(3). See also Rev. Proc. 94-27, I.R.B. 94-15, 17.
[33] Sec. 280A(d)(1). Use by the taxpayer's family, as defined in Sec. 267(c)(4), other individuals under a reciprocal-use arrangement, and anyone when a fair rental is not charged is counted as a day of personal use by the taxpayer (see Sec. 280A(d)(2) and Chapter I6).

deductible. This depends, of course, on the amount of Jana's total itemized deductions. Assuming that Jana's total itemized deductions exceed the standard deduction and that Jana is in the 31% marginal tax bracket, the after-tax interest rate of the home equity loan drops from 10% to 6.9% [10% × (1 − 0.31)].

STUDENT LOAN INTEREST. If certain requirements are met, individuals may take a *for* AGI deduction for interest paid on qualified education loans. The maximum annual interest deduction for qualified student loans is $2,500. Furthermore, the deduction is phased out ratably for individuals with modified AGI of $40,000 to $55,000 ($60,000 to $75,000 for individuals filing joint returns).[34]

▶ **EXAMPLE I7-21** ▶ During 2001, Ryan paid a total of $1,800 in interest on a loan incurred for qualified education expenses. Ryan is single and reports modified AGI of $46,000 for the year. Since his modified AGI of $46,000 is $6,000 greater than $40,000, the total potential deduction of $2,500 is reduced by 40% ($6,000/$15,000). Ryan may take a *for* AGI deduction of $1,500. ◀

In order to qualify for this deduction, the interest must be payable on a loan incurred solely to pay qualified higher education expenses. If a taxpayer takes out a loan to pay for higher education expenses as well as for other purposes, none of the interest on the loan qualifies. Higher education expenses include tuition, fees, books and equipment, and room and board incurred during a time the taxpayer, the taxpayer's spouse, or the taxpayer's dependent is a student at a qualified higher education institution on at least a half-time basis. However, these qualified expenditures are reduced by amounts excluded from income under an employer educational assistance program or from United States savings bonds, as well as any scholarship or allowance that is excluded from income. Furthermore, in order to prevent a double deduction, no deduction is allowed to an individual for whom a dependency exemption may be taken on another's tax return or for any amount that is deductible under any other provision of the Code. The deduction is only allowed for the first 60 months in which the qualified interest payments are required. This 60-month period begins when the interest payments are first required.

TIMING OF THE INTEREST DEDUCTION

Section 163 allows a deduction for all interest paid or accrued during the tax year. This generally means that cash-method taxpayers deduct interest in the year it is paid, whereas accrual-method taxpayers deduct interest as it accrues. However, there are exceptions to this general rule.

ADDITIONAL COMMENT
Points paid on the refinancing of an existing mortgage must be written off over the life of the new mortgage.

PREPAID INTEREST. If a cash method taxpayer prepays interest and the prepayment relates to a loan that extends beyond the end of the tax year, generally the payment must be capitalized and amortized over the periods to which the interest relates (i.e., the accrual method is applied to cash method taxpayers). As previously discussed, there is one exception to this rule involving interest paid in the form of points charged in connection with the purchase or improvement of the taxpayer's principal residence. If these points represent prepaid interest, they may be deducted in the year paid.[35]

INTEREST PAID WITH LOAN PROCEEDS. Assuming the interest is otherwise deductible, if an individual borrows money from a third party rather than from the original lending institution and uses the funds to make a payment on a previously outstanding loan, the individual generally may deduct the interest portion of the payment. However, if the taxpayer borrows the funds used to pay the interest on the first loan from the same lender to whom the interest is due, and either the purpose of the second loan is to pay the

---

[34] Modified AGI includes income that is excluded (1) under the foreign earned exclusion, (2) for qualified adoption expenses, or (3) from United States savings bonds used to pay higher education tuition and fees. Taxable social security amounts are included but a deduction for IRA contributions may be taken.

[35] Sec. 461(g). In order for the exception to apply, the home must be used to secure the loan, and the charging of points must be an established business practice in the area where the loan is granted. (See the discussion of the deductibility of points in this chapter under the heading Definition of *Interest* as well as the discussion in Chapter I6.)

interest on the first, or the borrower does not have unrestricted control of the funds, the borrower may not deduct the interest.[36]

DISCOUNTED NOTES. Lending institutions often discount notes. In effect, the borrower pays the interest by repaying more money than is received when the note is signed. A cash method taxpayer can deduct this interest at the time the note is repaid, whereas an accrual method taxpayer must deduct the interest as it accrues over the term of the loan.

> **EXAMPLE I7-22** ▶ On December 1, 2001, Stan borrows $1,000 from his credit union to use in his business. Under the terms of the contract, Stan actually receives $970 but is required to repay $1,000 on February 28, 2002 (three months later). Because Stan is a cash method taxpayer, he may deduct the full $30 interest in 2002 when the note is repaid. If he were an accrual method taxpayer, he could deduct $10 ($30 × 0.333) in 2001, and $20 ($30 × 0.667) in 2002. ◀

TYPICAL MISCONCEPTION
It is sometimes mistakenly assumed that any interest paid on loans between related taxpayers is not deductible. However, if the taxpayers are not governed by the Sec. 267 limitation and the interest is paid on a bona fide loan, it is deductible.

INTEREST OWED TO A RELATED PARTY BY AN ACCRUAL METHOD TAXPAYER. One of the purposes of Sec. 267 is to require related cash method lenders and accrual method borrowers to report the results of their joint transaction in the same year. Thus, an accrual method taxpayer must defer the deduction for any expense (including interest) accrued until the year in which the expense is actually paid and is reported as income by a cash method creditor who is related to the debtor. Section 267 also disallows losses on the sale of property between related parties. The disallowance of such losses is discussed in Chapter I6.

The relationships covered by this rule are quite extensive. Some of the more common relationships include the following:

- Members of a family (defined as an individual's brothers, sisters, spouse, ancestors, and lineal descendants)
- An individual and a C corporation in which the individual owns directly or indirectly more than 50% of the outstanding stock
- A corporation and a partnership which are both over 50% owned directly or indirectly by the same people
- A partnership and any partner of the partnership
- An S Corporation and any shareholder of the S Corporation[37]

> **EXAMPLE I7-23** ▶ During the current year, Lisa, a cash method taxpayer, loans some money to her 100%-owned corporation, which uses the accrual method of accounting. As of December 31 of the current year, the corporation owes Lisa $3,000 in interest. However, because of a shortage of funds, the corporation does not actually pay the interest until February 15 of the following year. Despite the fact that the corporation uses the accrual method of accounting, the corporation cannot deduct the $3,000 until the corporation actually pays the interest to Lisa in the subsequent year. The result would be the same if the corporation were an S Corporation even if Lisa owned 50% or less of the outstanding stock. ◀

IMPUTED INTEREST. Under certain circumstances, if a taxpayer charges less than an adequate rate of interest, the IRS is authorized to impute an interest charge. This may cause the lender to have additional interest income and the borrower to have additional interest expense. The deductibility of this imputed interest expense also depends on how the expense is classified (i.e. personal, investment, etc.). (See Chapter I11 for a discussion of imputed interest.)

The rules for deducting various types of interest are summarized in Topic Review I7-2.

---

[36] *H. C. Franklin v. CIR,* 50 AFTR 2d 82-5551, 82-2 USTC ¶9532 (5th Cir., 1982) and *Newton A. Burgess,* 8 T.C. 47 (1947). See also *Norman W. Menz,* 80 T.C. 1174 (1983). The IRS has also announced that it will disallow a deduction for interest paid with funds obtained through a second loan from the same lender (see IRS News Release 83-93, July 6, 1983).

[37] Secs. 267(b) and (e). The list of relationships is much more extensive than those mentioned. An S Corporation is one that meets certain requirements and has made an election to have its income taxed directly to its shareholders. A C Corporation is one that has not made an S election. (See Chapter C11 of the *Prentice Hall's Federal Taxation: Corporations, Partnerships, Estates, and Trusts* text or Chapter C11 of the *Prentice Hall's Federal Taxation: Comprehensive* text.)

Topic Review I7-2

Deductibility of Interest Expense

TYPE OF INTEREST	RULES
Business	Deductible in full as a *for* AGI deduction.
Passive	Subject to the passive loss limits (see Chapter I8).
Investment	Deductible as an itemized deduction to the extent of the taxpayer's net investment income for the year. Any amount not deductible is carried over to subsequent years.
Personal	Not deductible.
Qualified residence	(a) Must be attributable to debt secured by the taxpayer's principal residence and one other residence selected by the taxpayer. (b) Interest on up to $1,000,000 of home acquisition indebtedness is deductible as an itemized deduction. (c) Interest on home equity debt is deductible as an itemized deduction. Home equity debt is limited to the lesser of $100,000 or the excess of the FMV of the residence over the home acquisition indebtedness.
Student Loan Interest	(a) Payable on loan incurred to pay qualified higher education expenses. (b) Taken as a *for* AGI deduction. (c) Maximum deductible amount is $2,500. Amount is phased out ratably for AGI between $40,000 to $55,000 ($60,000 to $75,000 for married filing jointly).

CHARITABLE CONTRIBUTIONS

OBJECTIVE 7

Compute the amount of a charitable contribution deduction and identify limitations

Under Sec. 170, corporations and individuals who itemize their deductions can deduct **charitable contributions** to qualified organizations. With the exception of certain contributions made by corporations (explained later in this chapter), taxpayers take the deduction in the year the contribution is made, regardless of the taxpayer's method of accounting. The amount of the deduction depends on the type of charity receiving the contribution, the type of property contributed, and the applicable limitations.

QUALIFYING ORGANIZATION

ADDITIONAL COMMENT

In 1998, the deduction for charitable contributions totaled $105.3 billion which represented 16% of the total dollar amount of itemized deductions.

To be deductible for federal income tax purposes, a contribution must be made to or for the use of a qualified organization.[38] Contributions made directly to individuals, even though the individuals may be needy, are generally not deductible.[39] Under Sec. 170, qualified organizations include the following:

▶ The United States, the District of Columbia, a state or possession of the United States, or a political subdivision of a state or possession

▶ A corporation, trust, community chest, fund or foundation created or organized under the laws of the United States, a state, possession, or the District of Columbia[40]

▶ A post or organization of war veterans

▶ A domestic fraternal society, order, or association[41]

▶ Certain cemetery companies

Because of the restrictions and limitations examined later in this chapter, these qualifying organizations are further classified into public charities and private nonoperating foundations. Different restrictions and limitations apply to each type of organization.

---

[38] The Supreme Court has ruled that in order for a contribution to be for the use of a qualifying organization, the gift must be held either in a legally enforceable trust or in a similar legal arrangement. (See *U.S. v. Harold Davis,* 65 AFTR 2d 90-1051, 90-1 USTC ¶50,270 (USSC, 1990).)

[39] Under certain circumstances, a taxpayer may take a deduction (limited to $50 per month) for maintaining a student as a member of his or her household. The student may not be a dependent or relative of the taxpayer and must be placed in the taxpayer's home under an arrangement with a qualifying organization (see Sec. 170(g)).

[40] These organizations must be organized and operated exclusively for religious, charitable, scientific, literary, or educational purposes; to foster national or international amateur sports competition; or for the prevention of cruelty to children or animals.

[41] Furthermore, gifts to these organizations must be made by individuals and must be used exclusively for religious, charitable, scientific, literary, or educational purposes, or for the prevention of cruelty to children or animals.

> **REAL-WORLD EXAMPLE**
> The American Red Cross, Boy Scouts, United Fund, Goodwill, and Indiana University are examples of public charities.

Public charities include:

- Churches or a convention or association of churches
- Educational institutions that normally maintain a regular faculty, curriculum, and regularly enrolled students
- Organizations such as hospitals and medical schools whose principal function is medical care or medical education and research
- Government-supported organizations that exist to receive, hold, invest, and administer property for the benefit of a college or university
- Any qualified governmental unit
- Organizations that normally receive a substantial part of their support from either a governmental unit or the general public
- Certain private operating foundations[42]

Because several thousand organizations meet these requirements, the IRS publishes a list of many of the organizations that have applied for and received tax-exempt status.[43] Although this publication is frequently updated, an organization need not be listed in order to qualify.

TYPE OF PROPERTY CONTRIBUTED

If a taxpayer makes a contribution in cash, the amount of the deduction is easily determinable. However, if noncash property is donated, the amount of the contribution is not as easy to identify. In the case of noncash property, the amount of the donation depends on two factors: the type of property donated and the type of qualifying organization (public charity or private nonoperating foundation) to whom the property is given. Furthermore, a gift of property that consists of less than the donor's entire interest in the property is not usually considered a contribution of property. Thus, for example, no charitable contribution is made when an individual donates the use of a vacation home for a charitable fund-raising auction.[44]

> **SELF-STUDY QUESTION**
> Doug purchases an item having a FMV of $75 for $100 in a charity auction. How much can he deduct?
>
> **ANSWER**
> Doug can deduct only $25 because the cash paid must be reduced by the value of the property received.

CONTRIBUTION OF CAPITAL GAIN PROPERTY. In general, the amount of a donation of capital gain property is its FMV. Regulation Sec. 1.170A-1(c)(2) defines a property's FMV as the price at which the property would change hands between a willing buyer and a willing seller, neither being under any compulsion to buy or sell and both having reasonable knowledge of relevant facts. For purposes of charitable contributions **capital gain property** is defined as property held over one year on which a capital gain would be recognized if it were sold at its FMV on the date of the contribution. If a capital loss or a short-term capital gain would be recognized on the sale of the property, the property is considered to be ordinary income property for purposes of the charitable contribution deduction.

Contribution to a Private Nonoperating Foundation. The tax law provides an exception to this general rule for contributions of capital gain property to private nonoperating foundations. In general, a private nonoperating foundation is an organization that does not receive funding from the general public (e.g., the Carnegie Foundation). Private nonoperating foundations distribute funds to various charitable organizations that actually perform the charitable services. The amount of the contribution to a private nonoperating foundation is the property's FMV, reduced by the capital gain that would be recognized if the property were sold at its FMV on the date of the contribution. This means that generally the deductible amount of the contribution is the property's adjusted basis.[45]

---

[42] Sec. 170(b)(1)(E). The distinction between a private operating foundation and a private nonoperating foundation generally depends on the way the foundation spends or distributes its income and contributions. The details of this distinction are beyond the scope of this text.

[43] IRS, Pub. No. 78, Cumulative List of Organizations, 2000.

[44] Sec. 170(f)(3), Reg. Sec. 1.170A-7(a)(1) and Rev. Rul. 89-51, 1989-1 C.B. 89. Note, however, that certain transfers of partial interests in property do qualify (e.g., the contribution of certain remainder interests to a trust, the transfer of a remainder interest in a personal residence or a farm, or a contribution of an undivided interest in property). These exceptions are beyond the scope of this text.

[45] The amount of a contribution of appreciated stock made to a private nonoperating foundation remains at its FMV.

EXAMPLE I7-24 ▶ Betty purchases land in 1986 for $10,000. In the current year, she contributes the land to the United Way. At the time of the contribution, the FMV of the property is $25,000. Because the land is capital gain property donated to a public charity, the amount of the contribution is $25,000 (its FMV).

On the other hand, if Betty donates the land to Cherry Foundation, a private nonoperating foundation, the amount of the contribution is $10,000 ($25,000 − $15,000 capital gain that would be recognized if the land were sold). ◀

TYPICAL MISCONCEPTION

Many people do not understand that the unrelated use restriction applies only to tangible personal property. A gift of shares of stock (intangible property) would not be a gift of unrelated use property where the stock is sold by the donee.

Unrelated Use Property. A second exception applies to capital gain property (that is also tangible personal property) contributed to a public charity and used by the organization for purposes unrelated to the charity's function. In such cases, the amount of the contribution deduction is equal to the property's FMV minus the capital gain that would be recognized if the property were sold at its FMV. This amount generally is the property's adjusted basis. Tangible property is all property that is not intangible property (e.g., property other than stock, securities, copyrights, patents, and so on). Personal property is all property other than real estate. The taxpayer is responsible for proving that the property was not put to unrelated use. However, a taxpayer meets this burden of proof if at the time of the contribution the taxapyer reasonably anticipates that the property will not be put to unrelated use. The immediate sale of the property by the charitable organization is considered to be a use unrelated to its tax-exempt purpose.

EXAMPLE I7-25 ▶ Laura purchases a painting for $3,000. Several years later she contributes the painting to a local college. The FMV of the painting is $5,000 at the time the property is contributed. The painting is both tangible personal property and capital gain property. The college places the painting in the library for display and study by art students. Because the college does not use the painting for purposes unrelated to its function as an educational institution, the amount of Laura's contribution is equal to its FMV ($5,000). On the other hand, if the college had sold the painting immediately after receiving it, the presumption is that the property's use was unrelated to the college's tax-exempt purpose. In this case, Laura's contribution is only $3000. ◀

CONTRIBUTION OF ORDINARY INCOME PROPERTY

General Rule. If ordinary income property is contributed to a charitable organization, the deduction is equal to the property's FMV minus the amount of gain that would be recognized if the property were sold at its FMV on the date of the contribution. In most cases, this deduction is equal to the property's adjusted basis. This rule applies regardless of the type of charitable organization to which the property is donated.

REAL-WORLD EXAMPLE

A retired congressman was not entitled to a charitable contribution of his papers because the papers were ordinary income property and had no basis. *James H. Morrison*, 71 T.C. 683 (1979).

For this purpose **ordinary income property** includes any property that would result in the recognition of income taxed at ordinary income rates if the property were sold. Thus, ordinary income property includes inventory, works of art or manuscripts created by the taxpayer, capital assets that have been held for one year or less, and Sec. 1231 property to the extent a sale would result in the recognition of ordinary income due to depreciation recapture.[46]

EXAMPLE I7-26 ▶ During the current year Bart purchases land as an investment for $10,000. Five months later he contributes the land to the United Way. At the time of the contribution the property's FMV is $15,000. The amount of Bart's contribution is $10,000 ($15,000 − [$15,000 − $10,000]) because he held the land for less than one year. ◀

EXAMPLE I7-27 ▶ Paul purchased a truck a few years ago for $20,000. During the current year, Paul donates the truck previously used in his business to a local community college. At the time of the contribution, the truck's adjusted basis is $5,000 and its FMV is $8,000. Because Paul would have recognized a $3,000 gain (all ordinary income under Sec. 1245) if the truck were sold at its FMV, the amount of the contribution is $5,000 ($8,000 − $3,000), which is equal to the truck's adjusted basis. ◀

---

[46] Reg. Secs. 1.170A-4(b)(1) and 1.170A-4(d). Sec. 1231 property includes property used in a trade or business that is subject to depreciation. If it is sold at a gain, part or all of the gain is treated as ordinary income. Any remaining gain is subject to the Sec. 1231 rules. (See Chapter I13 for an explanation of the depreciation recapture and Sec. 1231 rules.)

Donation of Inventory by a Corporation. Under certain circumstances, a corporation's donation of inventory to certain public charities gives rise to a contribution that is valued at more than the adjusted basis of the inventory. One exception is available if the inventory is to be used by the charity solely for the care of the ill, needy, or infants.[47] Another exception involves the donation of scientific equipment constructed by the taxpayer and donated to a college, university, or qualified research organization to be used for research, experimentation, or research training in the physical or biological sciences. A third exception is available for contributions of computer technology and equipment that is donated to public libraries and elementary and secondary schools.[48] In all three cases, the amount of the charitable contribution is the property's FMV, reduced by 50% of the ordinary income that would be recognized if the property were sold at its FMV. However, the amount of the contribution is limited to twice the basis of the property.

EXAMPLE 17-28 ▶ During the current year, Able Corporation, a manufacturer of medical supplies, donates some of its inventory to the American Red Cross. The Red Cross intends to use the inventory for the care of the needy and ill. At the time of the contribution, the FMV of the inventory is $10,000. Able's basis in the inventory is $3,000. Because this transaction qualifies under the exception, the amount of Able's contribution (before any limitations are applied) is $6,500 [$10,000 − (0.50 × $7,000)] but the actual amount of the contribution is limited to $6,000 (2 × the $3,000 basis in the property). ◀

REAL-WORLD EXAMPLE
The donation of blood is considered a personal nondeductible service.

CONTRIBUTION OF SERVICES. When a taxpayer renders services to a qualified charitable organization, the taxpayer may only deduct the unreimbursed expenses incurred incident to rendering the services. These items include out-of-pocket transportation expenses, the cost of lodging and 50% of the cost of meals while away from home, and the cost of a uniform without general utility that is required to be worn in performing the donated services. The out-of-pocket expenses are deductible only if they are incurred by the taxpayer who actually renders the services to the charity. No deduction is allowed for traveling expenses while away from home unless there is no significant element of personal pleasure, recreation, or vacation in such travel. Instead of the actual costs of operating an automobile while performing the donated services, the law permits a deduction of 14 cents per mile.

EXAMPLE 17-29 ▶

REAL-WORLD EXAMPLE
The cost of newspaper advertising, paper, pencils, and other supplies purchased by volunteers in connection with their involvement in the Volunteer Income Tax Assistance Program (VITA) is deductible. Rev. Rul. 80-45, 1980-1 C.B. 54.

During the current year, Tony spends a total of 100 hours developing an accounting system for the local council of the Boy Scouts of America. As an accountant, Tony earns $200 per hour. During the year, Tony also drives his car a total of 500 miles in performing the services for the Boy Scouts of America. If he uses the automatic mileage method to compute the amount of the charitable contribution, he can deduct $70 (0.14 × 500). No deduction is available for the value of 100 hours of Tony's contributed services. ◀

DEDUCTION LIMITATIONS

OVERALL 50% LIMITATION. The charitable contribution deduction available for any tax year is subject to certain limitations. For individuals, the general overall limitation applicable to public charities is 50% of the taxpayer's AGI for the year.[49] Any contributions in excess of the overall limitation may be carried forward and deducted in the subsequent 5 tax years. In addition, the tax law imposes further limitations on contributions of capital gain property to either a public charity or a private nonoperating foundation and all types of property contributions to private nonoperating foundations.

---

[47] Sec. 170(e). These charitable organizations are known as Sec. 501(c)(3) charities.
[48] Sec. 170(e)(6) Qualified donations can also be made to certain private foundations and other charitable organizations if the equipment is then contributed to one of the target organizations (schools and public libraries) within a specified period of time. In addition to inventory, this exception includes the donation of computer equipment that is no more than three years old.
[49] A 10% of taxable income limitation is placed on corporate taxpayers. For purposes of this limitation, a corporation's taxable income is computed without regard to any deduction for charitable contributions, dividends received, a net operating loss carryback, or a capital loss carryback.

30% LIMITATION. Under certain circumstances a special 30% of AGI limitation applies. Contributions of capital gain property (capital assets held over one year on which a gain would be realized if sold) to public charities are generally valued at the property's FMV but are subject to an overall limit of 30% of AGI instead of a 50% limit. This limit does not apply, however, in the following situations:

▶ Capital gain property (which is tangible personal property) donated to a public charity that does not put the property to its related use. In such cases, the amount of the contribution is scaled down by the capital gain that would be recognized if the property were sold.

▶ The taxpayer elects to reduce the amount of the charitable contribution deduction by the capital gain that would be recognized if the property were sold.

> **KEY POINT**
> The generosity of Congress in permitting individuals to use FMV is tempered by the 30% of AGI limitation.

EXAMPLE I7-30 ▶ Joy donates a painting to the local university during a year in which she has AGI of $50,000. The painting, which cost $10,000 several years before, is valued at $30,000 at the time of the contribution. The university exhibits the painting in its art gallery. Because the painting is put to a use related to the university's purpose, the amount of Joy's contribution is $30,000. The amount of Joy's charitable deduction for the year, however, is limited to $15,000 (0.30 × $50,000 AGI) unless she elects to reduce the amount of the contribution by the long-term capital gain. ◀

The overall deduction limitation of 30% of AGI also applies to the contribution of all types of property other than capital gain property (e.g., cash and ordinary income property) to a private nonoperating foundation. However, the deductibility of certain contributions to this type of charity may be subject to even further restrictions.

> **REAL-WORLD EXAMPLE**
> The largest private nonoperating foundation ranked by the FMV of total assets is the Ford Foundation.

20% LIMITATION ON CAPITAL GAIN PROPERTY CONTRIBUTED TO PRIVATE NONOPERATING FOUNDATIONS. Contributions of capital gain property to private nonoperating foundations are limited to the lesser of 20% of the taxpayer's AGI or 30% of the taxpayer's AGI, reduced by any contributions of capital gain property donated to a public charity.

CONTRIBUTIONS FOR ATHLETIC EVENTS. If a taxpayer makes a contribution to a college or university and in return receives the right to purchase tickets to athletic events, only 80% of the payment may be deducted.

APPLYING THE DEDUCTION LIMITATIONS. Contributions subject only to the 50% of AGI limitation are accounted for before the contributions subject to the 30% of AGI limitation.

EXAMPLE I7-31 ▶ During a year when Ted's AGI is $70,000, he donates $22,000 to his church and $18,000 to a private nonoperating charity. The church contribution is initially subject to the 50% limitation and is fully deductible because the $22,000 contribution is less than the limitation amount of $35,000 (0.50 × $70,000). Ted's deduction for the contribution to the private nonoperating charity (a 30% charity) is limited to $13,000 (the lesser of the following three amounts):

The actual contribution	$18,000
The remaining 50% limitation after the contribution to Ted's church [(0.50 × $70,000) − $22,000]	$13,000
30% of AGI (0.30 × $70,000)	$21,000
◀

APPLICATION OF CARRYOVERS

As noted earlier, any contributions that exceed the 50% limitation may be carried over and deducted in the subsequent five years. These carryovers are subject to the limitations that apply in subsequent years. Thus, carryovers may be deducted only to the extent that the limitation of the subsequent year exceeds the contributions made during that year.

These general rules also apply with regard to the special limitations. For example, if property subject to the 30% limitation is donated during the current year and the amount of the contribution exceeds the limitation, the excess may be carried over to the five subsequent years subject to the 30% limitation in the carryover years. In the carryover year,

> **ADDITIONAL COMMENT**
> If a taxpayer has contribution carryovers that are about to expire, the taxpayer should consider reducing the current year's contribution so that the carryovers can be deducted.

a deduction may be taken for the excess contribution to the extent that the 30% limitation of the subsequent year exceeds the amount of the property donated during the subsequent year subject to the 30% limitation. Excess contributions of property subject to the 20% limitation may also be carried over to the subsequent five years. This carryover is also subject to the special restrictions noted above for the 30% limitation. The carryovers are used in chronological order.

EXAMPLE I7-32 ▶ Assume that for the years 1999 through 2001, Joan reports AGI and makes charitable contributions in the following amounts:

	1999	2000	2001
AGI	$40,000	$40,000	$60,000
Cash contributions subject to the 50% of AGI limitation	25,000	23,000	24,000
50% of AGI limitation	20,000	20,000	30,000

The amount of the charitable contribution deduction for each year and the order in which the deduction and carryovers are used are as follows:

	1999	2000	2001
Amount of deduction	$20,000	$20,000	$30,000
Amount of carryover			
From 1999	5,000	5,000	0
From 2000		3,000	2,000 ◀

SPECIAL RULES FOR CHARITABLE CONTRIBUTIONS MADE BY CORPORATIONS

The rules governing charitable contributions made by corporations are generally the same as those pertaining to contributions made by individuals. However, certain differences do exist.

ETHICAL POINT

A tax practitioner should not be a party to the backdating of a Board of Director's authorization of a charitable contribution pledge so that the corporation may improperly deduct the contribution in the earlier year.

PLEDGES MADE BY AN ACCRUAL METHOD CORPORATION. Generally, taxpayers may only deduct actual contributions (but not pledges) made during the tax year. This rule applies to both cash and accrual method taxpayers. A major exception to this general rule exists for accrual method corporations. Such corporations may elect to claim a charitable deduction for the year in which a pledge is made as long as the actual contribution is made by the fifteenth day of the third month following the close of the year in which the pledge is made.

LIMITATION APPLICABLE TO CORPORATIONS. Corporate charitable deductions are limited to 10% of the corporation's taxable income for the year. This amount is computed without regard to the dividends-received deduction, net operating loss or capital loss carrybacks, or any deduction for the charitable contribution itself. Excess contributions may be carried forward for five years and are deductible only if the current-year contributions are less than the current year's 10% limitation. The carryovers are used in chronological order.

SUMMARY OF DEDUCTION LIMITATIONS

The rules governing the deduction for charitable contributions are summarized in Topic Review I7-3.

STOP & THINK

Question: During the current year, Kim has pledged to contribute $10,000 to both the Boy Scouts of America (BSA) and to a private nonoperating foundation. She wants to satisfy those pledges before the end of the year in order to take a deduction this year. She has enough cash to satisfy one of the pledges, but must either sell or donate some land in order to satisfy the other. The land she has in mind has a fair market value of $10,000 and a cost basis of $2,000. She purchased the land four years ago. Kim estimates that she will have AGI of $300,000 and will be in the 39.6% marginal tax bracket. Assuming that both charities would gladly accept either contribution, how should Kim satisfy these pledges?

Topic Review I7-3

Deduction Rules for Charitable Contributions

```
Start
 │
 ▼
Cash contribution? ──Yes──▶ Public charity? ──Yes──▶ Amount of donation equals cash amount[a]
 │                               │
 │                               No
 │                               ▼
 │                          Amount of donation equals cash amount[b]
 No
 ▼
Contribution of capital gain property? ──Yes──▶ Public charity? ──Yes──▶ Tangible personal property? ──Yes──▶ Unrelated to donee's purpose? ──Yes──▶ Donation equals FMV less long-term capital gain recognized if sold[a]
 │                                                   │                           │                              │
 │                                                   No                          No                             No
 │                                                   ▼                           ▼                              ▼
 │                                          Donation equals FMV less        Donation equals FMV of property[d]
 │                                          long-term capital gain
 │                                          recognized if sold[c]
 No
 ▼
Ordinary income property? ──Yes──▶ Public charity? ──Yes──▶ Qualified property donated by a corporation[f] ──Yes──▶ Donation equals FMV less 50% of ordinary income recognized if sold. Limited to twice the basis of the property[e]
 │                                      │                               │
 │                                      No                              No
 │                                      ▼                               ▼
 │                             Donation equals FMV         Donation equals FMV
 │                             less gain recognized        less gain recognized
 │                             if sold[b]                  if sold[a]
 No
 ▼
Contribution is a donation of services. Deduction is limited to unreimbursed expenses.
```

[a] Limited to 50% of AGI.
[b] Limited to lesser of (1) 30% of AGI or (2) remaining 50% of AGI after accounting for donations to public charities.
[c] Limited to lesser of (1) 20% of AGI or (2) 30% of AGI less capital gain contributions to public charities.
[d] Taxpayer may elect to scale down the amount of donation by long-term capital gain. If the election is made, limited to 50% of AGI. If no election is made, limited to 30% of AGI.
[e] Limited to 10% of the corporation's taxable income without regard to any deduction for charitable contributions, dividends received, a net operating loss carryback or a capital loss carryback.
[f] Qualified property consists of either (1) inventory or property used in a trade or business which will be used by a Sec. 501 (c) (3) charity for the care of the ill, needy, or infants, (2) inventory constructed by the corporation which will be used by a qualified research institution in the physical or biological sciences, or (3) computer software and equipment donated to and used by elementary and secondary schools located in the United States and public libraries.

Solution: The amount of contribution of capital gain property to a public charity is the property's fair market value. Such contributions are subject to a 30% of AGI limitation. However, a contribution of capital gain property to a private non-operating private foundation is the property's fair market value, reduced by the gain that would be recognized if

Casualty and Theft Losses

Generally, losses on personal-use property are not deductible. However, under Sec. 165 individuals may deduct a casualty or theft loss on personal-use property as an itemized deduction on Schedule A of Form 1040. Individuals deduct casualty losses on business and investment properties held for the production of rents or royalties in arriving at AGI. Other casualty losses on investment property are itemized deductions. These casualty losses are studied in greater depth in Chapter I8.

Miscellaneous Itemized Deductions

OBJECTIVE 8

Identifying certain miscellaneous itemized deductions subject to the 2% of AGI limit

Taxpayers may deduct various types of expenses as miscellaneous itemized deductions. These deductions include employment-related expenses of employees, certain investment-related expenses, and the cost of tax advice. However, as explained in Chapter I9, generally these items are deductible only to the extent that, in the aggregate, they exceed 2% of AGI.

CERTAIN EMPLOYEE EXPENSES

Taxpayers may deduct certain employment-related expenses as itemized deductions on Schedule A. These expenses include *unreimbursed* expenditures for travel and transportation, dues to professional organizations, costs of job hunting, items of protective clothing or uniforms not suitable for everyday wear, union dues, subscriptions to trade journals, and so on. A more detailed discussion of this topic is included in Chapter I9.

EXPENSES TO PRODUCE INCOME

Under Sec. 212, individuals may deduct expenses incurred to produce income. If these expenses arise in an activity that produces either rental or royalty income, they are deductions *for* AGI (see the explanation in Chapter I6). However, if the expenses are incurred in generating other types of investment income, individual taxpayers deduct them on Schedule A as itemized deductions. These investment-related expenditures include items such as rental fees for safe-deposit boxes used to hold investment property, subscriptions to investment and trade journals, bank service charges on checking accounts used in an investment activity, and fees paid for consulting advice. These expenses are all subject to the 2% of AGI reduction. Certain investment income and expenses are earned and incurred by taxpayers in mutual funds and other publicly offered regulated investment companies. These items generally flow through and are reported by the shareholders or owners of the fund. Because typically these entities simply report the net income (income minus expenses) to the owners, Sec. 67(c)(2) exempts these investment-related expenses from the 2% of AGI limitation. Other types of flow-through entities (e.g., partnerships and S corporations) must report these expenses to their owners as separately stated items so that the 2% of AGI reduction may be applied to these expenses also.

ETHICAL POINT

If a client furnishes a handwritten list of his or her miscellaneous itemized deductions to a CPA, the CPA may in good faith rely on the information without verification. However, the CPA should not ignore the implications of information that is provided and should make reasonable inquiries if the information furnished appears to be incorrect, incomplete, or inconsistent.

COST OF TAX ADVICE

Section 212 provides individuals with a deduction for expenses incurred in connection with the determination, collection, or refund of any tax, including federal, state, local, and foreign income taxes as well as estate, gift, and inheritance taxes. These items include (1) tax return preparation fees, (2) appraisal fees incurred in determining the amount of a

REAL-WORLD EXAMPLE

A taxpayer claimed that it was necessary to take a leave of absence from his job in order to appear before the Tax Court, to type various legal papers, and to take notes during the trial. He was not allowed to deduct the so-called lost wages representing the amount of vacation time spent in defending the suit. *James P. Stuart,* 1987 PH T.C. Memo ¶87,386, 54 TCM 70.

casualty loss, certain capital improvements for a medical deduction, or the FMV of property donated to a qualified charity, (3) fees paid to an accountant for representation in a tax audit, (4) long-distance telephone calls responding to IRS questions, (4) costs of tax return preparation materials and books, and (5) legal fees incurred in planning the tax consequences dealing with estate planning. If an individual incurs these items in connection with the taxpayer's (1) trade or business (reported on Schedule C), (2) farm income (reported on Schedule F), or (3) an activity which produces rents or royalties (reported on Part I of Schedule E), they are *for* AGI deductions.[50] All other expenses incurred for tax advice are miscellaneous itemized deductions subject to the 2% of AGI limitation.

Fees that are not directly connected with the determination, collection, or refund of a tax or with the taxpayer's trade or business are personal expenses and are not deductible. Thus, legal fees incurred for drafting wills generally are not deductible. However, legal expenses incurred in tax fraud cases in connection with the filing of a fraudulent return generally are deductible.[51] Legal fees relating to a divorce generally are not deductible, unless they deal with tax-related items such as determining who will receive the exemption for dependent children. These fees are discussed in greater detail in Chapter I3.

REDUCTION OF CERTAIN ITEMIZED DEDUCTIONS

OBJECTIVE 9

Compute total itemized deductions for a taxpayer who is subject to the itemized deduction phase-out

ADDITIONAL COMMENT

The reduction in itemized deductions obscures the true marginal tax rate applicable to high-income taxpayers and can be thought of as a hidden tax rate.

Because of concerns with the budget deficit, Congress enacted Sec. 68 which provides for a reduction in the total amount of certain itemized deductions for high-income taxpayers. This reduction applies only to individuals with AGI in excess of a certain threshold amount. This AGI threshold amount for 2001 is $132,950 ($66,475 for married people filing separate returns), and will be adjusted by an inflation factor for subsequent years. The reduction of the itemized deductions is 3% of the amount that the individual's AGI for the year exceeds the threshold amount. However, two limitations apply. First, the reduction in the itemized deductions cannot exceed 80% of the total itemized deductions other than medical expenses, investment interest, casualty losses, and wagering losses. Second, the 3% reduction is applied after taking into account the other limitations on itemized deductions (e.g., the 2% of AGI limitation on miscellaneous itemized deductions).

EXAMPLE I7-33 ▶

During 2001, John and Sue (a married couple filing a joint return) report AGI of $250,000. In addition, their itemized deductions consist of $10,000 charitable contributions, $4,000 real property taxes, and $8,000 state income taxes. Because their AGI exceeds $132,950, their itemized deductions for the year are limited to $18,488 ($22,000 − $3,512), computed as follows:

AGI	$250,000
Threshold	(132,950)
Excess	$117,050
Times: Reduction percentage	× 0.03
Potential reduction	$3,512
Limit to reduction:	
Charitable contributions	$ 10,000
Property taxes	4,000
State income taxes	8,000
Total	$ 22,000
Times: Limitation percentage	× 0.80
Overall limit on reduction	$17,600

The 80% limitation does not apply because the $3,512 reduction is less than $17,600. ◀

---

[50] Rev. Rul. 92-29, 1992-1 C.B. 20. [51] Rev. Rul. 68-662, 1968-2 C.B. 69.

EXAMPLE I7-34 ▶ Assume the same facts as Example I7-33 except that the $10,000 charitable contributions were instead medical expenses in excess of 7.5% of AGI and that the state income taxes were instead a deductible casualty loss (i.e., the amount in excess of the 10% of AGI limitation). Now John and Sue's allowable itemized deductions for the year are $18,800 ($22,000 − $3,200), computed as follows:

AGI	$250,000
Threshold	(132,950)
Excess	$117,050
Times: Reduction percentage	× 0.03
Potential reduction	$3,512
Limit to reduction:	
Real property taxes	$ 4,000
Times: Limitation percentage	× 0.80
Overall limit on reduction	$3,200 ◀

STOP & THINK

Question: Joe is a general contractor who uses the cash method of accounting. He has been hired to do a job that will pay him $30,000. Under the terms of the agreement, Joe is to receive the full $30,000 when the job is complete. By December 15 of the current year, Joe estimates that the job can be completed with approximately seven more days of work. The person who hired Joe doesn't care if the job is completed in December of the current year or January of the subsequent year. Joe's AGI for the current year, excluding this job, will be $150,000. Joe and his wife, Kim, estimate that their state income taxes, residential interest, and charitable contributions for the current year total approximately $10,000. Because of a general economic slowdown, Joe estimates that his AGI for the subsequent year will be $90,000. What advice can you give Joe regarding when he should complete this job and collect the income?

Solution: For tax purposes, Joe should complete the job in January of the subsequent year for a couple of reasons. First, if their estimates are correct, Joe and Kim likely will be in the 31% marginal tax bracket for the current year and the 28% marginal tax bracket for the subsequent year. Second, if Joe is paid for the job in the current year, Joe and Kim's AGI will exceed the threshold amount, thus causing a reduction in their itemized deductions. This reduction increases their effective tax rate. On the other hand, if Joe and Kim report the $30,000 in income in the subsequent year, they will not have to reduce their itemized deductions of that year. Finally, since there is only a delay of a few days between collecting the income in the current year and delaying the collection into the subsequent year, present value issues regarding the receipt of the income don't need to be addressed.

TAX PLANNING CONSIDERATIONS

MEDICAL EXPENSE DEDUCTION

WORKING WITH THE 7.5% OF AGI FLOOR. As explained previously, a deduction for medical expenses is available to individuals only to the extent that those expenditures exceed 7.5% of the taxpayer's AGI for the year. Thus, many individuals find that no deduction is available, even though their medical expenses are relatively high. In these cases, some benefit may be obtained if a portion of the medical expenses can be bunched into one year. Orthodontic work, certain orthopedic treatment, noncosmetic elective surgery, and new eyeglasses are all examples of medical expenditures that may be either accelerated or delayed into a year in which other medical expenses are high or AGI is lower.

Generally, a deduction for medical expenses is allowed only in the year in which the expense is actually paid. The mere prepayment of future expenses usually does not accelerate the deduction. However, taxpayers may take a deduction in the earlier year of payment if there is a legal obligation to pay or if the prepayment is a requirement for the receipt of the medical care.[52] If the taxpayer has already received the medical treatment, but the taxpayer does not have sufficient cash to pay the bill, the taxpayer may preserve a deduction for the current year by either borrowing the cash to satisfy the bill or by using a credit card.

EXAMPLE I7-35 ▶ During the current year, Marty's estimated AGI is $50,000. Marty has already incurred $2,000 in medical expenses for himself and his family during the year. Because 7.5% of AGI for the year is $3,750, he receives no medical expense deduction. Marty plans to incur $4,000 in medical expenses for orthodontic work for his son next year. No other major medical expenses are anticipated, and Marty expects his AGI in the following year to remain the same. If these estimates are accurate, he will receive no medical deduction in either year. However, if the orthodontic work is started in the current year and Marty pays for the work, he will incur a total of $6,000 in medical expenses in the current year. Thus, $2,250 ($6,000 − $3,750) of the medical expenses may be deducted.

Mere prepayment in this case is not sufficient. Marty must have a portion of the orthodontic services performed in the earlier year. If he does not have sufficient cash to pay the bill in the current year, he could borrow the money or use a bank credit card.

KEY POINT
Even if the medical expenses exceed 7.5% of AGI the taxpayer may not benefit from the deduction if the medical expenses in addition to the other itemized deductions do not exceed the standard deduction.

MULTIPLE SUPPORT AGREEMENTS. An individual may deduct medical expenses incurred for him- or herself, his or her spouse, and any dependents. In cases where a multiple support agreement has been filed, the individual who is the subject of the agreement is treated as the dependent of the taxpayer who is entitled to the dependency exemption. Thus, in order to preserve the medical expense deduction, the taxpayer who is entitled to the dependency exemption should pay all medical expenditures for the dependent individual.

EXAMPLE I7-36 ▶ Amy, Bart, Clay, and Donna each provide 25% of the support of their father, Eric. Under the terms of a multiple support agreement, Bart, Clay, and Donna all agree to allow Amy to claim the dependency exemption with respect to Eric. During the year, $3,000 in medical expenses are incurred on Eric's behalf. If Amy pays these expenses, she may deduct them (subject to limitations). However, if Bart, Clay, or Donna pays these expenses, no one may claim the medical expenses as a deduction. ◀

INTEREST EXPENSE DEDUCTION

A taxpayer may deduct qualified residence interest incurred on a principal residence and one other qualified residence that is selected by the taxpayer. The taxpayer makes this choice annually. In order for the second residence to qualify, it must have been used personally by the taxpayer for more than the greater of 14 days or 10% of the rental days during the year. If this test is met, however, the Sec. 280A limitations on the rental of vacation homes also apply. As explained in Chapter I6, under these rules, taxpayers must allocate expenses between the rental use and the personal use of the property. Taxpayers may deduct the expenses allocated to the rental use only to the extent of the rental income. Of the expenses allocated to the personal use, only the taxes and interest (if the residence is selected and if the loan is secured by the residence) are deductible as itemized deductions.

If the personal use by the taxpayer does not meet the test mentioned above, the interest allocated to the personal use cannot qualify as residence interest and it becomes nondeductible personal interest. Furthermore, the rental income and expenses allocated to the rental use of the property generally are subject to the passive loss rules (see Chapter I8). Under these rules, individuals generally can deduct losses generated from a passive activity only to the extent of the individual's passive income. Certain individuals, however, may deduct up to $25,000 of losses from the rental of real estate. Thus, the two alternatives and their consequences are as follows:

---

[52] *Robert M. Rose v. CIR*, 26 AFTR 2d 70-5653, 70-2 USTC ¶9646 (5th Cir., 1970). See also Rev. Ruls. 75-302, 1975-2 C.B. 86, and 75-303, 1975-2 C.B. 87, both clarified by Rev. Rul. 93-72, 1993-2 C.B. 77.

- Meet the test. No loss from the rental portion of the property may be deducted. However, the interest allocated to the personal use portion may be fully deductible as qualified residence interest.
- Do not meet the test: The interest allocated to the personal use portion is nondeductible personal interest. However, all of the passive loss from the rental portion is deductible against passive income. Furthermore, certain individuals may deduct up to $25,000 additional passive loss.

The alternative a taxpayer chooses depends on several factors such as the amount of the taxpayer's passive income, the total amount of itemized deductions, and whether the loan is secured by the vacation home, etc.

DEDUCTION FOR CHARITABLE CONTRIBUTIONS

ELECTION TO REDUCE THE AMOUNT OF A CHARITABLE CONTRIBUTION.

The election to reduce the contribution of capital gain property to public charities by the long-term capital gain that would be recognized if the property were sold is an annual election that applies to all capital gain property donated to public charities during the year. Because the election increases the ceiling limitation from 30% to 50%, under certain circumstances a taxpayer may actually receive a larger deduction for the year than would normally be available if the election were not made.

SELF-STUDY QUESTION
What type of property lends itself to the "election to reduce"?

ANSWER
Property on which there is very little appreciation.

EXAMPLE I7-37 ▶ During the current year, Jane has AGI of $50,000. She donates a painting to the local university during the same year. The painting, valued at $30,000 at the time of contribution, cost her $25,000 several years before. The university displays the painting in its art museum. If Jane does not make the election, the amount of the contribution is equal to its FMV ($30,000). However, Jane's charitable contribution deduction for the year is limited to $15,000 ($50,000 × 0.30). If Jane makes the election to scale down the contribution amount, the deduction is reduced to $25,000 ($30,000 − $5,000 LTCG). The deduction limitation, however, increases to $25,000 for the year because the limitation is now based on 50% of AGI instead of 30%. In this case, Jane will receive a larger deduction for the year by making the election. However, the cost associated with this election is the loss of $5,000 of deduction because the total deduction is reduced from $30,000 to $25,000 if she makes the election. ◀

Many tax practitioners make this election only when preparing the taxpayer's final tax return. The election is made at this time because charitable contribution carryovers to the decedent's estate are not permitted.

ADDITIONAL COMMENT
To help determine the FMV of contributed property, taxpayers can read IRS Pub. No. 561, Determining the Value of Donated Property.

DONATION OF APPRECIATED CAPITAL GAIN PROPERTY.
Instead of selling substantially appreciated capital gain property and donating the cash proceeds, the taxpayer should donate the property directly to charity. If property is donated in this way, the donor receives a deduction equal to the FMV of the property and does not recognize any taxable gain on the disposition.

EXAMPLE I7-38 ▶ Colleen wishes to satisfy a pledge of $100,000 made to a local university. She owns $100,000 worth of marketable securities purchased ten years ago for $30,000. Because the securities are marketable, the university is indifferent as to whether Colleen donates cash or the securities. Although her marginal tax rate is 39.6%, Colleen would be subject to a tax rate of 20% on the sale of the securities. She has enough AGI to be able to deduct the full contribution in the current year. The following chart summarizes the cash flows to Colleen under two different alternatives:

	Donate Securities	Sell Securities and Donate Cash
Proceeds of sale	0	$100,000
Tax on gain	0	(14,000)[a]
Cash payment to charity		(100,000)
Tax savings from the contribution deduction	$39,600[b]	39,600
Net tax benefit	$39,600	$25,600

[a] ($100,000 − $30,000) × 0.20 = $14,000.
[b] $100,000 × 0.396 = $39,600.

◀

In order to take a tax loss on business or investment property, a taxpayer should not donate property that has decreased in value. Rather, the property should be sold and the cash proceeds donated.

Compliance and Procedural Considerations

MEDICAL EXPENSES

In certain cases, expenditures qualify as both a medical care expense and a dependent care expense (i.e., expenses for household and dependent care services that the taxpayer must pay to be gainfully employed). A taxpayer who incurs an expense that qualifies under both provisions may choose to take either a medical expense deduction or a tax credit under Sec. 21.[53] However, if a taxpayer takes a credit for these expenses, they are not deductible as medical expenses.

EXAMPLE I7-39 ▶ Joel's daughter, Debbie, is physically handicapped. As a result, Joel hires a nurse, who provides daily care while he is at work. During the year, Joel pays the nurse a total of $3,000. This amount qualifies for both the dependent care credit and the medical expense deduction. If Joel takes the dependent care credit, the $3,000 may not be deducted as a medical expense. Because of the limitations imposed on each, the determination of which treatment is more advantageous depends on items such as the taxpayer's AGI, other medical expenses, and total itemized deductions. ◀

CONTRIBUTION OF PROPERTY

ADDITIONAL COMMENT
On Form 8283, the charitable organization is required to acknowledge receipt of the gift and to file an information return if the property is sold or disposed of within two years.

REAL LIFE EXAMPLE
In one case the taxpayer, a CPA, failed to support a contribution with a qualified appraisal. As a result, his charitable deduction for art and printing supplies donated to a high school was denied. To substantiate the claimed $40,000 charitable deduction, the taxpayer submitted with Form 8283 an appraisal of the donated items made by the high school's principal. The principal, however, wasn't a "qualified appraiser." *D'Arcangelo*, TC Memo 1994-572 (1994).

When property other than cash is donated to a qualifying charity, proper determination of the property's FMV is a critical issue. Because of actual and perceived abuses in this area, the IRS often scrutinizes and, if necessary, challenges the valuation of contributed property. This is especially true of property for which no published market quotes exist. If contributions of property exceed $500, Form 8283 (see Appendix B), which requires information about the type, location, holding period, basis, and FMV of the property, must be submitted with the taxpayer's return. This information must also be retained by the taxpayer. If the noncash contributions exceed $5,000, the taxpayer must get an appraisal by a qualified appraiser and must submit an appraisal summary, signed by the appraiser and an authorized officer of the charitable organization, with Form 8283.[54] Taxpayers should keep a copy of completed Form 8283 and any attachments for their records. Publicly traded securities need not be appraised. Nonpublicly traded stock must be appraised only if its value exceeds $10,000.

CHARITABLE CONTRIBUTIONS

Individuals report their charitable contribution deductions on Schedule A of Form 1040. Out-of-pocket expenses and contributions by cash or check are all reported on line 15. All contributions of property are included on line 16. As previously mentioned, if noncash property contributions exceed $500, Form 8283 (Noncash Charitable Contributions) must be attached to the return. The IRS has announced that if taxpayers do not attach Form 8283 to their tax returns in support of their noncash contributions, the deduction will be disallowed.[55]

---

[53] A credit of 30% of expenses for household and dependent care services is allowed if the dependent is under age 13 or a spouse or dependent who is mentally or physically incapable of caring for himself or herself. The credit is reduced 1% for every $2,000 (or portion thereof) of AGI over $10,000. (See the discussion on Personal Tax Credits in Chapter I14 for a more detailed explanation of the child and dependent care credit.)

[54] Reg. Sec. 1.170A-13(c). However, the requirement for an appraisal may be waived for contributions of inventory for the care of the ill, needy, or infants if the contribution is made by a closely held corporation or a personal service corporation. See Notice 89-56, 1989-1 C.B. 698.

[55] IRS Announcement 90-25, I.R.B. 1990-8, 25.

If the contribution is made in cash, the taxpayer must retain evidence of the donation by keeping a cancelled check or a receipt from the charitable organization. In the absence of a cancelled check or receipt, other reliable written records showing the charity's name and the date and amount of the contribution will be accepted. If the contribution is in the form of noncash property, the taxpayer is required to maintain records containing the

- Name and address of the charity to which the contribution was made
- Date and location of the contribution
- Description of the property
- FMV of the property
- Method of determining the property's FMV
- Signed copy of the appraisal report if an appraiser was used[56]

ADDITIONAL COMMENT

If the taxpayer's total deduction for art is $20,000 or more, it is necessary to include an 8 × 10 inch color photograph or a color transparency no smaller than 4 × 5 inches.

For charitable contributions of $250 or more, no deduction is allowed unless the contribution is substantiated by a contemporaneous, written acknowledgment by the donee organization. Separate payments generally are treated as separate contributions for purposes of applying the $250 threshold. This acknowledgment must contain the following information:

- The amount of cash and a description of any property contributed
- Whether or not the organization provided any goods or services in consideration for the cash or property received, including a description and good faith estimate of the value of any goods or services provided by the organization.

The acknowledgment is considered contemporaneous if it is obtained by the earlier of the date the taxpayer files a return for the year in question or the extended due date for filing such a return. This substantiation requirement is waived if the donee organization files a return that contains the required information.[57]

Additionally, certain disclosure requirements must be met by charitable organizations for a quid pro quo contribution in excess of $75. This $75 limit is applied separately on each transaction. A quid pro quo contribution is a transaction that is partly a contribution and partly a payment for goods and services. In order for such payments to be deductible, the donee organization must provide the donor with a written statement indicating

- That the amount of the deduction is limited to the excess of the cash and value of the contributed property over the value of the goods and services provided by the charitable organization.
- A good faith estimate of the value of the goods and services provided to the donor by the charitable organization.

Failure to make the required disclosure subjects the charitable organization to a $10 per contribution penalty unless the failure is due to reasonable cause. The penalty is capped at $5,000 per fund-raising event.[58]

EXAMPLE I7-40

During the current year, Peter Smith (Soc. Sec. no. 276-31-7242) reports AGI of $100,000. Smith also makes the following charitable contributions during the year:

- Smith performs voluntary dental work three days each month in rural areas of the state. Smith drives a total of 4,000 miles on these trips during the year.
- Smith makes the following contributions by cash or check: $750 to the city library, $2,000 to the United Way, $500 to a local community college, and $4,000 to his church.
- Smith contributes a tract of land to a small rural town. The town plans to erect a public library on the site. Smith purchased the land in 1986 for $5,000. Its appraised value at the time of the contribution is $8,000.

Smith's contributions are reported on the partially completed Schedule A shown in Figure I7-1. The out-of-pocket expenses of $560 (4,000 miles × $0.14) and the contributions by cash or

---

[56] Reg. Sec. 1.170A-13.
[57] Sec. 170(f)(8) and Reg. Sec. 1.170A-13(f).
[58] Sec. 6115.

Schedule A—Itemized Deductions

SCHEDULES A&B (Form 1040)
Department of the Treasury
Internal Revenue Service (99)

(Schedule B is on back)
► Attach to Form 1040. ► See Instructions for Schedules A and B (Form 1040).

OMB No. 1545-0074
2000
Attachment Sequence No. 07

Name(s) shown on Form 1040: **Peter Smith**
Your social security number: **276 31 7242**

Medical and Dental Expenses

Caution. Do not include expenses reimbursed or paid by others.

1	Medical and dental expenses (see page A-2)	1
2	Enter amount from Form 1040, line 34	2
3	Multiply line 2 above by 7.5% (.075)	3
4	Subtract line 3 from line 1. If line 3 is more than line 1, enter -0-	4

Taxes You Paid
(See page A-2.)

5	State and local income taxes	5
6	Real estate taxes (see page A-2)	6
7	Personal property taxes	7
8	Other taxes. List type and amount ►	8
9	Add lines 5 through 8	9

Interest You Paid
(See page A-3.)

Note. Personal interest is not deductible.

10	Home mortgage interest and points reported to you on Form 1098	10
11	Home mortgage interest not reported to you on Form 1098. If paid to the person from whom you bought the home, see page A-3 and show that person's name, identifying no., and address ►	11
12	Points not reported to you on Form 1098. See page A-3 for special rules	12
13	Investment interest. Attach Form 4952 if required. (See page A-3.)	13
14	Add lines 10 through 13	14

Gifts to Charity
If you made a gift and got a benefit for it, see page A-4.

15	Gifts by cash or check. If you made any gift of $250 or more, see page A-4	15 7,810
16	Other than by cash or check. If any gift of $250 or more, see page A-4. You **must** attach Form 8283 if over $500	16 8,000
17	Carryover from prior year	17
18	Add lines 15 through 17	18 15,810 —

Casualty and Theft Losses

19	Casualty or theft loss(es). Attach Form 4684. (See page A-5.)	19

Job Expenses and Most Other Miscellaneous Deductions
(See page A-5 for expenses to deduct here.)

20	Unreimbursed employee expenses—job travel, union dues, job education, etc. You **must** attach Form 2106 or 2106-EZ if required. (See page A-5.) ►	20
21	Tax preparation fees	21
22	Other expenses—investment, safe deposit box, etc. List type and amount ►	22
23	Add lines 20 through 22	23
24	Enter amount from Form 1040, line 34	24
25	Multiply line 24 above by 2% (.02)	25
26	Subtract line 25 from line 23. If line 25 is more than line 23, enter -0-	26

Other Miscellaneous Deductions

27	Other—from list on page A-6. List type and amount ►	27

Total Itemized Deductions

28 Is Form 1040, line 34, over $128,950 (over $64,475 if married filing separately)?
☐ **No.** Your deduction is not limited. Add the amounts in the far right column for lines 4 through 27. Also, enter this amount on Form 1040, line 36.
☐ **Yes.** Your deduction may be limited. See page A-6 for the amount to enter.
► 28

For Paperwork Reduction Act Notice, see Form 1040 instructions.   Cat. No. 11330X   Schedule A (Form 1040) 2000

FIGURE 17-1 ► PARTIALLY COMPLETED SCHEDULE A

check of $7,250 (library, United Way, church, and community college) are totaled and reported on line 15. The property contribution of $8,000 is separately stated on line 16. Because Smith contributes property with a value exceeding $500, Form 8283, an appraisal summary, and signed statements by the qualified appraiser and an authorized official of the organization that received the property must be attached to the return. In addition, for the donations that separately exceed $250, Peter must obtain and retain written acknowledgments from the donee organizations in order for the contributions to be deductible. ◀

TAXES

Individuals generally report their deduction for property taxes on Schedule A of Form 1040. However, if the taxes are incurred in the taxpayer's business, they are reported on Schedule C. Taxes incurred for the production of rents and royalties are reported on Schedule E. Taxes incurred in the taxpayer's farming business are reported on Schedule F. State and local income taxes imposed on individuals are always reported on Schedule A even if the individual is self-employed.

Real estate brokers are required to report any real estate tax allocable to the purchaser of a residence. (See the discussion in this chapter regarding the allocation of real estate taxes between the seller and buyer of a residence.)[59] This information is reported by the broker on Form 1099-S (Proceeds from Real Estate Transactions).

EXAMPLE I7-41 ▶ During the year, Andrea incurs $1,500 in property taxes on a two-family house. Andrea lives in one unit and rents out the other. She also pays $100 in registration fees and $600 in personal property taxes on her automobile, based on its value. Andrea uses the automobile 80% of the time in an unincorporated business. During the current year, she also pays $2,000 in state income taxes, all of which is attributable to her income of the prior year from the unincorporated business.

Because one-half of the real estate taxes are attributable to property used to produce rental income, $750 (0.50 × $1,500) is reported on Schedule E, and the remaining personal-use portion ($750) is reported on Schedule A. Because 80% of the use of the automobile is in Andrea's business, $80 (0.80 × $100) of the registration fee is deductible as a business expense on Schedule C. The remaining $20 is not deductible because the registration fee is not a tax. However, $480 (0.80 × $600) of the personal property tax on the automobile is deductible as a business expense on Schedule C. The remaining $120 is deductible as a tax on Schedule A. Finally, even though the tax is related to Andrea's business income, all $2,000 of the state income tax is reported on Schedule A. Because the state income tax is paid in the current year, it is deductible in the current year. ◀

WHAT WOULD YOU DO IN THIS SITUATION?

GIVING TO BOTH: GOODWILL AND THE IRS

Much has been written about abusive practices concerning the valuation of noncash property donated to qualified charities. Under Sec. 170, both corporations and individuals may deduct the FMV of property contributed to charitable organizations. Of course, a number of valuation and percentage limitations and carryover rules are applicable to both individual and corporate taxpayers.

Assume your clients, Mr. and Mrs. Nicholas Nice, come into your office on December 27 for some year-end tax planning. Your review of their tax situation indicates that they have made substantial donations of clothing and household goods to Goodwill Industries. They have obtained proper documentation for donations made during the year but do not know how to qualify for taking a charitable deduction vis-à-vis valuation, forms, and the like. They do know that their original cost basis in the donated goods was $15,000 and that the goods were in usable condition at the time of the donation. What tax and ethical issues should be considered?

---

[59] Sec. 6045(e)(4) and NOTICE 93-4, 1993-1 C.B. 295.

Problem Materials

DISCUSSION QUESTIONS

I7-1 a. A taxpayer may deduct medical expenses incurred on behalf of which people?
b. In the case of children of divorced parents, must the parent who is entitled to the dependency exemption pay the medical expenses of the child to ensure that the expenses are deductible? Explain.
c. Who should pay the medical expenses of an individual who is the subject of a multiple support agreement?

I7-2 What is the definition of medical care for purposes of the medical care deduction?

I7-3 a. What is the definition of cosmetic surgery under the Internal Revenue Code?
b. Is the cost of cosmetic surgery deductible as a medical expense? Explain.

I7-4 a. If a taxpayer must travel away from his or her home in order to obtain medical care, which en route costs, if any, are deductible as medical expenses?
b. Are there any limits imposed on the deductibility of these expenses?

I7-5 What are the rules dealing with the deductibility of the cost of meals and lodging incurred while away from home in order to receive medical treatment as an outpatient?

I7-6 a. Which types of capital expenditures incurred specifically for medical purposes are deductible?
b. What limitations, if any, are imposed on the deductibility of these expenditures?

I7-7 Bill, a plant manager, is suffering from a serious ulcer. Bill's doctor recommends that he spend three weeks fishing and hunting in the Colorado Rockies. Can Bill deduct the costs of the trip as a medical expense?

I7-8 In what cases are medical insurance premiums paid by an individual not deductible as qualified medical expenses?

I7-9 What is the limit placed on medical expense deductions? When can a deduction be taken for medical care? What if the medical care is prepaid?

I7-10 a. Which taxes are specifically deductible for federal income tax purposes under Sec. 164?
b. If a tax is not specifically listed in Sec. 164, under what circumstances may it still be deductible?

I7-11 If Susan overpays her state income tax due to excess withholdings, can she deduct the entire amount in the year withheld? When Susan receives a refund from the state how must she treat that refund for tax purposes?

I7-12 What is an ad valorem tax? If a tax that is levied on personal property is not an ad valorem tax, under what circumstances may it still be deductible?

I7-13 When real estate is sold during a year, why is it necessary that the real estate taxes on the property be apportioned between the buyer and seller?

I7-14 a. Identify the different categories of interest expense an individual may incur. How is the classification of the interest determined?
b. Are these different categories of interest deductible? If so, how?

I7-15 At times, the term *points* is used to refer to different types of charges. Define the term and describe when points are deductible.

I7-16 In which year or years are points (representing prepaid interest on a loan) deductible?

I7-17 Why does Sec. 267 impose a restriction on the deductibility of expenses accrued and payable by an accrual-method taxpayer to a related cash-method taxpayer?

I7-18 a. What is the amount of the annual limitation placed on the deductibility of investment interest expense?
b. Explain how net investment income is calculated.
c. Is any disallowed interest expense for the year allowable as a deduction in another year? If so, when?

I7-19 Explain what acquisition indebtedness and home equity indebtedness are with respect to a qualified residence of a taxpayer, and identify any limitations on the deductibility of interest expense on this indebtedness.

I7-20 Explain what a qualified residence is for purposes of qualified residence interest.

I7-21 Why is interest expense disallowed if it is incurred to purchase or carry tax-exempt obligations?

I7-22 When is interest generally deductible for cash-method taxpayers? Explain if the general rule applies to prepaid interest, interest paid with loan proceeds, discounted notes, and personal interest. If the general rule does not apply, explain when these interest expenses are deductible.

I7-23 a. For purposes of the charitable contribution deduction, what is capital gain property? Ordinary income property?
b. What is the significance of classifying property as either capital gain property or ordinary income property?

I7-24 How is the *amount* of a charitable contribution of capital gain property determined if it is donated to a private nonoperating foundation? How does this determination differ if capital gain property is donated to a public charity?

I7-25 May an individual who is married and files a joint return deduct any charitable contributions if the itemized deductions total only $3,000 (of which $1,000 are qualified charitable contributions)?

I7-26 For individuals, what is the overall deduction limitation on charitable contributions? What is the limitation for corporations?

I7-27 If a taxpayer's charitable contributions for any tax year exceed the deduction limitations, may the excess contributions be deducted in another year? If so, in which years may they be deducted?

I7-28 How are charitable contribution deductions reported on the tax return for individuals? What reporting requirements must be met for the contribution of property?

I7-29 List some of the more common miscellaneous itemized deductions and identify any limitations that are imposed on the deductibility of these items.

I7-30 Certain itemized deductions of high-income taxpayers must be reduced. Which itemized deductions are subject to this reduction and when does the reduction apply?

ISSUE IDENTIFICATION QUESTIONS

I7-31 Wayne and Maria file a joint tax return on which they itemize their deductions and report AGI of $50,000. During the year they incurred $1,500 of medical expenses when Maria broke her leg. Furthermore, their dentist informed them that their daughter, Alicia, needs $3,000 of orthodontic work to correct her overbite. Wayne also needs a new pair of eyeglasses that will cost $300. What tax issues should Wayne and Maria consider?

I7-32 This year, Chuck took out a loan to purchase some raw land for investment. He paid $40,000 for the land, and he expects that within 5 years the land will be worth at least $75,000. Chuck is married, and his AGI for the year is $325,000. Chuck paid $3,200 in interest on the loan this year. Chuck has $2,600 in interest income and $1,300 in dividend income for the year. He plans to itemize his deductions, so he can use the interest expense to offset his investment income. What tax issues should Chuck consider?

I7-33 During the curent year, George made contributions totaling $40,000 to an organization called the National Endowment for the Preservation of Liberty (NEPL). Later during the year, the NEPL started giving money to a political candidate to help with his campaign expenses. What tax issues should George consider?

I7-34 During the current year, Bob has AGI of $100,000. He donates stock to his church that was purchased two years ago for $55,000. The FMV of the stock is $60,000. Bob has $5,000 of unused excess contributions from a prior year. What tax issues should Bob consider?

PROBLEMS

I7-35 *Medical Expense Deduction.* During 2001, Melanie is involved in an automobile accident and incurs the following expenditures:

Item	Amount
Doctor bills	$20,000
Hospital bills	15,000

Melanie is single and has no dependents. In 2001, her salary is $40,000, and itemized deductions other than medical expenses are $2,500. During the year Melanie also receives a reimbursement of $18,000 from the insurance company for medical expenses incurred in connection with the accident. What is Melanie's taxable income for 2001?

I7-36 *Reimbursement of Previously Deducted Medical Expenses.* Assume the same facts as in Problem I7-35. In addition, assume that in 2002, Melanie receives an additional $10,000 in a settlement of a lawsuit arising because of the automobile accident. $6,000 of the settlement is to pay Melanie for the medical expenses incurred because of the accident that were not covered by insurance. What is the proper tax treatment of this $10,000 settlement?

I7-37 *Medical Expense Deduction.* Dan lives in Duncan a small town in Arizona. Because of a rare blood disease, Dan is required to take special medical treatments once a month. The closest place these treatments are available to Dan is in Phoenix, 200 miles away. The treatments are provided on an outpatient basis but require him to stay overnight in Phoenix. During the year, Dan makes 12 trips to Phoenix by automobile to receive the treatments. The motel he always stays in charges $85 per night. For the year, Dan also spends a total of $250 for meals on these trips. $100 of this $250 is spent while en route to Phoenix. What is the amount of Dan's qualified medical expenses for the year?

I7-38 *Medical Expense Deduction.* Chad is divorced and has custody of Brett, his 14-year-old son. Chad's ex-wife has custody of their daughter, Sara. During the year, Chad incurs $3,000 for orthodontic work for Sara to correct a severe overbite and $2,000 in unreimbursed medical expenses associated with Brett's broken leg. Chad also pays $900 in health insurance premiums. Both Brett and Sara are covered under Chad's medical insurance plan. In addition, Chad incurs $400 for prescription drugs and $1,000 in doctor bills for himself. Chad's AGI is $40,000. What is Chad's medical expense deduction for the year assuming that his other itemized deductions exceed the standard deduction?

I7-39 *Medical Expense Deduction.* In 2001, Russ, a single taxpayer, was severely hurt in a construction accident. The accident left Russ's leg 70% paralyzed. After incurring $10,000 of medical expenses at the hospital, the doctor recommended that Russ install a jacuzzi at his home for therapy. The jacuzzi cost $9,000 to install and increased the value of his home by $5,000. He spent $400 maintaining the jacuzzi in 2001 and $500 in 2002. Russ also purchased a $2,000 wheelchair in 2001 but did not pay for the chair until 2002. In December 2001, Russ paid his physical therapist $4,000 for services to be performed in 2002. Russ paid $1,000 in medical insurance premiums in both 2001 and 2002. In 2002, the insurance company reimbursed Russ $5,000 for his hospital stay in 2001. His AGI for 2001 is $30,000. For 2002 his AGI is $35,000, not considering any of the above items. Russ has no other itemized deductions in either year.
a. What is the amount of his medical expense deduction in 2001?
b. What is the amount of his medical expense deduction in 2002?

I7-40 *Deduction of Taxes.* During 2001, Wendy has $1,400 in state income taxes withheld from her paycheck. Additionally, on April 15, 2001, she pays $300 in state income taxes when she files her state income tax return for 2000. In 2002 when she files her 2001 state income tax return, she will owe an additional $450 for her 2001 taxes. Wendy is a single, cash method taxpayer who has total (excluding state income taxes) itemized deductions for 2001 of $1,500. What is the amount of state income taxes Wendy may include as an itemized deduction for 2001?

I7-41 *Refund of Previously Deducted Taxes.* Assume the same facts as Problem I7-40, except that Wendy receives a $600 refund of 2001's state income taxes in 2002. What is the proper tax treatment of the refund?

I7-42 *Deduction of Taxes.* Dawn, a single, cash method taxpayer, paid the following taxes in 2001: Dawn's employer withheld $5,400 for federal income taxes, $2,000 for state income taxes, and $3,800 for FICA from her 2001 paychecks. Dawn purchased a new car and paid $600 in sales tax and $70 for the license. The car's FMV was $10,000 and it weighed 3,000 pounds. The county also assessed a property tax on the car. The tax was 2% of its value and $10 per hundredweight. The car is used 100% of the time for personal purposes. Dawn sold her house on April 15, 2001. The county's property tax on the home for 2001 is $1,850, payable on February 1, 2002. Dawn's AGI for the year is $50,000 and her other itemized deductions exclusive of taxes are $4,000.
a. What is Dawn's deduction for taxes in 2001?
b. Where on Dawn's tax return should she report her deduction for taxes?

I7-43 *Apportionment of Real Estate Taxes.* On May 1 of the current year, Tara sells a building to Janet for $500,000. Tara's basis in the building is $300,000. The county in which the building is located has a real property tax year that ends on June 30. The taxes are payable by September 1 of that year. On September 1, Janet pays the annual property taxes of $6,000. Both Tara and Janet are calendar-year, cash method taxpayers. The closing agreement does not separately account for the property taxes.
a. What amount of real property taxes may Janet deduct in the current year?
b. What amount of real property taxes may Tara deduct in the current year?
c. If no apportionment on the real property taxes is made in the sales agreement, what is Tara's total selling price of the building? Janet's basis for the building?

I7-44 *Classification of Interest Expense.* On January 1 of the current year, Scott borrowed $80,000, pledging the assets of his business as collateral. He immediately deposited the money in an interest-bearing checking account. Scott already had $20,000 in this account.

On April 1, Scott invests $75,000 in a limited real estate partnership. On July 1, he buys a new ski boat for $12,000. On August 1, he makes a $10,000 capital contribution to his unincorporated business. Scott repays $50,000 of the loan on November 30 of the current year. Classify Scott's interest expense for the year.

I7-45 *Investment Interest.* During the current year, David reports interest and dividend income of $18,000, net short-term capital gains of $6,000, and net long-term capital gains of $7,000. His AGI is $120,000. His investment expenses, exclusive of interest, are $5,000. During the year David also pays a total of $55,000 interest on debt incurred in his investment activities. David is married and files a joint return.
   a. What is the total amount of deduction David may take with respect to his investment interest expense if he does not make a special election?
   b. What is the treatment of any disallowed investment interest expense?
   c. What is the total amount of deduction David may take with respect to his investment interest expense if he elects to have his net capital gain taxed at the regular marginal tax rates?

I7-46 *Qualified Residence Interest.* During the current year, Tina purchases a beachfront condominium for $600,000, paying $150,000 down and taking out a $450,000 mortgage, secured by the property. At the time of the purchase, the outstanding mortgage on her principal residence is $700,000. This debt is secured by the residence and the FMV of the principal residence is $1,400,000. She purchased the principal residence in 1989. What is the amount of qualified indebtedness on which Tina may deduct the interest payments?

I7-47 *Qualified Residence Interest.* Several years ago, Magdelena purchased a new residence for $300,000. Currently, the outstanding mortgage on the residence is $260,000. The current fair market value of the home is $330,000. Magdelena wants to borrow a sizeable sum of money to pay for the college education costs of her two children and believes the interest would be deductible if she takes out a home equity loan. For each of the independent situations below, determine the amount of the loan on which Magdelena may deduct the interest as qualified residence interest.
   a. Magdelena borrows $50,000 as a home equity loan.
   b. Magdelena borrows $80,000 as a home equity loan.
   c. Alternatively, assume the current fair market value of her residence is $375,000 and she borrows $110,000 as a home equity loan
   d. Alternatively, assume the current outstanding balance of the mortgage Magdelena incurred to purchase the home is $1,200,000, the home's fair market value is $1,400,000, and she borrows $80,000 as a home equity loan.

I7-48 *Interest Between Related Parties.* King Corporation is an accrual-method taxpayer owned 60% by Jack and 40% by Kathy. The JR Partnership is owned 75% by Jack and 25% by Ron and uses the cash-method of accounting. On January 2 of the current year, King Corporation borrows $100,000 from the JR Partnership. Interest is charged at 9%, and both interest and principal are to be paid in full on December 31 of the current year. Because of a cash-flow problem arising late in the year, however, the loan and interest are not repaid until March 31 of the following year.
   a. What amount of interest expense may King Corporation deduct in the current year? in the following year?
   b. Assume the same facts except that on December 30 of the current year, King Corporation borrows cash from its bank to pay off the loan. What amount of interest expense may King Corporation deduct in the current year?

I7-49 *Timing of Interest Deduction.* On April 1 of the current year, Henry borrows $12,000 from the bank for a year. Because the note is discounted for the interest charge and Henry receives proceeds of $10,200, he is required to repay the face amount of the loan ($12,000) in four equal quarterly payments beginning on July 1 of the current year. Henry is a cash-method individual.
   a. What is the amount of Henry's interest expense deduction in the current year with respect to this loan?
   b. Assume the same facts except that the initial starting date when the repayments begin is April 1 of the following year. What is the amount of Henry's interest expense deduction in the current year?
   c. Assume the same facts as in Part b, except that Henry is an accrual method taxpayer. What is the amount of his interest expense deduction in the current year?

I7-50 *Itemized Deductions.* During 2001, Doug incurs the following deductible expenses: $2,100 in state income taxes, $2,000 in local property taxes, $800 in medical expenses, and $1,500 in charitable contributions. He is single, has no dependents, and has $35,000 AGI for the year. What is the amount of Doug's taxable income?

I7-51 *Computation of Taxable Income.* During 2001, James, a single, cash method taxpayer incurred the following expenditures:

Qualified medical expenses	$ 8,000
Investment interest expense	16,000
Other investment activity expenses	15,000
Qualified residence interest	12,000
Interest on loan on personal auto	2,000
Charitable contributions	3,000
State income tax paid	7,000
Property taxes	4,000
Tax return preparation and consulting fees	5,000

James's income consisted of the following items:

Salary	$70,000
Interest and Dividend income	20,000
Long-term Capital gains	23,000
Long-term Capital losses	(15,000)

a. Compute James's taxable income for the year (assuming that he makes an election to have the net capital gain taxed at the regular tax rates).
b. What is James' investment interest carryover (if any)?

I7-52 *Computation of Taxable Income.* Assume all the same facts as in Problem I7-51 except that James's salary income is $150,000 instead of $70,000 and that he does not make the election. Compute James's taxable income for the year.

I7-53 *Charitable Contributions: Services.* Donna is an attorney who renders volunteer legal services to a Legal Aid Society, which provides legal advice to low-income individuals. The Legal Aid Society is a qualified charitable organization. During the current year she spends a total of 200 hours in this volunteer work. Her regular billing rate is $150 per hour. In addition, she spends a total of $800 in out-of-pocket costs in providing these services. She receives no compensation and is not reimbursed for her out-of-pocket costs. What is Donna's charitable contribution for the year because of these activities?

I7-54 *Charitable Contribution Limitations.* In each of the following independent cases, determine the amount of the charitable contribution and the limitation that would apply. In each case, assume that the donee is a qualified public charity.
a. Sharon donates a tract of land to a charitable organization. She has held the land for seven years. Her basis in the land is $10,000 and its FMV is $40,000.
b. Assume the same facts in Part a, except that Sharon has held the land for only 11 months and that its FMV is $23,000.
c. Jack purchases a historical document for $50,000. He donates the historical document to a charitable organization two years later. The organization plans to use it for research and study. Its FMV at the time of the donation is $100,000.
d. Assume the same facts in Part c, except that the organization plans to sell the document and put the money into an endowment fund.
e. Valerie donates some inventory to a charitable organization. The inventory is purchased for $500 and its FMV is $1,200 at the time of the donation. She held the inventory for seven months.

I7-55 *Charitable Contributions to Private Nonoperating Foundations.* Assume the same facts as Problem I7-54, except that the qualified organization is a private nonoperating foundation. Determine the amount of the charitable contribution for Parts a through e.

I7-56 *Charitable Contributions—Tax Planning.* Dean makes a pledge of $30,000 to a local college. The college is willing to accept either cash or marketable securities in fulfillment of the pledge. Dean owns stock in Ajax Corporation worth $30,000. The stock was purchased five years ago for $10,000, Dean's marginal tax rate is 39.6%. Should Dean sell the stock and then donate the cash, or should he donate the stock directly? Compute the net tax benefit from each alternative and explain the difference.

I7-57 *Charitable Contribution Limitations.* During the current year, Helen donates stock worth $50,000 to her local community college. Two years ago the stock cost Helen $40,000. Her AGI for the current year is $100,000. Beginning next year, the bulk of her income will be from tax-exempt municipal securities. Thus, she is not interested in any carryover of excess charitable contribution. What is the maximum charitable contribution deduction Helen may take this year?

I7-58 *Charitable Contribution Limitations.* During the current year, Melissa reports AGI of $200,000. As part of some estate planning, she donates $30,000 to her alma mater, Middle State University, and $65,000 to a private nonoperating foundation.
a. What is the amount of Melissa's charitable deduction for the current year?
b. Assume the same facts in a. except that she donates $45,000 to Middle State University.

I7-59 *Corporate Charitable Contributions.* Circle Corporation, an accrual method taxpayer, manufactures and sells mainframe computers. In January of the current year, Circle Corporation donates a mainframe that was part of its inventory to City College. City College will use the computer for physical science research. Circle's basis in the mainframe is $300,000. The computer's FMV is $650,000. On December 15 of the current year, Circle also pledged stock to the Red Cross and promised delivery of the stock by March 1 of the following year. The stock's FMV is $100,000 and Circle's adjusted basis in the stock is $50,000. Circle's taxable income (before deducting any charitable contributions) for the current year is $4,000,000.
a. What is the amount of Circle's charitable contribution for the current year?
b. How much of the contribution can Circle deduct in the current year and how much may be carried over, if any?

I7-60 *Charitable Contribution Carryovers.* Bonnie's charitable contributions and AGI for the past four years were as follows:

	1998	1999	2000	2001
AGI	$50,000	$55,000	$58,000	$60,000
Contributions subject to the 50% limitation	40,000	29,000	25,000	10,000

What is the amount of the charitable deduction for each year and the order in which the deduction and carryovers are used?

TAX FORM/RETURN PREPARATION PROBLEMS

I7-61 Following is a list of information for Peter and Amy Jones for the current tax year. Pete and Amy are married and have three children, Aubrynne, Bryson, and Caden. They live at 1846 Joplin Way, Lakeville, MN 55022. Pete is a lawyer working for a Native American law firm. Amy works part-time in a genetic research lab. The Jones' Social Security numbers and ages are as follows:

Name	S.S. No.	Age
Peter	215-60-1989	32
Amy	301-60-2828	28
Aubrynne	713-84-5555	5
Bryson	714-87-2222	3
Caden	714-89-1684	1

Receipts

Pete's salary	$70,000
Amy's salary	32,000
Interest income on municipal bonds	2,400
Interest income on certificate of deposit (Universial Savings)	3,100
Dividends on GM stock	1,600

Disbursements

Eyeglasses and exam for Aubrynne	600
Orthodontic work for Bryson to correct a congenital defect	2,500

Medical insurance premiums	1,800
Withholding for state income taxes	7,200
Withholding for federal income taxes	16,000
State income taxes paid with last year's tax return (paid when the return was filed in the current year)	500
Property taxes on home	1,100
Property taxes on automobile	300
Interest on home	9,700
Interest on credit cards	200
Cash contribution to church	3,900

In addition to the above, Pete and Amy donate some stock to the local community college. The FMV of the stock at the date of the donation is $700. They purchased the stock 3 years before for $300.

Compute Pete and Amy's income tax liability for the current year using Form 1040, Schedules A and B, and Form 8283, if necessary.

I7-62 Kelly and Chanelle Chambers, ages 47 and 45, are married and live at 584 Thoreau Drive, Boston, MA 59483. Kelly's social security is 254-93-9483 and Chanelle's is 374-48-2938. The Chambers have two children; Emma, age 23, and Chet, age 19. Their social security numbers are 385-64-8496 and 385-68-9462, respectively. Emma is a single college student and earned $8,000 during the summer. Kelly and Chanelle help Emma through school by paying for her room, board, and tuition. Emma lives at home during the summer. Chet has a physical handicap and lives at home. He attends a local university and earned $4,000 working for a marketing firm.

Kelly is a commercial pilot for a small airline. His salary is $95,000, from which $19,000 of federal income tax and $8,000 of state income tax were withheld. Kelly also pays premiums for health, disability, and life insurance. $2,000 of the premium was for health insurance, $250 for disability, and $400 for life insurance.

Chanelle owns Alliance Networks, a sold proprietorship that does network consulting. During the year, Chanelle's gross revenues were $23,000. She incurred the following expenses in her business:

Liability insurance	$ 700
Software rental	5,400
Journals and magazines	150
Training seminars	1,200
Supplies	1,300
Donations to a political campaign fund	800

Kelly enjoys playing guitar and plays in a band. Kelly's band has developed a local following. This year, his gross revenues were $1,200 for playing shows and $700 on CD sales. He incurred the following expenses:

Studio rent expense	$1,300
Sound system repairs	200
CD production	500
New guitar and amplifier	800

Kelly's father passed away during the year. Kelly and Chantelle received $100,000 from the life insurance policy. Neither Kelly nor Chanelle paid any of the premiums.

Chanelle purchased 100 shares of Thurston Co. stock on May 1, 1991 for $1,000. Thurston Co. was declared bankrupt during the current year.

Chet's physician recommended that he see a physical therapist to help with his disability. Kelly paid the therapist $7,000 during the year because his insurance would not cover the bills.

Kelly and Chanelle went to Las Vegas and won $5,000 at the blackjack table. The next night, they lost $6,000.

Derek and Corinne gave $900 to their church and, during the year, they had the following other income and expenses:

Real estate taxes	$1,400
Property taxes on car (determined by value)	500
Home mortgage interest	9,000
Credit card finance charges	2,600

Tax return preparation fees ($600 is allocable to Corinne's business)	1,000
Sales tax on purchases during the year	6,200
Interest from a savings account	800
Interest from City of Boston Bonds	700
Dividend from 3M stock	400

Prepare Kelly and Chanelle's tax return Form 1040 and Schedules A, B, C, and SE for the current year.

CASE STUDY PROBLEMS

I7-63 Brian Brown, an executive at a manufacturing enterprise, comes to you on December 1 of the current year for tax advice. He has agreed to donate a small tract of land to the Rosepark Community College. The value of the land has been appraised at $53,000. Mr. Brown purchased the land 14 months ago for $50,000. Mr. Brown's estimated AGI for the current year is $100,000. He plans to retire next year and anticipates that his AGI will fall to $30,000 for all subsequent years. He does not anticipate making any additional large charitable contributions. He understands that there are special rules dealing with charitable contributions, and wants your advice in order to get the maximum overall tax benefit from his contribution. Because the college plans to use the property, selling the land is not an alternative. You are to prepare a letter to Mr. Brown explaining the tax consequences of the different alternatives. His address is 100 East Rosebrook, Mesa, Arizona 85203. For purposes of your analysis, assume that Mr. Brown is married and files a joint return. Also assume that Mr. Brown feels that an appropriate discount rate is 10%. In your analysis, use the tax rate schedules for the current year.

I7-64 For several years, you have prepared the tax return for Alpha Corporation, a closely held corporation engaged in manufacturing garden tools. On February 20 of the current year, Bill Johnson, the president of Alpha Corporation, delivered to your office the files and information necessary for you to prepare Alpha's tax return for the immediately preceding tax year. Included in this information were the minutes of all meetings held by Alpha's Board of Directors during the year in question.

Then on February 27, Bill stops by your office and hands you an "addendum" to the minutes of the director's meeting held December 15 of the tax year for which you are preparing the tax return. The addendum is dated the same day of the director's meeting, and authorizes a charitable contribution pledge of $20,000 to the local community college. With a wink and a big smile, Bill explains that the addendum had been misplaced. In reviewing the original minutes, you find no mention of a charitable contribution pledge.

What should you do? (See Appendix E and the *Statements on Standards for Tax Services* section in Chapter I15 (or C1 of *Comprehensive* volume) for a discussion of these issues.)

TAX RESEARCH PROBLEM

I7-65 Last year Mr. Smith was involved in an automobile accident, severely injuring his legs. As part of a long-term rehabilitation process, his physician prescribes a daily routine of swimming. Because there is no readily available public facility nearby, Smith investigates the possibility of either building a pool in his own back yard or purchasing another home with a pool. In the current year he finds a new home with a pool and purchases it for $175,000. He then obtains some estimates and finds that it would cost approximately $20,000 to replace the pool in the home he has just purchased. He also obtains some real estate appraisals, which indicate that the existing pool increases the value of the home by only $8,000. During the current year, Smith also expends $500 in maintaining the pool and $1,800 in other medical expenses. What is the total amount of medical expenses he may claim in the current year? Smith's AGI for the year is $60,000.

A partial list of research sources is

- Sec. 213
- Reg. Sec. 1.213-1(e)(1)(iii)
- *Richard A. Polacsek,* 1981 PH T.C. Memo ¶81,569, 42 TCM 1289
- *Paul A. Lerew,* 1982 PH T.C. Memo ¶82,483, 44 TCM 918
- *Jacob H. Robbins,* 1982 PH T.C. Memo ¶82,565, 44 TCM 1254

CHAPTER 8

LOSSES AND BAD DEBTS

LEARNING OBJECTIVES
After studying this chapter, you should be able to

1. Identify transactions that may result in losses
2. Determine the proper classification for losses
3. Calculate the suspended loss from passive activities
4. Identify what constitutes a passive activity loss
5. Determine when a taxpayer has materially participated in a passive activity
6. Identify and calculate the deduction for a casualty or theft loss
7. Compute the deduction for a bad debt
8. Compute a net operating loss deduction

CHAPTER OUTLINE

Transactions That May Result in Losses...8-2
Classifying the Loss on the Taxpayer's Tax Return...8-4
Passive Losses...8-7
Casualty and Theft Losses...8-17
Bad Debts...8-24
Net Operating Losses...8-29

Taxpayers often sustain losses on property that is sold, exchanged, or otherwise disposed of. If the taxpayer uses the property in a trade or business or holds the property for investment, the tax law generally provides a deduction for these losses. The tax law also provides a limited deduction for losses on personal-use property that is either stolen or damaged in a casualty. Other losses on personal-use property (e.g. a sale of a personal residence at a loss) are not deductible. A deduction is also provided for losses that taxpayers may incur because of uncollectible business or nonbusiness debts.

This chapter discusses the rules concerning with the deductibility of these types of losses.

TRANSACTIONS THAT MAY RESULT IN LOSSES

OBJECTIVE 1

Identify transactions that may result in losses

For a loss on property to be deductible, it must be both realized and recognized for tax purposes. Generally, *realization* occurs in a completed (closed) transaction evidenced by an identifiable event. Generally, taxpayers must recognize realized losses on business or investment property unless a specific provision holds otherwise (see page I8-7).

EXAMPLE I8-1 ▶ Anita purchased 500 shares of Data Corporation stock for $10,000 on February 22 of the current year. By October 31 of the same year, the price of the stock declines to $8,000. Even though Anita realizes an economic loss on the stock, no realization event has occurred, and she may not deduct the $2,000 loss. However, if Anita sells the stock for $8,000 on October 31, she realizes the loss for tax purposes in the current year. ◀

ADDITIONAL COMMENT

If property is used partly for business and partly for personal use, the loss attributable to the business portion is deductible but the loss on the personal-use portion is not unless the loss was sustained in a casualty.

KEY POINT

Anticipated losses, including those for which reserves have been established, are not deductible.

Losses on property may arise in a variety of transactions, including

▶ Sale or exchange of the property
▶ Expropriation, seizure, confiscation, or condemnation of the property by a government
▶ Abandonment of the property
▶ Worthlessness of stock or securities
▶ Planned demolition of the property in order to construct other property in its place
▶ Destruction of the property by fire, storm, or other casualty
▶ Theft
▶ Deductible business expenses exceeding business income, giving rise to a net operating loss (NOL)

SALE OR EXCHANGE OF PROPERTY

REAL-WORLD EXAMPLE

A taxpayer whose truck was repossessed was required to treat as an amount realized the unpaid indebtedness on the truck. The taxpayer failed to prove that he was required to pay a portion of the indebtedness after repossession. *Billie J. Ledbetter v. CIR*, 61 AFTR 2d 88-638, 88-1 USTC ¶9183 (5th Cir., 1988).

The amount of the loss a taxpayer incurs in a sale or exchange of property equals the excess of the property's adjusted basis over the amount realized for the property.[1] The amount realized for the property equals the sum of the money received plus the fair market value (FMV) of any other property received in the transaction. If the property sold or exchanged is subject to a mortgage or other liability, the amount realized also includes the amount of the liability transferred to the buyer.[2] The treatment of any selling costs depends on the type of property being sold or exchanged. If the property is inventory (i.e. property normally held for sale in the taxpayer's business), the selling costs are deductible expenses in the year in which they are paid or incurred. However, if the sale involves property that is not normally held for sale by the taxpayer, the selling costs reduce the amount realized from the sale or exchange.

---

[1] Sec. 1001.
[2] *Beulah B. Crane v. CIR*, 35 AFTR 776, 47-1 USTC ¶9217 (USSC, 1947); and Reg. Sec. 1.1001-2.

EXAMPLE I8-2 ▶ Four years ago, Louis purchased a plot of land as an investment for $50,000. Unfortunately, local economic conditions worsened after the land was purchased, and its value declined to $35,000. Becoming discouraged, Louis sells the property in the current year. At the time of the sale, the land is subject to a $10,000 mortgage. The terms of the sale are $25,000 paid in cash with the purchaser assuming the mortgage. Louis also incurs $2,000 in sales commissions. The amount realized is $33,000 ($25,000 cash + $10,000 mortgage assumed by the buyer − $2,000 commissions). The loss on the sale is $17,000 ($50,000 basis − $33,000 amount realized). ◀

Only losses a taxpayer incurs in the sale or exchange of property used in a trade or business or held for investment are deductible. Losses a taxpayer incurs in the sale or exchange of personal-use property are not deductible. Furthermore, the type of deduction a taxpayer may take for a loss realized on the sale or exchange of business or investment property depends on the type of property sold. For example, if the asset is a capital asset, the loss is a capital loss (see Chapter I5). If the sale is of property used in a trade or business (a Sec. 1231 asset), the type of loss depends on the total gain or loss realized on all the taxpayer's Sec. 1231 assets sold during the year (see Chapter I13). If the sale is of inventory, the loss is an ordinary loss.

EXPROPRIATED, SEIZED, OR CONFISCATED PROPERTY

A taxpayer may own property that is expropriated, seized, confiscated, or condemned by a government. In these cases, the taxpayer incurs a deductible loss if the property is used in a trade or business or is held for investment. However, the Tax Court has held that the confiscation, seizure, condemnation, or expropriation of property does not constitute a theft or a casualty. Rather, it is treated as a sale or exchange. Thus, no deductible loss arises if the seized property is personal-use property.[3] If the seized or condemned property is business or investment property, the classification of the loss depends on the type of property. (See the section in this chapter titled Classifying the Loss on the Taxpayer's Return.) A taxpayer may take the deduction only in the year in which the property is actually seized. It is irrelevant whether formal expropriation or nationalization occurs in a later year.[4] A gain is realized if the taxpayer receives compensation for the property in excess of its basis. Under certain circumstances this gain may be deferred. (See Chapter I12 for a discussion of the nonrecognition of gain in an involuntary conversion.)

REAL-WORLD EXAMPLE
Domestic confiscation losses may not be deductible even if the property was used in business. For example, a taxpayer who had been engaged in the business of trafficking in marijuana was arrested. As a result of the arrest, the taxpayer's truck and horse trailer were confiscated. The taxpayer was not entitled to a loss deduction, because losses from illegal activities are disallowed under Sec. 165. *Bill D. Holt,* 69 T.C. 75 (1977). See also Sec. 280E.

ABANDONED PROPERTY

If the taxpayer's property has become worthless or if it is not worth placing into a serviceable condition, the taxpayer may simply abandon the property. If the property still has basis, the taxpayer realizes a loss. The taxpayer may not deduct such losses if the property is personal-use property. However, business or investment property losses are deductible. Furthermore, because the abandonment of property is not a sale or exchange, the loss is an ordinary loss. The amount of the loss is the property's adjusted basis on the date of abandonment. The burden of proof to show that the property was actually abandoned rests with the taxpayer. If the property is depreciable (e.g., machinery and buildings), the taxpayer must actually physically abandon it in order to take the full amount of the loss.[5]

WORTHLESS SECURITIES

KEY POINT
Determining the year of worthlessness is essentially a factual problem, and the burden of proof is on the taxpayer.

A taxpayer may take a deduction for securities that become completely worthless during the tax year.[6] Because the deduction is only available in the year the security actually becomes worthless, a major problem for both the taxpayer and the IRS is determining the year in which the security becomes worthless. A mere decline in value is not sufficient to create a deductible loss if the stock has any recognizable value. Furthermore, the sale of the stock for a nominal amount such as $1 does not necessarily establish that the stock became

---

[3] *William J. Powers,* 36 T.C. 1191 (1961).
[4] Rev. Rul. 62-197, 1962-2 C.B. 66 as modified by Rev. Rul. 69-498, 1969-2 C.B. 31. See also *Estate of Frank Fuchs v. CIR,* 24 AFTR 2d 69-5077, 69-2 USTC ¶9505 (2nd Cir., 1969).
[5] Reg. Sec. 1.167(a)-8(a)(4).

[6] For this purpose, a *security* is defined in Sec. 165(g)(2) as stock in a corporation, the right to subscribe for or receive a share of stock in a corporation, or a bond, debenture, note, or certificate of indebtedness issued by a corporation or a government either in registered form or with interest coupons. Promissory notes issued by a corporation are generally not securities.

worthless in the year of the sale. The burden of proof rests with the taxpayer to show that the security is completely worthless and that the security became worthless during the year.

Once the year of worthlessness is determined, Sec. 165(g) provides that any loss incurred by an investor is treated as a loss from the sale of a capital asset on the last day of the tax year. Although this provision does not help in determining the year of worthlessness, it does establish a definite date for purposes of measuring whether the loss is short- or long-term. In some cases, this provision causes the loss to be long-term because the time period is extended to the end of the year in which the worthlessness occurs.

EXAMPLE I8-3 ▶ On February 20 of the current year, Control Corporation enters into bankruptcy with no possibility for the shareholders to receive anything of value. Because the amount of Control Corporation's outstanding liabilities exceeds the FMV of its assets on that date, the stock of the corporation becomes worthless. Janet, a calendar-year taxpayer, owns 500 shares of Control's common stock, which she had purchased for $10,000 through her broker on June 17 of the prior year. Under Sec. 165(g), the loss is treated as having arisen from the sale of a capital asset on the last day of the current year. Thus, Janet incurs a $10,000 long-term capital loss because the holding period for the stock is more than one year. On the other hand, if Janet had received the stock directly from Control Corporation in exchange for either money or other property, and if certain other requirements are met, the stock may qualify as Sec. 1244 stock. Individuals who sustain losses on Sec. 1244 stock receive ordinary loss treatment rather than capital loss treatment. (See the discussion in this chapter under the heading Losses on Sec. 1244 Stock.) ◀

Under certain circumstances, if the worthless securities are securities of an affiliated corporation that are owned by a domestic corporation, the loss is treated as having arisen from a sale of a noncapital asset. This allows the loss to be treated as an ordinary loss rather than as a capital loss.[7] For this exception to apply, the following percentage ownership requirements must be met:

▶ The domestic corporation that is deducting the loss must own at least 80% of the voting power of all classes of the affiliated corporation's stock (and 80% of all classes of nonvoting stock).

▶ More than 90% of the affiliated corporation's gross receipts for all its taxable years must be from nonpassive income.[8]

DEMOLITION OF PROPERTY

At times taxpayers, intent on building their own facilities, purchase land that contains an existing structure that must first be removed. Taxpayers may also demolish a structure they are currently using in order to construct new facilities. In both cases, taxpayers may not deduct any demolition costs or any loss sustained on account of the demolition. Instead, under Sec. 280B, taxpayers must add these amounts to the basis of the land where the demolished structure was located.

CLASSIFYING THE LOSS ON THE TAXPAYER'S TAX RETURN

OBJECTIVE 2

Determine the proper classification for losses

If a loss is deductible, the taxpayer must determine whether the loss is an ordinary loss or a capital loss. In addition, individual taxpayers must also identify the amount as either a deduction *for* or *from* AGI.

---

[7] As explained in Chapter 15, the deductibility of capital losses is limited. For corporate taxpayers, capital losses must initially be offset against capital gains of the current year, and any excess loss is not deductible but must be carried back 3 years and forward for 5 years. Individuals may offset capital losses against capital gains and any excess loss is deductible up to $3,000 per year as an offset to ordinary income. Capital losses in excess of this amount for an individual are carried forward for an indefinite period. Thus, taxpayers generally prefer ordinary losses rather than capital losses.

[8] Sec. 165(g)(3). *Nonpassive income* includes all income other than royalties, rents, dividends, interest, annuities, and gains from the sale or exchange of stocks and securities.

ORDINARY VERSUS CAPITAL LOSS

KEY POINT

The distinction between ordinary losses and capital losses is important because individuals can only offset $3,000 of capital losses against ordinary income each year. In addition, for individuals a maximum tax rate applies to net capital gains.

Whether a deductible loss is ordinary or capital depends on the type of property involved and the transaction in which the loss is sustained. To have a capital loss, a sale or exchange of a capital asset must occur. If both elements (i.e., a sale or exchange and a capital asset) are not present, the deduction is an ordinary loss. In general, all assets except inventory, notes and accounts receivable, and depreciable property and land used in a trade or business (i.e., property, plant, and machinery) are classified as **capital assets**.[9]

Because a casualty is not a sale or exchange, the destruction of a capital asset by a casualty creates an ordinary rather than a capital loss. Likewise, a deductible loss realized on the abandonment of property is an ordinary loss because an abandonment is not a sale or exchange.

EXAMPLE I8-4

BOOK-TAX DIFFERENCE

For book purposes, it makes no difference if a gain or loss is ordinary or capital. The full amount of the loss is deductible. However, since corporations may not deduct a capital loss in excess of its capital gains for the year, a book-tax timing (temporary) difference may arise.

On July 24 of the current year, Jermaine sells some investment property for $75,000. The property's adjusted basis is $85,000. The investment property is a capital asset. Jermaine realizes a $10,000 ($75,000 − $85,000) capital loss. If, instead, the property had been destroyed by fire and Jermaine had received $75,000 in insurance proceeds, the $10,000 loss would have been an ordinary loss since a casualty is not a sale or exchange.

Certain transactions, though not actually constituting a sale or exchange, are treated as a sale or exchange. For example, if a security owned by an individual investor becomes worthless during the year, the individual treats the loss as a loss from the sale of a capital asset on the last day of the tax year, even though no sale actually occurs. Thus, the loss is a capital loss. Likewise, the seizure or condemnation of property is treated as a sale or exchange.

SECTION 1231 PROPERTY. Whether a loss on a particular transaction is treated as a capital loss may also depend on the gains and losses reported from other property transactions for the tax year. For instance, under Sec. 1231, taxpayers must net certain gains and losses together. If the Sec. 1231 gains exceed the Sec. 1231 losses, both the gains and losses are treated as long-term capital gains and losses. However, if the losses equal or exceed the gains, both the gains and the losses are treated as ordinary. Section 1231 property includes real property or depreciable property used in a trade or business that is held for more than one year. (See Chapter I13 for a discussion of the netting procedure under Sec. 1231.)

HISTORICAL NOTE

Section 1244 was enacted in 1958 in order to encourage investment in small business enterprises. This was the same year that the original S corporation provisions were enacted.

LOSSES ON SEC. 1244 STOCK. Taxpayers generally recognize capital gain or loss on the sale of stock or securities. The tax law provides an exception for losses from the sale or worthlessness of small business corporation (Sec. 1244) stock. Taxpayers may deduct these losses as ordinary losses up to a maximum of $50,000 per tax year ($100,000 for married taxpayers filing a joint return). Any remaining loss for the year is capital loss.

To qualify the loss as ordinary under Sec. 1244, the following requirements must be met:

- The stock must be owned by an individual or a partnership.
- The stock must have been originally issued by the corporation to the individual or to a partnership in which an individual is a partner.[10]
- The stock must be stock in a domestic (U.S.) corporation.
- The stock must have been issued for cash or property other than stock or securities. Stock issued for services rendered is not eligible for Sec. 1244 treatment.

---

[9] Sec. 1221. The definition of a capital asset is more fully examined in Chapter I5.

[10] Stock received in certain reorganizations of corporations in exchange for Sec. 1244 stock is also considered Sec. 1244 stock. Section 1244 does not apply to stock that the individual has received through other means such as purchase in a secondary market, exchange, gift, or inheritance.

- The corporation must not have derived over 50% of its gross receipts from passive income sources during the five tax years immediately preceding the year of sale or worthlessness.[11]
- The amount of money and property contributed to both capital and paid-in surplus may not exceed $1 million at the time the stock is issued.

Note that the last test listed above is made *at the time the stock is issued*. Thus, even though at the time the loss is realized the corporation has capital and paid-in surplus in excess of the $1 million limit, the individual may still report an ordinary loss as long as the test is met when the stock is issued.

STOP & THINK

Question: Tony, a single taxpayer, incorporated Waffle, Inc. three years ago by contributing $70,000 in exchange for the stock. Waffle, Inc. owns and operates a small restaurant. Unfortunately, Waffle, Inc.'s business never really became profitable. Tony has been trying to sell the Waffle, Inc. stock since July of last year, but because the corporation had become insolvent, he couldn't find any buyers. In February of the current year Waffle, Inc. was judged to be bankrupt. Tony didn't receive anything for his stock. What issues should Tony's tax advisor address with regard to the Waffle, Inc. stock?

Solution: Tony's tax advisor must determine (1) the amount of any realized loss, (2) the year in which the loss is recognized, and (3) the character of the realized loss. The Waffle, Inc. stock is considered a security under Sec. 165. Whenever a security becomes completely worthless and it is determined that the owner will receive nothing for it, the owner realizes a loss to the extent of the security's basis ($70,000). The loss is deemed to be realized in the year in which the security becomes worthless. While the stock was judged to be worthless by the bankruptcy court in February of the current year, the fact that Tony could not find any buyers last year because the corporation was insolvent may indicate that the stock really became worthless last year. This determination is important because its loss must be taken in the year in which the stock becomes worthless. Furthermore, the stock is deemed to become worthless on the last day of that year. Since Tony received the stock directly from the corporation in exchange for contributed cash, Waffles, Inc.'s gross receipts are from business operations, and the capitalization is less than $1,000,000, the stock qualifies as Sec. 1244 stock. Thus, $50,000 of the loss is characterized as ordinary loss. The remaining $20,000 is a long-term capital loss.

DISALLOWANCE POSSIBILITIES

Losses taxpayers incur in certain transactions and activities may be disallowed or deferred. These include

- Transfers of property to a controlled corporation in exchange for stock of the corporation (see the discussion in Chapter C2 of *Prentice Hall's Federal Taxation: Corporations, Partnerships, Estates, and Trusts* text and Chapter C2 of the *Comprehensive* volume)
- Exchanges of property for other property that is considered to be like-kind to the property given up (see the discussion in Chapter I12)
- Property sold to certain related parties (see the discussion in Chapter I6)
- Wash sale transactions (see the discussion in Chapter I6)
- Losses limited because the losses exceed the amount for which the taxpayer is at risk (see the discussion in Chapter C9 of *Prentice Hall's Federal Taxation: Corporations, Partnerships, Estates, and Trusts* text and Chapter C9 of the *Comprehensive* volume)

In addition, individuals and certain corporations may be limited on the amount of deductible losses because of the passive loss rules

Topic Review I8-1 contains a summary of loss transactions.

---

[11] For this purpose, passive income sources include royalties, rents, dividends, interest, annuities, and sales or exchanges of stocks and securities. If the corporation has not been in existence for a full five years, the gross receipts test is applied to the shorter period. If the corporation has not been in existence for an entire taxable year, the test is applied to the time period up to the date of the loss (see Sec. 1244(c)(2)).

Topic Review I8-1

Transactions That May Result In Losses

TYPE OF TRANSACTION	RESULT
Sale or exchange	Taxpayers may not deduct a loss on personal-use property. The tax treatment of a loss on business or investment property depends on the type of property. Losses on capital assets result in capital losses. Losses on Sec. 1231 assets are subject to the Sec. 1231 netting rules discussed in Chapter I13.
Seizure, expropriation, confiscation, or condemnation	Treated as a sale or exchange.
Abandonment	Not treated as a sale or exchange. No deduction is allowed for a loss on personal-use property. Business or investment property is given ordinary loss treatment.
Worthless securities	Treated as a loss from the sale of the securities on the last day of the year in which the securities become worthless. This generally will result in a capital loss. However, if the requirements of Sec. 1244 are met, at least part of the loss may be treated as an ordinary loss. (See Sec. 1244 stock below.) A loss on worthless securities of an affiliated corporation results in an ordinary loss.
Demolition	No deductible loss is allowed. Instead, losses and costs of demolition are added to the basis of the land where the demolished structure was located.
Sec. 1244 stock	An ordinary loss is allowed for individuals up to $50,000 per year ($100,000 for married filing jointly). The remaining loss is capital. The stock must have been originally issued to the individual for property or cash, and the corporation must meet the requirements to be a small business corporation.

PASSIVE LOSSES

HISTORICAL NOTE
Before the passive activity loss limits became effective in 1987, most tax shelters were concentrated in the areas of real estate, oil and gas, equipment leasing, farming, motion pictures, timber, and research and development. Many tax shelters took advantage of liberal depreciation rules during the early 1980's such as the rapid depreciation of real estate over a 15-year period.

Before 1987, taxpayers had been able to reduce their income tax liability on income from one business or investment activity with deductions, losses, and credits arising in another activity. Thus, taxpayers often invested in activities, called **tax shelters**, that would spin off tax deductions and credits. Many of these tax shelters were simply *passive investments* because they did not require the taxpayer's involvement or participation. In some situations, however, tax shelters had real economic substance i.e., a taxpayer's investment in this type of shelter was not based solely on the tax benefits that the activity generated. In many cases, however, tax shelters had no real economic substance other than the creation of deductions and credits that enabled taxpayers to reduce and sometimes eliminate the income tax liability from their other business activities. In an effort to prevent these perceived and real abuses, Congress enacted Sec. 469, which restricts the current use of losses and credits that arise in rental activities as well as activities in which the taxpayer does not materially participate. These activities are described as passive activities. (See the Definition of a Passive Activity section in this chapter for an extended discussion of what constitutes a passive activity.)

COMPUTATION OF PASSIVE LOSSES AND CREDITS

OBJECTIVE 3
Calculate the suspended loss from passive activities

In enacting the passive loss rules, Congress did not want to prevent taxpayers from currently deducting or using losses and credits generated in active business endeavors of the taxpayer. At the same time, Congress realized that certain investments (such as investments that generate interest or dividend income) normally give rise to taxable income, which could itself be sheltered by losses and credits that arise in other passive activities. Thus, Sec. 469 requires taxpayers to classify their income into three categories: *active income* (such as wages, salaries, and active business income), *portfolio (or investment) income*, and *passive income*. **Portfolio income** includes dividends, interest, annuities, and royalties (and allocable expenses and interest expense) that are not derived in the ordinary course of a trade or business. Gains and losses on property that produces these types of income also are included in portfolio income if the disposition of the property does not occur in the ordinary course of business.[12] Portfolio income becomes part of net investment income, which is used in computing the deduction limit for investment interest expense. (See Chapter I7 for a discussion of the investment interest expense limitation.)

PASSIVE INCOME AND LOSSES. Taxpayers compute income and loss in the passive category separately for each passive activity in which they have invested. In general, for any tax year, losses generated in one passive activity may be used to offset income from other passive activities, but may not offset either active or portfolio income.

EXAMPLE I8-5 ▶ During the year, Kasi, a CPA, reports $100,000 of active business income from his CPA practice. He also owns two passive activities. From activity A, which he earned $10,000 of income, and from activity B, he incurred a $15,000 loss. Kasi may use $10,000 of the loss from activity B to offset the $10,000 of income from activity A. However, Kasi may not deduct the $5,000 excess loss from Activity B in the current year, even though he has $100,000 of active business income. ◀

CARRYOVERS

KEY POINT
Excess passive activity losses are not "lost" because they can be carried over to future years.

Passive activity losses that are disallowed as deductions for the year in which they are incurred are carried over indefinitely and treated as losses allocable to that activity in the following tax years. These losses, known as **suspended losses,** may offset passive activity income of the subsequent year, but generally may not offset other types of income. If a taxpayer has invested in several passive activities, and for the year some of the activities generate income while others generate losses, the loss carried over for each loss activity is a pro rata portion of the total passive loss for the year.

EXAMPLE I8-6 ▶ Tammy reports the following income and loss for the year:

Salary	$200,000
Loss from activity X	(40,000)
Loss from activity Y	(10,000)
Income from activity Z	30,000

X, Y, and Z are all passive activities. The losses generated in activities X and Y offset the income from activity Z, but none of the salary income is offset. Thus, Tammy has a net passive loss for the year of $20,000 ($40,000 + $10,000 − $30,000), which must be carried over to subsequent years. The amount of the carryover attributable to each activity is as follows:

Activity X: $\quad \$20,000 \times \dfrac{\$40,000}{\$50,000} = \$16,000$

Activity Y: $\quad \$20,000 \times \dfrac{\$10,000}{\$50,000} = \$ 4,000$ ◀

TAXABLE DISPOSITION OF INTEREST IN A PASSIVE ACTIVITY. When a taxpayer disposes of a passive activity in a taxable transaction, the economic gain or loss generated by the activity can be computed, and the suspended losses of that activity may be deducted against the taxpayer's other income. However, the amount of the total net economic loss from the asset that is disposed of must first offset any passive income from other passive activities.[13]

EXAMPLE I8-7 ▶ During the current year, Pam realizes $6,000 of taxable income from activity A, $1,000 of loss from activity B, and $8,000 of taxable income from activity C. All three activities are passive activities with regard to Pam. In addition, $30,000 of passive losses from activity C are carried over from prior years. During the current year, Pam sells activity C for a $15,000 taxable gain. Pam reports salary income of $90,000 for the year. Because activity C is disposed of in a fully taxable transaction, Pam may deduct $2,000 of loss against the salary income:

---

[12] Sec. 469(e)(1). Gain or loss on property dispositions occuring in the ordinary course of business is either passive or active business income, depending on the taxpayer's level of involvement (i.e., material participation) in the activity.

[13] Sec. 469(g). Income from the activity for prior years may also be taken into account in arriving at the net income from all passive activities for the year if it is necessary to prevent avoidance of the passive loss rules.

Income for the year from C	$ 8,000	
Gain from the sale of C	15,000	
Suspended losses from C	(30,000)	
Total loss from C		($7,000)
Income for the year from A	$ 6,000	
Loss for the year from B	(1,000)	5,000
Pam's deduction against salary income		($2,000) ◄

BOOK-TAX DIFFERENCE

Since passive losses are not limited under financial accounting rules, the limitation and carryover of passive losses for tax purposes will create a timing (temporary) difference between book and tax. However, most taxpayers subject to the passive loss rules do not use financial accounting rules.

If the taxpayer sells the passive activity to a related party, the suspended loss is not deductible until the related party sells the activity to a nonrelated person. The definition of *related persons* includes spouse, brothers and sisters, ancestors, lineal descendants, and corporations or partnerships in which the individual has a greater than 50% ownership.[14]

Although the death of a taxpayer is not a taxable disposition of the asset, some of the suspended losses may be deducted when a taxpayer dies. The amount of the deduction allowed is the amount by which the suspended losses exceed the increase in basis of the property. These losses generally are deducted on the decedent's final income tax return. Any suspended losses up to the amount of the increase in basis are lost.[15]

EXAMPLE 18-8 ▶ At the time that John died during the current year, he owned passive activity property with an adjusted basis of $20,000 and a FMV of $35,000. There were $25,000 in suspended losses attributable to the property. Because the increase in the basis of the property is $15,000 ($35,000 − $20,000), $15,000 of the suspended losses are lost. However, $10,000 ($25,000 suspended losses − $15,000 increase in basis) of the suspended losses are deductible on John's final income tax return. ◄

In general, the suspended losses of a passive activity become deductible only when the taxpayer completely disposes of his or her interest in the activity. However, in Treasury Reg. 1.469-4(g) the government has stated that taxpayers may treat the disposition of a substantial part of an activity as the disposition of a separate activity. This treatment is only available, however, if the taxpayer can establish with reasonable certainty the amount of income, deductions, credits, and suspended losses and credits that are allocable to that part of the activity.

CARRYOVERS FROM A FORMER PASSIVE ACTIVITY. The determination of whether an activity is passive with respect to a taxpayer is made annually. Thus, an activity that previously was considered passive may not be passive with respect to the taxpayer for the current year. This is called a **former passive activity**. Any loss carryover from a former passive activity is deductible against the current year's income of that activity even though the activity is not a passive activity in the current year. However, any suspended loss in excess of the activity's income for the year is still subject to the carryover limitations. Since the activity is no longer passive for the year, the current year's loss is deductible against active business income.

EXAMPLE 18-9 ▶ Kris owns activity A, which, for the immediately preceding tax year, was considered a passive activity with regard to Kris. $10,000 in losses from activity A were disallowed and carried over to the current year. Because of Kris' increased involvement in activity A in the current year, it is not considered passive with regard to Kris for that year. During the current year, activity A generates a $5,000 loss. During the current year, Kris also has an investment in activity B, a passive activity. Her share of activity B's income is $7,000. Kris reports $60,000 in salary. Because for the current year activity A is not a passive activity, the $5,000 current year loss is fully deductible against her salary. However, the $10,000 loss carryover from the prior year is deductible only against the $7,000 of income from passive activity B. The $3,000 ($10,000 − $7,000) excess is carried over to the subsequent year. ◄

---

[14] Other relationships described in Secs. 267(b) and 707(b) are also considered related parties for this purpose.

[15] Sec. 469(g)(2). Generally, the basis of inherited property is its FMV on the date of death (see Chapter 15).

Credits. Credits generated in a passive activity are also limited and may be used only against the portion of the tax liability that is attributable to passive income. This amount is determined by comparing the tax liability on all income for the year with the tax liability on all income excluding the passive income.

EXAMPLE I8-10 ▶ Dale invests in a passive activity. For the year, he must report $10,000 of taxable income from the passive activity. Dale's share of tax credits generated by the passive activity is $5,000. Assume Dale's precredit tax liability on all income (including the $10,000 from the passive activity) is $25,000, and his precredit tax liability on all income excluding the passive activity income is $22,000. He may use only $3,000 ($25,000 − $22,000) of the tax credits generated by the passive activity. The remaining $2,000 of tax credits is carried forward and may be used in a subsequent year against the portion of the tax liability attributable to passive activity income in that year. However, these credits may never offset any portion of the tax liability attributable to nonpassive activities. (See Chapter I14 for a discussion of credits and their carryovers.) ◀

DEFINITION OF A PASSIVE ACTIVITY

OBJECTIVE 4

Identify what constitutes a passive activity loss

The term *passive activity* includes any rental activity or any trade or business in which the taxpayer does not materially participate.[16] The definition of a passive activity is based on two critical elements: an identification of exactly what constitutes an activity and a determination of whether the taxpayer has materially participated in that activity.

IDENTIFICATION OF AN ACTIVITY. Identifying whether an activity is either passive or active becomes critical for several reasons. Whether a taxpayer materially participates in an activity is determined separately for each activity. Suspended losses of a passive activity are deductible when the taxpayer's ownership of the activity is completely terminated. As explained in a subsequent section of this chapter, taxpayers may deduct currently up to $25,000 of passive losses from rental real estate activities. Thus, taxpayers must not combine losses from passive business and rental real estate activities into one activity.

The way taxpayers combine or separate operations into activities can significantly impact the deductibility of losses that are generated. Taxpayers may treat one or more activities as a single activity only if they constitute an "appropriate economic unit."[17] Although this determination is made by examining all the relevant facts and circumstances, the following factors are given the greatest weight:

ADDITIONAL COMMENT

Tax year 1991 gave a clearer review of the impact of the passive loss provisions that were enacted in 1986. Net losses of limited partnerships, the types that are used as tax shelters, declined to $16.7 billion in 1991 from $35.5 billion in 1986.

▶ Similarities and differences in the types of business
▶ The extent of common control
▶ The extent of common ownership
▶ The geographical location, and
▶ Any interdependencies between the operations (i.e. the extent to which they purchase or sell goods between the activities, have the same customers, are accounted for with a single set of books, etc.).

Not all of these factors are necessary for a taxpayer to treat more than one operation as a single activity. Furthermore, a taxpayer may use any reasonable method of applying the relevant facts and circumstances in grouping the activities.

EXAMPLE I8-11 ▶ Carla owns a bakery and a movie theater in each of two different shopping malls, one located in Baltimore and the other in Philadelphia. Depending on other relevant facts and circumstances, a reasonable grouping of the operations may result in any of the following:

---

[16] Secs. 469(c)(1) and (c)(2). Sec. 469(c)(6) also includes investment (production of income) activities under Sec. 212 as a passive activity. Section 469(j)(8) defines the term *rental activity* as any activity where payments are principally for the use of tangible property. Pursuant to the Regulations, there are six exceptions to this general rule. These exceptions include providing the use of tangible property where the average period of customer use is seven days or less, the average period of customer use is 30 days or less and significant personal services are provided by the owner in conjunction with the use of the property, extraordinary personal services are provided by the owner in conjunction with the use of the property, the rental of the property is incidental to a nonrental activity of the taxpayer, the property is customarily made available during defined business hours for nonexclusive use by various customers, or the property is provided for use in a nonrental activity conducted by a partnership, S corporation, or joint venture in which the taxpayer owns an interest. The details of these exceptions are beyond the scope of this text. See Reg. Sec. 1.469-1(e)(3)(iii).

[17] Reg. Sec. 1.469-4.

- One activity involving all four operations
- Two activities: a bakery activity and a theater activity
- Two activities: a Baltimore activity and a Philadelphia activity
- Four activities

Under the Treasury Regulations, taxpayers apparently have some degree of flexibility in determining how different business operations are grouped into activities. However, once the activities are established, taxpayers must be consistent in grouping their activities in subsequent years unless material changes in the facts and circumstances clearly make the groupings inappropriate.

In identifying separate activities, taxpayers generally may not group rental operations with trade or business operations. However, a combination is allowed if either the rental operation is insubstantial in relation to the business operation or vice versa. Unfortunately, the Treasury Regulations do not give any guidance with regard to what is insubstantial. Furthermore, because of the special rules dealing with real estate rental activities (explained later in this chapter), rental activities involving real estate may not be combined with rental activities involving personal property.

EXAMPLE I8-12

Sandy owns a building in which she (1) operates a restaurant and (2) leases out apartments to tenants. Generally the tenants sign apartment leases of one year or longer. Of the total gross income derived from the building, 15% comes from the apartment rentals and 85% comes from the restaurant operation. If the apartment rental operation is considered insubstantial in relation to the restaurant operation, the two may be combined into one activity. If it is not insubstantial, the two operations are considered two separate activities: a business activity and a rental real estate activity.

Partnerships and S corporations (pass-through entities) must identify their business and rental activities by applying these rules at the partnership or S corporation level and then should report the results of their operations by activity to the partners or shareholders. Each partner or shareholder must then take these activities and, using these same rules, combine them where appropriate with operations conducted either directly or through other pass-through entities. In fact, many real estate passive activities are held as either partnerships or S corporations.

OBJECTIVE 5

Determine when a taxpayer has materially participated in a passive activity

MATERIAL PARTICIPATION. Once each activity has been identified, taxpayers must determine whether the activity is passive or active. If the taxpayer does not **materially participate** in the activity, it is deemed to be a passive activity with respect to that taxpayer. Pursuant to the Treasury Regulations,[18] taxpayers materially participate in an activity if they meet at least one of the following tests:

- The individual participates in the activity for more than 500 hours during the year.
- The individual's participation in the activity for the year constitutes substantially all of the participation in the activity by all individuals, including individuals who do not own any interest in the activity.
- The individual participates in the activity for more than 100 hours during the year, and that participation is more than any other individual's participation for the year (including participation by individuals who do not own any interest in the activity).
- The individual participates in "significant participation activities" for an aggregate of more than 500 hours during the year.[19] Thus, an individual who spends over 100 hours each in several separate significant participation activities may aggregate the time spent in these activities in order to meet the 500-hour test.
- The individual materially participated in the activity in any five years during the immediately preceding ten taxable years. These five years need not be consecutive.

---

[18] Temp. Reg. Sec. 1.469-5T(a).
[19] A significant participation activity is a trade or business in which the individual participates for more than 100 hours during the year but for which the individual does not meet the material participation test alone (i.e., with respect to that activity, the individual does not meet one of the other material participation tests.). See Temp. Reg. Sec. 1.469-5T(c).

ADDITIONAL COMMENT

A taxpayer may be a material participant in an activity one year and a passive investor the next year. A taxpayer must satisfy one of the material participation tests each year to be treated as a material participant.

▶ The individual materially participated in the activity for any three years preceding the year in question, and the activity is a personal service activity.[20]

▶ The individual participates in the activity on a regular, continuous, and substantial basis during the year, taking into account all the relevant facts and circumstances.

Note that the first four tests are based on the number of hours the taxpayer spent in the activity during the current year. The fifth and sixth tests are based on the material participation of the taxpayer in prior years and are designed to prevent taxpayers from asserting that retirement income is passive and offsetting it with passive losses from tax shelters. To determine whether a taxpayer materially participates in an activity, the participation of the taxpayer's spouse is taken into account.

LIMITED PARTNERSHIPS. A limited partner has a limited liability for his or her investment in the partnership without assuming any active involvement; thus, the material participation test is not met and the limited partner's investment is generally considered passive. However, a limited partner can meet the material participation test if the individual meets either the 500 hour test or the fifth and sixth tests above (prior year tests). It is rare for a limited partner to meet the material participation test because limited partners are generally not involved in the operation of the business. Thus, most income and deductions from limited partnerships are considered passive.

ADDITIONAL COMMENT

Congress excluded a working interest in an oil or gas property from the material participation requirement in those cases where the taxpayer's liability is not limited because Congress concluded that financial risk was a more relevant standard. At the time (1986) the oil and gas industry was suffering severe hardship due to the worldwide decline in oil prices.

WORKING INTEREST IN AN OIL AND GAS PROPERTY. A working interest is an interest that is responsible for the cost of development or operation of the oil and gas property. This type of interest in an oil and gas property is not a passive activity as long as the taxpayer's liability in the interest is not limited. Thus, even though a taxpayer may not materially participate in the activity, the passive loss rules do not apply. This is so even if the taxpayer holds the interest through an entity such as a partnership.

TAXPAYERS SUBJECT TO PASSIVE LOSS RULES

The passive loss limitation rules apply to

▶ Individuals, estates, trusts

▶ Any closely held C corporation

▶ Any personal service corporation

▶ Certain publicly traded partnerships

Because the income and losses of partnerships and S corporations are taxed directly to the partners and shareholders, the passive loss rules do not apply to these entities.[21] Rather, the passive loss limitations apply directly at the partner or shareholder level. Thus, the situation may arise where one partner or shareholder is subject to the passive loss rules with regard to an activity conducted by the partnership or S corporation while the partners or shareholders are not.

Generally, regular corporations (i.e., C corporations) are not subject to the passive loss limitation rules. However, in order to prevent certain individuals from avoiding the passive loss rules through the use of a regular corporation, the rules also apply to closely held C corporations and personal service corporations.

ADDITIONAL COMMENT

Because a closely held C corporation's passive losses may offset its income from active business operations, some tax professionals advise their clients to transfer their investments that generate passive losses to their profitable corporations.

CLOSELY HELD C CORPORATIONS. The passive loss rules apply to closely held C corporations but only on a limited basis. A **closely held C corporation** is a C corporation where more than 50% of the stock is owned by five or fewer individuals at any time during the last half of the corporation's taxable year.[22] Without this special rule involving

---

[20] A personal service activity involves rendering personal services in the fields of health, law, engineering, architecture, accounting, actuarial science, performing arts, or consulting. It also includes any other trade or business in which capital is not a material income-producing factor. See Temp. Reg. Sec. 1.469-5T(d).

[21] An S corporation is a corporation that has elected for federal income tax purposes to be treated basically like a partnership. Thus, the income or losses and separately stated items of an S corporation flow through to the shareholders and are reported on their individual tax returns.

[22] Secs. 469(j)(1), 465(a)(1)(B), and 542(a)(2).

closely held C corporations, taxpayers would be motivated to transfer their investments (both portfolio investments and passive activities) to a C corporation where the portfolio income could be offset by the corporation's passive losses. Thus, as applied to a closely held C corporation, the passive loss rules prevent passive activity losses from offsetting portfolio income. However, a closely held C corporation's passive losses may offset its income from active business operations.

▶ **EXAMPLE I8-13** ▶ All of the outstanding stock of Delta Corporation is owned equally by individuals Allen and Beth. During the current year, Delta generates $15,000 taxable income from its active business operations. It also earns $10,000 of interest and dividends from investments and reports a $30,000 loss from a passive activity. Because Delta is a closely held C corporation, the $15,000 of taxable income from the active business is offset by $15,000 of the passive loss. However, the $10,000 of portfolio income may not be offset. Thus, for the current year, Delta reports $10,000 of taxable income from its portfolio income and has a $15,000 passive loss carryover. ◀

PERSONAL SERVICE CORPORATION. A **personal service corporation (PSC)** is a regular C corporation whose principal activity is the performance of personal services that are substantially performed by owner-employees.[23] However, a corporation is not a PSC unless owner-employees own more than 10% of the value of the stock. In contrast with a non-PSC closely held C corporation, the passive loss limitation rules apply in their entirety. If a corporation is both a PSC and a closely held C corporation, the more restrictive rules for PSCs apply. Thus, passive losses of a PSC may not offset the PSC's active business income or portfolio income.

MATERIAL PARTICIPATION BY PSCs AND CLOSELY HELD C CORPORATIONS. Special rules apply for determining whether closely held C corporations or PSCs materially participate in an activity. These corporations materially participate in an activity only if one or more shareholders who own more than 50% in value of the outstanding stock materially participate in the activity. In addition, a closely held C corporation (other than a PSC) materially participates in an activity if it meets *all* of the following tests with regard to an activity:

1. A substantial portion of the services of at least one full-time employee is in the active management of the activity.
2. A substantial portion of the services of at least three full-time nonowner employees is directly related to the activity.
3. The Sec. 162 business deductions of the activity exceed 15% of the activity's gross income for the period.[24]

PUBLICLY TRADED PARTNERSHIPS

In many cases, a **publicly traded partnership (PTP)** is treated for tax purposes as a corporation. For purposes of the passive loss rules, a PTP is defined as any partnership if interests in the partnership are either traded on an established securities market or readily tradable on a secondary market.[25] If a PTP is treated for tax purposes as a corporation, the passive loss rules generally do not apply. However, if a PTP meets certain gross income requirements it may still be treated as a partnership, causing its items of income, loss, and credit to flow through to the partners.[26] If this is the case, the passive loss rules apply at the partner level separately to the flow through items from each PTP. Thus, partners treat losses from a PTP as separate from any other type of income (passive, active business, or

---

[23] Secs. 469(j)(2) and 269A(b)(1). For this purpose any employee who owns any stock of the corporation is an owner-employee. This stock ownership is determined by using the Sec. 318 constructive ownership rules as modified by Sec. 469(j)(2).

[24] Secs. 469(h)(4) and 465(c)(7). Tests 1 and 2 must be met for the 12-month period ending on the last day of the tax year. Test 3 must be met for the tax year. Furthermore, the Sec. 404 deductions are also included in the 15% of gross income test.

[25] Sec. 469(k)(2). See Chapter C10 of *Prentice Hall's Federal Taxation:*
Corporations, Partnerships, Estates, and Trusts and Chapter C10 of the *Comprehensive* volume for a definition and discussion of publicly traded partnerships.

[26] Sec. 7704(c). For the taxable year and all preceding years beginning after Dec. 31, 1987, at least 90% of the PTP's gross income consists of dividends, interest, real property rents, income from certain gas, oil, mineral or timber activities, and gains from the sale of real estate or certain capital assets. Furthermore, certain other PTPs may also elect to continue to be treated as a partnership rather than as a corporation.

portfolio), as well as separate from any income from other PTPs. Partners can only carry these losses forward and offset them against income generated by that particular PTP in a subsequent year. Furthermore, the loss may not offset any portfolio income that the PTP might generate. Any net income from PTPs is treated as portfolio income.

EXAMPLE I8-14 ▶ Mark owns interests in partnerships A and B, both of which are PTPs that are treated as partnerships. During the current year, Mark's share of the income from A is $2,000. Mark's share of B's loss is $1,200. B also generated some portfolio income. Mark's share of B's portfolio income is $800. The $1,200 loss from B may not offset any of B's $800 portfolio income. Furthermore, it may not offset any of the $2,000 income from A. The $2,000 income from A is treated as portfolio income. Thus, Mark reports $2,800 portfolio income and has a $1,200 suspended loss from B. In a subsequent year, Mark's share of any income from B can be offset by the $1,200 of suspended loss that is carried forward. ◀

Partners may deduct suspended losses from a PTP only in the year the partner disposes of his or her interest in the PTP. Partners do not recognize a loss in the year that the PTP itself sells a passive activity.

RENTAL REAL ESTATE TRADE OR BUSINESS

KEY POINT
Up to $25,000 of passive losses attributable to rental real estate can be deducted each year against income from nonpassive sources such as salary, interest, and dividends.

In general, rental activities are considered passive activities. However, the passive activity loss rules do not apply to certain taxpayers that are involved in real property trades or businesses. Instead, these activities are treated as active businesses. A real property trade or business involves the development, redevelopment, construction, reconstruction, acquisition, conversion, rental, operation, management, leasing, or brokering of real property.

This exception applies to taxpayers if both the following requirements are met:

▶ More than one-half of the personal services the taxpayer performs in all trades or businesses during the year must be performed in real property trades or businesses in which the taxpayer materially participates.

▶ The taxpayer must perform more than 750 hours of work during the taxable year in real property trades or businesses in which the taxpayer materially participates.

In meeting these tests, personal services a taxpayer renders in his or her capacity as an employee are not treated as performed in real property trades or businesses unless the employee owns at least 5% of the employer. Furthermore, for married taxpayers filing a joint return, the exception applies only if one of the spouses separately meets both requirements. The time spent in the activity by both spouses is used in determining whether or not the material participation test is met.

EXAMPLE I8-15 ▶ Anwar and Anya are married and file a joint return. Anwar's only job is renting and maintaining four large apartment complexes that he owns. Anwar and Anya manage the buildings themselves. During the current year, Anya spent 500 hours keeping records and corresponding with tenants. Anwar spent 700 hours during the year maintaining and repairing the apartments. Even though all of Anya and Anwar's personal services are connected with a real property trade or business in which they materially participate, this rental activity is considered passive because neither Anwar nor Anya alone spends more than 750 hours doing services related to the rental activity. ◀

In order for a closely held C corporation to meet this rental real estate business exception, the corporation must derive more than one-half of its gross receipts from real property businesses in which it materially participates.

Any deduction allowed under the previously discussed exception for taxpayers who are involved in real property trades or businesses is not taken into consideration in determining the taxpayer's AGI for purposes of the phase-out of the $25,000 deduction available for taxpayers who actively participate in a rental real estate activity. (See the following section in this chapter for a discussion of the $25,000 active participation exception.)

OTHER RENTAL REAL ESTATE ACTIVITIES

Many rental real estate activities are not considered rental real estate businesses, and are therefore subject to the passive loss rules. However, if an individual taxpayer meets certain requirements, the taxpayer still may deduct up to $25,000 of annual losses from these passive rental real estate activities against other income. In order to meet this exception, an individual must do both of the following:

▶ *Actively* participate in the activity[27]
▶ Own at least 10% of the value of the activity for the entire tax year

KEY POINT
Active participation is different from material participation, and is a lesser standard of involvement.

ACTIVE PARTICIPATION. A taxpayer can achieve *active participation*, as opposed to material participation, without regular, continuous, and material involvement in the activity and without meeting any of the material participation tests. However, the taxpayer still must participate in the making of management decisions or arranging for others to provide services in a significant and bona fide sense. This includes approving new tenants, deciding on rental terms, approving expenditures, and other similar decisions. Active participation may be achieved even if the taxpayer hires a rental agent and others provide the services.[28] In general, a limited partner is not able to participate actively in any activity of a limited partnership.

ADDITIONAL COMMENT
In calculating AGI to determine the amount of the $25,000 that is phased out, married taxpayers filing joint returns must include the income of both spouses. This provision results in a marriage penalty where both spouses have income.

LIMITATION ON DEDUCTION OF RENTAL REAL ESTATE LOSS. Taxpayers must first apply rental real estate losses against other net passive income for the year. Taxpayers may then reduce their portfolio or active business income up to $25,000. The $25,000, however, is reduced by 50% of the taxpayer's AGI in excess of $100,000. For this purpose, AGI is determined without regard to any passive activity loss or to any loss allowable to taxpayers who materially participate in real property trades or businesses (e.g., a real estate developer). Thus, if a taxpayer has AGI of $150,000 or more, all of the rental real estate losses must be suspended and carried over with the taxpayer's other passive losses.

EXAMPLE I8-16 ▶

During the current year, Penny, a married individual who files a joint return, reports the following items of income and loss:

Salary income	$120,000
Activity A (passive)	15,000
Activity B (nonbusiness rental real estate)	(50,000)

Penny owns over 10% and actively participates in Activity B. Her AGI for the year is as follows:

Salary		$120,000
Passive income from Activity A	$15,000	
Minus: Passive loss from Activity B ($50,000, but limited to $15,000)	(15,000)	–0–
Minus: Maximum rental real estate loss (from Activity B)	$25,000	
Reduced by phase-out: [($120,000 − $100,000) × 0.50]	(10,000)	
Deductible amount (but not to exceed actual loss)		(15,000)
AGI		$105,000

Penny may deduct $30,000 of the loss from Activity B during the year ($15,000 as an offset to the passive income from Activity A + $15,000 deductible against portfolio or active business income). Penny has $20,000 ($50,000 − $30,000) of suspended passive losses from Activity B that are carried over to the following year. ◀

---

[27] In order for a deduction to be taken in the current year for a loss sustained in a prior year, the taxpayer must actively participate in the activity during both years. See Sec. 469(i)(1).

[28] S. Rept. No. 99-313, 99th Cong., 2d Sess., pp. 737–738 (1986). However, a lessor under a net lease will probably not be deemed to achieve active participation.

The $25,000 limit applies to the sum of both deductions and credits. Thus, in order to properly apply the limit, taxpayers must convert the credits into deduction equivalents. A *deduction equivalent* is an amount that if taken as a deduction, would reduce the tax liability by an amount equal to the credits. The amount of deduction equivalents can be computed by dividing the amount of the credit by the taxpayer's marginal tax rate. If the sum of the deductions and the deduction equivalents exceeds the $25,000 limit, the deductions are used first.

EXAMPLE I8-17 ▶ Hal owns over 10% and actively participates in activity A, which is a passive real estate rental activity. Hal's marginal tax rate is 28% and he has AGI of less than $100,000. For the year, activity A generates a $20,000 net loss and $10,000 in tax credits (which amounts to $35,714 in deduction equivalent {$10,000/.28}). After deducting the $20,000 net loss against his active business and portfolio income, Hal has a remaining real estate deduction under the limit of $5,000 ($25,000 − $20,000). Thus, Hal may use $1,400 ($5,000 × 0.28) of the credits. The remaining $8,600 ($10,000 − $1,400) of tax credits must be carried over to subsequent years. ◀

If deductions and credits exceeding the $25,000 limit arise from more than one passive activity, they must be allocated between the activities.

EXAMPLE I8-18 ▶ Mary has AGI of less than $100,000 and a 28% marginal tax rate. During the year she reports a $30,000 loss from activity A and a $10,000 loss from activity B. Additionally, activity A generates $5,000 of tax credits. Both activities A and B are passive real estate rental activities in which Mary actively participates and owns over 10% of each activity. The $25,000 deduction is first allocated to the losses. Because the sum of the losses ($40,000) exceeds the limit, the deductible loss must be allocated ratably between the activities as follows:

Activity A: $25,000 × $30,000 ÷ $40,000 = $18,750
Activity B: $25,000 × $10,000 ÷ $40,000 = $6,250

Activity A has an $11,250 ($30,000 − $18,750) suspended loss, and activity B has a $3,750 ($10,000 − $6,250) suspended loss. In addition, activity A has $5,000 of suspended tax credits. ◀

A summary of the passive activity loss rules is presented in Topic Review I8-2.

STOP & THINK

Question: Jana is a business woman who has successfully invested in various stock and bond funds. Now she is considering diversifying her holdings by investing in real estate. One of the alternatives she is considering is purchasing an interest in a limited partnership that invests in real estate. A friend is also urging Jana to go into a partnership with him in order to purchase a small office building they would rent out. Assume that the size of Jana's investment in the two alternatives would be exactly the same and that Jana estimates the economic results to be equivalent (e.g., she expects both to spin off equivalent losses for the first few years and then begin turning a profit.) What tax issues should Jana consider when making her investment decision?

Solution: In comparing alternatives such as these, of course, the most important considerations should be the non-tax factors such as cash flow from the investment, the capital appreciation of the assets, the marketability of the investment, and the risk. For example, as a limited partner, Jana will not personally be liable for debts of the partnership or lawsuits filed against the partnership. Purchase of the office building as a general partner with her friend will cause her to be personally liable. Additionally, in comparing these two alternatives, certain tax issues may come into play. Both alternatives are investments in rental real estate. However, Jana is not eligible to deduct up to $25,000 of the passive losses from the limited partnership because she will not actively participate in the partnership. On the other hand, if she is involved in management decisions regarding the office building, she will be actively participating and will be eligible for the $25,000 passive loss deduction exception. Of course, the benefit of this exception is phased out if her AGI exceeds $100,000.

Topic Review I8-2

Passive Losses

TOPIC	SUMMARY
Taxpayers covered	Individuals, estates, trusts, closely held C corporations, personal service corporations, certain publicly traded partnerships.
Definition	Any trade or business activity in which the taxpayer does not materially participate. Includes all rental activities except for certain rental real estate activities and exceptions contained in regulations. Does not include working interests in oil and gas property.
Limitation	Passive losses are deductible against passive income, but not against active or portfolio income. Disallowed losses are carried over to subsequent years (suspended losses). Losses must be accounted for separately by activity. Activities are identified by examining the taxpayer's undertakings.
Suspended losses	Must be allocated and attributed among the passive activities that generated the losses.
Disposition of interest	Suspended losses may be deducted in the year of a taxable disposition. For inherited property, suspended losses in excess of the increase in basis may be deducted on the final return of a decedent. Losses up to the amount of the basis increase are lost.
Material participation	Must be regular, continuous, and substantial. The regulations contain seven separate tests; four based on current-year participation; two based on participation in prior years; and one based on facts and circumstances.
Real property trades or businesses	Passive activity loss rules do not apply to taxpayers who materially participate in real property trade or business activities constituting more than 750 hours. Additionally, more than one-half of the taxpayer's personal services must be performed in real property trades or businesses in which the taxpayer materially participates.
Rental of real estate	Individuals may deduct losses up to $25,000 against active and portfolio income if they actively particpate in the activity. This is a lesser standard than material participation, but the taxpayer must still participate in management decisions or arranging for others to provide services. The deduction phases out at a 50% rate for AGI in excess of $100,000.

CASUALTY AND THEFT LOSSES

OBJECTIVE 6

Identify and calculate the deduction for a casualty or theft loss

Taxpayers may deduct losses incurred in connection with business or investment property but deductions for losses on personal-use property are generally disallowed. However, under Sec. 165, taxpayers may take a limited deduction if the loss on personal-use property arises from a fire, storm, shipwreck, other casualty, or theft. In other words, losses on personal-use property are deductible only if the loss results from a casualty. In order for an event to qualify as a casualty, certain requirements must be met.

CASUALTY DEFINED

According to the IRS, a deductible **casualty loss** is one that has occurred in an identifiable event that was sudden, unexpected, or unusual.[29]

IDENTIFIABLE EVENT. Because the event that causes the loss must be *identifiable*, the act of losing or misplacing property is generally not considered a casualty.

However, in some cases taxpayers have been able to prove that the loss of the property was the result of an identifiable event.

---

[29] IRS *Publication No. 547* (Nonbusiness Disasters, Casualties, and Thefts), 2000, p. 1.

EXAMPLE I8-19 ▶ One evening Troy and his wife, Lynn, go to the theater. Troy accidentally slams the car door on Lynn's hand. The impact breaks the flanges holding the diamond in her ring. As a result, the diamond falls from the ring and is lost. In this case, a deductible casualty loss has occurred.[30] ◀

KEY POINT
The taxpayer has the burden of proof to establish that a loss was caused by a casualty. The taxpayer should gather as much evidence as possible. Newspaper clippings, police reports, photographs, and insurance reports can be helpful in establishing the cause of the loss.

SUDDEN, UNEXPECTED, OR UNUSUAL EVENTS. According to the IRS, a *sudden event* is one that is swift, not gradual or progressive. An *unexpected event* is one that is ordinarily unanticipated and not intended. An *unusual event* is one that is not a day-to-day occurrence and that is not typical of the activity in which the taxpayer is engaged.

Thus, the IRS has ruled that a deductible casualty loss was sustained when a taxpayer went ice fishing and his automobile fell through the ice.[31] A taxpayer whose automobile was damaged as the result of an accident also sustained a deductible casualty loss. However, a taxpayer may not deduct losses incurred in an accident caused by the taxpayer's willful negligence or willful act.[32] Damage sustained as the result of an accident in an automobile race was held to be nondeductible because accidents occur often and are not unusual events in automobile races.[33]

ADDITIONAL COMMENT
Sudden, unexpected, or unusual events must also be accompanied by an external force. For example, a blown engine in an automobile is a sudden event but because no external force caused the event, the loss is not a casualty loss.

The following are a few examples of events that have been held to constitute a deductible casualty loss:

▶ Rust and water damage to furniture and carpets caused by the bursting of a water heater
▶ Damage to the exterior paint of a residence caused by a severe, sudden, and unexpected concentration of chemical fumes in the air
▶ Loss caused by fire (unless the taxpayer sets the fire, in which case no deduction is available)
▶ Damage to a building caused by an unusually large blast at a nearby quarry or a jet sonic boom[34]
▶ Death of trees just a few days after a sudden infestation of pine beetles[35]

The following are examples of events that have been held *not* to be a casualty:

▶ Water damage to the walls and ceiling of a taxpayer's personal residence as the result of the gradual deterioration of the roof[36]
▶ Trees dying because of gradual suffocation of the root systems
▶ The loss of trees and shrubs because of disease[37]
▶ Damage to carpet and clothing caused by moths and carpet beetles[38]
▶ Damage to a road due to freezing, thawing, and gradual deterioration[39]
▶ Damage to a residence caused by the gradual sinking of the land underneath the home[40]
▶ Damage caused by drought because it occurs through progressive deterioration
▶ The steady weakening of a building caused by normal wind and weather conditions
▶ The rusting and deterioration of a water heater[41]

ETHICAL POINT
A client loses his diamond ring while fishing and wants to deduct the loss as a casualty. The CPA should not sign the tax return unless he or she believes that the client's position has a realistic possibility of being sustained on its merits if challenged, which is doubtful in this situation.

---

[30] *John P. White*, 48 T.C. 430 (1967), *acq.* 1969-2 C.B. xxv. In another case, the taxpayer convinced the Tax Court to allow a deduction for a lost diamond, even though the taxpayer could not remember a specific blow to the ring. In this instance, the taxpayer obtained an expert witness to testify that the flanges of the ring were strong enough and in good enough repair that the loss of the diamond had to have been caused by a sudden, unexpected blow rather than by progressive deterioration.
[31] Rev. Rul. 69-88, 1969-1 C.B. 58.
[32] *Willie C. Robinson*, 1984 PH T.C. Memo ¶84,188, 47 TCM 1510 and Reg. Sec. 1.165-7(a)(3).
[33] Ltr. Rul. 8227010 (March 30, 1982) contains the above examples.
[34] *Ray Durden*, 3 T.C. 1 (1944), *acq.* 1944 C.B. 8 and Rev. Rul. 60-329, 1960-2 C.B. 67.
[35] Rev. Rul. 79-174, 1979-1 C.B. 99. See also *Charles A. Smithgall v. U.S.*, 47 AFTR 2d 81-695, 81-1 USTC ¶9121 (D.C.-Ga., 1980). However, the IRS has ruled in Ltr. Rul. 8544001 (July 12, 1985) that no casualty loss results when the time interval between the infestation and the death of the trees was too long.
[36] *Lauren Whiting*, 1975 PH T.C. Memo ¶75,038, 34 TCM 241.
[37] *William R. Miller*, 1970 PH T.C. Memo ¶70,167, 29 TCM 741 and Rev. Rul. 57-599, 1957-2 C.B. 142. See also *Howard F. Burns v. U.S.*, 6 AFTR 2d 6036, 61-1 USTC ¶9127 (6th Cir., 1960).
[38] Rev. Rul. 55-327, 1955-1 C.B. 25. See also *J. P. Meersman v. U.S.*, 18 AFTR 2d 6152, 67-1 USTC ¶9125 (6th Cir., 1966).
[39] *Howard Stacy*, 1970 PH T.C. Memo ¶70,127, 29 TCM 542. However, the breaking up of a road over a 4-month period because of extreme weather conditions was held to be a casualty. See *Emmett J. O'Connell v. U.S.*, 29 AFTR 2d 72-596, 72-1 USTC ¶9312, (D.C. Cal., 1972). See also *Stephen L. Shaffer*, 1983 PH T.C. Memo ¶83,677, 47 TCM 285.
[40] *Henry W. Berry*, 1969 PH T.C. Memo ¶69,162, 28 TCM 802. See also *David McDaniel*, 1980 PH T.C. Memo ¶80,557, 41 TCM 563.
[41] IRS Publication No. 547 (Nonbusiness Disasters, Casualties, and Thefts), 2000, contains the above examples.

At times it is very difficult to determine under the particular facts whether the necessary incidents of suddenness, unexpectedness, or unusualness exist. For example, damage caused by the sudden infestation of pine beetles in some instances has been held to be a casualty, but in other instances it has not constituted a casualty.[42]

THEFT DEFINED

Under Sec. 165, a taxpayer may also deduct a loss sustained as the result of a theft. This includes theft of business, investment, or personal-use property. The Treasury Regulations state that "the term theft shall be deemed to include, but shall not necessarily be limited to, larceny, embezzlement, and robbery."[43] A determination whether other actions also constitute theft often depends on whether criminal intent was involved and the action is illegal under the state law where the action has occurred. Thus, the IRS has stated that blackmail, extortion, and kidnapping for ransom may also constitute theft.[44]

REAL-WORLD EXAMPLE

Taxpayer received a letter stating that a certain party was imprisoned in Mexico for bankruptcy. That party was alleged to have $375,000 in bills hidden in the secret compartment of a trunk checked in a customs house in the U.S. Taxpayer was told that he would be given one-third of the amount in the trunk if he went to Mexico and paid $8,300 to release the prisoner. Taxpayer went to Mexico, paid the $8,300, and later found that he had been swindled. The loss of $8,300 was a deductible theft loss. *Curtis H. Muncie*, 18 T.C. 849 (1952).

DEDUCTIBLE AMOUNT OF CASUALTY LOSS

The amount of a casualty loss deduction depends on the amount of the loss sustained, any insurance or other reimbursement received; and, in the case of personal-use property, the limitations imposed under the tax law.

MEASURING THE LOSS. In general, the amount of loss sustained in a casualty is the amount by which the property's FMV is reduced as a result of the casualty. This is measured by comparing the property's FMV immediately before and immediately after the casualty.[45] Any reduction in the FMV of the taxpayer's surrounding but undamaged property is disregarded.

EXAMPLE I8-20 ▶ Gail purchased a vacation home for $110,000. Shortly after she purchased the property, a mudslide completely destroyed several neighboring cabins. There was no damage to Gail's cabin. After the slide, an appraisal reveals that the FMV of the cabin has declined to $80,000 because of fears that other mudslides might occur. The $30,000 reduction in the FMV of the cabin does not constitute a deductible casualty loss. ◀

ADDITIONAL COMMENT

A loss cannot be deducted unless the damaged property is owned by the taxpayer. Therefore, a taxpayer cannot deduct amounts he or she paid to another individual for damage he or she caused to the other individual's property.

Actual market value, not sentimental value, is used to compute the reduction in the FMV. Additionally, the cost of protecting property to prevent damage from a casualty is not a deductible loss.

If the property involved in the casualty is only partially destroyed, the amount of the loss is the lesser of the reduction in the property's FMV or the taxpayer's adjusted basis in the property.

EXAMPLE I8-21 ▶ Troy purchased a home for $25,000 several years ago. Through the years, the value of the home appreciated until it was appraised at $125,000 in the current year. Shortly after the appraisal, a flood sweeps through the area, severely damaging Troy's home and reducing its value to $90,000. Troy does not have any flood insurance. His loss is limited to the $25,000 basis in the home even though the economic loss is $35,000 ($125,000 − $90,000). ◀

TYPICAL MISCONCEPTION

It is sometimes thought that a taxpayer's loss should be based on the total economic loss rather than just the property's basis. It should be remembered that a taxpayer has not paid a tax on the appreciation in value, and therefore, should not be entitled to a deduction for a loss on the unrealized gain.

If business or investment property is totally destroyed in a casualty, the amount of the loss is the taxpayer's adjusted basis in the property, even if it is greater than the property's FMV. However, if personal-use property is totally destroyed, the amount of the loss is limited to the lesser of the reduction in the property's FMV or the property's adjusted basis.

---

[42] Rev. Rul. 79-174, 1979-1 C.B. 99 and *George K. Notter*, 1985 PH T.C. Memo ¶85,391, 50 TCM 614. A graphic illustration of the controversy that may arise when determining whether an event is a casualty can be made by comparing the following two cases. In one case the taxpayer was washing dishes. Seeing a glass of water on the windowsill, he quickly dumped the contents down the drain and turned on the garbage disposal, not realizing that his wife's rings were in the glass. Damage to the rings in this case was deemed to be a casualty (*William H. Carpenter*, 1966 PH T.C. Memo ¶66,228, 25 TCM 1186). In the second case, the taxpayer gathered up some tissues from the night stand and flushed them down the toilet, not knowing that his wife's rings were wrapped in one of them. This event was held not to be a casualty (*W.J. Keenan, Jr. v. Bowers*, 39 AFTR 849, 50-2 USTC ¶9444 (D.C.-S.C., 1950)).

[43] Reg. Sec. 1.165-8(d).

[44] Rev. Rul. 72-112, 1972-1 C.B. 60 and IRS *Publication No. 547* (Nonbusiness Disasters, Casualties, and Thefts), 2000, p. 1.

[45] Reg. Sec. 1.165-7(a)(2).

EXAMPLE I8-22 ▶ A machine that Beth uses in her business is completely destroyed by fire. At the time of the fire, the adjusted basis of the machine is $5,000 and its FMV is $3,000. Because the machine is business property, Beth's loss is $5,000. If the machine were a personal-use asset, the amount of the loss would be $3,000. ◀

Generally, taxpayers must establish the reduction in the FMV of the property by an appraisal. If an appraisal is difficult or impossible to obtain, the cost of the repairs may be used instead. All of the following requirements must be met before this alternative can be used:

▶ The repairs will bring the property back to its condition immediately before the casualty.
▶ The cost of the repairs is not excessive.
▶ The repairs do no more than repair the damage incurred in the casualty.
▶ The repairs do not increase the value of the property over its value immediately before the casualty.

If more than one property is destroyed in the same casualty, the loss on each property must be calculated separately.[46] Thus, each property's basis is compared with the reduction in the FMV of that property, rather than aggregating the basis and FMV amounts for all the properties destroyed in the casualty.

If the taxpayer receives insurance or any other type of recovery, the amount of the loss must be reduced by these amounts. In some cases these payments may actually exceed the taxpayer's basis in the property, causing the realization of a gain. If certain requirements are met, taxpayers may defer or exclude the recognition of these gains. (See the detailed discussion of involuntary conversions in Chapter I12.)

LIMITATIONS ON PERSONAL-USE PROPERTY

The deductibility of casualty losses on personal-use property is subject to two limitations: the losses sustained in each separate casualty are reduced by $100, and the total amount of all net casualty losses for personal-use property is reduced by 10% of the taxpayer's AGI for the year. For property destroyed in the same casualty, only $100 is deducted from all the properties (i.e., $100 is not deducted from each separate property).

EXAMPLE I8-23 ▶ A windstorm blows over a large tree in front of Cathy's house, damaging the house and totally destroying her automobile. After the insurance reimbursement, the loss on the house amounts to $3,000, and the loss on the automobile is $2,500. Because the losses occur in the same casualty, the total amount of the loss is reduced to $5,400 ($3,000 + $2,500 − $100). If the damage to the car was sustained in a separate event such as an automobile accident, the total amount of the casualty losses incurred by Cathy during the year would have been $5,300 ($3,000 + $2,500 − $200). This $5,300 or $5,400 loss is then further reduced by 10% of Cathy's AGI for the year. ◀

EXAMPLE I8-24 ▶ As the result of a storm, Liz incurs a $4,500 casualty loss on personal-use property during the current year. She also sustains a $600 theft loss. Liz's AGI for the year is $50,000. She receives no tax deduction for the casualty and theft losses because they do not exceed the following limitations:

KEY POINT
Many taxpayers will not be able to deduct their casualty losses because of the $100 floor and 10% of AGI limitation.

	Storm	Theft	Total
Loss before limitations	$4,500	$600	$5,100
Minus: $100 floor	(100)	(100)	(200)
	$4,400	$500	$4,900
Minus: 10% of AGI (0.10 × $50,000)			(5,000)
Deductible loss			0 ◀

---

[46] Reg. Sec. 1.165-7(b)(2). For personal-use property, losses on real property and improvements to the property are computed in the aggregate. Thus, no separate basis need be apportioned to the improvements. See Reg. Secs. 1.165-7(b)(2)(ii) and 1.165-7(b)(3) Example (3).

ADDITIONAL COMMENT

Sometimes individuals fail to file insurance claims for damage to their personal automobile for fear that their insurance rates will increase, and hoping instead to deduct the loss. Because of this limitation, no deduction is available.

As a result of these limitations, many taxpayers who sustain casualty and theft losses on personal-use property do not receive a tax deduction. Furthermore, if the property is covered by insurance, no deduction is available for a casualty loss of personal-use property unless the taxpayer timely files an insurance claim for the loss. This disallowance relates only to the portion of the loss that was covered by the insurance.

The rules concerning deductibility of losses described above are summarized as follows:

Result of Casualty		Business	Investment	Personal-Use
Total Destruction	Amount of Casualty[a]	Basis	Basis	Lesser of: basis or decline in FMV, reduced by $100 and 10% of AGI
	Type	For AGI	From AGI (For AGI if Rental)	From AGI
Partial Destruction	Amount of Casualty[a]	Lesser of: basis or decline in FMV	Lesser of: basis or decline in FMV	Lesser of: basis or decline in FMV, reduced by $100 and 10% of AGI
	Type	For AGI	From AGI (For AGI if Rental)	From AGI

[a] All amounts are first reduced by any insurance reimbursement.

NETTING CASUALTY GAINS AND LOSSES ON PERSONAL-USE PROPERTY

TYPICAL MISCONCEPTION

The concept of a gain on a casualty is sometimes confusing. Nevertheless, if the insurance proceeds exceed the basis, a gain results.

Casualty gains and losses incurred during the year on personal-use assets are netted against each other rather than being combined with casualty gains and losses on business and investment property. For purposes of the netting process, the losses should be reduced by any insurance reimbursements and the $100 limitation, but not the 10% of AGI floor. If the gains exceed the losses for the year, all the gains and losses are treated as capital gains and losses.

▶ **EXAMPLE I8-25**

During the current year, Pat incurs the following casualty gains and losses on personal-use assets. Assets W and X are destroyed in one casualty, and asset Y is destroyed in another. Pat acquired assets X and Y in the current year, whereas she acquired asset W several years ago.

Asset	Reduction in FMV	Adjusted Basis	Insurance	Holding Period
W	$10,000	$3,000	$10,000	More than 12 months
X	4,000	5,000	2,000	Less than one year
Y	2,000	3,000	0	Less than one year

Pat realizes a $7,000 ($10,000 − $3,000) gain on asset W because the insurance proceeds received for the asset exceed its basis. She realizes a $2,000 ($4,000 reduction in FMV − $2,000 insurance) loss on asset X. This loss is reduced to $1,900 because of the $100 reduction for personal casualty losses. She realizes a $2,000 loss on asset Y. Because this loss of $2,000 is realized as a result of the second casualty, the $100 limitation is deducted, resulting in a $1,900 loss from that casualty. Pat realizes a $3,200 [$7,000 − ($1,900 + $1,900)] net casualty gain for the year. Thus, the gain or loss on each asset is treated as a capital gain or loss. Pat must report a $7,000 long-term capital gain on asset W, a $1,900 short-term capital loss on asset X, and a $1,900 short-term capital loss on asset Y. ◀

If the casualty losses on personal-use property exceed the casualty gains for the year, the net loss is further reduced by 10% of AGI. All of these calculations (the netting process and reductions) are done on Form 4684. If any loss remains after the netting and reductions, the loss is reported as an itemized deduction on Schedule A of Form 1040.

CASUALTY GAINS AND LOSSES ATTRIBUTABLE TO BUSINESS AND INVESTMENT PROPERTY

Taxpayers must net casualty gains and losses on business and investment property. (See Chapter I13 for a discussion of the netting procedure under Sec. 1231.) If the losses exceed the gains, the business losses and losses on investment property that generate rents or royalties are *for* AGI deductions. Losses on other investment property (e.g., the theft of a security) are itemized deductions but are not subject to the 2% of AGI floor or the 3% overall reduction of itemized deductions. Losses on business and investment property are not subject to the $100 or 10% of AGI limitations.

WHEN LOSSES ARE DEDUCTIBLE

In general, taxpayers must deduct casualty losses in the tax year in which the loss is sustained. In the following instances, however, taxpayers may deduct the loss in another year:

- Theft losses
- Insurance or other reimbursements that are reasonably expected to be received in a subsequent year
- Certain disaster losses (discussed later in this chapter)

THEFT. Taxpayers must deduct a theft loss in the tax year in which the theft is discovered. This rule is equitable and practical because a taxpayer may not discover a theft until a subsequent year.

REAL-WORLD EXAMPLE
In 1961, taxpayer gave two diamond rings to an acquaintance for safekeeping. In 1965 taxpayer was entitled to a casualty loss deduction after several fruitless attempts to locate the acquaintance and after reporting the matter to the police. *Virginia M. Cramer*, 55 T.C. 1125 (1971).

EXAMPLE I8-26 ▶ Dale owns a hunting lodge in upstate New York. Sometime after his last trip to the lodge in November 2001, someone breaks into the lodge and steals several guns and paintings. Dale discovers the theft when he returns to the lodge on May 19, 2002. Dale's insurance does not cover the entire cost of the items. The loss is deductible in 2002, even though the theft may have occurred in 2001. ◀

REAL-WORLD EXAMPLE
A taxpayer had property confiscated by the Cuban government in 1960. The taxpayer left the country and could have filed for indemnity but did not because she expected to return. Later, the government took away the right of indemnity in 1961. Since she did not file for indemnity from the Cuban government when she had the chance, she was not allowed a casualty or theft loss. *Vila v. U.S.*, 23 AFTR2d 69-1311 (1969).

INSURANCE AND OTHER REIMBURSEMENTS. Taxpayers must subtract any reimbursement received as compensation for a loss in arriving at the amount of the loss. This is necessary even when the taxpayer has not yet received the reimbursement, as long as there is a reasonable prospect that it will be received in the future. Thus no deduction is allowed in the year of loss if in that year a reasonable expectation of full recovery exists.[47] If full recovery is not anticipated, a loss may be deducted in the year the casualty occurs for the estimated unrecovered amount. As previously mentioned, no deduction is allowed to the extent the personal-use property is covered by insurance and the taxpayer does not file a timely insurance claim.

EXAMPLE I8-27 ▶ In December of the current year, Andrea suffers a $10,000 casualty loss when her personal automobile is struck by a city bus. Although she does not receive any reimbursement from the insurance company by December 31, there is a reasonable expectation that the full amount of the loss will be recovered. Andrea may not deduct a casualty loss in the current year. ◀

EXAMPLE I8-28 ▶ Assume the same facts as in Example I8-27, except that Andrea reasonably anticipates that her reimbursement from the insurance company will amount to only $7,000. In this case, her casualty loss in the current year is $3,000 (before reduction by the limitations). ◀

If the taxpayer does not receive the full amount of the anticipated recovery in the subsequent year, he or she may deduct the unrecovered portion. However, rather than filing an amended return for the year of loss, the taxpayer deducts the loss in the subsequent year. Thus in some cases, the income tax consequences for a single casualty loss may be spread over two years.

---
[47] Reg. Sec. 1.165-1(d)(2)(i).

EXAMPLE I8-29 ▶ During the current year, Javier's home is damaged by an exceptionally severe blast at a nearby stone quarry owned by Acme Corporation. Although the amount of the damage is properly appraised at $20,000, Javier can reasonably anticipate a recovery of only $15,000 from Acme Corporation at the end of the current year. He does not receive any recovery from Acme during the current year. Unfortunately, in the subsequent year Acme Corporation is declared bankrupt, and Javier does not receive any reimbursement. Javier's AGI is $40,000 in the current year and $45,000 in the subsequent year. During the current year, Javier may deduct $900 {$5,000 loss reasonably anticipated in the current year − [$100 limitation + (0.10 × $40,000)]}. In the subsequent year, Javier may deduct an additional casualty loss of $10,500 [$15,000 additional loss − (0.10 × $45,000)]. ◀

If a subsequent recovery is received for a loss that is previously deducted, the reimbursement is included in income in the year of recovery. An amended return is not filed. However, the amount that the taxpayer must include in income is limited to the amount of tax benefit the taxpayer received for the previous deduction.

EXAMPLE I8-30 ▶ During the current year, Becky's automobile sustains $5,000 in damages when it is struck by another automobile. The driver of the other automobile is at fault and is uninsured, and there is no reasonable prospect that Becky will recover any of the loss. Becky's AGI for the current year is $35,000. Becky deducts $1,400 ($5,000 loss − [$100 + $3,500]). During the subsequent year, the other driver reimburses Becky for the full amount of the damage. Because Becky received a tax benefit of only $1,400 for the loss in the year of the accident, only $1,400 must be included in gross income in the subsequent year, even though she receives a $5,000 reimbursement. Becky does not file an amended return for the year of the accident. ◀

REAL-WORLD EXAMPLE

In 1999, losses due to Hurricane Floyd in portions of North Carolina qualified as disaster losses.

DISASTER LOSSES. Under certain circumstances, a taxpayer may elect to deduct a casualty loss in the year preceding the year in which the loss actually occurs. This election is available to taxpayers who suffer losses attributable to a disaster that occurs in an area subsequently declared by the President of the United States as a disaster area.[48] Thus, an individual can elect to deduct a disaster loss occurring in 2002 on his or her 2001 tax return or report it in the regular way on his or her 2002 return. An amended return (Form 1040X) must be filed unless the prior year's return has not been filed when the disaster occurs. This allows taxpayers the possibility of receiving financial help from potential tax refunds by filing an amendment to the prior year's return.

Casualty loss deduction rules are summarized in Topic Review I8-3.

STOP & THINK

Question: Due to unusually heavy rainfall in the Pacific Northwest during the current year, many homes, roads and other property are destroyed. Because of the tremendous destruction, the President of the United States declares the area a disaster area. One of the properties totally destroyed in a mudslide is Jack's mountain cabin in Oregon. Jack uses the cabin exclusively for vacationing. The value of the cabin is $110,000. Unfortunately, the cabin is not insured against a mudslide. What issues must be considered in determining the year in which to take the casualty loss?

Solution: Since the property was destroyed in a disaster and is located in an area which the President subsequently declared as a disaster area, Jack may take the casualty deduction either in the year of the casualty or in the previous year. The year which is most beneficial is based on several factors. The destroyed property was personal use property, causing the deduction to be an itemized deduction subject to the 10% of AGI limitation. Thus, Jack must compare his estimated AGI for the current year with his AGI in the last year. He also should consider his other itemized deductions, including any other casualty losses. In addition, his marginal tax rates in the two years must be compared. Jack must also consider the time value of money, since by taking the deduction on his prior year return, he will receive the tax benefit earlier than if he takes the deduction on the current year return.

---

[48] Sec. 165(i). Additionally, the same treatment may apply under Sec. 165 to taxpayers who live in a disaster area and who are ordered by a state or local government to move from or relocate their residence because the disaster caused the residence to be unsafe. In order to qualify for this treatment, the order to move must come from the state or local government within 120 days of the date that the President determines the area to be a disaster area. If the property destroyed in a presidentially declared disaster area is the taxpayer's principal residence and the casualty results in a gain, a portion of the gain may be excluded if certain conditions are met (see Chapter I12).

Topic Review I8-3

Casualty Losses

TYPE OF PROPERTY	LIMITATION AND TREATMENT
Personal-use	The amount of the loss is the lesser of the property's adjusted basis or the reduction of the asset's FMV. This amount is reduced by any insurance reimbursement. If the insurance reimbursement exceeds the property's basis, a gain is realized. To the extent the property is insured, a claim must be filed or the loss is disallowed.
	The amount of loss incurred in each separate casualty event during the year is reduced by $100.
	All casualty gains and losses for the year are netted. If the gains exceed the losses, all gains and losses are treated as capital gains and losses. If the losses exceed the gains, the net loss is reduced by 10% of AGI. Any remaining loss is an itemized deduction.
Business or investment	If the property is totally destroyed, the amount of the loss is the adjusted basis of the property. If only partially destroyed, the amount of the loss is the lesser of the property's adjusted basis or the reduction of the asset's FMV. This amount is reduced by any insurance reimbursement. A gain is realized if the insurance reimbursement exceeds the property's basis.
	For property held one year or less, the losses and gains are ordinary losses and gains. For property held over one year, the casualty gains and losses for the year are netted. The treatment depends on the total of the taxpayer's other Sec. 1231 transactions (see Chapter I13). Business casualty losses and losses on investment property that generate rents or royalties are not subject to the $100 or 10% of AGI limitations.

BAD DEBTS

OBJECTIVE 7

Compute the deduction for a bad debt

In addition to losses on property, taxpayers may also sustain losses because of uncollectible debts. In dealing with a deduction for bad debts, taxpayers must address the following requirements and issues:

- A bona fide debtor-creditor relationship must exist between the taxpayer and some other person or entity.
- The taxpayer must have basis in the debt.
- The debt must actually have become worthless during the year.
- The type and timing of a bad debt deduction depend on whether the debt is a business or nonbusiness bad debt.
- Generally, only the specific write-off method of accounting may be used in deducting the bad debt.
- A partial or complete recovery of a debt that was previously deducted may occur. In many cases a recovery of this type causes income recognition in the year of the recovery.

KEY POINT
The tax provisions that deal with deductions for losses and the tax provisions that deal with the deductions for bad debts are mutually exclusive, and an amount properly deductible as a loss cannot be deducted as a bad debt or visa versa.

BONA FIDE DEBTOR-CREDITOR RELATIONSHIP

Only items constituting bona fide debt are eligible to be deducted as a bad debt. A bona fide debt is one that arises from a valid and enforceable obligation to pay a fixed or determinable sum of money and results in a debtor-creditor relationship.[49]

KEY POINT
The fact that the debtor is a related party does not preclude deduction of a bad debt, but the taxpayer should be able to document the debt as being bona fide.

RELATED-PARTY TRANSACTIONS. Determining whether a bona fide loan transaction has actually taken place is especially critical when the transaction is between the taxpayer and a family member or other related party (e.g., a controlled corporation). All the facts and circumstances surrounding the transaction must be carefully examined because a gift does not constitute a debt. The taxpayer's intent is critical here. For example, if the taxpayer's intent is to provide property, cash, or services to someone else without receiv-

---
[49] Reg. Sec. 1.166-1(c).

ing any consideration in return, a gift—not a loan—has been made. Some tests used to determine the taxpayer's intent include the following:

- Does a note or other written instrument exist which evidences an obligation to repay?[50]
- Have the parties established a definite schedule of repayment?
- Is a reasonable rate of interest stated?
- Would a person who is unrelated to the debtor make the loan?[51]

EXAMPLE I8-31

REAL-WORLD EXAMPLE

Taxpayer advanced $8,500 to his son-in-law who operated a livestock auction barn. Taxpayer was entitled to a bad debt deduction upon default because notations on the checks indicated that they were loans and undisputed testimony indicated that repayment was to be made within 90 days. *Giffin A. Andrew*, 54 T.C. 239 (1970).

During the current year Maria loaned $20,000 to her son Sam, who used the money in his business. Although no written note or contract was signed, Sam orally promised to repay Maria as soon as his business became profitable. No rate of interest was stated. Unfortunately, the business failed and Sam went out of business in the subsequent year. He never repaid the loan principal or interest.

In this case, no valid debt exists because neither an interest rate nor a repayment schedule was established. An unrelated person would not have made a loan to Sam under these conditions. In addition, Maria does not receive any consideration in return for the "loan." Since the facts indicate that the transaction is actually a gift, Maria may not claim a bad debt deduction because of Sam's failure to repay. ◀

Tax advisers should also closely examine other related party transactions. For example, a loan from a shareholder to a controlled corporation may actually be an additional contribution to capital disguised as a loan. Thus, a transfer of cash by a shareholder who owns a controlling (i.e., more than 50%) interest in the stock of a corporation may indicate a capital contribution rather than a loan. Likewise, a loan from a corporation to a controlling shareholder may actually be a disguised dividend or a salary payment.

THIRD PARTY DEBT. Generally, a taxpayer may deduct a bad debt only when a debtor-creditor relationship exists. However, in some cases a taxpayer will guarantee or endorse someone else's obligation. If the taxpayer is forced to pay the third party's debt under the terms of the guarantee, the guarantor may actually be treated as the creditor. If the original debtor does not repay the taxpayer who guarantees and pays the debt, the guarantor may deduct the loss. Any accrued interest that the guarantor pays may also be deductible as a bad debt. However, the interest is not deductible as interest when paid by the guarantor because it accrued on someone else's debt. Here, too, the taxpayer's intent determines whether the guarantee and payment constitute a gift.

EXAMPLE I8-32

Ron is the sole shareholder and a full-time employee of Zip Corporation. In order for Zip Corporation to obtain a bank loan, Ron personally signs a guarantee that the loan would be repaid. Unfortunately, Zip Corporation defaults on the loan and Ron is required to repay the loan. In this case, Ron signed the guarantee to preserve his job and enhance his investment in Zip Corporation. Although Ron receives no direct consideration for having signed the note, he does receive indirect consideration in the form of continued job security and protection of his investment. Because the loan guarantee was motivated by a business or investment purpose, Ron may deduct the bad debt. ◀

TYPICAL MISCONCEPTION

It is sometimes mistakenly assumed that a cash method taxpayer can take a bad debt deduction on a debt that arose from services rendered by the taxpayer.

TAXPAYER'S BASIS IN THE DEBT

For a bad debt to be deductible, the creditor must have basis in the debt. This basis may be acquired in different ways. If a taxpayer loans money, the taxpayer's basis in the debt is the amount loaned. If the debt arises because the taxpayer provides property or services

---

[50] A written note or other instrument is an evidence of a bona fide debtor-creditor relationship. However, if the note or other instrument is registered or has interest coupons and is issued by a corporation or a government, the bad debt provisions of Sec. 166 do not apply. Instead, the worthless security provisions of Sec. 165 (previously discussed) apply.

[51] *Jean C. Tyler v. Tomlinson*, 24 AFTR 2d 69-5426, 69-2 USTC ¶9559 (5th Cir., 1969). See also, *C. L. Hunt*, 1989 PH T.C. Memo ¶89,335, 57 TCM 919, where certain loans that the taxpayer made to his children were treated as bona fide loans, whereas others were treated as gifts. In that case, the children had been trading in silver futures and were required to make margin calls. Because they could not make the calls, the children's positions were involuntarily liquidated. Up to the date of the liquidation, the taxpayer had made loans to the children that were payable on demand and were subject to the prime rate of interest. These loans were evidenced by promissory notes. After the liquidation, the taxpayer continued to make loans to the children. However, these loans were not evidenced by notes. The loans up to the time of the liquidation were treated as bona fide loans and the subsequent loans were treated as gifts.

for the other party, basis is established only if the taxpayer has previously included the FMV of the property or services in income. This often depends on the taxpayer's method of accounting. An accrual method taxpayer generally reports income in the year the services are performed or the property is provided. (See the discussion in Chapter I11.) Thus, an accrual method taxpayer has a basis in either a note receivable or an open account receivable equal to the amount included in gross income (i.e., the FMV of the services). A cash method taxpayer, however, reports income only in the year in which payment in the form of cash or property is received. Because a note constitutes the receipt of property, a cash method taxpayer reports income (and establishes basis) in the year the note is received. However, if the cash-method taxpayer does not receive a note and the receivable is an open account item, the taxpayer reports no income until the receivable is collected. Thus, the taxpayer has no basis in the receivable and does not receive a bad debt deduction if the receivable is not collected.

EXAMPLE I8-33 ▶ In October of the current year, Jim performs some legal services for Joy. Jim bills Joy for $1,000. Joy does not sign a note for the debt. As a cash method taxpayer, Jim does not include the $1,000 in his current year's income. After repeated efforts to collect the fee, Jim discovers in June of the subsequent year that Joy has left the city and cannot be found. Jim may not deduct a bad debt for the uncollected amount in the subsequent year because he has not taken the amount into income and he has no basis in the debt. If Joy had signed a note for the debt, Jim would have reported income in the current year in an amount equal to the note's FMV and could have deducted the loss when the note became uncollectible in the subsequent year. ◀

DEBT MUST BE WORTHLESS

To deduct a bad debt, the taxpayer must show that the debt is worthless. This determination is made by reference to all the pertinent evidence, including the general financial condition of the debtor and whether the debt is secured by collateral.

In proving the worthlessness of a debt, a taxpayer does not need to take legal action if the surrounding circumstances indicate that legal action probably would not result in the collection of the debt. Simply showing that legal action is not warranted is sufficient proof that the debt is worthless.[52] Indications that an unsecured debt is worthless include bankruptcy of the debtor, disappearance or death of a debtor, and repeated unsuccessful attempts at collection. Furthermore, if the surrounding circumstances warrant it, a taxpayer may deduct a worthless debt even before the debt comes due. As will be explained later in this chapter, a nonbusiness debt must be totally worthless before a deduction is allowed. However, a current deduction is allowed for a partially worthless business bad debt.

KEY POINT
It is important to make a distinction between business and nonbusiness bad debts because the tax treatment varies according to the type of debt.

NONBUSINESS BAD DEBTS

The distinction between a business bad debt and a nonbusiness bad debt is important because the character of the debt determines its tax treatment. A business bad debt gives rise to an ordinary deduction, whereas a nonbusiness bad debt is treated as a short-term capital loss. All loans made by a corporation are assumed to be associated with the corporation's business; therefore, the provisions for nonbusiness bad debts do not apply to corporations.

TYPICAL MISCONCEPTION
Assume that a taxpayer lends money to a friend to be used in the friend's business. If the friend does not repay the loan, the debt is a nonbusiness bad debt unless the taxpayer is in the business of lending money. This type of debt is occasionally improperly classified as a business debt.

DEFINITION OF A NONBUSINESS BAD DEBT. A *nonbusiness debt* is defined as any debt other than (1) a debt created or acquired in connection with a trade or business of the taxpayer, or (2) a debt the loss from the worthlessness of which is incurred in the taxpayer's trade or business. This determination depends on an examination of the facts and circumstances surrounding the debt in question.

A debt incurred in a taxpayer's business continues to be a business debt for that taxpayer even though at the time the debt goes bad, the taxpayer has ceased conducting that particular business. This is situation (1) above. If another taxpayer acquires a business, any outstanding debt at the time the business is acquired continues to be business debt as

---
[52] Reg. Sec. 1.166-2.

long as the purchaser continues the business. This is situation (2) above. The debt is a nonbusiness debt if the person who owns the debt when it becomes worthless is not engaged in the business in which the debt is incurred either at the time the debt arose or when it becomes worthless.

EXAMPLE I8-34 ▶ Matt, an individual who uses the accrual method of accounting, is engaged in the grocery business. During 2001, he extends credit to Jeff on an open account. In 2002, Matt sells his business to Joan, but retains Jeff's account. Jeff's account becomes worthless in 2002. Even though Matt is no longer engaged in the grocery business at the time the debt becomes worthless, he may deduct the loss as a business bad debt in 2002. If Joan purchases Jeff's account upon acquiring the grocery business, Joan is entitled to a business bad debt deduction in 2002 because the debt was incurred in the trade or business in which Joan is currently engaged. ◀

ETHICAL POINT

A tax practitioner should serve as an advocate for his or her client. Thus, a tax practitioner may resolve doubt in favor of the client as long as there is reasonable support for his or her position.

In addition, classification as a business debt requires a proximate relationship between the debt and the taxpayer's business.[53] According to the Supreme Court, this relationship exists if a business motive is the taxpayer's dominant motivation in incurring the debt. This determination must be made on a case-by-case basis. For example, when an individual stockholder who is also an employee of the corporation loans money to the corporation, is the loan a business or nonbusiness debt? Because an employee is considered to be engaged in the business of working for a corporation, a loan made to the corporation in an attempt to protect the employment relationship may be held to be a business debt. However, if the individual's dominant motive is to protect his or her stock investment, the loan is a nonbusiness debt.[54]

EXAMPLE I8-35 ▶ Lisa is an individual engaged in the advertising business. If clients occasionally need additional funds to meet their cash-flow obligations, Lisa sometimes lends them money. Lisa's dominant motive for making the loans is to retain the clients. She has no ownership interests in these clients. Under these facts, if any of these loans becomes worthless, it would be considered a business bad debt.[55] ◀

KEY POINT

The nonbusiness bad debt of an individual is treated as a short-term capital loss regardless of how long the debt was outstanding.

TAX TREATMENT. Individuals deduct nonbusiness debts that become wholly worthless during the year as short-term capital losses. The length of time the debt is outstanding has no bearing on this treatment.

Individuals generally prefer an ordinary deduction over a short-term capital loss because the tax deduction attributable to net capital losses is limited to $3,000 each year. Any loss in excess of this limit is carried over to subsequent years to be included in the capital gain and loss netting process in those years (see Chapter I5).

EXAMPLE I8-36 ▶ During 2000, Kim loaned her friend $10,000. The friend used the funds to invest in commodities futures. The transaction had all the characteristics of a bona fide debt rather than a mere gift to a friend. Unfortunately, the commodities market prices declined, and Kim's friend incurred substantial losses. In 2001, Kim's friend declared personal bankruptcy and Kim was unable to collect any of the loan. Kim did not recognize any other capital gains or losses during 2001. The $10,000 bad debt loss recognized in 2001 is treated as a short-term capital loss. Thus, Kim may deduct only $3,000 in 2001. The remaining $7,000 is carried over indefinitely to 2002 and subsequent years. ◀

TYPICAL MISCONCEPTION

Partial worthlessness means that a debt is still partially recoverable. The term is sometimes erroneously applied to debt where there has been a partial recovery even though there is no prospect for further recovery.

PARTIAL WORTHLESSNESS. As previously noted, taxpayers may not deduct a partially worthless nonbusiness debt. Thus, no deduction is allowed for a nonbusiness debt that is still partially recoverable during the year.

EXAMPLE I8-37 ▶ Gordon, an individual, made a $5,000, five-year interest-bearing loan to a small company in 1999. Gordon was not in the trade or business of making commercial loans. In 2001, Gordon received word from the attorney who was appointed trustee of the company that bankruptcy proceedings had been filed. The trustee indicated that although final disposition of the case

---

[53] Reg. Sec. 1.166-5(b)(2).
[54] *John M. Trent v. CIR*, 7 AFTR 2d 1599, 61-2 USTC ¶9506 (2nd Cir., 1961). See also *Charles L. Hutchinson*, 1982 PH T.C. Memo ¶82,045, 43 TCM 440 and *U.S. v. Edna Generes*, 29 AFTR 2d 72-609, 72-1 USTC ¶9259 (USSC, 1972).
[55] *Stuart Bart*, 21 T.C. 880 (1954), *acq.* 1954-1 C.B. 3.

will not occur until 2002, Gordon can reasonably expect to receive only 20 cents for every $1 invested. Because this is a nonbusiness bad debt that is still partly recoverable in 2001, Gordon may not deduct the partial loss as a short-term capital loss in 2001. ◀

BUSINESS BAD DEBTS

The tax treatment of losses from business bad debts differs substantially from the treatment of nonbusiness bad debts. As previously discussed, a business bad debt provides an ordinary loss deduction. Furthermore, taxpayers may also deduct a business debt that has become only partially worthless during the year.

▶ **EXAMPLE I8-38** ▶ Assume the same facts as in Example I8-37 except that Gordon's loan is made for business reasons (e.g., to provide assistance to a customer in financial difficulty). Because 80% of the loan is reasonably expected to be unrecoverable during 2001, Gordon may deduct $4,000 (0.80 × $5,000) as an ordinary loss in 2001. In 2002, when Gordon receives the $500 settlement, he may deduct an additional $500 of ordinary loss. ◀

ACCOUNTING FOR THE BUSINESS BAD DEBT

BOOK-TAX DIFFERENCES

In general, for tax purposes, only the specific write-off method of accounting for bad debts can now be used. However, a corporation or other taxpayer would probably be required to use the reserve method for financial reporting purposes. This book-tax difference is one of the most common so-called M-1 adjustments in filing a Form 1120 for corporate taxpayers.

In general, two basic methods are available to account for business bad debts: the specific write-off method and the reserve method. Except for certain specialized industries, however, only the specific write-off method may be used for tax purposes. Under the specific write-off method, the taxpayer deducts each bad debt individually as it becomes worthless and is written off as an expense. Taxpayers use this method for (1) business bad debts that are either totally or partially worthless and (2) nonbusiness bad debts that are totally worthless. However, as previously noted, no deduction is available for partially worthless nonbusiness bad debts.

In the case of a partially worthless business bad debt, taxpayers may only deduct the worthless part of the debt. The taxpayer must prove to the satisfaction of the IRS the amount of the debt that has become worthless.

RECOVERY OF BAD DEBTS

A taxpayer may collect a debt that was previously written off for tax purposes. Since the taxpayer previously deducted the uncollectible debt, the taxpayer must report the recovery as income in the year it is collected. The amount of the income that must be reported depends on the tax benefit rule discussed in Chapter I4.

DEPOSITS IN INSOLVENT FINANCIAL INSTITUTIONS

KEY POINT

If the loss is treated as a casualty loss, it is subject to a $100 floor, and total net casualty losses for the year are deductible only to the extent that they exceed 10% of AGI.

At their election, qualified individuals may treat losses on deposits in qualified bankrupt or insolvent financial institutions as a personal casualty loss in the year in which the loss can be reasonably estimated. The recognized loss is the difference between the taxpayer's basis in the deposit and a reasonable estimate of the amount that the taxpayer will receive. This treatment allows the individual an ordinary loss deduction, but subjects the loss to the personal casualty loss limitations. In lieu of this election, qualified individuals may elect to treat these losses as if they were incurred in a transaction entered into for profit (but not connected with a trade or business). This election is available only with respect to deposits that are not insured under federal law, and is limited to $20,000 ($10,000 if married and filing separately) per institution per year. This limitation is reduced by any insurance proceeds expected to be received under state law. This election also allows the individual an ordinary loss deduction but subjects the loss to the $20,000 limitation as well as the 2% of AGI floor on miscellaneous itemized deductions. If neither of these elections is made, the taxpayer may claim the loss as a nonbusiness bad debt (a capital loss) in the year of worthlessness or partial recovery, whichever comes last.

A qualified individual is any individual *except* one who

▶ Owns at least 1% of the outstanding stock of the financial institution

▶ Is an officer of the financial institution

- Is a relative of an officer or a 1% owner of the financial institution[56]

Qualified financial institutions include banks, federal or state chartered savings and loans and thrift institutions, and federal or state insured credit unions.

This election applies to all losses sustained by the individual in the same institution and cannot be revoked unless the taxpayer receives IRS permission.[57]

The treatment of business and nonbusiness bad debts is summarized in Topic Review I8-4.

STOP & THINK

Question: Jim had $100,000 in deposits in a savings account at a bank in Page, Arizona. The bank collapsed and Jim did not receive anything for his deposits. The bank was chartered by the state of Arizona and was not insured by federal law. Jim is not sure what his options are in deducting this loss on his tax return. What can Jim do to take advantage of this loss on his tax return? He has an AGI of $110,000 and no capital gains for the current year.

Solution: Jim can treat the loss in one of three different ways: (1) as a casualty loss, (2) as a loss incurred in a transaction entered into for profit (but not a business loss), or (3) as a nonbusiness bad debt. If Jim elects to treat the loss as a casualty, the loss will be reduced by $100 and 10% of AGI (.1 × $110,000 = $11,000). Thus, he would be allowed an itemized deduction of $88,900 ($100,000 − $11,100). Second, if he elects to treat the loss as a loss incurred in a transaction entered into for profit, he would be allowed a $20,000 itemized deduction, reduced by 2% of AGI, or $2,200. Thus, his total deduction would be $17,800. Third, if neither of the above elections is made, Jim may claim the loss as a nonbusiness bad debt which would be limited to an ordinary deduction of $3,000 since he has no other capital gains or losses in the current year. In this case Jim should elect to treat the loss as a casualty loss. In other situations where Jim reports large short-term capital gains, the third option may be more beneficial since the loss is treated as a short-term capital loss which can offset (without reduction) the other short-term capital gains.

NET OPERATING LOSSES

OBJECTIVE 8
Compute a net operating loss deduction

A **net operating loss** (NOL) under Sec. 172 generally involves only business income and expenses and occurs when taxable income for any year is negative because business expenses exceed business income. A deduction for the NOL arises when a taxpayer carries the NOL to a year in which the taxpayer has taxable income. Thus, an NOL for one year becomes a deduction against taxable income of another year. This is accomplished in one of two ways:

- The year's NOL is carried back and deducted from the income of a previous year. This procedure provides for a refund of some of the taxes previously paid for the prior year.
- The year's NOL is carried forward and deducted from the income of a subsequent year. This procedure provides a reduction in the taxable income of the subsequent year, thus reducing the tax liability associated with that year.

The NOL deduction is intended to mitigate the inequity caused by the interaction of the progressive rate structure and the requirement to report income on an annual basis. This inequity arises between taxpayers whose business income fluctuates widely from year to year and those whose business income remains relatively constant.

KEY POINT
If taxpayers were not entitled to a deduction for net operating losses, taxpayers would actually pay a tax on an amount that exceeded their economic income over a period of time. The NOL deduction permits taxpayers to offset taxable income with losses incurred in other years.

EXAMPLE I8-39 ▶

Julie and Ken are both married (not to each other) and both file a joint return with their respective spouses. Over a two-year period they both report a total of $140,000 in taxable income. However, Julie and her husband report $70,000 of taxable income each year; Ken and his wife report $200,000 of taxable income in the first year and a $60,000 loss in the second year. Without the NOL provisions, Julie would report a $27,448 ($13,724 + $13,724) total tax

---

[56] Sec. 165(l). A *relative* is defined as a sibling, spouse, aunt, uncle, nephew, niece, ancestor, or lineal descendant.

[57] The rules dealing with this special election are found in Notice 89-28, (1989-1 C.B. 667).

Topic Review I8-4

Bad Debts

TYPE OF DEBT	RESULTS
Nonbusiness	Deductible as a short-term capital loss.
	Deductible only when the debt is totally worthless.
	The taxpayer must have basis in the debt.
Business	Deductible as an ordinary loss.
	Except for certain specialized exceptions, the specific write-off method must be used. The reserve method is not available.
	May deduct partial worthlessness.
	Must have basis in the debt.

liability for the two years, whereas Ken would report a total tax liability of $54,524 (taxable income of $200,000).[58] However, Ken can carryback the $60,000 loss to recover a portion of the taxes paid on the $200,000 in the prior year. Based on 2001 rates, Ken would recover $20,277 of the $54,524 paid, resulting in a net tax liability for both years of $34,247 ($54,524 − $20,277). Although the total tax liability over the two years for the two couples is still unequal, the ability to carryover NOL's provides some degree of fairness. ◀

COMPUTING THE NET OPERATING LOSS

The starting point in calculating an individual's NOL is generally taxable income. As mentioned earlier in this chapter, individuals may deduct three basic types of expenses to arrive at the amount of taxable income: business-related expenses, investment-related expenses, and certain personal expenses. The NOL, however, generally attempts to measure only the economic loss that occurs when business expenses exceed business income. Thus, taxpayers must make several adjustments to taxable income to arrive at the amount of the NOL for any particular year.[59] These include adjustments for an NOL deduction, a capital loss deduction, the deduction for personal exemptions, and the excess of nonbusiness deductions over nonbusiness income.

ADDITIONAL COMMENT
If taxpayers were permitted to calculate the NOL for the current year by including NOL carryovers from earlier years, it would be possible to extend the carryover period beyond the statutorily established 20-year carryforward period.

ADD BACK ANY NOL DEDUCTION. Under certain circumstances, a taxpayer might have taken a deduction for an NOL arising from another tax year in computing the taxable loss for the current loss year. To allow this deduction to create or increase the NOL of the current loss year would provide an unwarranted benefit. Thus, taxable income for the current loss year must be increased for this deduction.

ADD BACK ANY CAPITAL LOSS DEDUCTION. To compute taxable income, individuals may deduct up to a maximum of $3,000 capital losses in excess of capital gains in any year. Any capital loss in excess of this limit can be carried over and deducted in a subsequent tax year, subject to the same limitation. Because capital losses have their separate carryover provisions, taxpayers must add back any deduction associated with these losses to taxable income to arrive at the NOL for the current loss year. To make this adjustment, several steps must be followed:

Step 1: A taxpayer must separate nonbusiness capital gains and losses from business capital gains and losses. The nonbusiness gains and losses are then netted, while the business gains and losses are netted separately.

Step 2: If the nonbusiness capital gains exceed the nonbusiness capital losses, the excess, along with other types of nonbusiness income, is first used to offset any nonbusiness ordinary deductions. Any nonbusiness capital gain remaining is then used to offset any business capital loss in excess of the business capital gain for the year.[60]

---

[58] Using the 2001 tax rate schedules.
[59] In the case of a corporation, these adjustments are minor.
[60] Reg. Sec. 1.172-3. If the nonbusiness deductions exceed the nonbusiness income, the excess is added back. This adjustment is discussed later in the chapter.

Step 3: If both groups of transactions result in net losses, the capital loss deduction provided by these transactions must be added back. For purposes of the NOL, no deduction is allowed for either business or nonbusiness net capital losses.

Step 4: If the taxpayer's nonbusiness capital losses exceed the nonbusiness capital gains, the losses may not be offset against the taxpayer's excess business capital gains. Allowing this offset would provide an indirect deduction for a nonbusiness economic loss.[61]

> **EXAMPLE I8-40** ▶ During the current year, Nils recognizes a short-term capital loss of $10,000 on the sale of an investment capital asset. He also recognizes a $5,000 long-term capital gain on the sale of a business capital asset. For taxable income purposes, the loss is netted against the gain, leaving a $5,000 net short-term capital loss. This loss provides a $3,000 deduction from taxable income, with the remaining $2,000 being carried forward to the following year. To compute the NOL, however, none of the $10,000 nonbusiness capital loss is deductible. Thus, the $3,000 deduction as well as the $5,000 loss that offset the business capital gain must be added back. ◀

ADD BACK THE DEDUCTION FOR PERSONAL EXEMPTIONS. Because the deduction for personal and dependency exemptions is strictly a personal deduction, it must be added back to arrive at the year's NOL.

ADDITIONAL COMMENT
An excess of nonbusiness deductions over nonbusiness income cannot increase the NOL. However, an excess of nonbusiness income over nonbusiness expenses can reduce the NOL.

ADD BACK EXCESS OF NONBUSINESS DEDUCTIONS OVER NONBUSINESS INCOME. Because nonbusiness deductions do not reflect an economic loss from business, they are not deductible in arriving at the NOL. However, these deductions do offset any nonbusiness income reported during the year. Nonbusiness income includes sources of income such as dividends and interest, as well as nonbusiness capital gains in excess of nonbusiness capital losses. Wages and salary, even if they are earned in part-time employment, are considered business income. Nonbusiness deductions include itemized deductions such as charitable contributions, medical expenses, and nonbusiness interest and taxes. Casualty losses on personal-use assets, however, are treated as business losses and are excluded from this adjustment.[62] If a taxpayer does not have itemized deductions in excess of the standard deduction, the standard deduction is used as the amount of the nonbusiness deductions.

Following are several independent examples demonstrating these required adjustments. In each case, assume that Nancy is a single taxpayer.

> **EXAMPLE I8-41** ▶ During 2001, Nancy, who is single, reports the following taxable income:

Gross income from business		$123,000	
Minus: Business expenses		(147,000)	($24,000)
Plus: Interest income			700
Dividend income			400
AGI			($22,900)
Minus: Greater of itemized deductions or standard deduction:			
Interest expense		$6,000	
Taxes		4,000	
Casualty loss (reduced by the $100 floor)		1,000	
Total itemized deductions		$11,000	
		or	
Standard deduction		4,550	(11,000)
Minus: Personal exemption			(2,900)
Taxable income			($36,800)

---

[61] Sec. 172(d)(2). Note that all deductible nonbusiness capital losses involve investment property because capital losses on personal-use assets are not deductible in arriving at taxable income. To make the adjustment for any capital loss, the exclusion under Sec. 1202 for gains from small business stock is not allowed (see Chapter I5).
[62] Sec. 172(d)(4)(C).

Nancy's NOL for the year is computed as follows:

Taxable income			($36,800)
Nonbusiness deductions:			
Itemized deductions	$11,000		
Minus: Casualty loss	(1,000)	$10,000	
Minus: Nonbusiness income:			
Interest	$700		
Dividends	400	(1,100)	
Plus: Excess of nonbusiness deductions over nonbusiness income			8,900
Plus: Personal exemption			2,900
Net operating loss			($25,000)[a]

[a] Note that the NOL equals the total of the $24,000 net business loss and the $1,000 casualty loss.

EXAMPLE I8-42 ▶ During 2001, Nancy, who is single, reports the following taxable income:

Gross income from business		$123,000	
Minus: Business expenses		(147,000)	($24,000)
Plus: Interest income			700
Dividend income			400
AGI			($22,900)
Minus: Greater of itemized deductions or standard deduction:			
Interest expense		$ 2,000	
		or	
Standard deduction		4,550	(4,550)
Minus: Personal exemption			(2,900)
Taxable income			($30,350)

Nancy's NOL for the year is computed as follows:

Taxable income			($30,350)
Nonbusiness deductions:			
Standard deduction		$4,550	
Minus: Nonbusiness income:			
Interest	$700		
Dividends	400	(1,100)	
Plus: Excess of nonbusiness deductions over nonbusiness income			3,450
Plus: Personal exemption			2,900
Net operating loss			($24,000)[a]

[a] Note that the NOL equals the net business loss for the year.

EXAMPLE I8-43 ▶ During 2001, Nancy, who is single, reports the following taxable income:

Gross income from business		$123,000	
Minus Business expenses		(147,000)	($24,000)
Plus: Interest income			700
Dividend income			400
Salary			6,000
Nonbusiness LTCG			10,000
AGI			($6,900)
Minus: Greater of itemized deductions or standard deduction:			
Interest expense		$ 6,000	
Taxes		4,000	
Casualty (reduced by the $100 floor)		1,000	
Total itemized deductions		$11,000	
		or	
Standard deduction		4,550	(11,000)
Minus: Personal exemption			(2,900)
Taxable income			($20,800)

Nancy's NOL for the year is computed as follows:

Taxable income			($20,800)
Plus: Nonbusiness deductions:			
Itemized deductions	$11,000		
Minus: Casualty loss	(1,000)	$10,000	
Minus: Nonbusiness income:			
Interest	$700		
Dividends	400		
LTCG	10,000	(11,100)	
Excess of nonbusiness deductions over nonbusiness income			0
Plus: Personal exemption			2,900
Net operating loss			($17,900)a

aNote that the NOL can also be calculated as follows:

Loss from business	($24,000)
Salary	6,000
Casualty loss	(1,000)
Excess of nonbusiness income ($11,100) over nonbusiness deductions ($10,000)	1,100
NOL	($17,900)

CARRYBACK AND CARRYOVER PERIODS

Under Sec. 172, an NOL is initially carried back for two years and is deductible as an offset to the taxable income of the carryback years. Except as noted below, taxpayers must carry the loss back first. If any loss remains, taxpayers may then carry it forward for a period of 20 years.[63] Furthermore, in both the carryback and carryforward periods, the loss must be deducted from the years in chronological order. Thus, if an NOL is sustained in 2001, it first must be carried to 1999, then to 2000, followed by 2002, 2003, and so on until the loss is completely used. Any NOL that is not used during the carryover period expires and is of no further tax benefit.

If the NOL is carried back to a prior year, the taxpayer must file for a refund of taxes previously paid. If the NOL deduction is carried forward, it reduces the taxable income and the tax liability for the carryover year.

> **ADDITIONAL COMMENT**
> An election to forgo the carryback period for the NOL of any year is irrevocable.

ELECTION TO FORGO CARRYBACK PERIOD. A taxpayer may elect not to carryback the NOL and to carry the loss forward. This election, which is made with respect to the entire carryback period, does not extend the carryforward period beyond 20 years. This allows a taxpayer some degree of flexibility in using the NOL deduction to the greatest advantage. (See the Tax Planning Considerations section in this chapter for a discussion of this topic.)

LOSS CARRYOVERS FROM TWO OR MORE YEARS. At times, a taxpayer might have NOL carryovers that are incurred in two or more taxable years. Often these losses are carried to the same years in the carryover period. If such is the case, the loss of the earliest year is always completely used first before deducting any of the loss incurred in a subsequent year. Because of the limited carryover period, this rule is beneficial to the taxpayer.

RECOMPUTATION OF TAXABLE INCOME IN THE CARRYOVER YEAR

When the NOL deduction is carried back to a prior year, that year's taxable income must be recomputed. Because the NOL is attributable to a taxpayer's trade or business, it is deductible *for* AGI. As a result, the recomputation of taxable income for the carryback year may affect the deductible amount of certain itemized deductions because some of the deductions (e.g., the deductions for medical expenses, charitable contributions, and casu-

---

[63] For NOLs arising in a farming businss, in a qualified small business attributable to a Presidentially declared disaster, or in a casualty or theft sustained by an individual, the carry back period is extended to three years. These NOLs are taken after the regular NOL. Certain "specified liability losses" are entitled to a 10-year carryback. Sec. 172(b)(1)(C) and (f).

alty losses) are limited or measured by reference to the taxpayer's AGI. All of these deductions except the deduction for charitable contributions must be recomputed using the reduced AGI amount.[64]

Once the tax refund for the carryback year is determined, the amount of the NOL available to be deducted in subsequent carryover years must be calculated. This is done by adjusting the recomputed income of the prior carryover year. Although certain differences exist, these adjustments are similar to those mentioned above.

The rules for computing and deducting NOLs are presented in Topic Review I8-5.

TAX PLANNING CONSIDERATIONS

BAD DEBTS

> **KEY POINT**
> If there is uncertainty as to the year in which a debt became worthless, it is possible that the issue will not be settled within the normal three-year statute of limitations. For this reason, a taxpayer may claim a deduction for a worthless debt at any time within seven years.

In order to deduct a bad debt, a taxpayer must show that the debt is worthless. At times the IRS might assert that the debt being written off is either not yet worthless or that it became worthless in a previous year. If the taxpayer is unable to overcome the IRS's assertion concerning the year of worthlessness, the taxpayer might be barred from filing an amended return for the prior year because of the statute of limitations.[65] Thus, taxpayers should carefully document all efforts at collection and other facts that show the debt is worthless.

As previously mentioned, a third-party guarantor of a loan who is required to repay the debt may, under certain circumstances, be entitled to a bad debt deduction. The guarantor must demonstrate that he or she received reasonable consideration in the form of cash or property in exchange for guaranteeing the debt. If proper consideration is not received, the guarantee and subsequent payment of the loan by the guarantor is considered to be a gift rather than a loan. Reasonable consideration is also deemed to have been received if the taxpayer enters into the agreement for a good faith business purpose or in accordance with normal business practice. However, if the taxpayer guarantees the debt of a spouse or a relative, the consideration must be received in the form of cash or property.

In the case of an outright loan between related taxpayers, the lender should always make sure to retain proper documentation to substantiate the fact that the transaction is a loan. If the taxpayer does not keep such documentation, the IRS may assert that the transaction is a gift.

CASUALTIES

A deduction is allowed for stolen property, but no deduction is allowed for lost property. Thus, taxpayers should always carefully document losses of property through theft (e.g., the filing of police reports or claims with the taxpayer's insurance company). In addition, pictures and written appraisals may be helpful to prove the amount of the loss.

NET OPERATING LOSSES

> **ADDITIONAL COMMENT**
> Normally, a taxpayer would want to carry back the NOL because he or she will receive a refund in a short time period from the filing of the amended return. The carryover of the NOL involves waiting for a year or more to receive a tax benefit.

If a net operating loss is incurred, the taxpayer should carefully analyze whether to elect to forgo the carryback period. Situations under which a taxpayer might elect to only carry the loss deduction forward include the following:

▶ A taxpayer might anticipate being in a higher marginal tax rate in future years than in the carryback years. If such is the case, the value of the deduction is higher in the carryforward years than in the carryback years. Taxpayers should consider, however, cash flows and the time value of money (e.g., the tax benefits from a refund of taxes are immediately available only if the NOL is carried back).

---

[64] Reg. Sec. 1.172-5(a)(3)(ii).

[65] However, the statute of limitations for claims for a refund or credit because of a bad debt is extended from three years to seven years under Sec. 6511(d)(1), thus giving the taxpayer additional time if this is the case.

Topic Review I8-5

Net Operating Losses

ITEM	RULES
Computation of NOL (adjustments to taxable income)	Add back any NOL deduction carried to the current year. Add back any capital loss deduction. Add back the deduction for personal and dependency exemptions. Add back the excess of nonbusiness deductions over nonbusiness income. For this purpose, casualty losses on personal-use property are treated as business losses.
Carryover period	May be carried back two years and forward twenty years. (certain exceptions apply) Must be carried to the carryover years in chronological order: first carried back to the second prior year, then to the first prior year, then to the first succeeding year, etc. An election may be made to forgo the carryback. This does not extend the carryforward period. If losses from two or more years are carried to the same year, the losses from the earliest year are completely used first.

▶ General business and other tax credits that are nonrefundable (i.e., the credits are limited to the tax liability or some percentage thereof) may be reduced or eliminated for the carryback years because these credits must be recomputed based on the adjusted tax liability after applying the NOL carryback. (See Chaper 14 for a discussion of tax credits.)

COMPLIANCE AND PROCEDURAL CONSIDERATIONS

ADDITIONAL COMMENT

Instant access for downloading Federal income tax forms, instructions, publications, etc. is available on the World Wide Web (http://www.irs.ustreas.gov).

CASUALTY LOSSES

If a taxpayer sustains a casualty loss in a location that the President of the United States declares a disaster area, he or she may make an election to deduct the loss in the year preceeding the year in which the loss occurred. A taxpayer makes this election by either filing the return for the previous year and including the loss in that year (if the return has not already been filed) or filing an amended return or claim for refund for that year.[66] The return should clearly include all the following information:

▶ That the election is being made
▶ The date of the disaster giving rise to the loss
▶ The city, county, and state in which the damaged property is located

The taxpayer must make the election before the due date of the return for the year in which the disaster actually occurs. Although the Regulations state that the election may not be revoked more than 90 days after it is made, the Tax Court has held that this part of the Regulation is invalid.[67]

NET OPERATING LOSSES

When a taxpayer carries an NOL deduction back to a prior year, the taxpayer claims a refund of taxes by either filing an amended return on Form 1040X or filing for a quick refund on Form 1045. Corporations use Form 1139. If Form 1045 is used, the IRS must act on the application for refund within 90 days of the later of the date of the application and the last day of the month in which the return of the loss year must be filed.[68] Form

---

[66] Reg. Sec. 1.165-11(e).
[67] *Chester Matheson*, 74 T.C. 836 (1980), *acq.* 1981-2 C.B. 2.
[68] IRS, *Instructions for Filing Form 1045*, Revised, 2000.

1045 must be filed within a year after the end of the year in which the NOL arose. Additional information such as pages 1 and 2 of Form 1040 for the year of loss, a copy of the application for an extension of time to file the return for the year of loss, and copies of forms or schedules for items refigured in the carryback years must be attached.

WORTHLESS SECURITIES

As explained earlier in this chapter, securities that become worthless during the taxable year are deemed to have become worthless on the last day of the year. In many cases, this treatment causes the loss to be treated as a long-term capital loss. If the loss from the worthless security is long term, the taxpayer reports it in Part II of Schedule D (Form 1040) along with the other long-term gains and losses for the year. The taxpayer reports short-term capital losses in Part I of Schedule D.

WHAT WOULD YOU DO IN THIS SITUATION?

A client comes to you with an idea to treat a loan that he made to one of his children two years ago as a bad debt. The loan is evidenced by a properly executed note with stated interest and payment dates. However, the client has not collected any loan payments or interest during the two-year period. The child is insolvent and has declared bankruptcy. Before leaving your office, the client also mentions in passing that the child is in London on vacation with other members of the family and will stay in Europe for six weeks. What would you do about classifying this loan as a bad debt?

PROBLEM MATERIALS

DISCUSSION QUESTIONS

I8-1 What is the closed transaction doctrine, and why does it exist for purposes of recognizing a loss realized on holding property?

I8-2 When property is disposed of, what factors influence the amount of the deductible loss?

I8-3 Describe the usual tax consequences that apply to a worthless security.

I8-4 Under what circumstances will a loss that is realized on a worthless security not be treated as a capital loss?

I8-5 What two general requirements must be met for a transaction to result in a capital loss?

I8-6 What requirements must be met for stock to be considered Sec. 1244 stock?

I8-7 What tax treatment applies to gains and losses on Sec. 1244 stock?

I8-8 Describe a situation where a loss on the sale of business or investment property is not currently deductible, and explain why.

I8-9 a. What is a passive activity?
b. Who is subject to the passive loss limitation rules?

I8-10 a. For purposes of the passive loss rules, what is a closely held C corporation?
b. In what way do the passive loss rules differ from the regular passive loss rules when applied to closely held C corporations?

I8-11 Why is it important to identify exactly what constitutes an activity for purposes of the passive activity rules?

I8-12 a. If a taxpayer is involved in several different business operations during the year, how is the determination made as to how many activities these operations constitute for purposes of the passive activity loss rules?
b. Can a business operation and a rental operation ever be combined into one activity? Explain.

I8-13 Which of the following activities are considered passive for the year? Explain. Consider each situation independently.
a. Laura owns a rental unit that she rents out to students. The rental unit is Laura's only business and she spends approximately 875 hours per year managing, collecting the rent, advertising, and performing minor repairs. At times

she must hire professionals such as plumbers to do the maintenance. Is the rental unit a passive activity with respect to Laura?

b. Kami is a medical doctor who works four days a week in a medical practice that she and five other doctors formed. Last year she and her partners formed another partnership that owns and operates a medical lab. The lab employs ten technicians, one of whom also acts as manager. During the year Kami spent 120 hours in meetings, reviewing records, etc., for the lab. Is the lab a passive activity with respect to Kami?

c. Assume the same facts in part b. In addition, assume that the same group of doctors have formed two other partnerships. One is a medical supply partnership. Kami spent 150 hours working for this partnership. The medical supply partnership has five full-time employees. Kami also spent 250 hours during the year working for the other partnership. This partnership specializes in providing medical services to individuals from out of town who are staying at local hotels and motels. This partnership hires two full-time and six part-time nurses. Are the lab and the two other partnerships passive activities with respect to Kami?

I8-14 Explain the difference between materially participating and actively participating in an activity. When is the active participation test used?

I8-15 a. What requirements must be met in order for a taxpayer to deduct up to $25,000 of passive losses from rental real estate activities against active and portfolio income?
b. What requirements must be met in order for a real estate rental activity to be considered a real estate business that is not subject to the passive loss rules?

I8-16 Are the suspended losses under the passive loss rules lost forever? Explain.

I8-17 What tests must be met to qualify a loss as deductible under the casualty loss provisions? Discuss the application of each of these tests.

I8-18 Explain how a taxable gain on property can be realized because of a casualty event such as a fire or theft. How are these gains treated?

I8-19 During the current year, Rulon's toilet overflowed because of a mechanical problem. Rulon was outside playing croquet, and by the time he returned inside, the water had flooded the basement, causing damage to the carpet, walls, and ceiling. The cost of repairing the damage was $9,000. Rulon has homeowners insurance that will cover half of the damage. However, because he has already had claims this year, Rulon does not want to report the incident to his insurance company for fear of a large increase in insurance rates. Instead, Rulon wants to deduct the loss as a casualty loss on his tax return. His AGI for this year is $50,000, and he has other itemized deductions of $6,000. Rulon is widowed. What amount of the casualty loss may he deduct?

I8-20 Compare and contrast the computational rules for deducting casualty losses on personal-use property with casualty losses incurred on business or investment property.

I8-21 Under what circumstances may a loss arising from a casualty or theft be deducted in a year other than the year in which the loss occurs?

I8-22 For individuals, how are casualty losses on personal-use property reported on the tax return? How are casualty losses on business property reported?

I8-23 Is the $100 floor on personal-use casualty losses imposed on each individual loss item if more than one item of property is destroyed in a single casualty? Is the floor imposed before or after the casualty gains are netted against the casualty losses?

I8-24 Steve loans $50,000 to his best friend, John. John uses the money to open a pizza parlor next to the local high school. Three years later, when John still owed Steve $15,000, John closed the pizza parlor and declared bankruptcy. Discuss the appropriate tax treatment for Steve.

I8-25 Dana is an attorney who specializes in family law. She uses the cash method of accounting and is a calendar-year taxpayer. During the current year, she represented a client in a lawsuit and billed the client $5,000 for her services. Although she made repeated attempts during the current and subsequent year, Dana was unable to collect the outstanding receivable. Finally in November of the subsequent year she found out that the individual has moved without leaving any forwarding address. Dana's attempts to locate the individual were futile. What is the amount of deduction that Dana may take with respect to this bad debt?

I8-26 Under what circumstances may a taxpayer deduct a bad debt even though another party to the transaction is the creditor?

I8-27 What is the definition of a nonbusiness debt? What is the character of the deduction for a nonbusiness bad debt?

I8-28 a. What alternatives do individuals have in deducting a loss on a deposit in a qualifed financial institution?
b. Explain when it might be better to elect one over the other.

I8-29 A taxpayer collects a debt that was previously written off as a bad debt. What tax consequences arise if the recovery is received in a subsequent tax year?

I8-30 What is an NOL deduction, and why is it allowed?

I8-31 List the adjustments to an individual taxpayer's negative taxable income amount that must be made in computing an NOL for the year. What is the underlying rationale for requiring these adjustments for individuals?

I8-32 a. What is the NOL carryback and carryover period?
b. Does a taxpayer have any choice in deciding the years to which the NOL should be carried?
c. Explain the circumstances under which a taxpayer might elect not to use the regular carryback or carryover period.

I8-33 Can a casualty loss on a personal-use asset create or increase an NOL? Explain.

I8-34 If an NOL is carried back to a prior year, what adjustments must be made to the prior year's taxable income? What are the possible results of the adjustments?

ISSUE IDENTIFICATION QUESTIONS

I8-35 On January 12 of the current year, Barney Corporation, a publicly-held corporation, files bankruptcy. During the bankruptcy proceedings it is determined that creditors will only receive 10% of what they are owed and that the shareholders will receive nothing. Sheryl, a calendar-year taxpayer, purchased 1,000 shares of Barney Corporation common stock for $7,000 on February 22 of the prior year. What tax issues should Sheryl consider?

I8-36 Five years ago, Cora incorporated Gold, Inc., by contributing $80,000 and receiving 100% of the Gold common stock. Cora is single. Gold, Inc. experienced financial difficulties. On December 22 of the current year, Cora sold all of her Gold, Inc. stock for $5,000. What tax issues should Cora consider?

I8-37 In a rage because of personal difficulties, Evan drove recklessly and crashed his automobile doing $8,000 damage. Fortunately, no one was injured. Since Evan received two speeding tickets during the past year, he is concerned about losing his insurance if he files an insurance claim. What tax issues should Evan consider?

I8-38 Dan, a full-time employee of Beta, Inc., also owns 10% of its outstanding stock. The other 90% is owned by his three brothers. During the year, the president of Beta came to Dan, expressing grave concern about whether the company had the financial resources to remain in business. He mentioned specifically that a bank was threatening to force Beta to file bankruptcy if it didn't repay its $100,000 loan in full. After some negotiation, Dan agreed to loan Beta the $100,000 for one year until permanent financing could be obtained. A reasonable interest rate was set and a payment schedule was documented. Unfortunately, business did not improve, Beta discontinued its business and did not repay the loan. What tax issues should Dan consider?

PROBLEMS

I8-39 *Sec. 1244 Losses.* During the current year Sally sells her entire interest in Central Corporation common stock for $10,000. She is the sole shareholder, and originally organized the corporation several years ago by contributing $80,000 in exchange for her stock, which qualifies as Sec. 1244 stock. Since its incorporation, Central has been involved in the manufacture of items that protect personal computers from static electricity. Unfortunately, this market is extremely competitive, and Central Corporation incurs substantial losses throughout its existence.
a. Assuming Sally is single, what are the amount and the character of the loss recognized on the sale of the Central Corporation stock?
b. Assuming Sally is married and files a joint return, what are the amount and the character of the loss recognized on the sale of the Central Corporation stock?
c. How would your answer to Part a change if Sally had originally purchased the stock from another shareholder rather than organizing the corporation?
d. How might Sally have structured the transaction in Part a to receive a greater tax advantage?

I8-40 *Amount and Character of Loss Transactions.* On February 2 of the current year, Madison Corporation files for bankruptcy. At the time, it estimates that the total FMV of its assets is $800,000, whereas the total amount of its outstanding debt amounts to $1,000,000. Madison has been engaged for several years in a gold mining operation in Montana.
a. At the time of the bankruptcy Madison is owned 100% by Barry, who purchased the stock from an investor for $300,000 several years ago. Barry is married and files a joint return. What are the amount and character of the loss sustained by Barry upon Madison's bankruptcy?

b. How would your answer to Part a change if Barry originally organized Madison Corporation capitalizing it with $300,000? Madison Corporation qualifies as a small business corporation.
c. How would your answer to Part a change if Barry were a corporation instead of an individual?
d. How would your answer to Part b change if Barry were a corporation instead of an individual?

I8-41 *Character of Losses.* During the current year, Joe sold the following stocks:

Stock	Gain (Loss)	When Acquired
Acme	$6,000	5 years ago
Beta	(3,000)	3 years ago
Canary	25,000	8 years ago
Delta	(8,000)	8 months ago
Echo	2,000	3 months ago

In addition, on July 22, Joe received word that his Foxtrot, Inc. stock had gone bankrupt during the year and that Joe's entire $5,000 investment is lost. Joe purchased Foxtrot on January 14 of the prior year. All of the above corporations are large publicly-held companies. Joe asked his attorney to begin collection procedures on a $4,000 loan that was made to a friend two years ago, but the attorney informed Joe that the friend had skipped town and could not be found. Compute Joe's short-term and long-term capital gains and losses from the above transactions.

I8-42 *Passive Losses.* In the current year Alice reports $150,000 of salary income, $20,000 of income from activity X, and $35,000 and $15,000 losses from activities Y and Z, respectively. All three activities are passive with respect to Alice and are purchased during the current year. What is the amount of loss that may be deducted and that must be carried over with respect to each of these activities?

I8-43 *Passive Losses.* In the current year Clay reports income and losses from the following activities:

Activity X	$ 28,000
Activity Y	(10,000)
Activity Z	(20,000)
Salary	100,000

Activities X, Y, and Z are all passive with respect to Clay. Activity Z has $40,000 in passive losses which are carried over from the prior year. In the current year Clay sells activity Z for a taxable gain of $30,000.
a. What is the amount of loss that Clay may deduct and that must be carried over in the current year?
b. Based solely on the amounts above, compute Clay's AGI for the current year.

I8-44 *Passive Losses: Rental Real Estate.* During the current year, Irene, a married individual who files a joint return, reports the following items of income and loss:

Salary	$130,000
Activity X (passive)	10,000
Activity Y (nontrade or business rental real estate)	(30,000)
Activity Z (nontrade or business rental real estate)	(20,000)

Irene actively participates in activities Y and Z and owns 100% of both Y and Z.
a. What is Irene's AGI for the year?
b. What is the amount of losses that may be deducted and must be carried over with respect to each activity?

I8-45 *Passive Losses.* In 2000, Mark purchased two separate activities. Information regarding these activities for 2000 and 2001 is as follows:

| | 2000 | | | 2001 | |
Activity	Status	Income (Loss)	Activity	Status	Income (Loss)
A	Passive	($24,000)	A	Active	$10,000
B	Passive	(8,000)	B	Passive	20,000

The 2000 losses were suspended losses for that year. During 2001, Mark also reports salary income of $120,000 and interest and dividend income of $20,000. Compute the amount (if any) of losses attributable to activities A and B that are deductible in 2001 and any suspended losses carried to 2002.

I8-46 *Passive Losses.* During the current year, Juan has AGI of $125,000 before taking into account any passive activity losses. He also actively participates and owns 100% of activity A, which is a real estate rental activity. For the year, activity A generates a net loss of $6,000 and $3,000 in tax credits. Juan is in the 31% tax bracket. What is the amount of suspended loss and credit from activity A that must be carried to subsequent years?

I8-47 *Passive Losses.* In 2001, Julie, a single individual, reported the following items of income and deduction:

Salary	$126,000
Dividend income	14,000
Long-term capital gain from sales of stock	22,000
Short-term capital losses from sales of stock	(17,000)
Loss from a passive real estate activity	(20,000)
Interest expense on loan to purchase stock	(21,000)
Qualified residence interest on residence	(12,000)
Charitable contributions	(8,000)
Property taxes on residence	(5,000)
Tax return preparation fees	(2,500)
Unreimbursed employee business expenses	(2,000)

Julie owns 100% and is an active participant in the real estate activity. What is Julie's taxable income in 2001?

I8-48 *Casualty Losses.* Antonio, a mechanic, owns his own auto repair business. In the current year a fire starts in his garage, destroying the following property:

Asset	Adjusted Basis	FMV Before Casualty	FMV After Casualty	Insurance Recovery
A	$18,000	$15,000	—0—	$12,000
B	12,000	14,000	$6,000	7,000
C	18,000	11,000	2,000	1,000

Assets A and B are both machines that Antonio had used in his business for several years. Asset C is Antonio's personal automobile. Because of the fire, Antonio has to close the garage for 2 weeks. He estimates $10,000 lost in income while he is closed, none of which is compensated by insurance. Antonio's AGI for the year, not including the items mentioned above, is $40,000. What are the amount and character of Antonio's deduction as a result of the items noted above?

I8-49 *Theft Losses.* On December 17 of the current year, Kelly's business office safe is burglarized. The theft is discovered a few days after the burglary. $3,000 cash for the cash registers is stolen. A diamond necklace and a ring that Kelly frequently wore are also stolen. The necklace cost Kelly $2,300 many years ago and is insured for its $6,000 FMV. Kelly purchased the ring for $3,000 just two weeks before the burglary. Unfortunately, the ring and the cash are not insured. Kelly's AGI for the year, not including the items noted above, is $70,000.
a. What is Kelly's deductible theft loss in the current year?
b. What is Kelly's deductible theft loss in the current year if the theft is not discovered until January of the following year?

I8-50 *Casualty Losses: Year of Deduction.* Jerry sprayed all of the landscaping around his house with a pesticide in June 2001. Shortly thereafter, all of the trees and shrubs unaccountably died. The FMV and the adjusted basis of the plants were $15,000. Later that year, the pesticide manufacturer announced a recall of the particular batch of pesticide that Jerry used. It also announced a program whereby consumers would be repaid for any damage caused by the improper mixture. Jerry is single and reports $38,000 AGI in 2001 and $42,000 AGI in 2002.
a. Assume that in 2001 Jerry files a claim for his losses and receives notification that payment of $15,000 will be received in 2001. Jerry receives full payment for the damage in 2002. How should the loss and the reimbursement be reported?

b. How will your answer to Part a change if in 2002 the manufacturer files bankruptcy and Jerry receives $1,500 in total and final payment for his claim?

c. How will your answer to Part a change if the announcement and the reimbursement do not occur until late in 2002, after Jerry has already filed his tax return for 2001?

I8-51 *Personal-Use Casualty Losses.* In the current year Ned completely destroys his personal automobile (purchased two years earlier for $28,000) in a traffic accident. Fortunately none of the occupants are injured. The FMV of the car before the accident is $18,000; after the accident it is worthless. Ned receives a $14,000 settlement from the insurance company. Later in the same year his house is burglarized and several antiques are stolen. The antiques were purchased a number of years earlier for $8,000. Their value at the time of the theft is estimated at $12,000. They are not insured. Ned's AGI for the current year is $60,000. What is the amount of Ned's deductible casualty loss in the current year, assuming the thefts are discovered in the same year?

I8-52 *Casualty Losses.* During 2001, Pam incurred the following casualty losses:

Asset	FMV Before	FMV After	Basis	Insurance
Business 1	$18,000	$ 0	$15,000	$ 4,000
Business 2	25,000	10,000	8,000	3,000
Business 3	20,000	0	18,000	19,000
Personal 1	12,000	0	20,000	2,000
Personal 2	8,000	5,000	10,000	0
Personal 3	9,000	0	6,000	8,000

All of the items were destroyed in the same casualty. Before considering the casualty items, Pam reports business income of $80,000, qualified residential interest of $6,000 property taxes on her personal residence of $2,000, and charitable contributions of $4,000. Compute Pam's taxable income for 2001. Pam is single.

I8-53 *Business Bad Debt.* Elaine is a physician who uses the cash method of accounting for tax purposes. During the current year, Elaine bills Ralph $1,200 for office visits and outpatient surgery. Unfortunately, unknown to Elaine, Ralph moves away leaving no payment and no forwarding address. What is the amount of Elaine's bad debt deduction with respect to Ralph's debt?

I8-54 *Nonbusiness Bad Debt.* During 2000, Becky loans her brother Ken $5,000, which he intends to use to establish a small business. Because Ken has no other assets and needs cash to expand the business, the agreement provides that Ken will repay the debt if (and when) sufficient funds are generated from the business. No interest rate is agreed upon. The business is unsuccessful, and Ken is forced to file for bankruptcy in 2001. By the end of 2001, it is estimated that the creditors will receive only 20% of the amount owed. In 2002 the bankruptcy proceedings are closed, and the creditors receive 10% of the amount due on the debt. What is Becky's bad debt deduction for 2001? For 2002?

I8-55 *Bad Debt Deduction.* Assume the same facts as in Problem I8-54, except that Becky and Ken are not related and that under the terms of the loan Ken agrees to repay Becky the $5,000 plus interest (at a reasonable stated rate) over a five-year period. What is Becky's bad debt deduction for 2001? For 2002?

I8-56 *Net Operating Loss Deduction.* Jeff and Julie are married and file a joint income tax return. Jeff owns an unincorporated landscaping business; Julie is employed as a bank loan officer. They have no dependents. During 2001, they report the following items of income and expense:

Revenue from landscaping business	$ 60,000
Expenses of landscaping business	141,000
Julie's salary	45,000
Dividends	1,200
LTCG on stock	3,000
Interest on personal residence	6,000
Itemized deductions for state and local taxes	7,500

a. What is Jeff and Julie's taxable income or loss for 2001?
b. What is Jeff and Julie's NOL for 2001?

I8-57 *Net Operating Loss Deduction.* Assume the same facts as in Problem I8-56, except that in addition to the other itemized deductions Jeff and Julie suffer a $4,500 deductible casualty loss (after limitations).
  a. What is Jeff and Julie's taxable income or loss for 2001?
  b. What is Jeff and Julie's NOL for 2001?

I8-58 *Net Operating Loss Deduction.* Assume the same facts as in Problem I8-56, except that instead of $7,500 itemized deductions for state and local taxes, Jeff and Julie's itemized deductions consist of a $7,500 casualty loss (after limitations).
  a. What is Jeff and Julie's taxable income or loss for 2001?
  b. What is Jeff and Julie's NOL for 2001?

I8-59 During 2001, Kim, a single taxpayer, reports the following:

Revenue from business	$ 65,000
Expenses from business	105,000

Kim also worked part time during the year, earning a salary of $12,000. She reported dividends of $1,000 and interest of $500; but she had a long-term capital loss of $5,000 on the sale of some stock she had held for investment. Her itemized deductions total $3,000.
  a. What is Kim's taxable income for 2001?
  b. What is Kim's NOL for 2001?

TAX FORM/RETURN PREPARATION PROBLEMS

I8-60 Heather and Nikolay Laubert are married and file a joint income tax return. Their address is 3847 Jackdaw Path, Madison, WI 53493. Nikolay's social security number is 968-84-8532, and Heather's is 498-65-5432. Nikolay is a mechanical engineer, and Heather is a highly renowned speech therapist. She is self-employed. They report all their income and expenses on the cash method. For 2000, they report the following items of income and expense:

Gross receipts from Heather's business	$110,000
Rent on Heather's office	12,000
Receivables written off during the year (received in Heather's business)	1,300
Subscriptions to linguistic journals for Heather	250
Salary for Heather's secretary-receptionist	22,000
Nikolay's salary	78,000
Qualified medical expenses	12,000
Property taxes on their personal residence	4,200
State income tax refund received this year (the tax benefit was received in the prior year from the state income tax deduction)	400
State income taxes withheld on Nikolay's salary	4,600
Federal income taxes withheld on Nikolay's salary	12,000
Heather's estimated tax payments	20,000
Interest paid on residence	11,000
Income tax preparation fee for the prior year's return paid this year ($500 is allocated to preparation of Schedule C)	940

Heather and Nikolay sold the following assets:

Asset	Acquired	Sold	Sales Price	Cost
KNA stock	2/15/98	3/13/00	$14,000	$ 8,000
AEN stock	3/2/00	7/7/00	20,000	22,000
KLN stock	6/8/98	4/10/00	13,000	17,000
Motorcycle	5/3/96	9/12/00	2,500	6,000

Heather owned the KLN stock and sold it to her brother, Jacob. Heather and Nikolay used the motorcycle for personal recreation.

In addition to the items above, they donate Miner Corporation stock to their church. The FMV of the stock on the date it is donated (8/18/00) is $6,200. It cost $2,700 when purchased on 3/12/90. Heather and Nikolay's home is burglarized during the year. The burglar stole an entertainment system (FMV $3,500; cost $5,000), an antique diamond ring and pendant (FMV $12,000; cost $10,000), and a painting (FMV $1,500; cost

$1,300). The insurance company pays $1,500 for the entertainment system, $4,000 for the jewelry, and $500 for the painting. Complete Heather and Nikolay's Form 1040, Schedules A, C, D, and SE, and Form 4684.

I8-61 Kara and Brandon Arnold are married and file a joint return. Their Social Security numbers are 587-64-5235 and 588-54-8623, respectively. Kara and Brandon have one son, Henry, age 3. His social security is 587-45-3197. They live at 356 Welcome Lane, Woodbury, WA 84653. They report their income on the cash method. During 2000, they report the following items:

Salary	$103,000
Interest income from money market accounts	600
Dividend income from Davis Corp. stock	700
Cash contributions to church	6,000
Rental of a condominium in Lutsen:	
Rental income (30 days)	12,000
Interest expense	7,000
Property taxes	3,200
Maintenance	1,700
Depreciation (entire year)	7,500
Insurance	2,000
Days of personal use	16

During the year the following events also occur:

a. In 1998 Brandon had loaned a friend $3,000 to help pay medical bills. During 2000 he discovers that his "friend" has skipped town.
b. On June 20, 2000, Brandon sells Kim Corporation stock for $16,000. He purchased the stock on December 12, 1998 for $22,000.
c. On September 19, 2000, Kara discovers that the penny stock of Roberts, Inc. she purchased on January 2 of the prior year is completely worthless. She paid $5,000 for the stock.
d. Instead of accepting the $60 the repairperson offers for their old dishwasher, they donate it to Goodwill on November 21, 2000. They purchased the dishwasher for $750 on March 30, 1995. The new dishwasher cost $900.
e. Kara and Brandon purchased a new residence for $250,000. As part of the closing costs, they pay two points, or $3,800 on the $200,000 mortgage, which is interest rather than loan processing fees. This payment enables them to obtain a more favorable interest rate for the term of the loan. They also paid $8,400 in interest on their mortgage on their personal residence.
f. They paid $4,100 in property taxes on their residence and $7,500 in state income taxes.
g. On July 20, 2000 Kara and Brandon donated an antique automobile to the local community college. The value of the automobile was $10,200. They bought the car November 10, 1996 for $1,000 and fixed it up themselves. They estimate that they put in approximately $6,000 worth of labor into the project. The college auctioned the car for $9,700.
h. $16,450 in federal income tax was withheld during the year.

Complete Kara and Brandon's Form 1040, Schedules A, B, D, and E, Form 4684, and Form 8283.

CASE STUDY PROBLEMS

I8-62 Dr. John Brown is a physician who expects to make $150,000 this year from his medical practice. In addition, Dr. Brown expects to receive $10,000 dividends and interest income.

Last year, on the advice of a friend, Dr. Brown invested $100,000 in Limited, a limited partnership. He spends no time working for Limited. Limited's operations did not turn out exactly as planned, and Dr. Brown's share of Limited's losses last year amounted to $15,000. Dr. Brown has already been informed that his share of Limited's losses this year will be $10,000.

In January of the current year, Dr. Brown set up his own laboratory. Originally he intended to have the lab only do the work for his own practice, but other physicians in the area were impressed with the quick turnaround and convenience that the lab provided, and began sending their work. This year Dr. Brown estimates that the lab will generate $30,000 of taxable income. The work in the lab is done by 2 full-time qualified laboratory technicians. A part-time bookkeeper is hired to keep the books. Dr. Brown has spent 320 hours to date establishing and managing the lab. He plans to hire another technician, who will also manage the lab so that it can operate on its own.

In November, Dr. Brown calls you requesting some tax advice. Specifically, he would like to know what actions he should take before the end of the year in order to reduce his tax liability for the current year.

Write a memo to Dr. Brown, detailing your suggestions. His address is: Dr. John Brown, 444 Physician's Drive, Suite 100, Anytown, USA, 88888.

I8-63 In preparing the tax return for one of your clients, Jack Johnson, you notice that he has listed a deduction for a large business bad debt. Jack explains that the loan was made to his corporate employer when the corporation was experiencing extreme cash flow difficulties. In fact, Jack was very concerned at the time he made the loan that the corporation would go bankrupt. This would have been extremely bad, because not only would he have lost his job, but he also would have lost the $80,000 he had invested in the common stock of the corporation.

You know that if the loan is a business loan Jack will receive an ordinary deduction. However, if the loan is a nonbusiness debt, it becomes a short-term capital loss (and Jack can only currently deduct $3,000).

After thoroughly reviewing all of the facts you do a complete search of the relevant judicial and administrative authority. There you find that the courts are split as to whether under these circumstances the loan should be treated as a business or nonbusiness bad debt.

What position should you take on Jack's federal income tax return? (See the *Statements on Standards for Tax Services* section in Chapter I15 and Appendix E for a discussion of this issue.)

TAX RESEARCH PROBLEM

I8-64 Early in 2001, Kay meets Dan through a business associate. Dan tells Kay that he is directing a business venture that purchases poorly managed restaurants in order to turn them around and make them profitable. Dan mentions that he is currently involved in acquiring a real "gold mine" but needs to raise additional cash in order to purchase it. On the strength of Dan's representations, Kay loans Dan $30,000 for the venture. An agreement is written up between Kay and Dan, wherein Dan agrees to repay Kay the entire amount over a 5-year period plus 14% interest per annum on the unpaid balance. Later in the year, however, Kay discovers that Dan had never intended to purchase the restaurant and, in fact, had used most of the money for his own benefit. Upon making this discovery, Kay sues Dan for recovery of the money, alleging that Dan falsely, fraudulently, and deceitfully represented that the money would be invested and repaid, in order to cheat and defraud Kay out of her money. Unfortunately for Kay, she is never able to recover any amount of the loan. Discuss the tax treatment that Kay may claim with regard to the loss.

A partial list of research sources is

- *Robert S. Gerstell*, 46 T.C. 161 (1966)
- *Michele Monteleone*, 34 T.C. 688 (1960)

CHAPTER 9

EMPLOYEE EXPENSES AND DEFERRED COMPENSATION

LEARNING OBJECTIVES

After studying this chapter, you should be able to

1. Determine the proper classification and deductibility of travel and transportation expenses
2. Determine the proper deductible amount for entertainment expenses under the 50% disallowance rule
3. Identify deductible moving expenses and determine the amount and year of deductibility
4. Describe the requirements for deducting education expenses
5. Determine whether the expenses of an office in home meet the requirements for deductibility and apply the gross income limitations
6. Discuss the tax treatment and requirements for various deferred compensation arrangements

CHAPTER OUTLINE

Classification of Employee Expenses...9-2
Travel Expenses...9-4
Transportation Expenses...9-9
Entertainment Expenses...9-12
Reimbursed Employee Business Expenses...9-16
Moving Expenses...9-18
Education Expenses...9-20
Office in Home Expenses...9-23
Deferred Compensation...9-26

This chapter discusses the tax consequences that arise from two types of expenditures:

▶ Expenditures incurred by an employee in connection with his or her job
▶ Deferred compensation payments made to employees

Employees routinely incur expenses in connection with their jobs, such as travel, entertainment, professional journals, etc. The tax law considers employee expenses to be incurred in connection with a trade or business and therefore, are deductible under Sec. 162. However, employee expenses are subject to a myriad of special rules and limitations. Because of the large number of taxpayers who are employees and importance of the topic, this chapter discusses the rules as well as tax planning opportunities.

Deferred compensation refers to methods of compensating employees that are based on their current service but the actual payments are deferred until future periods. Deferred compensation arrangements are very popular and widely used in business. The two principal types of deferred compensation methods are qualified plans and nonqualified plans. Qualified plans, such as pension and profit-sharing plans, have very favorable tax benefits but also impose strict eligibility and coverage requirements. Nonqualified plans, while not as tax advantageous as qualified plans, are very useful for highly compensated employees. Both of these types of deferred compensation arrangements are discussed later in this chapter.

CLASSIFICATION OF EMPLOYEE EXPENSES

ADDITIONAL COMMENT

"The income tax has made more liars out of the American people than golf has. Even when you make a tax form on the level, you don't know when its through if you are a crook or a martyr." Will Rogers.

Employee expenses, for purposes of the tax law, are divided into two classifications: *reimbursed* employee expenses and *unreimbursed* employee expenses. Reimbursed employee expenses are expenses incurred by the employee that are reimbursed by the employer. IRC Section 62(a)(2) provides that an employee may deduct reimbursed employee expenses *for* AGI. This presumes, of course, that the employee has included the reimbursement in his gross income. Unreimbursed employee expenses are generally deductible by employees, but are deductible *from* AGI.

Some of the more frequently encountered employee expenses discussed in this chapter include

▶ Travel
▶ Transportation
▶ Moving
▶ Entertainment
▶ Education
▶ Office in home

Each of these types of employee expenses are discussed later in this chapter.

NATURE OF THE EMPLOYMENT RELATIONSHIP

KEY POINT

The business expenses of a self-employed individual and the reimbursed business expenses of an employee are deductible *for* AGI. The unreimbursed business expenses of an employee are deductible *from* AGI.

An individual who provides services for another person or entity may be classified either as an employee or as a self-employed individual (also referred to as an independent contractor). If the individual is classified as self-employed, expenses are deductible *for* AGI under Sec. 162, and are reported on Schedule C of Form 1040. Conversely, expenses of employees are deductible either *for* or *from* AGI depending on whether such expenses are reimbursed or unreimbursed (see discussion above). In addition to the deductibility of expenses, the proper classification is also important due to employment taxes, such as social security taxes. As is discussed below, self-employed taxpayers must pay both the employee and employer share of social security taxes.

EMPLOYER-EMPLOYEE RELATIONSHIP DEFINED. The Treasury Regulations provide that an employer-employee relationship generally exists where the employer has the right to control and direct the individual who provides services with regard to the end result and the means by which the result is accomplished.[1]

EXAMPLE I9-1 ▶ Carmen is a nurse who assists a group of doctors in a clinic. Carmen is under the direct supervision of the doctors and is told what procedures to perform and when to perform them. Therefore, Carmen is classified as an employee. ◀

EXAMPLE I9-2 ▶ Carol is a live-in nurse who is paid by the patient and receives instructions from the patient's doctor regarding such items as medications and diet. Carol is directly responsible for the delivery of nursing care and is in control of the end result. Thus, Carol is self-employed. ◀

> **ADDITIONAL COMMENT**
> Anyone in a trade or business making payments of $600 or more to an independent contractor during a year must file Form 1099-MISC.

IMPORTANCE OF PROPER CLASSIFICATION. As mentioned above, proper classification is important both to employers and employees. If an individual is classified as an employee, the employer must match the Social Security and Medicare taxes that are paid by the employee. In addition, employers are generally liable for unemployment taxes for its employees. Thus, an employer must pay these employment taxes to the government in addition to the wages, which means that the cost of an employee generally is higher than for a non-employee. If an individual is determined to *not* be an employee, the individual is considered to be self-employed (also called an independent contractor). Amounts paid to a self-employed individual are not considered to be wages and the payor is not responsible for any employment taxes. However, the self-employed individual must pay both the employee and employer portions of Social Security and Medicare taxes. This tax is referred to as the self-employment tax. As can be seen from the above discussion, employment taxes are shifted from the employer to the self-employed individual if the individual is not considered to be an employee.

Individuals may prefer to be classified as employees because the employee portion of the Social Security and Medicare taxes (7.65% in 2001) is only one-half of the self-employment tax rate (15.3% in 2001). Of the 7.65%, 6.2% (12.4% for self-employed individuals) is for the old age, survivors and disability insurance (OASDI) portion of the FICA tax and is assessed on a maximum income amount of $80,400 (2001). The remaining 1.45% (2.9% for self-employed individuals) portion of the FICA tax is for hospital insurance and has no ceiling limitation.[2]

LITIGATION ISSUES AND ADMINISTRATIVE ENFORCEMENT. The determination as to whether an individual who performs services is either an employee or an independent contractor has been a major area of contention between the IRS and taxpayers. In Rev. Rul. 87-41, 1987-1 CB 296, the IRS enumerated 20 factors as guides for determining whether an individual is an employee or an independent contractor. These factors are designed to help determine whether the person or persons for whom the services are performed exercises sufficient **control** over the individual for such individual to be classified as an employee. Some of the factors include; instructions, set hours of work, work on employer's premises, and method of payment (hourly versus commission, for example).

Substantial litigation has occurred in the interpretation of these factors. For example, truck drivers who were owner-operators and were engaged under contract by an interstate trucking company were considered independent contractors because they selected their own routes and were paid a percentage of the company's receipts for shipment.[3] However, drivers for a moving van company were considered employees because the company exercised control over their assignments.[4]

> **KEY POINT**
> Even if the employee expenses exceed 2% of AGI, the employee may not derive a tax benefit if the deductible employee expenses, when added to the other itemized deductions, do not exceed the standard deduction.

LIMITATIONS ON UNREIMBURSED EMPLOYEE EXPENSES

2% NONDEDUCTIBLE FLOOR. IRC Section 67 imposes a nondeductible floor of 2% of AGI to the following types of itemized deductions:

---

[1] Reg. Sec. 31.3401(c)-1(b).
[2] For years before 1994, a ceiling limitation applied to earnings and self-employment income subject to the hospital insurance portion of the FICA tax ($135,000 in 1993). See Chapter I14 for a discussion of these rules.
[3] Rev. Rul. 76-226, 1976-1 CB 332
[4] *R. N. Smith v. U.S.*, 78-1 USTC ¶9263 (CA-5, 1978).

9-4 Individuals ▼ Chapter 9

ADDITIONAL COMMENT
Unreimbursed employee business expenses are reported by the taxpayer first on Form 2106, then carried to Schedule A as a miscellaneous itemized deduction.

1) Unreimbursed employee business expenses,
2) Investment expenses, and
3) Other miscellaneous itemized deductions (i.e., tax return preparation fees)

All of these types of expenses are referred to as **miscellaneous itemized deductions** in Sec. 67.[5] Unreimbursed employee expenses that are classified as miscellaneous itemized deductions include

- The cost and maintenance of special clothing (e.g., uniforms for an airline pilot)
- Job-hunting expenses for seeking employment in the same trade or business (e.g., employment agency fees)
- Professional journals, professional dues, union dues, small tools and supplies.

Investment expenses include expenses connected with the earning of investment income, such as publications and safe deposit box rentals. Other miscellaneous itemized deductions include items such as fees for tax return preparation and appraisal fees for charitable contributions.

EXAMPLE I9-3 ▶

Charles incurs $3,000 unreimbursed employee expenses in 2001. Charles also incurs $1,000 of investment counseling fees and $500 for the preparation of his 2000 tax return and pays these amounts in 2001. Charles's AGI is $100,000. The total of miscellaneous itemized deductions is $4,500 ($3,000 + $1,000 + $500). Charles is limited to a $2,500 itemized deduction ($4,500 − $2,000) because of the application of the 2% nondeductible floor (0.02 × $100,000 AGI = $2,000). ◀

SELF-STUDY QUESTION
Before the Tax Reform Act of 1986, unreimbursed employee business expenses were not subject to the 2% nondeductible floor. Why did Congress decide to subject these expenses to this floor?

EXCEPTIONS TO THE 2% FLOOR. The 2% floor only applies to certain miscellaneous itemized deductions. Thus, most itemized deductions, such as charitable contributions, mortgage interest and real estate taxes on a principal residence, are not subject to the 2% nondeductible floor.

EXAMPLE I9-4 ▶

ANSWER
Prior law required extensive recordkeeping with regard to items that were commonly small expenditures. These small amounts presented significant administrative and enforcement problems for the IRS. The use of a floor also takes into account the fact that some expenses are sufficiently personal in nature that they might be incurred apart from any business activities.

In the current year Carmelia, who is single, incurs $1,500 of unreimbursed employee expenses, $3,000 of charitable contributions, and $4,000 of mortgage interest and real estate taxes on her principal residence. She has no other miscellaneous itemized deductions or investment expenses, and her AGI is $100,000. The $1,500 of employee expenses are not deductible because the 2% nondeductible floor ($2,000 in this case) is higher than the $1,500 of expenses. The $3,000 of charitable contributions and $4,000 of mortgage interest and real estate taxes are fully deductible as itemized deductions because Carmelia's total itemized deductions of $7,000 exceed the standard deduction amount ($4,550 for a single taxpayer in 2001). The charitable contributions, mortgage interest, and real estate taxes are not subject to the 2% nondeductible floor. ◀

TRAVEL EXPENSES

OBJECTIVE 1

Determine the proper classification and deductibility of travel and transportation expenses

DEDUCTIBILITY OF TRAVEL EXPENSES

The deductibility of travel expenses depends on the nature of the expenditure and whether the employee receives a reimbursement from the employer. The following rules apply to the deductibility of travel expenses.

- If the taxpayer is engaged in a trade or business as a self-employed individual or is engaged in an activity for the production of rental and royalty income, the travel-related expenditures are deductible *for* AGI and the 2% nondeductible floor is not applicable.

---

[5] The 2% disallowance applies before considering the 3% scale down of total itemized deductions under Sec. 68 for upper-income individuals with AGI in excess of $132,950 (2001). See Chapter I7 for a discussion of these rules. The 2% floor does not apply to certain other miscellaneous itemized deductions, including impairment-related work expenses for handicapped employees, amortizable bond premiums, certain short sale expenses, terminated annuity payments, and gambling losses to the extent of winnings.

- If the taxpayer is an employee and incurs travel expenses in connection with his job, the expenses are deductible either *for* AGI or *from* AGI depending on whether the expenses are reimbursed by the employer.
- Personal travel expenses are not deductible.

REIMBURSED EXPENSES: If business travel expenses are reimbursed and the reimbursement is included in the employee's gross income, the expenses are deductible *for* AGI.

UNREIMBURSED EXPENSES: Generally, if business travel expenses are not reimbursed by the taxpayer's employer, the expenses are a deduction *from* AGI subject to the 2% floor.

The tax rules for reporting reimbursed and unreimbursed employee business expenses are discussed in more detail later in this chapter. Table I9-1 illustrates these tax consequences.

DEFINITION OF TRAVEL EXPENSES

Travel expenses include transportation, meals, lodging, and other reasonable and necessary expenses incurred by a taxpayer while "away from home" in the pursuit of a trade or business or an employment-related activity. The term *travel expense* is more broadly defined in the IRC than is the term **transportation expense**. If an individual is not away from home, expenses related to local transportation are classified as transportation expenses rather than travel expenses. Transportation expenses for employees are deductible under certain conditions and are discussed later in this chapter.

ADDITIONAL COMMENT
Before 1987, travel and transportation costs were deductible *for* AGI whereas most other unreimbursed employee business expenses were deductible *from* AGI. Congress changed the law to move unreimbursed travel and transportation costs to deductions *from* AGI to make them conform to the other business expenses. All of these expenses constitute costs of earning income.

EXAMPLE I9-5 ▶ Ahmed is away from home overnight on a job-related business trip and incurs air fare, hotel, and taxi fares amounting to $800. Because Ahmed is away from home, the $800 is deductible as travel expenses. ◀

EXAMPLE I9-6 ▶ Charlotte uses her personal automobile to make deliveries of company products to customers in the same local area of her employer's place of business. Charlotte's automobile expenses are classified as transportation expenses (rather than travel expenses) because she was not away from home when they were incurred. As is discussed later in this chapter, transportation expenses are deductible but are subject to strict recordkeeping rules. If Charlotte stopped to eat lunch alone during her delivery activities, the meals are not deductible as they are neither travel nor transportation expenses. ◀

▼ **TABLE I9-1**
Classification of Travel Expenses

Situation Facts	Deductible *for* AGI	Deductible *from* AGI	Not Deductible
1. Cindy is a self-employed attorney who incurs travel expenses related to her business.	X[a]		
2. Jose, who lives in Dallas, is the owner of several apartment buildings in Denver. Periodically he travels to Denver to inspect and manage the properties.	X[a]		
3. Clay is an employee who is required to travel to company facilities throughout the U.S. in the conduct of his management responsibilities. Clay is not reimbursed by his employer.		X[b]	
4. Same as Situation 3, except that Clay is fully reimbursed by his employer and includes the reimbursement in his gross income.	X[a]		
5. Colleen is a student who travels to her parents' home during the holidays.			X

[a] The 2% nondeductible floor is not applicable.
[b] The 2% nondeductible floor is applicable and the expenses are only deductible in excess of the floor.

HISTORICAL NOTE
The partial disallowance of business meals (and entertainment) was enacted because Congress believed that prior law had not focused sufficiently on the personal consumption element of deductible business meal and entertainment expenses. Congress felt that taxpayers who could arrange business settings for personal consumption were unfairly receiving a federal tax subsidy for such consumption.

TYPICAL MISCONCEPTION
There is a tendency to erroneously assume that a taxpayer's tax home is the location of the primary personal residence.

REAL-WORLD EXAMPLE
A taxpayer was employed by a traveling circus with headquarters in Chicago. The Tax Court held that the taxpayer's home was wherever he happened to be with the circus. Therefore, the cost of his meals and lodging was not deductible. *Nat Lewis,* 1954 PH T.C. Memo ¶54,233, 13 TCM 1167.

GENERAL QUALIFICATION REQUIREMENTS

To qualify as a travel expense deduction, the following requirements must be met:

▶ The purpose of the trip must be connected with a trade or business or be employment-related (e.g., personal vacation trips or commuting to and from a job location are nondeductible personal expenses).[6]

▶ The taxpayer must be away from his tax home overnight or for a sufficient duration to require sleep or rest before returning home

AWAY-FROM-TAX-HOME REQUIREMENT. Travel expenses are deductible if the taxpayer is temporarily away from his tax home overnight. While this seems simple enough, there has been considerable debate as to what the words actually mean. There are three important aspects of determining the deductibility of travel expenses; (1) where is the taxpayer's home, (2) how is *temporarily* distinguished from *indefinite* or *permanent*, and (3) how the term "overnight" is interpreted.

Taxpayer's home: The IRS's position is that a person's tax home is the location of his principal place of employment regardless of where the family residence is maintained. Thus, a taxpayer who works permanently or for an indefinite period of time away from his or her family residence is *not* considered to be away from home and, therefore, travel expenses are not deductible. In this situation, the taxpayer's *tax home* is considered to be his work location.

Temporary vs Indefinite: The determination of whether a taxpayer is away from home temporarily or indefinitely is based upon the length of time the taxpayer is at such location. Work assignments of more than one year are treated as indefinite.[7] Work assignments for one year or less are classified as either temporary or indefinite depending on the facts and circumstances of each case. If an employee is reassigned only for a temporary period, then his tax home does not change and the travel expenses are deductible. However, if the assignment is for an indefinite period, the individual's tax home shifts to the new location. The following bulleted items and examples are taken from Rev. Rul. 93-86[8] and are used to illustrate the IRS's position concerning whether a taxpayer is away from home temporarily for purposes of deducting travel expenses:

▶ A taxpayer accepts away from home employment where it is realistically expected that the work will be completed in six months. The actual employment period lasts ten months. Because the employment period is realistically expected to last (and does in fact last) for one year or less, the IRS's position is that the employment is temporary and the taxpayer's travel expenses are deductible.

▶ A taxpayer accepts away from home employment where it is realistically expected that the work will be completed in 18 months but the work is actually completed in ten months. In such case the IRS's position is that the employment is treated as indefinite, regardless of whether it actually exceeds one year or not.

▶ A taxpayer accepts away from home employment where it is realistically expected that the work will be completed in nine months. After eight months the taxpayer is asked to remain for seven more months or a total period of more than one year. Based on these facts, the IRS's position is that the employment is temporary for eight months and the travel expenses are deductible for the eight-month period. The job is considered indefinite for the remaining seven months and no travel expense deduction is allowed for the travel expenses during this period.

Overnight test: To satisfy the overnight test, a taxpayer must show that it was reasonable for him to need and to obtain sleep or rest during release time on such trips in order to meet the demands of his job.[9] Generally, costs of meals on one-day business

---

[6] Travel expenses incurred in the production or collection of income are also deductible from AGI under Sec. 212(1), even though the travel is not connected with employment or with the conduct of a trade or business. See Rev. Rul. 84-113, 1984-2 C.B. 60.

[7] Sec. 162(a). See also Rev. Rul. 99-7, 1999-1 C.B. 361.
[8] Rev. Rul. 93-86, 1993-2 C.B. 71.
[9] Rev. Rul. 75-168, 1975-1 C.B. 58.

trips are not deductible since the taxpayer was not away from home overnight. The Supreme Court held that a taxpayer who took short rest stops on long one-day business trips was not allowed to deduct his meals.[10] However, whether it is reasonable to need sleep or rest depends on the specific circumstances. A railroad conductor was allowed to deduct lodging, meals, and tips incurred during a six-hour layover on a total trip of 16 hours.[11]

BUSINESS VERSUS PLEASURE

Travel expenses are deductible only if they are incurred in the pursuit of a trade or business activity or are related to the taxpayer's employment. Thus, if a taxpayer takes a trip that is *primarily personal* in nature but some business is transacted, the only deductions allowed are those that are directly related to the business activity.[12] In such event, all of the traveling expenses to and from the destination are treated as nondeductible personal expenditures. However, if the trip is *primarily related* to business or employment, all of the traveling expenses to and from the destination are deductible, and meals and lodging, local transportation, and incidental expenses are allocated to the business and personal activities respectively. In effect, an all-or-nothing approach is applied to the deductibility of traveling expenses to and from the destination depending upon the primary purpose for making the trip.

In determining the primary purpose for a trip, the amount of time spent on personal activities compared to the time spent on business activities is an important factor. However, the fact that a taxpayer may spend slightly more time on personal activities than business activities will not automatically prohibit the deductibility of the transportation expenses to and from the destination. The taxpayer must clearly show that the purpose of the trip was *primarily business*.

> **SELF-STUDY QUESTION**
> A student accepts employment in another state during his summer vacation. Would the cost of his meals and lodging at the job location be deductible?
>
> **ANSWER**
> No, the student did not travel to the job because of the employer's business needs. *Peter F. Janss v. CIR*, 2 AFTR 2d. 5927, 58-2 USTC ¶9873 (8th Cir., 1958).

EXAMPLE I9-7 ▶ Dana travels to New York on a business trip for her employer. She is not reimbursed for the travel expenses. Dana spends three days in business meetings and vacations for two days. Because the trip is primarily business, the traveling expenses to and from the destination (e.g., airfare) are fully deductible by Dana. If Dana's meals, lodging, and incidental expenses amount to $100 per day, only $300 ($100 × 3 business days) of such travel expenses is also deductible. The deductible business meal expenses are reduced by 50%, and the total amount of deductible travel expenses are subject to the nondeductible 2% floor on miscellaneous itemized deductions. A proration of the meals, lodging, and incidental expenses based on the number of days may not be appropriate if the expenses are uneven or are directly related to either business or personal activities. ◀

EXAMPLE I9-8 ▶ Assume that the facts in Example I9-7 are reversed (i.e., that two days are employment-related and three days are personal). Because more time was spent on personal activities, the general rule would hold that the trip is primarily personal and the traveling expenses to and from the destination are not deductible. Thus, only $200 ($100 × two business days) of travel expenses related to meals, lodging, and incidental expenses are deductible (subject to the limitations previously discussed). None of the traveling expenses to and from the destination (i.e., the airfare) are deductible. ◀

EXAMPLE I9-9 ▶ Carroll, who lives and works in St. Louis, is required by his employer to attend a sales meeting in San Francisco. The meeting lasts two days. Carroll decides to take three days of vacation and sightsee in the San Francisco area. Even though Carroll spent more days on personal activities than business activities, Carroll's airfare would be deductible if he can clearly show that the primary purpose of the trip was business. ◀

---

[10] *Correll v. U.S.*, 389 U.S. 299 (1968).
[11] *Williams v. Patterson*, 286 F2d 333 (5th Cir. 1961) and Rev. Rul. 75-170, 1975-1 C.B. 60.
[12] Reg. Sec. 1.162-2(b)(1).

REAL-WORLD EXAMPLE

A movie executive's wife accompanied him on business trips in the U.S. and abroad. She helped promote the movie company's image of a "family-type movie company." She also helped arrange his personal schedule. A deduction for her costs was allowed. *U.S. v. Roy O. Disney*, 24 AFTR 2d 69-5123, 69-2 USTC ¶9494 (9th Cir., 1969). However, as a result of the Revenue Reconciliation Act of 1993, the wife's travel costs would no longer be deductible unless she were an employee.

The IRS has ruled that the incremental expenses of an additional night's lodging and an additional day's meals that are incurred to obtain "excursion" air fare rates with respect to employees whose business travel extends over Saturday night are deductible business expenses.[13] The reimbursement for these expenses is deductible by the employer (subject to the 50% disallowance for meals). The employer is not required to report the reimbursement on the employee's Form W-2 as gross income or withhold employment taxes.

Stringent rules are applied if the taxpayer is accompanied by family members because of the likelihood that the trip is primarily for personal reasons. No deduction is permitted for travel expenses of a spouse or dependent (or other person accompanying the taxpayer) unless the person is an employee, the travel is for a bona fide business purpose, and the expenses would be otherwise deductible.[14]

FOREIGN TRAVEL

Due to the potential for abuse, special rules apply to foreign travel and foreign convention expenses.[15] Travel expenses related to foreign conventions, seminars, or similar types of meetings are disallowed unless it can be shown that the meeting is directly related to the taxpayer's trade or business (including employment) activity and that it is reasonable for the meeting to be held outside North America. In addition, complex expense allocation rules are applied to business trips made outside the United States.[16]

SELF-STUDY QUESTION

Would the cost of going on a safari in Africa be deductible if the taxpayer were in the business of selling guns?

ANSWER

In an actual case, the Court held that the safari expenses were not sufficiently connected to the taxpayer's gun-selling business. Therefore, the safari costs were not deductible. *Vincent W. Eckel*, 1974 PH T.C. Memo ¶74,033, 33 TCM 147.

ADDITIONAL LIMITATIONS ON TRAVEL EXPENSES

IRC Section 274 also provides several limitations on the deductibility of certain types of travel expenses, including the following:

▶ Travel deductions are disallowed if the expenses are deductible only as a form of education. For example, a French language professor cannot deduct travel expenses to France if the purpose of the trip is to maintain a general familiarity with the French language and customs.

▶ Deductions allowed for luxury water travel (i.e., ocean liners, cruise ships, or other forms of water transportation) are limited to twice the highest per diem amount allowable for a day of domestic travel by employees in the executive branch of the federal government.

▶ Travel deductions to attend a convention, seminar, or meeting are not allowed if they are related to income-producing activities coming under Sec. 212. Expenses to attend a convention, seminar, or meeting are deductible if directly connected with a taxpayer's trade or business. However, expenses to attend such meetings on a U.S. cruise ship are deductible but only to a maximum amount of $2,000.

EXAMPLE I9-10 ▶ Dawn travels on a cruise ship to attend a business meeting in Bermuda. The round-trip cost of the cruise is $4,000, and the travel is for a period of four days. If the daily per diem amount is $150 for a government employee, the travel expenses related to the cruise ship are limited to $1,200 ($300 per day × 4 days travel). ◀

EXAMPLE I9-11 ▶ Danielle is an investor in the stock market who attends investment counseling seminars. During the current year, she incurs $4,000 travel expenses to attend the seminars. None of the travel expenses are deductible because the expenses are related to income-producing activities coming under Sec. 212. If Danielle was employed as a stockbroker (rather than an investor) and attended investment seminars, her travel expenses would be deductible. ◀

---

[13] Ltr. Rul. 9237014 (June 10, 1992).
[14] Sec. 274(m)(3).
[15] Secs. 274(c) and (h).
[16] Reg. Sec. 1.274-4. No allocation of total expenses is made to the personal-use (nondeductible) element if an individual is away from home for seven days or less or if less than 25% of the time is devoted to personal purposes. In all other cases, all of the foreign travel expenses (including transportation costs) must be apportioned between business and personal activities based on the relative percentage of time devoted to each activity.

TRANSPORTATION EXPENSES

The deductibility and classification of transportation expenses also depends on the nature of the expenditure, as follows:

- Trade or business-related transportation expenses are deductible *for* AGI and are not subject to specific limitations.
- Transportation expenses related to the production of rental and royalty income (e.g., an owner-investor in rental properties) are deductible *for* AGI and are not subject to specific limitations.
- Reimbursed employee transportation expenses are deductible *for* AGI (assuming that an adequate accounting is made to the employer, see discussion of reimbursed employee business expenses on page I9-16).
- Unreimbursed employee transportation expenses are deductible *from* AGI as itemized deductions subject to the 2% nondeductible floor for miscellaneous itemized deductions.
- Commuting expenses are nondeductible personal expenses.

DEFINITION AND CLASSIFICATION

> **KEY POINT**
> The primary difference between travel expenses and transportation expenses for tax purposes is that travel expenses are broad in nature and include transportation, lodging, meals, and other necessary expenses, whereas transportation expenses include only the cost of transportation.

Transportation costs include taxi fares, automobile expenses, airfares, tolls, parking fees, and so on incurred in a trade or business or employment-related activity. Generally speaking, transportation costs are those incurred for "local transportation" and are not treated as travel expenses because the away from home requirements have not been met. The cost of commuting to and from an employee's job location are nondeductible personal expenditures regardless of the length of the trip. Both unreimbursed employment-related travel and transportation expenses for employees are subject to the 2% floor on miscellaneous itemized deductions. If a reimbursement is received, such expenses would be deductible *for* AGI.

> **EXAMPLE I9-12**

Eurie's employer requires her to call on several customers at different locations in the metropolitan area during the course of the workday. Her transportation expenses (e.g., auto expenses, tolls, and parking) are deductible as transportation expenses because they are related to providing services as an employee. If Eurie is required to travel away from home overnight, the transportation costs are included with meals and lodging and deducted as a travel expense. In either situation, the unreimbursed employment-related expenses are treated as miscellaneous itemized deductions and are subject to the 2% nondeductible floor limitation. If the expenses were reimbursed by Eurie's employer and an adequate accounting is made to the employer, the expenses would be deductible *for* AGI.

> **EXAMPLE I9-13**
>
> **ADDITIONAL COMMENT**
> The IRS takes the position that the hauling of equipment, tools, etc., in an automobile for business purposes does not make the commuting expenses deductible. This position is based on the Supreme Court's decision in *Donald W. Fausner v. CIR*, 32 AFTR 2d 73-5202, 73-2 USTC ¶9515 (USSC, 1973). The Court held that it was not possible to allocate the automobile expenses between nondeductible commuting expenses and deductible business expenses. However, if the taxpayer incurs additional costs, such as in renting a trailer, these additional costs are deductible.

David accepts a permanent job with a company located 80 miles from his principal residence. He decides not to move to the new location. None of David's transportation costs are deductible because they are personal commuting expenses. (Note: Because the job is a permanent assignment, it is for an indefinite period rather than a temporary period and the transportation expenses are not deductible as travel expenses.)

The following exceptions or unusual circumstances should be noted:

- Transportation expenses incurred to go from one job to another are deductible if an employee has more than one job. If the employee goes home between jobs, the deduction is only the amount it would have cost him to go directly from the first location to the second.[17]
- Certain transportation expenses related to income-producing activities are deductible under Sec. 212. Expenses are deductible *for* AGI if they are related to the production of rental or royalty income; expenses connected with other investment-related activities are deductible as miscellaneous itemized deductions subject to the 2% floor.

---

[17] IRS, *Publication No. 917* (Business Use of a Car), 2000, p. 3

- Transportation expenses related to medical treatment may be deductible from AGI as a medical expense (subject to the limitations on the deductibility of medical expenses discussed in Chapter I7).
- Transportation expenses related to charitable activities may be deductible as a charitable contribution (subject to the limitations on the deductibility of charitable contributions discussed in Chapter I7).
- Transportation expenses incurred in going between the taxpayer's residence and a temporary work location outside the metropolitan area are deductible.[18] Further, assuming a taxpayer has at least one regular work location (such as his primary office location), transportation expenses are deductible in going between the taxpayer's residence and a temporary work location, regardless of the distance.[19] Thus, a CPA who is employed by a CPA firm and who maintains a regular work location (e.g., an office is provided at the CPA firm work location) may deduct transportation expenses for trips from home to clients in the metropolitan area. Unreimbursed transportation costs for an employee are deductible *from* AGI as unreimbursed employee expenses that are subject to the 2% nondeductible floor. Transportation expenses for a self-employed individual are deductible *for* AGI.

EXAMPLE I9-14 ▶ As shown in Figure I9-1 below, Dick has two jobs that are 10 miles apart. Dick lives 5 miles from the first job site and 8 miles from the second job site. If Dick drives directly from one job to the other, he may deduct the automobile costs associated with the 10-mile trip. If he goes home from the first job before driving to the second job, the deduction is still limited to 10 miles, even though he actually travels 13 miles. ◀

EXAMPLE I9-15 ▶ Diana owns a duplex, which she rents to tenants. She periodically drives from her place of business to this income-producing property to collect the rents and to inspect the property. The transportation expenses are deductible *for* AGI as an expense related to the production of rental income under Sec. 212. ◀

EXAMPLE I9-16 ▶ Donna, an accountant who is employed by a CPA firm, travels from her home to an audit client located in the local metropolitan area. The firm maintains an office for Donna at their business location. She is not reimbursed for her transportation costs. The transportation costs are deductible *from* AGI as unreimbursed employee expenses that are subject to the 2% nondeductible floor. If Donna were instead a self-employed CPA operating a business from her home, her transportation expenses would be deductible *for* AGI. ◀

FIGURE I9-1 ▶ ILLUSTRATION FOR EXAMPLE I9-14

TREATMENT OF AUTOMOBILE EXPENSES

An employee or self-employed person may deduct actual automobile expenses, including gas, oil, repairs, depreciation, interest, property taxes, license fees, insurance, and so on based on the percentage of business miles to total miles. Detailed records to support the expenses are necessary in order to properly claim the deduction. To help reduce the burden of detailed recordkeeping, an alternative method, the standard mileage rate method, is available to taxpayers.

---

[18] Rev. Rul. 99-7, 1999-1 C.B. 361.

[19] Rev. Rul. 94-47, 1994-2 C.B. 18.

The standard mileage rate method permits a deduction based on a standard mileage rate of 34.5 cents per mile for the year 2001.[20] Parking and tolls for business purposes are allowed as an addition to this deduction as well as interest expense on an automobile loan and personal property taxes on the automobile. The following restrictions apply when the standard mileage rate is used:

> The standard mileage rate method cannot be used if two or more automobiles are used simultaneously for business purposes.

> If a taxpayer changes from the standard mileage rate method rate in one year to the actual expense method in a later year, the basis of the used automobile must be reduced by 15 cents per mile for 2001 (14 cents for 2000, 12 cents per mile for years 1997–1999) for any year or years in which the standard mileage rate method was used. The modified accelerated cost-recovery system (MACRS) rules (discussed in Chapter I10) cannot be used for computing depreciation in the year of the change and for the remaining useful life of the automobile. In such case, only the straight-line method under the alternative depreciation system (ADS) may be used (see Chapter I10).

> A change to the standard mileage rate method is not allowed for an automobile that was previously depreciated under the MACRS rules or where an election was made under Sec. 179 to expense part or all of the automobile's cost in the year of acquisition. (See Chapter I10 for a discussion of the Sec. 179 election.)

> The actual expense method is based on the ratio of business or employment-related miles to total miles. (See Chapter I10 for a discussion of specific restrictions on the computation of depreciation where mixed business- and personal-use automobiles are acquired.)

ADDITIONAL COMMENT

It should be remembered that in many cases the taxpayer can choose between the automatic mileage method and calculating the actual costs of operating the car. Although the automatic mileage method has the advantage of convenience, a calculation of the actual costs might produce a larger deduction.

STOP & THINK

Question: Assume a taxpayer uses his car (original cost, $20,000) in his business, drives a total of 25,000 miles per year, and can substantiate 80% of the mileage as business use. In general, will the taxpayer benefit more from the standard mileage method of deducting automobile expenses or from the actual expenses method?

Solution: In general, the actual expenses method will yield a higher deduction. The American Automobile Association estimates that it costs approximately $0.41 per mile to operate a car in the United States. Therefore, the actual cost of operating the automobile would be approximately $10,250 (25,000 miles × $0.41). The deductible amount for tax purposes would be 80% of $10,250, or $8,200 for the actual expense method. Compare this amount with the standard mileage amount of $6,900 (25,000 miles × 80% business usage × $0.345/mile) and the actual expenses method yields a higher deduction. Of course, each individual situation is different and the actual results can vary based on circumstances, such as the amount of repairs, depreciation, and so on.

EXAMPLE I9-17 ▶ Danielle owns two automobiles that are used at the same time in her small unincorporated business. One automobile is driven by an employee of the business and Danielle drives the other vehicle for business use. Danielle cannot use the standard mileage rate method for either automobile because both cars are used in the business simultaneously. ◀

EXAMPLE I9-18 ▶ Doug used the standard mileage rate method in 2000, the year the automobile was acquired for use in his unincorporated business. The automobile was used in the business for the entire year. If the actual expense method is used for 2001 and later years, the automobile's adjusted basis (for depreciation purposes) must be reduced by 14 cents per mile for its 2000 business usage. Thus, if the automobile originally cost $20,000 in 2000 and was used 10,000 miles for business purposes during the initial year, the adjusted basis for computing depreciation in 2001 is reduced to $18,600 [$20,000 − (0.14 × 10,000)]. The remaining $18,600 basis must be depreciated using straight-line depreciation over the automobile's estimated useful life if the actual expense method is used. ◀

---

[20] Rev. Proc. 2000-48. For the taxable year 2000, the standard mileage rate was 32.5 cents per mile.

EXAMPLE I9-19

KEY POINT
The Tax Reform Act of 1984 imposed a "contemporaneous" records test for substantiating expenses for automobiles and certain other activities. Public outcry caused Congress to repeal this requirement in 1985. Now the business use of an automobile can be substantiated either by keeping adequate records or by sufficient corroborating evidence, oral or written.

Edith uses her automobile 50% of the time for business and employment-related use and 50% for personal use. These percentages are substantiated by records that document the total usage for the automobile. During 2001, Edith drives 3,000 miles per month or a total of 36,000 miles for the year. If the standard mileage rate method is used, she can deduct $6,210 [(0.345 × 36,000 miles) × 50%] for the business and employment-related use. Additionally, Edith may deduct any business-related parking fees and tolls. ◀

REIMBURSEMENT OF AUTOMOBILE EXPENSES

An employee is entitled to deduct actual automobile expenses (or amounts derived under the standard mileage rate method if applicable) in excess of reimbursed amounts received from the employer. The computation is made on Form 2106 (Employee Business Expenses) and is reported on Schedule A of Form 1040.

EXAMPLE I9-20

ADDITIONAL COMMENT
The kind of written record that could corroborate the business use of an automobile would include account books, diaries, logs, trip sheets, expense reports, or written statements from witnesses.

Elizabeth, who makes an adequate accounting to her employer, receives a $2,000 (20,000 miles at 10 cents per mile) reimbursement in 2001 for employment-related business miles. She incurs the following expenses related to both business and personal use:

Gas and oil	$4,400
Repairs and maintenance	2,700
Depreciation	3,000
Insurance	1,900
Total	$12,000

Elizabeth also spent $100 on parking fees and tolls that were all related to business. Elizabeth drives a total of 32,000 miles during the year. Thus, 62.5% (20,000 ÷ 32,000) of the $12,000 in automobile expenses is deductible. After subtracting the employer's $2,000 reimbursement, Elizabeth may deduct $5,600 [($12,000 × 0.625) + 100 − $2,000] as a miscellaneous itemized deduction (subject to the 2% nondeductible floor). Alternatively, if 2001 is the first year she used the car in her business, she could have claimed a deduction using the standard mileage rate method. In this case the $7,600 ($7,500 + 100) of actual expenses is greater than the $7,000 permitted under the standard mileage rate method [(32,000 miles × 62.5% × $0.345) + $100 business-related tolls]. ◀

ENTERTAINMENT EXPENSES

OBJECTIVE 2

Determine the proper deductible amount for entertainment expenses under the 50% disallowance rule

Entertainment of business customers and clients is a routine and, in many cases, an essential practice in business. Because entertainment expenses are considered ordinary and necessary practices of a business, they are deductible under either Sec. 162 or Sec. 212. However, the nature of entertainment expenses lend themselves to abuse by taxpayers. There certainly is an element of personal pleasure in taking a client to a hockey game or a Philharmonic orchestra performance and allowing taxpayers to deduct such expenses creates serious enforcement problems for the IRS.

For the reasons above, Congress enacted Sec. 274, which is strictly a disallowance section and contains classification rules, restrictive tests, and specific recordkeeping requirements. To deduct entertainment expenses, taxpayers must first show that the expenditure qualifies for a deduction under Sec. 162 (trade or business expense) or Sec. 212 (investment-type expense). Then the various requirements of Sec. 274 must be adhered to in order for an entertainment expense to be deductible. Over the years, Congress has continued to tighten the rules for the deductibility of entertainment expenses.

50% DISALLOWANCE FOR MEAL AND ENTERTAINMENT EXPENSES

Sec. 274(n) provides that any expense incurred for either business meals or entertainment must be reduced by 50%.[21] Business meals may be deductible either as travel expenses or

---
[21] For pre-1994 tax years, the disallowance was 20%.

as entertainment, depending on the nature of the expenditure. In either case, the 50% limit applies to the cost of food and beverages including tips and taxes but is not applicable to transportation expenses incurred going to and from a business meal. Further, any portion of a business meal that is considered lavish or extravagant is disallowed.[22] In such a situation, the 50% reduction rule is applied to the allowable portion of the business meal.

> **EXAMPLE 19-21** ▶ Krishna, a self-employed individual, pays $80 for a business meal plus $4 sales tax and a $16 tip. The total cost of the meal is $100. If $40 of the meal is considered lavish or extravagant, Krishna could deduct $30 ($60 × 0.50). ◀

If an employee incurs entertainment or business meal expenses that are fully reimbursed by the employer, it is the employer rather than the employee who is limited to a deduction for 50% of the expenses. Assuming the reimbursement is made pursuant to an accountable plan (see discussion later in this chapter), the employee would not include the reimbursement in income and would not be allowed a deduction.

> **EXAMPLE 19-22** ▶ Gordon incurs employment-related entertainment expenses of $1,000 and is fully reimbursed by his employer pursuant to an accountable plan. The employer may deduct $500 [$1,000 − ($1,000 × 0.50)] of entertainment expenses. Gordon would not include the $1,000 reimbursement in gross income and would not be allowed to deduct the $1,000 as a deduction. Thus, there is no overall tax effect to Gordon. ◀

ADDITIONAL COMMENT

Entertainment expenses are not considered "directly related" if there are substantial distractions. Therefore, if a meeting takes place at a sporting event, theater, or night club, the entertainment cannot be "directly related." This type of entertainment could qualify as an "associated with" expense. An example of a "directly related" expense would be the costs related to a hospitality room at a convention.

CLASSIFICATION OF EXPENSES

If an individual is engaged in a trade or business (but not as an employee), allowable entertainment expenses are deductible *for AGI*. Employees, however, may deduct entertainment expenses only as a miscellaneous itemized deduction (subject to the 2% nondeductible floor) unless the expenses are reimbursed. The tax rules for reimbursements of employee business expenses are discussed more fully later in this chapter.

> **EXAMPLE 19-23** ▶ Helen is a self-employed attorney who entertains clients and prospective clients. To the extent that these expenditures meet the Sec. 274 requirements, they are deductible by Helen as a *for AGI* expense on Schedule C of Form 1040 because Helen is engaged in a trade or business activity. The entertainment expenses are subject to the 50% limit but are not subject to the 2% nondeductible floor because the entertainment is deductible when determining AGI as a trade or business expense. ◀

CRITERIA FOR DEDUCTION. To be deductible as an entertainment expense, an expenditure must be either **directly related** to the active conduct of a trade or business or **associated with** the active conduct of a trade or business. Different restrictions apply to each of these categories. The Regulations under Sec. 274 provide the substantive rules for the two types of entertainment expenses.

"Directly Related" Expenses. To meet the requirements for a "directly related" entertainment expense, some business benefit must be expected from the business conducted other than goodwill and the expense must be incurred in a clear business setting (i.e., where there are no substantial distractions). In other words, business in anticipation of a business benefit must actually be conducted during the entertainment period.

ADDITIONAL COMMENT

With respect to the "associated with" type of expense, there is *no* requirement that the business discussion last for any specified period, or that more time be devoted to business than to entertainment.

"Associated With" Expenses. To qualify an expense as an "associated with" entertainment expenditure, the taxpayer must show a clear business purpose, such as obtaining new business or encouraging the continuation of an existing business relationship. An added restriction is placed on "associated with" entertainment in that the entertainment must directly precede or follow a bona fide business discussion. This means that the entertainment generally must occur on the same day that business is discussed.

> **EXAMPLE 19-24** ▶ Holly is a lawyer who hosts a birthday party in her home. Most of the guests are law partners or clients. No formal business discussions are conducted either before or immediately following

---

[22] Sec. 274(k).

the party. The expenditures for the birthday party are not deductible because they do not meet either the "directly related" or "associated with" tests.

Substantiation Requirements. In addition to both the directly related and associated with requirements, Sec. 274 imposes stringent substantiation requirements for entertainment expenses. In order to deduct entertainment expenses, taxpayers are required to substantiate each expenditure for which a deduction is claimed. Lack of documentation alone will cause the disallowance of a deduction.

BUSINESS MEALS

Business meals related to travel or entertainment activities are subject to the same business-connection requirements as other types of entertainment expenses. Thus, an entertainment deduction is allowed only if the meal meets the "directly related" or "associated with" tests previously discussed. In addition, the expense must not be lavish or extravagant under the circumstances, and the taxpayer (or an employee of the taxpayer) must generally be present when the food or beverages are furnished. These requirements do not apply to a business meal associated with travel where the taxpayer claims a deduction only for his or her own expenses.

> **REAL WORLD EXAMPLE**
> One common way business people document a business meal is to write on the back of the credit card receipt the other person(s) at the meal and the topic discussed. Then all of the necessary substantiation requirements are present on the one piece of paper: date, time, place, amount, people present, and business discussed.

EXAMPLE I9-25 ▶ Hank is a salesman for a manufacturing supply company. Hank meets Harold, a purchasing agent who is a substantial customer, for lunch during a normal business day. Business is actually conducted during the lunch, and the lunch expenses are not lavish or extravagant under the circumstances. Hank is fully reimbursed by his employer for the $30 lunch expenses after an adequate accounting of the expenses is submitted. The business meal qualifies as "directly related" entertainment because the entertainment involved the actual conduct of business where some business benefit is reasonably expected and a business discussion was conducted during the meal. Hank's employer may deduct $15 ($30 × 0.50) of entertainment expenses because the meal was not lavish or extravagant. ◀

EXAMPLE I9-26 ▶ Assume the same facts as in Example I9-25, except that the purchasing agent is a prospective customer and no business is actually discussed either during, directly preceding, or immediately following the meal. Thus, no deduction is allowed because no business is discussed either before, during, or after the meal. ◀

The Regulations provide that the surroundings in which food or beverages are furnished must be in an atmosphere where there are no substantial distractions to the discussion (e.g., a floor show).[23]

WHAT WOULD YOU DO IN THIS SITUATION?

You have recently acquired a new individual tax client, Joe Windsack, who is a manufacturer's representative for a local tool and die company. You have been engaged by Windsack to prepare his individual income tax return for the current year. Before the current tax year is over, you are at a party where Windsack is also a guest. You overhear Windsack bragging to a group of people that he substantially reduces his income tax liability by overstating meal and entertainment expenses. He indicated that he overstates the deductions in several ways, (1) when he goes out to lunch or dinner that is personal in nature, such as with his family, he always uses a credit card and fictitiously writes the name of a client or prospective client on the charge card receipt, (2) when he goes out to lunch with several colleagues from his office (not business related), he charges the entire amount on his credit card (for everyone at the table), collects the cash from his colleagues for the cost of their meals, and then writes the entire amount off as a business-related meal, and (3) whenever he goes to any entertainment event, such as a ballgame, he always says that he took a client to the game with him and deducts the cost of the ticket as a business expense. When Windsack brings his tax information to you a couple of months later and you see a substantial amount of meal and entertainment expenses, what should you do?

---

[23] Reg. Sec. 1.274-2(f)(2)(i)(b).

EXAMPLE I9-27 ▶ Harry is a salesman who takes a customer to a local nightclub to watch a floor show and to have a few drinks. No business is discussed either before, during, or after the entertainment. The expenses for the beverages and floor show are not deductible because neither of the business meal requirements are met (i.e., the floor show produced substantial distractions, and no business was discussed). Even if business was actually discussed, no deduction would be allowed because there were substantial distractions. ◀

ENTERTAINMENT FACILITIES AND CLUB DUES

KEY POINT
Subject to a very few exceptions, no deduction is permitted for costs related to yachts, swimming pools, fishing camps, tennis courts, bowling alleys, vacation resorts, etc. This highly visible type of entertainment contributed to the public perception that the tax system was unfair.

No deduction is permitted for costs (e.g., depreciation, maintenance, repairs, and so on) related to the maintenance of facilities that are used for entertainment, amusement, or recreation. Facilities include yachts, hunting lodges, beach cottages, and so on.

No deduction is permitted for any type of club dues (including business, social, athletic, luncheon, and sporting clubs, as well as airline and hotel clubs).[24] Professional, civic and public service organizations (e.g., business leagues, trade associations, chambers of commerce, boards of trade, and real estate boards) are generally not subject to the dues disallowance rules. Initiation fees that are paid only upon joining a club are treated as nondeductible capital expenditures. While club dues are not deductible, other business expenses (e.g., business meals) are deductible if the general requirements for entertainment deductions are met.

EXAMPLE I9-28 ▶ Heidi is a self-employed CPA who entertains clients at her country club. Her club expenses include the following:

Annual dues	$4,000
Meal and entertainment charges related to business use	3,000
Personal-use meal charges	2,500
Initiation fee	10,000
Total expenses	$19,500

The only expense that is deductible is 50% of the specific business charges relating to the meals and entertainment. Thus, Heidi may deduct $1,500 ($3,000 × 0.50) *for* AGI as a business expense because she is a self-employed CPA. ◀

BUSINESS GIFTS

Business gifts are subject to an annual ceiling amount of $25 per donee.[25] Amounts in excess of the $25 limit per donee are disallowed. The following rules and exceptions apply to determine the business gift deduction:

▶ Multiple gifts to each donee are aggregated for purposes of applying the $25 per donee annual limitation. Husbands and wives and other family members are treated as a single donee.

▶ Husbands and wives who make gifts to a particular donee are treated as a single taxpayer and are subject to a single $25 limit.

▶ Incidental costs such as gift wrapping, mailing, and delivery of gifts and certain imprinted gift items costing $4 or less are excluded.

▶ Employee achievement awards made for length of service or safety that are under $400 per individual are excluded.[26]

▶ A gift from an employee to his or her supervisor does not qualify as a business gift because such gifts are personal rather than business related and are, therefore, not deductible.

EXAMPLE I9-29 ▶ Jack, an employee, makes the following gifts during the year, none of which are reimbursed by his employer:

---

[24] Sec. 274(a)(3).
[25] Sec. 274(b)(1).
[26] Sec. 274(j). The total limit including both qualified and nonqualified plan awards is $1,600 per individual (see Chapter I4).

9-16 Individuals ▼ Chapter 9

REAL-WORLD EXAMPLE
A taxpayer who had deducted the full cost of two wedding gifts, both of which were in excess of $25 apiece, was able to deduct only $25 for each gift. *Jack R. Howard,* 1981 PH T.C. Memo ¶81,250, 41 TCM 1554.

Jack's immediate supervisor	$20
Jack's secretary	15
Jeff (a customer of Jack's)	24
Jeff's wife (a noncustomer)	26
Gift-wrapping for the gift to Jeff	6
Total	$91

Jack's total deduction for business gifts is $46 ($15 + $25 + $6) and is classified as a miscellaneous itemized deduction subject to the 2% nondeductible floor because Jack is an employee. The $20 gift to Jack's immediate supervisor is not deductible. The gifts of $24 and $26 to Jeff and Jeff's wife must be aggregated and are limited to $25. The gift-wrapping charge is fully deductible because it is an incidental cost. ◀

LIMITATIONS ON ENTERTAINMENT TICKETS

In addition to the general 50% meals and entertainment limitation, the cost of a ticket for any entertainment activity or facility is limited to the ticket's face value. Thus, the 50% limit applies to the face value of the ticket. Further restrictions are placed on the rental of skyboxes that are leased for more than one event.[27]

EXAMPLE I9-30 ▶ Able Corporation acquires four tickets to a football game for $500 that are used for entertaining customers. The face amount of the tickets is only $100. Able's deduction for entertainment is initially limited to the $100 face value of the tickets. The deductible amount is $50 ($100 × 0.50) after applying the 50% limit on entertainment expenses. ◀

REIMBURSED EMPLOYEE BUSINESS EXPENSES

The tax treatment of reimbursements received by an employee from his employer for employment-related expenses depends upon whether the reimbursement is made pursuant to an **accountable** or **nonaccountable** plan. An accountable plan is a reimbursement arrangement that meets both of the following two tests.[28]

ADDITIONAL COMMENT
While reimbursed business expenses under an accountable plan are technically deductions for AGI, they do not actually appear on the employee's tax return as a deduction. This is because the reimbursement itself is not included on the Form W-2.

1. Substantiation—the employee must make an adequate accounting of expenses to his employer, which means that each business expense must be substantiated (an expense report, for example); and

2. Return of excess reimbursement—within a reasonable period of time, the employee is required to return to the employer any portion of the reimbursement in excess of the substantiated expenses.

If both of these tests are not met, all amounts paid to an employee are treated as paid under a nonaccountable plan.

ACCOUNTABLE PLAN. Under an accountable plan, reimbursements are excluded from the employee's gross income and the expenses are not deductible by the employee. Because of this netting of reimbursement and expense, nothing is reported on the employee's return. In the event, however, that an excess reimbursement is not returned to the employer, the excess reimbursement is included in the employee's gross income.

EXAMPLE I9-31 ▶ Antoine is an employee of the Bluechip Corporation, which maintains an accountable plan for purposes of reimbursing employee expenses. During the current year, Antoine went on a busi-

---

[27] Sec. 274(l)(2). The cost of a skybox is disallowed to the extent that it exceeds the cost of the highest-priced nonluxury box seat tickets multiplied by the number of seats in the skybox (e.g., if a skybox contains 30 seats and the cost of the highest-priced nonluxury box seat for a particular event is $40, the deduction for the skybox is limited to $1,200 ($40 × 30). The deduction would be also reduced by the 50% limitation applicable to entertainment expenses.

[28] Reg. Sec. 1.62-2(c).

ness trip and incurred $1,500 of expenses as follows: airfare, $800; lodging, $450; meals, $200; and tips, $50. Bluechip reimbursed him $1,500. Because the reimbursement is pursuant to an accountable plan, Antoine will not include the $1,500 reimbursement in his gross income and he is not allowed to deduct any of the business expenses. ◀

EXAMPLE I9-32 ▶ Using the same facts as in Example I9-31, assume Bluechip advanced Antoine $1,800 for his business trip and his expenses were the same as above. If Antoine returned the excess $300 to Bluechip within a reasonable period of time, the result would be the same as in Example I9-31. However, if Antoine did not return the excess reimbursement (even though he is required to under the terms of the plan), Antoine must include the $300 in his gross income. ◀

If an employee receives a reimbursement that is not as much as his expenses, a proration is required.

EXAMPLE I9-33 ▶ Fred, an employee, incurs employment-related expenses of $4,500 consisting of $1,200 business meals, $1,800 local transportation, and $1,500 entertainment of customers. He receives a $3,000 reimbursement from his employer that is intended to cover all of the expenses. Since the reimbursement is less than the amount of expenses, Fred must prorate the expenses as follows:

Expense	Total Amount	Reimbursed Expense [a]	Unreimbursed Expense
Business meals	$1,200	$ 800	$ 400
Local transportation	1,800	1,200	600
Entertainment	1,500	1,000	500
Total	$4,500	$3,000	$1,500

The reimbursed expenses of $3,000 are not deductible by Fred and the $3,000 reimbursement is not reportable as income. The $1,500 of unreimbursed expenses are deductible *from* AGI (subject to 2% of AGI) as follows:

Business meals ($400 × 50%)	$200
Local transportation	600
Entertainment ($500 × 50%)	250
	$1,050

[a] Reimbursements are allocated to each expense category on a prorata basis. For example, the $800 for business meals is computed, $\frac{\$1,200}{\$4,500} \times \$3,000$. ◀

KEY POINT
Why does the government require reimbursements from nonaccountable plans to be included in the employee's gross income? Because these types of plans are often referred to as "expense accounts paid to employees as additional compensation."

NONACCOUNTABLE PLAN. Under a nonaccountable plan, reimbursements are included in the employee's gross income and the expenses are deductible by the employee as miscellaneous itemized deductions, subject to the 2% of AGI floor and the 50% disallowance for meals and entertainment expenses.

EXAMPLE I9-34 ▶ Use the same facts as in Example I9-31 except that Bluechip does not require its employees to submit an accounting of expenses incurred. Bluechip's plan is a nonaccountable plan. Antoine must include the $1,500 in his gross income and may deduct the expenses as miscellaneous itemized deductions, subject to the 2% of AGI floor, in the amount of $1,400 [$800 + 450 + (200 × 50%) + 50]. ◀

PER DIEM ALLOWANCES FOR MEALS AND LODGING. The IRS permits employers and employees to use optional "per diem allowances" for meals and lodging expenses in lieu of actual expenses. The use of per diem allowances is intended to simplify the burden of keeping detailed records for taxpayers who incur significant travel expenses. Special tables have been issued by the IRS that provide fixed per diem amounts for lodging as well as meals and incidental expenses (M&IE). The per diem allowances vary in amount depending on the city in which the travel took place. The tables list many cities in the United States as well as many cities in foreign countries. Thus, a taxpayer must only substantiate the time, place, and business purpose of the trip and then is permitted to use the per diem allowances. The per diem system is permitted only for payments under an accountable plan, the expenses must be reasonably expected to be incurred, and the amount of expenses should be in reasonable proximity to the expected actual expense amount.[29] A full discussion of this topic is outside the scope of this textbook.

EXAMPLE I9-35 ▶ Peyton Boying is an employee of UT, Inc. UT, Inc. maintains an accountable plan for reimbursing employees for their business expenses. Peyton travels extensively in the United States for business purposes. Instead of requiring Peyton to keep actual records of his travel expenses, UT, Inc. reimburses Peyton the per diem amounts as allowed by the IRS. Assuming Peyton traveled exclusively in low-cost localities (see footnote below) and was away from home for 100 days, UT, Inc. could reimburse Peyton in the amount of $12,400 (100 days × $124) without the necessity of Peyton keeping detailed records of his actual travel expenses. The amount that Peyton actually spent is irrelevant as the IRS will accept the per diem amounts. ◀

Table I9-2 summarizes the concepts relating to employee business expenses and reimbursements.

▼ TABLE I9-2
Treatment of Employee Reimbursements

TYPE OF PLAN	TAX EFFECT
ACCOUNTABLE PLAN	
Reimbursement = Expense	No effect, amounts are netted and not reported on employee's return.
Reimbursement > Expense	Not permissible under plan, but should it occur, excess reimbursement is included in employee's gross income.
Reimbursement < Expense	Expenses are prorated to amount of reimbursement. Reimbursed expenses–no effect; Unreimbursed expenses are deductible as miscellaneous itemized deductions subject to 2% of AGI.
NONACCOUNTABLE PLAN	
Reimbursements	Always included in employee's gross income.
Expenses	Deductible as miscellaneous itemized deductions subject to 2% of AGI.

MOVING EXPENSES

ADDITIONAL COMMENT
In 1996, moving expenses deducted on tax returns totaled $1.6 billion.

Moving expenses are generally nondeductible personal expenditures. However, Sec. 217 allows a limited deduction for moving expenses for employees and self-employed people. The underlying rationale for this deduction is that such moves are similar to business expenditures because they are either employment-related or connected with a trade or business.

EXAMPLE I9-36 ▶ Ken retires from his job and moves from Ohio to Arizona. His moving expenses are nondeductible personal expenditures because the move is not employment-related and he is not moving to look for a new job. ◀

---

[29] The IRS tables for per diem allowances paid on or after October 1, 2000 may be found in Rev. Proc. 2000-39, I.R.B. 2000-41. The rate for high-cost localities (specifically identified by the IRS) is $201 per day (including $42 for M&IE); low-cost localities are $124 per day (including $34 for M&IE). Further, self-employed individuals who are not reimbursed for their travel expenses may use the M&IE rate, but must substantiate lodging with actual receipts.

Employee Expenses and Deferred Compensation ▼ Individuals 9-19

OBJECTIVE 3
Identify deductible moving expenses and determine the amount and year of deductibility

Two conditions must be met for a moving expense to be deductible:[30]

- *Distance requirement.* The new job location must be at least 50 miles farther from the taxpayer's old residence than the old residence was from the former place of employment. If an individual has no former place of employment, the new job must be at least 50 miles from the old residence.

- *Time requirement.* A new or transferred employee must be employed on a full-time basis at the new location for at least 39 weeks during the 12-month period immediately following the move. More stringent requirements must be met by self-employed people who either work as an employee at the new location or continue to be self-employed. Such individuals are subject to a 78-week minimum work period during the first two years following the move. At least 39 of the 78 weeks must be in the first 12-month period. A waiver of the time requirements is permitted for both employees and self-employed individuals if the taxpayer becomes disabled, dies, or is involuntarily terminated (other than for willful misconduct). Unemployed or retired individuals are generally not able to deduct moving expenses because they do not meet the 39 or 78 week test.

ADDITIONAL COMMENT
The time requirement test ensures that taxpayers cannot use temporary jobs as a pretext for deducting the cost of moving for personal reasons.

EXAMPLE I9-37 ▶ Ellen is employed by the Able Company in Dallas, Texas. She lives 30 miles from her place of employment in Dallas. If Ellen accepts a new job in Houston, the new job location is 270 miles from her former residence in Dallas. The 50-mile distance requirement is satisfied because the distance from her old residence to her new job in Houston exceeds the distance from her old residence to her old job by 240 miles (270 − 30). In addition, to meet the time requirement, Ellen must be employed on a full-time basis in Houston for at least 39 weeks during the 12-month period immediately following the move. ◀

EXAMPLE I9-38 ▶ Assume the same facts as in Example I9-37, except that Ellen accepts a new job and moves to a new residence in a small town outside of Dallas. Her new job location is 55 miles from her former residence. The 50-mile distance requirement is not met because the distance from her old residence to her new job is 55 miles and the distance from her old residence to her old job is 30 miles; thus, the excess distance is only 25 miles. ◀

ADDITIONAL COMMENT
The individual need not be employed at the location that he or she is leaving. For example, a graduating college student who has not been employed for the most recent four years could deduct moving costs if the distance requirement is satisfied and if he or she has been employed at the *new* location for the minimum time period.

EXPENSE CLASSIFICATION
Moving expenses of an employee or a self-employed individual are deductible *for* AGI.[31] Thus, a taxpayer may receive a tax benefit from the deduction of moving expenses even if the standard deduction is used in lieu of itemizing deductions.

DEFINITION OF MOVING EXPENSES
DIRECT MOVING EXPENSES. Only direct moving expenses are deductible. These expenses are deductible without limit as long as they are reasonable in amount and include:

- The cost of moving household goods and personal effects from the former residence to the new residence (e.g., moving van).

- The cost of traveling (including lodging but excluding meals) from the former residence to the new residence. If the trip is by personal automobile, a deduction of 12 cents per mile (or actual expenses) is allowed for each automobile that is driven.

- The expenses of moving household goods and personal effects do not include storage charges in excess of 30 days, penalties for breaking leases, mortgage penalties, expenses of refitting drapes, or losses on deposits and club memberships.[32]

KEY POINT
The standard mileage rate for purposes of the moving expense deduction is only 10 cents per mile, compared to the 2000 standard business mileage rate of 32.5 cents per mile.

EXAMPLE I9-39 ▶ Gail, a resident of California and a college student in that state, graduates from college and accepts a new position with an accounting firm in Atlanta. Thus, Gail is an employee of the Atlanta firm. Because the move meets the distance requirement (i.e., more than 50 miles), Gail

---

[30] The requirements for deducting moving expenses are contained in Sec. 217 and the Treasury Regulations thereunder.

[31] Sec. 62(a)(15). For years before 1994 moving expenses were deductible *from* AGI as an itemized deduction (not subject to the 2% nondeductible floor).

[32] Reg. Sec. 1.217-2(b)(3). In-transit storage charges for up to 30 consecutive days are allowable moving expenses.

qualifies for the deduction if she also meets the 39-week time requirement. Gail incurs the following expenses pursuant to the move: moving van, $1,200; lodging en route, $400; automobile expenses, $300 (2,500 miles × $0.12 cents per mile); and tolls and parking, $25. Assuming these expenses are reasonable, they qualify as direct moving expenses and are deductible without limitation. The cost of any meals incurred by Gail en route is not deductible.

Otherwise allowable expenses of any individual other than the taxpayer are taken into account only if the individual has both the former residence and the new residence as his principal place of abode and is a member of the taxpayer's household.

EXAMPLE I9-40 ▶ Assume the same facts as in Example I9-39 except that Gail's son Paul is a member of her household. Additional automobile expenses (including tolls and parking) of $275 are incurred during the move because Paul owns an automobile which is driven to the new location. The $275 of additional automobile expenses are deductible as moving expenses because Paul is a member of Gail's household and his principal place of abode includes both the former and the new residences.

KEY POINT

Indirect moving expenses are not deductible after December 31, 1993. In the Revenue Reconciliation Act of 1993, Congress eliminated the deduction for costs associated with pre-move househunting trips, temporary quarters, and selling the old residence. Congress felt that a deduction was not justified for expenses that were not directly related to the move.

NONDEDUCTIBLE INDIRECT MOVING EXPENSES. In addition to the disallowed moving expenses previously discussed (e.g., meals en route, storage charges etc.), the following indirect or moving-related expense items are not deductible:[33]

▶ Househunting trips including meals, lodging, and transportation.
▶ Temporary living expenses at the new job location.
▶ Qualified expenses related to a sale, purchase, or lease of a residence (e.g., attorney's fees, points, or payments to a lessor to cancel a lease).

TREATMENT OF EMPLOYER REIMBURSEMENTS

Moving expense reimbursements made by an employer, either paid directly or through reimbursement, are excluded from the employee's gross income as a qualified fringe benefit under Sec. 132 to the extent that the expenses meet the requirements for deductibility (i.e., the reimbursement is for moving expenses that are otherwise deductible under Sec. 217). Moving expense reimbursements must be included in gross income if the employee actually deducted the expenses in a prior tax year or if the expenses are otherwise not deductible under Sec. 217.[34]

EXAMPLE I9-41 ▶ In 2001, Ralph incurs $2,400 of moving expenses related to moving household effects and traveling to his new residence. He also incurs $2,600 of nondeductible moving-related expenses (e.g., househunting trips and temporary living expenses). Ralph receives a $5,000 reimbursement from his employer. Of the total reimbursement, $2,400 is excluded from gross income as a Sec. 132 fringe benefit. However, $2,600 of the reimbursement for nondeductible moving-related expenses is included in Ralph's gross income under Sec. 82. None of the $2,400 of moving expenses may be deducted by Ralph because they were reimbursed by his employer.

EDUCATION EXPENSES

OBJECTIVE 4

Describe the requirements for deducting education expenses

Generally, education expenses are considered personal expenses and, therefore, are not deductible despite the obvious benefits that accrue to society from the pursuit of such activities. However, education expenses that are necessary in the pursuit of an employment-related or trade or business activity are deductible. It would be inequitable if such educational expenditures were not deductible because they are incurred to produce income from employment or business activities. Educational expenses incurred by employees or self-employed individuals may be contrasted with scholarship and fellow-

---

[33] Before 1994, indirect moving expenses were deductible subject to a $1,500 limit for househunting trips and temporary living expenses and a $3,000 overall limitation was applied to all indirect moving expenses.

[34] Sec. 82 and Sec. 132(a).

ADDITIONAL COMMENT

Attendance at a convention or professional meeting is one of the most common deductible education expenses. Almost every profession or occupation has its own society or association. Often these organizations sponsor local, regional, or national meetings. Training sessions or other types of educational activities are normally included on the program.

ship grants under Sec. 117 and educational assistance payments under Sec. 127 made by employers. Both of these latter types of payments generally can be excluded from gross income. (See Chapter I4 for a discussion of scholarship and fellowship grants and educational assistance payments.) Further, several recent provisions have been enacted to provide individuals with some reductions in taxation for education expenses. The primary two provisions are in the form of tax credits, the HOPE Scholarship Credit and the Lifetime Learning Credit. Both of these credits are discussed in Chapter I14. Finally, a new type of Individual Retirement Account for education was also created, this new IRA is discussed later in this chapter.

The discussion below focuses on the deductibility of education expenses. The other tax incentives for education are discussed elsewhere in the textbook.

CLASSIFICATION OF EDUCATION EXPENSES

Depending on the nature of the education-related activity, educational expenses may be either personal and nondeductible, deductible *for* AGI, deductible *from* AGI (as a miscellaneous itemized deduction), or reimbursed by an employer and excluded from gross income. Table I9-3 illustrates the tax consequences that are accorded to various types of education expenses depending on the facts and circumstances and the type of expenditure for each case.

GENERAL REQUIREMENTS FOR A DEDUCTION

An employee may generally deduct education expenses if either of the following two requirements are met:[35]

TYPICAL MISCONCEPTION

Education costs include more than the cost of books, tuition, registration fees, and supplies. Transportation costs and travel costs are also included.

▶ The expenditure is incurred to maintain or improve skills required by the individual in his or her employment, trade, or business; or

▶ The expenditure is incurred to meet requirements imposed by law or by the employer for retention of employment, rank, or compensation rate.

▼ **TABLE I9-3**
Classification and Tax Treatment of Educational Expenses

Situation Facts	Classification and Tax Treatment
▶ Jeremy is a college student who is not classified as an employee and is pursuing a general course of study.	▶ The expenses are nondeductible personal expenditures regardless of whether Jeremy or his parents pay them.
▶ Irene is an employee who incurs certain employment-related educational expenses including travel, transportation, tuition, and books. Her expenses are not reimbursed by her employer.	▶ If the expenses meet the two general deduction requirements, the education expenses are deductible *from* AGI as a miscellaneous itemized deduction (subject to the 2% nondeductible floor).
▶ Jesse is an employee who receives educational assistance payments from his employer to reimburse him certain educational expenses incurred in attending college at the undergraduate level.	▶ Educational assistance payments up to $5,250 per year are excluded from Jesse's gross income and are deductible by the employer as trade or business expenses if the requirements of Sec. 127 are met.[36]
▶ Jackie is a self-employed CPA who incurs education expenses including travel, transportation, books, registration fees, and so on to attend a continuing education conference.	▶ All of the education expenses are deductible *for* AGI as trade or business expenses.
▶ Jim is an employee who incurs education expenses for a continuing education course related to his employment, and the expenses are reimbursed by the employer.	▶ The reimbursement is deductible by the employer as a trade or business expense. There is no tax effect to the employee because the education expenses are offset by the reimbursement.

---

[35] The Sec. 127 exclusion is applicable for expenses paid by an employer for courses beginning on or before December 31, 2001. Qualified expenses include tuition, fees, and related expenses. Graduate-level courses do not qualify for the exclusion.

[36] Reg. Sec. 1.162-5

Even if one of the two requirements above are met, education expenses are not deductible if:

- The education is required to meet minimum educational requirements for qualification in the taxpayer's employment; or
- The education qualifies the taxpayer for a new trade or business (or employment activity).

The deductibility of education expenses has been a frequent source of controversy and litigation because of the uncertainty in interpreting the above Regulations. The principal area of disagreement has been the interpretation of the term "qualifies the taxpayer for a new trade or business." If a taxpayer undertakes education and that education will *qualify* her for a new trade or business, then her expenses will not be deductible. For example, several courts have disallowed deductions to IRS agents and accountants for educational expenses incurred in obtaining a law degree, even though such training would be helpful in the taxpayer's employment.[37] The courts reasoned that the taxpayers were qualifying for a new profession (i.e., the practice of law). However, the IRS has ruled that a practicing dentist may deduct educational expenses in becoming an orthodontist under the theory that a dentist becoming an orthodontist is not a new trade or business.[38]

> **ETHICAL POINT**
> A client asks advice from his CPA as to whether certain educational expenses are deductible. The CPA should inform the client that the advice reflects professional judgment based on an existing situation. The CPA should use cautionary language to the effect that the advice is based on facts as stated and authorities that are subject to change.

STOP & THINK

Question: The Regulations clearly provide that if the education "qualifies" a taxpayer for a new trade or business, the cost of such education is not deductible. If taken to the extreme, could the IRS argue that *any* course would qualify an individual for a new trade or business? For example, if a person took a basket weaving course, could not the IRS argue that the person is now qualified for the new trade or business of basket weaving? How can a taxpayer support his position that the education does not qualify him for a new trade or business in order to meet the deductibility requirements?

Solution: This is a difficult question and many commentators have written that the Regulations are unfairly harsh toward taxpayers. The courts have required that the IRS be "reasonable" in its interpretations of qualification of a new trade or business. The best way for a taxpayer to support his position is to find a case where the facts are approximately the same as the taxpayer's and where the court has upheld the taxpayer's position in that case.

> **ADDITIONAL COMMENT**
> The same course could be deductible as a qualified educational expense or not depending on the particular situation of the student. For example, a CPA enrolled in a taxation course to update his or her tax knowledge could deduct the expense. On the other hand, a non-CPA taking the course as part of a series of courses meeting the requirements to sit for the CPA exam could not deduct the expense. The CPA has already met the minimum education requirements for the profession and the non-CPA has not.

Generally, a taxpayer must be employed or self-employed to be eligible for an education expense deduction. However, some courts have permitted individuals to qualify if they are unemployed for a temporary period.[39] School teachers have generally qualified for an education expense deduction in situations where the public school system requires advanced education courses as a condition for retention of employment or renewal of a teaching certificate or where state law imposes similar requirements. However, college instructors who are working on a doctorate in a college where the Ph.D. is the minimum degree for holding a permanent position generally have not been permitted to deduct the expenditures made to obtain the degree.[40]

EXAMPLE I9-42 ▶ Jane is a self-employed dentist who incurs education expenses attending a continuing education conference on new techniques in her field. Such expenditures are incurred to maintain or improve her skills as a practicing dentist (a trade or business activity). All of her educational expenses are deductible *for* AGI because Jane is engaged in a trade or business activity. ◀

EXAMPLE I9-43 ▶ Juan is a business executive who incurs education expenses in the pursuit of an MBA degree in management. None of the expenses are reimbursed by Juan's employer. The expenses are deductible because they are incurred to maintain or improve Juan's skills as a manager and do not qualify Juan for a new trade or business. All of Juan's education expenses (e.g., travel,

---

[37] *Jeffry L. Weiler*, 54 T.C. 398 (1970).
[38] Rev. Rul. 74-78, 1974-1 C.B. 44.
[39] *Robert J. Picknally*, 1977 PH T.C. Memo ¶77,321, 36 TCM 1292. The IRS has conceded that a deduction may be warranted in periods where the cessation of business activity was for periods of a year or less (Rev. Rul. 68-591, 1968-2 C.B. 73).
[40] *Kenneth C. Davis*, 65 T.C. 1014 (1976).

transportation, tuition, books, and word processing) are deductible *from* AGI as a miscellaneous itemized deduction (subject to the 2% nondeductible floor). ◀

EXAMPLE I9-44 ▶ Janet is a high school teacher who is required by state law to complete a specified number of additional graduate courses to renew her provisional teaching certificate. None of the expenses are reimbursed by Janet's employer. The educational expenses are deductible *from* AGI as a miscellaneous itemized deduction (subject to the 2% nondeductible floor) because the expenditures are incurred to meet the requirements imposed by law to retain her job and do not qualify her for a new trade or business. ◀

EXAMPLE I9-45 ▶ Jean is an accountant with a public accounting firm who incurs expenses in connection with taking the CPA examination (e.g., CPA review course fees, travel, and transportation). None of the expenses are reimbursed by Jean's employer. Even though the expenditures may improve her employment-related skills, they are not deductible because they are incurred to meet the minimum educational standards for qualification in Jean's accounting position.[41] ◀

EXAMPLE I9-46 ▶ Joy is a tax accountant who incurs expenses to obtain a law degree. Despite the fact that the law school courses may be helpful to Joy to maintain or improve her skills as a tax practitioner, such expenses are not deductible because the taxpayer is qualifying for a new trade or business. If Joy were not a degree candidate at the law school and merely took a few tax law courses for continuing education, the educational expenses would be deductible because they are incurred to maintain or improve Joy's skills as a tax specialist and do not qualify her for a new trade or business. In such a case, the expenses are deductible *for* AGI if Joy is self-employed and *from* AGI as a miscellaneous itemized deduction (subject to the 2% nondeductible floor) if Joy is an employee. ◀

KEY POINT

The deduction for travel expenses is not permitted if the travel itself is the educational activity. Therefore, a high school teacher who teaches Spanish cannot deduct expenses incurred in living in Madrid during the summer.

OFFICE IN HOME EXPENSES

OBJECTIVE 5

Determine whether the expenses of an office in home meet the requirements for deductibility and apply the gross income limitations

Employees or self-employed individuals who use a portion of their home for trade or business or employment-related activities should be entitled to a deduction because the property is used for trade or business or employment-related activities. However, it is often difficult to determine whether a taxpayer is using a portion of the home for business or personal use.

For over twenty years, there has been an ongoing controversy in the tax law as to the deductibility of office in home expenses. Because of the possibility of abuse by taxpayers, the IRC, Treasury Regulations, and the courts[42] have been extremely strict as to who qualifies to deduct office in home expenses. In order to promote fairness and consistency in the tax law, Congress, effective for tax years beginning after December 31, 1998, liberalized the definition of an office in home that qualifies for a tax deduction.

GENERAL REQUIREMENTS FOR A DEDUCTION

Employees and self-employed individuals are permitted to deduct office in home expenses only if the office is exclusively used on a regular basis under any of the following conditions:

▶ The office is used as the principal place of business for *any* trade or business of the taxpayer;

▶ The office is used as a place for meeting or dealing with patients, clients, or customers in the normal course of business; or

▶ If the office in home is located in a separate structure which is not attached to the dwelling unit, the office is used in connection with the taxpayer's trade or business.[43]

In addition to meeting any of these tests, an employee further must prove that the exclusive use is for the convenience of the *employer*. It is not enough that it is merely appropriate or helpful to the employee.

ADDITIONAL COMMENT

Approximately 24 million individuals, or 23% of the work force, work at least part-time at home.

REAL-WORLD EXAMPLE

Most teachers have been denied a home office deduction because the home office is not the principal place of business. Also, most teachers cannot demonstrate that their office in the home is for the convenience of the employer because the employer typically provides an office at the school.

---

[41] Rev. Rul. 69-292, 1969-1 C.B. 84.
[42] See, for example, *CIR v. Nader E. Soliman*, 71 AFTR2d 93-463, 93-1 USTC 50,014 (USSC, 1993).
[43] Sec. 280A(c)(1).

The first condition above has caused the major controversy in this area. Taxpayers are required to prove that the office is used exclusively as the "principal place of business". Under prior law, the principal place of business was interpreted to mean the "most important or significant place for the business", or more precisely, where the primary services were performed. Thus, a physician who performed medical services at a hospital but maintained an office in home to perform administrative duties was not allowed a deduction for the office because the principal place of business was interpreted to be the hospital.

EXAMPLE I9-47 ▶ In the *Soliman* case, Dr. Soliman was a self-employed anesthesiologist who performed medical services at three hospitals, none of which provided him with an office. He spent approximately two hours per day in his office in home where he maintained patient records and correspondence and he performed billing procedures. The office was not used as a place for meeting with or dealing with patients, clients, or customers in the normal course of his business. The U.S. Supreme Court denied a deduction for Dr. Soliman's office in home because it concluded that the essence of professional service rendered by the doctor was the actual medical treatment in the hospitals. A second factor considered by the court was the amount of time spent at the office relative to the total work effort. The effect of this case was to deny a deduction for an office in home for any type of taxpayer in a trade or business where the primary services were performed outside of the office (such as plumbers, electricians). This case was highly criticized. ◀

To combat the perceived unfairness of the *Soliman* case, Congress expanded the definition of "principal place of business" for tax years beginning after December 31, 1998. An office in home now qualifies as a taxpayer's principal place of business if:

1. the office is used by the taxpayer for *administrative or management* activities of the taxpayer's trade or business, and
2. there is no other fixed location of the trade or business where the taxpayer conducts substantial administrative or management activities of the trade or business.[44]

KEY POINT
The office-in-home deduction is available only where the office is being used for trade or business purposes. No deduction is permitted if the office is used to carry on investment activities.

Thus, the new law essentially allows a deduction for an office in home even though the taxpayer provides his primary service away from the office. The above tests are clearly intended for self-employed taxpayers. However, they also apply to employees except that the additional "convenience of the employer" test will still apply.

EXAMPLE I9-48 ▶ David is a self-employed electrician who performs his electrical services at the location of his customers. He also maintains an office where he does his administrative and management duties. David is permitted a deduction for an office in home even though his primary duties of providing electrical services are performed away from his office. ◀

EXAMPLE I9-49 ▶ Barbara is an employee of DRK, Inc. and is provided with an office on DRK's premises. However, Barbara's job requires significant administrative work after normal working hours and she prefers to perform these duties in her office at home. Barbara may not deduct the costs of her office in home because she uses her office at home for *her* convenience, not her employer's convenience. ◀

As can be seen from the discussion above, the deduction for an office in home is generally restricted to self-employed taxpayers and employees who are not provided with an office by their employer. If a self-employed taxpayer maintains an office in home, the expenses are deductible *for* AGI. Employees must deduct the office in home expenses as miscellaneous itemized deductions, subject to the 2% nondeductible floor.

---

[44] Ibid. For years before 1999, this new definition of principal place of business does not apply. Thus, the restrictive rules promulgated by *Soliman* apply to these years.

DEDUCTION AND LIMITATIONS

The deduction for home office expenses is computed using the following two categories of expenses:

1. Expenses directly related to the office, and
2. Expenses indirectly related to the office.

Direct expenses include operating expenses (supplies, etc.) that are used in the business as well as other expenses that relate solely to the office, such as painting and wallpaper. Indirect expenses are the prorata share of expenses that benefit the entire house or apartment, such as mortgage interest (or rent), real estate taxes, insurance, utilities, and maintenance. The office in the home expense is the sum of the direct expenses plus the prorata share (generally based on square footage) of indirect expenses.

EXAMPLE I9-50 ▶ Julie works as a full-time employee for a local company. She also operates a mail order business out of her home and maintains an office in her home that is used exclusively for business. The size of her home in total is 2,400 square feet and her office is 300 square feet. During the current year, the following expenses were incurred in connection with the office in her home:

Painting of office	$ 600
Decorations in office	900
Mortgage interest (total)	3,200
Real estate taxes (total)	1,800
Insurance (total)	600
Utilities (total)	2,400
Depreciation (total)	800

Julie's home office expense for the current year would be computed as follows:

Direct expenses:		
Painting	$600	
Decorations	900	$1,500
Indirect expenses:		
Mortgage interest	3,200	
Real estate taxes	1,800	
Insurance	600	
Utilities	2,400	
Depreciation	800	
	8,800	
Business percentage (300/2,400)	12.5%	1,100
Total expense for office in home		$2,600

◀

TYPICAL MISCONCEPTION

Where a taxpayer is not entitled to an office-in-home deduction, the taxpayer can still deduct directly related business expenses (e.g., the cost of office supplies, and an MACRS deduction on filing cabinets and other equipment).

The total allowable office in home expenses may not exceed the taxpayer's gross income from the business (or rental) activity.[45] This ceiling limitation on otherwise qualifying office in home deductions is intended to prevent taxpayers from recognizing tax losses if the business (or rental) activity does not produce sufficient amounts of gross income. Expenses disallowed because of the gross income limitation can be carried forward but are subject to the gross income limitation in the later year and are subject to specific ordering rules.[46]

Employee expense classifications and deduction limitations are summarized in Topic Review I9-1.

---

[45] Sec. 280A(c)(5).
[46] See Prop. Reg. Sec. 1.280A-2 for the ordering rules. These rules are similar, but not identical to the ordering rules for hobby losses under Sec. 183.

Topic Review I9-1

Classification and Deductibility of Employee Expenses

Type of Expenditure	50% Disallowance	For or From AGI	Other Limitations
Miscellaneous itemized deductions	Applies to unreimbursed meals and entertainment	From AGI	Subject to 2% of AGI nondeductible floor.
Reimbursed travel expenses (adequate accounting is made)	Applies to the employer for meals portion of the travel only	For AGI	2% of AGI nondeductible floor applies only to employee expenses that exceed the reimbursement.
Unreimbursed travel expenses	Applies to meals portion of travel only	From AGI	Subject to the 2% of AGI nondeductible floor. Employee must be away from his or her tax home overnight.
Automobile expenses	Not applicable	From AGI	Subject to the 2% of AGI nondeductible floor. The standard mileage rate method may be used.
Moving expenses	Not applicable because meals are not deductible	For AGI;	Indirect moving-related expenses are not deductible.
Entertainment expenses	Applies to all entertainment expenses	From AGI	Subject to the 2% of AGI nondeductible floor. Club dues and initiation fees are not deductible.
Education expenses	Applies to meal portion of education expenses	From AGI	Qualifying expenses are subject to the 2% of AGI nondeductible floor.
Office-in-home	Not applicable	From AGI; If trade- or business-related, the expenses are for AGI	Employment-related expenses (other than real estate taxes and interest) are subject to the 2% of AGI nondeductible floor. Gross income limitations apply to allowable expenses.

DEFERRED COMPENSATION

OBJECTIVE 6

Discuss the tax treatment and requirements for various deferred compensation arrangements

Various types of benefit plans providing favorable tax treatment are available to employees and self-employed individuals. These tax benefits are provided to stimulate savings accumulations for retirement as a supplement to the social security system. Favorable tax consequences generally include the following benefits:

▶ Deferral of taxes on amounts contributed to retirement plans until the individual retires or receives a distribution from the plan;

▶ An immediate deduction for contributions to qualified retirement plans for the employer or self-employed individual;

▶ Deferral of taxation on income earned on retirement plan assets;

The following types of *deferred compensation arrangements* are discussed here:

▶ Qualified pension and profit-sharing plans;

▶ Nonqualified deferred compensation arrangements, including restricted property and employee stock option plans;

▶ Self-employed (H.R. 10) retirement plans and individual retirement accounts (IRAs).

QUALIFIED PENSION AND PROFIT-SHARING PLANS

The federal tax law provides favorable tax benefits for *qualified* pension and profit-sharing plans. A **qualified plan** is one that must meet strict requirements, such as not discriminating in favor of highly compensated individuals, be formed and operated for the exclusive benefit of employees, and meet specified vesting and funding requirements. In a qualified plan, both the employer and employee receive significant tax benefits, as follows:

EMPLOYER: receives an immediate tax deduction for pension and profit-sharing contributions made on behalf of employees.

EMPLOYEE: is not taxed on either employer or employee contributions or earnings of the plan assets until funds are withdrawn from the plan at retirement.[47]

ADDITIONAL COMMENT

The Staff of the Joint Committee on Taxation estimates the revenue loss resulting from the deferral of taxes on contributions and earnings for qualified pension and profit-sharing plans for the period from 1994 through 1998 will approximate $311.1 billion. The provision is designed to encourage employers to establish pension plans for their employees. The employer receives a deduction for the contribution, but the employee is not taxed currently. The repeal of this provision would substantially reduce the budget deficit.

TYPES OF PLANS. Qualified plans[48] include

▶ Pension plans
▶ Profit-sharing plans (including Sec. 401(k) plans)
▶ Stock bonus plans, including employee stock ownership plans (ESOPs)

Pension Plans. The features that distinguish a *qualified pension plan* include the following:

▶ Systematic and definite payments are made to a pension trust (without regard to profits) based on formulas or actuarial methods.
▶ A pension plan may provide for incidental benefits such as disability, death, or medical insurance benefits.

A pension plan may be either contributory or non-contributory. Under a **non-contributory pension plan,** the contributions are made solely by the employer. Under a **contributory pension plan,** the employee also makes voluntary contributions that supplement those made by the employer.

Pension plans may also be either defined benefit plans or defined contribution plans. In a **defined contribution pension plan,** a separate account is established for each participant and fixed amounts are contributed based on a specific formula (e.g., a specified percentage of compensation). The retirement benefits are based on the value of a participant's account (including the amount of earnings that accrue to the account) at the time of retirement.

EXAMPLE I9-51 ▶ Alabama Corporation establishes a qualified pension plan for its employees that provides for employer contributions equal to 8% of each participant's salary. Retirement payments to each participant are based on the amount of accumulated benefits in the employee's account at the retirement date. The pension plan is a defined contribution plan, because the contribution rate is based on a specific and fixed percentage of compensation. ◀

KEY POINT

All qualified plans can be classified into two broad categories. They are either defined contribution plans or defined benefit plans. An understanding of the distinction between these two broad categories is important because some rules will apply to one type of plan but not the other.

Defined benefit plans establish a contribution formula based on actuarial techniques that are sufficient to fund a fixed benefit amount to be paid upon retirement. For example, a defined benefit plan might provide fixed retirement benefits equal to 40% of an employee's average salary for the five years before retirement.

A distinguishing feature of a defined benefit plan is that forfeitures of unvested amounts (e.g., due to employee resignations) must be used to reduce the employer contributions that would otherwise be made under the plan. In a defined contribution plan, however, the forfeitures related to unvested amounts may either be reallocated to the other participants in a nondiscriminatory manner or used to reduce future employer contributions.

---

[47] An employee may not be liable for federal income taxes but may be subject to Social Security taxes and possibly local or city income taxes.

[48] Qualified plans are generally covered in Secs. 401-416 of the IRC.

Profit-Sharing Plans. A qualified **profit-sharing plan** may also be established by an employer in addition to, or in lieu of, a qualified pension plan arrangement. Profit-sharing plans include the following distinguishing features:

- A definite, predetermined formula must be used to allocate employer contributions to individual employees and to establish benefit payments.
- Annual employer contributions are not required, but substantial and recurring contributions must be made to satisfy the requirement that the plan be permanent.
- Employees may be given the option to receive cash that is fully taxable as current compensation or to defer taxation on employer contributions by having such amounts contributed to the profit-sharing trust. Plans of this type are called Sec. 401(k) plans.[49]
- Forfeitures arising under the plan may be reallocated to the remaining participants to increase their profit-sharing benefits, provided that certain nondiscrimination requirements are met.
- Lump-sum payments made to an employee before retirement may be provided following a prescribed period for the vesting of such amounts.
- Incidental benefits such as disability, death, or medical insurance may also be provided in a profit-sharing arrangement.

Stock Bonus Plan. A **stock bonus plan** is a special type of defined contribution plan whereby the investments of the plan are in the employer-company's own stock. The employer makes its contribution to the trust either in cash or in stock. If in cash, the amounts are invested in the company's stock. The stock is allocated and subsequently distributed to the participants. Stock bonus plan requirements are similar to profit-sharing plans. An **employee stock ownership plan (ESOP)** is a type of qualified stock bonus plan.[50] An ESOP, funded by a combination of employer and employee contributions and plan loans, invest primarily in employer stock. The stock is held for the benefit of the employees. ESOPs are attractive because the employer is allowed to reduce taxable income by deducting any dividends that are paid to the participants (or their beneficiaries) in the year such amounts are paid and are taxable to the participant. For employer securities acquired by the ESOP, the dividends-paid deduction is limited to dividends paid on employer stock acquired with an ESOP loan.

QUALIFICATION REQUIREMENTS FOR A QUALIFIED PLAN

> **ADDITIONAL COMMENT**
>
> The tax law with respect to qualified pension and profit-sharing plans is extremely complex. A detailed study of these provisions is beyond the scope of this text.

Qualified pension, profit-sharing, and stock bonus plans must meet complex qualification rules and requirements to achieve and maintain their favored qualifying status. A summary of the important requirements are discussed below.

- Section 401(a) requires that the plan must be for the employee's exclusive benefit. For example, the trust must follow prudent investment rules to ensure that the pension benefits will accrue for the employees' benefit.
- The plan may not discriminate in favor of highly compensated employees. Highly compensated employees are employees who meet either of two tests, (1) own more than 5% of the corporation's stock in either the current or prior year, or (2) receive compensation of greater than $85,000 in the prior year.[51]
- Contributions and plan benefits must bear a uniform relationship to the compensation payments made to covered employees. For example, if contributions for the benefit of the participants are based on a fixed percentage of the employee's compensation (e.g., 4%), the plan should not be disqualified despite the fact that the contributions for highly-compensated employees are greater on an actual dollar basis than those for lower paid individuals.

---

[49] Sec. 401(k).
[50] Secs. 409(a) and 4975(e)(7).
[51] Sec. 414(q). The $85,000 amount is subject to annual indexing for inflation. Alternatively, an employer may elect to define a highly-compensated group as employees earning more than $85,000 *and* the top 20% group of employees based on compensation.

- Certain coverage requirements that are expressed in terms of a portion of the employees covered by the plan must be met.
- An employee's right to receive benefits from the employer's contributions must vest (i.e., become nonforfeitable) after a certain period or number of years of employment. The vesting requirement is intended to ensure that a significant percentage of employees will eventually receive retirement benefits. Employer-provided benefits must be 100% vested after 5 years of service.[52] In all cases, any employee contributions to the plan must vest immediately.

EXAMPLE I9-52 ▶ Ken is a participant in a noncontributory qualified pension plan that provides for no vesting until an employee completes five years of service. Ken terminates his employment with the company after four years of service. Because Ken has not met the minimum vesting requirements, he is not entitled to receive any of the employer contributions that are made on his behalf. If the plan adopted the alternative three- to seven-year vesting schedule (see footnote 46), 40% of the employer-provided benefits would be vested at the time of his termination and would provide Ken with future retirement benefits. ◀

TAX TREATMENT TO EMPLOYEES AND EMPLOYERS

ADDITIONAL COMMENT

Most employees choose to contribute amounts to their qualified retirement plans on a pre-tax basis because of the time value of money. A current deduction (and the related tax savings) is more valuable than a deduction at retirement.

Employer contributions to a qualified plan are immediately deductible (subject to specific limitations on contribution amounts), and earnings on pension fund investments are tax-exempt to the plan. Amounts paid into a plan by or for an employee are not taxable until the pension payments are received, normally at retirement. At the election of the employee, amounts may be treated as having been made from either pre-tax or after-tax earnings. If amounts contributed to a qualified plan by an employee are made on a pre-tax basis, the taxable portion of the employee's earnings is reduced by the contribution amount. This has the effect of permitting a deduction for the contribution amount. When amounts are withdrawn at retirement, the entire distribution is subject to taxation.

EXAMPLE I9-53 ▶ Larry is an employee of Cisco Corporation, which maintains a Sec. 401(k) plan. Larry contributes 5% of his gross salary into the plan on a pre-tax basis. During the current year, Larry's gross salary is $80,000 so his Sec. 401(k) contribution is $4,000. Since Larry's contribution is made on a pre-tax basis, his taxable salary for the current year will be $76,000. In effect, Larry is able to deduct the $4,000 from his salary in the current year. When Larry retires and begins withdrawing amounts from the plan, the entire amount withdrawn will be subject to income taxation. ◀

Conversely, an employee may elect to contribute to a qualified plan on an after-tax basis. If, in Example I9-53, Larry contributed to the Sec. 401(k) plan on an after-tax basis, his taxable salary would have been $80,000. The $4,000 contributed to the plan is treated as an investment in the plan and is considered a tax-free return of capital when this amount is withdrawn at retirement.[53]

EMPLOYEE RETIREMENT PAYMENTS. An employee's retirement benefits are generally taxed under the Sec. 72 annuity rules (see Chapter I3). If the plan is noncontributory (i.e., no employee contributions are made to the plan), all of the pension benefits when received by the employee are fully taxable. If the plan is contributory, each payment is treated, in part, as a tax-free return of the employee's contributions and the remainder is taxable. The excluded portion is based on the ratio of the employee's investment in the contract to the expected return under the contract. However, the total amount that may be excluded is limited to the amount of the employee's contributions to the plan. If the employee dies before the entire investment in the contract is recovered, the unrecovered amount is allowed as an itemized deduction in the year of death.

---

[52] Sec. 411(a). An alternative vesting schedule may also be used that provides for 20% vesting after three years and increases by 20% per year until the employee is fully vested after seven years.

[53] Amounts contributed to a qualified plan on an after-tax basis are treated as an investment in the contract under the annuity rules of Sec. 72. Amounts withdrawn during retirement are taxed under the general rules of Sec. 72. See Chapter I3 for a discussion of taxation of annuities.

EXAMPLE I9-54 ▶ Kevin retires in 2001 and receives annuity payments for life from his employer's qualified pension plan of $24,000 per year beginning in 2002. Kevin's investment in the contract (represented by his contributions) is $100,000, and the total expected return (based on his life expectancy) is $300,000. The exclusion ratio is one-third, so that $8,000 ($24,000 × 0.333) is excluded from Kevin's income and $16,000 ($24,000 − $8,000) is taxable in 2002. After Kevin receives payments for 12.5 years, his investment in the contract is recovered ($8,000 × 12.5 = $100,000), and all subsequent payments are fully taxable. (See Chapter I3 for a discussion of the annuity formula and related rules.) ◀

ADDITIONAL COMMENT

Many individuals have the option of taking their retirement savings from traditional pensions, profit-sharing plans, and 401(k)s as a lump sum or an annuity. Those who want to take a lump-sum distribution can delay taxes by transferring the money directly into a tax-deferred IRA.

KEY POINT

For purposes of the limitation on employer contributions, all defined contribution plans maintained by one employer are treated as a single defined contribution plan. Furthermore, under some circumstances a group of employers can be treated as a single employer.

If an employee age 59½ or older receives a lump-sum distribution from a qualified plan, a five-year forward income-averaging technique is generally available through 1999 to mitigate the effects of receiving a large amount of income in the year of the distribution.[54]

LIMITATION ON EMPLOYER CONTRIBUTIONS. The Code places the following limitations on the amounts an employer may contribute to qualified pension, profit-sharing, and stock bonus plans:

▶ Defined contribution plan contributions in 2001 are limited to the lesser of $35,000 or 25% of the employee's compensation.[55]

▶ Defined benefit plans are restricted to an annual benefit to an employee equal to the lesser of $140,000 for 2001 or 100% of the participant's average compensation for the highest three years.[56]

▶ An overall maximum annual employer deduction of 15% of compensation paid or accrued to plan participants is placed on profit-sharing and stock bonus plans.[57] If an employer has more than one type of qualified plan (e.g., a defined benefit pension plan and a profit-sharing plan), a maximum deduction of 25% of compensation is allowed.

The distinguishing features and major requirements for qualified pension and profit-sharing plans are summarized in Topic Review I9-2.

Topic Review I9-2

Qualified Pension and Profit-Sharing Plans

DISTINGUISHING FEATURES AND MAJOR REQUIREMENTS

▶ Employer contributions and earnings on contributed amounts are not taxed to employees until distributed or made available. The contributions are immediately deductible by the employer.
▶ Pension plans can be established as either defined contribution or defined benefit plans in which systematic and definite payments are made to a pension trust. Incidental benefits (e.g., death and disability payments) can be provided under the plan.
▶ Profit-sharing plans require the use of a predetermined allocation formula and substantial and recurring contributions must be made although annual employer contributions are not required and the contributions need not be based on profits. Section 401(k) plans can be established where employees have the option to receive cash or to have such amounts contributed to the profit-sharing trust. The employer may also establish an ESOP where the plan is funded by a contribution of the employer's stock.
▶ Qualified plans must be created for the employees' exclusive benefit.
▶ The plans may not discriminate in favor of highly compensated employees.
▶ Contributions and plan benefits must bear a uniform relationship to the compensation of covered employees.
▶ Minimum vesting requirements must be met (e.g., 100% vesting after five years).
▶ Employee benefits are taxed under the Sec. 72 annuity rules.
▶ Total employer contributions to the plan are subject to specific ceiling limitations.

---

[54] Sec. 402(e). Under the Small Business Act of 1996, the five-year forward averaging provision has been repealed for tax years beginning after December 31, 1999.
[55] Sec. 415(c). The deduction limit was $30,000 for both 1999 and 2000 and is subject to cost-of-living adjustments. Such adjustments are rounded to the next lowest multiple of $5,000.
[56] Sec. 415(b)(1). The benefit amount for 2000 was $135,000. These amounts are subject to indexing each year.
[57] Sec. 404(a)(3)(A).

KEY POINT

Although the nonqualified plans are not subject to the same restrictions imposed upon qualified plans, they do not receive the same tax benefits as are available under qualified plans. For example, the employer may not be able to deduct amounts that are set aside or placed in an escrow account.

NONQUALIFIED PLANS

Nonqualified deferred compensation plans are often used by employers to provide incentives or supplementary retirement benefits for executives. Common forms of nonqualified plans include the following:

- An unfunded, nonforfeitable promise to pay fixed amounts of compensation in future periods.[58]
- Restricted property plans involving property transfers (usually in the form of the employer-company stock), where the property transferred is subject to a substantial risk of forfeiture and is nontransferable.[59]

DISTINGUISHING CHARACTERISTICS OF NONQUALIFIED PLANS. Nonqualified plans are not subject to the same restrictions imposed on qualified plans (such as the nondiscrimination and vesting rules), although nonqualified plans may have some vesting rules. Thus, such plans are particularly suitable for use in executive compensation planning. In general, nonqualified plans impose certain restrictions on the outright transfer of the plan's benefits to the employee. This avoids immediate taxation under the constructive receipt doctrine, which does not apply if the benefits are not yet credited, set apart, or made available so that the employee may draw on them. The amount is taxed to the employee upon the lapse of such restrictions, and the employer receives a corresponding deduction in the same year.

UNFUNDED DEFERRED COMPENSATION PLANS. **Unfunded deferred compensation plans** are often used to compensate highly compensated employees who desire to defer the recognition of income until future periods (e.g., a professional athlete or a business executive who receives a signing bonus may prefer to defer the recognition of income from the bonus). In general, if the promise to make the compensation payment in a future period is nonforfeitable, the agreement must not be funded (e.g., the transfer of assets to a trust for the employee's benefit) or evidenced by a negotiable note. The employer, however, may establish an *escrow account* on behalf of the employee. Such an account is used to accumulate and invest the deferred compensation amounts. If the requirements for deferral are met, the employee is taxed when the amounts are actually paid or made available, and the employer receives a corresponding deduction in the same year.[60]

EXAMPLE I9-55 ▶ In 2001, Kelly signs an employment contract to play professional football for the Chicago Skyhawks. The contract includes a $500,000 signing bonus that is payable in five annual installments beginning in 2008. The bonus agreement is nonforfeitable and is unfunded. The Skyhawks have agreed to place sufficient amounts of money into an escrow account to fund the future payments to Kelly. None of the $500,000 bonus is deductible by the employer or taxable to Kelly when the agreement is signed in 2001. The Skyhawks do not receive a deduction for any amounts that are deposited into the escrow account during the 2001–2007 period. In 2008, Kelly receives $100,000 taxable compensation (interest, if any, that accrued and was paid to Kelly is also taxable) upon receipt of the initial payment, and the Skyhawks receive a corresponding tax deduction. ◀

RESTRICTED PROPERTY PLANS. **Restricted property plans** are used to attract and retain key executives. Under such arrangements, the executive generally obtains an ownership interest (i.e., stock) in the corporation. Restricted property plans are governed by the income recognition rules contained in Sec. 83. Under these rules, the receipt of restricted property in exchange for services rendered is not taxable if the property is nontransferable and subject to a substantial risk of forfeiture.

The employee is treated as receiving taxable compensation based on the amount of the property's fair market value (FMV) (less any amount paid for the property) at the earlier of the time the property is no longer subject to a substantial risk of forfeiture or is trans-

---

[58] Rev. Rul. 60-31, 1960-1 C.B. 174.
[59] Sec. 83.
[60] Reg. Sec. 1.451-2(a).

ferable. The employer receives a corresponding compensation deduction at the same time the income is taxed to the employee.

EXAMPLE I9-56 ▶ In the current year, Allied Corporation transfers 1,000 shares of its common stock to employee Karen as compensation pursuant to a restricted property plan. The FMV of the Allied stock is $10 per share on the transfer date. The restricted property agreement provides that the stock is nontransferable by Karen until the year 2006 (i.e., Karen cannot sell the stock to outsiders until year 2006). The stock is also subject to the restriction that if Karen voluntarily leaves the company before the year 2006, she must transfer the shares back to the company and will receive no benefit from the stock other than from the receipt of dividends. The FMV of the stock is $100 per share in year 2006 when the forfeiture and nontransferability restrictions lapse. Because the stock is both nontransferable and subject to a substantial risk of forfeiture from the issue date to year 2006, the tax consequences from the stock transfer are deferred for both Karen and Allied Corporation until the lapse of the nontransferability or forfeiture restrictions in year 2006. In year 2006, Karen must report ordinary (compensation) income of $100,000 ($100 × 1,000 shares), and Allied Corporation is entitled to a corresponding compensation deduction of the same amount. Karen is taxed currently on the dividends she receives because they are not subject to any restrictions. ◀

KEY POINT
If an employee makes the election to be taxed immediately, he or she should be aware of the adverse consequences of leaving the company before the forfeiture restrictions lapse. The employee will not receive the property, and no deduction is allowed on the forfeiture.

Election to Be Taxed Immediately. An exception which permits an employee to elect (within 30 days after the receipt of restricted property) to recognize income immediately upon receipt of the restricted property is provided in Sec. 83(b). If the election is made, the employer is entitled to a corresponding deduction at the time the income is taxed to the employee. This election is frequently made when the fair market value of the restricted property is expected to increase significantly in the future and the future gain would be taxed as long-term capital gain. Because the current rate of tax on long-term capital gains has been reduced to 20%, one would expect that more taxpayers would make the Sec. 83(b) election.

EXAMPLE I9-57 ▶ Assume the same facts as Example I9-56, except that Karen elects to recognize income on the transfer date. Karen must include $10,000 ($10 × 1,000 shares) in gross income as compensation in the current year, and Allied Corporation is entitled to a corresponding deduction in the same year. Karen will report no income in 2005 when the restrictions lapse and her basis in the Allied Corporation stock remains at $10,000. If Karen sells the stock for $100,000 in the year 2006 after the restrictions lapse, Karen reports a $90,000 ($100,000 − $10,000) long-term capital gain on the sale.[61] If Karen voluntarily leaves the company before the forfeiture restrictions lapse, no deduction is allowed when the forfeiture occurs, despite the fact that Karen is previously taxed on the stock's value on the transfer date (i.e., $10,000 of income is recognized by Karen in the current year). In such event, Allied Corporation must include $10,000 in gross income in the year of the forfeiture (i.e., the amount of the deduction that is taken in the year of the transfer to the extent of any previous tax benefit). ◀

Nonqualified plan features and requirements are summarized in Topic Review I9-3.

EMPLOYEE STOCK OPTIONS

Stock option plans are used by corporate employers to attract and retain key management employees. Both stock option and restricted property arrangements using the employer's stock permit the executive to receive a proprietary interest in the corporation. Thus, an executive may identify more closely with shareholder interests and the firm's long-run profit-maximization goals. The tax law currently includes two types of stock-option arrangements: the incentive stock option and the nonqualified stock option.[62] Each type is treated differently for tax purposes.

As will be seen in the discussions below, both types of plans have their respective advantages and disadvantages. Incentive stock option arrangements generally are preferred when long-term capital gain rates are low as compared to ordinary income rates.

---

[61] Sec. 1223. The holding period originates on the day following the transfer date because Karen made the election to be taxed immediately under Sec. 83(b).

[62] The incentive stock option rules are provided in Sec. 422, whereas the rules governing nonqualified stock options are contained in Reg. Sec. 1.83-7.

Topic Review I9-3

Nonqualified Plans

DISTINGUISHING FEATURES AND MAJOR REQUIREMENTS

1. The employee is taxed upon the lapse of restrictions imposed on the availability or withdrawal of funds and the employer receives a corresponding deduction in the same year.
2. Nonqualified plans may discriminate in favor of highly compensated employees and no minimum vesting rules are required.
3. Restricted property (usually employer stock) may be offered to executives where the incidents of taxation are deferred if the property is nontransferable and subject to a substantial risk of forfeiture. An election may be made under Sec. 83(b) to recognize income immediately upon the receipt of the restricted property.
4. Restrictions must be imposed to avoid immediate taxation to the employee under the constructive receipt doctrine.
5. To avoid immediate taxation, restricted property plans must be both nonforfeitable and subject to a substantial risk of forfeiture.

KEY POINT

The incentive stock option has the disadvantage of not providing a compensation deduction for the employer. Before January 1, 1987, this disadvantage was offset by the fact that the employee was eligible for a 60% long-term capital gain deduction. With the repeal of the long-term capital gain deduction, the incentive stock option lost much of its appeal. However, the maximum 20% tax rate for net long-term capital gains may help to increase the popularity of incentive stock options.

KEY POINT

Incentive stock options can be a valuable tax planning tool because the earliest that they are generally taxed is when they are exercised. Also, when an employee realizes profits from stock options those profits in certain cases may qualify as capital gains.

Thus, because the long-term capital gain rate has been decreased to 20% and marginal tax rates for ordinary income are rather high (39.6%), interest should increase in incentive stock option arrangements. However, an employer is more favorably treated under the nonqualified stock-option rules (i.e., the employer receives a tax deduction for the compensation related to a nonqualified stock option but does not receive a corresponding deduction if an incentive stock-option plan is adopted) and may therefore still prefer to continue to use nonqualified stock options.

INCENTIVE STOCK OPTION PLANS.
Employer Requirements. An **incentive stock option (ISO)** must meet the following plan or employer requirements:[63]

- The option price must be equal to or greater than the stock's FMV on the option's grant date.
- The option must be granted within ten years of the date the plan is adopted, and the employee must exercise the option within ten years of the grant date.
- The option must be both exercisable only by the employee and nontransferable except in the event of death.
- The employee cannot own more than 10% of the voting power of the employer corporation's stock immediately before the option's grant date.
- The total FMV of the stock options that become exercisable to an employee in any given year may not exceed $100,000 (e.g., an employee can be granted ISOs to acquire $200,000 of stock in one year, provided that no more than $100,000 is exercisable in any given year).
- Other procedural requirements must be met (e.g., shareholder approval of the plan).

Employee Requirements. In addition to the above plan requirements, the employee must meet the following requirements:

- The employee must not dispose of the stock within two years of the option's grant date nor within one year after the option's exercise date.
- The employee must be employed by the issuing company on the grant date and continue such employment until within three months before the exercise date.

If an employee meets the requirements listed above, no tax consequences occur on the grant date or the exercise date. However, the excess of the FMV over the option price on the exercise date is a tax preference item for purposes of the alternative minimum tax (see Chapter I14). When the employee sells the optioned stock, a long-term capital gain or loss

---

[63] Sec. 422.

is recognized. If the employee meets the two requirements, the employer does not receive a corresponding compensation deduction. If the requirements are not met, the option is treated as a nonqualified stock option.

EXAMPLE I9-58 ▶ American Corporation grants an incentive stock option to Kay, an employee, on January 1, 2001. The option price is $100, and the FMV of the American stock is also $100 on the grant date. The option permits Kay to purchase 100 shares of American stock. Kay exercises the option on June 30, 2003, when the stock's FMV is $400. Kay sells the 100 shares of American stock on January 1, 2005, for $500 per share. Because Kay holds the stock for the required period (at least two years from the grant date and one year from the exercise date) and because Kay is employed by American Corporation on the grant date and within three months before the exercise date, all of the requirements for an ISO have been met. No income is recognized on the grant date or the exercise date, although $30,000 [($400 − $100) × 100 shares] is a tax preference item for the alternative minimum tax in 2003. Kay recognizes a $40,000 [($500 − $100) × 100 shares] long-term capital gain on the sale date in 2005. American Corporation is not entitled to a compensation deduction in 2005 or in any other year. ◀

EXAMPLE I9-59 ▶ Assume the same facts as Example I9-58, except that Kay disposes of the stock on August 1, 2003, thus violating the one-year holding period requirement. Kay must recognize ordinary income on the sale date equal to the spread between the option price and the exercise price, or $30,000 [($400 − $100) × 100 shares]. The $30,000 spread between the FMV and the option price is no longer a tax preference item because the option ceases to qualify as an ISO. American Corporation can claim a $30,000 compensation deduction in 2003. Kay also recognizes a $10,000 [($500 − $400 adjusted basis) × 100 shares] short-term capital gain on the sale date, which represents the appreciation of the stock from the exercise date to the sale date. The gain is short-term because the holding period from the exercise date to the sale date does not exceed one year. ◀

KEY POINT

With ISO the employee does not recognize income when the option is exercised; income is recognized only when the stock is sold. With nonqualified stock options, income is recognized when the option is exercised or on the grant date and when the stock is sold at a gain.

NONQUALIFIED STOCK OPTION PLANS. Stock options that do not meet the plan requirements for incentive stock options are referred to as **nonqualified stock options**. The tax treatment of nonqualified stock options depends on whether the option has a **readily ascertainable fair market value** (e.g., whether the option is traded on an established options exchange).

Readily Ascertainable Fair Market Value. If a nonqualified stock option has a readily ascertainable FMV (e.g., the option is traded on an established options exchange), the employee recognizes ordinary income on the grant date equal to the difference between the stock's FMV and the option's exercise price. The employer receives a compensation deduction on the grant date equal to the same amount of income that is recognized by the employee. In such case, no tax consequences occur on the date the option is exercised, and the employee recognizes capital gain or loss upon the sale or disposition of the stock.

No Readily Ascertainable Fair Market Value. If a nonqualified stock option has no readily ascertainable FMV, no tax consequences occur on the grant date. On the exercise date the employee recognizes ordinary income equal to the spread between the FMV of the stock and the option price, and the employer receives a corresponding compensation deduction. When the stock option is exercised, the employee's basis in the stock is equal to the option price plus the amount reported as ordinary income on the exercise date. Capital gain or loss is recognized upon the subsequent sale of the stock by the employee.

The alternative minimum tax does not apply to nonqualified stock options regardless of whether the option has a readily ascertainable FMV. Table I9-4 illustrates the tax consequences to employees and employers for such options.

As illustrated in Table I9-4, Kim reports a total gain of $11,000 from the option transaction under both circumstances. However, the character of her profit (i.e., ordinary income or capital gain) and the timing of the profit recognition (i.e., grant date or exercise date) depends on whether the option's FMV is readily ascertainable.

The distinguishing features and major requirements for employee stock options are summarized in Topic Review I9-4.

TABLE I9-4
Taxation of Nonqualified Stock Options

Situation Facts	Readily Ascertainable FMV	No Readily Ascertainable FMV
Grant date: On January 1, 2001, Kim is granted a nonqualified stock option to purchase 100 shares of stock from Apple Corporation (Kim's employer) at $90 per share. The stock's FMV is $100 on the grant date.	Ordinary income of $1,000 is recognized [($100 − $90) × 100 shares] by Kim in 2001. Apple Corporation receives a corresponding $1,000 compensation deduction in 2001.	No tax consequences to Kim or Apple Corporation.
Exercise date: On January 31, 2002, Kim exercises the option and acquires the 100 shares of Apple Corporation stock for the $90 option price when the FMV is $190.	No tax consequences to Kim or Apple Corporation.	Kim recognizes ordinary income in 2002 of $10,000 [($190 − $90) × 100 shares], and Apple Corporation receives a $10,000 compensation deduction.
Sale date: On February 1, 2003, Kim sells the stock for $200 per share and realizes $20,000 ($200 × 100 shares).	Kim recognizes a $10,000 ($20,000 − $10,000 basis) long-term capital gain.[a]	Kim recognizes a $1,000 ($20,000 − $19,000 basis) long-term capital gain.[b]

[a] Kim's basis includes the amount paid for the optioned stock of $9,000 plus ordinary income of $1,000 recognized on the grant date. Kim's holding period commences on the January 1, 2001 grant date for determining whether the gain is long-term.

[b] Kim's basis includes the $9,000 paid for the option stock plus the $10,000 ordinary income recognized on the exercise date. Kim's holding period commences on the January 31, 2002 exercise date for determining whether the gain is long-term.

ADDITIONAL COMMENT
If you are self-employed and establish a Keogh plan, you must include any employees in the plan.

PLANS FOR SELF-EMPLOYED INDIVIDUALS

Self-employed individuals, such as sole proprietors and partners who practice a trade or business, are not classified as employees and are subject to special retirement plan rules known as **H.R. 10 plans** (also called **Keogh plans**). Retirement plans of self-employed people are generally subject to the same contribution and benefit limitations as other qualified corporate plans. An employee who is covered under a qualified pension or profit-sharing plan for wages earned as an employee and who is also self-employed may establish an H.R. 10 plan for earned income derived from self-employment activities.

Topic Review I9-4

Employee Stock Options

DISTINGUISHING FEATURES AND MAJOR REQUIREMENTS

- For an incentive stock option (ISO) plan no tax consequences occur on the grant or the exercise date (except for the recognition of a tax preference item under the AMT provisions on the exercise date). Capital gain or loss is recognized by the employee upon the sale or exchange of the stock. No deduction is allowed to the employer.
- ISOs and nonqualified stock options may be issued to highly compensated employees without regard to nondiscrimination rules.
- If a nonqualified stock option has a readily ascertainable FMV, the employee recognizes ordinary income equal to the spread between the FMV of the stock and the option price on the grant date and the employer receives a corresponding deduction. If the option has no readily ascertainable FMV, income is recognized on the exercise date equal to the spread between the FMV of the stock and the option price and a corresponding deduction is available to the employer.
- For an ISO, the option price must be equal to or greater than the FMV of the stock on the grant date, employees cannot own more than 10% of the voting power of the employer's stock, and restrictions are placed on the total FMV of stock options that may be issued.
- To qualify under the ISO rules, a two-year holding period from the grant date is required (and at least one year after the exercise date) and the employee must continue to be employed by the company until within three months of the exercise date.

KEY POINT

Keogh plans can be either defined benefit or defined contribution plans. Many individuals avoid the defined benefit type of Keogh plan due to the extra paperwork and administrative costs.

For a **defined contribution H.R. 10 plan**, a self-employed individual in 2001 may contribute the smaller of $35,000 or 25% of earned income from the self-employment activity.[64] *Earned income* refers to net earnings from self-employment. To compute the limitations for 2001, only $170,000 of earned income may be taken into account for any one individual.[65] For purposes of the 25% calculation, earned income is reduced by the contribution made on behalf of the self-employed individual.

EXAMPLE I9-60

Larry is a self-employed CPA whose 2001 net earnings from his trade or business (before the H.R. 10 plan contribution but after the deduction for one-half of the self-employment taxes paid under Sec. 164(f) [see Chapter I14]) is $100,000. The 25% contribution limitation is computed as follows: $100,000 - 0.25x = x$, where x equals Larry's net earned income after the contribution deduction. Thus, under this formula, Larry's net earned income is $80,000. Therefore, Larry may contribute $20,000 to the plan for 2001 ($80,000 × 0.25), because this amount is less than the $30,000 ceiling. Larry must also provide coverage for all of his eligible full-time employees under the general rules provided in the law for qualified plans (e.g., nondiscrimination, vesting, and so on).[66]

KEY POINT

A Keogh plan must be created no later than the last day of your tax year.

An H.R. 10 plan must be established before the end of the tax year, but contributions may be made up to the due date for the tax return (including extensions). All H.R. 10 pension contributions made by a self-employed individual for *employees* are deductible for AGI on Schedule C. The H.R. 10 contribution for the self-employed individual is deductible *for* AGI on page 1 of Form 1040.

INDIVIDUAL RETIREMENT ACCOUNTS (IRAS)

REAL WORLD EXAMPLE

The IRA savings provisions were originally enacted in 1974 to provide a tax-favored retirement savings arrangement to individuals who were not covered under a qualified plan. Beginning in 1982, Congress extended IRA availability to all taxpayers. It was hoped that the extended availability would increase the level of savings and provide a discretionary retirement savings plan that was uniformly available. However, Congress in the Tax Reform Act of 1986 restricted the availability of IRAs because there was no discernible impact on aggregate personal savings.

The tax law relating to IRA's was changed significantly by the Taxpayer Relief Act of 1997 (TRA 1997).[67] For tax years beginning after December 31, 1997, there are three types of IRA's that are available to taxpayers:

▶ Traditional IRA
▶ Roth IRA
▶ Education IRA

The Roth IRA and Education IRA were both created by the TRA 1997 and are effective beginning in 1998.

TRADITIONAL IRA

Traditional IRAs have been in the law for nearly 25 years and taxpayers may make either deductible or nondeductible contributions to the IRA. A contribution to a traditional IRA that is deductible has two principal benefits, (1) the amount contributed to the IRA (maximum $2,000 per year) is deductible on the taxpayer's return, and (2) the income earned on the investments in the IRA is not subject to current taxation. However, when amounts are withdrawn from the IRA at retirement, such amounts are fully subject to taxation. Nondeductible contributions to a traditional IRA may not be deducted on the taxpayer's return, but such contributions are not subject to taxation when withdrawn from the IRA. While contributions are not subject to taxation, any earnings are subject to taxation when withdrawn.

Individuals may make deductible contributions equal to the lesser of $2,000 or 100% of compensation only if either of the following conditions exists:

▶ The individual is *not* an active participant in an employer-sponsored retirement plan, including tax-sheltered annuities, government plans, simplified employee pension plans, and H.R. 10 plans; or

---

[64] Sec. 415(c)(1). A 15% deduction limit applies if the defined contribution plan is a profit sharing plan.
[65] Secs. 401(a)(17) and 404(l). The $170,000 ceiling is applicable for 2001. The ceiling was also $170,000 for 2000 and is adjusted for inflation in increments of $10,000.
[66] Sec. 401(d).
[67] Before 1987, virtually all taxpayers could establish and deduct contributions to an IRA (maximum $2,000) even though the taxpayer was covered under an employer-sponsored plan. However, effective for 1987 and subsequent years, the Tax Reform Act of 1986 severely curtailed the availability of deductible IRAs for taxpayers who were covered (or their spouses) under an employer-sponsored plan. These restrictive rules imposed by the Tax Reform Act of 1986 were partially repealed by the Taxpayer Relief Act of 1997.

Employee Expenses and Deferred Compensation ▼ Individuals 9-37

▶ Individuals who are active participants in an employer-sponsored retirement plan must have an AGI equal to or below the following applicable dollar limits for 2001:[68] $33,000 for an unmarried taxpayer; $53,000 for a married couple filing a joint return; zero for a married individual filing separately. If an individual has AGI above these amounts, the deductible IRA contribution amounts are phased out on a pro rata basis as AGI increases from $33,000 to $43,000 for unmarried taxpayers and from $53,000 to $63,000 for married taxpayers filing a joint return.

EXAMPLE I9-61 ▶ Laura is an unmarried taxpayer who is not an active participant in an employer-sponsored retirement plan or other qualified plan. In 2001, Laura's AGI is $60,000, consisting of earned income from wages. Laura is not subject to the dollar limitation because she is not an active participant in a qualified plan and may, therefore, contribute and deduct up to $2,000 to a traditional IRA. Laura's AGI is reduced to $58,000 ($60,000 − $2,000) because the amount is deductible *for* AGI. ◀

EXAMPLE I9-62 ▶ Judy is an unmarried taxpayer who is an active participant in her employer's qualified retirement plan. In 2001, Judy's AGI is $40,000, consisting of earned income from wages of $35,000 and interest and dividends of $5,000. Since she is an active participant in a qualified plan and her AGI is over $33,000, her deductible contribution to a traditional IRA is subject to the phaseout. Since the ceiling amount is exceeded by $7,000 ($40,000 − $33,000), the maximum IRA contribution is reduced by 70% ($7,000/$10,000). Thus, the maximum that Judy can contribute and deduct to her IRA in 2001 is $600 ($2,000 − $1,400). ◀

ADDITIONAL COMMENT

Banks, savings and loan associations, insurance companies, and stock brokerage firms make IRAs available to taxpayers. Usually, the amounts are invested in long-term savings accounts. However, self-directed plans are offered by some stock brokerage firms. In this type of IRA, the taxpayer can specify how the contributions will be invested.

If a taxpayer's AGI exceeds the above limits, the taxpayer may make a nondeductible contribution of up to $2,000 to a traditional IRA. The benefit of making a nondeductible contribution to an IRA is that the earnings of the IRA investments grow tax-free. Thus, even though the *earnings* of the nondeductible IRA will be taxed when distributed, the ability to allow investments to compound before-tax is a major advantage for taxpayers. However, as will be seen in the discussion of Roth IRAs below, if a taxpayer can qualify for a Roth IRA rather than a traditional nondeductible IRA, the choice clearly favors a Roth IRA. The maximum amount of a nondeductible contribution that may be made to a traditional IRA is $2,000 minus the amount that is allowed as a deduction. Also, a taxpayer may elect for all of his contributions to be nondeductible even though the contributions are otherwise eligible to be deducted.

EXAMPLE I9-63 ▶ Using the same facts as in Example I9-62, Judy is permitted to make a nondeductible contribution to her IRA of $1,400 ($2,000 − $600). She also could elect to designate all $2,000 as a nondeductible contribution even though she is eligible to deduct the $600. ◀

Two special rules apply to married couples relative to traditional IRAs. First, if only one spouse is employed and this working spouse is otherwise eligible to make IRA contributions, the nonworking spouse may contribute up to $2,000 per year to an IRA (a so-called spousal IRA). Thus, a total of $4,000 may be deductible by a married couple ($2,000 to each spouse's IRA) even though only one spouse has earned income. It should be noted that even though only the working spouse must have earned income, such working spouse must have at least $4,000 of earned income in order to contribute $4,000 to the two IRAs. Second, if one spouse is covered under a qualified retirement plan but the other spouse is not covered, the non-covered spouse may contribute to a traditional deductible IRA. However, the contribution to a traditional deductible IRA is phased out at adjusted gross incomes between $150,000 and $160,000. This rule, enacted under the TRA 1997, significantly increases the AGI threshold amounts for making deductible contributions to an IRA.

EXAMPLE I9-64 ▶ Gary and Babs are a married couple. Gary is covered under a qualified retirement plan at his job and earned $170,000 in 2001. Babs is employed as a secretary and earned $10,000. They file a

---

[68] Sec. 219(g). The phaseout limits for unmarried individuals increase from $33,000 in 2001 to $34,000 in 2002 and gradually phasing up to $50,000 by 2005. For married taxpayers filing a joint return, the $53,000 limit in 2001 increases to $54,000 in 2002 and gradually phases up to $80,000 by 2007.

joint return, have interest and dividend income of $20,000, and their AGI, therefore, is $200,000. Neither Gary nor Babs is entitled to deduct contributions to a traditional IRA because their AGI exceeds $160,000. However, both Gary and Babs are allowed to make nondeductible contributions of $2,000 each to the IRA.

EXAMPLE I9-65 ▶ Assume the same facts as in Example I9-64 but that Gary's income is $100,000 and their AGI is $125,000. Babs may contribute and deduct $2,000 to a traditional IRA because their AGI is less than $150,000. However, Gary may not make a deductible contribution because he is covered under a qualified plan and their AGI exceeds $53,000. Gary is permitted to make a $2,000 contribution to a nondeductible IRA. ◀

The following significant tax rules apply to traditional IRAs:

ADDITIONAL COMMENT

A contribution to an IRA for the year 2000 can be made as late as the due date for filing the 2001 return.

▶ An IRA plan may be established between the end of the tax year and the due date for the tax return (not including any extensions that are permitted). Any deductible contributions made during this time are treated as a deduction for the prior year. Contributions are deductible if made by the due date for the tax return (i.e., contributions for 2001 must be made no later than April 15, 2002). Contributions to nondeductible IRAs also must be made by April 15th of the following year.

▶ Distributions from a traditional IRA are taxed under the annuity rules in Sec. 72. Normally distributions from an IRA are fully subject to taxation. However, if nondeductible contributions are made to an IRA, these amounts would represent the investment in the contract in calculating the exclusion ratio.

▶ Withdrawals by a participant before age 59½ are both includible in income and subject to a nondeductible 10% penalty tax.[69]

ADDITIONAL COMMENT

Some financial advisers recommend the following approach when someone can only afford to have limited amounts set aside for retirement. Have pre-tax dollars withheld from salary up to the employer-matching amount in 401(k) plans, then place $2,000 in a Roth IRA. This maximizes employer contributions and places the maximum amount allowable into the much favored Roth IRA.

▶ Withdrawals must begin no later than April 1 of the year following the end of the tax year in which the individual reaches age 70½. IRA contributions that were deducted over the years on the taxpayer's returns are fully taxable as ordinary income when the amounts are distributed.

▶ A nondeductible 6% penalty is levied on excess contributions to an IRA.[70]

ROTH IRA

The Roth IRA[71] is a new type of IRA that is referred to as a "backloaded IRA" because the tax benefits come at the end, not at the beginning, of the IRA. Contributions to a Roth IRA are nondeductible but all distributions from the IRA, including earnings, are nontaxable. The maximum amount that may be contributed to a Roth IRA is $2,000. However, taxpayers who are eligible for both a Roth IRA and a traditional IRA, may only contribute a total of $2,000 to both types of IRAs. As with traditional IRAs, Roth IRAs are also subject to AGI phaseout limitations, although the limitation amounts are higher that with traditional IRAs. Roth IRAs are available for tax years beginning after December 31, 1997.

All taxpayers may contribute up to $2,000 to a Roth IRA, however, this amount is phased out for single taxpayers if their AGI is between $95,000 and $110,000 ($150,000 and $160,000 for married couples filing a joint return). The principal advantage of the Roth IRA is the nontaxability of qualified distributions. One requirement of a qualified distribution is that the distribution must meet a five year holding period. More specifically, the distribution may not be made before the end of the five-tax-year period beginning with the first tax year for which a contribution was made to the Roth IRA. In addition to satisfying the five-year test, a qualifying distribution must also meet one of the following:

---

[69] Sec. 72(t). The amount subject to the 10% penalty is the portion of the amount that must be included in gross income. Exceptions to the 10% penalty are provided in the event of death, disability, and certain non-lump-sum distributions. The TRA 1997 also added two additional exceptions, (1) withdrawals used to pay qualified higher education costs for taxpayer, spouse, children or grandchildren, and (2) up to $10,000 to buy or build the principal residence for a "first time homebuyer".
[70] Sec. 4973(b).
[71] Sec. 408A.

- made on or after the date on which the individual attains age 59½,
- made to a beneficiary (or the individual's estate) on or after the individual's death,
- attributable to the individual being disabled, or
- a distribution for first-time homebuyer expenses (maximum of $10,000).

An important aspect of distributions from a Roth IRA is a special ordering rule for determining the taxability of nonqualifying withdrawals. Under this rule, distributions are treated as being made from contributions first and, thus, are nontaxable. After all contributions have been withdrawn, any remaining amounts are considered taxable and subject to the 10% penalty.

EXAMPLE 19-66 ▶ Ray and Sandy are married and Ray is covered under his employer's qualified retirement plan. Their AGI on a joint return is $130,000. Ray can contribute $2,000 to a Roth IRA. Alternatively, however, if their AGI was $156,000, Ray would be limited to a maximum contribution of $800. Since their AGI exceeds the threshold of $150,000 by $6,000, the $2,000 contribution is reduced by 60% ($6000/$10,000), or $1,200. ◀

EXAMPLE 19-67 ▶ Bob, age 60 in 2001, contributes $2,000 each year to a Roth IRA in 2001, 2002, and 2003. On November 30, 2005, the value of the Roth IRA is $9,000. Bob has experienced some financial setbacks and needs to withdraw the money from the Roth IRA. If Bob withdraws $6,000 in 2005 and waits until January, 2006 to withdraw the remaining $3,000, none of the distributions are taxable. This result occurs because the first $6,000 is treated as coming from contributions. The remaining $3,000 is nontaxable because Bob has met the five-year test and is over age 59½. Conversely, if Bob withdraws the entire $9,000 in 2005, $3,000 must be included in his income because the five-year test was not met. ◀

A final aspect of Roth IRAs is the ability to "rollover" funds from an existing deductible IRA into a Roth IRA. However, since the taxpayer received a deduction for the contribution into the deductible IRA, any rollover amount must be included in gross income in the year the rollover occurred. More specifically, if a taxpayer's AGI does not exceed $100,000 and does not file as married filing separately, the taxpayer is eligible to rollover any amount of funds from a deductible IRA into a Roth IRA. Such rollover amount is includible in the taxpayer's income, but is not subject to the 10% penalty for early withdrawals. If the rollover was made before January 1, 1999, individuals could have elected to include the amounts in gross income ratably over a four-year period beginning with the year of rollover.

EXAMPLE 19-68 ▶ Mikael has a traditional IRA that has a balance of $60,000 on June 30, 2000. He is single and has AGI of $80,000. Mikael is eligible to rollover the $60,000 to a Roth IRA. If he completes the rollover in 2000, he will be required to include the $60,000 in his gross income for 2000. He is not subject to the 10% early withdrawal penalty on such rollover. ◀

Below is a discussion of some of the important tax rules for Roth IRAs:

- Like traditional IRAs, Roth IRAs must be established by the due date of the tax return (not including extensions). Similarly, contributions to a Roth IRA also must be made by the due date of the return (i.e., April 15, 2002 for 2001 contributions).
- Contributions to a Roth IRA are never deductible.
- Contributions to a Roth IRA are subject to special modified AGI limitations.
- Contributions to a Roth IRA can be made after the owner has reached age 70½. Similarly, no distributions are required at any age from a Roth IRA. (Remember: owners of traditional IRAs must begin taking distributions in the year after the taxpayer has reached age 70½).
- Withdrawals from a Roth IRA are not taxable if such withdrawals are "qualified distributions." If a withdrawal is not a qualified distribution, the amount is taxed under special ordering rules and subject to the 10% penalty.
- A taxpayer whose AGI is $100,000 or less may rollover his traditional IRA to a Roth IRA. However, the total amount rolled over from a traditional deductible IRA must be included in the taxpayer's gross income.

STOP & THINK

Question: Both nondeductible contributions to a traditional IRA and contributions to a Roth IRA are similar in the sense that neither provide a tax deduction at the date of contribution. Which of the two types would be most advantageous to taxpayers?

Solution: Clearly, if a taxpayer qualifies for a Roth IRA, that type of IRA is superior to a nondeductible contribution to a traditional IRA. The reason is that distributions from a Roth IRA are totally excluded from gross income while only the principal portion of nondeductible contributions to a traditional IRA are excludable. In other words, the earnings generated in a Roth IRA are excluded from gross income whereas earnings associated with nondeductible contributions to a traditional IRA are subject to taxation. Generally, a nondeductible contribution to a traditional IRA will not be advantageous unless the taxpayer's AGI exceeds $160,000.

For a discussion of the decision whether to invest in a traditional deductible IRA or a Roth IRA, see the Tax Planning Considerations later in this chapter. Also, for a more detailed analysis including computations, see Chapter I18 of this *Individuals* textbook.

Topic Review I9-5 contains a table which summarizes the eligibility rules for traditional and Roth IRAs.

EDUCATION IRA

The TRA 1997 created an additional type of IRA specifically intended to help low and middle income taxpayers save for education expenses. A contributor can make a *nondeductible* contribution of up to $500 per year into an Education IRA until the beneficiary reaches age 18.[72] The contributor need not be related to the beneficiary and there is no limit on the number of Education IRAs that can be set up by a contributor. Distributions to the beneficiary are excluded from gross income provided that the distribution does not exceed *qualified higher education expenses* (tuition, fees, books, supplies, equipment, and room and board) during the year of distribution.

Similar to other IRAs, there are phaseout limits based on AGI. The $500 annual contribution is phased out for married taxpayers filing joint returns with AGI from $150,000 to $160,000 ($95,000 to $110,000 for other taxpayers). In addition, beneficiaries claiming an exclusion from an Education IRA are not permitted to claim either the HOPE Scholarship Credit or the Lifetime Learning Credit in the same year.[73] Since these credits currently are more favorable than the Education IRA, it is unclear how many taxpayers will opt for this type of IRA.

ADDITIONAL COMMENT
Any number of people may contribute funds to an Education IRA for one child. But all of the contributions may not total more than $500 for that child.

Topic Review I9-5

Traditional and Roth IRAs—Eligibility

If 2001 AGI Is	Eligible For IRA (Joint Returns)				Traditional IRA (Nondeductible)*
	Traditional IRA (Deductible)			**Roth IRA**	
	A	B	C		
Up to $53,000	Yes	Yes	Yes	Yes	Yes
$53,000–$63,000	Yes	Partially	Yes	Yes	Yes
$63,000–$150,000	Yes	No	Yes	Yes	Yes
$150,000–$160,000	Yes	No	Partially	Partially	Yes
Over $160,000	Yes	No	No	No	Yes

A If neither spouse is an active participant in an employer-sponsored plan
B For the IRA of a spouse who is an active participant in an employer-sponsored plan
C For the IRA of a spouse who is not an active participant in an employer-sponsored plan.

* If AGI is not above $160,000, a nondeductible IRA will not be advantageous.

---

[72] Sec. 530.   [73] Sec. 25A(e)(2).

EXAMPLE I9-69 ▶ Ben and Barbara are married and have five children. Their AGI is $100,000 and they want to begin saving for their children's college costs. They decide to establish individual Education IRAs for each of their children. Ben and Barbara can put up to $500 per year into each of the five IRAs. The contributions are nondeductible, however, the IRA investments will grow tax-free and may be distributed tax-free to each of their children as long as the qualified higher education expenses of each beneficiary (child) exceeds the amount of the distribution. ◀

SIMPLIFIED EMPLOYEE PENSIONS

Due to the administrative complexity associated with qualified pension and profit-sharing plans, small businesses often establish simplified employee pension (SEP) plans for their employees. In a SEP, the employer makes contributions to the IRAs of its employees.[74] The following is a summary of the tax rules that apply to a SEP:

▶ The employer receives an immediate tax deduction for contributions made under the plan. The annual deductible contributions for each participant are limited to the lesser of 15% of the participant's compensation (up to a ceiling of $170,000) and the dollar limitations for defined contribution plans.[75]

▶ Contributions are treated as being made on the last day of the tax year if they are made by the due date of the tax return (including extensions).

▶ Employer contributions must be nondiscriminatory.

▶ Distributions from a SEP are subject to taxation based on the IRA rules (previously discussed) including the penalty tax for premature distributions.

▶ A self-employed person (i.e., a partner or sole proprietor) may establish a SEP rather than using an H.R. 10 plan arrangement because of reduced administrative complexity associated with a SEP.

SIMPLE RETIREMENT PLANS

Another more recent type of retirement savings plan for small businesses is called the savings incentive match plan for employees (SIMPLE).[76] This type of plan can be adopted by employers who have 100 or fewer employees who received at least $5,000 in compensation from the employer in the preceding year. A SIMPLE plan may be set up either as an IRA for each employee or part of a qualified cash or deferred arrangement (401(k) plan). Essentially, employees are allowed to make elective contributions in 2001 of up to $6,500 ($6,000 in 2000) per year and employers are required to make matching contributions.

The unique features of the SIMPLE plans are (1) that elective contributions by employees must be matched by the employer or the employer has the option of making nonelective contributions, (2) that all contributions to an employee's SIMPLE account must be fully vested and (3) the SIMPLE plans are not subject to the special nondiscrimination rules generally applicable to qualified plans. This last feature is important in that there is no requirement that a set number of employees *participate* in the plan, the only requirement is that all employees who had $5,000 in compensation in the previous year and are reasonably expected to have $5,000 in compensation in the current year must be eligible to participate.

TAX PLANNING CONSIDERATIONS

MOVING EXPENSES

To be eligible for the moving expense deduction, the moving expenses must be paid in connection with the commencement of work by the taxpayer as a full-time employee or self-employed individual. Therefore, it is important to secure full-time employment or to carry on a trade or business as a self-employed individual at the new location. Taxpayers who are approaching retirement are eligible for a moving expense deduction only if they

---

[74] Sec. 408(k).
[75] Sec. 402(h)(2).
[76] Sec. 408(p).

continue to work in the new location before their actual retirement (e.g., 39 weeks in the 12-month period following the move).

EXAMPLE I9-70 ▶ Louis decides to quit his job and return to school as a full-time graduate student. Louis incurs substantial long-distance moving expenses that would otherwise be deductible to relocate to the university where the education is to be taken. No deduction is allowed unless Louis is employed on a full-time basis or is engaged in a self-employment activity at the new location. ◀

REIMBURSED AMOUNTS. Moving expense reimbursements are often greater than the amounts allowable as a deduction. This is caused by the common practice of reimbursing nondeductible items (e.g., an employer may reimburse an employee for the cost of certain indirect moving expenses such as househunting trips, which do not qualify as deductible moving expenses). This results in an increase in the employee's gross income to the extent of the excess reimbursement. From a tax planning standpoint, the employer may provide an additional payment to compensate the employee for the additional tax cost associated with the move (commonly referred to as a "gross-up").

EXAMPLE I9-71 ▶ Austin Corporation has a policy of reimbursing transferred employees for 30% of their moving reimbursement that exceeds their deductible expenses to cover the federal and state tax costs associated with the excess reimbursement. Kathy, an employee, is transferred by the company to a new job location and incurs $6,000 of deductible moving expenses and receives an $8,000 reimbursement. Austin also will make an additional payment to Kathy of $600 (0.30 × $2,000) to cover the additional federal and state income tax costs. Kathy must include $2,600 ($2,000 + $600) of the reimbursement in gross income. ◀

PROVIDING NONTAXABLE COMPENSATION TO EMPLOYEES

Employers should consider the tax consequences to employees when changes in fringe benefit and deferred compensation arrangements are evaluated. For example, it is preferable for an employer to pay for fringe benefit items such as group term life insurance (up to $50,000 in coverage), health and accident insurance, employee parking, and so on rather than to give cash raises of a comparable amount. Such payments are nontaxable to the employee up to certain limits, whereas a comparable salary increase is fully taxable. Both types of payments are deductible by the employer.

Consideration should also be given to increased deferred compensation benefit programs for employees, particularly highly compensated individuals. The use of nonqualified deferred compensation plans, restricted property, and stock options result in tax deferrals and may result in the eventual recognition of capital gains that may be used to offset capital losses or that are taxed at a maximum 20% marginal tax rate.

All eligible employees should consider establishing an individual retirement account (IRA) because of the available tax deferral benefits. Even if a premature withdrawal (i.e., before age 59½ occurs), the time value of the deferred benefits for the plan contributions and the earnings may be greater than the penalty tax imposed.

REAL WORLD EXAMPLE

Banks and other financial institutions in their ads sometimes compare the accumulated wealth in an IRA to the accumulated wealth in a fully taxable investment. Although the IRA is generally advantageous, the ads sometimes overstate the advantages because they fail to deduct the tax that will be paid when amounts are withdrawn from the IRA.

ROLLOVER OF TRADITIONAL IRA TO ROTH IRA

Taxpayers have the ability to rollover amounts from a traditional IRA to a Roth IRA. However, if such a rollover is made, the taxpayer must include the amount in gross income in the year of the rollover. If the rollover was made before January 1, 1999, the taxpayer could have included the amount in gross income on a ratable basis over four years. The principal benefit of the rollover is that once the amounts are in the Roth IRA, no further taxes are due on these amounts upon distribution (assuming the five-year test is met). The essential question, therefore, is whether it is advantageous to rollover amounts from a traditional IRA to a Roth IRA and pay the tax now or keep the traditional IRA intact and pay the tax when regular distributions are made.

The decision rests on several factors, including (1) the marginal tax rate at retirement, (2) age of taxpayer, and (3) payment of tax from rollover from post-tax funds. First, if a taxpayer's marginal tax rate at retirement is expected to be lower than the current tax rate, a rollover may not be advantageous. Second, younger taxpayers are more likely to benefit from a rollover because they have more years to accumulate earnings tax-free and may be in a lower tax bracket today than at retirement. Finally, if the taxes that accrue from the rollover must be paid from the rollover funds, a rollover will probably not be in the taxpayer's favor. In other words, taxpayers should have sufficient funds from other sources to pay the tax, then the entire amount of rollover into the Roth IRA will have maximum ability to grow on a tax-free basis.

Each case must be analyzed based on the unique factors of that particular situation. However, for most taxpayers, it is generally advantageous to rollover funds from a traditional IRA to a Roth IRA. Of course, as is pointed out earlier in this chapter, the individual must have AGI of $100,000 or less (before the rollover distribution) to qualify for the rollover.

COMPLIANCE AND PROCEDURAL CONSIDERATIONS

SUBSTANTIATING TRAVEL AND ENTERTAINMENT EXPENSES

KEY POINT
It is extremely important to be able to substantiate travel and entertainment expenses. The *Cohan* Rule that permits a reasonable deduction when substantiation is lacking does not apply to travel and entertainment expenses (see Chapter I6).

Travel and entertainment expenses are disallowed if the taxpayer does not maintain adequate records or documentary proof of the expenditures.[77] Normally, documentation includes expense statements (diary or account book) and proof of the amount, time, place, and business purpose. Strict substantiation rules are enacted in the law to curb widespread abuses in the so-called expense account living practices engaged in by some taxpayers.

To make compliance easier, the IRS formulated the following administrative procedural rules:

▶ If an employee makes an adequate accounting of the expenditures to the employer, it is not necessary to submit a detailed statement on the employee's tax return unless the expenses exceed the reimbursements.

▶ The standard mileage rate may be used to compute automobile expenses in lieu of actual expenses and is reported on Form 2106 (Employee Business Expenses).

▶ Taxpayers may elect an optional method for computing deductions for business travel and meal expenses in lieu of using actual costs. If a per diem allowance is paid by an employer in lieu of reimbursing actual expenses, the reimbursement is deemed to be substantiated if it does not exceed a federal per diem rate for the travel locality. In lieu of using actual expenses an employee or self-employed individual may use the applicable federal per diem rate. The taxpayer must still provide documentation of time, place, and business purpose for the expenditures.

ETHICAL POINT
The CPA has a responsibility to make sure that proper documentation has been furnished by the taxpayer to substantiate travel and entertainment expenses according to the provisions in Sec. 274(d). The CPA cannot rely on the use of estimates for these expenses despite the fact that the *AICPA's Statements on Responsibilities in Tax Practice No. 4* (see Appendix E) permits the use of estimates if it is impractical to obtain exact data and the estimated amounts appear to be reasonable.

REPORTING EMPLOYEE BUSINESS EXPENSES

Form 2106 (Employee Business Expenses) is used to report employee business expenses (see Appendix B). Part I of Form 2106 is a recap of travel and transportation expenses. Part II includes a computation of automobile expenses using either actual expenses or the standard rate mileage method. Employer reimbursements must be included in the employee's wages on Form W-2 if an adequate accounting of the expenses is not made. Employer withholding of federal income tax is also required for nonaccountable plan reimbursements. Form 2106-EZ may be used by employees who do not receive an employer reimbursement, and where the standard mileage rate is used for the current year and for the year the taxpayer's automobile was first placed in service.

Moving expenses are reported on Form 3903 (Moving Expenses) instead of Form 2106 because they are treated differently from other employee expenses (e.g., unreimbursed moving expenses are deductible *for* AGI). Expenses such as entertainment, union dues, business gifts, and education expenses are reported on Schedule A of Form 1040 as itemized deductions (see Appendix B).

---

[77] Sec. 274(d).

A filled-in copy of Form 2106 is shown in Figure I9-2. It includes the computations relating to the information in Example I9-72.

EXAMPLE I9-72 ▶

Eric Graber, SSN 231-54-9876, is single and employed as a salesman by the Houston Corporation. Eric is required to use his personal automobile for employment-related business. He uses only one automobile for business purposes. During 2000, Eric drives his automobile 80% of the time for business use and incurs the following total expenses:

Gas and oil	$3,000
Repairs	600
Depreciation	2,300
Insurance	1,400
Parking and tolls (all business related)	250
Total	$7,550

During the year, Eric drives a total of 30,000 miles, of which 24,000 are business miles. Of the 6,000 personal miles, 2,000 miles are commuting to and from work. Eric receives a reimbursement of 15 cents per business mile from his employer. Eric also incurred $4,000 of unreimbursed employment-related travel and entertainment expenses. These expenses include the following:

Airfare	$2,500
Car rental	250
Business meals at which business was discussed	150
Laundry	100
Lodging	200
Entertainment of customers	800
Total	$4,000

Step 1, line 1: Vehicle expense (24,000 × $0.325)	$7,800
Step 2, line 7: (24,000 miles × $0.15)	$3,600
Section C, line 23: Actual Expenses:	
Gas and oil	$3,000
Repairs	600
Insurance	1,400
Total	$5,000
Section C, line 28: Depreciation ($2,300 × .80)	$1,840

◀

ADDITIONAL COMMENT

Many of the provisions related to employee business expenses are very complex. It has been said of the general complexity of the tax law that: "If Patrick Henry thought taxation without representation was bad, he should have seen taxation with representation."

REPORTING MOVING EXPENSES

Employer reimbursements for qualifying moving expenses reduce the otherwise deductible amount for the employee. Reimbursements for nondeductible moving expenses are included in gross income and should be included in total wages on the employee's Form W-2 and reported on page 1 (line 7) of Form 1040. Employers should complete Form 4782 (Employee Moving Expense Information) which summarizes the moving expense payments made to the employee and to third parties. The form is provided to an employee to properly report his moving expenses and reimbursements. Form 3903 (Moving Expenses) is used to compute the allowable moving expenses and is attached to the employee's tax return (see Appendix B). Moving expenses are deductible *for* AGI on line 26 of page 1 of the 2000 Form 1040. Moving expenses are not subject to federal income tax withholding if it is reasonable to believe that an employee will be entitled to a deduction for such amounts. Reimbursements in excess of the deductible amounts, however, are subject to the withholding of income and social security taxes.

A taxpayer may deduct moving expenses, even though the tests for qualification have not been met (e.g., the 39-week test). If the individual subsequently fails to satisfy the requirements, gross income for the subsequent year must be increased by the previous tax benefit.[78] Another alternative is to wait until the tests have been met and then file an amended return (Form 1040X–see Appendix B) for the prior year.

KEY POINT

If a taxpayer who is an employee moves in early December, the earliest that the 39-week test could be met would be early September of the following year. This is well after the April 15 due date for the individual return. The taxpayer may nevertheless deduct the moving expenses in the earlier year.

---

[78] Secs. 217(d)(2) and (3).

Employee Expenses and Deferred Compensation ▼ **Individuals 9-45**

Form **2106**	**Employee Business Expenses**	OMB No. 1545-0139
Department of the Treasury Internal Revenue Service (99)	► See separate instructions. ► Attach to Form 1040.	**2000** Attachment Sequence No. **54**

Your name: **Eric Grabar**
Occupation in which you incurred expenses: **Salesman**
Social security number: **231 54 9876**

Part I — Employee Business Expenses and Reimbursements

Step 1 Enter Your Expenses

		Column A Other Than Meals and Entertainment	Column B Meals and Entertainment
1	Vehicle expense from line 22 or line 29. (Rural mail carriers: See instructions.)	7,800	////
2	Parking fees, tolls, and transportation, including train, bus, etc., that **did not** involve overnight travel or commuting to and from work	250	////
3	Travel expense while away from home overnight, including lodging, airplane, car rental, etc. **Do not** include meals and entertainment	3,050	////
4	Business expenses not included on lines 1 through 3. **Do not** include meals and entertainment		////
5	Meals and entertainment expenses (see instructions)	////	950
6	**Total expenses.** In Column A, add lines 1 through 4 and enter the result. In Column B, enter the amount from line 5	11,100	950

Note: If you were not reimbursed for any expenses in Step 1, skip line 7 and enter the amount from line 6 on line 8.

Step 2 Enter Reimbursements Received From Your Employer for Expenses Listed in Step 1

| 7 | Enter reimbursements received from your employer that were **not** reported to you in box 1 of Form W-2. Include any reimbursements reported under code "L" in box 13 of your Form W-2 (see instructions) | 3,600 | //// |

Step 3 Figure Expenses To Deduct on Schedule A (Form 1040)

| 8 | Subtract line 7 from line 6. If zero or less, enter -0-. However, if line 7 is greater than line 6 in Column A, report the excess as income on Form 1040, line 7 | 7,500 | 950 |

Note: If **both columns** of line 8 are zero, you cannot deduct employee business expenses. Stop here and attach Form 2106 to your return.

| 9 | In Column A, enter the amount from line 8. In Column B, multiply line 8 by 50% (.50). (Employees subject to Department of Transportation (DOT) hours of service limits: Multiply meal expenses by 60% (.60) instead of 50%. For details, see instructions.) | 7,500 | 475 |
| 10 | Add the amounts on line 9 of both columns and enter the total here. **Also, enter the total on Schedule A (Form 1040), line 20.** (Fee-basis state or local government officials, qualified performing artists, and individuals with disabilities: See the instructions for special rules on where to enter the total.) ► | | 7,975 |

For Paperwork Reduction Act Notice, see instructions.   Cat. No. 11700N   Form **2106** (2000)

FIGURE I9-2   ►   PAGE 1 OF FORM 2106 FOR EXAMPLE I9-72

Form 2106 (2000) Page **2**

Part II — Vehicle Expenses

Section A—General Information (You must complete this section if you are claiming vehicle expenses.)

		(a) Vehicle 1	(b) Vehicle 2
11	Enter the date the vehicle was placed in service	/ /	/ /
12	Total miles the vehicle was driven during 2000	30,000 miles	miles
13	Business miles included on line 12	24,000 miles	miles
14	Percent of business use. Divide line 13 by line 12	80 %	%
15	Average daily roundtrip commuting distance	8 miles	miles
16	Commuting miles included on line 12	2,000 miles	miles
17	Other miles. Add lines 13 and 16 and subtract the total from line 12	4,000 miles	miles

18	Do you (or your spouse) have another vehicle available for personal use?	☒ Yes ☐ No
19	If your employer provided you with a vehicle, is personal use during off-duty hours permitted?	☐ Yes ☐ No ☐ Not applicable
20	Do you have evidence to support your deduction?	☒ Yes ☐ No
21	If "Yes," is the evidence written?	☒ Yes ☐ No

Section B—Standard Mileage Rate (See the instructions for Part II to find out whether to complete this section or Section C.)

22	Multiply line 13 by 32½¢ (.325)	22	7,800

Section C—Actual Expenses

			(a) Vehicle 1	(b) Vehicle 2
23	Gasoline, oil, repairs, vehicle insurance, etc.	23	5,000	
24a	Vehicle rentals	24a		
b	Inclusion amount (see instructions)	24b		
c	Subtract line 24b from line 24a	24c		
25	Value of employer-provided vehicle (applies only if 100% of annual lease value was included on Form W-2—see instructions)	25		
26	Add lines 23, 24c, and 25	26	5,000	
27	Multiply line 26 by the percentage on line 14	27	4,000	
28	Depreciation. Enter amount from line 38 below	28	1,840	
29	Add lines 27 and 28. Enter total here and on line 1	29	5,840	

Section D—Depreciation of Vehicles (Use this section only if you owned the vehicle and are completing Section C for the vehicle.)

			(a) Vehicle 1	(b) Vehicle 2
30	Enter cost or other basis (see instructions)	30		
31	Enter amount of section 179 deduction (see instructions)	31		
32	Multiply line 30 by line 14 (see instructions if you elected the section 179 deduction)	32		
33	Enter depreciation method and percentage (see instructions)	33		
34	Multiply line 32 by the percentage on line 33 (see instructions)	34		
35	Add lines 31 and 34	35	1,840	
36	Enter the limit from the table in the line 36 instructions	36	5,000	
37	Multiply line 36 by the percentage on line 14	37	4,000	
38	Enter the **smaller** of line 35 or line 37. Also enter this amount on line 28 above	38	1,840	

Form **2106** (2000)

FIGURE 19-2 ▶ PAGE 2 OF FORM 2106 FOR EXAMPLE 19-72

REPORTING OFFICE IN HOME EXPENSES

Form 8829 (Expenses for Business Use of Your Home) must be used to figure the allowable expenses for business use that are reported on Schedule C (Profit or Loss from Business) and the carryover of any nondeductible amounts from prior years. Form 4562 (Depreciation and Amortization) must also be used to compute depreciation on the office portion of the residence. These tax forms are reproduced in Appendix B.

QUALIFICATION OF PENSION AND PROFIT-SHARING PLANS

The reporting requirements to establish and maintain a qualified pension or profit-sharing plan are too complex for this text. However, it should be noted that it is generally advisable for a taxpayer to obtain advance approval of the plan from the district director of the IRS by requesting a determination letter that all requirements for qualification have been met. A new determination letter should generally be requested when any material (e.g., substantial) modification is made to a plan. Material changes are frequently required when major tax legislation is enacted. In addition, several reports must be filed with the IRS and the U.S. Department of Labor.

PROBLEM MATERIALS

DISCUSSION QUESTIONS

I9-1 Why is it important to distinguish whether an individual is an employee or an independent contractor (self-employed)?

I9-2 Matt, a CPA, is employed full-time as a tax accountant for a major company. He also operates a small tax practice in his spare time. Matt incurs local transportation and unreimbursed travel expenses for both his employment and business activities. How does Matt report these expenses on his tax return?

I9-3 Determine whether the following expenses are either deductible *for* AGI or *from* AGI or nondeductible on an employee's return. Indicate whether the expenses are subject to the 2% nondeductible floor for miscellaneous itemized deductions and whether the 50% meals and entertainment deduction limit applies.
   a. Reimbursed business meals (an adequate accounting is made to the employer and any excess reimbursement must be repaid)
   b. Automobile expenses associated with commuting to and from work
   c. Legal expenses incurred to prepare the taxpayer's income tax return
   d. Unreimbursed travel and transportation expenses (including meals)
   e. Unreimbursed entertainment expenses
   f. Qualified moving expenses of an employee
   g. Education-related expenses involving tuition and books

I9-4 Which of the following deduction items are subject to the 2% nondeductible floor applicable to miscellaneous itemized deductions?
   a. Investment counseling fees
   b. Fees for tax return preparation
   c. Unreimbursed professional dues for an employee
   d. Gambling losses
   e. Interest on a personal residence
   f. Unreimbursed employee travel expenses
   g. Reimbursed employee travel expenses (an adequate accounting is made to the employer and any excess reimbursement must be re-paid)
   h. Safe-deposit box rental expenses for an investor

I9-5 In each of the following cases involving travel expenses, indicate how each item is reported on the taxpayer's tax return. Include any limitations that might affect its deductibility.
   a. Marilyn, who lives in Houston, owns several apartments in Denver. To supervise the management of these properties, Marilyn incurs travel expenses including airfare, lodging, and meals while traveling to and from the apartment site.
   b. Marc is an employee who incurs travel expenses as a salesperson. The expenses are fully reimbursed by his employer after an adequate accounting has been made.
   c. Assume the same facts as in Part b, except that the expenses are not reimbursed.
   d. Kay is a self-employed attorney who incurs travel expenses (including meals) to prepare a court case in a nearby city.

I9-6 Kelly is an employee who incurs $2,000 of business meal expenses in connection with business entertainment and travel, none of which are reimbursed by her employer. $500 of the business meal costs are lavish or extravagant. How much can Kelly deduct before applying the 2% nondeductible floor on miscellaneous itemized deductions?

I9-7 Latoya is a college professor who takes a nine-month leave of absence from her employment at a college in Ohio and accepts a visiting professorship (temporary assignment) at a college in Texas. Latoya leaves her husband and children in Ohio and incurs the following expenses in connection with the temporary assignment:

Airfare to and from the temporary assignment	$ 1,000
Living expenses in the new location (including meals of $1,000)	8,000
Personal clothing	1,500
Total	$10,500

a. Which (if any) of these items can Latoya deduct?
b. Would your answer to a. change if Latoya, after completing the nine month assignment, resigned her position in Ohio and accepted a full-time assignment with the college in Texas?

I9-8 Larry is an investor in real estate who attends several investment counseling seminars on how to invest in real estate. In the current year, Larry incurs $4,000 of travel expenses and registration fees related to attending the real estate investment seminars. He deducts the expenses on his income tax return as a *for* AGI expense related to the production of income. Are the travel expenses and registration fees deductible? Should they be classified as *for* AGI or *from* AGI?

I9-9 If an employee receives a specific monthly amount from his or her employer as a reimbursement for employment-related entertainment, travel, and transportation expenses, why is it necessary to allocate a portion of the total reimbursement to each expense category?

I9-10 If an employee receives a reimbursement of 15 cents a mile from her employer for employment-related transportation expenses, is the employee permitted to deduct the difference between the standard mileage rate and the reimbursement rate as an unreimbursed employee expense? What other alternative is available for claiming the transportation deduction?

I9-11 If an employee (or self-employed individual) uses the standard mileage rate method for the year in which an automobile is acquired, may the actual expense method be used in a subsequent year? If so, what restrictions are imposed (if any) on depreciation methods? What adjustments to basis are required?

I9-12 What reporting procedures should be followed by an employee who deducts unreimbursed employee expenses on his or her tax return?

I9-13 Discuss the reporting procedures that should be followed by an employee to report employment-related expenses on his or her tax return under the following conditions:
a. Expenses are less than reimbursements, and no accounting is made to the employer.
b. Expenses equal reimbursements, and an adequate accounting is made to the employer.
c. Expenses exceed reimbursements, and an adequate accounting is made to the employer.
d. Expenses are less than reimbursements. An adequate accounting is made to the employer and the employee is required to repay any excess amount.

I9-14 Why were distance and time requirements legislated as conditions for eligibility for a moving expense deduction?

I9-15 Does it matter whether a moving expense is incurred by an employee, a self-employed individual, or an unemployed person?

I9-16 Len incurs $2,000 of deductible moving expenses in the current year and is fully reimbursed by his employer in the same year.
a. How are the expense deduction and the reimbursement reported on Len's tax return if he uses the standard deduction?
b. What tax consequences occur if the reimbursement is $2,000 but only $1,200 of the $2,000 of moving expenses are tax deductible?

I9-17 Why are strict recordkeeping requirements required for the deduction of entertainment expenses?

I9-18 Louis incurs "directly related" entertainment expenses of $4,000, but he is reimbursed by his employer for only $3,000 after an adequate accounting is made.
a. How are these amounts reported on Louis's tax return?
b. What are the tax consequences if Louis is unable to provide adequate documentation of the expenditures during the course of an IRS audit of his tax return?

I9-19 Latesha is a self-employed attorney who entertains clients and potential clients in her home.
a. What requirements must be met to qualify the outlays as deductible entertainment expenses?
b. If the expenses qualify, are they classified as "directly related" or "associated with" entertainment?

I9-20 Liz is an employee who entertains customers. In the current year, Liz incurs $6,000 in business meal expenses that are connected with entertainment. Liz's expenses are not lavish or extravagant. She itemizes her deductions in the current year.

a. If none of these expenses are reimbursed by Liz's employer, what amounts are deductible and how are they classified?
b. How are these amounts reported by Liz and her employer if all of her expenses are reimbursed and an adequate accounting is made by Liz?

I9-21 Atlantic Corporation provides a cafeteria for its employees. The meal charges are set at a sufficiently high level that the employees are not taxed on the subsidized eating facilities. Are Atlantic's cafeteria-related costs subject to the 50% disallowance for business meals?

I9-22 Lynn is a salesperson who entertains clients at business luncheons. A business relationship exists for the entertainment, and there is a reasonable expectation of business benefit. However, no business discussions are generally conducted before, during, or immediately following the meals. Do the business meal expenditures qualify as entertainment expenses?

I9-23 If an individual belongs to a country club and uses the facility primarily for business entertainment of customers, what portion of the club dues is deductible?

I9-24 Bass Corporation purchases 10 tickets to the Super Bowl in January 2001 for entertaining its customers. Due to unusually high demand, the tickets have to be purchased from scalpers for $6,000 (10 × $600). The face value of the tickets is only $900 (10 × $90). What amount is deductible by Bass in 2001?

I9-25
a. Discuss the two requirements for an employee expense reimbursement plan to be treated as an accountable plan.
b. How are expenses and reimbursements treated under an accountable plan?
c. How are expenses and reimbursements treated under a nonaccountable plan?

I9-26 Martin is a tax accountant employed by a public accounting firm. He incurs the following expenses:

CPA review course	$ 400
Law school tuition and books	4,000
Accounting continuing education course (travel, fees, and transportation (including meals of $200)	600
Total	$5,000

Martin is a degree candidate at the law school. Which (if any) of these expenditures qualify as deductible education expenses? How are they reported?

I9-27 Why are public school teachers generally allowed a deduction for education expenses related to graduate school or advanced courses?

I9-28 Discuss whether each of the following individuals is entitled to an office-in-home deduction (assume all expenses are incurred in tax years beginning after December 31, 1998):

a. Maggie is a self-employed management consultant who maintains an office in her home exclusively used for client meetings and other business-related activities. Maggie has no other place of business and her office is the most significant place for her business. She has substantial income from the consulting practice.
b. Marty is a college professor who writes research papers for academic journals in his office at home which is used exclusively for this purpose. Although Marty has an office at his place of employment, he finds it very convenient to maintain an office at home to avoid distractions from students and colleagues. Marty receives no income from the publication of the research articles for the year in question.
c. Bobby operates his own sole proprietorship as an electrician. He maintains an office at home where he keeps his books, takes phone calls from customers, and does the payroll for his five employees. All of his electrical work is done at the location of his customers.

I9-29 Compare and contrast the tax advantages accruing to employers and employees from the establishment of a qualified pension or profit-sharing plan versus a nonqualified deferred compensation arrangement (e.g., a restricted property plan).

I9-30 What is the difference between a defined benefit pension plan and a defined contribution pension plan?

I9-31 Austin Corporation is proposing the establishment of a pension plan that will cover only employees with salaries in excess of $100,000. No other employees are covered under comparable qualified plans. What problems (if any) do you envision regarding the plan's qualification with the IRS?

I9-32 Babson Corporation is proposing the creation of a qualified profit-sharing plan for its employees. The proposed plan provides for vesting of employer contributions after 20 years because the company wants to discourage employee turnover and does not feel that short-term employees should qualify for benefits. Will this plan qualify? Why or why not?

I9-33 Explain how distributions from a qualified pension plan, which are made in the form of annuity payments, are reported by an employee under the following circumstances:
a. No employee contributions are made to the plan.
b. The pension plan provides for matching employee contributions.

I9-34 Discuss the limitations and restrictions that the Code places on employer contributions to qualified pension and profit-sharing plans.

I9-35 Why are nonqualified deferred compensation plans particularly well-suited for use in executive compensation arrangements?

I9-36 If a newly formed corporation is considering going public and anticipates substantial future appreciation in its stock, would it be advisable for an executive receiving restricted property to elect to recognize income immediately under Sec. 83(b)? Contrast the tax consequences of a restricted property arrangement for both the employer and employee when this election is made versus when it is not made. Consider the effect of the subsequent lapsing of the restrictions and the employee's sale of the stock.

I9-37 List and discuss the qualification requirements for an incentive stock option plan (ISO). Describe the advantages and disadvantages of ISOs compared to nonqualified stock option plans.

I9-38 What difference does it make if a nonqualified stock option has a readily ascertainable FMV on the grant date?

I9-39 Is a self-employed individual, who is also employed and covered by an employer's qualified pension plan, eligible to establish an H.R. 10 or an SEP plan his or her self-employment income?

I9-40 What limitations are placed on self-employed individuals for contributions made to defined contribution H.R. 10 plans? Must self-employed individuals cover their full-time employees if an H.R. 10 plan is established?

I9-41 Would you be more favorably inclined to advise a 50-year-old individual or a 30-year-old individual to establish a traditional deductible IRA? Why? A traditional nondeductible IRA? Why? Consider any tax problems involved if the IRA funds are needed before age 59½.

I9-42 Discuss the essential differences between a traditional IRA and a Roth IRA.

I9-43 Your client, Charley Long, age 40, has requested your advice with respect to his IRA. He has a traditional IRA with a balance of $80,000 and his current AGI is $50,000. He expects his income to increase slightly when he retires at age 65. Charley has been reading about Roth IRAs and wants your advice as to whether he should rollover the $80,000 from his traditional IRA into a Roth IRA. He has sufficient outside money to pay any taxes due on the rollover. What advice would you give Charley?

I9-44 Sally, who is single and age 40, has previously made deductible IRA contributions for years before 1987 but has not been eligible to make deductible IRA contributions since that time because she is covered under her employer's plan. Her AGI is $60,000. She is interested in making IRA contributions in the current year, what advice would you give her?

I9-45 The owner of an unincorporated small business is considering whether to establish a simplified employee pension (SEP) plan for its employees.
a. What nontax factors might make an SEP attractive as an alternative to establishing a qualified pension or profit-sharing plan?
b. Is the owner of the small business eligible to make contributions on his or her behalf to the SEP?
c. Would you advise the owner to establish a salary reduction agreement SEP? Explain.

ISSUE IDENTIFICATION QUESTIONS

I9-46 Georgia is an executive who recently completed an assignment with her employer at an away-from-home location. It was realistically expected that the assignment would be completed in 15 months but the actual time period was only 11 months. Georgia incurred $15,000 of away-from-home expenses during the 11-month period none of which were reimbursed by her employer. What tax issues should Georgia consider?

I9-47 Jeremy is an executive for Columbia Corporation, which is going through a restructuring of its corporate headquarters operations. Columbia has offered to relocate Jeremy from its New York headquarters to its divisional operation in South Carolina and will reimburse him for both direct and indirect moving expenses. What tax issues should Jeremy consider?

I9-48 Juan, a self-employed medical doctor, maintains an office in his home where he maintains patient records and performs billing procedures. Most of his time is spent visiting patients and performing surgical procedures in the operating room at several local hospitals. Juan intends to deduct his expenses of his office in his home. What tax issues should Juan consider?

I9-49 David is on the audit staff of a national accounting firm. He has been with the firm for three years and is a CPA. David has applied and been accepted into a prestigious MBA program. The program is two years in duration. David has decided to resign from the accounting firm even though the firm has indicated that it would very much like David to return to work for the firm after he receives his MBA degree. David is somewhat interested in returning to public accounting but will certainly look at all of his options when he completes the program. David wants to deduct his education expenses, what are the relevant tax issues in this case?

PROBLEMS

I9-50 *Employment-Related Expenses.* Matt incurs the following employment-related expenses in the current year:

Actual automobile expenses	$1,000 — 2%
Moving expenses (deductible under Sec. 217)	1,000
Entertainment expenses	2,000 — 2%
Travel expenses (including $500 of business meals)	2,500 — "
Professional dues and subscriptions	500 — "
Total	$7,000

Matt's AGI is $100,000 before the above expenses are deducted. None of the expenses listed above are reimbursed by Matt's employer. He has no other miscellaneous itemized deductions and does not use the standard deduction.
a. What is the amount of Matt's deduction for employment-related expenses?
b. How are these items reported in Matt's tax return?

I9-51 *Travel and Entertainment.* Monique is a self-employed manufacturer's representative who solicits business for clients and receives a commission based on sales. She incurs the following expenditures during the current year:

Airfare and lodging while away from home overnight	$ 4,000
Business meals while traveling at which business is discussed	1,000 500
Local transportation costs for automobile, parking, tolls, etc. (business-related)	2,000
Commuting expenses	1,000
Local entertainment of customers	2,000 1000
Total	$10,000

a. Which of the expenditures listed above (if any) are deductible by Monique?
b. Are each of these items classified as *for* AGI or *from* AGI deductions?
c. How would your answers to Parts a and b change if Monique were an employee rather than self-employed and none of the expenses were reimbursed by her employer?

I9-52 *Unreimbursed Employee Expenses.* In the current year Mary incurs $3,600 of unreimbursed employment-related travel and entertainment expenses. These expenses include the following:

Airfare	$1,500
Taxi fare	100
Meals eaten alone while away from home on business	150 *from* 300
Laundry	50
Lodging	650
Business meals with customers at which business is discussed	500 250
Entertainment of customers	500 250
Total	$3,600

Mary also pays $1,000 of investment counseling fees and $500 of tax return preparation fees in the current year. Mary's AGI is $70,000.
a. What is the total amount of Mary's deductible expenses?
b. Are the deductible expenses classified as *for* AGI or *from* AGI?

I9-53 *Travel Expenses.* Marilyn is a business executive who accepts a temporary out-of-town assignment in Atlanta for a period of ten months. Marilyn leaves her husband and children in Miami and rents an apartment in Atlanta during the ten-month period. Marilyn incurs the following expenses, none of which are reimbursed by her employer:

Airfare to and from Atlanta	$ 800
Airfare for weekend trips to visit her family	8,000
Apartment rent	10,000
Meals in Atlanta	8,500
Entertainment of customers	2,000
Total	$29,300

a. Which of the expenditures listed above (if any) are deductible by Marilyn (before any limitations are applied)?
b. Are each of these expenditures classified as *for* AGI or *from* AGI deductions?
c. If Marilyn's AGI is $120,000, what is the amount of the deduction for the expenditures?
d. Do the tax consequences change if Marilyn's assignment is for a period of more than one year and is for an indefinite period rather than a temporary period?
e. Do the tax consequences in Parts a through c change if it was realistically expected that the work would be completed in ten months but after the ten-month period Marilyn is asked to continue for seven more months and if an additional $10,000 of travel expenses are incurred during the extended period?

I9-54 *Business/Personal Travel Expenses.* In the current year Mike's AGI is $50,000. Mike has no miscellaneous itemized deductions other than the employment-related expenses on the list below. Mike attends a professional trade association convention in Los Angeles. He spends three days at the meeting and two days vacationing before the meeting. Mike was unable to obtain excursion airfare rates (i.e., staying over a Saturday night) despite the fact that he was on vacation immediately before the meeting. Mike's total expenses, of which the business-related expenses are fully reimbursed by his employer after an adequate accounting is made, include the following:

Airfare	$ 450
Meals ($50 per day)	250
Hotel ($100 per day)	500
Entertainment of customers (business is discussed)	500
Total	$1,700

a. How much can Mike deduct for employment-related expenses?
b. How is the reimbursement reported on Mike's tax return?
c. Is the reimbursement fully deductible by Mike's employer?

I9-55 *Employment-Related Expenses and Reimbursements.* Maxine incurs the following employment-related business expenses in the current year:

Professional dues and subscriptions	$1,000
Airfare and lodging	2,000
Local transportation for employment-related business activities	1,000
Customer entertainment (business lunches where business is discussed)	1,000
Total	$5,000

After making an adequate accounting of the expenses, Maxine receives a fixed reimbursement of $3,000 from her employer. Assume that Maxine's AGI is $60,000, she has other miscellaneous itemized deductions of $1,000, and she does not use the standard deduction.
a. What amount of the expenses are deductible by Maxine?
b. Are each of these expenditures classified as *for* AGI or *from* AGI deductions?
c. How would your answers to Parts a and b change if Maxine instead received a $6,000 reimbursement?

I9-56 *Miscellaneous Itemized Deductions.* In the current year, Melissa, a single employee whose AGI is $100,000 before any of the items below, incurs the following expenses:

Safe deposit box rental for investments	$ 100
Tax return preparation fees	500
Moving expenses (deductible under Sec. 217)	2,000
Mortgage interest on Melissa's principal residence	12,000
Real estate taxes on Melissa's principal residence	1,800
Unreimbursed employment-related expenses (other than business meals and entertainment)	6,000
Unreimbursed employment-related expenses for business meals and entertainment (business is discussed)	1,200
Total	$23,600

a. What is the amount of Melissa's total miscellaneous itemized deductions (after deducting the 2% floor)?
b. What is the amount of Melissa's total itemized deductions?
c. What is the amount of Melissa's total itemized deductions if her AGI, after all adjustments above, is instead $150,000?

I9-57 *Transportation Expenses.* Jose, an employee of a law firm, maintains an office at the principal business location of his firm. He frequently travels from his home to client locations within and outside the metropolitan area. Jose is not reimbursed for his transportation expenses and has incurred the following:

Transportation expenses associated with trips to clients within the metropolitan area	$2,000
Transportation expenses associated with trips to clients located outside the metropolitan area	3,000
Total	$5,000

a. What is the amount of Jose's deduction for transportation expenses?
b. How is the deduction reported on Jose's tax return?
c. What is the amount of Jose's deduction for transportation expenses and its classification if he is self-employed and operates his office from his home? Assume that the requirements of Sec. 280A are satisfied.

I9-58 *Auto Expenses.* Michelle is an employee who must use her personal automobile for employment-related business trips. During 2001, Michelle drives her car 60% for business use and incurs the following total expenses (100% use of car):

Gas and oil	$4,000
Repairs	400
Depreciation	4,900
Insurance and license fees	1,300
Parking and tolls (business related)	100
Total	$10,700

Michelle drives 20,000 business miles during 2001 and receives a reimbursement of 10 cents per mile from her employer. Assume that the 2% nondeductible floor on miscellaneous itemized deductions is not applicable and that an adequate accounting is made to Michelle's employer.
a. What amount is deductible if Michelle elects to use the standard mileage method?
b. What amount is deductible if Michelle uses the actual cost method?
c. Can taxpayers switch back and forth between the mileage and actual methods each year?

I9-59 *Entertainment Expenses.* Milt, a self-employed attorney, incurs the following expenses in the current year:

Dues paid to the local chamber of commerce	$ 1,000
Business lunches for clients and prospective clients (Milt does not believe in conducting business discussions during lunch)	4,000
Entertainment of professional associates in his home (immediately following business meetings)	2,000
Country club dues (the club is used exclusively for business)	2,500
Entertainment of clients and prospective clients at the country club	1,500
Total	$11,000

a. Which of the expenditures listed above (if any) are deductible by Milt?
b. Are each of these items classified as *for* AGI or *from* AGI deductions?

I9-60 *Entertainment Expenses.* Beach Corporation purchases tickets to sporting events and uses them to entertain customers. In the current year Beach Corporation purchases the following tickets:

100 tickets to football games (face value of the tickets is $3,600)	$6,000
A skybox rented for six athletic events (seating capacity of the skybox is 30, and the highest price of a nonluxury box seat is $40)	18,000

What amount of the entertainment expenses is deductible in the current year?

I9-61 *Reimbursed Employee Expenses.* Latrisha is an employee of the Cooper Company and incurs significant employment-related expenses. During the current year, she incurred the following expenses in connection with her job:

Travel:	Airfare	$ 5,850
	Lodging	1,800
	Meals	1,200
Entertainment of customers		2,400
Total		$11,250

a. Determine the amount of deductible expenses for both Latrisha and the Cooper Company and, for Latrisha, whether they are deductible *for* AGI or *from* AGI assuming Cooper Company maintains an accountable plan for employee expense reimbursements, if the reimbursements are alternatively:

1. $11,250
2. $9,000
3. $14,000

b. What would be the result in a. for each of the three situations if the plan was a nonaccountable plan?

I9-62 *Moving Expenses.* Michael graduates from New York University and on February 1, 2001 accepts a position with a public accounting firm in Chicago. Michael is a resident of New York. In March, Michael travels to Chicago to locate a house and starts to work in June. He incurs the following expenses, none of which are reimbursed by the public accounting firm:

Automobile expense enroute (1,000 miles at 12 cents per mile-standard mileage rate)	$ 120
Cost of meals en route	100
Househunting trip travel expenses	1,400
Moving van expenses	3,980
Commission on the sale of Michael's New York condominium	3,500
Points paid to acquire a mortgage on Michael's new residence in Chicago	1,000
Temporary living expenses for one week in Chicago (hotel and $100 in meals)	400
Expenses incurred in decorating the new residence	500
Total expenses	$11,000

a. What is Michael's moving expense deduction?
b. How are the deductible expenses classified on Michael's tax return?
c. How would your answer to Part a change if all of Michael's expenses were reimbursed by his employer?

I9-63 *Education Expenses.* For each of the following independent situations, determine whether any of the expenditures qualify as deductible education expenses. Are the expenditures classified as *for* AGI or *from* AGI deductions?
a. Law school tuition and books for an IRS agent who is pursuing a law degree: $2,000.
b. Continuing professional accounting education expenses of $1,900 for a self-employed CPA: travel, $1,000 (including $200 meals); registration fees, $800; books, $100.
c. MBA education expenses totaling $5,000 for a business executive of a major corporation: tuition, $4,000; transportation, $800; and books, $200.
d. Tuition and books acquired for graduate education courses required under state law for a schoolteacher in order to renew a provisional certificate: $1,000.
e. Bar review courses for a recent law school graduate: $1,000.

I9-64 *Office-in-Home.* Nancy is a self-employed artist who uses 10% of her residence as a studio. The studio portion is used exclusively for business and is frequented by customers on a regular basis. Nancy also uses her den as an office (10% of the total floor space of her home) to prepare bills and keep records. However, the den is also used by her children as a TV room. Nancy's income from the sale of the artwork amounts to $40,000 in the current year. She also incurs $2,000 of expenses directly related to the business other than home office expenses (e.g., art supplies and selling expenses). Nancy incurs the following expenses in the current year related to her residence:

Real estate taxes	$ 2,000
Mortgage interest	5,000
Insurance	500
Depreciation	3,500
Repairs and utilities	1,000
Total	$12,000

a. Which of the expenditures above (if any) are deductible? Are they *for* AGI or *from* AGI deductions?
b. Would your answer to Part a change if Nancy's income from painting were only $2,500 for the year? What is the amount of the office-in-home deduction and the amount of the carryover (if any) of the unused deductions? (Assume that Nancy is not subject to the hobby loss restrictions.)

I9-65 Darrell is a self-employed consultant who uses 15% of his home exclusively as an office. Darrell operates completely out of his home office and makes all of his appointments from the office as well as keeping his books and records in the office. Darrell's gross income from his consulting business is $60,000 in 2001. He incurs $6,000 of expenses that are directly-related to his business, such as computer and office supplies. Below are expenses that relate to Darrell's residence for 2001:

Real estate taxes	$ 4,000
Mortgage interest	6,000
Insurance	1,000
Depreciation	4,000
Repairs and utilities	1,000
Total	$16,000

a. Which of the above expenditures (if any) are deductible? Are they *for* AGI or *from* AGI deductions?
b. How would your answer change if Darrell was an employee of a consulting company and maintained an office at home in order to take work home with him so he did not have to spend so many hours at his consulting company office?

I9-66 *Deferred Compensation Plan Requirements.* Identify whether each of the following plan features is associated with a qualified pension plan, a qualified profit-sharing plan, an employee stock ownership plan, a nonqualifed plan, or none of these plans.
a. Annual employer contributions are not required, but substantial and recurring contributions must be made based on a predetermined formula.
b. Annual, systematic, and definite employer contributions are required without regard to profits but based on actuarial methods.
c. Forfeitures must be used to reduce contributions that would otherwise be made under the plan.
d. The plan may discriminate in favor of highly compensated individuals.
e. The trust is funded with the contribution of employer stock, which is subsequently distributed to employees.

I9-67 *Taxability of Pension Payments.* Pam is a participant in a qualified pension plan. She retires on January 1, 2001 at age 63, and receives pension payments beginning in January 2001. Her pension payments, which will be received monthly for life, amounts to $1,000 per month. Pam contributed $30,000 to the pension plan on a pre-tax basis, and the number of anticipated payments based on Pam's age of 63 years in 260 months (see IRS table in Chapter I3) from the date she starts receiving payments.
a. What gross income will Pam recognize in 2001 and each year thereafter?
b. How would your answer to Part a change if Pam made contributions to the plan on an after-tax basis?
c. If, in part b., Pam dies in December 2002 after receiving pension payments for two full years, what tax consequences occur in the year of death?

I9-68 *Restricted Property.* In 2001, Bear Corporation transfers 100 shares of its stock to its employee Patrick. The stock is valued at $10 per share on the issue date. The stock is subject to the following restrictions:

- Patrick cannot transfer the stock by sale or other disposition (except in the event of death) for a five-year period.
- The stock must be forfeited to Bear Corporation if Patrick voluntarily terminates his employment with the company within a five-year period.

In year 2006, the Bear stock is worth $100 per share when the restrictions expire.
a. Assuming that no Sec. 83(b) election is made, what are the tax consequences to Patrick and Bear Corporation in 2001?
b. What are the tax consequences to Patrick and Bear Corporation if Patrick makes a valid Sec. 83(b) election in 2001?
c. What are the tax consequences to Patrick and Bear Corporation if Patrick forfeits the stock back to the company in 2002 when the stock is worth $20 per share if an election was made under Sec. 83(b)? What would happen if no Sec. 83(b) election were made?
d. What are the tax consequences to Patrick and Bear Corporation upon the lapse of the restrictions in year 2006 if an election has been made under Sec. 83(b)? What would the results be if no Sec. 83(b) election were made?
e. What are the tax consequences to Patrick and Bear Corporation if Patrick sells the Bear stock in year 2007 for $120 per share if a Sec. 83(b) election is made? if no Sec. 83(b) election is made?

I9-69 *IRAs.* On February 15, 2002, Phong, who is single and age 30, establishes an IRA and contributes $2,000 to the account. Phong's adjusted gross income is $36,000 in both 2001 and 2002. Phong is an active participant in an employer-sponsored retirement plan.
a. What amount of the contribution is deductible? In what year is it deductible?
b. How is the deduction (if any) reported (i.e., *for* AGI or *from* AGI)?
c. What tax treatment is accorded to Phong if he withdraws the $2,000 contribution from the IRA in 2003 due to a need for cash to make a down payment for a new car.
d. How would your answer to Part a change, if at all, if Phong were not an active participant in an employer-sponsored retirement plan?
e. How would your answer to Part a change if Phong were married and files a joint return with his spouse, who has no earned income? (Assume their combined AGI is $45,000.)

I9-70 *IRAs.* Phil, age 30, is married and files a joint return with his spouse. On February 15, 2002, Phil establishes a spousal IRA with a $4,000 contribution, $2,000 for himself and $2,000 for his wife. Phil's spouse earns $1,000 in 2001 from a part-time job, and their combined AGI is $40,000. Neither Phil nor his spouse is an active participant in an employer-sponsored retirement plan.
a. What amount of the contribution is deductible?
b. To what year does the contribution apply? (Assume that an election is made to treat Phil's spouse as having no compensation.)
c. Is the deduction reported as *for* AGI or *from* AGI?
d. How would your answer to Part a change, if at all, if Phil and his spouse were active participants in an employer-sponsored retirement plan?
e. If a portion of the contribution is nondeductible in Part d, is it possible for Phil to make a deductible and a nondeductible contribution in the same year? Explain.
f. How would your answer to Part a change if Phil and his spouse's combined AGI were $70,000 in 2001 and 2002 and Phil were an active participant in an employer-sponsored retirement plan?

I9-71 *Roth IRA.* Chatham Mae is single, age 35, and wants to make a contribution to an IRA for the year ended December 31, 2001. She is an active participant in a qualified retirement plan sponsored by her employer. Her AGI for 2001 is $100,000 before considering any IRA contribution.
a. What type of IRA, if any, is Chatham Mae eligible to make a contribution for 2001? If she is eligible to contribute to an IRA, what is the maximum amount that she can contribute?
b. Assume Chatham Mae makes contributions of $2,000 per year for six years to a Roth IRA. In 2007, she withdraws $15,000 to payoff her car loan. Her financial advisor suggested she withdraw the money from the IRA for two major reasons, (1) to eliminate her debt, and (2) no tax would be due on distributions from a Roth IRA after five years. Chatham Mae wants to verify the accuracy of her advisor's advice. What would be the tax consequences of this withdrawal? Alternatively, what if Chatham Mae withdrew the $15,000 to purchase a house (she is a first-time homebuyer)?

c. Alternatively to b. above, assume Chatham Mae has a traditional deductible IRA that has a balance of $50,000. She has been able to deduct all of her contributions to the IRA in prior years. Her financial advisor has recommended that she rollover the funds from her traditional IRA to a Roth IRA in 2001. What are the tax consequences of this rollover in 2001?

I9-72 **H.R. 10 Plans.** Paula is a self-employed doctor who is considering whether to establish a defined contribution H.R. 10 plan. Paula's only employee is a full-time nurse who has been employed by Paula for seven years. Paula's net earnings from self-employment (before the H.R. 10 plan contribution but after the deduction for one-half of self-employment taxes paid) is expected to be $100,000 during the current year and in future years.
a. If the H.R. 10 plan is established, what is the maximum amount Paula can contribute for the nurse's benefit?
b. What is the maximum amount Paula can contribute for herself? Is the amount reported as a *for* AGI or *from* AGI deduction?
c. Is Paula's nurse required to be included in the plan?
d. What are the tax consequences if Paula makes a premature withdrawal from the plan before reaching age 59½?

I9-73 **Stock Options.** Bell Corporation grants an incentive stock option to Peggy, an employee, on January 1, 2001, when the option price and FMV of the Bell stock is $80. The option entitles Peggy to buy 10 shares of Bell stock. Peggy exercises the option and acquires the stock on April 1, 2003, when the stock's FMV is $100. Peggy, while still employed by the Bell Corporation, sells the stock on May 1, 2005, for $120 per share.
a. What are the tax consequences to Peggy and Bell Corporation on the following dates: January 1, 2001; April 1, 2003; and May 1, 2005? (Assume all incentive stock option qualification requirements are met.)
b. How would your answer to Part a change if Peggy instead sold the Bell stock for $120 per share on May 1, 2003?

I9-74 **Stock Options.** Bender Corporation grants a nonqualified stock option to Penny, an employee, on January 1, 2001 that entitled Penny to acquire 10 shares of Bender stock at $80 per share. On this date, the stock has a $100 FMV and the option has a readily ascertainable FMV. Penny exercises the option on January 1, 2002 (when the FMV of the stock is $150) and acquires 10 shares of the stock for $80 per share. Penny later sells the Bender stock on January 1, 2004, for $200 per share.
a. What are the tax consequences to Penny and Bender Corporation on the following dates: January 1, 2001; January 1, 2002; and January 1, 2004?
b. How would your answer to Part a change if the Bender stock were instead closely-held and the option had no readily ascertainable FMV?

TAX FORM/RETURN PREPARATION PROBLEMS

I9-75 In the current year Dennis Johnson (SSN 277-33-7263) incurs the following unreimbursed employee business expenses:

Airplane and taxi fares	$ 4,000
Lodging away from home	5,000
Meals while away from home	1,000
Automobile expenses (related to 100% of the use of his personal automobile):	
Gasoline and oil	1,500
Repairs	500
Insurance	400
Depreciation	1,500
Parking and tolls (includes both business and personal use)	100
Total	$14,000

Johnson receives a $7,800 reimbursement for the travel expenses. He did not receive any reimbursement for the auto expenses. He uses his personal automobile 80% for business use. Total business miles amount to 20,000. Johnson's AGI is $40,000, and he has no other miscellaneous itemized deductions.

a. Calculate Johnson's expense deduction using Form 2106 (Employee Business Expenses) based on actual automobile expenses and other employee business expenses.
b. Calculate Johnson's expense deduction using the standard mileage rate method and other employee business expenses. (Assume that none of the restrictions on the use of the standard mileage rate method are applicable.)

I9-76 George Large (SSN 414-33-5688) and his wife Marge Large (SSN 555-81-9495), want you to prepare their income tax return based on the information below:

George Large worked as a salesman for Toyboat, Inc. He received a salary of $50,000 ($6,000 of income taxes withheld) plus an additional $5,000 to cover his employee business expenses. George must make an adequate accounting to his employer and return any excess reimbursement. Additionally, Toyboat provides George with medical insurance worth $3,500 per year. George drove his car 20,000 miles during the year. His log indicates that 17,000 miles were for sales calls to prospective customers at the customers' offices. George uses the standard mileage rate method. George is a professional basketball fan. He purchased two season tickets for a total of $2,000. He takes a customer to every game, and they usually discuss business at the games. George also takes clients to business lunches. His log indicates that he spent $1,500 on these business meals. George also took a five-day trip to the Toyboat headquarters in Musty, Ohio. He was so well-prepared that he finished his business in three days, so he spent the other two days sightseeing. He had the following expenses during each day of his trip:

Airfare	$200
Lodging	$85/day
Meals	$50/day
Taxicabs	$20/day

Marge Large is self-employed. She repairs rubber toy boats in the basement of their home, which is 25% of the house's square footage. She had the following income and expenses:

Income from rubber toy boat repairs	$12,000
Cost of materials	5,000
Contract labor	3,500
Long-distance phone calls (business)	500

The Large's home cost a total of $150,000, of which the cost of the land was $20,000. The FMV of the house is $225,000. The house is depreciable over a 39 year recovery period. The Larges incurred other expenses:

Utility bills for the house	$2,000
Real estate taxes	2,500
Mortgage interest	4,500
Cash charitable contributions	2,500

Prepare Form 1040, Schedules A and C for Form 1040, and Form 2106 for the current year. (Assume no depreciation for this problem and that no estimated taxes were paid by the Larges.)

CASE STUDY PROBLEMS

I9-77 Ajax Corporation is a young high-growth company engaged in the manufacture and distribution of automotive parts. Its common stock has doubled in value since the company was listed on the NASDAQ exchange about two years ago. Ajax currently has a high debt/equity ratio due to the issuance of debt to finance its capital expansion needs. Despite rapid growth in assets and profitability, Ajax has severe cash flow problems and a poor working capital ratio. The company urgently needs to attract new executives to the organization and to provide financial incentives to existing top management because of recent turnover and high growth. Approximately 55% of the common stock is owned by Andrew Ajax, who is the CEO, and his immediate family. None of the other officers own stock in the company.

You are a tax consultant for the company who has been asked to prepare suggestions after reviewing the compensation system. Your discussions with several top management individuals reveal the following aspects of corporate strategy and philosophy:

- The company needs to expand the equity capital base because of its concern for the high risk caused by large amounts of debt.

- Improvement in cash flow and liquidity would enhance its stock price and enable the company to continue its high growth rate.
- Top management feels that employee loyalty and productivity would be improved if all employees owned some stock in the company. The company currently offers a qualified pension plan to its employees and executives that provides only minimal pension benefits. No other deferred compensation or bonus arrangements are currently being offered.
- Andrew Ajax feels that the top management group should own a substantial amount of Ajax stock to ensure that the interests of management correspond with the shareholder interests (i.e., the maximization of shareholder wealth).

The following types of compensation arrangements have been discussed:

- Sec. 401(k) and ESOP plans for employees.
- Encourage all employees and executives to independently fund their retirement needs beyond any Social Security benefits by establishing IRA plans.
- Provide restricted property arrangements (using Ajax stock) to attract new top level executives and to retain existing executives.
- Offer nonqualified or incentive stock options to existing and new executives.

Required: Prepare a client memo that recommends revisions to Ajax Corporation's existing compensation system for both its employee and executive groups. Your recommendations should discuss the pros and cons of different deferred compensation arrangements and should consider both tax and nontax factors.

I9-78 Steve is part owner and manager of a small manufacturing company that makes keypads for alarm systems. The keypads are sold to several different alarm companies throughout the country. Steve must travel to several cities each year to meet with current customers and to attract new business. When you meet with Steve to obtain information to prepare his current year tax return, he tells you that he has spent about $5,000 during the current year on airfare and taking his customers out to dinner to discuss business. Because he took most of his trips in the summer and fall, and it is now April of the following year, Steve cannot remember the exact time and places of the business dinners and did not retain any receipts for the cash used to pay the bills. However he remembers the names of the customers he went to see and the business topics that were discussed. As Steve's tax consultant, what is your responsibility regarding the treatment of the travel and entertainment expenses under the mandates of the AICPA's *Statements on Standards for Tax Services*? Prepare a client letter explaining to Steve the requirements under Sec. 274(d) for sufficient substantiation of travel and entertainment expenses. (See the *Statements on Standards for Tax Services* section in Chapter I15 for a discussion of these issues and Appendix E.)

TAX RESEARCH PROBLEM

I9-79 Charley Long is a truck driver, the 18-wheeler variety. He works for Fishy Co., a seafood company in Mobile, Alabama, and drives a company truck. Charley's job entails leaving Mobile at 4:00 PM each day (five days per week) and delivering fresh fish to restaurants and wholesale fish distributors in Mississippi and Louisiana. His last stop, in Lafayette, Louisiana, is generally around 12:00 midnight. It normally takes Charley about five hours to get back to Mobile.

Charley's routine is varied. Sometimes, he drives straight back to Mobile from Lafayette. On other occasions, he will pull off at a truck stop and sleep in his cab before returning to Mobile. His cab is equipped with sleeping facilities, although small and sparse. Finally, on other occasions, Charley will spend the night in a motel along the road. The Fishy Co. has no preference as to what Charley does and has given him permission to either drive back or stay overnight. However, the company does not reimburse him for his food and lodging expenses.

When Charley drives straight back to Mobile, Charley will eat one meal. When he sleeps overnight (either in his cab or in a motel) he will eat two meals, a late dinner and breakfast. He spends an average of $6.00 for dinner and $4.00 for breakfast. The cost of his motel averages $50.00 per night. When Charley sleeps in the cab, he generally sleeps about 4-5 hours and then drives on to Mobile.

During the current year, Charley incurred the following expenses:

Meals incurred on nonstop trips	$ 900
Meals incurred when: slept in cab	600
slept in motel	400
Lodging	2,000
TOTAL	$3,900

The IRS has disallowed all of the above expenses on the grounds that they are not bona fide travel expenses but personal expenses. Would you advise Charley to contest this issue?

A partial list of research sources is:

- Sec. 162(a)(2) and Reg. Sec. 1.162-2(a)
- *U.S. v. Correll*, 389 U.S. 299 (1967)
- *Williams v. Patterson*, 286 F.2d 333 (5th Cir. 1961)
- Rev. Rul. 75-168, 1975-1 C.B. 58 and Rev. Rul. 75-432, 1975-2 C.B. 60

CHAPTER 10

DEPRECIATION, COST RECOVERY, AMORTIZATION, AND DEPLETION

LEARNING OBJECTIVES
After studying this chapter, you should be able to

1. Classify property and calculate depreciation under the pre-ACRS rules
2. Classify property and calculate cost recovery under the ACRS rules
3. Classify property and calculate depreciation under the MACRS rules
4. Calculate amortization for intangible assets and understand the difference between amortizable and non-amortizable assets
5. Apply cost and percentage depletion methods and understand the treatment for intangible drilling costs

10-2 Individuals ▼ Chapter 10

CHAPTER OUTLINE

Depreciation and Cost Recovery...10-2
Amortization...10-13
Depletion, Intangible Drilling and Development Costs...10-17
Tax Planning Considerations...10-20
Compliance and Procedural Considerations...10-21

The tax law allows taxpayers to deduct a reasonable allowance for the exhaustion, wear and tear, and obsolescence of property used in a trade or business or held for the production of income.[1] The purpose of allowing a depreciation deduction is to enable taxpayers to recover the cost of an asset under the return of capital doctrine. Depreciation, therefore, is the systematic allocation of the cost of an asset over its estimated economic life. *Depreciation* relates to deductions for most tangible property, *amortization* relates to deductions for intangible property, and *depletion* relates to deductions for natural resources (oil and gas, coal, etc.). While the concepts of depreciation, amortization, and depletion are similar to those in financial accounting, the income tax rules are unique. This chapter discusses the income tax rules relating to depreciation, amortization, and depletion.

DEPRECIATION AND COST RECOVERY

TYPICAL MISCONCEPTION

It is easy to forget that the depreciation or cost-recovery system that applies to any one asset is the system that was in effect when the property was placed in service. Property acquired in 1986 is not affected by the MACRS rules that became effective in 1987.

REAL-WORLD EXAMPLE

Harrah's Club in Reno, Nevada, restores antique autos and displays them. The restoration costs cannot be depreciated because the autos have an indefinite life as museum pieces. *Harrah's Club v. U.S.*, 43 AFTR 2d 79-745, 81-2 USTC ¶9677 (Ct. Cls., 1981).

HISTORICAL NOTE

Before 1954, except for the limited use of a declining-balance method, taxpayers were required to use the straight-line method.

ADDITIONAL COMMENT

Property is considered to be "placed in service" when it is in a condition or state of readiness and is available for a specifically assigned function. This can be important in attempting to determine the first year that a depreciation deduction is available.

GENERAL CONSIDERATIONS

Taxpayers must use specific depreciation methods depending on *when* an asset is placed into service. Three separate depreciation and cost recovery systems are currently in place. These three distinct systems are the result of tax law changes in 1981 and 1986. The systems that taxpayers must use are as follows:

▶ Property placed into service prior to 1981

Taxpayers must use the rules contained in Sec. 167 and these rules basically follow financial accounting principles.

▶ Property placed into service after December 31, 1980 and before January 1, 1987

Taxpayers must the Accelerated Cost Recovery System (ACRS) as provided in Sec. 168.

▶ Property placed into service after December 31, 1986

Taxpayers must the Modified Accelerated Cost Recovery System (MACRS) as provided in Sec. 168.

The primary emphasis in this chapter is placed upon the MACRS rules because most assets placed into service before 1987 are now fully depreciable.

The terms *depreciation* and *cost recovery* are used interchangeably in this text. The rules in Sec. 167 (or pre-ACRS) and the MACRS rules under Sec. 168 both refer to depreciation. However, the deduction under ACRS is referred to as cost recovery. In 1981, Congress initiated the original ACRS system to achieve a number of objectives, including a stimulus for private investment, improving business productivity, simplifying taxpayer compliance, and facilitating IRS administration of the tax law. Therefore, less importance was placed on the financial accounting concept of matching costs and revenues, which is the primary theory that governed the Sec. 167 depreciation rules. The primary objective of Congress in 1981 was to allow businesses and investors to recover the cost of capitalized expenditures over a period of time that is substantially shorter than the property's economic useful life. Thus, the term *cost recovery* rather than *depreciation* was used under the ACRS system. The post-1986 MACRS rules more closely follow the concept of economic useful life and, therefore, the MACRS rules refer to depreciation rather than cost recovery.

COMMON RULES OF ALL SYSTEMS. Regardless of the particular system of depreciation that is required to be used (i.e., MACRS, ACRS, etc.), there are certain rules that are common to all systems of depreciation. These common rules are discussed below.

▶ As discussed above, depreciation may only be claimed on property used in a trade or business or for the production of income. Thus, personal-use assets, such as a personal-use automobile or the taxpayer's personal residence, are not depreciable.

---

[1] Sec. 167(a).

- No depreciation is permitted for land or other assets that have an indefinite life. Assets such as works of art are generally not depreciable.
- Depreciation for the first year is permitted only in the year the asset is placed into service. For example, a taxpayer may purchase a depreciable asset in December, 2000, but not place it into service until January, 2001. In this case, depreciation is not allowed until 2001.
- Regardless of the depreciation system, consistency is required. Taxpayers must consistently use the method selected in the year the asset was placed into service unless a change of accounting method is requested from the IRS.
- The basis of the property being depreciated must be reduced by the amount of depreciation that is allowable for each taxable year. An important aspect of depreciation is determining the amount of depreciation that is *allowed* and *allowable*. The depreciation allowed is the actual depreciation that is claimed by the taxpayer for a particular taxable year. Allowable depreciation is the amount of depreciation to be claimed under the tax law by using the slowest possible method (i.e., straight-line using the longest permissible recovery period). If a taxpayer does not take any depreciation during a particular year, the basis of the property must be reduced by the amount of depreciation that should have been taken during the year (i.e., the allowable depreciation).

EXAMPLE I10-1 ▶

ADDITIONAL COMMENT

A recent case held that a professional musician could depreciate a nineteenth-century violin bow. The IRS had argued the bow had an indeterminate life but the court ruled that the recovery period under ACRS represented the useful life of the bow. *Simon v. Comm.*, 95-2 USTC ¶50,552 (CA-2, 1995).

Maria acquires a machine in the current year for $50,000 to be used in her business and elects straight-line depreciation under MACRS. The machine is classified as seven-year property for tax purposes. Maria properly takes depreciation in the first two years the asset is used in her business in the amount of $10,714 ($3,571 in Year 1 assuming the half-year convention and $7,143 in Year 2). However, because of a net operating loss in Year 3, Maria did not take any depreciation on the tax return. The allowable depreciation in Year 3 was $7,143. Even though Maria did not claim the $7,143 of depreciation in Year 3, the basis of the machine must still be reduced by that amount. Thus, at the end of Year 3, the basis of the machine would be $32,143 ($50,000 minus the allowable accumulated depreciation of $17,857). This is the case even though she did not actually claim any depreciation in Year 3. Obviously, Maria should amend her tax return for Year 3 and claim the allowable depreciation. This would increase her net operating loss for Year 3 which either can be carried back two years or forward 20 years. ◀

TYPES OF PROPERTY. Before examining the depreciation rules, it is necessary to define certain terms relating to the various types of property. For both property law and income tax purposes, there are two basic types of property, tangible and intangible. **Tangible property** refers to property that has physical substance, such as land, buildings, natural resources, equipment, etc. **Intangible property** refers to property that does not have physical substance, such as goodwill, patents, and stocks and bonds. The cost of tangible property (other than land, of course) is systematically written off through depreciation or depletion. Natural resources, such as oil and gas reserves, are recovered through depletion. Intangible property is written off through amortization.

Tangible property is further classified as either real property or personal property. **Real property** (often referred to as real estate or realty) is defined as land or any structure permanently attached to the land, such as buildings. **Personal property** is any tangible property that is not real property, and includes items such as equipment, vehicles, furniture, etc. It is important to distinguish between personal property and personal-use property. **Personal-use property** is any property, tangible or intangible, real or personal, that is used by the taxpayer for his own personal use rather than in a trade or business or for the production of income.

ADDITIONAL COMMENT

The IRS recently issued a private letter ruling that required an airline to capitalize engine overhauls rather than expensing such amounts in the current year. The IRS position requires capitalization because the overhauls involve replacement or reconditioning of a large portion of the engine's parts. This ruling has been severely criticized by the airlines industry, saying that the decision could negatively impact passenger safety.

CAPITALIZATION VERSUS EXPENSE. A frequent dilemma for taxpayers is whether an expenditure should either be capitalized (and depreciated) or expensed entirely in the current year. As is discussed in Chapter I6, if an expenditure either improves the efficiency of an asset or extends the life of an asset beyond the end of the year, the expenditure should generally be capitalized. However, most taxpayers have established materiality limits in order to justify the expensing of small expenditures that technically should be considered a capital expenditure. Since the capitalization-expense decision many times is subjective in nature, disputes between the IRS and taxpayers are common.

CONVERSION OF PERSONAL-USE PROPERTY. If personal-use property is either converted to business use or held for the production of income (e.g., a rental house), the property's basis for depreciation purposes is the lesser of its adjusted basis or its fair market value (FMV) determined as of the conversion date.[2] This lower of cost or market rule is intended to prevent taxpayers from depreciating the portion of the cost that represents a nondeductible loss on a personal-use asset.

EXAMPLE I10-2 ▶ Marty acquires a personal residence for $115,000 in 1998. In 2001, he converts the property to rental use because he is unable to sell the house due to a depressed local real estate market. The property's FMV is only $100,000 when it is converted to rental status in 2001. The $15,000 ($115,000 − $100,000) decline in value represents a nondeductible personal loss and is not depreciable. The depreciable basis is $100,000 (minus the portion of the property's FMV that represents land that is not depreciable). ◀

OBJECTIVE 1

Classify property and calculate depreciation under the MACRS rules.

DEPRECIATION METHODS

As mentioned previously, the method of depreciation required for income tax purposes depends on the date the asset was placed into service. Assets placed into service prior to 1987 must use the old depreciation methods that were in place during those years.[3] For assets placed into service after 1986, the MACRS system of depreciation is required for most assets. There are several unique features of the MACRS system that are different from depreciation methods used for financial accounting purposes. These features include the following:

▶ Salvage value is not considered in the computation of the depreciation amount.

▶ Specific asset classes are used. Both tangible personal property and real property must be placed into specific asset classes, based on the type of property. Asset classes merely refer to the number of years over which the asset must be depreciated.

▶ Fewer depreciation methods are used and the methods are built into the MACRS tables. Both accelerated and straight-line methods are used in MACRS, however, accelerated methods are not permissible for real property. The MACRS tables are summarized in Appendix C.

▶ The term "convention" in the tax law refers to the assumption as to when an asset is either placed into service or disposed of and is used extensively in the MACRS system. The **half-year convention** is required for all tangible personal property and assumes that all asset acquisitions or dispositions are made at the midpoint of the tax year, regardless of when the actual acquisition or disposition is made. For real estate, the *mid-month convention* is used and assumes that all asset acquisitions or dispositions are made at the midpoint of the month in which the transaction occurs.

EXAMPLE I10-3 ▶ Ted, a calendar-year taxpayer, purchases a machine for his business on March 1, 2001. For depreciation purposes, under the half-year convention, the machine is treated as if it were placed into service on July 1, 2001 and one-half year's depreciation is allowable in 2001. The half-year convention assumes all asset acquisitions and dispositions occur at the midpoint of the tax year. ◀

EXAMPLE I10-4 ▶ Bob, a calendar-year taxpayer, purchases a building for his business on March 5, 2001. For depreciation purposes, under the mid-month convention, the building is treated as if it were placed into service on March 15, 2001 and 9½ months of depreciation is allowable in 2001. ◀

TANGIBLE PERSONAL PROPERTY: CLASSIFICATION AND RECOVERY RATES. Tangible personal property, such as equipment, furniture, computers, etc., generally are

---

[2] Reg. Sec. 1.167(g)-1.
[3] For assets placed into service between 1981 and 1986, taxpayers were required to use the ACRS method; for assets placed into service before 1981, a pre-ACRS method was required. The pre-ACRS methods more closely resemble depreciation methods used for financial statement purposes.

Depreciation, Cost Recovery, Amortization, and Depletion ▼ Individuals 10-5

depreciable under MACRS if used in a trade or business or held for the production of income. Certain types of property are excluded from being depreciated under MACRS, including:

- Property depreciated under a method not expressed in terms of years, such as the units of production method, and the taxpayer elects to not depreciate the property under MACRS;
- Intangible assets, such as goodwill or copyrights;
- Films, video tapes, or sound recordings.[4]

For property depreciated under MACRS, each property acquired must be classified into one of six categories and depreciation computed using the percentages contained in Table I10-1. The classification of assets is based upon the determination of a class life from a listing of assets published by the IRS.[5]

The following classifications apply to personal property placed in service after December 31, 1986 under the MACRS system.[6]

ADDITIONAL COMMENT
The depreciable life of an automobile has been extended from 3 years to 5 years under the MACRS rules.

KEY POINT
Most depreciable personal property is classified as 7-year property under MACRS.

- 3-Year   Property with a class life of 4 years or less, including tractor units, race horses over 12 years old, and special tools.
- 5-Year   Property with a a class life of more than 4 years but less than 10 years including automobiles, light and heavy-duty, general purpose trucks, computers, and research and experimental (R&E) equipment.
- 7-Year   Property with a class life of 10 years or more but less than 16 years, including office furniture and equipment, horses, single-purpose agricultural or horticultural structures, and property with no class life and not classified elsewhere. Most types of machinery are included in this class.
- 10-Year   Property with a class life of more than 16 years, but less than 20 years, including barges, vessels, and petroleum and food processing equipment.
- 15-Year   Property with a class life of more than 20 years, but less than 25 years, including billboards, service station buildings, and land improvements.
- 20-Year   Property with a class life of 25 or more years, including utilities and sewers.

KEY POINT
Remember that salvage value is not taken into consideration under the MACRS system.

The depreciation rates for the 3-year, 5-year, and 7-year recovery classes are provided in Table I10-1 (See also Table 1 in Appendix C). The rates in Table I10-1 are based on the 200% DB method switching to straight-line when it yields a larger amount. A half-year convention is used in the year of acquisition and zero salvage value is assumed. In the year of disposition, the amount calculated from the table must be reduced by one-half in order to properly apply the half-year convention.

EXAMPLE I10-5 ▶

In March, 2001, Mary acquires and places into service a business machine which cost $20,000. The machinery has a 7-year recovery period under the MACRS rules. The depreciation deduction for 2001 is $2,858 (0.1429 × $20,000). The rate that is applied from Table I10-1 (0.1429) is based on the 200% DB method and assumes a half-year convention and zero salvage value. The MACRS depreciation deduction for the year of acquisition can also be computed by applying the accelerated depreciation rate (using the half-year convention) to the basis of the assets. Thus the depreciation deduction for 2001 is $2,857 ($20,000 ÷ 7 years × 200% DB × 0.50 year). Minor differences between the two calculations are due to rounding. ◀

KEY POINT
Remember, the mid-quarter convention does *not* apply to real property.

Use of the Mid-Quarter Convention. As mentioned previously, the MACRS system generally requires the use of the half-year convention. However, the MACRS system requires the use of the mid-quarter convention if the aggregate basis of all personal property placed in service during the last three months of the year exceeds 40% of the cost of all personal property placed in service during the tax year.[7] Therefore, if the test is met, the mid-quarter convention must be used instead of the half-year convention and special mid-quarter tables must be used to compute depreciation under this convention. (See Tables 2-5 in

---

[4] Sec. 168(f).
[5] To determine the class life of assets, see Rev. Proc. 87-56, modified by Rev. Proc. 88-22, which sets forth the class life of property for depreciation purposes.
[6] Sec. 168(e)(1).
[7] Sec. 168(d)(3).
[8] Sec. 168(d)(3)(B) and Reg. Sec. 1.168(d)-1(b)(3).

SELF-STUDY QUESTION

In Table I10-1, how has the 0.2000 first-year cost recovery rate for five-year property been calculated?

ANSWER

The 0.2000 rate is calculated by multiplying the double declining-balance rate of 0.4000 by ½ year of depreciation.

▼ TABLE I10-1
MACRS Rates for Tangible Personal Property (using half-year convention)

Recovery Year	Recovery Classes		
	3-Year	5-Year	7-Year
1	0.3333	0.2000	0.1429
2	0.4445	0.3200	0.2449
3	0.1481	0.1920	0.1749
4	0.0741	0.1152	0.1249
5	—	0.1152	0.0893
6	—	0.0576	0.0892
7	—	—	0.0893
8	—	—	0.0446

Source: Table 1 of Rev. Proc. 87-57, 1987-2 C.B. 687.

Appendix C). Property placed in service and disposed of during the same tax year is not taken into account.[8] Also, property expensed under Sec. 179 is excluded in computing the 40% test for the applicability of the mid-quarter convention.[9]

The 40% rule prevents taxpayers from using the half-year convention and thereby obtaining one-half year's depreciation in the year of acquisition when a substantial portion of the assets are acquired during the last quarter of the tax year.

EXAMPLE I10-6 ▶ Michael, a calendar-year taxpayer, acquires 5-year tangible personal property in 2001 and places it in service on the following schedule:

Date Placed in Service	Acquisition Cost
January 20	$100,000
April 18	200,000
November 5	300,000
Total	$600,000

Because more than 40% of the property acquired during the year is placed in service in the last three months, the mid-quarter convention will apply for all property placed in service during the year. (See Tables 2 through 5 in Appendix C for the percentages that are used to make this calculation.)

Property Placed in Service	Year 1 Depreciation	
January 20	$100,000 × 35% =	$ 35,000
April 18	200,000 × 25% =	50,000
November 5	300,000 × 5% =	15,000
Total	$600,000	$100,000

Note that if the half-year convention had been applied in this example, $120,000 (0.2000 × $600,000) of depreciation could have been claimed. Generally, if larger depreciation deductions are desired, care should be exercised on asset acquisitions to prevent the application of the mid-quarter convention. ◀

STOP & THINK *Question:* A common misconception of the mid-quarter convention is that it always yields a smaller depreciation deduction than the half-year convention. Consider the following situation where a business has placed into service the following assets (all 7-year property under MACRS) during the current year:

---

[9] PLR 9126014 (March 29, 1991). Section 179 is discussed later in this chapter.

February	$300,000
June	10,000
November	200,000

The business needs an additional $10,000 of equipment (also 7-year property) in the current year, but the purchase could be delayed until early January of the next year. Assuming the business wants to *maximize* its depreciation deduction in the current year, should the business purchase the additional $10,000 of equipment in the current year or delay the purchase until next year?

Solution: The business should purchase the equipment in the current year even though it will require the use of the mid-quarter convention.

Mid-quarter Test
Currently (before the purchase): $200,000/$510,000 = 39.2%

With the purchase: $210,000/$520,000 = 40.4%

Therefore, if the business purchases the additional $10,000 in the current year, the mid-quarter convention will apply. The depreciation for the current year assuming the purchase is made is:

First quarter:	$300,000 × 25% =	$75,000
Second quarter:	10,000 × 17.85% =	1,785
Fourth quarter:	210,000 × 3.57% =	7,497
	TOTAL	$84,282

Compare this amount with the depreciation that would result under the half-year convention ($510,000 × 14.29% = $72,879) assuming the purchase *was not* made. (The mid-quarter convention produces a higher depreciation deduction even if the half-year convention is computed on $520,000, i.e., $520,000 × 14.29% = $74,308). It is clear that the mid-quarter convention actually maximizes depreciation for the current year. You should notice that the mid-quarter convention yields more than the half-year convention for the reason that virtually all of the equipment that was purchased (other than the fourth quarter) was in the first quarter and this equipment is depreciated using a 25% rate versus a 14.29% rate under the half-year convention.

ADDITIONAL POINT
You must manually make the adjustment for the depreciation factor found in the MACRS table for assets sold during the year.

Year of Disposition. The MACRS system allows depreciation to be taken in the year of disposition using the same convention that applied on acquisition (e.g., half-year, mid-month, or mid-quarter convention). Therefore, if property is disposed of during the year in which the half-year convention is applicable, the depreciation for the year of disposition will be one-half of the amount computed by using the table percentages.

EXAMPLE I10-7 ▶ Assume the same facts as in Example I10-6, except that the equipment purchased on April 18 is disposed of on August 14 in the following year. The mid-quarter convention must be used because it is used in the year of acquisition. Thus, $37,500 of depreciation is claimed in the year of disposition [($200,000 × 0.30) × (7.5 ÷ 12)]. (See Table 3 in Appendix C.) ◀

EXAMPLE I10-8 ▶ Michelle acquires machinery in 2001 that qualifies as seven-year MACRS property and has a $100,000 basis for depreciation. The half-year convention is applied in the year of acquisition. In December 2002 the machinery is sold. Michelle's depreciation deduction in 2002 is $12,245 [$100,000 × (0.2449 × 0.50)] for the equipment (see Table I10-1). ◀

KEY POINT
All depreciable real property can be classified in one of two classes residential rental or nonresidential, real property.

REAL PROPERTY: CLASSIFICATION AND RECOVERY RATES . The MACRS recovery periods that apply to real property placed in service in years after 1986 have been lengthened as follows:

▶ Residential rental property: 27.5 years
▶ Nonresidential real property: 39 years[10]

---

[10] Sec. 168(c)(1). A 31.5-year recovery period applies to property placed in service on or after January 1, 1987 and before May 13, 1993. Certain exceptions permit the continued use of the 31.5-year recovery period for binding contracts entered into before May 13, 1993, and where the construction of the property commenced before May 13, 1993. See Table 9 in Appendix C for the 39-year property depreciation tables.

> **ADDITIONAL COMMENT**
> The recovery period for nonresidential real property was extended from 31.5 years to 39 years to offset the revenue loss from liberalizing the passive activity loss rules affecting real estate.

> **KEY POINT**
> Depreciable real property placed in service after 1986 must be depreciated using the straight-line method.

> **ADDITIONAL COMMENT**
> For purposes of determining whether at least 80% of the gross rental income is rental income from dwelling units, a taxpayer living in any part of the building includes the fair rental value of his unit in the gross rental income.

Depreciation must be calculated using the straight-line method. A mid-month convention is used in the year of acquisition and in the year of disposition. The tables for computing depreciation for real property are located in Tables 7, 8 and 9 in Appendix C.

A common transaction for taxpayers owning buildings is the depreciation of subsequent capital improvements. Capital improvements are depreciated over the full life of the improvement, not over the remaining life of the building. Thus, the cost of a new roof on an office building must be depreciated over 39 years even though the building may have been placed into service several years ago.

Real properties are divided into two categories: residential rental property and nonresidential real property. **Residential rental property** is defined as property from which at least 80% of the gross rental income is rental income from dwelling units.[11] Dwelling units include houses, apartments, and manufactured homes that are used for residential purposes but not hotels, motels, or other establishments for transient use. Nonresidential real property is any real property other than residential rental property.

STRAIGHT-LINE (METHOD) ELECTION UNDER MACRS. Instead of using the accelerated methods previously described under the MACRS rules, taxpayers may elect to use the straight-line method for tangible personal property. If the straight-line election is made, the taxpayer must use either the same depreciation period or an extended period based on the alternative depreciation system.[12]

ALTERNATIVE DEPRECIATION SYSTEM. The MACRS system provides an alternative depreciation system (ADS) that is required for certain property and is also available for all other depreciable assets if the taxpayer so elects.[13] The principal type of property for which the ADS is *required* is any tangible property which is used predominantly outside the United States. The recovery periods are specified under the ADS and, many times, are longer than the recovery periods under MACRS. Under the ADS, assets must be depreciated using the class life as set forth in Rev. Proc. 87-56. Personal property with no specific class life is assigned a 12-year life and real property is assigned a 40-year life. Further, the ADS requires the use of the straight-line method with a half-year, mid-quarter, or mid-month convention, whichever is applicable. The election of the ADS is generally made by taxpayers who want to use the straight-line method over a longer recovery period. These taxpayers frequently have net operating losses or are subject to the alternative minimum tax (see Chapter I14 for a discussion of the alternative minimum tax).

The ADS is an elective provision made on a year-by-year basis. Once the election is made for specified property, it is irrevocable. Also, for personal property, the ADS election applies to all property within a class (all five-year property, for example); for real property, the ADS election may be made on an individual property basis.

EXAMPLE I10-9 ▶ In May, 2001, Bob Roaster purchased an office building for $300,000 ($50,000 allocated to the land) as rental property. Because he has substantial net operating losses from other business ventures, Roaster elects to depreciate the building using the ADS. Depreciation expense for 2001, using the mid-month convention and a 40-year life is $3,906 ($250,000 ÷ 40 years × 7.5/12). If Roaster had not elected the ADS, his depreciation would have been $4,013 [$250,000 × .01605 (from Table 9, Appendix C)]. The difference is small because the recovery period is 39 years under regular MACRS and 40 years under the ADS. ◀

The alternative depreciation system is also used to compute earnings and profits (E&P) for a corporation and to compute the alternative minimum tax for both individuals and corporations (see Chapter I14).

A comparison of the ACRS and MACRS rules is presented in Topic Review I10-1.

---

[11] Secs. 168(e)(2)(A) and 167(j)(2)(B).
[12] Sec. 167(j)(2)(B).
[13] Sec. 168(g). See Tables 10–12 in Appendix C.

Topic Review I10-1

Comparison of MACRS and ADS

	MACRS	ADS
Recovery Periods:		
Automobiles	5 years	5 years
Computers	5 years	5 years
Office furniture and equipment	7 years	10 years
Residential rental property	27.5 years	40 years
Nonresidential real property	31.5 or 39 years	40 years
Conventions:		
Personal property	Half-year or mid-quarter[a]	Half-year or mid-quarter[a]
Real property	Mid-month	Mid-month
Depreciation in year of sale:		
Personal property	Yes	Yes
Real property	Yes	Yes

[a] If more than 40% of personal property is placed in service during the last quarter of year.

SECTION 179 EXPENSING ELECTION

ADDITIONAL COMMENT

In the case of a partnership, the partnership and each partner are individually subject to the annual $20,000 limitation.

In lieu of capitalizing the cost of new or used tangible personal business property, taxpayers may elect to expense up to $24,000 (2001) of the acquisition cost as an ordinary deduction in the year of acquisition.[14] To qualify for the deduction, the property must actually be placed into service during the year. The immediate expensing election is not applicable to real estate. The election is made on an annual basis, and the taxpayer must select the assets to which the $24,000 write-off applies. The MACRS rules apply to any amount of an asset's cost that is not expensed under Sec. 179.

The amount that may be expensed under Sec. 179 was increased in 1997 as follows:

▼ **TABLE I10-2**
Section 179 Expense Amounts

Tax Year Beginning In	Maximum Sec. 179 Expense
1996	$17,500
1997	18,000
1998	18,500
1999	19,000
2000	20,000
2001	24,000
2002	24,000
2003 and after	25,000

EXAMPLE I10-10 ▶ Tanya acquires and places into service a business machine (tangible personal property qualifying under Sec. 179) for $36,000 in July 2001. The machine has a 7-year MACRS recovery period. Tanya elects to immediately expense $24,000 of the asset's cost under Sec. 179. Tanya's remaining basis for calculating the MACRS depreciation deduction is $12,000 ($36,000 − $24,000). Tanya's 2001 regular depreciation allowance is $1,715 ($12,000 × 0.1429). Tanya's total depreciation deductions for 2001 are $25,715 ($24,000 expensed under Sec. 179 + $1,715 MACRS depreciation). ◀

---

[14] Sec. 179. The amount was increased from $10,000 to $17,500 for property placed in service in tax years beginning after December 31, 1992 and before January 1, 1997.

ADDITIONAL COMMENT

Married taxpayers who file separate tax returns are each entitled to a maximum $12,000 ($24,000 ÷ 2) limitation under Sec. 179.

SELF-STUDY QUESTION

Are corporations entitled to the election to expense up to $24,000 under Sec. 179?

ANSWER

Yes, but larger corporations will not receive the benefit from it because the ceiling is reduced when the cost of qualified property exceeds $200,000.

The following limitations and special rules apply to the Sec. 179 election:

- The property must be purchased for use in an active trade or business as distinguished from property that is acquired for the production of income (e.g., personal property used in a rental activity held by an investor does not qualify).
- The property cannot be acquired from a related party under Sec. 267 or by gift or inheritance.
- The Sec. 179 tax benefits are recaptured if the property is no longer predominantly used in a trade or business (e.g., the property is converted to personal use) at any time.[15] In the year of recapture, the taxpayer must include in gross income the amount previously expensed reduced by the amount of depreciation that would have been allowed for the period the property was held for business use.[16]
- If the total cost of qualified property placed into service during the year is more than $200,000, the $24,000 ceiling is reduced on a dollar-for-dollar basis by the excess amount. Thus, no deduction is permitted for the 2001 tax year in which $224,000 or more of Sec. 179 property is placed into service.
- A second limitation on the total Sec. 179 deduction is that it cannot exceed the taxpayer's taxable income (before deducting the Sec. 179 expense) from the trade or business.[17] Any acquisition cost that is unable to be deducted because of the limitation based on taxable income is carried forward for an unlimited number of years and is added to the other amounts eligible for the Sec. 179 deduction in the future year. The carryover amount is subject to the taxable income limitation in the carryover year.

EXAMPLE I10-11 ▶ Pam owns an unincorporated manufacturing business. In 2001, she purchases and places in service $213,000 of qualifying equipment for use in her business. Pam's taxable income from the business (before deducting any Sec. 179 amount) is $4,000. The $24,000 ceiling amount is initially reduced by $13,000 ($213,000 − $200,000) to reflect the fact that the qualified property placed in service during the year exceeded $200,000. The remaining $11,000 Sec. 179 deduction is further reduced by $7,000 ($11,000 − $4,000) to reflect the taxable income limitation. Pam's Sec. 179 deduction is $4,000; $7,000 is available for use as a carryover to 2002. The cost basis of the equipment for MACRS purposes is reduced by $11,000 in 2001 despite the fact that only $4,000 was immediately deductible under Sec. 179. ◀

MACRS RESTRICTIONS

ETHICAL POINT

The personal use of a corporate automobile by a shareholder-employee may be a constructive dividend. Personal use by a non-shareholder-employee results in additional taxable compensation to the employee and may present an ethical dilemma for the tax consultant.

PERSONAL-USE ASSETS. The personal use portion of an asset's cost is not depreciable. For example, if a taxpayer owns a duplex and uses one unit as a personal residence, only the portion of the unit that is rented to tenants qualifies for depreciation.

LISTED PROPERTY RULES. Because Congress was concerned about taxpayers claiming large depreciation deductions (using accelerated methods) on certain types of assets that are conducive to mixed business/personal use, restrictions are placed on assets that are classified as *listed property*. Listed property includes automobiles, computers and peripheral equipment, cellular telephones, and property generally used for purposes of entertainment, recreation, or amusement (for example, a video recorder). If a listed property's business usage is greater than 50% of its total usage, the taxpayer may use the regular MACRS tables for the business-use portion of the asset's cost. However, if the business use is 50% or less, the taxpayer must use the alternative depreciation system (e.g., five-year straight-line cost recovery period for automobiles and computers).

EXAMPLE I10-12 ▶ Patrick acquires an automobile for $10,000 in June 2001. It is used 60% for business. The depreciation deduction on the business-use portion of the automobile's cost is based on the MACRS system and five-year recovery class because the automobile is predominantly used in business

---

[15] Sec. 179(d)(10).
[16] Reg. Sec. 1.179-1(e).
[17] Sec. 179(b)(3). Under Reg. Sec. 1.179-2(c)(5)(iv), employees are considered to be engaged in the active conduct of the trade or business from their employment. Thus, a small business person who is also an employee may include wages and salary derived from employment in determining taxable income for purposes of this limitation. Such amounts are considered derived from the conduct of a trade or business. For an individual, taxable income is also computed without regard to the deduction for one-half of self-employment taxes paid under Sec. 164(f) (see Chapter I14).

(i.e., more than 50%). The MACRS depreciation allowance in 2001 is $1,200 ($10,000 × 0.20 MACRS rate × 0.60 business percentage use). See Table I10-1 for the MACRS rate.

EXAMPLE I10-13 ▶

ADDITIONAL COMMENT

The restrictions on automobiles were enacted in 1984 because of a concern that the tax system was underwriting the acquisition of automobiles whose cost and luxury far exceeded what was required for business needs.

Paula acquires an automobile for $10,000 in 2001. It is used only 40% for business. Paula must use the alternative depreciation system (ADS) to claim depreciation allowances on the business portion of the automobile. The business portion is $4,000 ($10,000 × 0.40). Paula's depreciation allowance in 2001 is $400 [($4,000 ÷ 5 years) × 0.50] the half-year convention. ◀

Additional restrictions apply to employees who acquire listed property (e.g., an automobile, personal computer, and so on) for use in employment-related activities. In addition to the "more than 50% test," the use must be for the convenience of the employer and be required as a condition of employment.[18] This rule is strictly interpreted by the IRS.

EXAMPLE I10-14 ▶

ADDITIONAL COMMENT

An automobile for purposes of the listed property restrictions is defined as any 4-wheeled vehicle manufactured primarily for use on public streets and rated at 6,000 pounds or less unloaded gross vehicle weight. At one time the Jeep Wagoneer was advertised as not being subject to the listed property limitation or luxury automobile limitation because its weight was slightly over the weight limit. Ambulances, hearses, and taxis are excluded.

Raul, a college professor, acquired a personal computer for use at home. He used the computer 60% of the time on teaching- and research-related activities associated with his job. The remaining usage was for personal activities. Raul's employer finds that it is helpful for employees to own a personal computer but does not require them to purchase a computer as a condition of employment. Raul meets the first requirement (i.e., the 60% business usage is greater than the 50% threshold). However, the second requirement for employees (that the use must be for the convenience of the employer and required as a condition of employment) is not met. Thus, no depreciation may be taken because the employment-related use is not deemed to be business use. ◀

RECAPTURE OF EXCESS COST-RECOVERY DEDUCTIONS. For listed property, if the MACRS rules were used and the business-use percentage decreases to 50% or less in a subsequent year, the property is subject to depreciation recapture. The depreciation deductions for all years are recomputed using the alternative depreciation system. The excess depreciation that has been taken is recaptured as ordinary income by including the excess amount in the taxpayer's gross income in the year the business-use percentage first falls to 50% or below.[19] Once the business use falls to 50% or below, the alternative depreciation system must be used for the current year and for all subsequent years, even if the business-use percentage increases to more than 50% in a subsequent year.

EXAMPLE I10-15 ▶

ADDITIONAL COMMENT

The limitations on luxury automobiles mean that the depreciation deductions are limited during the normal five-year recovery period on business automobiles costing more than $15,300 (for 2001).

Peggy, a self-employed attorney, acquires an automobile in 2001 for $10,000. The automobile's business usage is 60% in 2001 but declines to 40% in 2002. In 2001, Peggy is eligible to use the regular MACRS depreciation rates because the business use was greater than 50%. The MACRS deduction in 2001 is $1,200 ($10,000 cost × 0.60 business use × 0.20). The straight-line depreciation method using the five-year life specified for the alternative depreciation system and the half-year convention would have resulted in a deduction of only $600 [($10,000 cost × 0.60 business use ÷ 5 years) × 0.50 year] in 2001. Thus, $600 ($1,200 − $600) of the previously claimed depreciation is recaptured as ordinary income in 2002. Peggy's depreciation deduction for 2002 and subsequent years is limited to the straight-line method and a five-year recovery period. Her depreciation deduction for 2002 is $800 [($10,000 cost × 0.40 business use) ÷ 5 years]. ◀

LIMITATIONS ON LUXURY AUTOMOBILES. Additional MACRS depreciation deduction restrictions are placed on the purchase of so-called luxury automobiles.[20] The limitations apply even if such automobiles are used 100% of the time for business. The MACRS depreciation for automobiles placed into service in 2001 is subject to a $3,060 ceiling limitation for the first year, $4,900 for the second year, $2,950 for the third year, and $1,775 for each succeeding year in the recovery period.[21] In the years following the

---

[18] Sec. 280F(d)(3). Any other property used for transportation (e.g., a pickup truck) qualifies as listed property if the nature of the property lends itself to personal use. See Sec. 280F(b)(4).
[19] Sec. 280F(b)(3).
[20] Sec. 280F. The term "luxury automobile" may be an overstatement as the limitations apply to automobiles acquired in 2000 which cost in excess of $15,300.

[21] Sec. 280F(a)(2). The ceiling imitation for the first year includes any amounts that are immediately written off under Sec. 179. The Sec. 280F limitations restrict the deductibility of lease payments for automobiles in the same way that depreciation is restricted.

end of the depreciation period (e.g., in year six and subsequent years), additional depreciation up to $1,775 per year is allowed in taxable years commencing after the end of the recovery period until the business use portion of the automobile is fully depreciated. Luxury automobile limitations for the past several years are contained in Table 6 of Appendix C. These amounts are adjusted for inflation each year. These ceilings are reduced by the percentage of personal use and also apply to amounts that are expensed under Sec. 179. The effect of these ceilings is to extend the basic MACRS depreciation period from six to seven years or longer depending on the automobile's acquisition cost.

EXAMPLE I10-16 ▶

TYPICAL MISCONCEPTION

It is sometimes mistakenly believed that the $24,000 expensing allowance can be used to boost the first-year write-off on luxury automobiles.

ADDITIONAL COMMENT

The amount that can be deducted for leased automobiles is also limited.

Phil acquires an automobile for $20,000 in 2001. The automobile is used 80% for business and 20% for personal activities during the year. Table I10-3 lists the depreciation amounts for a six-year period, assuming that the 80% business use continues for the life of the automobile and that no amount is expensed under Sec. 179. At the end of the regular six-year depreciation period, the unrecovered cost in the business use portion of the automobile may be recovered in year 2007 and succeeding years at an annual rate not to exceed $1,420 ($1,775 × 0.80). ◀

▼ **TABLE I10-3**
Depreciation Amounts for Example I10-16

	MACRS Deduction Before Limitation	Ceiling Limit	Deduction Allowed
2001			
Regular calculation ($20,000 × 0.80 × 0.20)	$3,200		
Ceiling limit ($3,060 × 0.80)		$2,448	$2,448
2002			
Regular calculation ($20,000 × 0.80 × 0.32)	5,120		
Ceiling limit ($4,900 × 0.80)		3,920	3,920
2003			
Regular calculation ($20,000 × 0.80 × 0.192)	3,072		
Ceiling limit ($2,950 × 0.80)		2,360	2,360
2004			
Regular calculation ($20,000 × 0.80 × 0.1152)	1,843		
Ceiling limit ($1,775 × 0.80)		1,420	1,420
2005			
Regular calculation ($20,000 × 0.80 × 0.1152)	1,843		
Ceiling limit ($1,775 × 0.80)		1,420	1,420
2006			
Regular calculation ($20,000 × 0.80 × 0.0576)	922		
Ceiling limit ($1,775 × 0.80)		1,420	922
2007 and later years until fully depreciated			
Ceiling limit ($1,775 × 0.80)		1,420	1,420

ADDITIONAL COMPUTATIONS FOR LEASED LUXURY AUTOMOBILES. If a taxpayer leases an automobile for business purposes, the deduction for rental payments is reduced to reflect the limitations on depreciation deductions that are imposed on owners of automobiles under Sec. 280F. If these restrictions were not applied to leased automobiles, the limitations could be avoided by leasing instead of purchasing an automobile. The leasing restriction is accomplished by requiring taxpayers to include in their gross income an "inclusion amount" obtained from an IRS table.[22] This amount is based on the automobile's FMV and the tax year in which the lease commences, and is prorated for the percentage of business use and number of days used during the year. A partial lease inclusion table is provided in Table 17 in Appendix C.

EXAMPLE I10-17 ▶ On April 1, 2000 Jim leases and places into service an automobile with a FMV of $40,000. Business use is 60%. The "inclusion amount" for the initial year of the lease (2000) from the IRS lease inclusion table is $202 (see table in Appendix C). This amount is prorated for the number of days the automobile is leased ($275/365$) and is then multiplied by the percentage of business use (60%). Jim is entitled to deduct 60% of the lease payments but must include $91 [($202 × $275/365$) × 60%] in his gross income for the current year. In 2001, the second year of the lease, the inclusion amount is $443. Thus, Jim must include $266 ($443 × 60%) in his gross income for the second year. Subsequent years follow the same procedures. ◀

Special elections and restrictions are summarized in Topic Review I10-2.

AMORTIZATION

OBJECTIVE 2

Calculate amortization for intangible assets and understand the difference between amortizable and non-amortizable assets

An amortization deduction is allowed for a variety of intangible assets. While the amortization period varies greatly depending on the type of asset, a characteristic of all intangible assets is that they are amortized on a *straight-line basis*. The major intangible assets that may be amortized are as follows:

▶ Goodwill and Other Purchased Intangibles, Sec. 197
▶ Research and Experimental Expenditures, Sec. 174
▶ Start-up Expenditures, Sec. 195
▶ Organizational Expenditures, Sec. 248
▶ Pollution Control Facilities, Sec. 169

Several of the above intangibles are discussed below.

SEC. 197 INTANGIBLES

ADDITIONAL COMMENT
The only way goodwill will appear on a balance sheet is if the business was purchased.

Sec. 197 was enacted in 1993 to provide greater certainty as to the amortization of many acquired intangible assets and to specifically allow the amortization of *purchased goodwill*. An amortization deduction is permitted for certain acquired Sec. 197 intangible assets. The amortization is deducted on a ratable basis over a 15-year period beginning with the month of acquisition.[23] In general, Sec. 197 applies only to intangible assets that are *acquired* in connection with the conduct of a trade or business or an activity engaged in for the production of income. For example, Sec. 197 does not apply to an intangible asset that is internally created by the taxpayer, such as a patent resulting from the taxpayer's research and development lab. Internally-created patents and copyrights both have definite and limited lives and are therefore amortizable over the defined period.[24] Internally created patents are generally amortized over 17 years; internally created copyrights over 28 years.

---

[22] The latest lease inclusion table at the date of printing of this textbook is contained in Rev. Proc. 2000-18, 2000-9 I.R.B. 722. The luxury depreciation amounts for 2001 are based on changes to the Consumer Price Index.
[23] Sec. 197(a). The amortization rules apply to property acquired after August 13, 1993 unless an election is made to apply Sec. 197 to all property acquired after July 25, 1991. Final regulations under Sec. 197 were adopted on January 25, 2000 in T.D. 8865.
[24] Reg. Sec. 1.167(a)-3.

Topic Review I10-2

Special Elections and Restrictions

SECTION 179 EXPENSING ELECTION

Deduction: $24,000 for 2001 on the purchase of new or used tangible personal business property used in the conduct of a trade or business.
Limitations:
  Asset purchases: The $24,000 limit is reduced by the excess of qualified purchases over $200,000.
  Taxable income limitation: Limited to taxable income before the Sec. 179 deduction.
Basis reduction: The depreciable basis is reduced by the amount of the Sec. 179 deduction.
Recapture: Occurs when the asset is no longer predominantly used in a trade or business.
  The recapture amount equals the excess of the Sec. 179 expense amount minus the amount that would have been claimed as depreciation if no Sec. 179 election were made.

BUSINESS USE RESTRICTION

Listed property: Business use must be more than 50% to use the regular MACRS rules. If business use is less than 50%, the alternative depreciation system's straight-line method must be used.
Recapture: If business use falls below 50%, the taxpayer must recompute depreciation using the alternative depreciation system's straight-line method and recapture the difference between the prior depreciation taken and straight-line depreciation. The straight-line method is continued for the remaining useful life even if business use subsequently exceeds 50%.

LUXURY AUTOMOBILE LIMITATIONS

Sum of depreciation and Sec. 179 expense limits:

	2000 and 2001
1st year	$3,060
2nd year	4,900
3rd year	2,950
4th and later years	1,775

LEASED LUXURY AUTOMOBILE LIMITATIONS

An "inclusion amount" is added to gross income based on the automobile's FMV on the date placed in service to approximate the depreciation restrictions. Special tables that are revised annually are used to calculate the inclusion amount. A partial lease inclusion table is provided in Appendix C.

EXAMPLE I10-18 ▶ On January 1, 2001, Central Corporation receives patent approval on an internally created process improvement. Legal costs associated with the patent are $100,000 and the patent has a legal life of 17 years. The patent does not qualify as a Sec. 197 intangible. The patent has a definite and limited life and is amortizable ratably over its legal life of 17 years beginning with the month of its creation. ◀

ADDITIONAL COMMENT

In the 1993 *Newark Morning Ledger Co. v. U.S.* case the U.S. Supreme Court held that a taxpayer could depreciate intangible assets if the asset could be valued and if it had a limited life. The case was a victory for taxpayers but promised disputes over valuation of intangibles. To eliminate potential battles, Congress in the Revenue Reconciliation Act of 1993 required a 15-year amortization of certain intangible assets such as goodwill, information base, know-how, customer lists, etc.

DEFINITION OF A SEC. 197 INTANGIBLE ASSET. Sec. 197 intangibles (i.e., intangible assets that are subject to 15-year ratable amortization) include the following:

▶ Goodwill and going concern value. Conceptually, goodwill is an intangible asset that is neither separately identified or valued but possesses characteristics that allow a business to earn greater returns than would be possible without such characteristics. The characteristics that make-up goodwill include many items, such as valued employees, superior management team, loyal customer base, strategic location, etc. For income tax purposes, however, goodwill is determined in a much more practical manner. **Goodwill** is defined as the value of a trade or business that is attributable to the expectancy of continued customer patronage, whether due to the name or reputation of the trade or business or to any other factor.[25] Going concern value is the added value that attaches to acquired property because it is an integral part of a going concern.

---

[25] Reg. Sec. 1.197-2(b)(1).

- Intangible assets relating to the workforce, information base, know-how, customers, suppliers, or similar items, (e.g., the portion of the purchase price of an acquired business that is attributable to an existing employment contract for a key employee) may be amortized over a 15-year period. An example of an information base intangible would be a customer list. Know-how related intangibles include patents, copyrights, formulas, and processes.
- Licenses, permits, or other rights granted by a governmental unit or agency (e.g., the capitalized cost of acquiring a radio broadcasting license).
- Covenants not to compete. A covenant not to compete represents an agreement between a buyer and seller of a business that the seller (i.e., the selling corporation and/or its shareholders) will not compete with the buyer for a limited period. The covenant may also be limited to a geographic area.
- Franchises, trademarks, and tradenames. A franchise includes any agreement that gives one of the parties the right to distribute, sell, or provide goods, services, or facilities, within a specified area.

EXAMPLE I10-19

During the current year, Chicago Corporation acquires all of the net assets of Coastal Corporation for $1,000,000. The following intangible assets are included in the purchase agreement:

Assets	Acquisition Cost
Goodwill and going concern value	$100,000
Licenses	55,000
Patents	45,000
Covenant not to compete for five years	100,000

All of the intangible assets above qualify as Sec. 197 intangible assets and are amortizable on a ratable basis over 15 years beginning with the month of the acquisition. This 15-year amortization period applies to the convenant not to compete even though the convenant is only for five years.

STOP & THINK

Question: When one company purchases the assets of another company, the purchasing company may acquire goodwill. Since purchased goodwill is a Sec. 197 intangible asset and may be amortized over 15 years, the determination of the cost of goodwill is important. How is the "cost" of goodwill determined when the purchasing company purchases many assets in the acquisition?

Solution: The IRS requires that taxpayers use the "residual method" as prescribed in Sec. 1060. Under this method, all of the assets except for goodwill are valued. The total value of these assets are then subtracted from the total purchase price and the residual value is the amount of the purchase price that is allocated to goodwill.

ADDITIONAL COMMENT

Sec. 1231 generally allows gains to be treated as long-term capital gains and losses to be deducted as ordinary losses. Sec. 1245 requires gains to be classified as ordinary income to the extent depreciation, amortization or depletion was claimed as an ordinary deduction in prior periods. (See Chapter I13).

CLASSIFICATION AND DISPOSITION OF INTANGIBLE ASSETS. A Sec. 197 intangible asset is treated as depreciable property so that Sec. 1231 treatment is accorded the disposition if the intangible asset is held for more than one year.[26] Gain from the disposition of a Sec. 197 intangible is subject to depreciation recapture under Sec. 1245 (see Chapter I13).[27] A loss on the disposition of a Sec. 197 intangible asset, however, is not deductible if other intangibles acquired in the same asset acquisition of a trade or business are retained. In such case, the bases of the retained Sec. 197 intangibles are increased by the unrecognized loss.[28]

EXAMPLE I10-20

Assume the same facts as in Example I10-19 except that after five years the covenant not to compete expires when its adjusted basis is $66,667 [$100,000 − (0.333 × $100,000)]. The loss is not deductible and the $66,667 disallowed loss is allocated to the retained Sec. 197 assets based on their respective FMVs.

---

[26] Sec. 197(f)(7).
[27] Sec. 1245(a)(2)(C).
[28] Sec. 197(f)(1).

EXAMPLE I10-21 ▶ Assume the same facts as in Example I10-20 except that after one year the patent is sold for $50,000. In the initial year, $3,000 of amortization was deducted. The recognized gain is $8,000 ($50,000 − $42,000) and $3,000 of the gain is recaptured as ordinary income under Sec. 1245. The remaining $5,000 of gain is classified as Sec. 1231 gain. ◀

RESEARCH AND EXPERIMENTAL EXPENDITURES

In general, research and experimental (R&E) expenditures, as defined in Sec. 174, include experimental and laboratory costs incidental to the development of a product.[29] Sec. 174 was enacted to clarify the income tax treatment of research and experimental expenditures. Without statutory guidance, the decision to either capitalize or currently expense such expenditures would be in doubt. The Regulations define items that do and do not qualify as research and experimental expenditures. These items are summarized in Table I10-4. For income tax purposes, the following alternatives are available for R&E expenditures:

- Expense in the year paid or incurred
- Defer and amortize the costs as a ratable deduction over a period of 60 months or more
- Capitalize and write off the costs only when the research project is abandoned or is worthless[30]

A taxpayer must make an election to expense or defer and amortize the costs in the initial year the R&E expenditures are incurred. If no election is made, the costs must be capitalized. The taxpayer must continue to use the same accounting method for the R&E expenditures unless IRS approval to change methods is obtained.

The following points are significant regarding the computation of the deduction for R&E expenditures:

- Most taxpayers elect to expense the R&E expenditures because they prefer the immediate tax benefit.
- The deferral and amortization method is desirable if the taxpayer is currently in a low tax rate situation or expects initial NOLs during a start-up period.
- If the deferral and amortization method is used, the amortization period of 60 or more months commences with the month in which the benefits from the expenditures are first realized.

> **TYPICAL MISCONCEPTION**
>
> It is sometimes mistakenly believed that if a company constructs a new building to be used entirely as a research facility, the entire cost of the building can be expensed. However, the expensing election applies only to the depreciation allowances on the building.

▼ **TABLE I10-4**
Research and Experimental Expenditures

Items That Qualify	Items That Do Not Qualify[a]
▶ Costs incident to the development of an experimental or pilot model, a plant process, a product, a formula, an invention ▶ Costs associated with product improvements ▶ Costs of obtaining a patent, such as attorney fees ▶ Research contracted to others ▶ Depreciation or cost-recovery amounts attributable to capitalized R&E items (e.g., research laboratory and equipment)	▶ Expenditures for ordinary testing or inspection of materials or products for quality control purposes ▶ Efficiency surveys and management studies ▶ Marketing research, advertising, and so on ▶ Cost of acquiring another person's patent, model, production, or process ▶ Research incurred in connection with literary, historical, or similar projects

[a] Certain of these expenses may be deductible as trade or business expenses under Sec. 162, subject to amortization under Sec. 197, or treated as start-up expenditures under Sec. 195.

---

[29] Reg. Sec. 1.174-2(a)(2). The Regulations define the term "product" to include any pilot model, formula, invention, technique, patent, or similar product.

[30] Sec. 174.

- ▶ R&E expenses include depreciation allowances related to capitalized expenditures. Thus, if the deferral and amortization method is used, depreciation allowances are deferred as part of the R&E expenditures that are amortized over a period of at least 60 months. Capital expenditures made in connection with R&E activities cannot be expensed when they are incurred merely because an election to expense R&E costs are made.
- ▶ A 20% tax credit applies to certain incremental research expenditures, even if they are immediately expensed under Sec. 174. (See Chapter I14 for a discussion of the research activities credit.)

EXAMPLE I10-22 ▶

In 2001 Control Corporation leases a research laboratory to develop new products and to improve existing products. Control Corporation, a calendar-year taxpayer that uses the accrual method of accounting, incurs the following expenditures during 2001:

Laboratory supplies and materials	$ 40,000
Laboratory equipment	60,000[a]
Utilities and rent	50,000
Salaries	50,000
Total expenditures	$200,000

[a] The MACRS recovery period is 5 years at a 20% rate for the initial year.

REAL-WORLD EXAMPLE

An airline company made payments to an aircraft manufacturer to help defray the cost of designing, developing, producing, and testing a supersonic transport prototype aircraft. These payments were considered R&E expenditures. Rev. Rul. 69-484, 1969-2 C.B. 38.

Assume the benefits from the R&E expenditures are first realized in January, 2002. If Control Corporation elects to expense the R&E expenditures, the deduction in 2001 is $152,000 ($40,000 laboratory supplies and materials + $12,000 depreciation on the equipment + $50,000 utilities and rent + $50,000 salaries). If the deferral and amortization method is elected, none of the expenditures above are deductible in 2001 because the benefits of the R&E activities are not first realized until January, 2002. If the 60-month minimum amortization period is elected, the monthly amortization commencing in January, 2002 is $2,533 ($152,000 ÷ 60 months). The $48,000 ($60,000 − $12,000) of laboratory equipment cost is depreciated over the remaining MACRS recovery period beginning in 2002. ◀

DEPLETION, INTANGIBLE DRILLING AND DEVELOPMENT COSTS

OBJECTIVE 3

Apply cost and percentage depletion methods and understand the treatment for intangible drilling costs

The exploration, development, and operation of oil and gas properties require an outlay of various types of expenditures. These expenditures must be properly classified to determine the correct income tax treatment of such expenditures. Below are the four major types of expenditures of an oil and gas property and their income tax treatment.

- ▶ Payments for the mineral interest. These costs are capitalized and recovered through depletion.
- ▶ Intangible drilling and development costs (e.g., labor and other operating costs to clear land, erect a derrick, and drill the well). Taxpayers elect to either capitalize or immediately write off these expenditures.
- ▶ Tangible asset costs (e.g., machinery, pipe). These expenditures must be capitalized and depreciated under the MACRS rules.
- ▶ Operating costs after the well is producing. These expenditures are deductible under Sec. 162 as ordinary and necessary business expenses.

KEY POINT

A depletion deduction is available in the case of mines, oil and gas wells, other natural resources, and timber. However, the percentage depletion method is not available in the case of timber.

DEPLETION METHODS

Depletion is similar to depreciation but refers to natural resources, such as oil and gas, timber, and coal. Depletion is the using up of natural resources by the process of mining (coal, for example) or drilling (oil and gas) and is calculated under the **cost depletion method** or the **percentage depletion method** for each period. The method that is used in any year is the one that results in the largest deduction. Thus, percentage depletion may be used in one year and cost depletion may be used in the following year.

Depletion is allowed to the taxpayer who has an **economic interest** in the property. The person who typically has an economic interest in the property is the owner of the natural resource (i.e., the oil, gas, coal, etc.). Thus, depletion may be claimed by the persons who either own the natural resource property or retain a royalty interest. A mining company that only mines coal from a property and does not own (or lease) the underlying coal is not considered to hold an economic interest and, therefore, is not allowed a depletion deduction. The landowner who owns the coal would be entitled to the depletion deduction.

ADDITONAL COMMENT

Note that a taxpayer must use the greater of cost depletion or percentage depletion. If percentage depletion is used, the adjusted basis of the property is reduced by the percentage depletion amount.

COST DEPLETION METHOD. The cost depletion method is similar to the units-of-production method of depreciation. The adjusted basis of the asset is divided by the estimated recoverable units to arrive at a per-unit depletion cost. This per-unit cost is then multiplied by the number of units sold to determine the cost depletion deduction.[31] If percentage depletion is used in any one year because it is greater than the cost depletion amount, the property's adjusted basis for purposes of determining cost depletion in the following year and the gain or loss on disposition of the property is reduced by the amount of percentage depletion claimed. If the original estimate of recoverable units is subsequently determined to be incorrect, the per-unit cost depletion rate must be revised and used on a prospective basis to determine cost depletion in future years.[32] It is not proper to file an amended return for the years in which the incorrect estimated unit cost was used.

EXAMPLE I10-23

Ralph acquires an oil and gas property interest for $100,000 in 2001. The estimate of recoverable units is 10,000 barrels of oil. The per-unit cost depletion amount is $10 ($100,000 ÷ 10,000). If 3,000 units are produced and 2,000 units are sold in 2001, the cost depletion amount is $20,000 (2,000 units × $10 per unit). If cost depletion is used because it exceeds the percentage depletion amount, the cost basis of the property is reduced to $80,000 ($100,000 − $20,000) at the beginning of 2002. If the estimate of remaining recoverable units is revised downward from 8,000 units in 2002 (10,000 − 2,000 units sold in 2001) to 5,000 units (including the 1,000 barrels produced but not sold in 2001), the property's $80,000 adjusted basis is divided by 5,000 units to arrive at a new per-unit cost depletion amount of $16 for 2002. This process is continued each year until the cost of the oil and gas property interest is fully depleted.

REAL-WORLD EXAMPLE

Taxpayers are entitled to a depletion deduction if they have an economic interest in the property. This economic interest may be in the form of a royalty interest where a landowner receives a certain amount per unit extracted from her land, such as $10 for each barrel of oil. The landowner would be entitled to a depletion deduction based on the royalty income received.

PERCENTAGE DEPLETION METHOD. Percentage depletion generally offers substantial tax benefits for taxpayers in the natural resources industry. The purpose of allowing percentage depletion is to encourage persons to invest and/or operate in an industry that is both capital intensive and high risk but is also vital to our national interests. Percentage depletion may be used by taxpayers for a wide variety of natural resources, such as oil and gas, coal, gold, etc. However, the percentage depletion method has not been available to *large* oil and gas producers since 1974, but is still available to *small* oil and gas producers and royalty owners under a specific exemption in the law.[33] Percentage depletion is computed by multiplying the percentage depletion rate times the gross income from the property. However, the depletion amount may not exceed 50% of the taxable income from the property before depletion is deducted (100% for oil and gas properties).[34] Percentage depletion may not be calculated on any lease bonus, advance royalty, or other amount payable without regard to production from the property.

When using either cost depletion or percentage depletion, the amount of the depletion deduction reduces the basis of the natural resource property. Once the basis of depletable property has been reduced to zero, a taxpayer may no longer claim depreciation using the cost depletion method. However, the taxpayer may continue to claim percentage depletion, even though subsequent percentage depletion will not reduce the basis of the property below zero. It should be apparent that percentage depletion is a very advantageous method because the amount of depletion that is allowed over the life of the property may exceed the property's cost.[35]

---

[31] Sec. 612.
[32] Sec. 611(a).
[33] Sec. 613A(c). To be classified as a small oil and gas producer or royalty owner, the maximum depletable quantity is based on average daily production of not more than 1,000 barrels of oil or 6 million cubic feet of natural gas.
[34] Sec. 613(a).
[35] Depletion in excess of the adjusted basis of the property is a tax preference item under Sec. 57(a)(1).

Percentage depletion rates vary by the type of mineral. Depletion rates for selected minerals are as follows:

Mineral	Depletion Rate
Oil and gas	15%[36]
Coal, asbestos	10%
Gold, silver, copper, iron ore	15%
Sulphur and uranium	22%
Gravel, stone	5%

EXAMPLE I10-24 ▶ Carmen acquires an oil and gas property interest for $400,000 in the current year with 200,000 barrels of estimated recoverable oil. During the year, 10,000 barrels of oil are sold for $250,000. Intangible drilling and development costs amount to $100,000 and are expensed in the current year. Other expenses are $50,000. Cost depletion is $20,000 (10,000 × $2) in the current year. The computation of percentage depletion is as follows:

(1) Percentage depletion before taxable income limitation	
$250,000 × 0.15	$ 37,500
(2) Taxable income ceiling:	
Gross income	$250,000
Minus: Intangible drilling costs	(100,000)
Other expenses	(50,000)
Taxable income before depletion	$100,000
(3) Percentage depletion (lesser of (1) or (2))	$37,500

Carmen's depletion deduction is $37,500 because the percentage depletion amount is greater than the $20,000 of cost depletion. The adjusted basis of the property is reduced by $37,500, the amount of depletion actually claimed. ◀

HISTORICAL NOTE

An Arab oil embargo to the United States in 1973 created a situation where oil prices increased significantly. Consequently, most domestic U.S. oil producers reported huge profits. This situation contributed to the repeal of the percentage depletion allowance for large oil and gas producers.

KEY POINT

The use of the percentage depletion method permits recovery of more than the cost of the property.

TREATMENT OF INTANGIBLE DRILLING AND DEVELOPMENT COSTS

Intangible drilling and development costs (IDCs) may either be deducted as an expense or capitalized.[37] IDCs apply only to oil, gas, and geothermal wells and basically include all expenditures, other than the acquisition costs of the underlying property, that are incurred for the drilling and preparation of wells. If the IDCs are capitalized, the amounts are added to the property's basis for determining cost depletion, and the costs are written off through cost depletion. For a well that is nonproductive (i.e., a dry hole), an ordinary loss is allowed for any IDC costs that have been capitalized and not recovered through depletion. The amount of depletion claimed in a tax year equals the greater of the percentage depletion and cost depletion amounts. If IDCs are capitalized and cost depletion is thereby increased, little or no tax benefit may result because the percentage depletion may still produce a greater deduction than cost depletion. Therefore, it is generally preferable to expense the IDCs if the percentage depletion is expected to be more than the cost depletion and is used to compute the depletion allowance.

EXAMPLE I10-25 ▶ Penny acquires certain rights to oil and gas property in the current year for $1,000,000. In the current year Penny incurs $300,000 of IDCs. If the IDCs are capitalized, the basis for cost depletion purposes is $1,300,000. Assume that the cost depletion amounts are $100,000 in the current year if the IDCs are expensed and $130,000 if IDCs are capitalized. If the percentage depletion amount is $150,000, percentage depletion will be used because it is greater than either of the cost depletion amounts. Thus, the expensing of the IDCs permits the taxpayer to deduct the entire $300,000 of IDCs in the current year plus $150,000 of percentage depletion. ◀

---

[36] For small producers and royalty owners of oil and gas properties, there is a further limitation: the percentage depletion deduction may not exceed 65% of taxable income from all sources before the depletion deduction, Sec. 631A(d)(1).

[37] Sec. 263(c).

TAX PLANNING CONSIDERATIONS

ADDITIONAL COMMENT

A taxpayer who is attempting to report a profit in three out of five years in an attempt to avoid the hobby loss rules might want to use the alternative depreciation system.

ALTERNATIVE DEPRECIATION SYSTEM UNDER MACRS

In some instances, it may be preferable to elect to use the alternative depreciation system rather than the regular MACRS rules. For example, a taxpayer who anticipates losses during the next few years or who currently has NOL carryovers may elect to use the alternative depreciation system, which employs the straight-line method of depreciation over a longer recovery period.

EXAMPLE I10-26 ▶ Delta Corporation has substantial NOL carryovers that will expire if not used during the next few years. Delta Corporation anticipates it will not have taxable income for each of the next seven years if the regular MACRS rules are used to depreciate its fixed asset additions. In the current year, Delta Corporation acquires new machinery and equipment at a cost of $100,000. Depreciation deductions using the MACRS rules and a seven-year recovery period are $14,290 (0.1429 × $100,000). Depreciation deductions under the straight-line method using the alternative depreciation system (a 12-year life) and the half-year convention are only $4,167 [($100,000 ÷ 12 years) × 0.50 year]. The alternative depreciation system election increases taxable income in the current year by $10,123 and allows Delta Corporation to offset additional loss carryovers (which might otherwise expire) against this income amount. ◀

KEY POINT

In general, the option to capitalize or to expense applies only to drilling or development expenditures having no salvage value. For example, the cost of oil well pumps, oil storage tanks, and pipe lines would not be eligible for immediate expensing.

IDCs: CAPITALIZATION VERSUS EXPENSING ELECTION

Although most taxpayers elect to expense intangible drilling costs (IDCs), sometimes capitalization and amortization are preferable because of the effect of IDCs on the depletion deduction.

If IDCs are expensed, taxable income from the property is reduced. This may result in a smaller percentage depletion deduction because the percentage depletion claimed is limited to 100% of pre-depletion taxable income.

EXAMPLE I10-27 ▶ Gross income from an oil and gas property is $500,000. Expenses of $450,000 are incurred including $200,000 of IDCs. The percentage depletion deduction (before the 100% limitation) is $75,000 (0.15 × $500,000). The percentage depletion limitation is $50,000 (1.00 × $50,000

WHAT WOULD YOU DO IN THIS SITUATION?

Your CPA firm has a long-standing tax client named Widgets R Us, Incorporated (WRU). WRU has been a worldwide leader in widget technology for years and continues to expand its global market share of Class A Crystal Widgets through a substantial program of basic research and development of widget crystallization processes. You have always advised WRU as to which of these expenditures qualify as research and experimental (R&E) expenditures. In addition, you have always given timely advice as to when to expense rather than capitalize these expenditures.

You are having your monthly tax conference with Ms. Ima Worthmore, president of WRU, and Mr. Stan Cunning, tax counsel of WMU, and Ms. Worthmore relates to you a conversation she had with the local manager of a competitor CPA firm, Ms. Ruth Less. Ms Less told Ms. Worthmore that she had discovered that WRU was one of the top spenders on research and development in the area and that her firm was "certified" to practice before the IRS and had experienced great success in gaining better R&E write-offs for comparable firms. Ms. Less went on to say that, "For you, for this one year only, we offer to prepare your tax returns on a contingent basis. We promise to save you at least $1 million dollars from what you are now paying the IRS through our better use of R&E write-offs and our fee will only be 30% of the tax savings!"

Ms. Worthmore was excited that WRU might pay such a considerably less amount of taxes under the plan of Ruth Less and is somewhat perturbed at you because you had not brought this tax opportunity to her attention. She wants your firm to provide her with a counteroffer. How do you ethically respond to your client's request to match or better Ms. Ruth Less' proposal?

net income before depletion). Thus, the percentage depletion that is allowed is limited to the lesser of the percentage depletion earned ($75,000) or the limitation ($50,000), or $50,000. If the IDCs are capitalized, the percentage depletion deduction limitation is $250,000 (1.00 × $250,000 net income before depletion) and the taxpayer could claim the full $75,000 of percentage depletion earned. ◀

If the IDCs are capitalized, the property's basis for cost depletion purposes is increased and the IDCs are amortized as part of the cost depletion. However, if cost depletion is less than percentage depletion, the benefits from IDC amortization may be lost because percentage depletion is used.

EXAMPLE I10-28 ▶ Assume the same facts as in Example I10-27, except that the IDCs are capitalized and assume that cost depletion is increased from $20,000 to $45,000 due to the capitalization of the IDCs. Because percentage depletion is $75,000 and cost depletion is only $45,000, percentage depletion is used and the benefits from capitalizing IDCs (i.e., $25,000 increase in cost depletion) are lost. The election to capitalize the IDCs did result in an increase in the amount of percentage depletion from $50,000 to $75,000. ◀

USE OF UNITS OF PRODUCTION DEPRECIATION

Many times, the MACRS depreciation system requires taxpayers to use a recovery period that is much longer than the actual useful life of the asset. For example, assume a taxpayer uses a machine in her business that is required to be classified as 7-year property under MACRS. However, the machine is operated 24 hours a day, seven days a week and will completely wear out in two years. The use of the 7-year recovery period substantially understates the depreciation for the machine. Under Sec. 168(f), taxpayers may exclude property from the MACRS system if the property is depreciated under the unit-of-production method or any other method not expressed in terms of years. Therefore, if a taxpayer can express the useful life of the machine in terms of some other base than years (such as machine hours, units produced, etc.), it may be possible for the taxpayer to depreciate the machine over a much shorter period than the seven years required under MACRS.

STRUCTURING A BUSINESS COMBINATION

REAL-WORLD EXAMPLE

A taxpayer purchased a business that owned retail franchises. It was the opinion of the IRS that the amounts paid in excess of the value of the net assets represented a nondepreciable "indivisible asset." However, the taxpayer was able to show that retail franchises have limited useful lives, and was able to amortize the excess costs. *Super Food Services, Inc. v. U.S.*, 24 AFTR 2d 69-5309, 69-2 USTC ¶ 9558 (7th Cir., 1969).

Tax planning needs to be conducted to ensure favorable tax consequences for the acquiring company if the assets of the acquired company are purchased as part of a business combination. The sales agreement must specify the amounts that have been paid for the tangible depreciable and nondepreciable assets and the intangible assets and the reporting requirements of Sec. 1060 must be complied with. Under the requirements of Sec. 1060, both the transferor and the transferee are bound by their written agreement as to the allocation of the purchase price to individual assets unless the IRS determines that such allocation is not appropriate. The amounts paid for the tangible assets should be documented by appraisals and evidence of negotiations between the buyer and seller. Within reason, the purchaser should attempt to allocate as much of the total price to the tangible depreciable assets. The purchaser should also consider allocating part of the purchase price to amortizable Sec. 197 intangible assets such as goodwill, a covenant not to compete, patents, copyrights, licenses, and customer lists because such asset costs are recovered over a 15-year period.

COMPLIANCE AND PROCEDURAL CONSIDERATIONS

IDC ELECTION PROCEDURES

The IDC election is made in the initial year that the expenditures are incurred. No formal statement or form is required. The expensing election is made by merely deducting the IDCs on the tax return.[38] If the costs are capitalized, cost depletion merely reflects the capitalized IDC costs.

---
[38] Reg. Sec. 1.612-4(d).

REPORTING COST RECOVERY, DEPRECIATION, DEPLETION, AND AMORTIZATION DEDUCTIONS

If an individual is engaged in a trade or business as a sole proprietor, depreciation, cost recovery, depletion, and amortization deductions are initially computed and reported on Form 4562 (Depreciation and Amortization) and the totals are then carried to Schedule C. Depletion and depreciation on rental properties are reported on Schedule E instead of Schedule C if the taxpayer is an investor. Depreciation on employee business property is reported on Form 2106. Separate Form 4562s are required for each different activity.

The election to expense property under Sec. 179 is made by claiming the deduction on Part I of Form 4562. The taxpayer must specify the items of property and the portion of the cost for each asset being expensed. Form 4562 is not required of individuals and non-corporate taxpayers (including S corporations) when filing their 2000 tax returns if the depreciation deduction is for assets, other than listed property, placed in service before 2000. In such cases, the depreciation deduction is entered directly on Form 1040 or other equivalent tax forms. However, even though a Form 4562 may not be required to be filed with the return, detailed depreciation records must still be maintained by the taxpayers to support the deduction.

EXAMPLE I10-29 ▶ George Jones, SSN 277-32-6542, is a building trade contractor who owns the following properties:

- Specialized utility repair truck (5-year property that is not listed property under Sec. 280F(d)(4)), costing $20,000, acquired on February 15, 2000.
- Office equipment (7-year property), costing $23,000, acquired on May 10, 2000. The election to expense under Sec. 179 is made for $20,000.
- Patent, costing $10,000, that was acquired on June 1, 2000 when it had a remaining legal life of 17 years.
- ACRS deduction for assets placed into service before 1987 is $2,000.
- MACRS deduction for assets placed into service before 2000 is $8,000.

Jones has taxable income (before the Sec. 179 deduction and the deduction for one-half of self-employment taxes paid under Sec. 164(f)) of $60,000. The cost-recovery, depreciation, and amortization amounts are reported on Form 4562 and Schedule C, respectively, and are shown in Figures I10-1 and I10-2. ◀

RESEARCH AND EXPERIMENTAL EXPENDITURES

The election to expense or to defer R&E expenditures is made by attaching a statement to the tax return for the first tax year in which the expenditures are incurred.[39] As previously discussed in the text, the capitalization method is not an election and applies only if no election is made in the initial year. Once a method has been adopted, the taxpayer is required to obtain the permission of the IRS to change to another method.

ADDITIONAL COMMENT
Once the election to expense R&E expenditures has been made, it is applicable to all R&E expenditures paid or incurred in the current year and all subsequent years.

PROBLEM MATERIALS

DISCUSSION QUESTIONS

I10-1 Which of the following assets are subject to either amortization, depreciation, or cost recovery?
  a. An automobile held for personal use.
  b. Excess amounts paid in a business combination that are attributable to goodwill.
  c. Excess amounts paid in a business combination that are attributable to customer lists that have a limited useful life.
  d. A patent that has been created internally and has a legal life of 17 years.
  e. Land that is being held for investment purposes.
  f. A covenant not to compete which is entered into by the buyer and seller of a business.

I10-2 Rick is a sole proprietor who has a small business that is currently operating at a loss. He would like to discontinue depreciating the fixed assets of the

---
[39] Reg. Sec. 1.174-3(b)(1).

Form **4562** Department of the Treasury Internal Revenue Service (99)	**Depreciation and Amortization** (Including Information on Listed Property) ▶ See separate instructions. ▶ Attach this form to your return.	OMB No. 1545-0172 **2000** Attachment Sequence No. **67**
Name(s) shown on return George Jones	Business or activity to which this form relates Building Trade Contractor	Identifying number 277-32-6542

Part I — Election To Expense Certain Tangible Property (Section 179)
Note: *If you have any "listed property," complete Part V before you complete Part I.*

1	Maximum dollar limitation. If an enterprise zone business, see page 2 of the instructions	1	$20,000
2	Total cost of section 179 property placed in service. See page 2 of the instructions	2	43,000
3	Threshold cost of section 179 property before reduction in limitation	3	$200,000
4	Reduction in limitation. Subtract line 3 from line 2. If zero or less, enter -0-	4	-0-
5	Dollar limitation for tax year. Subtract line 4 from line 1. If zero or less, enter -0-. If married filing separately, see page 2 of the instructions	5	20,000

(a) Description of property	(b) Cost (business use only)	(c) Elected cost
6 Office Equipment	23,000	20,000
Truck	20,000	-0-

7	Listed property. Enter amount from line 27	7	
8	Total elected cost of section 179 property. Add amounts in column (c), lines 6 and 7	8	20,000
9	Tentative deduction. Enter the smaller of line 5 or line 8	9	20,000
10	Carryover of disallowed deduction from 1999. See page 3 of the instructions	10	
11	Business income limitation. Enter the smaller of business income (not less than zero) or line 5 (see instructions)	11	20,000
12	Section 179 expense deduction. Add lines 9 and 10, but do not enter more than line 11	12	20,000
13	Carryover of disallowed deduction to 2001. Add lines 9 and 10, less line 12 ▶	13	

Note: *Do not use Part II or Part III below for listed property (automobiles, certain other vehicles, cellular telephones, certain computers, or property used for entertainment, recreation, or amusement). Instead, use Part V for listed property.*

Part II — MACRS Depreciation for Assets Placed in Service Only During Your 2000 Tax Year (Do not include listed property.)

Section A — General Asset Account Election

14 If you are making the election under section 168(i)(4) to group any assets placed in service during the tax year into one or more general asset accounts, check this box. See page 3 of the instructions ▶ ☐

Section B — General Depreciation System (GDS) (See page 3 of the instructions.)

(a) Classification of property	(b) Month and year placed in service	(c) Basis for depreciation (business/investment use only—see instructions)	(d) Recovery period	(e) Convention	(f) Method	(g) Depreciation deduction
15a 3-year property						
b 5-year property		20,000	5 yr.	HY	MACRS	4,000
c 7-year property		3,000	7 yr.	HY	MACRS	429
d 10-year property						
e 15-year property						
f 20-year property						
g 25-year property			25 yrs.		S/L	
h Residential rental property			27.5 yrs. 27.5 yrs.	MM	S/L	
i Nonresidential real property			39 yrs. 	MM MM	S/L S/L	

Section C — Alternative Depreciation System (ADS) (See page 5 of the instructions.)

16a Class life					S/L	
b 12-year			12 yrs.		S/L	
c 40-year			40 yrs.	MM	S/L	

Part III — Other Depreciation (Do not include listed property.) (See page 5 of the instructions.)

17	GDS and ADS deductions for assets placed in service in tax years beginning before 2000	17	8,000
18	Property subject to section 168(f)(1) election	18	
19	ACRS and other depreciation	19	2,000

Part IV — Summary (See page 6 of the instructions.)

20	Listed property. Enter amount from line 26	20	
21	**Total.** Add deductions from line 12, lines 15 and 16 in column (g), and lines 17 through 20. Enter here and on the appropriate lines of your return. Partnerships and S corporations—see instructions	21	34,429
22	For assets shown above and placed in service during the current year, enter the portion of the basis attributable to section 263A costs	22	

For Paperwork Reduction Act Notice, see page 9 of the instructions.   Cat. No. 12906N   Form **4562** (2000)

FIGURE I10-1 ▶ FORM 4562

Form 4562 (2000)   Page **2**

Part V   **Listed Property** (Include automobiles, certain other vehicles, cellular telephones, certain computers, and property used for entertainment, recreation, or amusement.)

Note: *For any vehicle for which you are using the standard mileage rate or deducting lease expense, complete **only** 23a, 23b, columns (a) through (c) of Section A, all of Section B, and Section C if applicable.*

Section A—Depreciation and Other Information (Caution: *See page 7 of the instructions for limits for passenger automobiles.*)

23a   Do you have evidence to support the business/investment use claimed? ☐ Yes ☐ No   23b If "Yes," is the evidence written? ☐ Yes ☐ No

(a) Type of property (list vehicles first)	(b) Date placed in service	(c) Business/ investment use percentage	(d) Cost or other basis	(e) Basis for depreciation (business/investment use only)	(f) Recovery period	(g) Method/ Convention	(h) Depreciation deduction	(i) Elected section 179 cost
24 Property used more than 50% in a qualified business use (See page 6 of the instructions.):								
		%						
		%						
		%						
25 Property used 50% or less in a qualified business use (See page 6 of the instructions.):								
		%				S/L –		
		%				S/L –		
		%				S/L –		

26   Add amounts in column (h). Enter the total here and on line 20, page 1   **26**

27   Add amounts in column (i). Enter the total here and on line 7, page 1   **27**

Section B—Information on Use of Vehicles

Complete this section for vehicles used by a sole proprietor, partner, or other "more than 5% owner," or related person.
If you provided vehicles to your employees, first answer the questions in Section C to see if you meet an exception to completing this section for those vehicles.

	(a) Vehicle 1	(b) Vehicle 2	(c) Vehicle 3	(d) Vehicle 4	(e) Vehicle 5	(f) Vehicle 6
28 Total business/investment miles driven during the year (**do not** include commuting miles— see page 1 of the instructions)						
29 Total commuting miles driven during the year						
30 Total other personal (noncommuting) miles driven						
31 Total miles driven during the year. Add lines 28 through 30						
	Yes No	Yes No	Yes No	Yes No	Yes No	Yes No
32 Was the vehicle available for personal use during off-duty hours?						
33 Was the vehicle used primarily by a more than 5% owner or related person?						
34 Is another vehicle available for personal use?						

Section C—Questions for Employers Who Provide Vehicles for Use by Their Employees

Answer these questions to determine if you meet an exception to completing Section B for vehicles used by employees who **are not** more than 5% owners or related persons. See page 8 of the instructions.

	Yes	No
35 Do you maintain a written policy statement that prohibits all personal use of vehicles, including commuting, by your employees?		
36 Do you maintain a written policy statement that prohibits personal use of vehicles, except commuting, by your employees? See page 8 of the instructions for vehicles used by corporate officers, directors, or 1% or more owners		
37 Do you treat all use of vehicles by employees as personal use?		
38 Do you provide more than five vehicles to your employees, obtain information from your employees about the use of the vehicles, and retain the information received?		
39 Do you meet the requirements concerning qualified automobile demonstration use? See page 8 of the instructions		

Note: *If your answer to 35, 36, 37, 38, or 39 is "Yes," do not complete Section B for the covered vehicles.*

Part VI   **Amortization**

(a) Description of costs	(b) Date amortization begins	(c) Amortizable amount	(d) Code section	(e) Amortization period or percentage	(f) Amortization for this year
40 Amortization of costs that begins during your 2000 tax year (See page 8 of the instructions.):					
Patent	6-1-2000	10,000	167	17 yr.	343

41   Amortization of costs that began before 2000   **41**

42   **Total.** Add amounts in column (f). See page 9 of the instructions for where to report   **42**   343

Form **4562** (2000)

FIGURE I10-2   ▶   FORM 4562 (CONTINUED)

SCHEDULE C
(Form 1040)

Department of the Treasury
Internal Revenue Service (99)

Profit or Loss From Business
(Sole Proprietorship)

▶ Partnerships, joint ventures, etc., must file Form 1065 or Form 1065-B.
▶ Attach to Form 1040 or Form 1041.   ▶ See Instructions for Schedule C (Form 1040).

OMB No. 1545-0074

2000

Attachment Sequence No. 09

Name of proprietor: **George Jones**

Social security number (SSN): **277 32 6542**

A Principal business or profession, including product or service (see page C-1 of the instructions)
Building Trade Contractor

B Enter code from pages C-7 & 8 ▶

C Business name. If no separate business name, leave blank.

D Employer ID number (EIN), if any

E Business address (including suite or room no.) ▶ **1998 Natchamp Blvd.**
City, town or post office, state, and ZIP code **Lexington, KY 40506**

F Accounting method: (1) ☑ Cash   (2) ☐ Accrual   (3) ☐ Other (specify) ▶

G Did you "materially participate" in the operation of this business during 2000? If "No," see page C-2 for limit on losses   ☐ Yes   ☐ No

H If you started or acquired this business during 2000, check here ▶ ☐

Part I Income

1	Gross receipts or sales. Caution. If this income was reported to you on Form W-2 and the "Statutory employee" box on that form was checked, see page C-2 and check here ▶ ☐	1
2	Returns and allowances	2
3	Subtract line 2 from line 1	3
4	Cost of goods sold (from line 42 on page 2)	4
5	**Gross profit.** Subtract line 4 from line 3	5
6	Other income, including Federal and state gasoline or fuel tax credit or refund (see page C-2)	6
7	**Gross income.** Add lines 5 and 6 ▶	7

Part II Expenses. Enter expenses for business use of your home only on line 30.

8	Advertising	8	19	Pension and profit-sharing plans	19
9	Bad debts from sales or services (see page C-3)	9	20	Rent or lease (see page C-4):	
			a	Vehicles, machinery, and equipment	20a
10	Car and truck expenses (see page C-3)	10	b	Other business property	20b
			21	Repairs and maintenance	21
11	Commissions and fees	11	22	Supplies (not included in Part III)	22
12	Depletion	12	23	Taxes and licenses	23
13	Depreciation and section 179 expense deduction (not included in Part III) (see page C-3)	13 **34,429**	24	Travel, meals, and entertainment:	
			a	Travel	24a
			b	Meals and entertainment	
14	Employee benefit programs (other than on line 19)	14	c	Enter nondeductible amount included on line 24b (see page C-5)	
15	Insurance (other than health)	15			
16	Interest:		d	Subtract line 24c from line 24b	24d
a	Mortgage (paid to banks, etc.)	16a	25	Utilities	25
b	Other	16b	26	Wages (less employment credits)	26
17	Legal and professional services	17	27	Other expenses (from line 48 on page 2)	27 **343**
18	Office expense	18			

28	**Total expenses** before expenses for business use of home. Add lines 8 through 27 in columns ▶	28
29	Tentative profit (loss). Subtract line 28 from line 7	29
30	Expenses for business use of your home. Attach **Form 8829**	30
31	**Net profit or (loss).** Subtract line 30 from line 29. • If a profit, enter on **Form 1040, line 12,** and **also** on **Schedule SE, line 2** (statutory employees, see page C-5). Estates and trusts, enter on Form 1041, line 3. • If a loss, you **must** go to line 32.	31
32	If you have a loss, check the box that describes your investment in this activity (see page C-5). • If you checked 32a, enter the loss on **Form 1040, line 12,** and **also** on **Schedule SE, line 2** (statutory employees, see page C-5). Estates and trusts, enter on Form 1041, line 3. • If you checked 32b, you **must** attach **Form 6198.**	32a ☐ All investment is at risk. 32b ☐ Some investment is not at risk.

For Paperwork Reduction Act Notice, see Form 1040 instructions.   Cat. No. 11334P   Schedule C (Form 1040) 2000

FIGURE I10-3   ▶ FORM 1040, SCHEDULE C

Schedule C (Form 1040) 2000 Page **2**

Part III — Cost of Goods Sold (see page C-6)

33 Method(s) used to value closing inventory: **a** ☐ Cost **b** ☐ Lower of cost or market **c** ☐ Other (attach explanation)

34 Was there any change in determining quantities, costs, or valuations between opening and closing inventory? If "Yes," attach explanation ☐ Yes ☐ No

35 Inventory at beginning of year. If different from last year's closing inventory, attach explanation **35**

36 Purchases less cost of items withdrawn for personal use **36**

37 Cost of labor. Do not include any amounts paid to yourself **37**

38 Materials and supplies **38**

39 Other costs **39**

40 Add lines 35 through 39 **40**

41 Inventory at end of year **41**

42 **Cost of goods sold.** Subtract line 41 from line 40. Enter the result here and on page 1, line 4 **42**

Part IV — Information on Your Vehicle.
Complete this part **only** if you are claiming car or truck expenses on line 10 and are not required to file Form 4562 for this business. See the instructions for line 13 on page C-3 to find out if you must file.

43 When did you place your vehicle in service for business purposes? (month, day, year) ▶ ___/___/___

44 Of the total number of miles you drove your vehicle during 2000, enter the number of miles you used your vehicle for:

a Business _____ **b** Commuting _____ **c** Other _____

45 Do you (or your spouse) have another vehicle available for personal use? ☐ Yes ☐ No

46 Was your vehicle available for use during off-duty hours? ☐ Yes ☐ No

47a Do you have evidence to support your deduction? ☐ Yes ☐ No

b If "Yes," is the evidence written? ☐ Yes ☐ No

Part V — Other Expenses. List below business expenses not included on lines 8–26 or line 30.

Patent Amortization 343

48 Total other expenses. Enter here and on page 1, line 27 **48** 343

Schedule C (Form 1040) 2000

FIGURE I10-4 ▶ FORM 1040, SCHEDULE C (CONTINUED)

business for the next few years in order to carry the deductions over to a future period. What tax consequences would result if Rick implements the plan to discontinue depreciation and then sells some of the depreciable assets several years later?

I10-3 Rita acquired a personal residence two years ago for $120,000. In the current year she purchases another residence and attempts to sell her former residence. Due to depressed housing conditions in the town where she used to live, Rita is unable to sell the house. Her former residence is now being offered for sale at $100,000 (its current FMV according to real estate appraisal experts). Rita has decided to rent the house rather than "give it away." She states that the rental for an indefinite period will permit her to write off the original $120,000 investment over its useful life and to, therefore, recoup her investment. What restrictions in the tax law may prevent her from accomplishing this objective? Explain.

I10-4 Daytona Corporation, a manufacturing corporation, acquires the following business assets in the current year:
- Furniture
- Plumbing fixtures
- Land
- Goodwill and a trademark acquired in the acquisition of a business
- Automobile
- Heavy truck
- Machinery
- Building used in manufacturing activities

a. Which of the assets above are eligible for depreciation under the MACRS rules or amortization under Sec. 197?
b. What recovery period should be used for each of the assets above that come under the MACRS rules or under Sec. 197?

I10-5 Robert, a sole proprietor who uses the calendar year as his tax year, acquires a business machine on June 1, 2001 for $10,000 and sells certain business equipment on the same date for $2,000. No other property was acquired in 2001. The equipment that is sold was acquired on January 5, 1997 for $20,000.
a. What amount (if any) of depreciation deductions should be allowed under MACRS for the newly acquired machine and for the equipment that is sold in 2001 assuming both assets are 7-year property and the expensing election under Sec. 179 was not made.
b. How would your answer in a. change if the business machine was acquired on December 1, 2001 rather than June 1, 2001?

I10-6 Is a depreciation deduction allowed under the MACRS rules for depreciable real estate (used in a business or held for investment) in the year the property is sold? If so, explain how it is calculated.

I10-7 Jose is considering acquiring a new luxury automobile costing $44,000 that will used 100% use in his business. The salesperson at the automobile dealership states that Jose will be entitled to both of the following tax benefits in the initial year (2001):
- A deduction for $24,000 of the acquisition cost under Sec. 179.
- A $4,000 ($20,000 × 0.20) MACRS depreciation deduction.

a. Are the salesperson's assertions relative to the tax benefits accurate? Explain.
b. How would your answer to Part a differ (if any) if the automobile were used only 60% for business purposes?
c. How would your answer to Part a differ (if any) if Jose instead was to lease the automobile?

I10-8 Explain why the straight-line MACRS method might be preferable over the regular MACRS method under the following circumstances:
a. Ray incurs NOLs in his business for a number of years and has NOL carryovers he would like to use.
b. Rhonda's marginal tax rate is 15% but is expected to increase to 36% in three years.

I10-9 Rudy is considering whether to make the election under Sec. 179 to expense $24,000 (2001) of the acquisition cost related to certain fixed asset additions. What advantages are associated with the Sec. 179 election?

I10-10 Your client is a self-employed attorney who is considering the purchase of a $25,000 automobile that will be used 80% of the time for business and a $4,000 personal computer that will be used 100% of the time for business, but is located in his home.
a. What depreciation methods and recovery periods may be used under MACRS for the automobile and the personal computer?
b. How would your answer to Part a change if your client were an employee and the computer and automobile were not required as a condition of employment?
c. What tax consequences occur in Part a if the business use of the personal computer or the automobile decreases to 50% or less in a succeeding year? Explain.

I10-11 Sarah enters into a three-year lease of an automobile in the current year that is used exclusively in her business. The automobile's FMV was $40,000 at the inception of the lease. Sarah made ten monthly lease payments of $600 each during the current year. Is Sarah able to avoid the luxury automobile restrictions on depreciation by leasing instead of purchasing the automobile? Explain. (The inclusion amount for Sarah's automobile under the current Rev. Proc. is $202.)

I10-12 What difference does it make for income tax purposes whether an intangible asset (1) is acquired in connection with a business acquisition, (2) is acquired by the purchase of an individual asset (e.g., a patent), or (3) is created internally? Explain.

I10-13 In January of the current year, Park Corporation incurs $34,000 of legal costs associated with the obtaining of a patent that was developed internally and has a legal life of 17 years. Park also acquired for cash the net assets of Central Corporation on January 1, for $1,000,000. The following assets are specified in the purchase agreement:

Land	$200,000
Goodwill and going concern value	100,000
Covenant not to compete	50,000
Licenses	125,000
Customer lists	25,000
Inventory	100,000
Equipment and other tangible depreciable business assets	400,000
Total	$1,000,000

a. What tax treatment should be accorded the intangible assets?

b. Assuming that you were advising Park Corporation during the negotiations before the drafting of the purchase agreement, what suggestions would you make regarding the allocation of the total purchase price to the individual assets? How could the purchase price of individual assets be substantiated?

I10-14 Why do most taxpayers prefer to currently expense research and experimental expenditures?

I10-15 In a business combination, why does the buyer generally prefer to allocate as much of the purchase price to short-lived depreciable assets, ordinary assets such as inventory, and Sec. 197 intangible assets?

I10-16 Explain the difference between cost depletion and percentage depletion. Which of these two methods will generally provide the largest deduction?

I10-17 Simon acquires an interest in an oil property for $50,000. Intangible drilling costs (IDCs) in the initial year are $10,000. Cost depletion is $5,000 if the IDCs are expensed and $6,000 if the costs are capitalized. Percentage depletion is $15,000 if the IDCs are expensed and $20,000 if the costs are capitalized. The difference in the percentage depletion amounts is due to the 100% taxable income limitation.

a. What method (i.e., immediate write-off or capitalization and amortization) should be elected for the treatment of the IDCs in the initial year if Simon wants to maximize his deductions?

b. Why are intangible drilling costs expensed by most taxpayers?

ISSUE IDENTIFICATION QUESTIONS

I10-18 Georgia Corporation acquires a business automobile for $30,000 on December 31 of the current year but does not actually place the automobile into service until January 1 of the following year. What tax issues should Georgia Corporation consider?

I10-19 Paula is planning to acquire by purchase or by lease a $50,000 luxury automobile. She anticipates that the business use will be 60% for the first two years but will decline to 40% in years three through five. Currently, Paula's marginal tax rate is 15% but she anticipates that her marginal tax rate will be 36% after a few years. What tax issues should Paula consider relative to the decision to purchase or lease the automobile?

I10-20 In the current year Coastal Corporation acquires all of the net assets of Acorn Corporation for $2,000,000. The purchase agreement allocated the following amounts to the individual assets and liabilities:

Land and building	$1,400,000
Accounts receivable	200,000
Inventory	300,000
Goodwill	400,000
Patents (remaining legal life of ten years)	100,000
Covenant not to compete	200,000
Liabilities	(600,000)
Total	$2,000,000

What tax issues should Coastal Corporation consider relative to the asset acquisitions?

I10-21 Weiskopf, a sole proprietor and a calendar-year taxpayer, purchased $100,000 of equipment during the current year, as follows:

	Cost	Recovery Period
March 1	$25,000	7 years
September 18	$40,000	7 years
October 2	$35,000	5 years

Weiskopf's CPA, to maximize the depreciation deduction, elected to take Sec. 179 depreciation on the March 1 property of $20,000. What tax issue should be considered with respect to the total depreciation deduction for the current year?

PROBLEMS

I10-22 *Allowed Versus Allowable Depreciation.* Sandy acquires business machinery (which qualifies as 7-year MACRS property) on July 15, 1999 for $10,000. In 1999, Sandy claims a $1,429 depreciation deduction, but Sandy fails to claim any depreciation deduction in 2000 or 2001. The machine is sold on July 1, 2001 for $6,000.
a. What is the adjusted basis of the machine on the sale date?
b. How much gain or loss is recognized on the sale of the machine?

I10-23 *Conversion of Personal Asset to Business Use.* Sid purchased an automobile for personal use on January 18, 1999 for $10,000. On January 1, 2001, Sid starts a small business and begins to use the automobile exclusively in the business. The automobile's FMV on this date is $6,000. MACRS depreciation deductions are taken in 2001 based on a 5-year recovery period.
a. What is the automobile's basis for depreciation purposes when converted to business use in 2001?
b. What is Sid's depreciation deduction in 2001?

I10-24 *MACRS Depreciation.* Small Corporation acquires and places in service the following business assets in 2001 (no other assets were placed in service during the year):
- Light truck costing $10,000 (on December 15) with a 5-year MACRS recovery period
- Machinery costing $50,000 (on February 1) with a 7-year MACRS recovery period
- Land costing $60,000 (on July 1)
- Building costing $100,000 (on December 1) with a 39-year MACRS recovery period
- Equipment costing $40,000 (acquired on December 24, but not placed in service until January of the following year) with a 5-year MACRS recovery period

a. What is the MACRS depreciation deduction for each asset in the current year (assume Sec. 179 was not elected for any asset)?
b. What is the MACRS deduction for each asset in the current year if the machinery is instead acquired on November 1?
c. Assume the facts in Part a. If Small Corporation sells the machinery on June 15, 2003 and sells the building on October 20, 2003, compute the depreciation deductions for 2002 and 2003 and the adjusted basis for these two assets at the respective dates of sale.

I10-25 *MACRS Depreciation.* Ted is in the real estate business and owns rental property. On May 12, 2001, Ted purchased a small apartment building for $180,000. In addition, Ted purchased 5-year recovery period personal property costing $30,000 on April 1, 2001, and 7-year recovery period personal property costing $40,000 on November 1 of 2001. (Assume that Ted does not elect the Sec. 179 expensing election and uses the MACRS rules.) What is the amount of the MACRS depreciation deduction for each asset in 2001 and 2002?

I10-26 *Sec. 179 Expensing Election and MACRS Depreciation.* Tish acquires and places in service a business machine with a 7-year MACRS recovery period in July 2001. The machine costs $30,000, and Tish elects to expense the maximum amount allowable under Sec. 179. The total cost of qualifying property placed in service during the year amounts to $214,000. Tish's taxable income (before deducting the Sec. 179 amount and one-half of self-employment taxes paid) is $4,000.
a. What is the amount Tish can deduct under Sec. 179 in 2001?
b. What is the amount of MACRS depreciation deduction for the machine in 2001?

I10-27 *ACRS and MACRS Dispositions.* Tampa Corporation disposes of the following assets in 2001:

	Date Acquired	Date Sold	Original Cost Basis	Depreciation/ Cost-Recovery Method	Recovery Period (Years)
Auto	1/1/99	12/1/01[a]	9,000	MACRS	5
Equipment	1/6/99	9/1/01[a]	20,000	MACRS	7
Building	4/1/86	12/10/01	100,000	ACRS	19

[a] Assume that the half-year convention was used in the year of acquisition and Sec. 179 expense election was not made.

What is the amount of cost recovery or depreciation deduction for each asset in 2001?

I10-28 *Sec. 179 and MACRS Depreciation.* Thad acquires a machine for use in his business on April 1, 2001 for $32,000. The MACRS rules with a 7-year recovery period are used, and Thad elects to expense $24,000 of the acquisition cost under Sec. 179.
  a. What is the machine's basis for regular depreciation purposes and the depreciation deduction in 2001?
  b. Assume Thad depreciates the machine in 2001 and 2002 and then sells the machine on October 5, 2003 for $15,000. Compute Thad's depreciation deductions for 2002 and 2003, the adjusted basis of the machine on October 5, 2003, and the gain or loss on the sale.

I10-29 *Sec. 179 and Mid-Quarter Convention.* Todd acquired two pieces of equipment for use in his business during the year as follows:

Item	Date Acquired	Recovery Period	Cost
Equipment A	April, 2001	5-year	$50,000
Equipment B	November, 2002	7-year	$50,000

Todd elects to expense $24,000 of the acquisition cost under Sec. 179 and wants to maximize the amount of depreciation for the year. Compute Todd's depreciation in order to yield the highest depreciation possible. (Hint: The mid-quarter convention is calculated after taking Sec. 179 on any asset or assets)

I10-30 *Straight-Line Depreciation.* Long Corporation has been unprofitable for several years and has substantial NOL carryovers. Therefore, the company policy has been to use the straight-line ACRS or MACRS rules for property acquisitions. The following assets are acquired, held, or sold in 2001:

	Date Acquired	Date Sold	Original Cost Basis	Selling Price	Depreciation Method	Recovery Period (Years)
Equipment	6/1/01	—	$40,000	—	SL	7
Light truck	7/1/98	12/1/01	30,000	$12,000	SL	5
Furniture	3/1/99		10,000		SL	7
Automobile	7/1/99	12/1/01	12,000	10,000	SL	5

Assume the expensing election under Sec. 179 is not made.
  a. What is the depreciation deduction for each asset in 2001?
  b. What amount of gain or loss is recognized on the properties sold in 2001?

I10-31 *Mixed Personal/Business Use.* Trish, a self-employed CPA and calendar-year taxpayer, acquires an automobile and a personal computer in 2001. Pertinent data include the following:

Asset	Date Acquired	Original Cost Basis	Portion of Business Usage	Sec. 179 Election
Automobile	1/1/01	$11,000	60%	No
Personal computer	7/1/01	4,000	40%	No

For each asset calculate the MACRS current year depreciation deduction.

I10-32 *Employee Listed Property.* Assume the same facts as in Problem I10-31, except that Trish is an employee and uses the automobile and personal computer on employment-related activities. While both assets are helpful to Trish in performing her job duties, her employer does not require employees to purchase a car or a personal computer as a condition of employment. What is the amount of depreciation for each asset?

I10-33 *Recapture of Depreciation Deductions Due to Personal Use.* Tammy acquires an automobile for $10,000 on July 1, 1999. She uses the automobile partially for business purposes during the 1999–2001 period. The percentage of business use is as follows: 1999–70%; 2000–70%; 2001–40%. The MACRS rules with a 5-year recovery period are used in 1999 and 2000.
a. What is the amount of the MACRS depreciation deduction for 1999? 2000? 2001?
b. What is the amount of recapture of previously claimed depreciation deductions (if any) that must take place in 2001?

I10-34 *Luxury Auto Limitations.* Lutz Corporation acquires a luxury automobile on July 1, 2001 for $20,000 that is used 100% for business-use. The Sec. 179 expensing election is not made but the company chooses to claim the maximum amount of MACRS depreciation deductions available. What is the depreciation deduction amount for 2001, 2002, 2003, and any subsequent years?

I10-35 *Luxury Auto Limitations.* Tracy acquires a luxury automobile on March 1, 2001, that is used 80% of the time in his business and 20% of the time for personal use. The automobile cost $30,000, and no amounts are expensed under Sec. 179. What is the depreciation amount for 2001–2003 and any subsequent years?

I10-36 *Luxury Auto Limitations—Leasing.* Troy enters into a 3-year lease of a luxury auto on January 1, 2000, for use 80% in business and 20% for personal use. The FMV of the automobile at the inception of the lease is $40,500 and twelve monthly lease payments of $600 were made in 2000 and 2001.
a. What is the amount of lease payments that are deductible in 2000 and 2001?
b. What portion, if any, of the "inclusion amount" must be included in gross income in 2000 and 2001?
c. How would your answers to Parts a and b change if the FMV of the auto were instead $15,000 and the monthly lease payments were $200.

I10-37 *Goodwill.* On January 1 of the current year, Palm Corporation acquires the net assets of Vicki's unincorporated business for $600,000. The tangible net assets have a $300,000 book value and $400,000 FMV. The purchase agreement states that Vicki will not compete with Palm Corporation by starting a new business in the same area for a period of five years. The stated consideration received by Vicki for the covenant not to compete is $50,000. Other intangible assets included in the purchase agreement are as follows:

- Goodwill: $70,000
- Patents (12-year remaining legal life): $30,000
- Customer list: $50,000

a. How would Vicki's assets be recorded for tax purposes by Palm Corporation?
b. What is the amortization amount for each intangible asset in the current year?

I10-38 *R&E Expenditures.* Park Corporation incurs the following costs in the initial year of doing business:

Materials and supplies for research laboratory	$ 80,000
Utilities and depreciation on research laboratory and equipment	40,000
Costs of acquiring another person's patent for a new product	20,000
Market research salaries for surveys relative to proposed new products	60,000
Labor and supplies for quality control tests	50,000
Research costs subcontracted to a local university	35,000
Total	$285,000

Park's controller states that all of these costs are qualifying R&E expenditures and that the company policy is to expense such amounts for tax purposes in the year they are incurred. Which of these expenditures are deductible as R&E costs under Sec. 174?

I10-39 *R&E Expenditures.* In 2001, Phoenix Corporation acquires a new research facility and hires several scientists to develop new products. No new products are developed until 2002, although the following expenditures were incurred in 2001:

Laboratory materials	$ 40,000
Research salaries	80,000
Overhead attributable to the research facility	30,000
R&E equipment placed into service (5-year MACRS recovery period)	100,000
Total	$250,000

a. What is Phoenix Corporation's deduction for R&E expenditures in 2001 and 2002 if the expensing method is elected?
b. How would your answer to Part a change if the deferral and amortization method were elected and the amortization period were 60 months?

I10-40 *Cost Depletion.* Tina acquires an oil and gas property interest for $200,000 in the current year. The following information about current year operations is supplied for purposes of computing the amount of Tina's depletion and IDC deductions:

Estimated recoverable units	20,000
Units produced	6,000
Units sold	4,000
IDCs	$20,000
Percentage depletion (after limitations)	$25,000

a. What is the cost depletion amount if the IDCs are expensed?
b. What is the cost depletion amount if the IDCs are capitalized?
c. How much depletion is deducted on the tax return?
d. Should the IDCs be capitalized or expensed? Explain.

I10-41 *Percentage Depletion.* Tony has owned an oil and gas property for a number of years. The following information is provided about the property's operations in the current year:

Gross income	$500,000
Minus: Expenses (including IDCs of $100,000)	(300,000)
Taxable income (before depletion)	$200,000
Cost depletion (if IDCs are expensed)	$ 20,000
Cost depletion (if IDCs are capitalized)	$ 30,000

a. What is the percentage depletion amount if the IDCs are expensed?
b. What is the percentage depletion amount if the IDCs are capitalized?
c. What is the depletion deduction amount assuming that the IDCs are expensed?
d. Based on the information above, which method should be used for the IDCs? Explain.

TAX FORM/RETURN PREPARATION PROBLEMS

I10-42 Thom Jones (SSN 277-31-7253) is an unincorporated manufacturer of widgets. He uses the LCM method to value his inventory and has the following transactions during the year:

Sales (less returns and allowances)	$800,000
Costs of goods sold	500,000
Office expenses	10,000
Depreciation and Sec. 179 deduction (see the schedule below)	
Legal services	4,000
Salary expenses	36,000
Travel expenses	30,000
Repairs	20,000

Mr. Jones's depreciation schedule is as follows:

Office furniture held for business use is purchased on April 15, 2000 and an election is made to expense the maximum amount possible under Sec. 179.	$30,000
Depreciation on other recovery property acquired and placed into service on August 1, 1999:	
5-year recovery period property (computers-not listed property)	6,000
7-year recovery period property (equipment)	14,000
Depreciation on assets purchased prior to 2000	28,000

Complete Form 4562 and Schedule C of Form 1040 for 2000 for Mr. Jones.

I10-43 John and Ellen Brite (SSN 265-32-1497 and 571-07-7345, respectively) own an unincorporated specialty electrical lighting retail store, Brite-On. Brite-On had the following assets on January 1, 2000:

Assets	Cost
Building purchased April 1, 1986	$100,000
7-year recovery period equipment purchased January 10, 1996	30,000
Inventory valued using FIFO method:	
Inventory: 4,000 light bulbs	$5/bulb

The Brites purchased a competitor's store on March 1, 2000 for $89,000. The purchase price included the following:

	FMV
Store building	$60,000
Land	18,000
5-year recovery period equipment	11,000
Inventory: 3,000 light bulbs	$6/bulb

On June 30, 2000 the Brites sold the 7-year recovery period equipment for $12,000. Brite-On leased a $30,000 car for $500/month beginning on January 1, 2000. The car is used 100% for business and the car was driven 14,000 miles during the year. Brite-On sold 8,000 light bulbs at $15/bulb during the year. Also, Brite-On made additional purchases of 4,000 light bulbs in August and September, 2000 at $7/bulb. Brite-On had the following revenues (in addition to the sales of light bulbs) and additional expenses:

Service revenues	$40,000
Interest on business loans	4,000
Auto expenses (gas, oil, etc.)	3,800
Taxes and licenses	3,300
Utilities	2,800

John and Ellen also had some personal expenses:

Medical bills	$ 4,500
Real property taxes	3,800
Home mortgage interest	9,000
Charitable contributions (cash)	600

They had interest income on a bank savings account of $275. John and Ellen made four $5,000 quarterly estimated tax payments.

Additional Facts:
- Assume that an election is made under Sec. 179 to expense the cost of the 5-year equipment that was acquired in 2000.
- The latest IRS lease inclusion table requires the Brites to include $119 in their gross income due to the leased automobile restrictions.

Complete Forms 4562, 4797, and 1040, pages 1 and 2 and Schedules A and C for 2000. (Omit any self-employment tax computation.)

CASE STUDY PROBLEMS

I10-44 Able Corporation is a manufacturer of electrical lighting fixtures. Able is currently negotiating with Ralph Johnson, the owner of an unincorporated business, to acquire his retail electrical lighting sales business. Johnson's assets that are to be acquired include the following:

Assets	Adjusted Basis	FMV
Inventory of electrical fixtures	$ 30,000	$ 50,000
Store buildings	80,000	100,000
Land	40,000	100,000
Equipment: 7-year recovery period	30,000	50,000
Equipment: 5-year recovery period	60,000	100,000
Total	$240,000	$400,000

Mr. Johnson indicates that a total purchase price of $1,000,000 in cash is warranted for the business because of its high profitability and strategic locations and Able has agreed that the business is worth $1,000,000. Despite the fact that both parties attribute the excess payment to be for goodwill, Able would prefer that the $600,000 excess amount be designated as a 5-year covenant not to compete so that he can amortize the excess over a 5-year period.

You are a tax consultant for Able who has been asked to make recommendations as to the structuring of the purchase agreement and the amounts to be assigned to individual assets. Prepare a client memo to reflect your recommendations.

I10-45 The Margate Corporation acquired an automobile with an acquisition cost of $30,000 for use in its business in 1999. During this time, Margate Corporation was experiencing a seasonal decline in sales. Several employees were laid off and the automobile was not immediately needed for any of the sales personnel. Instead of letting the new automobile sit in the corporate lot, the president decided to permit a corporate officer to use the automobile for personal use. The officer used the automobile in 1999 and 2000 only. In 2001, Margate Corporation has hired you as their new CPA (tax consultant). You learn about the officer's personal use of the corporate automobile that took place for the two prior years without proper accounting of the automobile to the IRS. As Margate Corporation's tax consultant, what actions (if any) should you take regarding the proper treatment of the automobile? What are your responsibilities as a CPA regarding this matter under the rules of the AICPA's *SSTS* No. 6? (See the *Statements on Standards for Tax Services (SSTS)* section in Chapter I15 and Appendix E for a discussion of *SSTS* No. 6.)

TAX RESEARCH PROBLEM

I10-46 The Mumme Corporation is a very successful and profitable manufacturing corportation. The corporation just completed the construction of new corporate offices, primarily for its top executives. The president and founder of the corporation, Mr. Timothy Couch, is an avid collector of artwork and has instructed that the lobby and selected offices be decorated with rare collections of art. These expensive works of art were purchased by the corporation in accordance with Couch's directives. Couch jusified the purchase of these artworks on the premise that (1) they are excellent investments and should increase in value in the future, (2) they provide an appropriate and impressive office atmosphere when current and prospective customers visit the corporation's offices, and (3) the artwork is depreciable property and the corporation will be able to take sizable writeoffs against its income. The Financial Vice-President of the corporation has requested your advice as to whether the works of art are, in fact, depreciable property. Prepare a research memorandum for the Financial Vice-President on this issue.

A partial list of research sources is provided below.

- *Rev. Rul. 68-232*, 1968-1 C.B. 70
- *Shauna C. Clinger*, 60 T.C.M. 598 (1990).
- *Simon v. Comr.*, 103 T.C. 247 (1994), *aff'd*, 95-2 USTC ¶50,552 (2d Cir. 1995) *nonacq.* 1996-2 C.B.I.
- *Liddle v. Comr.*, 103 T.C. 285 (1994), *aff'd*, 95-2 USTC ¶50,488 (3rd Cir. 1995)

CHAPTER 11

ACCOUNTING PERIODS AND METHODS

LEARNING OBJECTIVES

After studying this chapter, you should be able to

1. Explain the rules for adopting and changing an accounting period
2. Explain the differences among cash, accrual, and hybrid accounting
3. Determine whether specific costs must be included in inventory
4. Determine the amount of income to be reported from a long-term contract
5. Compute the gain to be reported from an installment sale
6. Compute the amount of imputed interest in a transaction
7. Determine the tax treatment of duplications and omissions that result from changes of accounting methods

11-2 Individuals ▼ Chapter 11

CHAPTER OUTLINE

Accounting Periods...11-2
Overall Accounting Methods...11-7
Inventories...11-11
Special Accounting Methods...11-15
Imputed Interest...11-22
Change in Accounting Methods...11-26

An **accounting method** is a system of rules and procedures that is used to determine the year in which income and expenses are reported for tax purposes. The accounting methods used in computing income for tax purposes generally must be the same as those used in keeping the taxpayer's books and records and determine *when* income and expenses are reported, not whether they are reported. Although the accounting methods used by a taxpayer do not necessarily affect the amount of income reported over the life of a business, they do affect the tax burden in two ways. First, selecting the appropriate accounting method can accelerate deductions or defer income recognition in order to postpone tax payments, and second, because of the progressive tax rate structure, taxpayers can save taxes by spreading income over several accounting periods rather than having income bunched into one period.

EXAMPLE I11-1 ▶ Jane, a taxpayer using the cash method of accounting, has a 28% marginal tax rate for 2001 and expects to have a 15% marginal tax rate in 2002. Jane plans to make a charitable contribution of $1,000 in January 2002. A contribution in 2002 will reduce Jane's tax by $150 (0.15 × $1,000), whereas a contribution in 2001 will reduce Jane's tax by $280 (0.28 × $1,000). Obviously Jane may wish to accelerate the contribution in order to reduce her tax liability. ◀

ACCOUNTING PERIODS

OBJECTIVE 1

Explain the rules for adopting and changing an accounting period

Taxable income is computed on the basis of the taxpayer's annual **accounting period**, which is ordinarily 12 months (either a calendar year or a fiscal year). A **fiscal year** is a 12-month period that ends on the last day of any month other than December. The tax year must coincide with the year used to keep the taxpayer's books and records. Taxpayers who do not have books (e.g., an individual with wage income) must use the calendar year.[1] A taxpayer with a seasonal business may find a fiscal year to be advantageous. During the slow season, inventories may be lower and employees are available to take inventory and perform other accounting duties associated with the year-end. The tax year is elected on the first tax return that is filed by a taxpayer and cannot be changed without consent from the IRS.[2]

A partnership generally must use the same tax year of the partners who own the majority (greater than 50%) of partnership income and capital. If a majority of partners do not have the same year, the partnership must use the tax year of its principal partners (those with more than a 5% interest in the partnership). If the principal partners do not have the same tax year, the partnership must use the taxable year that results in the least aggregate deferral of income to the partners.[3] An exception is made for partnerships that can establish to the satisfaction of the IRS a business purpose for having a different year.

The purpose of the strict rules for selecting accounting periods is to prevent partners from deferring partnership income by choosing a different tax year for the partnership. For example, calendar-year partners might select a partnership year that ends on January 31. Because partnership income is considered to be earned by the partners on the last day of the partnership's tax year, reporting the profits would thus be deferred 11 months because the partnership year ends after the partner's year. (See the section entitled Required Payments and Fiscal Years in this chapter for further discussion of the calendar-year requirement.)

A similar rule generally requires S corporations and personal service corporations to adopt a calendar year unless the corporation has a business purpose for electing a fiscal year.[4] Taxpayers willing to make required payments or distributions may choose a fiscal year. (See the Required Payments and Fiscal Years section in this chapter.)

STOP & THINK

Question: The tax rules related to accounting periods essentially require most partnerships, S corporations, and personal service corporations to report on the calendar

---
[1] Sec. 441(g).
[2] Reg. Sec. 1.441-1(b)(4).
[3] Temp. Reg. Sec. 1.706-1T.
[4] Sec. 1378(a).

year basis. Of course, almost all individual taxpayers also report on the calendar year basis. What impact does this have on accountants?

Solution: The principal impact is a compression of tax compliance work into the "accounting busy season." A substantial portion of auditing and other accounting work also takes place shortly after the year end. As a result, these services are also compressed into the accounting busy season. The accounting profession has sought to have these tax rules changed, but has, at least so far, been unsuccessful.

An improper election to use a fiscal year automatically places the taxpayer on the calendar year.[5] Thus, if the first return is filed late because of oversight, the option to choose a fiscal year is lost.

EXAMPLE I11-2 ▶ City Corporation receives its charter in 1999 but does not begin operations until 2001. Tax returns are required for 1999 and 2000 as well as for 2001. Timely returns are not filed because the City's officers are unaware that returns must be filed for inactive corporations. Thus, City Corporation must use the calendar year. City Corporation may petition the IRS for approval to use a fiscal year. ◀

ADDITIONAL COMMENT
The use of a 52-53-week year aids in budgetary matters and statistical comparisons because a four-week period, unlike a calendar month, is a uniform, fixed period.

REAL-WORLD EXAMPLE
Merrill Lynch & Company uses a 52-53-week year ending on the last Friday in December.

TYPICAL MISCONCEPTION
It is sometimes mistakenly believed that a tax year can end on a day in the middle of the month.

While most tax years end on the last day of a month, the tax law allows taxpayers to use a tax year that always ends on the same day of the week, such as the last Friday in October. This means that the tax years will vary in length between 52 and 53 weeks. Taxpayers who regularly keep their books over a period that varies from 52 to 53 weeks may elect the same period for tax purposes. A 52-53-week taxable year must end either the last time a particular day occurs during a calendar month (e.g., the last Friday in October) or the occurrence of the particular day that is closest to the end of a calendar month (e.g., the Saturday closest to the end of November).[6] Under the first alternative, the year may end as many as six days before the end of the month, but must end within the month. Under the second alternative, the year may end as many as three days before or after the end of the month.

The 52-53-week year is especially useful to businesses with inventories. For example, a manufacturer might choose a 52-53-week year that ends on the last Friday in December to permit inventory to be taken over the weekend without interfering with the company's manufacturing activity. Similarly, wage accruals would be eliminated for a company with a weekly payroll if the payroll period always ends on Friday.

Although the 52-53-week year may actually end on a day other than the last day of the month, it is treated as ending on the last day of the calendar month for "effective date" changes in the tax law that would otherwise coincide with the year-end.

EXAMPLE I11-3 ▶ Eagle Corporation has adopted a 52-53-week year. Eagle's tax year begins on December 29, 2001. Assume that a new tax rate schedule applies to tax years beginning after December 31, 2001. The new tax rate schedule is applicable to Eagle because, in the absence of the 52-53-week year, its tax period would have started on January 1, 2002. ◀

REQUIRED PAYMENTS AND FISCAL YEARS

Virtually all C corporations (other than personal service corporations) have flexibility in choosing an accounting period. Other taxpayers, such as partnerships and S corporations, may use a fiscal year if they have an acceptable business purpose. However, most of these businesses are unable to meet the rather rigid business purpose requirements outlined by the IRS. As a result, these businesses report using the calendar year concentrating most tax work during the early months of the year. Concern over this problem led Congress to enact Sec. 444 which allows partnerships, S corporations, and personal service corporations (such as incorporated medical practices) to elect a taxable year that results in a tax deferral of three months or less (e.g., a partnership with calendar-year partners may elect a September 30 year end). This is called the **Sec. 444 election**. Furthermore, partnerships,

---

[5] *Q.A. Calhoun v. U.S.*, 33 AFTR 2d 74-305, 74-1 USTC ¶9104 (D.C. Va., 1973).

[6] Sec. 441(f).

S corporations, and personal service corporations may continue using the fiscal year they were using when the current law was passed in 1986 even if that fiscal year results in a deferral beyond three months.

Partnerships and S corporations making the Sec. 444 election, however, must make annual required payments by April 15 of the following year. The purpose of the required payment is to offset the tax deferral advantage obtained when fiscal years are used.

The amount of the required payment is determined by multiplying the maximum tax rate for individuals plus 1% (i.e., 40.6% in 2001) times the previous year's taxable income times a deferral ratio.[7] The deferral ratio is equal to the number of months in the deferral period divided by the number of months in the taxable year. An adjustment is made for deductible amounts distributed to the owners during the year. If the amount due is $500 or less, no payment is required.

> **ADDITIONAL COMMENT**
> The American Institute of Certified Public Accountants and accounting firms lobbied extensively for the provision that permits partnerships, S corporations, and personal service corporations to continue to use a fiscal year if annual required payments are made.

EXAMPLE I11-4 ▶ ABC Partnership begins operations on October 1, 2001 and elects a September 30 year-end under Sec. 444. The partnership's net income for the fiscal year ended September 30, 2002 is $100,000. ABC must make a required payment of $10,150 ($100,000 × 40.6% × 3/12) on or before April 15, 2003. ◀

The owners of businesses making such payments do not claim a credit for the amount paid. Instead, the partnership or S Corporation subtracts the previous year's required payment from the current year's required payment. If the result is negative, then the entity is entitled to a refund.

EXAMPLE I11-5 ▶ Assume the same facts as in Example I11-4 except that ABC Partnership's required payment for the year ended September 30, 2003 is $6,000. ABC is entitled to a refund of the difference of $4,150 ($10,150 − $6,000). ◀

Personal service corporations may elect a fiscal year if they make minimum distributions to shareholders during the deferral period.[8] Personal service corporations are incorporated medical practices and other similar businesses owned by individuals who provide their services through the corporation. In general, the rules prevent a distribution pattern that creates a tax deferral. This is achieved by requiring that the deductible payments made to owners during the deferral period be at a rate no lower than during the previous fiscal year.

EXAMPLE I11-6 ▶ Austin, Inc. is a personal service corporation of attorneys with a fiscal year ending September 30. For the year ended September 30, 2001 the company earned a profit of $480,000 before any salary payments to the owners. The entire profit, however, was paid out as wages to the owners, resulting in a taxable income of zero. To avoid penalty, Austin must pay salaries to its owners of no less than $120,000 ($480,000 × 3/12) during the period October 1, 2001 to December 31, 2001. ◀

An option allows personal service corporations to compute the amount of the minimum distribution by using a three-year average of income and distributions.

CHANGES IN THE ACCOUNTING PERIOD

> **KEY POINT**
> The use of a natural business year helps in the matching of revenue and expense because the business is normally in a maximum state of liquidity and the problems associated with making estimates involving uncompleted transactions are reduced to a minimum.

Once adopted, an accounting period cannot normally be changed without approval of the IRS.[9] The IRS will usually approve a change only if the taxpayer can establish a substantial business purpose for the change (e.g., changing to a natural business year).[10] A natural business year ends at or soon after the peak income earning period (e.g., the natural business year for a department store that has a seasonal holiday business may be on January 31). A business without a peak income period may not be able to establish a natural business year and may, therefore, be precluded from changing its tax year. In general, at least 25% of revenues must occur during the last two months of the year in order to qualify as a natural business year.

---

[7] Sec. 7519(b).
[8] Sec. 280H(k).
[9] Sec. 442.
[10] Rev. Proc. 74-33, 1974-2 C.B. 489 and Rev. Proc. 87-32, 1989-2 C.B. 32.

EXAMPLE I11-7 ▶ USA Department Store's sales reach their peak during the holiday season in December. During January the department store further reduces its inventory through storewide clearance sales. USA elects a "natural" business year-end of January 31 because its inventory levels are lowest at the end of January. Also, USA meets the prescribed test because at least 25% of its revenues for the year occur in December and January. ◀

In a few instances IRS approval is not required to change to another accounting period.

REAL-WORLD EXAMPLE

J.C. Penney, K mart, and Wal-Mart all use an accounting period ending January 31.

▶ A newly married person may change tax years to conform to that of his or her spouse so that a joint return may be filed. The election must be made in either the first or second year after the marriage date.[11]

▶ A change to a 52-53-week year that ends with reference to the same calendar month in which the former tax year ended.[12]

▶ A taxpayer who erroneously files tax returns using an accounting period other than that on which his or her books are kept is not required to obtain permission to file returns for later years based on the way the books are kept.[13]

▶ A corporation meeting the following specified conditions may change without IRS approval: (1) There has been no change in its accounting period within the past ten calendar years, (2) the resulting year does not have a net operating loss (NOL), (3) the taxable income for the resulting short tax year when annualized is at least 90% of the taxable income for the preceding full tax year, and (4) there is no change in status of the corporation (such as an S corporation election).[14]

▶ An existing partnership can change its tax year without prior approval if the partners with a majority interest have the same tax year to which the partnership changes or if all principal partners who do not have such a tax year concurrently change to such a tax year.[15]

There is one instance, however, when a change in tax years is required: A subsidiary corporation filing a consolidated return with its parent corporation must change its accounting period to conform with its parent's tax year.

Application for permission to change accounting periods is made on Form 1128, Application for Change in Accounting Period, on or before the due date of the return including extensions. The application must be sent to the Commissioner of the IRS, Washington, D.C.

The IRS may establish certain conditions for the taxpayer to meet before it approves the change to a new tax year. For example, the IRS has ruled that if the short period that results from a change involves a NOL greater than $50,000, the taxpayer may have to forgo a carryback of the loss.[16]

RETURNS FOR PERIODS OF LESS THAN 12 MONTHS

Most income tax returns cover an accounting period of 12 months. On two occasions, however, a taxpayer's accounting period may be less than 12 months: when the taxpayer's first or final return is filed and when the taxpayer changes accounting periods.

Taxpayers filing an initial tax return and executors filing a taxpayer's final return or corporations filing their last return are not required to annualize the year's income, nor are personal exemptions or tax credits prorated. These returns are prepared and filed, and taxes are paid as though they are returns for a 12-month period ending on the last day of the short period. An exception permits the final return of a decedent to be filed as though the decedent lived throughout the entire tax year.[17]

---

[11] Reg. Sec. 1.442-1(e). A statement should be attached to the resulting short period return indicating that the change is being made.
[12] Reg. Sec. 1.441-2(c)(2). A statement should be attached to the first return filed under the election indicating that the change is being made.
[13] Rev. Rul. 58-256, 1959-1 C.B. 215.
[14] Reg. Sec. 1.442-1(c). A statement should be attached to the return indicating that each condition is met.
[15] Reg. Sec. 1.442-1(b)(2).
[16] Rev. Proc. 2000-11, I.R.B. 2000-3.
[17] Reg. Sec. 1.443-1(a)(2).

EXAMPLE I11-8 ▶ ABC Partnership, which has filed its returns on a calendar-year basis, terminates on June 30, 2001. ABC's final return is due on October 15, 2001. ◀

EXAMPLE I11-9 ▶ Joy, a single individual who has filed her returns on a calendar-year basis, dies on June 30, 2001. Joy's final return is due on April 15, 2002. ◀

Taxpayers who change from one accounting period to another must annualize their income for the resulting short period. This prevents income earned during the resulting short period from being taxed at lower rates. Income is annualized as follows:

1. Determine modified taxable income. Individuals must compute their taxable income for the short period by itemizing their deductions (i.e., the standard deduction is not allowed) and personal and dependency exemptions must be prorated.[18]
2. Multiply modified taxable income by the following fraction:

$$\frac{12}{\text{Number of months in short period}}$$

3. Compute the tax on the resulting taxable income using the appropriate tax rate schedule.
4. Multiply the resulting tax by the following fraction:

$$\frac{\text{Number of months in short period}}{12}$$

EXAMPLE I11-10 ▶ Pat, a single taxpayer, obtains permission to change from a calendar year to a fiscal year ending on June 30, 2001. During the six months ending June 30, 2001, Pat earns $25,000 and has $5,000 in itemized deductions.[19]

Gross Income	$25,000
Minus: Itemized deductions	(5,000)
Personal exemption [(6 ÷ 12) × $2,900]	(1,450)
Modified taxable income	$18,550
Annualized income [(12 ÷ 6) × $18,550]	$37,100
Tax on annualized income	$ 6,872
Current tax [(6 ÷ 12) × $6,872]	$ 3,436

◀

Topic Review I11-1 summarizes the available accounting periods and the rules for changing accounting periods.

STOP & THINK

Question: Why are taxpayers required to annualize when they change tax years? What provision of the tax law creates this need?

Solution: A change of tax years results in a shortened filing period during the period the change takes place. For example, a taxpayer who changes from a calendar year to a June 30 year end reports income for only a 6-month period on the first return following the change. Less income is reported, and that income would be taxed at lower rates without annualization. Annualization is necessary because of the progressive tax rate structure.

---

[18] The exemptions are prorated as follows: exemptions × (number of months in the short period ÷ 12).

[19] An alternative method to compute the tax is provided in Sec. 443(b)(2) and Reg. Sec. 1.443-1(b)(2) whereby the taxpayer can elect to compute the tax for a 12-month period beginning on the first day of the short period and then convert the tax to a short-period tax.

Topic Review I11-1

Accounting Periods and Changes

AVAILABLE YEARS

- Available tax years include the calendar year, a fiscal year (a year that ends on the last day of any month other than December), and a 52-53-week year (a year that always ends on the same day of the week).
- A partnership must use the tax year of its partners unless the partnership can establish a satisfactory business purpose for having a different year or if the partnership makes required payments.
- Similar rules generally require S corporations and personal service corporations to adopt a calendar year unless the corporation has a business purpose for electing a fiscal year. Taxpayers willing to make required payments or distributions may choose a fiscal year ending on September 30, October 31, or November 30.

CHANGE IN ACCOUNTING PERIODS

- Once adopted, an accounting period normally cannot be changed without approval by the IRS. The IRS is more likely to approve a change to a natural business year. In general, at least 25% of revenues must occur during the last two months of the year in order to qualify as a natural business year.
- Taxpayers who change from one accounting period to another must annualize their income for the resulting short period. This prevents income earned during the resulting short period from being taxed at lower rates.

OVERALL ACCOUNTING METHODS

OBJECTIVE 2

Explain the difference between cash, accrual, accounting and hybrid accounting

A taxpayer's method of accounting determines the year in which income is reported and expenses are deducted. Taxable income must be computed using the method of accounting regularly used by the taxpayer in keeping his or her books if that method clearly reflects income.[20] Permissible overall accounting methods are

- Cash receipts and disbursements method (often called the cash method of accounting)
- Accrual method
- A combination of the first two methods, often called the hybrid method

KEY POINT

The Code provides the IRS with broad powers in ascertaining whether the taxpayer's accounting method clearly reflects income. It entitles the IRS to more than the usual presumption of correctness.

New taxpayers may generally choose any of the accounting methods listed above. However, the accrual method must be used for sales and cost of goods sold if inventories are an income-producing factor to the business. An exception permits businesses with inventories to use the cash method if their average annual gross receipts for the three preceding tax years do not exceed $1 million.[21] The fact that an overall accounting method is used in one trade or business does not mean that the same method must be used in a second trade or business or for nonbusiness income and deductions.

EXAMPLE I11-11 ▶ Troy, a practicing CPA, also owns an appliance store. The fact that Troy uses the accrual method of reporting income from the appliance store, where inventories are an income-producing factor, does not preclude Troy from reporting income from his service-based accounting practice by using the cash method. Troy could also use the cash method for reporting nonbusiness income (such as dividends) and nonbusiness expenses (such as itemized deductions). ◀

REAL-WORLD EXAMPLE

It has been held that the cash method of accounting can be used where inventories are inconsequential. *Michael Drazen,* 34 T.C. 1070 (1960).

The term *method of accounting* is used to include not only overall methods of accounting listed above but also the accounting treatment of any item.[22]

CASH RECEIPTS AND DISBURSEMENTS METHOD

Most individuals and service businesses use the cash receipts and disbursements method of accounting. Taxpayers cannot use the cash method in a business for sales and cost of

---

[20] Sec. 446.
[21] Rev. Proc. 2000-22, I.R.B. 2000-20, 1008. This Revenue Procedure has been modified and superseded by Rev. Proc. 2001-10, I.R.B. 2001-2, 272.
[22] Reg. Sec. 1.446-1(a)(1). Examples of accounting methods for specific items include Sec. 174, relating to research and experimentation expenses; Sec. 451, relating to reporting income from long-term contracts; and Sec. 453, relating to reporting income from installment sales.

goods sold if inventories are an income-producing factor.[23] However, as noted above, businesses with inventories are permitted to use the cash method if their average annual gross receipts for the three preceding tax years do not exceed $1 million. C corporations and partnerships with a corporate partner may use the cash method only if their average annual gross receipts for the three preceding tax years do not exceed $5 million or if the business meets the requirements associated with providing personal services (i.e., if it is owned by professionals who are using the business to provide professional services).[24] Thus, a law or accounting firm can use the cash method even if its average receipts exceed $5 million.

Under the cash receipts and disbursements method of accounting, a taxpayer is required to report income for the tax year in which payments are actually or constructively received. While it might seem that receipts under the cash method of accounting should only be recognized if the taxpayer receives cash, this is not the case. The Regulations clearly provide that gross income under the cash method includes cash, property, or services.[25] Thus, if a CPA accepts a set of golf clubs as payment from a client for services rendered, the CPA must include the fair market value of the golf clubs in his gross income. However, an accounts receivable or other unsupported promise to pay is considered to have no value and, as a result, no income is recognized until the receivable is collected. Expenses are deducted in the year paid. Because the recognition of expense is measured by the flow of cash, a taxpayer can determine the year in which an expense is deductible by choosing when to make the payment. Individual taxpayers do not have the same opportunity to determine the year in which income is recognized, because the constructive receipt rule requires taxpayers to recognize income if a payment is available, even if actual payment has not been received. (See Chapter I3 for a discussion of constructive receipt.)

> **KEY POINT**
> A taxpayer using the cash method is entitled to certain deductions that do not involve current year cash disbursements, such as depreciation, depletion, and losses.

CAPITALIZATION REQUIREMENTS FOR CASH-METHOD TAXPAYERS. Taxpayers who use the cash receipts and disbursements method are required to capitalize fixed assets and to recover the cost through depreciation or amortization. The Regulations state that prepaid expenses must be capitalized and deducted over the life of the asset if the life of the asset extends substantially beyond the end of the tax year.[26] Typically, capitalization is required only if the life of the asset extends beyond the close of the tax year following the year of payment.[27]

EXAMPLE I11-12 ▶ On July 1, 2001, Acme Corporation, a cash basis, calendar-year taxpayer, pays an insurance premium of $3,000 for a policy that is effective July 1, 2001 to June 30, 2002. The full $3,000 is deductible in 2001. ◀

EXAMPLE I11-13 ▶ Assume the same facts as in Example I11-12, except that the premium covers a three-year period beginning July 1, 2001 and ending June 30, 2004. Acme Corporation may deduct $500 in 2001, $1,000 in 2002 and 2003, and $500 in 2004. ◀

One notable exception to the one-year rule denies a deduction for prepaid interest. Cash-method taxpayers must capitalize such amounts and allocate interest over the prepayment period. A special rule allows homeowners to deduct points paid on a mortgage used to buy or improve a personal residence. The payment must be an established business practice in the area and not exceed amounts generally charged for such home loans. (See Chapter I7 for a discussion of the deductibility of points.)

To be deductible, a payment must be more than just a refundable deposit. A taxpayer who has an option of cancelling delivery and receiving a refund of amounts prepaid is not normally entitled to deduct the amount of the deposit.

Payments can be made either by a check that is honored in due course or by the use of a credit card.[28] Payment by credit card is considered to be the equivalent of borrowing

---

[23] Reg. Sec. 1.471-1. However, Sec. 448(b) permits farmers to use the cash method even though they have inventories. Sec. 448(a) denies tax shelters the right to use the cash method even if they do not have inventories.
[24] Secs. 448(b) and (c).
[25] Reg. Sec. 1.446-1(c)(1)(i).
[26] Reg. Sec. 1.461-1(a)(1).
[27] *Bonaire Development Co.*, 76 T.C. 789 (1981), and *Martin J. Zaninovich v. CIR*, 45 AFTR 2d 80-1442, 80-1 USTC ¶9342 (9th Cir., 1980).
[28] Rev. Rul. 78-39, 1978-1 C.B. 73.

funds to pay the expense. However, a taxpayer's note is not the equivalent of cash, so if a cash method taxpayer gives a note in payment, he or she cannot take the deduction until the note is paid, even if the note is secured by collateral.[29]

ACCRUAL METHOD

There are two tests used to determine when an item of income must be reported or an expense deducted: the **all-events test** and the **economic performance test**.

ADDITIONAL COMMENT
The phrase *reasonable accuracy* means that approximate amounts are ascertainable. Although the word *accuracy* means exactness or precision, when it is used with the word *reasonable* it implies something less than an exact amount.

ALL-EVENTS TEST. An accrual-method taxpayer reports an item of income when "all events" have occurred that fix the taxpayer's right to receive the item of income and the amount can be determined with reasonable accuracy.[30] Similarly, an expense is deductible when all events have occurred that establish the fact of the liability and the amount of the expense can be determined with reasonable accuracy. For deductions, the all-events test is not satisfied until economic performance has taken place.

ECONOMIC PERFORMANCE TEST. Economic performance (of services or property to be provided to a taxpayer) occurs when the property or services are actually provided by the other party.

EXAMPLE I11-14 ▶ The owner of a professional football team provides medical benefits for injured players through insurance coverage. Economic performance occurs over the term of the policy rather than when the team enters into a binding contract with the insurance company or during the season when the player earns the right to medical benefits. Thus, a one-year premium is deductible over the year of the insurance coverage rather than over the term of the player's contract under which the benefit is earned. ◀

Similarly, if a taxpayer is obligated to provide property or services, economic performance occurs in the year the taxpayer provides the property or service.

EXAMPLE I11-15 ▶ Assume the same facts as in Example I11-14 except that medical benefits are required under the terms of a player's contract. Also, the team decides to pay medical costs directly. Economic performance occurs as the team actually provides the benefits. Thus, the deduction is permitted only as medical care is provided. ◀

REAL-WORLD EXAMPLE
Before the economic performance test was added to the tax law, a company engaged in strip mining coal was able to deduct the future land reclamation costs as the coal was mined because the liability was certain and the cost could be estimated. *Ohio River Collieries*, 77 T.C. 1369 (1981).

The requirement that economic performance take place before a deduction is allowed is waived if all of the following five conditions are met:
▶ The all-events test, without regard to economic performance, is satisfied.
▶ Economic performance occurs within a reasonable period (but in no event more than 8½ months) after the close of the tax year.
▶ The item is recurring in nature, and the taxpayer consistently treats items of the same type as incurred in the tax year in which the all-events test is met.
▶ The taxpayer is not a tax shelter.
▶ Either the amount is not material or the earlier accrual of the item results in a better matching of income and expense.[31]

EXAMPLE I11-16 ▶ To promote sales, Bass Corporation (a used car sales company) offers coupons to customers for three free car washes. Bass purchases the coupons from a local car wash. The coupons must be used within six months after the purchase of an automobile. If Bass uses the cash method, it could deduct the cost of the coupons at the time the payment for the coupons is made to the car wash. Under the accrual method and assuming the five conditions listed above are met, Bass could deduct the cost of the coupons as they are given to customers (instead of having to wait until the coupons are used). ◀

---

[29] *Frank D. Quinn Exec. v. CIR*, 24 AFTR 927, 40-1 USTC ¶9403 (5th Cir., 1940).
[30] Reg. Sec. 1.451-1(a). See Chapter I3 for a discussion of the all-events test as it applies to gross income.
[31] Sec. 461(h).

TYPICAL MISCONCEPTION

It is sometimes mistakenly believed that taxpayers can deduct warranty expenses and bad debts using the allowance method instead of the direct write-off method.

Reserves for items such as product warranty expense are commonly encountered in financial accounting. The all-events and economic performance tests prevent the use of such reserves for tax purposes. This is because the amount of such expense is not usually determinable with sufficient accuracy. Under prior law, taxpayers were permitted to use the allowance method for bad debts, but that method is no longer allowed for tax purposes.

HYBRID METHOD

Taxpayers may use a combination of accounting methods as long as income is clearly reflected. Taxpayers with inventories are required to use the accrual method to report sales and purchases if their average gross receipts for the three preceding years exceeds $1 million. These taxpayers may use the cash method to report other items of income and expense. To ensure that income is clearly reflected, certain restrictions have been placed on combining accounting methods.

KEY POINT

A taxpayer who uses the cash method in computing gross income from his or her business must use the cash method in computing expenses of such business.

Taxpayers who use the cash method of accounting in determining gross income from a trade or business must use the cash method for determining expenses of the same trade or business. Similarly, taxpayers who use the accrual method of accounting for expenses must use the accrual method in computing gross income from the trade or business.

The basic rules relating to accounting methods, the all-events test, and economic performance are summarized in Topic Review I11-2.

STOP & THINK

Question: If an accountant does tax work for an automobile dealer, in exchange for free use of an automobile, does the accountant have to report any income? Does it make a difference whether the accountant uses the automobile in her business? When is any taxable income reported?

Solution: The rental value of the automobile must be included in gross income. If the automobile is used in the accountant's business, a portion of the rental value is deductible as a business expense. Although it is not entirely clear, it seems that an accrual basis accountant would report income as tax services are provided to the dealer. A cash basis taxpayer would report income over the time the automobile is used.

Topic Review I11-2

Accounting Methods

AVAILABLE METHODS

▶ Permissible overall accounting methods are the cash receipts and disbursements method, the accrual method, and the hybrid method.

▶ The cash method is available to taxpayers without inventories and to taxpayers with inventories whose average gross receipts during the three preceding years was $1 million or less. C corporations whose average gross receipts fall between $1 and $5 million thresholds may use the cash method if they do not have inventories. C corporations (other than personal service corporations) may not use the cash method if their average gross receipts in the three preceding tax years exceed $5 million.

ALL-EVENTS TEST AND ECONOMIC PERFORMANCE TEST

▶ An accrual-method taxpayer reports an item of income when all events have occurred that fix the taxpayer's right to receive the item of income and when the amount of the item can be determined with reasonable accuracy.

▶ An expense is deductible when all events have occurred that establish that there is a liability and when the amount of the expense can be determined with reasonable accuracy. The all-events test is not satisfied until economic performance has taken place.

▶ Economic performance takes place when property or services are actually provided.

Accounting Periods and Methods ▼ Individuals 11-11

INVENTORIES

OBJECTIVE 3

Determine whether specific costs must be included in inventory

In general, manufacturing and merchandising companies are required to use the accrual method of accounting for purchases and sales of merchandise. The inventory method used by a taxpayer must conform to the best accounting practice in the trade or business, and it must clearly reflect income. However, best accounting practices (synonymous with generally accepted accounting principles) and clear reflection of income (which is determined by the IRS) occasionally conflict. The Supreme Court has held that the standard of clear reflection of income prevails in a case where the two standards conflict. In the *Thor Power Tool Co.* case, the company for both tax and financial accounting purposes wrote off the cost of obsolete parts for both tax and financial accounting purposes even though the parts were kept on hand and their selling price was not reduced.[32] Regulation Sec. 1.471-4(b) states that obsolete or other slow-moving inventory cannot be written down unless the selling price is also reduced.

KEY POINT

Taxpayers cannot always use inventory methods for tax purposes that conform with generally accepted accounting principles.

Although the company's practice conformed with generally accepted accounting principles, it did not, according to the Supreme Court, clearly reflect income. Hence, generally accepted accounting principles are used only when the Regulations do not specify the treatment of an item or, alternatively, when the Regulations provide more than one alternative accounting method.

Taxpayers who value inventory at cost may write down goods that are not salable at their normal price (e.g., damaged, obsolete, or shopworn goods) only after the selling price has been reduced. Items may be valued at a bona fide selling price reduced by the direct cost of disposal.[33] The option to write down this type of merchandise is available even if the taxpayers use the LIFO inventory method.

EXAMPLE I11-17 ▶

KEY POINT

The uniform capitalization rules, included in the Tax Reform Act of 1986, require the capitalization of significant overhead costs that previously were expensed.

Stone Corporation publishes books for small academic audiences in Sanskrit and other ancient languages. There is typically one printing of a few hundred or perhaps a thousand copies of each book. Stone may sell a few copies a year of each book. Only after several years can the Corporation determine whether they will ever sell all copies of a given work. Based upon the *Thor Power Tool Co.* case, Stone Corporation cannot write off unsold copies unless they are destroyed or otherwise disposed of, and they cannot write down unsold copies unless the selling price is reduced below cost. ◀

DETERMINATION OF INVENTORY COST

Inventories may be valued at either cost or at the lower of cost or market value. Taxpayers who use the LIFO inventory valuation method (discussed later in this chapter) may not use the lower of cost or market method. In the case of merchandise purchased, cost is the invoice price less trade discounts, plus freight and other handling charges.

ETHICAL POINT

The UNICAP rules must be followed by taxpayers. To bring a business into compliance with these rules, the taxpayer may need to make certain estimates. SRTP No. 4 provides that a CPA may use a client's estimates if such use is generally acceptable or if it is impractical to obtain exact data. If a change in the overhead application rate is contemplated, it may be desirable to request IRS approval.

Unlike financial accounting, purchasing costs (e.g., salaries of purchasing agents), warehousing costs, packaging, and administrative costs related to these functions must be allocated between cost of goods sold and inventory. The costs that must be included in inventory are found in Sec. 263A and are referred to as the Uniform Capitalization rules (UNICAP). This requirement is applicable only to taxpayers whose average gross receipts for the three preceding years exceed $10 million.[34]

In the case of goods manufactured by the taxpayer, cost is determined by using the UNICAP rules, which may be thought of as an expanded version of the full absorption costing method. Thus, direct costing and prime costing are not acceptable inventory methods. Direct labor and materials along with manufacturing overhead must be included in inventory. Under UNICAP, the following overhead items are included in inventory:

▶ Factory repairs and maintenance, utilities, rent, insurance, small tools, and depreciation (including the excess of tax depreciation over accounting depreciation)

▶ Factory administration and officers' salaries related to production

---

[32] *Thor Power Tool Co. v. CIR*, 43 AFTR 2d 79-362, 79-1 USTC ¶9139 (USSC, 1979).

[33] Reg. Sec. 1.471-2(c).

[34] Sec. 263A(b)(2)(B).

- Taxes (other than the income tax)
- Quality control and inspection
- Rework, scrap, and spoilage
- Current and past service costs of pension and profit-sharing plans
- Service support such as purchasing, payroll, and warehousing costs

Nonmanufacturing costs (e.g., advertising, selling, and research and experimental costs) are not required to be included in inventory. Interest must be inventoried if the property is real property, long-lived property, or property requiring more than two years (one year in the case of property costing more than $1 million) to produce.

KEY POINT

Identifying the appropriate additional overhead costs to capitalize can be confusing and extremely time consuming.

The main difference between full absorption costing traditionally used for financial accounting purposes and UNICAP costing required for tax purposes is that UNICAP expands the list of overhead costs to include certain indirect costs that have not always been included in overhead for financial accounting purposes. For example, for financial accounting purposes, the costs of operating payroll and personnel departments have sometimes been considered sufficiently indirect or remote to justify omitting them from manufacturing overhead. This is true even though much of the effort of the payroll and personnel departments was directed toward manufacturing operations. For simplicity and other reasons, overhead costs included in inventory for financial purposes are often limited to those incurred in the factory. UNICAP requires that costs associated with these departments be allocated between manufacturing and nonmanufacturing functions (e.g., sales, advertising, research and experimentation).

EXAMPLE I11-18 ▶ Best Corporation manufactures traditional style rocking chairs in a small factory with 34 employees. The office staff consists of four employees who handle payroll, receivables, hiring, and other office responsibilities. The sales staff includes three employees who travel the region selling to furniture and craft stores. The remaining 27 employees all work in the factory. Under UNICAP, factory costs including the wages of the 27 factory workers are generally all manufacturing costs. The costs associated with the sales staff are not manufacturing costs. This would include their compensation along with related costs such as travel. Office expenses including the wages paid to the four office workers can be allocated between manufacturing overhead and sales. Reasonable allocation methods are acceptable. One possibility might be to allocate office overhead between sales and manufacturing on a basis as simple as the number of employees in sales (3) and the number in manufacturing (27). Thus, 90% of the cost of the office operation could be treated as manufacturing-related and 10% sales-related. In such case, 90% of the office expenses would be allocated to manufacturing and 10% deducted as a period cost (i.e., selling expenses). The office expenses allocated to manufacturing would in turn be allocated between cost of sales and ending inventory. This allocation could be done on a basis as simple as multiplying the allocated office expenses by the number of chairs in ending inventory and dividing by the total number of chairs made during the year. ◀

A manufacturer may use standard costs to value inventory if any significant variance is reallocated pro rata to ending inventory and cost of goods sold.[35] Taxpayers may determine inventory costs by the following methods: specific identification method; first-in, first-out method (FIFO); last-in, first-out method (LIFO); or average cost method. A few taxpayers, such as an automobile or large appliance dealer, may find it practical to determine the specific cost of items in inventory. Most taxpayers, however, must rely on a flow of goods assumption (e.g., FIFO or LIFO). A discussion of the LIFO method is presented below.

LIFO METHOD. Many taxpayers use the LIFO cost flow assumption because, during inflationary periods, LIFO normally results in the lowest inventory value and hence the lowest taxable income. Once LIFO has been elected for tax purposes, the taxpayer's financial reports must also be prepared using LIFO.[36] This requirement to conform financial reporting often discourages companies from electing LIFO because lower earnings must be reported to shareholders. However, taxpayers may make footnote disclosure of the amount

---

[35] Reg. Sec. 1.471-11(d)(3).
[36] Sec. 472(c).

Accounting Periods and Methods ▼ **Individuals 11-13**

of net income that would have been reported under FIFO or other inventory methods.[37] Taxpayers may adopt LIFO by attaching a completed Form 970 (or by a statement acceptable to the IRS) to the return for the tax year in which the method is first used.

STOP & THINK

Question: As noted, many publicly held companies do not use LIFO inventory valuation. This is, in part, attributed to the fact that LIFO ordinarily results in lower reported income for accounting purposes than FIFO, and management prefers to report higher profits. Many small, closely-held companies also use FIFO even though their earnings are not reported to the public. Why wouldn't closely-held companies use LIFO?

Solution: There are a variety of reasons. Some businesses are very interested in how their financial statements look to banks and other lenders and to potential investors. In some industries, such as electronics, FIFO may actually provide lower inventory values. Also, LIFO cannot be used with lower of cost or market. As a result, some businesses may elect FIFO to be eligible to use lower of cost or market.

Perhaps, however, the main reason is that LIFO is more complex, and small businesses prefer to simplify their accounting. The advent of computers, accounting software, and bar codes may be having some impact on inventory valuation choices. Nevertheless, many accounting packages only track units on hand and sales revenue. They do not track inventory value (cost). Thus, the company must assign a value to inventory at year end, and the complexity of LIFO remains a deterrent.

REAL-WORLD EXAMPLE

An automobile dealer, using the dollar-value LIFO method in maintaining its inventory, was required to use one pool for new automobiles and a separate pool for new trucks. *Fox Chevrolet, Inc.,* 76 T.C. 708 (1981).

Recordkeeping under LIFO can be cumbersome. For this reason, taxpayers are permitted to determine inventories using "dollar-value" pools and government price indexes rather than by maintaining a record of actual costs.[38] Retailers use appropriate categories in the Consumer Price Index; other taxpayers use categories in the Producer Price Index. Taxpayers using the index method must divide their inventories into one or more pools (groups of similar items). Thus, a department store might create separate pools for automobile parts, appliances, clothing, furniture, and other products. Dividing inventory into pools can be critical because of the different inflation rates associated with various goods and because, if a particular pool is depleted, the taxpayer loses the right to use the lower prices associated with past layers. An important exception permits taxpayers with average annual gross receipts of $5 million or less for the current and two preceding tax years to use the **simplified LIFO method**.[39] The simplified LIFO method uses a single LIFO pool, thereby avoiding problems with multiple pools.

EXAMPLE I11-19 ▶

In 2001 King Department Store changes its inventory method from FIFO to LIFO. Because King's gross receipts have never exceeded $5 million, the simplified LIFO method is available. King's year-end inventories under FIFO are as follows:

2000	$100,000
2001	$130,000

Assume the 2000 price index is 120% and the 2001 index is 125%. King must convert its 2001 inventory to 2000 prices.

$$\frac{120\%}{125\%} \times \$130{,}000 = \$124{,}800$$

A base period inventory of $100,000 is established. The increase in inventory (the 2001 layer) is valued at 2001 prices.

Base inventory (2000)	$100,000
Plus: 2001 layer [(125% ÷ 120%) × ($124,800 − $100,000)]	25,833
2001 ending inventory	$125,833

Assume the 2002 inventory valued under FIFO is $136,000 and the 2002 price index is 130%. The 2002 inventory is converted to 2000 prices.

---

[37] Reg. Sec. 1.472-2(e).
[38] Sec. 472(f).
[39] Sec. 474(c).

$$\frac{120\%}{130\%} \times \$136,000 = \$125,538$$

The 2002 increase in inventory (the 2002 layer) is valued at 2002 prices.

Base inventory (2000)	$100,000
2001 layer	25,833
2002 layer	800[a]
2002 ending inventory	$126,633

[a] [(130% ÷ 120%) × ($125,538 − $124,800)].

ADDITIONAL COMMENT

For tax purposes the lower of cost or market method must ordinarily be applied to each separate inventory item, but for financial accounting purposes it can be applied using an aggregate approach.

LOWER OF COST OR MARKET METHOD. Inventory may be valued at the **lower of cost or market.** This option is available to all taxpayers other than those who determine cost using the LIFO method.[40] The term *market* refers to replacement cost. On the date an inventory is valued, the replacement cost of each item in the inventory is compared with its cost. The lower figure is used as the inventory value. The lower of cost or market method must ordinarily be applied to each separate item in the inventory.

Recall the *Thor Power Tool,* case (discussed earlier in this chapter) in which the Supreme Court distinguished market value from expected selling price. **Market value** is the price at which the taxpayer can replace the goods in question. Replacement cost is used in the lower of cost or market determination. Obsolete or other slow-moving inventory can be written down below replacement cost only if the selling price has been reduced.

CYCLE INVENTORY VALUATION. Computer technology, including bar codes and software developments, enables businesses to maintain real-time perpetual inventory records. Many businesses, especially those with multiple locations, do not attempt to count all inventory items on the last day of the taxable period. Instead they count inventory following a scheduled cycle. At year-end, businesses adjust quantities shown in perpetual records for shrinkage since the most recent physical count utilizing estimates based on past experiences. The IRS challenged this practice unsuccessfully arguing that the adjustments failed the "all events" test which requires that amounts must be determined with reasonable accuracy.[41] In midst of the litigation, Congress specifically permitted the method in instances where "the taxpayer makes proper adjustment to such inventories and its estimation method [for] actual shrinkage."[42]

WHAT WOULD YOU DO IN THIS SITUATION?

INVENTORY VALUATION

Jack is a new tax client. He says he and his previous accountant did not get along very well. Jack owns an automobile dealership with sales of $12 million. He has provided you with most of the information you need to prepare his tax return, but he has not yet given you the year-end inventory value. You have completed much of the work on his return, but cannot complete it without the inventory figure. You have called Jack three times about the inventory. Each time he has interrupted, and asked you what his tax liability will be at alternative inventory levels. What problem do you see?

---

[40] Reg. Secs. 1.471-2(b) and (c).
[41] *Wal-Mart Stores Inc. v. CIR,* 82 AFTR 2d 5601, 98-2 USTC ¶50,645 (8th Cir., 1998), *Dayton Hudson Corp. v. CIR,* 82 AFTR 2d 5610, 98-2 USTC ¶50,644 (8th Cir., 1998), and *Kroger Co.,* 1997 RIA T.C. Memo ¶97,002, 73 TCM 1637.
[42] Sec. 471(b).

SPECIAL ACCOUNTING METHODS

The term *method of accounting* is used to include not only overall methods of accounting (i.e., cash, accrual, and hybrid) but also the accounting treatment of specific items. Special rules have been established for two types of transactions that cover long periods of time. One rule applies to installment sales (a sale in which final payment is not received until a subsequent tax year) and a separate set of rules applies to long-term contracts (construction and similar contracts that are not completed in the same year they are started). These special rules permit taxpayers to report income from this type of transaction when they have the wherewithal to pay the tax (i.e., the year in which payment is received).

LONG-TERM CONTRACTS

OBJECTIVE 4
Determine the amount of income to be reported from a long-term contract

Long-term contracts include building, installation, construction, or manufacturing contracts that are not completed in the same tax year in which they began.[43] A manufacturing contract is long-term only if the contract involves the manufacture of either a unique item not normally carried in finished goods inventory or items that normally require more than 12 calendar months to complete. Contracts for services (architectural, accounting, legal, and so on) do not qualify for long-term contract treatment.[44]

EXAMPLE I11-20 ▶ Diamond Corporation manufactures two types of airplanes: small, general aviation planes that require approximately six months to complete and large jet aircrafts sold to airlines that require two years to complete. Diamond maintains an inventory of the small planes but manufactures the large planes to contract specification. Diamond can use long-term contract accounting only for the large planes. Assume Diamond also offers aircraft design assistance to the government and others who seek such services. The long-term contract method of accounting is not available for such services. ◀

HISTORICAL NOTE
The use of the completed contract method was severely restricted in the Tax Reform Act of 1986 because Congress found that several large corporations, particularly those with large defense contracts, had significant deferred taxes attributable to this method. Many of these companies had extremely low or negative tax rates for several years.

The accounting method selected by a taxpayer must be used for all long-term contracts in the same trade or business.[45] In general, the income and expenses associated with long-term contracts may be accounted for by using either the **percentage of completion method** or the **modified percentage of completion method**. In limited instances (explained below), taxpayers may use the **completed contract method**. Under the percentage of completion method, income from a project is reported in installments as the work progresses. Under the completed contract method, income from a project is recognized upon completion of the contract. The modified percentage of completion method is a hybrid that combines two methods (discussed below). Alternatively, taxpayers may use any other accounting method (e.g., the accrual method) that clearly reflects income.

ADDITIONAL COMMENT
In general, a construction contract must involve what has historically been thought of as construction which includes erecting buildings, building dams, roads, and power plants.

COSTS SUBJECT TO LONG-TERM CONTRACT RULES. Direct contract costs are subject to the long-term contract rules. Labor, materials, and overhead costs must be allocated to the contract and accounted for accordingly. Thus, under the completed contract method, such costs are capitalized and deducted from revenue in the year the contract is completed. Selling, marketing and advertising expenses, expenses for unsuccessful bids and proposals, and research and development costs not associated with a specific contract may be deducted currently.

In general, administrative overhead must be allocated to long-term contracts. (See the earlier list of overhead items that must be included in inventory.) This is not required of taxpayers (other than homebuilders) using the completed contract method, but as noted below, the use of the completed contract method is limited.

As previously mentioned, interest must be capitalized if the property being produced is real property, long-lived property, or property requiring more than two years (one year in

---

[43] Reg. Sec. 1.451-3(b).
[44] Rev. Proc. 71-21, 1971-2 C.B. 549, does establish rules for service contracts that extend into the year following the receipt of payment. These rules are discussed in Chapter I3.
[45] Reg. Sec. 1.451-3(a)(1).

the case of property costing more than $1 million) to produce. Interest costs directly attributable to a contract and those that could have been avoided if contract costs had not been incurred must be allocated to long-term contracts.

COMPLETED CONTRACT METHOD. Under the completed contract method of accounting, income from a contract is reported in the taxable year in which the contract is completed. This is true without regard to whether the contract price is collected in advance, upon completion of the contract, or in installments. Costs associated with the contract are accumulated in a work-in-progress account and deducted upon completion. Several courts are in conflict with regard to determining when a contract is completed. Some courts have required total completion and acceptance of the contract.[46] Other courts have held the contract to have been completed when the only work remaining consists of correcting minor defects or furnishing incidental parts.[47]

The use of the completed contract method may only be used in two limited circumstances. First, the method can be used by smaller companies (those whose average gross receipts for the three preceding tax years is $10 million or less) for construction contracts that are expected to take two years or less to complete and second, for home construction contracts.[48] It cannot be used by larger companies for manufacturing, or for other long-term contracts other than construction or for construction contracts expected to last longer than two years.

> **KEY POINT**
> In general, taxpayers with long-term contracts must compute income under the percentage of completion method for contracts entered into after July 10, 1989.

PERCENTAGE OF COMPLETION METHOD. Under the percentage of completion method of reporting income, the taxpayer reports a percentage of the gross income from a long-term contract based on the portion of work that has been completed. The portion of the total contract price reported in a given year is determined by multiplying the total contract price by the percentage of work completed in the year. The percentage is determined by dividing current year costs by the expected total costs.

> **KEY POINT**
> After a taxpayer has adopted an accounting method for long-term contracts, he or she must continue to use that method unless permission to change methods is granted.

MODIFIED PERCENTAGE OF COMPLETION METHOD. At the beginning of a contract, it is difficult to estimate total costs. For this reason, taxpayers may elect to defer reporting any income from a contract until they have incurred at least 10% of the estimated total cost.[49] This is called the modified percentage of completion method. Under this method, if a contract has just been started as of the end of the year, the taxpayer does not have to estimate the profit on the contract during that year. The next year the taxpayer will report profit on all work that has been completed, including work done during the first year. Of course, this assumes that at least 10% of the work has been completed as of the end of the taxable year. If more than 10% of the costs are incurred during the first year, the modified percentage of completion method is identical to the regular percentage of completion method.

The completed contract method, the percentage of completion method, and the modified percentage of completion method are compared in Example I11-21.

EXAMPLE I11-21 ▶ In 2001, a contractor enters into a contract to construct a bridge for $1,400,000. At the outset, the contractor estimates that it will cost $1,200,000 to build the bridge. Actual costs in 2001 are $540,000 (45% of the $1,200,000 total estimated costs). Actual costs in 2002 are less than expected and amount to $600,000. The profits reported in both years of the contract are illustrated below.

	2001	2002
Completed contract		
Revenue	0	$1,400,000
Costs incurred	0	(1,140,000)
Gross profit	0	$ 260,000

---

[46] E. E. Black Limited v. Alsup, 45 AFTR 1345, 54-1 USTC ¶9340 (9th Cir., 1954), and Thompson-King-Tate, Inc. v. U.S., 8 AFTR 2d 5920, 62-1 USTC ¶9116 (6th Cir., 1961).
[47] Ehret-Day Co., 2 T.C. 25 (1943), and Nathan Wohlfeld, 1958 PH T.C. Memo ¶58,128, 17 TCM 677.
[48] Sec. 460(e).
[49] Sec. 460(a).

Percentage of completion		
Revenue	$630,000[a]	$770,000[b]
Costs incurred	(540,000)	(600,000)
Gross profit	$ 90,000	$170,000

[a] 540,000/1,200,000 × $1,400,000 = $630,000.
[b] $1,400,000 − $630,000 = $770,000.

In Example I11-21, the modified percentage of completion method results in the same income being reported each year as the percentage of completion method because more than 10% of the estimated costs were incurred during the first year. Note that the completed contract method defers reporting income until the contract is completed, causing all income from the project to be reported in a single year. Thus, the tax is deferred but the taxpayer may end up being taxed at higher rates. As noted, the completed contract is available only for home construction contracts and to certain smaller contractors for projects of two years or less.

LOOK-BACK INTEREST. Certain contracts (or portions of a contract) accounted for under either the regular or modified percentage of completion method are subject to a **look-back interest** adjustment. When a contract is completed, a computation is made to determine whether the tax paid each year during the contract is more or less than the tax that would have been paid if the actual total cost of the contract had been used rather than the estimated cost.[50] Interest is paid on any additional tax that would have been paid. The taxpayer receives interest on any additional tax that was paid.

Look-back interest is applicable only to contracts completed more than two years after the commencement date. Furthermore, look-back interest is applicable only if the contract price equals or exceeds either 1% of the taxpayer's average gross receipts for the three taxable years preceding the taxable year the contract was entered into or $1 million.[51]

Taxpayers may elect a "de minimis" exception to the "look-back" interest computation. If elected, the exception is applicable to all contracts completed within a year, and the election to use the exception can be revoked only with IRS approval. Under the exception, if income reported each year on a contract is within 10% of the recomputed "look-back income," no interest computation is made for the contract. Whether reported income is within 10% of recomputed income is determined separately for each completed contract.

EXAMPLE I11-22 ▶ The contractor in Example I11-21 is exempt from the look-back rule because the contract is completed within two years after the commencement date. On the other hand, if the contract took more than two years to complete, interest would be owed on the underpaid taxes for the first and subsequent contract years. The underreported income for the first year would be $33,158 [($260,000 profit × $540,000 first year's costs ÷ $1,140,000 total costs) − $90,000 first year reported income]. Assuming a 35% tax bracket, the underpaid tax for the first year is $11,605. Upon completion of the contract, interest would be paid on this amount and underpaid taxes for other years. Even if elected, the "de-minimis" exception would be inapplicable as the reported income in the first year of the contract ($90,000) is not within 10% of the income that would have been reported if actual costs had been used in the computation ($123,158 = $33,158 + $90,000). ◀

INSTALLMENT SALES METHOD

OBJECTIVE 5

Compute the gain to be reported from an installment sale

In general, the gain or loss from the sale of property is reported in the year the property is sold. If the sales proceeds are collected in years after the sale, the taxpayer may find it difficult to pay the tax on the entire amount of the gain in the year of sale. To reduce the burden, the tax law permits taxpayers to spread the gain from installment sales over the collection period. The installment method is applicable only to gains and is used to report income from an installment transaction unless the taxpayer elects not to use the install-

---

[50] Sec. 460(b)(3).   [51] Sec. 460(b)(3).

11-18 Individuals ▼ Chapter 11

KEY POINT
The installment sales method allows either a cash or an accrual method taxpayer to spread the gain from the sale of property over the period during which payments are received.

ment method. An **installment sale** is any disposition of property where at least one payment is received after the close of the taxable year in which the disposition occurs. The installment method is *not* applicable to sales:

► inventory, or
► marketable securities[52]

COMPUTATIONS UNDER SEC. 453. Income under the installment sales method is computed as follows:

SELF-STUDY QUESTION
A taxpayer sells 100 shares of Ford Motor Company stock for a gain of $800 on December 30, 2000. The taxpayer received the proceeds from the sale from the stockbroker on January 5, 2001. Can the taxpayer use the installment sales method?

ANSWER
No, the method is not applicable to sales of publicly traded property.

TYPICAL MISCONCEPTION
The selling price is sometimes confused with the contract price.

STEP 1: Compute the gross profit from the sale.

Selling price	$xx,xxx
Minus: Adjusted basis	(x,xxx)
Selling expenses	(x,xxx)
Depreciation recapture[53]	(x,xxx)
Gross profit	$ x,xxx

STEP 2: Determine the contract price.

Contract price (greater of the gross profit from above or the selling price reduced by any existing mortgage assumed or acquired by the purchaser) $xx,xxx

STEP 3: Compute the gross profit percentage.

$$\text{Gross profit percentage} = \frac{\text{Gross profit}}{\text{Contract price}} = xx\%$$

STEP 4: Compute the gain to be reported in the year of sale.

Collections of principal received during year (exclusive of interest)	$xx,xxx
Plus: Excess mortgage (if any)[a]	x,xxx
Total $xx,xxx	
Times: Gross profit percentage	× xx%
Net gain recognized in year of sale	$ x,xxx
Plus: Depreciation recapture	x,xxx
Gain reported in year of sale	$ x,xxx

ADDITIONAL COMMENT
On the sale of a capital asset a taxpayer might elect not to use the installment sales method and report the entire gain in the year of sale if he or she has capital losses that could be used to offset the gain.

STEP 5: Compute the gain to be reported in subsequent years.

Collections of principal received	$ x,xxx
Times: Gross profit percent	× xx%
Gain reported in each of the subsequent years	$ x,xxx

[a] Mortgage − Basis − Selling expense − Depreciation recapture = Excess mortgage.

Note that depreciation recapture (see Chapter I13) must be reported in the year of the sale even if no payment is received.

EXAMPLE I11-23 ► Gina, a cash basis taxpayer, sells equipment for $200,000. The equipment originally cost $70,000, and $10,000 of MACRS depreciation has been deducted before the sale. The $10,000 of depreciation must be recaptured as ordinary income under Sec. 1245. The buyer assumes the existing mortgage of $50,000, pays $10,000 down, and agrees to pay $10,000 per year for 14 years plus interest at a rate acceptable to the IRS. Selling expenses are $13,000. Using the steps listed above, calculations are made as follows:

---

[52] Sec. 453(b)(2) and (k).

[53] For a discussion of depreciation recapture, see Chapter I13.

STEP 1: Compute the gross profit from the sale.

	Selling price	$200,000
Minus:	Adjusted basis	(60,000)
	Selling expenses	(13,000)
	Depreciation recapture	(10,000)
	Gross profit	$117,000

STEP 2: Determine the contract price.

Greater of gross profit of $117,000 or selling price minus mortgage assumed by purchaser ($150,000 5 $200,000 2 $50,000) — $150,000

STEP 3: Compute the gross profit percentage.

$$\text{Gross profit percentage} = \frac{\text{Gross profit (\$117,000)}}{\text{Contract price (\$150,000)}} = 78\%$$

STEP 4: Compute the gain to be reported in the year of sale.

	Principal received during year	$ 10,000
Plus:	Excess mortgage	0
	Total amount realized	$ 10,000
	Times: Gross profit percentage	
	Gross profit	$ 7,800
Plus:	Depreciation recapture	10,000
	Gain reported in year of sale	$ 17,800

STEP 5: Compute the gain to be reported in subsequent years.

Principal received	$ 10,000
Times: Gross profit percentage	
Gain reported in each subsequent year	$ 7,800

Thus, the total gain reported is $127,000 [$17,800 + ($7,800 × 14)]. This is equal to the gross profit of $117,000 (which is the amount of Sec. 1231 gain reported on the sale) plus the $10,000 of depreciation recapture). As a cash basis taxpayer Gina will report the interest income as it is collected. See Figure I11-1 at the end of this chapter which illustrates this computation on Form 6252, Installment Sale Income. ◀

REAL-WORLD EXAMPLE

When an installment obligation is assigned as collateral for a loan, the transaction is treated as a disposition of the obligation. Rev. Rul. 65-185, 1965-2 C.B. 153.

DISPOSITION OF INSTALLMENT OBLIGATIONS. A taxpayer who sells property on the installment basis may decide not to hold the obligation until maturity. For example, the holder may sell the obligation to a financial institution for the purpose of raising cash. Alternatively, the holder may not be able to collect the full amount of the installments because of the inability of the buyer to make payments. Thus, the holder must determine the adjusted basis of the obligation in order to compute the gain or loss realized on the disposition. The adjusted basis of an installment obligation is equal to the face amount of the obligation reduced by the gross profit that would be realized if the holder collects the face amount of the obligation. In general, this means the adjusted basis of an obligation is equal to

$$\text{Face amount} \times (100\% - \text{Gross profit percentage})$$

EXAMPLE I11-24 ▶ Assume the same facts as in Example I11-23 except that Gina immediately sells a single $10,000 installment to a bank for $9,700. Gina reports a gain of $7,500 computed as follows:

	Selling price	$9,700
Minus:	Adjusted basis of installment	(2,200)[a]
	Recognized gain	$7,500

[a] $10,000 face amount × (100% − 78% gross profit percentage) = $2,200

Gina would have reported a gain of $7,800 had she decided not to sell the installment but to collect the face amount. Because the obligation is discounted by $300 ($10,000 − $9,700), the reported gain is reduced by $300. If the installment had not been sold immediately, the bank would probably also pay to Gina an amount for the accrued interest. In such a situation Gina would report the gain from the sale and the accrued interest as income. ◄

EXAMPLE I11-25 ▶ Assume that Gina in Example I11-24 is unable to collect the final $10,000 installment because the individual who purchases the property declares bankruptcy. Gina would be entitled to a bad debt deduction of $2,200, the basis of the installment. Gina does not receive a bad debt deduction for the accrued interest because the interest has not been included in her gross income. ◄

KEY POINT

A donor of property does not normally recognize gain, but a gift of certain installment obligations causes the recognition of gain.

Certain dispositions of installment obligations, such as gifts, are taxable events.[54] The main objective of this rule is to prevent income from being shifted from one taxpayer to another. Thus, if a corporation distributes an installment obligation as a dividend or if a father gives his daughter an installment obligation, gain or loss is recognized. In general, the gain or loss recognized is equal to the difference between the FMV of the obligation and its adjusted basis. In the case of a gift, the gain recognized is equal to the difference between the face of the obligation and its adjusted basis. However, certain exceptions to this rule exist. Transfers to controlled corporations under Sec. 351, certain corporate reorganizations and liquidations, transfers on the taxpayer's death, transfers incident to divorce, distributions by partnerships, and contributions of capital to a partnership are exceptions to this rule. In these cases, the recipients of the obligations report income when the installments are collected.

REPOSSESSIONS OF PROPERTY SOLD ON THE INSTALLMENT BASIS. In general, the repossession of property sold on the installment basis is a taxable event. The gain or loss recognized is generally equal to the difference between the value of the repossessed property (reduced by any costs incurred as a result of the repossession) and the adjusted basis of any remaining installment obligations.

EXAMPLE I11-26 ▶ Yuji sells stock of a non–publicly traded corporation with a $7,000 adjusted basis for $10,000. Yuji receives a $1,000 down payment, and the balance of $9,000 is due the following year. In the year of the sale Yuji reports a capital gain of $300 (0.30 × $1,000) under the installment method of accounting. Yuji is unable to collect the $9,000 note, and after incurring legal fees of $500, he repossesses the stock. When Yuji repossesses the stock it is worth $8,700. The adjusted basis of the note is $6,300 (0.70 × $9,000). Yuji must report a capital gain of $1,900 ($8,700 − $500 − $6,300). The basis of the stock to Yuji is its FMV at the time it is repossessed ($8,700). ◄

The amount of gain recognized from the repossession of real property is limited to the lesser of (1) the gross profit in the remaining installments reduced by the costs incurred as a result of the repossession or (2) the cash and FMV of other property received from the buyer in excess of the gain previously recognized.[55] In the case of the repossession of either real or personal property, the gain or loss retains the same character as the gain or loss on the original sale.

EXAMPLE I11-27 ▶ Assume the same facts as in Example I11-26, except that the property sold is land. Yuji reports a capital gain of $700, which is the lesser of $2,200 [(0.30 × $9,000) − $500] or $700 ($1,000 − $300). The basis of the land is $7,500 [$9,000 − (0.30 × $9,000) unrealized profit + $700 gain previously recognized + $500 legal fees]. ◄

INSTALLMENT SALES FOR MORE THAN $150,000. Special rules apply to nondealers who sell property for more than $150,000. The special rules do not apply to sales of personal use property, to sales of property used or produced in the trade or business of farming, or to sales of timeshares or residential lots.

First, if the taxpayer borrows funds using the installment obligations as security, the amount borrowed is treated as a payment received on the installment obligation.[56] This

---

[54] Sec. 453B(a).
[55] Sec. 1038.
[56] Sec. 453A(d).

prevents the taxpayer from using the installment method to defer tax and yet obtain cash by borrowing against the installment obligation. Second, if the installment method is used, interest must be paid to the government on the deferred tax.[57] This rule, however, applies only to deferred principal payments over $5 million.[58]

INSTALLMENT SALES BETWEEN RELATED PERSONS. Installment sales between related persons are subject to the same rules as other installment sales except when the property is resold by the related purchaser. The primary purpose of the resale rule is to prevent the original owner from deferring gain recognition by selling the property to a related person who, in turn, resells the property.

Sec 453(e) requires the first seller to treat amounts received by the related person (second seller) as having been personally received. Thus, the first seller would be required to report the gain in the year (or years) in which proceeds are received by the second seller. This acceleration provision is applicable only if the resale takes place within two years of the initial sale. For purposes of Sec. 453(e), the term *related person* includes a spouse, children, grandchildren, and parents. Controlled corporations, partnerships, estates, and trusts are also covered.

> **KEY POINT**
> Installment sales between related parties cannot be used to defer the recognition of gain by the original owner when the related purchaser receives cash.

DEFERRED PAYMENT SALES

The installment sale rules are not applicable to all sales involving future payments. The installment method cannot be used when the sale of property produces a loss. Also a taxpayer can elect out of the installment method when a sale results in a gain. The manner in which these transactions are reported depends on the taxpayer's accounting method. For accrual method taxpayers, the total *amount receivable* from the buyer (exclusive of interest) is treated as part of the amount realized. Thus, the entire gain or loss is reported in the year of sale. For cash method taxpayers, the FMV of the installment obligation is treated as part of the amount realized in the year of sale. The amount realized, however, cannot be considered to be less than the FMV of the property sold minus any other consideration received (e.g., cash).[59]

> **EXAMPLE I11-28**
> USA Corporation, an accrual method taxpayer, sells land for $100,000. USA receives $50,000 down and a $50,000 note payable in 12 months plus 14% interest. Assume the basis of the land is $80,000 and that it is a capital asset. Because of the buyer's poor credit, the value of the note is only $45,000. USA affirmatively elects not to report the installment sale on the installment method. USA reports a capital gain of $20,000 ($100,000 − $80,000). If USA collects the face of the note at maturity, no additional gain or loss is recognized. If USA sells the note for $45,000, a $5,000 capital loss is recognized.

> **EXAMPLE I11-29**
> Assume the same facts as in Example I11-28, except that USA is a cash method taxpayer. If the FMV of the land is $100,000 (the stated selling price), the treatment of the transaction is exactly the same as it is using the accrual method. If the FMV of the land is assumed to be $95,000 (cash received plus FMV of the note received), USA recognizes a $15,000 ($95,000 − $80,000) capital gain in the year of the sale. If USA collects the face of the note at maturity, $5,000 of ordinary income is recognized. If USA sells the note for $45,000, no gain or loss is recognized.

> **ADDITIONAL COMMENT** *skip*
> A contingent payment sale is a sale or other disposition of property in which the aggregate selling price cannot be determined by the close of the tax year in which the sale took place.

INDETERMINATE MARKET VALUE. In certain transactions, the value of obligations received cannot be determined (e.g., a mineral interest is sold for an amount equal to 10% of the value of future production). Under the Regulations, the value of obligations with an **indeterminate market value** is assumed to be no lower than the value of the property sold less the value of other property received.[60] Hence, if the value of property sold is determinable, the recognized gain equals the excess of the value of the property sold over its basis. On occasion, however, neither the value of the obligation received nor the value of property sold can be determined.

Temporary regulations specify how these types of transactions are to be treated.[61] The basic rules relating to special accounting methods are summarized in Topic Review I11-3.

---

[57] The interest computation is described in Sec. 453A(c).
[58] Sec. 453A(b)(2)(B).
[59] Temp. Reg. Sec. 15A.453-1(d)(2)(ii)(A).
[60] Reg. Sec. 1.453-1(d)(3)(iii).
[61] Temp. Reg. Sec. 15A.453-1(c).

11-22 Individuals ▼ Chapter 11

Topic Review I11-3

Special Accounting Methods

LONG-TERM CONTRACTS

▶ Long-term contracts include building, installation, construction, or manufacturing contracts that are not completed in the same tax year in which they are entered into. A manufacturing contract is long-term only if the contract involves the manufacture of either a unique item not normally carried in inventory or an item that normally requires more than 12 calendar months to complete.

▶ Long-term contracts may be reported under the regular or the modified percentage of completion method. Under both methods income is reported as work is completed, except that under the modified percentage of completion method no income is reported until at least 10% of the work is completed.

▶ The completed contract method is available only for home construction contracts, for construction contracts expected to take two years or less to complete, and for use by smaller companies (those whose average gross receipts for the three preceding tax years are $10 million or less).

INSTALLMENT METHOD

▶ Under the installment method gain is reported as the sales proceeds are collected. The installment method is generally not available for sales of inventory or publicly traded property. Furthermore, the method is available only for gains.

▶ Gain is reported as sales proceeds are collected. However, both depreciation recapture and any mortgage in excess of basis must be reported in the year of sale. Gain recognition is also accelerated in certain situations if the seller borrows against the installment obligation or if a related buyer resells the property within two years.

IMPUTED INTEREST

OBJECTIVE 6

Compute the amount of imputed interest in a transaction

KEY POINT

Imputed interest is important because it alters the amount of gain on the sale and causes an interest expense deduction for the buyer and interest income for the seller.

TYPICAL MISCONCEPTION

Some people mistakenly assumed that the imputed interest rules do not apply if the property is sold for a loss.

Before the enactment of Sec. 1274 and the amendment of Sec. 483, property could be sold on an installment basis in a contract providing for little or no interest. Instead of charging interest, the seller charged a higher price for the property. If the property sold was a capital asset, the result of the arrangement was to reduce the interest income reported by the seller and to increase the amount of favorably taxed capital gain. Sections 483 and 1274 now *impute* interest in a deferred payment contract where no interest or a low rate of interest is provided. Another impact of the **imputed interest rules** on sellers is to reallocate payments received between interest (which is fully taxable) and principal (only the gain portion of which is taxable). The result is often an increase in the income reported in early years and a decrease in later years. The rules are generally applicable to both buyers and sellers. In certain instances, the buyer may want interest to be imputed in order to increase his interest deduction in early years.

The following transactions are exempt from the imputed interest rules:

▶ Debt subject to original issue discount provisions (basically bonds issued for less than face where amortization of the discount is required under Sec. 1274, see Chapter I5)

▶ Sales of property for $3,000 or less

▶ Any sales where all of the payments are due within six months

▶ Sales of patents to the extent the payment is contingent on the use or disposition of the patent

▶ Certain carrying charges for personal property or educational services covered by Sec. 163(b) when the interest charge cannot be ascertained

▶ Charges for the purchase of personal-use property (purchaser only)[62]

---

[62] Sec. 483(d). The rule lowers the basis of a personal-use asset in order to increase any gain on the future sale of the property.

EXAMPLE I11-30 ▶ Joan is involved in several transactions during the current year. No interest is stated on any of the transactions. The terms of the transactions and the applicability of the imputed interest rules are summarized below:

Transaction	Imputation of Interest
Purchases furniture costing $8,000 for her residence. Full price is payable within four months.	Not applicable because property is for personal use. Also, all payments are due within six months.
Sells a boat for $2,000. Payment is due in a year.	Not applicable because sales price is not more than $3,000.
Sells land for $100,000. Payment is due in five years.	Interest must be imputed because no exception is applicable.
Purchases a newly issued bond for $650 (face of $1,000).	Not applicable because transaction is subject to the original isue discount rules in Sec. 1274. Also, the price is not more than $3,000. ◀

IMPUTED INTEREST COMPUTATION

In order to avoid the imputation of interest, the stated interest rate must be at least equal to 100% of the applicable federal rate (110% of the applicable federal rate in the case of sale–lease back arrangements). Lower rates are specified for two types of transactions: (1) If the stated principal amount for qualified debt obligations that are issued in exchange for property under Sec. 1274A does not exceed $2,800,000, the interest rate is limited to 9% compounded semiannually; and (2) the interest rate is limited to 6% compounded semiannually in the case of sales of land between related individuals (unless the sales price exceeds $500,000).

The **applicable federal rate** is determined monthly and is based on the rate paid by the federal government on borrowed funds. The rate varies with the terms of the loan. Loans are divided into short-term (not over three years), mid-term (over three years but not over nine years), and long-term (over nine years).

EXAMPLE I11-31 ▶ Kasi sells land for $100,000 to Bill, an unrelated person. The sales price is to be paid to Kasi at the end of five years in a single installment with no stated interest. Kasi paid $60,000 for the land. Assume the current federal rate is 10%. Because the amount of the stated principal is less than $2,800,000, interest is imputed at a rate not to exceed 9% compounded semiannually. As a result, the effective rate is 9.2025% (9% compounded semiannually), and the present value factor is .64393 (1 ÷ 1.092025^5). Thus, the present value of the final payment is $64,393 (0.64393 × $100,000). Kasi reports a $4,393 ($64,393 − $60,000) gain on the sale of the land and $35,607 ($100,000 − $64,393) interest income instead of a $40,000 gain and no interest income. The buyer is treated as incurring $35,607 in interest and has a $64,393 basis in the land. Whether the interest is deductible depends on a variety of other factors (see Chapter I7). ◀

ACCRUAL OF INTEREST

ADDITIONAL COMMENT
The $2,000,000 limit on the stated principal is subject to inflation adjustments for calendar years beginning after 1989.

Is imputed interest reported under the cash or the accrual method? In other words, is imputed interest reported when it accrues or when it is paid? In general, imputed interest is reported as it accrues. However, there are some major exceptions, as follows:

▶ Sales of personal residences
▶ Most sales of farms for $1 million or less
▶ Sales involving aggregate payments of $250,000 or less
▶ Sales of land between related persons unless the sales price exceeds $500,000[63]

In addition, if the borrower and lender jointly elect, and if the stated principal does not exceed $2,000,000, accrual of interest is not required. This election is not available if the

---
[63] Sec. 1274(c)(4).

lender is an accrual method taxpayer or a dealer with respect to the property sold or exchanged.[64]

EXAMPLE I11-32 ▶ Assume the same facts as in Example I11-31. Because the aggregate payments do not exceed $250,000, the transaction is exempt from the requirement that interest be accrued. As a result, Kasi reports interest income and Bill reports interest expense in the fifth year when the final payment is made on the transaction. Under the installment method, $4,393 gain on the sale is recognized in the fifth year. ◀

GIFT, SHAREHOLDER, AND OTHER LOANS

Imputed interest rules are not limited to installment transactions. Sec. 7872 applies to transactions involving related parties whose taxes are lowered as a result of low interest or interest-free loans. These situations include

▶ *Gift loans.* For example, parents in higher tax brackets may loan money to their children without charging interest. If the children invest the borrowed money and are taxed on the income at a lower rate, the family has reduced its total tax liability in the absence of imputed interest rules.

▶ *Corporation shareholder loans.* In the absence of imputed interest rules, taxes may be saved by a corporation that makes an interest-free loan to a shareholder. If the corporation had invested the money and paid out the resulting income as a dividend, it would have first been taxed on the profit. By making the interest-free loan, the corporation could, in the absence of imputed interest rules, reduce its taxes by avoiding the otherwise taxable income.

▶ *Compensation-related loans.* Employers may loan money to employees without charging interest. Without the requirement to impute interest, this could produce tax savings if the employer was unable to deduct additional compensation because of the reasonable compensation limitation or if the employee was unable to deduct the interest, say, because the borrowed funds were used to purchase personal use property.

▶ *Other tax avoidance loans.* Any other low-interest or interest-free loan that produces tax savings may be subject to the imputed interest rules. For example, a club may offer its members a choice of either paying dues or making a large refundable deposit. The club can invest the money and earn interest perhaps equal to the dues. In the absence of imputed interest rules, the member avoids taxes by not having to report the income that would have been earned if the member personally invested the funds. The club is indifferent between the alternatives because both the dues and the interest income are taxable.

In general, interest is imputed on the above loans by applying the applicable federal rates discussed earlier. The resulting interest income is taxable to the lender. Whether the interest expense is deductible by the borrower is determined by applying the usual interest deduction rules (see Chapter I7).

The imputation process involves a second step. The lender is treated as returning the imputed interest to the borrower. This is necessary because the interest was not actually paid. For example, in the case of a gift loan, the lender is treated as giving the imputed interest back to the borrower. This would not normally have income tax implications, but if the imputed interest were large enough, it could result in a gift tax. In the case of the corporation-shareholder loan, the corporation is treated as paying the imputed interest back to the shareholder as a dividend. Typically, this does not increase the corporation's

---

[64] Sec. 1274A(c).

tax, but it results in the recognition of dividend income to the shareholder. For compensation-related loans, the second step is to impute compensation paid by the employer and received by the employee. The compensation is taxable to the employee and, if reasonable in amount, is deductible by the employer.

There are several important exceptions intended to limit the application of imputed interest in situations where tax avoidance may be immaterial:

- Interest is not imputed on gift loans between two individuals totaling $10,000 or less, except when the borrowed funds are used to purchase income-producing property.
- If the gift loans between two individuals total $100,000 or less, the imputed interest is limited to the borrower's "net investment income" as defined by Sec. 163(d)(4). (See Chapter I7 for a discussion of net investment income). If the net investment income is $1,000 or less, it is not necessary to impute interest.
- Interest is not imputed on compensation-related and corporate shareholder loans totaling $10,000 or less.

These exceptions do not apply when tax avoidance is one of the principal purposes of the loans.

EXAMPLE I11-33 ▶ Linda made interest-free gift loans to each of her four children: Andy, Bob, Cathy, and Donna. Andy borrowed $9,000 to purchase an automobile. Bob borrowed $25,000 to buy stock. Bob's net investment income is $800. Cathy also borrowed $25,000 to buy stock, but her net investment income is $1,100. Donna borrowed $120,000 to purchase a residence, and her net investment income is $500. Tax avoidance is not a motive for any of the loans. Imputation of interest is not required for the loans to Andy or Bob. The loan to Andy is exempt because the amount is less than $10,000, and the loan to Bob is exempt because his net investment income is under $1,000. Imputation of interest is required for the loans to Cathy and Donna. In the case of Cathy, the amount of imputed interest is limited to her net investment income of $1,100. The imputed interest for Donna, however, is not limited to her net investment income because the amount of the loan is over $100,000. ◀

The imputed interest rules are summarized in Topic Review I11-4.

Topic Review I11-4

Imputed Interest

PURPOSE

The imputed interest rules are intended to prevent taxpayers from reducing their taxes by charging little or no interest on installment payment transactions and loans.

APPLIES TO

In most cases applies to both parties, the debtor and the creditor. The result is to impute interest income to the lender and interest expense to the borrower. Several exceptions exempt small transactions from imputed interest. For example, sales involving payments of $3,000 or less are generally exempt as are loans of less than $10,000.

RATE

Interest is imputed at the applicable federal rate if the stated interest rate is lower. The applicable federal rate is the rate the federal government pays on borrowed funds and is determined monthly. In general, the current rate at the time of the transaction is used throughout the term of the loan. The rate varies with the term of the loan. Loans are divided into short-term (not over three years), mid-term (over three years but not over nine years), and long-term (over nine years).

CHANGE IN ACCOUNTING METHODS

In general, a new taxpayer elects an accounting method by simply applying the selected method when computing income for the initial tax return.[65] If a particular item does not occur in the first year, the accounting method is elected the first year in which the item occurs.

EXAMPLE I11-34 ▶

OBJECTIVE 7

Determine the tax treatment of duplications and omissions that result from changes of accounting methods

Gordon opened a beauty shop several years ago. Because he had no inventory, no inventory method was selected. In the current year, Gordon expanded his business to offer beauty supplies to his customers. Gordon can delay electing the FIFO inventory method until the current year, the first year in which he has an inventory. ◀

In general, once an accounting method is chosen, it cannot be changed without IRS approval. There are a few exceptions. For example, taxpayers may adopt the LIFO inventory method without prior IRS approval.[66] Once such methods are adopted, however, they cannot be changed without IRS approval.

As previously noted, the term *accounting method* indicates not only the overall accounting method used by the taxpayer, but also the treatment of any item of income or deduction.[67] A change of accounting methods should not be confused with the correction of an error. Errors include mathematical mistakes, posting errors, deductions of the wrong amount for an expense, omission of an item of taxable income, or incorrect computation of a credit. An error is normally corrected by filing an amended return for the tax year or years in which the error occurs. In general, there is a three-year statute of limitations on the correction of errors. After three years, the tax year is closed and changes cannot be made.[68]

Taxpayers wishing to change accounting methods must file Form 3115 with the IRS in Washington, DC on or before the due date of the tax return including extensions. A duplicate copy of Form 3115 must be filed with the tax return for the year. A taxpayer who amends the original income tax return within six months of its due date may request a change of accounting methods with the amended return.[69]

In general, taxpayers initiate a change in accounting methods from an incorrect to a correct method are exempt from penalty and from retroactive application of the new reporting method. Although changes in accounting methods require IRS approval, the IRS states that approval will automatically be granted for a wide variety of changes if the taxpayer meets specific requirements that include proper filing of both Form 3115 and the current year's tax return, agreeing to take into account the Sec. 481(a) adjustment (as described below), not being under examination, and not having changed the same method of accounting within the last four years.[70] Although the IRS retains the right to again change any method of accounting adopted under these procedures it states that such changes will not be retroactive except in rare or unusual circumstances. Examples of situations where retroactive application may occur include misstatement or omission of material facts, change in material facts, and changes in applicable authority.

REAL-WORLD EXAMPLE

The write-down of soil aggregate to its market value by a paving company was a change in accounting method rather than the mere correction of an accounting error. The soil aggregate was included in its election to adopt the LIFO inventory method, and the use of this method required that the soil aggregate be included at cost regardless of market value. *First National Bank of Gainesville, Trustee,* 88 T.C. 1069 (1987).

REAL-WORLD EXAMPLE

An extension of time to file the application for change of accounting method was granted because of the death of the accountant in charge of filing the application. Rev. Rul. 79-417, 1979-2 C.B. 202.

AMOUNT OF CHANGE

A change in accounting methods usually results in duplications or omissions of items of income or expense.

EXAMPLE I11-35 ▶

Bonnie, a practicing CPA, has been reporting income using the cash method. In the current year, Bonnie obtains permission to change to the accrual method. At the beginning of the cur-

---

[65] Reg. Sec. 1.446-1(e)(1).
[66] A taxpayer may adopt LIFO by merely determining year-end inventory by that method and attaching Form 970 to the tax return for the year (Reg. Sec. 1.472-3(a)).
[67] Reg. Sec. 1.446-1(e)(2)(ii)(b).
[68] Exceptions are applicable when the taxpayer omits from the return an amount of income that is over 25% of the gross income stated on the return (6 years) or where fraud occurs (no limitation).

[69] The extension will be granted if the taxpayer (a) files the original income tax return on time, (b) uses the new method of accounting on the amended return, (c) attaches the application to change methods to the amended return, (d) files a copy of the application with the national office no later than when the original is filed with the amended return, and (e) writes at the top of the application "FILED PURSUANT TO §301.9100-2." Rev. Proc. 99-49, I.R.B. 1999-52, 725.
[70] 1997-2 C.B. 455.

rent year, Bonnie has $80,000 of receivables that have not been reported in prior years. The receivables were not reported in prior years because they were not collected. Although the receivables are collected in the current year, they are not taxable because, under the accrual method, Bonnie now reports income as it is earned and the income is not earned in the current year. In this case, the income was earned in prior years.

Also, assume Bonnie has accounts payable of $15,000 at the beginning of the current year. The accounts payable were not deducted in prior years because the expenses had not been paid. Furthermore, the accounts payable are not deductible in the current year even if they are paid. This is because the expenses were incurred in prior years. Obviously, the IRS expects to collect the tax on the $80,000 of receivables, and Bonnie is entitled to deduct the $15,000 of payables. In the absence of any special provision, both amounts would be omitted from the computation of taxable income. If the change is from the accrual method to the cash method, both amounts would be reported twice (in the year prior to the change because they had accrued and in the year of the change because they are collected or paid). Thus, a special provision is also needed for duplications.

REPORTING THE AMOUNT OF THE CHANGE

The net amount of the change must be taken into account.[71] A positive adjustment is added to income, whereas a negative adjustment is subtracted from income. This adjustment can, of course, be made in the year of the change. If the amount is small, recognizing the full amount of the net adjustment in the year of the change is both simple and equitable. Reporting a large positive adjustment in one year could push the taxpayer into a higher marginal tax bracket and result in a significant tax increase. Because the extra income is due to changing accounting methods, not increasing cash flows, the taxpayer may not have the wherewithal to pay the additional tax.

As a result, there are alternative methods that may be used to report the amount of the change. The methods that are available depend on whether the change is voluntary (a change that is initiated by the taxpayer) or involuntary (a change from an unacceptable to an acceptable method that is required by the IRS).

In the case of an involuntary change, several alternative methods are available to the IRS.[72]

In the case of voluntary changes, taxpayers must agree to report the adjustment over a period not to exceed four years. When the amount of the adjustment is $25,000 or less, taxpayers may elect to include the full amount in the current year.[73] In the case of a change spread over four years, equal portions of the change are reported in each of the four years beginning with the year of the change.

EXAMPLE I11-36 ▶ In 2001 Diana obtains permission to change from the accrual to the cash method of reporting income. The change results in a $30,000 negative adjustment to income. The IRS requires Diana to spread the adjustment over four years. As a result, she may deduct $7,500 in 2001 and $7,500 per year through year 2004. Note that because the amount of the adjustment is spread over the current and future years, the tax savings associated with the deduction are deferred. ◀

In general, the amount of the adjustment cannot be spread over a period longer than the method being changed has been used.

OBTAINING IRS CONSENT

REAL-WORLD EXAMPLE
A pipeline company was required to capitalize reconditioning costs on its natural gas pipelines instead of expensing these costs. *Mountain Fuel Supply Co. v. U.S.*, 28 AFTR 2d 71-5833, 71-2 USTC ¶9681 (10th Cir., 1971).

Most changes in accounting method require IRS approval. Sec. 446(e) states that a taxpayer changing the method of accounting "on the basis of which he regularly computes his income in keeping his books" must obtain consent before computing taxable income under the new method. This implies that a taxpayer who has been computing taxable income on a method other than that used in computing book income does not need approval to conform the computation of taxable income to the method regularly used on the taxpayer's books. This conclusion is supported by Sec. 441(a), which requires that the same method of accounting be used in computing taxable income as is used in keeping the

---

[71] Sec. 481.
[72] Sec. 481(a), (b)(1), (b)(2), and (c).
[73] Rev. Rul. 97-37, 1997-2 C.B. 455.

books. The alternative might be to require the taxpayer to conform his or her book accounting method with the tax accounting method. The answer may well be in how one defines "books." The IRS has ruled that a reconciliation of taxable income with accounting income was a part of the taxpayer's auxiliary records.[74] Hence, the taxpayer was using the same accounting method for book and tax reporting. As a result, a taxpayer who changes the method of accounting used for financial reporting may not be required to change the method of accounting used for tax reporting as long as financial income and book income are reconciled.

TAX PLANNING CONSIDERATIONS

ACCOUNTING PERIODS

KEY POINT
C corporations and estates have more flexibility than S corporations and partnerships in the selection of a tax year.

New corporations often routinely adopt a calendar year. Consideration should be given, however, to adopting a tax year for the initial reporting period that ends before the amount of taxable income exceeds the amount that is taxed at the lowest tax rates (e.g., when taxable income is $50,000 or less). This is less critical for a corporation suffering losses because the NOLs may be carried forward for a 20-year period.

In the past, taxpayers were able to defer income by selecting different tax years for partners and partnerships or S corporations and shareholders. Current law limits this opportunity. Nevertheless, partnerships and S corporations may adopt a tax year that differs from that of their owners if that year qualifies as a natural business year (i.e., at least 25% of revenues occur during the last two months of the year). Furthermore, deferral is possible in the case of estates, because they are not subject to similar restrictions on the choice of tax years.

ACCOUNTING METHODS

KEY POINT
The election to use an accounting method is made by filing the first tax return on the basis of that method.

New businesses should consider the tax implications of electing an accounting method. For example, taxpayers may benefit from the LIFO inventory method because LIFO typically reduces gross profit and defers the payment of taxes during inflationary periods. Similarly, service companies usually choose the cash method of reporting income because it permits receivables to be reported when collected rather than when the income is earned. Choosing an accounting method requires an understanding not only of the available accounting methods, but also the nature of the taxpayer's business. Will a specific election be to the tax advantage of the taxpayer? LIFO inventory is often recommended because, during inflationary periods, it tends to reduce inventory values and increase the cost of goods sold. In certain industries, such as the computer industry, however, costs are declining, and LIFO actually may result in a higher inventory value.

In other industries, inventories may fluctuate widely from one year to the next because of changing demand, shortages of materials, strikes, or other causes. LIFO layers may have to be depleted simply to continue business operations. This can cause one of two things to happen: (1) incurring extra recordkeeping costs of LIFO for little or no benefit because the inventories are depleted before they produce significant tax deferrals or (2) depleting low-cost layers from years past, resulting in a substantial increase in taxable income in the year of occurrence.

INSTALLMENT SALES

Taxpayers normally choose the installment method of reporting income from casual sales of property. By spreading the gain from a sale over more than one tax year, the taxpayer normally remains in lower tax brackets and defers the tax. A taxpayer with low current taxable income may elect not to use the installment sale method in order to take advantage of the lower current tax rates.

---

[74] Rev. Rul. 58-601, 1958-2 C.B. 81.

Form 6252 — Installment Sale Income (2000)

Form 6252
Department of the Treasury
Internal Revenue Service

Installment Sale Income
► See separate instructions. ► Attach to your tax return.
► Use a separate form for each sale or other disposition of property on the installment method.

OMB No. 1545-0228
2000
Attachment Sequence No. **79**

Name(s) shown on return: **Gina Green**
Identifying number: **123-45-6789**

1. Description of property ► **Equipment**
2a. Date acquired (month, day, year) ► **7/01/98**   b. Date sold (month, day, year) ► **8/31/00**
3. Was the property sold to a related party after May 14, 1980? See instructions. If "No," skip line 4 .... ☐ Yes ☒ No
4. Was the property you sold to a related party a marketable security? If "Yes," complete Part III. If "No," complete Part III for the year of sale and the 2 years after the year of sale .... ☐ Yes ☒ No

Part I — Gross Profit and Contract Price. Complete this part for the year of sale only.

Line	Description	Amount	Total
5	Selling price including mortgages and other debts. Do not include interest whether stated or unstated		200,000
6	Mortgages and other debts the buyer assumed or took the property subject to, but not new mortgages the buyer got from a bank or other source	50,000	
7	Subtract line 6 from line 5	150,000	
8	Cost or other basis of property sold	70,000	
9	Depreciation allowed or allowable	10,000	
10	Adjusted basis. Subtract line 9 from line 8	60,000	
11	Commissions and other expenses of sale	13,000	
12	Income recapture from Form 4797, Part III. See instructions	10,000	
13	Add lines 10, 11, and 12		83,000
14	Subtract line 13 from line 5. If zero or less, stop here. Do not complete the rest of this form		117,000
15	If the property described on line 1 above was your main home, enter the amount of your excluded gain. Otherwise, enter -0-. See instructions		
16	**Gross profit.** Subtract line 15 from line 14		117,000
17	Subtract line 13 from line 6. If zero or less, enter -0-		-0-
18	**Contract price.** Add line 7 and line 17		150,000

Part II — Installment Sale Income.
Complete this part for the year of sale **and** any year you receive a payment or have certain debts you must treat as a payment on installment obligations.

19	Gross profit percentage. Divide line 16 by line 18. For years after the year of sale, see instructions	78%
20	**For year of sale only:** Enter amount from line 17 above; otherwise, enter -0-	-0-
21	Payments received during year. See instructions. Do not include interest, whether stated or unstated	10,000
22	Add lines 20 and 21	10,000
23	Payments received in prior years. See instructions. Do not include interest, whether stated or unstated	
24	**Installment sale income.** Multiply line 22 by line 19	7,800
25	Part of line 24 that is ordinary income under recapture rules. See instructions	10,000
26	Subtract line 25 from line 24. Enter here and on Schedule D or Form 4797. See instructions	17,800

Part III — Related Party Installment Sale Income.
Do not complete if you received the final payment this tax year.

27. Name, address, and taxpayer identifying number of related party _____
28. Did the related party resell or dispose of the property ("second disposition") during this tax year? ☐ Yes ☐ No
29. If the answer to question 28 is "Yes," complete lines 30 through 37 below unless one of the following conditions is met. Check the box that applies.
   a. ☐ The second disposition was more than 2 years after the first disposition (other than dispositions of marketable securities). If this box is checked, enter the date of disposition (month, day, year) ► __/__/__
   b. ☐ The first disposition was a sale or exchange of stock to the issuing corporation.
   c. ☐ The second disposition was an involuntary conversion and the threat of conversion occurred after the first disposition.
   d. ☐ The second disposition occurred after the death of the original seller or buyer.
   e. ☐ It can be established to the satisfaction of the Internal Revenue Service that tax avoidance was not a principal purpose for either of the dispositions. If this box is checked, attach an explanation. See instructions.

30. Selling price of property sold by related party
31. Enter contract price from line 18 for year of first sale
32. Enter the **smaller** of line 30 or line 31
33. Total payments received by the end of your 2000 tax year. See instructions
34. Subtract line 33 from line 32. If zero or less, enter -0-
35. Multiply line 34 by the gross profit percentage on line 19 for year of first sale
36. Part of line 35 that is ordinary income under recapture rules. See instructions
37. Subtract line 36 from line 35. Enter here and on Schedule D or Form 4797. See instructions

For Paperwork Reduction Act Notice, see back of form.   Cat. No. 13601R   Form **6252** (2000)

FIGURE I11-1 ► REPORTING INSTALLMENT SALE INCOME ON FORM 6252 (BASED ON EXAMPLE I11-23)

Compliance and Procedural Considerations

REPORTING INSTALLMENT SALES ON FORM 6252

Form 6252 (Installment Sale Income) is used to report income under the installment method from sales of real property and casual sales of personal property other than inventory. Figure I11-1 illustrates how an installment sale transaction is reported. The illustration is based on Example I11-23. A separate Form 6252 is normally used for each installment sale. Form 6252 is used in the year of the sale and any year in which the taxpayer receives a payment from the sale. Taxpayers who do not wish to use the installment method may report the transaction on either Schedule D or on Form 4797.

PROCEDURES FOR CHANGING TO LIFO

The LIFO method may be adopted in the initial year that inventories are maintained by merely using the method in that year. In addition, advance approval (e.g., within 180 days following the start of the year) from the IRS is not required for an adoption of the LIFO method in the initial year that inventories are maintained on the LIFO method. However, Form 970 should be filed along with the taxpayer's tax return for the year of the change.[75] The application must include an analysis of the beginning and ending inventories. Further, if a taxpayer is changing to the LIFO method from another method (e.g., FIFO), advance approval from the IRS is also not required. Form 970 must be filed with the return and the beginning inventory for LIFO purposes is the same as under the former inventory method.[76]

If the former inventory is valued based on the lower of cost or market (LCM) method, an adjustment is required to restate the beginning inventory to cost because the LCM method cannot be used under LIFO. Generally, the beginning LIFO inventory is the same as the closing inventory for the prior year, except for the required restatement of previous writedowns to market. This adjustment to the beginning inventory can be spread ratably over the year of the change and the next two years.[77]

EXAMPLE I11-37 ▶ Delaware Corporation elects to change to the LIFO inventory method for 2001. In 2000 Delaware's inventories are valued using the LCM method based on the FIFO cost-flow assumption. The FIFO cost for the ending inventory in 2000 is $50,000, and its LCM amount is $35,000. The initial inventory for 2001 under LIFO must be restated to its cost, or $50,000. The $15,000 ($50,000 cost − $35,000 LCM value) difference can be included in taxable income over the current year and next two years. $5,000 is added to taxable income in 2001, 2002, and 2003. ◀

Problem Materials

DISCUSSION QUESTIONS

I11-1 Do accounting rules determine the amount of income to be reported by a taxpayer?

I11-2 How does a taxpayer's tax accounting method affect the amount of tax paid?

I11-3 Most individuals use the calendar year as their tax year. What requirement, if any, in the tax law causes this?

I11-4 Why is it desirable for a new taxpayer to select an appropriate tax year?

---

[75] An acceptable election is considered to have been made even if Form 970 is not filed as long as all of the information required by Reg. Sec. 1.472-3(a) is provided by the taxpayer.

[76] Reg. Sec. 1.472-2(c).

[77] Sec. 472(d).

I11-5 What restrictions apply to partnerships selecting a tax year?

I11-6 Does a similar restriction apply to S corporations? Explain.

I11-7 How could the 52-53 week year prove to be beneficial to taxpayers? Explain.

I11-8 Under what circumstances can an individual taxpayer change tax years without IRS approval?

I11-9 Is there any instance in which a change in tax years is required? Explain.

I11-10 a. In what situations will a tax year cover a period of less than 12 months?
b. Under what conditions is a taxpayer required to annualize income?
c. Does annualizing income increase or decrease the taxpayer's tax liability? Explain.

I11-11 When is a final tax return due for an individual who uses a calendar year and who dies during the year?

I11-12 a. Is it correct to say that businesses with inventories must use the accrual method?
b. What other restrictions apply to taxpayers who are choosing an overall tax accounting method?
c. Why is the cash method usually preferred to the accrual method?

I11-13 a. Does the term *method of accounting* refer only to overall methods of accounting? Explain.
b. Does a taxpayer's accounting method affect the total amount of income reported over an extended time period?
c. How can the use of an accounting method affect the total amount of tax paid over time?

I11-14 a. When are expenses deductible by a cash method taxpayer?
b. Are the rules that determine when interest is deductible by a cash method taxpayer the same as for other expenses?
c. Is a cash method taxpayer subject to the same rules for depreciable assets as accrual method taxpayers? –yes

I11-15 Who may use the completed contract method of reporting income from long-term contracts?

I11-16 When is a cash method taxpayer allowed to deduct deposits?

I11-17 What constitutes a payment in determining when a cash-basis taxpayer is entitled to deduct an expense?

I11-18 What is meant by economic performance?

I11-19 What conditions must be met if the economic performance test is to be waived for an accrual-method taxpayer?

I11-20 When is an accrual method taxpayer permitted to deduct estimated expenses? Explain.

I11-21 What is the significance of the *Thor Power Tool Co.* decision?

I11-22 a. How are overhead costs treated in determining a manufacturing company's inventory?
b. Do retailers have a similar rule?
c. Are these rules the same as for financial accounting? If not, explain.

I11-23 What transactions are subject to the long-term contract method of reporting?

I11-24 a. What conditions must be met in order to use the installment method?
b. Why would a taxpayer elect not to use the installment method?

I11-25 What is the impact of having the entire gain on an installment sale consist of ordinary income from depreciation recapture?

I11-26 What impact does the gifting of an installment obligation have on the donor?

I11-27 What treatment is given to an installment sale involving related people?

I11-28 What is the primary impact of the imputed interest rules on installment sales?

I11-29 What changes in accounting method can be made without IRS approval?

I11-30 Can the IRS require a taxpayer to change accounting methods?

I11-31 Explain the purpose of the four-year method used in computing the tax resulting from a net adjustment due to a change in accounting methods.

I11-32 If a taxpayer changes the method of accounting used for financial reporting purposes, must the taxpayer also change his or her method of accounting for tax purposes?

ISSUE IDENTIFICATION QUESTIONS

I11-33 Judy's Cars, Inc. sells collectible automobiles to consumers. She employs the specific identification inventory valuation method. Prices are negotiated by Judy and individual customers. Judy accepts trade-ins when she sells an automobile. Judy negotiates the allowance for trade with the customer. Occasionally, Judy finds that it can take two or three years to sell a given automobile. Judy now has four automobiles that she has held for over two years. She expects to eventually sell those automobiles, but expects that they will sell for less than their original cost. What tax issues should Judy consider?

I11-34 Lana operates a real estate appraisal service business in a small town serving local lenders. After noting that lenders must pay to bring in a surveyor from out of town, she completes

I11-35 John owns a small farm on a lake. A local developer offers John $400,000 cash for his farm. The developer believes John's farm will be very attractive to home buyers because it is on a lake. After John turns down the initial offer, the developer offers to pay John $250,000 plus an amount equal to 10% of the selling price for the homes that are developed and sold. Identify the tax issues John should consider if he accepts the offer.

a course and obtains a surveyor's license that enables her to provide this service also. She now provides both services as a proprietor. What tax issues should Lana consider?

I11-36 Lee is starting a small lawn service. On the advice of his accountant, Lee has formed a corporation and made an S corporation election. The accountant has asked Lee to consider electing a fiscal year ending on the last day in February. The accountant pointed out that Lee's business is likely to slow down in the winter. Also, the accountant indicated that the February year end would permit the accountant to do Lee's accounting work after the busy season in accounting is over. What tax issues should Lee consider?

PROBLEMS

I11-37 *Allowable Taxable Year.* For each of the following cases, indicate whether the taxpayer has selected an allowable tax year in an initial year. If the year selected is not acceptable, indicate what an acceptable year would be.
a. A corporation selects a January 15 year-end.
b. A corporation selects a March 31 year-end.
c. A corporation selects a year that ends on the last Friday in March.
d. A partnership selects a year that ends on December 31 and has three equal partners whose years end on March 31, April 30, and June 30.
e. An S corporation selects a December 31 year-end.

I11-38 *Change in Accounting Period.* In which of the following instances is a taxpayer permitted to change accounting periods without IRS approval?
a. A calendar-year taxpayer who wishes to change to a year that ends on the last Friday in December.
b. ABC Partnership has filed its tax return using a fiscal-year ending on March 31 for over 40 years. The partnership wishes to change to a calendar year-end that coincides with its partners' year-end.
c. Iowa Corporation, a newly acquired subsidiary, wishes to change its year-end to coincide with its parent.

I11-39 *Annualization.* Each of the following cases involves a taxable year of less than 12 months. In which situations is annualization required?
a. A new corporation formed in September elects a calendar year.
b. A calendar-year individual dies on June 15.
c. Jean, who has been using a calendar year, marries Hank, a fiscal-year taxpayer. Soon after the marriage, Jean changes her tax year to coincide with her husband's tax year.
d. A calendar-year corporation liquidates on April 20.

I11-40 *Short Period Return.* Lavanya, a single taxpayer, is a practicing accountant. She obtains permission to change her tax year from the calendar year to a year ending July 31. Her practice income for the seven months ending July 31 is $40,000. In addition, Lavanya has $3,000 of interest income and $6,308 of itemized deductions. She is entitled to one exemption. What is her tax for the short period?

I11-41 *Cash Basis Expenses.* How much of the following expenses are currently deductible by a cash basis taxpayer?
a. Medical prescriptions costing $20 paid by credit card (medical expenses already exceed the 7.5% of AGI floor).
b. Prepaid interest (not related to points) of $200 on a residential loan.
c. Taxpayer borrows $300 from the bank to make a charitable contribution. The $300 is paid to the charitable organization before the end of the tax year.
d. Taxpayer gives a note to his church indicating an intent to contribute $300.
e. A calendar-year individual mails a check for $200 to his church on December 31. The check is postmarked December 31 and clears the bank on January 4.

I11-42 *Economic Performance.* In light of the economic performance requirement, how much is deductible by the following accrual-basis corporate taxpayers in 2001?

a. Camp Corporation sells products with a one-year warranty. In 2001 Camp estimates that the warranty costs on products sold during the year will amount to $80,000. In 2001 Camp performs $38,000 of warranty work on products sold during 2000 and $36,000 of warranty work on products sold in 2001.
b. Data Corporation agrees to pay $10,000 per year for two years to a software developer. The developer has completed all work on the software and delivers the product to Data before the end of 2001.
c. In 2001 Palm Corporation pays $5,000 to a supplier to guarantee delivery of raw materials. The $5,000 is refundable if Palm decides not to acquire the materials.
d. In 2001 North Corporation pays a $1,000 security deposit on space it rents for a new office. In addition, North pays 2001 rent of $18,000. The security deposit is refundable if the property is returned in good condition.

I11-43 *Manufacturing Inventory.* Which of the following costs must be included in inventory by a manufacturing company?
a. Raw materials
b. Advertising
c. Payroll taxes for factory employees
d. Research and experimental costs
e. Factory insurance
f. Repairs to factory equipment
g. Factory utility costs
h. Factory rent

I11-44 *Single Pool LIFO.* Prime Corporation begins operations in late 2001. Prime decides to use the single pool LIFO method. Year-end inventories under FIFO are as follows:

2001	$110,000
2002	134,000
2003	125,000

The price index for 2001 is 130%; for 2002, 134%; and 2003, 140%. What are 2002 and 2003 inventories?

I11-45 *Installment Sale.* In 2001 Ace Construction Company sells a used crane to Go Construction Company. The crane, which cost $87,000 in 1993, sells for $80,000. Ace has deducted the entire cost of the crane under MACRS depreciation. Ace receives $20,000 down and is to receive $20,000 per year plus 10% interest for four years. Under the Sec. 1245 depreciation recapture rules, the entire gain is taxable as ordinary income. There is no applicable installment obligation. How much of the gain is taxable in 2001? 2002?

I11-46 *Installment Sale.* In 2001 Fast Corporation sells land held as an investment. The land, which cost $87,000 in 1997, sells for $180,000. Fast incurs selling expenses of $12,000. The mortgage on the property at the time of the sale is $100,000. The buyer assumes the mortgage, pays $20,000 down, and agrees to pay $20,000 per year for three years plus interest at an acceptable rate to the IRS. How much of the gain is taxable in 2001? 2002?

I11-47 *Installment Sale Collections.* During 2001, Bear Corporation collects $240,000 of 2001 installment sales, $150,000 of 2000 installment sales, and $40,000 of 1999 installment sales. Actual 2001 sales total $450,000. The gross profit percentage is 32% for 2001, 33% for 2000, and 35% for 1999. What gross profit must Bear report in 2001?

I11-48 *Installment Sale.* On December 31, 2001, Dan sells unlisted stock with a cost of $14,000 for $20,000. Dan collects $5,000 down and is scheduled to receive $5,000 per year for three years plus interest at a rate acceptable to the IRS.
a. How much gain must Dan recognize in 2001? Assume Dan uses the installment method to report the gain.
b. In early January 2002, Dan sells the three installments for a total of $13,800. How much gain or loss must Dan recognize from the sale?

I11-49 *Repossession.* Liz sells for $50,000 stock not listed on any exchange having a $36,000 adjusted basis. Liz receives $10,000 down and a one-year interest-bearing note for the balance. Liz is unable to collect the balance, and after incurring $1,000 in legal fees, repossesses the stock. When Liz repossesses the stock, it is worth $49,000.
a. How much gain must Liz recognize in the year of the sale?
b. How much gain must Liz recognize when she repossesses the stock?

c. What is the basis of the stock after the repossession?
d. How would your answers to Parts b and c differ if the property sold were land instead of stock?
e. What would be the basis of the land?

I11-50 *Deferred Payment Sale.* Joe sells land with a $40,000 adjusted basis for $32,000. He incurs selling expenses of $3,000. The buyers pay $8,000 down and agree to pay him $8,000 per year for three years plus interest at a rate acceptable to the IRS. Because of the buyers' poor credit rating, the installments are worth only $20,000 ($7,200, $6,600, and $6,200, respectively).
a. What gain or loss is reported in the year of the sale? Assume Joe is an accrual method taxpayer.
b. How would the answer to Part a change if Joe had instead been a cash method taxpayer? Assume the land is worth $32,000.
c. How would your answer to Part a change if Joe had been a cash method taxpayer and the land were worth only $28,000?
d. What is the tax impact of collecting the installments in Parts a through c?

I11-51 *Imputed Interest.* On January 30, 2001, Amy sells land to Bob for a stated price of $200,000. The full $200,000 is payable on January 30, 2003. No interest is stated. Amy, a cash-method taxpayer, purchased the land in 1997 for $130,000.
a. How much interest income must be reported by Amy on the sale? Assume a 9% rate compounded semiannually. The present value factor is 0.83856.
b. In what year is the interest reported?
c. How much gain is reported by Amy on the sale?
d. In what year is the gain reported?
e. What is Bob's basis in the land?

I11-52 *Change of Accounting Method.* Dana owns a retail store and is a cash method taxpayer. She changes to the accrual method in 2002. Dana's business income for 2002 is $30,000 computed on the accrual method. Her books show the following:

	December 31, 2001	December 31, 2002
Accounts receivable	$ 6,000	$ 5,300
Accounts payable	15,200	11,800
Inventory	12,000	12,400

a. What adjustment is necessary to Dana's income?
b. How should Dana report the adjustment?

I11-53 *Required Payment.* BCD Partnership has, for many years, had a March 31 year end. The Partnership's net income for the fiscal year ended March 31, 2002 is $400,000. Because of its fiscal year, BCD has $100,000 on deposit with the IRS from 2001.
a. How much must BCD add to the deposit?
b. When must BCD make the addition?
c. Will the partners receive any credit for the deposit? That is, are they permitted to treat the amount as estimated payments?

I11-54 *Imputed Interest.* Lorenzo sells land to Jan, an unrelated person, for $500,000. Jan pays $200,000 down and agrees to pay the remaining $300,000 one year after the purchase. No interest is provided for in the contract of sale. Lorenzo had purchased the land for $400,000 several years earlier. Assume the applicable rate is 8% compounded semiannually and the relevant present value factor is 0.92456.
a. What is Jan's basis in the land?
b. How much interest income must Lorenzo report and when?
c. How much gain must Lorenzo report from the sale?
d. Is the installment method available to Lorenzo?

I11-55 *Imputed Interest.* Jane loans $80,000 to John, her son, to permit him to purchase a principal residence. The loan principal is secured by John's residence, but the agreement does not specify any interest. The applicable federal rate for the year is 8%. John's net investment income is $800.
a. How much interest is imputed on the loan each year?
b. Assume that the amount of the loan is $125,000. How much interest is imputed on the loan?

c. Is John allowed to deduct the imputed interest?
d. What other tax implications are there for the loan?

I11-56 *Long-Term Contract.* King Construction Company is engaged in a road construction contract to build a highway over a three-year period. King will receive $11,200,000 for building five miles of highway. King estimates that it will incur $10,000,000 of costs before the contract is completed. As of the end of the first year King incurred $3,000,000 of costs allocated to the contract.
a. How much income from the contract must King report during the first year?
b. Assume King incurs an additional $5,000,000 of costs during the second year. How much income is reported during that year?
c. Assume that King incurs an additional $2,500,000 of costs in the third and final year of the contract. How much does King report during the third year?
d. Will King receive or pay look-back interest? Explain.

TAX FORM/RETURN PREPARATION PROBLEM

I11-57 Barbara B. Kuhn (Social Security number 987-65-4321) purchases a fourplex on January 8, 1997 for $175,000. She allocates $25,000 of the cost to the land, and she deducts MACRS depreciation totaling $16,364. Barbara sells the fourplex on January 6, 2000, for $225,000. The buyer assumes the existing mortgage of $180,000, pays $15,000 down, and agrees to pay $15,000 per year for two years plus 12% interest. Barbara incurs selling expenses of $18,000. Complete Form 6252.

CASE STUDY PROBLEMS

I11-58 Lavonne just completed medical school and residency. She plans to open her medical practice soon. She is not familiar with the intricacies of accounting methods and periods. On advice of her attorney, she plans to form a professional corporation (a form of organization permitted under the laws of most states that does not have the usual limited liability found with business corporations, but is taxed as a corporation). She has asked you whether she should elect a fiscal year and whether she should use the cash or accrual method of reporting income. Discuss whether the options are available to her and the implications of available choices.

I11-59 Don owns an office building that he purchased several years ago. He purchased the building for $400,000, allocated $280,000 of the purchase price to the structure, and over the years properly deducted $110,000 of depreciation. The depreciation will have to be recaptured as ordinary income on the sale. There is a $90,000 mortgage on the property. Don has an offer to purchase the building from an individual who says he will pay $100,000 down and $100,000 per year for five years. There is no mention of interest. As the mortgage is nonassumable, Don will pay off the mortgage using most of the down payment. Don is age 61, and proceeds from the sale along with a pension from his employer will provide for his retirement. Don plans to retire next year. He currently has a 28% marginal tax rate. Discuss the tax implications of the sale. Is there anything Don can do to improve his situation?

I11-60 Troy Tools manufactures over one hundred different hand tools used by mechanics, carpenters, and plumbers. Troy's cost accounting system has always been very simple. The costs allocated to inventory have included only materials, direct labor, and factory overhead. Other overhead costs such as costs of the personnel department, purchasing, payroll, and computer services have never been treated as manufacturing overhead even though many of the activities of the departments relate to the manufacturing operations. You are preparing Troy's tax return for the first time and determine that the company is not following the uniform capitalization rules prescribed in the tax law. You have explained to the company's president that there is a problem, and she is reluctant to change accounting methods. She says allocating these costs to the many products the company makes will be a time-consuming and expensive process. She feels that the cost of determining the additional amounts to include in inventory under the uniform capitalization rules will probably be more than the additional tax that the company will pay. What is the appropriate way to handle this situation? (See the *Statements on Standards for Tax Services* section in Chapter I15 for a discussion of these issues.)

TAX RESEARCH PROBLEMS

I11-61 Eagle and Hill Corporations discuss the terms of a land sale in December 2001, and they agree to a price of $230,000. Eagle wants to use the installment sale method, but is not sure Hill is a reliable borrower. As a result, Eagle requires Hill to place the entire purchase price in escrow to be released in five yearly installments by the escrow agent. Is the installment method available to Eagle?

A partial list of research sources is

- Rev. Rul. 77-294, 1977-2 C.B. 173
- Rev. Rul. 79-91, 1979-1 C.B. 179
- *H. O. Williams v. U.S.*, 46 AFTR 1725, 55-1 USTC ¶9220 (5th Cir., 1955)

I11-62 Texas Corporation disassembles old automobiles for the purpose of reselling their components (i.e., different types of metals, plastics, rubber, and other materials). Texas sells some of the items for scrap, but must pay to dispose of environmentally hazardous plastics and rubber. At year-end, Texas Corporation has a difficult time determining the cost of the individual parts that are stacked in piles. In fact, it would be very expensive to even weigh some of the materials on hand. Texas has followed the practice of having two experienced employees estimate the weight of different stacks and then pricing them based on quotes found in trade journals. If Texas must pay to dispose of an item, it is assigned a value of zero. In other words, Texas does not value its inventory using standard FIFO or LIFO methods. Is such a practice acceptable?

A partial list of research sources is

- Reg. Secs. 1.471-2(a) and 1.471-3(d)
- *Morrie Chaitlen*, 1978 PH T.C. Memo ¶78,006, 37 TCM 17
- *Justus & Parker Co.*, 13 BTA 127 (1928)

I11-63 Apple Corporation has never been audited before the current year. An audit is now needed from a CPA because the company is in a rapid expansion period and is planning to issue stock to the public in a secondary offering. A CPA firm has been doing preliminary evaluations of the Apple Corporation's accounts and records. One major problem involves the valuation of inventory under GAAP. Apple Corporation has been valuing its inventory under the cost method and no write-downs have been made for obsolescence. A review of the inventory indicates that obsolescence and excess spare parts in the inventory are two major problems. The CPA states that for GAAP the company will be required to write down its inventory by 25% of its stated amount, or $100,000, and charge this amount against net income from operations for the current period. Otherwise, a "clean opinion" will not be rendered. The company controller asks your advice regarding the tax consequences from the obsolescence and spare parts inventory write-downs for the current year and the procedures for changing to the LCM method for tax purposes. Apple Corporation is on a calendar year, and the date of your contact with the company is December 1 of the current year.

A partial list of research sources is

- Secs. 446 and 471
- Reg. Secs. 1.446-1(e)(3), 1.471-2 and 1.471-4
- *American Liberty Pipe Line Co. v. CIR,*, 32 AFTR 1099, 44-2 USTC ¶9408 (5th Cir., 1944)
- *Thor Power Tool Co. v. CIR*, 43 AFTR 2d 79-362, 79-1 USTC ¶9139 (USSC, 1979)

CHAPTER 12

PROPERTY TRANSACTIONS: NONTAXABLE EXCHANGES

LEARNING OBJECTIVES
After studying this chapter, you should be able to

1. Understand the tax consequences arising from a like-kind exchange
2. Determine the basis of property received in a like-kind exchange
3. Determine whether gain from an involuntary conversion may be deferred
4. Determine the basis of replacement property in an involuntary conversion
5. Determine when a gain resulting from the sale of a principal residence is excluded

Chapter 12

CHAPTER OUTLINE

Like-Kind Exchanges...12-2
Involuntary Conversions...12-10
Sale of Principal Residence...12-16

Taxpayers who sell or exchange property for an amount greater or less than their basis in that property have a realized gain or loss on the sale or exchange. Almost any transfer of property is treated as a sale or other disposition (see Chapter I5). The realized gain or loss must be recognized unless a specific Code section provides for nonrecognition treatment. If the realized gain or loss is not recognized at the time of the transaction, the nonrecognized gain or loss may be deferred in some cases and excluded in others.

The general rules related to the computation of realized and recognized gains or losses are covered in Chapter I5. This chapter discusses three of the most common transactions that may result in *nonrecognition* of a realized gain or loss:

- Like-kind exchanges under Sec. 1031 (deferred gain or loss)
- Involuntary conversions under Sec. 1033 (deferred gain)
- Sales of a personal residence under Sec. 121 (excluded gain)

KEY POINT

The transactions examined in this chapter override the normal rule that provides for the recognition of realized gains and realized losses on property used in a business or held for investment.

Nonrecognition of gain treatment for like-kind exchanges, involuntary conversions, and the sale of a residence may be partially justified by the fact that taxpayers may lack the wherewithal to pay the tax despite the existence of a realized gain. For example, a taxpayer who realizes a gain due to an involuntary conversion of property (damage from fire, storm, etc.) may have to use the amount received to replace the converted property.

A typical requirement in a nontaxable exchange is that the taxpayer is required to maintain a continuing investment in comparable property (e.g., a building is exchanged for another building). In essence, a change in form rather than a change in substance occurs.

A transaction generally considered to be nontaxable may be taxable in part. In a like-kind exchange, for example, the taxpayer may also receive money or property that is not like–kind property. If non-like-kind property or money is received, the realized gain is taxable to the extent of the sum of the money and the fair market value (FMV) of the non–like-kind property received.[1]

LIKE-KIND EXCHANGES

OBJECTIVE 1

Understand the tax consequences arising from a like-kind exchange

"No personal property"

Section 1031(a) provides that "No gain or loss shall be recognized on the exchange of property held for productive use in a trade or business or for investment if such property is exchanged solely for property of like-kind which is to be held either for productive use in a trade or business or for investment."[2]

In a **like-kind exchange**, both the property transferred and the property received must be held either for productive use in the trade or business or for investment.

EXAMPLE I12-1 ▶ Tom owns land used in his trade or business. He exchanges the land for other land, which is to be held for investment. No gain or loss is recognized by Tom because he has exchanged property used in a trade or business for like-kind property to be held for investment. ◀

EXAMPLE I12-2 ▶ Dawn's automobile is held only for personal use. She exchanges the automobile, which has a $10,000 basis, for stock of AT&T with a $12,000 FMV. The stock will be held for investment. A $2,000 gain is recognized because the automobile is not used in Dawn's trade or business or held for investment. The exchange is not a like-kind exchange because neither personal-use assets nor stock qualify as like-kind property. ◀

REAL-WORLD EXAMPLE

An exchange or trade of professional football player contracts qualifies as a like-kind exchange. Rev. Rul. 71-137, 1971-1 C.B. 104.

Section 1031 is not an elective provision. If the exchange qualifies as a like-kind exchange, nonrecognition of gain or loss is mandatory. To qualify for like-kind exchange treatment, a direct exchange must occur and the property exchanged must be like-kind. A taxpayer who prefers to recognize a loss on an exchange must structure the transaction to avoid having the exchange qualify as a like-kind exchange.

ADDITIONAL COMMENT

The mandatory nonrecognition of loss under Sec. 1031 can be avoided by selling the old property in one transaction and buying the new property in a separate, unrelated transaction.

LIKE-KIND PROPERTY DEFINED

CHARACTER OF THE PROPERTY. To be a nontaxable exchange under Sec. 1031, the property exchanged must be like-kind. The Treasury Regulations specify that "the words

---

[1] Sec. 1031(b).

[2] Sec. 1031(a).

'like-kind' have reference to the nature or character of the property and not to its grade or quality."[3] Thus, exchanges of real property qualify even if the properties are dissimiliar.

EXAMPLE I12-3 ▶ Eric owns an apartment building held for investment. Eric exchanges the building for farmland to be used in his trade or business. The exchange is a like-kind exchange because both the building and the farmland are classified as real property and both properties are used either in business or held for investment. ◀

EXAMPLE I12-4 ▶ Trail Corporation exchanges improved real estate for unimproved real estate, both of which are held for investment. The exchange is a like-kind exchange.[4] ◀

ADDITIONAL COMMENT
Real property is often referred to as real estate.

LOCATION OF THE PROPERTY. Transfers of real property located in the U.S. and real property located outside the U.S. after July 9, 1989, are not like-kind exchanges. Exchanges of personal property predominantly used in the United States and personal property used outside of the United States that occur after June 8, 1997, are not like-kind exchanges. To determine where the property is predominantly used, the two-year period ending on the date the property is exchanged is analyzed. For property received, the location of predominant use is determined by analyzing the use during the two-year property after the property is received.

PROPERTY MUST BE THE SAME CLASS. An exchange is not a like-kind exchange when property of one class is exchanged for property of a different kind or class.[5] For example, if real property is exchanged for personal property (or vice versa), no like-kind exchange occurs.[6]

EXAMPLE I12-5 ▶ Gail exchanges an office building with a $400,000 adjusted basis for an airplane with a $580,000 FMV to be used in business. This is not a like-kind exchange because the office building is real property and the airplane is personal property. Gail must recognize a $180,000 ($580,000 − $400,000) gain. ◀

EXAMPLE I12-6 ▶ Gary exchanges a business truck for another truck to use in his business. This is an exchange of like-kind property. ◀

ADDITIONAL COMMENT
The rules in the Regulations dealing with exchanges of personal property are not interpreted as liberally as the rules relating to real property.

PROPERTY OF A LIKE CLASS. The Treasury Regulations provide that personal property of a **like class** meets the definition of *like-kind*.[7] Like class property is defined as depreciable tangible personal properties within the same General Asset Class or within the same Product Class.[8] Property within a General Asset Class consists of depreciable tangible personal property described in one of the asset classes provided in Rev. Proc. 87-56 for depreciation.[9] Some of the General Asset Classes are as follows:

- Office furniture, fixtures, and equipment (Asset Class 00.11)
- Information systems such as computers and peripheral equipment (Asset Class 00.12)
- Automobiles and taxis (Asset Class 00.22)
- Buses (Asset Class 00.23)
- Light general purpose trucks (Asset Class 00.231)
- Heavy general purpose trucks (Asset Class 00.242)
- Vessels, barges, tugs, and similar water-transportation equipment except those used in marine construction (Asset Class 00.28)

For purposes of the like-kind exchange provisions, a single property may not be classified in more than one General Asset Class or more than one Product Class. Furthermore, property in any General Asset Class may not be classified in a Product Class. A property's General Asset Class or Product Class is determined as of the exchange date.

---

[3] Reg. Sec. 1.1031(a)-1(b).
[4] *Ibid.*
[5] *Ibid.*
[6] Real property includes land and property attached to land in a relatively permanent manner. Personal property that is affixed to real property in a relatively permanent manner is a fixture and is considered part of the real property. Personal property is all property that is not real property or a fixture.
[7] Reg. Sec. 1.1031(a)-2.
[8] Reg. Sec. 1.1031(a)-2(b).
[9] 1987-2 C.B. 674.

EXAMPLE I12-7 ▶ Wint transfers a personal computer used in his trade or business for a printer to be used in his trade or business. The exchange is a like-kind exchange because both properties are in the same General Asset Class (00.12). ◀

EXAMPLE I12-8 ▶ Renee transfers an airplane (Asset Class 00.21) that she uses in her trade or business for a heavy general purpose truck to use in her trade or business. The properties are not of a like class because they are in different General Asset Classes. The heavy general purpose truck is in Asset Class 00.242. ◀

Example I12-8 is taken from the Treasury Regulations, which further state: "Because each of the properties is within a General Asset Class, the properties may not be classified within a Product Class. The airplane and heavy general purpose truck are also not of a like kind. Therefore, the exchange does not qualify for nonrecognition of gain or loss under Sec. 1031."[10]

If two properties are not within a General Asset Class, it still may be possible to be considered like-kind if the properties are within the same Product Class. Property in a Product Class consists of depreciable tangible personal property listed in a 4-digit product class in Division D of the *Standard Industrial Classification (SIC)* codes set forth in the *Standard Industrial Classification Manual*.[11] The Regulations state that an exchange of a grader for a scrapper is an exchange of properties of like class because neither property is in a General Asset Class and both properties are listed in the same Product Class (SIC code 3533).[12]

There are no like classes for intangible personal property, nondepreciable personal property, or personal property held for investment. To have a like-kind exchange of property held for investment, the property must be exchanged for like-kind property. To determine whether an exchange of intangible personal property is a like-kind exchange, one must consider the type of right involved as well as the underlying property to which the intangible property relates. An exchange of a copyright for a novel for a copyright on a different novel is a like-kind exchange, but the exchange of a copyright on a novel for a copyright on a song is not a like-kind exchange.[13]

ADDITIONAL COMMENT
An exchange can be a like-kind exchange for one party to the transaction but not qualify as a like-kind exchange for the other party.

NON–LIKE-KIND PROPERTY EXCHANGES. An exchange of inventory or securities does not qualify as a like-kind exchange.[14]

EXAMPLE I12-9 ▶ Antonio, a dealer in farm equipment, exchanges a new combine for other property in the same General Asset Class to be used in Antonio's trade or business. Because Antonio is a dealer, the new combine is inventory and the exchange does not qualify as a like-kind exchange. ◀

EXAMPLE I12-10 ▶ Nancy owns Able Corporation stock as an investment. Nancy exchanges the stock for antiques to be held as investments. This exchange is taxable because stock does not qualify as like-kind property. ◀

In most cases, to qualify as a like-kind exchange of personal property, the property must be nearly identical. For example, livestock of different sexes are not like-kind property.[15] An exchange of gold bullion held for investment for silver bullion held for investment is not a like-kind exchange. Silver and gold are intrinsically different metals and primarily are used in different ways.[16] Currency exchanges are not like-kind exchanges,[17] and the exchange of a partnership interest for an interest in another partnership is not a like-kind exchange.[18]

---

[10] Reg. Sec. 1.1031(a)-2(b)(7) Ex. 2.
[11] Reg. Sec. 1.1031(a)-2(b)(3).
[12] Reg. Sec. 1.1031(a)-2(b)(7) Ex. 3.
[13] Reg. Sec. 1.1031(a)-2(c)(1).
[14] Sec. 1031(a)(2). An exchange of stock is not a like-kind exchange. However, an exchange of stock is a nontaxable exchange if the exchange is related to a tax-free reorganization.
[15] Sec. 1031(e).
[16] Rev. Rul. 82-166, 1982-2 C.B. 190.
[17] Rev. Rul. 74-7, 1974-1 C.B. 198.
[18] Sec. 1031(a)(2).

EXCHANGE OF SECURITIES. The like-kind exchange rules do not apply to stocks, bonds, or notes.[19] However, Sec. 1036 provides that no gain or loss is recognized on the exchange of common stock for common stock or preferred stock for preferred stock in the same corporation. Common stock for preferred stock of the same corporation or any kind of stock in different corporations may not be exchanged tax-free. Sec. 1036 applies even if voting common stock is exchanged for nonvoting common stock of the same corporation. The nontaxable exchange of stock of the same corporation may be between two stockholders or a stockholder and the corporation.[20]

EXAMPLE I12-11 ▶ Kelly owns common stock of Best Corporation. Best issues class B common stock to Kelly in exchange for her common stock. No gain or loss is recognized because this is an exchange of common stock for common stock in the same corporation. ◀

EXAMPLE I12-12 ▶ Shirley owns 100 shares of Top Corporation common stock. The stock has a $40,000 adjusted basis and a $50,000 FMV. Bob owns 100 shares of Star Corporation common stock with a $50,000 FMV. If Shirley and Bob exchange their stock, the exchange is taxable, and Shirley has a $10,000 ($50,000 − $40,000) recognized gain. The exchange is neither a like-kind exchange nor an exchange of stock for stock of the same corporation. ◀

A DIRECT EXCHANGE MUST OCCUR

To qualify as a like-kind exchange, a direct exchange of property must occur.[21] Thus, the sale of property and the subsequent purchase of like-kind property does not qualify as a like-kind exchange unless the two transactions are interdependent.

EXAMPLE I12-13 ▶ Karen sells a lathe used in her business to Rashad for an amount greater than the lathe's adjusted basis. After the sale, Karen purchases another lathe from David. The gain is recognized because these two transactions do not qualify as an exchange of like-kind property. ◀

KEY POINT

Transfers of property in a three-party exchange must be part of a single, integrated plan. It is important that the taxpayers can show their intent to enter into a like-kind exchange even though contractual interdependence is not necessary to the finding of an exchange.

A sale and a subsequent purchase may be treated as an exchange if the two transactions are interdependent. The IRS indicates that a nontaxable exchange may exist when the taxpayer sells property to a dealer and then purchases like-kind property from the same dealer.[22]

THREE-PARTY EXCHANGES

The typical two-party exchange is not always practical. If both parties do not own like-kind property that meets each other's needs, a three-party exchange might be necessary. A three-party exchange is also useful when the taxpayer is willing to exchange property for like-kind property but is not willing to sell the property to a prospective buyer. The taxpayer's unwillingness to sell the property may be motivated by the desire to avoid an immediate tax on a gain resulting from the sale of the property. Therefore, the taxpayer may arrange to have the prospective buyer purchase property from a third party that fulfills the taxpayer's needs. The three-party exchange can be an effective way of allowing the taxpayer to consummate a like-kind exchange.

EXAMPLE I12-14 ▶ Kathy owns a farm in Nebraska, which Dick offers to purchase. Kathy is not willing to sell the farm but is willing to exchange the farm for an apartment complex in Arizona. The complex is available for sale. Dick purchases the apartment complex in Arizona from Allyson and transfers it to Kathy in exchange for Kathy's farm. The farm and the apartment complex each have a $900,000 FMV. For Kathy, the transaction qualifies as a like-kind exchange because it is a direct exchange of business real property (the farm) for investment real estate (the apartment complex). For Dick, the exchange is not a like-kind exchange. ◀

In the example above, the exchange is convenient for all the parties. However, it is not always this convenient to execute a three-party exchange. For example, Kathy may want

---

[19] Reg. Sec. 1.1031(a)-1(a)(1)(ii).
[20] Reg. Sec. 1.1036-1(a).
[21] Sec. 1031(a).
[22] Rev. Rul. 61-119, 1961-1 C.B. 395.

to own an apartment complex in Arizona, but the property she prefers may not be currently available. In this case, a nonsimultaneous exchange may occur.

NONSIMULTANEOUS EXCHANGE. As a result of the Tax Reform Act of 1984, a nonsimultaneous exchange is a like-kind exchange if the exchange is completed within a specified time period. The property to be received in the exchange must be identified within 45 days after the date of the transfer of the property relinquished in the exchange. The replacement property must be received within the earlier of 180 days after the date the taxpayer transfers the property relinquished in the exchange or the due date for filing a return (including extensions) for the year in which the transfer of the relinquished property occurs.[23]

> **ADDITIONAL COMMENT**
> The property to be received in the exchange can be identified as late as 45 days after the transfer of the property given up in the exchange.

EXAMPLE I12-15 ▶ On May 5, 2001, Joal transfers property to Lauren, who transfers cash to an escrow agent. The escrow agent is to purchase suitable like-kind property for Joal. Joal does not have actual or constructive receipt of the cash during the delayed period. To be a like-kind exchange for Joal, the suitable like-kind property must be identified by June 19, 2001 (45 days after the transfer) and Joal must receive the property by November 1, 2001 (180 days after the transfer). ◀

EXAMPLE I12-16 ▶ Assume the same facts as Example I12-15 except that the transfer by Joal occurs on November 10, 2001. To be a like-kind exchange for Joal, the suitable like-kind property must be identified by December 25, 2001 and Joal must receive the property by April 15, 2002 unless Joal files an automatic four-month extension for the filing of his return (i.e., the due date is extended until August 15, 2002). In such a case, the property must be received no later than 180 days following the transfer of the property relinquished in the exchange, or by May 8, 2002 (i.e., 180 days after November 10, 2001). ◀

RECEIPT OF BOOT

Taxpayers who want to exchange property do not always own property of equal value. To complete the exchange, non–like-kind property or money may be given or received. Cash and non–like-kind property constitute **boot**.

Gain is recognized to the extent of the boot received. However, the amount of recognized gain is limited to the amount of the taxpayer's realized gain.[24] In effect, the realized gain serves as a ceiling for the amount of the recognized gain. The receipt of boot as part of a nontaxable exchange does not cause a realized loss to be recognized.[25]

> **TYPICAL MISCONCEPTION**
> In calculating the amount of gain to be recognized when boot is received, it is important not to apply financial accounting principles, which use a proportionate approach.

EXAMPLE I12-17 ▶ Mario exchanges business equipment with a $50,000 adjusted basis for $10,000 cash and business equipment with a $65,000 FMV. The realized gain is $25,000 ($75,000 − $50,000). Because the $10,000 of boot received is less than the $25,000 of realized gain, the recognized gain is $10,000. ◀

EXAMPLE I12-18 ▶ Mary exchanges business equipment with a $70,000 adjusted basis for $20,000 cash and business equipment with a $65,000 FMV. Her realized gain is $15,000 ($85,000 − $70,000). Because the $20,000 of boot received is more than the $15,000 of realized gain, only $15,000 of gain is recognized. ◀

Taxing part or all of the gain when cash is received in like-kind exchanges is consistent with the wherewithal-to-pay concept. However, boot may not always be in the form of a liquid asset. If non-like-kind property other than cash is received as boot, the amount of the boot is the property's FMV.

> **TYPICAL MISCONCEPTION**
> It is possible to erroneously assume that the receipt of boot causes the recognition of loss.

EXAMPLE I12-19 ▶ Jane exchanges land held as an investment with a $70,000 basis for other land with a $100,000 FMV and a motorcycle with a $2,000 FMV. The acquired land is to be held for investment, and the motorcycle is for personal use. Personal-use property is non-like-kind property and constitutes boot. The realized gain is $32,000 [($100,000 + $2,000) − $70,000]. The amount of boot received is equal to the FMV of the motorcycle. The recognized gain is $2,000, the lesser of the amount of boot received ($2,000) or the realized gain ($32,000). ◀

---

[23] Secs. 1031(a)(3)(A) and (B).
[24] Sec. 1031(b).

[25] Sec. 1031(c).

Property Transactions: Nontaxable Exchanges ▼ Individuals 12-7

EXAMPLE I12-20 ▶ Assume the same facts in Example I12-19 except that Jane uses the motorcycle in a business. The motorcycle is boot, and a $2,000 gain is still recognized because the exchange of real property for personal property is not a like-kind exchange. ◀

SELF-STUDY QUESTION
Why is the relief of a liability treated as if one has received cash?

ANSWER
If it were not treated as such, a taxpayer could receive cash shortly before the exchange by borrowing from a bank, using the property as collateral. Then, if the taxpayer is relieved of the debt in the like-kind exchange, he or she would still have the cash without having paid a tax on the gain.

PROPERTY TRANSFERS INVOLVING LIABILITIES. If a liability is assumed (or the property is taken subject to a liability), the amount of the liability is considered money received by the taxpayer on the exchange.[26] One who assumes the debt or takes the property subject to a liability is treated as having paid cash, while the party that is relieved of the debt is treated as having received cash. If each party assumes a liability of the other party, only the net liability given or received is treated as boot.[27]

EXAMPLE I12-21 ▶ Mary exchanges land with a $550,000 FMV that is used in her business for Doug's building, which has a $450,000 FMV. Mary's basis in the land is $400,000, and the land is subject to a liability of $100,000, which Doug assumes. Mary's realized gain is $150,000 [($450,000 + $100,000) − $400,000]. Because assumption of the $100,000 liability is treated as boot, Mary recognizes a $100,000 gain. ◀

EXAMPLE I12-22 ▶ Matt owns an office building with a $700,000 basis, which is subject to a liability of $200,000. Susan owns an apartment complex with a $900,000 FMV, which is subject to a $150,000 liability. Matt and Susan exchange buildings. Matt's realized gain is $250,000 [($900,000 + $200,000) − ($700,000 + $150,000)]. Matt receives boot of $50,000 ($200,000 − $150,000) and recognizes a $50,000 gain. ◀

BASIS OF PROPERTY RECEIVED

OBJECTIVE 2

Determine the basis of property received in a like-kind exchange

LIKE-KIND PROPERTY RECEIVED. The basis of property received in a nontaxable exchange is equal to the adjusted basis of the property exchanged increased by gain recognized and reduced by any boot received or loss recognized on the exchange.[28]

Basis of property received in a nontaxable exchange = Basis of property exchanged − Boot received + Gain recognized − Loss recognized[29]

EXAMPLE I12-23 ▶

ADDITIONAL COMMENT
In effect the formula used to calculate the basis of the new property involves nothing more than journalizing the transaction and adjusting the basis of the new property by an amount needed to make the entry balance.

Chuck, who is in the business of racing horses, exchanges a racehorse with a $30,000 basis for $10,000 cash and a trotter with an $80,000 FMV. Chuck's realized gain is $60,000 [($80,000 + $10,000) − $30,000], and $10,000 of the gain is recognized because the boot received is less than the realized gain. Chuck's basis for the replacement property (i.e., the trotter) is $30,000 ($30,000 basis of property exchanged − $10,000 of boot received + $10,000 of gain recognized). ◀

The basis of the like-kind property received can also be computed by subtracting the unrecognized gain from its FMV or by adding the unrecognized loss to its FMV. Chuck's $30,000 basis for the trotter in Example I12-23 may be computed by subtracting the $50,000 of unrecognized gain from the $80,000 FMV.

EXAMPLE I12-24 ▶

KEY POINT
The basis adjustment is the mechanism that ensures that gain or loss is temporarily postponed rather than permanently excluded.

Pam, who operates a circus, exchanges an elephant with a $15,000 basis for $3,000 cash and a tiger with a $10,000 FMV. The $2,000 realized loss [($10,000 + $3,000) − $15,000] is not recognized. The receipt of boot does not cause a realized loss to be recognized. Pam's basis for the replacement property (i.e., the tiger) is $12,000 ($15,000 basis of property exchanged − $3,000 boot received). ◀

As indicated earlier, realized gains and losses resulting from nontaxable exchanges are deferred. This deferral is reflected in the basis of property received and is illustrated in the

---

[26] Sec. 1031(d). If a liability is assumed, the taxpayer agrees to pay the debt. If property is taken subject to the liability, the taxpayer is responsible for the debt only to the extent that the property could be used to pay the debt.

[27] Reg. Sec. 1.1031(b)-1(c).

[28] Sec. 1031(d).

[29] A loss is recognized only when the taxpayer transfers boot with a basis greater than its FMV. Transfers of non–like-kind property (i.e. boot) are discussed in a separate section of this chapter.

two preceding examples. In Example I12-23, the $50,000 ($60,000 − $10,000) unrecognized gain may be recognized when the trotter is sold or exchanged in a taxable transaction, because the basis of the replacement property is less than its FMV by the amount of the deferred gain. For example, if the trotter is sold in a taxable transaction for its $80,000 FMV, the $50,000 ($80,000 − $30,000 basis) of previously unrecognized gain would be recognized. In Example I12-24, the $2,000 unrecognized loss is reflected in the basis of the tiger. If Pam sells the tiger for its $10,000 FMV, a $2,000 loss ($10,000 − $12,000 basis) is recognized.

If more than one item of like-kind property is received, the basis is allocated among the properties in proportion to their relative FMVs on the date of the exchange.

EXAMPLE I12-25 ▶ Saul, who operates a zoo, exchanges a boa constrictor with a $300 basis for a python with a $400 FMV and an anaconda with a $600 FMV. The $700 realized gain [($400 + $600) − $300] is not recognized. The total bases of the properties received is $300. This amount is allocated to the properties (i.e., the python and the anaconda) based on their relative FMVs. Saul's basis for the python is $120 [($400 ÷ $1,000) × $300], and the basis for the anaconda is $180 [($600 ÷ $1,000) × $300]. ◀

NON–LIKE-KIND PROPERTY RECEIVED. The basis of non–like-kind property received is "an amount equivalent to its FMV at the date of the exchange."[30]

EXAMPLE I12-26 ▶
KEY POINT
Steve had basis of $20,000 before the exchange. Since he recognized gain of $5,000, the total basis of the two assets should be $25,000.

Steve exchanges a punch press with a $20,000 adjusted basis for a press brake with a $50,000 FMV and $5,000 of marketable securities. Steve's realized gain is $35,000 [($50,000 + $5,000) − $20,000], and $5,000 of the realized gain is recognized due to the receipt of boot. Steve's basis for the marketable securities is $5,000, and the basis for the press brake is $20,000 ($20,000 basis of property exchanged − $5,000 boot received + $5,000 gain recognized). ◀

STOP & THINK

Question: Chris Reedy owns 40 houses that he uses as rental property. All houses have a FMV greater than their adjusted basis. Chris wishes to diversify his investments and is considering selling ten of his houses and using the proceeds to purchase other types of investment assets such as stocks, bonds, commercial parking lots and land near town that he expects to increase in value. He asks you for advice.

ADDITIONAL COMMENT
The running of the two-year holding period is suspended during any period in which the property holder's risk of loss is substantially diminished.

Solution: If he sells the ten houses, he will have a gain and must pay taxes on the gain. He could defer the gain by exchanging the houses for like-kind property. Stocks and bonds are not like-kind property, but the commercial parking lots and the land should qualify as like-kind property, therefore the tax law encourages him to exchange the houses for the commercial parking lot and/or the land.

EXCHANGES BETWEEN RELATED PARTIES

Prior to 1990, related taxpayers could often use the like-kind exchange provisions to lower taxes because the tax basis for the property received is determined by the basis of the property exchanged. Related taxpayers could take advantage of the shift in tax basis to transfer a gain on a subsequent sale to a related party.[31] However, exchanges of property between related parties are not like-kind exchanges under current law if either party disposes of the property within two years of the exchange. Any gain resulting from the original exchange is recognized in the year of the subsequent disposition.[32] Dispositions due to death or involuntary conversion, or for non–tax avoidance purposes are disregarded.[33]

EXAMPLE I12-27 ▶ Melon Corporation, which is 100% owned by Linda, owned land with a basis of $200,000 that was held for investment. Rick wanted to purchase the land for $900,000. Linda owned an office building with a basis of $750,000 and a FMV of $900,000. Instead of selling the land to Rick, Melon Corporation exchanged the land for Linda's office building in December, 2000.

---

[30] Reg. Sec. 1.1031(d)-1(c).
[31] The definition of *related parties* is the same as those for Sec. 267(a) which is discussed in Chapter I6, and includes brothers, sisters, parents, children, and corporations where the taxpayer owns at least 50% in value. See Sec. 1031(f)(3).
[32] Sec. 1031(f)(1)(C).
[33] Secs. 1031(f)(2).

ADDITIONAL COMMENT

If Linda in Example 12-27 sells the land to Rick for $910,000, she has a $150,000 recognized gain on the exchange and a $10,000 recognized gain on the sale.

Two months later, Linda sells the land to Rick for $900,000. The exchange of the land for the office building is not a like-kind exchange because one of the related parties disposes of the property within two years of the exchange. In 2001, Melon's recognized gain on the exchange of the land is $700,000 ($900,000 − $200,000) and Linda's recognized gain on the exchange of the office building is $150,000 ($900,000 − $750,000). Because Linda's basis for the land is now $900,000, no gain is recognized on the sale of the land to Rick. ◀

If the parties in Example I12-27 were not related, a like-kind exchange occurred in 2000 and Linda's gain on the sale of the land to Rick is $150,000 ($900,000 − $750,000). Of course, the exchange is not a like-kind exchange if Linda does not hold the land for investment or for use in her trade or business after receiving it from Melon.

TRANSFER OF NON–LIKE-KIND PROPERTY

In all of the preceding examples that include a transfer of boot, the transferor (i.e., the taxpayer) received boot. If the taxpayer transfers non–like-kind property, gain or loss equal to the difference between the FMV and the adjusted basis of the non–like-kind property surrendered must be recognized. However, if the non–like-kind property is a personal use asset, the loss is not recognized.

EXAMPLE I12-28 ▶ Shirley exchanges land with a $30,000 basis and marketable securities with a $10,000 basis to David for land with a $60,000 FMV in a transaction that otherwise qualifies as a like-kind exchange. The FMV of the marketable securities and the land surrendered by Shirley is $14,000 and $46,000 respectively. Because the non–like-kind property that Shirley transfers has a FMV greater than its basis, she recognizes $4,000 ($14,000 − $10,000) of gain. Shirley's basis for the land received is $44,000 ($30,000 + $10,000 + $4,000), which is the basis of both assets exchanged plus the gain recognized on the exchange. ◀

EXAMPLE I12-29 ▶ Paul exchanges timberland held as an investment for undeveloped land with a $200,000 FMV. Paul's basis for the timberland is $125,000. His tractor with a $6,000 basis and a $4,000 FMV is also transferred. Because the non–like-kind property (i.e., the tractor) that Paul transfers has a FMV less than its basis, he recognizes a $2,000 ($4,000 − $6,000) loss. Paul's basis for the undeveloped land is $129,000 ($125,000 + $6,000 − $2,000). ◀

In Example I12-29, Paul recognizes a loss on the non–like-kind property he surrenders, despite receiving property in the aggregate with a FMV greater than the total adjusted basis of the transferred assets. Paul is actually making two exchanges. His exchange of timberland with a basis of $125,000 for undeveloped land with a $196,000 FMV is a like-kind exchange, but his exchange of the tractor with a basis of $6,000 for undeveloped land with a $4,000 FMV is a taxable exchange. In Example I12-30, Ed also makes two exchanges. He has a realized and recognized gain as well as a realized but unrecognized loss.

EXAMPLE I12-30 ▶ Ed owns equipment used in business with a $20,000 adjusted basis and a $15,000 FMV and marketable securities with a $10,000 basis and an $18,000 FMV. Ed exchanges the marketable securities and the equipment for business equipment in the same General Asset Class with a $33,000 FMV. Although the net realized gain is $3,000 [$33,000 − ($20,000 + $10,000)], Ed recognizes an $8,000 gain because he has transferred non–like-kind property with a $10,000 basis and an $18,000 FMV. The $5,000 realized loss on the transfer of equipment is not recognized due to the nonrecognition of gain or loss rules of Sec. 1031. Ed's basis for the equipment received is $38,000 ($20,000 + $10,000 + $8,000). ◀

KEY POINT

A taxpayer who exchanges like-kind property and non-like-kind property is actually making two exchanges.

ADDITIONAL COMMENT

The holding period is relevant only when the asset is a capital asset or a Sec. 1231 asset.

HOLDING PERIOD FOR PROPERTY RECEIVED

LIKE-KIND PROPERTY. The holding period of like-kind property received in a nontaxable exchange includes the holding period of the property exchanged if the like-kind property surrendered is a capital asset or an asset that is Sec. 1231 property. In essence, the holding period of the property exchanged carries over to the holding period of the like-kind property received.[34] The rule regarding the holding period carryover is consistent with the notion of a continuing investment in the underlying property that has been transferred.

---

[34] Sec. 1223(1) and Reg. Sec. 1.1223-1(a).

BOOT. The holding period for the boot property received begins the day after the date of the exchange.[35]

EXAMPLE I12-31 ▶ Mario owns a Van Gogh painting he acquired on May 1, 1990 as an investment. He exchanges the painting on April 10, 2001, for a Picasso sculpture and marketable securities to be held as investments. The holding period for the sculpture begins on May 1, 1990, and the holding period for the marketable securities starts on April 11, 2001. ◀

The like-kind exchange provisions are summarized in Topic Review I12-1.

INVOLUNTARY CONVERSIONS

OBJECTIVE 3

Determine whether gain from an involuntary conversion may be deferred

Taxpayers who realize a gain due to the involuntary conversion of property may elect to defer recognition of the entire gain if qualifying replacement property is acquired within a specified time period at a cost equal to or greater than the amount realized from the involuntary conversion. No gain is recognized if the property is converted "into property similar or related in service or use to the property so converted."[36]

The opportunity provided in Sec. 1033 to defer recognition of the gain reflects the fact that the taxpayer maintains a continuing investment and may lack the wherewithal to pay the tax on the gain that would otherwise be recognized. Furthermore, the involuntary conversion is beyond the taxpayer's control.

Note that the gain is deferred, not excluded. The basis of the replacement property is the property's cost reduced by the amount of gain deferred. The tax treatment for an involuntary conversion is similar to the tax treatment of a like-kind exchange.

KEY POINT

Unlike the like-kind exchange provisions which are mandatory, the involuntary conversion provisions are elective. Further, the involuntary conversion rules apply only to gains, not losses.

EXAMPLE I12-32
ADDITIONAL COMMENT

Property involved in an involuntary conversion need not be used in a trade or business or held for investment to qualify for the deferral of gain.

▶ Lenea's warehouse with a $500,000 basis is destroyed by a hurricane. She collects $650,000 from the insurance company and purchases a new warehouse for $720,000. Lenea may elect to defer recognition of the $150,000 gain ($650,000 − $500,000). If the election is made, the basis of the new warehouse is $570,000 ($720,000 − $150,000). The $150,000 gain is merely deferred rather than excluded, because an immediate sale of the replacement property at its $720,000 FMV results in a recognized gain equal to the deferred gain on the involuntarily converted property. For example, if the new warehouse is sold for $720,000, the recognized gain is $150,000 ($720,000 − $570,000). ◀

Topic Review I12-1

Section 1031—Like-Kind Exchanges

▶ Gains and losses are not recognized for like-kind exchanges.
▶ Nonrecognition of gains and losses is mandatory if the exchange is a like-kind exchange.
▶ Section 1031 applies to exchanges of property used in a trade or business or held for investment.
▶ Property exchanged and received must be like-kind.
▶ Subject to certain time constraints, a nonsimultaneous exchange may qualify as a like-kind exchange.
▶ Some gain may be recognized if the taxpayer receives or gives non–like-kind property (boot) in an otherwise like-kind exchange.
▶ A loss may be recognized if the taxpayer transfers non–like-kind property (boot) in an otherwise like-kind exchange.
▶ The basis of property received in an exchange is the basis of the property exchanged less the boot received plus the gain recognized and less any loss recognized.
▶ The nonrecognized gain or loss is deferred.
▶ The holding period of like-kind property received includes the holding period of the property exchanged.

---

[35] Sec. 1223 and Reg. Sec. 1.1223-1(a).   [36] Sec. 1033(a)(1).

TYPICAL MISCONCEPTION
Occasionally, taxpayers fail to realize that Sec. 1033 applies only to gains, not losses.

Section 1033 does not apply to losses realized from an involuntary conversion. A taxpayer may not elect to defer recognition of a loss resulting from an involuntary conversion.

EXAMPLE I12-33 ▶ Barry's offshore drilling rig with an $800,000 basis is destroyed by a typhoon. He collects $700,000 from the insurance company and purchases a new drilling rig for $760,000. The $100,000 loss ($700,000 − $800,000) is recognized as a casualty loss, and the basis of the new drilling rig is its purchase price of $760,000. ◀

INVOLUNTARY CONVERSION DEFINED

ADDITIONAL COMMENT
Typically, an involuntary conversion consists of either a casualty or a condemnation.

For Sec. 1033 to apply, property must be compulsorily or involuntarily converted into money or other property. An **involuntary conversion** may be due to theft, seizure, requisition, condemnation, or destruction of the property. The destruction of the property may be complete or partial.[37] For purposes of Sec. 1033, destruction of property does not have to meet the "suddenness" test if the cause of destruction otherwise falls within the general concept of a casualty.[38]

An involuntary conversion occurs when a governmental unit exercises its power of eminent domain to acquire the taxpayer's property without the taxpayer's consent. Furthermore, the threat or imminence of requisition or condemnation of property may permit a taxpayer to defer recognition of gain from the sale or exchange of property under the involuntary conversion rules. Taxpayers who transfer property due to such a threat must be careful to confirm that a decision to acquire their property for public use has been made.[39] Written confirmation of potential condemnation is particularly helpful.[40]

EXAMPLE I12-34 ▶ Bruce owns an automobile dealership near a state university campus. On a number of occasions, the president of the university expressed an interest in acquiring Bruce's property for additional parking space. The president is not certain about the availability of funds for the purchase, and the university is reluctant to have the property condemned for its use. Based on the university's interest in the property, Bruce sells the property to the Jet Corporation. The threat or imminence of conversion does not exist merely because the property is being considered for acquisition. The sale does not constitute an involuntary conversion.[41] ◀

THREAT OF CONDEMNATION. If a threat of condemnation exists and the taxpayer has reasonable grounds to believe that the property will be condemned, Sec. 1033 applies even if the taxpayer sells the property to an entity other than the governmental unit that is threatening to condemn the property.[42]

EXAMPLE I12-35 ▶ At its regular meeting on Tuesday night, the city commission authorized the city attorney to start the process of condemning two lots owned by Beth for use as a public park. On Wednesday afternoon, Beth sells the two lots to Marty at a gain. The sale of property to Marty is an involuntary conversion, and Beth may elect to defer recognition of the gain if she satisfies the Sec. 1033 requirements. ◀

ADDITIONAL COMMENT
If the property in Example I12-35 is later condemned, Marty may be able to defer part or all of the gain.

CONVERSION MUST BE INVOLUNTARY. The conversion must be involuntary. For example, an involuntary conversion does not occur when a taxpayer pays someone to set fire to his or her building.[43] An involuntary conversion also does not occur when a taxpayer who is developing a subdivision, reserves certain property for a school site, and later sells the property to the school district under condemnation proceedings. In this situation, the taxpayer was required to reserve property for a school site in order to receive zoning approval for development of the subdivision.[44]

---

[37] Reg. Sec. 1.1033(a)-1.
[38] Rev. Rul. 59-102, 1959-1 C.B. 200.
[39] Rev. Rul. 63-221, 1963-2 C.B. 332, and *Joseph P. Balistrieri*, 1979 PH T.C. Memo ¶79,115, 38 TCM 526.
[40] Rev. Rul. 63-221, 1963-2 C.B. 332.
[41] *Forest City Chevrolet*, 1977 PH T.C. Memo ¶77,187, 36 TCM 768.
[42] Rev. Rul. 81-180, 1981-2 C.B. 161, and *Creative Solutions, Inc. v. U.S.*, 12 AFTR 2d 5229, 1963-2 USTC ¶9615 (5th Cir., 1963).
[43] Rev. Rul. 82-74, 1982-1 C.B. 110.
[44] Rev. Rul. 69-654, 1969-2 C.B. 162.

> **REAL-WORLD EXAMPLE**
> Because of mounting losses and declining property values, a taxpayer decided to burn down his building to collect the fire insurance proceeds. Although the building was converted into money (insurance proceeds) as a result of its destruction, this conversion was not involuntary within the meaning of Sec. 1033. Rev. Rul. 82-74, 1982-1 C.B. 110.

Although the typical involuntary conversion generally results from a casualty or condemnation, Sec. 1033 provides that certain transactions involving livestock are to be treated as involuntary conversions.[45] For example, the destruction or sale of livestock because of disease is an involuntary conversion.

TAX TREATMENT OF GAIN DUE TO INVOLUNTARY CONVERSION INTO BOOT

Gain may be deferred if the property is involuntarily converted into money or property that is not similar or related in service or use to the converted property.[46] The taxpayer must make a proper replacement of the converted property within a specific time period and elect to defer the gain.

REALIZED GAIN. The taxpayer's realized gain is the excess of the amount received due to the involuntary conversion over the adjusted basis of the property converted. The total award or proceeds received are reduced by expenses incurred to determine the amount realized (e.g., attorney's fees incurred in connection with determining the settlement to be received from a condemnation). If the payment of the award or proceeds is delayed, any amounts paid as interest are not included in determining the amount realized.[47] Amounts received as interest on an award for property condemned are taxed as ordinary income even if the interest is paid by a state or political subdivision.[48]

EXAMPLE I12-36 ▶ Richard's property with a $100,000 basis is condemned by the city of Phoenix. Richard receives a $190,000 award and pays $1,000 legal expenses for representation at the condemnation proceedings and $800 for an appraisal of the property. The amount realized is $188,200 [$190,000 − ($1,000 + $800)]. The gain realized is $88,200 ($188,200 − $100,000). Part or all of the realized gain may be deferred if the requirements of Sec. 1033 are satisfied and an election is made to defer the gain. ◀

> **ADDITIONAL COMMENT**
> The gain recognized is limited to the lesser of the gain realized or the excess of the amount realized from the conversion over the cost of the qualified replacement property.

GAIN RECOGNIZED. To defer the entire gain, the taxpayer must purchase replacement property with a cost equal to or greater than the amount realized from the involuntary conversion. If the replacement property is purchased for an amount less than the amount realized, that portion of the realized gain that is equal to the excess of the amount realized from the conversion over the cost of the replacement property must be recognized.[49]

EXAMPLE I12-37 ▶ Bob owns a restaurant with a $200,000 basis. The restaurant is destroyed by fire, and he receives $300,000 from the insurance company. Bob's realized gain is $100,000 ($300,000 − $200,000). He purchases another restaurant for $275,000. Bob may elect to defer $75,000 of the gain under Sec. 1033; $25,000 ($300,000 − $275,000) of Bob's gain must be recognized because he failed to reinvest all of the $300,000 insurance proceeds in a suitable replacement property. ◀

EXAMPLE I12-38 ▶ Stacey owns a racehorse with a $450,000 basis used for breeding purposes. The racehorse is killed by lightning, and she collects $800,000 from the insurance company. Stacey's realized gain is $350,000 ($800,000 − $450,000). She purchases another racehorse for $430,000. The entire $350,000 of gain is recognized, because the cost of the replacement property is $370,000 ($800,000 − $430,000) less than the amount realized from the involuntary conversion. ◀

> **OBJECTIVE 4**
> Determine the basis of replacement property in an involuntary conversion

BASIS OF REPLACEMENT PROPERTY. If replacement property is purchased, the basis of the replacement property is its cost less any deferred gain. If the taxpayer elects to defer the gain, the holding period of the replacement property includes the holding period of the converted property.[50]

---

[45] Secs. 1033(d) and (e). If a taxpayer sells or exchanges more livestock than normal because of a drought, the sale or exchange of the excess amount is treated as an involuntary conversion. The livestock must be other than poultry and be held by the taxpayer for draft, breeding, or dairy purposes.
[46] Sec. 1033(a)(2).
[47] *Flushingside Realty & Construction Co.*, 1943 PH T.C. Memo ¶43,286, 2 TCM 259.
[48] *Spencer D. Stewart v. CIR.*, 52 AFTR 2d 83-5885, 83-2 USTC ¶9573 (9th Cir., 1983).
[49] Sec. 1033(a)(2)(A).
[50] Sec. 1223(1)(A).

EXAMPLE I12-39 ▶ Tracy owns a yacht that is held for personal use and has a $20,000 basis. The yacht is destroyed by a storm, and Tracy collects $24,000 from the insurance company. She purchases a new $35,000 yacht for personal use and elects to defer the $4,000 ($24,000 − $20,000) gain. The basis of the new yacht is $31,000 ($35,000 − $4,000). The holding period for the new yacht includes the holding period of the yacht that was destroyed. ◀

SEVERANCE DAMAGES. If a portion of the taxpayer's property is condemned, the taxpayer may receive **severance damages** as compensation for a decline in the value of the retained property. For example, if access to the retained property becomes difficult or if the property is exposed to greater damage from flooding or erosion, its value may decline.

The IRS considers severance damages to be "analogous to the proceeds of property insurance; they represent compensation for damages to the property."[51] Amounts received as severance damages reduce the basis of the retained property, and any amount received in excess of the property's basis is treated as gain.[52]

EXAMPLE I12-40 ▶ Cindy owns a 500-acre farm with a $200 basis per acre ($100,000 basis). The state condemns ten acres across the northwest corner of her farm to build a major highway. Cindy receives a condemnation award of $500 per acre for the ten acres. The highway separates the farm into a 25-acre tract and a 465-acre tract. Because her ability to efficiently use the 25-acre tract for farming is reduced, the state pays additional severance damages of $90 per acre for the 25 acres. Cindy's gain realized from condemnation of the ten acres is $3,000 [$5,000 − ($200 × 10 acres)]. The $2,250 ($90 × 25 acres) of severance damages reduce the basis of the 25-acre tract from $5,000 ($200 × 25 acres) to $2,750 [($200 × 25) − $2,250]. The reduction in basis is applied solely to the 25 acres because of its decline in value as farmland. ◀

REAL-WORLD EXAMPLE

Seven of the 18 holes of a golf course were condemned. Although 11 holes remained, it was anticipated that the course would have to be reduced to 9 holes. Therefore, $21,000 of the condemnation award was allocated to severance damages to reflect the decline in value of the two lost holes. *Marco S. Marinello Associates, Inc.*, 1975 PH T.C. Memo ¶75,078, 34 TCM 392.

The Sec. 1033 provisions concerning nonrecognition of gain may apply to severance damages. For instance, if severance damages are used to restore the retained property, only that portion of severance damages not spent for restoration reduces the basis of the retained property. A taxpayer who uses severance damages to purchase adjacent farmland to replace the portion of the farm condemned may use Sec. 1033 to defer a gain due to the receipt of the severance damages.[53]

TAX TREATMENT OF GAIN DUE TO AN INVOLUNTARY CONVERSION DIRECTLY INTO SIMILAR PROPERTY

ADDITIONAL COMMENT

The direct conversion of property into similar property is rarely encountered.

Nonrecognition of gain is mandatory if property is involuntarily converted directly into similar property rather than money.[54] The basis of the replacement property is the same as the basis of the converted property, and the holding period for the converted property carries over to the replacement property.[55]

EXAMPLE I12-41 ▶ Ed's farm with a $200,000 basis is condemned by the state. The state transfers other farmland with a $280,000 FMV to Ed. The $80,000 ($280,000 − $200,000) of realized gain is not recognized, and the basis of the farmland received is $200,000. Nonrecognition of gain is mandatory. Direct conversions are rarely encountered because the usual payment procedure for insurance companies and governmental agencies involves a payment of cash. ◀

REPLACEMENT PROPERTY

To qualify for nonrecognition of gain due to an involuntary conversion, the taxpayer must acquire qualified replacement property. With some exceptions, the **replacement property** must be "similar or related in service or use to the property so converted."[56] Taxpayers who own and use the property must use the functional use test although

---

[51] Rev. Rul. 53-271, 1953-2 C.B. 36.
[52] Rev. Rul. 68-37, 1968-1 C.B. 359.
[53] Rev. Ruls. 69-240, 1969-1 C.B. 199, 73-35, 1973-1 C.B. 367, and 83-49, 1983-1 C.B. 191.
[54] Sec. 1033(a).
[55] Sec. 1033(b).

[56] Secs. 1033(a)(2)(A) and 1033(f). The replacement of property requirement is modified when proceeds from the involuntary conversion of livestock may not be reinvested in property similar or related in use to the converted livestock because of soil contamination or other environmental contamination. Sec. 1033(f) permits the livestock to be replaced with other property, including real property, used for farming purposes.

replacement may be made with like-kind property in certain cases. A taxpayer who owns and leases the property that is involuntarily converted may use the taxpayer-use test.

FUNCTIONAL-USE TEST. The **functional-use test** is more restrictive than the like-kind test. To be considered similar or related in service or use, the replacement property must be functionally the same as the converted property. For example, the exchange of a business building for land used in business qualifies as a like-kind exchange. Replacing a building with land does not qualify as replacement property under the involuntary conversion rules. The building must be replaced with a building that is functionally the same as the converted building.

EXAMPLE I12-42 ▶

REAL-WORLD EXAMPLE

The replacement of bowling alleys destroyed in a fire with a recreational billiards center did not pass the functional-use test. Rev. Rul. 76-319, 1976-2 C.B. 242.

Julie owns a movie theater that is destroyed by fire. She uses the insurance proceeds to purchase a skating rink. The converted property has not been replaced with property that is similar or related in service or use under the functional-use test. The election to defer gain under Sec. 1033 is not available. ◀

REPLACEMENT WITH LIKE-KIND PROPERTY. If real property held for productive use in a trade or business or for investment is condemned, a proper replacement may be made by acquiring like-kind property.[57] This exception to the functional use test applies only to real property used in a trade or business or held for investment but not to real property held as inventory.

EXAMPLE I12-43 ▶

Ken owns a building used in his business that is condemned by the state to widen a highway. He uses the proceeds to purchase land to be held for investment. The land is a qualified replacement property because the condemned building is real property used in a trade or business, and the like-kind exchange rule may be applied to the condemnation. ◀

EXAMPLE I12-44 ▶

REAL-WORLD EXAMPLE

A nursery with its trees and shrubs was condemned, and the taxpayer replaced the condemned property with land and greenhouses. The replacement was considered to have been made with like-kind property. *Evert Asjes, Jr.*, 74 T.C. 1005 (1980).

Assume the same facts as in Example I12-43 except that the building is destroyed by a violent windstorm. Ken's purchase of the investment land is not qualified replacement property because the more flexible like-kind exchange rules apply only to condemnations. He must purchase property with the same functional use as the business building. ◀

If business or investment property is involuntarily converted as a result of a Presidentially declared disaster after 1994, the taxpayer may replace the property with any tangible property that is held for productive use in a trade or business.

TAXPAYER-USE TEST. The **taxpayer-use test** applies to the involuntary conversion of rental property owned by an investor. This test permits greater flexibility than the functional use test. The principal requirement is that the owner-investor must lease out the replacement property that is acquired. However, the lessee is not required to use the leased property for the same functional use.[58]

EXAMPLE I12-45 ▶

Sally owns an apartment complex that is rented to college students. The apartment complex is destroyed by fire. She uses the insurance proceeds to purchase a medical building that is leased to physicians. This is a qualified replacement property by Sally under the taxpayer-use test, and the gain, if any, may be deferred if an election is made under Sec. 1033. ◀

STOP & THINK

Question: Greg Stacey's motel is destroyed by fire on March 10 of the current year. The basis of the property is $400,000 and he receives $2,000,000 from the insurance company. Greg is concerned about the possibility of having to pay income tax on the $1,600,000 gain and is aware of the tax rules relating to involuntary conversions. Greg is considering replacing the destroyed motel by building either a new motel or an ice skating rink on the vacant lot. The cost of a new motel or an ice skating rink is expected to be $2,500,000, and he expects to borrow 60% of the cost. What tax advice would you give him?

---

[57] Sec. 1033(g)(1).

[58] Rev. Rul. 64-237, 1964-2 C.B. 319.

REAL-WORLD EXAMPLE

Taxpayer owned land and a warehouse held for rental purposes. Upon the condemnation of this property, taxpayer invested the proceeds in a gas station on land already owned by the taxpayer which was also held for rental purposes. The taxpayer-use test applied, and the taxpayer was able to defer the gain. Rev. Rul. 71-41, 1971-1 C.B. 223.

Solution: Greg may defer the $1,600,000 gain if the involuntary conversion requirements are met and he makes a proper election. The principal issue in this case is whether the replacement property is considered to be "similar in service or use" to the converted property. Because the functional-use test is applicable in this case, an ice skating rink is not similar property and the gain of $1,600,000 must be recognized. Conversely, the new motel is similar property and, since Greg is reinvesting an amount greater than $2,000,000, none of the gain is recognized. His basis in the new motel is $900,000 ($2,500,000 − deferred gain of $1,600,000). The fact that he borrows money and does not spend the $2,000,000 insurance proceeds does not prevent him from electing to defer the gain. The tax requirement is only that he must reinvest an amount equal to or greater than the $2,000,000 insurance proceeds. In this case, the tax law clearly encourages the taxpayer to build a new motel rather than an ice skating rink.

OBTAINING REPLACEMENT PROPERTY

The general rule is that the taxpayer must purchase the replacement property.[59] Taxpayers may purchase replacement property indirectly by purchasing control (i.e., 80% or more of the stock) of a corporation that owns the replacement property.[60] However, this exception is not applicable to the purchase of like-kind property to replace condemned real property used in a trade or business or held for investment.[61]

EXAMPLE I12-46 ▶ Hank's airplane, used in business, is hijacked and taken to a foreign country. He uses the insurance proceeds to purchase 80% of the Fast Corporation stock. Fast Corporation owns an airplane which is qualified replacement property. The involuntary conversion requirements are satisfied if Hank elects to defer any gain realized. ◀

EXAMPLE I12-47 ▶ Lynn's farm is condemned by the state for public use. She uses the proceeds to purchase 80% of Vermont Corporation stock. Vermont Corporation owns eight parking lots. A qualified replacement property has not been obtained through the stock purchase because the parking lots are not functionally the same as the farm. ◀

TIME REQUIREMENTS FOR REPLACEMENT

TYPICAL MISCONCEPTION

The first taxable year in which any part of the gain on the conversion is realized is the year in which the insurance proceeds are received not the year in which the involuntary conversion took place.

To qualify for nonrecognition of gain treatment, the converted property must be replaced within a specified time period. The general rule is that the period begins with the date of disposition of the converted property and ends "two years after the close of the first taxable year in which any part of the gain upon the conversion is realized."[62] If the involuntary conversion is due to condemnation or requisition, or the threat of such, the replacement period begins on the date of the threat or imminence of the requisition or condemnation. The replacement period may be extended by obtaining permission from the IRS.[63]

EXAMPLE I12-48 ▶ On December 8, 2001, Craig's business property was destroyed by fire. Craig receives insurance proceeds in 2002 and elects to defer recognition of the gain. He must replace the property between December 8, 2001, and December 31, 2004. The two-year time period includes 2004 because the gain is realized when the insurance proceeds are received in 2002. ◀

KEY POINT

The replacement period is three years instead of two years on the condemnation of real property used in a business or held for investment.

The replacement period is longer if the involuntary conversion is due to the condemnation of real property (excluding inventory) held for productive use in a trade or business or for investment. The replacement period ends three years after the close of the first tax year in which any part of the gain is realized.[64] This provision for a longer replacement period applies to the same type of real property that may be replaced with like-kind property.

---

[59] To qualify as a purchase of property or stock under Sec. 1033(a)(2)(A)(ii), the unadjusted basis of the property or stock must be its cost within the meaning of Sec. 1012 without considering the basis adjustment for the deferred gain. Property acquired by inheritance, gift, or a nontaxable exchange does not qualify as replacement property (see Reg. Sec. 1.1033(a)-2(c)(4)).

[60] Sec. 1033(a)(2)(A) and Reg. Sec. 1.1033(a)-2(c).
[61] Sec. 1033(g)(2).
[62] Sec. 1033(a)(2)(B).
[63] Sec. 1033(a)(2)(B)(ii).
[64] Sec. 1033(g)(4).

12-16 Individuals ▼ Chapter 12

EXAMPLE I12-49 ▶ Beth owns a building used in her dry cleaning business. In 2001, the state condemns the building and awards Beth an amount greater than the adjusted basis of the building. Beth may replace the property with like-kind property, and the replacement period ends on December 31, 2004. ◀

The involuntary conversion rules are summarized in Topic Review I12-2.

SALE OF PRINCIPAL RESIDENCE

OBJECTIVE 5

Determine when a gain resulting from the sale of a principal residence is excluded

Congress uses the tax law to encourage home ownership in many ways: (1) Real estate taxes and interest on a mortgage used to acquire a principal or second residence are deductible (see Chapter I7), (2) part or all of the interest on home equity debt may be deductible and (3) taxpayers may elect to exclude up to $250,000 ($500,000 on a joint return) of gain from the sale of a principal residence.

Individuals who sell or exchange their personal residence after May 6, 1997, may exclude up to $250,000 of gain if it was owned and occupied as a principal residence for at least two years of the five-year period before the sale or exchange. A married couple may exclude up to $500,000 when filing jointly if both meet the use test, at least one meets the ownership test and neither spouse is ineligible for the exclusion because he or she sold or exchanged a residence within the last two years.[65]

The Sec. 121 exclusion is available regardless of age, and taxpayers do not have to purchase a replacement residence. Any gain not excluded is capital gain because a personal residence is a capital asset. A loss on the sale or exchange of a personal residence is not deductible because the residence is personal-use property.[66]

EXAMPLE I12-50 ▶ Maki, who is single and 35 years old, sells her principal residence that she purchased four years ago and realizes a $230,000 gain. Maki may exclude the entire gain regardless of her age or whether she purchases a new principal residence. ◀

EXAMPLE I12-51 ▶ Assume the same facts as in Example I12-50 except the realized gain is $320,000. Maki may exclude $250,000 and recognize a $70,000 LTCG. ◀

Topic Review I12-2

Section 1033: Involuntary Conversions

1. Section 1033 applies only to gains, not losses.
2. Nonrecognition of gain under Section 1033 is elective. (Nonrecognition of gain is mandatory in a direct conversion, but direct conversions seldom occur.)
3. Section 1033 applies to involuntary conversions of all types of properties.
4. Some gain may be recognized if the taxpayer replaces the involuntarily converted property with property that costs less than the amount realized in the involuntary conversion.
5. The nonrecognized gain is deferred.
6. The basis of property acquired to replace the involuntarily converted property is the cost of the property less the deferred gain.
7. Property acquired to replace the involuntarily converted property generally must be functionally related property.
8. The required replacement period generally begins with the date of disposition of the converted property and ends two years after the close of the first taxable year in which any part of the gain on the conversion is realized. (A three-year period applies to condemnations of real property used in a trade or business or held for the production of income.)

---

[65] Sec. 121(a) and (b).

[66] Reg. Secs. 1.165-9(a) and 1.262-1b)(4).

EXAMPLE I12-52 ▶ Assume the same facts as in Example I12-51 except Maki is married to Yixin, and they have owned and occupied the residence for the last four years. They may exclude the entire $320,000 gain. ◀

ADDITIONAL COMMENT
The elimination of taxes on up to $500,000 of gain from the sale of a personal residence has been a great benefit for many taxpayers who had very large built-in gains.

KEY POINT
The reason that recordkeeping will be reduced is the sales price for most homes is less than $250,000 ($500,000 on a joint return). If the sale price is less than $250,000, clearly no taxable gain would result and no records are necessary to prove the basis of the home.

Prior to the Taxpayer Relief Act of 1997, taxpayers could defer gain resulting from sale of a personal residence if they purchased another principal residence within two years at a cost greater than the adjusted sales price. Taxpayers who were at least 55-years-old could exclude up to $125,000 of gain resulting from the sale of a personal residence. The deferral provision of Sec. 1034 has been repealed; the exclusion has been increased to $250,000 or $500,000; and taxpayers may exclude gain regardless of age.

Today, the rules for excluding gain resulting from the sale of a personal residence are more favorable for most taxpayers than the old rules because Congress wanted to eliminate the need for homeowners to maintain records for long periods of time. However, taxpayers who expect to sell their homes for more than $250,000, or $500,000 if a joint return is filed, still need to maintain records. Also, taxpayers who convert their personal residence to business property or rental property will need to know the property's correct adjusted basis to compute depreciation.

DETERMINING THE REALIZED GAIN. Gain realized is the excess of the amount realized over the property's adjusted basis.[67] The amount realized on the sale of the property is equal to the selling price less selling expenses.[68] Selling expenses include commissions, advertising, deed preparation costs, and legal expenses incurred in connection with the sale.[69]

EXAMPLE I12-53 ▶ Kirby sells his personal residence, which has a $100,000 basis, to Maxine. To make the sale, Kirby pays a $7,000 sales commission and incurs $800 of legal costs. Maxine pays $30,000 cash and assumes Kirby's $90,000 mortgage. The amount realized is $112,200 [($30,000 + $90,000) − ($7,000 + $800)]. The realized gain is $12,200 ($112,200 − $100,000). ◀

ADJUSTED BASIS OF RESIDENCE. The original basis of a principal residence is a function of how the residence is obtained. It could be purchased, received as a gift or inherited. The cost of a residence includes all amounts attributable to the acquisition including commissions and other purchasing expenses paid to acquire the residence.[70] Capital improvements, but not repairs, increase the adjusted basis of the residence. The costs of adding a room, installing an air conditioning system, finishing a basement and landscaping are capital improvements. Expenses incurred to protect the taxpayer's title in the residence are also capitalized. Under Sec. 1034 which was repealed in 1997, a taxpayer who deferred gain on the sale of a principal residence was required to reduce the basis of the replacement residence by the amount of the deferred gain.[71]

EXAMPLE I12-54 ▶ In 1996, Susan paid $200,000 to purchase a new residence. She paid a realtor $4,000 to help locate the house and paid legal fees of $1,200 to make certain that the seller had legal title to the property. As a result of the purchase, she deferred a gain of $50,000 from the sale a former residence in 1995. In 1997, she added a new porch to the house at a cost of $6,000 and installed central air conditioning at a cost of $5,200. Since purchasing the house, she has paid $1,500 for repairs. The adjusted basis of her house is $166,400 [$200,000 + $4,000 + $1,200 − $50,000 + $6,000 + $5,200]. ◀

REAL-WORLD EXAMPLE
One taxpayer plans to make good use of the multiple exclusion allowance. He has purchased two houses; one to live in and one to rent out. After a certain number of years he will sell his personal residence and move into the rental house. After at least two more years he will then sell the second house. Except for the depreciation on the rental house, the gain from both houses will be tax-free up to $500,000 each.

MULTIPLE USE OF THE EXCLUSION. Previously under Sec. 121, a taxpayer was limited to the exclusion once in their lifetime. A married taxpayer whose spouse had taken the exclusion could not use the exclusion even if the taxpayer filed as married filing separately. The exclusion is now determined on an individual basis. An individual may claim the exclusion even if the individual's spouse used the exclusion within the past two years. Also, for a married couple filing a joint return when each spouse maintains a separate

---

[67] Reg. Sec. 1.1034-1(b)(5).
[68] Reg. Sec. 1.1034-1(b)(4).
[69] Reg. Sec. 1.1034-1(b)(4)(i).
[70] Reg. Sec. 1.1034-1(c)(4).
[71] Sec. 1034(e).

principal residence, the $250,000 exclusion is available for the sale or exchange of each spouse's principal residence.

> **EXAMPLE I12-55** ▶ Krista who has owned and used a house as her principal residence for the last seven years marries Eric in January of 2000. Eric sold his residence in October of 2000 and excluded a $145,000 gain. Krista sells her residence in December of 2001 and realizes a gain of $378,000. She may exclude $250,000 of the gain.
>
> Assuming that Krista and Eric use her residence in the above example for a two-year period starting in January 2001, they could exclude up to $500,000 if she waits to sell the house until January, 2003. ◀

PRINCIPAL RESIDENCE DEFINED

For Sec. 121 to apply, taxpayers must sell property that qualifies as their principal residence. Whether property is used as the taxpayer's principal residence is determined on a case-by-case basis.[72]

> **EXAMPLE I12-56** ▶
> **KEY POINT**
> A taxpayer may own two or more residences, but only one of them qualifies as the principal residence.
>
> Len, a 40-year-old college professor, owns and occupies a house in Oklahoma. During the summer, he lives in a cabin in Idaho. After owning the cabin for eight years, Len sells it for $50,000 and realizes a gain. Gain on the sale of the cabin in Idaho must be recognized because Len's principal residence is in Oklahoma. ◀

Condominium apartments, houseboats, and housetrailers may qualify as principal residences.[73] Stock held by a tenant-stockholder in a cooperative housing corporation is a principal residence if the dwelling that the taxpayer is entitled to occupy as a stockholder is used as his or her principal residence.[74]

DETERMINING WHETHER THE PROPERTY IS THE TAXPAYER'S PRINCIPAL RESIDENCE. To qualify for the favorable tax treatment provided by Sec. 121, the residence must be the taxpayer's principal residence.[75] Controversy often exists as to whether a residence qualifies as the taxpayer's principal residence, and the IRS will not issue rulings or determination letters concerning whether property qualifies under Secs. 121.[76]

Property that is not being used as a principal residence when sold may have lost its character as the taxpayer's residence. A taxpayer's residence that is abandoned before its sale does not qualify as the taxpayer's principal residence.[77] In a case where taxpayers had not occupied their residence for more than ten years, the court ruled that the residence was not their principal residence. The taxpayers were in the process of remodeling the property when they received and accepted an unsolicited offer.[78]

KEY POINT
A residence can be rented and retain its designation as the taxpayer's principal residence. However, the taxpayer should be able to show that he or she was trying to sell the property.

While attempting to sell the residence, the taxpayer may rent the property to another party. This action may jeopardize the taxpayer's ability to exclude the gain, although temporary rental before the sale does not always indicate a conversion to business use.[79]

> **EXAMPLE I12-57** ▶
> **ADDITIONAL COMMENT**
> When a residence retains its designation as the principal residence, the taxpayer may deduct depreciation and other rental expenses during the rental period.
>
> In December 2000, Sandy discovered that her "dream house" was available for purchase. Sandy purchased the house and immediately occupied it as her new principal residence. She lives in a college town and knows that the market for housing becomes active in the spring. She lists her vacated house for sale with a realtor and agrees to allow two college students to rent the property on a month-to-month basis. Sandy retains the right to show the house to prospective buyers while the students are tenants. In April 2001, she sells the property. Because the conversion to rental property status is temporary, the residence is still Sandy's principal residence. ◀

If rental of the property constitutes abandonment of the residence, it is no longer the taxpayer's principal residence.

---

[72] Reg. Sec. 1.1034-1(c)(3). Even though Sec. 1034 has been repealed, the definition of a *principal residence* is still contained in the Treasury Regulations under Sec. 1034.
[73] Rev. Rul. 64-31, 1964-1 C.B. 300.
[74] Reg. Sec. 1.1034-1(c)(3).
[75] Sec. 121(a).
[76] Rev. Proc. 92-3, 1992-1 C.B. 561.
[77] *William C. Stolk v. CIR*, 13 AFTR 2d 535, 64-1 USTC ¶9228 (2nd Cir., 1964).
[78] *Ann K. Demeter*, 1971 PH T.C. Memo ¶71,209, 30 TCM 863.
[79] Rev. Rul. 78-146, 1978-1 C.B. 260.

EXAMPLE I12-58 ▶ In 1995, Sam and his wife moved from their residence in New Orleans to a home in Mobile. After renting the house in New Orleans for six years, they sell it in 2001. Section 121 will not apply to the sale of the residence in New Orleans because the extended rental period constitutes an abandonment of the principal residence.[80] ◀

ADDITIONAL COMMENT
The taxpayer does not have to be occupying the old residence at the date of sale. The taxpayer may have already moved to a new residence and be renting the old residence temporarily before its sale.

SALE OF MORE THAN ONE PRINCIPAL RESIDENCE WITHIN A TWO-YEAR PERIOD

The new exclusion provided by Sec. 121 applies to only one sale or exchange every two years. A portion of the gain may be excluded in certain circumstances even if the two-year requirement is not satisfied.

If a principal residence is sold within two years of a previous sale or exchange of a residence, part of the gain may be excluded if the sale or exchange is due to a change in employment, health or unforseen circumstances. The portion of the gain excluded is based on a ratio with a denominator of 730 days and the numerator being the shorter of:

1) the period during which the ownership and use tests were met during the five-year period ending on the date of sale, or

2) the period of time after the date of the most recent prior sale or exchange for which the exclusion applied until the date of the current sale or exchange.[81]

The amount excluded is $250,000 or $500,000 times the above ratio.

EXAMPLE I12-59 ▶ Winnie, who is single, sold her principal residence in Detroit on November 1, 2001, and excluded the $127,000 gain because she owned and used the residence for two of the last five years. Winnie purchased another residence in Cleveland on October 1, 2001, that she occupies until June 12, 2002, when she receives a job offer from a new employer in Dallas. She moves to Dallas on June 12 and rents a townhouse. She sells the residence in Cleveland on November 15, 2002, and realizes a gain of $40,000. Winnie may exclude all of the gain because (254/730) of $250,000 is more than the $40,000 realized gain. She owns and uses the residence in Cleveland for 254 days, and the period between the sale of the residence in Detroit and the sale in Cleveland is 379 days. ◀

ADDITIONAL COMMENT
If Winnie's gain in Example I2-59 is $100,000, she may exclude $86,986 (254/730 × $250,000).

OWNERSHIP AND USE TESTS If a principal residence is sold before satisfying the ownership and use tests, part of the gain may be excluded if the sale is due to a change in employment, health, or unforseen circumstances. The portion of the gain excluded is determined by multiplying the amount of the exclusion (i.e., $250,000 or $500,000) by a fraction whose numerator is the number of days the use and ownership tests were met and the denominator is 730 days.

EXAMPLE I12-60 ▶ Tim, a single taxpayer who purchased his home on January 1, 2001, for $500,000, recently became ill and sells his home in order to move closer to a relative who can care for him. Tim sells his principal residence on September 14, 2001, for $620,000 realizing a gain of $120,000. Because he owned and occupied the residence for 256 days and the sale was due to a change in his health, he may exclude $87,671 ($250,000 × 256/730) ◀

For purposes of the two-year ownership rule, a taxpayer's period of ownership includes the period during which the taxpayer's deceased spouse owned the residence. When a taxpayer receives a residence from a spouse or an ex-spouse incident to a divorce, the taxpayer's period of owning the property includes the time the residence was owned by the spouse or ex-spouse.[82]

EXAMPLE I12-61 ▶ Sachie receives an $800,000 residence owned for six years by, Richard, her former spouse as part of a divorce settlement. Richard's basis for the residence is $430,000. They lived in the house for five years prior to the divorce. Three months after transfer of the residence to Sachie, she sells it for $825,000, and $250,000 of her $395,000 realized gain is excluded. Sachie must recognize a $145,000 LTCG. ◀

---

[80] Rene A. Stiegler, Jr., 1964 PH T.C. Memo ¶64,057, 23 TCM 412.
[81] Sec. 121(c).
[82] Sec. 121(d)(2) and (3).

12-20 Individuals ▼ Chapter 12

STOP & THINK

Question: Rebecca's uncle told her that she could purchase his house for $150,000 in five years provided that she could pay at least $30,000 of the purchase price in cash. Rebecca has $15,000 and is considering two alternative methods to obtain the remaining $15,000 in five years. The first alternative is to purchase $15,000 of non-dividend paying stock that she expects to increase in value to $30,000 within five years. The second alternative is to purchase an $80,000 residence by paying $15,000 and borrowing $65,000. Payments on the mortgage will be interest only for five years and amount to $450 per month. Insurance, property taxes and other home ownership expenses average $90 per month. She expects the house to be worth $95,000 at the end of five years. She will rent an apartment for $540 per month if she buys the stock. Ignoring transaction costs and assuming that she does not itemize deductions, should Rebecca purchase the stock or the house?

Solution: The $15,000 gain resulting from sale of the stock is LTCG and probably taxed at 20%. If the rate is 20%, she must pay taxes of $3,000 and has only $27,000 available to use to purchase her uncle's house. She will have a gain of $15,000 if she sells the house but the gain is excluded. She has $30,000 of cash and is able to buy her uncle's house. The tax law encourages Rebecca to buy a principal residence.

INVOLUNTARY CONVERSION OF A PRINCIPAL RESIDENCE

Ordinarily, the involuntary conversion of a principal residence is governed by Sec. 1033, discussed earlier in this chapter. A gain due to an involuntary conversion of a personal residence may be deferred if the requirements of Sec. 1033 are satisfied. The functional use test must be satisfied regardless of the type of involuntary conversion.

For purposes of Sec. 121, the destruction, theft, seizure, requisition, or condemnation of property is treated as a sale.[83] Thus, taxpayers may exclude a gain of up to $250,000 or $500,000 due to the involuntary conversion of a principal residence if the use and ownership test is satisfied. Taxpayers normally prefer to exclude gain if the use and ownership tests are satisfied rather than defer gain under the involuntary conversion provisions.

If taxpayers make a proper and timely replacement of the residence subject to the involuntary conversion, gain may be excluded up to $250,000, or $500,000, and the remaining gain may be deferred. For purposes of applying the involuntary conversion provisions, the amount realized due to the involuntary conversion is reduced by any gain excluded under Sec. 121.[84]

EXAMPLE I12-62 ▶ The Koch's principal residence, with an adjusted basis of $200,000, has been used and owned by them for nine years. The house is destroyed by a hurricane and the Kochs receive insurance proceeds of $820,000. Four months later, they purchase another residence for $900,000. The Kochs have a realized gain of $620,000 and may exclude $500,000 under Sec. 121. The remaining $120,000 gain may be deferred and the basis of their replacement residence is $780,000 ($900,000 − $120,000). ◀

Because the amount realized is reduced by the gain excluded, the Kochs could have deferred the $120,000 gain in the above example by investing $320,000 in a replacement residence.

If gain due to the involuntary conversion of a principal residence is deferred under Sec. 1033, the holding period of the replacement residence includes the holding period of the converted property for purposes of satisfying the use and ownership tests of Sec. 121.[85] The Kochs satisfy the use and ownership requirements for Sec. 121 with respect to their new residence in Example I12-62 because gain is deferred under Sec. 1033.

A loss due to a condemnation of a personal residence is not recognized. If the loss is due to a casualty, the loss is deductible and is treated like other casualty losses of non-business property (see Chapter I8).

---

[83] Sec. 121(d)(5)(A).
[84] Sec. 121(d)(5)(B).

[85] Sec. 121(d)(8).

ADDITIONAL COMMENT

Because of the tremendous damage and hardships produced by Hurricane Andrew in Florida and the flooding of the Mississippi River, Congress responded with substantial tax relief for taxpayers who received insurance proceeds for damaged personal property, and made the favorable tax treatment retroactive to disasters after August 31, 1991.

PRESIDENTIALLY DECLARED DISASTER OF A PRINCIPAL RESIDENCE. Special treatment is provided when a taxpayer's principal residence or any of its contents is compulsorily or involuntarily converted and the residence is located in an area which is determined by the President to be in an area that warrants assistance by the federal government under the Disaster Relief and Emergency Assistance Act. Part of the gain resulting from the receipt of insurance proceeds is excluded if the President's declaration is after August 31, 1991.[86]

No gain is recognized due to the receipt of insurance proceeds for damaged personal property located in the residence if the property was unscheduled property for the purpose of such insurance. Although proceeds received for property that is not separately scheduled are excluded from gross income, other proceeds received, including those received for scheduled property, are treated as being received as a common fund for a single item of property. Separately scheduled property typically consists of items such as computers, jewelry, artwork, and pianos.

EXAMPLE I12-63 ▶ Nora's principal residence, with an adjusted basis of $70,000, was destroyed by a flood in May 2001. The area was declared by the President to be a federal disaster area. All of the contents of her home, including a Steinway grand piano with a basis of $25,000 and a FMV of $30,000, were destroyed. Nora received the following payments from the insurance company in July 2001: $200,000 for the house, $25,000 for personal property contents with an adjusted basis of $15,000, and $30,000 for the piano, which was separately scheduled property in the insurance policy. The $10,000 ($25,000 − $15,000) gain on the unscheduled personal property is excluded from gross income. The $135,000 gain attributable to the house and the piano is excluded under Sec. 121. ◀

TAX PLANNING CONSIDERATIONS

AVOIDING THE LIKE-KIND EXCHANGE PROVISIONS

In some cases, a taxpayer may prefer a taxable exchange to a nontaxable like-kind exchange. For instance, if the gain is taxed as a capital gain and the taxpayer has capital losses to offset the gain, the taxpayer may prefer to recognize the gain during the current year. If gain on the exchange is recognized instead of deferred, the basis of the property received in the exchange is higher.

EXAMPLE I12-64 ▶ Connie owns land with a $20,000 basis. The land is held as an investment. Connie exchanges the land for a duplex with a $100,000 FMV. Because the exchange qualifies as a like-kind exchange, no gain is recognized and Connie's basis for the duplex is $20,000. If the exchange does not qualify as a like-kind exchange (e.g., the land is a personal-use asset), Connie recognizes an $80,000 capital gain. Connie's basis for the duplex is $100,000. The basis of the duplex, except for the portion allocable to land, is eligible for depreciation. ◀

If an exchange qualifies as a like-kind exchange, no loss on the exchange is recognized. A taxpayer who prefers to recognize a loss should avoid making a like-kind exchange. It may be advantageous to sell the property to recognize the loss and then purchase the replacement asset in two independent transactions. If the sale and purchase transactions are with the same party, the IRS may maintain that the like-kind exchange rules apply because the two transactions are in substance a like-kind exchange (i.e., the judicial doctrine of substance over form might be applied).

---

[86] Sec. 1033(h)(1)(A) The Revenue Reconciliation Act of 1993 granted retroactive tax relief for taxpayers because of the mass destruction in Florida caused by Hurricane Andrew and the flooding in several midwest states that occurred in 1993.

SALE OF A PRINCIPAL RESIDENCE

ELECTION PROVISION. When the requirements of Sec. 121 are satisfied, gain is excluded unless the taxpayer elects not to have Sec. 121 apply.[87] It is unlikely that a taxpayer will ever have an incentive to elect not to apply Sec. 121.

IDENTIFYING THE PRINCIPAL RESIDENCE. In view of the advantages of excluding gain on the sale of a principal residence, a taxpayer contemplating a sale should satisfy all requirements of Sec. 121. A taxpayer who owns and occupies more than one residence may have difficulty identifying the principal residence. The *principal residence* is the one that the taxpayer occupies most of the time.[88]

EXAMPLE I12-65 ▶ Paula, a business consultant, owns residences in Boston and Philadelphia. She plans to sell both residences in two years and purchase a new residence in California. The Boston residence has a FMV that is $200,000 greater than its basis. The residence in Philadelphia has not appreciated. Paula should plan her activities in a manner that will allow her to occupy the Boston residence more than the Philadelphia residence so the Boston residence will qualify as her principal residence. ◀

PROPERTY CONVERTED TO BUSINESS USE. If a residence is converted to business use at the time of the sale, it does not qualify as a principal residence.[89] A principal residence converted to business use may subsequently become the taxpayer's principal residence if the business use is discontinued for a period of time.[90]

EXAMPLE I12-66 ▶ Brad, a college professor, uses 20% of his residence as an office from 1975 until 2001. Brad deducted expenses related to the office portion of the residence for the years 1975 through 1980. After 1980, no deduction was allowed because Brad no longer met the eligibility requirements for an office-in-home deduction. (See Chapter I9 for a discussion of the office-in-home deduction.) If Brad sold the property before 1981, only 80% of the property would have qualified as a principal residence and 20% would be considered business property. Alternatively, if he sells the residence in 2001, he may exclude up to $250,000 of gain. The entire residence is considered to be his principal residence because the business use has been discontinued. The basis of the residence is reduced by the depreciation allowed from 1975 through 1980. ◀

The Taxpayer Relief Act of 1997 created a major change for the sale of a principal residence when depreciation has been allowed or allowable for periods attributable to periods after May 6, 1997. Only the gain in excess of the amount of depreciation after May 6, 1997, is eligible to be excluded under Sec. 121.[91]

Note that under the new law, a taxpayer such as Brad in Example I12-66 will not be able to exclude all of the gain under Sec. 121 if depreciation was allowed after May 6, 1997, even if the residence is being used solely as a residence at the time of sale.

EXAMPLE I12-67 ▶ Ilena purchased a residence on June 1, 1997, for $150,000 and uses 20% of the residence as an office for her consulting business until she sells the residence in November of the current year for $200,000. She must treat the transaction as the sale of two assets and may exclude the $40,000 gain on the sale of the residence ($160,000 − $120,000). Because 20% of the house is not being used as a principal residence, the gain on the portion of the house used for the consulting business must be recognized. The amount of the gain is $40,000 less the adjusted basis which is $30,000 less depreciation allowed. ◀

EXAMPLE I12-68 ▶ Bobbi purchased a house in 1986 and used it as her principal residence until March 1, 1997, when she rented the house to the Allens while she lived with her mother. On November 1, 2000, the Allens' lease expired and she moved back into the house. She sells the house on July 12, 2001, and realizes a gain of $210,000. She may not exclude any of the gain because she has not used the property as her principal residence for two of the last five years. ◀

---

[87] Sec. 121(f).
[88] Rev. Rul. 77-298, 1977-2 C.B. 308.
[89] Reg. Sec. 1.1034-1(a)(3)(ii).
[90] Rev. Rul. 82-26, 1982-1 C.B. 114.
[91] Sec. 121(d)(6).

EXAMPLE I12-69 ▶ Assume the same facts as in I12-68 except that Bobbi sells the house on December 12, 2002. Because she has used the property as her principal residence for two of the last five years, she may exclude the excess of the $210,000 gain over depreciation allowed after May 6, 1997. ◀

COMPLIANCE AND PROCEDURAL CONSIDERATIONS

REPORTING OF INVOLUNTARY CONVERSIONS

ADDITIONAL COMMENT
The failure to include gain from an involuntary conversion in gross income is deemed to be an election even though the details are not reported.

The election to defer recognition of the gain from an involuntary conversion is made by not reporting the gain as income for the first year in which gain is realized. All details pertaining to the involuntary conversion (including those relating to the replacement of the converted property) should be reported for the taxable year or years in which any of the gain is realized.[92]

A taxpayer who elects to defer recognition of the gain but does not make a proper replacement of the property within the required period of time must file an amended return for the year or years for which the election was made. An amended return may be needed if the cost of the replacement property is less than expected at the time of the election. All details pertaining to the replacement of converted property must be reported in the year in which replacement occurs.[93]

EXAMPLE I12-70 ▶ Bob's property, with a $40,000 adjusted basis, was destroyed by a storm in 2000. Bob received $45,000 insurance proceeds in 2000 and planned to purchase property similar to the converted property in 2001 at a cost of $47,000. Bob elected to defer recognition of the gain in 2000. In 2001 the replacement property is purchased for $44,500. Bob must file an amended return for 2000 and recognize a $500 ($45,000 − $44,500) gain. ◀

ADDITIONAL COMMENT
The replacement period may be extended if special permission is obtained from the IRS.

A taxpayer who either is ineligible or does not want to defer the gain must report the gain in the usual manner. If a taxpayer does not elect to defer the gain in the year the gain is realized and the replacement period has not expired, a subsequent election may be made. In such an event, a refund claim should be filed for the tax year in which the gain was realized and previously recognized.[94]

Taxpayers who do not initially elect to defer the gain from an involuntary conversion may later make the election, but the election may not subsequently be revoked. The Tax Court has ruled that the Treasury Regulations allow the filing of an amended return for a year in which the election is made only if proper replacement is not made within the specified time period or the replacement is made at a cost lower than anticipated at the time of the election.[95] The IRS takes the position that taxpayers who designate qualifying property as replacement property may not later designate other qualifying property as the replacement property.[96]

EXAMPLE I12-71 ▶ In 1999 Troy collected $200,000 from an insurance company as the result of the destruction of rental property with a $140,000 basis. He made the election to defer the gain realized in 1999 and attached a supporting schedule of details regarding the involuntary conversion including a designation of replacement property to be acquired in 2000. In 2000 Troy purchased the designated replacement rental property for $225,000. In 2001 Troy purchases other rental property for $400,000 and now wants to designate that property as the replacement property for the property destroyed in 1999. Troy may not designate the property acquired in 2001 as the replacement property because the rental property purchased in 2000 was already designated as such. ◀

---

[92] Reg. Sec. 1.1033(a)-2(c)(2).
[93] Ibid.
[94] Ibid.
[95] *John McShain*, 65 T.C. 686 (1976).
[96] Rev. Rul. 83-39, 1983-1 C.B. 190.

REPORTING OF SALE OR EXCHANGE OF A PRINCIPAL RESIDENCE

Prior to 1998, Form 2119 was used to report the sale or exchange of a principal residence, however the form was eliminated in 1998. Taxpayers only have to report the sale if any of the gain is not excluded. If the taxpayer does not qualify to exclude all of the gain or elects not to exclude the gain, the entire gain realized is reported on Schedule D either on line 1, if residence is held for one year or less, or on line 8. On the line below where the entire gain is shown, the taxpayer should indicate on the following line the amount of the gain that is being excluded as a loss (i.e., show in parentheses).

Publication 523, Selling Your Home provides the following worksheet that may be used to determine if any gain is recognized. If the taxpayer has to utilize the exceptions to the two-year ownership and use tests, a different worksheet is provided.

Worksheet 2. Gain (or Loss), Exclusion, and Taxable Gain

Part 1–Gain (or Loss) on Sale
1. Selling price of home . . . . _____
2. Selling expenses . . . . _____
3. Subtract line 2 from line 1 . . . . _____
4. Adjusted basis of home sold. (From Worksheet 1, line 15.) . . . . _____
5. Subtract line 4 from line 3. This is the **gain (or loss)** on the sale. If this is a loss, stop here . . _____

Part 2–Exclusion and Taxable Gain
6. Maximum exclusion. (See *Amount of Exclusion* in this chapter.) . . . . _____
7. Enter any depreciation claimed on the property for periods after May 6, 1997. If none, enter zero _____
8. Subtract line 7 from line 5. (If the result is less than zero, enter zero.) . . . . _____
9. Subtract line 7 from line 6 . . . . _____
10. Enter the smaller of line 8 or 9. This is your exclusion. If you are reporting the sale on the installment method, enter this amount on line 15 of Form 6252 . . . . _____
11. Subtract line 10 from line 5. This is your taxable gain. Report it on Schedule D (Form 1040) as described under *Reporting the Gain* in this chapter. If the amount on this line is zero, do not report the sale or exclusion on your tax return . . . . _____

PROBLEM MATERIALS

DISCUSSION QUESTIONS

I12-1 Evaluate the following statement: The underlying rationale for the nonrecognition of a gain or loss resulting from a like-kind exchange is that the exchange constitutes a liquidation of the taxpayer's investment.

I12-2 Why might a taxpayer want to avoid having an exchange qualify as a like-kind exchange?

I12-3 Debbie owns office equipment with a basis of $300,000 acquired on May 10, 1994. Debbie exchanges the equipment for other office equipment owned by Doug on July 23, 2001. Doug's equipment has an FMV of $500,000. Both Debbie and Doug use the equipment in their businesses.
  a. What is Debbie's basis for the office equipment received in the exchange and when does the holding period start for that equipment?
  b. If Debbie and Doug are related taxpayers, explain what action could occur that would cause the exchange not to qualify as a like-kind exchange.

I12-4 Kay owns equipment used in her business and exchanges the equipment for other like-kind equipment and marketable securities.
  a. Will Kay's recognized gain ever exceed the realized gain?
  b. Will Kay's recognized gain ever exceed the FMV of the marketable securities?
  c. What is the basis of the marketable securities received?
  d. When does the holding period of the marketable securities begin?

I12-5 Demetrius sells word processing equipment used in his business to Edith. He then purchases new word processing equipment from Zip Corporation.

a. Do the sale and purchase qualify as a like-kind exchange?
b. When may a sale and a subsequent purchase be treated as a like-kind exchange?

I12-6 When determining whether property qualifies as like-kind property, is the quality or grade of the property considered?

I12-7 What is personal property of a like class that meets the definition of like-kind?

I12-8 When does a nonsimultaneous exchange qualify as a like-kind exchange?

I12-9 Burke is anxious to purchase land owned by Kim for use in his trade or business. Kim's basis for the land is $150,000 and Burke has offered to pay $800,000 if she will sell within the next 10 days. Kim is interested in selling but wants to avoid recognizing gain. What advice would you give?

I12-10 Lanny wants to purchase a farm owned by Jane, but Jane does not want to recognize a gain on the transfer of the appreciated property. Explain how a three-party exchange might be used to allow Lanny to obtain the farm without Jane having to recognize a gain.

I12-11 Does the receipt of boot in a transaction that otherwise qualifies as a like-kind exchange always cause the exchange to be at least partially taxable?

I12-12 When must a taxpayer who gives boot recognize a gain or loss?

I12-13 What is the justification for Sec. 1033, which allows a taxpayer to elect to defer a gain resulting from an involuntary conversion? May a taxpayer elect under Sec. 1033 to defer recognition of a loss resulting from an involuntary conversion?

I12-14 Must property be actually condemned for the conversion of property to be classified as an involuntary conversion? Explain.

I12-15 What are severance damages? What is the tax treatment for severance damages received if the taxpayer does not use the severance damages to restore the retained property?

I12-16 The functional use test is often used to determine whether the replacement property is similar or related in service or use to the property converted. Explain the functional use test.

I12-17 In what situations may a gain due to an involuntary conversion of real property be deferred if like-kind property is purchased to replace the converted property?

I12-18 Prior to the Taxpayer Relief Act of 1997, taxpayers could defer a gain on the sale of a principal residence sold before May 7, 1997, if they purchased and occupied a new principal residence within two years before or after the sale and the cost of the new residence was at least equal to the adjusted sales price of the old residence. Some taxpayers who were at least 55 years old had a once-in-a-lifetime exclusion up to $125,000 if they owned and used the property as a principal residence for at least three years of the five-year-period ending on the date of sale. Discuss why current law with respect to the sale of a personal residence is more favorable than the law prior to the Taxpayer Relief Act of 1997.

I12-19 One reason Congress expanded the exclusion of gain on the sale of a principal residence and eliminated the deferral provision was to eliminate the need for many taxpayers to keep records of capital improvements that increase the basis of their residence. Why might taxpayers still need to maintain such records to substantiate the adjusted basis of their principal residence?

I12-20 Steve maintains that the cost of wallpapering his three-bedroom house is a capital expenditure while Martha maintains that the cost of wallpapering her three-bedroom house is an expense. Steve uses his house as his personal residence while Martha's house is rental property. Explain why Steve and Martha view the cost of wallpapering differently.

I12-21 The Nelsons purchased a new residence in 1988 for $200,000 from David who owned and used the residence as rental property. When the Nelsons wanted to purchase the property, it was being rented to tenants who had four months remaining on their lease. The Nelsons paid the tenants $1,000 to relinquish the lease and vacant the property. They deferred a $70,000 gain on the sale of a principal residence on December 10, 1987. In 1990, they added a family room to the house at a cost of $45,300. In 1994, they suffered hail damage to the roof and received $6,000 from the insurance company. They did not repair the damaged roof, and no casualty loss was allowed. What is their adjusted basis for the house today?

I12-22 What requirements must be satisfied by an unmarried taxpayer under Sec. 121 to be eligible for the election to exclude a gain up to $250,000 on the sale or exchange of a principal residence?

ISSUE IDENTIFICATION QUESTIONS

I12-23 John owns 25% of the ABC Partnership and Jane owns 25% of the XYZ Partnership. The ABC Partnership owns a farm and produces corn and the XYZ Partnership owns a farm and produces soybeans. John and Jane agree to exchange their partnership interests. What tax issues should John and Jane consider?

I12-24 Chauvin Oil Corporation operates primarily in the United States and owns an offshore drilling rig with an adjusted basis of $400,000 that it uses near Louisiana. Chauvin, Inc. exchanges the rig for a new rig with a FMV of $1,000,000, and Chauvin also pays $250,000. Chauvin plans to expand its drilling operations to offshore sites near Finland. What tax issues should the Chauvin Corporation consider?

I12-25 Jaharta, Inc. owns land used for truck farming and cattle raising. The California Division of Highways condemned 36 acres of Jaharta's land to build a new highway. Jaharta owned a 50% interest in property being used for apricot, prune, and walnut orchards. Jaharta used the proceeds received as a result of the condemnation to purchase the remaining interest in the property being used for orchards.

PROBLEMS

I12-26 *Like-Kind Property.* Which of the following exchanges qualify as like-kind exchanges under Sec. 1031?
a. Acme Corporation stock held for investment purposes for Mesa Corporation stock also held for investment purposes
b. A motel used in a trade or business for an apartment complex held for investment
c. A pecan orchard in Texas used in a trade or business for an orange grove in Florida used in a trade or business
d. A one-third interest in a general partnership for a one-fourth interest in a limited partnership
e. Inventory for equipment used in a trade or business
f. Unimproved land held as an investment for a warehouse used in a trade or business
g. An automobile used as a personal-use asset for marketable securities held for investment

I12-27 *Like-Kind Property.* Which of the following exchanges qualify as like-kind exchanges under Sec. 1031?
a. A motel in Texas for a motel in Italy
b. An office building held for investment for an airplane to be used in the taxpayer's business
c. Land held for investment for marketable securities held for investment
d. Land held for investment for a farm to be used in the taxpayer's business

I12-28 *Like-Kind Exchange: Boot.* Determine the realized gain or loss, the recognized gain or loss, and the basis of the equipment received for the following like-kind exchanges:

Basis of Equipment Exchanged	FMV of Boot Received	FMV of Equipment Received
$40,000	$-0-	$75,000
50,000	10,000	70,000
60,000	25,000	65,000
70,000	30,000	60,000
80,000	20,000	50,000

I12-29 *Like-Kind Exchange: Personal Property.* Beach Corporation owns a computer with a $30,000 adjusted basis. The computer is used in the company's trade or business. What is the realized and recognized gain or loss for each of the following independent transactions?
a. The computer is exchanged for a used computer with a $70,000 FMV plus $12,000 cash.
b. The computer is exchanged for a used computer with a $18,000 FMV plus $7,000 cash.
c. The computer is exchanged for marketable securities with a $61,000 FMV.

I12-30 *Like-Kind Exchange: Personal Property.* Boise Corporation exchanges a machine with a $14,000 basis for a new machine with an $18,000 FMV and $3,000 cash. The machines are used in Boise's business and are in the same General Asset Class.
a. What are Boise Corporation's recognized gain and the basis for the new machine?
b. How would your answer to Part a change if the corporation's machine is also subject to a $6,000 liability, and the liability is assumed by the other party?

I12-31 *Exchange of Personal Property.* Lithuania Corporation operates a ferry service and owns four barges. Lithuania exchanges one of the barges with an adjusted basis of $350,000 for a used smaller barge with a FMV of $444,000 and a $26,000 computer. Without considering the exchange, Lithuania Corporation's taxable income is $700,000.
a. What is the realized gain on the exchange?
b. What is the recognized gain?
c. What is the basis of the new barge?
d. What is the basis of the computer?
e. Assume that the recognized gain is $26,000 and the gain is not capital gain. What is the increase in Lithuania's tax liability as a result of the exchange?

I12-32 *Like-Kind Exchange: Liabilities.* Paul owns a building used in his business with an adjusted basis of $400,000 and an $750,000 FMV. He exchanges the building for a building owned by David. David's building has a $950,000 FMV but is subject to a $200,000 liability. Paul assumes David's liability and uses David's building in his business.
a. What is Paul's realized gain?
b. What is Paul's recognized gain?
c. What is Paul's basis for the building received?

I12-33 *Like-Kind Exchange: Liabilities.* Helmut exchanges his apartment complex for Heidi's farm, and the exchange qualifies as a like-kind exchange. Helmut's adjusted basis for the apartment complex is $600,000 and the complex is subject to a $180,000 liability. The FMV of Heidi's farm is $770,000 and the farm is subject to a $100,000 liability. Each asset is transferred subject to the liability. What is Helmut's recognized gain and the basis of the new farm?

I12-34 *Like-Kind Exchange: Liabilities.* Sheila owns land with a basis of $100,000 and FMV of $220,000. The land is subject to an $80,000 liability. Sheila plans to exchange the land for land owned by Tony that has a $250,000 FMV but is subject to a liability of $150,000. Sheila plans to assume Tony's debt and Tony will assume her $80,000 debt. Because the exchange is not of equal value, how much cash must Tony transfer to equalize the exchange?

I12-35 *Like-Kind Exchange: Transfer of Boot.* Wayne exchanges unimproved land with a $50,000 basis and marketable securities with a $10,000 basis for an eight-unit apartment building having a $150,000 FMV. The land and marketable securities are held by Wayne as investments, and the apartment building is held as an investment. The marketable securities have a $25,000 FMV. What is his realized gain, recognized gain, and the basis for the apartment building?

I12-36 *Like-Kind Exchange: Related Parties.* Bob owns a duplex used as rental property. The duplex has a basis of $86,000 and $300,000 FMV. He transfers the duplex to Cindy, his sister, in exchange for a triplex that she owns. The triplex has a basis of $279,000 and a $300,000 FMV. Two months after the exchange, Cindy sells the duplex to a business associate for $312,000.
a. What is Bob's realized and recognized gain on the exchange?
b. What is Cindy's realized and recognized gain on the exchange?

I12-37 *Like-Kind Exchange: Related Parties.* Assume the same facts as in I12-36 except Cindy sells the duplex to a nonrelated individual more than two years after the exchange with Bob. Ignore any changes in adjusted basis due to depreciation that would have occurred after the exchange.
a. What is Bob's realized and recognized gain on the exchange?
b. What is Cindy's realized and recognized gain on the exchange?
c. What is Cindy's realized and recognized gain on the sale?

I12-38 *Involuntary Conversion.* Duke Corporation owns an office building with a $400,000 adjusted basis. The building is destroyed by a tornado. The insurance company paid $750,000 as compensation for the loss. Eight months after the loss, Duke uses the insurance proceeds and other funds to acquire a new office building for $682,000 and machinery for one of the company's plants at a $90,000 cost. Assuming that Duke elects to defer as much of the gain as possible, what is the recognized gain, the basis for the new office building, and the basis for the machinery acquired?

I12-39 *Involuntary Conversion: Replacement Period.* The Madison Corporation paid $3,000 for several acres of land in 1992 to use in its business. The land is condemned and taken by the state in March 2001. The company receives $25,000 from the state. Whenever pos-

sible, the corporation elects to minimize taxable income. For each of the following independent cases, what is the recognized gain or loss in 2001 on the conversion and the tax basis of the replacement property (whenever the property is replaced)?
a. The land will not be replaced.
b. Replacement land will be purchased in July 2002 for $22,500.
c. Replacement land will be purchased in July 2003 for $28,500.
d. Replacement land will be purchased in July 2004 for $23,600.

I12-40 *Involuntary Conversion of Real Property.* On April 27, 2001, an office building owned by Newark Corporation, an offshore drilling company that is a calendar-year taxpayer, is destroyed by a hurricane. The basis of the office building is $600,000, and the corporation receives $840,000 from the insurance company.
a. To defer the entire gain due to the involuntary conversion, what amount must the corporation pay for replacement property?
b. To defer the gain due to the involuntary conversion, by what date must the corporation replace the converted property?
c. If Newark replaces the office building by purchasing a 900,000 gallon storage tank at an $810,000 cost, may it defer any of the gain due to the involuntary conversion?
d. How would your answers to Parts b and c change if the office building had been condemned by the state? Explain.

I12-41 *Involuntary Conversion: Different Methods of Replacement.* On September 3, 2001, Federal Corporation's warehouse is totally destroyed by fire. $800,000 of insurance proceeds are received, and the realized gain is $300,000. Whenever possible, Federal elects to defer gains. For each of the following independent situations, what is the amount of gain recognized? Explain why the gain is not deferred, if applicable.
a. On October 23, 2001, Federal purchases a warehouse for $770,000.
b. On February 4, 2002, Federal purchases 100% of the Park Corporation, which owns a warehouse. Federal pays $895,000 for the stock.
c. On March 10, 2002, Federal receives a capital contribution from its majority shareholder. The shareholder transfers a warehouse to the corporation. The warehouse's FMV is $975,000. The shareholder's basis in the warehouse is $635,000.
d. On November 20, 2003, Federal purchases an apartment complex for $900,000.
e. On March 26, 2004, Federal purchases a warehouse for $888,000.

I12-42 *Severance Damages.* Twelve years ago, Marilyn purchased two lots in an undeveloped subdivision as an investment. Each lot has a $10,000 basis and a $40,000 FMV when the city condemns one lot for use as a municipal sewage treatment plant. As a result of the condemnation, Marilyn receives $40,000 from the city. Because the value of the other lot is reduced, the city pays $7,500 severance damages. She does not plan to replace the condemned lot.
a. What is her recognized gain due to the condemnation?
b. What is her recognized gain from the receipt of the severance damages?
c. What is her basis for the lot she continues to own?

I12-43 *Sale of a Principal Residence.* Marc, age 45, sells his personal residence on May 15, 2001, for $70,000. He pays $5,000 in selling expenses and $600 in repair expenses. He has lived in the residence since 1980, when he purchased it for $40,000. In 1984, he paid $4,000 to install central air conditioning. If Marc purchases a new principal residence in December of the current year for $62,000, what is the realized gain, recognized gain, and the basis for the new residence?

I12-44 *Sale of a Principal Residence.* Mr. and Mrs. Rusbarsky purchased a residence on June 12, 1998, for $200,000. On March 12, 2001, they sell the residence for $300,000, and selling expenses amount to $11,000. They purchase another house in a new subdivision for $275,000. Determine the gain realized and recognized.

I12-45 *Sale of a Principal Residence.* On January 10, 2001, Kirsten married Joe. Joe sold his personal residence on October 25, 2000, and excluded the entire gain of $175,000. Although they had originally planned to live in the house that Kirsten had received as a gift from her parents in 1992, they decided to purchase a larger house, and Kirsten sold her house and realized a $370,000 gain.
a. If they file a joint return, how much of the $370,000 gain may be excluded?
b. If Kirsten files as married filing separately, how much of the $370,000 gain may be excluded?

I12-46 *Involuntary Conversion of Principal Residence.* Mr. and Mrs. Mahan own and live in a house, with an adjusted basis of $200,000, that was purchased in 1994. The house is destroyed by a tornado on March 10 of the current year, and the Mahans receive insurance proceeds of $275,000. They purchase another residence for $322,000 four months later.
  a. May they exclude the $75,000 gain, and if so, what is the basis of the residence purchased in July?
  b. May they defer the $75,000 gain, and if so, what is the basis of the residence purchased in July?

I12-47 *Sale of a Principal Residence.* Mr. and Mrs. Kitchens purchased their first home in Ohio for $135,000 on October 1, 2000. Because Mr. Kitchens' employer transferred him to Utah, they sold the house for $160,000 on January 10, 2001. How much of the gain is recognized?

I12-48 *Sale of a Principal Residence.* Prior to the Taxpayer Relief Act of 1997, taxpayers could defer a gain on the sale of a principal residence sold before May 7, 1997. To defer all of the gain, the taxpayer had to make a timely purchase of a replacement residence that cost more than the adjusted sales price of the residence sold. The basis of the replacement residence was reduced by the gain deferred.

Answer the following questions to demonstrate why Beverley and George might prefer the law prior to the Taxpayer Relief Act if they sell their principal residence for $900,000, with an adjusted basis of $200,000. Selling expenses of $20,000 were paid. They owned and occupied the home for 20 years and file a joint return. The amount realized is equal to the adjusted sales price, and they purchase a new residence for $1,000,000 two weeks after the sale.
  a. Under current law, what is the gain recognized and the basis of their new residence?
  b. If the sale had occurred prior to May 7, 1997, what is the gain recognized and the basis of their new residence?
  c. Which law might they prefer?

I12-49 *Sale of a Principal Residence.* Ray and Ellie have each owned a principal residence for more than five years. Ray's residence has an adjusted basis of $100,000 and a FMV of $325,000, while Ellie's residence has an adjusted basis of $300,000 and a FMV of $490,000. They plan to marry and will purchase another house.
  a. Should they sell their houses before the marriage in order to minimize their taxes?
  b. Will your answer to a change if the FMV of Ellie's house is $690,000.

I12-50 *Definition of a Principal Residence.* Ken's parents lived with him until 1999 in a house on 23rd Street purchased by Ken in 1998 for $30,000. In 1999 Ken married Beth and moved to a rented apartment. In 2001 they purchase a house on 42nd Street for $90,000 and Ken sells the house on 23rd Street for $60,000 when his parents move into a nursing home. Ken pays $4,000 selling expenses and $1,000 repair expenses. How much of the realized gain on the sale of the house on 23rd Street is recognized?

I12-51 *Sale of a Principal Residence: Rental Property.* For the last several years, Mr. and Mrs. Cockrell have rented their furnished basement to local college students. When determining their taxable income each year, they have deducted a portion of the utilities, property taxes, interest, and depreciation based on the fact that 15% of the house is used for rental purposes. The original basis of the property is $100,000, and depreciation of $4,000 has been allowed on the rental portion of the property. During the current year, Mr. and Mrs. Cockrell sell the house for $300,000. No selling expenses or fixing-up expenses are incurred. They plan to purchase a new principal residence and will no longer rent any portion of their house to college students.
  a. What is the amount realized on the sale of the principal residence?
  b. What is the realized and recognized gain on the sale of the principal residence?
  c. What is the amount realized on the sale of the portion of the residence not considered to be the principal residence?
  d. What is the realized and recognized gain on the sale of the portion of the residence not considered to be the principal residence?

I12-52 *Multiple Sales of a Principal Residence.* Consider the following information for Mr. and Mrs. Di Palma:
  - On June 10, 2000, they sold their principal residence for $80,000 and incur $6,000 of selling expenses. The basis of the residence, acquired in 1992, is $50,000.

- On June 25, 2000, they purchased a new principal residence for $90,000 and occupied it immediately.
- May 10, 2001, they purchase their neighbor's residence for $115,000 and occupy the residence immediately.
- August 29, 2001, they sell the residence purchased on June 25, 2000, for $148,000. They pay $7,000 of selling expenses.

a. What is the realized gain on the sale of the residence in 2000?
b. What is the recognized gain on the sale of the residence in 2000?
c. What is the realized gain on the sale of the residence in 2001?
d. What is the recognized gain on the sale of the residence in 2001?

I12-53 *Multiple Sales of a Principal Residence.* Consider the following information for Mr. and Mrs. Gomez:
- On May 26, 2000, they sold their principal residence, acquired in 1991, for $200,000. They paid $8,000 of selling expenses. Their basis in the residence was $70,000.
- On July 25, 2000, they purchased a new principal residence for $250,000.
- On June 2, 2001, Mr. Gomez, a bank officer, is transferred to another bank in the northern part of the state and they vacate their house.
- On July 1, 2001, they purchase a new principal residence for $420,000.
- On October 6, 2001, they sell the residence that was purchased on July 2, 2000 for $520,000. They pay $30,000 of selling expenses.

a. What is the realized gain on the sale of the residence in 2000?
b. What is the recognized gain on the sale of the residence in 2000?
c. What is the realized gain on the sale of the residence in 2001?
d. What is the recognized gain on the sale of the residence in 2001?

COMPREHENSIVE PROBLEM

I12-54 Paden, who is single and has been employed as an accountant for 27 years with Harper, Inc., lost his job due to company downsizing. His last day of employment is July 31, 2001, and Harper provides a $9,000 severance payment. The severance payments are based on an employee's time of employment. During the year, Paden received a salary of $36,000. Harper also paid $1,500 of Paden's medical insurance premiums.

In May, 2001, Paden, who had always wanted to be associated with a football team, applied for the head coaching job at Hawk University in Iowa and, much to his surprise, received the job. In June and July, Paden paid $4,500 to take courses in sports management at the local university. Hawk University is substantially short of funding and Paden paid $1,400 for entertainment expenses related to his job and $500 for supplies. No reimbursement was received.

On August 1, he sold his house for $329,000 and paid a sales commission of $14,000. He inherited the house 20 years ago when his mother died. Her basis for the house was $37,000 and the FMV when she died was $50,000. Property taxes for the 2001 calendar year amount to $3,600, and property taxes were apportioned at the closing. Property taxes are payable on October 1. He paid $12,000 of interest on home equity debt of $150,000.

To move to Iowa, he drove 200 miles and spent $25 for meals during the trip. Movers charged $4,150 to move his household items. He purchased a new house in Iowa for $150,000 on August 15 and borrowed $110,000. He also agreed to pay all property taxes for 2000. Real property taxes for the home in Iowa will be paid on January 30, 2002 and amount to $1,500. Interest on the $110,000 debt during the current year is $1,475. To obtain the loan, Paden paid points of $1,000.

He contributed common stock (basis of $1,000 and FMV of $6,000) held as an investment for three years to Hawk University and cash of $1,765 to the First United Methodist Church. He paid personal property taxes of $435 for his car.

Paden sold 200 shares of Dell Corporation stock on April 10 for $100 per share. His basis was $145 per share. On May 1, he purchased 300 shares of Dell at $89 per share.

Determine:
1. Gross income without considering the sale of his house or the Dell Corporation stock.
2. Recognized gain due to the sale of his house.
3. Net capital gain
4. Adjusted gross income
5. Total amount of itemized deductions

6. Taxable income
7. Basis of his house in Iowa
8. If the sales price for his home was $470,000 instead of $370,000, would his taxable income increase by more than $100,000. If yes, explain.

TAX FORM/RETURN PREPARATION PROBLEMS

I12-55 On October 29, 2000, Miss Joan Seely (SSN 123-45-6789) sells her principal residence for $150,000 cash. She purchased the residence on May 12, 1993 for $85,000. She spent $12,000 for capital improvements in 1994. To help sell the house, she pays $300 on October 2, 2000, for minor repairs made on that date. The realtor's commission amounts to $7,500. On February 3, 2001, she purchases a new principal residence for $130,000. Her old residence is never rented out or used for business. Complete the worksheet on page I12-24 for Miss Seely for 2000.

I12-56 At the beginning of the current year, Donna Harp was employed as a cinematographer by Farah Movie, Inc., a motion picture company in Los Angeles, California. In June, she accepted a new job with Ocala Production in Orlando, Florida. Donna is single and her social security number is 223-77-6793. She sold her house in California on August 10 for $500,000. She paid a $14,000 sales commission. The house was acquired on March 23, 1987, for $140,000.

The cost of transporting her household goods and personal effects from California to Orlando amounted to $2,350. To travel from California to Florida, she paid travel and lodging costs of $370 and $100 for meals.

On July 15, she purchased a house for $270,000 on 1225 Minnie Lane in Orlando. To purchase the house, she incurred a 20-year mortgage for $170,000. To obtain the loan, she paid points of $3,400. The $3,600 of property taxes for the house in Orlando were prorated with $1,950 being apportioned to the seller and $1,650 being apportioned to the buyer. In December of the current year she paid $3,600 for property taxes.

Other information related to her return:

Salary from Farah Movie, Inc.	$30,000
Salary from Ocala Production, Inc.	50,000
Federal income taxes withheld by Farah	6,000
Federal income taxes withheld by Ocala	12,000
FICA taxes withheld by Farah	2,295
FICA taxes withheld by Ocala	3,825
Dividend income	10,000
Interest paid for mortgage:	
Home in California	6,780
Home in Orlando	3,800
Property taxes paid in California	4,100
Sales taxes paid in California and Florida	3,125
State income taxes paid in California	2,900
Interest income from Sun National Bank	1,800

Prepare Form 1040 including Schedules A, B, and D and Form 3903.

I12-57 Jim Sarowski (SSN 344-77-9255) is 70 years old and single. He received social security benefits of $16,000. He works part-time as a greeter at a local discount store and received wages of $7,300. Federal income taxes of $250 were withheld from his salary. Jim lives at Rt. 7 in Daingerfield, Texas.

In March of the current year, he purchased a duplex at 2006 Tennessee Street to use as rental property for $100,000, with 20% of the price allocated to land. During the current year, he had the following receipts and expenditures with respect to the duplex:

Rent receipts	$8,800
Interest paid	5,900
Property taxes	1,400
Insurance	800
Maintenance	300

Other expenditures during the current year:

Contributions to the church	$2,600
Personal property taxes	225
Sales tax	345

On July 24 of the current year, he exchanged ten acres of land for a car with a $16,500 FMV to be held for personal use. The land was purchased on November 22, 1990, for $18,000 as an investment. Because of some pollution problems in the area, the value of the land declined.

On December 1 of the current year, he sold his residence, which had been his home for 30 years, for $475,000. Sales commissions of $16,000 were paid, and the adjusted basis for his home is $110,000. He plans to rent an apartment and does not plan to purchase another home. His only other sale of a principal residence occurred 32 years ago.

Prepare Forms 1040 and 4562 and Schedules D and E.

CASE STUDY PROBLEMS

I12-58 The Electric Corporation, a publicly held corporation, owns land with a $1,600,000 basis that is being held for investment. The company is considering exchanging the land for two assets owned by the Quail Corporation: land with a FMV of $3,000,000 and marketable securities with a $1,000,000 FMV. Both assets will be held by the Electric Corporation for investment, although the corporation is considering the possibility of developing the land and building residential houses. The president of the corporation has hired you to prepare a report explaining how the exchange will affect the corporation's reported net income and its tax liability. The corporation has a tax rate of 34%.

TAX RESEARCH PROBLEMS

I12-59 For the last nine years, Mr. and Mrs. Orchard live in a residence located on eight acres. In January of the current year they sell the home and two acres of land. The purchaser of the residence does not wish to own the entire eight acres of land. In December they sell the remaining 6 acres of land to another individual for $60,000. The house and the land have never been used by the Orchards in a trade or business or held for investment. The realized gains resulting from the two sales are computed as follows:

	House and Two Acres January Sales	Eight Acres December Sale
Selling price	$140,000	$60,000
Minus: selling expenses	(8,000)	(3,000)
Amount realized	$132,000	$57,000
Minus: Basis	(80,000)	(18,000)
Realized gain	$ 52,000	$39,000

In March they purchase a new residence for $225,000. As a result of the sales described above, what is the amount of realized gain that must be recognized during the current year?

A partial list of research sources is

- Sec. 1034
- Reg. Sec. 1.1034-1(c)(3)
- Rev. Rul. 76-541, 1976-2 C.B. 246

I12-60 George, age 68, decides to retire from farming and is considering selling his farm. The farm has a $100,000 basis and a $400,000 FMV. George's two sons are not interested in farming. Both sons have large families and would like to own houses suitable for their needs. The Iowa Corporation is willing to purchase George's farm. George's tax advisor suggests that Iowa Corporation should buy the two houses the sons want to own for $400,000 and then exchange the houses for George's farm. After the exchange, George could make a gift of the houses to the sons.

a. If the transactions are executed as suggested by the tax advisor, George's recognized gain will be $300,000. The transaction does not qualify as a like-kind exchange. Explain why.

b. George wants the exchange to qualify as a like-kind exchange and still help his sons obtain the houses. What advice do you have for him?

A partial list of research sources is

- *Dollie H. Click*, 78 T.C. 225 (1982)
- *Fred S. Wagensen*, 74 T.C. 653 (1980)

I12-61 On March 3, 1998, Jeremy, who was 53 years old, purchased a principal residence for $90,000. He has never been married. Except for two months in 1998 when Jeremy was on vacation in Hawaii, he owned and used the house as his principal residence until January 4, 2000, when he suffered a massive stroke. He was in the hospital until February 10, 2000, when he was moved to a nursing home because he was incapable of self-care.

If he sells the house on April 12, 2001, for $160,000, may Jeremy exclude the gain? A partial list of research sources is

- Sec. 121(d)(7)

CHAPTER 13

PROPERTY TRANSACTIONS: SECTION 1231 AND RECAPTURE

LEARNING OBJECTIVES

After studying this chapter, you should be able to

1. Identify Sec. 1231 property
2. Understand the tax treatment for Sec. 1231 transactions
3. Apply the recapture provisions of Sec. 1245
4. Apply the recapture provisions of Sec. 1250
5. Describe other recapture applications

13-2 Individuals ▼ Chapter 13

CHAPTER OUTLINE

History of Sec. 1231...13-2
Overview of Basic Tax Treatment for Sec. 1231...13-3
Section 1231 Property...13-5
Involuntary Conversions...13-6
Procedure for Sec. 1231 Treatment...13-7
Recapture Provisions of Sec. 1245...13-8
Recapture Provisions of Sec. 1250...13-11
Additional Recapture for Corporations...13-16
Recapture Provisions—Other Applications...13-17

Chapter 15 states that all recognized gains and losses must eventually be designated as either capital or ordinary. However, gains or losses on certain types of property are designated as Sec. 1231 gains or losses, which are given preferential treatment under the tax law. Ordinary loss treatment is accorded to a net Sec. 1231 loss, which is defined as the excess of Sec. 1231 losses over Sec. 1231 gains.[1] Net Sec. 1231 gain, which is the excess of Sec. 1231 gains over Sec. 1231 losses, is generally treated as long-term capital gain.[2] However, as with many provisions of the tax law, the preferential treatment of Sec. 1231 gains has been gradually diminished, principally by the so-called "depreciation recapture rules" and the five-year lookback rule. This chapter discusses the important rules dealing with Sec. 1231 gains and losses and depreciation recapture.

HISTORY OF SEC. 1231

During the depressed economy of the early and mid-1930s, business property was classified as a capital asset. Many business properties were worth less than their adjusted basis. Instead of selling business properties, taxpayers found it advantageous to retain assets that had declined in value because they could recover the full cost as depreciation. Capital losses had only limited deductibility during this period. To encourage the mobility of capital (i.e., the replacement of business fixed assets), the Revenue Act of 1938 added business property to the list of properties not considered to be capital assets.

During the period from 1938 to 1942, gains and losses on the sale or exchange of business property were treated as ordinary gains and losses. Favorable capital gain treatment was eliminated and taxpayers with appreciated business properties were reluctant to sell the assets because of the high tax cost. This restriction on the mobility of capital was more significant than usual because business assets had to be shifted into industries that were more heavily involved in the production of military goods. Furthermore, taxpayers were often forced to recognize ordinary gains because the government used the condemnation process to obtain business property for the war effort. In 1942, Congress created the predecessor of Sec. 1231, which allowed taxpayers to treat net gains from the sale of business property as capital gains and net losses as ordinary losses. Before 1987, only 40% of an individual's net capital gain might be subject to tax because of the 60% long-term capital gain deduction.

KEY POINT

If a taxpayer has gains, it is preferable to have the gains treated as capital gains; if a taxpayer has losses, it is preferable to have the losses treated as ordinary losses. Because Sec. 1231 property receives the preferable treatment for both net gains and losses, it has been said that this property enjoys the best of both worlds.

The Tax Reform Act of 1986 eliminated the 60% long-term capital gain deduction for net long-term capital gains. Favorable long-term capital gain treatment was reinstated into the tax law in 1991 in the form of a 28% maximum tax rate applying to net capital gains for noncorporate taxpayers. The Taxpayer Relief Act of 1997 significantly increased the preferential tax treatment by reducing the maximum rate to 20% for net capital gain that is adjusted net capital gain. However, to qualify for the 20% rate, the holding period was increased to greater than 18 months. Finally, the IRS Restructuring and Reform Act of 1998 eliminated the more than 18-month holding period requirement.

It may also be advantageous to have gains classified as capital or Sec. 1231 if taxpayers have capital losses or capital loss carryovers because of the limitations imposed on the deductibility of capital losses. Furthermore, there are other situations where it may be important for the property to be Sec. 1231 property (e.g., a contribution of appreciated property to a charitable organization).

---

[1] Secs. 1231(c)(4) and (a)(2).
[2] Secs. 1231(c)(3) and (a)(1). There are several exceptions to this rule that are covered later in this chapter.

OVERVIEW OF BASIC TAX TREATMENT FOR SEC. 1231

NET GAINS

At the end of the tax year, Sec. 1231 gains are netted against Sec. 1231 losses. If the overall result is a net Sec. 1231 gain, the gains and losses are treated as long-term capital gains (LTCGs) and long-term capital losses (LTCLs) respectively.[3] For the sake of expediency, it is often stated that a net Sec. 1231 gain is treated as a LTCG. For tax years beginning after 1984, however, a portion or all of the net Sec. 1231 gain may be treated as ordinary income because of a special five-year lookback rule (see discussion below).

EXAMPLE I13-1 ▶ Dawn owns a business that has $20,000 of Sec. 1231 gains and $12,000 of Sec. 1231 losses during the current year. Because the Sec. 1231 gains exceed the Sec. 1231 losses, the gains and losses are treated as LTCGs and LTCLs. After the gains and losses are offset, there is an $8,000 net long-term capital gain (NLTCG). ◀

EXAMPLE I13-2 ▶ Assume the same facts as in Example I13-1 except that Dawn also recognizes a $7,000 LTCG from the sale of a capital asset. After considering the $8,000 net Sec. 1231 gain, which is treated as a LTCG, Dawn has a $15,000 NLTCG ($8,000 + $7,000). ◀

NET LOSSES

If the netting of Sec. 1231 gains and losses at the end of the year results in a net Sec. 1231 loss, the Sec. 1231 gains and losses are treated as ordinary gains and losses.[4] For expediency, it is often stated that the net Sec. 1231 loss is treated as an ordinary loss.

EXAMPLE I13-3 ▶ David owns an unincorporated business and has $30,000 of Sec. 1231 gains and $40,000 of Sec. 1231 losses in the current year. Because the losses exceed the gains, they are treated as ordinary losses and gains. ◀

EXAMPLE I13-4 ▶ Assume the same facts as in Example I13-3 except that David receives a $37,000 salary as a corporate employee. David has no other income, losses, or deductions affecting his adjusted gross income (AGI). The Sec. 1231 gains and losses are treated as ordinary gains and losses, and David's AGI is $27,000 ($37,000 salary − $10,000 of ordinary loss). The $40,000 of ordinary losses offsets the $30,000 of ordinary gains and $10,000 of David's salary. ◀

TYPICAL MISCONCEPTION

It is sometimes erroneously thought that each Sec. 1231 gain should be treated as a LTCG and each Sec. 1231 loss as an ordinary loss. However all Sec. 1231 gains and losses must be combined to determine whether the Sec. 1231 gains and losses are LTCGs and LTCLs or ordinary gains and losses.

One important advantage of Sec. 1231 is illustrated in Example I13-4. Because the Sec. 1231 gains and losses are treated as ordinary, the $10,000 net Sec. 1231 loss is fully deductible in the current year. If the gains and losses were classified as long-term capital gains and losses, David would have a $10,000 NLTCL. Only $3,000 of the $10,000 NLTCL would have been deductible against David's other income. As explained in Chapter I5, only $3,000 of net capital losses may be deducted from non-capital gain income per year.

ADDITIONAL COMMENT

A taxpayer's share of a Sec. 1231 loss from a partnership or S Corporation may be subject to the passive activity loss rules.

FIVE-YEAR LOOKBACK RULE The Tax Reform Act of 1984 reduced the benefits of Sec. 1231. For tax years beginning after 1984, any net Sec. 1231 gain is ordinary gain to the extent of any nonrecaptured net Sec. 1231 losses from the previous five years.[5] This provision is referred to as the *five-year lookback rule*. In essence, net Sec. 1231 losses previously deducted as ordinary losses are recaptured by changing what would otherwise be a LTCG into ordinary income.

EXAMPLE I13-5 ▶ In 2001, Craig recognizes $25,000 of Sec. 1231 gains and $15,000 of Sec. 1231 losses. In 1997, Craig reported $14,000 of Sec. 1231 losses and no Sec. 1231 gains. No other Sec. 1231 gains or losses were recognized by Craig during the 1998–2000 period. The $10,000 ($25,000 − $15,000) of net Sec. 1231 gain in 2001 is treated as ordinary income due to the $14,000 of nonrecaptured net Sec. 1231 losses. ◀

---

[3] Sec. 1231(a)(1).
[4] Sec. 1231(a)(2).
[5] Sec. 1231(c)(1).

HISTORICAL NOTE
Congress reduced the benefits of Sec. 1231 by requiring the recapture of any nonrecaptured net Sec. 1231 loss. This recapture is required because taxpayers have a certain amount of control over the timing of the recognition of Sec. 1231 gains or losses. Taxpayers had attempted to recognize Sec. 1231 losses in one year and Sec. 1231 gains in another year to avoid the netting process.

To determine the amount of nonrecaptured net Sec. 1231 losses, compare the aggregate amount of net Sec. 1231 losses for the most recent preceding five tax years with the amount of such losses recaptured as ordinary income for those preceding tax years. The excess of the aggregate amount of net Sec. 1231 losses over the previously recaptured loss is the nonrecaptured net Sec. 1231 loss. In Example I13-5, $4,000 of nonrecaptured net Sec. 1231 losses remain that can be recaptured in 2002. In 2002, the preceding five-year period includes 1997 through 2001.

TAX RATE FOR NET SEC. 1231 GAIN

In general, Sec. 1231 gains are taxed similarly to the taxation of capital gains. Thus, a Sec. 1231 gain will be subject to a maximum tax rate of 20% (or 10% if the taxpayer's regular tax rate is 15%). Sec. 1231 property must have a holding period of more than one year. Recall from Chapter 5 that adjusted net capital gain (ANCG) is net capital gain (NCG) determined *without* regard to:

(1) the 28% rate gain, and

(2) unrecaptured section 1250 gain–taxed at no more than 25% as explained later.

ANCG might be taxed at 20% or 10%.[6] If Sec. 1231 property is sold at a gain, the Sec. 1231 gain is LTCG if there are no Sec. 1231 losses or nonrecaptured Sec. 1231 losses. However, all or part of this gain is unrecaptured Section 1250 gain if the asset is a building. Thus, net Sec. 1231 gain might be taxed today at 10%, 15%, 20% or 25% depending on the taxpayer's tax rate and whether or not the gain is unrecaptured section 1250 gain.

EXAMPLE I13-6 ▶ Savannah, whose tax rate is 31%, sells land at a gain of $10,000 and other land at a gain of $15,000. Both tracts of land qualify as Sec. 1231 property. She has no other transactions involving capital assets or 1231 property and no nonrecaptured Sec. 1231 losses. Savannah has net Sec. 1231 gain of $25,000 that is NLTCG and her NCG is $25,000. Her ANCG is $25,000 taxed at a rate of 20%. ◀

EXAMPLE I13-7 ▶ Assume the same facts as in Example 13-6 except Savannah also has a $7,000 loss from the sale of a third tract of land that is Sec. 1231 property. Her net Sec. 1231 gain is $18,000. Her NCG is $18,000 and her ANCG is $18,000 taxed at a rate of 20%. ◀

EXAMPLE I13-8 ▶ Grace, whose tax rate is 15%, sells land that is Sec. 1231 property at a gain of $2,000. She has no other transactions involving capital assets or 1231 property and no nonrecaptured Sec. 1231 losses. The $2,000 gain is taxed at 10%. ◀

ADDITIONAL COMMENT
The Sec. 1231 property in Examples I13-6, I13-7 and I13-8 is land and none of the gain is unrecaptured Section 1250 gain.

APPLYING THE FIVE-YEAR LOOKBACK RULE. As explained earlier, net Sec. 1231 gain is ordinary income to the extent of nonrecaptured Sec. 1231 losses. Net Sec. 1231 gain is recharacterized as ordinary income under the five-year lookback rule in the following order:

(1) Net Sec. 1231 gain in the 25% group (unrecaptured Sec. 1250 gain)
(2) Net Sec. 1231 gain in the 20% group

EXAMPLE I13-9 ▶ Chris has nonrecaptured net Sec. 1231 losses of $20,000 at the beginning of the current year when he recognizes gains from the sale of two assets used in his trade or business and held more than one year. Asset #1 has a $14,000 gain and the entire gain is unrecaptured Sec. 1250 gain. Asset #2 has a Sec. 1231 gain of $15,000. All of the gain resulting from the sale of asset #1 is ordinary income and $6,000 of the gain from the sale of asset #2 is ordinary income because of the five-year lookback rule. The remaining $9,000 gain from the sale of asset #2 is taxed at 20%, or possibly 10%. ◀

---

[6] The rates could be as low as 18% or 8% for tax years beginning after Dec. 31, 2000, if the holding period is more than five years.

SECTION 1231 PROPERTY

SECTION 1231 PROPERTY DEFINED

OBJECTIVE 1
Identify Sec. 1231 property

Section 1231 property includes the following types of property:
- Real property or depreciable property used in a trade or business that is held for more than one year.
- Timber, coal, or domestic iron ore.
- Livestock.
- Unharvested crops.

Each of these types of Sec. 1231 assets are discussed below.

REAL OR DEPRECIABLE PROPERTY USED IN TRADE OR BUSINESS

KEY POINT
Inventory, free publications of the U.S. government, and copyrights, literary, musical, or artistic compositions are not capital assets.

As noted in Chapter I5, the Code does not provide a definition of a capital asset. Instead, Sec. 1221 provides a list of noncapital assets. This list includes both depreciable property and real property used in a trade or business.[7] These properties are treated as Sec. 1231 properties if held for more than one year. Depreciable property and real property used in a trade or business and held for **one year or less** are neither capital assets nor Sec. 1231 property. Any gain or loss resulting from the disposition of such assets is ordinary.

EXAMPLE I13-10 ▶ The Prime Corporation owns land held as an investment and land used as an employee parking lot. The land held as an investment is a capital asset. The land used as a parking lot is real property used in a trade or business and is not a capital asset. The land used as a parking lot is a Sec. 1231 asset if held for more than one year. ◀

EXAMPLE I13-11 ▶ Dale, a self-employed plumber, owns an automobile held for personal use and a truck used in his trade. The automobile is a capital asset because it is held for personal use, but the truck is a Sec. 1231 asset if held for more than one year. As described later, a portion or all of any gain realized on the sale of the truck may be taxed as ordinary income due to the Sec. 1245 depreciation recapture provisions. ◀

KEY POINT
Only property used in a trade or business is included in the definition of Sec. 1231 property. Gains and losses on property held for investment may be included only if the result of a condemnation or casualty.

Certain types of property do not qualify as Sec. 1231 property, even if used in a trade or business. For example, inventory is not Sec. 1231 property. Thus, a sale of inventory results in ordinary gain or loss. Publications of the U.S. Government received other than by purchase at its regular sale price; a copyright; literary, musical, or artistic compositions; letters or memorandums; or similar properties held by certain taxpayers are not classified as Sec. 1231 property.[8]

EXAMPLE I13-12 ▶ Carl, who owns a recording studio, writes a musical composition to be sold to a record company. Because the musical composition is created by the personal efforts of the taxpayer, the musical composition is not Sec. 1231 property, and the sale results in ordinary gain from the sale of an ordinary asset. ◀

REAL-WORLD EXAMPLE
Christmas trees can be included in the definition of Sec. 1231 property, and this opportunity to convert ordinary income into capital gains has resulted in the use of Christmas tree tax shelters.

TIMBER. Section 631 allows taxpayers to elect to treat the cutting of timber as a sale or exchange of such timber. To be eligible to make this election, the taxpayer must own the timber or hold the contract right on the first day of the year and for more than one year. Furthermore, the timber must be cut for sale or for use in the taxpayer's trade or business.[9]

The gain or loss is determined by comparing the timber's adjusted basis for depletion with its fair market value (FMV) on the first day of the tax year in which it is cut. If the timber is eventually sold for more or less than its FMV (determined on the first day of the year the timber is cut), the difference is ordinary gain or loss.

---

[7] Sec. 1221(2).
[8] Sec. 1231(b)(1).
[9] Sec. 631(a) and Reg. Sec. 1.631-1.

13-6 Individuals ▼ Chapter 13

EXAMPLE I13-13 ▶ Vermont Corporation owns timber with a $60,000 basis for depletion. The timber, acquired four years ago, is cut during the current year for use in the corporation's business. The FMV of the timber on the first day of the current year is $200,000. Vermont Corporation may elect to treat the cutting of the timber as a sale or exchange and recognize a $140,000 ($200,000 − $60,000) gain. ◀

If the election is made to treat the cutting of timber as a sale or exchange, the timber is considered Sec. 1231 property.[10] Thus, the $140,000 of gain in Example I13-13 is a Sec. 1231 gain. If the taxpayer does not make the election, the character of any gain or loss depends on whether the timber is held for sale in the ordinary course of the taxpayer's trade or business, held for investment, or held for use in a trade or business.

SELF-STUDY QUESTION

Is the possible inclusion of timber and coal or domestic iron ore in the definition of Sec. 1231 property favorable to the taxpayers who produce these items?

ANSWER

Yes, it can result in income being taxed at rates applicable for long-term capital gain instead of ordinary income from the sale of inventory.

COAL OR DOMESTIC IRON ORE. An owner who disposes of coal (including lignite) or domestic iron ore while retaining an economic interest in it must treat the disposal as a sale.[11] The coal or iron ore is considered Sec. 1231 property.[12] The owner must own and retain an economic interest in the coal or iron ore in place.[13] An economic interest is owned when one acquires by investment any interest in mineral in place and seeks a return of capital from income derived from the extraction of the mineral.[14]

ADDITIONAL COMMENT

Livestock includes cattle, hogs, horses, mules, donkeys, sheep, goats, fur-bearing animals, and other mammals, but excludes poultry, fish, frogs, and reptiles.

LIVESTOCK. Livestock held by the taxpayer for draft, breeding, dairy, or sporting purposes is considered Sec. 1231 property if held for 12 months or more from the date of acquisition. However, cattle and horses must be held for 24 months or more from the date of acquisition to qualify as Sec. 1231 property.[15]

ADDITIONAL COMMENT

The treatment of unharvested crops as a Sec. 1231 asset is largely a rule of convenience. If the taxpayer were not permitted to treat the crops in this fashion, it would be necessary to allocate the selling price between the land and crops.

UNHARVESTED CROPS AND LAND. An unharvested crop growing on land used in a trade or business is considered Sec. 1231 property if the crop and the land are both sold at the same time to the same person and the land is held more than one year.[16] Section 1231 does not apply to the sale or exchange of an unharvested crop if the taxpayer retains any right or option to reacquire the land.[17]

If Sec. 1231 applies to the sale or exchange of an unharvested crop sold with the land, no deductions are allowed for expenses attributable to the production of the unharvested crop.[18] Instead, costs of producing the crop must be capitalized.

INVOLUNTARY CONVERSIONS

Gains and losses from involuntary conversions of property used in a trade or business generally are classified as Sec. 1231 gains and losses. Involuntary conversions of capital assets that are held in connection with a trade or business or in a transaction entered into for profit also generally qualify for Sec. 1231 treatment. The property that is involuntarily converted must be held for more than one year. Certain involuntary conversions are treated differently for income tax purposes. For example, the tax rules are different for condemnations and casualties, even though both are involuntary conversions of property.

CONDEMNATIONS

Gains and losses resulting from condemnations of Sec. 1231 property and capital assets held more than one year are classified as Sec. 1231 gains and losses. As indicated above, the capital assets must be held in connection with a trade or business or with a transaction entered into for profit.[19]

---

[10] Sec. 1231(b)(2) and Reg. Sec. 1.631-1(d)(4).
[11] Sec. 631(c) and Reg. Sec. 1.631-3(a)(1).
[12] Sec. 1231(b)(2) and Reg. Sec. 1.631-3(a)(2).
[13] Reg. Sec. 1.631-3(b)(4).
[14] Reg. Sec. 1.611-1(b)(1).
[15] Sec. 1231(b)(3).
[16] Sec. 1231(b)(4) and Reg. Secs. 1.1231-1(c)(5) and 1(f).
[17] Reg. Sec. 1.1231-1(f).
[18] Sec. 268 and Reg. Sec. 1.268-1.
[19] Secs. 1231(a)(3)(A) and (4)(B).

EXAMPLE I13-14 ▶ Kathryn owns land with a $20,000 basis and a $30,000 FMV as well as a capital asset with a $40,000 basis and a $26,000 FMV. Both assets are used in her trade or business and have been held for more than one year. As a result of the state exercising its powers of requisition or condemnation, Kathryn is required to transfer both properties to the state for cash equal to their FMVs. No other transfers of assets occur during the current year. The $10,000 gain due to condemnation of the land is a Sec. 1231 gain and the $14,000 loss due to condemnation of the capital asset is a Sec. 1231 loss. ◀

OTHER INVOLUNTARY CONVERSIONS

TYPICAL MISCONCEPTION
The inclusion of gains and losses from condemnations in the netting of the other involuntary conversions is a common error.

Gains or losses resulting from an involuntary conversion arising from fire, storm, shipwreck, other casualty, or theft are not classified as Sec. 1231 gains or losses if the recognized losses from such conversions exceed the recognized gains.[20] In such a case, the involuntary conversions are treated as ordinary gains and losses. However, if the gains from such involuntary conversions exceed the losses, both are classified as Sec. 1231 gains and losses.

EXAMPLE I13-15 ▶ Jose owns equipment having a $50,000 basis and a $42,000 FMV and a building having a $30,000 basis and a $35,000 FMV which are used in Jose's trade or business. The straight-line method of depreciation is used for the building. Both assets are held for more than a year. As a result of a fire, both assets are destroyed, and Jose collects insurance proceeds equal to the assets' FMV. No other transfers of assets occur during the current year. Because the $8,000 ($42,000 − $50,000) recognized loss exceeds the $5,000 ($35,000 − $30,000) recognized gain, the recognized loss and gain are both treated as ordinary. ◀

PROCEDURE FOR SEC. 1231 TREATMENT—Losses

OBJECTIVE 2
Understand the tax treatment for Sec. 1231 transactions

After determining the recognized gains and losses from transfers of property qualifying for Sec. 1231 treatment, it is necessary to determine whether any gain must be recaptured as ordinary income under Secs. 1245 and 1250. The recaptured gain, discussed later in this chapter, is not eligible for Sec. 1231 treatment. After eliminating the gain recaptured as ordinary income due to the recapture of depreciation, the procedure for analyzing Sec. 1231 transactions is as follows:

STEP 1. Determine all gains and losses resulting from casualties or thefts of Sec. 1231 property and non–personal-use capital assets held for more than one year. Gains and losses are netted and treated as Sec. 1231 gains and losses if the gains exceed the losses.

If the losses exceed the gains, both are treated as ordinary losses and gains and do not, therefore, enter into the Sec. 1231 netting procedure. Recall from Chapter I8 that business casualty losses are deductible *for* AGI and other casualty losses are deductible *from* AGI.

KEY POINT
Gains that are recaptured under Secs. 1245 and 1250 are not eligible for Sec. 1231 treatment.

STEP 2. Combine the following gains and losses to determine whether Sec. 1231 gains exceed Sec. 1231 losses or vice versa:

▶ Net casualty and theft <u>gains</u> resulting from Step 1, if any
▶ Gains and losses resulting from the sale or exchange of Sec. 1231 property
▶ Gains and losses resulting from the condemnation of Sec. 1231 property and non–personal-use capital assets held more than one year.

If a net Sec. 1231 loss is the result, the losses and gains are treated as ordinary losses and gains. If a net Sec. 1231 gain is the result, the gains and losses are treated as LTCGs and LTCLs, although a portion or all of the capital gain may be recaptured as ordinary income as outlined in Step 3 (five-year lookback rule) below.

---

[20] Sec. 1231(a)(4)(C).

STEP 3. If a net Sec. 1231 gain is the result of Step 2, determine if the taxpayer has any nonrecaptured net Sec. 1231 losses. Nonrecaptured net Sec. 1231 losses are the excess of aggregate net Sec. 1231 losses for the preceding five years over losses previously recaptured as ordinary income due to the recapture provision of Sec. 1231. Net Sec. 1231 gains to the extent of any nonrecaptured net Sec. 1231 losses are treated as ordinary income. Sec. 1231 gain that is unrecaptured Sec. 1250 gain is first treated as ordinary income to the extent of nonrecaptured net Sec. 1231 losses. Any net Sec. 1231 gain in excess of nonrecaptured net Sec. 1231 loss is treated as a LTCG.

EXAMPLE I13-16 ▶ The following gains and losses pertain to Danielle's business assets that qualify as Sec. 1231 property. Danielle does not have any nonrecaptured net Sec. 1231 losses from previous years, and the portion of gain recaptured as ordinary income due to the depreciation recapture provisions has been eliminated.

Gain due to an insurance reimbursement for fire damage	$10,000
Loss due to condemnation	19,000
Gain due to the sale of Sec. 1231 property	22,000

The $10,000 casualty gain is classified as a Sec. 1231 gain because gains resulting from casualties or thefts of Sec. 1231 property exceed losses. Danielle has $32,000 ($10,000 + $22,000) of Sec. 1231 gains and a $19,000 Sec. 1231 loss. Danielle's $13,000 net Sec. 1231 gain is treated as a LTCG. No portion of the $13,000 LTCG is recaptured as ordinary income because Danielle does not have any nonrecaptured net Sec. 1231 losses during the preceding five-year period. ◀

EXAMPLE I13-17 ▶ Assume the same facts as in Example I13-16 except that Danielle has a $10,000 loss because of the fire instead of a $10,000 gain. The $10,000 casualty loss is an ordinary loss, not a Sec. 1231 loss because losses resulting from casualties or thefts of Sec. 1231 property exceed gains. Because the loss is a business loss, it is deductible *for* AGI. Due to the $19,000 condemnation loss and the $22,000 of Sec. 1231 gain, she has a $3,000 net Sec. 1231 gain that is treated as a LTCG. ◀

EXAMPLE I13-18 ▶ The following gains and losses recognized in 2001 pertain to Fred's business assets that were held for more than one year. The assets qualify as Sec. 1231 property.

Gain due to an insurance reimbursement for a casualty	$15,000
Gain due to a condemnation	25,000
Loss due to the sale of Sec. 1231 property	12,000

A summary of Fred's net Sec. 1231 gains and losses for the previous five-year period is as follows:

Year	Sec. 1231 Gain	Sec. 1231 Loss	Cumulative Nonrecaptured Net Sec. 1231 Losses (from 5 Prior Years)
1996	$ 5,000		—0—
1997		$2,000	$2,000
1998		6,000	8,000
1999	13,000		—0—
2000		9,000	9,000

The $15,000 gain due to the insurance reimbursement for a casualty is treated as a Sec. 1231 gain. The $25,000 gain from the condemnation is also a Sec. 1231 gain. Fred's net Sec. 1231 gain in 2001 is $28,000 [($15,000 + $25,000) − $12,000]. However, $9,000 of the Sec. 1231 gain is recaptured as ordinary income due to the $9,000 of nonrecaptured Sec. 1231 loss from 2000. The remaining $19,000 of net Sec. 1231 gain is a LTCG. ◀

RECAPTURE PROVISIONS OF SEC. 1245

OBJECTIVE 3

Apply the recapture provisions of Sec. 1245

In 1962, Congress enacted Sec. 1245, which substantially reduced the advantages of Sec. 1231. A gain from the disposition of Sec. 1245 property is treated as ordinary income to the extent of the total amount of depreciation (or cost-recovery) deductions allowed since January 1, 1962. The gain recaptured as ordinary income cannot exceed the amount of the realized gain.

EXAMPLE I13-19 ▶

TYPICAL MISCONCEPTION

It is sometimes thought that only tangible property is subject to Sec. 1245 recapture. In fact, both tangible and intangible personal property are included.

Adobe Corporation sells equipment used in its trade or business for $95,000. The equipment was acquired several years ago for $110,000 and is Sec. 1245 property.[21] The equipment's adjusted basis is $60,000 because $50,000 of depreciation was deducted. The entire $35,000 ($95,000 − $60,000) gain is treated as ordinary income because the total amount of depreciation taken ($50,000) is greater than the $35,000 realized gain. ◀

The recapture provisions of Sec. 1245 apply to the total amount of depreciation (or cost recovery) allowed or allowable for Sec. 1245 property. It makes no difference which method of depreciation is used.[22]

Generally, the entire gain from the disposition of Sec. 1245 property is recaptured as ordinary income because the total amount of depreciation (or cost recovery) is greater than the gain realized. A portion of the gain will receive Sec. 1231 treatment if the realized gain exceeds total depreciation or cost recovery.

EXAMPLE I13-20 ▶

Assume the same facts as in Example I13-19 except that the asset is sold for $117,000. Because the $57,000 ($117,000 − $60,000) realized gain is greater than the $50,000 of total depreciation, $50,000 of the gain is ordinary income and the remaining $7,000 is a Sec. 1231 gain. ◀

PURPOSE OF SEC. 1245 — Gains

ADDITIONAL COMMENT

Section 1245 does not apply to losses because in these cases the taxpayers have taken too little depreciation rather than too much depreciation.

The purpose of Sec. 1245 is to eliminate any advantage taxpayers would have if they were able to reduce ordinary income by deducting depreciation and subsequently receive Sec. 1231 treatment when the asset was sold. For individuals, Sec. 1245 recapture prevents net Sec. 1231 gain from being treated as LTCG and being taxed at a maximum 20% rate. An increase in the maximum tax rates for high-income individuals in 1993 and subsequent years from 31% to 36% or 39.6% increased the negative effect of the Sec. 1245 recapture provisions for such individuals. The conversion of Sec. 1231 gain to Sec. 1245 ordinary income also prevents taxpayers from possibly using capital losses.

EXAMPLE I13-21 ▶

KEY POINT

On the sale of Sec. 1245 property, a portion of the gain is treated as Sec. 1231 gain only if the property is sold for more than the original cost. This is very unlikely for factory equipment, trucks, office equipment, and other Sec. 1245 property.

During the current year, Coastal Corporation has capital losses of $50,000 and no capital gains for the current year or the preceding three years. The corporation owns equipment purchased several years ago for $90,000, and depreciation deductions of $48,000 have been allowed. If Coastal sells the equipment for $72,000, the entire $30,000 ($72,000 − $42,000) gain, which is due to the depreciation deductions, is Sec. 1245 ordinary income. Without Sec. 1245, the $30,000 gain is a Sec. 1231 gain that could be offset by $30,000 of the corporation's capital loss. ◀

Note that Sec. 1245 does not apply to losses. If Coastal Corporation sells the equipment in Example I13-21 for $40,000, a $2,000 ($40,000 − $42,000 basis) Sec. 1231 loss is recognized.

KEY POINT

Property must be depreciable or amortizable to be considered Sec. 1245 property.

SECTION 1245 PROPERTY. Section 1245 property is certain property subject to depreciation and, in some cases, amortization. The most common example of Sec. 1245 property is depreciable personal property such as equipment. Automobiles, livestock, railroad grading, and single-purpose agricultural or horticultural structures are Sec. 1245 properties as well as intangible assets that are subject to amortization under Sec. 197 (see Chapter I10).[23] Except for certain buildings placed in service after 1980 and before 1987, buildings and structural components are generally not Sec. 1245 property.[24]

EXAMPLE I13-22 ▶

Buckeye Corporation owns the following assets acquired before 1981: equipment, a patent, an office building (including structural components), and land. The equipment and patent are Sec. 1245 property. The office building and the land are not Sec. 1245 property. ◀

---

[21] Throughout this chapter, property is considered to be placed in service when it is purchased or acquired. The term *Sec. 1245 property* is used here to refer to either recovery property under the ACRS or MACRS rules or nonrecovery property that falls outside of the ACRS or MACRS rules.

[22] As explained later in this chapter, the method of cost recovery used determines whether certain real property is treated as Sec. 1245 recovery property.

[23] Sec. 1245(a)(3).

[24] Sec. 1245(a)(3)(B)(i). Tangible real property "used as an integral part of the manufacturing, production, extraction, or furnishing of transportation, communication, electrical energy, gas, water, or sewage disposal services" is Sec. 1245 property.

REAL WORLD EXAMPLE

Pipelines, electric transmission towers, blast furnaces, greenhouses, and oil tanks are examples of real property that are included in the definition of Sec. 1245 property.

In many cases, taxpayers are allowed preferential treatment with respect to amortizing certain costs. For example, taxpayers may elect to expense up to $15,000 of the cost of making any business facility more accessible to handicapped and elderly people,[25] or to amortize pollution control facilities over 60 months[26] and reforestation expenditures over 84 months.[27] If taxpayers have amortized the costs of any real property under the special provisions, Sec. 1245 applies to the gain resulting from the disposition of such property.[28]

If taxpayers elect to expense certain depreciable property under Sec. 179, the amount deducted is treated as a depreciation deduction for purposes of the Sec. 1245 recapture provisions.[29]

EXAMPLE I13-23 ▶ Compact Corporation purchased $90,000 of 5-year equipment on March 10, 2000, and elected to expense $20,000 under Sec. 179. Compact sells the equipment on July 30, 2001, for $95,000. Regular depreciation allowed under MACRS for 2000 and 2001 is $14,000 and $11,200 (½ year) respectively. The adjusted basis of the equipment on the date of sale is $44,800 ($90,000 − $20,000 − $25,200 depreciation). The realized gain is $50,200 ($95,000 − $44,800), and $45,200 ($20,000 + $25,200) of the gain is Sec. 1245 ordinary income. The remaining $5,000 is Sec. 1231 gain. ◀

TYPICAL MISCONCEPTION

The categorization of nonresidential real estate acquired between 1981 and 1986 on which an accelerated depreciation method was used, as Sec. 1250 property rather than as Sec. 1245 property is a common error.

APPLICATION OF SEC. 1245 TO NONRESIDENTIAL REAL ESTATE. Most real property is not affected by Sec. 1245. However, Sec. 1245 does apply to nonresidential real estate that qualified as recovery property under the ACRS rules (i.e., placed in service after 1980 and before 1987) unless the taxpayer elected to use the straight-line method of cost recovery.[30] Section 1245 does not apply to nonresidential real estate acquired after 1986, because only straight-line depreciation may be used for nonresidential real estate acquired after 1986 (see Chapter I10).

EXAMPLE I13-24 ▶ Brad sells the following two warehouses during the current year:

	Warehouse 1	Warehouse 2
Year of purchase	1985	1985
Cost	$720,000	$900,000
Cost recovery—straight line ACRS	570,000	
Cost recovery—ACRS statutory rates (accelerated)		730,000
Adjusted basis	150,000	170,000
Selling price	700,000	800,000

KEY POINT

Taxpayers acquiring nonresidential real property between 1981 and 1986 were confronted with choosing between straight-line ACRS and ACRS using the statutory rates. In making the decision, these taxpayers should have considered the number of years the property would be held, the estimated selling price, the present value of the additional depreciation deductions, and any preferential treatment for net capital gains.

Both warehouses were acquired after 1980 and qualified as recovery property under ACRS. The $550,000 ($700,000 − $150,000) gain on the sale of Warehouse 1 is a Sec. 1231 gain. Section 1245 does not apply because the straight-line method of cost recovery is used. Section 1245 applies to the sale of Warehouse 2 because ACRS is used and the property is nonresidential real estate. Therefore, the $630,000 ($800,000 − $170,000) gain is ordinary income because the $630,000 gain is less than the $730,000 total ACRS cost-recovery allowance. ◀

If the properties in Example I13-24 were acquired before 1981 or after 1986, they would not be subject to the Sec. 1245 recapture rules regardless of the method of depreciation used. However, nonresidential real estate (e.g., a warehouse) acquired after 1963 and before 1981 is subject to the Sec. 1250 recapture rules, and a portion of the gain from its disposition may be treated as ordinary income.

The Sec. 1245 recapture rules are summarized in Topic Review I13-1.

---

[25] Sec. 190.
[26] Sec. 169(a).
[27] Sec. 194(a).
[28] Sec. 1245(a)(3)(C). The Sec. 1245 rules recapture amortization deductions claimed on real property under Secs. 169, 179, 185, 188, 190, 193 and 194.
[29] Sec. 1245(a)(2)(C). The maximum amount deductible under Sec. 179 is $20,000 in 2001, $24,000 in 2002 and 2003, and $25,000 in 2004 and after.
[30] Sec. 1245(a)(5), before being eliminated by the Tax Reform Act of 1986.

Property Transactions: Section 1231 and Recapture ▼ Individuals 13-11

Topic Review I13-1

Section 1245 Recapture

- Section 1245 affects the character of the gain, not the amount of gain.
- Section 1245 does not apply to assets sold or exchanged at a loss.
- Section 1245 ordinary income is never more than the realized gain.
- Section 1245 recapture applies to the total depreciation or amortization allowed or allowable but not more than the realized gain.
- Section 1245 property includes depreciable personal property and amortizable intangible assets (e.g., a patent).
- Section 1245 property includes nonresidential real estate placed in service after 1980 and before 1987 under the ACRS rules **unless** the taxpayer elected to use the straight-line method of cost recovery.
- Section 1245 does not apply to nonresidential real estate acquired after 1986 because only straight-line depreciation may be used.

RECAPTURE PROVISIONS OF SEC. 1250

OBJECTIVE 4

Apply the recapture provisions of Sec. 1250

In 1964, Sec. 1250 was enacted to extend the recapture concept to include most depreciable real property. Unlike Sec. 1245, where the recapture is based upon the total amount of depreciation (or cost recovery) allowed, Sec. 1250 applies solely to additional depreciation. **Additional depreciation**, also referred to as **excess depreciation**, is the excess of the actual amount of accelerated depreciation (or cost-recovery deductions under ACRS) over the amount of depreciation that would be deductible under the straight-line method. For property held a year or less, additional depreciation is the total amount of depreciation taken on the property.[31] Although Sec. 1250 was enacted in 1964, it is no longer necessary to consider additional depreciation for pre-1970 years.[32]

PURPOSE OF SEC. 1250

Section 1250 has the effect of converting a portion of the Sec. 1231 gain into ordinary income when real property is sold or exchanged. The incremental benefits from using accelerated depreciation or ACRS cost recovery may be recaptured when the property is sold. Noncorporate taxpayers can avoid Sec. 1250 recapture by either using the straight-line method of depreciation or cost recovery or holding the Sec. 1250 property for its entire useful life or recovery period.

When the Sec. 1250 recapture rules are applied solely to the additional depreciation amount instead of total depreciation claimed (as is the case for Sec. 1245 property), real property that is not Sec. 1245 property gets more favorable treatment. Despite a number of changes making Sec. 1250 more restrictive, Sec. 1250 still affords taxpayers more favorable tax treatment than Sec. 1245.

SECTION 1250 PROPERTY DEFINED

Section 1250 property is any depreciable real property other than Sec. 1245 property and includes the following:[33]

- All other depreciable real property except nonresidential real estate that qualifies as recovery property (i.e., placed in service after 1980 and before 1987) unless the straight-line method of cost recovery is elected
- Low-income housing
- Depreciable residential rental property

ADDITIONAL COMMENT

Elevators and escalators were defined as Sec. 1245 property if placed in service before 1987, but as Sec. 1250 property if placed in service after 1986.

---

[31] Sec. 1250(b)(1).
[32] Recapture of additional depreciation allowed before 1970 is avoided under Sec. 1250(a)(3) if the property is held for more than ten years.
[33] Sec. 1250(c).

> **KEY POINT**
> An apartment building is the most common type of property classified as residential real estate.

For noncorporate taxpayers depreciation recapture is not required on real property placed in service after 1986 because such property must be depreciated under the straight-line modified ACRS rules.[34]

EXAMPLE I13-25 ▶ Frances sells an office building during the current year for $800,000. The office building was purchased in 1980 for $700,000 and depreciation of $500,000 has been allowed using an accelerated method of depreciation. If the straight-line method was used, depreciation would be $420,000. The office building is Sec. 1250 property. Her realized gain is $600,000 and $80,000 is Sec. 1250 ordinary income due to excess depreciation. The remaining $520,000 gain is Sec. 1231 gain. ◀

As explained below, $420,000 of the gain in Example 13-25 is taxed at 25% and $100,000 is taxed at 20% if there are no Sec. 1231 losses, unrecaptured Sec. 1231 losses, and no capital gains and losses from other transactions. Recall from Chapter 5 that the tax rate on LTCG may be 20% or 10%.

UNRECAPTURED SECTION 1250 GAIN

For sales of real property after May 6, 1997, some or all of the Sec. 1231 gain may be LTCG that is unrecaptured Sec. 1250 gain taxed at a rate of 25%. Unrecaptured Sec. 1250 gain is the amount of LTCG, not otherwise treated as ordinary income, which would be taxed as ordinary if Sec. 1250 provided for the recapture of all depreciation and not just additional depreciation. When a taxpayer sells Sec. 1250 property at a gain, any gain due to excess depreciation is ordinary income. Any remaining gain is Sec. 1231 gain and may be LTCG, however any of the LTCG due to depreciation other than excess depreciation is unrecaptured Sec. 1250 gain.

An individual taxpayer who uses straight-line depreciation for Sec. 1250 property does not have any additional depreciation that would be recaptured as ordinary gain under Sec. 1250. Today however, all of the Sec. 1231 gain to the extent of straight-line depreciation is unrecaptured Sec. 1250 gain subject to a maximum tax rate of 25%. In Example 13-25, $420,000 of the gain is unrecaptured Sec. 1250 gain because $420,000 more of the gain would be taxed as ordinary income if all depreciation had been recaptured.

EXAMPLE I13-26 ▶ Linnie owns a building used in her trade or business that was placed in service in 1987. She has no Sec. 1231 losses, nonrecaptured Sec. 1231 losses or capital gains and losses. The building cost $400,000 and depreciation-to-date amounts to $160,000. If she sells the building for $350,000, her $110,000 gain ($350,000 − $240,000) is Sec. 1231 gain and there is no depreciation recapture under Sec. 1250 because straight-line depreciation was allowed. ◀

> **SELF-STUDY QUESTION**
> In Example I13-24, how much of the $550,000 Sec. 1231 gain resulting from the sale of warehouse #1 is unrecaptured Sec. 1250 gain?
>
> **ANSWER**
> All $550,000

The $110,000 Sec. 1231 gain in the above example is LTCG and is taxed at a rate of 25% because it is unrecaptured Sec. 1250 gain.

Prior to the Taxpayer Relief Act of 1997, the $110,000 gain recognized by Linnie was subject to a maximum rate of 28%. Although the law was changed to lower the rate on capital gains to 20% or even 10%, Congress did not extend such favorable treatment to real property subject to depreciation. The maximum rate was reduced from 28% to 25%, not to 20%.

EXAMPLE I13-27 ▶ Assume the same facts as above except Linnie sells the building for $500,000. Her Sec. 1231 gain is $260,000 ($500,000 − $240,000), and $160,000 of the gain is taxed at 25% because it is unrecaptured Sec. 1250 gain. The remaining $100,000 of gain is taxed at 20%. ◀

> **ADDITIONAL COMMENT**
> When a building is sold at a gain, different tax rates might apply to portions of the gain: rate for ordinary income, 25% for unrecaptured Sec. 1250 gain and 20% (or 10%) for ANCG.

RECAPTURE RULES FOR RESIDENTIAL RENTAL PROPERTY

All residential rental property is Sec. 1250 property. For a building or structure to qualify as residential rental property, 80% or more of the gross rental income from the building

---

[34] As explained in the Additional Recapture for Corporations section for this chapter, corporations may have depreciation recapture under Sec. 291(a) despite the use of straight-line depreciation.

or structure must be rental income from dwelling units. Residential rental property does not include any unit in a hotel, motel, inn, or other establishment if more than one-half of the units are used on a transient basis.[35]

For depreciable residential rental property, Sec. 1250 recapture applies only to additional depreciation allowed after 1975.[36]

EXAMPLE I13-28 ▶

ADDITIONAL COMMENT
If the selling price in Example 13-28 is $600,000, all of the gain is Sec. 1250 ordinary income.

Selling Price	$600,000
Adjusted Basis	391,000
Realized Gain	$209,000
Ordinary Gain	$209,000

Buddy sells an apartment complex used as residential rental property and placed in service on January 1, 1976. The cost of the apartment complex is $900,000, and the complex is sold on January 1, 2001, for $700,000. Depreciation claimed by Buddy on the property is as follows:

Time Period	Depreciation Allowed	Straight-Line Depreciation	Additional Depreciation
Jan. 1, 1976–Jan. 1, 2001	$509,000	$286,000	$223,000

On the date of sale, the adjusted basis of the apartment is $391,000 ($900,000 − $509,000) and the realized gain is $309,000 ($700,000 − $391,000). All $223,000 of additional depreciation allowed is recaptured as ordinary income because the additional depreciation is less than the realized gain. The remaining $86,000 ($309,000 − $223,000) of gain is a Sec. 1231 gain, that is taxed at 25% because it is unrecaptured Sec. 1250 gain. ◀

RESIDENTIAL RENTAL PROPERTY THAT IS RECOVERY PROPERTY

For residential rental property that is cost-recovery property (i.e., property placed in service after 1980 and before 1987), all of the **additional depreciation** is recaptured as ordinary income to the extent of gain. Additional depreciation is the excess of the ACRS deduction using the percentages provided in the ACRS tables over a hypothetical cost recovery amount based upon the straight-line ACRS method using the length of the recovery period (i.e., 15, 18, or 19 years).

EXAMPLE I13-29 ▶ Joel purchased depreciable residential rental property for $700,000 on January 1, 1986. The property is 19-year recovery property and accelerated cost recovery was used. Joel sells the property for $800,000 during the current year.

Cost Recovery Deductions Allowed	Cost Recovery with Straight-Line	Additional Depreciation
$406,000	$333,200	$72,800

Joel's realized gain is $506,000 [$800,000 − ($700,000 − $406,000)] and $72,800 is recaptured as Sec. 1250 ordinary income. The remaining $433,200 of gain is Sec. 1231 gain. $333,200 may be taxed at 25% because it is unrecaptured Sec. 1250 gain. ◀

There is a difference between Sec. 1250 ordinary income and unrecaptured Sec. 1250 gain. Sec. 1250 ordinary income could be taxed at 39.6% for noncorporate taxpayers while unrecaptured Sec. 1250 gain is LTCG taxed at a maximum rate of 25%. To have unrecaptured Sec. 1250 gain, the property must have a holding period greater than one year.

EXAMPLE I13-30 ▶ Kim, whose tax rate is 36%, owns an office building purchased for $1,000,000 on April 10 of last year. The building is sold on March 28 of the current year for $990,000 when its adjusted basis is $966,850. The $23,150 gain is not Sec. 1231 gain and none of the gain is unrecaptured Sec. 1250 gain because the holding period is not more than one year. The $23,150 gain is ordinary taxed at 36%. If the holding period was more than one year, the Sec. 1231 gain of $23,150 is LTCG that is unrecaptured Sec. 1250 gain taxed at 25%. ◀

---

[35] Reg. Sec. 1.167(j)-3(b)(1)(i).
[36] For additional depreciation after December 31, 1969, and before January 1, 1976, the recapture percentage is 100% minus 1% for each full month over 100 months the property is held. If the residential rental property is held for at least 200 months, none of the additional depreciation is recaptured for the 1970-1975 period. Secs. 1250(a)(1)(B)(v) and (a)(2)(B)(iii).

RECAPTURE RULES FOR NONRESIDENTIAL REAL ESTATE

Depreciable nonresidential real property is Sec. 1250 property except when the property is placed in service after 1980 and before 1987 and accelerated cost recovery was allowed. If the property is placed in service after 1980 and before 1987, the property is Sec. 1245 property if accelerated cost recovery is used.[37] There is no depreciation recapture if the noncorporate taxpayer elected to use the straight-line method of cost recovery[38] for nonresidential ACRS property.[39]

EXAMPLE I13-31 ▶ The AB partnership purchased an office building in 1981 and a warehouse in 1982. The statutory percentages provided in the ACRS table are used to determine cost-recovery deductions for the office building. The straight-line method is used to determine cost-recovery deductions for the warehouse. The office building is subject to the Sec. 1245 recapture rules, and the warehouse is Sec. 1250 property. Even though the warehouse is Sec. 1250 property, the gain realized on the sale is Sec. 1231 gain because the straight-line ACRS method was used. However, the Sec. 1231 gain realized on the sale at the warehouse is unrecaptured Sec. 1250 gain to the extent of depreciation allowed, if the warehouse is sold after May 6, 1997. ◀

PRE-ACRS NONRESIDENTIAL REAL ESTATE. All additional depreciation allowed after December 31, 1969, is subject to recapture as ordinary income under Sec. 1250.[40] The recaptured amount is limited to the realized gain.

EXAMPLE I13-32 ▶ Wayne sells his manufacturing plant during the current year. The plant was purchased in 1972 for use in his business. Additional depreciation (excess of accelerated depreciation under ACRS over straight-line) of $375,000 has been taken on the building. Information pertaining to the sale is as follows:

	Original Cost	Total Depreciation	Adjusted Basis	Selling Price
Plant	$3,000,000	$2,400,000	$600,000	$1,100,000
Land	300,000		300,000	900,000

The realized gain from the sale of the plant is $500,000 ($1,100,000 − $600,000) and $375,000 of the gain is recaptured as ordinary income under Sec. 1250. The remaining $125,000 of gain is Sec. 1231 gain taxed at 25% because it is unrecaptured Sec. 1250 gain. The $600,000 of realized gain from the sale of the land is a Sec. 1231 gain. ◀

EXAMPLE I13-33 ▶ Assume the same facts as in Example I13-32 except that the selling price of the plant is $850,000. All of the $250,000 realized gain ($850,000 − $600,000) is recaptured as ordinary income because the $375,000 of additional depreciation is greater than the $250,000 of realized gain. ◀

TYPICAL MISCONCEPTION
It is easy to forget that the amount recaptured as ordinary income under either Sec. 1245 or Sec. 1250 can never exceed the realized gain.

RECAPTURE FOR ACRS NONRESIDENTIAL REAL ESTATE. Section 1245 applies to nonresidential real property (1) if ACRS statutory rates were used to determine the cost-recovery deductions (as opposed to straight-line rates) and (2) if the property was placed in service after December 31, 1980, and before January 1, 1987. For Sec. 1245 recovery property, all gain to the extent of the lesser of the gain realized or the cost recovery deductions claimed is ordinary income. If the straight-line method of cost recovery is elected, the property is Sec. 1250 and none of the cost-recovery deductions are recaptured under Sec. 1250.[41]

---

[37] Sec. 1245(a)(5), before amendment by the Tax Reform Act of 1986.
[38] The cost of 18-year recovery property may be recovered under Sec. 168(b)(3)(A) over a period of 18, 35, or 45 years.
[39] Sec. 1245(a)(5)(C), before being repealed by the Tax Reform Act of 1986.
[40] Secs. 1250(a)(1)(B)(v) and (a)(2)(B)(v).
[41] An exception is provided for corporate taxpayers under Sec. 291 (See the Additional Recapture for Corporations section in this chapter.)

EXAMPLE I13-34 ▶

SELF-STUDY QUESTION

If the asset in Example I13-29 is an office building, how much ordinary income must Joel recognize?

ANSWER

$406,000
The office building is Sec. 1245 property. Joel must recognize ordinary income of $406,000 and a $100,000 Sec. 1231 gain.

Larry owns the following two buildings that are used in his business. Both buildings were purchased in 1982 and qualify as recovery property under the ACRS rules. Larry uses the ACRS statutory rates to determine cost-recovery deductions for Building 1 and the straight-line method for Building 2.

	Original Cost	Cost-Recovery Deductions	Adjusted Basis
Building 1	$1,000,000	$420,000	$580,000
Building 2 (SL)	1,000,000	300,000	700,000

If Building 1 is sold for $1,200,000, the realized gain is $620,000 ($1,200,000 − $580,000). Section 1245 applies, and $420,000 is recaptured as ordinary income. The remaining $200,000 is Sec. 1231 gain. If Building 2 is sold for $1,200,000, the realized gain is $500,000 ($1,200,000 − $700,000). None of the gain is Sec. 1245 ordinary income because the straight-line cost recovery method is used, and Sec. 1245 does not apply unless the ACRS statutory rates are used. $300,000 of the Sec. 1231 gain realized on the sale of Building 2 is unrecaptured Sec. 1250 gain, thus $300,000 may be taxed at 25%, and $200,000 at 20%. ◀

LOW-INCOME HOUSING

Congress has provided incentives for the construction and rehabilitation of low-income housing. For tax years after 1986, a low-income housing credit is available to owners of qualified low-income housing projects.[42]

The depreciation recapture provisions of Sec. 1250 also favor low-income housing. The recapture percentage applied to the amount of additional depreciation allowed for low-income housing after 1975 is 100% less one percentage point for each full month the property is held for more than 100 months.[43] If the low-income housing unit is held for 16 years and 8 months, none of the additional depreciation is subject to recapture as ordinary income. To illustrate the more favorable treatment provided in Sec. 1250 for low-income housing, consider Example I13-35.

EXAMPLE I13-35 ▶

SELF-STUDY QUESTION

If building 2 in Example I13-35 is a manufacturing plant, what is the character of the $650,000 gain?

ANSWER

Sec. 1245 ordinary income.

ADDITIONAL COMMENT

All of the Sec. 1231 gain in Example I13-35 may be taxed at 25%.

On January 1, 1985, Priscilla acquired two apartment buildings for $3,000,000 each. Building 1 qualifies as low-income housing, and building 2 is residential rental property but not low-income housing. Accelerated depreciation is used for both buildings, and $300,000 in additional depreciation has been deducted with respect to each building. Each building is sold on January 1, 2001, for $2,650,000.

Apartment Building	Cost	Total Depreciation	Adjusted Basis
Building 1 (low-income)	$3,000,000	$1,000,000	$2,000,000
Building 2	3,000,000	1,000,000	2,000,000

Gain realized from the sale of each apartment building is $650,000 ($2,650,000 − $2,000,000). Whereas 100% of the additional depreciation for building 2 is recaptured as ordinary income under Sec. 1250, only 8% of the additional depreciation for building 1 is recaptured as ordinary income. The low-income housing unit has been held for 192 months. For the first 100 months, the recapture percentage is 100%. Then the recapture percentage decreases by 1% each month for the next 92 months. $24,000 (.08 × $300,000 additional depreciation) of the $650,000 gain realized from the sale of building 1 is recaptured as ordinary income. The remaining $626,000 ($650,000 − $24,000) of gain is Sec. 1231 gain. Of the $650,000 gain realized from the sale of building 2, $300,000 is recaptured as ordinary income and $350,000 is Sec. 1231 gain. ◀

The Sec. 1250 recapture rules for noncorporate taxpayers are summarized in Topic Review I13-2.

---

[42] Sec. 42.   [43] Secs. 1250(a)(1)(B)(i), (ii), (iii), and (iv).

Topic Review I13-2

Section 1250 Recapture for Noncorporate Taxpayers

- Section 1250 affects the character of the gain, not the amount of gain.
- Section 1250 does not apply to assets sold or exchanged at a loss.
- Section 1250 ordinary income is never more than the realized gain.
- Section 1250 ordinary income is never more than the *additional* depreciation allowed. (Note, that this statement is not true for corporate taxpayers.)
- Section 1250 property includes depreciable real property unless the real property is nonresidential real estate placed in service in 1980 and before 1987 under the ACRS rules and the straight-line method is not elected.
- Section 1250 ordinary income does not exist if the straight-line method of depreciation is used. (Note that this statement is not true for corporate taxpayers because of the additional recapture requirements under Sec. 291.)

ADDITIONAL RECAPTURE FOR CORPORATIONS

KEY POINT

Section 291 has no effect on Sec. 1245 property because gain is already recaptured to the extent of all depreciation.

ADDITIONAL COMMENT

Corporations are subject to an additional 20% depreciation recapture rule under Sec. 291 on sales of Sec. 1250 property.

Corporations are subject to additional recapture rules under Sec. 291 if depreciable real estate is sold or otherwise disposed of. This recapture is in addition to the normal recapture rules under Sec. 1250. The additional ordinary income that is recaptured effectively reduces the amount of the Sec. 1231 gain.

The additional recapture amount under Sec. 291 is equal to 20% of the difference between the amount that would be recaptured if the property was Sec. 1245 property and actual recapture amount under Sec. 1250.[44]

EXAMPLE I13-36

SELF-STUDY QUESTION

If the taxpayer in Example I13-36 is a noncorporate taxpayer, how much of the gain is Sec. 1250 ordinary income?

ANSWER

$85,000

In 1980 Orlando Corporation purchased an office building for $500,000 for use in its business. The building is sold during the current year for $480,000. Total depreciation allowed for the building is $245,000. Total depreciation of $160,000 would have been allowed if the straight-line method of depreciation has been used. The property's adjusted basis is $255,000 ($500,000 − $245,000) and the realized gain is $225,000 ($480,000 − $255,000). Under Sec. 1250, the ordinary income recaptured amount is equal to 100% of the additional depreciation, which is $85,000 ($245,000 − $160,000). Under Sec. 1245, the ordinary income recapture amount would be $225,000. The amount of Sec. 1250 ordinary income under Sec. 291 is $28,000 [0.20 × ($225,000 − $85,000)]. To summarize, the total amount recaptured as Sec. 1250 ordinary income is $113,000 ($85,000 + $28,000) and the Sec. 1231 gain is $112,000 ($225,000 − $113,000). ◀

EXAMPLE I13-37

SELF-STUDY QUESTION

If the taxpayer in Example I13-37 was a noncorporate taxpayer, how much of the gain is Sec. 1250 ordinary income?

ANSWER

Zero

Pacific Corporation purchased an office building in 1981 for $800,000 for use in its trade or business. The building is sold during the current year for $850,000. Pacific elected to use the straight-line method of cost recovery and $320,000 cost-recovery deductions have been allowed. The realized gain is $370,000 ($850,000 − $480,000). Because the straight-line method was elected, none of the gain is ordinary income under Sec. 1250 if Sec. 291 is not considered. If the building were instead Sec. 1245 recovery property, $320,000 of the gain would be treated as ordinary income. The amount of Sec. 1250 ordinary income under Sec. 291 is $64,000 [0.20 × ($320,000 − $0)]. The remaining $306,000 ($370,000 − $64,000) gain is Sec. 1231 gain. ◀

For corporations, none of the Sec. 1231 gain is unrecaptured Sec. 1250 gain.

SUMMARY OF SEC. 1231, 1245 AND 1250 GAINS

Sec. 1231 property is depreciable property and nondepreciable real property used in one's trade or business and held for more than one year. Net Sec. 1231 gain, the excess of Sec.

---

[44] Sec. 291(a)(1).

1231 gain over Sec. 1231 loss, is LTCG unless the five-year lookback rule applies in which case the gain is ordinary to the extent of the nonrecaptured net Sec. 1231 loss. Net Sec. 1231 loss, the excess of Sec. 1231 loss over Sec. 1231 gain, is ordinary.

Sec. 1245 applies to depreciable personal property and amortizable intangible assets. It also applies to certain nonresidential real property placed in service during ACRS if accelerated cost recovery is used. Gain to the extent of depreciation is ordinary income. All of the gain resulting from the sale of Sec. 1245 property is ordinary income unless the asset is sold for more than its original basis.

Sec. 1250 property is depreciable real property, and gain is ordinary income to the extent of additional depreciation, the excess of accelerated depreciation over straight-line. After 1986, the straight-line method must be used for real property and thus noncorporate taxpayers will not have any Sec. 1250 ordinary income on the sale of depreciable real property placed in service after 1986. Unfortunately, Congress made the sale and exchange of buildings more complicated in 1997 when it created the concept of unrecaptured Sec. 1250 gain that is taxed at 25%. When a noncorporate taxpayer sells depreciated buildings at a gain, any gain to the extent of straight-line depreciation is Sec. 1231 gain but is taxed at 25% because it is unrecaptured Sec. 1250 gain.

To further illustrate Sec. 1231, 1245 and 1250, refer to Topic Review I13-3 where a noncorporate taxpayer with a 36% tax rate sells various assets during the current year. Each asset was purchased in 1994 and the selling price is $450,000 for each of the first three assets. All assets are used in a trade or business. There are no other gains and losses and no unrecaptured Sec. 1231 losses.

ADDITIONAL COMMENT

If the taxpayer in Topic Review I13-3 is a corporation, the character of the gain is the same for assets 1, 2, 4 and 5. For asset 3, $10,000 of the gain is Sec. 1250 ordinary income under Sec. 291 and $40,000 is Sec. 1231 gain. For asset 6, $20,000 is Sec. 1250 ordinary income under Sec. 291 and $280,000 is Sec. 1231 gain.

RECAPTURE PROVISIONS—OTHER APPLICATIONS

OBJECTIVE 5

Describe other recapture applications

The Secs. 1245 and 1250 recapture provisions take precedence over other provisions of the tax law.[45] Unless an exception or limitation is specifically stated in Secs. 1245 or 1250, gain is recognized under Secs. 1245 or 1250 despite the existence of provisions elsewhere in the Code that allow nonrecognition of gain.[46]

GIFTS OF PROPERTY SUBJECT TO RECAPTURE

A gift of appreciated depreciable property does not result in the recapture of depreciation or cost-recovery deductions under Secs. 1245 or 1250.[47] The donee must consider the recapture potential when disposing of the property. The recapture amount for the donee is computed by including the recaptured amount attributable to the donor.[48]

EXAMPLE I13-38 ▶ Ashley makes a gift of equipment with an $8,200 FMV to Helmut. Ashley paid $10,000 for the equipment and deducted $4,000 of depreciation before making the gift. Ashley does not have to recapture any depreciation when making the gift. Helmut's basis for the equipment is $6,000 and the potential depreciation recapture carries over to Helmut. ◀

EXAMPLE I13-39 ▶ Assume the same facts as in Example I13-38 except that Helmut uses the equipment in a trade or business, deducts $1,500 of depreciation, and sells the equipment for $7,100. When determining the amount of depreciation subject to recapture, Helmut must also consider the depreciation allowed to Ashley. The entire $2,600 [$7,100 − ($6,000 − $1,500)] of gain is recaptured as ordinary income because it is less than the $5,500 ($4,000 + $1,500) of depreciation claimed. ◀

---

[45] Secs. 1245(d) and 1250(i).
[46] Reg. Secs. 1.1245-6(a) and 1.1250-1(c)(1).
[47] Secs. 1245(b)(1) and 1250(d)(1).
[48] Reg. Secs. 1.1245-2(a)(4) and 1.1250-2(d).

Topic Review I13-3

Section 1231, 1245 and 1250—Comparison of Various Assets

The taxpayer is a noncorporate taxpayer with a 36% tax rate who sells each of the first three assets for $450,000. Each asset was purchased in 1994 and is used in a trade or business. There are no other gains and losses and no nonrecaptured Sec. 1231 losses.

	ORIGINAL BASIS	ADJUSTED BASIS	TAX TREATMENT
1. Land	$400,000	$400,000	$50,000 Sec. 1231 gain taxed at 20%
2. Equipment	600,000	400,000	$50,000 Sec. 1245 ordinary income taxed at 36%. All gain is due to depreciation.
3. Building	500,000	400,000	$50,000 Sec. 1231 gain which is unrecaptured Sec. 1250 gain taxed at 25%

For assets 4, 5 & 6, assume the selling price is $700,000.

	ORIGINAL BASIS	ADJUSTED BASIS	TAX TREATMENT
4. Land	$400,000	$400,000	$300,000 Sec. 1231 gain taxed at 20%
5. Equipment	600,000	400,000	$200,000 Sec. 1245 ordinary income taxed at 36% and $100,000 Sec. 1231 gain taxed at 20%
6. Building	500,000	400,000	$300,000 Sec. 1231 gain with $200,000 taxed at 20% and $100,000 of unrecaptured Sec. 1250 gain taxed at 25%

TRANSFER OF PROPERTY SUBJECT TO RECAPTURE AT DEATH

KEY POINT
Death is one of the few ways to avoid the recapture provisions.

The transfer of appreciated property at death does not cause a recapture of depreciation deductions to the decedent's estate under Secs. 1245 and 1250.[49] In addition, recapture potential does not carry over to the person who receives the property from the decedent.

EXAMPLE I13-40 ▶ Nancy dies while owning a building with a $900,000 FMV. The building is Sec. 1245 property acquired in 1985 for $800,000 on which cost-recovery deductions of $680,000 have been claimed. Pam inherits the building from Nancy. Pam's basis for the building is $900,000, and the $680,000 of cost-recovery deductions are not recaptured. If Pam immediately sells the building, there is no depreciation recapture attributable to the $680,000 of cost-recovery deductions taken by the decedent. ◀

CHARITABLE CONTRIBUTIONS

As discussed in Chapter I7, the deduction for a charitable contribution of ordinary income property is generally limited to its adjusted basis (i.e., the amount of the contribution deduction is equal to the FMV of the property less the amount of gain that would not have been LTCG [or Sec. 1231 gain] if the contributed property had been sold by the taxpayer at its FMV).[50] Thus, the contribution deduction for recapture property is generally scaled down to reflect the ordinary income that would be recognized if the property were sold rather than contributed to the charity.

EXAMPLE I13-41 ▶ Ralph makes a gift of an organ to a church. The organ is used in Ralph's trade or business and has a $6,300 FMV. Ralph paid $10,000 for the organ, and $8,000 depreciation has been claimed. If the organ were sold for its $6,300 FMV, the realized and recognized gain would be $4,300 ($6,300 − $2,000) and all of the gain would be ordinary income due to the recapture of depreciation under Sec. 1245. The charitable contribution deduction is limited to $2,000 ($6,300 − $4,300), because none of the $4,300 gain would be taxed as a LTCG if the organ were sold. ◀

---

[49] Secs. 1245(b)(2) and 1250(d)(2).

[50] Sec. 170(e)(1)(A).

LIKE-KIND EXCHANGES

A taxpayer who receives boot (i.e., non–like-kind property) in a transaction that otherwise qualifies as a like-kind exchange recognizes gain equal to the lesser of the realized gain and the amount of boot received. If the property is Sec. 1245 or 1250 property, the gain is first considered to be ordinary income up to the maximum amount of the gain that is subject to the recapture provisions.

ADDITIONAL COMMENT

If the FMV of the organ in Example I13-41 is $11,000, the charitable contribution deduction is limited to $3,000, the $11,000 FMV less $8,000. If the organ is sold for $11,000, $8,000 of the gain is ordinary income.

EXAMPLE I13-42 ▶

REAL-WORLD EXAMPLE

A taxpayer's exchange of yachts used for business was a nontaxable transaction under Sec. 1031. Because no gain was recognized on the transaction, no gain could be subject to the recapture rules. *J. Wade Harris,* 1975 PH T.C. Memo ¶75,276, 34 TCM 1192.

Virginia owns a duplex that is residential rental property. The duplex cost $300,000 in 1979 and has a $140,000 adjusted basis. Additional depreciation of $22,000 has been deducted. Virginia exchanges the duplex for a four-unit apartment building with a $250,000 FMV and $25,000 in cash. Gain realized on the exchange is $135,000 [($250,000 + $25,000) − $140,000)], and the recognized gain is $25,000. Gain recognized is the lesser of the $25,000 boot received or the $135,000 of gain realized. Because additional depreciation is recaptured as ordinary income under Sec. 1250, $22,000 of the gain is ordinary income and $3,000 of the gain is Sec. 1231 gain which may be taxed at 25% because it is unrecaptured Sec. 1250 gain. ◀

If gain is not recognized in a like-kind exchange, the recapture potential carries over to the replacement property (i.e., any recapture potential associated with the property exchanged attaches to the property received in the exchange).[51]

EXAMPLE I13-43 ▶

Melissa owns a Chevrolet pickup truck used in her trade or business that cost $10,000 and has a $6,000 adjusted basis due to $4,000 in depreciation deductions she has claimed. The truck is exchanged for a Ford pickup truck with a $9,000 FMV. The Ford truck is used in Melissa's business. Melissa does not recognize any portion of the $3,000 realized gain because the exchange qualifies as a like-kind exchange and no boot is received. Her basis for the Ford truck is $6,000 (i.e., a substituted basis).

After deducting $2,000 of depreciation, Melissa sells the Ford truck for $7,300. All of the recognized gain of $3,300 ($7,300 − $4,000) is ordinary income. The depreciation recapture amount under Sec. 1245 is equal to the total $6,000 in depreciation (including $4,000 on the Chevrolet pickup truck) but the recognized gain is only $3,300.[52] ◀

INVOLUNTARY CONVERSIONS

If an involuntary conversion of Sec. 1245 property occurs and all or a portion of the gain is not recognized,[53] the amount of gain that is considered to be Sec. 1245 ordinary income is limited. Ordinary income under Sec. 1245 may not exceed the sum of (1) the recognized gain and (2) the FMV of acquired property that is not Sec. 1245 property but is qualifying property under Sec. 1033.[54] A similar provision exists for the involuntary conversion of Sec. 1250 property.[55]

EXAMPLE I13-44 ▶

REAL-WORLD EXAMPLE

Taxpayer received insurance proceeds in excess of the adjusted basis of a business automobile upon the destruction of the auto in an accident. The taxpayer did not use Sec. 1033 to defer the gain and the court held that the gain was subject to recapture under Sec. 1245. *Anthony Astone,* 1983 PH T.C. Memo ¶83,747, 47 TCM 632.

Joan owns an office building with a $600,000 adjusted basis. The building was originally purchased in 1978, and additional depreciation amounts to $60,000. The building is destroyed by fire, and she receives insurance proceeds of $800,000. Joan purchases another office building for $750,000 and elects to defer as much of the gain as possible. Joan must recognize $50,000 of the $200,000 ($800,000 − $600,000) realized gain because the cost of the replacement property is $50,000 ($800,000 − $750,000) less than the insurance proceeds. The amount of ordinary income under Sec. 1250 is limited to $50,000 because Sec. 1250 property is purchased to replace the Sec. 1250 property destroyed by the fire. ◀

INSTALLMENT SALES

As discussed in Chapter I11, gain resulting from an installment sale is generally recognized as payments are received. Thus, the gain may be spread over more than one accounting period. An installment sale of depreciable property may result in all of the recaptured gain being taxed in the year of the sale.[56] Recapture income is "the aggregate

---

[51] Reg. Sec. 1.1245-2(c)(4).
[52] Reg. Sec. 1.1245-2(a)(4).
[53] As discussed in Chapter I12, one may elect to defer recognition of the gain if the Sec. 1033 requirements are satisfied.
[54] Sec. 1245(b)(4) and Reg. Sec. 1.1245-4(d)(1).
[55] Sec. 1250(d)(4) and Reg. Sec. 1.1250-3(d).
[56] Sec. 453(i)(1).

WHAT WOULD YOU DO IN THIS SITUATION?

You recently graduated with an advanced degree in taxation and have accepted a job with a CPA firm in the tax department. One of the firm's clients, a wealthy individual, was in need of cash and decided to sell some assets to raise the cash. The client asked the firm to advise him, from a tax standpoint, which assets he should sell. The client is in the 39.6% tax bracket. You suggested in a written memo that the client sell one of the client's jet airplanes. The plane you recommended to be sold had originally cost $16 million and now had an adjusted basis of $6 million. A buyer had offered to buy the plane for $12 million on the installment basis, paying $4 million per year for three years plus interest at 9%. The principal reason for selling that particular plane is that it would raise $12 million over three years, but the tax could be spread over three years by using the installment sale method. The client took your advice and sold the plane in the current year.

Later, when preparing the client's tax return, you realize that depreciation recapture must be recognized in the year of sale, even if the property is sold under the installment sale method. Thus, *all* of the gain on the sale of the plane must be recognized in the year of sale, not spread over three years. You go to your manager and tell him about your major mistake. Your manager, who reviewed your original memo, indicates that he thinks that the two of you should not tell anyone about the mistake as it will negatively impact both of your careers. The manager thinks that because the client has such a large amount of income, reporting the entire gain on the sale of the plane on the client's return might not be detected by the client. Thus, the manager instructs you to prepare the current year return with the entire $6 million of gain and not tell anyone about the mistake. What should you do in this situation?

amount which would be treated as ordinary income under Sec. 1245 or 1250 for the taxable year of the disposition if all payments to be received were received in the taxable year of disposition."[57] Recapture income must be recognized in the year of sale, even if no payments are received.

EXAMPLE I13-45 ▶

KEY POINT

In the case of an installment sale of Sec. 1245 or 1250 property, it is possible to report a large taxable gain even though the taxpayer has not yet received the cash to pay the tax on such gain.

Pat owns equipment with a $100,000 acquisition cost and a $42,000 adjusted basis. Depreciation of $58,000 has been allowed. During the current year, Pat sells the property for $30,000 cash and a $60,000 ten-year interest-bearing note. The realized gain is $48,000 ($90,000 − $42,000), and the recapture income amount is $48,000 (the lesser of total depreciation deductions of $58,000 or the $48,000 of realized gain). The $48,000 of gain is all recognized as ordinary income in the current year, despite the fact that the transaction qualifies as an installment sale and only $30,000 of cash is received in the year of sale. ◀

If gain realized from the installment sale exceeds the recapture income, the excess gain is reported under the installment method.[58] The amount of recapture income recognized is added to the adjusted basis to determine the gross profit ratio.

EXAMPLE I13-46 ▶

SELF-STUDY QUESTION

What method of cost recovery is Bob using in Example I13-46?

ANSWER

Accelerated cost recovery. The office building is subject to Sec. 1245 recapture.

Bob owns an office building acquired for $700,000 in 1986 and subject to the Sec. 1245 recapture rules. After claiming $560,000 of cost recovery deductions, Bob sells the building to Judy in 2001 for $1,000,000. Bob receives $200,000 in cash and an $800,000 interest-bearing note. The note is to be paid with annual principal payments of $100,000 beginning in 2002. The total amount of realized gain is $860,000 ($1,000,000 − $140,000). In 2001, Bob recognizes $560,000 of Sec. 1245 ordinary income. The gross profit ratio is determined by adding $560,000 recapture income to the $140,000 basis. The gross profit ratio is 30% [($1,000,000 − $700,000) ÷ $1,000,000]. In addition to recognizing $560,000 of ordinary income, Bob recognizes $60,000 (0.30 × $200,000) Sec. 1231 gain in 2001 because a $200,000 cash down payment was received in the year of the sale. In 2002 and in each subsequent year, $30,000 (0.30 × $100,000) of Sec. 1231 gain is recognized as the cash payments on the principal are received. ◀

---

[57] Sec. 453(i)(2).

[58] Sec. 453(i)(1)(B).0.

SECTION 179 EXPENSING ELECTION

In lieu of capitalizing the cost of new or used tangible personal business property, taxpayers may elect to expense up to $24,000 of the acquisition cost in 2001[59] (see Chapter I10). If the property is subsequently converted to nonbusiness use, previous tax benefits derived from the immediate expensing election must be recaptured and added to the taxpayer's gross income in the year of the conversion.[60] The recaptured amount equals the difference between the amount expensed under Sec. 179 and the total depreciation that would otherwise have been claimed for the period of business use.

EXAMPLE I13-47 ▶ Joel purchased business equipment last year for $18,100 and elected to expense the entire amount under Sec. 179. In the current year, he converts the equipment to nonbusiness use. Depreciation of $3,620 (0.20 × $18,100) based on a five-year recovery period under the MACRS rules would have been allowed during the period the equipment was held for business use if Joel had not elected to expense the $18,100 cost. Joel must include $14,480 ($18,100 − $3,620) in his gross income for the current year. This amount represents the previous tax benefit obtained from the immediate expensing election. ◀

CONSERVATION AND LAND CLEARING EXPENDITURES

Taxpayers engaged in the business of farming may deduct expenditures paid or incurred during the taxable year for soil and water conservation or the prevention of erosion. The expenditures must be made with respect to land used in farming and would be capital expenditures except for this provision.[61]

KEY POINT
There is no recapture of conservation costs if the farmland is held for at least 10 years.

The deductions for conservation expenditures may be partially or fully recaptured as ordinary income if the farmland is disposed of before the land is held for more than nine years.[62] The amount of deductions recaptured as ordinary income under Sec. 1252 is a percentage of the aggregate deductions allowed for conservation expenditures. The amount of ordinary income recognized under Sec. 1252 is limited to the lesser of the taxpayer's realized gain or the applicable recapture percentage times the total conservation expenditures.

The recapture percentage is 100% if the farmland is disposed of within five years after the date it is acquired. The percentage declines by 20 percentage points for each additional year the property is held. If the land is disposed of after being held for more than nine years, none of the expenses are recaptured.[63]

EXAMPLE I13-48 ▶ Paula owns farmland with a $400,000 basis. She has deducted $50,000 for soil and water conservation expenditures. After farming the land for six years and five months, Paula sells the land for $520,000. The realized gain is $120,000 ($520,000 − $400,000) and the recapture percentage is 60%, because the farmland is disposed of within the seventh year after it was acquired. The amount of ordinary income due to recapture under Sec. 1252 is $30,000, the lesser of the $120,000 realized gain or the $30,000 (0.60 × $50,000) recapture amount. ◀

INTANGIBLE DRILLING COSTS AND DEPLETION

ADDITIONAL COMMENT
Intangible drilling and development costs represent the major cost of operations and can provide investors with working interests in oil and gas properties with a first-year write-off of substantially all of their investment.

Taxpayers may elect to either expense or capitalize intangible drilling and development costs (IDC).[64] If the election to expense is not made, the costs are capitalized and recovered through additional cost depletion deductions. Intangible drilling and development costs include "all expenditures made by an operator for wages, fuel, repairs, hauling, supplies, etc., incident to and necessary for the drilling of wells and the preparation of wells for the production of oil or gas."[65]

Part or all of the gain from the sale of oil and gas properties may be recaptured as ordinary income due to the recapture of the IDC deduction and the deduction for depletion. However, the amount of ordinary income recognized from the recapture of IDC and depletion is limited to the gain realized from the disposition of the property.[66]

---

[59] Secs. 179(a) and (b)(1).
[60] Sec. 179(d)(10) and Reg. Sec. 1.179-1(e).
[61] Sec. 175(a).
[62] Sec. 1252(a)(1).
[63] Sec. 1252(a)(3).
[64] Sec. 263(c).
[65] Reg. Sec. 1.612-4(a).
[66] Sec. 1254(a)(1).

EXAMPLE I13-49 ▶ In 1993 Marty purchased undeveloped property for the purpose of drilling for oil and gas. Intangible drilling and development costs of $400,000 were paid in 1993. Marty elected to expense the IDC. During the current year, Marty sells the property and realizes a $900,000 gain. $300,000 of cost depletion was allowed. Marty must recognize $700,000 of ordinary income because of the recapture of IDC ($400,000) and the recapture of depletion ($300,000). The remaining $200,000 ($900,000 − $700,000) gain is Sec. 1231 gain. ◀

EXAMPLE I13-50 ▶ In 1995 Tina acquired oil and gas properties for $700,000. During 1995, she elected to expense $200,000 of IDC. Total depletion allowed was $80,000. During the current year, Tina sells the property for $840,000 and realizes a $220,000 [($840,000 − ($700,000 − $80,000)] gain. The amount of ordinary income due to recapture is $220,000, because both IDC and depletion must be recaptured only to the extent of the gain. ◀

GAIN ON SALE OF DEPRECIABLE PROPERTY BETWEEN RELATED PARTIES

All gain recognized on the sale or exchange of property between related parties is ordinary income if the property is subject to depreciation in the hands of the transferee (i.e., the person who purchases the property). The sale or exchange may be direct or indirect.[67]

EXAMPLE I13-51 ▶ Phil owns a building with a $500,000 adjusted basis and $800,000 FMV. The building, which cost $700,000, is used in his business, and the straight-line method of depreciation is used. $200,000 of depreciation deductions were allowed. If the building is sold to Phil's 100%-owned corporation for $800,000, the $300,000 realized gain ($800,000 − $500,000) is treated as ordinary income under Sec. 1239, because the property is subject to depreciation in the hands of the transferee and the corporation and Phil are related parties. ◀

A sale or exchange of property could be subject to depreciation recapture under Sec. 1245 or 1250 as well as the Sec. 1239 related party rules. If so, recapture under Sec. 1245 or 1250 is considered before recapture under Sec. 1239.[68]

EXAMPLE I13-52 ▶ Assume the same facts as in Example I13-51 except that Phil sells equipment to the corporation instead of a building. All of the $300,000 realized gain is treated as ordinary income. The recapture amount under Sec. 1245 is $200,000, and Sec. 1239 applies to the remaining $100,000 gain. ◀

REAL-WORLD EXAMPLE
A taxpayer sold a secret formula for typing correction fluid to a corporation that was a related party. The gain on the sale was treated as a capital gain, not as ordinary income under Sec. 1239, because the secret formula was not depreciable. *Bette C. Graham v. U.S.*, 43 AFTR 2d 79-1013, 79-1 USTC ¶9274 (D.C. Tx., 1979).

PURPOSE OF SEC. 1239. Without Sec. 1239, a taxpayer could transfer appreciated depreciable property to a related party and recognize a Sec. 1231 gain on the sale. Net Sec. 1231 gain is treated as LTCG. The related purchaser of the property would receive a step up in the depreciation basis of the property to its FMV and be able to claim a larger amount of depreciation. In Example I13-51, Phil might prefer to recognize a $300,000 Sec. 1231 gain if the 100%-owned corporation was able to obtain a step-up in the property's basis to $800,000. Because Sec. 1239 applies, Phil must recognize $300,000 of ordinary income rather than Sec. 1231 gain. This rule prevents an individual taxpayer from receiving favorable Sec. 1231 gain treatment and prevents all taxpayers having large capital loss carryovers from using a related party to recognize a Sec. 1231 or capital gain which can be offset against their capital losses.

RELATED PARTIES. A person is related (1) to any corporation if the individual owns (directly or indirectly) more than 50% of the value of the outstanding stock and (2) to any partnership in which the person has a capital or profits interest of more than 50%.[69] Constructive ownership rules apply when determining whether the person owns more than 50% of the corporation or has more than a 50% interest in the partnership. Thus, an individual is considered to own stock that is owned by other family members and related entities (e.g., corporations, partnerships, estates, and trusts).

---

[67] Sec. 1239(a).
[68] Reg. Sec. 1.1245-6(f).
[69] Sec. 1239(c).

EXAMPLE I13-53 ▶ Tony sells a truck, which he has used for nonbusiness purposes, to the Able Corporation for $15,000. The adjusted basis of the truck is $12,000 on the date of the sale.

Tony owns 30% of the Able stock and his spouse owns 40% of the Able stock. Tony and Able are related parties because Tony is deemed to own 70% of the Able stock under the constructive ownership rules and $3,000 of ordinary income must be recognized under Sec. 1239 unless the overriding recapture rules of Sec. 1245 apply. ◀

A person is related to any trust in which such a person or the person's spouse is a beneficiary.[70] Section 1239 also applies to a sale or exchange of depreciable property between two corporations if the same individual owns more than 50% of each corporation.[71]

TAX PLANNING CONSIDERATIONS

For noncorporate taxpayers, net Sec. 1231 gains are generally preferable to ordinary gains because of the possible lower tax rate applicable to net capital gains. The tax rate could be 10%, 15%, 20% or 25%. For corporate taxpayers, however, after 1986 it usually does not make any difference whether a gain is classified as Sec. 1231 or ordinary unless the corporation has capital losses. Corporations do have a 35% alternative tax rate on net capital gains.

EXAMPLE I13-54 ▶ Western Corporation has taxable income of $550,000 without considering the sale of equipment for $400,000 during the current year. The equipment originally cost $500,000 and has a $350,000 adjusted basis after deducting depreciation. The corporation has no other gains and losses during the year or any capital loss carryovers from previous years. For Western Corporation, it does not make any difference whether the gain is Sec. 1245 ordinary income or Sec. 1231 gain. The effect on the corporation's taxable income and tax liability is the same regardless of how the gain is classified. ◀

The avoidance of the recapture provisions is important to both corporate and noncorporate taxpayers if capital loss carryovers exist. For example, if Western Corporation has a capital loss carryforward of $40,000 in Example I13-54, the corporation's taxable income is increased by $10,000 ($50,000 − $40,000) if the $50,000 gain is Sec. 1231 gain. However, because the gain is Sec. 1245 ordinary income, the corporation's taxable income is increased by $50,000. The $40,000 capital loss carryforward is not deductible unless it can be offset by a capital gain or a net Sec. 1231 gain.

AVOIDING THE RECAPTURE PROVISIONS

In view of the pervasiveness of the recapture provisions discussed in this chapter, recapture is difficult to avoid. In some cases, recapture can be avoided by holding the property a specific length of time before disposing of it (e.g., the recapture of conservation and land clearing expenses can be avoided by holding the farmland for more than nine years).[72] Contributing appreciated property to a qualified charitable organization cannot be used to circumvent the recapture provisions because in such case the amount of the charitable contribution is reduced by the amount of the gain that would not be a LTCG if the property were sold by the taxpayer.[73]

Although it is often difficult to avoid the recapture provisions, taxpayers may dispose of the property and defer recapture if the disposition is a nontaxable exchange. In a like-kind exchange where no boot is received, the recapture potential is carried over to the property received in the exchange. In a tax-free incorporation under Sec. 351, the recapture potential is transferred to the corporation receiving the recapture property. Sec. 351

---

[70] Sec. 1239(b)(2).
[71] Rev. Rul. 79-157, 1979-1 C.B. 281.
[72] Sec. 1252(a)(1).
[73] Sec. 170(e)(1)(A).

is discussed in Chapter I16. Recapture may also be avoided in situations involving a transfer of property to a partnership in exchange for a partnership interest.

Proper timing of the asset's disposition may be advantageous. Disposition may be delayed until the taxpayer's tax rate is low or the property can be sold in the same year that the taxpayer has an NOL that is about to expire.

Taxpayers can shift the recapture potential to other taxpayers by making a gift of property subject to recapture. The recapture potential remains with the property and must be considered when the donee disposes of the property.

RESIDENTIAL RENTAL PROPERTY. Noncorporate taxpayers can avoid the recapture provisions for residential rental property by using the straight-line method of depreciation.[74] The recapture provisions do not apply to residential rental property acquired after 1986 because only the straight-line depreciation method may be used. Recapture can also be avoided if the asset is fully depreciated at the date of disposal because no additional depreciation or cost recovery exists.

EXAMPLE I13-55 ▶ Vincent owns a building used as residential rental property. The building was purchased before 1981 and is not ACRS recovery property. Vincent could avoid depreciation recapture at the time of disposing of the asset by using the straight-line method of depreciation. If Vincent uses an accelerated method of depreciation, recapture is avoided if the disposition does not occur until the asset is fully depreciated. ◀

EXAMPLE I13-56 ▶ Assume the same facts as in Example I13-55 except that Vincent purchased the building after 1980 and before 1987 and the building is ACRS recovery property. Vincent could avoid recapturing cost recovery deductions when he disposes of the asset by using the straight-line method of cost recovery. If Vincent uses the accelerated method of cost recovery and disposes of the residential rental property at a gain, he cannot avoid recapture unless the asset's cost is fully recovered (i.e., no additional cost recovery exists). ◀

KEY POINT
For noncorporate taxpayers, there is no recapture on either residential or nonresidential real property placed in service after 1986 because the property can be depreciated only by using the straight-line method.

NONRESIDENTIAL REAL PROPERTY. For noncorporate taxpayers, the Sec. 1250 recapture provisions do not apply to nonresidential real property acquired after 1986 because only the straight-line method may be used. However, to avoid recapture on the disposition of appreciated nonresidential real property acquired after 1980 and before 1987 noncorporate taxpayers must use the straight-line method of depreciation. Nonresidential real property acquired before 1987, which is recovery property subject to ACRS, is subject to the Sec. 1245 recapture rules unless the straight-line method is used. If the accelerated method of cost recovery is used, recapture cannot be avoided by waiting until the asset's cost is fully recovered before disposing of the asset.

EXAMPLE I13-57 ▶ Christine purchased an office building in 1986 for $225,000 for use in her trade or business. The property is ACRS recovery property, and she uses the accelerated method to compute the cost-recovery deductions. Cost-recovery deductions taken before the sale of the building amount to $140,000. If she sells the building for $250,000, $140,000 of the $165,000 ($250,000 − $85,000) realized gain is recaptured as ordinary income under Sec. 1245. The remaining gain of $25,000 is Sec. 1231 gain. Recapture could have been avoided if Christine had instead used the straight-line method of cost recovery. If the straight-line method were used instead, she would report a smaller realized gain, all of which is Sec. 1231 gain. ◀

EXAMPLE I13-58 ▶ Bryce purchased an office building in 1986 for $300,000 for use in his trade or business. The property is 19-year recovery property, and he used the accelerated method of cost recovery. If Bryce sells the building for $250,000 after all of the cost has been recovered (i.e., the adjusted basis is zero), the realized gain of $250,000 is recaptured as ordinary income under Sec. 1245. ◀

---

[74] Corporate taxpayers must consider Sec. 291(a). (See the Additional Recapture for Corporations section in this chapter.)

Property Transactions: Section 1231 and Recapture ▼ **Individuals 13-25**

TRANSFER PROPERTY AT DEATH. One of the most effective ways to avoid the recapture provisions is to transfer the property at death. No recapture occurs at the time of the transfer, and the basis of property received from a decedent is generally the FMV of the property at the date of the decedent's death.[75] The property's recapture potential does not carry over to the beneficiary as in the case of a gift made to a donee.

COMPLIANCE AND PROCEDURAL CONSIDERATIONS

ADDITIONAL COMMENT

Form 4797 has four major parts. In completing this form one should normally begin with Part III on page 2, where the recapture is calculated. Note that the total amount recaptured from line 31 is carried forward to Part II, where it is combined with other ordinary gains and losses. Any unrecaptured gain from line 32 is carried forward to Part I, where it is netted with other Sec. 1231 gains and losses.

Form 4797, Supplemental Schedule of Gains and Losses, is used to report gains and losses from sales or exchanges of assets used in a trade or business (see Figures I13-1 through I13-3). The form is also used to report gains or losses resulting from involuntary conversions, other than casualties or thefts, of property used in the trade or business and capital assets held more than a year. If gains or losses due to casualties or thefts of property used in a trade or business or property held to produce income are recognized, they are reported on Form 4684, Casualties and Thefts (see Figure I13-3). If such casualties or thefts occur, Form 4684 is prepared either before or at the same time as Form 4797.

REPORTING SEC. 1231 GAINS AND LOSSES ON FORM 4797

Part I of Form 4797, which is reproduced in Figure I13-1, is used to report gains and losses resulting from

▶ The sale or exchange of Sec. 1231 property

▶ An involuntary conversion, other than a casualty or theft, of Sec. 1231 property

▶ An involuntary conversion, other than a casualty or theft, of capital assets held more than one year and used to produce income.

As indicated on lines 3 through 6 in Part I of Form 4797, gains and losses recorded on other forms and in Part III of Form 4797 are reported in Part I. The netting of Sec. 1231 gains and losses occurs in Part I of Form 4797. All gains and losses are recorded in column (g). If line 7(g) has a loss, Sec. 1231 losses exceed Sec. 1231 gains and the net loss is reported on line 11 as ordinary loss. If there is no nonrecaptured net section 1231 losses, the amount on line 7(g) is transferred to Schedule D. If the taxpayer does have nonrecaptured net Sec. 1231 losses, that amount is reported on line 8. Gains reported on line 7(g) will be recharacterized as ordinary income to the extent of the nonrecaptured net Sec. 1231 losses and reported as ordinary income on line 12.

Ordinary gains and losses recognized including those recorded on other forms and in Parts I and III of Form 4797 are reported on lines 11 through 17 in Part II of Form 4797.

REPORTING GAINS RECAPTURED AS ORDINARY INCOME ON FORM 4797

Part III of Form 4797, reproduced in Figure I13-2, is used to determine and report ordinary income due to the recapture provisions of Secs. 1245, 1250, 1252, 1254, and 1255. Part III is completed before Parts I and II. To illustrate the use of Part III, assume an individual sells equipment (7-year recovery) used in a trade or business for $60,000 on April 30, 2000. The equipment cost $58,000 on March 10, 1998 and depreciation deductions through the date of sale of $27,565 were allowed. The $29,565 ($60,000 − $30,435) total gain is reported on line 24. The $3,000 of depreciation allowed is reported on lines 25(a) and also on (b) because the depreciation allowed is less than the realized gain. On line 30, total gains resulting from the sale of all properties ($29,565 in this illustration) reported in Part III are combined. The total amount of ordinary income due to the recapture provisions ($27,565 in this illustration) is reported on line 31 and then reported as

---

[75] Sec. 1014(a).

Form **4797**	**Sales of Business Property**	OMB No. 1545-0184
Department of the Treasury Internal Revenue Service (99)	(Also Involuntary Conversions and Recapture Amounts Under Sections 179 and 280F(b)(2)) ▶ Attach to your tax return. ▶ See separate instructions.	**2000** Attachment Sequence No. **27**

Name(s) shown on return | Identifying number

1 Enter the gross proceeds from sales or exchanges reported to you for 2000 on Form(s) 1099-B or 1099-S (or substitute statement) that you are including on line 2, 10, or 20 (see instructions) **1**

Part I — Sales or Exchanges of Property Used in a Trade or Business and Involuntary Conversions From Other Than Casualty or Theft—Most Property Held More Than 1 Year (See instructions.)

(a) Description of property	(b) Date acquired (mo., day, yr.)	(c) Date sold (mo., day, yr.)	(d) Gross sales price	(e) Depreciation allowed or allowable since acquisition	(f) Cost or other basis, plus improvements and expense of sale	(g) Gain or (loss) Subtract (f) from the sum of (d) and (e)
2						

3 Gain, if any, from Form 4684, line 39 .... **3**
4 Section 1231 gain from installment sales from Form 6252, line 26 or 37 .... **4**
5 Section 1231 gain or (loss) from like-kind exchanges from Form 8824 .... **5**
6 Gain, if any, from line 32, from other than casualty or theft **6** 2,000
7 Combine lines 2 through 6. Enter the gain or (loss) here and on the appropriate line as follows: .. **7** 2,000

Partnerships (except electing large partnerships). Report the gain or (loss) following the instructions for Form 1065, Schedule K, line 6. Skip lines 8, 9, 11, and 12 below.
S corporations. Report the gain or (loss) following the instructions for Form 1120S, Schedule K, lines 5 and 6. Skip lines 8, 9, 11, and 12 below, unless line 7 is a gain and the S corporation is subject to the capital gains tax.
All others. If line 7 is zero or a loss, enter the amount from line 7 on line 11 below and skip lines 8 and 9. If line 7 is a gain and you did not have any prior year section 1231 losses, or they were recaptured in an earlier year, enter the gain from line 7 as a long-term capital gain on Schedule D and skip lines 8, 9, and 12 below.

8 Nonrecaptured net section 1231 losses from prior years (see instructions) **8**
9 Subtract line 8 from line 7. If zero or less, enter -0-. Also enter on the appropriate line as follows (see instructions): **9**
S corporations. Enter any gain from line 9 on Schedule D (Form 1120S), line 15, and skip lines 11 and 12 below.
All others. If line 9 is zero, enter the gain from line 7 on line 12 below. If line 9 is more than zero, enter the amount from line 8 on line 12 below, and enter the gain from line 9 as a long-term capital gain on Schedule D.

Part II — Ordinary Gains and Losses

10 Ordinary gains and losses not included on lines 11 through 17 (include property held 1 year or less):

11 Loss, if any, from line 7 .... **11** ( )
12 Gain, if any, from line 7 or amount from line 8, if applicable **12**
13 Gain, if any, from line 31 .... **13** 27,565
14 Net gain or (loss) from Form 4684, lines 31 and 38a **14**
15 Ordinary gain from installment sales from Form 6252, line 25 or 36 .... **15**
16 Ordinary gain or (loss) from like-kind exchanges from Form 8824 .... **16**
17 Recapture of section 179 expense deduction for partners and S corporation shareholders from property dispositions by partnerships and S corporations (see instructions) **17**
18 Combine lines 10 through 17. Enter the gain or (loss) here and on the appropriate line as follows: .. **18** 27,565
  a For all except individual returns: Enter the gain or (loss) from line 18 on the return being filed.
  b For individual returns:
   (1) If the loss on line 11 includes a loss from Form 4684, line 35, column (b)(ii), enter that part of the loss here. Enter the part of the loss from income-producing property on Schedule A (Form 1040), line 27, and the part of the loss from property used as an employee on Schedule A (Form 1040), line 22. Identify as from "Form 4797, line 18b(1)." See instructions .... **18b(1)**
   (2) Redetermine the gain or (loss) on line 18 excluding the loss, if any, on line 18b(1). Enter here and on Form 1040, line 14 .... **18b(2)** 27,565

For Paperwork Reduction Act Notice, see page 7 of the instructions. Cat. No. 13086I Form **4797** (2000)

FIGURE I13-1 ▶ PART I AND PART II OF FORM 4797

Form 4797 (2000) — Page 2

Part III — Gain From Disposition of Property Under Sections 1245, 1250, 1252, 1254, and 1255

19 (a) Description of section 1245, 1250, 1252, 1254, or 1255 property: | (b) Date acquired (mo., day, yr.) | (c) Date sold (mo., day, yr.)

A Equipment — 3-10-98 — 4-30-00
B
C
D

These columns relate to the properties on lines 19A through 19D. ▶		Property A	Property B	Property C	Property D
20	Gross sales price (Note: See line 1 before completing.)	60,000			
21	Cost or other basis plus expense of sale	58,000			
22	Depreciation (or depletion) allowed or allowable	27,565			
23	Adjusted basis. Subtract line 22 from line 21	30,435			
24	Total gain. Subtract line 23 from line 20	29,565			
25	If section 1245 property:				
a	Depreciation allowed or allowable from line 22	27,565			
b	Enter the smaller of line 24 or 25a	27,565			
26	If section 1250 property: If straight line depreciation was used, enter -0- on line 26g, except for a corporation subject to section 291.				
a	Additional depreciation after 1975 (see instructions)				
b	Applicable percentage multiplied by the smaller of line 24 or line 26a (see instructions)				
c	Subtract line 26a from line 24. If residential rental property or line 24 is not more than line 26a, skip lines 26d and 26e				
d	Additional depreciation after 1969 and before 1976				
e	Enter the smaller of line 26c or 26d				
f	Section 291 amount (corporations only)				
g	Add lines 26b, 26e, and 26f				
27	If section 1252 property: Skip this section if you did not dispose of farmland or if this form is being completed for a partnership (other than an electing large partnership).				
a	Soil, water, and land clearing expenses				
b	Line 27a multiplied by applicable percentage (see instructions)				
c	Enter the smaller of line 24 or 27b				
28	If section 1254 property:				
a	Intangible drilling and development costs, expenditures for development of mines and other natural deposits, and mining exploration costs (see instructions)				
b	Enter the smaller of line 24 or 28a				
29	If section 1255 property:				
a	Applicable percentage of payments excluded from income under section 126 (see instructions)				
b	Enter the smaller of line 24 or 29a (see instructions)				

Summary of Part III Gains. Complete property columns A through D through line 29b before going to line 30.

30	Total gains for all properties. Add property columns A through D, line 24	29,565
31	Add property columns A through D, lines 25b, 26g, 27c, 28b, and 29b. Enter here and on line 13	27,565
32	Subtract line 31 from line 30. Enter the portion from casualty or theft on Form 4684, line 33. Enter the portion from other than casualty or theft on Form 4797, line 6	2,000

Part IV — Recapture Amounts Under Sections 179 and 280F(b)(2) When Business Use Drops to 50% or Less
(See instructions.)

		(a) Section 179	(b) Section 280F(b)(2)
33	Section 179 expense deduction or depreciation allowable in prior years		
34	Recomputed depreciation. See instructions		
35	Recapture amount. Subtract line 34 from line 33. See the instructions for where to report		

Form 4797 (2000)

FIGURE I13-2 ▶ PART III OF FORM 4797

13-27

Name(s) shown on tax return. Do not enter name and identifying number if shown on other side. | Identifying number

SECTION B—Business and Income-Producing Property

Part I Casualty or Theft Gain or Loss (Use a separate Part I for each casualty or theft.)

19 Description of properties (show type, location, and date acquired for each):
    Property **A** _____
    Property **B** _____
    Property **C** _____
    Property **D** _____

Properties (Use a separate column for each property lost or damaged from one casualty or theft.)

	A	B	C	D

20 Cost or adjusted basis of each property 20

21 Insurance or other reimbursement (whether or not you filed a claim). See the instructions for line 3
    Note: If line 20 is **more than** line 21, skip line 22.   21

22 Gain from casualty or theft. If line 21 is **more than** line 20, enter the difference here and on line 29 or line 34, column (c), except as provided in the instructions for line 33. Also, skip lines 23 through 27 for that column. See the instructions for line 4 if line 21 includes insurance or other reimbursement you did not claim, or you received payment for your loss in a later tax year   22

23 Fair market value **before** casualty or theft . . .   23
24 Fair market value **after** casualty or theft   24
25 Subtract line 24 from line 23   25
26 Enter the **smaller** of line 20 or line 25   26
    Note: If the property was totally destroyed by casualty or lost from theft, enter on line 26 the amount from line 20.
27 Subtract line 21 from line 26. If zero or less, enter -0-   27
28 Casualty or theft loss. Add the amounts on line 27. Enter the total here and on line 29 or line 34 (see instructions)   28

Part II Summary of Gains and Losses (from separate Parts I)

(a) Identify casualty or theft	(b) Losses from casualties or thefts		(c) Gains from casualties or thefts includible in income
	(i) Trade, business, rental or royalty property	(ii) Income-producing and employee property	

Casualty or Theft of Property Held One Year or Less

29 _____   ( ) ( )
    _____   ( ) ( )
30 Totals. Add the amounts on line 29 . . . . 30 ( ) ( )
31 Combine line 30, columns (b)(i) and (c). Enter the net gain or (loss) here and on Form 4797, line 14. If Form 4797 is not otherwise required, see instructions 31
32 Enter the amount from line 30, column (b)(ii) here. Individuals, enter the amount from income-producing property on Schedule A (Form 1040), line 27, and enter the amount from property used as an employee on Schedule A (Form 1040), line 22. Estates and trusts, partnerships, and S corporations, see instructions 32

Casualty or Theft of Property Held More Than One Year

33 Casualty or theft gains from Form 4797, line 32 33
34 _____   ( ) ( )
    _____   ( ) ( )
35 Total losses. Add amounts on line 34, columns (b)(i) and (b)(ii) . . . 35 ( ) ( )
36 Total gains. Add lines 33 and 34, column (c) 36
37 Add amounts on line 35, columns (b)(i) and (b)(ii) 37
38 If the loss on line 37 is **more than** the gain on line 36:
  a Combine line 35, column (b)(i) and line 36, and enter the net gain or (loss) here. Partnerships (except electing large partnerships) and S corporations, see the note below. All others, enter this amount on Form 4797, line 14. If Form 4797 is not otherwise required, see instructions 38a
  b Enter the amount from line 35, column (b)(ii) here. Individuals, enter the amount from income-producing property on Schedule A (Form 1040), line 27, and enter the amount from property used as an employee on Schedule A (Form 1040), line 22. Estates and trusts, enter on the "Other deductions" line of your tax return. Partnerships (except electing large partnerships) and S corporations, see the note below. Electing large partnerships, enter on Form 1065-B, Part II, line 11 . . 38b
39 If the loss on line 37 is **less than** or **equal to** the gain on line 36, combine lines 36 and 37 and enter here. Partnerships (except electing large partnerships), see the note below. All others, enter this amount on Form 4797, line 3 39

Note: Partnerships, enter the amount from line 38a, 38b, or line 39 on Form 1065, Schedule K, line 7. S corporations, enter the amount from line 38a or 38b on Form 1120S, Schedule K, line 6.

Form **4684** (2000)

FIGURE I13-3 ▶ SECTION B OF FORM 4684

ordinary income on line 13 in Part II. The excess of the gain over the amount of ordinary income is reported on line 32. The portion of this gain not due to casualty or theft ($2,000 in this illustration) is a Sec. 1231 gain and is reported on line 6 of Part I of Form 4797. If any of the gain is due to casualty or theft, that portion of the gain is reported on Section B of Form 4684.

REPORTING CASUALTY OR THEFT GAIN OR LOSS ON FORM 4684

Section A of Form 4684 is used to report gains and losses resulting from a casualty or theft of personal-use property. These gains and losses are not Sec. 1231 transactions, and Sec. A of Form 4684 is not discussed in this chapter.

Section B of Form 4684, reproduced in Figure I13-3, is used to report gains and losses resulting from a casualty or theft of property used in a trade or business or held for the production of income. Note that a separate Part I is used for each different casualty or theft. Gains are reported on line 22, and losses are reported on line 27. For properties held a year or less, the gains and losses are reported on lines 29 through 32 of Part II. These gains and losses are either recorded as ordinary gains and losses on line 14 of Part II of Form 4797 or as itemized deductions on Schedule A of Form 1040.

For properties held more than a year, the gains and losses are reported on lines 33 and 34. If gains exceed losses, the net gain is reported on line 39 and then on line 3 of Part I of Form 4797 (i.e., the gains and losses are treated as Sec. 1231 gains and losses). If the losses exceed the gains, all or part of the gains and losses are reported as ordinary in Part II of Form 4797 and/or on Schedule A of Form 1040.

PROBLEM MATERIALS

DISCUSSION QUESTIONS

I13-1 Explain how the gain on the sale or exchange of land could be classified as either ordinary income, a Sec. 1231 gain, or a LTCG, depending on the facts and circumstances.

I13-2 Why were taxpayers reluctant to sell appreciated business property between 1938 and 1942? What effect did this reluctance have on the tax law?

I13-3 Alice owns timber, purchased six years ago, with an adjusted basis of $50,000. The timber is cut for use in her furniture business on October 1, when the FMV of the timber is $200,000. The FMV of the timber on January 1 is $190,000. May Alice treat any of the gain as Sec. 1231 gain? If so, how much?

I13-4 Explain how the gain from an involuntary conversion of business property held more than one year is taxed if the involuntary conversion is the result of a condemnation. Explain the tax treatment if the involuntary conversion is due to a casualty.

I13-5 When is livestock considered Sec. 1231 property?

I13-6 When is a net Sec. 1231 gain treated as ordinary income?

I13-7 Carlie has a Sec. 1231 gain of $10,000 and no Sec. 1231 losses during the current year. Explain why the gain might be taxed at (a) 20%, (b) 36%, (c) 25%, or (d) 10%.

I13-8 Why is it unlikely that gains due to the sale of equipment will be treated as Sec. 1231 gains?

I13-9 Hank sells equipment used in a trade or business for $25,000. The equipment costs $30,000 and has an adjusted basis of $25,500. Why is it important to know the holding period?

I13-10 Jackie purchases equipment during the current year for $800,000 that has a seven-year MACRS recovery period. She expects to sell the property after three years. Jackie anticipates that her marginal tax rate in the year of sale will be significantly higher than her current marginal tax rate. Why might it be advantageous for her to use the straight-line method of depreciation?

I13-11 Karen purchased a computer three years ago for $4,500 to use exclusively in her business. She expensed the entire cost of the computer under Sec. 179. If she sells the computer during the current year for $1,622, what is the amount and character of her recognized gain?

I13-12 Sheila owns a motel that is used in a trade or business. If she sells the motel, the gain will be Sec. 1245 ordinary income. During what period of time was the motel placed into service?

I13-13 How may a taxpayer avoid having additional depreciation?

I13-14 Marty sells his fully depreciated building at a gain to an unrelated party. The building is purchased before 1981. Is any of the gain taxed as ordinary income?

I13-15 Which of the following assets (assume all assets have a holding period of more than one year) do not qualify as Sec. 1231 property: inventory, a pig held for breeding, land used as a parking lot for customers, and marketable securities?

I13-16 When is an office building subject to the depreciation recapture rules of Sec. 1245?

I13-17 Does a building that is 60% rented for residential use and 40% for commercial use qualify as residential rental property?

I13-18 Roger owns an apartment complex with a FMV of $2 million. If he sells the apartment complex, $700,000 of the gain is ordinary income. If he dies before selling the apartment complex and his estate sells the property for $2 million, how much ordinary income must the estate recognize?

I13-19 Rashad owns a duplex that is used 100% as residential rental property. Under what conditions, if any, will any gain that he recognizes be Sec. 1245 ordinary income?

I13-20 John and Karen are unrelated individuals. John sold land that is Sec. 1231 property held for three years and recognized a $50,000 gain. Karen sold a building that is Sec. 1231 property held for three years and recognized a $50,000 gain. Straight-line depreciation was used. John and Karen both have a 31% tax rate, no other transactions involving capital assets or 1231 assets, and no nonrecaptured Sec. 1231 losses. Except for the sales of different assets, their tax situation is exactly the same. As a result of selling his Sec. 1231 property, will John pay more, less or the same amount of taxes than Karen as a result of selling her Sec. 1231 property? Explain.

I13-21 Why may a corporation recognize a greater amount of ordinary income due to the sale of Sec. 1250 property than a noncorporate taxpayer?

I13-22 Assume a taxpayer sells equipment used in a trade or business for a gain that is less than the depreciation allowed. If the taxpayer is a corporation, will a greater amount of Sec. 1245 income be recognized than if the taxpayer is an individual? Explain.

I13-23 Dale owns business equipment with a $100,000 FMV and an adjusted basis of $60,000. The property was originally acquired for $150,000. Which one of the following transactions would result in recognition of $40,000 ordinary income by Dale due to the depreciation recapture rules of Sec. 1245?
  a. He makes a gift of the property to a daughter.
  b. He contributes the property to a qualified charitable organization.
  c. He disposes of the equipment in an installment sale and receives $10,000 cash in the year of sale.

I13-24 Carlos owns an office building with a $700,000 acquisition cost, a $250,000 adjusted basis, and a $500,000 FMV. The office building was acquired before 1981, and additional depreciation amounts to $110,000. Carlos makes a gift of the building to a charitable organization. What is the amount of his charitable contribution deduction?

I13-25 Ted owns a warehouse that cost $650,000 in 1984 and is subject to depreciation recapture under Sec. 1245. The warehouse, which has an adjusted basis of $300,000, is destroyed by a tornado and Ted receives $510,000 from the insurance company. Within nine months, he pays $450,000 for a new warehouse and an election is made to defer the gain under Sec. 1033. What is the amount and character of Ted's recognized gain?

I13-26 When a taxpayer disposes of oil, gas, or geothermal property, part or all of the gain may be recaptured as ordinary income. Explain how the recapture amount is determined for oil and gas and geothermal properties.

I13-27 William owns two appreciated assets, land and a building, which have been used in his trade or business for several years. The straight-line method of depreciation is used for the building. If he sells the two assets to his 100%-owned corporation, will William have to recognize any ordinary income? Explain.

ISSUE IDENTIFICATION QUESTIONS

I13-28 Six years ago Joelle started raising chinchillas. She separates her chinchillas into two groups, a breeding group and a market group. During the year, she had the following sales of chinchillas from her market group: 400 to producers of fur products; 100 to pet stores; and 25 to individuals to use as pets. From her breeding stock, she sold six chinchillas to Rebecca, an individual who is starting a chinchilla ranch, and five to Fur Pelts, a producer of fur products. All 11 chinchillas from the breeding group have been held for at least 22 months, and the five sold to Fur Pelts were poor performers.

I13-29 Green Acres, Inc. owns 1,400 acres adjacent to land owned by the U.S. government. The government, wanting to sell timber from its land, had to assure prospective bidders of access to the timber. The government entered into an agreement with Green Acres for a logging road easement across land owned by Green Acres. The government agreed to pay

$2 per thousand board feet of timber removed up to a maximum of $130,000. Bidders for the rights to obtain the government's timber had to agree to pay the fee to Green Acres as part of their bids for the timber. Stanley Lumberyard, Inc. provided the highest bid and paid $80,000 to Green Acres during the first year of cutting and removing the timber and $50,000 during the second year. What tax issues should Green Acres and Stanley Lumberyard consider?

I13-30 Sarah, who has been in the business of erecting, maintaining, and renting outdoor advertising displays for 18 years, has an offer to purchase her business. Two basic types of advertising displays are used in her business: structure X and structure Y. Structure X consists of a single sign face nailed to a wooden support frame and attached to wooden poles 30 feet long. Its structure is rather easy to dismantle and move from one location to another. In contrast, structure Y is a permanent sign that is designed to withstand winds of up to 100 miles per hour. None of the Structure Y signs have ever been moved. What tax issues should Sarah consider?

I13-31 Sylvester owns and operates an unincorporated pizza business that delivers pizza to customers. Three years ago, he acquired an automobile for $10,000 to provide delivery service. Recently, Sylvester hired an employee who prefers to use his personal automobile to make the deliveries. Thus, Sylvester decided to permit his 18-year old daughter to use the automobile for her personal use. The automobile's adjusted basis is $3,080 and its FMV is $4,700. What tax issues should Sylvester consider?

PROBLEMS

I13-32 *Sec. 1231, 1245, and 1250 Transactions.* All assets listed below have been held for more than one year. Which assets might be classified as Sec. 1231, Sec. 1245, or Sec. 1250 property? An asset may be classified as more than one type of property.
a. Land on which a factory is located
b. Equipment used in the factory
c. Raw materials inventory
d. Patent purchased to allow use of a manufacturing process
e. Land held primarily for sale
f. Factory building acquired in 1986 (the straight-line ACRS recovery method is used)

I13-33 *Sec. 1231 Gains and Losses.* Vivian's AGI is $40,000 without considering the gains and losses below. Determine her revised AGI after the inclusion of any applicable gains or losses for the following independent cases. Assume she has no unrecaptured net Sec. 1231 losses at the beginning of the year.

	Case A	Case B	Case C	Case D
Sec. 1231 gain	$15,000	$10,000	$30,000	$ 5,000
Sec. 1231 loss	5,000	18,000	38,000	12,000
LTCG	—0—	—0—	4,000	—0—
LTCL	—0—	—0—	—0—	4,200

I13-34 *Sec. 1231 Gains and Losses.* Edith, who has no other sales or exchanges and no nonrecaptured Sec. 1231 losses, sells three tracts of land that are used in her trade or business. Her tax rate is 36%.
Asset #1–$10,000 gain and holding period of 20 months
Asset #2–$12,000 loss and holding period of 25 months
Asset #3–$ 5,000 gain and holding period of 13 months
a. What is the increase in her taxes as a result of the three sales?
b. If the holding period for Asset #2 is nine months, what is the decrease in her taxes as a result of the three sales?

I13-35 *Sec. 1231 Transactions.* Which of the following transactions or events is treated as a Sec. 1231 gain or loss? Assume all assets are held for more than one year.
a. Theft of uninsured diamond ring, with an $800 basis and a $1,000 FMV.
b. Gain due to condemnation of land used in business.
c. Loss on the sale of a warehouse.
d. Gain on the sale of equipment. The gain recognized amounts to $4,000 and the depreciation deductions allowed amount to $10,000.

I13-36 *Capital Loss Versus Sec. 1231 Loss.* Vicki has an AGI of $60,000 without considering the sale of a nondepreciable asset for $23,000. The asset was acquired six years ago and has an adjusted basis of $35,000. She has no other sales or exchanges. Determine her AGI for the following independent situations:
a. The asset is a capital asset.
b. The asset is Sec. 1231 property.

I13-37 *Ordinary Income Versus Sec. 1231 Gain.* At the beginning of 2001, Silver Corporation has a $95,000 capital loss carryforward from 2000. During 2001, the corporation sells land, held for four years, and realizes a $80,000 gain. Silver has no unrecaptured Sec. 1231 losses, and it made no other sales during the current year. Determine the amount of capital loss carryforward that Silver can use in 2001 if
a. The land is Sec. 1231 property.
b. The land is not a capital asset or Sec. 1231 property.

I13-38 *Sec. 1231 Transactions.* During the current year, Sean's office building is destroyed by fire. After collecting the insurance proceeds, Sean has a $50,000 recognized gain. The building was acquired in 1978, and the straight-line method of depreciation has been used. He does not plan to acquire a replacement building. Consider the following independent cases and determine his net capital gain. For each case, include the $50,000 casualty gain described above.
a. Land used in his trade or business and held more than a year is condemned by the state. The recognized gain is $60,000.
b. Assume the same facts as in Part a, except the condemnation results in a $60,000 loss.
c. An apartment building used as residential rental property and held more than one year is destroyed by a sudden, unexpected mudslide. The building is not insured, and the loss amounts to $200,000.

I13-39 *Nonrecaptured Net Sec. 1231 Losses.* Consider the following summary of Sec. 1231 gains and losses recognized by Janet during the period 1996–2001. If Janet has no capital gains and losses during the six-year period, determine her net capital gain for each year.

	Sec. 1231 Gains	Sec. 1231 Losses
1996	$ 9,000	$ 7,000
1997	20,000	24,000
1998	12,000	20,000
1999	9,000	5,000
2000	25,000	13,200
2001	10,000	17,000

I13-40 *Nonrecaptured Net Sec. 1231 Losses.* Dillion has a tax rate of 31% and $40,000 of net nonrecaptured Sec. 1231 losses at the start of the year. During the year, he recognizes a Sec. 1231 gain of $53,000 from the sale of land. As a result of the sale, how much does Dillion's tax liability increase?

I13-41 *Sec. 1245.* The Pear Corporation owns equipment with a $300,000 adjusted basis. The equipment was purchased six years ago for $650,000. If Pear sells the equipment for the selling prices given in the three independent cases below, what are the amount and character of Pear's recognized gain or loss?

Case	Selling Price
A	$407,000
B	790,000
C	245,000

I13-42 *Sec. 1245.* Elizabeth owns equipment that cost $500,000 and has an adjusted basis of $230,000. If the straight-line method of depreciation had been used, the adjusted basis would be $300,000.
a. What is the maximum selling price that she could sell the equipment for without having to recognize Sec. 1245 ordinary income?
b. If she sold the equipment and had to recognize $61,000 of Sec. 1245 ordinary income, what was the selling price?

I13-43 *Secs. 1231, 1245, and 1250.* Betty is in the business of breeding and racing horses. Except for the transactions below, she has no other sales or exchanges and she has no unrecaptured Sec. 1231 losses. Consider the following transactions that occur during the year:

- A building with an adjusted basis of $300,000 is destroyed by fire. Insurance proceeds of $500,000 are received, but Betty does not plan to replace the building. The building was built 12 years ago at a cost of $430,000 and straight-line depreciation has been used. The building was used to provide lodging for her employees.
- Four acres of the farm are condemned by the state to widen the highway and Betty receives $50,000. The adjusted basis of the four acres is $15,000 and the land was inherited from her mother 15 years ago. She does not plan to purchase additional land.
- A racehorse purchased four years ago for $200,000 was sold for $550,000. Total depreciation allowed using the straight-line method amounts to $160,000.
- Equipment purchased three years ago for $200,000 is exchanged for $100,000 of IBM common stock. The adjusted basis of the equipment is $120,000. If straight-line depreciation had been used, the adjusted basis would be $152,000.
- A pony, with an adjusted basis of $20,000 and FMV of $35,000, that her daughter uses only for personal use is injured while attempting a jump. Because of the injury, the uninsured pony has to be destroyed by a veterinarian.

a. What amount of Sec. 1245 ordinary income must be recognized?
b. What amount of Sec. 1250 ordinary income must be recognized?
c. Will the loss resulting from the destruction of her daughter's pony be used to determine net Sec. 1231 gains or losses?
d. After all of the netting of gains or losses is completed, will the gain resulting from the involuntary conversion of the building be treated as LTCG?
e. What is the amount of the net Sec. 1231 gain or loss?
f. What is the amount of her unrecaptured Sec. 1250 gain?

I13-44 *Sale of Business and Personal-Use Property.* Arnie, a college student, purchased a new truck in 1999 for $6,000. He used the truck 70% of the time as a distributor for the local newspaper and 30% of the time for personal use. The truck has a five-year recovery period, and he claimed depreciation deductions of $840 in 1999 and $1,344 in 2000. Arnie sells the truck on June 20, 2001, for $3,000.
a. What is the amount of allowable depreciation in 2001?
b. What are the amount and character of Arnie's realized and recognized gain or loss?

I13-45 *Like-Kind Exchange of Sec. 1245 Property.* General Corporation owns equipment which cost $70,000 and has a $44,000 adjusted basis. General exchanges the equipment for other equipment with a $42,000 FMV and marketable securities with a $30,000 FMV. Determine the following:
a. Realized gain
b. Recognized gain
c. Gain treated as ordinary income
d. Gain treated as Sec. 1231 gain
e. Basis of marketable securities received
f. Basis of equipment received

I13-46 *Like-Kind Exchange of Sec. 1245 Property.* Leroy owns a truck used in his trade or business that cost $50,000 and has an adjusted basis of $34,000. The truck is exchanged for a new truck that is like-kind property with a FMV of $40,000. Prior to selling the new truck two years later, Leroy is allowed depreciation of $13,000 for the new truck. Determine:
a. Gain realized on the exchange?
b. Gain recognized on the exchange?
c. Basis of truck received?
d. Gain recognized, and the character of the gain, if the sales price of the truck is $41,000?
e. Gain recognized, and the character of the gain, if the sale price of the truck is $52,000?

I13-47 *Purpose of Sec. 1245.* Assume the year is 1986 when noncorporate taxpayers are allowed to deduct 60% of net capital gains to determine their AGI. Martin owns equipment used in his trade or business that was purchased in 1979 for $200,000. Allowed depreciation deductions amount to $160,000. Martin sells the equipment in 1986 for $110,000. No other sales or exchanges are made in 1986 or the preceding five years.

a. Determine the increase in Martin's 1986 AGI as a result of the sale if Sec. 1245 did not exist.
b. Given that Sec. 1245 does exist, what is the increase in his AGI as a result of the sale?
c. How would your answers to Parts a and b change if the asset were sold in 2001?

I13-48 *Secs. 1231 and 1250.* Charles owns an office building and land that are used in his trade or business. The office building and land were acquired in 1978 for $800,000 and $100,000, respectively. During the current year, the properties are sold for $900,000 with 20% of the selling price being allocated to the land. The assets as shown on the taxpayer's books before their sale are as follows:

Building	$800,000	
Accumulated depreciation	590,000[a]	$210,000
Land		100,000

[a] If the straight-line method of depreciation had been used, the accumulated depreciation would be $440,000.

a. What is the recognized gain due to the sale of the building?
b. What is the character of the recognized gain due to the sale of the building?
c. What is the recognized gain and character of the gain due to the sale of the land?
d. If the taxpayer is a corporation, how will the answers to Parts a–c change?

I13-49 *Sec. 1250.* Maggie owns a motel that is operated as a trade or business adjacent to an interstate highway. The motel was purchased in March 1965 for $2,000,000, and she used an accelerated method of depreciation. The motel is sold during the current year for $975,000. The adjusted basis of the motel is $600,000. Additional depreciation is deducted as follows:

	Additional Depreciation
March 1965 to January 1, 1970	$ 95,000
January 1, 1970 to current date	205,000

a. What is the amount of realized gain?
b. What is the amount, if any, of ordinary income that Maggie must recognize as a result of the additional depreciation deducted before January 1, 1970?
c. What is the amount of ordinary income that Maggie must recognize as a result of selling the motel?

I13-50 *Sec. 1250.* Ken purchased an office building on January 1, 1980, for $360,000 (40-year life and a $32,000 salvage value) and he elected to use the sum-of-the-years' digits method of depreciation. Prior to 1981, salvage value was considered when computing depreciation. Total depreciation allowed at the time of sale is $248,000. If the building is sold on January 1, 2001, for $340,000, what is the amount of gain recognized and the character of the gain?

I13-51 *Sec. 1250.* Assume the same facts as Problem I13-50 except that the taxpayer is a corporation instead of an individual. What is the amount and character of the corporation's recognized gain or loss?

I13-52 *Sec. 1250 Residential Rental Property.* Assume the same facts as Problem I13-50 except that the building is an apartment complex that qualifies as residential rental property. What is the amount and character of Ken's recognized gain or loss?

I13-53 *Sec. 1250 Residential Rental Property.* Assume the same facts as in Problem I13-51 except that the building is an apartment complex that qualifies as residential rental property. What is the amount and character of the corporation's recognized gain or loss?

I13-54 *Sec. 1250 Residential Rental Property.* Jesse owns a duplex that he uses as residential rental property. The duplex cost $100,000 in 1986, and 10% of the cost was allocated to the land. Total cost-recovery deductions allowed amount to $81,000. The statutory percentages were used to compute cost-recovery deductions. If the straight-line method of cost recovery were used instead, $76,000 of cost-recovery deductions would have been allowed.
a. What is the amount of recognized gain and the character of the gain if Jesse sells the duplex for $125,000?
b. What is the amount of recognized gain in the year of sale and the character of the gain if Jesse sells the property under the installment sale method? Terms of the installment

I13-55 *Sec. 1250.* Rosemary owns an office building placed in service before 1981 that cost $625,000 and has an adjusted basis of $227,000. If the straight-line method of depreciation were used, the adjusted basis would be $300,000.
   a. What is the maximum selling price that she could sell the building for without having to recognize Sec. 1250 ordinary income?
   b. If she sold the building and had to recognize $51,000 of Sec. 1250 ordinary income, what was the selling price?

I13-56 Consider three office buildings placed in service as shown below and answer the following true-false questions. Assume all assets are sold by a noncorporate taxpayer at a gain and there are no other sales or exchanges or nonrecaptured Sec. 1231 loss unless told otherwise. None of the buildings are fully depreciated when sold.

	Placed in Service
Building #1	Before 1981
Building #2	After 1980 and before 1987
Building #3	After 1986

1. Some or all of the gain on sale of #1 is ordinary if accelerated depreciation was used.
2. If the straight-line method of depreciation was used for #1, some or all of the gain may be taxed at 25%.
3. Gain on the sale of #2 could be Sec. 1245 ordinary income.
4. Gain on the sale of #2 could be Sec. 1231 gain.
5. Part of the gain on the sale of #2 could be Sec. 1245 ordinary income and part could be Sec. 1231 gain.
6. If the straight-line method of depreciation was used for #2, some or all of the gain may be taxed at 25%.
7. Some or all of the gain on the sale of #3 could be Sec. 1245 ordinary income.
8. Some or all of the gain on the sale of #3 could be taxed at 25%.
9. Some of the gain on the sale of #3 could be Sec. 1250 ordinary income.
10. If the taxpayer has a nonrecaptured Sec. 1231 loss of $30,000 and the gain on the sale of #3 is $40,000, all $40,000 of the gain is taxed as ordinary income.

I13-57 Assume the same facts as in Problem 56 except the taxpayer is a corporate taxpayer and answer the ten true-false questions.

I13-58 *Recapture of Soil and Water Conservation Expenditures.* Bob owns farmland with a $600,000 basis, and he elects to expense $100,000 of expenditures incurred for soil and water conservation purposes. After farming for seven years and four months, Bob sells the farmland for $825,000.
   a. What is the amount of the recognized gain and the character of the gain?
   b. What is the amount of recognized gain and the character of the gain if the farmland is sold for $615,000?

I13-59 *Recapture of Intangible Drilling Costs.* Jeremy purchased undeveloped oil and gas property in 1994 and paid $300,000 for intangible drilling and development costs. He elected to expense the intangible drilling and development costs in 1994. During the current year, Jeremy sells the property, which has an $800,000 adjusted basis, for $900,000. What is the amount of gain treated as ordinary income under Sec. 1254 because of the election to expense intangible drilling and development costs?

I13-60 *Recapture of Intangible Drilling Costs and Depletion.* In 1997, Jack purchased undeveloped oil and gas property for $900,000 and paid $170,000 for intangible drilling and development costs. He elected to expense the intangible drilling and development costs. During the current year he sells the property for $950,000 when the property's adjusted basis is $700,000. Depletion of $200,000 was allowed on the property.
   a. What is the realized gain and how much of the gain is ordinary income?
   b. For Jack to have a Sec. 1231 gain, the selling price must exceed what amount?

I13-61 *Related Party Transactions.* Ed operates a storage business as a sole proprietorship and owns the following assets acquired in 1977:

Warehouse		$400,000
Minus: Accumulated depreciation (straight-line method)		(230,000)
Adjusted basis		$170,000
Land		65,000

The FMV of the warehouse and the land are $500,000 and $200,000, respectively. Ed owns 75% of the stock of the Crane Corporation. If he sells the two assets to Crane at a price equal to the FMV of the assets, determine the following:

a. Recognized gain due to sale of the building and character of the gain.
b. Recognized gain due to the sale of the land and character of the gain.

I13-62 *Timing of Sec. 1231 Transactions.* Russ has never recognized any Sec. 1231 gains or losses. In December 2001, Russ is considering the sale of two Sec. 1231 assets. The sale of one asset will result in a $20,000 Sec. 1231 gain while the sale of the other asset will result in a $20,000 Sec. 1231 loss. Russ has no other capital or Sec. 1231 gains and losses in 2001 and does not expect to have any other capital or Sec. 1231 gains and losses in 2001. He is aware that it might be advantageous to recognize the Sec. 1231 gain and the Sec. 1231 loss in different tax years. However, he does not know whether he should recognize the Sec. 1231 gain in 2001 and the Sec. 1231 loss in 2002 or vice versa. His marginal tax rate for each year is expected to be 31%. Advise the taxpayer with respect to these two alternatives:

a. Recognize the $20,000 Sec. 1231 loss in 2001 and the $20,000 Sec. 1231 gain in 2002.
b. Recognize the $20,000 Sec. 1231 gain in 2001 and the $20,000 Sec. 1231 loss in 2002.

I13-63 *Timing of Sec. 1231 Transaction.* Holly has recognized a $9,000 STCL. She has no other recognized capital gains and losses in 2001. She is considering the sale of a Sec. 1231 asset held for four years at a $5,000 gain in 2001. She had not recognized any Sec. 1231 losses during the previous five years and does not expect to have any other Sec. 1231 transactions in 2001. Her marginal tax rate for 2001 is 31%. What is the amount of increase in her 2001 taxes if Holly recognizes the $5,000 Sec. 1231 gain in 2001?

TAX FORM/RETURN PREPARATION PROBLEMS

I13-64 George Buckner, Soc. Sec. no. 267-31-7251, sells an apartment building during the current year for $1,750,000. The building was purchased on January 1, 1978, for $2,000,000. An accelerated method of depreciation has been used, and depreciation of $1,140,000 has been taken. If the straight-line method of depreciation had been used, depreciation of $800,000 would have been allowed. The figures given above do not include the purchase price or the selling price of the land. Mr. Buckner's adjusted basis for the land is $200,000, and the sales price is $350,000. Mr. Buckner, who owns and operates a taxi business, sells one of the automobiles for $1,800. The automobile's adjusted basis is zero, and the original cost is $15,000. The automobile was purchased on April 25, 1994. Mr. Buckner has no other gains and losses during the year, and nonrecaptured net Sec. 1231 losses amount to $32,000. Prepare Form 4797 for the current year.

I13-65 Julie Hernandez is single and has no dependents. She operates a dairy farm and her social security number is 510-88-6387. She lives at 1325 Vermont Street in Costa, Florida. Consider the following information for her tax return for the current year:

- Schedule C was prepared by her accountant and the net profit from the dairy operations for the current year is $48,000.
- Itemized deductions amount to $3,185.
- Dividend income amounts to $280.
- State income tax refund received during the year is $125. She did not itemize her deductions last year.
- In June, a burglar broke into her house and stole the following two assets, which were acquired in 1987:

	Basis	FMV	Insurance Proceeds Received
Painting	$2,000	$10,000	$9,000
Sculpture	1,700	1,500	0

The following assets used in her business were sold during the year:

	Acquisition Date	Original Cost	Depreciation to Date of Sale	Date of Sale	Selling Price
Tractor	June 10, 1990	$25,000	$25,000	Oct. 20	$ 8,300
Barn	May 23, 1980	90,000	36,000[a]	May 13	87,000
Land	May 23, 1980	15,000	—0—	May 13	27,000
Cows	Sept. 7, 1998	20,000	13,000	Nov. 8	21,000

[a] $25,000 if the straight-line method had been used.

In August, three acres of the farm were taken by the state under the right of eminent domain for the purpose of building a highway. The basis of the three acres is $1,500 and the state paid the FMV, $22,000, on February 10. The farm was purchased on August 12, 1971.

Nonrecaptured net Section 1231 losses from the five most recent tax years preceding the current year amount to $7,000. Estimated taxes paid during the year amount to $32,000.

Prepare Forms 1040, 4684 Section A, 4797, and Schedule D for the current year. (Do not consider self-employment taxes discussed in Chapter I14.)

CASE STUDY PROBLEMS

I13-66 Your client, Kent Earl, whose tax rate is 39.6%, owns a bowling alley and has indicated that he wants to sell the business for $1,000,000 and purchase a minor league baseball franchise. His business consists of the following tangible assets:

	Acquisition Date	Original Cost	Adjusted Basis
Equipment	1987	$600,000	$150,000
Building	1978	900,000	400,000[a]
Land	1978	100,000	100,000
Inventory	Current year	50,000	50,000

[a] $480,000 if straight-line depreciation had been used.

Because you have another client, Tom Quick, who is interested in purchasing a business, you informed Tom of Kent's interest in selling. Tom wants to purchase the bowling alley, and the price sounds right to him. The bowling alley business has been very profitable in the last few years because Kent has developed a loyal group of customers by promoting bowling leagues during the week days and a special Saturday afternoon session for children in the elementary school grades. Kent and Tom have come to you and want to know how the transaction should be handled for the best tax results. You know, of course, that the $1,000,000 purchase price will have to be allocated among the assets and it will be necessary to estimate the FMV of all assets. Because FMV is often subjective, Kent and Tom recognize that some flexibility might exist in allocating the purchase price. For example, it might be just as easy to justify a FMV of $300,000 or $325,000 for the equipment.

a. What advice do you have for Kent with respect to the allocation (i.e., should he be interested in allocating more to some assets than others)? Explain the reasoning for your advice.
b. Would your advice to Kent be different if he had a large amount of capital losses and no nonrecaptured net Sec. 1231 losses?
c. What advice do you have for Tom with respect to the allocation (i.e., should he be interested in allocating more of the purchase price to some assets than to others)? Explain the reasoning for your advice.
d. What advantages might result from having Kent sign an agreement not to compete (i.e., operate a bowling alley)?
e. Should you have a concern about the ethical implications of advising both Kent and Tom?

I13-67 Assume the same facts as in Case Study Problem I13-66 except you have the following market values as a result of an appraisal:

Equipment	$ 250,000
Building	500,000
Land	140,000
Inventory	110,000
Total	$1,000,000

Tom insists that $150,000 of the purchase price should be allocated to inventory and $100,000 should be allocated to land. He refuses to complete the purchase unless the allocation is made as he requests. What action should you take with respect to Tom's request? (See Chapter I10 for a discussion of valuation issues in the purchase and sale of a business.)

TAX RESEARCH PROBLEM

I13-68 Berkeley Corporation has a policy of furnishing new automobiles to the athletic department of the local university. The automobiles are used for short periods of time by the extremely popular head basketball coach. When the automobiles are returned to Berkeley Corporation, they are sold to regular customers. The owner of Berkeley Corporation maintains that any such cars held for more than one year should qualify as Sec. 1231 property. Do you agree?

Research sources include
- Rev. Rul. 75-538, 1975-2 C.B. 34.

CHAPTER 14

SPECIAL TAX COMPUTATION METHODS, TAX CREDITS, AND PAYMENT OF TAX

LEARNING OBJECTIVES

After studying this chapter, you should be able to

1. Calculate the alternative minimum tax
2. Describe what constitutes self-employment income and compute the self-employment tax
3. Describe the various business and personal tax credits
4. Understand the mechanics of the federal withholding tax system and the requirements for making estimated tax payments

CHAPTER OUTLINE

Alternative Minimum Tax...14-2
Self-Employment Tax...14-7
Overview of Tax Credits...14-9
Personal Tax Credits...14-9
Miscellaneous Credits...14-16
General Business Credits...14-17
Refundable Credits...14-22
Payment of Taxes...14-24

Chapter I2 discussed the basic tax computation for individuals using the tax table and tax rate schedules. This chapter completes the discussion of the tax computation by examining three principal topics:

1. Two special methods of tax computation, the alternative minimum tax and self-employment tax,
2. Various tax credits that are available to reduce a taxpayer's tax liability, and
3. Methods for payment of an individual's tax liability, including the pay-as-you-go withholding rules and estimated tax payment requirements.

ALTERNATIVE MINIMUM TAX

OBJECTIVE 1

Calculate the alternative minimum tax

Over the years, Congress has used the income tax law for a variety of purposes other than just the raising of revenue to fund government operations, such as enacting provisions to promote economic and social goals. As the number of special tax provisions increased, many taxpayers were able to carefully plan their financial affairs so as to use these special tax provisions to substantially reduce or eliminate their entire income tax liability. As a result, a new set of rules were implemented in 1969 to ensure that all taxpayers would pay at least a minimum amount of income tax. Thus was born what is known today as the **alternative minimum tax (AMT)**.

The original minimum tax was referred to as an add-on minimum tax because it was added to the taxpayer's regular income tax liability. The amount of the tax was 10% times the taxpayer's tax preferences in excess of a $30,000 statutory exemption. The present AMT system, originally created in 1978, is no longer an add-on tax but is actually a separate and parallel tax system. Taxpayers are first required to compute their regular income tax liability and then compute their tax under the AMT system. The AMT system essentially requires taxpayers to adjust their regular taxable income by a number of adjustments and preferences, then subtract an exemption amount to arrive at the AMT base. The AMT base is then multiplied by the special AMT rates to compute the AMT. Taxpayers are required to pay the *greater* of (1) the regular income, or (2) the AMT.

The present AMT applies to individuals, corporations, estates, and trusts.[1] Most individual taxpayers are actually not subject to the AMT because their regular income tax is greater than the AMT. This is caused primarily because many taxpayers do not have substantial adjustments and preferences and the AMT exemption is liberal in amount (i.e., $45,000 for married individuals filing a joint return and $33,750 for single individuals).

EXAMPLE I14-1 ▶ Ricardo and Sue are married and file a joint return for the current year with taxable income of $30,000 and tax preferences and adjustments of $12,000 for AMT purposes. Their alternative minimum taxable income (AMTI) is $42,000 ($30,000 + $12,000), but the alternative minimum tax base is zero because of the $45,000 exemption. Thus, their tax liability is based on the regular tax computation and no AMT liability is owed. ◀

EXAMPLE I14-2 ▶ Assume the same facts for Ricardo and Sue above except that they have tax preferences and adjustments of $50,000. Their alternative minimum taxable income (AMTI) is $80,000 ($30,000 + $50,000). Their regular tax would be $4,500 ($30,000 × 15%). The total tax computed under the AMT system would be $9,100 ($80,000 minus the AMT exemption of $45,000 yields the AMT base of $35,000; $35,000 × AMT tax rate of 26% equals $9,100). Thus, Ricardo and Sue must pay $9,100 in tax since it is greater than their regular tax of $4,500. ◀

COMPUTATIONAL ASPECTS

The formula for computing the alternative minimum tax for individuals for the tax year is to apply a two-tiered graduated rate schedule to the AMT tax base. The tax base consists of the following items:[2]

---

[1] The AMT applicable to corporations is discussed in *Prentice Hall's Federal Taxation: Corporations, Partnerships, Estates, and Trusts* text and in the *Comprehensive* volume.

[2] Sec. 55(b)(1).

Special Tax Computation Methods, Tax Credits, and Payment of Tax ▼ **Individuals 14-3**

ADDITIONAL COMMENT

Some tax advisors recommend accelerating income into a year in which the taxpayer is subject to the AMT because the income will be taxed at a 26% or a 28% rate rather than a possibly higher rate in a later year.

TAXABLE INCOME
Plus: Tax preference items[3]
Plus: Personal and dependency exemptions
 The standard deduction if the taxpayer does not itemize
Plus or minus: Adjustments required because different rules are used for calculating the alternative minimum taxable income as compared with taxable income (e.g., special AMT limitations on certain itemized deductions)

EQUALS: ALTERNATIVE MINIMUM TAXABLE INCOME (AMTI)
Minus: Exemption amount ($45,000 for a married couple filing a joint return and surviving spouses, $33,750 for single individuals, and $22,500 for a married individual filing separately). The exemption amount is reduced by 25% of AMTI in excess of $150,000 for a married couple filing a joint return and surviving spouses, $112,500 for single individuals, and $75,000 for a married individual filing separately.[4]

EQUALS: ALTERNATIVE MINIMUM TAX BASE
Times: Tax rate (26% of first $175,000; 28% of amounts in excess of $175,000)[5]

EQUALS: TENTATIVE MINIMUM TAX
Minus: Regular tax

EQUALS: ALTERNATIVE MINIMUM TAX

EXAMPLE I14-3 ▶

KEY POINT

For purposes of the alternative minimum tax, no deduction is allowed for personal exemptions or the standard deduction.

ADDITIONAL COMMENT

In the Revenue Reconciliation Act of 1993, Congress created a two-tier alternative minimum tax schedule in order to make the individual income tax system more progressive.

Rita, a single taxpayer, has taxable income of $138,200, a regular tax liability of $37,432, a positive AMT adjustment due to limitations on itemized deductions of $30,000, and tax preferences of $40,000 in 2001. Rita's alternative minimum tax for 2001 is calculated as follows:

Taxable income		$138,200
Plus:	Tax preferences	40,000
Plus:	Personal exemption	2,900
Plus:	Adjustments related to itemized deductions	30,000
Alternative minimum taxable income		$211,100
Minus:	Exemption	(9,100)[a]
Alternative minimum tax base		$202,000
Tax on first $175,000: $175,000 × 0.26 =		$ 45,500
Tax on excess over $175,000: $27,000 × 0.28 =		$7,560
Tentative minimum tax		$ 53,060
Minus:	Regular tax	(37,432)
	Alternative minimum tax	$ 15,628

Rita will pay a total of $53,060 ($37,432 regular tax + $15,628 AMT).

[a] $33,750 − [0.25 × ($211,100 − $112,500)].

◀

TAX PREFERENCE ITEMS

Tax preferences are provisions in the Internal Revenue Code (IRC) granting favorable treatment to taxpayers. For example, accelerated depreciation allowed for real property placed in service before 1987 is a tax preference item. (See Chapter I10 for a discussion of ACRS depreciation.) To compute the tax base for the AMT, the tax preferences designated in Sec. 57 must be added to taxable income. Some of the most common tax preference items include the following:

ADDITIONAL COMMENT

Most taxpayers will not have tax preference items. Over the years, tax preference items have diminished in importance while adjustments create most AMT.

▶ Excess of accelerated depreciation (or ACRS cost recovery) claimed over a hypothetical straight-line depreciation amount for real property placed in service before 1987 computed on an item-by-item basis.

---

[3] Sec. 57.
[4] Sec. 55(d)(3).
[5] The AMT rate on net capital gains has been reduced from the 26%/28% rates to 20%/10% to correspond with the reduction in rates on net capital gains for regular tax purposes. This reduction is effecive for tax years ending after May 6, 1997.

- Tax-exempt interest on certain private activity bonds.
- Exclusion of gain on the sale of certain small business stock. The exclusion is 42% of the gain on the disposition of qualified small business stock under Sec. 1202[6] (See Chapter I15).

It should be noted, however, that not all items receiving preferential treatment are tax preference items. For example, most municipal bond interest income is exempt from the federal income tax but is not a tax preference item. Only tax-exempt interest on private activity bonds (e.g., bonds issued by a municipality to fund certain nongovernmental activities such as industrial parks) issued after August 7, 1986 are subject to the AMT.

EXAMPLE I14-4

Richard, a single taxpayer, has the following tax preference items for the current year:
- $15,000 ACRS cost-recovery deduction on real property placed in service before 1987 and held for investment. The straight-line ACRS deduction would have been $10,000.
- $10,000 of tax-exempt interest on private activity bonds.

Richard's total tax preferences are $15,000, consisting of $5,000 excess cost recovery deductions and $10,000 tax-exempt interest on the private activity bonds.

AMT ADJUSTMENTS

As previously discussed, AMTI equals taxable income as modified by certain adjustments and increased by tax preference items. For most individual taxpayers AMT adjustments represent itemized deductions that are not allowed in computing AMTI or timing differences relating to the deferral of income or the acceleration of deductions under the regular tax rules. These adjustments generally increase the AMT tax base, although the AMT tax base may be reduced when the timing differences reverse. Some of the more important adjustments are discussed below.

ADDITIONAL COMMENT

Some tax advisors recommend that cash basis taxpayers prepay their local property taxes or state income taxes before the end of the year in order to reduce the current year's tax liability. However, if the taxpayer is subject to the AMT, this may not be a valid strategy.

LIMITATION ON ITEMIZED DEDUCTIONS. Only certain itemized deductions are allowed in computing AMTI. Additionally, the standard deduction is not allowed if an individual does not itemize deductions. The following items are deductible for AMT purposes:

- Casualty and theft losses in excess of 10% of AGI
- Charitable contributions (but not in excess of the 20%, 30%, and 50% of AGI limitation amounts)
- Medical expenses in excess of 10% of AGI (a 7.5% ceiling applies to the regular tax computation)
- Qualified housing interest and certain other interest up to the amount of qualified net investment income included in the AMT base
- Estate tax deduction on income in respect of a decedent
- Gambling losses

Some of the more significant itemized deductions that are not deductible for the AMT include miscellaneous itemized deductions (e.g., unreimbursed employee expenses), state, local, and foreign income taxes, and real and personal property taxes. The 3% reduction of itemized deductions of high-income taxpayers does not apply to the AMT.

EXAMPLE I14-5

Robin, a single taxpayer, has AGI of $100,000 and the following itemized deductions in 2001:

Charitable contributions	4,000
Medical expenses in excess of 7.5% of AGI ($10,000 actual expenses − $7,500)	2,500
Mortgage interest on Robin's personal residence	18,600
Real estate taxes	4,000
State income taxes	6,000
Personal casualty loss, net of insurance, in excess of 10% of AGI ($22,000 actual loss − $10,000) and $100 floor	$12,000

---

[6] Sec. 57(a)(7). The 42% rate was formerly 50%. The Taxpayer Relief Act of 1997 reduced this tax preference item to 42% effective for tax years ending after May 6, 1997. For stock acquired after December 31, 2000, the 42% rate is reduced to 28%.

Special Tax Computation Methods, Tax Credits, and Payment of Tax ▼ **Individuals 14-5**

From the information above, Robin's taxable income is $50,000 ($100,000 minus itemized deductions and personal exemption of $2,900). Assume she also has $20,000 of tax preferences for AMT purposes. Robin's AMT adjustments for disallowed itemized deductions include $2,500 of medical expenses, because the 10% AMT limitation eliminates the medical expense deduction [$10,000 − (0.10 × $100,000 AGI) = $0] and $10,000 of real estate and state income taxes ($4,000 + $6,000). Thus, Robin's total AMT adjustment for disallowed itemized deductions is $12,500 ($2,500 + $10,000). Robin's AMTI is $85,400 ($50,000 taxable income + $20,000 tax preferences + $12,500 disallowed itemized deductions + her $2,900 personal exemption). ◀

AMT ADJUSTMENTS DUE TO TIMING DIFFERENCES. Other adjustments are required when the rules for calculating taxable income permit the taxpayer to temporarily defer the recognition of income or to accelerate deductions. This temporary benefit is caused by applying different accounting methods that result in timing differences when income or expenses are recognized. The most common AMT adjustments for individuals that represent timing differences include:

▶ For real property placed in service after 1986 and before January 1, 1999, the difference between the MACRS depreciation claimed using the property's actual recovery period and a hypothetical straight-line depreciation amount calculated using a 40-year life (see Chapter I10 for a discussion of the alternative depreciation system).[7]

▶ For personal property placed in service after 1986, the difference between the MACRS deduction and the amount determined by using the 150% declining balance method under the alternative depreciation system with a switch to the straight-line method.[8]

▶ For research and experimental (R&E) expenditures, the difference between the amount expensed and the deduction that would have been allowed if the expenditures were capitalized and amortized over a ten-year period.[9]

EXAMPLE I14-6 ▶ Rob has the following AMT adjustments caused by timing differences in 2001:

▶ Depreciation in 2001 on residential rental property costing $100,000 and placed in service in January, 1999 is $3,636 using the straight-line method, a 27½-year recovery period, and based on MACRS rules. The depreciation in 2001 for AMT purposes is $2,500 based on the straight-line method and a 40-year recovery period under the alternative depreciation system. Thus, the positive AMT adjustment is $1,136 ($3,636 − $2,500). (See footnote 7 for real property placed in service after December 31, 1998)

▶ Depreciation on an automobile used in business costing $10,000 and placed in service in 2001 is $2,000 based on the MACRS rules (i.e., 200% DB method, a half-year convention, and a five-year recovery period). The depreciation for AMT purposes is $1,500 based on the alternative depreciation system (i.e., 150% DB method, half-year convention and a five-year recovery period). Thus, the positive AMT adjustment is $500 ($2,000 − $1,500).

▶ R&E expenditures amounting to $50,000 are expensed in the current year. For AMT purposes, the R&E deduction would be $5,000 ($50,000 ÷ 10 years) since the expenditures are capitalized and amortized over a 10-year period. Thus, the positive AMT adjustment is $45,000 ($50,000 − $5,000).

Rob's total positive AMT adjustment to his taxable income in 2001 to arrive at AMTI is $46,636 ($1,136 + $500 + $45,000). ◀

ADDITIONAL COMMENT

For corporate taxpayers only, there is a 0.12% environmental tax imposed on the excess of the corporation's modified alternative minimum taxable income over $2 million.

CREDIT THAT REDUCES THE AMT. As we will discuss later in this chapter, there are a number of credits that are allowed to reduce a taxpayer's regular tax liability. However, for purposes of the AMT, only the foreign tax credit is allowed to reduce the tentative minimum tax. Further, the foreign tax credit that may be deducted from the AMT is a specially computed credit, called the "alternative minimum tax foreign tax credit." It is basically computed using the various amounts used in computing alternative minimum tax-

---

[7] For real property being depreciated under the straight-line method and placed in service after 1998, the Taxpayer Relief Act of 1997 eliminates this adjustment.

[8] For personal property not being depreciated under the 200% declining balance method (i.e., 15-year and 20-year property) and placed into service after 1998, the Taxpayer Relief Act of 1997 effectively eliminates this adjustment for such property.

[9] Sec. 56(b)(2). However, this adjustment does not apply if the taxpayer materially participates in the activity, Sec. 56(b)(2)(D).

able income instead of taxable income. Thus, the AMT is likely to apply to a taxpayer who uses credits (other than the foreign tax credit) to reduce his regular tax liability.

STOP & THINK

Question: What are the most common characteristics of taxpayers who are subject to the AMT?

Solution: While each situation is certainly unique, there are certain taxpayers who are more likely to be subject to the AMT. First, taxpayers who have materially invested in real estate before January 1, 1999 are likely candidates for the AMT because they will have a large positive adjustment caused from the differences in depreciation. Second, as discussed above, taxpayers who use credits to reduce their regular tax liability may well be subject to the AMT because only the foreign tax credit can reduce the AMT. Third, taxpayers who have very large itemized deductions, primarily from large state and local taxes, may be subject to the AMT because state and local taxes are not deductible for AMT purposes.

AMT CREDIT. Under Sec. 53, taxpayers are allowed an AMT credit which can be used against their *regular tax liability*. Basically, if a taxpayer pays AMT in a taxable year, that amount of AMT is eligible to be used as a credit against the taxpayer's regular tax liability in a future year. While this may seem unusual at first glance, the underlying reasoning for the AMT credit is as follows: since the AMT is caused primarily by adjustments that will reverse in the future and the taxpayer will actually pay a higher regular tax in those future years, the imposition of a prior year AMT and the current year regular tax essentially would constitute double taxation. Thus, a taxpayer who has paid AMT in prior years, but is not subject to the AMT in the current year, may be entitled to an AMT credit against his regular tax liability in the current year.[10]

SUMMARY ILLUSTRATION OF THE AMT COMPUTATION

The AMT formula is illustrated in the following example:

EXAMPLE I14-7 ▶ Roger and Kate are married and file a joint return. They have the following items (including $25,000 in tax preference items from interest income earned on private activity bonds) that are used to compute taxable income in 2000:

Gross income:		
Salary		$ 60,000
Dividends and interest		10,000
Business income		30,000[a]
AGI		$100,000
Minus: Itemized deductions:		
State and local property taxes	$10,000	
Mortgage interest on their personal residence	12,000	
Charitable contributions	3,000	(25,000)
Minus: Personal and dependency exemptions ($2,900 × 2)		(5,800)
Taxable income		$ 69,200

[a] MACRS depreciation deductions of $70,000 on personal property placed in service after 1986 were claimed in arriving at business income. Only $50,000 of depreciation would be claimed under the alternative depreciation system using the 150% declining balance method.

Roger's AMT is computed as follows:

ADDITIONAL COMMENT

In some circumstances, the AMT applies to unsuspecting taxpayers. In a recent case, *D.R. Klaussen*, TC Memo. 1998-241 (affd, CA-10), the taxpayers had 12 personal exemptions and were subject to the AMT even though they had no tax preferences or adjustments.

---

[10] Detailed discussion of the rules for computing the AMT credit is beyond the scope of this book. See Sec. 53 for additional information.

Special Tax Computation Methods, Tax Credits, and Payment of Tax ▼ **Individuals 14-7**

Taxable income			$ 69,200
Plus: Tax preferences			25,000
Personal and dependency exemptions			5,800
AMT adjustments:			
Excess depreciation		$20,000	
State and local property taxes		10,000	30,000
AMTI			$130,000
Minus: AMT exemption			(45,000)
Tax base			$ 85,000
Times: Tax rate			
Tentative minimum tax ($85,000 × 26%)			$ 22,100
Minus: Regular tax (based on taxable income of $69,200)			(13,500)
Alternative minimum tax			$ 8,600[a]

[a] An AMT credit may be available in future years to offset any regular tax that is owed. However, the AMT credit applies only to the AMT that results from timing differences such as depreciation adjustments and not from exclusions (e.g., personal exemptions and taxes).

The total tax liability for Roger and Kate is $22,100 ($13,500 + $8,600). ◀

SELF-EMPLOYMENT TAX

OBJECTIVE 2

Describe what constitutes self-employment income and compute the self-employment tax

Most individuals are classified as employees and are not subject to the self-employment tax. Employees are covered under the Federal Insurance Contributions Act (FICA) through the payment of payroll taxes. The employer must withhold the employee's share of the FICA tax and provide a matching amount. Employees are not subject to an additional employment tax upon the filing of their federal income tax return.

The self-employment tax is imposed to finance Social Security coverage for self-employed individuals. Thus, the distinction between a self-employed individual (often referred to as an independent contractor) and an employee is important because no employer FICA contribution is required if the payee is deemed to have independent contractor status. Independent contractors are subject to self-employment tax on the amount of net earnings from the self-employment activity. Employees who have a small business in addition to their regular employment (e.g., an accountant, who is an employee for a large corporation, also prepares tax returns as a consultant) may be subject to the self-employment tax on the consulting income in addition to the FICA tax on wages.

COMPUTING THE TAX

ETHICAL POINT

An employer must have a reasonable basis for treating a worker as an independent contractor or meet the general common law rules for determining whether an employer-employee relationship exists. Otherwise, the employer is liable for federal and state income tax withholding, FICA and FUTA taxes, interest, and penalties associated with the misclassification.

HISTORICAL NOTE

The ceiling amount on income from self-employment was $7,800 in 1971.

Self-employed individuals are subject to the self-employment (SE) tax if their net earnings are $400 or more.[11] The SE tax rate is a total of 15.3%, comprised of 12.4% for old-age, survivors, and disability insurance (OASDI) up to a ceiling amount of $80,400 in 2001 ($76,200 in 2000), and 2.9% for hospital insurance (HI), commonly referred to as Medicare taxes. No ceiling amount applies to the HI portion. Note that the SE tax rates are exactly twice the rates for employees under FICA (e.g., 6.2% for OASDI up to a ceiling amount of $80,400 in 2001, and 1.45% for HI). For employee wages, the 6.2% and 1.45% (total of 7.65%) must be matched by the employer. This matching requirement for employers effectively equalizes Social Security taxes for employees and self-employed individuals.

One-half of the self-employment tax imposed is allowed as a *for* AGI deduction and is reported on page 1 of Form 1040.[12] Net earnings from self-employment are determined by multiplying self-employment income by 0.9235 (which is equivalent to 100% of self-employment income minus one-half of self-employment taxes, or 7.65%, resulting in net earnings from self-employment of 92.35%) to compute the amount that is subject to self-employment tax.

---

[11] Sec. 6017. [12] Sec. 164(f).

EXAMPLE I14-8 ▶

ADDITIONAL COMMENT
The Revenue Reconciliation Act of 1993 eliminated the wage cap on the hospital insurance component of wages. Though presented as a tax increase for high-income individuals, it also increases the tax burden for employers of high-income individuals.

Rose has $90,000 of earnings from self-employment in 2001. Her net earnings from self-employment is $83,115 ($90,000 × 0.9235). The OASDI portion of the tax is $9,970 ($80,400 × 0.124). The amount of self-employment income that is subject to the hospital insurance portion of the tax is $83,115 and the HI tax is $2,410 ($83,115 × 0.029). Thus, the total self-employment tax reported on Schedule SE is $12,380. Rose also receives a *for* AGI tax deduction of $6,190 ($12,380 × 0.50), which is reported on page 1 of Form 1040. ◀

If an individual is an employee and also has income from self-employment, the tax base for computing the self-employment tax is reduced by the wages that are subject to the FICA tax. The self-employment tax base for the OASDI component is equal to the lesser of the primary ceiling ($80,400 in 2001) reduced by the FICA wages or the self-employment income multiplied by 0.9235.

EXAMPLE I14-9 ▶

Sandy receives wages as an employee of $35,000 in 2001 that are subject to FICA tax. In addition, Sandy has a small consulting practice that generates $10,000 of income from self-employment. The tentative tax base for computing the self-employment tax is $9,235 ($10,000 × 0.9235) net earnings from self-employment. Thus, the tax base for computing the OASDI portion of the tax is the lesser of $9,235 net earnings from self-employment or $45,400 ($80,400 ceiling − $35,000 FICA wages). Sandy's self-employment tax for the OASDI portion is $1,145 ($9,235 × 0.124) and the HI component is $268 ($9,235 × 0.029). The total amount of self-employment tax is therefore $1,413 ($1,145 + $268) and Sandy also receives a *for* AGI deduction of $707 ($1,413 × 0.50), which is reported on page 1 of Form 1040. ◀

EXAMPLE I14-10 ▶

Assume the same facts as in Example I14-9 except that Sandy's wages are $100,000. Sandy's taxable self-employment income for the OASDI portion of the tax is zero because her FICA wages exceed the $80,400 primary ceiling amount. However, she is subject to self-employment tax with respect to the HI portion. The tax base for the HI portion is the $9,235 net earnings from self-employment because no ceiling amount is applicable. The HI portion of the self-employment tax is $268 ($9,235 × 0.029) and Sandy also receives a *for* AGI deduction for $134 ($268 × 0.50). ◀

KEY POINT
In the case of married taxpayers filing joint returns, it is important on Schedule SE of Form 1040 to fill in the name and Social Security number of the spouse with the self-employment income. This information is used to establish benefit eligibility.

WHAT CONSTITUTES SELF-EMPLOYMENT INCOME

Individuals who carry on a trade or business as a proprietor or partnership are considered to render services as independent contractors and are, therefore, subject to the self-employment tax. If an individual has two separate self-employment activities, the *net* earnings from each activity are aggregated. However, where a husband and wife file a joint return and both have self-employment income, the self-employment tax must be computed separately.

EXAMPLE I14-11 ▶

Russ and Ruth are married and file a joint return. Russ has $13,000 net earnings from a consulting business and a $4,000 net loss from a retail store that is operated as a sole proprietorship. Ruth has wages of $50,000 from her employer that are subject to FICA taxes. Russ's net earnings from self-employment are $8,312 ($9,000 × 0.9235). No reduction in the self-employment tax base is allowed for Ruth's wages as an employee because Ruth is not self-employed and the tax is computed separately for Russ and Ruth. ◀

ADDITIONAL COMMENT
For some self-employed taxpayers, the amount of self-employment tax exceeds the amount of income tax for the year. For example, a married couple with two children and $17,000 of self-employment income would not owe any income tax, but would have a $2,402 (17,000 × .9235 × 15.3%) self-employment tax liability.

Among the items that constitute earnings that are subject to the self-employment tax are:

▶ Net earnings from a sole proprietorship
▶ Director's fees[13]
▶ Taxable research grants
▶ Distributive share of partnership income plus guaranteed payments from the partnership

The self-employment tax is computed on Schedule SE of Form 1040 (see Appendix B). The rules for computing the self-employment tax are summarized in Topic Review I14-1.

---

[13] Rev. Rul. 57-246, 1957-1 C.B. 338. It is a factual question whether an officer who also serves as a director is performing services as an employee or as an independent contractor. The courts have recognized that an individual can perform services as a director and also perform employment-related services but the director fees may be recharacterized by the courts if the fees are in reality compensation for services rendered as an employee. See *Peter H. Jacobs* 1993 RIA T.C. Memo ¶ 93, 570, 66 TCM 1470.

Topic Review I14-1
Self-Employment Tax Summary

- The self-employment tax is imposed on net earnings from self-employment over $400.
- The tax base for computing the self-employment tax is generally the amount of self-employment income multiplied by 0.9235.
- A $80,400 (2001) ceiling applies to the old age survivors and disability (OASDI) portion. However, no ceiling applies to the hospital insurance (HI) portion of the tax.
- Self-employment tax is computed separately for married individuals filing joint returns.
- One-half of the self-employment tax that is imposed is allowed as a business deduction *for* AGI.
- The self-employment tax rate is 15.3% which includes 12.4% for the OASDI portion and 2.9% for the hospital insurance (HI) portion.

OVERVIEW OF TAX CREDITS

OBJECTIVE 3
Describe the various business and personal tax credits

USE AND IMPORTANCE OF TAX CREDITS

Tax credits are often used to implement tax policy objectives. For example, tax credits are provided to increase employment, encourage energy conservation and research and experimental activities, encourage certain socially desired activities, and provide tax relief for low-income taxpayers and working couples with dependent children. Tax credits are also used to mitigate the effects of double taxation on income from foreign countries. Credits may be classified into two broad categories, **nonrefundable** and **refundable.** Nonrefundable credits may only be used to offset a taxpayer's tax liability. Refundable credits, on the other hand, not only offset a taxpayer's tax liability but if the credits exceed the tax liability, the excess will be paid (refunded) directly to the taxpayer. Topic Review I14-2, located at the end of this section, provides a summary of selected tax credits and the rationale for their inclusion in the tax law. Note that most tax credits are nonrefundable. The principal refundable credits include taxes withheld on wages and the earned income credit.

VALUE OF A CREDIT VERSUS A DEDUCTION

Tax credits are extremely valuable for taxpayers as they reduce the tax liability on a dollar-for-dollar basis. This is in contrast to a tax deduction which reduces taxable income and the value of a tax deduction is limited to the taxpayer's marginal tax rate. Thus, tax deductions are more valuable to high-income taxpayers than lower-income taxpayers because their marginal tax rate is higher. Tax credits, however, benefit all taxpayers in the same amount regardless of their marginal tax rate.

EXAMPLE I14-12 ▶ If Tasha's marginal tax rate is 15%, a $100 deduction produces a tax benefit of $15 ($100 × 0.15). If Sean's marginal tax rate is 36%, a $100 deduction produces a tax benefit of $36 ($100 × 0.36). However, a tax credit provides the same benefit to both Tasha and Sean. ◀

CLASSIFICATION OF CREDITS

ADDITIONAL COMMENT
The total amount of tax credits claimed by individual taxpayers increased by 14.9% in 1996.

As mentioned earlier, credits may be classified into two general categories, refundable and nonrefundable credits. Table I14-1 lists and further classifies the various types of major credits available under the tax law. The reason why it is important to properly classify the credits is that limitations are imposed on credits depending on the classification.

PERSONAL TAX CREDITS

As a result of tax legislation in the last few years, the number of personal tax credits has increased significantly. These credits are allowed as an offset against an individual's tax liability before all other nonrefundable credits (i.e., the miscellaneous credits and the gen-

TABLE I14-1
CLASSIFICATION OF MAJOR TAX CREDITS

NONREFUNDABLE CREDITS

Personal Credits
- Child and dependent care credit – Sec. 21
- Credit for the elderly and disabled – Sec. 22
- Adoption credit – Sec. 23
- Child tax credit – Sec. 24
- Residential mortgage credit – Sec. 25
- HOPE scholarship credit – Sec. 25A
- Lifetime learning credit – Sec. 25A

Miscellaneous Credits
- Foreign tax credit – Sec. 27
- Nonconventional source fuel credit – Sec. 29
- Credit for qualified electric vehicles – Sec. 30

General Business Credits
- Research credit – Sec. 41
- Low income housing credit – Sec. 42
- Disabled access credit – Sec. 44
- Rehabilitation credit – Sec. 47
- Business energy credit – Sec. 48
- Work opportunity credit – Sec. 51
- Welfare-to-work credit – Sec. 51A
- Empowerment zone employment credit – Sec. 1396

REFUNDABLE CREDITS

- Tax withheld on wages – Sec. 31
- Earned income credit – Sec. 32

---

eral business credits).[14] Most of the personal tax credits have been enacted for social welfare rather than economic reasons. The more important personal tax credits are discussed below.

CHILD TAX CREDIT

Taxpayers are allowed a nonrefundable credit of $500 for each qualifying child under the age of 17.[15] This credit was first allowed in 1998 in the amount of $400, but was increased to $500 for 1999 and thereafter. The credit is phased out when the taxpayer's modified AGI reaches $110,000 ($75,000 for single taxpayers and $55,000 for married taxpayers filing separately) at a rate of $50 for each $1,000, or fraction thereof, that modified AGI exceeds the above thresholds.

A qualifying child must be a dependent of the taxpayer and must be the taxpayer's son or daughter (or a descendent of either), a stepchild, or an eligible foster child. Further, the child must also be a U.S. citizen, a U.S. national, or a resident of the U.S.[16]

---

[14] Sec. 26. See detailed discussion below on limitation on personal credits.
[15] Sec. 24.
[16] Sec. 24(c).

In general, the child tax credit is limited to the taxpayer's income tax liability. More specifically, the sum of the child tax credit and all other nonrefundable personal credits is limited to the excess of the taxpayer's regular tax liability over the taxpayer's tentative minimum tax liability. However, there are situations in which the child tax credit may be treated as a refundable credit. While not discussed in detail in this textbook, the child tax credit (or portion thereof) may be a refundable credit under certain circumstances for families with three or more children and is computed in connection with the earned income credit.

CHILD AND DEPENDENT CARE CREDIT

The child and dependent care credit provides relief for taxpayers who incur child and dependent care expenses because of employment activities.[17] To qualify for the credit, an individual must meet two requirements: qualifying child or dependent care expenses must be incurred to enable the taxpayer to be gainfully employed, and the taxpayer must maintain a household for a dependent under age 13 or an incapacitated dependent or spouse.[18]

ADDITIONAL COMMENT
The dollar amount of the child and dependent care credit amounted to $2.5 billion in 1996.

EXAMPLE I14-13 ▶ Tim and Tina are married and have two children under age 13. They incur child care expenses (e.g., a housekeeper and nurse) to enable both Tim and Tina to work on a full-time basis. The child care expenditures are eligible for the child and dependent care credit because Tim and Tina incurred the child care expenses to enable the taxpayers to be gainfully employed. Alternatively, if Tina was not employed but incurred the child care expenses to play tennis and other social activities, the expenditures would not be eligible for the child and dependent care credit. ◀

ADDITIONAL COMMENT
Qualifying child care expenses include amounts spent to send a child to nursery school or kindergarten, but not first grade.

QUALIFYING EMPLOYMENT-RELATED EXPENSES. Eligible expenses include amounts spent for housekeeping, nursing, cooking, baby-sitting, etc. in the taxpayer's home but do not include expenses for a chauffeur or gardener. If the child or dependent care is provided outside the home by a dependent care facility (e.g., a day care facility), the amounts will generally qualify only if the dependent care facility provides care for more than six individuals. Employment-related expenses do not include amounts paid for services outside of the taxpayer's household at a camp where the qualifying individual stays overnight. In addition, amounts paid for services outside of the taxpayer's household (e.g., adult day care) that are spent for the care of an incapacitated dependent or spouse qualify only if the individual lives in the taxpayer's home for at least eight hours a day.

EXAMPLE I14-14 ▶ Tony is divorced and has two children under age 13. He is employed and incurs child care expenses at a preschool nursery for one of the children. He also has a live-in nanny who provides housekeeping services and a gardener to care for his yard. The expenditures for the preschool nursery and the live-in nanny qualify because these services constitute eligible household services and care of a qualifying individual. However, the payments to the gardener do not constitute qualifying household services. ◀

The following special rules also apply:

▶ The maximum amount of child and dependent care expenses that qualify for the credit is $2,400 for one qualifying individual and $4,800 for two or more individuals. These ceilings are reduced by the aggregate amount excludable from gross income due to the exclusion under Sec. 129 relating to dependent care assistance programs. No carryover is permitted for expenses that exceed these maximum amounts.

▶ Payments to a relative qualify unless the relative is a dependent or a child (under age 19) of the taxpayer.[19]

▶ The maximum child and dependent care expenses cannot exceed the individual's earned income. For married individuals, the limitation is applied to the earned income of the spouse with the smaller amount of earned income.

---

[17] Sec. 21. The complete title of this credit is *Expenses for Household and Dependent Care Services Necessary for Gainful Employment*.
[18] Secs. 21(b)(1) and (e)(1). Maintaining a household means that the individual (or the individual and spouse if married) must provide over one-half of the cost of maintaining the home. Married individuals must generally file a joint return to obtain the credit.
[19] Sec. 21(e)(6).

▶ A spouse who either is a full-time student or is incapacitated is deemed to have earned income of $200 per month.[20] The amount is increased to $400 per month if there are two or more qualifying individuals (e.g., children under age 13) in the household.

EXAMPLE I14-15 ▶

KEY POINT

The percentage used to calculate the credit varies from 20% to 30% depending on the taxpayer's AGI.

Troy and Tracy are married and incur qualifying child care expenses of $4,000 to take care of their two children, ages 1 and 3. Tracy's earned income is $20,000, and Troy's earned income from a part-time job is $3,000. The limitation on qualifying child care expenses is $3,000. Although the overall limitation of $4,800 is not exceeded, the earned income limitation applies because Troy's earned income ($3,000) is less than the child care expenses ($4,000). Therefore, the amount of eligible child-care expenses is limited to $3,000. ◀

COMPUTATION OF THE CREDIT RATE AND AMOUNT. The credit is 30% of the qualifying expenses (after the ceiling limitations of $2,400 or $4,800 have been applied). However, the credit rate is reduced by one percentage point for each $2,000 (or fraction thereof) of adjusted gross income (AGI) in excess of $10,000 but goes no lower than 20%. The minimum credit (20%) is applied once a taxpayer's AGI exceeds $28,000.

EXAMPLE I14-16 ▶

Vincent and Vicki are married, file a joint return, and have three children under age 13. Vincent and Vicki's employment-related earnings are $25,000 and $10,000, respectively. Their AGI is $35,000. They incur $8,000 of child care expenses during the current year. The eligible child care expenses are limited to $4,800, because Vincent and Vicki have more than one child who is qualified and this limitation is less than Vicki's earned income or the actual expenses incurred. Because their AGI is greater than $28,000, the minimum 20% credit rate is applicable. The child and dependent care credit is $960 (0.20 × $4,800). ◀

DEPENDENT CARE ASSISTANCE. An employee may exclude amounts up to $5,000 from gross income for dependent care assistance payments made by the individual's employer and provided to the employee.[21] The exclusion amount is limited to the earned income of the employee (or in the case of a married taxpayer, the lesser of the employee's earned income or the earned income of the spouse). To avoid a double benefit, the otherwise eligible expenses for purposes of computing the child and dependent care credit are reduced by the amount of assistance that is excluded from gross income.[22]

EXAMPLE I14-17 ▶

Assume the same facts as in Example I14-16 except that Vincent was reimbursed $4,000 by his employer under a qualified dependent care assistance program and this amount was excluded from his gross income. Since $4,000 was excluded under a Sec. 129 qualified dependent care assistance program, expenses eligible for the child and dependent care credit must be reduced. Thus, the eligible child care expenses are reduced to $800 ($4,800 − $4,000) and the child care credit is $160 (0.20 × $800). ◀

ADDITIONAL COMMENT

The tax credit for the credit for the elderly or disabled has been declining in recent years and amounted to only $32 million in 1996, down 32% from 1995.

TAX CREDIT FOR THE ELDERLY AND DISABLED

A limited, personal, nonrefundable credit is provided for certain low-income elderly individuals who have attained age 65 before the end of the tax year and individuals who retired because of a permanent and total disability and who receive insubstantial Social Security benefits. Most elderly taxpayers are ineligible for the credit because they receive Social Security benefits in excess of the ceiling limitations that apply to the credit (e.g., an initial amount of $5,000 per year for a single taxpayer) or they have AGI amounts in excess of the limitations, which effectively reduces or eliminates the allowable credit.

The maximum credit is 15% times an initial amount of $5,000 ($7,500 for married individuals filing jointly if both spouses are 65 or older).[23] This initial amount is reduced by:

▶ Social Security, railroad retirement, or Veterans Administration pension or annuity benefits that are excluded from gross income

---

[20] Sec. 21(d)(2). To qualify as a full-time student, the individual must enroll in an educational institution on a full-time basis for at least five calendar months of the year (Reg. Sec. 1.44A-2(b)(3)(B)(ii)).

[21] Sec. 129. (See Chapter I4 for a discussion of the requirements for exclusion.)

[22] Sec. 21(c).

[23] Sec. 22(c)(2). The initial ceiling amount is $5,000 if one spouse filing a joint return is less than age 65 and the limitation is $3,750 for a married individual filing a separate return. Unless married individuals are living apart for the entire year, they must file a joint return in order to obtain the credit.

- One-half of AGI in excess of $7,500 for a single individual ($10,000 for married taxpayers filing a joint return).[24] All types of taxable income items are included in AGI (e.g., salaries, taxable pension and taxable Social Security benefits, and investment income).

EXAMPLE I14-18 ▶ Wayne and Tammy are both 67 years old and file a joint return. They have AGI of $11,000 and receive nontaxable Social Security payments of $3,000 during the current year. Their tax credit for the elderly is computed as follows:

Initial ceiling amount		$7,500
Minus: Nontaxable social security	$3,000	
One-half of AGI in excess of $10,000 (0.50 × [$11,000 − $10,000])	500	(3,500)
Total credit base		$4,000
Times: Credit percentage		
Tax credit		$ 600

The $600 credit is allowed only to the extent that Wayne and Tammy's total personal tax credits do not exceed the actual tax due before credits. ◀

ADOPTION CREDIT

A nonrefundable credit has been enacted for qualified adoption expenses for tax years beginning after 1996. The amount of the credit is limited to a maximum of $5,000 ($6,000 for a child with special needs) and generally is allowable in the year the adoption is finalized. However, if the adoption expenses are paid or incurred in a year subsequent to the year the adoption is finalized, the credit is allowable in such later year. If adoption expenses are paid *prior* to the year the adoption is finalized, such expenses are deductible in the year the adoption is finalized. Further, there is a phase-out of the credit based on AGI. For taxpayers with AGI between $75,000 and $115,000, the credit is ratably phased out and is fully phased out when a taxpayer's AGI reaches $115,000.[25] The credit, except in the case of special needs adoptions, expires with respect to expenses paid or incurred after December 31, 2001.[26]

Qualified adoption expenses include reasonable and necessary adoption fees, court costs, attorney fees, and other expenses that are directly related to the legal adoption by the taxpayer of an eligible child. An eligible child is defined as a child who has not reached 18 years old when the adoption takes place or is physically or mentally incapable of self-care.

EXAMPLE I14-19 ▶ Oscar and Betty began adoption proceedings in June, 2000 to adopt an infant child. They incurred attorney fees and adoption agency fees in 2000 of $3,000. In 2001, they incurred an additional $4,000 of qualified adoption expenses when the adoption became final. Oscar and Betty's AGI in 2001 is $100,000. The adoption credit is allowable in 2001 in the amount of $1,875, computed as follows:

Total qualified adoption expenses in 2000 and 2001	$7,000
Maximum credit	5,000
Phase-out percentage ($25,000/$40,000)	62.5%
Amount of credit disallowed	3,125
Amount of credit allowed	1,875

Oscar and Betty only can use $5,000 of expenses (maximum) and must claim the expenses in 2001, the year the adoption becomes final. Finally, the adoption is limited based upon the level of their AGI. ◀

---

[24] The AGI ceiling is $5,000 for married individuals filing a separate return. To obtain the credit, however, a separate return can be filed only if both spouses live apart for the entire tax year.

[25] For purposes of the phase-out of the credit, AGI must be modified. AGI for this purpose is determined without regard to the exclusions from gross income for foreign earned income under Sec. 911 and after the application of the rules relating to the taxation of Social Security, as well as selected other items. See Sec. 23.

[26] The Tax Relief Act of 2000 which, at the date of this writing has not been passed by Congress, would extend the credit through December 31, 2005 *and* would increase the amount of the credit to $10,000 ($12,000 for special needs adoptions).

The adoption credit, when combined with other personal credits, is limited to the taxpayer's regular tax liability. The portion of the credit which is limited may be carried forward for up to five years.

HOPE SCHOLARSHIP CREDIT

Two credits are available to assist taxpayers who incur higher education expenses for themselves, their spouses, and dependents. The two credits are the "HOPE scholarship credit" and the "lifetime learning credit".[27] The Hope scholarship credit (HOPE credit) is discussed first, then the lifetime learning credit is discussed.

Taxpayers are allowed up to a $1,500 credit for tuition and related expenses paid during the taxable year for each qualified student. Qualified tuition and related expenses include only tuition and fees required for enrollment and do not include books, room and board, student activity fees, and other expenses unrelated to an individual's academic course of instruction. The HOPE credit applies to expenses paid after December 31, 1997 for education furnished in academic periods beginning after such date. Below are a number of requirements and limitations that exist for the HOPE credit:

▶ The $1,500 credit is allowed only for a maximum of two years per student and is computed by taking 100% of the first $1,000 of tuition and fees *plus* 50% of the second $1,000 of tuition and fees.

▶ Qualified tuition and related expenses eligible for the HOPE credit are limited to the first two years of postsecondary education. The first two years of postsecondary education is measured at the *beginning* of the taxable year. If a student has not completed the first two years of postsecondary education by the beginning of the taxable year, qualified tuition and related fees are eligible for the HOPE credit. The first two years is determined based on whether the educational institution awards the student two years of academic credit at that institution.

▶ If a taxpayer pays qualified education expenses in one year but the expenses relate to an academic period that begins during January, February, or March of the next taxable year, the academic period is treated as beginning during the taxable year in which the payment is made. Thus, a payment of tuition in December, 2001 for the Spring Semester, 2002 (which begins in January, 2002) would be eligible for the HOPE credit in 2001.

▶ An eligible student must carry at least ½ of the normal full-time load for the course of study the student is pursuing.

▶ The HOPE credit is not available to any student who has been convicted of a federal or state felony offense for possession or distribution of a controlled substance as of the end of the taxable year for which the credit is claimed.

▶ Qualified tuition and related expenses eligible for the credit must be reduced by amounts received under other sections of the tax law, such as scholarships (Sec. 117), employer-sponsored educational reimbursement plans (Sec. 127), Education IRAs (Sec. 530), or other provisions of the tax law.

▶ The allowable credit (including both the HOPE credit and the lifetime learning credit) is reduced for taxpayers who have modified AGI above certain amounts. The phaseout for taxpayers filing joint returns is $80,000 to $100,000 ($40,000 to $50,000 for other taxpayers). The HOPE credit and lifetime learning credit are ratably phased-out for joint filers using the formula below:

$$\text{Sum of HOPE credit and lifetime learning credit} \times \frac{\text{Modified AGI} - \$80,000}{\$20,000}$$

---

[27] Sec. 25A. Both credits are contained in Sec. 25A, the HOPE credit is specifically described in Sec. 25A(b) while the lifetime learning credit is described in Sec. 25A(c). The various definitions contained in Sec. 25A apply to both credits.

For taxpayers other than joint filers, the $80,000 is replaced with $40,000 and the $20,000 is replaced with $10,000.

It is important to understand that the HOPE credit applies to each student. Thus, parents who have two children in their first two years of college may claim up to a $1,500 credit for each child.

ADDITIONAL COMMENT

The education expenses for the HOPE and lifetime learning credits must be incurred at an educational institution that is eligible to participate in Department of Education student aid programs.

LIFETIME LEARNING CREDIT

The lifetime learning credit is computed differently than the HOPE credit and is less restrictive, however, most of the definitions regarding eligible students and qualified expenses are identical with the HOPE credit. The credit is 20% of a maximum of $5,000 per year of qualified tuition and fees paid by the taxpayer for one or more eligible students. However, unlike the HOPE credit, the $5,000 limitation is imposed at the taxpayer level, not on a per student basis. Below are some important requirements for the lifetime learning credit.

▶ The definition of qualified tuition and related expenses are the same as for the HOPE credit above.

▶ The lifetime learning credit is available for an unlimited number of years and may be used for undergraduate, graduate, and professional degree expenses.

▶ The maximum amount of expenses eligible for the credit is $5,000, however, this amount increases to $10,000 in 2003 and later years.

▶ The lifetime learning credit applies only to expenses paid after June 30, 1998 for education furnished in academic periods beginning after such date.

▶ The lifetime learning credit and HOPE credit may not be taken in the same tax year with respect to the same student's tuition and related expenses, i.e., no doubling-up is permitted. For example, if Son A's tuition for the academic year is $10,000 and is used to claim $1,500 HOPE credit, none of the $10,000 may be used for the lifetime learning credit with respect to Son A. However, if Son B also has tuition expenses in the same tax year, either the lifetime learning credit or the HOPE credit is allowed for Son B.

▶ The lifetime learning credit may be claimed for any course (degree or nondegree) at a college or university that helps an individual acquire or improve their job skills, such as credit or noncredit courses that qualify as continuing professional education (CPE). Also, the requirement that a student take at least ½ of a full load does not apply to the lifetime learning credit.

EXAMPLE I14-20 ▶ Mark and Jane are married, file a joint return, and have three dependent children in college, Ron, Rhonda, and Ray. All three children attend State U. Mark and Jane's modified AGI is $85,000 in 2001 and the classification of each of the three children for each semester is as follows: Ron was a junior during the Spring Semester, 2001 and a senior in Fall Semester, 2001; Rhonda was a sophomore during the Spring Semester, 2001 and a junior in Fall Semester, 2001; Ray was in high school until the Fall Semester, 2001. Below are the expenses incurred in calendar year 2001 for the three children's college expenses:

		Spring Semester, 2001 (Paid in January, 2001)	Fall Semester, 2001 (Paid in August, 2001)
Ron:	Tuition and fees	$1,500	$1,550
	Books	300	300
	Room and board	3,500	3,700
Rhonda:	Tuition and fees	1,500	1,550
	Books	275	325
	Room and board	4,000	4,200
Ray:	Tuition and fees		1,550
	Books		325
	Room and board		3,700

Mark and Jane are allowed to claim the HOPE credit and the lifetime learning credit for 2001 as follows:

HOPE credit: Only Rhonda and Ray qualify for the credit because the HOPE credit is limited to the first two years of postsecondary education. Rhonda qualifies because she has not completed two years of postsecondary education as of the beginning of the taxable year. Thus, the tentative HOPE credit is $2,775, $1,500 for Rhonda and $1,275 for Ray [100%($1,000) + 50%($1,550 − $1,000)]. Only tuition and fees qualify for the HOPE credit, the books and room and board are not qualified education expenses.

Lifetime learning credit: Ron qualifies for the credit. His tuition and fees for the year total $3,050 and the tentative lifetime learning credit is $610 [20% × ($3,050)]. Only tuition and fees qualify for the credit, the books and room and board are not qualified education expenses.

Since Mark and Jane have modified AGI above $80,000, the above credits of $3,385 ($2,775 + $610) are partially phased-out as follows:

$$\$3,385 \times \frac{\$85,000 - \$80,000}{\$20,000} = \$846$$

Thus, the total HOPE and lifetime learning credits for 2001 are $2,539 ($3,385 − $846). ◀

LIMITATION ON PERSONAL CREDITS

Sec. 26 imposes limitations of the amount of nonrefundable personal credits for individual taxpayers (see Table I14-1 for a listing of such credits). For tax years beginning in 2000 and 2001, the nonrefundable personal credits may not exceed the *sum* of the taxpayer's regular tax liability plus the AMT imposed by Sec. 55(a). Thus, for these two years only, the nonrefundable personal credits may offset both the regular tax and the alternative minimum tax. For other years, under the general rules of Sec. 26, nonrefundable personal credits may not exceed the excess of (1) the taxpayer's regular tax liability for the taxable year, over (2) the tentative minimum tax for the taxable year (without regard to the alternative minimum tax foreign tax credit). These general rules will presumably go back into effect in 2002 unless Congress passes new law or extends the law in effect for 2000 and 2001.

MISCELLANEOUS CREDITS

The miscellaneous credits, with the exception of the foreign tax credit, are specialized types of tax credits. For this reason, only the foreign tax credit is discussed in this textbook.

FOREIGN TAX CREDIT

KEY POINT
The foreign tax credit is available only on income, war profits, and excess profits taxes or taxes paid in lieu of such taxes. It is sometimes difficult to determine whether a particular foreign tax falls into the qualifying category.

U.S. citizens, resident aliens, and U.S. corporations are subject to U.S. taxation on their worldwide income.[28] To reduce double taxation, the tax law provides a foreign tax credit for income taxes paid or accrued to a foreign country or a U.S. possession.[29]

Taxpayers may elect to take a deduction for the taxes paid or accrued in lieu of a foreign tax credit.[30] In general, the foreign tax credit results in a greater tax benefit because (as previously discussed) a credit is fully offset against the tax liability, while a deduction merely reduces taxable income.

---

[28] Certain exceptions are provided by treaty agreements between the United States and foreign countries whereby certain types of foreign-source income may be exempt from taxation in the foreign country.

[29] Under Sec. 911, U.S. citizens and resident aliens may elect to exclude from gross income up to $78,000 (2001) of foreign-earned income and certain housing cost amounts. This amount increases to $80,000 for 2002 and thereafter. The foreign taxes that are attributable to the excluded income cannot be taken as a credit. (See Chapter I4 for a discussion of these exclusions.)

[30] Sec. 164(a)(3).

Special Tax Computation Methods, Tax Credits, and Payment of Tax ▼ **Individuals 14-17**

ADDITIONAL COMMENT
In 1996, 2.1 million tax returns claimed $3.1 billion in foreign tax credits.

Computation of Allowable Credit. The **foreign tax credit** amount equals the lesser of the foreign taxes paid or accrued in the tax year or the portion of the U.S. income tax liability attributable to the income earned in all foreign countries.[31] This limitation, which restricts the claiming of foreign tax credit if the effective foreign tax rate on the foreign earnings exceeds the effective U.S. tax rate on these earnings, may result in double taxation if the unused credit cannot be used as a carryback or carryover (see discussion under the next heading). The foreign tax credit limitation is based on the following formula:

$$\frac{\text{Foreign source taxable income}}{\text{Worldwide taxable income}} \times \frac{\text{U.S. income tax}}{\text{before credits}} = \frac{\text{Foreign tax credit}}{\text{limitation}}$$

EXAMPLE I14-21 ▶ Edison Corporation has $200,000 U.S. source taxable income and $100,000 of foreign source taxable income from country A. Total worldwide taxable income is $300,000 ($200,000 + $100,000). Country A levies a total of $40,000 in foreign income taxes upon the foreign source taxable income (i.e., a 40% effective tax rate). The U.S. tax before credits is $100,250 on the $300,000 of taxable income. Using the formula given above, the overall foreign tax credit limitation is computed as follows:[32]

$$\frac{\$100,000}{\$300,000} \times \$100,250 = \$33,417$$

Because the foreign tax payments ($40,000) exceed the U.S. tax attributable to the foreign source income ($33,417), the limitation applies. Thus, $6,583 ($40,000 − $33,417) of foreign tax credit cannot be used in the current year. ◀

STOP & THINK

Question: Since a credit is generally much more valuable than a deduction, under what circumstances would it be more beneficial for a taxpayer to take a deduction for foreign taxes in lieu of the foreign tax credit?

Solution: If a taxpayer has foreign source taxable income from one country and an equal loss from another foreign country, the foreign tax credit limitation is zero because the net foreign source taxable income is zero. Because none of the taxes paid in the foreign country in which taxable income was produced can be claimed as a credit, the taxpayer may choose to deduct them unless the credits are carried back or forward.

Treatment of Unused Credits. Unused foreign tax credits are carried back two years and then forward for five years to years where the limitation is not exceeded (i.e., the foreign tax payment is lower than the U.S. taxes attributable to the foreign source income in the carryback or carryover years). The unused credits are lost if they are not used by the end of the five-year carryover period.

GENERAL BUSINESS CREDITS

The tax credits commonly available to businesses are grouped into a special credit category called the **general business credit** and are summarized in Table I14-1 on page 14-10. The general business credits are combined for the purpose of computing an overall dollar limitation on their use because these credits are nonrefundable. The general business credit may not exceed the *net income tax* minus the greater of the tentative minimum tax

---

[31] Sec. 904.
[32] Certain types of income may have a separate foreign tax credit limitation. These types of income include passive income, high withholding tax interest, financial services income, shipping income, dividends from noncontrolled foreign (Sec. 902) corporations, dividends from domestic international sales corporations (DISCs), and foreign trade income from a foreign sales corporation. See Chapter C16 of *Prentice Hall's Federal Taxation: Corporations, Partnerships, Estates, and Trusts* for a more detailed discussion of these separate limitations.

or 25% of the *net regular tax liability* above $25,000.[33] If the general business credits exceed the tax limits, effective for tax years beginning after December 31, 1997, they may be carried back one year and carried forward 20 years.[34]

During the carryover years, the unused credits from prior years are first applied (commencing with the earliest carryover year) before the current year credits that are earned are used (i.e., a first-in, first-out [FIFO] method is applied). This method permits the use of credits from the earliest of the carryover years and may prevent such carryovers from expiring.

EXAMPLE I14-22 ▶ Eastern Corporation has unused general business tax credits of $10,000 in 2000 that are carried forward to 2001. Eastern earns $5,000 of additional credits in 2001 and has a $12,000 limitation. The $12,000 of credits that are used consist of the $10,000 carryover from 2000 and $2,000 from 2001. The remaining $3,000 ($5,000 − $2,000) of 2001 credits are carried forward to 2002. ◀

The more important general business credits are discussed below.

CREDIT FOR INCREASING RESEARCH ACTIVITIES

HISTORICAL NOTE
The research credit was enacted in 1981 because Congress was concerned about the substantial relative decline in total U.S. expenditures for research and development.

The tax law provides two means of encouraging research and experimental activities: (1) research and experimental expenditures may be either deducted immediately or capitalized and amortized over a period of 60 months or more under Sec. 174 (see Chapter I10 for a discussion of these rules) or (2) a tax credit for qualified research expenses is available under Sec. 41. Before July 1, 1995, the research credit was allowed in an amount equal to the sum of:

▶ 20% of qualified research expenses incurred in a tax year in excess of a base amount[35] for that tax year, plus

▶ 20% of basic research payments in excess of a base amount for that year.

The tax law allows taxpayers to elect to compute the credit in two alternative ways: (1) in a manner substantially similar to the law that existed prior to July 1, 1995, or (2) to elect to compute the credit under an alternative method that employs a three-tiered credit regime with reduced credit rates and fixed-based percentages. The second alternative is intended to benefit taxpayers whose base amount has gotten very high because of dramatically higher sales. Because the computation of the research credit is very complex, the details are not presented in this textbook. Readers are directed to Sec. 41 for additional details. The research credit is scheduled to expire on June 30, 2004.[36]

DISABLED ACCESS CREDIT

A nonrefundable tax credit is available to eligible small businesses for expenditures incurred to make existing business facilities accessible to disabled individuals. Eligible access expenditures include payments for the purpose of removing architectural, communication, physical or transportation barriers that prevent a business from being accessible or usable by disabled individuals. Expenditures made in connection with new construction are not eligible for the credit. The disabled access credit is equal to 50% of eligible expenditures that exceed $250 but do not exceed $10,250.[37] Thus, the annual credit limitation is $5,000. The basis of the property is reduced by the allowable credit. An eligible small business is any business that either (1) had gross receipts of $1 million or less in the preceding year or, (2) in the case of a business failing the first test, had no more than 30 full-time employees in the preceding year and makes a timely election to claim the credit.

---

[33] Sec. 38(c). The term *net income tax* is the sum of the regular tax plus the alternative minimum tax reduced by other nonrefundable credits. The term *net regular tax liability* means the regular tax liability reduced by nonrefundable credits. See Example I14-27 for an example of this calculation.

[34] For tax years prior to 1998, the carryback period was three years and the carryforward period was 15 years.

[35] The base amount is defined in Sec. 41(c)(2) as the product of the fixed-base percentage and the taxpayer's average annual gross receipts for the four tax years before the current (credit) year. All taxpayers are limited to a minimum base amount that may not be less than 50% of the qualified research expenses for the current year. The fixed-based percentage is the ratio of the taxpayer's total qualified research expenses to its total gross receipts for a specified base period (see Sec. 41(c)(3)).

[36] The research credit had expired effective June 30, 1999. However, the credit was retroactively restored and extended through June 30, 2004 by the Tax Relief Extension Act of 1999.

[37] Sec. 44.

EXAMPLE I14-23 ▶ Crane Corporation had 14 employees during the preceding tax year and $2 million of gross receipts. During the current year, Crane installed concrete access ramps at a total cost of $14,000. Crane is an eligible small business because the company had 30 or fewer full-time employees during the preceding year even though its gross receipts exceed the threshold amount (i.e., $1 million). Only $10,000 of eligible expenditures qualify for the credit, thereby limiting it to $5,000 ($10,000 × 0.50). The depreciable basis of the property is reduced by the credit amount to $9,000 ($14,000 − $5,000). ◀

The disabled access credit is also one of the items included in the general business credit. Thus, the limitation is based on the taxpayer's tax liability, and the carryback and carryover of excess credits are governed by the Sec. 38 rules.

TAX CREDIT FOR REHABILITATION EXPENDITURES

Congress has provided incentives for the rehabilitation of older industrial and commercial buildings and certified historic structures. A credit for rehabilitation expenditures is available subject to the following special rules and qualification requirements:[38]

REAL-WORLD EXAMPLE

Taxpayers incurred substantial rehabilitation expenditures on an old factory building, but the tax credit was not allowed because the taxpayers did not use the straight-line depreciation method. *Frank DeMarco,* 87 T.C. 518 (1986).

▶ The credit is 10% for structures that were originally placed in service before 1936 and 20% for certified historic structures.[39]

▶ The credit applies only to trade or business property and property held for investment that is depreciable. Residential rental property does not qualify unless the building is a certified historic structure.

▶ At least 75% of the external walls, including at least 50% utilization of external walls, and at least 75% of the building's internal structural framework must remain in place.[40]

▶ Straight-line depreciation generally must be used with the applicable Sec. 168 recovery periods with respect to rehabilitation expenditures. The regular MACRS depreciation rules apply to the portion of the property's basis that is not eligible for the credit.

▶ The basis of the property for depreciation is reduced by the full amount of the credit taken.[41]

▶ The rehabilitation expenditures must exceed the greater of the property's adjusted basis or $5,000.

▶ The rehabilitation credit is recaptured at a rate of 20% per year if there is an early disposition of the property.

EXAMPLE I14-24 ▶ During the current year, Ted rehabilitates a certified historic structure used in his business at a cost of $40,000. The adjusted basis of the certified historic structure is $38,000 at the time the property is rehabilitated. The property qualifies for the rehabilitation credit because

▶ It is used in Ted's trade or business and is depreciable.

▶ The property is a certified historic structure.

▶ The amount of the expenditure exceeds the greater of the property's $38,000 adjusted basis or the $5,000 statutory minimum.

The credit is $8,000 (0.20 × $40,000). The basis of the rehabilitation expenditures for depreciation purposes is reduced by the full amount of the credit to $32,000 ($40,000 − $8,000). If the property is disposed of after one year, $1,600 of the credit (0.20 × $8,000) is earned and $6,400 ($8,000 − $1,600) is recaptured. ◀

BUSINESS ENERGY CREDITS

To encourage energy conservation measures, additional credits are available to businesses that invest in energy-conserving properties (e.g., solar and geothermal property).[42] The business energy credit is 10%. The construction, reconstruction, or erection of the prop-

---

[38] Sec. 47.
[39] Secs. 47(a)(1) and (2). A certified historic structure must be certified by the Department of Treasury and must be located in a registered historic district or listed in the *National Register.*
[40] Sec. 47(c)(1)(A). The percentage requirements for rehabilitation do not apply to a certified historic structure.
[41] Sec. 50(c)(1).
[42] Sec. 48(a)(2).

erty must be completed by the taxpayer and its original use must commence with the taxpayer. This credit is part of the general business credit and is subject to the same limitations on deductibility and carryback and carryover rules as other general business credits.

WORK OPPORTUNITY CREDIT

A work opportunity tax credit (WOTC) is available on an elective basis and is intended to reduce unemployment for individuals who are considered economically disadvantaged. The WOTC has been allowed to expire several times but has been repeatedly restored by Congress. The current WOTC is scheduled to expire for individuals beginning work after December 31, 2002.[43] This constant reshuffling of effective dates creates considerable uncertainty and complexity for taxpayers. However, Congress presumably wants to allow the credit on a year-by-year basis in order to evaluate its effectiveness in creating employment opportunities for economically disadvantaged individuals.

The WOTC includes the following targeted groups:[44]

(1) Qualified IV-A (Aid to Families with Dependent Children) recipient,
(2) Qualified veteran,
(3) Qualified ex-felon,
(4) High-risk youth,
(5) Vocational rehabilitation referral,
(6) Qualified summer youth employee,
(7) Qualified food stamp recipient, or
(8) Qualified SSI recipient.

ADDITIONAL COMMENT
The employer must receive or request the certification in writing no later than the employee's first day of work.

The credit is 40% of the first $6,000 of qualified wages paid to employees hired from one or more of the eight targeted groups. The new credit imposes a minimum employment period for qualified employees: employment for at least 180 days (20 days for qualified summer youth employee) or completes at least 400 hours of service for the employer (120 hours for a qualified summer youth employee). To qualify for the credit, the employer must obtain a certification from a local jobs service office of a state employment security agency stating that the unemployed individual is a qualified member of a targeted group. Further, an employee is not eligible for the credit if such employee was formerly employed by the employer at any time (i.e., a rehire). A disadvantage associated with the WOTC is that the employer's deduction for wages must be reduced by the amount of the credit.

EXAMPLE I14-25 ▶ Jet Corporation hires two individuals in the current year, one a qualified ex-felon and the other a qualified food stamp recipient. Both individuals are properly certified by the state agency. One of the individuals is paid $8,000 of wages during the year, and the second individual is paid $4,000. The amount of wages eligible for the work opportunity credit is $10,000 ($6,000 ceiling limit for the first employee plus $4,000 actual wages paid to the second employee). The credit is $4,000 (40% × $10,000). Jet must reduce its $12,000 deduction for wages paid to the two individuals by $4,000 in the current year. ◀

The WOTC is one of the items included in the general business credit. Thus, the limitation is based on the taxpayer's tax liability, and the carryback and carryover of excess credits are governed by the Sec. 38 rules.

WELFARE-TO-WORK CREDIT

A new credit was enacted in 1997 to encourage employers to hire individuals who are on welfare.[45] The credit is 35% of the qualified of the qualified first-year wages plus 50% of the qualified second year wages for "long-term family assistance recipients" up to a maximum of $10,000 of wages during the applicable tax years. Thus, the maximum credits

---

[43] The Work Opportunity Credit has been extended several times over the past several years. Tha Tax Relief Act of 2000, which has yet to be passed by Congress, extends the WOTC another 30 months to July 1, 2004.

[44] Sec. 51.
[45] Sec. 51A.

are $3,500 for the first year and $5,000 for the second year. First- and second-year wages refer to the periods beginning with the date employment begins. This credit expires for exployees who begin work for the employer after December 31, 2001.[46]

Long term family assistance recipients generally include members of a family that has been receiving family assistance for at least the 18-month period ending on the hiring date or no more than two years after a family is no longer eligible for assistance because they have reached the maximum duration for such assistance. If an employer takes the welfare-to-work credit for a recipient, the employer is not permitted to claim the work opportunity credit under Sec. 51 for such recipient.

EMPOWERMENT ZONE EMPLOYMENT CREDIT

The empowerment zone employment credit is an attempt to provide economic revitalization of distressed urban and rural areas. Empowerment zones and enterprise zones that have a condition of pervasive poverty, unemployment, and general distress are designated by the Secretary of Housing and Urban Development and the Secretary of Agriculture.

Employers are eligible for a 20% tax credit on the first $15,000 of wages per employee including training and educational costs paid to full- and part-time employees who are residents of an empowerment zone provided that the employer's trade or business and the employee's principal place of abode are within the empowerment zone.[47]

Qualified wages do not include wages taken into account for purposes of the targeted jobs credit (discussed above). The empowerment zone employment credit is one of the items included in the general business credit and the employer's deduction for wages is also reduced by the amount of the credit.

EXAMPLE I14-26 ▶ Ace Corporation is located in a designated empowerment zone and employs two eligible individuals who reside in the empowerment zone. One of the individuals is paid $12,000 in wages (plus $4,000 of training expenses are incurred for the employee) and the second employee is paid $10,000 in wages. $15,000 of wages and training expenses for the first employee and $10,000 of wages for the second employee are qualified wages. The credit is $5,000 ($25,000 × 0.20). Ace Corporation must reduce its $26,000 deduction for wages and training expenses by $5,000 (the credit amount for the year). ◀

LIMITATION BASED UPON TAX LIABILITY

As mentioned previously on page I14-16 and footnote 31, there is an overall dollar limitation of the general business credit based on the tax liability of the taxpayer. The general business credit may not exceed the *net income tax* minus the greater of the tentative minimum tax or 25% of the *net regular tax liability* above $25,000.[48] This complicated limitation is demonstrated in the example below.

EXAMPLE I14-27 ▶ Steve's general business tax credit includes a $40,000 research credit and a $10,000 work opportunity credit. Steve's regular tax liability (before credits) is $45,000, and his tentative minimum tax is $10,000 (thus, Steve is not subject to the AMT). Nonrefundable tax credits also include a $2,000 child and dependent care credit (a nonrefundable personal tax credit) and a $1,000 foreign tax credit. Steve's dollar limitation on the general business tax credit is initially limited by the amount of net income tax of $42,000 ($45,000 regular tax minus $3,000 other nonrefundable credits). This amount is reduced by the $10,000 tentative minimum tax because this amount is greater than the net regular tax ceiling of $4,250 [0.25 × ($45,000 regular tax − $3,000 nonrefundable credits − $25,000)]. Thus, the limitation upon the $50,000 of general business tax credits ($40,000 + $10,000) is $32,000 ($42,000 − $10,000). ◀

ADDITIONAL COMMENT

The general business credit fell from $4.8 billion in 1985 to $0.6 billion in 1996. The decrease is attributable to the phasing out in 1986 of the major component of the general business credit, the investment tax credit.

---

[46] The welfare-to-work credit expired on June 30, 1999 but was restored retroactively to July 1, 1999 and extended through December 31, 2001 by the Tax Relief Extension Act of 1999.

[47] Sec. 1396.

[48] The limitation discussed above actually must be separated into two parts, (1) all general business credits other than the empowerment zone credit, and (2) the empowerment zone credit. See Sec. 38(c) for details.

REFUNDABLE CREDITS

As mentioned earlier, refundable credits not only may offset a taxpayer's income tax liability but, if the refundable credits exceed the taxpayer's tax liability, such excess will be refunded by government to the taxpayer. The principal type of refundable credit is the earned income credit, which is discussed below.

EARNED INCOME CREDIT

The earned income credit is refundable and, as such, the earned income credit is a special type of "negative income tax" or welfare benefit for certain low-income families. The credit is based on earned income that includes wages, salaries, tips, and other employee compensation plus net earnings from self-employment and is designed to encourage low-income individuals to become gainfully employed.[49]

ADDITIONAL COMMENT
The earned income credit was claimed on 19.7 million tax returns in 1996 and amounted to $29.4 billion. This compares with 14.4 million returns and $13.4 billion in 1992.

KEY POINT
The Revenue Reconciliation Act of 1993 dramatically increased the benefits available from the earned income credit, which follows President Clinton's campaign promise to provide tax relief to the working poor.

ELIGIBILITY RULES. The credit is available to individuals with qualifying children and to certain individuals without children if the earned income and AGI thresholds are met.[50] The earned income credit applies to married individuals only if a joint return is filed. Individuals without children are eligible only if the following requirements are met:

▶ The individual's principal place of abode is in the United States for more than one-half of the tax year.

▶ The individual (or spouse if married) is at least age 25 and not more than age 64 at the end of the tax year.

▶ The individual is not a dependent of another taxpayer for the tax year.[51]

A taxpayer will become ineligible for the earned income credit if the taxpayer has excessive investment income. Excessive investment income is defined as disqualified income that exceeds $2,450 for the taxable year 2001 ($2,400 for 2000). Disqualified income includes:

1. Dividends;
2. Interest (both taxable and tax-free); and
3. Net rental income.
4. Capital gain net income.

COMPUTATION OF THE CREDIT AMOUNT. The earned income credit percentages and the maximum amount of earned income used to compute the credit for 2001 are summarized in Table I14-2. The basic percentage rate and the maximum amount of earned income used to compute the credit depend on the number of qualifying children (from none to two or more). The maximum allowable credit is then reduced by a phase-out percentage (see Table I14-3).[52]

EXAMPLE I14-28 ▶ Vivian is eligible for the earned income credit and has one qualifying child. In the current year, she has $15,400 of earned income from wages and $3,600 of alimony. The wages are considered earned income, the alimony is not earned income but is included in modified AGI. Vivian's AGI is $19,000. The tentative credit is $2,424 (0.34 × the first $7,130 of earned income). This amount is reduced by $944 [0.1598 × ($19,000 − $13,090)]. The allowable credit is therefore $1,480 ($2,424 − $944), and this amount is refundable to Vivian.[53] ◀

---

[49] See Chapter I2 for a discussion of the relationship between the child tax credit and the earned income credit.
[50] Sec. 32(c). A qualifying child must be the taxpayer's child, stepchild, foster child, or a descendent of the taxpayer's child. The child must share the same principal place of abode with the taxpayer for more than one-half of the tax year and the child must be less than age 19 or be a full-time student under age 24 or be permanently and totally disabled.
[51] Sec. 32(c)(1)(A).
[52] The percentages are adjusted annually for inflation.
[53] Sec 32(b)(1). $19,000 is used in the formula because modified AGI of $19,000 is greater than $13,090 of earned income. Modified AGI is defined as the individual's AGI decreased by certain items, principally net capital losses (not over $3,000), net losses from nonbusiness rents and royalties, and 50% of net losses from a trade or business.

Topic Review I14-2

Summary of Selected Tax Credits

TAX CREDIT ITEM	RATIONALE
PERSONAL CREDITS	
Child and dependent care credit[b]	To provide equitable relief for parents and other individuals who are employed and who must incur expenses for household and dependent care services
Tax credit for the elderly[b]	To provide tax relief for elderly taxpayers who are not substantially covered by the Social Security system
Adoption credit[b]	To provide relief for taxpayers who incur expenses in the adoption of children
Child tax credit	To reduce the tax burden on families with dependent children.
Residential mortgage interest credit[b]	To encourage qualified first-time home buyers to purchase a principal residence (this credit is not discussed in the text due to its limited applicability)
HOPE scholarship credit and lifetime learning credit	To assist students and families of students with the cost of postsecondary education.
MISCELLANEOUS CREDITS	
Foreign tax credit	To mitigate the effects of double taxation on foreign source income
Qualified electrical vehicles credit[a]	To encourage energy conservation (this credit is not discussed in the text due to its limited applicability)
GENERAL BUSINESS CREDITS	
Credit for increasing research activities[a]	To encourage research and development activities to enhance our technological base
Low-income housing credit[a]	To encourage construction, rehabilitation, and ownership of qualified low-income housing projects (this credit is not discussed in the text due to its limited applicability)
Disabled access credit[a]	To encourage small businesses to provide access for disabled
Rehabilitation expenditure credit[a]	To encourage the rehabilitation of older buildings including certified historic structures
Business energy credits[a]	To encourage energy conservation measures and the use of fuel other than petroleum
Work opportunity[a]	To encourage employers to hire unemployed people from disadvantaged groups
Welfare-to-work[a]	To encourage employees to hire persons who are on welfare
Empowerment zone employment credit[a]	To reduce the level of unemployment in distressed urban and rural areas.
REFUNDABLE CREDITS	
Earned income credit[b]	To provide special tax breaks for certain low-income individuals who have earned income (e.g., salary and wages) and dependent children or other incapacitated individuals living in the household

[a]Part of the general business credit.
[b]Personal tax credits.

▼ TABLE I14-2
2001 Earned Income Credit Table

Number of Qualifying Children	Basic Percentage	Maximum Amount of Earned Income to Compute Credit	Maximum Tentative Credit
None	7.65%	$ 4,760	$ 364
One	34.0%	7,130	2,424
Two or more	40.0%	10,020	4,008

▼ TABLE I14-3
2001 Earned Income Credit Phase-Out Table

Number of Qualifying Children	Phase-Out Begins at[a]	Phase-Out Percentage	Phase-Out Ends at
None	$ 5,950	7.65%	$10,710
One	13,090	15.98%	28,260
Two or more	13,090	21.06%	32,121

[a] Larger of modified AGI or earned income.

PAYMENT OF TAXES

OBJECTIVE 4

Understand the mechanics of the federal withholding tax system and the requirements for making estimated tax payments.

The IRS collects federal income taxes during the year either through withholding on wages or quarterly estimated tax payments. If the withholdings and estimated taxes are less than the amount of tax computed on the tax return, the taxpayer must pay the balance of the tax due when the tax return is filed. If there has been an overpayment of tax, the taxpayer may either request a refund or choose to apply the overpayment to the following year's quarterly estimated taxes.

Substantial penalties are imposed if an employer fails to withhold federal income tax and pay such amounts to the IRS.[54] In addition, a taxpayer may be subject to a nondeductible penalty upon an underpayment of estimated tax.[55]

WITHHOLDING OF TAXES

REAL-WORLD EXAMPLE

A teacher claimed a credit for Social Security taxes that had been withheld from his salary. He believed that the Social Security tax was illegally withheld because he did not authorize the collection of the tax. The Tax Court held that the Social Security tax is mandatory for designated employees and does not allow a person to elect not to contribute. *Richard L. Feldman*, 1967 PH T.C. Memo ¶67,091, 26 TCM 444.

An employer must withhold federal income taxes and FICA taxes from an employee's wages. No withholdings are required if an employer-employee relationship does not exist (e.g., an individual who performs services as an independent contractor). Generally, unless a specific exemption is provided under the IRC, withholding is required on all forms of remuneration paid to an employee. Thus, salaries, fees, bonuses, dismissal payments, commissions, vacation pay, and taxable fringe benefits are subject to withholding.[56] Special rules include for the following:

▶ *More than one employer during the same year.* Each employer must withhold FICA and federal income taxes without regard to the fact that the employee has more than one employer. This requirement may result in an overwithholding of FICA taxes if the ceiling amount on the OASDI portion of the tax is exceeded. In the event of an overwithholding of FICA taxes, the employee may credit the excess amount as an additional payment of tax on line 61 on page 2 of Form 1040. However, the excess FICA contributions related to the matching employer contributions are not refundable or creditable against the tax liabilities of either employer.

▶ *Exemptions for certain employment activities.* Certain employees such as agricultural laborers, ministers, household employees, newspaper carriers under age 18, and tips of less than $20 per month from an employer are exempt from income tax withholding. Note, however, that the earnings of such individuals are fully taxable and that an employer may be liable for FICA tax payments on these earnings.[57]

---

[54] Sec. 3403. Employers are liable for payment of the full amount of withholdings that must be withheld and paid to the IRS. In addition, responsible individuals (e.g., corporate officers, directors, and consultants) may be held personally liable for payment of the tax. (See *Renate Schiff v. U.S.*, 69 AFTR 2d 92-804, 92-1 USTC ¶50,248 (D.C. NV, 1992), *Ted E. Tsouprake v. U.S.*, 69 AFTR 2d 92-821, 92-1 USTC ¶50,249 (D.C. FL, 1992), and *Ralph M. Guito, Jr. v. U.S.*, 67 AFTR 2d 91-1066, 92-1 USTC ¶ 50,231 (D.C. FL, 1991).

[55] Sec. 6654.
[56] Reg. Sec. 31.3401(a)-1(a)(2).
[57] Reg. Sec. 31.3401(a)(10)-1(a). An employer is liable for FICA tax payments for domestic servants if $1,200 or more is paid to an individual in any calendar year.

▶ *Exemptions for certain fringe benefits.* Fringe benefits such as moving expense reimbursements, payments under a self-insured medical reimbursement plan, meals and lodging, travel expense reimbursements, and payments under a qualified educational assistance program are not subject to withholding if it is reasonable to believe that an employee can deduct the item or the item is nontaxable. Any excess reimbursements are subject to withholding. For example, the portion of moving expenses that is not deductible by an employee (e.g., nondeductible indirect moving expenses) is subject to withholding.

▶ *Backup withholding.* Backup withholding rules were enacted to prevent abusive noncompliance situations. Taxpayers who give false information to avoid backup withholding are subject to both civil and criminal penalties.[58] A 31% withholding rate is required on most types of payments that are reported on Form 1099 (e.g., interest, dividends, royalties, etc.) under the following circumstances:

▶ The taxpayer does not provide the payor with the taxpayer identification number in the required manner.

▶ The taxpayer is required to certify that he or she is not subject to backup withholding but fails to do so.

▶ The IRS notifies the payor that the taxpayer gave an incorrect taxpayer identification number.

▶ The IRS notifies the payor that the taxpayer has failed to report the item of income on his or her return.[59]

▶ *Special rules for lump-sum pension plan or annuity payments.* Federal income tax withholding is mandatory for such payments unless the individual elects to have no tax withheld.[60] These requirements are intended to increase the level of taxpayer compliance and alleviate the need for retired people to pay quarterly estimated taxes, which would otherwise be necessary to avoid an underpayment penalty.

If the pension payments are periodic (i.e., received as an annuity), the withholding is figured using the same procedures that are used for salary and wages. The retiree merely fills out a withholding certificate (Form W-4P). If this form is not filled out, the withholding is based on the tables for a married individual claiming three withholding allowances.[61] A 10% withholding rate is generally used for nonperiodic payments (e.g., lump-sum distributions). Withheld amounts are based on the taxable portion of a pension payment.[62]

EXAMPLE I14-29 ▶

HISTORICAL NOTE
The withholding of federal income taxes by employers began during World War II.

Roy, a married taxpayer with four dependents, retires in the current year and receives taxable pension income from a qualified pension plan of $600 per month. He also receives a lump-sum distribution of $50,000 from a qualified profit-sharing plan. The trustees of both plans notify Roy that amounts will be withheld unless he elects not to have any amount withheld. If Roy elects not to have any taxes withheld, he may be required to make quarterly estimated tax payments to the extent that the pension payments are taxable to avoid an underpayment penalty. If Roy does not make an election and files two withholding certificates, regular withholding procedures will apply to the periodic pension payments and a 10% withholding rate will apply to the lump-sum distribution. ◀

▶ *Special rules for supplemental wage payments.* If an employee receives supplemental wage payments (in addition to regular wage payments), the withholding amount is determined under either of two methods:[63]

▶ Concurrent payments—if the supplemental wages are included in the payment of regular wages, the tax is withheld as if the total was a single wage payment for the payroll period.

---

[58] Sec. 6682.
[59] Sec. 3406.
[60] Sec. 3405. Withholding is imposed at a 20% rate on any distribution eligible for tax deferral rollover treatment (e.g., a distribution from a qualified pension plan to an IRA) unless the funds are transferred directly to the eligible plan (see Sec. 3405(c)).
[61] Sec. 3405(a)(4).
[62] Pension payments are subject to tax under the Sec. 72 annuity rules (see Chapter I3).
[63] Reg. Sec. 31.3402(g)-1(a).

- Separate payments—if the supplementary wages are paid separately, the tax withheld is either a flat 28% or by aggregating the supplemental wage payment with wages paid within the same calendar year for the last preceding payroll period or the current payroll period.

Supplemental wages payments include items such as bonuses, commissions, overtime, accumulated sick pay, severance pay, awards, prizes, back pay, and retroactive pay increases.

WITHHOLDING ALLOWANCES AND METHODS. Every employee must file an employee's withholding allowance certificate (Form W-4), which lists the employee's marital status and number of withholding allowances and becomes the basic source of input for the computation of the amount to be withheld. If an employee's circumstances change (e.g., a married taxpayer is divorced or the amount of allowances claimed is reduced), an amended Form W-4 must be filed within 10 days. In general, the employee's Form W-4 is not sent to the IRS unless the number of withholding allowances exceeds 10 or an employee claims an exemption from withholding when his earnings are more than $200 per week.[64] This procedure is intended to prevent employees from avoiding the withholding of income tax on amounts that are otherwise due.

The following procedural rules apply to withholding:

- A $500 civil penalty is imposed for filing false statements (e.g., claiming excessive numbers of withholding allowances).[65]

- An employee may claim an exempt status on Form W-4 if he or she has no income tax liability in the prior year and anticipates none in the current year. High school or college students with jobs earning less than the minimum dollar amount required to file a tax return should take advantage of this exemption. Otherwise, it may be necessary to file a return to obtain a tax refund in the following year. In such a case, the student has, in effect, made an interest-free loan to the government.

- Income tax withholding tables result in a lower amount being withheld if the taxpayer is married.

- An individual may request that additional amounts be withheld if it is anticipated that taxes will be owed at the end of the year and the person does not want to make quarterly estimated payments. It is also possible to claim fewer withholding allowances in order to increase the amount withheld.

- Each additional withholding allowance that is claimed reduces the amount withheld.

Withholding allowances on Form W-4 may be claimed for the same number of personal and dependency exemptions that will be taken on the employee's tax return for the year. An additional special withholding allowance that reflects the standard deduction may be claimed by a taxpayer who has one job or, if married, has a spouse who is unemployed.[66] Additional withholding allowances may be claimed if an individual who has deductions, losses, or credits from a wide variety of sources, including itemized deductions, alimony payments, moving expenses, and losses from a trade or business, rental property, or farm. Tables and a worksheet are provided to compute the amount of the additional withholding allowances.[67]

> **REAL-WORLD EXAMPLE**
> It has been held that the employer's withholding of federal income taxes is not an improper taking of property without due process in violation of the Fifth Amendment. *Michael O. Campbell v. Amax Coal Co.*, 610 F.2d 701, 45 AFTR 2d 80-564, 80-1 USTC ¶9185 (10th Cir., 1980).

EXAMPLE I14-30 ▶ Sam and Sally are married and have three dependent children. They file a joint return. Sally is not employed, and Sam does not claim additional withholding allowances for unusually large deductions or tax credits. Sam may claim six allowances (two personal exemptions [for Sam and Sally]) plus three dependency exemptions plus one special withholding allowance to reflect the standard deduction). The special allowance is available because Sally is not employed and Sam has only one job. ◀

---

[64] Reg. Sec. 31.3402(f)(2)-1.
[65] Sec. 6682(a).
[66] Sec. 3402(f)(1)(E).

[67] Married taxpayers who are both employed may allocate withholding allowances as they see fit as long as the same allowance is not claimed more than once.

STOP & THINK

Question: Many taxpayers believe that they must claim the same number of withholding allowances for withholding purposes as the number of personal exemptions on their income tax return. Why is this not correct?

Solution: While the starting point for determining withholding allowances is taxpayer's marital status and number of personal exemptions, taxpayers are allowed to claim more or less withholding allowances based on their individual situations. According to the IRS, taxpayers may claim additional withholding allowances for two principal reasons: (1) a taxpayer has high deductions, losses, or credits, or (2) an unmarried taxpayer qualifies for head of household filing status. The withholding tables are constructed by assuming that the taxpayer's deductions will be equal to the standard deduction. Therefore, if a taxpayer has much higher itemized deductions than the standard deduction, the withholding tables may prescribe too much tax to be withheld and the taxpayer would have a large refund at the end of the year. To alleviate this situation, taxpayers are allowed to claim additional withholding allowances so as to prevent a large overpayment. Similarly, the withholding tables only have two categories of marital status, single or married. Thus, if an unmarried taxpayer qualifies for the head of household status, the "single" withholding tables may cause over-withholding of tax.

COMPUTATION OF FEDERAL INCOME TAX WITHHELD. The computation of the amount to be withheld is made by using wage bracket tables or by an optional percentage method of withholding. Both methods produce approximately the same results. Wage bracket tables are available for daily, weekly, biweekly, and monthly payroll periods. Separate tables are used for single (including heads-of-household) and married individuals. The wage bracket table for married persons using a monthly payroll period for wages from $0 through $3,239.99 is located in the 2001 Tax Tables and Rate Schedules on page T-15.

EXAMPLE I14-31 ▶ Henry is married and claims six withholding allowances. His monthly salary is $3,000. The federal income tax withheld per month for 2001 using the wage bracket table on page T-15 is $155. ◀

ESTIMATED TAX PAYMENTS

ADDITIONAL COMMENT
The IRS does not mail reminder statements for the required quarterly estimated payments.

Certain types of income are not subject to withholding (e.g., investment income, rents, income from self-employment, and capital gains). Taxpayers who earn this type of income must make quarterly estimated tax payments.

The purpose of the estimated tax system is to ensure that all taxpayers have paid enough tax by the end of the tax year to cover most of their tax liability. Thus, estimated

WHAT WOULD YOU DO IN THIS SITUATION?

THE NANNY TAX: DON'T PAY NOW, WORRY LATER

You are a CPA engaged in tax practice and one of your clients is Mr. Throckmorton D. Princeton IV, J.D. He is a senior partner in the prestigious employment litigation firm of Huey, Dewey and Fooey. Mr. Princeton is known for his ruthless style of litigation services.

Things were really rosy for Mr. Princeton until last week, when there was some speculation in the press about his being appointed to a cabinet-level position by the President. A TV news magazine show looked into Mr. Princeton's domestic worker situation. It appears that Mr. Princeton has long engaged in the practice of hiring part-time workers in his household to clean his house, tend to his gardens, walk his dogs, cook his meals, service his car, and nurse him when he is ill. All told, he used over twenty-five people at one time or another over the past year. These workers were all paid as little as possible, and all were asked to sign a contract with Mr. Princeton that declared that they were to be classified as independent contractors. The total amount paid out to these workers added up to $50,000. No payroll taxes of any kind were paid by Mr. Princeton, although he did file Forms 1099 with the IRS. What tax and ethical issues should be considered?

tax payments may also be required if insufficient tax is being withheld from an individual's salary, pension, or other income (although many taxpayers prefer to file an amended Form W-4 instead and request additional withholding amounts or reduce the number of withholding allowances). The amount of estimated tax is the taxpayer's tax liability (including self-employment tax and alternative minimum tax) reduced by withholdings, tax credits, and any excess FICA amounts.[68]

ADDITIONAL COMMENT

Red Skelton on the IRS: "I get even with them. I send in an estimated tax form, but I don't sign it. If I've got to guess what I'm making, let them guess who's making it."

REQUIRED ESTIMATED TAX PAYMENTS. For calendar-year individuals, required quarterly payments are due by April 15, June 15, September 15 of the current year, and January 15 of the following year. The estimated tax payments must be the lesser of the following amounts to avoid the imposition of a penalty[69] on the underpaid amount:

▶ 90% of the tax liability shown on the return for the current year;

▶ 100% of the tax liability shown on the return for the prior year if the taxpayer's AGI for such prior year was $150,000 or less. If the taxpayer AGI is greater than $150,000, no penalty will be imposed if the taxpayer pays estimated tax payments in the current year equal to a percentage of the preceding year's income tax liability, as follows:

CURRENT YEAR	PRECEDING YEAR	PERCENT OF PRECEDING YEAR'S INCOME TAX LIABILITY
2000	1999	108.6%
2001	2000	110%

▶ 90% of the tax liability shown on the return for the current year computed on an annualized basis.

Further, no penalty is imposed if (1) the estimated tax for the current year is less than $500 or (2) the individual had no tax liability for the prior year.

It should be noted that no penalty is imposed for failure to file quarterly estimated tax payments, even though the IRC includes specific filing requirements. A penalty is imposed only if the taxpayer fails to meet the minimum payment requirements or one of the previously mentioned exceptions does not apply.

EXAMPLE I14-32 ▶ Sarah does not make quarterly estimated tax payments for 2001, even though she has a substantial amount of income not subject to withholding. Her taxable income in 2001 is $140,000. Her actual tax liability (including self-employment taxes and the alternative minimum tax) for 2001 is $40,000. Withholdings from her salary are $30,000. She pays the $10,000 balance due to the IRS with the filing of the return on April 3, 2002. Sarah's tax liability for 2000 was $27,000. There is no penalty for failure to make the quarterly estimated tax payments because she meets one or more of the exceptions relating to the minimum payment requirement. Although the first exception is not met because her $30,000 of withholdings (plus zero estimated tax payments) is less than 90% of her $40,000 tax liability for 2001 ($30,000 ÷ $40,000 = 75%), she meets the second exception because the $30,000 of withholdings is more than 100% of her $27,000 tax liability for 2000. If Sarah's AGI for 2000 was more than $150,000, the second exception safe harbor amount would be 110% (instead of 100%) of the prior year's tax or $29,700 ($27,000 × 1.10). Because the $30,000 of withholding is still more than 110% of her $27,000 tax liability, Sarah would also meet the second exception and would not be subject to the underpayment penalty. ◀

Form 2210 (see Appendix B) should be completed and submitted with the tax return if a possible underpayment of tax is indicated. This form is used to determine whether one of the exceptions is applicable and, if not, to compute the amount of the underpayment penalty. The actual computation of the underpayment penalty is not shown here because of the length and complexity of the rules. Topic Review I14-3 summarizes the withholding tax and estimated payment requirements.

---

[68] Excess FICA payments will occur if an employee has more than one employer during the year and the total FICA payments exceed in the aggregate the ceiling on FICA taxes.

[69] Sec. 6654.

Topic Review I14-3

Withholding Taxes and Estimated Payments

WITHHOLDING OF TAXES

	FICA	INCOME TAX
When to withhold	All employee earnings up to $80,400 (in 2001) per employer. No ceiling applies to the 1.45% hospital insurance portion of the tax.	All employee wages, salaries, fees, bonuses, commissions, taxable fringe benefits, and so on.[a]
Amount to withhold	7.65% of FICA wages including 1.45% for the hospital insurance portion of the tax. 1.45% for amounts in excess of $80,400 is withheld from the employee's earnings.	Determined by using withholding tables or the percentage method based on an individual's filing status and number of exemptions.

[a] Exceptions are provided for certain nontaxable fringe benefits.

ESTIMATED TAX PAYMENTS

▶ To avoid an underpayment penalty, the estimated tax payments and withholdings for the year must be equal to or exceed any one of the following:
90% of the tax liability shown on the return for the current year, or 100% of the tax liability shown on the return for the prior year (110% if AGI for the prior year 2000 exceeds $150,000), or 90% of the tax liability shown on the return for the current year computed on an annualized basis.

▶ The underpayment penalty is not deductible for income tax purposes.

▶ Form 2210 should be completed and submitted with the tax return if an underpayment is indicated.

TAX PLANNING CONSIDERATIONS

AVOIDING THE ALTERNATIVE MINIMUM TAX

KEY POINT
The alternative minimum tax can be avoided or its impact lessened by various tax strategies.

Taxpayers with substantial amounts of tax preference items and a corresponding low regular tax liability may be subject to the AMT. These taxpayers need to engage in tax planning in order to minimize or avoid the AMT. Because a liberal exemption is provided for most individuals (i.e., $45,000 for married individuals filing a joint return and $33,750 for single taxpayers and heads-of-households), the timing of certain income and deduction items may result in the full use of the exemption in each year. For example, planning to avoid the AMT may be accomplished by delaying the payment of certain itemized deductions (e.g., state and local taxes) that reduce the regular income tax but do not reduce the AMT. A cash method of accounting taxpayer who defers the payment of state income taxes into the following year triggers an increase in the regular tax for the current year. This increase can eliminate the AMT liability. However, it is necessary to consider the tax effects for both the current and following years because state income taxes are deductible for purposes of the regular tax calculation when the payment is made in the following year. This reduction may affect the AMT calculation in such a year and increase the amount of tax that is owed.

Certain tax-exempt investments generate additional tax preferences for the investor such as interest on private activity bonds. Before such investments are acquired, an investor should determine the impact on his or her AMT.

AVOIDING THE UNDERPAYMENT PENALTY FOR ESTIMATED TAX

Many taxpayers find it difficult to estimate their taxes for the purposes of making quarterly estimated payments and are uncertain whether their withholdings and estimated tax will equal or exceed 90% or more of their actual tax liability for the year. A common planning technique to avoid a possible underpayment tax penalty is to make estimated tax payments and withholdings in an amount that is at least 100% (or 110%[70] if AGI was in excess of $150,000 for the prior year) of the actual tax liability for the prior year, thereby meeting one of the exceptions that prevents the underpayment penalty from being imposed. This technique is commonly referred to as a "safe estimate."

EXAMPLE I14-33 ▶ Yong expects his federal income tax withholdings to be $14,000 for 2001 and estimates that his income tax liability will be $24,000. Yong's actual federal income taxes were $20,000 in 2000. If estimated taxes of at least $6,000 are paid during the year, Yong's estimated taxes plus withholding will be at least 100% of his prior year's tax liability ($14,000 + $6,000 = $20,000) and no underpayment penalty is due despite the fact that there is a $4,000 ($24,000 − $20,000) balance due of the actual tax liability. If Yong's AGI was in excess of $150,000 for 2000, his estimated taxes plus withholding must be at least 110% of his 2000 tax liability or $22,000 (1.10 × $20,000) to avoid the underpayment penalty. Thus, his estimated tax payments must be at least $8,000. ◀

CASH-FLOW CONSIDERATIONS

KEY POINT
A taxpayer should avoid making estimated payments that exceed the actual tax liability because the taxpayer is making an interest-free loan to the IRS. Nevertheless, many taxpayers deliberately have excess amounts withheld from their wages or make excessive estimated payments in order to receive a refund. These taxpayers view this strategy as a forced saving plan.

Assuming that the underpayment penalty can be avoided, it is generally preferable to have an underpayment of tax to the government at the time for filing the return rather than to receive a refund resulting from an overpayment of tax. No interest is paid on a refund if the IRS pays the refund within 45 days from the later of the due date of the return or its filing date.[71] In addition, the IRS has, in effect, received an interest-free loan from the taxpayer during the period such overpayment is made. To avoid an overpayment, a taxpayer may file an amended W-4 form and claim additional withholding allowances if the requirements are met (e.g., the taxpayer has unusually large itemized deductions, tax credits, alimony payments, etc.).

If an individual anticipates that her estimated tax payments and withholdings are insufficient to avoid the underpayment penalty, it may be preferable to increase amounts withheld before the end of the tax year (e.g., amounts withheld in the fourth quarter) to avoid the penalty rather than to increase the estimated tax payments. This technique may be advantageous because the penalty is calculated on a quarterly basis, and the withholdings are spread evenly over the year, despite the fact that such increased withholding amounts are paid near the end of the year. The end result is cash-flow savings to the taxpayer. Another alternative means to avoid the underpayment penalty is to accelerate certain deductions (e.g., real estate taxes on a personal residence), by paying such amounts before the end of the tax year. Additionally, otherwise deductible contributions to an IRA made between the end of the tax year and the due date for the tax return may be treated as a deduction for the prior year, thereby avoiding the underpayment penalty (see Chapter I9).

USE OF GENERAL BUSINESS TAX CREDITS

Business tax credits (e.g., the disabled access credit and the work opportunity credit) are combined for the purpose of computing an overall limitation based on the taxpayer's tax liability. Also, an individual's personal tax credits (e.g., the child and dependent care credit) and the foreign tax credit are deducted from the tax liability before the limitations are applied to the general business tax credit. Similarly, the nonrefundable personal tax credits reduce the tax liability before the foreign tax credit limitation is applied. Therefore, it is necessary to consider the priority and interrelated aspects of these credits to ensure that a particular credit is fully used.

FOREIGN TAX CREDITS AND THE FOREIGN EARNED INCOME EXCLUSION

Individuals who accept foreign job assignments should consider the federal income tax implications because U.S. citizens are subject to U.S. tax on their worldwide income. Assuming that certain requirements and limitations are met, an individual may elect to take either a foreign tax credit or a foreign-earned income exclusion of $76,000 (2000)

---

[70] The 110% is applicable if the preceding year is 2000. If the preceding year is 1999, the percentage is 108.6%. See the text discussion for more details.

[71] Sec. 6611(e).

with respect to salaries, allowances, and other forms of earned income that are earned while on extended non-U.S. assignments.[72] Any taxes that are paid or accrued with respect to the excluded income are not available as a foreign tax credit. In general, the exclusion is preferable if the effective foreign tax rate is less than the effective U.S. tax rate because the foreign tax credit that can be claimed does not equal the gross U.S. tax owed on the income. If the effective foreign tax rate on the earned income exceeds the effective U.S. tax rate, U.S. taxpayers ordinarily elect not to use the exclusion. Instead, the excess tax credits on earned income are used to offset the U.S. taxes owed on other types of foreign income. Detailed coverage of foreign tax credits and the exclusion is contained in Chapter C16 of the *Prentice Hall's Federal Taxation: Corporations, Partnerships, Estates and Trusts* text.

CHILD AND DEPENDENT CARE CREDIT

ADDITIONAL COMMENT

If the employer provides a child care assistance plan, the taxpayer may lose the benefit of the child and dependent care credit because it is necessary to reduce the amount of expenses eligible for the credit dollar-for-dollar by the amount excluded from gross income under the employer's child care plan.

The child and dependent care credit is increasingly important because a greater percentage of both spouses are now in the labor force as well as the large number of single parent families. Nonworking spouses who are considering employment should evaluate the tax consequences arising from the child and dependent care credit.

It should be noted that certain child and dependent care expenses may qualify as a medical expense (e.g., nursing care for a disabled dependent). Therefore, it is necessary to compare the marginal tax benefit from the additional child and dependent care credit with the marginal tax benefit from the additional medical expense deduction to determine whether the credit is worth more than the deduction. Expenditures in excess of the child and dependent care ceiling amounts ($2,400 for one child or dependent and $4,800 for two or more children or dependents) may also qualify as medical expenses.

EXAMPLE I14-34 ▶

REAL WORLD EXAMPLE

Many taxpayers do not comply with the tax law when they hire people to care for their children. Zoe Baird withdrew as attorney general nominee when it was disclosed that she had hired illegal aliens to care for her children and had failed to withhold the FICA tax from the employee's wages and to pay the employer's FICA tax.

Stacey, a single taxpayer, maintains a household for an incapacitated dependent parent and two children under age 13. Stacey has AGI from alimony of $20,000 and could earn an additional $15,000 working as a secretary. To enable Stacey to be employed, assume that she would incur $4,000 of eligible child care expenses for the children and an additional $4,000 of nursing expenses for the care of her disabled parent. Before considering the tax effects, Stacey's net increase in income from being employed would only be $7,000 ($15,000 earnings − $8,000 of child and dependent care expenses). The tax credit for child and dependent care expenses is $960 ($4,800 × 0.20). The rate is scaled down from 30% to 20% because Stacey's AGI is $35,000 (i.e., the credit rate is reduced by one percentage point for each $2,000 of AGI in excess of $10,000 until it reaches 20% when AGI exceeds $28,000). A portion of the qualified nursing care expenses (i.e., $8,000 − $4,800 = $3,200) that is not used as child and dependent care expenditures may be deducted as medical expenses if they exceed the 7.5% of AGI floor. If Stacey itemizes her deductions and has other medical expenses equal to or greater than 7.5% of AGI and has an average tax rate of 20%, the value of the additional medical deductions is $640 (0.20 × $3,200). Stacey's additional net cash flows from working are only $4,453, consisting of the following:

Gross earnings from employment		$15,000
Minus:	Federal income tax on earnings ($15,000 × 0.20)	(3,000)[a]
	Actual child and dependent care expenses	(8,000)
	FICA taxes (0.0765 × $15,000)	(1,147)
Plus:	Child and dependent care credit	960
	Medical expense tax benefit	640
Cash flow from employment		$ 4,453

[a] A 20% average tax rate was used because more than one tax rate is used to compute Stacey's tax liability.

Consideration should also be given to additional incremental work-related expenditures (e.g., clothing, meals, and commuting expenses) that are not deductible. The income tax and cash flow consequences arising from an employee assistance program for child care or medical expenses should also be considered if a plan is offered to employees. ◀

---

[72] Sec. 911(a). The foreign income exclusion requirements are discussed in Chapter I4.

Compliance and Procedural Considerations

ALTERNATIVE MINIMUM TAX FILING PROCEDURES

Form 6251 is used by individuals to compute the AMT, and corporations must use Form 4626 (see Appendix B for both forms). Form 6251 must be completed and attached to an individual's tax return in any of the following situations:

▶ An AMT tax liability actually exists.

▶ The taxpayer has tax credits that are limited by the tentative minimum tax.

▶ The AMT base exceeds the exemption amounts and an individual has AMT adjustment or tax preference items.

IRS Publication 909 contains detailed information regarding filing considerations for individuals.

ADDITIONAL COMMENT
The Revenue Reconciliation Act of 1993 raised the AMT rate from 24% to 26% on the first $175,000 of AMTI over the exemption amount and 28% on amounts over $175,000. Because the rate on net capital gains was capped at 28%, taxpayers whose income is primarily from net capital gains are more likely to fall into an AMT position.

WITHHOLDING AND ESTIMATED TAX

Taxpayers who have income taxes withheld from wages, pensions, and so on should receive a Form W-2 (or Form 1099-R for pensions) by January 31. These forms should be attached to the tax return to substantiate the amount of the withholdings. If the form is incorrect, the taxpayer should request a corrected form from the payor.

If an individual makes quarterly estimated tax payments, Form 1040A or Form 1040EZ may not be used. Married individuals may make either joint estimated tax payments or separate estimated tax payments. If joint estimated tax payments are made and the married individuals subsequently file separate returns (e.g., in the case of a divorce that is pending or a divorce completed before the end of the year), the joint estimated tax payments are divided in proportion to each spouse's individual tax if no agreement is reached concerning an appropriate division.

EXAMPLE I14-35 ▶ Allen and Alice make joint estimated tax payments during 2001 of $10,000. Allen and Alice are separated in February 2002 and Alice refuses to file a joint return with Allen. Allen's tax liability for 2001 on his separate return is $20,000 and Alice's tax liability on her separate return is $5,000. If no agreement is reached concerning the allocation of the joint estimated payments of $10,000, Alice is entitled to claim $2,000 of the estimated tax payments on her return [($5,000 ÷ $25,000) × $10,000]. The remaining $8,000 is apportioned to Allen. ◀

GENERAL BUSINESS TAX CREDITS

The computation of the business energy credit is made on Form 3468. Individuals must transfer the totals to page 2 of Form 1040. Form 3800 must be filed if any other general business credits are claimed.

PERSONAL TAX CREDITS

KEY POINT
The earned income credit is available even in cases where the taxpayer has no tax liability. The refund of taxes not even paid or incurred is often called a negative income tax.

Personal tax credits are reported on page 2 of Form 1040. These credits are deducted from the taxpayer's tax liability before other credits. The credits section on page 2 of Form 1040 limits the deduction for personal tax credits to the amount of the tax due. Form 2441 (see Appendix B) must be filed to claim the child and dependent care credit. Taxpayers who claim the child and dependent care credit must also include the care provider's name, address, and taxpayer identification number on their tax return. If the caregiver will not provide the required information, the taxpayer has the option to supply the name and address of the caregiver on Form 2441 and attach a statement explaining that the caregiver has refused to provide his or her identification number (TIN). Schedule R of Form 1040 (see Appendix B) is filed to claim the credit for the elderly. An elderly individual may elect to have the IRS compute the tax and the amount of the tax credit.[73]

---

[73] Sec. 6014. See Form 1040 instructions for more reporting details.

The earned income credit is refundable to an individual even if no tax is owed. The IRS will automatically compute the credit amount.[74] However, tax tables to assist in the process are included in IRS instructions to Forms 1040 and 1040A. Schedule EIC of Form 1040 (see Appendix B) is used to compute the credit if Form 1040 is used. If an individual expects to be eligible for the earned income credit, he or she can obtain advance payments of the credit amount by filing Form W-5 (Earned Income Credit Advance Payment Certificate) with his or her employer, who will increase the employee's pay by the amount of the credit. Individuals who receive advance payments must file Form 1040 or Form 1040A to obtain the credit even if they are not required to file a tax return. Taxpayers who are eligible for the earned income credit can not use Form 1040-EZ.

The foreign tax credit for individuals is computed on Form 1116 (see Appendix B). The foreign tax credit amount so determined is entered on page 2 of Form 1040.

PROBLEM MATERIALS

DISCUSSION QUESTIONS

I14-1 Why are most taxpayers not subject to the alternative minimum tax (AMT)?

I14-2 Does the AMT apply if an individual's tax liability as computed under the AMT rules is less than his or her regular tax amount?

I14-3 Which of the following are tax preference items for purposes of computing the individual AMT?
a. Net long-term capital gain
b. Excess depreciation for real property placed in service before 1987
c. Straight-line depreciation on residential real estate acquired in 1992
d. Appreciated element for charitable contributions of capital gain real property

I14-4 Which of the following are individual AMT adjustments?
a. Itemized deductions that are not allowed in computing AMTI
b. Excess of MACRS depreciation over depreciation computed under the alternative depreciation system for real property placed in service after 1986.
c. Excess of MACRS depreciation over depreciation computed under the alternative depreciation system for personal property placed in service after 1986
d. Tax-exempt interest earned on State of Michigan general revenue bonds.

I14-5 Which of the following itemized deductions are deductible when computing the alternative minimum tax for individuals?
a. Charitable contributions
b. Mortgage interest on a personal residence
c. State and local income taxes
d. Interest related to an investment in undeveloped land where the individual has no investment income
e. Medical expenses amounting to 8% of AGI

I14-6 Why are most individuals not subject to the self-employment tax?

I14-7 Tony, who is single and 58 years old, is considering early retirement. He currently has $70,000 salary and $50,000 of profits from a consulting business. What advice would you give Tony relative to the need to make Social Security tax payments if he retires and continues to be actively engaged as a consultant during his retirement?

I14-8 Theresa is a college professor who wants to work for a consulting firm during the summer. She will be working on special projects involving professional development programs. What advantages might accrue to the consulting firm if the engagement is set up as a consulting arrangement rather than an employment contract?

I14-9 Ted and Tina are both self-employed and file a joint return in 2001. Ted has self-employment income of $20,000 and receives a $30,000 salary from his employer. Tina's has no salary and self-employment income of $10,000.
a. How much self-employment tax is due for Ted and Tina on a joint return?
b. How much, if any, of the self-employment tax payments may be deducted on Ted and Tina's income tax return?

I14-10 Discuss the underlying rationale for the following tax credit items:
a. Foreign tax credit
b. Research credit

---

[74] Sec. 6695(g) requires preparers to meet due diligence requirements with respect to the earned income credit (EIC). If the EIC is incorrectly computed or overlooked, the *preparer* could be subject to a $100 penalty.

c. Business energy credit
d. Work opportunity credit
e. Child and dependent care credit
f. Earned income credit
g. HOPE scholarship credit
h. Disabled access credit
i. Empowerment Zone employment credit
j. Adoption credit

I14-11 If Congress is considering a tax credit or deduction as an incentive to encourage certain activities, is a $40 tax credit more valuable than a $200 tax deduction for a taxpayer with a 15% marginal rate? a 28% marginal rate?

I14-12 What are the more significant tax credit items included in the computation of the general business tax credit?

I14-13 Discuss the limitations that have been imposed on the claiming of the general business tax credit including the following:
a. Overall ceiling limitation based on the tax liability
b. Priority of general business and personal credits
c. Carryback and carryover of unused credits (including the application of the FIFO method).

I14-14 Wayne is considering a foreign assignment for two years. He will earn approximately $90,000 in the foreign country and will be eligible for the foreign tax credit or the earned income exclusion. The effective tax rate on Wayne's earnings if fully taxable under U.S. law would be 30%. The effective tax rate for the foreign salary is 20% under the foreign country's laws.
a. Discuss in general terms the computation of the foreign tax credit and its limitation.
b. Would Wayne be better off electing the foreign tax credit or the earned income exclusion? Explain.

I14-15 King Corporation is expanding its business and is planning to hire four additional employees at an annual labor cost of $12,000 each. What will the tax consequences be if King hires employees who are eligible for the work opportunity tax credit?

I14-16 Queen Corporation has been in business since 1979. During the preceding year the company had 25 full-time employees and gross receipts of $8,000,000. During the current year Queen spent $10,000 to install access ramps for disabled individuals. Is Queen Corporation eligible for the disabled access credit? If so, what is the credit amount and the basis reduction (if any) for the depreciable property?

I14-17 Discuss the special tax rules that apply to the tax credit for rehabilitation expenditures including the following:
a. Types of eligible expenditures
b. Applicable tax credit rates
c. Restrictions on depreciation methods
d. Calculation of basis for expenditures
e. Potential recapture of the credit

I14-18 What types of business property qualify for the business energy credit?

I14-19 What is the underlying reason for enactment of most of the personal tax credits?

I14-20 Discuss the difference between a refundable tax credit and a nonrefundable tax credit. Give at least one example of each type of credit.

I14-21 If an individual is unemployed and has no earned income, is it possible to receive a child and dependent care credit for otherwise qualifying child and dependent care expenses? Explain.

I14-22 Discuss the major differences between the HOPE scholarship credit and the lifetime learning credit. Include in your discussion the type of taxpayers that would likely qualify for each of the credits.

I14-23 What is the maximum child and dependent care credit available to an individual who has $6,000 of qualifying child care expenses and two or more qualifying children or incapacitated dependents?

I14-24 Vivian is a single taxpayer with two children who qualify for the child and dependent care credit. She incurred $5,000 of qualifying child care expenses during the current year. She also received $3,000 in reimbursements from her employer from a qualified employee dependent care assistance program. What is the maximum child and dependent care credit available to Vivian if her AGI is $21,000?

I14-25 The adoption credit is intended to assist taxpayers with the financial burden of adopting children.
a. Discuss how the credit is computed.
b. Why did Congress impose a phase-out of the credit for taxpayers based on AGI?

I14-26 Alice is single, 37 years old, and has two qualifying children, ages 3 and 6. She receives $2,500 alimony and $8,000 of wages resulting in $10,500 of AGI in 2001. Is Alice eligible for the earned income credit? If so, is it possible for her to receive advance payments of the credit amounts rather than receiving a tax refund when the tax return is filed?

I14-27 Why are most elderly people unable to qualify for the tax credit for the elderly?

I14-28 If an employer fails to withhold federal income taxes and FICA taxes on wages or fails to make payment to the IRS, what adverse tax consequences may result? May corporate officers or other corporate officials be held responsible for the underpayment?

I14-29 Jet Corporation reimburses Tracy, an employee, for certain moving expenses. The reimbursement is $6,000. However, only $4,000 is deductible on Tracy's income tax return. Should Jet Corporation withhold federal income tax on the reimbursed amounts? If so, how much?

I14-30 When Vicki retires during the current year, she will receive a monthly pension of $800 and a fully taxable lump-sum distribution of $50,000 from

her employer's qualified profit-sharing plan. She does not want the trustee of either plan to withhold any federal income tax because she expects that it will be difficult for her to live on the pension income and the investment income from the lump-sum distribution.
a. What procedures should Vicki follow if she does not want the trustees to withhold on the periodic pension payments or the lump-sum distribution?
b. What are the possible tax consequences that might occur if Vicki does not file estimated tax payments?
c. What percentage rate is used to determine the amount withheld from periodic pension payments and lump-sum distributions?

I14-31 Although Virginia is entitled to five personal and dependency exemptions, she claims only one withholding allowance on Form W-4.
a. Is it permissible to claim fewer allowances than an individual is entitled to?
b. Why would an individual claim fewer allowances?

I14-32 Mario is a college student who had no income tax liability in the prior year and expects to have no tax liability for the current year.
a. What steps should Mario take to avoid having amounts being withheld from his summer employment wages?
b. What are the cash-flow implications to Mario if the employer withholds federal income taxes?

I14-33 What is backup withholding? What is its purpose?

I14-34 Under what circumstances may an individual claim additional withholding allowances on Form W-4?

I14-35 In April 2001, Vincent anticipates that his actual tax liability for 2001 tax year will be $12,000 and that the federal income taxes withheld from his salary will be $9,000. Thus, when he files his 2001 income tax return in 2002, he will have a $3,000 balance due. His actual federal income tax liability for 2000 was $8,000 and his AGI for 2000 was less than $150,000.
a. Is Vincent required to make estimated tax payments in 2001?
b. If no estimated tax payments are made, will Vincent be subject to an underpayment penalty if the actual tax liability for the 2001 tax year is $12,000? Why or why not?
c. Will Vincent be subject to an underpayment penalty if his actual tax liability for 2001 is instead $25,000? Why?

I14-36 What tax planning strategy can you suggest to avoid the penalty for underpayment of estimated tax for an individual who has increasing levels of income each year and is uncertain regarding the amount of his or her estimated taxable income for any given year?

I14-37 From a cash-flow perspective, why is it generally preferable to have an underpayment of tax (assuming there is no underpayment penalty imposed) rather than an overpayment of tax?

I14-38 Why do many taxpayers intentionally overpay their tax through withholdings so as to obtain a tax refund?

ISSUE IDENTIFICATION QUESTIONS

I14-39 Daryl is an executive who has an annual salary of $120,000. He is considering early retirement so that he can pursue a career as a management consultant. Daryl estimates that he could earn approximately $80,000 annually from his consulting business. What tax issues should Daryl consider?

I14-40 Jennifer recently received a check for $30,000 and securities with an FMV of $200,000 from her former husband pursuant to a divorce. The $30,000 represents alimony and the securities were transferred pursuant to the property settlement. What tax issues should Jennifer consider?

I14-41 Coastal Corporation is planning an expansion of its production facilities and is considering whether to hire additional employees from economically disadvantaged groups so as to be able to avail itself of the targeted jobs credit. The company plant is not located in an Empowerment Zone. New employees are paid approximately $18,000 per year. If economically disadvantaged employees are hired, additional job training expenses of $5,000 per employee will be required. What tax issues should Coastal consider with regard to the hiring and training of its new employees?

PROBLEMS

I14-42 *AMT Computation.* William, a married taxpayer who files a joint return with his spouse, reports the following items in 2001:

Taxable income	$70,000
Tax preferences	20,000
AMT adjustments related to itemized deductions	30,000
Regular tax liability	13,724

a. What is William's AMT liability in the current year?
b. What is William's AMT liability in the current year if he is instead a single taxpayer and his regular tax liability is $16,217 rather than $13,724?

I14-43 *AMT Computation.* Jose, a single taxpayer with no dependents, has AGI of $180,000 and reports the following items in 2001:

Taxable income	$130,000
Tax preferences	40,000
AMT adjustments related to itemized deductions	30,000
Regular tax liability	34,817

What is Jose's AMT liability in the current year?

I14-44 *AMT Tax Preferences.* Allison, a single taxpayer, reports the following items on her federal income tax return in the current year:

Excess depreciation on real property placed in service in 1986	$20,000
Excess depreciation on personal property placed in service in 1995	10,000
Net long-term capital gain	20,000
Tax-exempt municipal bond interest (private activity bonds)	30,000

What is the amount of Allison's tax preferences for purposes of computing the AMT in the current year?

I14-45 *AMT Adjustments and Computation of Tax.* Allen, a single taxpayer, reports the following items on his 2001 federal income tax return:

Adjusted gross income	$75,000
Taxable income	48,000
Regular tax liability	9,924
Tax preferences	20,000
Itemized deductions including:	
Charitable contributions	7,500
Medical expenses (before AGI floor)	10,000
Mortgage interest on personal residence	10,000
State income taxes	5,000
Real estate taxes	8,000

a. What is the amount of Allen's AMT adjustments related to the itemized deductions?
b. What is Allen's AMT liability for the current year?

I14-46 *Self-Employment Tax.* In the current year, Amelia receives wages of $40,000 and net earnings from a small unincorporated business of $50,000. What is the amount of Amelia's self-employment tax and *for* AGI deduction relative to her self-employment tax?

I14-47 *Self-Employment Tax.* Arnie and Angela are married and file a joint return in the current year. Arnie is a partner in a public accounting firm. His share of the partnership's income in the current year is $40,000, and he receives guaranteed payments of $30,000. Angela receives wages of $50,000 from a large corporation. What is each taxpayer's self-employment tax amount?

I14-48 *Self-Employment Tax.* Anita, a single taxpayer, reports the following items for the current year:

Salary (subject to withholding)	$20,000
Director's fees	10,000
Consulting fees	10,000
Expenses related to consulting practice	(15,000)

a. What is the amount of Anita's self-employment tax?
b. How would your answer to Part a change if Anita's salary were instead $78,000?

I14-49 *Computation of Tax Credits.* Becky's tentative tax credits for the current year include the following:

Special Tax Computation Methods, Tax Credits, and Payment of Tax ▼ **Individuals 14-37**

Work opportunity credit	$ 1,000
Child and dependent care credit	960
Research credit	14,000
Business energy credit	600
Total	$16,560

Becky's regular tax liability before credits is $14,000. Assume that there is no alternative minimum tax liability.
a. What is the amount of allowable personal tax credits?
b. What is the amount of allowable business tax credits?
c. What treatment is accorded to the unused tax credits for the current year?

I14-50 *Child and Dependent Care Credit.* In each of the following independent situations, determine the amount of the child and dependent care tax credit. (Assume that both taxpayers are employed.)
a. Brad and Bonnie are married and file a joint return. Brad and Bonnie have earned income of $40,000 and $14,000, respectively. Their combined AGI is $52,000. They have two children ages 10 and 12 and employ a live-in nanny at an annual cost of $9,000.
b. Assume the same facts as in Part a, except that Brad and Bonnie employ Bonnie's mother as the live-in nanny. Bonnie's mother is not claimed as a dependent by her children.
c. Bruce is divorced and has two children ages 10 and 16. He has AGI and earned income of $27,000. Bruce incurs qualifying child care expenses of $8,000 during the year which were incurred equally for both children. Bruce's employer maintains an employee dependent care assistance program. $1,000 was paid to Bruce from this program and excluded from Bruce's gross income.
d. Buddy and Candice are married and file a joint return. Their combined AGI is $50,000. Buddy earns $46,000, and Candice's salary from a part-time job is $4,000. They incur $5,000 of qualifying child care expenses for a day-care facility for their two children, ages 2 and 4.

I14-51 *Adoption Credit.* Brad and Valerie decided to adopt a child and contacted an adoption agency in August 2000. After extensive interviews and other requirements (such as financial status, etc.), Brad and Valerie were approved as eligible parents to adopt a child. The agency indicated that it might take up to two years to find a proper match. In November, 2001, the adoption became final and Brad and Valerie adopted an infant daughter (not a special needs child). Below is a list of expenses that they incurred:

2000:	Agency fees (first installment)	$5,000
	Travel expenses for interviews, etc.	1,500
	Publications for prospective adoptive parents	300
	Legal fees connected with the adoption	1,000
	Kennel fees for dog while on adoption trips	250
2001:	Agency fees (final installment)	$3,000
	Travel expenses	400
	Court costs for adoption	200
	Kennel fees	100
	Nursery furniture (baby's room) and supplies	2,000

Brad and Valerie's AGI for 2000 was $70,000 and in 2001 was $90,000.
a. Compute Brad and Valerie's qualified adoption expenses for 2000 and 2001.
b. Compute Brad and Valerie's adoption credit. What year(s) may the credit be taken?
c. Would your answer to b. change if the adopted child was a special needs child?

I14-52 *HOPE Scholarship Credit and Lifetime Learning Credit.* John and Mary, a married couple who file a joint return, have two dependent children in college, Jeff and Brooke. Jeff attends Pepper College, a private, liberal arts college, and Brooke attends State U. During 2001, Jeff was a sophomore during the Spring Semester, 2001 and a junior during the Fall Semester, 2001. Brooke was a freshman during the Fall Semester, 2001 and was in high school during the Spring Semester, 2001. Below are the college expenses paid by John and Mary for Jeff and Brooke during 2001:

	Spring Semester, 2001 (Paid in January, 2001)		Fall Semester, 2001 (Paid in August, 2001)	
	Jeff	Brooke	Jeff	Brooke
Tuition	$4,500		$4,800	$1,200
Laboratory fees	500		500	0
Student activity fees	100		100	100
Books	400		350	400
Room and board	3,000		3,200	3,500

a. Compute any education credits that John and Mary may claim in 2001 assuming that neither Jeff nor Brooke receive any type of financial assistance and John and Mary's modified AGI is less than $80,000.
b. Would your answer in a. change if Jeff received an academic scholarship of $2,500 for each semester in 2001?
c. How would your answer in a. change if John and Mary's modified AGI for 2001 was $90,000?
d. How would your answer in a. change if Jeff was a junior during the Spring Semester, 2001 and a senior during the Fall Semester, 2001?

I14-53 *Tax Credit for the Elderly.* Caroline, age 66 and single, receives the following income items for the current year:

Social Security payments	$ 3,000
Fully taxable pension	4,000
Dividend and interest income	4,500
Total	$11,500

Caroline's tax liability (before credits) is $300 in the current year.
a. What is Caroline's tentative tax credit for the elderly (before the tax liability limitation is applied) in the current year?
b. What is the amount of Caroline's allowable tax credit for the elderly in the current year?

I14-54 *Business Tax Credit Carrybacks and Carryovers.* In 2001, Large Corporation, which was incorporated in 1995, has an unused general business tax credit of $40,000 in 1998. The following schedule shows the amount of business tax credits earned and used for the period 1995–2001:

	Credits Earned During the Year	Credit Limitation for the Carryback or Carryover Year
1995	$40,000	$40,000
1996	30,000	40,000
1997	25,000	25,000
1998	60,000	20,000
1999	20,000	22,000
2000	15,000	20,000
2001	15,000	15,000

The excess credits for 1998 were carried back to 1996.
a. How much of the unused 1998 credit is used in the carryback period?
b. What is the amount of the unused credit that is carried foward to 1999? In what years are the credits used?
c. What is the amount of the general business credit carryovers to 2002? Identify the tax years in which the credit carryovers are earned.

I14-55 *Foreign Tax Credit.* Laser Corporation, a U.S. corporation, has a foreign office that conducts business in France. Laser pays foreign taxes of $40,000 on foreign-source taxable income of $100,000. Its U.S.-source taxable income is $200,000, total U.S. taxable income of $300,000, and the total U.S. tax liability (before reductions for the foreign tax credit) is $100,250. What is Laser's foreign tax credit? What is Laser's foreign tax credit carryback or carryover?

I14-56 *Work Opportunity Credit.* Last Corporation hires two economically disadvantaged youths (qualified for the work opportunity credit) in August of the current year. Each employee receives $8,000 of wages in the current year. Salaries and wages paid to other

employees in the current year are $50,000. Last Corporation has a regular tax liability of $50,000 in the current year before deducting its tax credits assuming the appropriate deduction is claimed for the youths' salaries. Its tentative minimum tax is $10,000. Business tax credits other than the work opportunity credit amount to $50,000 in the current year.
a. What is Last Corporation's tentative work opportunity credit (before limitations) in the current year?
b. What is Last Corporation's total general business credit that is used in the current year? What amount is available for carryover or carryback?
c. What is Last Corporation's deduction for salaries and wages paid to the two youths?

I14-57 *Empowerment Zone Employment Credit.* Acorn Corporation operates its business in an Empowerment Zone and John, one of its employees, lives in the zone. In the current year John received $12,000 in wages. In addition, Acorn incurred $4,000 of training expenses related to John's employment.
a. What is Acorn Corporation's tentative Empowerment Zone credit (before any limitations on the general business credit are considered)?
b. What is Acorn Corporation's deduction for wages paid to John?

I14-58 *Rehabilitation Tax Credit.* Bob acquires a certified historic structure in the current year to be used as an office for his business. He pays $20,000 for the building (exclusive of the land) and spends $40,000 for renovation costs.
a. What is the rehabilitation tax credit (before limitations)?
b. What depreciation method(s) must be used for the property?
c. What is the basis of the building for MACRS depreciation purposes?

I14-59 *Earned Income Credit.* Carolyn has a dependent child, age 6, who lived with her for the entire year. She has earned income of $12,000 of wages and $4,000 of alimony in the current year. Her AGI is $16,000.
a. What is Carolyn's tentative earned income credit (before the phase-out reduction is applied)?
b. What is Carolyn's allowable earned income credit?
c. If Carolyn has no income tax liability (before the earned income credit is subtracted), is she entitled to a tax refund in the current year?

I14-60 *Earned Income Credit.* Jose is single with no qualifying children. He has $7,800 of wages during the current year and is otherwise eligible for the earned income credit. Jose has $200 of interest income and no *for* AGI deductions. His AGI is $8,000.
a. What is Jose's tentative earned income credit before the phase-out reduction is applied?
b. What is Jose's allowable earned income credit?
c. If Jose has no income tax liability (before the earned income credit is subtracted), is he entitled to a refund for the current year?
d. Would your answer to b. change if Jose had dividend and interest income of $2,500 during the taxable year?

I14-61 *Penalties for Nonpayment of Withholding and FICA Taxes.* Lake Corporation has some severe cash-flow problems. You are the company's financial and tax consultant. The treasurer of the company has informed you that the company has failed to make FICA and federal income tax withholding payments for both the employer and employee contributions to the IRS for a period of approximately six months.
a. What advice can you give to the company treasurer regarding the nonpayment of taxes?
b. Can the liability for payment of the taxes extend to parties other than the corporation? Explain.

I14-62 *Exemptions from Withholding.* Which of the following categories of individuals or income are exempt from the federal withholding tax requirements?
a. Domestic servants
b. Independent contractors
c. Newspaper carriers over age 18
d. Bonuses
e. Commissions
f. Vacation pay
g. Tips under $20 per month from a single employer
h. Nontaxable fringe benefits
i. Pensions

I14-63 *Withholding Exemptions.* Barry is a college student who is employed as a waiter during the summer. He earns approximately $1,500 during the summer and estimates that he will not be required to file a tax return and will have no federal income tax liability. Last year, however, he made $6,000 and was required to file a return and pay $400 in taxes. Barry is single and is supported by his parents. He has no dependents and does not have any other sources of income or deductions.
  a. Can Barry claim an exempt status on Form W-4 for withholding purposes?
  b. Can Barry claim more than one exemption on Form W-4 (e.g., additional withholding allowances or the standard deduction allowance) to minimize the amount withheld? Explain.

I14-64 *Witholding Allowances.* Bart's spouse is not employed. They plan to file a joint return. Bart obtains a new job and is asked to fill out a Form W-4. His monthly gross earnings will be $3,000. Bart, who has four dependent children, can claim three additional withholding allowances because he is obligated to pay substantial alimony to his ex-wife.
  a. What is the correct number of withholding allowances that he may claim on Form W-4?
  b. What is the amount of federal income tax to be withheld using the wage bracket tables (see withholding table on page T-15)?
  c. What disclosure procedures must Bart's employer follow if Bart claims more than ten allowances?

I14-65 *Estimated Tax Requirements.* Anna does not make quarterly estimated tax payments even though she has substantial amounts of income that are not subject to withholding. In 2000, Anna's tax liability was $18,000. This year, in 2001, Anna's actual tax liability is $30,000, although only $18,200 was withheld from her salary. Anna's AGI for 2000 was not over $150,000.
  a. Is Anna subject to the underpayment penalty? Why?
  b. If Anna's withholdings were only $15,000, would she be subject to the underpayment penalty? Why?
  c. If Anna is subject to an underpayment penalty, can she deduct this amount as interest? Explain.

I14-66 *Estimated Tax Underpayment Penalty.* Anne's estimated tax payments for 2001 are $14,000 and her withholdings amount to $12,000. Anne's actual tax liability for 2000 and 2001 are $25,000 and $30,000, respectively. Her income is earned evenly throughout the current year. Anne's AGI for 2000 was $160,000. Is Anne subject to the underpayment penalty? Explain.

COMPREHENSIVE PROBLEM

I14-67 Chuck's tax file reveals the following information for 2001:

Salary		$55,000
Net income from consulting (before deducting one-half of self-employment taxes paid)		40,000
Net loss from an unincorporated business		(10,000)
Itemized deductions:		
State and local taxes	$6,000	
Mortgage interest on personal residence	8,000	
Contributions	2,000	
General business tax credits		1,000
Estimated taxes paid ($2,000) and withholdings (10,584) from salary		12,584
Actual income tax liability for 2000		9,500
AGI for 2000		70,000
Personal and dependency exemptions		1
Filing status: single		

  a. Is Chuck subject to the self-employment tax? If so, what are the self-employment tax liability and the amount of self-employment taxes that may be deducted on Chuck's income tax return?
  b. Compute Chuck's taxable income for 2001, his total tax liability, and the balance due or refund when the return is filed.
  c. Is Chuck subject to the estimated income tax underpayment penalty? Explain.

TAX FORM/RETURN PREPARATION PROBLEMS

I14-68 Warren (SSN 123-45-6789) and Alice (SSN 987-65-4321) Williams have the following tax credits for 2000:

General business credits	$12,140
Child and dependent care credit	960
Total	$13,100

Warren and Alice Williams have two children, 5 and 7, and incur $5,000 of qualifying child care expenses ($2,500 for day care and $2,500 for a nurse). Warren had earned income of $50,000; Alice's earned income was $25,000 and their AGI is $116,988. Their itemized deductions are $14,200, taxable income is $91,588, and regular tax liability (before credits) is $19,944. Disregard any limitations that might be imposed by the tentative minimum tax.

Complete Form 2441, Form 3800 and the Tax Credits section on page 2 of Form 1040.

I14-69 Harold Milton (SSN 574-45-5477) is single and had the following income and deductions for 2000:

Salary	$177,000	State income taxes	18,000
Interest income	12,000	Mortgage interest expense	
Dividend income	3,000	on residence	19,000
IRA contribution	2,000	Interest expense on car loan	3,000
Tax-exempt interest		Real estate taxes	
from private activity		on residence	2,000
bonds issued in 1990	24,000	Miscellaneous deductions	
Charitable contributions	27,000	(before the 2% AGI floor)	7,000
		Income taxes withheld	20,000
		Estimated tax payments	
		($2,500 per quarter)	10,000

Complete Form 1040, Schedule A, Form 6251 and Form 2210. Milton had AGI in 1999 of $200,000 and his 1999 income tax liability was $46,000. (Note: Milton is eligible to use the Short Method on Form 2210)

CASE STUDY PROBLEMS

I14-70 Barbara was divorced in 1998. However, the final property settlement and determination of alimony payments was not made until February, 2001 because of extended litigation. Barbara received a $20,000 payment of back alimony in March 2001 and will receive monthly alimony payments of $2,000 for the period April through December, 2001. In 2000, Barbara's income consisted of $15,000 salary and $2,000 of taxable interest income. She uses the standard deduction and has no dependents. In 2000, Barbara's tax liability was $1,900. She expects to continue working at an annual salary of $15,000 and have $2,000 of interest income in 2001. Her monthly alimony payments of $2,000 are also expected to continue for an indefinite period.

In early April 2001 Barbara requests your advice regarding the payment of quarterly estimated taxes for 2001. Prepare a memo to your client that discusses these requirements, including any possible penalties for not making quarterly payments and nontax issues such as cash-flow and investment income decisions.

I14-71 Chips-R-Us is a computer technology corporation that designs hardware and software for use in large businesses. The corporation regularly pays individuals to install programs and give advice to different companies that buy their software. In the current year, Simone, a computer expert, was sent to a customer of Chips-R-Us by the corporation to perform computer services. Simone is not a regular employee of the corporation and the corporation did not train Simone for the task. Simone keeps track of the time spent on the job at the customer and reports to the corporation, which pays Simone for her services. The corporation specifies the work to be done for their client. The corporation can also replace Simone with another individual if her work is not satisfactory. Chips-R-Us treats Simone as an independent contractor for employment tax purposes. In the current year the IRS challenges the corporation that it has failed to remit FICA taxes and income taxes that should have been withheld with respect to Simone's employment. Chips-R-Us refuses to pay the amount, stating that it is not required to do so because Simone is not an employee of the corporation. What will be the likely outcome of the IRS's decision concerning the status of Simone as an employee or independent contractor? Who may be liable for payment of the employment taxes, interest, and penalties to the government? What ethical responsibilities should be followed in the remittance of taxes on behalf of an employee?

TAX RESEARCH PROBLEM

I14-72 Lean Corporation was incorporated in 1981 by Bruce Smith, who has served as an officer and member of the Board of Directors. Carl Jones has served as the secretary-treasurer of the company as a convenience to his friend Bruce Smith. He acted as a part-time bookkeeper but did not run the everyday business affairs and paid only the bills he was instructed to pay. Carl was an authorized signatory for the corporate bank accounts but had no final control over expenditures.

Beginning in the last quarter of 2000, the company failed to pay all of the taxes withheld from employees and the employer's share of FICA taxes to the IRS. Despite this delinquency, the corporation continued to pay other creditors, including its employees, in preference to the IRS.

In January, 2001, Lean Corporation entered into an installment agreement with the IRS to keep current on its withholding taxes and to make payments on the past due balance until paid in full. The company subsequently defaulted on the agreement in April, 2001. During this period, Bruce Smith was serving as chief financial officer and was a member of the Board of Directors. He had the authority to make policy decisions. He was responsible for negotiating the installment agreement with the IRS and the decision to default on the agreement.

Who is liable for the penalty for the nonpayment of the payroll tax withholdings?

A partial list of research sources is

- Sec. 6672
- *Ernest W. Carlson v. U.S.*, 67 AFTR 2d 91-1104, 91-1 USTC ¶50,262 (D.C. UT, 1991)

CHAPTER 15

TAX RESEARCH

LEARNING OBJECTIVES
After studying this chapter, you should be able to

1. Describe the steps in the tax research process
2. Explain how the facts affect the tax consequences
3. Identify the sources of tax law and understand the authoritative value of each
4. Use tax services to research an issue
5. Use a citator to assess authorities
6. Understand the basics of computerized tax research
7. Understand the guidelines to which CPAs in tax practice should adhere
8. Prepare work papers and communications to clients

CHAPTER OUTLINE

Overview of Tax Research...15-2
Steps in the Tax Research Process...15-3
Importance of the Facts to the Tax Consequences...15-5
The Sources of Tax Law...15-7
Tax Services...15-25
Citators...15-28
Computers as a Research Tool...15-34
Statements on Responsibilities in Tax Practice...15-34
Sample Work Papers and Client Letter...15-38

This chapter introduces the reader to the tax research process. Its major focus is the sources of the tax law (i.e., the Internal Revenue Code and other tax authorities) and the relative weights given to each source. The chapter describes the steps in the tax research process and places particular emphasis on the importance of the facts to the tax consequences. The chapter also describes frequently used tax services and computer-based tax research resources and how to use a citator.

The end product of the tax research process—written communication of the results in a client letter—also is discussed. This text uses a hypothetical set of facts to provide a comprehensive illustration of the research process. Sample work papers demonstrating how to document the results of the research efforts are included in Appendix A. In addition, a supplemental explanation of the computerized tax research process and available resources is available for download at *www.prenhall.com/phtax*. The text also discusses the American Institute of Certified Public Accountants' (AICPA's) *Statements on Standards for Tax Services*, which provide guidance for CPAs in tax practice. These statements are reproduced in Appendix E.

OVERVIEW OF TAX RESEARCH

Tax research is the process of solving a tax-related problem by applying tax law to a specific set of facts. Sometimes this activity involves researching several issues. In addition, tax research often is conducted to determine tax policy. For example, policy-oriented research would determine the extent (if any) to which the amount contributed to charitable organizations would likely change if such contributions were no longer deductible. This type of tax research usually is performed by economists to assess the effects of government actions.

Tax research also can be conducted to determine the tax consequences to a particular taxpayer of specific transactions. For example, client-oriented research would determine whether Smith Corporation could deduct a particular expenditure as a trade or business expense. This type of research generally is conducted by accounting and law firms for the benefit of their clients. This text considers only the latter type of research.

Client-oriented tax research is performed in one of two contexts:

ADDITIONAL COMMENT
Closed-fact situations allow the tax advisor the least amount of flexibility. Because the facts are already established, the tax advisor must develop the best solution possible within certain predetermined constraints.

1. **Closed-fact or tax compliance situations:** The client contacts the tax advisor after a transaction has occurred or a question arises while the tax return preparer is preparing the client's tax return. In such situations, the tax consequences can be costly because the facts cannot be modified to obtain more favorable results.

EXAMPLE I15-1 ▶ Tom informs Carol, his tax advisor, that on November 4 of the current year, he sold land held as an investment for $500,000 cash. His basis in the land was $50,000. On November 9, Tom reinvested the sales proceeds in another plot of investment land costing $500,000. This is a closed-fact situation. Tom wants to know the amount and the character of the gain (if any) he must recognize. Because Tom solicits the tax advisor's advice after the sale and reinvestment occur, the opportunity for tax planning is limited. For example, the opportunity to defer taxes by using a like-kind exchange or an installment sale has been lost. ◀

ADDITIONAL COMMENT
Open-fact or tax-planning situations give a tax advisor flexibility to structure transactions to accomplish the client's objectives. In this type of situation, a creative tax advisor can save taxpayers dollars through effective tax planning.

2. **Open-fact or tax-planning situations:** Before structuring or concluding a transaction, the client contacts the tax advisor to discuss tax planning opportunities. Tax-planning situations generally are more difficult and challenging because the tax advisor must bear in mind the client's tax and nontax objectives. Most clients will not be interested in a transaction that minimizes their taxes if it is inconsistent with their nontax objectives.

EXAMPLE I15-2 ▶ Diane seeks advice from Carol, her tax advisor, about how to minimize her estate taxes while passing the the greatest value of property to her descendants. Diane is a widow with three children and five grandchildren and at present owns property valued at $10 million. This is an open-fact situation. Carol could advise Diane to leave all but a few hundred thousand dollars of her property to a charitable organization so that her estate would owe no estate taxes. Although this recommendation would minimize Diane's estate taxes, Diane is likely to reject it because she wants her children or grandchildren to be her primary beneficiaries. Thus, reducing estate taxes to zero is inconsistent with her objective of allowing her descendants to receive as much after-tax wealth as possible. ◀

When conducting research in a tax-planning context, the tax professional should keep a number of points in mind. First, the objective is not to minimize taxes per se but rather to maximize the after-tax return. For example, if the federal income tax rate is a constant 40%, an investor should not buy a tax-exempt bond yielding 5% when he or she could buy a corporate bond of equal risk that yields 9% before tax and 5.4% after tax. This is the case even though his or her explicit taxes (actual tax liability) would be minimized by investing in the tax-exempt bond.[1] Second, taxpayers do not engage in unilateral transactions; thus, the tax ramifications for all parties to the transaction are relevant. For example, in the executive compensation context, employees may prefer to receive incentive stock options (because income recognition is postponed until they sell the stock), but the employer may prefer to grant a different type of option (because he or she is entitled to no tax deduction with respect to incentive stock options). Thus, the employer might grant a different number of options if it uses one type of stock option as compensation versus another. Third, taxes are but one cost of doing business. In deciding where to locate a manufacturing plant, for example, factors more important to some businesses than the amount of state and local taxes paid might be the proximity to raw materials, good transportation systems, the cost of labor, the quantity of skilled labor available, and the quality of life in the area. Fourth, the time for tax planning is not restricted to the beginning date of an investment, contract, or other arrangement. Instead, the time extends throughout the life of the activity. As tax rules change or as business and economic environments change, the tax advisor needs to reevaluate whether the taxpayer should hold on to an investment and must consider the transaction costs of making changes.

One final note: the tax advisor should always bear in mind the financial accounting implications of proposed transactions. An answer that may be desirable from a tax perspective may not always be desirable from a financial accounting perspective. Though interrelated, the two fields of accounting have different orientations and different objectives. Tax accounting is oriented primarily to the Internal Revenue Service (IRS). Its objectives include calculating, reporting, and predicting one's tax liability according to legal principles. Financial accounting is oriented primarily to stockholders, creditors, managers, and employees. Its objectives include determining, reporting, and predicting a business's financial position and operating results according to Generally Accepted Accounting Principles. Success in any tax practice, especially at the managerial level, requires consideration of both sets of objectives and orientations.

ADDITIONAL COMMENT

It is important to consider nontax objectives as well as tax objectives. In many situations, the nontax considerations outweigh the tax considerations. Thus, the plan eventually adopted by a taxpayer may not always be the best when viewed strictly from a tax perspective.

STEPS IN THE TAX RESEARCH PROCESS

OBJECTIVE 1

Describe the steps in the tax research process

In both open- and closed-fact situations, the tax research process involves six basic steps:

1. Determine the facts.
2. Identify the issues (questions).
3. Locate the applicable authorities.
4. Evaluate the authorities and choose those to follow where the authorities conflict.
5. Analyze the facts in terms of the applicable authorities.
6. Communicate conclusions and recommendations to the client.

---

[1] For an excellent discussion of explicit and implicit taxes and tax planning see Myron S. Scholes, Mark A. Wolfson, Merle Erickson, Edward L. Maydew, and Terry Shevlin, *Taxes and Business Strategy,* Second Edition (Upper Saddle River, NJ: Prentice Hall Inc, 2001). See also Chapter I18 of the *Individuals* volume. An example of an implicit tax is the excess of the before-tax earnings on a taxable bond over the risk-adjusted before-tax earnings on a tax-favored investment (e.g., a municipal bond).

FIGURE I15-1 ▶ STEPS IN THE TAX RESEARCH PROCESS

Although the above outline suggests a lock-step procedure, the tax research process often is circular. That is, it does not always proceed step-by-step. Figure I15-1 illustrates a more accurate process, and Appendix A provides a comprehensive example of this process.

In a closed-fact situation, the facts have already occurred, and the tax advisor's task is to analyze them to determine the appropriate tax treatment. In an open-fact situation, by contrast, the facts have not yet occurred, and the tax advisor's task is to plan for them or shape them so as to produce a favorable tax result. The tax advisor performs the latter task by reviewing the relevant legal authorities, particularly court cases and IRS rulings, all the while taking into consideration the facts of those cases or rulings that produced favorable results compared with those that produced unfavorable results. For example, if a client wants to realize an ordinary loss (as opposed to a capital gain) from the sale of several plots of land, the tax advisor might consult cases involving similar land sales. The advisor might attempt to distinguish the facts of those cases in which the taxpayer realized an ordinary loss from the facts of those cases in which the taxpayer realized a capital gain. The advisor then might structure the transaction accordingly.

Often, the research pertains to a gray area (i.e., it involves a question for which no clearcut, unequivocally correct answer exists). In such situations, probing a related issue might lead to a solution pertinent to the central question. For example, in researching whether the taxpayer may deduct a loss as ordinary instead of capital, the tax advisor might research the related issue of whether the presence of an investment motive precludes classifying a loss as ordinary. The solution to the latter issue may be relevant to the question of whether the taxpayer may deduct the loss as ordinary.

Identifying the issue(s) to be researched often is the most difficult step in the tax research process. In some instances, the client defines the issue(s) for the tax advisor, such as where the client asks, "May I deduct the costs of a winter trip to Florida recommended by my physician?" In other instances, the tax advisor, after reviewing the documents submitted to him or her by the client, defines the issue(s) himself or herself. The ability to do so presupposes a firm grounding in tax law.[2]

ADDITIONAL COMMENT

The steps of tax research provide an excellent format for a written tax communication. For example, a good format for a client memo includes (1) statement of facts, (2) list of issues, (3) discussion of relevant authority, (4) analysis, and (5) recommendations to the client of appropriate actions based on the research results.

TYPICAL MISCONCEPTION

Many taxpayers think the tax law is all black and white. However, most tax research deals with gray areas. Ultimately, when confronted with tough issues, the ability to develop strategies that favor the taxpayer and then to find relevant authority to support those strategies will make a successful tax advisor.

---

[2] Often, in an employment context, supervisors indicate the questions to be researched and the authorities that might be relevant to the tax consequences.

Once the tax advisor locates the applicable legal authorities, he or she might have to turn to the client for additional information. Example I15-3 illustrates the point. The example assumes that all relevant tax authorities are in agreement.

EXAMPLE I15-3 ▶ Mark calls his tax advisor, Al, and states that (1) he incurred a loss on renting his beach cottage during the current year and (2) he wonders whether he may deduct the loss. He also states that he, his wife, and their minor child occupied the cottage only eight days during the current year.

This is the first time Al has dealt with the Sec. 280A vacation home rules. On reading Sec. 280A, Al learned that a loss is *not* deductible if the taxpayer used the cottage as a residence for personal purposes for longer than the greater of (1) 14 days or (2) 10% of the number of days the unit was rented at a fair rental value. He also learned that the property is *deemed* to be used by the taxpayer for personal purposes on any days on which it is used by any member of his or her family (as defined in Sec. 267(c)(4)). The Sec. 267(c)(4) definition of family members includes brothers, sisters, spouse, ancestors, or lineal descendants (i.e., children and grandchildren).

Mark's eight-day use is not long enough to make the rental loss nondeductible. However, Al must inquire about the number of days, if any, Mark's brothers, sisters, or parents used the property. (He already has information about use by Mark, his spouse, and his lineal descendants.) In addition, Al must find out how many days the cottage was rented to other persons at a fair rental value. On obtaining such additional facts, Al proceeds to determine how to calculate the deductible expenses. Al then reaches his conclusion concerning the deductible loss, if any, and communicates it to Mark. This example assumes the passive activity and at-risk rules restricting a taxpayer's ability to deduct losses from real estate activities will not pose a problem for Mark. (See Chapter I8 of *Prentice Hall's Federal Taxation: Individuals* for a comprehensive discussion of these topics.) ◀

Many firms require that a researcher's conclusions be communicated to the client in writing. Members or employees of such firms can answer questions orally, but their oral conclusions must be followed up with a written communication. According to the AICPA's *Statements on Standards for Tax Services* (reproduced in Appendix E),

> Although oral advice may serve a client's needs appropriately in routine matters or in well-defined areas, written communications are recommended in important, unusual, or complicated transactions. The member may use judgment about whether, subsequently, to document oral advice in writing.[3]

IMPORTANCE OF THE FACTS TO THE TAX CONSEQUENCES

OBJECTIVE 2

Explain how the facts affect the tax consequences

Many terms and phrases used in the Internal Revenue Code (IRC) and other tax authorities are vague or ambiguous. Many of their provisions conflict or are difficult to reconcile, posing to the researcher the dilemma of deciding which rules are applicable and which tax results are proper. For example, a condition that a taxpayer must satisfy to claim another person as a dependent is to provide more than half of such person's support.[4] Neither the IRC nor the Treasury Regulations define "support." Consequently, if the taxpayer purchased a used automobile costing $5,000 for an elderly parent whose only source of income is $4,800 in Social Security benefits, the question of whether the expenditure constitutes support would arise. The tax advisor would have to consult court opinions, revenue rulings, and other IRS pronouncements to ascertain the legal meaning of the term "support."

In other instances, the legal language is quite clear, but a question arises as to whether the taxpayer's transaction conforms to the specific pattern of facts necessary to obtain a particular tax result. Ultimately, the peculiar facts of a transaction or event determine its tax consequences. A change in the facts can significantly change the consequences. Consider the following illustrations:

---

[3] AICPA, *Statement on Standards for Tax Services*, No. 8, "Form and Content of Advice to Clients," 2000, Para. 6.

[4] Sec. 152(a).

Illustration One

Facts: A holds stock, a capital asset, that he purchased two years ago at a cost of $1,000. He sells the stock to B for $920. What are the tax consequences to A?
Result: Under Sec. 1001, A realizes an $80 capital loss. He recognizes this loss in the current year. A must offset the loss against any capital gains recognized during the year. Any excess loss is deductible from ordinary income up to a $3,000 limit.
Change of Facts: A is B's son.
New Result: Under Sec. 267, A and B are related parties. Therefore, A may not recognize the realized loss. However, B may use the loss if she subsequently sells the stock at a gain.

Illustration Two

Facts: C donates ten acres of land that she purchased two years ago for $10,000 to State University. The fair market value (FMV) of the land on the date of the donation is $25,000. C's adjusted gross income is $100,000. What is C's charitable contribution deduction?
Result: Under Sec. 170, C is entitled to a $25,000 charitable contribution deduction (i.e., the FMV of the property unreduced by the unrealized long-term gain).
Change of Facts: C purchased the land 11 months ago.
New Result: Under the same IRC provision, C is entitled to only a $10,000 charitable contribution deduction (i.e., the FMV of the property reduced by the unrealized short-term gain).

Illustration Three

Facts: Acquiring Corporation pays Target Corporation's shareholders one million shares of Acquiring voting stock. In return, Target's shareholders tender 98% of their Target voting stock. The acquisition is for a bona fide business purpose. Acquiring continues Target's business. What are the tax consequences of the exchange to Target's shareholders?
Result: Under Sec. 368(a)(1)(B), Target's shareholders are not taxed on the exchange, which is solely for Acquiring voting stock.
Change of Facts: Acquiring purchases the remaining 2% of Target's shares with cash as part of the same transaction.
New Result: Under the same IRC provision, Target's shareholders are now taxed on the exchange, which is not solely for Acquiring voting stock.

ABILITY TO DESIGN A FACTUAL SITUATION FAVORING THE TAXPAYER

TYPICAL MISCONCEPTION

Many taxpayers believe tax practitioners spend most of their time preparing tax returns. In reality, providing tax advice that accomplishes the taxpayer's objectives is one of the most important responsibilities of a tax advisor. This latter activity is tax consulting as compared to tax compliance.

Based his or her research, a tax advisor might recommend to a taxpayer how to structure a transaction or plan an event so as to increase the likelihood that related expenses will be deductible. For example, suppose a taxpayer is given a temporary task in a location (City Y) different from the location (City X) of his or her permanent employment. Suppose also that the taxpayer wants to deduct the meal and lodging expenses incurred in City Y as well as the cost of transportation thereto. To do so, the taxpayer must establish that City X is his or her tax home and that he or she temporarily works in City Y. (Section 162 provides that a taxpayer may deduct travel expenses while "away from home" on business. A taxpayer is deemed to be "away from home" if his or her employment at the new location does not exceed one year, i.e., it is "temporary.") Suppose the taxpayer wants to know the tax consequences of his or her working in City Y for ten months and then, within that ten-month period, finding permanent employment in City Y. What can tax research reveal?

Tax research is likely to uncover an IRS ruling that states that, in such circumstances, the employment will be deemed to be temporary until the date on which the realistic expectation about the temporary nature of the assignment changes.[5] After this date, the employment will be deemed to be permanent, and travel expenses relating to it will be nondeductible. Based on this finding, the tax advisor might advise the taxpayer to postpone his or her permanent job search in City Y until the end of the ten-month period and simply treat his or her assignment as temporary. So doing would lengthen the period of time during which he or she is deemed to be "away from home" on business and thus increase the amount of meal, lodging, and transportation costs deductible as travel expenses.

---

[5] Rev. Rul., 1993-2 C.B. 71.

THE SOURCES OF TAX LAW

OBJECTIVE 3

Identify the sources of tax law and understand the authoritative value of each

The language of the IRC is general; that is, it addresses in generic terms the tax treatment of broad categories of transactions and events. The reason for this approach is that Congress can neither foresee nor provide for every detailed transaction or event. Even if it could, doing so would render the statute narrow in scope and inflexible in application. Because of this generality, interpretations of the IRC—both administrative and judicial—are necessary. Administrative interpretations are found in Treasury Regulations, revenue rulings, and revenue procedures. Judicial interpretations are presented in court opinions. The term *tax law* as used by most tax advisors encompasses administrative and judicial interpretations in addition to the IRC. It also includes committee reports issued by the Congressional committees involved in the legislative process.

THE LEGISLATIVE PROCESS

All tax legislation begins in the House of Representatives as a bill. The committee responsible for initiating statutory changes dealing with taxation is the Ways and Means Committee. After the Ways and Means Committee approves the bill, it submits it to the floor of the House for consideration by the full membership. Legislation approved by a majority vote in the House then goes to the Senate, where it is considered by the Senate Finance Committee. The bill moves from the Finance Committee to the full Senate. Upon being approved by the Senate, the bill goes to the President for approval or veto, provided the House and Senate versions of the bill are in complete agreement. If the President signs the bill, it becomes law. If the President vetoes the bill, Congress can override the veto by a vote of at least two-thirds of the members of each chamber.

Often, the House and Senate versions are not in agreement. When this disagreement occurs, (1) the bill goes to a conference committee[6] consisting of members of each chamber, (2) the conference committee resolves the differences, and (3) a compromise version of the bill goes back to the House and Senate for approval. For example, in 1998 the House and Senate disagreed over what the taxpayer must do to shift the burden of proof to the IRS. The House proposed that the taxpayer assert a "reasonable dispute" regarding a taxable item. The Senate proposed that the taxpayer introduce "credible evidence" regarding the item. A conference committee was appointed to resolve the differences. This committee ultimately adopted the Senate proposal, which was later approved by both chambers.

Before drafting statutory changes, both the House and the Senate hold hearings in which interested parties testify. Often the Secretary of the Treasury or another Treasury Department official offers extensive testimony. Generally, persons testifying express their opinions concerning provisions that should or should not be enacted. The U.S. Government Printing Office publishes the statements made at the hearings in Congressional documents.

Most major legislation also is accompanied by committee reports. These reports, published by the U.S. Government Printing Office as separate publications and as part of the *Cumulative Bulletin,* explain Congress's purpose in drafting legislation.[7] Because committee reports provide clues as to Congressional intent, they can be valuable aids in interpreting the IRC, especially where the statutory language in question has not been interpreted by the courts.

ADDITIONAL COMMENT

Committee reports can be helpful in interpreting new legislation because they indicate the intent of Congress. With the proliferation of tax legislation, committee reports have become especially important because the Treasury Department often is unable to draft the needed regulations in a timely manner.

EXAMPLE I15-4 ▶ As mentioned earlier, in 1998 Congress passed legislation concerning shifting the burden of proof to the IRS. This legislation was codified in Sec. 7491. The question arises as to what constitutes "credible evidence." (Remember, the taxpayer must introduce "credible evidence" to shift the burden of proof to the IRS). Section 7491 does not define the term. Because the provision is relatively new, few courts have had an opportunity to interpret what "credible evidence" means. In the absence of relevant statutory or judicial authority, the researcher might

---

[6] The size of a conference committee can vary. It is made up of an equal number of members from the House and the Senate.

[7] The *Cumulative Bulletin* is described in the discussion of revenue rulings on page I15-12.

look to the committee reports to ascertain what Congress intended by the term. Senate Report No. 105-174 states that "credible evidence" means evidence of a quality, which, "after critical analysis, the court would find sufficient upon which to base a decision on the issue if no contrary evidence were submitted."[8] This language suggests that Congress intended the term to mean evidence of a kind sufficient to withstand judicial scrutiny. Such a meaning should be regarded as authoritative in the absence of other authority. ◀

THE INTERNAL REVENUE CODE

The IRC, which comprises Title 26 of the United States Code, is the foundation of all tax law. First codified (i.e., organized into a single compilation of revenue statutes) in 1939, the tax law was recodified in 1954. The IRC was known as the Internal Revenue Code of 1954 until 1986, when its name was changed to the Internal Revenue Code of 1986. Whenever changes to the IRC are approved, the old language is deleted and new language added. Thus, the IRC is organized as an integrated document, and a researcher does not have to read through the applicable parts of all previous tax bills to find the current version of the law.

The IRC contains provisions dealing with income taxes, estate and gift taxes, employment taxes, alcohol and tobacco taxes, and other excise taxes. Organizationally, the IRC is subdivided into subtitles, chapters, subchapters, parts, subparts, sections, subsections, paragraphs, subparagraphs, and clauses. Subtitle A contains rules concerning income taxes, and Subtitle B deals with estate and gift taxes. A set of provisions concerned with one general area constitutes a subchapter. For example, the topics of corporate distributions and adjustments appear in Subchapter C, and topics concerning partners and partnerships appear in Subchapter K. Figure I15-2 presents the organizational scheme of the IRC.

A section is the organizational category to which tax advisors most often refer. For example, they speak of "Sec. 351 transactions," "Sec. 306 stock," and "Sec. 1231 gains and losses." Although a tax advisor need not know all the IRC sections, paragraphs, and parts, he or she must be familiar with the IRC's organizational scheme to read and interpret it correctly. The language of the IRC is replete with cross-references to titles, paragraphs, subparagraphs, and so on.

EXAMPLE I15-5 ▶ Section 7701, a definitional section, begins, "When used in this title . . ." and then provides a series of definitions. Thus, a definition in Sec. 7701 applies for all of Title 26; that is, it applies for purposes of the income tax, estate and gift tax, excise tax, and so on. ◀

EXAMPLE I15-6 ▶ Section 302(b)(3) allows taxpayers whose stock holdings are completely terminated in a redemption (a corporation's purchase of its stock from one of its shareholders) to receive capital gain treatment on the excess of the redemption proceeds over the stock's basis instead of ordinary income treatment on the entire proceeds. Section 302(c)(2)(A) states, "In the case of a distribution described in subsection (b)(3), section 318(a)(1) shall not apply if. . . ." Further, Sec. 302(c)(2)(C)(i) indicates "Subparagraph (A) shall not apply to a distribution to any entity unless. . . ." Thus, in determining whether a taxpayer will receive capital gain treatment for a stock redemption transaction, a tax advisor must be able to locate and interpret various cross-referenced IRC sections, subsections, paragraphs, subparagraphs, and clauses. ◀

TREASURY REGULATIONS

The Treasury Department issues regulations that expound upon the IRC. Treasury Regulations often contain examples with computations that provide valuable assistance in understanding the statutory language.[9]

Because of frequent statutory changes, the Treasury Department does not always update the regulations in a timely manner. Consequently, when consulting a regulation, a tax advisor should check its introductory or end note to determine when the regulation was adopted. If the regulation was adopted before the most recent revision of the applica-

> **ADDITIONAL COMMENT**
> According to Sheldon S. Cohen, in *The Wall Street Journal's* weekly tax column, a bound volume of the Internal Revenue Code in 1952 measured three-fourths of an inch thick. Treasury Regulations could fit in one bound volume measuring one-half of an inch thick. In 2000, a bound volume of the Internal Revenue Code measured four and one-half inches thick, and Treasury Regulations fit into six bound volumes measuring nine and three-quarters inches thick.

---

[8] S. Rept. No. 105-174, 105th Cong., 1st Sess. (unpaginated) (1998).
[9] Treasury Regulations are formulated on the basis of Treasury Decisions (T.D.s) The numbers of the Treasury Decisions that form the basis of a Treasury Regulation usually are found in the notes at the end of the regulation.

> **Overall Scheme**
>
> Title 26. All matters concerned with taxation
>
> Subtitle A. Income taxes
>
> Chapter 1. Normal taxes and surtaxes
>
> Subchapter A. Determination of tax liability
>
> Part I. Tax on individuals
>
> Sec. 1. Tax imposed
>
> **Scheme for Sections, Subsections, etc.**
>
> Sec. 165 (h) (2) (A) (i) and (ii)
>
> Section | Paragraph | Clauses
> Subsection | Subparagraph

FIGURE I15-2 ▶ ORGANIZATIONAL SCHEME OF THE INTERNAL REVENUE CODE

ble IRC section, the regulation should be applied with the understanding that it does not reflect this revision. Thus, for example, one would have to substitute a revised dollar amount stated in the IRC for an out-of-date amount stated in the regulation.

PROPOSED, TEMPORARY, AND FINAL REGULATIONS. Generally, Treasury Regulations are first issued to the public in proposed form. The public is given the opportunity to comment on them and suggest changes. Individuals most likely to comment are tax accountants and tax attorneys. Organizations such as the American Bar Association, the Tax Division of the AICPA, and the American Taxation Association also comment on proposed regulations. In general, such comments suggest that the proposed treatment affects the taxpayer more adversely than what Congress anticipated. In drafting final regulations, the Treasury Department usually considers the remarks and somewhat modifies the proposed regulations.

Proposed regulations are just that—proposed. Consequently, they carry no more weight than the arguments of the IRS in a court brief. They do, nonetheless, represent the Treasury Department's official interpretation of the IRC. In finalizing regulations, the Treasury Department generally responds to taxpayer comments concerning rules as proposed. If the response is favorable, it usually finalizes the rules with minor revisions. If the response is unfavorable, it finalizes them with major revisions or allows them to expire.

Immediately after a major statutory change, the Treasury Department often issues **temporary regulations** (which usually are effective upon publication) to guide taxpayers and their advisors on procedural or computational matters. For example, in 1992 the Treasury Department issued temporary regulations to advise taxpayers on the tax treatment of employee fringe benefits. In the same year, it issued temporary regulations to instruct them on the calculation of adjusted gross income. Temporary regulations have the same authoritative weight as final regulations. According to the Technical Amendments and Miscellaneous Revenue Act of 1988, temporary regulations may remain effective for up to three years. Also, a temporary regulation must be issued concurrently as a proposed regulation.

The Treasury Department drafts final regulations after the public has had an opportunity to comment on the proposed regulations. Most of the time, the final version of the regulation differs at least slightly from the proposed version. For changes to the IRC enacted after July 29, 1996, the Treasury Department generally is precluded from issuing regulations with retroactive effect. Final regulations, however, can be effective on the date proposed or the date on which the temporary regulations preceding them were published in the *Federal Register*.

INTERPRETATIVE AND LEGISLATIVE REGULATIONS. In addition to being classified as proposed, temporary, or final, Treasury Regulations are categorized as interpretative or legislative. **Interpretative regulations** are issued under the general authority of Sec. 7805 and, as the name implies, merely make the statutory language easier to understand and apply. In addition, they often provide illustrations as to how to perform various computations. **Legislative regulations**, by contrast, are written where Congress delegates its rule-making authority to the Treasury Department. Because Congress believes it lacks the expertise necessary to deal with a highly technical matter, it instructs the Treasury Department to articulate substantive tax principles relating to the matter.

Whenever the statute contains language such as "The Secretary shall prescribe such regulations as he may deem necessary" or "under regulations prescribed by the Secretary," the regulations interpreting such a statute are legislative. The consolidated tax return regulations are the clearest example of legislative regulations. In Sec. 1502, Congress delegated to the Treasury Department authority to issue regulations that determine the tax liability of a group of affiliated corporations filing a consolidated tax return. As a precondition to filing such a return, the corporations must consent to follow the consolidated return regulations.[10] Such consent generally precludes the corporations from arguing in court that the regulatory provisions should be overturned.

AUTHORITATIVE WEIGHT. Final regulations are presumed to be valid and to have almost the same authoritative weight as the IRC. Despite this presumption, taxpayers occasionally argue that a regulation is invalid and, consequently, should not be followed. A court will not conclude that an interpretative regulation is invalid unless, in its opinion, such regulation is "unreasonable and plainly inconsistent with the revenue statutes."[11] Thus, a court is unlikely to invalidate a legislative regulation because it recognizes that Congress has abdicated its rule-making authority with respect to such regulation to the Treasury Department. Nevertheless, the courts have invalidated legislative regulations where, in their opinion, the regulations exceeded the scope of power delegated to the Treasury Department,[12] were contrary to the statute,[13] or were unreasonable.[14]

In assessing the validity of Treasury Regulations, some courts apply the **legislative reenactment doctrine**. Under this doctrine, a regulation is deemed to receive Congressional approval whenever the statute under which the regulation was issued is reenacted without amendment.[15] Underlying this doctrine is the rationale that, if Congress believed that the regulation offered an erroneous interpretation of the statute, it would have amended the statute to conform to its belief. Congress's failure to amend the statute signifies approval of the regulation.[16] This doctrine is predicated upon the power of Congress under the Constitution to lay taxes. The power implies that, if Congress is dissatisfied with the manner in which either the executive or the judiciary have interpreted its tax statutes, it can invalidate these interpretations through new legislation.

KEY POINT
The older a regulation becomes, the less likely a court is to invalidate the regulation. The legislative reenactment doctrine holds that if a regulation did not reflect the intent of Congress, lawmakers would have changed the statute in subsequent legislation to obtain their desired objectives.

STOP & THINK

Question: You are researching the manner in which a deduction is calculated. You consult the Treasury Regulations for guidance because the IRC states that the calculation is to be done "in a manner prescribed by the Secretary." After studying these authorities, you conclude that another way of doing the calculation arguably is correct under an intuitive approach. This approach would result in a lower tax liability for the client. Should you follow the Treasury Regulations or use the intuitive approach and argue that the regulations are invalid?

---

[10] Sec. 1501.
[11] *CIR v. South Texas Lumber Co.*, 36 AFTR 604, 48-1 USTC ¶5922 (USSC, 1948). In *U.S. v. Douglas B. Cartwright, Executor*, 31 AFTR 2d 73-1461, 73-1 USTC ¶12,926 (USSC, 1973), the Supreme Court concluded that a regulation dealing with the valuation of mutual fund shares for estate and gift tax purposes was invalid.
[12] *McDonald v. CIR*, 56 AFTR 2d 5318, 85-2 USTC ¶9494 (5th Cir., 1985).
[13] *Jeanese, Inc. v. U.S.*, 15 AFTR 2d 429, 65-1 USTC ¶9259 (9th Cir., 1965).
[14] *United States v. Vogel Fertilizer Co.*, 49 AFTR 2d 82-491, 82-1 USTC ¶9134 (USSC, 1982).
[15] *United States v. Homer O. Correll*, 20 AFTR 2d 5845, 68 USTC ¶9101 (USSC, 1967).
[16] One can rebut the presumption that Congress approved of the regulation by showing that Congress was unaware of the regulation when it reenacted the statute.

Solution: Because of the language "in a manner prescribed by the Secretary," the Treasury Regulations dealing with the calculation are legislative. Whenever it calls for legislative regulations, Congress explicitly authorizes the Treasury Department to write the "rules." Thus, such regulations are more difficult than interpretative regulations to be overturned by the courts. Grounds for overruling legislative regulations include exceeding the scope of the power that Congress delegated, being contrary to the statute, and being unreasonable. If based on your research, you do not believe the Treasury Regulations would be overturned by a court, you should follow them.

> **ADDITIONAL COMMENT**
> Citations serve two purposes in tax research: first, they substantiate propositions; second, they enable the reader to locate underlying authority.

CITATIONS. Citations to Treasury Regulations are relatively easy to understand. One or more numbers appear before a decimal place, and several numbers follow the decimal place. The numbers immediately following the decimal place indicate the IRC section being interpreted. The numbers preceding the decimal place indicate the general subject matter of the regulation. Numbers that often appear before the decimal place and their general subject matter are as follows:

Number	General Subject Matter
1	Income tax
20	Estate tax
25	Gift tax
301	Administrative and procedural matters
601	Procedural rules

The number following the IRC section number indicates the number of the regulation, such as the fifth regulation. No relationship exists between this number and the subsection of the IRC being interpreted. An example of a citation to a final regulation is as follows:

Reg. Sec. 1.165 – 5

Income tax   IRC section   Fifth regulation

Citations to proposed or temporary regulations are in the same format. They are referenced as Prop. Reg. Sec. or Temp. Reg. Sec. For temporary regulations the numbering system following the IRC section number always begins with the number of the regulation and an upper case T (e.g., -1T).

Section 165 addresses the broad topic of losses and is accompanied by several regulations. According to its caption, the topic of Reg. Sec. 1.165-5 is worthless securities, which also is addressed in subsection (g) of IRC Sec. 165. Parenthetical information following the caption to this regulation indicates that the regulation was last amended December 6, 1972 by Treasury Decision (T.D.) 7224. Section 165(g) was last revised in 1991.

When referencing a regulation, the researcher should fine tune the citation as much as possible to indicate the precise wording that provides the basis for his or her conclusion. An example of such a detailed citation is Reg. Sec. 1.165-5(i), Ex. 2(i), which refers to paragraph (i) of Example 2, found in paragraph (i) of the fifth regulation interpreting Sec. 165.

ADMINISTRATIVE INTERPRETATIONS

The IRS interprets the IRC through various pronouncements. These pronouncements are referred to generally as **administrative interpretations**. After consulting the IRC and the Treasury Regulations, tax advisors are likely next to consult administrative interpretations. Some of the most important of these interpretations are discussed below.

> **TYPICAL MISCONCEPTION**
> Even though revenue rulings do not have the same weight as regulations or court cases, one should not underestimate their importance. Because a revenue ruling is the official published position of the IRS, in audits the examining agent will place considerable weight on any applicable revenue rulings.

REVENUE RULINGS. In **revenue rulings**, the IRS indicates the tax consequences of a particular transaction in which several taxpayers might engage. For example, a revenue ruling might indicate whether the exchange of stock for stock derivatives is tax-free.

The IRS issues more than 100 revenue rulings a year. These rulings do not rank as high as Treasury Regulations or court cases in the hierarchy of authorities. They simply represent the IRS's view of the tax law. Taxpayers do not have to follow revenue rulings if they have substantial authority for different treatment.[17] However, the IRS presumes that the tax treatment specified in a revenue ruling is correct. Consequently, if an examining agent discovers in an audit that a taxpayer did not adopt the position prescribed in a revenue ruling, the agent will contend that the taxpayer's tax liability should be adjusted to reflect that position.

Soon after it is issued, a revenue ruling appears in the weekly *Internal Revenue Bulletin* (cited as I.R.B.), published by the U.S. Government Printing Office. Revenue rulings also are published in the *Cumulative Bulletin* (cited as C.B.), a bound publication issued semiannually by the U.S. Government Printing Office. An example of a citation to a revenue ruling appearing in the *Cumulative Bulletin* is as follows:

Rev. Rul. 80-265, 1980-2 C.B. 378.

This is the 265th ruling issued during 1980, and it appears on page 378 of Volume 2 of the 1980 *Cumulative Bulletin*. Before the issuance of the appropriate volume of the *Cumulative Bulletin*, citations are given to the *Internal Revenue Bulletin*. An example of such a citation follows:

Rev. Rul. 98-1, I.R.B. 1998-2, 1.

The ruling is the first issued during 1998. It was published on page 1 of the *Internal Revenue Bulletin* for the second week of 1998. Once a revenue ruling is published in the *Cumulative Bulletin*, the citation to the *Cumulative Bulletin* should be used. Thus, the I.R.B. citation is a temporary one.

REVENUE PROCEDURES. As the name suggests, **revenue procedures** are IRS pronouncements that usually deal with the procedural aspects of tax practice. For example, in a revenue procedure the IRS provides guidance concerning the reporting of tip income. Another revenue procedure describes the requirements for reproducing paper substitutes for informational returns such as Form 1099.

Revenue procedures are published first in the *Internal Revenue Bulletin* and later in the *Cumulative Bulletin*. An example of a citation to a revenue procedure appearing in the *Cumulative Bulletin* is as follows:

Rev. Proc. 97-19, 1997-1 C.B. 644.

This item was published in Volume 1 of the 1997 *Cumulative Bulletin* on page 644. It was the nineteenth revenue procedure issued in 1997.

In addition to revenue rulings and revenue procedures, the *Cumulative Bulletin* includes IRS notices, as well as texts of proposed regulations, treaties and tax conventions, committee reports, and Supreme Court decisions.

LETTER RULINGS. **Letter rulings** are initiated by taxpayers who write and ask the IRS to explain the tax consequences of a particular transaction.[18] The IRS provides its explanation in the form of a letter ruling, that is, a personal response to the individual or corporation requesting an answer. Only the taxpayer to whom the ruling is addressed may rely on it as authority. Nevertheless, letter rulings are significant to other taxpayers and to tax advisors because they offer insight into the IRS's position concerning the tax treatment of particular transactions.

SELF-STUDY QUESTION
Are letter rulings of precedential value for third parties?

ANSWER
No. A letter ruling is binding only on the taxpayer to whom the ruling was issued. Nevertheless, letter rulings can be very useful to third parties because they provide insight as to the IRS's opinion about the tax consequences of various transactions.

---

[17] Chapter C15 discusses in depth the authoritative support taxpayers and tax advisors should have for positions they adopt on a tax return.

[18] Chapter C15 further discusses letter rulings.

Originally the public did not have access to letter rulings issued to other taxpayers. As a result of Sec. 6110, enacted in 1976, letter rulings (with any confidential information deleted) are accessible to the general public and have been reproduced by the major tax services. An example of a citation to a letter ruling appears below:

Ltr. Rul. 8511075 (March 17, 1985).

The numbering system for all letter rulings consists of seven digits.[19] The first two digits indicate the year in which the ruling was made public, in this case, 1985. The next two digits denote the week in which it was made public, here the eleventh. The last three numbers indicate the ruling for the week, here the seventy-fifth. The date in parentheses denotes the date of the ruling.

OTHER INTERPRETATIONS

Technical Advice Memoranda. When the IRS audits a taxpayer's return on a complicated, technical matter, the IRS district or appeals office may refer the matter to the IRS national office in Washington, DC for technical advice concerning the appropriate tax treatment. The answer from the national office, in the form of a **technical advice memorandum**, is made available to the public as a letter ruling.[20] Researchers can recognize which letter rulings are technical advice memoranda because they generally begin with language such as, "In response to a request for technical advice. . . ." An example of a citation to a technical advice memorandum is as follows:

T.A.M. 9801001 (January 1, 1998).

This item represents the first technical advice memorandum issued in the first week of 1998. The memorandum is dated January 1, 1998.

Information Releases. If the IRS wants to disseminate information to the general public, it will issue an **information release**. Information releases are written in lay terms and are dispatched to thousands of newspapers throughout the country. The IRS, for example, may issue an information release to announce the standard mileage rate applicable to business travel. An example of a citation to an information release is as follows:

I.R. 86-70 (June 12, 1986).

This item signifies the seventieth information release issued in 1986. The release is dated June 12, 1986.

Announcements and Notices. The IRS also disseminates information to tax practitioners in the form of **announcements** and **notices**. These pronouncements generally are more technical than information releases, and they frequently address current tax developments. After a major tax act, and before the Treasury Department has had an opportunity to issue proposed or temporary regulations, the IRS may issue an announcement or notice to clarify the measure. The IRS is bound to follow the announcement or notice just as it is bound to follow a revenue procedure or revenue ruling. Examples of citations to announcements and notices are as follows:

Announcement 98-1, I.R.B. 1998-2, 38.
Notice 98-1, I.R.B. 1998-3, 42.

The first citation is to the first announcement issued in 1998. It can be found on page 38 of the second *Internal Revenue Bulletin* for 1998. The second citation is to the first notice issued in 1998. It can be found on page 42 of the third *Internal Revenue Bulletin* for 1998. While notices appear in both the *Internal Revenue Bulletin* and the *Cumulative Bulletin*, announcements appear only in the first of these publications.

> **ADDITIONAL COMMENT**
>
> A technical advice memorandum is published as a letter ruling. Whereas a taxpayer-requested letter ruling deals with prospective transactions, a technical advice memorandum deals with past or consummated transactions.

> **ADDITIONAL COMMENT**
>
> Announcements are used to summarize new tax legislation or publicize procedural matters. Announcements generally are aimed at tax practitioners and are "the equivalent of revenue rulings and revenue procedures" [Rev. Rul., 1987-2 C.B. 287].

---

[19] Sometimes a letter ruling is cited as PLR (private letter ruling) instead of Ltr. Rul.

[20] Technical advice memoranda are discussed further in Chapter C15.

JUDICIAL DECISIONS

Judicial decisions are an important source of tax law. Judges are reputed to be unbiased individuals who decide questions of fact (the existence of a fact or the occurrence of an event) or questions of law (the applicability of a legal principle or the proper interpretation of a legal term). Judges do not always agree on the tax consequences of a particular transaction or event. Therefore, tax advisors often must reach their conclusions against the background of conflicting judicial authorities. For example, a U.S. district court decision may differ from a Tax Court decision, or different circuit courts may disagree on the same issue.

OVERVIEW OF THE COURT SYSTEM. In tax matters, there are three trial courts: the U.S. Tax Court, the U.S. Court of Federal Claims (formerly the U.S. Claims Court), and U.S. district courts. The taxpayer may begin litigation in any of the three. Court precedents are important in deciding where to begin litigation (see page I15-21 for a discussion of precedent). Also important is when the taxpayer must pay the deficiency the IRS contends is due. A taxpayer who wants to litigate either in a U.S. district court or in the U.S. Court of Federal Claims must first pay the deficiency. The taxpayer then files a claim for refund, which the IRS will deny. This denial must be followed by a suit for a refund of the taxes. If the taxpayer wins the refund suit, he or she receives a refund of the taxes in question plus interest. If the taxpayer begins litigation in the Tax Court, on the other hand, he or she need not pay the deficiency until the case has been decided. If the taxpayer loses in the Tax Court, he or she must pay the deficiency plus any interest and penalties.[21] A taxpayer who thinks that a jury trial would be especially favorable should litigate in a U.S. district court, the only forum where a jury trial is possible.

Regardless of which party loses at the trial court level, such party can appeal the decision. Appeals of Tax Court and U.S. district court decisions are made to the Court of Appeals for the taxpayer's circuit (i.e., geographical area). There are eleven numerical circuits plus the circuit for the District of Columbia. The map in Figure I15-3 shows the states that lie in the various circuits. California, for example, is in the Ninth Circuit. When referring to these appellate courts, instead of saying, for example, "the Court of Appeals for the Ninth Circuit," one generally says "the Ninth Circuit." All decisions of the U.S. Court of Federal Claims are appealable to one court—the Court of Appeals for the Federal Circuit—irrespective of the taxpayer's geographical location.[22] The only cases the Federal Circuit hears are those that originate in the U.S. Court of Federal Claims.

The party losing at the Court of Appeals level can petition the Supreme Court to hear the case by a **writ of certiorari**. If the Supreme Court agrees to consider the case, it grants certiorari.[23] In recent years, the Court has heard only about six to ten tax cases per year. Figure I15-4 and Table I15-1 provide an overview and summary of the court system with respect to tax matters.

THE U.S. TAX COURT. The U.S. Tax Court was created in 1942 as a successor to the Board of Tax Appeals. It is a court of national jurisdiction that hears only tax-related cases. All taxpayers, regardless of their state of residence, may litigate in the Tax Court. It has 19 judges, including one chief judge.[24] The President, with the consent of the Senate, appoints the judges for a 15-year term and may reappoint them for an additional term. The judges, specialists in tax-related matters, periodically travel to roughly 100 cities throughout the country to hear cases. In most instances, only one judge hears a case.

The Tax Court issues both regular and memorandum (memo) decisions. The chief judge decides whether to publish each opinion as a memo or regular decision. Generally, the first time the Tax Court decides a particular legal issue, its decision appears as a regu-

---

SELF-STUDY QUESTION
What are some of the factors that a taxpayer should consider when deciding in which court to file a tax-related claim?

ANSWER
(1) Each court's published precedent pertaining to the issue, (2) desirability of a jury trial, (3) tax expertise of each court, and (4) when the deficiency must be paid.

ADDITIONAL COMMENT
Because the Tax Court deals only with tax cases, it presumably has a higher level of tax expertise than do other courts. Tax Court judges are appointed by the President, in part, due to their considerable tax experience. In June 2000, the Tax Court judges faced a backlog of about 16,200 cases. This is an improvement over its 27,000 cases in 1998.

---

[21] Revenue Procedure 84-58, 1984-2, C.B. 501, provides procedures for taxpayers to make remittances or apply overpayments to stop the accrual of interest on deficiencies.
[22] The Court of Claims was reconstituted as the United States Court of Claims in 1982. In 1992, this court was renamed the U.S. Court of Federal Claims.
[23] The granting of certiorari signifies that the Supreme Court is granting an appellate review. The denial of certiorari does not necessarily mean that the Supreme Court agrees with the lower court's decision. It simply means the court has decided not to hear the case.
[24] The Tax Court also periodically appoints, depending on budgetary constraints, a number of trial judges and senior judges who hear cases and render decisions with the same authority as the regular Tax Court judges.

Tax Research ▼ Individuals 15-15

The Thirteen Federal Judicial Circuits

See 28 U.S.C.A. § 41

FIGURE I15-3 ▶ MAP OF THE GEOGRAPHICAL BOUNDARIES OF THE CIRCUIT COURTS OF APPEALS

Source: Reprinted with permission from *West's Federal Reporter,* Third Series, Copyright © by West Publishing Company.

Appellate Courts:
- U.S. Supreme Court[a]
- Court of Appeals for taxpayer's geographical jurisdiction (First through Eleventh Circuits and D.C. Circuit)
- Court of Appeals for Federal Circuit

Courts of Original Jurisdiction (Trial Courts):
- U.S. Tax Court — *Do Not Pay Deficiency First*
- U.S. District Court for taxpayer's district — *Pay Deficiency First*
- U.S. Court of Federal Claims — *Pay Deficiency First*

[a] Cases are heard only if the Supreme Court grants a writ of certiorari.

FIGURE I15-4 ▶ OVERVIEW OF COURT SYSTEM—TAX MATTERS

▼ TABLE I15-1
Summary of Court Sytem—Tax Matters

Court(s) (Number of)	Number of Judges on Each	Personal Jurisdiction	Subject Matter Jurisdiction	Determines Questions of Fact	Trial by Jury	Precedents Followed	Where Opinions Published
U.S. district courts (over 200)	1	Local	General	Yes	Yes	Same court Court for circuit where situated U.S. Supreme Court	*Federal Supplement* *American Federal Tax Reports* *United States Tax Cases*
U.S. Tax Court (1)	19	National	Tax	Yes	No	Same court Court for taxpayer's circuit U.S. Supreme Court	*Tax Court of the U.S. Reports* *CCH Tax Court Memorandum Decisions* *RIA Tax Court Memorandum Decisions*
U.S. Court of Federal Claims (1)	16	National	Claims against U.S. Government	Yes	No	Same court Federal Circuit Court U.S. Supreme Court	*Federal Reporter* (pre-1982) *U.S. Court of Federal Claims* *American Federal Tax Reports* *United States Tax Cases*
U.S. Courts of Appeals (13)	about 20	Regional	General	No	No	Same court U.S. Supreme Court	*Federal Reporter* *American Federal Tax Reports* *United States Tax Cases*
U.S. Supreme Court (1)	9	National	General	No	No	Same Court	*U.S. Supreme Court Reports* *Supreme Court Reporter* *United States Reports, Lawyers' Editon* *American Federal Tax Reports* *United States Tax Cases*

lar decision. **Memo decisions** usually deal with a factual variation of a previously-decided issue. Regular and memo decisions have the same precedential value.

At times, the chief judge determines that a particular case deals with an important matter that the entire Tax Court should consider. In such a situation, the words *reviewed by the court* will appear at the end of the majority decision. Any concurring or dissenting opinions will appear after the opinion of the majority.[25]

Other language sometimes appearing at the end of a Tax Court decision is *Entered under Rule 155*. These words signify that the court has reached a decision concerning the appropriate tax treatment of an item but has left the computation of the exact amount of the deficiency to the two litigating parties.

Small Cases Procedure. The Tax Court has a special policy concerning small cases. Taxpayers have the option of having their cases heard under the **small cases procedure** if the amount in question for a particular year does not exceed $50,000.[26] Such procedures are less formal than the regular Tax Court procedures, and taxpayers can appear without an attorney.[27] The cases are heard by special commissioners instead of by one of the 19 Tax Court judges. For the losing party, a disadvantage of the small cases procedure is that the decision cannot be appealed. The opinions in the small cases are not published and have no precedential value.

Acquiescence Policy. The IRS has adopted a policy of announcing whether, in future cases involving similar facts and similar issues, it will follow federal court decisions that are adverse to it. This policy is known as the IRS **acquiescence policy**. If the IRS wants taxpayers to know that it will follow an adverse decision in future cases involving similar facts and issues, it will announce its "acquiescence" in the decision. Conversely, if it wants taxpayers to know that it will not follow the decision, it will announce its "nonacquiescence." The IRS does not announce its acquiescence or nonacquiescence in every adverse decision.

The IRS publishes its acquiescences and nonacquiescences as "Actions on Decision" first in the *Internal Revenue Bulletin,* then in the *Cumulative Bulletin.* Before 1991, the IRS published acquiescences and nonacquiescences in regular Tax Court decisions only. In 1991, it broadened the scope of its policy to include adverse U.S. Claims Court, U.S. district court, and U.S. circuit court decisions.

In cases involving multiple issues, the IRS may acquiesce in some issues but not others. In decisions supported by extensive reasoning, it may acquiesce in the result but not rationale (*acq. in result*). Further, it may retroactively revoke an acquiescence or nonacquiescence. The footnotes to the relevant announcement in the *Internal Revenue Bulletin* and *Cumulative Bulletin* indicate the nature and extent of IRS acquiescences and nonacquiescences.

These acquiescences and nonacquiescences are important for taxpayers. If a taxpayer bases his or her position on a decision in which the IRS has nonacquiesced, he or she can expect an IRS challenge in the event of an audit. In this situation, the taxpayer's only recourse may be litigation. On the other hand, if the taxpayer bases his or her position on a decision in which the IRS has acquiesced, he or she can expect little or no challenge. In either case, the examining agent will be bound by the IRS position.

Published Opinions and Citations. Regular Tax Court decisions are published by the U.S. Government Printing Office in a bound volume known as the *Tax Court of the United States Reports.* Soon after a decision is made public, it also is published by

---

SELF-STUDY QUESTION

What are some of the considerations for litigating under the small cases procedure of the Tax Court?

ANSWER

The small cases procedure gives the taxpayer the advantage of having his or her "day in court" without the expense of an attorney. But if the taxpayer loses, the decision cannot be appealed.

ADDITIONAL COMMENT

The only cases with respect to which the IRS will consider publishing an acquiescence or nonacquiescence are decisions that the government loses. Because the majority of cases, particularly Tax Court cases, are won by the government, the IRS will potentially acquiescence to only a small number of cases.

ADDITIONAL COMMENT

If a particular case is important, the chief judge will instruct the other judges to review the case. If a case is reviewed by the entire court, the phrase *reviewed by the court* is inserted immediately after the text of the majority opinion. A reviewed decision provides an opportunity for Tax Court judges to express their dissenting opinions.

---

[25] A judge who issues a concurring opinion agrees with the basic outcome of the majority's decision but not with its rationale. A judge who issues a dissenting opinion believes the majority reached an erroneous conclusion.

[26] Sec. 7463. The $50,000 amount includes penalties and additional taxes but excludes interest.

[27] Taxpayers can represent themselves in regular Tax Court proceedings also, even though they are not attorneys. Where taxpayers represent themselves, the words *pro se* appear after the taxpayer's name.

Research Institute of America (RIA) and CCH Incorporated (CCH) in their looseleaf reporters of Tax Court decisions. An official citation to a Tax Court decision is as follows:[28]

J. Simpson Dean, 35 T.C. 1083 (1961).

The citation indicates that this case appears on page 1083 in Volume 35 of the official *Tax Court of the United States Reports* and that the case was decided in 1961.

Regular decisions of the Board of Tax Appeals (predecessor of the Tax Court) were published by the U.S. Government Printing Office in the *United States Board of Tax Appeals Reports* from 1924 to 1942. An example of a citation to a Board of Tax Appeals case is as follows:

J. W. Wells Lumber Co. Trust A., 44 B.T.A. 551 (1941).

This case is found in Volume 44 of the *United States Board of Tax Appeals Reports* on page 551. It is a 1941 decision.

If the IRS has acquiesced or nonacquiesced to a federal court decision, the IRS's action should be denoted in the citation. At times, the IRS will not announce its acquiescence or nonacquiescence until several years after the date of the decision. An example of a citation to a decision in which the IRS has acquiesced is as follows:

Estate of John A. Moss, 74 T.C. 1239 (1980), *acq*. 1981-1 C.B. 2.

The case appears on page 1239 of Volume 74 of the *Tax Court of the United States Reports* and the acquiescence is reported on page 2 of Volume 1 of the 1981 *Cumulative Bulletin*. The IRS acquiesced to this 1980 decision in 1981. A citation to a decision in which the IRS has nonacquiesced is as follows:

Warren Jones Co., 60 T.C. 663 (1973), *nonacq*. 1980-1 C.B. 2.

The case appears on page 663 of Volume 60 of the *Tax Court of the United States Reports*. The nonacquiescence is reported on page 2 of Volume 1 of the 1980 *Cumulative Bulletin*. The IRS nonacquiesced in this 1973 decision in 1980.

Tax Court memo decisions are not published by the U.S. Government Printing Office. The decisions are available in bound form from RIA in *RIA T.C. Memorandum Decisions* and from CCH in *CCH Tax Court Memorandum Decisions*. In addition, soon after an opinion is issued, it is published in loose-leaf form by RIA and CCH. The following are citations to a Tax Court memo decision:

Edith G. McKinney, 1981 PH T.C. Memo ¶81,181, 41 TCM 1272.

McKinney is found at Paragraph 81,181 of Prentice Hall's (now RIA's)[29] 1981 *PH T.C. Memorandum Decisions* reporter, and in Volume 41, page 1272, of CCH's *Tax Court Memorandum Decisions*. The 181 in the PH citation denotes that the case is the Tax Court's 181st memo decision of the year. A more recent citation is based on the same format but refers to RIA's memo decisions.

Paul F. Belloff, 1992 RIA T.C. Memo ¶92,346, 63 TCM 3150.

ADDITIONAL COMMENT
Once the IRS has acquiesced in a federal court decision, other taxpayers generally will not need to litigate the same issue. However, the IRS can change its mind and revoke a previous acquiescence or nonacquiescence. References to acquiescences or nonacquiescences in federal court decisions can be found in the citators.

KEY POINT
To access all Tax Court cases, a tax advisor must refer to two different publications. The regular opinions are found in the *Tax Court of the United States Reports*, published by the U.S. Government Printing Office, and the memo decisions are published by both RIA (formerly PH) and CCH in their own court reporters.

---

[28] In a citation to a Tax Court case, only the name of the plaintiff (taxpayer) is listed. The defendant is understood to be the Commissioner of Internal Revenue whose name usually is not shown in the citation. In cases litigated outside the Tax Court, the name of the plaintiff is listed first and the name of the defendant second. For non-Tax Court cases, the Commissioner of Internal Revenue is referred to as *CIR* in our footnotes and text.

[29] For several years the Prentice Hall Information Services division published its *Federal Taxes 2nd* tax service and a number of related publications, such as the *PH T.C. Memorandum Decisions*. Changes in ownership occurred, and in late 1991 Thomson Professional Publishing added the former Prentice Hall tax materials to the product line of its RIA tax publishing division. Some products such as the *PH T.C. Memorandum Decisions* still have the Prentice Hall name on the spine of older editions.

U.S. DISTRICT COURTS. Each state has at least one U.S. district court, and more populous states have more than one. Each district court is independent of the others and is thus free to issue its own decisions, subject to the precedential constraints discussed later in this chapter. Many different types of cases—not just tax cases—are heard in this forum. A district court is the only forum in which the taxpayer may have a jury decide questions of fact. Depending on the particular taxpayer and the circumstances involved, a jury trial might or might not be beneficial.[30]

District court decisions are officially reported in the *Federal Supplement* (cited as F. Supp.) published by West Publishing Co. (West). However, some decisions are not officially reported and are referred to as **unreported decisions**. Decisions by U.S. district courts on the topic of taxation also are published by RIA and CCH in secondary reporters that include only tax-related cases. RIA's reporter is called *American Federal Tax Reports* (cited as AFTR),[31] and CCH's reporter is known as *U.S. Tax Cases* (cited as USTC). Even though a case is not officially reported, it nevertheless may be published in the AFTR and USTC. An example of a complete citation to a U.S. district court decision is as follows:

Margie J. Thompson v. U.S., 429 F. Supp. 13, 39 AFTR 2d 77-1485, 77-1 USTC ¶9343 (DC Eastern District PA., 1977).

ADDITIONAL COMMENT

A citation, at a minimum, should contain the following information: (1) the name of the case, (2) the reporter that publishes the case along with both a volume and page (or paragraph) number, (3) the year the case was decided, and (4) the court that decided the case.

In the example above, the **primary citation** is to the *Federal Supplement*. The case appears on page 13 of Volume 429 of this reporter. **Secondary citations** are to *American Federal Tax Reports* and *U.S. Tax Cases*. The same case is found in Volume 39 of the second series of the AFTR, page 77-1485 (meaning page 1485 in the volume containing 1977 cases) and in Volume 1 of the 1977 USTC at Paragraph 9343. The parenthetical indicates that the case was decided in 1977 by the U.S. District Court for the Eastern District of Pennsylvania. Because some judicial decisions have greater precedential weight than others (e.g., a Supreme Court decision versus a district court decision), information relating to the identity of the adjudicating court is useful.

ADDITIONAL COMMENT

The U.S. Court of Federal Claims adjudicates claims (including suits to recover federal income taxes) against the U.S. Government. This court usually hears cases in Washington, D.C., but will hold sessions in other locations as the court deems necessary.

U.S. COURT OF FEDERAL CLAIMS. The U.S. Court of Federal Claims, another trial court that addresses tax matters, has nationwide jurisdiction. Originally, this court was named the U.S. Court of Claims (cited as Ct. Cl.), and its decisions were appealable to the U.S. Supreme Court only. In a restructuring, effective October 1, 1982, the reconstituted court was named the U.S. Claims Court (cited as Cl. Ct.), and its decisions became appealable to the Circuit Court of Appeals for the Federal Circuit. In October 1992, the court's name was again changed to the U.S. Court of Federal Claims (cited as Fed. Cl.).

Beginning in 1982, U.S. Claims Court decisions were reported officially in the *Claims Court Reporter*, published by West from 1982 to 1992.[32] An example of a citation to a U.S. Claims Court decision appears below:

Benjamin Raphan v. U.S., 3 Cl. Ct. 457, 52 AFTR 2d 83-5987, 83-2 USTC ¶9613 (1983).

The *Raphan* case appears on page 457 of Volume 3 of the *Claims Court Reporter*. Secondary citations are to Volume 52, page 83-5987 of the AFTR, second series, and to Volume 2 of the 1983 USTC in Paragraph 9613.

---

[30] Taxpayers prefer to have a jury trial if they think a jury will be sympathetic to their case.

[31] The *American Federal Tax Reports* (AFTR) is published in two series. The first series, which includes opinions issued up to 1957, is cited as AFTR. The second series, which includes opinions issued after 1957, is cited as AFTR 2d. The *Margie Thompson* decision cited as an illustration of a U.S. district court decision appears in the second *American Federal Tax Reports* series.

[32] Before the creation in 1982 of the U.S. Claims Court (and the *Claims Court Reporter*), the opinions of the U.S. Court of Claims were reported in either the *Federal Supplement* (F. Supp.) or the *Federal Reporter, Second Series* (F.2d). The *Federal Supplement* was the primary source of U.S. Court of Claims opinions from 1932 through January 19, 1960. From January 20, 1960, to October 1982, such opinions were reported in the *Federal Reporter, Second Series*.

Effective with the 1992 name change, decisions of the U.S. Court of Federal Claims are now reported in the *Federal Claims Reporter*. An example of a citation to an opinion published in this reporter is presented below:

Jeffrey G. Sharp v. U.S., 27 Fed. Cl. 52, 70 AFTR 2d 92-6040, 92-2 USTC ¶50,561 (1992).

The *Sharp* case appears on page 52 of Volume 27 of the *Federal Claims Reporter*, on page 6040 of the 70th volume of the AFTR, second series, and in Paragraph 50,561 of Volume 2 of the 1992 USTC reporter. Note that, even though the name of the reporter published by West has changed, the volume numbers continue in sequence as if there had been no name change.

CIRCUIT COURTS OF APPEALS. Trial court decisions are appealable by the losing party to the court of appeals for the circuit in which the litigation originated. Generally, if the case began in the Tax Court or a U.S. district court, the case is appealable to the circuit for the taxpayer's residence as of the appeal date. For a corporation, the case is appealable to the circuit for the corporation's principal place of business. As mentioned above, the Federal Circuit handles all appeals of cases originating in the U.S. Court of Federal Claims.

There are 11 geographical circuits designated by numbers, the circuit for the District of Columbia, and the Federal Circuit. A map of the circuits and their jurisdictions appears in Figure I15-3, displayed earlier in this chapter. The 11 numbered circuits and the D.C. Circuit hear appeals of persons or firms from their locality. In October 1981, the Eleventh Circuit was created by moving Alabama, Georgia, and Florida from the Fifth to the new Eleventh Circuit. The Eleventh Circuit voluntarily adopted the policy that it will follow as precedent all decisions made by the Fifth Circuit during the time the states currently constituting the Eleventh Circuit were part of the Fifth Circuit.[33]

EXAMPLE I15-7 ▶ In 2000, the Eleventh Circuit first considered an issue in a case concerning a Florida taxpayer. In 1980, the Fifth Circuit had ruled on this issue in a case involving a Louisiana taxpayer. Because Florida was part of the Fifth Circuit in 1980, under the policy adopted by the Eleventh Circuit, it will follow the Fifth Circuit's earlier decision. Had the Fifth Circuit's decision been rendered in 1982—after the creation of the Eleventh Circuit—the Eleventh Circuit would not have been bound by the Fifth Circuit's decision. ◀

As the later discussion of precedential value points out, different circuits may reach different conclusions concerning the same issue.

Circuit court decisions—regardless of topic (e.g., civil rights, securities law, and taxation)—are now reported officially in the *Federal Reporter, Third Series* (cited as F.3d), published by West. The third series began in October 1993 after the volume number for the second series reached 999. The primary citation to a circuit court opinion should be to the *Federal Reporter*. Tax decisions of the circuit courts also appear in the *American Federal Tax Reports* and *U.S. Tax Cases*. Below is an example of a citation to a 1994 circuit court decision:

Leonard Greene v. U.S., 13 F.3d 577, 73 AFTR 2d 94-746, 94-1 USTC ¶50,022 (2nd Cir., 1994).

The *Greene* case appears on page 577 of Volume 13 of the *Federal Reporter, Third Series*. It also is reported in Volume 73, page 94-746 of the AFTR, second series, and in Volume 1, Paragraph 50,022, of the 1994 USTC. Parenthetical information indicates that the Second Circuit decided the case in 1994. (A *Federal Reporter, Second Series* citation can be found in footnote 33 of this chapter.)

---

[33] *Bonner v. City of Prichard*, 661 F.2d 1206 (11th Cir., 1981).

ADDITIONAL COMMENT

A judge is not required to follow judicial precedent beyond his or her jurisdiction. Thus, the Tax Court, the U.S. district courts, and the U.S. Court of Federal Claims are not required to follow the others' decisions, nor is a circuit court required to follow the decision of a different circuit court.

SUPREME COURT. Whichever party loses at the appellate court level can request that the U.S. Supreme Court hear the case. The Supreme Court, however, hears very few tax cases. Unless the circuits are divided on the proper treatment of a tax item, or the issue is deemed to be of great significance, the Supreme Court probably will not hear the case.[34] Supreme Court decisions are the law of the land and supersede earlier cases. As a practical matter, a Supreme Court ruling on an interpretation of the IRC has the same effect as if its interpretative language was added to the IRC. If Congress does not agree with the Court's interpretation, it can amend the statutory language to achieve a contrary result. From time to time, Congress has responded to Supreme Court decisions by amending the IRC.[35] If the Supreme Court decides that a particular statute is unconstitutional, the provision is invalid.

All Supreme Court decisions, regardless of the subject matter, are published in the *United States Supreme Court Reports* (cited as U.S.) by the U.S. Government Printing Office, the *Supreme Court Reporter* (cited as S.Ct.) by West, and the *United States Reports, Lawyers' Edition* (cited as L. Ed.) by Lawyer's Co-Operative Publishing Co. In addition, the AFTR and USTC reporters published by RIA and CCH, respectively, contain Supreme Court decisions concerned with taxation. An example of a citation to a Supreme Court opinion appears below:

U.S. v. Maclin P. Davis, 397 U.S. 301, 25 AFTR 2d 70-827, 70-1 USTC ¶9289 (1970).

According to the primary citation, this case appears in Volume 397, page 301, of the *United States Supreme Court Reports*. According to the secondary citation, it also is reported in Volume 25, page 70-827, of the AFTR, second series, and in Volume 1, Paragraph 9289, of the 1970 USTC.

Table I15-2 provides a summary of how court decisions, revenue rulings, revenue procedures, and other administrative interpretations should be cited. Primary citations are to the reporters published by West or the U.S. Government Printing Office, and secondary citations are to the AFTR and USTC reporters.

SELF-STUDY QUESTION

Is it possible for the Tax Court to intentionally issue conflicting decisions?

ANSWER

Yes. If the Tax Court issues two decisions that are appealable to different circuit courts and these courts have previously reached different conclusions on the issue, the Tax Court follows the respective precedent in each circuit and issues conflicting decisions. This is a result of the *Golsen* Rule.

PRECEDENTIAL VALUE OF VARIOUS DECISIONS.

Tax Court. The Tax Court is a court of national jurisdiction. Consequently, it generally rules uniformly for all taxpayers, regardless of their geographical location. It follows Supreme Court decisions and its own earlier decisions. It is not bound by cases decided by the U.S. Court of Federal Claims or a U.S. district court, even if the district court is the court for the taxpayer's jurisdiction.

In 1970, the Tax Court adopted what has become known as the *Golsen* Rule.[36] Under the *Golsen* Rule, the Tax Court departs from its general policy of ruling uniformly for all taxpayers and instead follows the decisions of the court of appeals to which the case in question is appealable. Stated differently, the *Golsen* Rule holds that the Tax Court rules consistently with decisions of the circuit court for the taxpayer's jurisdiction.

EXAMPLE I15-8 ▶

In 1999, the year in which an issue was first litigated, the Tax Court decided that an expenditure was deductible. The government appealed the decision to the Tenth Circuit Court of Appeals and won a reversal. This is the only appellate decision regarding the issue. If and when the Tax Court encounters this issue again, it will hold, with one exception, that the expenditure is deductible. The exception applies to taxpayers in the Tenth Circuit. Under the *Golsen* Rule, these taxpayers will be denied the deduction. ◀

---

[34] *Vogel Fertilizer Co. v. U.S.,* 49 AFTR 2d 82-491, 82-1 USTC ¶9134 (USSC, 1982), is an example of a case the Supreme Court heard to settle a split in judicial authority. The Fifth Circuit, the Tax Court, and the Court of Claims had reached one conclusion on an issue, while the Second, Fourth, and Eighth Circuits had reached another.

[35] For an example of an instance in which Congress enacted legislation to achieve a result contrary to that of a Supreme Court decision, see *U.S. v. Marian A. Byrum,* 30 AFTR 2d 72-5811, 72-2 USTC ¶12,859 (USSC, 1972).
[36] The *Golsen* Rule is based on the decision in *Jack E. Golsen,* 54 T.C. 742 (1970).

TABLE I15-2
Summary of Tax-related Primary Sources—Statutory and Administrative

Source Name	Publisher	Materials Provided	Citation Example
U.S. Code, Title 26	Government Printing Office	Internal Revenue Code	Sec. 441(b)
Code of Federal Regulations, Title 26	Government Printing Office	Treasury Regulations (final)	Reg. Sec. 1.461-1(c)
		Treasury Regulations (temporary)	Temp. Reg. Sec. 1.62-1T(e)
Internal Revenue Bulletin	Government Printing Office	Treasury Regulations (proposed)	Prop. Reg. Sec. 1.671-2(e)
		Treasury decisions	T.D. 8756 (January 12, 1998)
		Revenue rulings	Rev. Rul. 98-1, I.R.B. 1998-2, 1
		Revenue procedures	Rev. Proc. 97-37, I.R.B. 1997-33, 18
		Committee reports	S.Rept. No. 105-33, 105th Cong., 1st Sess., p. 308 (1997)
		Public laws	P.L. 105-34, Sec. 224(a), enacted August 6, 1997
		Announcements	Announcement 98-1, I.R.B. 1998-2, 38
		Notices	Notice 98-1, I.R.B. 1998-3, 42
Cumulative Bulletin	Government Printing Office	Treasury Regulations (proposed)	Prop. Reg. Sec. 1.671-2(e)
		Treasury decisions	T.D. 8756 (January 12, 1998)
		Revenue rulings	Rev. Rul. , 1974-1 C.B. 105
		Revenue procedures	Rev. Proc. 77-28, 1977-2 C.B. 537
		Committee reports	S.Rept. No. 105-33, 105th Cong., 1st Sess., p. 308 (1997)
		Public laws	P.L. 105-34, Sec. 224(a), enacted August 6, 1997
		Notices	Notice 88-74, 1988-2 C.B. 385

Summary of Tax-related Primary and Secondary Sources—Judicial

Reporter Name	Publisher	Decisions Published	Citation Example
U.S. Supreme Court Reports	Government Printing Office	U.S. Supreme Court	U.S. v. Maclin P. Davis, 397 U.S. 301 (1970)
Supreme Court Reports	West Publishing Company	U.S. Supreme Court	U.S. v. Maclin P. Davis, 90 S. Ct. 1041 (1970).
Federal Reporter (1st-3d Series)	West Publishing Company	U.S. Court of Appeal Pre-1982 Court of Claims	Leonard Green v. U.S., 13 F.3d 577 (2nd Cir., 1994)
Federal Supplement Series	West Publishing Company	U.S. District Court	Margie J. Thompson v. U.S., 429 F.Supp. 13 (DC Eastern District PA, 1977)
U.S. Court of Federal Claims	West Publishing Company	Court of Federal Claims	Jeffery G. Sharp v. U.S., 27 Fed. Cl. 52 (1992)
Tax Court of the U.S. Reports	Government Printing Office	U.S. Tax Court regular	Henry D. Duarte, 44 T.C. 193 (1965), acq. 1967-2 C.B. 3
Tax Court Memorandum Decisions	CCH Incorporated	U.S. Tax Court memo	Paul F. Beloff, 63 TCM 3150 (1992).
RIA Tax Court Memorandum Decisions	Research Institute of America	U.S. Tax Court memo	Paul F. Beloff, 1992 RIA T.C. Memo ¶92,346.
American Federal Tax Reports	Research Institute of America	Tax: all federal courts except Tax Court	U.S. v. Maclin P. Davis, 25 AFTR 2d 70-827 (USSC, 1970)
U.S. Tax Cases	CCH Incorporated	Tax: all federal courts except Tax Court	Ruddick Corp. v. U.S., 81-1 USTC ¶9343 (Ct. Cls., 1981)

U.S. District Court. Because each U.S. district court is independent of the other district courts, the decisions of each have precedential value only within its own jurisdiction (i.e., only with respect to subsequent cases brought before that court). District courts must follow decisions of the U.S. Supreme Court, the circuit court to which the case is appealable, and the district court's own earlier decisions on the same issue.

EXAMPLE I15-9 ▶ The U.S. District Court for Rhode Island, the Tax Court, and the Eleventh Circuit have ruled on a particular issue. Any U.S. district court within the Eleventh Circuit must follow that circuit's decision. Similarly, the U.S. District Court for Rhode Island must rule consistently with its previous ruling. Tax Court decisions are not binding on the district courts. Thus, all district courts other than the one for Rhode Island and those within the Eleventh Circuit are free to decide the issue independently. ◀

U.S. Court of Federal Claims. In deciding issues, the U.S. Court of Federal Claims must rule consistently with U.S. Supreme Court cases, cases decided by the Circuit Court of Appeals for the Federal Circuit, and its own earlier decisions, including decisions rendered when the court had a different name. It need not follow decisions of other circuit courts, the Tax Court, or U.S. district courts.

EXAMPLE I15-10 ▶ Assume the same facts as in Example I15-9. In a later year, the same issue is litigated in the U.S. Court of Federal Claims. This court is not bound by any of the authorities that have addressed the issue. Thus, it has complete flexibility to reach its own conclusion. ◀

Circuit Courts of Appeals. A circuit court is bound by U.S. Supreme Court cases and earlier cases decided by that particular circuit. If neither the Supreme Court nor the circuit in question has already decided an issue, the circuit court has no precedent that it must follow, regardless of whether other circuits have ruled on the point. In such a situation, the circuit court is said to be writing on a clean slate. In issuing a decision, the judges may adopt the view expressed in another circuit's opinion if they deem it appropriate.

EXAMPLE I15-11 ▶ Assume the same facts as in Example I15-9. Any circuit other than the Eleventh would be writing on a clean slate if it faced the same issue. After reviewing the Eleventh Circuit's decision, another circuit might or might not rule in the same way. ◀

In such a case of "first impression" for the court, when the court has had no precedent on which to base a decision, a tax practitioner might look at past decisions of the court to see which other circuits the court has found to be "persuasive."

Forum Shopping. Not surprisingly, courts often disagree as to the appropriate tax treatment of the same item. This disagreement gives rise to differing precedents within the various jurisdictions (what is called a "split in judicial authority"). Because taxpayers have the flexibility of choosing where to file a lawsuit, these circumstances afford them the opportunity to **forum shop.** Forum-shopping involves choosing where among the courts to file a lawsuit based on differing precedents.

An example of a split in judicial authority concerned the issue of when it became too late for the IRS to question the proper tax treatment of items that "flowed through" an S corporation's return to a shareholder's return. The key question was this: if the time for assessing a deficiency (statute of limitations) with respect to the corporation's, but not the shareholder's, return had expired, was the IRS precluded from collecting additional taxes from the shareholder? In *Kelley*,[37] the Ninth Circuit Court of Appeals ruled that the IRS would be barred from collecting additional taxes from the shareholder if the statute of limitations for the *S corporation's* return had expired. In *Bufferd*,[38] *Fehlhaber*,[39] and

---

[37] *Daniel M. Kelley v. CIR*, 64 AFTR 2d 89-5025, 89-1 USTC ¶9360 (9th Cir., 1989).
[38] *Sheldon B. Bufferd v. CIR*, 69 AFTR 2d 92-465, 92-1 USTC ¶50,031 (2nd Cir., 1992).
[39] *Robert Fehlhaber v. CIR*, 69 AFTR 2d 92-850, 92-1 USTC ¶50,131 (11th Cir., 1992).

Green,[40] three other circuit courts ruled that the IRS would be barred from collecting additional taxes from the shareholder if the statute of limitations for the *shareholder's* return had expired. The Supreme Court affirmed the *Bufferd*[41] case, establishing that the statute of limitations for the shareholder's return governed. This action brought about certainty and uniformity in the judicial system.

Dictum. At times, a court may comment on an issue or a set of facts not central to the case under review. A court's remark not essential to the determination of a disputed issue, and therefore not binding authority, is called *dictum*. An example of dictum is found in *Central Illinois Public Service Co.*[42] In this case, the U.S. Supreme Court addressed whether lunch reimbursements received by employees constitute wages subject to withholding. Justice Blackman remarked in passing that earnings in the form of interest, rents, and dividends are not wages. This remark is dictum because it is not essential to the determination of whether lunch reimbursements are wages subject to withholding. Although not authoritative, dictum may be cited by taxpayers to bolster an argument in favor of a particular tax result.

STOP & THINK

Question: You have been researching whether a certain amount received by your new client can be excluded from her gross income. The IRS is auditing the client's tax return for two years ago, which another firm prepared. In a similar case decided a few years ago, the Tax Court allowed an exclusion, but the IRS nonacquiesced in the decision. The case involved a taxpayer from the Fourth Circuit. Your client is a resident of Maine, which is in the First Circuit. Twelve years ago, in a case involving another taxpayer, the U.S. district court for the client's district ruled that this type of receipt is not excludable. There has been no other litigation. To sustain an exclusion, must your client litigate? Explain. If your client litigates, in which trial court should she begin her litigation?

Solution: Because of the IRS's nonacquiescence, your client's exclusion is not likely to be sustained unless she litigates. She would not want to litigate in her U.S. district court because it would be bound by its earlier decision, which is unfavorable to taxpayers. A good place to begin would be the Tax Court because of its earlier pro-taxpayer position. No one can predict how the U.S. Court of Federal Claims would rule because no precedent that it must follow exists.

TAX TREATIES

ADDITIONAL COMMENT
A tax treaty carries the same authoritative weight as a statute. A tax advisor should be aware of provisions in tax treaties that will affect a taxpayer's worldwide tax liability.

The United States has concluded **tax treaties** with numerous foreign countries. These treaties address tax and other matters. A tax advisor addressing the U.S. tax consequences of a U.S. corporation's business operations in another country should determine whether a treaty exists between that country and the United States. If one does, the tax advisor should ascertain the applicable provisions of the treaty. (See Chapter C16 of this text for a more extensive discussion of treaties.)

TAX PERIODICALS

KEY POINT
Tax articles can be used to help *find* answers to tax questions. Where possible, the underlying statutory, administrative, or judicial sources referenced in the tax article should be cited as authority and not the author of the article. The courts and the IRS will place little, if any, reliance on mere editorial opinion.

Tax periodicals assist the researcher in tracing the development of, and in analyzing tax law. These periodicals are especially useful when they trace the legislative history of a recently enacted statute, and there is little or no administrative or judicial authority on point.

Tax experts write articles on recent court decisions, proposed regulations, new tax legislation, and other matters. Frequently, those who write articles of a highly technical nature are attorneys, accountants, or professors. Among the periodicals that provide in-depth coverage of tax-related developments are the following:

---

[40] *Charles T. Green v. CIR*, 70 AFTR 2d 92-5077, 92-2 USTC ¶50,340 (5th Cir., 1992).
[41] *Sheldon B. Bufferd v. CIR*, 71 AFTR 2d 93-573, 93-1 USTC ¶50,038 (USSC, 1993).
[42] *Central Illinois Public Service Co. v. CIR*, 41 AFTR 2d 78-718, 78-1 USTC ¶9254 (USSC, 1978).

The Journal of Taxation
The Tax Adviser
Practical Tax Strategies
Taxes—the Tax Magazine
Tax Law Review
Tax Notes
The Journal of Corporate Taxation
The Journal of Partnership Taxation
The Journal of Real Estate Taxation
The Review of Taxation of Individuals
Estate Planning Journal

The first six journals are generalized; that is, they deal with a variety of topics. As their titles suggest, the next five are specialized; they deal with specific subjects. All these publications (other than *Tax Notes*, which is published weekly) are published either monthly or quarterly. Daily newsletters, such as the *Daily Tax Report*, published by the Bureau of National Affairs (BNA), are used by tax professionals when they need updates more timely than can be provided by monthly and quarterly publications.

Tax periodicals and tax services are secondary authorities. The IRC, Treasury Regulations, IRS pronouncements, and court opinions are primary authorities. In presenting research results, the tax advisor should always cite primary authorities.

TAX SERVICES — Skip

OBJECTIVE 4

Use tax services to research an issue

Multivolume commentaries on the tax law are published by various publishers. These commentaries are known as **tax services**. Each tax service is encyclopedic in scope. Most come in looseleaf form so that information concerning current developments can be easily added. The organizational scheme of each service differs. Some are updated more frequently than others. Each has its own special features and unique way of presenting material. The best way to become familiar with the various tax services is to use them in researching hypothetical or actual problems.

Organizationally, there are two types of tax services: "annotated" and "topical." An **annotated tax service** is organized by IRC section. The IRC-arranged subdivisions of this service are likely to encompass several topics. A **topical tax service** is organized by broad topic. The topically-arranged subdivisions of this service are likely to encompass several IRC sections. The principal annotated tax services are *United States Tax Reporter* and *Standard Federal Tax Reporter*. The main topical services are *Federal Tax Coordinator 2d, Law of Federal Income Taxation (Mertens), Tax Management Portfolios, and CCH Federal Tax Service*. Each of these services is discussed below.

ADDITIONAL COMMENT

Tax services often are consulted at the beginning of the research process. A tax service helps identify the tax authorities pertaining to a particular tax issue. The actual tax authorities, and not the tax service, are generally cited as support for a particular tax position.

KEY POINT

Both the *United States Tax Reporter* and the *Standard Federal Tax Reporter* services are organized by IRC section. Many tax advisors find both of these services easy to use. The other major tax services are organized by topic.

UNITED STATES TAX REPORTER

United States Tax Reporter, published by RIA, is a multi-volume series devoted to income, estate, gift, and excise taxes. It is organized by IRC section (i.e., its commentary begins with Sec. 1 of the IRC and proceeds in numerical order through the last section of the IRC). Researchers familiar with the IRC section applicable to their problem can begin their research by turning directly to the paragraphs discussing this section. For each IRC section, a code-based paragraph sequencing is used for the IRC text, the Treasury Regulations text, committee reports, editorial explanations, and digests of cases and rulings, so the researcher does not have to learn a different numbering system. Thus, a researcher who knows which IRC section addresses the issue (e.g., Sec. 280A) can go immediately to whichever volume provides commentary on that section. Another technique for beginning research is first to think of key words that capture the flavor of the problem and then to consult the index. The topical index appears in a separate volume. It refers the researcher to the paragraph number(s) of the service where the topics of interest are discussed.

For each IRC section, the *United States Tax Reporter* service reproduces verbatim the statutory language and the Treasury Regulations, provides an editorial explanation of the provisions, and furnishes brief summaries of cases and rulings interpreting the applicable IRC section. It provides citations to the full text of each case or ruling. The summaries are categorized into fairly explicit topical areas, such as the deductibility, as a medical expense, of the cost of special food and beverages and food supplements.

The *United States Tax Reporter* service is updated weekly. The most recent developments are highlighted in Volume 16 in a cross-reference table and periodically moved into the body of the text. The cross-reference table is organized by paragraph number. To determine whether any recent developments affect a particular question, the researcher should look in the table for entries for the paragraph number where he or she found helpful information in the main body of the service. Because of the need to consult the cross-reference table, the researcher should note the paragraph numbers that prove fruitful as the research proceeds. The supplementary index in the Index Volume (Volume 1) of the service is updated monthly to reflect recent developments. Supplementary tables of cases and rulings in the Tables Volume (Volume 2) provide information on new authorities that have been incorporated into the main body of the service.

STANDARD FEDERAL TAX REPORTER

REAL WORLD EXAMPLE
The 1913 CCH explanation of the federal tax law was a single 400-page volume. The current *Standard Federal Tax Reporter* is 25 volumes and over 95,000 pages in length.

CCH publishes the *Standard Federal Tax Reporter* (CCH service). This service also is organized by IRC section. Separate services devoted to excise taxes and estate and gift taxes are available, as well as the multivolume income tax service. The CCH service reproduces the IRC and Treasury Regulations. It summarizes and provides citations to other authorities in much the same way as does the *United States Tax Reporter* service.[43]

An index volume contains a topical index that lists references by paragraph number. Because the volumes are organized by IRC section number, a researcher who knows the number of the relevant IRC section can bypass the index.

Searching for any recent authorities on an issue is similar in approach to searching in the *United States Tax Reporter* service. The researcher should consult the Cumulative Index table in Volume 19 and search for entries applicable to the paragraph numbers in the main body of the service where he or she found relevant authorities. The CCH service publishes weekly supplements on current developments. Updates of court cases and revenue rulings are retained in Volume 19 until the end of the calendar year, when CCH publishes an entirely new service. Major events such as new legislation and Supreme Court decisions are integrated into the main body of the text throughout the year.

FEDERAL TAX COORDINATOR 2d

ADDITIONAL COMMENT
The RIA *Federal Tax Coordinator 2d* service is a more voluminous service than either the *United States Tax Reporter* or *Standard Federal Tax Reporter* services because it has more editorial commentary. The *Federal Tax Coordinator 2d* updates are integrated into the main body of the text. The service is not replaced each year. By contrast, both the *United States Tax Reporter* and *Standard Federal Tax Reporter* services compile their updates in one volume. CCH issues a new *Standard Federal Tax Reporter* service each year. The other services integrate the updates into the body of existing text at the beginning of each year.

The *Federal Tax Coordinator 2d* is published by RIA and is referred to in this text as the RIA service. It covers three major areas: income taxes, estate and gift taxes, and excise taxes. The RIA income tax service is a multivolume looseleaf publication organized by broad topic. For example, Volume K deals with deductions for taxes, interest, charitable contributions, medical expenses, and other items. The topic index, found in a separate volume, indicates the chapter and paragraph numbers of the main commentary where tax-related topics are discussed. Cross-reference volumes provide tables for finding where IRC sections, Treasury Regulations, revenue rulings, and court cases are discussed.

The RIA service reproduces all the IRC sections and Treasury Regulations applicable to a particular volume behind a tab marker titled "Code & Regs." Using detailed captions, the various volumes provide an editorial-type commentary about tax issues. References to cases, including citations, appear in footnote form. The RIA service does not compile in a single volume information about new developments for all topics. Although each volume has a tab marker titled "Developments," current developments for

---

[43] Examples of citations to these tax services are as follows: (2001) 6 *United States Tax Reporter* (RIA) ¶3025 and (2001) 8 *Std. Fed. Tax Rep.* (CCH) ¶21,966.02, where 6 and 8 represent the volume numbers, and the paragraph numbers refer to the cited passages in the volume. Because citations should be to primary authorities, citations to secondary authorities are rarely used.

that volume are included in the main body of the service. Separate volumes are devoted to proposed regulations, revenue rulings, and revenue procedures. The RIA service publishes current developments weekly.

LAW OF FEDERAL INCOME TAXATION (MERTENS)

ADDITIONAL COMMENT

Mertens is reputed to be the most scholarly of all tax services. It is the only service cited by the judiciary with any regularity.

The *Law of Federal Income Taxation,* published by the West Group, was originally edited by Jacob Mertens and usually is called "Mertens" by tax practitioners. Mertens generally is considered to be the most authoritative of all tax services. It is the service most frequently cited by the courts and, in fact, the only service cited by the judiciary with any regularity. Like the RIA *Federal Tax Coordinator 2d* service, Mertens is organized by general topic. Volume 7, for example, provides a comprehensive discussion of wages, travel, interest, taxes, and net operating losses. The commentary is in narrative form and reads like a treatise. References to the authorities appear in footnotes.

One volume of Mertens contains a topical index. References are to section numbers (assigned by the editors) instead of to paragraph numbers. Another volume, titled *Tables,* discloses where IRC sections, Treasury Regulations, and IRS rulings are discussed in the commentary volumes. The *Table of Cases* volume does the same with respect to cases.

Mertens is updated monthly to reflect current developments. Like the RIA *Federal Tax Coordinator 2d* service, the supplementary material for a particular volume is found in that volume. The new material is organized by the same Mertens' section numbers that have been assigned to topics in the main body of the service. The volume titled *Current Materials* contains in-depth articles on current developments as well as monthly updates that complement the supplementary materials included in the treatise volumes.

Mertens includes several volumes devoted exclusively to Treasury Regulations and revenue rulings. The text of these authorities do not appear in Mertens' main commentary volumes. Mertens' *Current Rulings Materials* volume contains a Code-Rulings Table that lists by IRC section the numbers of all revenue rulings, issued since 1954, that interpret a particular section. For example, for the period 1954 through 2000, the table lists one ruling under IRC Sec. 1034(b)(1) that interprets that subsection. The post-2000 table lists no rulings under IRC Sec. 1034(b)(1) that interpret that subsection.

The *Current Rulings Materials* volume also contains a Rulings Status Table. This table indicates how the status of every revenue ruling issued since 1954 has been impacted by IRS actions. Examples of IRS actions are revoking, modifying, amplifying, or superceding a ruling. The RIA and CCH citators provide essentially the same information in different formats.[44]

TAX MANAGEMENT PORTFOLIOS

ADDITIONAL COMMENT

The *Tax Management Portfolios* are popular with many tax advisors because they are very readable yet still provide a comprehensive discussion of the pertinent tax issues. However, because the published portfolios do not cover all areas of the tax law, another service may be necessary to supplement the gaps in the portfolio coverage.

BNA publishes booklets of approximately 150 pages each called *Tax Management Portfolios* (referred to as "BNA portfolios" by many practitioners and in this text). Each portfolio provides an in-depth discussion of a relatively narrow issue, such as involuntary conversions or the estate tax marital deduction. Thus, when the research question has been narrowed down to a very precise issue, consulting a BNA portfolio can be quite helpful.

BNA provides a notebook that contains an IRC section index and a key words list or topical index. Each index references appropriate page numbers.

Each portfolio contains a narrative discussion called "Detailed Analysis" and a compilation of practical aids called "Working Papers." The Detailed Analysis is supported by a wealth of footnotes in which are found numerous references to primary authorities. Working Papers contains excerpts from committee reports, copies of tax forms relevant to the Detailed Analysis, sample language for drafting letters, and other practical tools. At the end of each portfolio is a bibliography that lists primary and secondary sources pertinent to the analysis.

---

[44] Citators are discussed later in this chapter.

CCH FEDERAL TAX SERVICE

The newest of the major tax services is the *CCH Federal Tax Service,* currently published by CCH and formerly published by Matthew Bender & Company. This service is a multi-volume looseleaf publication that, like the RIA *Federal Tax Coordinator 2d* and Mertens services, is organized by broad topic. It provides analyses of broad topics such as the taxation of individuals and partnerships, sales and exchanges, and farming and natural resources.

The *CCH Federal Tax Service* does not reproduce the IRC and Treasury Regulations in the volumes with the topical analysis. Instead, it devotes separate volumes to the IRC and proposed, temporary, and final Treasury Regulations. An IRC section and the related Treasury Regulations appear together in the same volume.

The *CCH Federal Tax Service* is updated periodically to reflect current developments. In addition, a weekly newsletter is sent to subscribers as part of the service. The current developments material is combined with the analysis to which it relates.

Figure I15-5 provides an overview of one approach for using the tax services to research a tax question.

CITATORS

OBJECTIVE 5

Use a citator to assess authorities

Citators serve two functions: first, they give a history of the case (e.g., if the case under analysis is an appeals court decision, the citator indicates the trial court that heard the case and whether the Supreme Court reviewed the case); and second, they list other authorities (e.g., cases and revenue rulings) that cite the case in question. A citator of judicial decisions is included in the CCH service at no additional charge. The RIA citator is available separately from either of RIA's principal tax services.

CCH CITATOR

The CCH citator consists of two loose-leaf volumes, one for cases with names beginning with the letters A through M and the other for cases with names starting with the letters N through Z, revenue rulings, and other government promulgations. This citator analyzes every decision reported in CCH's *Standard Federal Tax Reporter,* its *Excise Tax Reporter,* and its *Federal Estate and Gift Tax Reporter* and selectively lists cases that cite the reported decision. (CCH editors decide which of these other cases influence the precedential weight of the reported decision.) With respect to rulings and other government promulgations, the Finding Lists section provides full histories of all actions affected by or affecting each ruling. For example, the list notes that a certain 1993 revenue ruling revokes a certain 1989 revenue ruling. An excerpt from the CCH citator appears in Figure I15-6.

Refer to Figure I15-6, and find the *Leonarda C. Diaz* case. The information in bold print with bullets to the left denotes that *Diaz* was a decision of the Second Circuit and the Tax Court and that the Second Circuit affirmed (upheld) the Tax Court's decision. The two cases listed beneath the Second Circuit decision (i.e., *Kuh* and *Damm*) cite the *Diaz* decision. The six cases listed beneath the Tax Court decision (i.e., *German, Jr., Orr, Zeidler, Schwerm, Wassenaar,* and *Toner*) cite the Tax Court's opinion in *Diaz.* The abbreviation *Dec.* appearing in some of the citations stands for *decision.* The CCH citator lists the decision numbers of the Tax Court cases.

The main CCH citator volumes are published once a year. The first of these volumes contains a "Current Citator Table," which lists court decisions recently cited, as well as additional citing cases for court decisions previously cited. Citator updates are issued quarterly. The *Diaz* decision has not been cited in any opinion issued since 2000, the year

```
┌─────────────────────────────────────────────────┐
│ 1. Consult the topical index for references to  │
│    the appropriate paragraph numbers, etc. in   │
│    the commentary section.                      │
└─────────────────────────────────────────────────┘
                        ↓
┌─────────────────────────────────────────────────┐
│ 2. Consult the paragraph numbers, etc. of the   │
│    commentary section. (This section contains   │
│    excerpts of relevant provisions of the IRC   │
│    and Treasury Regulations as well as editorial│
│    comments. The commentary also summarizes and │
│    cites cases and rulings.) Read the IRC,      │
│    Treasury Regulations, and the editorial      │
│    comments.                                    │
└─────────────────────────────────────────────────┘
                        ↓
┌─────────────────────────────────────────────────┐
│ 3. Refer to the supplementary material to       │
│    determine whether any relevant current       │
│    developments are not discussed in the main   │
│    body of the service.                         │
└─────────────────────────────────────────────────┘
                        ↓
┌─────────────────────────────────────────────────┐
│ 4. Read the full text of the primary            │
│    authorities referenced in Steps 2 and 3.     │
└─────────────────────────────────────────────────┘
                        ↓
┌─────────────────────────────────────────────────┐
│ 5. Use a citator to determine (1) the current   │
│    status of pertinent cases and rulings and    │
│    (2) other authorities (if any) that may be   │
│    on point. Read the additional authorities    │
│    (if any).                                    │
└─────────────────────────────────────────────────┘
                        ↓
┌─────────────────────────────────────────────────┐
│ 6. Evaluate the authorities; analogize if no    │
│    cases are on point; formulate your           │
│    conclusions.                                 │
└─────────────────────────────────────────────────┘
                        ↓
┌─────────────────────────────────────────────────┐
│ 7. Communicate conclusions and recommendations  │
│    to the client.                               │
└─────────────────────────────────────────────────┘
                        ↓
┌─────────────────────────────────────────────────┐
│ 8. At times the researcher may discover that    │
│    additional facts are needed or the issues    │
│    must be refined. In such situations, the     │
│    researcher may have to return to Step 1.     │
└─────────────────────────────────────────────────┘
```

FIGURE I15-5 ▶ USE OF TAX SERVICES TO RESEARCH A TAX QUESTION

in which the CCH citator was last published. The applicable page from the main citator table for the *Diaz* decision is reproduced here.

The entry "¶5504.195" appearing to the right of *Alfonso Diaz* denotes the number of the *Standard Federal Tax Reporter* paragraph that discusses the case. Usually, before consulting the citator, a researcher already would have read about this case in the paragraph and would have decided that it was relevant to his or her research. In such circumstances, the paragraph reference would not be particularly useful. In other circumstances, the reference would be useful. For example, if the researcher had heard about the case from a colleague and wanted to read more about it, he or she could readily locate the passage that discusses it.

Cases are listed in the CCH citator even where they have not been cited in other cases. For example, refer to the entry for *Frank Diaz*. This Tax Court memo decision is listed among the cases analyzed, even though no other published decision has referred to it. Moreover, the citator indicates whether the IRS Commissioner has acquiesced or nonacquiesced in a Tax Court decision. For example, refer to the entry for *Alfonso Diaz*. Note that the first Tax Court citation is followed by a capital "A," then another citation. The "A" indicates that the IRS Commissioner acquiesced in the Tax Court decision. The second citation indicates that the Commissioner's acquiescence is found on page 2 of Volume 2 of the 1972 *Cumulative Bulletin*.

DIA   93,302   ———CCH———

Diamond, Sol . . ¶5508.085, 8520.517, 21,005.123, 25,083.2683, 25,243.016, 25,243.08, 25,442.023
- CA-7—(aff'g TC), 74-1 USTC ¶9306; 492 F2d 286

Campbell, CA-8, 91-2 USTC ¶50,420
Rev. Proc. 93-27
Anderson, TC, Dec. 50,410(M), 69 TCM 1609, TC Memo. 1995-8
Banks, TC, Dec. 47,832(M), 62 TCM 1611, TC Memo. 1991-641
Arcia, TC, Dec. 52,701(M), 75 TCM 2287, TC Memo. 1998-178
Johnson, TC, Dec. 52,812(M), 76 TCM 194, TC Memo. 1998-275
AJF Transportation Consultants, Inc., TC, Dec. 53,220(M), TC Memo. 1999-16, 77 TCM 1244
Pacheco, CA-9, 90-2 USTC ¶50,458
Vestal, CA-8, 74-2 USTC ¶9501, 498 F2d 487
St. John, DC-III, 84-1 USTC ¶9158
Campbell, TC, Dec. 46,493(M), 59 TCM 236, TC Memo. 1990-162
McNulty, TC, Dec. 44,857(M), 55 TCM 1138, TC Memo. 1988-274
Greater Display & Wire Forming, Inc., TC, Dec. 44,802(M), 55 TCM 922, TC Memo. 1988-231
National Oil Co., TC, Dec. 43,557(M), 52 TCM 1223, TC Memo. 1986-596
Hirst, TC, Dec. 43,215(M), 51 TCM 1597, TC Memo. 1986-321
Mouriz, TC, Dec. 42,851(M), 51 TCM 392, TC Memo. 1986-43
Parker, TC, Dec. 42,129(M), 50 TCM 14, TC Memo. 1985-263
Kenroy, Inc., TC, Dec. 41,186(M), 47 TCM 1749, TC Memo. 1984-232
Bertolini Trucking Co., TC, Dec. 39,474(M), 45 TCM 44, TC Memo. 1982-643
Kessler, TC, Dec. 39,226(M), 44 TCM 624, TC Memo. 1982-432
Tooke, TC, Dec. 34,336(M), 36 TCM 396, TC memo. 1977-91
Pierson, TC, Dec. 34,009(M), 35 TCM 1256, TC Memo. 1976-281
- TC—Dec. 30,838; 56 TC 530

Manchester Music Co., Inc., DC-NH, 90-1 USTC ¶50,168, 733 FSupp 473
Miller, Jr., TC, Dec. 45,977(M), 57 TCM 1419, TC Memo. 1989-461
McNulty, TC, Dec. 44,857(M), 55 TCM 1138, TC Memo. 1988-274
Greater Display & Wire Forming, Inc., TC, Dec. 44,802(M), 55 TCM 922, TC Memo. 1988-231
National Oil Co., TC, Dec. 43,557(M), 52 TCM 1223, TC Memo. 1986-596
Goodwin, David C., TC, Dec. 36,413, 73 TC 215
Schaevitz, TC, Dec. 30,925(M), 30 TCM 823, TC Memo. 1971-197

Diamond, Solomon . . . . ¶8632.68
- TC—Dec. 25,981(M); 22 TCM 229; TC Memo. 1963-57

Diamond T Motor Car Co.: Allen v. . . . . . . ¶38,160.82
- CA-10—(rev'g DC), 61-1 USTC ¶9484; 291 F2d 115

Randall, CA-5, 76-2 USTC ¶9770, 542 F2d 270
Jefferson Bank and Trust, DC-Colo, 89-1 USTC ¶9221
Rodkey, DC-Okla, 87-1 USTC ¶9218
Nevada Rock & Sand Co., DC-Nev, 74-2 USTC ¶9617, 376 FSupp 161
Nomellini Construction Co., DC-Calif, 71-2 USTC ¶9510, 328 FSupp 1281
- DC-Colo—60-2 USTC ¶9557

Diamondhead Corp. v. Fort Hope Development, Inc. . . . . ¶40,720.1945
- DC-Ga—78-2 USTC ¶9718

Diamondstone, I. A. (See Kann, William L.)
DiAndre, Anthony F. . . . . ¶36,894.7255, 41,758.30
- SCt—Cert. denied, 3/19/93
- CA-10—(rev'g and rem'g unreported DC), 92-2 USTC ¶50,373; 968 F2d 1049

Stewart, DC-Ohio, 95-1 USTC ¶50,249
Russell, DC-Mich, 95-1 USTC ¶50,029
Jones, DC-Neb, 94-2 USTC ¶50,562, 869 FSupp 747
Schachter, DC-Calif, 94-1 USTC ¶50,242
Fostvedt, DC-Colo, 93-1 USTC ¶50,299, 824 FSupp 978
Jones, DC-Neb, 95-2 USTC ¶50,567, 898 FSupp 1360
May, DC-Mo, 95-2 USTC ¶50,605
Spence, DC-NM, 96-2 USTC ¶50,615
Spence, CA-10, 97-1 USTC ¶50,485
Roebuck, DC-NC, 99-2 USTC ¶50,627

DiAndrea, Inc. . . . ¶16,233.25, 21,817.108, 44,507.09
- TC—Dec. 40,697(M); 47 TCM 731; TC Memo. 1983-768

Johnson, TC, Dec. 47,836(M), 62 TCM 1629, TC Memo. 1991-645

Diaz, Alfonso . . . . ¶5504.195
- TC—Dec. 31,442; 58 TC 560; A. 1972-2 CB 2

Marrone, TC, Dec. 50,424(M), 69 TCM 1684, TC Memo. 1995-22
Sloan, TC, Dec. 50,305(M), 68 TCM 1489, TC Memo. 1994-628
Muniz, TC, Dec. 49,775(M), 67 TCM 2625, TC Memo. 1994-151
Drabiuk, TC, Dec. 50,692(M), 69 TCM 2890, TC Memo. 1995-260
Jackson, TC, Dec. 50,736(M), TC Memo. 1995-300, 70 TCM 12
Levin, TC, Dec. 51,326(M), 71 TCM 2938, TC Memo. 1996-211
American Underwriters, Inc., TC, Dec. 51,694(M), TC Memo. 1996-548, 72 TCM 1511
Schaas, TC, Dec. 52,529(M), 75 TCM 1613, TC Memo. 1998-25
Arcia, TC, Dec. 52,701(M), 75 TCM 2287, TC Memo. 1998-178
Meslow, TC, Dec. 52,302(M), TC Memo. 1997-466, 74 TCM 910
Neff Est., TC, Dec. 51,999(M), TC Memo. 1997-186, 73 TCM 2606
Swiatek, TC, Dec. 53,485(M), 78 TCM 223, TC Memo. 1999-257
Schirle, TC, Dec. 52,398(M), TC Memo. 1997-552, 74 TCM 1379
Kong, TC, Dec. 46,090(M), 58 TCM 378, TC Memo. 1989-560
Caglia, E. Bonnie, TC, Dec. 45,585(M), 57 TCM 1, TC Memo. 1989-143
Ettg, TC, Dec. 44,736(M), 55 TCM 720, TC Memo. 1988-182
Heller, TC, Dec. 44,083(M), 53 TCM 1486, TC Memo. 1987-376
Anastasato, TC, Dec. 43,309(M), 52 TCM 293, TC Memo. 1986-400
Stevenson, TC, Dec. 43,068(M), 51 TCM 1050, TC Memo. 1986-207
Wilhelm, TC, Dec. 42,813(M), 51 TCM 261, TC Memo. 1986-12
Branson, TC, Dec. 38,026(M), 42 TCM 281, TC Memo. 1981-338
Calloway, TC, Dec. 37,019(M), 40 TCM 495, TC Memo. 1980-211
Greenfield, TC, Dec. 35,253(M), 37 TCM 1082, TC Memo. 1978-251
Leong, TC, Dec. 34,232(M), 36 TCM 89, TC Memo. 1977-19
Dougherty, TC, Dec. 32,138, 60 TC 917
Hernandez, TC, Dec. 52,552(M), TC Memo. 1998-46, 75 TCM 1714

Diaz, Antonio A. v. Southern Drilling Corp. . . . . ¶41,699.45
- CA-5—(aff'g unreported DC), 71-1 USTC ¶9236

Diaz, Enrique . . ¶33,538.43, 39,475.65, 39,585.63, 42,688.377
- DC-Calif—90-1 USTC ¶50,209

Van Camp & Bennion, P.S., DC-Wash, 96-2 USTC ¶50,438

Diaz, Frank . . . . ¶29,412.9911
- TC—Dec. 42,922(M); 51 TCM 594; TC Memo. 1986-98

Diaz, Greg, Acting County Recorder for the City and County of San Francisco (See Chase Manhattan Bank, N.A. v. City & County of San Francisco)
Diaz, Humberto (See Flicker, Marvin)
Diaz, Juan (See Setal, Manuel G.)
Diaz, Leonarda C. . . . . ¶8632.3876
- CA-2—(aff'g TC), 79-2 USTC ¶9473; 607 F2d 995

Kuh, TC, Dec. 40,461(M), 46 TCM 1405, TC Memo. 1983-572
Damm, TC, Dec. 37,861(M), 41 TCM 1359, TC Memo. 1981-203
- TC—Dec. 35,436; 70 TC 1067

German, Jr., TC, Dec. 48,867(M), 65 TCM 1931, TC Memo. 1993-59
Orr, TC, Dec. 48,532(M), 64 TCM 882, TC Memo. 1992-566
Zeider, TC, Dec. 51,264(M), 71 TCM 2603, TC Memo. 1996-157
Schwerm, TC, Dec. 42,817(M), 51 TCM 270, TC Memo. 1986-16
Wassenaar, TC, Dec. 36,359, 72 TC 1195
Toner, TC, Dec. 35,877, 71 TC 772

Diaz, Miguel A. (See Powers (Belcher), Sandra L.)
Dibble, Leon N., Exr. . . . . ¶29,225.442
- BTA—Dec. 2320; 6 BTA 732; A. VI-2 CB 2

FIGURE I15-6   ▶   EXCERPT FROM THE CCH CITATOR

Reproduced with permission from CCH *Standard Federal Tax Reporter*, published and copyrighted by CCH Incorporated, 2700 Lake Cook Road, Riverwoods, IL 60015.

RESEARCH INSTITUTE OF AMERICA CITATOR 2nd SERIES

Like the CCH citator, the *Research Institute of America Citator 2nd Series*[45] (RIA citator) provides the history of each case and ruling and lists the cases and rulings that have cited the authority in question. The RIA citator, however, conveys more information than does the CCH citator. This information includes the following:

1. Whether the citing cases comment favorably or unfavorably on the cited cases, or whether they can be distinguished from the cited cases.[46]
2. The specific issue(s) in the cited case that is (are) referenced by the citing authorities.

> **ADDITIONAL COMMENT**
>
> The history of a case may be easier to find in CCH because each of the courts that tried the case is listed in a single volume in bold-face print.

The RIA citator (formerly, the Prentice Hall citator) consists of six hard-bound volumes and several cumulative supplements. The first hard-bound volume lists cases decided from 1863 through 1941; the second, cases decided from 1942 through September 30, 1948; the third, cases decided from October 1, 1948 through July 29, 1954; the fourth, cases decided from July 30, 1954 through December 15, 1977; the fifth, cases cited from December 15, 1977 through December 20, 1989; and the sixth, cases decided from January 4, 1990 to December 26, 1996. The softback cumulative supplements list cases decided from December 26, 1996 to the present month. Each year, a revised annual supplement is published. Each month, a revised monthly supplement is published. In analyzing a 1945 case, a researcher should consult every cumulative supplement and every main volume except the first. In analyzing a 1980 case, the researcher should consult every cumulative supplement and the last two bound volumes.

As mentioned earlier, the RIA citator reveals the manner in which the citing authorities comment on the case under analysis. The nature of the comment is indicated by symbols that appear to the left of the citing case names. The RIA citator also reveals the history of the case under analysis (i.e., whether it was affirmed, reversed, etc.)[47] This history is indicated by symbols that appear to the left of citations to the same case heard at different appellate levels (parallel citations). Figure I15-7 explains the meaning of the various symbols.

The RIA citator is especially useful if the cited case deals with more than one issue. As previously mentioned, the citator reports the issue(s) addressed in the cited case that is (are) referenced in the citing authority. The numbers to the left of this authority denote the specific issue(s) referenced. These numbers correspond to headnotes of the opinion as it appears in *American Federal Tax Reports*. A **headnote** is an editorial summary of a particular point of case law. Headnotes appear in case reporters immediately before the text of the opinions authored by the judges.

An excerpt from the 1978–1989 citator volume appears in the first column of Figure I15-8. Refer to it and locate the Tax Court decision for *Leonarda C. Diaz*. All the cases that cite the decision after 1977 and through 1989 are listed. (*Diaz* was decided by the Tax Court in 1978, so no earlier references will be found.) *Diaz* has been cited with respect to its first and second AFTR headnotes. If there are other AFTR headnotes, the case has not been cited with respect to them.

The "a" on the first line beneath the name of the case indicates that the Tax Court's decision was affirmed by the Second Circuit. The Tax Court's opinion has been explained and followed in various cases, but it has not been cited in an unfavorable manner. Thus, its authoritative weight is substantial.

The Second Circuit's decision appears as a separate entry. The letters "sa" signify that the circuit court affirmed the Tax Court decision in the *Diaz* case. The cases that have cited the circuit court's opinion are listed under the entry for such opinion. The appellate decision has not been questioned or criticized; thus, its authority is relatively strong.

---

[45] The *Research Institute of America Citator 2nd Series* is published currently by RIA. It originally was published by Prentice Hall's Information Services Division, which was acquired in 1990 by Maxwell Macmillan. *Prentice Hall* and/or *Maxwell Macmillan* appears on the spines and title pages of the older citators and will remain there because, unlike the CCH citator, the RIA citator is not republished each year.

[46] When a court distinguishes its conclusion in one case from an earlier decision, it points out that the two different outcomes are justifiable because the facts in the two cases are not the same.

[47] If a case is *affirmed*, the decision of the lower court is upheld. *Reversed* means the higher court arrived at the opposite decision of the court from which the case was appealed. *Remanded* signifies that the higher court sent the case back to the lower court with instructions to address certain matters not earlier addressed.

SYMBOLS USED IN CITATOR COURT DECISIONS
Judicial History

- **a**   affirmed by a higher court (Note: When available, the official cite to the affirmance is provided; if the affirmance is by unpublished order or opinion, the date of the decision and the court deciding the case are provided.)
- **App auth**   appeal authorized by the Treasury
- **adptd**   magistrate judge's decision is accepted and adopted by district court
- **adptg**   district court accepts and adopts magistrate judge's decision
- **App**   appeal pending (Note: Later volumes may have to be consulted to determine if appeal was decided or dismissed.)
- **cert gr**   petition for certiorari was granted by the U.S. Supreme Court
- **d**   appeal dismissed by the court or withdrawn by the party filing the appeal
- **(G)**   following an appeal notation, this symbol indicates that it was the government filing the appeal
- **m**   the earlier decision has been modified by the higher court, or by a later decision.
- **r**   the decision of the lower court has been reversed on appeal
- **rc**   related case arising out of the same taxable event or concerning the same taxpayer
- **reh den**   rehearing has been denied by the same court in which the original case was heard
- **reinst**   a dismissed appeal has been reinstated by the appellate court and is under consideration again
- **remd**   the case has been remanded for proceedings consistent with the higher court decision
- **remg**   the cited case is remanding the earlier case
- **revg & remg**   the decision of the lower court has been reversed and remanded by a higher court on appeal
- **s**   same case or ruling
- **sa**   the cited case is affirming the earlier case
- **sm**   the cited case is modifying the earlier case
- **sr**   the cited case is reversing the earlier case
- **sx**   the cited case is an earlier proceeding in a case for which a petition for certiorari was denied
- **(T)**   an appeal was filed from the lower court decision by the taxpayer
- **vacd**   the lower court decision was vacated on appeal or by the original court on remand
- **vacg**   a higher court or the original court on remand has vacated the lower court decision
- **widm**   the original opinion was withdrawn by the court
- **x**   petition for certiorari was denied by the U.S. Supreme Court
- **•**   Supreme Court cases are designated by a bold-faced bullet (•) before the case line for easy location

Certain notations appear at the end of the cited case line. These notations include:

- **(A) or acq**   the government has acquiesced in the reasoning or the result of the cited case
- **(NA) or nonacq**   the government has refused to acquiesce or to adopt the reasoning or the result of the cited case, and will challenge the position adopted if future proceedings arise on the same issue
- **on rem**   the case has been remanded by a higher court and the case cited is the resulting decision

Evaluation of Cited Cases

- **c**   the citing case court has adversely commented on the reasoning of the cited case, and has criticized the earlier decision
- **e**   the cited case is used favorably by the citing case court
- **f**   the reasoning of the court in the cited case is followed by the later decision
- **g**   the cited and citing cases are distinguished from each other on either facts or law
- **inap**   the citing case court has specifically indicated that the cited case does not apply to the situation stated in the citing case.
- **iv**   on all fours (both the cited and citing cases are virtually identical)
- **k**   the cited and citing case principles are reconciled
- **l**   the rationale of the cited case is limited to the facts or circumstances surrounding that case (this can occur frequently in situations in which there has been an intervening higher court decision or law change)
- **n**   the cited case was noted in a dissenting opinion
- **o**   the later case directly overrules the cited case (use of the evaluation is generally limited to situations in which the court notes that it is specifically overturning the cited case, and that the case will no longer be of any value)
- **q**   the decision of the cited case is questioned and its validity debated in relation to the citing case at issue

The evaluations used for the court decisions generally are followed by a number. That number refers to the headnoted issue in the American Federal Tax Reports (AFTR) or Tax Court decision to which the citing case relates. If the case is not directly on point with any headnote, a bracketed notation at the end of the citing case line directs the researcher to the page in the cited case on which the issue appears.

A blank may appear in the evaluation space. Generally, this means that the citing court didn't comment on any of the legal issues raised in the cited case.

FIGURE I15-7   ▶   ABBREVIATIONS USED IN RIA CITATOR 2ND SERIES

Source: Reproduced with permission from Research Institute of America, Inc.

ADDITIONAL COMMENT

The RIA citator has the advantage of providing the most references for a cited case. This point is apparent when one compares RIA's six volumes plus supplements with CCH's two volumes. Also, RIA numbers each tax issue litigated in a court case. This coding allows the tax advisor to identify cases dealing with the specific issue being researched. For example, if the advisor is interested in the first issue in the *Leonarda Diaz* Tax Court decision, the citator reproduced in Figure I15-8 denotes five cases that deal specifically with issue 1 of which three follow the *Diaz* reasoning.

1978–1989
Citator Volume

DiANDREA, YOLANDA, TRANSFEREE, 1983 PH TC Memo ¶ 83,768 See DiAndrea, Inc.)
DIAZ, ALFONSO & MARIA de JESUS, 58 TC 560, ¶ 58.57 PH TC
  Reilly, Peter W., Est. of, 76 TC 374, 76 PH TC 201 [See 58 TC 565, n. 2]
  e—Greenfield, Stuart & Eileen, 1978 PH TC Memo 78-1070 [See 58 TC 564]
  e—Calloway, Johnny T., 1980 PH TC Memo 80-952 [See 58 TC 564]
  e—Branson, David L., 1981 PH TC Memo 81-1199 [See 58 TC 564, 565]
  e—Cohen, Robert B. & Marilyn W., 1983 PH TC Memo 83-1042 [See 58 TC 564]
  e—Patton, Luther R., 1985 PH TC Memo 85-629 [See 58 TC 564]
  e—Malek, Theresa M. & Edward J., Sr., 1985 PH TC Memo 85-1905 [See 58 TC 574]
  e—Wilhelm, Mary R., 1986 PH TC Memo 86-39 [See 58 TC 564]
  e—Stevenson, Wayne E. & Marilyn J., 1986 PH TC Memo 86-866, 86-873 [See 58 TC 564]
  e—Anastasato, Pano & Janice, 1986 PH TC Memo 86-1811 [See 58 TC 564]
  e—Shih-Hsieh, Marilan, 1986 PH TC Memo 86-2429 [See 58 TC 562]
  e—Heller, Jacob W. & Esther R., 1987 PH TC Memo 87-1881 [See 58 TC 562]
  e—Ettig, Tobin R., 1988 PH TC Memo 88-953 [See 58 TC 564]
  e—Belli, Melia, 1989 PH TC Memo 89-1950 [See 58 TC 564]
  f—Kong, Young E. & Jeen K., 1989 PH TC Memo 89-2781 [See 58 TC 564-565]
  e-1—Caglia, E. Bonnie, 1989 PH TC Memo 89-689
DIAZ, FRANK & AMPARO R., 1986 PH TC Memo ¶ 86,098
DIAZ, LEONARDA C., 70 TC 1067, ¶ 70.95 PH TC
  a—Diaz, Leonarda C. v Comm., 44 AFTR2d 79-6027 (USCA 2)
  e—Stazer, Alan K. & Katalin V., 1981 PH TC Memo 81-505 [See 70 TC 1076]
  e—Damm, Marvin V. & Nina M., 1981 PH TC Memo 81-673 [See 70 TC 1074-1075]
  e—Stuart, Ian & Maria, 1981 PH TC Memo 81-1311, 81-1312 [See 70 TC 1076]
  e—Olsen, Randy B. & Deborah R., 1981 PH TC Memo 81-2409 [See 70 TC 1076]
  f—Kuh, Johannes L. & Adriana, 1983 PH TC Memo 83-2311 [See 70 TC 1075, 1076]
  f-1—Wassenaar, Paul R., 72 TC 1200, 72 PH TC 659
  f-1—Browne, Alice Pauline, 73 TC 726, 73 PH TC 402 [See 70 TC 1074]
  f-1—Rehe, William G. & Suzanne M., 1980 PH TC Memo 80-1426
  g-1—Schwerm, Gerald & Joyce J., 1986 PH TC Memo 86-54, 86-55
  e-1—Baist, George A. & Janice, 1988 PH TC Memo 88-2859
  f-2—Toner, Linda M. Liberi, 71 TC 778, 779, 781, 71 PH TC 435, 436, 437 [See 70 TC 1075]
  2—Toner, Linda M. Liberi, 71 TC 782, 783, 71 PH TC 437, 438
  n-2—Toner, Linda M. Liberi, 71 TC 790, 71 PH TC 441
  f-2—Robinson, Charles A. & Elaine M., 78 TC 552, 78 PH TC 290 [See 70 TC 1074]
  2—Gruman, David T., 1982 PH TC Memo 82-1700 [See 70 TC 1074]
DIAZ, LEONARDA C. v COMM., 44 AFTR2d 79-6027 (USCA 2, 6-25-79)
  sa—Diaz, Leonarda C., 70 TC 1067, ¶ 70.95 PH TC
  e—Stazer, Alan K. & Katalin V., 1981 PH TC Memo 81-505
  e—Damm, Marvin V. & Nina M., 1981 PH TC Memo 81-673
  e—Olsen, Randy B. & Deborah R., 1981 PH TC Memo 81-2409
  f—Kuh, Johannes L. & Adriana, 1983 PH TC Memo 83-2311
  e—Malek, Theresa M. & Edward J., Sr., 1985 PH TC Memo 85-1905
  f-1—Rehe, William G. & Suzanne M., 1980 PH TC Memo 80-1426
  g-1—Schwerm, Gerald & Joyce J., 1986 PH TC Memo 86-54, 86-55
  e-1—Baist, George A. & Janice, 1988 PH TC Memo 88-2859
DIAZ, MIGUEL A. & FELICIA N., 1981 PH TC Memo ¶ 81,069 (See Powers, Sandra L.)

1990–1996
Citator Volume

DiANDRE, ANTHONY F. v U.S., 70 AFTR 2d 92-5190, 968 F2d 1049, 92-2 USTC ¶ 50,373, (CA10, 7-7-92)
  x—Metro Denver Maintenance Cleaning, Inc. v. U.S., 507 US 1029, 113 S Ct 1843, 123 L Ed 2d 468, (US, 4-19-93), (T)
  e-1—Barnes, William R. v U.S., 73 AFTR 2d 94-1161, (CA3)
  e-1—Fostvedt, Robert J. v U.S., 71 AFTR 2d 93-1573, 824 F Supp 983, (DC CO)
  e-1—Jones, Terry L., et al v U.S., et al, 74 AFTR 2d 94-6706, 869 F Supp 753, (DC NE), [Cited at 71 AFTR2d 93-1573, 824 F Supp 983]
  g-1—Russell, Orval D. v. U.S., 75 AFTR 2d 95-496, (DC MI)
  e-1—Stewart, Daniel v. U.S., 75 AFTR 2d 95-2250, 95-2251, (DC OH)
  e-1—Jones, Terry L., et al v U.S., et al, 76 AFTR 2d 95-6607, 95-6615, 898 F Supp 1373, 1380, (DC NE), [Cited at 71 AFTR2d 93-1573, 824 F Supp 983]
  e-1—May, Joseph A. v. U.S., 76 AFTR 2d 95-7228, (DC MO)
  e-1—Cassity, James v. Great Western Bank, 76 AFTR 2d 95-8035, (DC CA)
  e-1—Spence, Raymond v. U.S., 78 AFTR 2d 96-5777, (DC NM)
DiANDREA, INC., 1983 PH TC Memo ¶ 83,768
  e-1—Johnson, Peter A., 1991 TC Memo 91-3185
DIAZ, ALFONSO & MARIA de JESUS, 58 TC 560, ¶ 58.57 PH TC, (A), 1972-2 CB 2
  Sanai, Farhin, 1990 PH TC Memo 90-2459, [See 58 TC 564-565]
  e—Hawkins, Robert Lavon & Pamela, 1993 RIA TC Memo 93-2734, [See 58 TC 564]
  e—Muniz, Rolando, 1994 RIA TC Memo 94-760, [See 58 TC 564]
  e—Sloan, Lorin G., 1994 RIA TC Memo 94-3427, [See 58 TC 564]
  e—Marrone, Anthony & Carol, 1995 RIA TC Memo 95-145, [See 58 TC 564]
  e—Wada, Takeshi & Young Sook, 1995 RIA TC Memo 95-1532, [See 58 TC 564]
  e—Drabiuk, Stanislaw & Jeanette, 1995 RIA TC Memo 95-1649, [See 58 TC 565]
  e—Jackson, Sammy Lee, 1995 RIA TC Memo 95-1875, [See 58 TC 564]
  e—Levin, Harris & Gayle, 1996 RIA TC Memo 96-1557, [See 58 TC 564]
  e—American Underwriters Inc, 1996 RIA TC Memo 96-3980, [See 58 TC 564]
DIAZ, BARBARA E., 1990 PH TC Memo ¶ 90,559, (See Taylor, Barbara E.)
DIAZ, ENRIQUE v. U.S., 71A AFTR 2d 93-3563, 90-1 USTC ¶ 50209, (DC CA, 3/19/90)
  g-1—Van Camp & Bennion, P.S. v. U.S., 78 AFTR 2d 96-5847, (DC WA)
DIAZ, LEONARDA C., 70 TC 1067, ¶ 70.95 PH TC
  a—Diaz, Leonarda C. v Comm., 44 AFTR 2d 79-6027, 607 F2d 995, (CA2)
  f—Wiertzema, Vance v U.S., 66 AFTR 2d 90-5371, 747 F Supp 1365, (DC ND), [See 70 TC 1074-1075]
  e—Barboza, David, 1991 TC Memo 91-1905, [See 70 TC 1074]
  e—Orr, J. Thomas, 1992 RIA TC Memo 92-2912, [See 70 TC 1073]
  e—German, Harry, Jr. & Carol, 1993 RIA TC Memo 93-261—93-262, [See 70 TC 1074-1075]
  e—Meredith, Judith R., 1993 RIA TC Memo 93-1247, [See 70 TC 1074, cited at 73 TC 726]
  e—Holmes, Lynn J., 1993 RIA TC Memo 93-1978, [See 70 TC 1072-1073]
  e—Kersey, Robert C., 1993 RIA TC Memo 93-3396, [See 70 TC 1072-1073]
  e—Zeidler, Gerald L. & Joy M., 1996 RIA TC Memo 96-1151, [See 70 TC 1074, cited at 73 TC 726]
DIAZ, LEONARDA C. v COMM., 44 AFTR 2d 79-6027, 607 F2d 995, (CA2, 6-25-79)
  e—Wiertzema, Vance v U.S., 66 AFTR 2d 90-5371, 747 F Supp 1363, (DC ND)
  e—Zeidler, Gerald L. & Joy M., 1996 RIA TC Memo 96-1151
DiBENEDETTO, FRANK R. v U.S., 35 AFTR 2d 75-1502, 75-1 USTC ¶ 9503, (DC RI, 11-7-74)
  e-1—Seachrist, Craig v Riggs, C.W., 67 AFTR 2d 91-453, (DC VA)
  e-1—Cook, Dean A. v U.S., 68 AFTR 2d 91-5053—91-5056, 765 F Supp 219, 221, (DC PA)
  e-1—Carlucci, Joseph P. v U.S., 70 AFTR 2d 92-6002, 793 F Supp 484, (DC NY)
  e-1—Padalino, Vincent v. U.S., 71A AFTR 2d 93-3016,

FIGURE I15-8 ▶ EXCERPTS FROM THE RIA CITATOR

Reproduced with permission from Research Institute of America, Inc.

More recent references to *Leonarda C. Diaz* are reported in the 1990–96 citator volume (see Figure I15-8, Column 2). Nine additional cases cite the Tax Court decision[48]; two additional cases cite the Second Circuit Court decision. Recall that the CCH citator indicates that in 1972 the IRS Commissioner acquiesced in the Tax Court decision in *Alphonso Diaz*. This acquiescence is denoted by the capital "A," which appears after the citation to the same decision in the 1990–1996 citator volume.

No additional cases citing each of the Leonarda C. Diaz decisions are listed in the 1997–2000 cumulative supplements.

COMPUTERS AS A RESEARCH TOOL

OBJECTIVE 6

Understand the basics of computerized tax research

Tax professionals are increasingly using computers to conduct their tax-related research. Tax services are increasingly shifting their resources to media accessible by computer. With the technological advances in computer hardware and software, large databases are becoming more accessible and less costly. In the coming years, computer-assisted tax research will become an even more important tool for the tax advisor. A supplement to this chapter, which discusses this development, is available for download at *www.prenhall.com/phtax*. It also presents an overview of tax resources on the Internet.

In the major computerized tax services, most of the primary authorities discussed in this chapter appear as databases. Typically, each authority constitutes a separate database. Thus, the Internal Revenue Code constitutes a separate database, as do Treasury Regulations, revenue rulings, revenue procedures, and other IRS pronouncements. Supreme Court opinions constitute a separate database, as do opinions of the Tax Court, the U.S. district courts, the Court of Federal Claims, and the circuit courts. Likewise, most of the secondary authorities discussed in this chapter appear as databases. Some authorities, however, are found exclusively in one service, while others are found exclusively in another. For example, the *Standard Federal Tax Reporter, Federal Tax Service,* and CCH citator are found exclusively in the CCH Internet Tax Research Network. The *U.S. Tax Reporter, Federal Tax Coordinator 2d,* and RIA citator are found exclusively in RIA's CHECK-POINT. The basic features of the computerized and print sources generally are the same, with the following notable exceptions:

▶ Computerized sources have no finding lists. Cross referencing is facilitated through hyperlinks.

▶ Computerized sources have no cumulative supplements. New developments information is integrated into the main text.

▶ On computer, primary sources pertinent to explanatory paragraphs are accessible through hyperlink.

▶ On computer, citator symbols are explicitly spelled out.

STATEMENTS ON STANDARDS FOR TAX SERVICES

OBJECTIVE 7

Understand the guidelines to which CPAs in tax practice should adhere

Tax advisors confronted with ethical issues frequently turn to a professional organization for guidance. Although the guidelines set forth by such organizations are not *legally* enforceable, they carry significant moral weight, may be cited in a negligence lawsuit as the proper "standard of care" for tax practitioners, and may provide grounds for the termination or suspension of one's professional license. One such set of guidelines is the

---

[48] The first listing under the citation to the Tax Court decision in *Leonarda C. Diaz* refers to the same case decided at the Second Circuit Court level.

Statements on Standards for Tax Services (SSTSs),[49] issued by the American Institute of Certified Public Accountants (AICPA) and reproduced in Appendix E. Inspired by the principles of honesty and integrity, these guidelines define standards of ethical conduct for CPAs engaged in tax practice. In the words of the AICPA:

> In our view, practice standards are the hallmark of calling one's self a professional. Members should fulfill their responsibilities as professionals by instituting and maintaining standards against which their professional performance can be measured. The promulgation of practice standards also reinforces one of the core values of the AICPA Vision—that CPAs conduct themselves with honesty and integrity.[50]

The SSTSs differ in one important way from the AICPA's predecessor standards, *Statements on Responsibilites in Tax Practice,* in that the SSTSs are *professionally* enforceable; that is, they may be enforced through a disciplinary proceeding conducted by the AICPA, which may terminate or suspend a practitioner from AICPA membership.

Statement No. 1 defines the circumstances under which a CPA should (or should not) recommend a tax return position to a taxpayer. It also prescribes a course of conduct that the CPA should follow when making such a recommendation. Specifically,

▶ A member should not recommend that a tax return position be taken with respect to any item unless the member has a good-faith belief that the position has a realistic possibility of being sustained administratively or judicially on its merits if challenged . . .

▶ [A] member may recommend a tax return position that the member concludes is not frivolous so long as the member advises the taxpayer to appropriately disclose . . .

▶ When recommending tax return positions and when preparing or signing a return on which a tax return position is taken, a member should, when relevant, advise the taxpayer regarding potential penalty consequences of such tax return position and the opportunity, if any, to avoid such penalties through disclosure.

The "realistic possibility standard" set forth in Statement No. 1 parallels that of Sec. 6694. (For a discussion of the latter IRC section, see Chapter C15.) However, it differs from the IRC standard in that it allows as support for a tax return position well-reasoned articles or treatises, in addition to primary tax authorities. The IRC standard allows as support for a tax return position only primary tax authorities.

Statement No. 3 addresses (1) whether tax practitioners can reasonably rely on information supplied to them by the taxpayer, (2) when they have a duty to examine or verify such information, (3) when they have a duty to make inquiries of the taxpayer, and (4) what information they should consider in preparing a tax return. Specifically,

▶ In preparing or signing a return, a member may in good faith rely, without verification, on information furnished by the taxpayer or by third parties. However, a member should make reasonable inquiries if the information furnished appears to be incorrect, incomplete, or inconsistent either on its face or on the basis of other facts known to a member . . .

▶ If the tax law or regulations impose a condition with respect to the deductibility or other tax treatment of an item . . . a member should make appropriate inquiries to determine to the member's satisfaction whether such condition has been met.

▶ When preparing a tax return, a member should consider information actually known to that member from the tax return of another taxpayer if the information is relevant to that tax return and its consideration is necessary to properly prepare that tax return . . .

Note that the duty to verify arises only when taxpayer-provided information appears "strange" on its face. Otherwise, the tax practitioner has no duty to investigate taxpayer facts and circumstances.

---

[49] AICPA, *Statements on Standards for Tax Services*, 2000, effective October 31, 2000. The SSTSs supercede the AICPA's *Statements on Responsibilities in Tax Practice, 1991 Revision.*

[50] Letter to AICPA members by David A. Lifson, Chair, AICPA Tax Executive Committee, and Gerald W. Padwe, Vice President, AICPA Taxation Section (April 18, 2000).

What Would You Do in This Situation?

Regal Enterprises and Macon Industries, unaffiliated corporations, have hired you to prepare their respective income tax returns. In preparing Regal's return, you notice that Regal has claimed a depreciation deduction for equipment purchased from Macon on February 22 at a cost of $2 million. In preparing Macon's return, you notice that Macon has reported gross income of $1.5 million from the sale of equipment to Regal on February 22. One of the two figures must be incorrect. How do you proceed to correct it?

Statement No. 4 defines the circumstances in which a tax practitioner may use estimates in the preparation of a tax return. In addition, it cautions the practitioner as to the manner in which he or she may use such estimates. Specifically,

▶ A member may advise on estimates used in the preparation of a tax return, but the taxpayer has the responsibility to provide the estimated data. Appraisals or valuations are not considered estimates . . .

▶ [A] member may use the taxpayer's estimates in the preparation of a tax return if it is not practical to obtain exact data and if the member determines that the estimates are reasonable based on the facts and circumstances known to the member. If the taxpayer's estimates are used, they should be presented in a manner that does not imply greater accuracy than exists.

Notwithstanding this Statement, the tax practitioner may not use estimates when such use is implicitly prohibited by the IRC. For example, Sec. 274(d) disallows deductions for certain expenses (e.g., meals and entertainment) unless the taxpayer can substantiate the expenses with adequate records or sufficient corroborating information. The documentation requirement effectively precludes the taxpayer from estimating such expenses and the practitioner from using such estimates.

Statement No. 6 defines a tax practitioner's duty when he or she becomes aware of (1) an error in the taxpayer's return, (2) the taxpayer's failure to file a required return, or (3) the taxpayer's failure to correct an error in a prior year's return. Specifically,

▶ A member should inform the taxpayer promptly upon becoming aware of an error in a previously filed return or upon becoming aware of a taxpayer's failure to file a required return. A member should recommend the corrective measures to be taken . . . The member is not obligated to inform the taxing authority, and a member may not do so without the taxpayer's permission, except when required by law.

▶ If a member is requested to prepare the current year's return and the taxpayer has not taken appropriate action to correct an error in a prior year's return, the member should consider whether to withdraw from preparing the return and whether to continue a professional or employment relationship with the taxpayer . . .

This Statement implies that the tax practitioner's primary duty is to the taxpayer, not the taxing authority. Furthermore, upon the taxpayer's failure to correct a tax-related error, the practitioner may exercise discretion in deciding whether or not to terminate the professional relationship.

Occasionally, the tax practitioner discovers a taxpayer error in the course of an administrative proceeding (e.g., an IRS audit or appeals conference). The practitioner may advise the client to disclose the error, and the taxpayer may refuse. Statement No. 7 provides guidance as to what to do in these situations. Specifically,

▶ If a member is representing a taxpayer in an administrative proceeding with respect to a return that contains an error of which the member is aware, the member should inform the taxpayer promptly upon becoming aware of the error. The member should recommend the corrective measures to be taken. . . . A member is neither obligated to inform the taxing authority nor allowed to do so without the taxpayer's permission, except where required by law.

- A member should request the taxpayer's agreement to disclose the error to the taxing authority. Lacking such agreement, the member should consider whether to withdraw from representing the taxpayer in the administrative proceeding and whether to continue a professional or employment relationship with the taxpayer.

Finally, Statement No. 8 addresses the quality of advice provided by the tax practitioner, what consequences presumably ensue from such advice, and whether the practitioner has a duty to update advice to reflect subsequent developments. Specifically,

- A member should use judgment to ensure that tax advice provided to a taxpayer reflect professional competence and appropriately serves the taxpayer's needs . . .
- A member should assume that tax advice provided to a taxpayer will affect the manner in which the matters or transactions considered would be reported on the taxpayer's tax returns . . .
- A member has no obligation to communicate with a taxpayer when subsequent developments affect advice previously provided with respect to significant matters except while assisting a taxpayer in implementing procedures or plans associated with the advice provided or when a member undertakes an obligation by specific agreement.

The Statement implies that practitioner-taxpayer dealings should be neither casual nor nonconsensual nor open-ended; rather, they should be professional, contractual, and definite.

From the foregoing emerges the following picture of the normative relationship between the tax advisor and his or her client: unlike an auditor, a tax advisor is an advocate. His or her primary duty is to the client, not the IRS. In fulfilling this duty, the advisor is bound by the highest standards of care. These standards include a good-faith belief that a tax return position has a realistic possibility of being sustained on its merits and on quality advice based on professional competence and client needs. Encompassed under the advisor's duty is the obligation to inform the client of the potential adverse consequences of a tax return position, how the client can avoid a penalty through disclosure, errors in a previously filed tax return, and corrective measures to be taken. Also encompassed is the obligation to determine by inquiry that the client satisfies conditions for taking a deduction, and to obtain information when material provided by the client appears incorrect, incomplete, or inconsistent. Excluded from the advisor's duty is the obligation to verify client-provided information when, based on the advisor's own knowledge, such information is not suspicious on its face. Also excluded is the obligation to update professional advice based on developments following its original conveyance. In preparing a tax return, the advisor may use estimates if obtaining concrete data is impractical and if the advisor determines that the estimates are reasonable. Although responsibility for providing the estimates resides with the client, responsibility for presenting them in a manner that does not imply undue accuracy resides with the advisor. Finally, the advisor may terminate a professional relationship if the client refuses to correct a tax-related error. On the other hand, unless legally bound, the advisor may not disclose the error to the IRS without the client's consent.

In addition to these obligations, the tax advisor has a strict duty of confidentiality to the client. Though not encompassed under the SSTSs, this duty is implied by the accountant-client privilege. (For a discussion of this privilege, see Chapter C15.)

STOP & THINK

ADDITIONAL COMMENT
The underpayment penalty rules under Sec. 6662 impose a higher standard for disregarding a rule, such as a Treasury Regulation. Under these rules, the taxpayer must have a reasonable basis rather than a nonfrivolous position, in addition to disclosure.

Question: As described in the Stop & Think box on page I15-10, you are researching the manner in which a deduction is calculated. The IRC states that the calculation is to be done "in a manner prescribed by the Secretary." After studying the IRC, Treasury Regulations, and committee reports, you conclude that another way of doing the calculations is arguably correct under an intuitive approach. This approach would result in a lower tax liability for the client. According to the *Statements on Standards for Tax Services*, may you take a position contrary to final Treasury Regulations based on the argument that the regulations are not valid?

Solution: You should not take a position contrary to the Treasury Regulations unless you have a "good-faith belief that the position has a realistic possibility of being sustained administratively or judicially on its merits." However, you can take a position that does not meet the above standard, provided you adequately disclose the position and the position is not frivolous. We need more information about the situation before we can determine whether the "good-faith belief" test is met. Chapter C15 discusses tax return preparer positions contrary to the Treasury Regulations.

SAMPLE WORK PAPERS AND CLIENT LETTER

OBJECTIVE 8

Prepare work papers and communications to clients

Appendix A presents a set of sample work papers, including a draft of a client letter and a memo to the file. The work papers indicate the issues to be researched, the authorities addressing the issues, and the researcher's conclusions concerning the appropriate tax treatment, with rationale therefor.

The format and other details of a set of work papers differ from firm to firm. The sample in this text offers general guidance concerning the content of work papers. In practice, work papers may include less detail.

PROBLEM MATERIALS

DISCUSSION QUESTIONS

I15-1 Explain the difference between closed-fact and open-fact situations.

I15-2 List the steps in the tax research process.

I15-3 Explain why the steps in the tax research process are sometimes circular.

I15-4 According the the AICPA's *Statements on Standards for Tax Services*, what duties does the tax practitioner owe the client?

I15-5 Explain what is encompassed by the term *tax law* as used by tax advisors.

I15-6 The U.S. Government Printing Office publishes both hearings on proposed legislation and committee reports. Distinguish between the two.

I15-7 Explain how committee reports can be used in tax research. What do they indicate?

I15-8 Has the tax researcher's job been simplified by the codification of the tax statutes? Explain.

I15-9 A friend notices that you are reading the Internal Revenue Code of 1986. Your friend inquires why you are consulting a 1986 publication, especially when tax laws change so frequently. What is your response?

I15-10 Does Title 26 contain statutory provisions dealing only with income taxation? Explain.

I15-11 Refer to IRC Sec. 301.
a. Which subsection discusses the general rule for the tax treatment of a property distribution?
b. Where should one look for exceptions to the general rule?
c. What type of Treasury Regulations would relate to subsection (e)?

I15-12 Why should tax researchers take note of the date on which a Treasury Regulation was adopted?

I15-13 a. Distinguish between proposed, temporary, and final regulations.
b. Distinguish between interpretative and legislative regulations.

I15-14 Which type of regulation is more difficult for a taxpayer to successfully challenge, and why?

I15-15 Explain the legislative reenactment doctrine.

I15-16 a. Discuss the authoritative weight of revenue rulings.
b. As a practical matter, what consequences are likely to occur if a taxpayer does not follow a revenue ruling and his or her return is audited?

I15-17 a. In which courts may litigation dealing with tax matters begin?
b. Discuss the factors that might be considered in deciding where to begin litigation.
c. Describe the appeals process in tax litigation.

I15-18 May a taxpayer appeal a case litigated under the Small Cases Procedure of the Tax Court?

I15-19 Explain whether the following decisions are of the same precedential value: (1) Tax Court regular decisions, (2) Tax Court memo decisions, (3) decisions under the Small Cases Procedures of the Tax Court.

I15-20 Does the IRS acquiesce in decisions of U.S. district courts?

I15-21 The decisions of which courts are reported in the AFTR 2d? In the USTC?

I15-22 Who publishes regular decisions of the Tax Court? Memo decisions?

I15-23 Explain the *Golsen* Rule. Give an example of its application.

I15-24 Assume that the only precedents relating to a particular issue are as follows:
Tax Court—decided for the taxpayer
Eighth Circuit Court of Appeals—decided for the taxpayer (affirming the Tax Court)
U.S. District Court for Eastern Louisiana—decided for the taxpayer
Fifth Circuit Court of Appeals—decided for the government (reversing the U.S. District Court of Eastern Louisiana)
a. Discuss the precedential value of the foregoing decisions for your client, who is a California resident.
b. If your client, a Texas resident, litigates in the Tax Court, how will the court rule? Explain.

I15-25 Under what circumstances might a tax advisor find the provisions of a tax treaty useful?

I15-26 Compare the tax services listed below (if they are found in your tax library) with respect to (a) how they are organized and (b) where current developments are reported.
a. *United States Tax Reporter*
b. *Standard Federal Tax Reporter*
c. *Federal Tax Coordinator 2d*
d. *Law of Federal Income Taxation* (Mertens)
e. BNA's *Tax Management Portfolios*
f. CCH's *Federal Tax Service*

I15-27 What two functions does a citator serve?

I15-28 Describe two types of information that can be gleaned from citing cases reported in the RIA citator but not the CCH citator.

I15-29 Explain how your research approach might differ if you use a computerized database instead of a print tax service (e.g., the CCH service).

I15-30 Compare the features of the electronic, CD-ROM, and Internet tax services. What are the relative advantages and disadvantages of each type of service? (In answering this question, consult the supplement to this chapter available for download at *www.prenhall.com/phtax*.)

I15-31 Compare the features of the computerized tax services with those of Internet sites maintained by noncommercial institutions. What are the relative advantages and disadvantages of each? Could the latter sites serve as a substitute for a commercial tax service? (In answering this question, consult the supplement to this chapter available for download at *www.prenhall.com/phtax*.)

I15-32 According to the *Statements on Standards for Tax Services*, what belief should a CPA have before taking a pro-taxpayer position on a tax return?

PROBLEMS

I15-33 *Interpretation of the IRC.* Under a divorce instrument executed in the current year, an ex-wife receives from her former husband cash of $25,000 per year for eight years. The instrument does not explicitly state that the payment is not includable in income.
a. Does the ex-wife have gross income? If so, how much?
b. Is the former husband entitled to a deduction? If so, is it for or from AGI?
Refer only to the IRC in answering this problem. Start with Sec. 71.

I15-34 *Interpretation of the IRC.* Refer to Sec. 385 and answer the questions below.
a. Whenever Treasury Regulations are issued under this section, what type are they likely to be: legislative or interpretative? Explain.
b. Assume Treasury Regulations under Sec. 385 have been finalized. Will they be relevant to estate tax matters? Explain.

I15-35 *Using the Cumulative Bulletin.* Consult any *Cumulative Bulletin*. In what order are revenue rulings arranged?

I15-36 *Using the Cumulative Bulletin.* Which IRC section does Rev. Rul. 85-44 interpret? (Hint: consult the 1985-1 *Cumulative Bulletin*.)

I15-37 *Using the Cumulative Bulletin.* Refer to the 1989-1 *Cumulative Bulletin*.
a. What time period does this bulletin cover?
b. What appears on page 1?
c. What items are found in Part I of the bulletin?
d. In what order are the items presented in Part I?
e. What items are found in Part II?
f. What items are found in Part III?

I15-38 *Using the Cumulative Bulletin.* Refer to the 1990-1 *Cumulative Bulletin*.
a. For the time period covered by the bulletin, in which cases did the IRS nonacquiesce?

b. What is the topic of Rev. Rul. 90-10?
c. Does this bulletin contain a revenue ruling that interprets Sec. 162? If so, specify.

I15-39 *Determination of Acquiescence.*
a. What official action did the IRS Commissioner take in 1986 concerning the Tax Court case of *John McIntosh*? (Hint: consult the 1986-1 *Cumulative Bulletin*.)
b. Did such action concern *all* the issues in the case? If not, explain. (Consult the headnote to the case before answering this question.)

I15-40 *Determination of Acquiescence.*
a. What original action (acquiescence or nonacquiescence) did the IRS Commissioner take concerning *Streckfus Steamers, Inc.*, 19 T.C. 1 (1952)?
b. Was the action complete or partial?
c. Did the IRS Commissioner subsequently change his mind? If so, when?

I15-41 *Determination of Acquiescence.*
a. What original action (acquiescence or nonacquiescence) did the IRS Commissioner take concerning *Pittsburgh Milk Co.*, 26 T.C. 707 (1956)?
b. Did the IRS Commissioner subsequently change his mind? If so, when?

I15-42 *Evaluating a Case.* Look up the decision in *Everett J. Gordon*, 85 T.C. 309 (1985), and answer the questions below.
a. Was the decision reviewed by the court? If so, was it unanimous? Explain.
b. Was the decision entered under Rule 155?
c. Consult a citator. Was the case heard by an appellate court? If so, which one?

I15-43 *Evaluating a Case.* Look up the decision for *Bush Brothers & Co.*, 73 T.C. 424 (1979), and answer the questions below.
a. Was the decision reviewed by the court? If so, was it unanimous? Explain.
b. Was the decision entered under Rule 155?
c. Consult a citator. Was the case heard by an appellate court? If so, which one?

I15-44 *Writing Citations.* Provide the proper citations (including both primary and secondary citations where applicable) for the authorities listed below. (For secondary citations, reference both the AFTR and USTC.)
a. *Ruth K. Dowell v. U.S.*, a 10th Circuit Court decision
b. *Thomas M. Dragoun v. CIR*, a Tax Court memo decision
c. *John M. Grabinski v. U.S.*, a District Court of Minnesota decision
d. *John M. Grabinski v. U.S.*, an Eighth Circuit Court decision
e. *Rebekah Harkness*, a 1972 Court of Claims decision
f. *Hillsboro National Bank v. CIR*, a Supreme Court decision
g. Rev. Rul. 78-129

I15-45 *Writing Citations.* Provide the proper citations (including both primary and secondary citations where applicable) for the authorities listed below. (For secondary citations, reference both the AFTR and USTC.)
a. Rev. Rul. 69-125
b. *Frank H. Sullivan*, a Board of Tax Appeals decision
c. *Lloyd Weaver*, a Tax Court decision
d. *Ralph L. Rogers v. U.S.*, an Ohio District Court decision
e. *Norman Rodman v. CIR*, a Second Circuit Court decision

I15-46 *Interpreting Citations.* Indicate which courts decided the cases cited below. Also indicate on which pages and in which publications the authority is reported.
a. *Lloyd M. Shumaker v. CIR*, 648 F.2d 1198, 48 AFTR 2d 81-5353 (9th Cir., 1981)
b. *Dean R. Shore*, 69 T.C. 689 (1978)
c. *Real Estate Land Title & Trust Co. v. U.S.*, 309 U.S. 13, 23 AFTR 816 (USSC, 1940)
d. *J. B. Morris v. U.S.*, 441 F. Supp. 76, 41 AFTR 2d 78-335 (DC TX, 1977)
e. Rev. Rul. 83-3, 1983-1 C.B. 72
f. *Malone & Hyde, Inc. v. U.S.*, 568 F.2d 474, 78-1 USTC ¶9199 (6th Cir., 1978)

I15-47 *Using a Tax Service.* Use the topical index of the *United States Tax Reporter* to locate authorities dealing with the deductibility of the cost of a facelift.
a. In which paragraph(s) does the *United States Tax Reporter* summarize and cite these authorities?
b. List the authorities.

c. Have there been any recent non-statutory developments concerning the tax consequences of facelifts? (*Recent* suggests authorities appearing in the cross-reference section.)
d. May a taxpayer deduct the cost of a facelift paid for in the current year? Explain.

I15-48 *Using a Tax Service.* Refer to Reg. Sec. 1.302-1 at ¶3022 of the *United States Tax Reporter*. Does this Treasury Regulation reflect today's version of the IRC? Explain.

I15-49 *Using a Tax Service.* Use the topical index of the *Standard Federal Tax Reporter* to locate authorities dealing with whether termite damage qualifies for a casualty loss deduction.
a. In which paragraph(s) does the *Standard Federal Tax Reporter* summarize and cite these authorities?
b. List the authorities.
c. Have there been any recent developments concerning the tax consequences of termite damage? (*Recent* suggests authorities appearing in the cumulative index section.)

I15-50 *Using a Tax Service.*
a. Locate in the *Standard Federal Tax Reporter* where Sec. 303(b)(2)(A) is reproduced. This provision states that Sec. 303(a) applies only if the stock in question meets a certain percentage test. What is the applicable percentage?
b. Locate Reg. Sec. 1.303-2(a) in the same service. Does this Treasury Regulation reflect today's version of the IRC with respect to the percentage test addressed in Part a? Explain.

I15-51 *Using a Tax Service.* The questions below deal with BNA's *Tax Management Portfolios.*
a. What is the number of the main portfolio that deals with tax-free exchanges under Sec. 1031?
b. On which page does a discussion of "boot" begin?
c. What are the purposes of Worksheets 1 and 5 of this portfolio?
d. Refer to the bibliography and references at the end of the portfolio. Indicate the numbers of the IRC sections listed as "secondarily" relevant

I15-52 *Using a Tax Service.* This problem deals with Mertens' *Law of Federal Income Taxation.*
a. Refer to Volume 5. What general topics does it discuss?
b. Which section of Volume 5 discusses the principal methods of determining depreciation?
c. In Volume 5, what is the purpose of the yellow and white sheets appearing before the tab labeled "Text"?
d. Refer to the Ruling Status Table in the Current Rulings Materials volume. What is the current status of Rev. Ruls. 79-433 and 75-335?
e. Refer to the Code-Rulings Tables in the same volume. List the numbers (e.g., Rev. Rul. 84-88) of all 1984 revenue rulings and revenue procedures that interpret Sec. 121.

I15-53 *Using a Tax Service.* The questions below deal with RIA's *Federal Tax Coordinator 2d.*
a. Use the topical index to locate authorities dealing with the deductibility of the cost of work clothing by ministers (clergymen). List the authorities.
b. Where does this tax service report new developments?

I15-54 *Using a Tax Service.* Refer to the *United States Tax Reporter* and *Standard Federal Tax Reporter*. Then, for each tax reporter, answer the following questions.
a. In which volume is the index located?
b. Is the index arranged by topic or IRC section?
c. If all you know is an IRC section number, how do you locate additional materials?
d. If all you know is the name of a court decision, how do you locate additional materials?

I15-55 *Using a Citator.* Trace *Biltmore Homes, Inc.*, a 1960 Tax Court memo decision, in both the CCH and RIA citators.
a. According to the RIA citator, how many times has the Tax Court decision been cited by other courts on Headnote Number 5?
b. How many issues were involved in the trial court litigation? (Hint: refer to the case headnote numbers.)
c. Did an appellate court review the case? If so, which one?
d. According to the CCH citator, how many times has the Tax Court decision been cited by other courts?
e. According to the CCH citator, how many times has the circuit court decision been cited by other courts on Headnote Number 5?

I15-56 *Using a Citator.* Trace *Stephen Bolaris,* 776 F2d 1428, in both the CCH and RIA citators.
a. According to the RIA citator, how many times has the Ninth Circuit's decision been cited?
b. Did the case address more than one issue? Explain.
c. Was the case ever cited unfavorably? Explain.
d. According to the CCH citator, how many times has the Ninth Circuit's decision been cited?
e. According to the CCH citator, how many times has the Tax Court's decision been cited on Headnote Number 1?

I15-57 *Interpreting a Case.* Refer to the *Levin Metals Corporation* case (92 T.C. 307).
a. In which year was the case decided?
b. What controversy was litigated?
c. Who won the case?
d. Was the decision reviewed at the trial level?
e. Was the decision appealed?
f. Has the case been cited in other cases?

I15-58 *Internet Research.* Access the IRS Internet site at *http://www.irs.gov* and answer the following questions: (In answering this question, consult the supplement to this chapter available for download at *www.prenhall.com/phtax*.)
a. What types of tax-related documents are available on this site?
b. What tax-rate schedules are available on this site?

I15-59 *Internet Research.* Access the IRS Internet site at *http://www.irs.gov* and indicate the titles of the following IRS forms: (In answering this question, consult the supplement to this chapter available for download at *www.prenhall.com/phtax*.)
a. Form 4506
b. Form 973
c. Form 8725

I15-60 *Internet Research.* Access the IRS Internet site at *http://www.irs.gov* and indicate the titles of the following state tax forms and publications: (In answering this question, consult the supplement to this chapter available for download at *www.prenhall.com/phtax*.)
a. Minnesota Form M-3
b. Illinois Schedule CR
c. New York Form CT-3-C

I15-61 *Internet Research.* Access Emory's *Federal Courts Finder* at *http://www.law.emory.edu/FEDCTS/* and answer the following questions: (In answering this question, consult the supplement to this chapter available for download at *www.prenhall.com/phtax*.)
a. What is the historical timespan of the underlying databases?
b. In what ways can they be accessed?
c. What 1995 Eleventh Circuit Court cases address the issue of the charitable deduction for estates?

COMPREHENSIVE PROBLEM

I15-62 Your client, a physician, recently purchased a yacht on which he flies a pennant with a medical emblem on it. He recently informed you that he purchased the yacht and flies the pennant to advertise his occupation and thus attract new patients. He has asked you if he may deduct as ordinary and necessary business expenses the costs of insuring and maintaining the yacht. In search of an answer, consult either CCH's *Standard Federal Tax Reporter* or RIA's *United States Tax Reporter* first in print, and then on computer (i.e., the CCH Internet Tax Research Network or RIA CHECKPOINT). Then compare the steps taken on each to find your answer.

CASE STUDY PROBLEM

I15-63 A client, Mal Manley, fills out his client questionnaire for the previous year and on it provides information for the preparation of his individual income tax return. The IRS has never audited Mal's returns. Mal reports that he made over 100 relatively small cash contributions totaling $24,785 to charitable organizations. In the last few years, Mal's charitable contributions have averaged about $15,000 per year. For the previous year, Mal's adjusted gross income was roughly $350,000, about a 10% increase from the year before.

Required: According to the *Statements on Standards for Tax Services,* may you accept at face value Mal's information concerning his charitable contributions? Now assume that the IRS recently audited Mal's tax return for two years ago and denied 75% of the charitable contribution deduction claimed thereon because the deduction was not substantiated. Assume also that for the previous year Mal indicates he contributed $25,000 (instead of $24,785). How does this change of fact affect your earlier decision?

TAX RESEARCH PROBLEMS

I15-64 In answering these questions, refer only to *Thomas A. Curtis, M.D., Inc.,* 1994 RIA TC Memo ¶94,015. The purpose of this question is to enhance your skills in interpreting the authorities that you locate in your research.
   a. What general controversy is litigated in this case?
   b. Which party—the taxpayer or the goverment—won the case?
   c. Why is the corporation listed as the plaintiff instead of Dr. and/or Ms. Curtis?
   d. What is the relationship between Ellen Barnert Curtis and Dr. Thomas A. Curtis?
   e. Approximately how many hours a week did Ms. Curtis work, and what were her credentials?
   f. For the fiscal year ended in 1989 what salary did the corporation pay Ms. Curtis? What amount did the court decide was reasonable?
   g. What dividends did the corporation pay for its fiscal years ending in 1988 and 1989?
   h. To which circuit would this case be appealable?
   i. According to *Curtis*, what five factors did the Ninth Circuit mention in *Elliotts, Inc.* as relevant in determining reasonable compensation?

I15-65 Josh contributes $5,000 toward the support of his widowed mother, aged 69. His mother, a U.S. citizen and resident, earns gross income of $2,000 and spends it all for her own support. In addition, Medicare pays $3,200 of her medical expenses. She does not receive support from sources other than those described above. Must the Medicare payments be included in the support that Josh's mother provides for herself?

Prepare work papers and a client letter (to Josh) dealing with the issue.

I15-66 Amy owns a vacation cottage in Maine. She predicts that use of the cottage during the current year will be as follows:

By Amy, solely for vacation	12 days
By Amy, making repairs ten hours per day and vacationing the rest of the day	2 days
By her sister, who paid fair rental value	8 days
By her cousin, who paid fair rental value	4 days
By her friend, who paid a token amount of rent	2 days
By three families from the Northeast, who paid fair rental value for 40 days each	120 days
Not used	217 days

Calculate the ratio for allocating the following expenses to the rental income to be received from the cottage: interest, taxes, repairs, insurance, and depreciation. The ratio will be used to determine the amount of expenses that are deductible and, thus, Amy's taxable income for the year.

Prepare for the tax manager to whom you report work papers in which you address the manner of calculation. Also, draft a memorandum to the file dealing with the results of your tax research.

I15-67 Look up *Summit Publishing Company,* 1990 PH T.C. Memo ¶90,288, 59 TCM 833, and *J.B.S. Enterprises,* 1991 PH T.C. Memo ¶91,254, 61 TCM 2829, and answer the following questions:
   a. What was the principal issue in these cases?
   b. What factors did the Tax Court consider in resolving the issue?
   c. How are the facts of these cases similar? How are they dissimilar?

CHAPTER 16

CORPORATIONS

LEARNING OBJECTIVES

After studying this chapter, you should be able to

1. Define a corporation
2. Calculate the corporate income tax liability and explain specific tax rules
3. Apply the nonrecognition of gain or loss rules for corporate formations
4. Understand the significance of earnings and profits
5. Determine the consequences of nonmoney distributions and stock redemptions
6. Understand the consequences of a corporate liquidation to the shareholders and the liquidating corporation

CHAPTER OUTLINE

Definition of a Corporation...16-2
Similarities and Differences Between Corporations and Individuals...16-3
Specific Rules Applicable to Corporations...16-3
Computation of Tax...16-8
Transfers of Property to Controlled Corporations...16-20
Capitalization of the Corporation...16-23
Earnings and Profits...16-25
Nonmoney Distributions...16-27
Stock Redemptions...16-28
Corporate Distributions in Complete Liquidation...16-31

ADDITIONAL COMMENT

In 1960, corporate taxes produced over 20% of federal tax revenues. By 1993, that percentage dropped to 10% and has remained at this low level.

A business may be organized and operated as a **sole proprietorship, C corporation, S corporation, partnership, limited liability partnership**, or **limited liability company**. These forms of organizations fall into two major types: taxpaying entities and flow-through entities. This latter category also is referred to as conduit or pass-through entities. Sole proprietorships and C corporations fall into the taxable category although sole proprietorships are subject to a single level of tax, whereas C corporations entail two levels of tax. Sole proprietorships are relatively simple because they do not require a separate legal entity. The individual business proprietor is taxed directly and reports business income and expenses on Schedule C of Form 1040 (U.S. Individual Income Tax Return). The C corporation also is taxed directly and reports its tax results on Form 1120 (U.S. Corporate Income Tax Return). In addition, the corporate shareholders are taxed if the C corporation distributes dividends to them or if the shareholders sell their stock at a gain. Thus, the C corporation organizational form creates two levels of taxation: once at the corporate level and again at the shareholder level. Despite its double taxation and sometimes complicated legal form, the corporation has the advantages of raising outside capital and limiting the shareholders' legal liability.

Flow-through entities, like a sole proprietorship, entail only one level of taxation at the ownership level. Accordingly, the entities themselves are not taxed, and the income and losses pass through to the shareholders of an S corporation, the partners of a partnership, or the members of a limited liability partnership or limited liability company. The owners then report the pass-through income or losses on their individual tax returns. Some of these entities, such as S corporations, limited liability companies, and limited partnerships, also have the advantage of limiting their owners' legal liability. Nevertheless, flow-through entities entail certain complexities and restrictions, which is one disadvantage of this form of organization.

This chapter explores the basic tax consequences of forming, operating, and liquidating a C corporation. Chapter I17 discusses the basic tax rules pertaining to flow-through entities, and Table I17-2 at the end of that chapter compares the alternative forms of business organizations. Detailed coverage of these two areas of taxation are reserved for this text's companion volume titled *Prentice Hall's Federal Taxation: Corporations, Partnerships, Estates, and Trusts*.

DEFINITION OF A CORPORATION

OBJECTIVE 1
Define a corporation

Under Treasury Regulations,[1] a business entity with two or more owners is classified as either a corporation or a partnership. An entity having only one owner is classified as a corporation or a sole proprietorship. A business entity is a corporation if it is organized under a federal or state statute that refers to the entity as incorporated or as a corporation, body corporate, body politic, joint-stock company, or joint-stock association. Corporations also include insurance companies, state-chartered banks, and a business entity wholly owned by a state or political subdivision. In short, if a business entity incorporates, it is a corporation.

On the other hand, if the business entity has two or more owners and forms itself as a partnership, limited liability company, or limited liability partnership, the entity can elect to be *taxed* as either a partnership or corporation. These so-called "check-the-box" election rules replace prior entity classification procedures that involved much subjective judgement and manipulation.

EXAMPLE I16-1 ▶

Al and Jane form a business entity that incorporates in Delaware. Because it is legally incorporated, the entity is taxed as a corporation. Bill and Max form a limited liability company in Florida. The limited liability company can elect to be taxed as a corporation or it can elect to be treated as a partnership for federal tax purposes. ◀

---
[1] Reg. Secs. 301.7701-1, -2, and -3.

SIMILARITIES AND DIFFERENCES BETWEEN CORPORATIONS AND INDIVIDUALS

SIMILARITIES

The computation of corporate taxable income is similar to the computation of taxable income for an unincorporated business operating as a sole proprietorship. For example, corporations can deduct ordinary and necessary business expenses under Sec. 162 and may exclude items such as tax-exempt interest and life insurance proceeds from gross income. Corporations also can deduct interest, depreciation, and other business-related expenses in a manner similar to unincorporated taxpayers.

Section 453(a) permits both corporate and noncorporate taxpayers to use the installment method of accounting to report income from an installment sale (see Chapter 11). The IRS in Rev. Proc. 2000-22 has provided guidance that will allow small businesses with $1,000,000 or less in gross receipts to use the cash method of accounting. Under the revenue procedure, eligible businesses won't be required to maintain inventories and can use the cash method of accounting. This exception applies to corporate taxpayers.[2]

ADDITIONAL COMMENT

According to a Tax Foundation estimate, Fortune 500 companies spend an average of $2.1 million per year on income-tax compliance. Approximately 70% is attributable to the federal income tax system, especially provisions relating to foreign-source income and the alternative minimum tax.

DIFFERENCES

One principal difference in computing corporate taxable income compared with an individual is that personal, consumption-type expenditures and exemptions apply solely to individuals. Certain specific differences should be noted before discussing the corporate provisions in greater detail:

- Computation of *adjusted gross income* (AGI) applies only to individuals.
- A corporation cannot use the standard deduction or deduct personal and dependency exemptions.
- Corporations receive a dividends-received deduction of 70%, 80%, or 100% for qualifying dividends, whereas individuals are taxed on their total dividends with no exclusion or deduction.
- Corporate charitable contributions are limited in any given year to 10% of taxable income (with certain adjustments described on page I16-6 of this chapter), whereas individual contributions generally are limited to 50% of AGI.

SPECIFIC RULES APPLICABLE TO CORPORATIONS

SELF-STUDY QUESTION

What are the major differences between the capital gain and loss taxation of individuals and corporations?

CAPITAL GAINS AND LOSSES

The rules for netting long- and short-term capital gains and losses, the treatment of Sec. 1231 (i.e., business fixed assets) gains and losses, and the long-term capital gain and loss holding periods are the same for both corporations and individuals. The netting process consists of the following procedural rules (See Schedule D of Form 1120–Capital Gains and Losses in Appendix B):

---

[2] I.R.B. 2000-16, 880. A business that qualifies for the small taxpayer exception of Rev. Proc. 2000-22, I.R.B. 2000-20, 1008 and wants to switch to cash accounting must follow the automatic change in accounting method provisions of Rev. Proc. 99-49, I.R.B. 1999-52, 725. Rev. Proc. 2000-22 has been modified and superseded by Rev. Proc. 2001-10, I.R.B. 2001-2, 272.

ANSWER
First, an individual can offset $3,000 of capital losses against ordinary income. Second, an individual has an indefinite carryover instead of a 3-year carryback and a 5-year carryover. Third, all corporate capital loss carrybacks and carryovers are treated as STCLs. Finally, a 20% maximum tax rate applies to most net capital gains (i.e., the excess of net long-term capital gain over net short-term capital loss) for noncorporate taxpayers.

▶ Long-term capital gains (LTCGs) are netted against long-term capital losses (LTCLs).
▶ Short-term capital gains (STCGs) are netted against short-term capital losses (STCLs).
▶ A net long-term capital gain (NLTCG) is then offset against a net short-term capital loss (NSTCL).
▶ A net long-term capital loss (NLTCL) is then offset against a net short-term capital gain (NSTCG).
▶ If a corporation reports both a NLTCG and a NSTCG after the netting procedure is completed, both the NSTCG and the NLTCG are taxed at the same rates as ordinary income.
▶ NSTCGs are netted against NLTCLs, and any excess amount is taxed at the same rates as ordinary income.
▶ NLTCLs and NSTCLs cannot be deducted from ordinary income.

EXAMPLE I16-2 ▶ Gulf Corporation has the following capital gains and losses during the current year:

LTCG	$15,000
LTCL	5,000
STCG	3,000
STCL	8,000

Gulf Corporation has a $10,000 NLTCG and a $5,000 NSTCL. The NLTCG is offset against the NSTCL, resulting in a $5,000 net capital gain that is taxed at the same rates as ordinary income. ◀

EXAMPLE I16-3 ▶ High Corporation has the following capital gains and losses during the current year:

LTCG	$15,000
LTCL	5,000
STCG	10,000
STCL	8,000

High Corporation has a $10,000 NLTCG and a $2,000 NSTCG. Both the $2,000 NSTCG and the $10,000 NLTCG are taxed at the same rates as ordinary income. ◀

EXAMPLE I16-4 ▶ Huge Corporation has the following capital gains and losses during 2001:

LTCG	$ 5,000
LTCL	15,000
STCG	8,000
STCL	10,000

Huge Corporation has a $10,000 NLTCL and a $2,000 NSTCL. Neither net loss is deductible against ordinary income in computing its 2001 taxable income. ◀

CORPORATE CAPITAL LOSS LIMITATIONS. Neither a NLTCL nor a NSTCL is deductible against ordinary income in the year it is incurred. Instead, they are eligible for a 3-year carryback and 5-year carryover and can be used as an offset against capital gains in those years.[3] For corporations, both the NSTCL and the NLTCL are treated as STCLs for purposes of the carryback and carryover rules. The corporate capital loss limitations and carryback-carryover rules differ from the rules applicable to noncorporate taxpayers (see the discussion in Chapter I5).[4]

EXAMPLE I16-5 ▶ Assume the same facts as in Example I16-4. The $10,000 NLTCL and the $2,000 NSTCL are not deductible in 2001. The $12,000 ($10,000 + $2,000) total loss is carried back initially to 1998 as a STCL. If the net gains in the carryback years (1998 through 2000) are insufficient to absorb the $12,000 STCL carryback from 2001, the excess is carried over for up to 5 years (2002 through 2006). ◀

---

[3] Secs. 1211(a) and 1212(a).
[4] Noncorporate taxpayers (e.g., individuals) can deduct up to $3,000 of net capital losses against ordinary income. Unused capital losses are carried over (but not carried back) for an indefinite time period and retain their character as long- or short-term capital losses.

DIVIDENDS-RECEIVED DEDUCTION

BOOK-TAX ACCOUNTING COMPARISON
The dividends-received deduction is strictly a tax concept. No such expense exists for financial reporting.

Corporations may deduct 80% of dividends received from a domestic corporation if the recipient corporation owns 20% or more of the voting power and value of the issuing corporation's stock.[5] If a corporation owns less than 20% of the distributing corporation's stock, the dividends-received deduction is 70%. The percentage increases to 100% if the dividend is received from an 80%-or-more-owned affiliated corporation for which a consolidated return election is not in effect. This seemingly liberal deduction mitigates the effects of triple taxation that otherwise would occur if one corporation paid dividends to another corporate shareholder, which in turn distributed such amounts to its shareholders.

The illustration below summarizes the amount of dividends-received deduction.

Percentage of Stock Owned	Dividends-Received Deduction
Less than 20%	70%
20% through 79.99%	80%
80% or more	100%

SELF-STUDY QUESTION
Calculate the maximum effective tax rate on dividends received from a corporation that is less than 20%-owned.

ANSWER
The maximum effective tax rate is 10.5% (30% dividend inclusion times the top corporate tax rate of 35%).

The 80% and 70% **dividends-received deductions** are subject to the following limitations:

▶ The dividends-received deduction is limited to 80% (or 70%) of taxable income (computed without regard to the net operating loss (NOL) deduction, the dividends-received deduction, and capital loss carrybacks to the limitation year).

▶ The limitation based on 80% (or 70%) of taxable income does not apply if the corporation has an NOL for the current year after deducting the dividends-received deduction determined under the general rules.

▶ The dividends-received deduction is not available if the stock is held 45 or fewer days out of the 91-day period that commences 45 days before the ex-dividend date.

ADDITIONAL COMMENT
Although corporations are allowed a dividends-received deduction, they are not allowed a dividends-paid deduction for purposes of computing taxable income.

EXAMPLE I16-6 ▶ King Corporation has the following income and expense items during the current year:

Net income from operations	$ 50,000
Dividend income from 20% (or more)-owned corporations	200,000

The dividends-received deduction determined under the general rule is $160,000 (0.80 × $200,000 dividends). The deduction limitation is $200,000 (0.80 × $250,000 taxable income before the dividends-received deduction). Because the limitation ($200,000) exceeds the dividends-received deduction computed under the general rule ($160,000), the entire $160,000 dividends-received deduction is allowed. ◀

EXAMPLE I16-7 ▶ Assume the same facts as in Example I16-6, except that the corporation incurred a $10,000 net loss from operations. The dividends-received deduction under the general rule is $160,000 (0.80 × $200,000 dividends). The limitation under the general rule is based on taxable income before the dividends-received deduction of $190,000 ($200,000 − $10,000). The limitation is $152,000 (0.80 × $190,000). No NOL results after deducting the entire 80% dividends-received deduction computed under the general rule as shown below:

Net loss from operations	$ (10,000)
Plus: Dividends received from 20% (or more) owned corporations	200,000
Minus: Dividends-received deduction (0.80 × $200,000)	(160,000)
Taxable income as computed under the general rule	$ 30,000

Because the dividends-received deduction is limited to $152,000, the actual taxable income for the year is $38,000 ($190,000 − $152,000). ◀

EXAMPLE I16-8 ▶ Assume the same facts as in Example I16-7, except that the loss from operations is $50,000. The dividends-received deduction under the general rule is $160,000 (0.80 × $200,000 dividends). The limitation is $120,000 (0.80 × $150,000 taxable income before the dividends-received deduction). The limitation does not apply, however, because a $10,000 NOL results after subtracting the dividends-received deduction computed using the general rule.

---

[5] The dividend-received deduction rules are in Secs. 243 and 246.

16-6 Individuals ▼ Chapter 16

ADDITIONAL COMMENT
Even though the dividends-received deduction creates (or increases) a NOL, the corporation gets the full benefit of the deduction because it can carry back or carry over the NOL.

Net loss from operations	$ (50,000)
Plus: Dividends received	200,000
Minus: Dividends-received deduction (0.80 × $200,000)	(160,000)
Taxable income	$ (10,000)

Therefore, the entire $160,000 dividends-received deduction is allowed. ◄

EXAMPLE I16-9 ▶ Lean Corporation acquires 5% of Madison Corporation's stock on June 1. Madison Corporation pays a cash dividend to all shareholders who own the Madison stock on June 15. Lean receives the dividend payment on June 20. On July 1, Lean sells the Madison stock. The dividends-received deduction is not allowed because Lean does not hold the Madison stock for the required 46 days out of the 91-day period that commences 45 days before the ex-dividend date (June 15). ◄

NET OPERATING LOSSES

The computation of a corporate **net operating loss** (NOL) does not involve making adjustments for nonbusiness deductions and capital gains and losses as is required for individuals (see Chapter I8 for a discussion of these adjustments for individuals). Thus, the corporate rules are fairly straightforward.[6] In computing a corporation's NOL, the full dividends-received deduction is allowed. However, no deduction is permitted for an NOL carryover or carryback from a preceding or succeeding year.

EXAMPLE I16-10 ▶ Maine Corporation's NOL for 2001 is computed from the following income and deduction items:

Operating income	$ 400,000
Plus: Dividends received from 20% (or more) owned corporations	300,000
Gross income	$ 700,000
Minus: Business operating expenses	(600,000)
Dividends-received deduction (0.80 × $300,000)	(240,000)
Net operating loss	$(140,000)

NOLs are carried back two years (beginning with the earliest tax year). Any excess amounts are carried forward up to 20 years to offset taxable income in those years. Maine's NOLs can be carried back to 1999 and 2000. Any remaining NOL is carried over to years 2002-2021.[7] ◄

KEY POINT
In making the decision whether to forgo the NOL carryback, the corporation should compare the current refund from the potential carryback to the present value of any future benefit from a carryover.

A corporation may elect to forgo the NOL carryback and instead carry the unused loss forward. For example, if the corporation has taxable income less than $75,000 in the carryback year(s) subject to tax rates less than 34%, the tax benefit may be of limited value because the NOL carryback offsets income taxed at these lower rates. The NOL might be more valuable if the carryback is forgone and the NOL is carried over to a year in which the marginal tax rate may be as high as 39%. However, in this case the tax savings are deferred, whereas a carryback produces an immediate tax savings. The election, if made, applies to all carryback years, and the NOL carries forward for 20 years.

ADDITIONAL COMMENT
Taxable income for purposes of determining the charitable contribution deduction limit is calculated without regard to NOL and capital loss carrybacks, but NOL carryovers are reflected in calculating taxable income.

CHARITABLE CONTRIBUTIONS

Some of the rules governing charitable contributions for individuals also apply to corporations (e.g., the restriction imposed on contributions of ordinary income property, which is discussed in Chapter I7).[8] The following rules apply solely to corporations:

▶ Under the general rule, a payment must be made before a contribution deduction is allowed. However, corporations using the accrual method of accounting may accrue a contribution deduction in the year preceding payment if the payment is authorized by the board of directors before the end of the tax year and the contribution is made within 2½ months of the end of the tax year.

---

[6] The NOL rules are in Sec. 172.
[7] NOLs incurred in tax years beginning before August 6, 1997 are carried back three years and forward 15 years. IRC Sec. 172(f) contains special rules that permit three-year or longer carryback periods. Corporate losses eligible for longer carrybacks include product liability losses and losses arising in Presidentially declared disaster areas.
[8] Rules pertaining to charitable contributions are in Sec. 170.

- An increased charitable contribution deduction is provided by Sec. 170(e) for certain corporate property contributions. The increased deduction is available for (1) property used to care for the ill, needy, or infants; (2) scientific research property used by colleges or universities for research and experimentation; and (3) computer technology, software, and peripherals donated to educational institutions for use in grades Kindergarten through 12. In each case the amount of the deduction equals the donor's adjusted basis for the property plus one-half of the excess of the property's FMV over its adjusted basis (not to exceed twice the property's adjusted basis).
- Corporate charitable contributions are limited to 10% of taxable income (computed without regard to the charitable contribution deduction, NOL and capital loss carry-*backs*, or the dividends-received deduction).
- Unused contributions are carried forward 5 years. In the carryover year, the current year's contributions are deducted first in applying the 10% limitation. Any unused limitation is then applied to contribution carryovers from the earliest year.

EXAMPLE I16-11 ▶ During 2001, Mesa Corporation reports the following results:

Taxable income (before deducting the dividends-received deduction and charitable contributions)	$130,000
Dividends-received deduction	10,000
Charitable contributions	20,000

Mesa has never incurred an NOL. The limitation on contributions is $13,000 ($130,000 × 0.10), and taxable income is $107,000 ($130,000 − $13,000 − $10,000). The $7,000 ($20,000 − $13,000) of unused contributions carries forward for 5 years (2002-2006). ◀

EXAMPLE I16-12 ▶ Assume that the same facts as in Example I16-11 for 2001 also apply to 2002, except that taxable income (before deducting the dividends-received deduction and charitable contributions) is $220,000. The contribution limitation therefore is $22,000 ($220,000 × 0.10). The $20,000 charitable contribution from 2002 initially applies against the $22,000 limitation, leaving a $2,000 unused charitable contribution limitation. Thus, $2,000 of the carryover from 2001 is used against this limitation, leaving a $5,000 carryover from 2001, which can be used in tax years 2003 through 2006. ◀

COMPENSATION DEDUCTION LIMITATION FOR PUBLICLY HELD CORPORATIONS

A publicly-held corporation is denied a deduction for compensation paid to its chief executive officer and its four highest-compensated officers if the compensation amount for any individual exceeds $1 million per year.[9] Includible compensation includes both cash and noncash benefits. The following types of compensation are not taken into account for purposes of the $1 million limitation:

- Remuneration payable on a commission basis
- Compensation based on individual performance goals (if approved by certain outside directors and shareholders)[10]
- Payments to a qualified retirement plan
- Tax-free employee benefits (such as employer-provided health care benefits and Sec. 132 fringe benefits)

EXAMPLE I16-13 ▶ Acorn Corporation is a publicly held company listed on the New York Stock Exchange. During the current year, its chief executive officer, Rodney, receives the following compensation from the corporation: salary, $1,200,000; commissions based on sales generated by Rodney, $400,000; payments to a qualified pension plan, $25,000; and tax-free fringe benefits, $10,000. The commissions, payments to the qualified pension plan, and tax-free fringe benefits are not

---

[9] Sec. 162 (m). A publicly held corporation is any corporation issuing any class of securities required to be registered under Section 12 of the Securities Exchange Act of 1934. The Conference Committee Report indicates that this generally is a corporation listed on a national securities exchange, or one that has at least $5 million or more of assets and 500 or more shareholders.

[10] See Reg. Sec. 1.162-27 for the requirements relating to the attainment of performance goals.

subject to the $1 million annual deduction limitation for Rodney's compensation. Thus, $200,000 ($1,200,000 − $1,000,000) of Rodney's salary is not deductible by Acorn Corporation even though Rodney is taxed on the entire $1,200,000. ◄

For a summary of the capital gain and loss, dividends-received deduction, net operating loss, charitable contribution deduction, and compensation deduction rules for corporations, see Topic Review I16-1.

COMPUTATION OF TAX

OBJECTIVE 2

Calculate the corporate income tax liability and explain specific tax rules

COMPUTATION OF TAXABLE INCOME

Table I16-1 illustrates the computation of *taxable income* for a C corporation.

COMPUTATION OF REGULAR TAX

The corporate tax rates reflect a stair-step pattern of progression as follows:[11]

If Taxable Income Is: Over...	But Not Over...	The Tax Is:	Of the Amount Over...
$0	$50,000	15%	$0
50,000	75,000	$7,500 + 25%	50,000
75,000	100,000	13,750 + 34%	75,000
100,000	335,000	22,250 + 39%	100,000
335,000	10,000,000	113,900 + 34%	335,000
10,000,000	15,000,000	3,400,000 + 35%	10,000,000
15,000,000	18,333,333	5,150,000 + 38%	15,000,000
18,333,333		6,416,667 + 35%	18,333,333

EXAMPLE I16-14 ► Able Corporation's taxable income for the current year is $100,000. Its regular tax liability is computed as follows:

0.15 × $50,000	=	$ 7,500
0.25 × $25,000	=	6,250
0.34 × $25,000	=	8,500
Total tax		$22,250

The total tax due on the $100,000 of taxable income is $22,250. This tax also can be computed directly from the tax rate schedule shown above (or inside back cover). ◄

The 15% and 25% tax rates on the first $75,000 of taxable income provide a $11,750 benefit to corporations as compared to a flat 34% rate, computed as follows:

Tax on $75,000 at 34%	$25,500
Minus: Tax on $75,000 from tax rate schedule	(13,750)
Benefit of lower rates	$11,750

Congress, however, wanted only small corporations to obtain this benefit, so it imposed a 5% surtax on taxable income between $100,000 and $335,000. This 5% surtax is reflected in the 39% (34% + 5%) marginal tax rate in the corporate tax rate schedule. Once taxable income reaches $335,000, the entire benefit is recaptured ($235,000 × 0.05 = $11,750). Therefore, corporations with taxable income from $335,000 to $10,000,000 pay a flat tax equal to 34% times taxable income.

---

[11] Sec. 11(b)(1).

Topic Review I16-1

Summary of Special Corporate Rules for Calculating Taxable Income

Capital Gains and Losses
- If a net loss results after netting long-term and short-term capital gains and losses, no amount can be deducted from ordinary income. Instead, net losses are carried back 3 years and forward 5 years as STCLs.
- The corporate net capital gain does not receive favorable tax treatment. The maximum 20% tax rate for net capital gains applies to individuals.

Dividends-Received Deduction
- The dividends-received deduction for corporate shareholders is 80% if the corporate investor owns 20% or more of the stock and is 70% if the corporate investor owns less than 20%. A 100% dividends-received deduction is available for dividends from 80%-or-more-owned affiliated group members not filing consolidated tax returns.
- The dividends-received deduction is limited to 80% (or 70% as the case may be) of taxable income (after adjustments for the NOL deduction, the dividends-received deduction, and capital loss carrybacks) unless the corporate shareholder has an NOL after deducting the full amount of the dividends-received deduction.

Charitable Contributions
- Accrual-basis corporate donors may accrue a contribution deduction at the end of the tax year if authorized by the board of directors and paid within 2½ months following the end of the tax year.
- Corporations are permitted increased donations for qualifying property used (1) to care for the ill, needy, or infants, (2) to conduct research or experimentation in colleges or universities, or (3) by educational institutions in grades kindergarten through 12.
- Contributions are limited to 10% of the taxable income (with certain adjustments).
- Unused charitable contributions are carried forward 5 years.

Other
- NOLs are carried back 2 years (beginning with the earliest year) and forward 20 years. However, the corporation may elect to forgo the 2-year carryback. Longer carryback periods are permitted for special losses (for example, product liability losses).
- Publicly held corporations are denied a deduction for compensation payments exceeding $1 million to certain key executives.

EXAMPLE I16-15 ▶ Ajax Corporation's taxable income for the current year is $335,000. Its tax liability is computed as follows:

0.15 × $ 50,000	=	$ 7,500
0.25 × $ 25,000	=	6,250
0.34 × $260,000	=	88,400
0.05 × $235,000	=	11,750
Total tax		$113,900

Alternatively, the $113,900 tax liability can be determined by multiplying 34% times $335,000. Thus, the benefit of the lower rates on the first $75,000 of taxable income is completely phased-out when taxable income reaches $335,000. ◀

KEY POINT
The corporation income tax is essentially a flat tax for large corporations.

A 35% rate applies to taxable income exceeding $10 million. An additional 3% surtax (reflected in the 38% rate) applies to taxable income from $15 million to $18,333,333, which eliminates the benefit of the 34% rate once taxable income equals or exceeds $18,333,333. Thus, a flat 35% rate applies to taxable income exceeding $18,333,333.

EXAMPLE I16-16 ▶ Ajax Corporation's taxable income for the current year is $18,333,333. Its tax liability is computed as follows:

0.34 × $10,000,000	=	$3,400,000
0.35 × $5,000,000	=	1,750,000
0.38 × $3,333,333	=	1,266,667
Total tax		$6,416,667

▼ **TABLE I16-1**
Computation of Corporate Taxable Income

Sales	$600,000
Minus: Cost of goods sold	(300,000)
Gross profit	$300,000
Plus: Other income	
Dividends from 25%-owned corporation	$100,000
Interest	10,000
Long-term capital gain	90,000
Gross income	$500,000
Minus: Deductions:	
Salaries	$ 80,000
Repairs	20,000
Bad debts	30,000
Taxes	10,000
Contributions (subject to the 10% corporate limitation discussed on page I16-7)	5,000
Depreciation	20,000
Pension and profit-sharing contributions	35,000
Total deductions	$200,000
Taxable income before special deductions	$300,000
Minus: Special deductions:	
Net operating loss deduction	(15,000)[a]
Dividends-received deduction	(80,000)[b]
Taxable income	$205,000

[a] This amount represents a net operating loss carried over from a prior year.
[b] 0.80 × $100,000 = $80,000 dividends-received deduction.

ADDITIONAL COMMENT

Most states impose an income tax on C corporations. Some states exempt S corporations from the corporate income tax.

Alternatively, at $18,333,333 of taxable income, a flat 35% rate applies (0.35 × $18,333,333 = $6,416,667). ◀

SPECIAL RULE FOR CERTAIN PERSONAL SERVICE CORPORATIONS. Personal service corporations are denied the benefits of the corporate graduated rates.[12] Thus, a flat 35% rate is imposed on a personal service corporation that performs services in the fields of health, law, engineering, architecture, accounting, actuarial science, performing arts, or consulting where substantially all of the stock is held by employees or retired employees, or by their estates.

COMPUTATION OF THE CORPORATE ALTERNATIVE MINIMUM TAX (AMT)

The corporate alternative minimum tax (AMT) is similar to that applicable to individuals (see Chapter I14 for a discussion of the AMT for individuals).[13] The AMT ensures that corporations with substantial economic income pay a minimum amount of federal income tax.[14] If a corporation's AMT liability is greater than its regular (income) tax liability, the excess amount is payable in addition to the regular tax.

The corporate AMT is 20% of alternative minimum taxable income (AMTI) less an exemption that is based on the entity's AMTI. The exemption amount for corporations is $40,000 reduced by 25% of the excess of AMTI over $150,000. The exemption is phased-out when AMTI exceeds $310,000 [$150,000 + (1.0/0.25 × $40,000)].

---

[12] Sec. 11(b)(2).
[13] The AMT rules are in Secs. 55–58.
[14] The Taxpayer Relief Act of 1997 has repealed the corporate AMT for *small corporations* for tax years beginning after December 31, 1997. For details, see the discussion below.

EXAMPLE I16-17 ▶ Allied Corporation has $200,000 of AMTI before the exemption. The $40,000 exemption is reduced by $12,500 [0.25 × ($200,000 − $150,000)] to $27,500 ($40,000 − $12,500). Thus, the tax base for the AMT is $172,500 ($200,000 − $27,500). ◀

ADDITIONAL COMMENT
For AMTI through $150,000, the exemption amount is $40,000. For AMTI of $310,000 or more, the exemption amount is $0. Thus, the reduction formula need be applied only when AMTI is between $150,000 and $310,000.

COMPUTATION OF AMTI. AMTI equals taxable income modified by certain adjustments and increased by tax preference items. Tax preferences are specific items that receive preferential tax treatment. As with the individual AMT, these tax preference items are *added* to taxable income to compute AMTI. However, because corporations are more likely to incur AMT adjustments than the specified tax preferences,[15] only AMT adjustments are discussed in this chapter.

AMT Adjustments. AMT adjustments are timing differences relating to deferred income or accelerated deductions. These adjustments generally increase the AMT tax base, although the netting of timing differences may result in an overall reduction of the AMT tax base when the timing differences reverse. When an AMT liability is paid, an AMT tax credit carryover is available to the corporation to reduce the regular tax liability in subsequent years if its regular tax exceeds its tentative minimum tax in those years. (See Chapter I14 for a detailed discussion of this topic.) The most common AMT adjustments include

▶ For real property placed in service after 1986 and before 1999, the difference between the MACRS income tax depreciation claimed and a hypothetical straight-line depreciation amount computed under the alternative depreciation system using a 40-year life (see Chapter I10 for a discussion of the alternative depreciation system).

▶ For personal property placed in service after 1986, the difference between the MACRS income tax depreciation deduction and the amount determined by using the 150% declining balance method under the alternative depreciation system.

▶ 75% of the excess of the adjusted current earnings (ACE) over AMTI (before the ACE adjustment and the alternative tax NOL deduction but after all other adjustments and tax preference items).[16]

EXAMPLE I16-18 ▶ In the current year, Camp Corporation has taxable income of $100,000, and its regular tax liability is $22,250. Camp's AMT adjustments other than ACE are $80,000, and it has $340,000 of adjusted current earnings. Camp Corporation's AMT liability is computed as follows:

Taxable income	$100,000
Plus: AMT adjustments other than ACE	80,000
AMTI (before ACE adjustment)	$180,000
Plus: ACE adjustment [0.75 × ($340,000 − $180,000)]	120,000
AMTI	$300,000
Minus: Exemption ($40,000 − [($300,000 − $150,000) × 0.25])	(2,500)
AMT base	$297,500
Times: AMT rate	× .20
Tentative minimum tax	$ 59,500
Minus: Regular tax	(22,250)
AMT liability	$ 37,250

ADDITIONAL COMMENT
Because of the AMT credit, the AMT essentially is a prepaid tax on preference items and adjustments; it affects the timing of the corporation's tax payments.

Thus, Camp's total current year tax liability is $59,500 ($22,250 regular tax + $37,250 AMT). In effect, the corporation pays the greater of the regular tax or the tentative minimum tax. Camp also carries over the $37,250 AMT payment to next year as an AMT credit. For example, if next year's regular tax liability is $30,000 and the tentative minimum tax is $20,000, Camp takes a $10,000 credit against next year's regular tax and carries over the remaining $27,250 ($37,250 − $10,000) AMT credit to the following year. ◀

---

[15] See Sec. 57 for a list of tax preferences. Also, see pages I14-3 and I14-4 for a discussion of tax preferences.

[16] The term *adjusted current earnings* is a concept based on the traditional earnings and profits definition found in Sec. 312. (See Chapter C5 of *Prentice Hall's Federal Taxation: Corporations, Partnerships, Estates, and Trusts* for a detailed discussion of this AMT adjustment.)

STOP & THINK

Question: Corporations that are subject to AMT typically must alter their tax planning to minimize their overall tax liability. How might a corporation change its tax planning concerning the timing of income and deductions when the AMT applies?

Solution: When subject to the regular tax, a corporation prefers to accelerate deductions into the current year and defer income until a future year. However, while this technique reduces the regular tax, it increases the AMT and for some corporations may result in no overall tax benefit to the corporation. Therefore, when the AMT applies, the corporation should consider reversing its planning by accelerating income and deferring deductions. The interplay of income tax planning and AMT planning thus creates a point at which the income tax is reduced to as low an amount as possible without triggering the AMT.

Exception to AMT for Small Corporations. For tax years beginning after 1997, the AMT does not apply to a small business corporation. A small business corporation is an entity whose average gross receipts for all three-year periods ending before the year in which the exemption is claimed is $7.5 million or less.[17] The average gross receipts calculation includes only tax years beginning after December 31, 1993, and ending before the tax year for which the AMT exemption is claimed. The $7.5 million maximum is reduced to $5 million for the corporation's first three-year period that begins after 1993 and ends before the tax year for which the AMT exemption is claimed. Thus, a corporation in existence on January 1, 1994 will apply a $5 million ceiling for the three-year period including 1994 through 1996, and a $7.5 million ceiling for the three-year period including 1995 through 1997 to determine whether it is eligible for an AMT exemption in 1998 or not. If the corporation does not qualify for the exemption in 1998, it can not qualify for the exemption in a later year (1999). Note that this test is based on gross receipts, not taxable income. Thus, a corporation with high gross receipts and high expenses could be subject to the AMT even though it might have low taxable income.

EXAMPLE I16-19

Little Corporation, a calendar year corporation that has been in existence since 1990, has gross receipts in periods beginning after December 31, 1993 as follows:

1994	$ 3,000,000
1995	4,000,000
1996	5,000,000
1997	9,000,000
1998	10,000,000

Average prior-year gross receipts for the two three-year periods are calculated as follows

1994-1996	$4,000,000 = [($3,000,000 + $4,000,000 + $5,000,000) ÷ 3]
1995-1997	$6,000,000 = [($4,000,000 + $5,000,000 + $9,000,000) ÷ 3]

Little Corporation qualifies as a small corporation in 1998 because its average gross receipts for 1994-1996 did not exceed $5 million, and its average gross receipts for 1995-1997 did not exceed $7.5 million. Thus, Little Corporation is not subject to the AMT in 1998. Little Corporation also will be exempt from the corporate AMT in 1999 if its average gross receipts for the three-year period including 1996-1998 is $7.5 million or less. [The $7.5 million ceiling applies to 2000 and later years.]

Unfortunately for Little Corporation, its average gross receipts for 1996-1998 are $8,000,000 ([$5,000,000 + $9,000,000 + $10,000,000] ÷ 3). Little Corporation is not eligible for the small corporation AMT exemption in 1999. It may be able to avoid the AMT by using the $40,000 statutory exemption. If the statutory exemption does not eliminate the need to pay the AMT, Little Corporation may end up paying a large enough regular tax liability to avoid the AMT. Failing to qualify for the small corporation exemption in 1999 precludes the exemption from being used in 2000 and later years.

---

[17] The exemption also applies to a noncorporate entity that elects to be taxed as a C corporation under the check-the-box rules. Gross receipts are calculated using the entity's tax year.

Corporations ▼ Individuals 16-13

Corporations created after 1997 are subject to a slightly different set of exemption rules. A new corporation is generally exempt from the corporate AMT for its first tax year regardless of its gross receipts for the year. To be exempt in its second tax year, the corporation's gross receipts must not have exceeded $5 million in its first tax year. To be exempt in its third tax year, the corporation's average gross receipts for its first two tax years must not exceed $7.5 million. To be exempt in its fourth tax year, a corporation's average gross receipts for its first three tax years must not exceed $7.5 million. For all succeeding tax years, a three-year look-back rule applies like the one used to determine eligibility for the exemption in a corporation's fourth year. Special rules apply if the corporation in question is aggregated with other corporations under Sec. 448(c)(2) [for example, a member of a controlled group], or is considered to be a successor to an existing corporation under Sec. 448(c)(3).

EXAMPLE I16-20 ▶ Assume the same facts as in Example I16-19 except that Little Corporation was created in 1998 and it reports the following gross receipts:

Year	Gross Receipts
1998	$ 3,000,000
1999	4,000,000
2000	5,000,000
2001	9,000,000
2002	10,000,000

Little Corporation is not aggregated with other corporations under Sec. 448(c)(2) or related to a predecessor corporation under the rules of Sec. 448(c)(3). Little Corporation is exempt from the corporate AMT in its first year (1998) without regard to its actual gross receipts. An exemption is available to Little in 1999 because its gross receipts for its first tax year were $5 million or less. An exemption is available to Little in 2000 because the average gross receipts for its first two tax years were $7.5 million or less ([$3,000,000 + $4,000,000] ÷ 2 = $3,500,000). The exemption continues to be available to Little in 2001 because its average gross receipts for the first three tax years were $7.5 million or less ([$3,000,000 + $4,000,000 + $5,000,000] ÷ 3 = $4,000,000). The exemption remains available to Little in 2002 because its average gross receipts for the previous three tax years were $7.5 million or less ([$4,000,000 + $5,000,000 + $9,000,000] ÷ 3 = $6,000,000). The exemption is lost by Little in 2003 because its average gross receipts for the previous three tax years were $8,000,000 ([$5,000,000 + $9,000,000 + $10,000,000]), and in excess of the $7.5 million ceiling. Little can not requalify for the exemption in 2003 and later years. Loss of the exemption may make Little subject to the AMT in 2003 and succeeding tax years. ◀

The AMT liability for a corporation that loses its exemption includes only preference items and adjustments involving transactions and investments taking place after the small corporation status is lost. The modifications required in making the AMT calculation for corporations having lost their small corporation status are beyond the scope of this book.

PENALTY TAXES

Two penalty taxes are imposed to avoid otherwise abusive tax planning practices: the accumulated earnings tax and the personal holding company tax. The computation of both penalty taxes involves a complex array of rules that are discussed in detail in the companion volume to this text, *Prentice Hall's Federal Taxation: Corporations, Partnerships, Estates, and Trusts*. Here, we present an overview of these complex subjects.

ACCUMULATED EARNINGS TAX. The **accumulated earnings tax** discourages companies from retaining excessive amounts of earnings if the funds are invested in assets unrelated to business needs.[18] Thus, a company may avoid the penalty tax if its earnings are reinvested in operating-type assets or retained for the reasonable needs of the business. If this tax were not imposed, closely held corporations might not pay dividends to their

---
[18] The basic rules for the accumulated earning tax are in Code Secs. 531–537.

ADDITIONAL COMMENT

When the highest marginal tax rate on individuals was considerably higher than the corporate tax rate, corporations commonly were used as tax shelters. From 1987 through 1992, corporate tax rates were higher than the individual tax rates, making the accumulated earnings tax and the personal holding company tax less important. In 1993 and subsequent years, the increase in the highest individual tax rate to 39.6% has increased the importance of the two penalty taxes to some degree because the top corporate tax rate is only 35%.

ADDITIONAL COMMENT

The accumulated earnings tax can be avoided by the payment of a large enough dividend or by making an S election. The accumulated earnings tax does not apply for the years the S election is in effect.

shareholders (thereby avoiding a double tax on the earnings). The retained earnings then could be reinvested in passive investments.

Reasonable needs of the business include

- Reasonably anticipated expansion of the business and plant replacement
- Acquiring the assets or stock (other than portfolio investments) of another business
- Providing working capital for the business
- Establishing a sinking fund to retire corporate debt
- Making investments or loans to suppliers or customers

The accumulated earnings tax generally is imposed on closely held corporations. However, the tax may be imposed on a publicly held corporation if effective control is in the hands of a few related shareholders.[19]

The accumulated earnings tax is imposed on a corporation's accumulated taxable income for a particular year. The accumulated earnings tax rate is 39.6%. Accumulated taxable income is computed as follows:

Taxable income
Plus: Dividends-received deduction
       Net operating loss deduction
Minus: Net capital losses
       Net long-term capital gains over net short-term capital
            losses (less federal income tax on such net gains)
       Federal income tax liability
       Charitable contributions exceeding the 10% limit
       Deductions for dividends paid or deemed paid[20]
       Accumulated earnings credit
Accumulated taxable income

The accumulated earnings credit equals the greater of (1) $250,000 minus the accumulated earnings and profits (E&P) at the beginning of the year[21] or (2) the amount of E&P for the tax year that are retained for the reasonable needs of the business. Reasonable needs of the business are determined at year-end and are reduced by accumulated E&P at the beginning of the year. Thus, only the amount of E&P that are retained to meet the increase in reasonable business needs can be claimed as a credit. (The E&P term is formally defined later in this chapter.)

EXAMPLE I16-21

Compact Corporation has taxable income of $100,000 in the current year. Compact's federal income tax liability is $22,250, and the corporation paid $10,000 in dividends to its shareholders. Compact claims a dividends-received deduction of $80,000 on $100,000 of dividend income. Accumulated E&P at the beginning of the year retained for the reasonable needs of the business is $200,000, and Compact Corporation's reasonable needs of the business at year-end amount to $220,000. The accumulated taxable income and the accumulated earnings credit are computed as follows:

Taxable income		$100,000
Plus: Dividends-received deduction		80,000
Minus: Federal income tax liability		(22,250)
Dividends-paid deduction		(10,000)
Accumulated earnings credit—the greater of:		
(1) $250,000 (statutory exemption) − $200,000		
(accumulated E&P at the beginning of the year)	$50,000	
	or	
(2) E&P retained for the increased reasonable		
needs of the business ($220,000 − $200,000)	$20,000	(50,000)
Accumulated taxable income		$ 97,750

---

[19] Sec. 532(c) and *Golconda Mining Corp. v. CIR*, 35 AFTR 2d 75-336, 74-2 USTC ¶9845 (9th Cir., 1974).

[20] Sec. 561. The deduction for dividends paid includes dividends actually paid during the tax year and consent dividends (e.g., a hypothetical dividend) where the shareholders agree to be taxed on such amounts. Under Sec. 563, dividends paid during the first 2½ months following the end of the tax year are considered paid on the last day of the preceding tax year.

[21] The $250,000 credit amount is reduced to $150,000 for service corporations engaged in the field of health, law, engineering, architecture, accounting, actuarial science, performing arts, or consulting.

The accumulated earnings tax is $38,709 (0.396 × $97,750) and is paid in addition to the corporation's regular tax. Compact's total federal tax liability is $60,959 ($22,250 + $38,709). ◀

An IRS auditor will likely look to Schedules L and M-2 of Form 1120 (U.S. Corporation Income Tax Return) to make an initial determination about the existence of an accumulated earnings tax problem. See Appendix C for a filled-in Form 1120. The auditor will look to Schedule L (the balance sheet) to identify the assets owned by the firm. A large amount of marketable securities, loans made to shareholders, and nonbusiness assets (for example, a boat or resort condominium owned by the corporation) may be indicative of excess earnings being retained in the business. Alternatively, these earnings could have been distributed by the corporation to the shareholders in the form of a dividend. The shareholders could have used the monies to personally purchase the securities and nonbusiness assets. Loans made to the shareholders may represent an attempt to avoid having the earnings be taxed as a dividend if they were distributed to the shareholders, or used to redeem a shareholder's stock. The IRS auditor will look at Schedule M-2 to see if the corporation has declared and paid any dividends to the shareholders during the tax year. The existence of recurring dividend payments may be an argument used by the firm to avoid the accumulated earnings tax.

ADDITIONAL COMMENT
The personal holding company tax is imposed on the basis of mechanical criteria, whereas the accumulated earnings tax uses a subjective standard of purpose to avoid the tax.

PERSONAL HOLDING COMPANY TAX. A company must meet both of the following tests to be classified as a **personal holding company**:[22]

▶ More than 50% of the value of outstanding stock must be owned by five or fewer individuals at some time during the last six months of the tax year.

▶ 60% or more of adjusted ordinary gross income must be personal holding company income. Personal holding company income consists of passive types of income including dividends, interest, and under certain circumstances, rental income.

Most closely held companies have difficulty avoiding the 50% stock ownership test because of special family stock attribution rules. For example, 20 family members (e.g., spouses, children, and grandchildren) owning stock in a family corporation may count as only one shareholder for purposes of applying the 50% and five or fewer shareholders tests.

ADDITIONAL COMMENT
The personal holding company tax can be a particular problem in a corporation's final year as it scales down its operations. The corporation may have discontinued its operations, sold its assets, and earned primarily investment income.

The personal holding company tax prevents closely held companies from converting an operating company into a nonoperating investment company by reinvesting substantial amounts of earnings into passive investments (e.g., stocks and bonds of other companies). The personal holding company tax forces a company to distribute its earnings to shareholders as dividends if the earnings are not invested in operating assets. This tax is imposed even if the corporation and shareholders have no tax-avoidance motive, whereas the intent to avoid tax on dividend distributions must be present under the accumulated earnings tax rules.

The accumulated earnings tax, however, cannot be imposed in the same year the corporation qualifies as a personal holding company. In many instances, a corporation that is gradually converting itself into a nonoperating company by reinvesting its earnings in passive investments will have an accumulated earnings tax problem before being subjected to the personal holding company tax. However, this is not always the case. For example, a newly-formed company that temporarily invests surplus funds in nonoperating assets may be classified as a personal holding company in its first year while the $250,000 accumulated earnings credit will temporarily shield the same company from the accumulated earnings tax.

Computation of Personal Holding Company Tax. The **personal holding company tax** is 39.6% times undistributed personal holding company income. Various adjustments are made to taxable income to arrive at the tax base. These adjustments are similar to those for the accumulated earnings tax as illustrated in Example I16-21 above.

---

[22] The basic rules for personal holding companies are in Secs. 541–547.

EXAMPLE I16-22

ADDITIONAL COMMENT

The personal holding company tax, like the accumulated earnings tax, can be avoided by paying a large enough dividend or by making an S election. The S election prevents the corporation from being classified as a personal holding company for the years it is in effect.

Crane Corporation has four shareholders who together own more than 50% of the value of the stock at all times during the current year. In addition, 60% or more of adjusted ordinary gross income is personal holding company income (dividends, interest, etc.). Therefore, Crane is classified as a personal holding company for the current year because the stock ownership and income tests are met. Crane receives a $25,000 dividend for which a $20,000 dividends-received deduction is claimed and pays $18,750 of dividends to its shareholders. Crane has $200,000 of taxable income and a $61,250 regular tax liability.

Crane Corporation's personal holding company tax is computed as follows:

Taxable income	$200,000
Adjustments:	
Federal income tax liability	(61,250)
Dividends-received deduction	20,000
Dividends-paid deduction[23]	(18,750)
Undistributed personal holding company income	$140,000
Times: Personal holding company tax rate	× 0.396
Personal holding company tax	$ 55,440

Crane's total federal tax liability is $116,690 ($61,250 + $55,440). The $55,440 personal holding company tax may be avoided if Crane pays all of the undistributed personal holding company income to its shareholders. Special rules allow personal holding companies to pay these dividends even after the corporation's year-end. The shareholders then pay an income tax levy on the dividend distribution.

Topic Review I16-2 presents a comparison of the accumulated earnings tax and personal holding company tax rules.

COMPUTATION OF TAX FOR CONTROLLED GROUPS

Shareholders of a single corporation could recognize substantial tax savings by splitting the corporation into two or more corporations. This tax savings results from splitting the income of the single corporation among the separate corporations, allowing the separate corporations to take advantage of the lower corporate tax rates. To prevent this type of manipulation, however, a **controlled group** must apportion the lower tax rates among the

---

WHAT WOULD YOU DO IN THIS SITUATION?

Scott, Steve, and Sean own 100% of the outstanding stock of Sofa Corporation for all of the current year. Sofa Corporation, a manufacturer of custom-made sofas, has never paid a dividend to its shareholders, preferring to retain its earnings for working capital, additional machinery, and marketable security investments. Scott and Steve would like to borrow money from Sofa before the end of the year because Scott is planning to open a florist shop as an additional business, and Steve needs a loan to pay off personal debts. For these reasons, Sofa Corporation will not pay a dividend in the current year. However, the company plans to start paying dividends next year. Sofa has accumulated E&P exceeding $250,000. As Sofa's tax consultant, you inform the shareholders of the possibility that the company will be subject to the accumulated earnings tax. The shareholders ask you if they should inform the IRS, voluntarily pay the tax, or just wait to be audited by the IRS.

a. What advice would you give the shareholders regarding the reporting of the potential accumulated earnings tax problem to the IRS and the payment of the tax? (See the *Statements on Responsibilities in Tax Practice* section in Chapter I15 and Appendix E.)

b. What advice would you give to the shareholders if the corporation instead reported low operating profits from its sofa-making activities and met the requirements for a personal holding company in the current year?

---

[23] Secs. 547 and 561. The dividends-paid deduction is available for dividends paid during the tax year, dividends paid within 2½ months following the end of the tax year (subject to certain limitations), consent dividends, and dividends paid within 90 days following a determination that a personal holding company tax liability is owed (i.e., deficiency dividends). Deficiency dividends are not allowed when computing the accumulated earnings tax.

Topic Review I16-2

Comparison of the Two Corporate Penalty Taxes

ITEM	ACCUMULATED EARNINGS TAX—SEC. 531	PERSONAL HOLDING COMPANY (PHC) TAX—SEC. 541
Reason for imposing the penalty tax	To discourage companies from retaining excessive amounts of earnings if the funds are invested in nonoperating assets. A primary purpose is to force dividend payments of excess earnings.	To prevent closely held companies from converting an operating company into a passive investment company. A primary purpose is to force dividend payments of passive income.
Nature of the tax formula	The tax base is taxable income plus or minus certain adjustments. The tax computation is inherently subjective because the accumulated earnings credit (which often reduces the tax base to zero) is based on the retention of earnings for the reasonable needs of the business, which is a subjective determination.	The determination of whether a corporation is a personal holding company and the computation of the penalty tax is a mechanical process. Once the corporation is determined to be a PHC, the tax base is taxable income plus or minus certain adjustments.
Computation of tax	Adjustments are made to taxable income for items such as the dividends-received deduction, the dividends-paid deduction, the federal income tax liability, and the accumulated earnings credit (see Example I16-21). The tax is 39.6% of accumulated taxable income for the tax year.	Adjustments are made to taxable income for items such as the dividends-received deduction, dividends-paid deduction, and the federal income tax liability to arrive at undistributed PHC income (see Example I16-22). The tax rate is 39.6% of undistributed PHC income for the tax year.

group members as if only one corporation existed.[24] An equal apportionment to each member is required unless all the controlled group's members consent to an unequal allocation of such amounts. A controlled group, as discussed below, is a group of corporations that are, in general, owned by the same shareholders.

EXAMPLE I16-23 ▶ West and East Corporations are members of a controlled group. West and East each have taxable income of $100,000. If each corporation were taxed separately, each corporation's tax liability would be $22,250, or a total of $44,500. However, because West and East are members of a controlled group, the reduced tax rate brackets must be apportioned to each corporation. The tax liability for each corporation assuming an equal apportionment is computed as follows:

	Corporation West	East
Tax on initial $50,000 of taxable income apportioned equally to West and East (0.15 × $25,000)	$ 3,750	$ 3,750
Tax on next $25,000 apportioned equally to West and East (0.25 × $12,500)	3,125	3,125
Tax on next $25,000 apportioned equally to West and East (0.34 × $12,500)	4,250	4,250
Tax on remaining $50,000 of taxable income for each corporation (0.39 × $50,000)	19,500	19,500
Tax on $100,000 of taxable income for each corporation	$30,625	$30,625

ADDITIONAL COMMENT

A controlled group of corporations must apportion not only the lower tax rates but also the $250,000 accumulated earnings credit and the $40,000 exemption for the alternative minimum tax.

---

[24] Sec. 1561.

The tax result of being a controlled group caused West and East Corporations to pay a total of $61,250 in income taxes. This amount is $16,750 ($61,250 − $44,500) more tax than if each were taxed as separate corporations. However, the total tax of $61,250 also would have been the total tax if West and East were, in fact, one corporation. ◄

If taxable income of the controlled group exceeds $10 million, a comparable allocation needs to occur to reflect the lower 34% rate applying to taxable income up to $10 million.

Controlled groups may be classified into three types: a brother-sister controlled group, a parent-subsidiary controlled group, and a combined group. These three types of groups are discussed below.

ADDITIONAL COMMENT
In practice, brother-sister corporations frequently occur with one or a small number of taxpayers owning several small, closely-held corporations.

BROTHER-SISTER CORPORATIONS. A **brother-sister controlled group** exists if the following conditions are met:

▶ Five or fewer individuals, estates, or trusts own at least 80% of the voting power or value of all classes of stock of each corporation.[25]

▶ The shareholders commonly own more than 50% of the total voting power or value of all classes of stock. The stock is counted for this test only to the extent that each shareholder owns an identical interest in each corporation.[26] The term *identical interest* means the smallest percentage of stock owned by the shareholder in any corporation in the brother-sister group.

EXAMPLE I16-24 ▶ The single classes of stock of First, Second, and Third Corporations are owned by Amir, Beth, Carol, Dawn, and Edith as shown below.

	Corporation			Identical
Individuals	First	Second	Third	Interest
Amir	40%	20%	20%	20%
Beth	30	30	60	30
Carol	10	40	10	10
Dawn	10	10	—	—
Edith	10	—	10	—
Total	100%	100%	100%	60%

The 80% test is met because five or fewer individuals own at least 80% of the First, Second, and Third stocks. This test is met because Amir, Beth, and Carol own 80% of the First stock and 90% of the Second and Third stocks. Dawn and Edith are not included for the 80% test because they do not have stock ownership in each of the three corporations. The 50% test also is met because common ownership exceeds 50% (60% total in the Identical Interest column). For the 50% test, the stock ownership of Dawn and Edith is not counted because they do not own shares in each of the three corporations. For example, if Dawn (but not Edith) owned the 10% interest in the Third stock, Dawn would be counted for the 80% test and the common ownership test would increase from 60% to 70%. ◄

PARENT-SUBSIDIARY CONTROLLED GROUPS. A **parent-subsidiary controlled group** exists if the following conditions are met:

▶ A common parent corporation owns at least 80% of the stock of at least one subsidiary corporation.[27]

▶ At least 80% of the stock of each other member of the controlled group is owned by other members of the controlled group.

---

[25] The 80% test is met if 80% or more of the total combined voting power of all classes of voting stock *or* at least 80% of the total value of all classes of stock of each corporation is held by five or fewer people on December 31. To be counted for the 80% test, a shareholder must own stock in each corporation of the brother-sister controlled group.

[26] Sec. 1563(a)(2).
[27] Sec. 1563(a)(1).

EXAMPLE I16-25 ▶ Federal Corporation owns 100% of the Apex Corporation stock and 30% of the Giant Corporation stock. Apex also owns 50% of the Giant stock. Each corporation has only one class of stock outstanding. Owning at least 80% of the Apex stock makes Federal the common parent corporation of the controlled group. Giant also is a member of the controlled group because at least 80% of the Giant stock is owned by members of the controlled group (Federal and Apex together own 80% [30% + 50%]). The parent-subsidiary controlled group consists of Federal, Apex, and Giant Corporations. ◀

COMBINED CONTROLLED GROUPS. A combined controlled group exists if the following two conditions are met by a group of three or more corporations:

▶ A common parent corporation owns at least 80% of at least one subsidiary corporation (a parent-subsidiary group), and

▶ The common parent corporation is a member of a group of corporations that constitute a brother-sister group.[28]

Using the facts from Example I16-25, a combined controlled group would exist if Federal Corporation was a member of a brother-sister controlled group that also included National Corporation which results from Viki owning 100% of the single classes of stock of Federal and National Corporations. Then, Federal, National, Apex, and Giant Corporations would constitute a combined controlled group and must share the various tax benefits.

BOOK-TAX ACCOUNTING COMPARISON

The corporations included in a consolidated tax return may differ from those included in consolidated financial statements. 80% stock ownership is needed to be part of a consolidated tax return while only 50% stock ownership is needed to be part of a consolidated financial statement.

CONSOLIDATED RETURNS

Corporations that are members of a parent-subsidiary affiliated group are eligible to file a consolidated tax return if an election is made under the consolidated return Treasury Regulations. Be aware, however, that the eligibility requirements for an affiliated group and a controlled group are slightly different (see Chapter C8 of the *Prentice Hall's Federal Taxation: Corporations, Partnerships, Estates, and Trusts* text for a detailed discussion of the requirements for filing a consolidated tax return). Moreover, brother-sister controlled groups never can file consolidated tax returns. Once the election is made, IRS permission must be obtained to discontinue filing on a consolidated basis.[29]

The consolidated return treats the affiliated group as a single entity, thereby allowing the following advantages: (1) net operating losses of one or more members can offset profits of other members; (2) capital losses of one or more members can offset capital gains of other members; and (3) profit and gains on transactions involving two or more group members are treated as taking place between divisions of a single entity and thus tax-deferred until a subsequent transaction occurs involving a group member and a taxpayer outside the affiliated group.

STOP & THINK

Question: P Corporation owns 100% of S-1 Corporation and P and S-1 Corporations each own 50% of S-2 Corporation. Both P and S-1 Corporations are highly profitable (subject to a flat 34% corporate tax rate). S-2 Corporation, however, has never earned a profit and has had a net operating loss (NOL) in each year of its existence. Would it be beneficial from a tax standpoint for P, S-1, and S-2 Corporations to commence filing a consolidated tax return?

Solution: Filing a consolidated return would be highly beneficial because S-2 Corporation's current year losses can offset current year profits earned by P and S-1 Corporations. Because S-2 Corporation has never earned a profit, it would not be able to use the NOL if it filed a separate return. In addition, S-2's prior year losses may be able to offset profits reported by S-1 in current year and future year consolidated tax returns. Therefore, filing a consolidated return allows the NOLs of one or more members of an affiliated group to offset the profits of other members and reduce the group's overall tax liability.

---

[28] Sec. 1563(a)(3).   [29] Reg. Sec. 1.1502-75(c).

TRANSFERS OF PROPERTY TO CONTROLLED CORPORATIONS

OBJECTIVE 3

Apply the nonrecognition of gain or loss rules for corporate formations

Section 351 permits shareholders of a corporation to defer recognition of gain or loss on the transfer of assets to the corporation. The transfer of property may be made when a new corporation is formed or may reflect additional capital contributions to an existing corporation. Without Sec. 351, a sole proprietorship or a partnership would have difficulty adopting the corporate form of organization for legal and/or tax purposes because the transfer of appreciated property would constitute a taxable transaction resulting in a recognized gain.

SECTION 351 NONRECOGNITION REQUIREMENTS

KEY POINT

The nonrecognition provisions of Sec. 351 are mandatory rather than elective if all conditions are met.

The deferral of gain or loss under Sec. 351 can be justified because the assets merely have been transferred to a corporation that is controlled by the transferors. In addition, the transferors do not have the wherewithal to pay the tax on the gains that otherwise would be recognized because the shareholders receive only stock of the transferee (controlled) corporation, rather than cash or liquid assets. Section 351 also prevents recognition of losses on transfers of property that have declined in value.

Gain or loss is not recognized if the following conditions are met:

▶ Property (other than services) is transferred to the corporation solely in exchange for stock of the transferee corporation.[30]

▶ Immediately after the exchange, the transferor-shareholders in aggregate control the transferee corporation by owning at least 80% of its stock.[31]

▶ If a transferor receives money or property (other than stock in the transferee corporation), the transferor recognizes gain (but not loss) equal to the lesser of the boot received (i.e., money plus the FMV of nonstock property received) or the realized gain.[32] In addition, a corporation that transfers appreciated property (other than its own stock or debt obligations) to the transferor-shareholders also recognizes gain on the exchange.[33]

▶ The character of any gain recognized by the transferor depends on the type of asset transferred as follows: capital gain on capital assets, Sec. 1231 gain on Sec. 1231 property, and ordinary income on other property (e.g., inventory).

▶ Depreciation recapture does not apply to a Sec. 351 transfer unless the transferor recognizes gain on the depreciable property that is transferred.[34]

EXAMPLE I16-26 ▶ Carlos and Fred combine their sole proprietorships by forming the Miami Corporation. Carlos transfers land and a building having a $50,000 adjusted basis and a $100,000 FMV to the corporation in exchange for 40% of the Miami stock. Fred transfers equipment with a $60,000 adjusted basis and a $150,000 FMV to the corporation in exchange for 60% of the Miami stock. Miami Corporation is controlled by Carlos and Fred because together they own at least 80% of Miami's single class of stock immediately after the exchange. Carlos and Fred recognize no gain because all of the Sec. 351 requirements are met and they received no property other than Miami stock. The depreciation recapture potential on the building and equipment carries over to Miami Corporation. ◀

---

[30] Section 351(d) provides that services do not qualify as property. Thus, if an individual transfers services in exchange for stock, the individual is not counted as a transferor for purposes of meeting the 80% control requirement unless the individual also transfers substantial other properties. In any event, the transfer of services results in the transferor recognizing ordinary income equal to the FMV of services rendered.

[31] Sec. 368(c). Control means the ownership of at least 80% of the total combined voting power of all classes of stock and at least 80% of the total number of shares of all other classes of stock.

[32] Sec. 351(b). The recognized gain calculation is done on an asset-by-asset basis.

[33] Secs. 351(f) and 311(b).

[34] Secs. 1245(b)(3) and 1250(d)(3). The corporation recognizes the depreciation recapture assumed from the transferor if it subsequently sells or disposes of the asset.

EXAMPLE I16-27 ▶ Gail and Gary form Michigan Corporation. Gail transfers inventory with a $50,000 adjusted basis and a $100,000 FMV to Michigan Corporation in exchange for 50% of the stock worth $80,000 and $20,000 cash. The cash represents borrowings by Michigan Corporation from a bank. Gary transfers equipment with a $150,000 adjusted basis and a $100,000 FMV in exchange for 50% of the stock worth $80,000 and a Michigan Corporation 10-year note valued at $20,000. Section 351 applies to the exchange because property is transferred by the two transferors who together control more than 80% of the Michigan stock immediately after the exchange. The tax consequences to Gail and Gary are as follows:

	Gail	*Gary*
FMV of stock received	$ 80,000	$ 80,000
Plus: Cash or note received	20,000	20,000
Amount realized	$100,000	$100,000
Minus: Adjusted basis of property transferred	(50,000)	(150,000)
Gain (loss) realized	$ 50,000	$ (50,000)
Gain (loss) recognized	$ 20,000	$ —0—

Gail's recognized gain is the lesser of the $20,000 boot she received or her $50,000 realized gain. Moreover, her gain is ordinary income because she transferred inventory. Because Gary realized a loss, he recognizes no gain or loss even though he received $20,000 of boot. ◀

ADDITIONAL COMMENT

When different classes of stock are received in a Sec. 351 exchange, the available basis must be allocated to the different classes in proportion to their relative FMVs when received.

BASIS CONSIDERATIONS

STOCK RECEIVED BY THE TRANSFEROR. In Sec. 351 transactions, substituted basis rules apply to stock received by the transferors and carryover basis rules apply to property transferred to the corporation. The basis formula for the transferor's stock is as follows:

Basis of the property transferred to the corporation
Plus: Any gain recognized by the transferor on the exchange (e.g., due to boot received)
Minus: Amount of money received (including any liabilities transferred to the corporation)
FMV of any nonmoney boot property received
Basis of the stock received[35]

Any boot property received takes a basis equal to its FMV.

EXAMPLE I16-28 ▶ George and Gina form New Corporation. George transfers land and a building with a $60,000 adjusted basis and a $100,000 FMV in exchange for 50% of New stock. Gina transfers equipment with a $120,000 adjusted basis and a $100,000 FMV for 50% of the New stock. George realizes a $40,000 gain, and Gina realizes a $20,000 loss. However, George and Gina recognize no gain or loss because Sec. 351 applies. George's basis in his New stock is $60,000, and Gina's basis in her New stock is $120,000. ◀

STOP & THINK

Question: In Example I16-28, George and Gina recognized no gain or loss. Why is this treatment a deferral rather than permanent nonrecognition?

Solution: George's $40,000 unrecognized gain is reflected in a $60,000 stock basis that is $40,000 *below* its $100,000 FMV. Thus, if George immediately sells his stock for its FMV, he recognizes the $40,000 deferred gain ($100,000 selling price − $60,000 adjusted basis in his stock). Similarly, Gina's $20,000 unrecognized loss is reflected in a $120,000 stock basis that is $20,000 *above* its $100,000 FMV. Thus, if Gina immediately sells her stock for its FMV, she recognizes the $20,000 deferred loss ($100,000 selling price − $120,000 adjusted basis in her stock). In short, the substituted basis rules ensure that nonrecognized gains and losses are merely deferred. However, the deferral can be made permanent if the stock is held until the shareholder's death at which time the stock's basis is adjusted up or down to its FMV.

---

[35] Sec. 358(a).

BOOK-TAX ACCOUNTING COMPARISON

Financial accounting requires that the corporation record the transferred assets at their fair market values.

PROPERTY RECEIVED BY TRANSFEREE CORPORATION. Carryover basis rules apply to the property received by the transferee corporation. The basis of property received by the transferee corporation is computed as follows:

Adjusted basis of property in the transferor's hands
Plus: Gain recognized by the transferor
Basis of property to the transferee corporation[36]

EXAMPLE I16-29 ▶ North Corporation receives property having a $60,000 adjusted basis in the transferor's hands and a $100,000 FMV in an exchange qualifying under Sec. 351. If no gain is recognized on the transfer, the $60,000 adjusted basis is used for the asset's basis on the corporation's books and the shareholder's stock basis. Assume that the transferor instead recognizes a $10,000 gain because she receives boot (e.g., cash) from the transferee corporation. North Corporation's basis of the property is $70,000 ($60,000 adjusted basis in the transferor's hands + $10,000 gain recognized by the transferor), and the transferor's basis is $70,000 for the stock. ◀

TREATMENT OF LIABILITIES

NONRECOGNITION OF GAIN. Section 357(a) permits the assumption of liabilities by the transferee corporation (or the corporation may take the property subject to the liability) without recognition of gain under the boot rules previously discussed. Thus, under the general rule, shareholders recognize no gain if they transfer liabilities to a controlled corporation. The shareholders, however, must reduce their stock basis by the amount of liabilities assumed or acquired. This rule is logical because, if a shareholder transfers net assets of $10,000 (i.e., gross assets of $100,000 and liabilities of $90,000), the contribution to capital is only $10,000 even though $100,000 in gross assets are transferred.

TYPICAL MISCONCEPTION

When a corporation assumes a shareholder's liabilities and the shareholder recognizes no gain, one can mistakenly assume that the shareholder's stock basis is not reduced by the liabilities assumed.

EXAMPLE I16-30 ▶ Ira transfers land with an $80,000 adjusted basis and a $100,000 FMV to Mega Corporation in exchange for 100% of its stock having a $60,000 FMV in a transaction qualifying under Sec. 351. The transferred property is subject to a $40,000 liability that the corporation assumes. The tax consequences to Ira are as follows:

FMV of stock received	$ 60,000
Plus: Liability assumed by the corporation	40,000
Amount realized	$100,000
Minus: Adjusted basis of property transferred	(80,000)
Gain realized	$ 20,000
Gain recognized	$ –0–
Adjusted basis of property transferred	$ 80,000
Minus: Liability assumed by corporation	(40,000)
Adjusted basis of stock received	$ 40,000

In addition, the corporation takes an $80,000 carryover basis in the land. ◀

EXCEPTIONS. Two exceptions require gain recognition upon the transfer of liabilities to the corporation. The first exception relates to the nature of the exchange. If the principal purpose for the assumption of the liabilities is tax avoidance or if the transaction does not have a bona fide business purpose, all of the transferor's liabilities assumed by the transferee corporation are treated as boot, causing potential gain recognition.[37]

EXAMPLE I16-31 ▶ Helen transfers land and a building with a $70,000 adjusted basis and a $100,000 FMV to Orlando Corporation in exchange for 100% of its stock in a transaction qualifying under Sec. 351. Shortly before the transfer, Helen obtains a $60,000 mortgage on the property and uses the funds to pay off personal debts. The corporation then assumes the $60,000 mortgage and issues stock worth $40,000. The mortgage assumption lacks business purpose and is intended to place cash in Helen's hands without recognizing gain under the boot rules. For this reason,

---

[36] Sec. 362(a).   [37] Sec. 357(b).

Helen must treat the entire $60,000 liability assumed as boot for determining the gain recognized. Thus, the tax consequences to Helen are as follows:

FMV of stock received	$ 40,000
Plus: Liability assumed by the corporation	60,000
Amount realized	$100,000
Minus: Adjusted basis of property transferred	(70,000)
Gain realized	$ 30,000
Gain recognized	$ 30,000
Adjusted basis of property transferred	$ 70,000
Plus: Gain recognized	30,000
Minus: Liability assumed by the corporation	(60,000)
Adjusted basis of stock received	$ 40,000

Although the total boot is $60,000 (the liability assumed), Helen's recognized gain does not exceed her realized gain. In addition, the stock basis equals its FMV because Helen recognizes the entire realized gain, leaving no gain to defer. Finally, Orlando's basis in the land and building is $100,000 ($70,000 adjusted basis in the transferor's hands + $30,000 gain recognized by the transferor). ◄

A second exception applies to excess liabilities. If a transferor's total liabilities assumed by the corporation exceeds the total basis of assets (including cash) transferred by that transferor, the transferor must recognize gain to the extent of the excess.[38] Without this rule, the shareholder would have a negative basis in the stock received. In addition, gain is recognized because the transferor has received a net economic benefit to the extent the liabilities assumed exceed the adjusted basis of the transferred assets.

REAL-WORLD EXAMPLE
Customer deposits representing obligations to perform future services were considered liabilities. Because these liabilities exceeded the basis of the assets transferred to the corporation, gain was recognized. *William P. Orr*, 78 T.C. 1059 (1982).

EXAMPLE I16-32 ▶ Jack transfers assets with a $60,000 adjusted basis and a $100,000 FMV, along with $75,000 of liabilities assumed by the transferee corporation in a transaction otherwise qualifying under Sec. 351. Jack recognizes a $15,000 gain because the liabilities assumed by the corporation exceed the basis of the assets transferred ($75,000 − $60,000). If the gain were not recognized, Jack's basis for his stock would be a negative $15,000 ($60,000 − $75,000). Jack's net economic benefit from the exchange also is $15,000 ($75,000 liabilities assumed by the corporation − $60,000 adjusted basis of assets transferred). Jack's basis in the stock received is zero ($60,000 adjusted basis of assets + $15,000 gain recognized − $75,000 liabilities assumed). Because Jack's realized gain is $40,000 and because he recognizes $15,000 of the gain, only $25,000 of the gain is deferred ($25,000 FMV of stock − $-0- basis). The corporation's basis in the assets is increased from $60,000 to $75,000 because of the $15,000 gain recognized by Jack. ◄

Topic Review I16-3 summarizes the general requirements relating to the transfer of property to controlled corporations.

CAPITALIZATION OF THE CORPORATION

ADDITIONAL COMMENT
The thin capitalization issue is primarily a problem for closely held corporations where the shareholders also are the ones holding the debt, and is not normally a problem for large publicly-held corporations.

A corporation may be capitalized with both equity securities (generally common or preferred stock) and long-term debt issued to the shareholders. Issuance of debt in the capital structure has the following advantages:

▶ The interest payments on the debt are deductible by the corporation, whereas dividends are not deductible.

---

[38] Sec. 357(c). Accounts receivable and accounts payable with a zero basis for a cash basis transferor are disregarded for purposes of applying the Sec. 357(c) rules. See Sec. 357(c)(3).

Topic Review I16-3

Sec. 351 Requirements, Gain Recognition Rules, and Basis Rules

- Nonrecognition treatment under Sec. 351 requires an exchange of property solely for stock, and the transferor-shareholders must control (i.e., 80% stock ownership) the corporation immediately after the exchange.
- Nonqualifying property (e.g., cash, nonmoney property, or debt obligations of the transferee corporation) received by the transferors is treated as boot received.
- The transferors recognize gain equal to the lesser of the boot received or the realized gain.
- Generally, the transferors recognize no gain if liabilities are transferred to a controlled corporation. Exceptions to the nonrecognition of gain rule apply if the principal purpose of the liability transfer is tax avoidance, if no bona fide business purpose exists, or if the total liabilities assumed by the corporation exceed the transferor's adjusted basis for the transferred assets.
- Substituted basis rules referencing the basis of the asset(s) transferred apply to the stock received by the transferors. Carryover basis rules apply to contributed property in the transferee corporation's hands.

- Redemptions of stock may result in dividend income treatment to the shareholders unless certain requirements are met (see page I16-28), whereas a repayment of debt is a tax-free return of capital.

If the corporation is too thinly capitalized (e.g., excessive amounts of debt are issued relative to the amount of equity capital), the IRS may attempt to recharacterize the debt as equity and deny an interest deduction to the corporation. IRC Section 385 provides the following guidelines (or factors) for determining whether debt is recharacterized as equity:

ADDITIONAL COMMENT
A safe-harbor rule sets parameters that characterize a transaction one way if met and that characterize a transaction another way if not met.

- The legal form of the instrument and actual adherence to its terms: For example, if a reasonable interest rate is stated, the interest is currently being paid, a definite maturity date is stated, and the notes actually are repaid when due, then the evidence supports the taxpayer's contention that the instrument is debt.
- Excessive debt-equity ratio: The courts have not prescribed any exact mathematical formula although a debt-equity ratio that does not exceed 3 to 1 is likely to be acceptable to the IRS.[39]
- Proportionality of debt and the shareholder's equity interests: If the shareholders own the same percentage of the debt as their percentage of common stock, the debt stands a greater likelihood of being reclassified as equity than if the debt is held by the shareholders disproportionately to the stock ownership.
- Convertibility of the debt into stock of the corporation or contingent interest payments based on corporate earnings: These features are more likely to be found in an equity issue rather than in debt instruments.

Under Sec. 385, the issuing corporation must characterize the instrument as debt or stock. The shareholders or debtholders are prohibited from treating the instrument inconsistently with the issuer's characterization unless they disclose the inconsistent treatment on their tax returns. The issuer's characterization is not binding on the IRS.

EXAMPLE I16-33 ▶ Palm Corporation is formed with $90,000 of debt consisting of three-year shareholder notes and $10,000 of common stock. The corporation issues $30,000 of notes to each shareholder, Hank, Harold, and Antonio, who also own equal interests in the common stock. The interest payments are contingent on the earnings of the company, and the notes were not repaid at maturity. All of the factors mentioned above (i.e., high debt-equity ratio, proportionality of debt and equity interests, contingent interest payments, and the failure to observe the obligation's legal form) indicate that the debt will likely be reclassified by the IRS as equity. If the debt

---

[39] Boris I. Bittker and James S. Eustice, *Federal Income Taxation of Corporations and Shareholders* (Boston: Warren Gorham Lamont, 1998), p. 4-41.

EARNINGS AND PROFITS

CALCULATION OF EARNINGS AND PROFITS

OBJECTIVE 4

Understand the significance of earnings and profits

Earnings and profits (E&P) measure a corporation's economic ability to pay dividends from its current and accumulated earnings without impairment of capital. If the corporation has no E&P, a distribution represents a tax-free return of capital, and possibly a capital gain, rather than a taxable dividend.

Current E&P is calculated by making various adjustments to the corporation's taxable income.[40] This computation and the addition to accumulated E&P are illustrated in Table I16-2.

EXAMPLE I16-34

Park Corporation, an accrual method taxpayer, reported $100,000 of taxable income in the current year. Its tax accountant made the following adjustments to determine its current E&P and addition to accumulated E&P:

Taxable income	$100,000
Plus:	
Tax-exempt bond interest	2,000
Key officer life insurance proceeds (nontaxable)	10,000
Dividends-received deduction	20,000
MACRS depreciation exceeding ADS depreciation	18,000
Percentage depletion exceeding cost depletion	10,000
	$160,000
Minus:	
Federal income taxes accrued[a]	(22,250)
Net capital losses	(5,000)
Key officer life insurance premiums (not deductible because the corporation is the beneficiary)	(2,000)
Charitable contributions exceeding the 10% limitation	(3,000)
Fine for overweight trucks on city streets	(5,000)
Current E&P	$122,750
Minus: Money distribution	(5,000)
Addition to accumulated E&P	$117,750

[a] An accrual method of accounting corporation reduces its E&P by its accrued federal income taxes for the tax year. A cash method of accounting corporation reduces its E&P by its actual federal income tax payments made during the tax year.

BOOK-TAX ACCOUNTING COMPARISON

E&P is similar to retained earnings in financial accounting although numerous differences exist between the two accounts. For example, issuance of a stock dividend usually reduces retained earnings but does not affect E&P.

SELF-STUDY QUESTION

Should Sue, an individual, consider transferring her $100,000 in municipal bonds to her controlled corporation?

ANSWER

No; although the interest income on the municipal bond is excludable from the corporation's taxable income, the tax-exempt interest creates E&P, which causes the cash distribution to Sue to be taxable as a dividend.

To arrive at E&P, taxable income is increased for nontaxable income—the tax-exempt bond interest and the life insurance proceeds—received by the corporation. Taxable income is also increased for deductions claimed when determining taxable income but not allowed when determining E&P. Two of these increases do not represent economic outlays—the dividends-received deduction and percentage depletion deducted in excess of cost depletion. A third item represents a timing difference that will turn around in a later tax year—the MACRS depreciation deducted in excess of the alternative depreciation system depreciation. Taxable income is reduced by negative adjustments for economic outlays that reduce E&P under Sec. 312 but which are not deductible when determining taxable income. These E&P reductions include federal income taxes, capital losses in excess of capital gains, key officer life insurance premiums, excess charitable contributions, and fines.

---

[40] These adjustments are enumerated in Sec. 312 and related Treasury Regulations.

▼ **TABLE I16-2**

Calculation of Earnings and Profits

Taxable income
Plus: Income excluded from taxable income:
              Tax-exempt interest income
              Life insurance proceeds where the corporation is the beneficiary
              Recoveries of bad debts and other prior-year deductions for which the corporation received no tax benefit
              Federal income tax refunds from prior years
Plus: Income deferred to a later year when computing taxable income:
              Deferred gain on installment sales
             Deferred gain on like-kind exchanges
Plus or
minus: Adjustments for items that must be recomputed:
              Income on long-term contracts must be based on percentage of completion method rather than completed contract method
              Excess of pre-ACRS accelerated depreciation over straight-line depreciation
              Excess of ACRS depreciation deductions claimed over straight-line ACRS calculation using an extended recovery period
              Excess of regular MACRS depreciation over depreciation calculated using the alternative depreciation system (ADS).
              Excess of percentage depletion claimed over cost depletion
Plus: Deductions not allowed in computing E&P:
              Dividends-received deduction
              NOL carryovers, charitable contribution carryovers, and capital loss carryovers from prior years used in the current year
Minus: Expenses and losses not deductible in computing taxable income:
              Federal income taxes
              Life insurance premiums where the corporation is the beneficiary
              Excess capital losses not deductible in current year
              Excess charitable contributions not deductible in current year
              Expenses related to production of tax-exempt income
              Nondeductible losses on sales to related parties
              Nondeductible penalties and fines
              Nondeductible political contributions

Current E&P (or E&P deficit)
Minus: Distributions to shareholders (but not in excess of current E&P)
Addition to accumulated E&P (if any)

CURRENT VERSUS ACCUMULATED E&P

Current and accumulated E&P must be differentiated because Sec. 316 provides specific tracing rules to determine whether a distribution is taxable as a dividend. For example, a distribution to shareholders is deemed to be made first out of current E&P and therefore results in a taxable dividend even if accumulated E&P at the beginning of the year is negative. Accumulated E&P represents the total of all prior years' undistributed current E&P amounts as of the first day of the tax year. Distributions are deemed to be made out of accumulated E&P only after the current E&P (if any) is exhausted.

EXAMPLE I16-35 ▶ Pacific Corporation, a calendar-year taxpayer, has a $100,000 accumulated E&P deficit as of January 1. It reports $30,000 of current E&P. The corporation makes a $40,000 distribution to its shareholders. Of the $40,000 distribution, $30,000 is a taxable dividend to the extent of current E&P, and the remaining $10,000 is a tax-free return of capital (to the extent that Pacific's shareholders have basis in their stock) because of the accumulated E&P deficit. The E&P deficit is not increased by the tax-free distribution. ◀

If a shareholder's stock basis is reduced to zero because of a tax-free return of capital distribution, any additional amounts received are treated as a capital gain.

EXAMPLE I16-36 ▶ Peach Corporation, a calendar-year taxpayer, has one shareholder, Georgia, who has owned her stock for several years. The corporation has $30,000 of current E&P and $20,000 of accumulated E&P at the beginning of the current year. Georgia's stock basis is $10,000. At the end of the current year, Peach distributes $65,000 to Georgia. The $65,000 distribution is treated as follows:

Taxable dividend out of current E&P	$30,000
Taxable dividend out of accumulated E&P	20,000
Total dividend	$50,000
Tax-free return of capital	10,000
Long-term capital gain	5,000
Total distribution	$65,000

In addition, Georgia's stock basis is reduced to zero because of the $10,000 return of capital. ◀

If the distributing corporation has a current E&P deficit and a positive accumulated E&P balance, the current deficit and accumulated E&P are netted on the distribution date.[41] The current E&P deficit for the year is prorated on a daily basis unless a nonratable allocation can be shown to be more appropriate.

EXAMPLE I16-37 ▶ Prime Corporation, a calendar-year taxpayer, has a $100,000 positive accumulated E&P balance on January 1, 2001 and a $36,500 current E&P deficit. Prime makes a $30,000 distribution to its shareholders on July 1 (the 182nd day of 2001). E&P as of July 1 is $81,800 [$100,000 accumulated E&P − (182/365 × $36,500 current E&P deficit)] because the current deficit is allocated ratably during the year unless the corporation can show that a nonratable allocation is more appropriate. Therefore, the $30,000 distribution is fully taxable as a dividend. ◀

NONMONEY DISTRIBUTIONS

OBJECTIVE 5

Determine the consequences of nonmoney distributions and stock redemptions

TAX CONSEQUENCES TO THE SHAREHOLDERS

Occasionally, a corporation distributes nonmoney property (i.e., assets other than its stock or stock rights) instead of money to its shareholders. If nonmoney property is distributed to the shareholders, the following tax consequences generally occur:

▶ The amount distributed equals the FMV of the property (reduced by any associated liabilities).

▶ The amount distributed is treated as a taxable dividend if the corporation has sufficient E&P.

▶ The basis of the distributed property equals its FMV (without reduction for any associated liabilities).

EXAMPLE I16-38 ▶

REAL-WORLD EXAMPLE

A distribution of $20 Double Eagle gold coins was a property distribution rather than a distribution of money because the gold coins were withdrawn from circulation and had numismatic value. *Warren C. Cordner v. U.S.*, 49 AFTR 2d 82-1353, 82-1 USTC ¶9275 (9th Cir., 1982).

Red Corporation distributes land and a building having a $50,000 adjusted basis and a $100,000 FMV to its sole shareholder, Irene. Red has current and accumulated E&P exceeding $100,000. The property is subject to a $40,000 mortgage, which Irene assumes. The amount distributed to Irene is $60,000 ($100,000 FMV of the property − $40,000 liability). Irene has a $60,000 taxable dividend because the corporation has sufficient E&P. Irene's basis in the real estate is its $100,000 FMV. ◀

TAX CONSEQUENCES TO THE DISTRIBUTING CORPORATION

As a general rule, the corporation recognizes no gain or loss when making a nonmoney distribution to its shareholders.[42] However, if a corporation distributes appreciated property to its shareholders, the corporation is treated as if it sold the property to the shareholder for its FMV immediately before the distribution, and the corporation recognizes

---

[41] Reg. Sec. 1.316-2(b).   [42] Sec. 311(a).

any realized gain.[43] On the other hand, a corporation does not recognize any loss when it makes a nonliquidating distribution of property even if a sale of the property would otherwise yield a deductible tax loss.

EXAMPLE I16-39 ▶ Rocket Corporation distributes $75,000 in cash along with land having a $50,000 adjusted basis and a $60,000 FMV to its shareholder Peter. Rocket Corporation recognizes $10,000 ($60,000 − $50,000) of gain on the distribution of the land. Alternatively, if the land had a $60,000 adjusted basis and a $50,000 FMV, the corporation would not recognize the $10,000 ($50,000 − $60,000) realized loss. ◀

If the property distributed is subject to a liability that exceeds its basis, the FMV of such property, for purposes of determining gain on the distribution, is the greater of the actual FMV or the amount of the liability.[44]

EXAMPLE I16-40 ▶ Assume the same facts as in Example I16-38 except that Rocket Corporation also transfers a $70,000 mortgage attaching to the land to its shareholder. Rocket recognizes a $20,000 ($70,000 − $50,000) gain on the distribution of the land because the liability exceeds the property's FMV. ◀

STOP & THINK

Question: So far we have been describing money and nonmoney distributions. What are the tax consequences if a corporation instead makes a pro rata stock dividend, that is, if it issues additional shares of its own single class of stock to existing shareholders?

Solution: The economic situation for the shareholders does not change as a result of the stock dividend. The shareholders still own the same proportion of the corporation, but they have additional shares of stock. Consequently, the shareholders recognize no income on receiving the stock dividend. Instead, they spread the basis of their old stock over the combined old and new stock, thereby causing the per share basis to decrease while the total basis remains unchanged. In addition, the corporation recognizes no gain or loss and does not reduce its E&P. Some stock dividends, such as when a shareholder owning common stock has the opportunity to elect to receive either additional common stock or cash, are taxable.[45] These distributions are beyond the scope of this text (see Chapter 4 of *Prentice Hall's Corporations, Partnerships, Estates and Trusts* text).

STOCK REDEMPTIONS

Two possible tax consequences can result when a corporation repurchases (redeems) some of its outstanding stock from a shareholder:

▶ The redemption is treated as a taxable dividend (to the extent of E&P)
▶ The redemption is treated as an exchange of the stock, generally resulting in capital gain or loss treatment by the shareholder.

The first consequence, taxable dividend treatment, prevents corporations from paying disguised dividends in the form of a stock redemption taxable as a capital gain. For example, the corporation might redeem 10% of its sole shareholder's stock rather than pay a cash dividend to the shareholder. After the redemption, the shareholder continues to own all of the outstanding stock, retains the same amount of control over the corporation, and has received a substantial distribution of money or other property. Taxing the redemption as an exchange would permit a reduced tax burden for the shareholder without requiring a reduction in his/her ownership interest.

The second consequence, exchange treatment, is significant because individual shareholders are generally subject to a 20% maximum tax rate on their net capital gain. In

---

[43] Sec. 311(b).
[44] Secs. 311(b)(2) and 336(b).
[45] Sec. 305(b).

addition, the exchange treatment is preferable if the shareholders have unused capital losses or capital loss carryovers that otherwise would be of limited tax benefit. Moreover, exchange treatment permits shareholders a tax-free recovery of their investment in the stock. A tax-free recovery of the shareholder's stock basis is not permitted if the distribution is a dividend.

EXAMPLE I16-41 ▶ Ajax Corporation has two equal shareholders, Rita and Harry. Each shareholder owns 10 shares of Ajax stock and has owned the stock for several years. Each share has a $100 basis and a $150 FMV. Ajax, which has sufficient E&P, redeems 5 shares from each shareholder at the $150 FMV. This redemption causes Rita and Harry each to recognize $750 ($150 FMV × 5 shares) of dividend income. Rita and Harry have dividend income because they each still own 50% of Ajax's stock after the redemption. Rita's $1,000 total basis for her stock is not reduced by receiving dividend treatment for the redemption. Her per share basis increases from $100 ($1,000 ÷ 10 shares) to $200 ($1,000 ÷ 5) per share with the redemption.

If instead, Ajax redeems 5 shares from Rita but none from Harry, Rita obtains exchange treatment and recognizes a $250 capital gain calculated as follows:

Proceeds of redemption ($150 × 5)	$750
Minus: Basis of stock redeemed ($100 × 5)	(500)
Capital gain	$250

The capital gain is generally taxed at the maximum 20% tax rate for long-term capital gains. Moreover, only $250 is taxed as contrasted with $750 under dividend treatment. Rita's $1,000 total basis for her stock is reduced to $500 by receiving capital gain treatment for the redemption and offsetting the $500 proceeds against the basis of the shares redeemed. Her per share basis remains at $100 ($500 ÷ 5 shares) after the redemption. Example I16-42 on page I16-30 explains why the first redemption causes dividend treatment while the second redemption provides exchange treatment. ◀

DETERMINING WHETHER A REDEMPTION IS A DIVIDEND OR CAPITAL GAIN

SELF-STUDY QUESTION

Why might a corporate shareholder prefer to have the redemption treated as a dividend rather than as an exchange?

ANSWER

The corporate shareholder would be eligible for the 70%, 80%, or 100% dividends-received deduction on the proceeds of the redemption that are taxed as a dividend.

A redemption is treated as an exchange subject to capital gain or loss treatment if any of the following conditions or tests are met:[46]

▶ The redemption is substantially disproportionate with respect to the shareholder's interest [Sec. 302(b)(2)].

▶ The redemption is not essentially equivalent to a dividend [Sec. 302(b)(1)].[47]

▶ The redemption results in a complete termination of the shareholder's interest [Sec. 302(b)(3)].

SUBSTANTIALLY DISPROPORTIONATE RULE. If a redemption is substantially disproportionate, capital gain or loss (rather than dividend income) treatment results. Constructive stock ownership rules apply to determine whether a redemption is disproportionate.[48] **Constructive stock ownership** means that the redeemed shareholder is considered to own the stock of certain related parties. These related parties include family members, partnerships and corporations in which an ownership interest is held, and trusts and estates in which a beneficial interest is held.

For a redemption to qualify as substantially disproportionate, Sec. 302(b)(2) provides that the following tests must be met immediately after the redemption:

▶ The shareholder must own less than 80% of his or her former percentage interest in the voting stock (including stock held by related parties).

▶ The shareholder also must own less than 80% of his or her former percentage interest in the common (voting and nonvoting) stock (including stock held by related parties).

---

[46] Sec. 302.
[47] For example, exchange treatment has been allowed where the redeemed shareholder's voting control, right to share in current earnings, and right to receive corporate assets upon liquidation have been significantly reduced. Ordinarily, this occurs when a shareholder's majority interest is converted to a 50% interest, a majority interest is converted to a minority (less than 50%) interest, or a minority interest is reduced. See, for example, Rev. Ruls. 75-502 and 76-364 cited in footnotes 50 and 51.
[48] Sec. 318.

▶ The shareholder must own less than 50% of the voting stock (including stock held by related parties).

A redemption of solely nonvoting stock will not qualify for capital gain treatment under Sec. 302(b)(2).

NOT ESSENTIALLY EQUIVALENT TO A DIVIDEND. This condition requires a subjective judgment as to whether a stock redemption causes a meaningful reduction in the shareholder interest in the corporation.[49] In deciding whether a meaningful reduction has occurred, the IRS looks at the shareholder's interest in the following rights: (1) voting power, (2) participation in earning and profits and (3) share of net assets upon liquidation.[50] This approach usually is applied if the redemption fails the objective tests for a substantially disproportionate redemption discussed above. Specifically, if a shareholder's interest falls below 50% after the redemption, but the redemption does not meet the 80% test, the shareholder may want to argue that the redemption is not essentially equivalent to a dividend. For example, reduction in ownership from 27 percent to 22 percent fails the 80% test under the substantially disproportionate rule (80% × 27% = 21.6%) but would be considered a meaningful reduction that is not essentially equivalent to a dividend.[51]

EXAMPLE I16-42 ▶ In Example I16-41, the redemption of both Rita and Harry's stock failed the substantially disproportionate test. For Rita and Harry to qualify their ownership must be less than 80% of their prior ownership percentage, or 40% (80% × 50% prior ownership) and be less than 50%. However, after the redemption, Rita and Harry each still own exactly 50% of the single class of stock, thereby failing both the 80% and 50% tests.

On the other hand, the redemption of only Rita's 5 shares qualifies for exchange treatment because, after the redemption, Rita owns 33⅓% (5 shares Rita still owns ÷ 15 total shares outstanding) of Ajax's single class of stock. Thus, Rita's post-redemption ownership is less than the 40% and 50% thresholds, thereby making the redemption substantially disproportionate. ◀

EXAMPLE I16-43 ▶ Jane owns 60 shares of Fast Corporation's single class of stock, and her mother owns 20 additional shares of Fast stock. The remaining 20 Fast shares are owned by Peter, who is unrelated to Jane or her mother. Fast Corporation redeems 30 shares of Jane's stock for $100,000. Jane's percentage interest before the redemption is 80% [(60 + 20 shares) ÷ 100 shares]. Immediately after the redemption, Jane's percentage interest is 71.4% [(30 + 20 shares) ÷ 70 shares]. To meet the 80% test, Jane's interest must be less than 64% (80% × 80%). Therefore, Jane does not meet the 80% test. Also, Jane does not meet the 50% test because she does not own less than 50% of the Fast stock after the redemption. Both tests must be met for the redemption to qualify as a substantially disproportionate redemption. Jane does not qualify for the Sec. 302(b)(1) "not essentially equivalent to a dividend" treatment since she has not reduced her stock interest to 50% or below. Therefore, the $100,000 received is treated as a dividend and is taxable to Jane to the extent Fast has sufficient E&P. ◀

COMPLETE TERMINATION. Under Sec. 302(b)(3), a complete termination of a shareholder's stock interest also qualifies for capital gain or loss treatment. At first glance, this rule appears to be redundant because the substantially disproportionate redemption rule also should apply to a redemption that results in a complete termination of a shareholder's interest. However, the complete termination provision is important because a special rule permits a waiver of the constructive ownership rules for family members. The constructive ownership rules are waived in a complete termination if the former shareholder files an agreement with the IRS that he or she will have no interest other than a creditor interest in the corporation for 10 years.[52]

---

[49] U.S. v. *Maclin P. Davis,* 25 AFTR 2d 70-827, 70-1 USTC ¶9289 (USSC, 1970).
[50] Rev. Rul. 75-502, 1975-2 C.B. 111.
[51] Rev. Rul. 76-364, 1976-2 C.B. 91.

[52] Sec. 302(c)(2). The former shareholder cannot serve as an officer, director, or employee for at least 10 years and must notify the IRS if additional stock is acquired (other than by bequest or inheritance). If such stock is subsequently acquired, it usually causes the redemption to be recharacterized as a dividend.

EXAMPLE I16-44 ▶

Assume the same facts as in Example I16-43 except that Fast Corporation redeems all 60 shares held by Jane for $200,000, and Jane's basis for her shares is $90,000. The constructive stock ownership rules are waived if Jane agrees not to acquire any interest in Fast Corporation for 10 years. Therefore, Jane's interest is deemed to be completely terminated, and the redemption is treated as a sale of stock qualifying for capital gain treatment. Jane has a capital gain of $110,000 ($200,000 − $90,000). If the waiver is not obtained because she remains as an employee of Fast, the substantially disproportionate tests are applied to determine whether the redemption qualifies as an exchange. Jane would be considered to own 50% of the stock (20 shares owned ÷ 40 outstanding shares) immediately after the redemption, and therefore the substantially disproportionate redemption test would not be met. The redemption does not qualify as a complete termination because Jane is deemed to own her mother's stock unless Jane obtains a waiver of the constructive ownership rules. Thus, without the waiver, the redemption would be treated as a dividend to Jane unless it could qualify under the Sec. 302(b)(1) not essentially equivalent to a dividend exception. ◀

REAL-WORLD EXAMPLE

All of a father's stock in a corporation was redeemed, and his children were the remaining shareholders. Then the father entered into a long-term contract with the corporation to perform consulting and advisory services. The contract represented an interest in the corporation and the family attribution rules were not waived. Rev. Rul. 70-104, 1970-1 C.B. 66.

REDEMPTION PROVISIONS FOR SPECIAL SITUATIONS

Two additional redemption rules cover special situations:

▶ Section 302(b)(4) provides exchange (rather than dividend) treatment for noncorporate shareholder redemptions in a partial liquidation of the distributing corporation. To qualify, the distribution must be made pursuant to the termination of an active trade or business of the distributing corporation[53] or be considered not essentially equivalent to a dividend at the corporate level.[54]

▶ Section 303 permits the executor of an estate or a beneficiary to have stock in a closely held corporation redeemed, whereby the redemption is treated as an exchange (rather than as a dividend) provided certain conditions are met.[55] The redemption amount is limited to the death taxes imposed and the amount of deductible funeral and administration expenses incurred.

CORPORATE DISTRIBUTIONS IN COMPLETE LIQUIDATION

OBJECTIVE 6

Understand the consequences of a corporate liquidation to the shareholders and the liquidating corporation

Sometimes shareholders may wish to terminate a corporation's existence. A complete liquidation is similar to a stock redemption except that all (rather than a portion) of the stock is redeemed. In a complete liquidation, the assets are either distributed in kind to the shareholders in exchange for their stock or sold and converted to cash, which is then distributed to the shareholders in exchange for their stock. The liquidated corporation usually is dissolved under state law.

Surprisingly, the reasons for a complete termination are not always associated with unprofitable operations. For example, a highly-successful closely held company may have management continuity problems because the key officer-shareholder group is approaching retirement age. Also, a parent corporation, as a matter of organizational management policy, may wish to liquidate a subsidiary and continue its operations as a separate division.

TYPICAL MISCONCEPTION

It is sometimes assumed that the liquidation of a corporation always is associated with the discontinuance of business activities. Sometimes, however, the business is operated as a limited liability company, partnership or sole proprietorship after the liquidation.

TAX CONSEQUENCES TO THE LIQUIDATING CORPORATION

DISTRIBUTION OF ASSETS. The liquidating corporation recognizes gains and losses on distributions of property.[56] A corporation that makes the liquidating distribution is treated as if it had sold the assets for their FMV to the shareholders. If the distributed

---

[53] Secs. 302(b)(4) and 302(e). The distributions must be made pursuant to a plan and must occur within the same tax year in which the plan is adopted or within the next succeeding tax year. Immediately after the distribution, the distributing corporation must be actively engaged in the conduct of at least one qualified trade or business.

[54] Reg. Sec. 1.346-1(a) provides examples of situations that are not essentially equivalent to a dividend at the corporate level and can qualify as a partial liquidation. Generally such a transaction results in a contraction of the corporation's assets, revenues and number of employees.

[55] Sec. 303.

[56] Sec. 336.

property is subject to a liability, the FMV of the property is treated as being the greater of the property's actual FMV or the amount of the liability.

EXAMPLE I16-45 ▶ Pursuant to a complete liquidation, Southern Corporation distributes the following assets to its shareholders:

- Inventory: $10,000 basis, $20,000 FMV
- Land held as an investment: $5,000 basis, $40,000 FMV, subject to a $30,000 liability
- Marketable securities: $20,000 basis, $15,000 FMV

Southern Corporation recognizes $10,000 ($20,000 − $10,000) of ordinary income on the distribution of the inventory, $35,000 ($40,000 − $5,000) of capital gain on the distribution of the land, and $5,000 ($15,000 − $20,000) of capital loss on the distribution of the marketable securities. ◀

SALE OF ASSETS. The tax consequences for an asset sale closely parallel a liquidating distribution. For example, if a corporation sells its assets pursuant to a complete liquidation and then distributes the money received from the sale to its shareholders, all gain or loss realized on the sale of the assets is recognized by the corporation.

LIMITATION ON LOSS RECOGNITION. Under the general rule, the corporation recognizes both gains and losses on liquidations. However, to prevent abuses, three special rules limit the recognition of losses in certain situations. First, a liquidating subsidiary corporation recognizes neither gain or loss when it distributes property to its parent corporation. In addition, a liquidating subsidiary corporation recognizes gain (but not loss) when it distributes property to minority shareholders. (The special rules applying to the liquidation of a subsidiary corporation can be found on the next page.) Second, a liquidating corporation recognizes no loss when it distributes property to a related person, unless the property is distributed ratably to all shareholders and the property was not acquired as a capital contribution or in a Sec. 351 transaction within the preceding five years. Finally, losses are not recognized when a sale, exchange, or distribution of property occurs, and the property in question was acquired as a capital contribution or in a Sec. 351 transaction where the principal purpose of the transfer was the recognition of loss. These special loss limitations are explained in greater detail Chapter C6 of *Prentice Hall's Federal Taxation: Corporations, Partnerships, Estates, and Trusts*.

TAX ATTRIBUTES. Tax attributes, such as NOL carryovers, earnings and profits, capital loss carryovers, and tax credits, disappear upon liquidation of the corporation.

TAX CONSEQUENCES TO THE SHAREHOLDERS

KEY POINT
An appraisal may be necessary to determine the FMV of the distributed assets.

Under the general rule for complete liquidations, shareholders are deemed to have sold their stock to the corporation in exchange for money or other property.[57] If the stock is a capital asset, the shareholder recognizes capital gain or loss equal to the difference between (1) the money plus the FMV of other property distributed to the shareholder and (2) the adjusted basis of the shareholder's stock.[58] The basis of property distributed to a shareholder is its FMV on the distribution date.[59]

EXAMPLE I16-46 ▶ Sun Corporation makes a liquidating distribution of land with a $70,000 adjusted basis and a $100,000 FMV to shareholder John, who surrenders his Sun stock to the corporation. Joan, another shareholder, receives $100,000 cash for her shares. John's adjusted basis in the Sun stock is $40,000. Joan's adjusted basis in her stock is $120,000. John recognizes a $60,000 ($100,000 − $40,000) capital gain. Joan recognizes a $20,000 ($120,000 − $100,000) capital loss. The tax basis of the land received by John is $100,000 (the land's FMV on the distribution date). ◀

---

[57] Sec. 331(a)(1).
[58] Certain losses on small business stock receive ordinary loss treatment if the requirements of Sec. 1244 are met (see Chapter I8).
[59] Sec. 334(a).

SECTION 332: LIQUIDATION OF A SUBSIDIARY CORPORATION

KEY POINT

Section 351 permits a parent corporation to incorporate a subsidiary corporation tax-free. Section 332 permits a parent corporation to liquidate a controlled subsidiary corporation without incurring adverse tax results where the subsidiary's property has significantly appreciated in value.

GAIN AND LOSS CONSIDERATIONS. Section 332 provides an exception to the general rule that gain or loss is recognized in a liquidating distribution. Under this exception (along with Sec. 337) neither the parent nor the subsidiary recognize gain or loss if a parent corporation liquidates an 80%-owned subsidiary corporation.[60] In a Sec. 332 liquidation, the subsidiary corporation usually is dissolved, and the assets and liabilities transfer to the parent corporation. Section 332's nonrecognition rules are mandatory (rather than elective) if their requirements are satisfied.

The subsidiary corporation must do either of the following:

▶ Distribute all its property to the parent corporation in complete liquidation of its stock within a single tax year.

▶ Make a series of liquidating distributions resulting in a complete liquidation over a 3-year period that commences with the close of the tax year in which the first liquidating distribution is made.

If a minority interest also is being liquidated, the general liquidation rules described above apply, and the subsidiary corporation recognizes gain (but not loss) on property distributed to a minority shareholder. In addition, the liquidation is taxable to the minority shareholder(s) with gain or loss being recognized under the general liquidation rules outlined above.

KEY POINT

A parent corporation whose basis for its subsidiary's stock exceeds the tax basis of its share of the subsidiary's net assets loses the tax benefit of the economic loss if the subsidiary is liquidated under the Sec. 332 rules.

BASIS CONSIDERATIONS. The basis of the subsidiary's assets carry over to the parent corporation, and the adjusted basis of the parent corporation's interest in the subsidiary stock disappears.[61] This carryover basis rule may create certain inequities because the parent corporation may have paid an amount for the subsidiary stock that is greater (or less) than the tax basis of the parent corporation's share of the subsidiary's net assets.

EXAMPLE I16-47 ▶

Tampa Corporation acquired 100% of Top Corporation's stock several years ago for $100,000. In the current year, Top is liquidated, and assets having a $50,000 tax basis are transferred to Tampa Corporation. No gain or loss is recognized by Tampa Corporation when receiving the liquidating distribution. Tampa's $100,000 basis for the Top stock disappears, and Tampa takes only a $50,000 basis in Top's assets. ◀

If these carryover basis rules apply, the parent corporation also inherits the tax attributes of the subsidiary.[62] For example, NOL and capital loss carryovers and the E&P balance of the liquidated subsidiary carry over to the parent corporation. In addition, the subsidiary does not recognize any gain under the depreciation recapture rules. Instead, this recapture potential carries over to the parent corporation.

Topic Review I16-4 summarizes the complete liquidation rules.

TAX PLANNING CONSIDERATIONS

CAPITAL STRUCTURE AND SECTION 1244

As mentioned earlier in the chapter, the use of long-term debt to capitalize a closely held C corporation is an excellent choice assuming the corporation is profitable. However, if the corporation is not successful and goes bankrupt, the corporate debt owed to the shareholders becomes worthless and is treated by any noncorporate shareholders as a nonbusiness bad debt. As is discussed in Chapter I8, nonbusiness bad debts are deductible as a short-term capital loss subject to the $3,000 per year limitation.

---

[60] Pursuant to Sec. 1504(a)(2), 80% ownership means the parent corporation must own at least 80% of the total combined voting power of all classes of stock entitled to vote and at least 80% of the total value of all classes of stock.

[61] Sec. 334(b)(1).
[62] Sec. 381.

Topic Review I16-4

Distributions in Complete Liquidation

SEC. 331 GENERAL LIQUIDATION RULES	LIQUIDATING CORPORATION	SHAREHOLDERS
Recognition of gain or loss	Gain or loss generally is recognized equal to the difference between the FMV of the property distributed and the property's adjusted basis.	Gain or loss is recognized equal to the difference between the amount of money plus the FMV of other property received and the basis of the shareholder's stock in the liquidating corporation.
Exception to the gain or loss rule	Losses are not recognized on certain distributions of property to related parties, or property acquired in a carryover basis transaction where the principal purpose for the transaction was tax avoidance.	Not applicable.
Basis considerations	Not applicable.	The basis of nonmoney property received is its FMV.
Tax attributes	Tax attributes (e.g., NOL carryovers and E&P) disappear when the liquidation is completed.	Not applicable.

SEC. 332 SUBSIDIARY CORPORATION LIQUIDATION RULES	SUBSIDIARY CORPORATION	PARENT CORPORATION
General requirements	The subsidiary corporation is dissolved, and its assets and liabilities are transferred to the parent corporation and minority shareholders.	Sec. 332 is mandatory. The parent corporation must own at least 80% of the subsidiary corporation's stock.
Recognition of gain or loss	No gain or loss is recognized on the transfer of assets to the parent. Gain but not loss is recognized on distributions to minority shareholders.	The parent corporation recognizes no gain or loss. Minority shareholders will recognize gain and loss.
Basis considerations	None.	The basis of the subsidiary's assets carry over to the parent corporation. Minority shareholders take a FMV basis in the assets they receive.
Tax attributes	No tax attributes remain after the liquidation.	Tax attributes (e.g., NOL carryovers and E&P) carry over to the parent corporation.

As an alternative to using debt, the shareholders could capitalize the corporation using stock (equity). Assuming the requirements are met, the corporation's stock would be considered Sec. 1244 stock (small business corporation stock, see Chapter I8 for details). Upon the worthlessness of the Sec. 1244 stock, each shareholder may deduct up to $50,000 ($100,000 on a joint return) as an ordinary loss. The ability to deduct up to $100,000 against ordinary income is superior to the capital loss treatment that applies to nonbusiness bad debts.

The two alternative capitalization methods clearly yield different results depending on whether the corporation is ultimately successful or unsuccessful. Thus, the decision as to the method of capitalization of a closely held corporation involves an evaluation of the potential profitability of the corporation at the beginning of the business. For example, if the owners of a new corporation believe the venture is going to be very profitable, debt may be the preferred method of capitalization because of the deductibility of the interest payments. Because no one would go into a business believing that the business is going to be unsuccessful, it may be difficult to advise a taxpayer to capitalize a corporation using substantially more equity than debt.

One major alternative to avoid some of the problems discussed above is to organize the corporation as either a partnership, an S corporation or a limited liability company rather than as a C corporation. These types of flow-through entities are discussed in Chapter I17.

DIVIDEND POLICY

Dividends paid from E&P are fully taxable to shareholders and are not deductible by the corporation. Thus, in a closely held corporation where ownership and management are not separated, the parties may wish to increase salary payments to shareholder-employees rather than increase dividends. A similar type of incentive may be present for a shareholder to lease property to a corporation instead of transferring it to the corporation as a capital contribution. Even though the increased salary or rental payments are taxable to the shareholders (as are dividends), these payments are deductible as business expenses by the entity as long as the amounts paid are reasonable.

> **ADDITIONAL COMMENT**
> Reasonableness of a salary payment is a question of fact to be determined for each case. No formula can be used to determine a reasonable amount of compensation.

EXAMPLE I16-48 ▶ Mario and Nancy are equal owners of Texas Corporation, which is highly profitable and has substantial E&P. Mario and Nancy are the key officers and each are paid a $100,000 salary. A reasonable salary for each would be $150,000. To increase cash distributions to the owners, additional salary payments of $50,000 should be made to both Mario and Nancy (rather than increasing the dividend payments by the same amount) because the corporation can deduct salary payments, whereas the dividend payments are not deductible. The salary payments result in only a single level of taxation, while the dividend payments result in double taxation. Consideration also should be given to payroll taxes because the additional $50,000 compensation may subject the employer and the two shareholders to additional payroll taxes (e.g., the 1.45% Medicare portion of the FICA tax). ◀

USE OF LOSSES

A corporation should plan to use its net operating loss and capital loss carryovers. For example, the sale of appreciated business assets may result in recognition of Sec. 1231 gain that can offset capital loss carryovers because net Sec. 1231 gains receive capital gain treatment. Alternatively, the sale or disposition of assets may result in the recognition of ordinary income because of the depreciation recapture rules. This ordinary income can offset expiring NOLs.

If a business anticipates net operating losses or capital losses during its start-up phase, an S election may be desirable because the losses can be used immediately by the shareholders. The S election may be terminated when the corporation becomes profitable and C corporation treatment is preferred. (See Chapter I17 for a discussion of S corporations.)

> **REAL-WORLD EXAMPLE**
> An accrual basis corporation that attempted to treat a contribution paid within 2½ months following year-end as a contribution in the earlier year had its contribution deduction denied because no written declaration of the resolution of the board of directors authorizing the contribution was attached to the return. *Donald G. Griswold*, 39 T.C. 620 (1962).

CHARITABLE CONTRIBUTIONS

Many owners of closely held corporations prefer to make charitable donations through their controlled corporation rather than as individuals because the corporation can deduct the contributions. Otherwise, to fund the contributed amounts, the controlled corporation may have to make nondeductible dividend payments to the shareholders. Also, an accrual basis corporation may accelerate a charitable contribution deduction if the board of directors approves the contribution before year-end, and the corporation pays the pledge within 2 1/2 months of the corporation's tax year-end.

DIVIDENDS-RECEIVED DEDUCTION

Corporate shareholders may deduct 80% (or 70%) of dividends received. However, this deduction is limited to 80% (or 70%) of taxable income unless the deduction creates or increases an NOL. Thus, a substantial scale-down of the dividends-received deduction may result if taxable income (other than the dividend income) is negative and if the final result is a small amount of taxable income being reported instead of an NOL. Therefore, if the limitation is expected to apply, the corporation should either accelerate deductions into the current year or postpone the recognition of income to a later year. Either action can result in the creation of an NOL that prevents the limitation on the dividends-received deduction from applying. (See Examples I16-7 and I16-8.)

16-36 Individuals ▼ Chapter 16

COMPLIANCE AND PROCEDURAL CONSIDERATIONS

FILING REQUIREMENTS

KEY POINT
All corporations must file an income tax return. The filing requirements are not based on certain minimum amounts of gross income, as in the case of individuals.

A corporation must file Form 1120 (U.S. Corporation Income Tax Return) even if the corporation exists for only part of the year. The basic return is supplemented with a separate Schedule D to report capital gains and losses. In addition, Form 4626 (Alternative Minimum Tax—Corporations) must be filed even if no alternative minimum tax is due. Certain small corporations are eligible to file a simplified Form 1120-A (U.S. Corporation Short-Form Income Tax Return) if their gross receipts, total income, and total assets are all less than $500,000. The Form 1120-A may not be filed in certain instances (e.g., the corporation is in the process of being liquidated or is a member of a controlled group).

The regular filing due date for the corporate return is the fifteenth day of the third month following the end of the tax year (e.g., March 15 for calendar-year corporations). The corporation can obtain an automatic 6-month extension by filing Form 7004 (Application for Automatic Extension of Time to File Corporation Income Tax Return). If an extension is obtained, the full amount of the estimated tax due must be paid on or before the due date of the return (e.g., March 15 for calendar-year corporations).

Quarterly estimated tax payments must be made on the fifteenth day of the fourth, sixth, ninth, and twelfth months of the tax year. In general, the total required estimated tax payments are the lesser of 100% of the corporation's tax liability for the current year or 100% of the tax shown on the preceding year's return.[63] However, a corporation may not base the quarterly payments of estimated tax on the preceding year's tax liability if that liability was zero.[64] The corporation is subject to a nondeductible underpayment penalty on the underpayment to the extent the quarterly payments are less than the required payments.

BOOK-TAX ACCOUNTING COMPARISON
The Schedule M-1 adjustments highlight the fact that financial accounting and tax accounting differ in many ways.

SCHEDULE M-1 AND M-2 RECONCILIATIONS

Schedule M-1 is used to reconcile financial accounting net income with taxable income before special deductions (the NOL and dividends-received deductions). Figure I16-1 shows a completed Schedule M-1 based on the following adjustments:

Net income per books	$100,000
Plus:	
Federal income tax liability	3,000
Net capital losses	2,000
Nondeductible premiums on key officers' life insurance	4,000
Minus:	
Tax-exempt interest income	(9,000)
Excess of tax depreciation over financial accounting depreciation	(75,000)
Taxable income (before special deductions)	$ 25,000

Schedule M-2 reconciles the beginning of the year balance in retained earnings (for financial accounting purposes) with the balance in the account at year-end. This reconciliation explains changes in the balance sheet reported on Schedule L or accounts for items

---

[63] Exceptions are provided for large corporations and corporations that earn their income unevenly during the tax year. Large corporations—those with taxable income exceeding $1 million in any of the three preceding tax years—must make quarterly estimated tax payments based on 100% of the tax shown on their current year return, although they are permitted to make their first-quarter payment based on 100% of the preceding year's tax liability [Sec. 6655(d)]. Section 6655(e) permits corporations to use an annualized income installment or seasonally-adjusted installment if it is less than the normally-required installment [Sec. 6655(e)].

[64] Rev. Rul. 92-54 1992-2 C.B. 320.

FIGURE I16-1 ▶ FORM 1120, SCHEDULE M-1

Schedule M-1	Reconciliation of Income (Loss) per Books With Income per Return (See page 18 of instructions.)			
1	Net income (loss) per books	100,000	7	Income recorded on books this year not included on this return (itemize): Tax-exempt interest $ 9,000
2	Federal income tax	3,000		
3	Excess of capital losses over capital gains	2,000		
4	Income subject to tax not recorded on books this year (itemize):			9,000
5	Expenses recorded on books this year not deducted on this return (itemize):		8	Deductions on this return not charged against book income this year (itemize):
a	Depreciation $		a	Depreciation $ 75,000
b	Contributions carryover $		b	Contributions carryover $
c	Travel and entertainment $ Premiums on Life Insurance 4,000	4,000	9	Add lines 7 and 8	84,000
6	Add lines 1 through 5	109,000	10	Income (line 28, page 1)—line 6 less line 9	25,000

of income, gain, or loss taken directly to retained earnings without being reported as part of net income. Figure I16-2 shows a completed Schedule M-2 based on the above facts and assuming a $140,000 balance for retained earnings on January 1, $100,000 of net income for financial accounting purposes, and the payment of a $40,000 cash dividend.

MAINTENANCE OF RECORDS FOR E&P

Companies are not required to compute E&P on the tax return. Therefore, many companies do not maintain adequate records for this account. Detailed records of items that make up current and accumulated E&P, however, should be maintained because the statute of limitations remains open indefinitely on this determination, and the taxpayer has the burden of proof. Thus, if the IRS determines that a company has current or accumulated E&P and treats a distribution as a taxable dividend rather than a tax-free return of capital, the taxpayer must show that the IRS determination is erroneous.

Form 5452 (Corporate Report of Nondividend Distributions) must be filed by any corporation that makes a return-of-capital distribution. This form requires a computation of E&P for the tax year and a schedule of differences between taxable income and E&P. This form also requires a year-by-year computation of accumulated E&P.

FIGURE I16-2 ▶ FORM 1120, SCHEDULE M-2

Schedule M-2	Analysis of Unappropriated Retained Earnings per Books (Line 25, Schedule L)			
1	Balance at beginning of year	140,000	5 Distributions: a Cash	40,000
2	Net income (loss) per books	100,000	b Stock	
3	Other increases (itemize):		c Property	
			6 Other decreases (itemize):	
			7 Add lines 5 and 6	40,000
4	Add lines 1, 2, and 3	240,000	8 Balance at end of year (line 4 less line 7)	200,000

PROBLEM MATERIALS

DISCUSSION QUESTIONS

I16-1 Under the present tax system, C corporation income is taxed twice, once when earned and again when the shareholders receive dividends or sell their stock. Nevertheless, the C corporation form is widely used in the United States, especially for large corporations. Why would an entity choose C corporation status instead of a flow-through organizational form?

I16-2 Anya is considering whether to become a limited partner in a real estate limited partnership by making an investment of $10,000. The limited partnership will generate substantial operating losses for the first five years. What are the tax consequences to Anya if the partnership elects to be taxed as a corporation? Is this election a good idea?

I16-3 Does a corporation really pay taxes? Who actually bears the corporate tax burden?

I16-4 If a corporation has a net Sec. 1231 loss and a net long-term capital gain are the gain and loss netted against each other? What difference does it make whether the items are netted or treated separately?

I16-5 Acorn Corporation has a $5,000 NSTCG and a $9,000 NLTCL in the current year. Last year, Acorn Corporation had a $3,000 NLTCG. No other capital gains or losses were reported in prior tax years.
a. Do the NSTCG and NLTCL have to be offset in the current year?
b. Is any portion of the NLTCL deductible in the current year?
c. What loss carryback or carryover rules should be applied to any unused capital losses incurred in the current year?

I16-6 C corporations are allowed a dividends-received deduction (DRD) for dividends received from domestic corporations.
a. What is the purpose of the DRD?
b. Does the taxable income limitation on the DRD serve any useful function?

I16-7 Under what circumstances might a corporation elect not to carry back an NOL to its prior tax years?

I16-8 What requirements must be met for an accrual-basis corporation to deduct a charitable contribution in a year before its payment?

I16-9 Acorn Corporation is publicly traded on the American Stock Exchange. Its chief executive officer, Carl, currently receives an annual salary of $1 million. The Board of Directors is considering increasing his compensation level by $200,000.
a. What are the income tax consequences to Acorn if Carl's salary is increased to $1,200,000?
b. What alternatives might be considered to increase Carl's annual compensation that would produce more favorable tax consequences for Acorn Corporation?

I16-10 Current tax law imposes a $1 million limitation on the deductibility of executive compensation. Should such a limitation be retained or repealed? Give reasons for your opinion.

I16-11 The current corporate tax structure contains phaseouts (via surtaxes) at various levels of taxable income that eliminate the benefits of lower tax brackets. Identify the two phaseouts contained in the corporate tax rate structure. How do these phaseouts affect a corporation's marginal and average tax rates? In your opinion, should phaseouts be retained in the tax law or repealed?

I16-12 Describe the basic structure of the alternative minimum tax (AMT), including a discussion of the differences between tax preference items and AMT adjustments.

I16-13 Current tax law contains a dual tax system, the regular tax and alternative minimum tax. In effect, a corporation pays the greater of the regular tax or the tentative minimum tax. Why did Congress enact such a dual system of taxation? How could Congress replace the dual system with a single tax system?

I16-14 How has Congress reduced the burden of the AMT for small corporations?

I16-15 Collins Corporation pays $30,000 in alternative minimum tax in the current year. What tax benefit (if any) is available for the AMT payment to reduce federal income taxes paid in a prior tax year, in the current tax year, or in a future tax year?

I16-16 The accumulated earnings tax is a penalty tax on corporations.
a. What is the purpose of the accumulated earnings tax?
b. Why does the "reasonable needs of the business" exception either reduce or eliminate the accumulated earnings tax burden for many corporations?

I16-17 Acme Corporation is a highly profitable closely held corporation that has never paid a dividend.

During the past five years, after-tax earnings of $200,000 per year have been retained in the business. All of the earnings have been reinvested in operating assets to finance an expansion of the business. Is the corporation subject to possible attack by the IRS regarding the imposition of the accumulated earnings tax because no dividends have been paid?

I16-18 The personal holding company tax is a penalty tax on corporations.
a. What is the purpose of the personal holding company tax?
b. Two tests are used to classify a corporation as a personal holding company. What are these tests, and how do they accomplish the purpose of the personal holding company tax?

I16-19 Why are controlled groups of corporations required to apportion the lower tax rates applicable to taxable income up to $75,000 among the group members?

I16-20 Discuss the underlying rationale for the nonrecognition of gain or loss in a Sec. 351 transaction.

I16-21 a. Ted Dupay transfers a building having a $75,000 FMV and a $45,000 adjusted basis to Gator Corporation. An advantage of the asset transfer coming under Sec. 351 is that Ted can defer his $30,000 ($75,000 FMV − $45,000 adjusted basis) realized gain. What disadvantages accrue to Gator Corporation with respect to the post-transfer tax consequences of the transaction?
b. Assume the same facts as in part (a) except that the building's FMV is instead $45,000 and its adjusted basis is $75,000. What disadvantage accrues to the transfer as presently structured? What advantages accrue to Gator Corporation with respect to the post-transfer consequences of the transaction? Are there any suggestions that you can offer to Ted to improve his tax consequences?

I16-22 Carmen transfers land and a building having a $60,000 adjusted basis and a $100,000 FMV to Bass Corporation in a transaction qualifying under Sec. 351. Immediately before the exchange, Carmen takes out a $50,000 mortgage on the property. The mortgage is assumed by the corporation, and the mortgage proceeds are used by Carmen to remodel her personal residence.
a. What are the likely tax consequences of the asset transfer?
b. What is the rationale for this result?

I16-23 Damien, Eric, and Fred form a new corporation. Each individual contributes $100,000 of property and receives a one-third ownership interest. Each individual is to receive $10,000 of common stock and a $90,000 20-year corporate note bearing an 8% annual interest rate.
a. What are the advantages of capitalizing the corporation with a high percentage of debt?
b. What are the income tax consequences to Damien, Eric, and Fred if they transfer appreciated property to the newly formed corporation in a transaction that qualifies under Sec. 351?
c. List the factors that might be used to determine whether the note is debt or equity.
d. What are the tax consequences if the 20-year notes are subsequently recharacterized as equity on an IRS audit of the corporation?

I16-24 Under current tax law, a corporation may deduct interest payments but not dividends paid to shareholders. What problems are created by this disparate treatment? Should the law be changed to either disallow the interest deduction or allow a dividends-paid deduction?

I16-25 Due to severe financial difficulties, Big Corporation has not paid a dividend to its shareholders for several years. Big has a $300,000 accumulated E&P deficit on January 1 of the current year but has sufficient liquidity to resume dividend payments. Current E&P is expected to be $10,000 in the current year and $50,000 in subsequent years.
a. What are the income tax consequences for the shareholders if Big makes a $50,000 cash distribution in the current year?
b. What are the income tax consequences for the shareholders if Big delays the initial $50,000 distribution until January 1 of next year?
c. In which year should Big make the $50,000 initial distribution?

I16-26 Why is it generally preferable to structure the redemption of a shareholder's stock so that it meets the mechanical substantially disproportionate test or the complete termination test rather than to rely on the not essentially equivalent to a dividend provision?

I16-27 If the requirements for a complete termination of a shareholder's interest are met, shouldn't the substantially disproportionate redemption requirements also be met? What is the major difference between these two provisions?

I16-28 How does the liquidation of a controlled subsidiary differ from the liquidation of a corporation owned by a single individual? What is the reason for the distinction?

I16-29 Why is Sec. 1244, which pertains to small business corporation stock, in the tax law?

I16-30 Why is it generally preferable to increase salaries, interest, or rental payments to employee-shareholders in a closely held corporation rather than to increase dividends?

I16-31 In many accounting firms, managers and partners review the corporate tax return prepared by others. Why is the Schedule M-1 an important tool for this review?

ISSUE IDENTIFICATION QUESTIONS

I16-32 Acorn Corporation is a very profitable closely held company that is owned solely by Helen, age 55, who plans to retire in 10 years. Management continuity is a problem because neither the existing employees nor Helen's children are interested in or capable of managing the company. Acorn has never paid a dividend and does not intend to do so in the future because dividends are not deductible by the corporation and would be taxable to the shareholders. Helen does not wish to expand the business and plans to have the corporation reinvest its earnings in investment securities. What tax issues should Helen consider?

I16-33 Hugo and Helga each own unincorporated businesses. They plan to form a corporation. Under the plan, they would transfer all of their business assets and liabilities to the corporation in exchange for all of the corporation's stock. Because Hugo's assets are substantially appreciated, a transfer of all of the assets and liabilities would result in an excess of liabilities over the adjusted basis of the assets. On the other hand, Helga has substantial unrealized losses on certain business properties (e.g., land and a building). Her tax accountant has recommended that she sell the properties to recognize capital or Sec. 1231 losses that could be used to offset capital or ordinary gains. The sales proceeds then could be invested in the new corporation. What tax issues should both individuals consider?

I16-34 Eastern Corporation is being formed by John and Joy with an initial capitalization of $500,000. Two alternative capitalization plans are being considered: (1) John and Joy, who are unrelated, each would receive $200,000 of 8% 15-year bonds and $50,000 of Eastern stock or (2) John and Joy each would receive $250,000 of Eastern stock. John's business assets that would be transferred to Eastern are highly appreciated, and he does not want to recognize any gain on the transfer of these assets. Organizational costs of $3,000 are expected to be incurred? What tax issues should John and Joy consider?

PROBLEMS

I16-35 *Capital Gains and Losses.* First Corporation, which is in its fifth year of operations, has the following capital gains and losses in the current year:

LTCG	$20,000
LTCL	8,000
STCG	16,000
STCL	40,000

Taxable income (exclusive of the capital gains and losses) is $60,000.
a. What is First Corporation's capital gain or loss position?
b. What is First Corporation's taxable income for the current year?
c. Explain the tax treatment for any unused capital losses.

I16-36 *Capital Loss Carrybacks and Carryovers.* Federal Corporation has the following net capital losses in 2001:

STCL	$ 80,000
LTCL	120,000

NLTCGs were incurred in 1998 through 2000 as follows:

1998	$20,000
1999	20,000
2000	60,000

a. What are the amount and character of the capital loss carryback to 1998 through 2000?
b. What treatment should be accorded to any unused capital losses after the carryback rules are applied?
c. What is the character of any unused capital loss carryovers?

I16-37 *Dividends-Received Deduction.* During the current year, Florida Corporation reports the following results:

Net income from operations	$100,000
Dividend income from a 20%-owned corporation (qualifying for the dividends-received deduction)	200,000

a. What is Florida Corporation's dividends-received deduction?
b. How would your answer to Part a change if Florida Corporation instead reported a $20,000 loss from operations?
c. How would your answer to Parts a and b change if the dividend income were instead from a 10%-owned corporation and the loss from operations in part b were instead $70,000?

I16-38 *Dividends-Received Deduction.* During the current year, Maine Corporation reports the following results:

Net income (loss) from operations	$(20,000)
Dividend income from a 10%-owned corporation	200,000
(qualifying for the dividends-received deduction)	

a. What is Maine Corporation's dividends-received deduction?
b. How would your answer to Part a change if Maine Corporation's dividend income were from a 25%-owned corporation and net income from operations were instead $90,000?

I16-39 *Net Operating Losses.* General Corporation reports the following results for its second year of operations (the current year):

Gross operating income	$300,000
Business operating expenses	500,000
Dividend income from a 20%-owned corporation	100,000
Dividends-received deduction	80,000

a. What is General Corporation's NOL for the current year?
b. What is the disposition of the NOL if General Corporation reported a $40,000 profit in its first tax year (last year) on which federal income taxes of $6,000 were paid and no special elections were made?
c. What is the best disposition of the NOL if General Corporation anticipates taxable income of $600,000 in its third year?
d. How would your answer to part (a) change if General Corporation also reported a $30,000 long-term capital gain and a $50,000 short-term capital loss?

I16-40 *Charitable Contributions.* On May 15 of the current year, the board of directors of Georgia Corporation authorized a $40,000 donation to a qualified charity. The corporation made the $40,000 payment to the charity on December 1 of the current year. It made no other charitable contributions during the year. Georgia Corporation reports the following results for the current year:

Taxable income (before deducting the dividends-received deduction and charitable contributions)	$250,000
Dividends-received deduction	10,000

a. What amount of charitable contributions are deductible in the current year?
b. How are any unused contributions treated?
c. How would your answer to Part a change, if at all, if Georgia incurs a $30,000 NOL in the next year that is carried back to the current year?

I16-41 *Corporate Tax Rates.* Calculate Ajax Corporation's regular tax liability for the following amounts of taxable income:
a. $90,000
b. $300,000
c. $5 million
d. $12 million
e. $17 million
f. $20 million
g. Alternatively, for Parts a, b, and c above, compute Ajax Corporation's regular tax liability if it were classified as a personal service corporation.

I16-42 *Corporate Tax Rates.* In December of the current year, Colorado Corporation is considering selling certain corporate assets that would result in the recognition of a $50,000 LTCG. The company controller estimates that the taxable income for the current year will be $60,000 (before considering the LTCG). She also estimates that taxable income for the following year will be $200,000 (before considering the LTCG).

a. What is Colorado Corporation's tax liability for the two years if the assets are sold in the current year?
b. What is Colorado Corporation's tax liability for the two years if the assets are sold in the following year?
c. Should Colorado Corporation sell the assets in the current year or in the following year? Explain.

I16-43 *Alternative Minimum Tax.* During an audit of Control Corporation, you have been assigned to review the company's current-year tax accrual (e.g., provision for federal income taxes and the related liability). Control Corporation was incorporated in 1994. The following tax information is made available for your review:

- Taxable income for income tax purposes is $150,000.
- Depreciation claimed for income tax purposes is $100,000. Depreciation that is deductible for AMT purposes is $60,000.
- Gain on the sale of a depreciable property included in taxable income was $30,000. Depreciation claimed for income tax purposes exceeded that claimed for AMT purposes by $11,000.
- Adjusted current earnings is $370,000.

Assume that Central Corporation is not eligible for the small corporation AMT exemption.
a. What is the total amount of Control Corporation's AMT adjustments for the current year?
b. Calculate the following amounts for Control Corporation:
  - Alternative minimum taxable income
  - AMT base
  - Tenative minimum tax
  - Alternative minimum tax
  - Total tax liability

I16-44 *Alternative Minimum Tax.* Ace Corporation, a calendar year corporation incorporated on January 1, 1996, has the following gross receipts:

1996	$2,000,000
1997	5,000,000
1998	8,000,000
1999	7,000,000
2000	10,000,000

Is Ace Corporation a small corporation that qualifies for the AMT exemption in 1999? in 2000? in 2001? If Ace fails the small corporation requirement in any year, can it again become a small corporation in a later year?

I16-45 DeSantiago Corporation, a calendar year corporation formed on January 1, 1999, reports gross receipts as follows:

Year	Gross Receipts
1999	$ 4,000,000
2000	5,000,000
2001	6,000,000
2002	7,000,000
2003	10,000,000

DeSantiago Corporation is not related to a predecessor corporation, or other members of a controlled group under Sec. 448.
a. For what years does DeSantiago Corporation qualify for a small corporation exemption from the AMT?
b. What are the tax consequences of DeSantiago becoming a "large" corporation under the AMT rules?
c. Assume DeSantiago Corporation fails to be a small corporation in 2003. Can DeSantiago requalify as a small corporation in a later year and again be exempt from the AMT?

I16-46 *Accumulated Earnings Tax.* The IRS is auditing Crane Corporation, a manufacturer of widgets, to ascertain whether the company is subject to the accumulated earnings tax in a prior tax year. Crane was owned by 20 shareholders who were unrelated and was not a personal holding company in the year in question. Crane reported the following results during the year in question:

Taxable income	$150,000
Federal income taxes	41,750
Dividends-received deduction	85,000
Dividend paid on June 1	20,000

The accumulated E&P balance on January 1 was $180,000, and the company can justify the retention of $80,000 of earnings earned in the year to meet its end-of-the-year reasonable business needs. All of the January 1 earnings were retained for the reasonable needs of the business.

a. What is Crane Corporation's accumulated taxable income?
b. What is Crane Corporation's accumulated earnings tax liability?

I16-47 *Personal Holding Company Tax.* Delta Corporation has been gradually converting its operating business into an investment company because its retained earnings have been used to make passive investments. The company is owned by three shareholders, and more than 60% of its income is personal holding company income. George, the president of Delta Corporation, however, feels that personal holding company status should not be detrimental because the company has paid dividends to its shareholders for several years and therefore should not be liable for any penalty tax.

Delta reports the following results for the current year:

Taxable income	$25,000
Federal income tax liability	3,750
Dividends paid	3,000
Dividends-received deduction	81,750

a. Do you agree or disagree with George? Explain.
b. What is the Delta Corporation's personal holding company tax liability for the current year?
c. How could Delta avoid being subject to the personal holding company tax?

I16-48 *Controlled Group.* Eagle and East Corporations are members of a brother-sister controlled group. Eagle's taxable income is $75,000, and East's taxable income is $50,000.
a. What is the total federal income tax liability for Eagle and East Corporations?
b. What is the total federal income tax liability for Eagle and East Corporations if they are not members of a controlled group?

I16-49 *Controlled Group.* Alfred, Barbara, and Cathy own stock in First, Second, and Third Corporations as follows:

Individuals	First	Second	Third
Alfred	40%	40%	40%
Barbara	30%	60%	30%
Cathy	30%	–0–	30%

Which corporations are members of a brother-sister controlled group?

I16-50 *Corporate Formation.* In the current year, Jack, Karen, Latoya, and Marc transfer the following property to Giant Corporation (an existing corporation), which is owned equally by the four transferors.

- Jack transfers land and a building with a $60,000 adjusted basis and a $100,000 FMV for additional Giant stock having an $80,000 FMV and $20,000 of marketable securities having an adjusted basis of $15,000 to Giant Corporation. $10,000 of MACRS straight-line depreciation was claimed by Jack on the building prior to the transfer.

- Karen transfers equipment with a $120,000 adjusted basis and a $100,000 FMV for additional Giant stock having an $80,000 FMV and a $20,000 20-year Giant Corporation note. $25,000 of MACRS depreciation was claimed by Karen on the equipment prior to the transfer.

- Latoya transfers inventory with a $70,000 adjusted basis and a $100,000 FMV for additional Giant stock having an $80,000 FMV and $20,000 cash.

- Marc transfers land with an $80,000 adjusted basis and a $100,000 FMV, subject to a $20,000 mortgage, which Giant Corporation assumes, for additional Giant stock having an $80,000 FMV.

a. What amount and character of gain or loss does Jack recognize? What is Jack's basis in the Giant stock and the marketable securities? What is Giant's basis in the land and building?
b. What amount and character of gain or loss does Karen recognize? What is Karen's basis in the Giant stock and note? What is Giant's basis in the equipment?
c. What amount and character of gain or loss does Latoya recognize? What is Latoya's basis in the Giant stock? What is Giant's basis in the inventory?
d. What amount and character of gain or loss does Marc recognize? What is Marc's basis in the Giant stock? What is Giant's basis in the land?
e. What amount and character of gain or loss does Giant Corporation recognize on the distribution of its stock, note, and other property to its shareholders?

I16-51 *Corporate Formation.* Gold Corporation receives land from Marty in a transaction qualifying for nonrecognition of gain or loss under Sec. 351. Marty's basis in the land was $80,000. The FMV of the land is $200,000. Marty receives $20,000 cash and 80% of Gold stock. Mary transfers inventory with a $50,000 adjusted basis and a $200,000 FMV to Gold in exchange for $200,000 of Gold Corporation's debt obligations. Mary acquired the remaining 20% of Gold stock for $50,000 in cash. Mary recognizes a $150,000 gain because she received debt obligations of Gold in addition to the Gold stock.
a. What is the basis of the land to Gold Corporation?
b. What is the basis of the inventory to Gold Corporation?
c. Under what circumstances might it be preferable for Sec. 351 *not* to apply?

I16-52 *Corporate Formations: Transfer of Liabilities.* Matt transfers land that was used in his business with a $600,000 adjusted basis and a $1,000,000 FMV to Hill Corporation in a transaction that otherwise qualifies under Sec. 351. The land is subject to an $800,000 mortgage, which Hill Corporation assumes. Matt receives 100% of the Hill stock.
a. What are the amount and character of the gain or loss recognized by Matt?
b. What is Matt's basis in the Hill Corporation stock?
c. What is Hill Corporation's basis in the land?

I16-53 *Debt/Equity.* Joe and Joy formed Huge Corporation five years ago with an initial total capitalization of $500,000. Joe received $80,000 of Huge stock and a $100,000, 12% 15-year Huge Corporation note. Joy received $20,000 of Huge stock and a $300,000 12% 15-year Huge Corporation note. During the next five years, the interest payments were made when due, and the corporation reinvested its retains earnings of $500,000 to finance operating needs. The IRS audits the company in the current year, and the IRS agent maintains that the debt should be reclassified as equity and that the interest payments on the notes should be treated as dividends.
a. List the factors that should be taken into consideration in determining whether the debt should be reclassified as equity.
b. Present arguments the taxpayer should make to the IRS agent as to why the debt should not be reclassified as equity.

I16-54 *Earnings and Profits (E&P).* During the current year, Nevada Corporation distributed $100,000 in cash to its sole shareholder. Because the corporation has a $300,000 accumulated E&P deficit at the beginning of the current year and only $10,000 of taxable income in the current year, Nevada's controller feels that the distribution should be treated as a tax-free return of capital to the shareholder. Your investigation reveals the following items that may have an effect on the computation of current E&P:

Federal income tax liability	$ 1,500
Dividends-received deduction	60,000
Excess of MACRS depreciation tax deduction over alternative depreciation system depreciation	40,000
Excess charitable contributions	9,000

a. What is Nevada Corporation's current E&P?
b. How much (if any) of the $100,000 cash distribution is taxable as a dividend to the sole shareholder?
c. What is the amount of Nevada Corporation's accumulated E&P (or accumulated E&P deficit) on the last day of the current year?

I16-55 *Earnings and Profits (E&P).* North Corporation has $200,000 of accumulated E&P at the beginning of the current year. North made cash distributions of $300,000 during the current year to its shareholders. The company's operating results for the current year were as follows:

Taxable income	$100,000
Tax-exempt bond interest	10,000
Dividends-received deduction	7,000
Federal income tax liability	22,250
Net capital losses	5,000

a. What is North Corporation's current E&P?
b. How much of the $300,000 distribution is taxable as a dividend?
c. What is North Corporation's accumulated E&P balance (or accumulated E&P deficit) at the end of the current year?

I16-56 *Earnings and Profits (E&P).* Ohio Corporation has a $40,000 accumulated E&P balance at the beginning of the year 2001 and a $73,000 current E&P deficit. The corporation makes a $60,000 cash distribution to its sole shareholder on April 30. The shareholder's tax basis in her Ohio stock at the beginning of the year 2001 is $15,000.
a. What amount of the $60,000 distribution is taxable as a dividend (assume that a ratable allocation of the deficit is used)?
b. What are the amount and character of any nondividend amounts received by the shareholder?
c. What is the amount of Ohio Corporation's accumulated E&P (or accumulated E&P deficit) on the last day of the year 2001?

I16-57 *Property Distributions.* Old Corporation has a severe liquidity shortage but desires to maintain its existing dividend payment policy. Therefore, Old distributes land that was being held as an investment to its two shareholders. The land has a $30,000 adjusted basis and a $100,000 FMV. Old Corporation has E&P of $300,000 (excluding the effects of the distribution). Nancy receives 50% of the land, and Palm Corporation receives the remaining 50%.
a. What amount of the distribution is taxable to Nancy and Palm Corporation?
b. What is the basis of the property to Nancy and Palm Corporation?
c. What are the income tax consequences of the distribution to Old Corporation?

I16-58 *Property Distributions.* Park Corporation distributes equipment with a $60,000 adjusted basis and a $70,000 FMV as a nonliquidating distribution to Pam. The equipment is subject to a $40,000 mortgage note assumed by Pam. Park Corporation has $300,000 of E&P (excluding the effects of the distribution).
a. How much gain (if any) does Park Corporation recognize on the distribution of the equipment?
b. What amount is taxable as a dividend to Pam?
c. What is Pam's basis in the equipment?

I16-59 *Stock Redemptions.* Private Corporation redeems some of its stock from Jane, a major shareholder in the company. Before the redemption Jane owns 50 of the 100 outstanding shares, and her daughter Jill owns 40 shares. The remaining ten shares are owned by unrelated individuals. Private Corporation redeems 40 of Jane's shares, having a $200,000 basis, for $600,000 in cash. Private Corporation has $900,000 of current and accumulated E&P. Jane's basis in her remaining ten shares of Private Corporation stock is $50,000.
a. What are the tax consequences of the redemption to Jane?
b. What is the basis of Jane's remaining ten shares of Private stock after her 40 shares are redeemed?
c. How would your answers to parts (a) and (b) change if Jane and Jill were not related?

I16-60 *Stock Redemption.* Prime Corporation redeems some of its stock from two of its shareholders on the same date. Frank and Sam own 50 and 20 shares, respectively, of the 100 shares outstanding before the redemption. The remaining 30 shares are owned by unrelated individuals. Prime redeems ten of Frank's shares having a $15,000 basis for $50,000. All of Sam's shares, having a $30,000 basis are redeemed for $100,000. Frank and Sam are father and son. Sam files an agreement with the IRS that he will have no interest in the corporation other than as a creditor for 10 years. Prime Corporation has current and accumulated E&P totaling $200,000.
a. What are the tax consequences of the redemption to Frank and Sam?

I16-61 *Corporate Liquidation.* Queen Corporation adopts a plan of complete liquidation on January 1 of the current year. The corporation sells the assets listed below during the current year, and this sale is followed by the payment of Queen's liabilities and a single liquidating distribution of $1,200,000 cash on December 12 of the current year to Ahmed (Queen's sole shareholder). Ahmed has a $400,000 basis for his Queen stock that he has held for seven years.

- Inventory costing $600,000 is sold to customers for $1,000,000.
- Depreciable fixed assets with a $2,000,000 adjusted basis are sold for $3,000,000. Depreciation recapture under Sec. 1245 is $800,000.
- Land held as a capital asset with a $4,000,000 adjusted basis is sold for $5,000,000.

a. What are the tax consequences to Queen Corporation of the liquidation?
b. What are the tax consequences to Ahmed upon receiving the liquidating distribution?
c. How would your answer to parts (a) and (b) change if the assets were instead distributed to Ahmed in exchange for his Queen stock and Ahmed then proceeded to sell the three assets for the prices shown.

I16-62 *Corporate Liquidation.* Tampa Corporation acquired 100% of Union Corporation's stock several years ago for $1,000,000. In the current year, Tampa liquidates Union Corporation, receiving all of its assets and liabilities. Tampa continues to operate it as a division. On the liquidation date, the tax basis and FMV of Union Corporation's assets are $800,000 and $2,000,000, respectively. Union Corporation also has $100,000 of liabilities outstanding that were owed to third parties and E&P of $125,000 on the liquidation date.

a. How much gain or loss does Union Corporation recognize as a result of the liquidation?
b. What is Tampa's basis for Union Corporation's assets?
c. What Union Corporation tax attributes (if any) carry over to Tampa Corporation?

TAX FORM/RETURN PREPARATION PROBLEMS

I16-63 Zane Corporation's financial accounting balance sheet as of the end of the current year is as follows:

Assets

Cash	$ 50,000
Accounts receivable	20,000
Inventory	10,000
Land	20,000
Buildings (net of $30,000 accumulated depreciation)	100,000
Equipment (net of $50,000 accumulated depreciation)	150,000
Total assets	$350,000

Liabilites & Owner's Equity

Accounts payable	$ 40,000
Mortgage payable	40,000
Capital stock	100,000
Retained earnings	170,000[a]
Total liabilities and stockholders' equity	$350,000

[a] The retained earnings balance at the beginning of the current year was $70,000. Beginning inventory was $15,000. Dividends were paid in the amount of $25,000.

Zane Corporation reports the following financial accounting operating results using the accrual method for the current year:

Sales	$550,000
Minus: Costs of goods sold	(350,000)
Gross profit	$200,000
Dividend income (from a 20%-owned domestic corporation)	75,000
Net long-term capital gains	150,000
Total income	$425,000

Expenses:
Salaries (including officer's salary of $40,000)	$140,000
Repairs	30,000
Bad debts	10,000
State and local taxes	25,000
Contributions	35,000
Depreciation (straight-line for financial accounting purposes)	40,000
Total expenses (before federal income tax expense)	$280,000
Operating profit	$145,000
Minus: Provision for federal income taxes	(40,000)
Net income	$105,000

All dividends qualify for the dividends-received deduction. In addition, the following items should be taken into account in the preparation of Form 1120:

Current-year estimated tax payments	$15,000
MACRS depreciation for income tax purposes	60,000

Prepare Form 1120 (U.S. Corporation Income Tax Return) for Zane Corporation. Disregard beginning-of-the-year balance sheet amounts other than retained earnings. Also, leave spaces blank on Form 1120 if information is not provided.

I16-64 Huge Corporation has the following balance sheet information at the beginning and end of the current year:

	Beginning of Year	End of Year
Cash	$ 40,000	$ 70,000
Accounts receivable	23,000	21,500
Inventories	26,000	53,000
Marketable securities	30,000	30,000
Investment in 100%-owned subsidiary	100,000	115,000
Depreciable assets	100,000	100,000
Accumulated depreciation	(20,000)	(30,000)
Total assets	$299,000	$359,500
Accounts payable	$ 50,000	$ 80,000
Short-term loans payable	20,000	35,000
Mortgage payable	80,000	79,000
Common stock	1,000	1,000
Additional paid-in capital	49,000	49,000
Retained earnings	99,000	115,500
Total liabilities and stockholders' equity	$299,000	$359,500

Huge Corporation had the following income and expense items for the year:

Sales	$720,000
Purchases	570,000
Dividend income from 100%-owned subsidiary corporation	30,000
Dividend income from less-than-20%-owned corporation	10,000
Salaries (including officers' salaries of $30,000)	90,000
Repairs	12,000
Contributions	60,000
State and local taxes	7,500
Interest	11,000
Financial accounting depreciation	10,000
MACRS depreciation	17,490
Federal income tax expense per books	10,000

In addition, Huge Corporation reported an NOL carryover of $12,000 from the preceding year and made current year estimated tax payments of $10,000.

Prepare Form 1120 (U.S. Corporation Income Tax Return) for Huge Corporation. Leave spaces blank on Form 1120 if information is not provided. Note: You need to prepare a schedule of net income per books to determine the number for Line 1 of Schedule M-1.

CASE STUDY PROBLEMS

I16-65 Frank, Paul, and Sam are considering whether to merge their respective unincorporated businesses and form a C corporation. Frank would transfer land and a building with a $50,000 adjusted basis and $100,000 FMV to the corporation in exchange for $100,000 of common stock in the newly-formed FPS Corporation. Paul would transfer inventory with an adjusted basis of $60,000 and $100,000 FMV to FPS Corporation for $50,000 of FPS stock and $50,000 of FPS 10-year notes. Sam will contribute equipment with an adjusted basis of $80,000 and $60,000 FMV along with legal services for the creation of the business with a $40,000 FMV in exchange for $100,000 of FPS stock.

Prepare a client memo that details the tax consequences of the transaction to the newly-formed corporation and to Frank, Paul, and Sam if the transaction is carried out as proposed.

I16-66 Beth, who is married, is the sole shareholder of Pet Store, Inc., which is a C corporation. She also manages the store. She wishes to expand the business, but the corporation needs additional capital for her to do so. Fortunately, she has saved $50,000 cash and plans to contribute it to the corporation. However, she doesn't know whether to contribute the cash in exchange for additional stock or lend the $50,000 to the corporation. Prepare a client memo that explains the tax consequences and requirements of each alternative so that Beth can make an informed decision.

TAX RESEARCH PROBLEM

I16-67 Ted is the sole shareholder of Zero Corporation. Before his retirement from the company, he transferred 100 shares of Zero stock by gift to his son. A few months later, Ted sold the remaining 1,900 shares to Zero Corporation for $2 million. The company has E&P exceeding $2 million. Ted's basis for his 2,000 shares before the two transfers was $80,000. Ted then filed for a waiver of the attribution rules under Sec. 318 and treated the redemption of Zero stock as a long-term capital gain. He also signed a consulting contract with the company that provides him with consulting income of $5,000 per month for five years. Three years later the IRS audits Ted's return and argues that the redemption should be treated as a dividend under Sec. 301. Have the requirements for Sec. 302(c)(2) been met that would permit a waiver of the family attribution rules?

A partial list of research sources is

- Secs. 302(c)(2) and (b)(3)
- Reg. Sec. 1.302-4
- *William M. Lynch v. CIR*, 58 AFTR 2d 86-5970, 86-2 USTC ¶9731 (9th Cir., 1986)

I16-68 Beth in Case Study Problem I16-66 also wants to know whether she can make a $50,000 contribution to capital of the corporation without having the corporation issue additional shares. If so, should she have the corporation issue the shares or not? Assume that Beth's basis in her current stock is $40,000 and that she files a joint return with her husband.

A partial list of research sources is

- Sec. 1244(d)(1)(B)
- Reg. Secs. 1.1244(c)-1(b) and 1.1244(d)-2(a)
- *Sol Lessinger v. CIR*, 63 AFTR 2d 89-1055, 89-1 USTC ¶9254 (2nd Cir., 1989)
- *James D. Pierce*, 1989 PH T.C. Memo ¶89,647, 58 TCM 865 (1989).

I16-69 Peter purchased 150 shares of Able Manufacturing Corporation stock for $75,000 in 1995. Able is a C corporation that has 40 shareholders. None of the other 60 shareholders own more than 5% of the 5,000 shares of stock that are outstanding. No events have taken place that have caused either the number of shares of stock that Peter owns, or the total basis of Peter's shares to change. Peter has become unhappy with Able's management. It is now Spring 2001 and Peter would like to sell part or all of his Able stock and reinvest the proceeds in the stock of another small corporation. His total unrealized gain is $300,000 at the present time. Peter has heard from his stockbroker that he may be eligible to exclude part of all of his profit on the Able Corporation shares from current taxation. He calls you and asks you what advice you can give him on reducing the tax cost of making the sale.

A partial list of research sources is

- Sec. 1202
- Sec. 1044
- Sec. 1045

CHAPTER 17

PARTNERSHIPS AND S CORPORATIONS

LEARNING OBJECTIVES
After studying this chapter, you should be able to

1. Determine the tax implications of a partnership formation
2. Apply the operating rules for partnerships
3. Understand the tax implications (to the partnership and its partners) of distributions to partners
4. Understand the requirements for electing and maintaining S corporation status
5. Apply the operating rules for S corporations
6. Determine the tax treatment of an S corporation's shareholders

CHAPTER OUTLINE

Types of Flow-Through Entities...17-2
Taxation of Partnerships...17-4
Partnership Elections...17-18
Taxation of S Corporations...17-19
Tax Planning Considerations...17-30
Compliance and Procedural Considerations...17-32

KEY POINT

Flow-through entities entail taxation only at the ownership level. This single level of taxation is achieved by (1) exempting the entity from taxation; (2) passing income, deductions, losses, and credits through to the owners; and (3) adjusting the basis of the owner's interest in the entity.

Flow-through or conduit business entities, such as partnerships, S corporations, limited liability companies, and limited liability partnerships, have the major advantage of entailing only one level of taxation.[1] These legal organizational forms thus represent an interesting blend of what tax theorists call the entity and aggregate theories of taxation. In some ways, they are treated as entities separate from their owners. For example, the entity files a tax return (for information purposes), makes elections pertaining to accounting periods and methods, and computes the results of business operations. In other ways, however, a flow-through entity is treated as a mere aggregation of its owners. For example, the entity is not taxed, and the entity's income, deductions, losses, and credits are allocated to the owners based on their proportionate ownership or some other allocation arrangement. These allocated items then flow through to the owners to be reported in their own tax returns.

Aside from exempting flow-through entities from entity-level taxation, the tax law preserves the single-level of taxation in another important way: basis adjustments made to the owner's interest in the entity. Each owner obtains an original basis in his or her ownership interest upon acquiring the interest via formation of the entity, purchase of the entity interest, gift of the entity interest, etc. Subsequently, the owner's basis increases if the entity earns income or if the owner contributes additional money or property to the entity. Conversely, the owner's basis decreases if the entity incurs a loss or if the entity distributes money or property to the owner. In short, the owner's basis increases as the entity expands, and the owner's basis decreases as the entity contracts. Without these basis adjustments, the owner could be subject to double taxation upon selling his or her interest or upon the dissolution of the entity.

EXAMPLE I17-1 ▶

Conduit Company is a flow-through entity with two owners, George and Flo. Each owner has a $10,000 original basis in the entity. In its first year of operations, Conduit Company earns $30,000, which is allocated $15,000 to each owner. Thus, each owner reports $15,000 in his or her individual tax return even though the company does not distribute the earnings to the owners. At the beginning of the second year, Flo sells her interest to Fred for $25,000. If Flo did not get an increased basis adjustment for her $15,000 of earnings, she would recognize a $15,000 ($25,000 selling price − $10,000 basis in the entity) gain on the sale of her interest, which taxes her twice on the $15,000. However, both George and Flo do increase their bases to $25,000 ($10,000 original basis + $15,000 share of entity earnings) at the end of the first year. Therefore, when Flo sells her interest for $25,000, she incurs no addition taxable gain ($25,000 selling price − $25,000 basis in the entity = $0 gain). ◀

The next section of this chapter briefly describes the four basic types of flow-through business entities. Afterward, the chapter provides more detail on the tax treatment of partnerships and S corporations.

TYPES OF FLOW-THROUGH ENTITIES

PARTNERSHIPS

Of the flow-through business entities, partnerships have been around the longest. The Code defines a **partnership** as "a syndicate, group, pool, joint venture, or other incorporated organization" that carries on any business, financial operation, or venture. The definition of a partnership, however, does not include a trust, estate, or corporation.[2] A partner is a member of such syndicate, group, pool, joint venture, or organization, and the partner can be an individual, corporation, trust, or estate. Unlike a corporation, which must file incorporation documents with the state, partnerships require no legal documentation although most states have laws that govern the rights and restrictions of partnerships. Moreover, most states model their laws on the Uniform Partnership Act (UPA) or

---

[1] Trusts and estates are also conduit entities. Trusts and estates are not generally used to conduct business activities. Income taxation of trusts and estates is discussed in Chapter C14 of the *Prentice Hall Federal Taxation of Corporations, Partnerships, Estates, and Trusts* text.
[2] Secs. 761(a) and 7701(a)(2).

the Uniform Limited Partnership Act (UPLA). A partnership must have at least two partners but can have an unlimited number beyond two.

A partnership can be either a general partnership or a limited partnership. In a general partnership, each partner has unlimited liability for partnership debts. Thus, these partners are at risk for more than their investment in the partnership. In a limited partnership, at least one partner must be a general partner, and at least one partner must be a limited partner. As in a general partnership, the general partners are liable for all partnership debts, but the limited partners are liable only to the extent of their investment plus any amount they commit to contribute to the partnership if called upon. Moreover, limited partners may not participate in the management of the partnership.

A major document for a partnership is the partnership agreement. In this agreement, the partners set out the terms of how the partnership will operate and how income, deductions, losses, and credits will be allocated to the partners. The partners, therefore, should take great care in drafting this agreement.[3]

A partnership files an annual information return with the IRS. This return, Form 1065 (U.S. Partnership Return of Income), reports the results of the partnership's operations and indicates the separate income, deduction, loss, and credit items that flow through to the partners. Form 1065 is included in Appendix B.

S CORPORATIONS

An **S corporation** is so designated because rules pertaining to this entity are located in Subchapter S of the Internal Revenue Code (IRC). S corporations are a special form of corporation treated by the tax laws as flow-through entities. Similar to partnerships, therefore, S corporations are not taxed, and income, deduction, loss, and credit items flow through to the shareholders. These entities, however, still are corporations so that corporate tax rules apply to them unless overridden by the Subchapter S provisions.[4] As with C corporations, the shareholders enjoy limited liability, but S corporations offer less flexibility than do partnerships. For example, the number and type of shareholders are limited, and the shareholders cannot agree to allocate income, deduction, loss, and credit items in a way that differs from their proportionate stock ownership.

To achieve S corporation status, the corporation must file an S election, and its shareholders must consent to that election. An electing S corporation files an information return, Form 1120S (U.S. Income Tax Return for an S Corporation), which reports the results of the corporation's operations and indicates the separate income, deduction, loss, and credit items that flow through to the shareholders.

LIMITED LIABILITY COMPANIES

ADDITIONAL COMMENT

An LLC is a new type of entity that has been legislatively adopted by all 50 states.

A qualifying **limited liability company** (LLC) combines the best features of a partnership and a corporation even though it is neither. Specifically, it is taxed like a partnership while providing the limited liability protection of a corporation. Moreover, this limited liability extends to all the LLC's owners, called members. Thus, the LLC is similar to a limited partnership with no general partners, and unlike an S corporation, it can have an unlimited number of members who can be individuals, corporations, estates, or trusts.

As mentioned in Chapter I16, an LLC may elect to be taxed as either a corporation or a partnership under the "check-the-box" Treasury Regulations.[5] Under these Regulations, effective on January 1, 1997, an LLC with more than one member is treated as a partnership unless the LLC affirmatively elects to be classified as a corporation. In most cases, LLCs will prefer to be classified as a partnership because of the tax advantages of that form of organization. Assuming the LLC elects its default partnership classification, it files Form 1065 (U.S. Partnership Return of Income). Nevertheless, an LLC is not legally a partnership; it just is taxed as one. A single member LLC is disregarded for tax purposes. As such, income earned by the LLC is generally taxed to its owner under the sole proprietorship rules. Alternatively, an LLC can elect to be taxed as a corporation

---

[3] Also see T. Thorne-Thomsen and J.B. Truskowski, "The Importance of Partnership Agreements," *Journal of Accountancy,* January, 1994, pp. 92-96.

[4] Sec. 1371(a)(1).

[5] Reg. Secs. 301.7701-1 through -4.

REAL WORLD EXAMPLE
All five of the "Big 5" accounting firms have converted from being a general partnership to a limited liability partnership (LLP).

LIMITED LIABILITY PARTNERSHIPS

under the check-the-box rules. S corporation status can be achieved by making an S election.

Many states also have statutes that allow a business to operate as an **limited liability partnership (LLP)**. This partnership form is particularly attractive to professional service partnerships, such as public accounting firms. As a result, many firms have adopted the LLP form, primarily to limit legal liability. Under state LLP laws, partners are liable for their own acts and the acts of individuals under their direction. However, LLP partners are not liable for the negligence or misconduct of other partners. Thus, from a liability perspective, an LLP partner is like a limited partner with respect to other partners' acts but like a general partner with respect to his own acts.

TAXATION OF PARTNERSHIPS[6]

OBJECTIVE 1

Determine the tax implications of a partnership formation

FORMATION OF A PARTNERSHIP

When a partnership is formed, the partners often contribute property (e.g., money, business equipment, and inventory previously used in a proprietorship) or services to the partnership. In exchange for this property and/or services, the partners receive an interest in the partnership. For each partner, a **partnership interest** is an investment security similar to corporate stock and thus is a capital asset.

KEY POINT
The nonrecognition provisions of Sec. 721 apply not only at the time of the formation of a partnership but also to subsequent capital contributions.

SECTION 721: NONRECOGNITION RULES. Section 721 prevents the recognition of gain or loss upon either the transfer of property in exchange for a partnership interest or subsequent transfers of property by the partners in exchange for a pro rata increase in their partnership interests. Without this nonrecognition provision, gain on a transfer of appreciated property would be recognized, and the partners might not have sufficient liquidity (e.g., cash) to pay the tax. In addition, the transfer of property to the partnership represents a mere change in ownership form, which is not a recognition event under the tax laws. Finally, the depreciation recapture rules do not apply if no gain is recognized under Sec. 721.

The following exceptions to the Sec. 721 nonrecognition rules should be noted:

▶ The Sec. 721 nonrecognition of gain or loss rules do not apply if the partner acts in a capacity other than as partner. For example, if a partner sells property to the partnership in an arm's-length transaction, the sale would be taxable.[7]

▶ If a partner contributes services instead of cash or property in exchange for an unrestricted partnership interest, the fair market value (FMV) of the services is taxed as compensation to the contributing partner because services do not qualify as property.[8]

▶ The contributing partner recognizes gain if liabilities transferred to the partnership exceed the partner's basis in the partnership.[9]

▶ The contributing partner recognizes gain if the partnership would be treated as an investment company had it incorporated under Sec. 351.[10]

KEY POINT
The substituted basis of the partnership interest is consistent with the nonrecognition of gain or loss.

BASIS OF A PARTNERSHIP INTEREST. If the Sec. 721 nonrecognition rules apply, Sec. 722 provides a substituted basis rule for determining the basis of a partnership interest. Disregarding the effect of any liabilities, the basis of the contributing partner's part-

---

[6] The rules described in this chapter apply generally to partnerships. However, a legislative change enacted in 1997 added special rules for electing large partnerships (those having at least 100 partners). A brief discussion of these rules is provided starting on page I17-16.
[7] Reg. Sec. 1.721-1(a).
[8] Reg. Sec. 1.721-1(b)(1).
[9] See Example I17-4 and the discussion of the partnership basis rules.
[10] Sec. 721(b). The partnership is considered to be an investment company if 80% or more of the transferred assets (excluding cash and nonconvertible debt obligations) consists of marketable stocks or securities. This restriction prevents investors from diversifying their portfolios by creating a partnership through a tax-free transfer of securities in exchange for a partnership interest.

nership interest equals the sum of money contributed plus the adjusted basis of other property transferred to the partnership.

EXAMPLE I17-2 ▶ Allen contributes business equipment having a $10,000 FMV and a $4,000 adjusted basis to the ABC Partnership in exchange for a 30% interest in the partnership. The basis of Allen's partnership interest is $4,000 (a substituted basis) because he recognizes no gain or loss under Sec. 721. ◀

If a contributing partner renders services to the partnership in exchange for a partnership interest, the contributing partner's basis equals the amount of income recognized from rendering the services (i.e., the FMV of the services).[11] The FMV basis is permitted because the partner recognizes ordinary income equal to the FMV of the services.

EXAMPLE I17-3 ▶ Angela contributes property having a $10,000 FMV and a $4,000 adjusted basis and renders services valued at $10,000 in exchange for a 60% interest in the ABC Partnership. Section 721 prevents gain from being recognized on the transfer of the property. However, Angela recognizes $10,000 of ordinary income for the services rendered. Thus, the basis of Angela's partnership interest equals $14,000 ($4,000 adjusted basis of the property plus the $10,000 FMV of the services). ◀

SELF-STUDY QUESTION

Bob, a partner in an equal three-person partnership, had a $10,000 basis in his partnership interest before the partnership borrowed $300,000 to purchase a building. What is Bob's basis after the loan is made?

ANSWER

It increases by one-third of the $300,000 borrowing or from $10,000 to $110,000. This characteristic could result in Bob being allocated partnership losses greater than his cash investment.

Section 752 Adjustment. A partner's basis for his or her partnership interest includes the partner's ratable share of partnership liabilities as well as the basis attributable to any property and services contributed to the partnership. In addition, the following rules apply if a partnership assumes a partner's liability or if the partner transfers property to the partnership subject to a liability:

▶ An increase in partnership liabilities is treated as a cash contribution by all partners, which increases their bases by their ratable share of the assumed liabilities.

▶ The partnership's assumption of a liability is treated as a cash distribution to the partner whose liability is assumed, which decreases his basis in the partnership.

EXAMPLE I17-4 ▶ Brad contributes a building to a newly-formed partnership, BCD Partnership, in exchange for a one-third interest in the partnership. The building has a $90,000 FMV, an $80,000 adjusted basis, and is subject to a $60,000 mortgage. The partnership assumes the mortgage but has no other liabilities. Carol and Dale each contribute $30,000 of cash for a one-third interest in the partnership. After the contributions, the partners have the following bases in their partnership interests:

	Brad	Carol	Dale
Adjusted basis of property or amount of cash contributed	$80,000	$30,000	$30,000
Plus: Share of mortgage assumed by the partnership ($60,000 × 1/3)	20,000	20,000	20,000
Minus: Decrease in Brad's personal liabilities	(60,000)	—0—	—0—
Basis in partnership interest	$40,000	$50,000	$50,000	◀

Under the general rules of Sec. 752, a partner's basis in the partnership interest increases by the partner's share of any changes in the partnership's liabilities during the year. For example, if total partnership liabilities (including accounts and notes payable, mortgages, bank loans, etc.) increase during the year from $100,000 to $200,000, the basis of a partner with a 50% interest in the partnership increases by $50,000 ($100,000 increase in liabilities × 0.50).

Negative Basis Rule. The basis of a partnership interest cannot be negative. Therefore, Sec. 731 requires recognition of gain in situations where a negative basis would otherwise occur.

EXAMPLE I17-5 ▶ Becky transfers property having a $100,000 FMV and a $20,000 adjusted basis, which is subject to a $60,000 mortgage, in exchange for a one-third interest in the BCD Partnership. The part-

---

[11] Reg. Sec. 1.722-1.

nership owes no other liabilities. Becky, Cindy, and Dan each have a one-third interest in the partnership. The $60,000 reduction in Becky's individual liabilities is treated as a distribution of money. Thus, Becky must recognize a $20,000 gain because the distribution exceeds her $40,000 basis in the partnership interest. Becky's basis in the partnership interest is zero after the distribution. The basis is computed as follows:

Adjusted basis of property transferred	$20,000
Plus: Becky's share of the mortgage assumed by the partnership ($60,000 × 1/3)	20,000
Minus: Decrease in Becky's individual liabilities	(60,000)
Tentative basis of Becky's partnership interest	($20,000)
Plus: Gain recognized by Becky (to the extent of negative basis)	20,000
Becky's basis in the partnership interest	$ —0—

STOP & THINK

Question: In Example I17-5, Becky transferred property subject to a liability exceeding the property's adjusted basis. How does the treatment of excess liabilites in a partnership differ from the treatment when such property is transferred to a corporation?

Solution: In the corporation situation, the shareholder recognizes gain to the extent that total liabilities exceed the total basis of property transferred by that shareholder. Thus, had Becky transferred the same property to a corporation in a Sec. 351 transaction, she would have recognized gain for the entire $40,000 ($60,000 mortgage - $20,000 adjusted basis) excess liability. In a partnership, however, the transferor partner recognizes gain only if the deemed money distribution associated with the liability exceeds the partner's basis in the partnership interest. In Example I17-5, Becky recognized only a $20,000 gain. Had she already had substantial basis in an existing partnership, she would not have recognized any gain.

HOLDING PERIOD FOR A PARTNERSHIP INTEREST. If a partner contributes only cash to the partnership in exchange for a partnership interest, the holding period begins on the date the interest is acquired. If the partner contributes property, the holding period for the partnership interest generally includes the holding period of the contributed property. However, if the contributed property is other than a capital asset or Sec. 1231 property, the holding period begins on the date the partnership interest is acquired.[12]

EXAMPLE I17-6 ▶ In the current year, Johanna contributes business machinery to the JK Partnership in exchange for a partnership interest. Johanna originally acquired the machinery in 1997. Because the machinery is Sec. 1231 property, Johanna's holding period for her partnership interest begins in 1997 (the date she acquired the machinery). If Johanna had contributed inventory instead of machinery, the holding period would begin on the inventory contribution date. ◀

ADDITIONAL COMMENT

When property that has been held for personal use is contributed to a partnership, the basis equals the lesser of the property's FMV or adjusted basis on the contribution date.

BASIS OF PARTNERSHIP ASSETS. Section 723 provides a carryover basis rule for property contributed to the partnership. The partnership's basis in the property is the same as that of the transferor partner, even if the contributing partner recognizes gain. Without this rule, partners could increase the basis of their property for depreciation and subsequent sale purposes merely by contributing appreciated property to a partnership. Because the carryover basis rule applies, the partnership's holding period for the property includes the period the property was held by the contributing partner.[13]

EXAMPLE I17-7 ▶ In the current year, Carlos contributes equipment with a $6,000 adjusted basis and an $8,000 FMV to the CDE Partnership and receives a one-third interest in the partnership. Carlos acquired the equipment in 1997. CDE's basis for the equipment is $6,000, its adjusted basis in the hands of the contributing partner. Carlos recognizes no gain due to the Sec. 721 nonrecognition rules. CDE's holding period for the equipment begins in 1997 because it includes Carlos' holding period for the property. ◀

---

[12] Reg. Sec. 1.1223-1(a).   [13] Sec. 1223(2) and Reg. Sec. 1.723-1.

An individual who contributes property encumbered with a liability to a partnership may have to recognize gain on the transfer when the discharge of the liability creates a negative basis situation (see Example I17-5). The adjusted basis of Becky's partnership interest in this example is reduced by this release from the liability, and is not increased by the gain Becky recognizes. No basis adjustment is allowed because the gain recognition is due to a distribution of money on the release from the liability and not from the contribution of the property to the partnership. For a similar reason, the basis of partnership property is not increased by the gain recognized by the partner.[14]

> **KEY POINT**
>
> For many items, the partnership must maintain separate sets of records for tax and financial accounting purposes.

FINANCIAL ACCOUNTING CONSIDERATIONS. Under generally accepted accounting principles (GAAP), the carryover basis and nonrecognition rules used in taxation do not apply. For example, if property is contributed to a partnership, its book value is recorded at the contributed property's FMV. This GAAP treatment results in a difference between the tax bases and financial accounting book values of contributed assets.

> **EXAMPLE I17-8**
> **BOOK-TAX ACCOUNTING COMPARISON**
>
> The difference between book value and tax basis also causes book and tax depreciation to differ if a partner contributes depreciable property.

Anwar contributes cash of $30,000 and Beth contributes land having a $30,000 FMV and a $20,000 adjusted basis to the AB Partnership. Each partner receives a 50% interest in the partnership. For financial accounting purposes, the land is recorded at $30,000. For tax purposes, the carryover basis of the land to the partnership is $20,000. No gain or loss is recorded for financial accounting purposes if the partnership later sells the land for $30,000. However, the partnership recognizes a $10,000 gain under the tax rules because the land's adjusted basis for tax purposes is only $20,000. The $10,000 precontribution gain is allocated to Anwar. (See the section titled Special Allocations on page I17-9 for a discussion of precontribution gains and losses.)

Topic Review I17-1 highlights the nonrecognition of gain or loss provisions and basis rules.

ORGANIZATIONAL AND SYNDICATION FEES. The costs of organizing a partnership are not immediately deductible but must be capitalized by the partnership and amortized over a period of not less than 60 months beginning with the month in which the partnership begins business.[15] **Organizational expenses** include legal and accounting fees incident to organizing the partnership, filing fees, etc.

The partnership must capitalize expenses attributable to syndicating the partnership. These expenses, however, are *not* amortizable. **Syndication fees** are expenses incurred to promote and market partnership interests (usually associated with tax-sheltered limited partnership interests). Examples of nondeductible syndication fees include brokerage and registration fees, legal fees of the underwriter and issuer, and printing costs associated with the prospectus and promotional materials.

OBJECTIVE 2

Apply the operating rules for partnerships

PARTNERSHIP OPERATIONS

The partnership tax return (Form 1065) provides information regarding the measurement and reporting of income, deductions, losses, and credits that pass through to the partners. Certain separately stated items (e.g., capital gains and losses, charitable contributions, and Sec. 1231 gains and losses) are segregated and passed through to the partners without losing their identity. Such items must be separately stated because their tax effect depends on the partner's particular tax situation. These items are reported on Schedules K and K-1 of the partnership return. Schedule K reports tax information for the entire partnership, and a separate Schedule K-1 summarizes the results for each partner.

> **ADDITIONAL COMMENT**
>
> Many states impose an income tax on each nonresident partner's share of income produced by the partnership in that state, which can cause a partner to file several state income tax returns where a partnership conducts business in those states.

Items that do not have special tax effect are netted at the partnership level and are reported on page 1 of Form 1065. The netting of such items results in partnership ordinary income or ordinary loss, which then is allocated to the partners depending on the profit and loss sharing ratios contained in the partnership agreement. Table I17-1 contains a list of commonly encountered separately stated items and items that make up partnership ordinary income or loss.

---

[14] Rev. Rul. 84-15, 1984 C.B. 158.
[15] These rules are contained in Sec. 709 and associated Treasury Regulations. The partnership makes the election to amortize organization costs by attaching a statement to the partnership's tax return that includes the month in which it begins business.

Topic Review I17-1

Section 721 Formations: Nonrecognition of Gain or Loss Rules

- A transfer of property in exchange for a partnership interest or pro rata increase in a partnership interest causes nonrecognition of gain or loss treatment.
- A partner's basis in her partnership interest is adjusted upward for the following:
  - Cash contributed to the partnership
  - Adjusted basis of noncash property contributed
  - FMV of services contributed
  - Sec. 752 adjustment for liabilities
  - Gain recognized under Sec. 731 due to the negative basis rule
- The partnership's basis in the transferred property carries over from the transferor partners.
- With limited exceptions for cash and ordinary income property, the partnership's holding period for the transferred property includes the contributing partner's holding period.
- The nonrecognition rules do not apply to services contributed. The contributing partner recognizes ordinary income equal to the FMV of the services, and the partner's basis in the partnership interest is increased by the amount of income recognized from rendering the services.
- The depreciation recapture rules do not apply to contributed property unless a gain is recognized, but the depreciation recapture potential carries over to the partnership.

▼ TABLE I17-1
Segregation of Ordinary Income and Separately Stated Items

	Separately Stated Items (Schedules K and K-1)	Partnership Ordinary Income (or Loss) (Page 1 of Form 1065)
Sales minus cost of goods sold (gross profit)		X
Salaries and wage expense		X
Guaranteed payments to partners[a]	X	X
Tax, bad debt, and repair expenses		X
Charitable contributions	X	
Investment interest income and expense	X	
Foreign income taxes paid or accrued	X	
Specially allocated income, deduction, loss, gain, and credit items that differ from the general profit and loss allocation ratios	X	
Tax-exempt interest income	X	
Capital gains and losses	X	
Sec. 1245 and 1250 depreciation recapture		X
Sec. 1231 gains or losses	X	
Tax credits	X	
Tax preference items	X	

[a] Guaranteed payments appear in both columns because the partnership deducts them to arrive at partnership ordinary income (or loss), and they are reported separately and are taxable to the partner who receives the payments.

As indicated earlier in Chapters I11 and I16, Rev. Proc. 2000-22 permits small businesses, that would normally be required to use the accrual method of accounting for tax purposes for the purchase and sale of merchandise, now to be able to use the cash method of accounting.[16] As such, the small business can also avoid the need to maintain invento-

---
[16] Rev. Proc. 2000-22, I.R.B. 2000-20, 1008. This Revenue Procedure was modified and superseded by Rev. Proc. 2001-10.

SPECIAL ALLOCATIONS

ries. Corporations eligible for this special exception generally need to have gross receipts of $1 million or less for all prior tax years. Rev. Proc. 2000-22 applies to partnerships and S corporations.

SPECIAL ALLOCATIONS

Section 704 permits partners some latitude to decide how income, deductions, losses, and credits are to be allocated among the individual partners. Special allocations are unique to partnerships and permit flexible arrangements among the partners for sharing specific income and loss items. A partner's distributive share of such items generally is determined by the partnership agreement. However, the special allocation provisions restrict the partners' freedom to shift tax benefits among individual partners. For example, the special allocation must have substantial economic effect (e.g., it cannot be a tax sham). In addition, a special allocation must be made for property contributed by the partners when determining the allocation of depreciation deductions and the amount of gain or loss recognized when the partnership eventually sells the property. Essentially, the allocation of the depreciation deductions and the amount of recognized gain or loss must take into account the difference between the partnership's basis for the contributed property and the property's FMV at the time of the contribution.

> **ADDITIONAL COMMENT**
> In general, partnership income or loss is allocated according to the provisions of the partnership agreement. The partnership agreement can be amended any time up to the due date for filing the partnership return.

EXAMPLE I17-9 ▶ Clay and Dana formed an equal partnership five years ago. Clay contributed cash of $100,000, and Dana contributed land having a $60,000 adjusted basis and a $100,000 FMV. The partnership's basis for the land is $60,000 (Dana's carryover basis). If the partnership sells the land in the current year for $110,000, it recognizes $50,000 ($110,000 − $60,000) of gain. If a special allocation of the gain were not required, $25,000 of the gain would be allocated to each Clay and Dana based on their equal profit and loss sharing ratios. The special allocation rules, however, require $45,000 of the gain to be allocated to Dana ($40,000 appreciation accruing before her transfer of property to the partnership plus $5,000, which is one-half of the $10,000 of post-contribution appreciation). The remaining $5,000 of post-contribution gain is allocated to Clay [($110,000 − $100,000) × 0.50]. ◀

ALLOCATION OF PARTNERSHIP INCOME, DEDUCTIONS, LOSSES, AND CREDITS TO PARTNERS

If any partner's interest in the partnership changes during the year (e.g., due to the sale of a partnership interest or the entry of a new partner who contributes property to the partnership in exchange for an interest), all of the partners must determine their distributive share of the partnership income, deductions, losses, and credits according to their varying interests in the partnership during the year.[17] Retroactive allocations (e.g., an allocation of deductions or losses incurred before admission of a new partner to the partnership) may not be made to new partners admitted during the partnership's tax year.

WHAT WOULD YOU DO IN THIS SITUATION?

Alex and Alicia plan to form a partnership with each partner making an equal capital contribution to the partnership. The partnership agreement will specify that the partners share equally in partnership profits and losses. Among other things, the partnership will invest in taxable and tax-exempt bonds. The partners expect the taxable and tax-exempt bonds each to generate $1,000 of interest per year. For the next several years, Alex expects to be in the 15% tax bracket and Alicia expects to be in the 39.6% tax bracket. Without a special allocation, each partner would be allocated $500 of each type interest. Instead, however, they want a special allocation in the partnership agreement that allocates (1) all $1,000 of taxable interest to Alex plus $75 of tax-exempt interest to compensate him for additional taxes on the extra $500 of taxable interest and (2) the remaining $925 of tax-exempt interest to Alicia. Alex and Alicia seek your advice on the propriety of this special allocation. Hint: Prepare a schedule of after-tax interest income to the partners with and without the special allocation.

---

[17] Sec. 706(d)(1).

EXAMPLE I17-10 ▶ Colleen and Dan are equal partners in the CDE Partnership, which uses the calendar year as its tax year. On December 1 of the current year, Ed contributes $50,000 cash for a one-third interest in the partnership. The partnership reports a $9,000 ordinary loss for the current tax year ending on December 31. The partners must report their shares of the partnership loss based on their varying interests. A daily allocation of the loss (assuming all months have 30 days) takes place as follows:[18]

Partner		Loss Allocation
Colleen	1/2 × $9,000 × 11/12	$4,125
	1/3 × $9,000 × 1/12	250
	Colleen's share	$4,375
Dan	Same as Colleen	4,375
Ed	1/3 × $9,000 × 1/12	250
	Total allocation	$9,000

Ed's loss is limited to his ratable (one-third) share of the loss incurred after his entry into the partnership, or $250. This result occurs even if the partnership agreement provides that Ed would receive one-third of all losses for the entire year. ◀

BASIS ADJUSTMENTS FOR OPERATING ITEMS

KEY POINT
Although the basis of C corporation stock is not likely to change over time, the basis of a partnership interest is subject to annual adjustment.

Under Sec. 705, the basis of each partnership interest is adjusted to reflect the partner's share of income and deduction items. This basis adjustment is necessary to ensure the single level of taxation of partnerships. Basis adjustments for income and deduction items are made currently regardless of whether an actual distribution is made to the partners. In addition, each partner's basis in the partnership interest is adjusted for capital contributions, withdrawals, and changes in liabilities that occur during the year. Each partner's basis is increased by the partner's distributive share of partnership ordinary income and separately stated income and gain items. The basis of the partnership interest is increased whether the income is taxable to the partners or is tax-exempt.[19]

A partner's basis is decreased (but not below zero) by partnership distributions and by the partner's distributive share of partnership ordinary loss, separately stated losses and deductions, and expenditures that are nondeductible in computing partnership ordinary income or loss (e.g., charitable contributions made by the partnership).

EXAMPLE I17-11 ▶ David and Edith form a partnership in the current year and share profits and losses equally. The partnership agreement provides for no special allocations. The following transactions occur during the year that affect David's basis in his partnership interest:

▶ David contributes land having a $60,000 basis and a $100,000 FMV in exchange for his initial partnership interest.

▶ The partnership liabilities increase from zero to $100,000 by the end of the tax year.

▶ The partnership earns $50,000 of ordinary income.

▶ The partnership earns $5,000 of tax-exempt interest income.

▶ The partnership incurs $10,000 of capital losses.

▶ David withdraws $20,000 in cash from the partnership.

▶ The partnership makes a $15,000 charitable contribution.

---

[18] Regulation Sec. 1.706-1(c)(2) provides for alternative allocation methods. The partners may elect to use the interim closing method as an alternative to the pro rata allocation method used in Example I17-10.

[19] If the partnership includes oil and gas properties, an increase in basis is made for the excess of percentage depletion claimed over the basis of the property subject to depletion, and a reduction in basis is made for the depletion deduction claimed under Sec. 611.

David's year-end basis is determined as follows:

Capital contribution of land (adjusted basis)		$ 60,000
Plus: Share of the increase in partnership liabilities ($100,000 × 0.50)		50,000
Share of ordinary income ($50,000 × 0.50)		25,000
Share of tax-exempt interest income ($5,000 × 0.50)		2,500
Minus: Share of capital losses ($10,000 × 0.50)		(5,000)
Withdrawals by David		(20,000)
Share of charitable contribution ($15,000 × 0.50)		(7,500)
David's basis at the end of the current year		$105,000

STOP & THINK

Question: Why do partners increase the basis of their partnership interests by their share of tax-exempt income?

Solution: Increasing the basis ensures that the tax-exempt income will retain its tax-free character when the income is subsequently distributed in the form of cash.

LIMITATIONS ON LOSSES AND RESTORATION OF BASIS

Although a partner's distributive share of the partnership's ordinary loss and any separately stated losses and deductions pass through to the partner, Sec. 704(d) limits deductibility of the losses to the partner's adjusted basis in his or her partnership interest as determined at the end of the partnership's tax year.[20] All positive and negative adjustments referred to in Example I17-11 (except the loss) are made before the limitation is considered. If the loss limitation rule did not apply, the partner's interest could have a negative basis. Any unused losses and deductions carry over indefinitely and are allowed in subsequent years when the partner again has a positive basis in her partnership interest.

EXAMPLE I17-12 ▶ Ellen, who has a 50% interest in the EF Partnership, has a $10,000 basis in her partnership interest at the end of 2001 (before deducting her share of losses). The EF Partnership incurs a $50,000 ordinary loss in 2001. Ellen's share of the loss is $25,000 ($50,000 × 0.50), but Ellen can deduct only $10,000 in 2001. The remaining $15,000 of loss carries over to 2002. The deductible loss reduces Ellen's partnership basis to zero at the end of 2001. ◀

EXAMPLE I17-13 ▶ Assume the same facts as in Example I17-12, except that in 2002 Ellen's share of partnership liabilities increases by $5,000, Ellen's share of 2002 ordinary income is $5,000, and Ellen makes a $5,000 additional capital contribution. Ellen's basis increases by a total of $15,000 due to the three items. Therefore, she deducts the $15,000 loss carryover from 2001 in 2002. The deduction reduces Ellen's partnership basis to zero at the end of 2002. A zero tax basis for a partnership interest does not necessarily mean that the interest is worthless. The FMV of the partnership's net assets or their financial accounting book value, nevertheless, may be substantial. ◀

BOOK-TAX ACCOUNTING COMPARISON
Although a partner's basis in the partnership may not go below zero, a partner's book capital account (equity) may be negative.

Topic Review I17-2 summarizes the special allocation and basis rules.

PASSIVE ACTIVITY LOSS LIMITATIONS. The passive activity loss limitations that were discussed in Chapter I8 apply to partners who do not materially participate in the business of the partnership. The passive activity loss rules are applied at the *partner* level, that is, each partner must determine whether he or she materially participates in the partnership. If a loss is determined to be passive, a partner may not deduct the loss against either earned income or portfolio income, but may deduct the loss only against other passive income. These rules are highly significant and play a major role in determining the deductibility of partnership losses by partners.

---

[20] Two other rules also restrict the deductibility of losses. The at-risk rules contained in Sec. 465 limit loss deductions to the partner's at-risk basis. In addition, Sec. 469 contains passive activity loss rules that disallow virtually all net passive activity losses. These restrictions are discussed in Chapter I8 of this text and in Chapter C9 of *Prentice Hall's Federal Taxation: Corporations, Partnerships, Estates, and Trusts.*

Topic Review I17-2

Allocation Rules and Basis Adjustments

- When a partner contributes property to a partnership, any unrecognized gain or loss must be allocated to the contributing partner when the partnership sells the property.
- Partnership income, gains, deductions, losses, and credits are allocated to the partners on a daily basis based on each partner's interest in the partnership.
- Special allocations of income, gains, deductions, losses, and credits are permitted as long as they have substantial economic effect.
- Basis in the partnership interest is increased by the partner's share of ordinary income, separately stated income items, and tax-exempt income. Basis is reduced by a partner's share of ordinary loss, separately stated deductions and losses, and nondeductible expenditures. Basis also is adjusted for capital contributions, withdrawals, and changes in partnership liabilities. Basis cannot be decreased below zero.
- Ordinary losses and separately stated deduction and loss items that exceed a partner's basis carry over indefinitely until the partner again has a positive basis in his or her partnership interest.

TRANSACTIONS BETWEEN A PARTNER AND THE PARTNERSHIP

Sometimes a partner may independently engage in transactions with the partnership. For example, a partner may sell property to the partnership rather than make a capital contribution of the property. In such transactions, the partner is treated as an outside independent party.[21] Thus, a partner recognizes gain or loss on the sale of property to the partnership, and the partnership receives a cost basis equal to the amount of consideration paid. Because the partner and the partnership are not truly independent parties, abuse of this provision is possible. For example, the partners might want to recognize losses by selling certain assets at a loss to the partnership while still retaining those assets in the partnership. Alternatively, a partner may wish to sell certain depreciable business assets (Sec. 1231 property) at a gain taxable to the partner at favorable capital gains rates while the partnership receives a stepped-up FMV basis in the assets for depreciation purposes. Section 707(b) forestalls such potential abuses by disallowing losses and by providing ordinary income (rather than capital gain) treatment under the following circumstances:

ADDITIONAL COMMENT
Defining a partner's interest in a partnership is not always an easy matter. These determinations become difficult if a partner has varying interests in different types of income.

- Losses are disallowed on sales or exchanges between a partner and the partnership if the partner owns more than a 50% interest in the partnership. A loss also is disallowed if a sale or exchange of property occurs between two partnerships in which the same partners own more than a 50% interest. The Sec. 267 constructive ownership rules apply to determine whether the 50% test is met. If the purchaser (i.e., the partner or the partnership) of the property later sells the asset to an outsider, the gain recognized is reduced by the previously disallowed loss.
- Gains are treated as ordinary income (rather than a capital gain) if the partner owns (directly or indirectly) more than a 50% interest in the partnership and if the exchanged asset is not a capital asset in the transferee's hands.[22] Again, the Sec. 267 constructive ownership rules apply.

EXAMPLE I17-14 ▶ Ira has a 60% interest in the HI Partnership. Ira sells land with a $100,000 adjusted basis to the partnership for its $60,000 FMV. Ira does not recognize the $40,000 ($60,000 − $100,000) loss, and the basis of the land to the partnership is $60,000 because Ira owns more than a 50% interest in the partnership. If the partnership later sells the land to an outsider for $110,000, the partnership recognizes only $10,000 of gain because the $50,000 ($110,000 − $60,000) realized gain is reduced by the $40,000 previously disallowed loss. ◀

---

[21] Rules for transactions between a partner and the partnership are found in Sec. 707.
[22] Gains also are converted to ordinary income if the sale is between two partnerships in which the same partners owns directly or indirectly more than a 50% interest in the partnership. In determining the 50% ownership rule, the Sec. 267 constructive ownership rules apply.

EXAMPLE I17-15 ▶ Helen has a 90% interest in the HI Partnership. Helen sells a building used in her business with a $60,000 adjusted basis to the HI Partnership for $100,000. After the purchase, the partnership continues to use the building in its business activities. Before the sale Helen had taken straight-line depreciation. Therefore, had Helen instead sold the building to an outsider, she would have recognized a $40,000 Sec. 1231 gain. Net Sec. 1231 gain is treated as capital gain so that the taxpayer may use the gain to offset capital losses. However, Helen's $40,000 gain is treated as ordinary income because the building is sold to a partnership in which she owns a more than 50% interest, and the building is not a capital asset to the partnership. The ordinary income does not qualify for a reduced tax rate, nor can it be used to offset capital losses. HI Partnership's basis in the building is $100,000. ◀

ADDITIONAL COMMENT
A partner generally has to make estimated tax payments to cover the income and self-employment taxes on a guaranteed payment.

GUARANTEED PAYMENTS. Even though a partner does not qualify as an employee of the partnership for tax purposes, the partnership agreement may provide for fixed salary payments that are not based on partnership income. Generally, the partnership deducts such payments as guaranteed payments to arrive at partnership ordinary income. They are includible in the partner's gross income in the tax year received. Guaranteed payments also can be made in lieu of interest payments on the amount of the partner's capital investment. Such payments also are deductible by the partnership to arrive at partnership ordinary income and are includible in the partner's gross income.

EXAMPLE I17-16 ▶ José owns a 40% interest in the JKL Partnership. The partnership agreement provides that José is to receive a fixed salary of $20,000 plus 10% interest on his average capital balance. No other guaranteed payments are made to the other partners. If his average capital balance for the year is $50,000, $5,000 (0.10 × $50,000) of interest would be paid as a guaranteed payment. If partnership ordinary income is $10,000 before deducting the guaranteed payments, the partnership ordinary loss is $15,000 ($10,000 income − $25,000 of guaranteed payments to José). José reports $25,000 of ordinary income for the year, consisting of the $20,000 salary and the $5,000 interest. He also reports a $6,000 ($15,000 × 0.40) ordinary loss. The other partners report in total a $9,000 ($15,000 × 0.60) ordinary loss. ◀

OBJECTIVE 3

Understand the tax implications (to the partnership and its partners) of distributions to partners

PARTNERSHIP DISTRIBUTIONS

A distribution of cash or property from the partnership to a partner generally is treated as a tax-free return of capital. This treatment closely parallels the tax-free consequences resulting from a capital contribution of property made in exchange for a partnership interest under Sec. 721.

A distribution may result in a reduction of a partner's capital interest in the partnership. This type of distribution is called as a **nonliquidating distribution**. The partnership may desire to liquidate a partner's entire interest due to retirement, death, or other business reasons. These distributions are called **liquidating distributions**. In such cases, the liquidating distribution is treated as a sale or exchange of the partnership interest.

Due to the complex nature of this topic, this chapter includes only an abbreviated coverage of these materials, and the discussion of liquidating distributions is omitted. Comprehensive coverage of these topics is included in Chapter C9 of *Prentice Hall's Federal Taxation: Corporations, Partnerships, Estates, and Trusts*.

KEY POINT
The adjusted basis of a property distributed by a partnership generally measures the taxability of the distribution. The difference between the property's FMV and basis can be important, however, in determining the property's basis when multiple properties are distributed by the partnership.

SELF-STUDY QUESTION
Carl, a partner with a $10,000 basis in the ABC Partnership, receives property having a FMV of $20,000 and a basis of $8,000 in a nonliquidating distribution. How much gain does Carl recognize?

NONLIQUIDATING DISTRIBUTIONS. As a general rule, neither the partner nor the partnership recognize gain or loss if the partnership distributes money or other property to the partner.[23] Such nonliquidating distributions generally are treated as tax-free returns of capital. If the amount of money received by the partner exceeds the partner's basis for the partnership interest, however, the partner recognizes gain to the extent of the excess.[24] If property other than money (e.g., land and machinery) is distributed to the partner, the basis of the partnership interest is reduced by the adjusted basis of the distributed assets. As previously mentioned, no gain or loss is recognized by the partnership or by the distributee partner even if the adjusted basis of the distributed property exceeds the partner's

---

[23] Distribution rules are found in Sec. 731.
[24] Exceptions apply if unrealized receivables and inventory items, referred to as Sec. 751 assets, remain in the partnership or are distributed to the partner. In such instances, the partnership and/or the partner may recognize gain on the distribution.

ANSWER
None; a partner recognizes gain only when the amount of cash distributed exceeds the basis of the partnership interest.

basis in his or her partnership interest. In this case, the basis of the property to the partner is reduced to equal the basis of the partnership interest. If the partnership distributes both money and property, the money distribution reduces the basis of the partnership interest before any adjustment is made for the property distribution.

EXAMPLE I17-17 ▶ Jane receives a nonliquidating distribution of $10,000 in money from the JK Partnership. At the distribution date, Jane's basis in her partnership interest is $8,000. Of the $10,000 distribution, $8,000 is a tax-free return of capital, which reduces Jane's basis to zero. The remaining $2,000 is a capital gain.[25] ◀

EXAMPLE I17-18 ▶ Jeff receives a nonliquidating distribution of land having a $6,000 adjusted basis and a $10,000 FMV from the JK Partnership. When the distribution is made, Jeff's basis in his partnership interest is $8,000. Neither Jeff nor the partnership recognize gain or loss when the distribution is made. Jeff's basis in his partnership interest is reduced by $6,000 (the adjusted basis of the property distributed). Thus, Jeff's basis in his partnership interest is $2,000 ($8,000 − $6,000) following the distribution. His basis in the land is $6,000. ◀

EXAMPLE I17-19 ▶ Jean receives a nonliquidating distribution of $5,000 cash plus land having a $6,000 adjusted basis and a $10,000 FMV from the JK Partnership. When the distribution is made, Jean's basis in her partnership interest is $8,000. Her basis initially is reduced by the $5,000 money distribution to reflect its tax-free return of capital treatment. The remaining $3,000 basis in her partnership interest is allocated to the land, and neither Jane nor the partnership recognize gain or loss on the distribution. Jean's basis for her partnership interest is zero after the distribution. ◀

Topic Review I17-3 summarizes the gain or loss recognition rules relating to nonliquidating distributions.

SALE OF A PARTNERSHIP INTEREST

RECOGNITION OF GAIN OR LOSS. A partnership interest is a capital asset similar to a corporate security. It may be sold or exchanged as existing partners retire or withdraw from the buisness. The remaining partners may acquire the selling partner's interest, or the interest may be sold to an outsider.

ADDITIONAL COMMENT
A sale of a partnership interest is treated as a sale even though the sale results in the termination of the partnership. For example, if one partner in a two-person partnership sells his or her interest to the other partner, the transaction is treated as a sale.

Capital gain or loss generally arises from the sale of a partnership interest because the interest is a capital asset in the hands of the selling partner. For most noncorporate partners, the long-term capital gain is taxed at a 20% maximum rate. In this case, a partnership is viewed as an entity separate and distinct from the partners. However, in some

---

Topic Review I17-3

Nonliquidating Distributions

▶ Generally, neither the partner nor the partnership recognize gain on loss when a nonliquidating distribution of money or other property is made. However, if the distributed money exceeds the distributee partner's basis in the partnership interest, the partner recognizes gain on the excess. For this purpose, any release from partnership liabilities is treated as a distribution of money to the partner.

▶ The partner's basis in the partnership interest is reduced (but not below zero) by the amount of money distributed. If the partnership distributes other property, the following two points apply.

▶ If the adjusted basis of distributed property does not exceed the partner's basis in the partnership interest (after reduction for money distributions), the basis of the distributed property carries over to the partner, and the partner's basis in the partnership interest is reduced by the distributed property's adjusted basis.

▶ If the adjusted basis of distributed property exceeds the partner's basis in the partnership interest (after reduction for money distributions), the distributed property takes a basis equal to the partner's remaining basis in the partnership interest, and the partner's basis in the partnership interest is reduced to zero.

---

[25] A portion of this gain may be converted to ordinary income if Jane's share of any Sec. 751 assets (i.e., unrealized receivables and substantially appreciated inventory items) held by the partnership changes as a result of the cash distribution.

circumstances a partner is considered to own a proportionate interest in each partnership asset (i.e., the partnership is viewed as a conduit), which results in part capital gain and part ordinary income treatment depending on the character of the underlying assets.

Under the general rules of Sec. 741, gain or loss is measured by the difference between the amount realized and the selling partner's adjusted basis in the partnership interest. The amount realized includes the partner's share of partnership liabilities from which the partner is released as a result of the sale. The basis of the partnership interest also is adjusted by the selling partner's distributive share of partnership income or loss, which must be computed up to the sale date.

EXAMPLE I17-20 ▶ On October 1, Jesse sells his interest in the JK Partnership to Paula, an outsider, for $150,000 cash plus the release from $30,000 of partnership liabilities. Jesse's basis in his partnership interest is $74,000 before taking into account his distributive share of partnership income for the period ending on the sale date and his share of any increase in partnership liabilities during the same period. For the current year, Jesse's share of the partnership income for the period up to the date of sale is $20,000, and his share of increased partnership liabilities is $6,000. Thus, Jesse's basis in his partnership interest is $100,000 ($74,000 basis on January 1 + $20,000 share of partnership income + $6,000 share of increased partnership liabilities). The amount realized on the sale is $180,000 ($150,000 selling price + $30,000 liabilities). Thus, Jesse recognizes an $80,000 gain on the sale, which is capital gain unless ordinary income is triggered under Sec. 751. (See Example I17-21 for a discussion of Sec. 751.) ◀

SECTION 751 ORDINARY INCOME TREATMENT. Ordinary income rather than capital gain treatment may result under Sec. 751 if a partnership has unrealized receivables or inventory items when a partnership interest is sold. A sale of Sec. 751 assets by the partnership results in ordinary income, which eventually flows through to the partners. Thus, this rule prevents a partner from converting ordinary income into capital gain by selling or liquidating the partnership interest. Section 751 assets include the following:

▶ Inventory items include the traditional definition of inventory plus any other property except capital assets or Sec. 1231 property

▶ Unrealized receivables for services rendered or goods delivered, such as accounts receivable of a cash method partnership (i.e., receivables having a zero basis)

▶ Unrealized receivables also include Sec. 1245 and 1250 depreciation recapture potential (i.e., amounts that would be recaptured as ordinary income if Sec. 1245 or 1250 property were sold by the partnership) or recapture potential under another Code section (for example, Secs. 617(d), 1252, 1254, 1278, or 1283)

EXAMPLE I17-21 ▶ Joy's basis in her partnership interest is $100,000, and the amount realized on its sale is $180,000, which results in an $80,000 gain. The cash method of accounting partnership has accounts receivable with a zero basis and a $30,000 FMV. Joy's share of these receivables is $10,000. Thus, $10,000 of the amount realized on the sale of the partnership interest is attributed to Joy's share of the accounts receivable. Because her share of the receivables has a zero basis and a $10,000 FMV, $10,000 ($10,000 − $0) of the gain is ordinary income to Joy as though she sold her share of the receivables. The remaining $70,000 ($170,000 − $100,000) of gain from the sale of Joy's partnership interest is a capital gain. ◀

OTHER SPECIAL TREATMENTS. As discussed in Chapter I5, IRC Sec. 1(h) provides for different tax rates that apply to gains recognized on certain property transactions involving a partnership. These rates are in addition to the conversion of capital gains into ordinary income that takes place under Sec. 751. First, a 28% rate applies to gain on the sale of collectibles and small business (Sec. 1202) stock. Second, a 25% rate applies to unrecaptured Sec. 1250 gain. These two special rules are in lieu of the 20% rate that generally applies to capital gains of a taxpayer whose taxable income is taxed at a 28% or higher rate.

OPTIONAL BASIS ADJUSTMENTS

Section 754 provides an election that permits a basis adjustment to the assets of a continuing partnership when a partnership interest is sold or exchanged or when certain distributions take place. This election, which is made at the partnership level, prevents inequities that might arise because the basis of partnership assets are not adjusted under general partnership tax accounting rules. The election is binding for all future years unless the IRS consents to a revocation of the election.

> **EXAMPLE I17-22** ▶ Jim acquires Antonio's one-third partnership interest in the ABC Partnership for $40,000. The partnership's balance sheet on the sale date includes the following:

	Adjusted Basis	FMV
Assets:		
Cash	$20,000	$ 20,000
Accounts receivable	10,000	10,000
Inventory	15,000	20,000
Depreciable assets	15,000	85,000
Total	$60,000	$135,000
Liabilities	$15,000	$ 15,000
Capital:		
Antonio	15,000	40,000
Beth	15,000	40,000
Carmen	15,000	40,000
Total	$60,000	$135,000

Jim's basis adjustment equals the difference between his basis for the partnership interest of $45,000 ($40,000 amount paid + $5,000 of ABC's liabilities) and his $20,000 ($60,000 × 1/3) basis in the underlying partnership assets. Thus, if the partnership makes the optional basis adjustment election with respect to the sale or if a previous election is in effect on the sale date, Jim steps up the basis of his share of partnership assets from $20,000 to $45,000. The election does not affect the remaining partners' underlying basis in partnership assets.

The election would be favorable only to Jim because his share of the appreciated partnership assets (inventories and depreciable assets) would be stepped up by $25,000, based on the relative amounts of appreciation for each asset. Jim then would be entitled to additional depreciation deductions on the increased basis. In addition, Jim would receive an increased basis for calculating gain on the sale of the inventory. If this election were not in effect and the inventory were sold, Jim would report $1,667 (1/3 × $5,000) gain from the sale of his one-third interest in the inventory even though he paid $6,657 (1/3 × $20,000) for such interest. ◀

ADDITIONAL COMMENT

A partner's basis in the partnership interest is referred to as the "outside basis," while his or her share of basis in the underlying partnership assets is referred to as the "inside basis."

Once the election is in effect, its application may be detrimental because a downward adjustment is required if the amount paid for a partnership interest is less than the adjusted basis of the assets (i.e., the assets have declined rather than appreciated in value).

ELECTING LARGE PARTNERSHIPS

The 1997 Tax Act added a new election for large partnerships. Partnerships meeting the large partnership definition can elect to be taxed as an "Electing Large Partnership". Four qualifications are outlined in Sec. 775 that must be met for a partnership to be taxed as an Electing Large Partnership. The partnership

ADDITIONAL COMMENT

The Electing Large Partnership provisions were enacted for two basic reasons; (1) to ease the reporting burden of partners who own a relatively small interest in a large partnership, and (2) to ease the computer-matching effort of the IRS.

▶ Must not be a service partnership
▶ Must not be engaged in commodity trading
▶ Must have at least 100 partners
▶ Must file an election to be taxed as an electing large partnership.

Sec. 775(b) defines a service partnership as one in which substantially all the partners perform substantial services in connection with the partnership activities or the partners are retired but in the past performed substantial services in connection with the partnership's activities. For example, a partnership that performs accounting services is prevented from being an electing large partnership. In addition, the partnership must have 100 or more partners excluding those partners who provide substantial services in connection with the partnership's business activities.

The calculation of an Electing Large Partnership's taxable income includes separately stated income and other income. However, the items that are separately stated under Sec.

772(a) for an Electing Large Partnership are much different from other partnerships. For example, under Sec. 773(b)(3), miscellaneous itemized deductions for an Electing Large Partnership are combined at the partnership level and subject to a 70% disallowance at the partnership level. After the 70% disallowance, the remaining miscellaneous itemized deductions are combined with other income items and passed through to the partner. Because the miscellaneous itemized deductions are combined with other partnership income, the deductions are not subject to the 2% nondeductible floor at the partner level. Charitable contributions that are made by an Electing Large Partnership are subject to a 10% of taxable income limit under Sec. 773(b)(2) that is similar to the limit applying to a C corporation.

Section 773(a)(3) requires an Electing Large Partnership to apply the Sec. 179 expensing deduction limitation at only the entity level instead of at both the partnership and partner levels. Under Sec. 773(a)(4), Sec. 1231 gains and losses are netted at the partnership level. Net Sec. 1231 losses are reported with other taxable income or loss and net Sec. 1231 gains are reported with capital gains and losses. The capital gains and losses are netted at the partnership level with only a single, net number reported to the partners. The capital gain or loss is treated as long-term, unless the net is a short-term capital gain, in which case it gets combined with ordinary income. Many of the partnership's tax credits are combined at the partnership level into a single number with the exception of the four credit categories that are listed below as being separately reported.

The separate items reported to the partners under Sec. 772(a) include:

▶ Taxable income or loss from passive loss limitation activities
▶ Taxable income or loss from other partnership activities
▶ Net capital gain or loss from passive loss limitation activities
▶ Net capital gain or loss from other partnership activities
▶ Tax exempt interest
▶ All net alternative minimum tax adjustments are computed separately for passive loss limitation activities and other activities.
▶ Separate credit passthroughs are used for only the: general credits, low income housing credit, rehabilitation credit, foreign income taxes, and producing fuel from a nonconventional source.
▶ Any other item the IRS determines should be separately stated.

EXAMPLE I17-23 ▶ The JLK Partnership makes an election to be an Electing Large Partnership. The partnership reports the following activities for 2001. It has no passive activities.

Ordinary income	$120,000
Sec 1231 gain	60,000
Tax-exempt income	12,000
Net long-term capital loss	40,000
Charitable contributions	30,000

JLK Partnership reports the following results to its partners:

Ordinary income	$106,000
Net long-term capital gain	20,000
Tax-exempt income	12,000

The partnership's net Sec. 1231 gain ($60,000) is treated as a long-term capital gain and offsets the net long-term capital loss ($40,000), thereby producing a $20,000 net long-term capital gain. Ordinary income is reduced only by the charitable contribution. However, the 10% contribution deduction limit restricts the deduction to $14,000 [($120,000 + $20,000) × 0.10]. The remaining $16,000 of contributions are carried forward. The partnership's ordinary income is $106,000 ($120,000 − $14,000). ◀

An Electing Large Partnership must provide a Schedule K-1 to its partners on or before March 15 following the close of the partnership tax year without regard to when the partnership tax return is due. Partnerships other than Electing Large Partnerships only need to provide the Schedule K-1 by the due date for the partnership's tax return. The March 15 date is different from the April 15 deadline that is otherwise applied to calendar year partnerships. Unlike other partnerships, an Electing Large Partnership does not terminate for tax purposes when a substantial change in ownership occurs. An Electing Large Partnership terminates only when the partners cease to conduct any business, financial operation or venture using the partnership form.

Partners of an Electing Large Partnership must report all items of partnership income, gain, loss, or deduction the same way that the partnership reports the item. Deviations from the required reporting will be "corrected" by the IRS in the same say that a math mistake is corrected. Electing Large Partnerships are subject to different audit rules than other partnerships. An Electing Large Partnership is subject to special audit rules and will be audited only at the partnership level.

PARTNERSHIP ELECTIONS

TAX YEAR RESTRICTIONS

When a partnership's tax year ends, each partner's distributive share of the partnership income (including guaranteed payments) is reported on each partner's Form 1040 (or Form 1120 for corporate partners). Thus, if the partnership's tax year ends on January 31, 2001 and the partners report on a calendar-year basis ending December 31, 2000, none of the partnership income for 2000 is reported on the partners' federal income tax returns until 2001. This situation results in an effective 11-month income deferral.

EXAMPLE I17-24 ▶ Kim is admitted to the ABC Partnership on April 1, 2000. Kim is a calendar-year taxpayer who previously was employed by the partnership from January 1, 2000, until her admission to the partnership on April 1, 2000. Kim's earnings as an employee for the three-month period are $8,000. She receives monthly distributions of $3,000 for the last nine months of the year that represent draws against her share of estimated partnership income for the year ending January 31, 2001. ABC's tax year ends on January 31, 2001, and Kim's distributive share of the partnership income for the period April 1, 2000, through January 31, 2001, is $60,000. Because distributions to a partner are treated as made on the last day of the partnership's tax year (January 31, 2001) and because the partnership tax year ends after December 31, 2000, Kim's income for 2000 is only $8,000 (her salary as an employee for the first three months of 2000). Kim's $60,000 share of the partnership income for the year ending January 31, 2001, is reported on her 2001 tax return. ◀

ADDITIONAL COMMENT

Partnerships having only individual partners usually have calendar tax years. The three-step test most often comes into play when the partnership has one or more fiscal year corporate partners.

In general, partnerships must use the calendar year. However, partnerships may elect a fiscal year if certain requirements are met. To prevent or minimize opportunities for the deferral of partnership income as illustrated in Example I17-24, Sec. 706 provides the following requirements on the selection of a tax year by the partners and the partnership:

▶ A partnership uses the tax year of the one or more partners who own a majority interest (more than 50%) in the partnership. This majority interest tax year rule is determined on the first day of the partnership's existing tax year.

▶ If partners having a majority interest in the partnership do not have the same tax year, the partnership uses the same tax year as *all* of its principal partners (a **principal partner** has a 5% or greater interest in the partnership).

▶ If the principal partners do not have the same tax year and no majority of its partners have the same tax year, the partnership uses the tax year that allows the "least aggregate deferral." (See Chapter C9 of *Prentice Hall's Federal Taxation: Corporations, Partnerships, Estates, and Trusts* for a detailed discussion of this requirement.)

EXAMPLE I17-25 ▶ ABC Partnership has one corporate partner, Ace Corporation, with a fiscal year-end of March 31. Ace Corporation has a 25% interest in the ABC Partnership. The other partners are individuals with a calendar year for tax purposes, none of whom has a 5% or more interest in the ABC Partnership. ABC Partnership must use a calendar year for tax purposes (the tax year of the individual partners who in aggregate own a majority interest). ◀

SELF-STUDY QUESTION

Ace and Buckeye, corporate partners in the ABC Partnership, have September 30 year-ends. Craig, an individual partner, uses the calendar year. Ace, Buckeye, and Craig have equal one-third interests in the partnership. What tax year must the newly-organized partnership adopt?

ANSWER

It must adopt a September 30 year-end because it must use the tax year of the two partners who own a majority (66 2/3%) interest.

The rules given above have three exceptions. First, a partnership with all calendar-year partners can adopt or change to a fiscal year if it can convince the IRS that a business purpose exists for the choice. For example, if the partnership owns a ski resort, it probably could make a good case for closing the partnership tax year on May 31, shortly after the ski season ends, rather than on December 31, which is in the middle of the ski season. However, the IRS must agree that a valid business purpose exists for using the fiscal year.

Second, a partnership may adopt or change to a fiscal year-end if the business recognizes 25% or more of its annual gross receipts in the last two months of the fiscal year, with this being the case for three consecutive 12-month periods. Third, a partnership may elect a maximum 3-month deferral if it agrees to make a special tax payment each year that approximates the income deferral benefit.[26] The net effect of these rules is to restrict any deferral opportunities for partnerships in choosing their tax accounting year-end.

(See Chapter I11 of this text and Chapter C9 of *Prentice Hall's Federal Taxation, Corporations, Partnerships, Estates, and Trusts* for a detailed discussion of partnership tax years.)

CASH METHOD OF ACCOUNTING RESTRICTIONS

A partnership may elect with its first tax return any method of accounting that clearly reflects income. Unlike the tax year election, partnerships may elect an accounting method without regard to the methods used by its partners. The two most commonly used methods are the cash method and the accrual method. Under the *cash method*, the partnership reports income as received and expenses when actually paid. Under the *accrual method*, the partnership reports income when earned even if the cash has not yet been received. Similarly, the partnership reports expenses when incurred, not when actually paid.

Congress understands that the cash method does not always reflect the economic realities of a business. However, Congress also concedes that the cash method is much simpler to use than the accrual method. Because of its simplicity, the cash method still is an option, but it has been restricted by Congress.

Partnerships that have a C corporation for a partner and that have average gross receipts exceeding $5 million during the prior three years are not allowed to use the cash method of accounting.[27] Tax shelters, no matter what their size, may not use the cash method under any circumstances. (See Chapter I11 for a discussion of permissible accounting methods.)

TAXATION OF S CORPORATIONS

OBJECTIVE 4

Understand the requirements for electing and maintaining S corporation status

QUALIFICATION REQUIREMENTS

To qualify as an S corporation, a business must meet the definition of a small business corporation.[28] To meet this definition, the entity[29]

▶ Must be a domestic (U.S.) corporation rather than a foreign corporation

▶ Must not be an ineligible corporation[30]

▶ Must not have more than 75 shareholders[31]

---

[26] Secs. 444 and 7519.
[27] Sec. 448(a)(2). Section 448(b) provides exceptions for farming businesses and certain qualified personal service corporations.
[28] These qualification rules are in Sec. 1361.
[29] An S corporation does not have to be a corporation. Under the check-the-box regulations that took effect on January 1, 1997, an S election can be made by a noncorporate entity that elects to be taxed as a corporation. See Reg. Sec. 301.7701-1, -2, and -3 that describes the tax consequences of a noncorporate entity electing to be taxed under the check-the-box rules. Most LLCs and partnerships will not make an S election because of the benefits available with the more liberal partnership tax rules.
[30] Ineligible corporations include insurance companies, certain financial institutions, U.S. possessions corporations, and Domestic International Sales Corporations.
[31] The numbers of shareholders permitted S corporations was formerly 35 shareholders. The number of shareholders was increased to 75 for tax years beginning after December 31, 1996.

ADDITIONAL COMMENT
Some states do not recognize the S election for state income tax purposes, which results in the payment of state income taxes by an S corporation.

- Must have only individuals, estates, certain kinds of trusts, and certain kinds of tax-exempt organizations as shareholders
- Must not have a nonresident alien as a shareholder
- Must issue only one class of stock

All of the above requirements must be met for the initial election to be made. Once an election is made, the requirements must be met on every day of each tax year that the S election is in effect. Otherwise, the election terminates.

SEVENTY-FIVE SHAREHOLDER LIMITATION. The S corporation rules place no restriction on the amount of an S corporation's assets or income. Nevertheless, most large, publicly-traded corporations have more than 75 shareholders and therefore are not eligible to be an S corporation.

The following operating rules apply to S corporations:

- A husband and wife (each owning stock individually or jointly) are treated as one shareholder. This rule might create problems in a divorce situation if both individuals continue their ownership interests because the divorce results in two shareholders rather than one shareholder.
- If one spouse dies, the estate of the deceased spouse is not counted as an additional shareholder. Thus, the death of a spouse does not create problems if the estate distributes the stock to the surviving spouse. However, additional shareholders are created if the estate distributes the stock to heirs who do not already own any stock in the S corporation.

EXAMPLE I17-26

SELF-STUDY QUESTION
At any one time, how many different individuals could be shareholders in a single S corporation?

ANSWER
The S corporation could have as many as 150 shareholders in the case of 75 married couples.

Adobe Corporation, a qualifying S corporation, has 75 shareholders, including Brad and Bonnie, who are married and are counted as one shareholder. Brad dies and his stock is willed to his two children, who do not already own Adobe stock. Before the distribution of the stock from the estate, the estate and Bonnie are counted as one shareholder, and the S corporation remains qualified under the 75-shareholder limitation. Adobe is disqualified as an S corporation when the stock is distributed to the two children because the corporation then has 76 shareholders.

TYPE OF SHAREHOLDER RESTRICTIONS. A qualifying shareholder must be an individual (other than a nonresident alien), estate, qualifying trust, or qualifying tax-exempt organization.[32] Thus, a C corporation or a partnership may not own stock in an S corporation. If a C corporation or partnership were permitted to own stock, the 75-shareholder limitation easily could be avoided through indirect ownership of the S corporation stock through another corporation or partnership having many shareholders or partners.

SUBSIDIARIES OF S CORPORATIONS. Although an S corporation may not have a corporate shareholder, it may own stock of a C corporation. If this stock ownership equals or exceeds 80%, however, the S corporation (parent) and the C corporation (subsidiary) are considered an affiliated group under Sec. 1504. Under tax law for years prior to 1997, the existence of an affiliated group would have terminated the S election. However, starting in 1997, being a member of an affiliated group no longer terminates the S election. Nevertheless, an S corporation may not file a consolidated return with its 80%-owned subsidiaries.[33] In addition, an S corporation may have a Qualified Subchapter S Subsidiary (QSSS).[34] The subsidiary is a QSSS if the parent S corporation owns 100% of the QSSS stock and elects to treat the QSSS as such. Under this election, the QSSS is not treated as a separate corporation for income tax purposes. Instead, all assets, liabilities, income, deductions, and credits of the QSSS are treated as those of the parent S corporation.

---

[32] Qualifying trusts include voting trusts, Sec. 678 grantor trusts, electing small business trusts, and qualified Subchapter S trusts. Qualifying tax-exempt organizations include qualified retirement plan trusts and charitable organizations. See Chapter C11 of *Prentice Hall's Federal Taxation: Corporations, Partnerships, Estates, and Trusts* for a discussion of these trusts.
[33] Sec. 1504(a)(8).
[34] Sec. 1361(b)(3).

ONE CLASS OF STOCK RESTRICTION. An S corporation can have only one class of stock outstanding. This requirement simplifies problems that otherwise would result from determining how corporate income and losses should be allocated to the shareholder.

The requirement for one class of stock, however, can be troublesome if an S corporation is thinly capitalized (i.e., significant amounts of debt exist in the capital structure) because the debt may in fact be equity and represent a second class of stock. To reduce the uncertainty regarding the second class of stock issue, a safe-harbor rule provides that straight debt shall not be treated as a second class of stock if it meets certain requirements. To qualify as straight debt, the interest rate cannot be contingent on profits,[35] the debt cannot be convertible into stock, and the creditor must be either a person otherwise eligible to be an S corporation shareholder or a person actively and regularly engaged in the business of lending money.

Aside from the debt issue, Treasury Regulations provide that a corporation is treated as having only one class of stock if all outstanding shares of stock confer identical rights to distribution and liquidation proceeds. This test is determined based on the corporate charter, articles of incorporation, bylaws, applicable state law, and any binding agreements relating to distribution or liquidation proceeds.[36] Nevertheless, shares of common stock can have different voting rights without violating the one-class-of-stock restriction.

> **ADDITIONAL COMMENT**
> If a corporation needs to issue preferred stock for estate planning reasons (e.g., freezing the value of the stock), the S corporation is not an available choice because the preferred stock is a second class of stock.

EXAMPLE I17-27 ▶ Dale is the sole owner of an S corporation. For estate tax planning purposes, Dale desires to make gifts of certain shares of the corporation's stock to his children while still retaining control over the company. S corporation common stock with limited or no voting rights may be issued to Dale in exchange for a capital contribution. Dale can subsequently make gifts of this new stock to his children without disqualifying the S election. ◀

ELECTION REQUIREMENTS

The corporation files an election for S corporation status, and all shareholders who own stock on the date the S election is filed must consent to the election.[37] The election and consent are filed with the IRS on Form 2553 (Election by a Small Business Corporation to Tax Corporation Income Directly to Shareholders). Shareholders who own stock during any part of the tax year including the election date must consent to the election if they own stock on any day preceding the election date even if they are not shareholders on the election date. A shareholder will receive an allocation of the S corporation's income or loss when they own the S corporation's stock during a portion of the tax year prior to the date on which the election was made and sell it before the election date.

A corporation may make the election in the tax year preceding the election year or on or before the fifteenth day of the third month of the election year. An election after the fifteenth day of the third month of the election year is treated as made for the next tax year. Once made, the election remains in effect until revoked or terminated.

The tax law, however, provides some relief for improper elections. First, if the corporation misses the deadline for making the S election, the IRS can treat the election as timely if the IRS determines that the corporation had reasonable cause for making the late election. Second, if the election was ineffective because the corporation inadvertently failed to qualify as a small business corporation or because it inadvertently failed to obtain shareholder consents, the IRS can nevertheless honor the election if the corporation and shareholders take steps to correct the deficiency within a reasonable time period.

> **ADDITIONAL COMMENT**
> Because of the higher top individual income tax rate of 39.6% in the Revenue Reconciliation Act of 1993, the S election and continued S corporation status is less favorable than under prior law. A C corporation has a top marginal tax rate of 34% or 35% which is substantially below the top tax rate applying to an individual owner of an S corporation.

EXAMPLE I17-28 ▶ Circle Corporation, a C corporation, uses the calendar year as its tax year. To file an S election for 2001, the election may be filed anytime in 2000 or during the period that starts on January 1, 2001, and ends on March 15, 2001. If Circle Corporation makes the election on March 31, 2001, the corporation remains a C corporation in 2001 and becomes an S corporation in 2002. However, if Circle Corporation can show reasonable cause for making the late election, the IRS may allow the election to be effective for 2001. ◀

---

[35] The interest rate, however, may vary with the prime rate or a similar factor unrelated to the debtor corporation.

[36] Reg. Sec. 1.1361-1(l).

[37] Election and termination rules are in Sec. 1362.

TERMINATION CONDITIONS

KEY POINT
An election to be taxed as an S corporation becomes effective only as of the beginning of a tax year, but a termination can become effective before the end of the normal tax year.

REVOCATION OF S CORPORATION STATUS. An S election may be terminated either voluntarily by the shareholders or involuntarily if the corporation fails to continue to meet the requirements for a small business corporation (e.g., if on any day in any year the S corporation has more than 75 shareholders or issues a second class of stock). Voluntary revocation is permitted if consents are obtained from shareholders owning more than 50% of the corporation's stock.

General Effective Date. Under the general rules, a revocation is effective for the entire tax year if the corporation files a statement on or before the fifteenth day of the third month of the tax year. If the corporation files the revocation after this date (e.g., after March 15 for a calendar-year S corporation), the effective date is the first day of the next tax year.

EXAMPLE I17-29 ▶ Shareholders owning more than 50% of the stock of a qualifying calendar-year S corporation consent to a voluntary revocation statement filed by the corporation on March 12, 2001. Because the corporation filed the revocation on or before March 15, it is taxed as a C corporation for all of 2001. If the corporation does not file the revocation until March 18, 2001, it continues to be taxed as an S corporation during 2001, and its special tax status is revoked for 2002. ◀

Specified Termination Date. The law provides an exception when the corporation and its shareholders specify a prospective termination date. In this case, the revocation takes effect as of the specified date. If a prospective date other than the first day of a tax year is specified, the revocation results in a short tax year for the final S corporation tax return and a short tax year for the initial C corporation tax return. In such a case, the income or loss is allocated between the two short years on a prorated daily basis.[38]

EXAMPLE I17-30 ▶ Assume the same facts as in Example I17-29, except that a prospective termination date of July 1, 2001, is specified. The termination is effective as of this date, and the corporation files an S corporation short-period return for the period January 1 through June 30, 2001 and files a C corporation short-period return for the period July 1 through December 31, 2001. The income or loss is prorated to each return on a daily basis. Unless extended, the S corporation return is due September 15, 2001, 15th day of the third month following the close of the short tax year, and the C corporation return is due March 15, 2002. ◀

INVOLUNTARY AND INADVERTENT TERMINATIONS. An S corporation may involuntarily lose its special tax status and revert to being a C corporation if it fails to meet the small business corporation requirements or if it has excessive amounts of passive (investment) income for each year in a three-year period (i.e., more than 25% of gross receipts).[39] However, if the IRS deems that the termination was inadvertent and the S corporation or its shareholders take the necessary steps within a reasonable time period to restore its small business corporation status, the S corporation status is considered to have been continuously in effect.

EXAMPLE I17-31 ▶ A calendar-year S corporation adds a seventy-sixth shareholder on June 4. The S corporation status terminates on June 3. The corporation files a short-period S corporation tax return for the period January 1 through June 3 and files a C corporation tax return for the period from June 4 through December 31. Income or loss is prorated to the two tax returns on a daily basis. ◀

---

[38] The first day of the C corporation tax year is the day on which the revocation occurs. Under Sec. 1377(a)(2), a special election may be made to use the interim closing method (i.e., the books are closed as of the termination date) if all affected shareholders consent to this method.

[39] The passive income restrictions apply solely to S corporations that were previously taxed as C corporations in pre-election years and have accumulated Subchapter C earnings and profits from those years on the last day of three consecutive S corporation tax years. Thus, a corporation that elects S corporation status in its initial tax year and continually retains such status is not subject to the restrictions. If the restrictions apply and the S corporation has passive income exceeding 25% of its gross receipts for three consecutive tax years, the S election automatically terminates on the first day of the fourth tax year. In addition, a penalty tax equal to 35% of the corporation's excess net passive income is imposed during each year of the three-year period.

EXAMPLE I17-32 ▶ Assume the same facts as in Example I17-31 except that the termination is deemed to be inadvertent and the violation of the 75-shareholder requirement is corrected within a reasonable time period. The S corporation status is considered to have been continuously in effect, and no C corporation tax return is required. A single S corporation tax return will be filed for the year. ◀

ELECTION AFTER TERMINATION. If an S corporation terminates its election either by ceasing to be a small business corporation or by revocation, the corporation may not reelect S corporation status for five years unless the IRS consents to an early reelection. For purposes of the five-year rule, tax years beginning before January 1, 1997 are not counted. Thus, for example, corporations whose election terminated before this date can reelect S corporation status at any time without IRS consent.

Topic Review I17-4 summarizes the S corporation qualification, election, and termination rules.

OBJECTIVE 5

Apply the operating rules for S corporations

S CORPORATION OPERATIONS

Income, gains, losses, deductions, and credits pass through to the S corporation's shareholders in a manner similar to the partnership rules. Some common separately stated items include

Topic Review I17-4

S Corporation Qualification, Election, and Termination Rules

Qualification Requirements
- An S corporation must be a domestic corporation.
- A maximum of 75 shareholders are allowed. A husband and wife count as one shareholder, and each beneficiary of a qualifying trust is a separate shareholder.
- Only individuals (citizens or resident aliens), estates, certain kinds of trusts, and certain kinds of tax-exempt organizations can be shareholders. No corporate or partnership shareholders are permitted.
- Only one class of stock generally may be issued and outstanding. Multiple classes of stock can be used if the only difference between the two classes is voting rights.
- Certain corporations that maintain special tax statuses are ineligible.
- If an S corporation has an 80%-or-more-owned subsidiary, it cannot file a consolidated tax return with that subsidiary. Special rules apply to a QSSS.

Election Requirements
- All shareholders on the S election date must consent and the corporation must file Form 2553. To be effective for the election year, the S election and consent form must be filed on or before the fifteenth day of the third month of the election year. Otherwise, the election is effective for the next tax year.
- The IRS can waive the election deadline if the corporation shows reasonable cause for late filing.
- The IRS can grant relief for improper elections if they are inadvertent and subsequently corrected.

Termination Rules
- To effect a voluntary revocation, consent must be obtained from shareholders owning more than 50% of the S corporation's stock. The revocation is effective for the entire year if made on or before the fifteenth day of the third month of the tax year. Otherwise, the termination is effective the first day of the next tax year unless a prospective termination date is specified.
- An involuntary revocation takes place if (1) the S corporation fails to meet any of the small business corporation requirements (e.g., it has more than 75 shareholders) or (2) it has excessive passive investment income in a three-year period (assuming the corporation has prior C corporation accumulated E&P). If the IRS deems the involuntary termination to be inadvertent, the S corporation status is considered to have been continuously in effect provided the corporation and shareholders correct the defect.
- Aside from the inadvertent termination exception, a corporation may not reelect S corporation status for five years after a termination or revocation. Tax years beginning before January 1, 1997 do not count for the five-year test.

- Short-term and long-term capital gains and losses
- Sec. 1231 gains and losses
- Charitable contributions
- Credits
- Interest on investment indebtedness (see Chapter I7 for a discussion of this item)
- AMT adjustments and tax preference items
- Foreign taxes paid or accrued
- Dividends and other portfolio income

(Table I17-1 on pp. I17-8 provides a list of comparable items for partnerships.) These separately stated items are segregated from the computation of ordinary income (or loss) because each item affects the tax returns of the various shareholders differently, depending on their particular tax situation. The residual income or loss amount (i.e., the amount remaining after removing the separately stated items) represents the S corporation's ordinary income (or loss). Separately stated items and S corporation ordinary income (or loss) pass through to the shareholders as of the last day of the S corporation's tax year.[40] The S corporation computes its ordinary income (or loss) on page 1 of Form 1120S (U.S. Income Tax Return for an S Corporation), and it reports all items on Schedule K of that return. Then for each shareholder, the corporation prepares a Schedule K-1, which reports each shareholder's share of the S corporation items. The shareholders use the Schedule K-1 information to prepare their individual tax returns (Form 1040).

The tax treatment of some S corporation items is similar to that for C corporations. For example, S corporations can amortize organizational expenditures over a period of at least 60 months under the general corporate taxation rules. However, S corporations are not entitled to other corporate deductions, such as the dividends-received deduction or the net operating loss deduction because dividends and net operating losses pass through to the S corporation's shareholders.

EXAMPLE I17-33

SELF-STUDY QUESTION

Compare the manner in which income of an S corporation is allocated among the shareholders to the manner in which partnership income is allocated among the partners.

ANSWER

In the case of an S corporation, the income must be allocated based on the percentage of stock owned on a daily basis. Partners have much greater flexibility. The partnership agreement serves as the basis for allocation, with special allocations being permitted. No special allocations are permitted for an S corporation.

Ajax Corporation, an electing S corporation owned equally by Linda and Hal, reports the following operating results for the current year (a non-leap year):

Sales	$10,000
Minus: Cost of goods sold	(2,000)
Gross profit	$ 8,000
Plus: Long-term capital gains	3,000
Total income	$11,000
Minus: Administrative expenses	(500)
Repairs	(500)
Sec. 1231 losses	(1,000)
Charitable contributions	(1,000)
Net income per books	$ 8,000

The individual items are reported on the S corporation tax return as follows:

	Ordinary Income	Separately Stated Items	Linda's K-1	Hal's K-1
Sales	$10,000			
Cost of goods sold	(2,000)			
Administrative expenses	(500)			
Repairs	(500)			
Total ordinary income	$7,000		$3,500	$3,500
Long-term capital gains		$3,000	1,500	1,500
Sec. 1231 losses		(1,000)	(500)	(500)
Charitable contributions		(1,000)	(500)	(500)

---

[40] Sec. 1363. Special rules apply if the S election terminates during the tax year. These rules are beyond the scope of this text.

Linda and Hal each report $3,500 of ordinary income plus 50% of each separately stated item on their individual tax returns. ◀

Income, gains, losses, deductions, credits, and other separately stated items are allocated to the shareholders based on the number of shares of stock owned on each day of the S corporation's tax year. Thus, if a shareholder sells S corporation stock during the year, ordinary income (or loss) and separately stated items are allocated on a daily basis to the seller and purchaser of the stock.[41]

EXAMPLE I17-34 ▶ Assume the same facts as in Example I17-33, except that Linda sells her stock to Marc on the 181st day of the tax year. According to Reg. Sec. 1.1377-1(a), income through the date of the transfer is allocated to Linda. Only $1,736 [0.50 × (181 ÷ 365)× $7,000] of the ordinary income and a similar portion of each separately stated item is reported by Linda. The ordinary income and separately stated items attributable to Linda's one-half interest for the remainder of the year are reported by Marc. The sale does not affect Hal's reporting of his share of the income. ◀

OBJECTIVE 6
Determine the tax treatment of an S corporation's shareholders

BASIS ADJUSTMENTS TO S CORPORATION STOCK

Usually, a shareholder's original basis for S corporation stock is either the amount paid for the stock or a substituted basis from a nontaxable transaction (e.g., a Sec. 351 tax-free corporate formation transaction).[42] Adjustments are subsequently made for ordinary income (or loss) and separately stated items that flow through to the shareholders, as well as additional capital contributions by shareholders and distributions to shareholders.[43]

EXAMPLE I17-35 ▶ Juan acquires 100 shares of Allied Corporation stock during the current year for $40,000. Allied Corporation is a qualifying calendar-year S corporation. Juan's share of Allied's current year ordinary income is $10,000. In addition, his share of separately stated items includes $4,000 of long-term capital gains and $2,000 of Sec. 1231 losses. Allied Corporation also distributes $5,000 cash to Juan on November 9. Juan's basis in the S corporation stock on December 31 is computed as follows:

Original basis (cost)		$40,000
Plus:	Share of ordinary income	10,000
	Share of long-term capital gains	4,000
Minus:	Share of Sec. 1231 losses	(2,000)
	Cash distribution to Juan	(5,000)
Basis of stock on December 31		$47,000	◀

The logic behind these basis adjustments can be explained by differentiating between the conduit (aggregate) and entity concepts. For example, C corporations are taxable as separate entities. Thus, corporate earnings are taxed at the corporate level, so no adjustments are made to a shareholder's C corporation stock basis for amounts earned by the corporation. The S corporation's shareholders would be subject to double taxation if the basis adjustments were not allowed because all corporate earnings (distributed and undistributed) flow through and are taxed to each of the shareholders on an annual basis.

KEY POINT
Adjustments to a shareholder's stock basis prevent double taxation of income or double deduction of losses.

EXAMPLE I17-36 ▶ Mary is the sole shareholder of Apple Corporation, an electing S corporation. Mary originally contributed $100,000 to the newly formed company. The funds were used to acquire various corporate assets. During the next 10 years, the corporation earned $900,000 of ordinary income and reinvested these earnings in corporate assets. After 10 years, Mary sells the stock for $1 million (its tax basis). Mary's gain on the sale of her stock is calculated as follows:

---

[41] If a special election is made under Sec. 1377(a)(2), the income is allocated according to the accounting methods used by the S corporation (instead of on a daily basis) when a shareholder terminates his or her interest during the tax year.

[42] The death or gift tax basis rules also may be used to determine the initial basis for S corporation stock.
[43] Sec. 1367.

	With Stock Basis Adjustments	If No Basis Adjustments Were Permitted
Selling price of the stock	$1,000,000	$1,000,000
Original capital contribution	$ 100,000	$ 100,000
Plus: Share of ordinary income (taxed to Mary)	900,000	
Minus: Adjusted basis of stock	($1,000,000)	($ 100,000)
Gain on sale (selling price minus adjusted basis)	$ –0–	$ 900,000

The $900,000 of earnings would be taxed twice to Mary if the positive basis adjustments were not permitted under the S corporation rules. With a C corporation, the $900,000 of earnings would be taxed at the corporate level and not to Mary. However, Mary would have an eventual $900,000 capital gain upon selling her stock after ten years. For an S corporation, a capital gain is recognized only if the stock's selling price exceeds the sum of its acquisition cost plus the accumulated earnings. ◀

S CORPORATION LOSSES AND LIMITATIONS

LIMITATIONS ON LOSS DEDUCTIONS. An ordinary loss and any separately stated loss and deduction items of an S corporation are allocated among the shareholders based on the number of shares of stock owned on each day of the S corporation's tax year.[44] The last day of the S corporation's tax year determines when the shareholders report the loss.[45]

EXAMPLE I17-37 ▶ Adobe Corporation is an S corporation whose tax year ends on January 31, 2001. All of its shareholders report their taxes using a calendar year. Adobe reports a $100,000 ordinary loss for the 12-month period ending on January 31, 2001. The shareholders report this loss on their calendar-year 2001 returns. ◀

KEY POINT
An S corporation shareholder gets debt basis, separate from stock basis, for amounts the shareholder lends directly to the corporation, but the shareholder gets no basis for corporate liabilities owed to third parties. This treatment differs from that of partnership liabilities.

A shareholder's deduction for ordinary losses and separately stated items cannot exceed his or her basis for the S corporation stock plus the debt basis for any shareholder loans made to the S corporation.[46] The following rules apply when determining the deductibility of ordinary loss and separately-stated loss items:

▶ A positive basis adjustment is made to the stock basis for ordinary income or separately stated income or gain items accruing during the year before the ordinary losses and separately stated loss and deduction items are used to reduce the stock basis.

▶ The shareholder's deduction for pass-through losses is limited to (1) stock basis after the above positive adjustments and after distributions but before negative adjustments for losses and deductions and (2) the shareholder's debt basis.[47]

▶ A shareholder's pass-through loss first reduces the shareholder's stock basis (but not below zero).

▶ If the loss exceeds the shareholder's stock basis, the remaining pass-through loss then reduces the shareholder's debt basis (but not below zero).

▶ If the loss exceeds both the stock and debt basis, the shareholder carries over the excess loss and deducts it in a subsequent year when the shareholder again has basis in stock or debt. The carryover period is indefinite but does not transfer to another taxpayer if the shareholder disposes of all of the stock or if the shareholder dies. Furthermore, if the S election is terminated, the loss must be used against any basis of the former S corporation stock by the end of a one-year post-termination transition period.

---

[44] Sec. 1366(a)(1).
[45] The same rule is applied for the reporting of ordinary income and separately stated income and gain items.
[46] Sec. 1366(d)(1). The deductible loss is treated as a deduction for AGI on an individual shareholder's tax return. S corporation shareholders also are subject to special limitations on losses and deductions that pass through from the S corporation (e.g., at-risk limitations under Sec. 465 and passive activity losses under Sec. 469 see Chapter C11 of *Prentice Hall's Federal Taxation: Corporations, Partnerships, Estates, and Trusts* for a discussion of these additional limitations).
[47] Secs. 1366(d)(1)(A) and 1367(a)(2).

EXAMPLE I17-38 ▶ Matt owns 20% of the stock of an electing S corporation. His basis in the stock is $20,000 at the end of 2001 after adjustments for separately stated income and gain items. Matt also loans the S corporation $10,000 during 2001. The S corporation incurs a $200,000 ordinary loss in 2001. Matt's share of the ordinary loss is $40,000 (0.20 × $200,000). Matt's deduction and carryover of the unused loss are as follows:

Basis in stock	$20,000
Minus: Ordinary loss applied against stock basis	(20,000)
Basis in stock after ordinary loss	$ –0–
Debt basis in loan	$10,000
Minus: Ordinary loss applied against debt basis	(10,000)
Debt basis in loan after ordinary loss	$ –0–
Share of ordinary loss	$40,000
Minus: Deduction in 2001 ($20,000 + $10,000)	(30,000)
Carryover of ordinary loss to 2002	$10,000 ◀

If a shareholder's basis is insufficient to absorb the entire amount of ordinary loss (and separately stated loss and deduction items), the flow-through of each item is determined on a pro rata basis. For example, if a shareholder's basis is $5,000 and he has a $6,000 ordinary loss and a $4,000 capital loss, his total deduction is limited to $5,000. This deduction consists of a $3,000 [($6,000 ÷ $10,000) × $5,000] ordinary loss and a $2,000 [($4,000 ÷ $10,000) × $5,000] capital loss. He also has a $3,000 ($6,000 − $3,000) ordinary loss and a $2,000 ($4,000 − $2,000) capital loss carryover.

RESTORATION OF BASIS. If a shareholder's debt basis in a loan made to the S corporation is reduced by a loss deduction, subsequent increases in basis resulting from S corporation income in a future year initially increase the debt basis until that basis reduction is fully restored. Any excess positive adjustment then increases the shareholder's stock basis.

EXAMPLE I17-39 ▶ Assume the same facts as in Example I17-38, except that in 2002 the S corporation's ordinary income is $140,000. Matt's share of the income is $28,000 (0.20 × $140,000). The $28,000 of income earned in 2002 permits Matt to deduct the $10,000 ordinary loss carryover from 2001. Stock and debt basis are adjusted as follows:

	Debt Basis	Stock Basis
Basis at beginning of year	$ –0–	$ –0–
Plus: Income for the year ($28,000)	10,000	18,000
Minus: Loss carryover from prior year utilized	–0–	(10,000)
Basis at end of year	$10,000	$ 8,000 ◀

If the debt basis is not fully restored, gain results when the loan is repaid. If the loan is in the form of a note, the repayment results in a capital gain because the note constitutes a capital asset.[48] However, ordinary income results if the loan is an unsecured advance.[49]

PASSIVE ACTIVITY LOSS LIMITATIONS. S corporation shareholders are subject to the passive activity loss limitations in the same manner as partners. Losses that pass through to a shareholder who does not materially participate in the S corporation's business may not be deducted against that shareholder's other earned income or against portfolio income (e.g., dividends and interest). Such passive losses can offset only other passive activity income. S corporation shareholders who materially participate (i.e., participate on a regular, continuous, and substantial basis) can avoid the passive activity loss limitations. (See Chapter I8 for a detailed discussion of the passive activity loss limitations rules.)

Topic Review I17-5 summarizes the basic tax rules for S corporation shareholders.

---

[48] Rev. Rul. 64-162, 1964-1 C.B. 304.

[49] Rev. Rul. 68-537, 1968-2 C.B. 372.

Topic Review I17-5

Basic Tax Rules for S Corporation Shareholders

- Ordinary losses and separately stated loss and deduction items are allocated to shareholders on a per share per day basis.
- The last day of the S corporation's tax year determines the year in which the shareholders report their share of income, gain, deductions, losses, credits, and other separately stated items.
- Basis cannot be reduced below zero. Positive basis adjustments are made for ordinary income and separately stated income or gain items before basis reductions for ordinary losses, separately stated loss and deduction items, and distributions.
- Losses initially reduce the shareholder's stock basis (but not below zero). Any excess losses then reduce the basis of debt owed by the S corporation to the shareholder.
- Unused losses are suspended and carried over until the shareholder again has basis to absorb the losses.
- Net positive basis adjustments in subsequent years initially increase the shareholder's debt basis until fully restored. Any additional net positive basis adjustments increase the basis of the shareholder's S corporation stock.

OTHER S CORPORATION CONSIDERATIONS

DISTRIBUTIONS OF CASH AND PROPERTY TO SHAREHOLDERS. A money or property distribution made by an S corporation to its shareholders is treated as a return of capital if the S corporation has no accumulated earnings and profits from pre-S corporation years.[50] As such, the amount of money or FMV of the nonmoney property distributed to a shareholder reduces the basis of the shareholder's S corporation stock. If distributions exceed the shareholder's stock basis, the excess is treated as a capital gain if the stock is a capital asset.[51]

The S corporation recognizes gain (but not loss) if it distributes nonmoney property to its shareholders.[52] The distribution is treated as if the corporation sold the property to the shareholders at its FMV. The gain then passes through to the shareholders whose basis for their S corporation stock is increased. The distributed property's FMV reduces the shareholders' S corporation stock basis.

> **ADDITIONAL COMMENT**
> Another important difference between partnerships and S corporations involves the tax consequences of property distributions. An S corporation recognizes gain if it distributes appreciated property to its shareholders, but a partnership would not recognize such gain.

EXAMPLE I17-40 ▶ Austin Corporation, an electing S corporation, distributes land (a capital asset) to its sole shareholder Sue. The land has a $10,000 basis and a $90,000 FMV. The S corporation recognizes an $80,000 capital gain, which passes through to Sue and increases the basis of her Austin stock. The basis of the land to Sue is $90,000 (its FMV). ◀

TAX YEAR RESTRICTIONS. S corporations must use a calendar year unless a business purpose (i.e., a natural business year) can be established for choosing a fiscal year-end.[53] These year-end restrictions prevent shareholders from deferring pass-through income for up to 11 months (e.g., if a January 31 fiscal year-end were permitted). Also, like a partnership, an S corporation may elect a maximum three-month deferral if it agrees to make a special tax payment each year that approximates the deferral benefit.

> **ADDITIONAL COMMENT**
> For purposes of calculating which shareholders own more than 2% of the outstanding stock, the Sec. 318 attribution rules apply.

TREATMENT OF FRINGE BENEFITS. S corporation shareholders who own more than 2% of the outstanding stock are not eligible for tax-free corporate employee fringe benefits, for the following statutory fringe benefits:

- The group term life insurance exclusion under Sec. 79 for premiums paid for up to $50,000 coverage

---

[50] The tax consequences of property distributions to shareholders are discussed in Chapter C11 of *Prentice Hall's Federal Taxation: Corporations, Partnerships, Estates, and Trusts*.
[51] Sec. 1368(b). The S corporation also can have accumulated E&P from a tax year in which it was taxed as a C corporation. The tax consequences of a distribution made by an S corporation having accumulated E&P are complex.

These rules are beyond the scope of this text but are discussed in Chapter C11 of *Prentice Hall's Federal Taxation: Corporations, Partnerships, Estates, and Trusts*.
[52] Sec. 311(b).
[53] Sec. 1378(b).

- The exclusion from income for premiums paid for accident and health insurance and medical reimbursement plans under Secs. 105 and 106[54]
- The exclusion for cafeteria plan benefits under Sec. 125;
- Employer provided fringe benefits under Sec. 132; and
- Meals and lodging furnished for the convenience of the employer under Sec. 119.

The fringe benefits listed above are included in the gross income of a more-than-2% shareholder as a guaranteed payment. The amount of the payment is deductible by the corporation. Amounts received by a shareholder owning 2% or less of the S corporation's stock are excluded by the shareholder and deductible by the corporation as they would be for employee of a C corporation.

EXAMPLE I17-41 ▶ Bass Corporation is an electing S corporation. Health insurance and group term life insurance premiums are paid by the corporation for its employee-owner group, all of whom own more than 2% of the Bass stock. The premiums are included in the gross income of the owner-employees and are deductible by the S corporation. An employee-shareholder, who owns more than 2% of the S corporation's stock and is treated as a partner under Sec. 1372(a), can deduct 60% in 2001 of the amount includible in gross income as being paid for medical insurance for himself, his spouse, and his dependents.[55] The premiums would not be included in the gross income of employees who did not own any Bass stock, or who owned 2% or less of the Bass stock. ◀

Not all S corporation fringe benefits are subject to special treatment for a more-than-2% shareholder. A partial list of fringe benefits not subject to special treatment includes:

- Stock options
- Qualified fringe benefits
- Nonqualified deferred compensation
- Compensation for injuries and sickness (Sec. 104)
- Educational assistance programs (Sec. 127)
- Dependent care assistance programs (Sec. 129)
- No-additional-cost fringe benefits, qualified employee discounts, working condition fringe benefits, de minimis fringe benefits, and on-premises athletic facilities.

Fringe benefits included in this list are reported by the employee under the general gross income inclusion rule applying to the fringe benefit and are deductible by the corporation under Sec. 162.

KEY POINT
The built-in gains tax was enacted in 1986 to prevent C corporations from avoiding double taxation in a corporate liquidation by electing S corporation status immediately before the liquidation.

CORPORATE TAX ON BUILT-IN GAINS. A 35% corporate tax on built-in gains applies if a corporation that previously was a C corporation elects to be an S corporation.[56] The built-in gains tax does not apply to a corporation that always has been an S corporation or that elected S corporation status before 1987. A built-in gain exists if the FMV of an asset exceeds its adjusted basis on the first day the S election is effective. If the corporation sells an asset with a built-in gain within the ten-year period beginning on the effective date for the election, the S corporation is taxed on the built-in gain. Built-in losses existing on the first day of the S election period can be used to reduce built-in gains. Any appreciation on the asset that occurs after conversion from a C corporation to an S corporation is subject to the regular S corporation pass-through rules but is not taxed under the built-in gains tax. Any asset not held on the first day of the S corporation election period also is exempt from the built-in gains tax.

EXAMPLE I17-42 ▶ Beach Corporation, an accrual method taxpayer incorporated six years ago (1995), elects to be taxed as an S corporation as of January 1 of last year (2000). On January 1 of last year, Beach owned land with a $50,000 basis and a $200,000 FMV. Beach sold the land this year for

---
[54] Rev. Rul. 91-26, 1991-1 C.B. 184. Rules similar to those applying to S corporation shareholders will apply to partners in a partnership. The payment is deductible by the partnership and includible in the partner's gross income.

[55] Sec. 162(l)(1) and (5).
[56] Sec. 1374. This discussion is only a sketch of these complex rules.

$225,000. Thus, Beach reports a total gain of $175,000 ($225,000 − $50,000). The first $150,000 of post-conversion appreciation is subject to the built-in gains tax at the corporate level and flows through to the shareholders. The remaining $25,000 of post-conversion appreciation also is subject to the regular S corporation pass-through rules but is not subject to the built-in gains tax. In addition, the built-in gains tax that is paid by the corporation flows through as a loss to the shareholders. ◀

TAX ON EXCESS NET PASSIVE INCOME A 35% excess net passive income tax applies when an S corporation has passive investment income for the tax year that exceeds 25% of its gross receipts and, at the close of the tax year, the S corporation has accumulated Subchapter C E&P. Subchapter C E&P is the earnings and profits the corporation earned when it was taxed as a C corporation.[57]

EXAMPLE I17-43 ▶ Acorn Corporation made an S election last year after having been a C corporation for several years. Acorn has accumulated Subchapter C E&P at the end of the current year. During the current year, Acorn's excess net passive income is $10,000 that is made up of dividends and interest. The excess net passive income tax is $3,500 ($10,000 × 0.35). The tax reduces (on a pro rata basis) the passive income items (e.g., dividends and interest) that pass through to its shareholders. ◀

STOP & THINK

Question: Suppose shareholders of an S corporation wanted to convert the business into a limited liability company (LLC). What tax obstacles might they encounter?

Solution: The shareholders would have to liquidate the corporation and recontribute the assets to the LLC. Because the S corporation must comply with general corporate tax rules, the liquidation will cause gain recognition at the corporate level for appreciated property distributed (IRC, Sec. 336). This gain will flow through to the shareholders and be taxable to them. In addition, the liquidation might trigger the corporate level tax on built-in gains (IRC, Sec. 1374). Thus, conversion from an S corporation to an LLC could have adverse tax consequences. Contrast these major tax obstacles above with the conversion of a partnership to an LLC. The IRS has ruled that the conversion of a partnership to an LLC is a nontaxable event.

The discussion about the sale of a partnership interest introduced the IRC Sec. 1(h) special recognition rules for sales of an interest in a passthrough entity. S corporations are subject to similar, but less-complicated, sale or exchange rules under Sec. 1(h) when their stock is sold or the corporation is liquidated. Three categories of gain are encountered when S corporation stock is sold or exchanged. These categories are: (1) ordinary income (for example, gain recognized under Secs. 304, 306, 341, or 1254), (2) collectibles gain, and (3) capital gain or loss. The capital gain or loss that is reported is the difference between the recognized gain or loss and the gain reported under categories (1) and (2). Unlike the partnership rules, there is no need to treat as ordinary income any portion of the unrecaptured Sec. 1250 gain.

TAX PLANNING CONSIDERATIONS

USE OF OPERATING LOSSES

Often, the decision to select a particular form of business organization involves both tax and nontax issues. For example, the corporate form may be preferred due to the availability of nontax attributes such as limited liability, the relative freedom to transfer ownership interests, and the ability to raise outside equity capital.

---

[57] Sec. 1375(a). These rules are discussed in greater detail in Chapter C11 of *Prentice Hall's Federal Taxation: Corporations, Partnerships, Estates, and Trusts.*

In many instances, however, the tax attributes dominate, making the partnership or S corporation form preferable to the C corporation. If the owners expect operating losses in the initial years of operation, they may prefer the partnership form to either the C corporation or the S corporation form of organization. In a C corporation, the operating losses do not benefit the shareholders directly and may be of no benefit if the corporation cannot generate sufficient profits in future years to offset the loss carryovers.[58] In a partnership, the losses pass through to the partners, limited by their basis for the partnership interest. The basis of a partner's interest, however, includes his or her share of partnership liabilities. In contrast, an S corporation's ability to pass through losses is limited to the shareholder's basis in the stock and any shareholder loans. Other S corporation liabilities are not included in determining the shareholder's loss limitation. Thus, the partnership form may provide its owners a greater opportunity to deduct losses than does the S corporation form.

EXAMPLE I17-44 ▶ Mary and Marty are considering whether to operate a new business venture as a C corporation, S corporation, or a partnership. Mary and Marty plan to invest $50,000 of equity and raise an additional $50,000 from outside creditors (e.g., accounts payable and a mortgage). They expect initial losses of $20,000 per year for five years. If a C corporation is used, the corporate losses are not deductible (i.e., the corporation has net operating loss carryovers of $100,000 after the five-year period). If an S corporation is formed, Mary and Marty can deduct only $50,000 due to the exclusion of general corporate debt from determining the basis for the shareholder's investment. The remaining $50,000 loss carries forward indefinitely at the sharholder level unless the shareholders lend $50,000 of additional funds to the corporation (instead of having the corporation borrow these amounts from outside creditors) or make $50,000 of additional capital contributions. If a partnership is formed, Mary and Marty can deduct the full $100,000 of losses because their basis includes their ratable share of the partnership's liabilities. Assuming Mary and Marty have sufficient other sources of income to absorb the losses, the value of these additional deductions in the first five years favors the partnership form of organization. A nontax factor that might influence the decision is the limited liability protection offered by the corporate entity. ◀

STOP & THINK

Question: Paul owns a business that produces $50,000 of annual profits. If the business were incorporated, it could justify the retention of all of its earnings and pay little or no dividends. Paul also has $100,000 of taxable income from other sources. Should Paul organize the business as an S corporation or as a C corporation?

Solution: Although many factors could be involved, one important tax factor is that Paul's income from the business could be taxed at a 39.6% rate if it is an S corporation. The tax rate on a C corporation is 15% on the first $50,000 of taxable income. Double taxation would result, however, if the profits were withdrawn as a dividend or as a capital gain when the stock was sold.

INCOME SHIFTING AMONG FAMILY MEMBERS

Subject to gift tax rules and restrictions, an attractive tax planning strategy is to shift income from higher tax bracket family members to children or others who are subject to lower tax rates. In an S corporation, parents may gift nonvoting common stock to their children age 14 and older (subject to the gift tax rules and restrictions). Thus, a portion of the S corporation income is taxed to the children even though the parents retain all voting rights for the corporate stock. A partnership interest also may be gifted to other family members. However, the IRS generally does not recognize the family member as a partner in a partnership where capital (e.g., inventory, plant, and equipment) is a material income-producing factor unless the individual is the real owner of the interest and has

---

[58] In a C corporation, net operating losses are carried back 2 years and forward 20 years. In a newly-formed corporation, the carryback rules do not apply.

dominion and control over it. In a service partnership (e.g., an accounting firm), the family member must provide vital or substantial services. If property is given to a child under age 14, the child's unearned income exceeding $1,500 in 2001 is taxed at the parents' higher tax rate. Therefore, if S corporation stock or a partnership interest is given to a child under age 14, the child's share of S corporation or partnership income generally is taxed to the child at the parents' highest marginal tax rate. Essentially, the tax planning technique of income shifting from higher tax bracket family members to children under age 14 no longer exists. These rules do not apply to children age 14 and older (see Chapter I2).

With an S corporation or a partnership, family members (e.g., children) can be hired as employees. Thus, income may be shifted to lower tax bracket family members. The under-age-14 rules discussed previously have no effect on earned income even if derived from a parent's business. In a partnership and an S corporation, the IRS will reallocate income to reflect the value of the services and capital contributions if unreasonable salaries are paid.[59]

▶ **EXAMPLE I17-45** ▶ Paul, the sole owner of an electing S corporation gifts 20% of the corporation's stock to his children age 14 and older. The S corporation's ordinary income is $100,000 after deducting a $10,000 salary paid to Paul. If a reasonable salary for Paul's services is $50,000, the IRS may reduce ordinary income to $60,000 ($100,000 − $40,000) and increase Paul's taxable compensation to $50,000. Thus, the share of income that passes through to the children is reduced from $20,000 (0.20 × $100,000) to $12,000 (0.20 × $60,000). ◀

OPTIONAL BASIS ADJUSTMENT ELECTION UNDER SEC. 754

ADDITIONAL COMMENT

The Sec. 754 election may be revoked only with the approval of the IRS District Director, and no application for revocation will be approved when the purpose is primarily to avoid stepping-down the basis of partnership assets.

A basis adjustment election under Sec. 754 usually is desirable for an incoming partner whose partnership interest cost more than the tax basis of his or her share of partnership's assets. The excess amount is added to the new partner's basis for his or her interest in the partnership's assets. If the partnership made a Sec. 754 election in a prior year, the election continues in effect and automatically applies to the current year. However, if the election was not previously made, all of the partners must agree to make the election because it is made at the partnership level rather than by the individual partner.

Therefore, before a sale is consummated, an incoming partner should attempt to obtain assurances from the remaining partners that the partnership will agree to make the election in the current year if the election is not already in effect. The election is made by attaching a statement to a timely filed tax return for the year the transaction occurs. A retroactive election cannot be made for prior years.[60] A Sec. 754 election, however, may have adverse effects in subsequent years if the amount paid for a partnership interest is less than the tax basis of partnership assets because the incoming partner must reduce her share of the basis of partnership assets. The Sec. 754 optional basis adjustment is beyond the scope of this text. Additional coverage can be found in Chapter C10 of *Prentice Hall's Federal Taxation of Corporations, Partnerships, Estates, and Trusts*.

COMPLIANCE AND PROCEDURAL CONSIDERATIONS

ADDITIONAL COMMENT

Most partnerships that have more than ten partners must select a partner to serve as the tax matters partner. This partner will be in charge of administrative matters in the event of a partnership audit.

PARTNERSHIP FILING REQUIREMENTS AND ELECTIONS

Partnerships must file Form 1065 (U.S. Partnership Return of Income) on or before the fifteenth day of the fourth month following the close of its tax year (by April 15 for a calendar-year partnership). The IRS can allow reasonable extensions of time up to six months although a partnership can obtain an automatic three-month extension by filing Form 8736 (Application for Automatic Extension of Time To File U.S. Return for a

---

[59] Secs. 1366(e) and 704(e).

[60] Reg. Sec. 1.754-1(b).

Partnership, REMIC, or for Certain Trusts). If the partnership needs an additional extension, it can file Form 8800 (Application for Additional Extension of Time To File U.S. Return for Partnership, REMIC, or for Certain Trusts). Penalties are imposed for failure to file a timely or complete partnership return.

> **REAL-WORLD EXAMPLE**
>
> A partnership reported its capital gain on a sale in one tax year rather than on the installment basis. The partners could not use the installment method because this is a partnership election. *George Rothenberg,* 48 T.C. 369 (1967).

PARTNERSHIP ELECTIONS. The partnership makes most elections affecting the computation of partnership income. These elections include

- Selection of a tax year
- Selection of an overall accounting method
- Inventory valuation method
- Depreciation methods
- Amortization method for organization expenses
- Optional basis adjustments under Sec. 754

An election made at the partnership level is binding on all partners.

Certain elections are made by each partner. The common elections are the partners' own accounting periods and methods and the election to take a credit or deduction for foreign income taxes.

REPORTING PARTNERSHIP ITEMS ON FORM 1065

The partnership ordinary income and deduction items are reported on page 1 of Form 1065. Schedule K summarizes all of the partners' shares of separately stated items (e.g., capital gains and losses, tax credits, and charitable contributions). Schedule K also includes guaranteed payments made to partners and the ordinary income or loss, even though both items are reported on page 1. A separate Schedule K-1 is prepared for each partner. The Schedule K-1 represents each partner's share of the Schedule K items, depending on the agreed upon ratio for sharing income, deduction, loss, and credit items. This schedule becomes the primary input for preparation of each partner's federal income tax return.

A partnership also must prepare a balance sheet (Schedule L), a reconciliation of income per books with income per tax (Schedule M-1), and an analysis of capital accounts (Schedule M-2).

S CORPORATION FILING REQUIREMENTS AND ACCOUNTING METHOD ELECTIONS

An S corporation must file its corporate tax return no later than the fifteenth day of the third month following the end of the tax year. The S corporation reports its results on Form 1120S (U.S. Income Tax Return for an S Corporation). An S corporation is allowed an automatic 6-month extension of time for filing its tax return by filing Form 7004 (Application for Automatic Extension of Time to File U.S. Corporation Income Tax Return).

The S corporation, rather than the shareholders, make the accounting method elections used to compute ordinary income or loss and the separately stated items. As with a partnership, these elections are made independently of the accounting method elections made by its shareholders.

REPORTING S CORPORATION ITEMS ON FORM 1120S

Page 1 of Form 1120S summarizes the ordinary income and deduction items for the S corporation. If the corporation owes any tax due to the excess net passive income tax or the built-in gains tax, such amounts are reported on page 1 of the return. Schedule K lists the separately stated items and ordinary income or losses for the S corporation, S corporation distributions, and selected other items. A Schedule K-1 is prepared for each shareholder reflecting his or her share of the ordinary income (loss) and separately stated items. The Schedule K-1 becomes the basis for preparing each shareholder's federal income tax return. The S corporation also must prepare a balance sheet (Schedule L) and a reconciliation of income per books with income per tax (Schedule M-1).

COMPARISON OF ALTERNATIVE FORMS OF BUSINESS ORGANIZATIONS

Table I17-2 provides a comparison of sole proprietorships, partnerships, S corporations, and C corporations. The partnership comments also apply to entities treated as partnerships for tax purposes such as LLCs or LLPs.

▼ **TABLE I17-2**
Comparison of Alternative Forms of Business Organizations

Attributes	Sole Proprietorship	Partnership	S Corporation	C Corporation
Application of the separate entity versus the conduit (flow-through) concepts.	Single level of taxation. The proprietor is the same person as the individual taxpayer. The sole proprietor reports proprietorship income, expenses, losses, and credits in his individual tax return.	Conduit with a single level of taxation. The partnership is not taxed. Instead, its income, gains, deductions, losses, and credits flow through to the partners to be taxed in their tax returns.	Conduit with a single level of taxation. Similar to a partnership in that its income, gains, deductions, losses, and credits flow through to the shareholders to be taxed in their tax returns. In special cases, the S corporation may pay entity level taxes on built-in gains and excess net passive income	Entity with double taxation. The corporation is taxed at the entity level, and its shareholders are taxed again when they receive dividends or sell their stock.
Applicable income tax rates	Individual tax rates apply to the proprietorship's income, which is included in the proprietor's total taxable income.	Individual tax rates apply to individual partners; corporate tax rates apply to corporate partners; and estate and trust tax rates apply to fiduciary partners.	Individual tax rates apply to individual shareholders; estate and trust tax rates apply to fiduciary shareholders	Corporate tax rates apply to the corporation's taxable income. Individual, corporate, or fiduciary tax rates apply to the shareholders depending on the type of shareholder.
Ownership restrictions	By definition, a sole proprietorship can have only one owner.	A partnership can have an unlimited number of partners, and these partners can be individuals, corporations, estates, or trusts.	An S corporation may have only 75 shareholders (with two spouses counting as one). Shareholders are limited to individuals, estates, certain trusts, and certain tax-exempt organizations.	A C corporation can have an unlimited number of shareholders of any type.
Personal liability	The sole proprietor is liable for debts of the proprietorship.	General partners have unlimited liability. Limited partners have liability to the extent of their investment.	Shareholders have limited liability.	Shareholders have limited liability.

▼ TABLE I17-2
Comparison of Alternative Forms of Business Organizations (Continued)

Attributes	Sole Proprietorship	Partnership	S Corporation	C Corporation
Other nontax factors	A sole proprietorship has management continuity problems and may have difficulty raising outside capital.	A partnership has management continuity problems and restrictions on the transfer of partnership interests. It may have difficulty raising outside capital although limited partners, who are pure investors, mitigate this problem.	S corporations have the same characteristics as C corporations. Problems, however, may arise if the state income tax law does not recognize the conduit form of taxation and taxes the S corporation as a C corporation.	Along with limited liability, C corporations have continuity of life, centralized management, and free transferability of ownership interests. These factors may outweigh the disadvantages of double taxation.
Basis	A sole proprietor has basis in the business's assets but has no basis in the entity.	A partnership has basis in its assets, and its partners have basis in their partnership interests. The partners' basis includes their share of partnership liabilities. Partners' basis is adjusted annually for their share of partnership transactions.	An S corporation has basis in its assets. Shareholders have basis in their stock and a separate debt basis in their loans to the corporation. A shareholder's basis does not include corporate level liabilities. A shareholder's stock basis is adjusted annually for their share of corporate transactions. Debt basis is adjusted downward for flow-through losses and increased for basis restorations.	A C corporation has basis in its assets, and shareholders have basis in their stock. Stock basis is adjusted upward only for additional contributions to the corporation and downward for distributions that exceed the corporation's E&P.
Treatment of losses	No limitations apply to the proprietor's NOLs assuming the at-risk and passive activity loss limitations do not apply. Unused proprietor NOLs carry back 2 years and carry over 20 years.	Partners' flow-through of loss deductions are limited to the basis of their partnership interests. At-risk and passive activity loss limitations also may apply.	Shareholders' flow-through of loss deductions are limited to their stock and debt basis. At-risk and passive activity loss limitations also may apply.	C corporation losses do not flow through to its shareholders. Unused corporate level NOLs carry back 2 years and carry over 20 years at the corporate level.
Choice of accounting methods	The sole proprietor can elect the cash or accrual method for business items. However, the accrual method for sales and purchases is required if inventory is a material income producing factor.	Partnerships can elect the cash or accrual method unless they are tax shelters or have a C corporation as a partner, in which case they must use the accrual method. Also, the accrual method for sales and purchases is required if inventory is a material income producing factor.	S corporations can elect the cash or accrual method unless they are tax shelters, in which case they must use the accrual method. Also, the accrual method for sales and purchases is required if inventory is a material income producing factor.	C corporations must use the accrual method unless they are personal service corporations or have gross receipts less than $5 million, in which case they can elect the cash or accrual method.

TABLE I17-2
Comparison of Alternative Forms of Business Organizations (Continued)

Attributes	Sole Proprietorship	Partnership	S Corporation	C Corporation
Choice of tax year	A sole proprietorship must use the same tax year as the sole proprietor, usually a calendar year.	The tax year is restricted to that of the majority partners, principal partners, or the least aggregate deferral. The partnership can use a fiscal year if it establishes a business purpose (e.g., a natural business cycle). Other special rules allow a tax year resulting in a maximum three-month deferral.	The tax year is restricted to a calendar year unless the corporation establishes a business purpose (e.g., a natural business cycle) for a fiscal year. Other special rules allow a tax year resulting in a maximum three-month deferral.	C corporations can use a calendar year or any fiscal year. Personal service corporations, however, face restrictions similar to those for S corporations.
Employment related tax considerations	A sole proprietor is not considered an employee of the business and must pay self-employment taxes on business earnings. Corporate fringe benefits, such as group term life insurance, are not available.	A partner is not considered an employee of the partnership and must pay self-employment taxes on business earnings. Corporate fringe benefits, such as group term life insurance, are not available.	Same as for partnerships for shareholders owning more than 2% of the corporation's stock. S corporation shareholders may be treated as employees, however, for social security tax purposes if they receive a salary.	A shareholder-employee may be treated as an employee for social security tax purposes and fringe benefits.

PROBLEM MATERIALS

DISCUSSION QUESTIONS

I17-1 Distinguish between the partnership, S corporation, and C corporation organization forms regarding the following:
  a. Incidence of taxation on business income of the organization
  b. Taxation of distributions to owners
  c. Application of the conduit and separate entity concepts of taxation

I17-2 Explain how the following business forms are taxed under the check-the-box rules. What alternative tax treatments are available other than the default classification?
  a. Corporation
  b. Limited liability company
  c. Limited liability partnership

I17-3 Paula transfers the following assets to a partnership:

  a. Land with a $60,000 adjusted basis and a $100,000 FMV in exchange for a 20% interest in the partnership
  b. A machine with a $50,000 adjusted basis and a $40,000 FMV. The partnership signs a note for $40,000 as consideration for the exchange.

Explain whether Paula recognizes gain or loss for either of these transactions, and discuss the reason for any difference in tax treatment.

I17-4 Peggy agrees to act as a broker to arrange debt financing for the PQR Partnership. In exchange, the PQR Partnership offers Peggy, as compensation for the brokerage services rendered, a 10% interest in the partnership having a $50,000 value. Discuss the tax implications of this offer to Peggy and the partnership.

I17-5 In the current year, Penny contributes machinery (Sec. 1231 property) that she acquired five years earlier and that has a $50,000 adjusted basis and an $80,000 FMV to a partnership in exchange for a partnership interest. What are Penny's basis and holding period for the partnership interest? What is the partnership's basis and holding period for the asset? Explain the reasons for these rules in the tax law.

I17-6 How is Mario's basis in his partnership interest affected by the following changes in partnership liabilities (assuming he has a 50% interest in the partnership)?
  a. Mario contributes a building with a $70,000 basis subject to a $50,000 mortgage, which the partnership assumes.
  b. The partnership's accounts payable increase by $50,000 during the tax year.
  c. The partnership pays off a $50,000 bank note that was outstanding for several years.

I17-7 What are the tax consequences to a partner who contributes liabilities that exceed the basis of an asset transferred to the partnership in exchange for a partnership interest?

I17-8 Why are certain special partnership income and deduction items (e.g., capital gains and losses and charitable contributions) reported separately on Schedule K rather than being included in ordinary income on page 1 of Form 1065?

I17-9 What inequities might result if partners were not required to make special allocations for pre-contribution gains and losses when a contribution of noncash property is made to a partnership?

I17-10 Indicate whether a partner's basis in the partnership interest increases (+), decreases (−), or is not affected (0) by the partner's share of the following operating items:
  a. Ordinary income
  b. Ordinary loss
  c. Tax-exempt income
  d. Capital losses
  e. Charitable contributions made by the partnership
  f. Distributions of property to the partners

I17-11 Phyllis owns a 30% interest in the PQR Partnership and has a $20,000 basis in her partnership interest (before adjustments for Phyllis's share of partnership income or loss). During the current year, the PQR Partnership reports a $100,000 ordinary loss and no change in partnership liabilities, and Phyllis materially participates in the business in the current year.
  a. What amount of the loss is deductible by Phyllis in the current year?
  b. What is Phyllis's basis in her partnership interest at the end of the current year?
  c. What happens to Phyllis's unused ordinary loss (if any)?
  d. What steps can be taken by Phyllis to accelerate the use of the loss carryover?

I17-12 Ralph sells an asset to the RST Partnership at a loss. In which of the following situations is the loss recognized?
  a. Ralph owns a 20% direct interest in the partnership, and his son also owns a 20% interest.
  b. Ralph owns a 35% direct interest in the partnership, and his daughter also owns a 35% interest.
  c. Ralph owns a 35% direct interest in the partnership, and his 100%-owned corporation also owns a 35% interest.

I17-13 Jose owns a 60% interest in the JKL Partnership. What are the amount and character of the recognized gain or loss in each of the following situations?
  a. Jose sells common stock held as an investment with a $1,000 adjusted basis and a $2,000 FMV to the partnership. The stock is held as an investment by the partnership.
  b. Jose sells a parcel of land held for investment purposes with a $10,000 adjusted basis and a $20,000 FMV to the partnership. The land is used in the partnership's business.
  c. Jose sells a building used in his business with a $100,000 adjusted basis and a $60,000 FMV to the partnership. The building is used in the partnership's business.

I17-14 Ursula is a 30% partner in the UV Partnership. The partnership agreement states that she shall receive 30% of partnership profits computed before considering guaranteed payments. However, she is not to receive less than $10,000.
  a. What is Ursula's income if the partnership earns $60,000? How much of her income is a guaranteed payment?
  b. What is Ursula's income if the partnership earns $20,000? How much of her income is a guaranteed payment?

I17-15 Explain the circumstances that cause a partner to recognize gain or loss if money or other property is distributed in a nonliquidating partnership distribution.

I17-16 Explain why a partner who sells his or her interest in the partnership for cash must include his or her share of the partnership liabilities in the amount realized from the sale.

I17-17 What are the tax consequences to a partner who sells his or her partnership interest if the partnership has Sec. 751 assets (i.e., unrealized receivables or inventory items)? What is the reason for this result?

I17-18 What is an electing large partnership? What requirements must be met by a partnership in order to make an election to use the simplified reporting rules available to electing large partnerships?

I17-19 What are the major differences between the reporting of business profits and losses earned by an electing large partnership having 200 partners and a regular partnership having two partners? capital gains and losses?

I17-20 What are the tax consequences to an S corporation and its shareholders if one of the requirements for a small business corporation is not met at some time in a tax year?

I17-21 An S corporation issues straight debt obligations to its shareholders. Is it possible for the debt to be treated as a second class of stock, which would terminate the S election? Explain.

I17-22 Andrew sells his Ajax Corporation stock to Angela on March 1. On March 15, Ajax Corporation elects S corporation status for the current year. Ajax is a calendar year taxpayer. Which shareholder(s) must consent to the election? Why? Which shareholder(s) receive an allocation of the S corporation's profits? For what time period is the allocation received?

I17-23 An S corporation's shareholder wants to voluntarily revoke the S election. What percentage of stock interests must agree to the revocation? When is the revocation first effective?

I17-24 Under what conditions will an S corporation involuntarily lose its special tax status and revert to being a C corporation? What remedies are available if the S corporation termination is deemed to be inadvertent?

I17-25 Indicate whether the following items are reported on the tax return of an S corporation as part of ordinary income (or loss) or as a separately stated item:
 a. Repairs
 b. Long-term capital gains
 c. Short-term capital losses
 d. Sec. 1231 gains
 e. Tax credits
 f. Tax preference items
 g. Salary paid to an S corporation shareholder

I17-26 Explain why the basis of S corporation stock is reduced by the stockholder's share of an ordinary loss.

I17-27 Anne's basis in her S corporation stock on January 1 of the current year is $10,000. On March 1 of the current year, Anne lends the corporation $8,000. Her share of the S corporation's ordinary loss for the current year (which has not yet ended) is expected to be $28,000. Anne expects her marginal tax rate to be 15% in the current year. She expects that her marginal tax rate will increase to 31% next year, and she anticipates substantial profits for the S corporation next year. Advise Anne regarding the deductibility of her share of the losses and the desirability of making additional capital contributions in either year.

I17-28 Allied Corporation, an S corporation, is considering making a distribution of land (acquired three years earlier and held for investment) having a $60,000 adjusted basis and a $130,000 FMV to its sole shareholder. The corporation has always been an S corporation. Explain the tax consequences to the corporation and to the shareholder if the land is distributed.

I17-29 Barry and Bart are considering whether to start a new manufacturing business. Alternative forms of business organization being considered include operating as a partnership, an S corporation, or a C corporation. Barry and Bart are calendar-year taxpayers but would like to use a January 31 year-end for the business to obtain an 11-month deferral of the income. Discuss the implications and restrictions of operating under each alternative form of business organization being considered.

I17-30 Assume the same facts as in Problem I17-29, except that Barry and Bart are instead considering the treatment of fringe benefits. Barry and Bart want to provide group term life insurance and accident and health insurance for themselves and their employees and plan to make the premium payments from business funds. Explain any restrictions that apply to each form of business organization.

I17-31 Explain the circumstances in which an S corporation is subject to taxation at the corporate level.

ISSUE IDENTIFICATION QUESTIONS

I17-32 Bert and Jose plan to combine their unincorporated businesses by forming a partnership. Bert has substantially appreciated business assets. Moreover, if he transfers all of the liabilities of the business and all of the assets, the liabilities will exceed the adjusted basis of the assets but not their FMV. Jose will render services to the partnership in addition to transferring all of his business assets. What tax issues should Bert and Jose consider?

I17-33 Helen and Helga are equal partners in the HH Partnership. However, Helen devotes most of her time managing the business and feels that she should be given additional compensation in the form of a guaranteed payment. Currently, the partnership is operating at a break-even point (i.e., zero ordinary income and no separately stated items of income or loss). The basis of each partner's partnership interest also is negligible. Helen has requested an $80,000 guaranteed payment as compensation for her additional efforts. What tax issues should Helen and Helga consider?

I17-34 Coastal Corporation has been a C corporation for several years and has substantial earnings and profits. Its tangible business assets are highly appreciated, and the corporation has paid no dividends for several years. The Board of Directors and its key shareholders are now recommending making an S election, selling the appreciated property, and paying a substantial cash distribution in the initial S corporation tax year. What tax issues should Coastal Corporation and its shareholders consider?

PROBLEMS

I17-35 *Formation of a Partnership.* Becky, Beth, and Bob form the BBB Partnership, and all the partners have an equal interest in the partnership. Becky contributes cash of $100,000; Beth contributes land (acquired five years earlier and held for business use) with a $50,000 adjusted basis and a $100,000 FMV; and Bob contributes cash of $60,000 and legal and brokerage services with a $40,000 FMV.
  a. What are the amount and character of the gain or loss Beth must recognize on the land transfer to the partnership?
  b. What are the amount and character of the income Bob must recognize due to the services he performed?
  c. What is the basis of each individual's partnership interest?
  d. Beth sells her partnership interest four months after it is acquired and recognizes a capital gain. Is the gain long-term or short-term? Explain.
  e. What is the partnership's basis for each asset acquired? When does its holding period commence for each asset?
  f. How is the land recorded on the partnership's books under generally accepted accounting principles?
  g. Assume that $9,000 of the legal services contributed by Bob relate to the organization of the partnership and $1,000 relate to Beth's transfer of the land to the partnership. How are these services reported for tax purposes by the partnership?

I17-36 *Formation of a Partnership and Treatment of Liabilities.* Bonnie, Carlos, and Dale form the BCD Partnership as equal partners. Bonnie contributes land and a building with a $50,000 adjusted basis and a $200,000 FMV that is subject to a $100,000 mortgage assumed by the partnership. The land and the building originally cost $200,000. The original basis for the building was $180,000. The original basis for the land was $20,000. Straight-line depreciation of $150,000 has been claimed on the building. Carlos contributes cash of $100,000, and Dale contributes land (a capital asset) with a $200,000 adjusted basis and a $100,000 FMV. All assets have been held for more than one year.
  a. What are the amount and character of Bonnie's recognized gain or loss on the transfer?
  b. What is Bonnie's basis in her partnership interest?
  c. What is Carlos's basis in his partnership interest?
  d. What are the amount and character of Dale's recognized gain or loss on the transfer?
  e. What is Dale's basis in his partnership interest?
  f. What is the basis for each of the contributed properties to the BCD Partnership?

I17-37 *Formation of a Partnership and Treatment of Liabilities.* In the current year, Dana transfers to the DE Partnership land and a building having a $20,000 adjusted basis and an $80,000 FMV that is subject to a $70,000 mortgage. The land and the building cost $100,000 when acquired by Dana in 1980, and the building has been depreciated in the amount of $80,000 by using the straight-line method. The land and building originally cost $15,000 and $85,000, respectively. Dana, who is active in the management of the partnership, receives a one-half interest in the partnership.
  a. What are the amount and character of Dana's recognized gain or loss on the transfer?
  b. What is Dana's basis in her partnership interest?
  c. When does Dana's holding period for the partnership interest begin?
  d. What is the basis of the contributed properties to the DE Partnership?

I17-38 *Formation of a Partnership and Loss Limitation.* Dan, who is active in the management of the partnership, contributes $10,000 to the newly formed DEF Partnership for a 10% interest in the partnership. No liabilities are transferred to the partnership by any of the partners. During the partnership's first year, DEF borrows $100,000 from a bank and is liable for accounts payable amounting to $100,000 at the end of its tax year. The DEF Partnership incurs a $400,000 ordinary loss during the year.
  a. How much of the ordinary loss may Dan deduct on his individual tax return?
  b. What is Dan's basis in his partnership interest at the end of the year?
  c. How much of the loss (if any) carries over to future years?

I17-39 *Expenses of Forming a Partnership.* The AEC Partnership, a calendar-year entity, is formed on July 1 of the current year and incurs the following expenditures on the date the partnership is formed:

Legal fees incident to the organization of the partnership	$3,000
Printing costs associated with the syndication of the partnership	6,000
Brokerage fees associated with underwriting efforts to sell limited partnership interests	5,000

  a. What is the appropriate tax treatment (i.e., capitalization, capitalization subject to amortization, or immediate expensing) for each of these items?
  b. How much amortization should be deducted for the current year?

I17-40 *Pass Through of Income and Separately Stated Items.* Damien and Donna are equal partners in the DD Partnership. The passive activity loss and the at-risk rules are not applicable to the partners. The partnership reports the following items on its Schedule K during the current year:

Ordinary loss	$10,000
Long-term capital gains	40,000
Research and experimentation credit	4,000
AMT tax preference items	6,000

Damien's basis in his partnership interest is $80,000 at the beginning of the current year. The DD Partnership's liabilities increased by $20,000 during the current year.
  a. What amounts should Damien report on his individual tax return as a result of DD Partnership's activities?
  b. What is Damien's basis in his partnership interest after taking into account the Schedule K items?

I17-41 *Special Allocations on Contributed Property.* Ed contributes land (a capital asset) having an $80,000 adjusted basis and a $100,000 FMV, and Gail contributes $100,000 cash to the EG Partnership. Ed and Gail each receive 50% interests in the partnership. Two years later the partnership sells the land (still a capital asset) for $110,000. What are the amount and character of the EG Partnership's gain or loss? How much of EG's gain or loss is allocated to Ed? To Gail?

I17-42 *Loss Allocations.* Alice and Bruce are equal partners in the calendar-year AB Partnership. On November 1 of the current year, Carl is admitted to the partnership by making a $100,000 cash contribution in exchange for a one-third interest in the partnership. Alice and Bruce's partnership interests are each reduced to one-third. The partnership agreement is amended to provide that Carl will receive a retroactive allocation of one-third of all partnership profits and losses incurred for the entire year. The AB Partnership reports a $90,000 ordinary loss for the tax year ending on December 31. How much of the partnership's loss is allocated to Alice, Bruce, and Carl?

I17-43 *Basis of a Partnership Interest.* Anita has a one-half interest in the AB Partnership. Anita's basis in her interest at the beginning of the current year is $75,000. During the year, the following events occur:
- Partnership liabilities increase by $50,000.
- Partnership earns $60,000 of ordinary income.
- Partnership recognizes $20,000 of capital losses.
- Partnership earns $10,000 of tax-exempt interest.
- Anita withdraws $20,000 in cash.
- Anita contributes land having a $30,000 adjusted basis and a $100,000 FMV as an additional capital contribution without increasing her interest in the partnership.

What is Anita's basis in her partnership interest at the end of the current year?

I17-44 *Partnership Losses and Basis.* Ken has a one-half interest in the KL Partnership. His basis in the partnership interest at the end of the current year (before deducting his share of partnership losses) is $40,000. His share of the partnership's ordinary loss in the current year is $180,000. Next year, Ken makes a $60,000 additional capital contribution, and the partnership's ordinary income is $100,000. Assume that no change occurs in Ken's partnership interest as a result of the capital contribution and that he materially participates in the business.

a. How much ordinary loss can Ken deduct in the current year?
b. What is Ken's basis in his partnership interest at the end of the current year?
c. How much ordinary income or loss does Ken report next year?
d. What is Ken's basis in his partnership interest at the end of next year?

I17-45 *Transactions Between the Partners and the Partnership.* Kevin has a 30% interest in the KLM Partnership. Louis (Kevin's son) also has a 30% interest. The remaining 40% interest is owned by an individual unrelated to either Kevin or Louis. Kevin sells the following assets to the partnership during the year:

- Common stock (a capital asset) having a $10,000 basis and a $20,000 FMV and selling price.
- Land (a Sec. 1231 asset) having a $100,000 adjusted basis and a $60,000 FMV and selling price.
- Machine having a $50,000 adjusted basis and a $70,000 FMV and selling price. The original cost of the machine was $60,000, and $10,000 in MACRS depreciation allowances have been taken.

a. What are the amount and character of Kevin's recognized gain or loss on the sale of the common stock? The land? The machine?
b. What gain or loss would the partnership recognize if it sells the land two years later for $90,000?

I17-46 *Guaranteed Payments.* Laura and Mark are equal partners in the LM Partnership. Laura receives a $35,000 guaranteed payment in the current year and withdraws $15,000 of her partnership capital in cash. Partnership ordinary income is $100,000 for the current year. What amounts must be included in Laura's gross income for the current year?

I17-47 *Nonliquidating Distributions.* Lynn's basis in her partnership interest is $9,000 when she receives a nonliquidating distribution of $5,000 cash and land having a $6,000 adjusted basis and a $12,000 FMV.
a. What are the amount and character of the income or gain Lynn must recognize on the distribution?
b. What is Lynn's basis in the land?
c. What is Lynn's basis in her partnership interest after the distribution?

I17-48 *Sale of a Partnership Interest.* The balance sheet of the ABC Partnership at November 30 of the current year is as follows:

	Adjusted Basis	FMV
Assets:		
Cash	$ 10,000	$ 10,000
Accounts receivable	20,000	20,000
Inventory	15,000	16,000
Land, buildings, and machinery	60,000	74,000[a]
Total	$105,000	$120,000
Liabilities and capital:		
Accounts payable	$ 5,000	$ 5,000
Notes payable	10,000	10,000
Allen's Capital (⅓)	30,000	35,000
Beth's Capital (⅓)	30,000	35,000
Candace's Capital (⅓)	30,000	35,000
Total	$105,000	$120,000

[a] Assume that $3,000 would be ordinary income under the depreciation recapture rules if the assets were sold.

All partners have an equal interest in the partnership. Allen sells his partnership interest to an outsider on November 30 of the current year for $35,000. Allen's share of the partnership income for the 11-month period ending November 30 is $3,000, and his basis in the partnership interest is $38,000 (which includes Allen's share of the income and partnership liabilities for the period ending November 30).
a. What amount is realized by Allen on the sale?
b. What are the amount and character of the gain or loss Allen must recognize on the sale?

I17-49 *Reporting Partnership Income.* Rita, a calendar-year taxpayer, is an employee of the RST Partnership, which has an April 30 year-end. The partnership pays Rita a salary of $3,000 per month for the period from January 1 through April 30, 2001. On May 1, she is admitted to the partnership and receives monthly drawings of $3,000 for the 12-month period ending April 30, 2002. The drawings reflect her approximate share of the partnership income for the period from May 1, 2001 through April 30, 2002. On April 30, 2002, Rita's share of the partnership ordinary income is $40,000.
a. What amount of income does Rita report on her 2001 individual tax return?
b. What amount of income does Rita report on her 2002 individual tax return?

I17-50 *Electing Large Partnerships.* JLK Partnership is an electing large partnership. The partnership reports the following operating results from the current year:

Ordinary income	$200,000
Net Sec. 1231 gain	25,000
Tax-exempt interest income	10,000
Net long-term capital gain	15,000
Charitable contributions	20,000
Miscellaneous itemized deductions	5,000

None of JLK's activities are passive activities. During the year, JLK made $75,000 of distributions to its partners. JLK has 125 partners.
a. What income, gains, losses, and deductions are reported by the JLK Partnership to its partners?
b. How are the items from part (a) reported by JLK's partners?

I17-51 *S Corporation Terminations.* Which of the following events will cause a termination of the S election for a calendar year corporation? When is the termination effective? (Assume that all other requirements for an S election are met and that the termination is not inadvertent.)
a. Best Corporation has 75 qualifying S corporation shareholders. Sam dies on October 13, and his stock is held by the estate for the rest of the year.
b. Assume the same facts as in Part a, except that the estate distributes the stock to Sam's child before the end of the tax year. Sam's child did not previously own any Best stock.
c. Best Corporation issues nonvoting common stock to Susan's two children during the current year. Susan's children did not previously own any Best stock.
d. Shareholders Susan, Ted, and Tim, who own 60% of the Best stock, file a revocation on October 1 to terminate the election as of this date. All three shareholders are calendar year taxpayers.

I17-52 *S Corporation Ordinary Income and Separately Stated Items.* The income statement for Central Corporation, an electing S corporation, reflects the following:

Sales	$200,000
Cost of goods sold	(60,000)
Repair expense	(5,000)
Depreciation expense	(10,000)
Salary expense	(30,000)
Long-term capital losses	(10,000)
Charitable contributions	(5,000)
Sec. 1231 losses	(8,000)
Net income per tax books	$ 72,000

a. What is Central's ordinary income (or loss) for the year?
b. Which of the items above appear as separately stated items on Schedule K?
c. Carol owns 50% of Central's stock, which has a $50,000 basis (before any of the items listed above are taken into account). What is Carol's adjusted basis for her stock after all adjustments are made for Carol's share of Central's ordinary income or loss and separately stated items?

I17-53 *Basis of S Corporation Stock.* Cathy is a 50% shareholder of City Corporation. City is an electing (calendar-year) S corporation. Cathy acquires her stock on January 1 of the current year for $50,000. In the current year, City reports the following results of operations, cash distributions, and salary payments:

Ordinary income allocable to Cathy	$30,000
Salary payments to Cathy	40,000
Long-term capital losses allocable to Cathy	5,000
Cash distributions to Cathy	10,000

a. What is Cathy's basis in her stock at the end of the current year?
b. What amounts should be included in Cathy's individual tax return for the current year?

I17-54 *S Corporation Losses and Stock Basis.* Chris owns one-third of the stock of Coastal Corporation, an electing S corporation, and he materially participates in the business. Coastal uses the calendar year as its tax year. On January 1 of the current year, Chris's basis in the stock is $25,000, and he has a $10,000 loan outstanding to the corporation. In the current year, Coastal Corporation reports a $180,000 ordinary loss.
a. What amount of loss can Chris deduct on his individual tax return?
b. What is Chris's basis in his stock and loan at December 31?
c. How much of the loss (if any) is carried forward to subsequent years?

I17-55 *S Corporation Basis for Stock and Loans.* Because of earlier losses, Cindy has a zero basis in her S corporation stock and a zero basis in her $10,000 loan to the corporation. During the current year, Cindy acquires additional shares of the S corporation stock for $8,000, and her share of the S corporation income is $7,000.
a. What is Cindy's basis in her loan and stock on December 31?
b. What are the tax consequences to Cindy if her loan (secured by a note) is fully repaid on January 1 of the following year?

I17-56 *S Corporation Distributions and Basis of Stock.* Control Corporation distributes $10,000 cash to shareholder Craig whose stock basis is $8,000. Craig's share of ordinary income for the current year is $1,000, and the corporation has no separately stated items. Control Corporation always has been an electing S corporation.
a. What are the tax consequences of the distribution (i.e., amount and character of income or gain to Control Corporation and Craig)?
b. What is Craig's stock basis at the end of the tax year?

I17-57 *S Corporation Distributions and Basis of Property.* Compact Corporation, an electing S corporation, distributes land used in its business to Clay, its sole shareholder. The land has an $80,000 adjusted basis and a $125,000 FMV. Clay's basis in the Compact stock is $150,000, which includes his share of ordinary income and separately stated items for the current year (other than any gains or losses recognized because of the distribution). Compact always has been an S corporation.
a. What are the tax consequences of the distribution to Compact Corporation and Clay?
b. What is the basis of the land to Clay?
c. How would your answer to part (a) change if the land instead had a $100,000 adjusted basis and a $75,000 FMV?

I17-58 *S Corporation Fringe Benefits.* Copper Corporation was formed two years ago and immediately elected S corporation status. In the current year, the corporation pays the following insurance premiums for its employees:

Group term life insurance for shareholder-employees, all of whom own more than 2% of the stock	$3,000
Accident, health, and medical reimbursement plan insurance premiums for shareholder-employees, all of whom own more than 2% of the stock	5,000
Group term life insurance premiums for employees who are not shareholders	1,000
Accident, health, and medical reimbursement plan insurance premiums for employees who are not shareholders	2,000

a. What tax consequences result from Copper Corporation's payment of the insurance premiums?
b. What are the tax consequences to the shareholder-employees and to the employees who are not shareholders?

I17-59 *S Corporation Built-In Gains Tax.* Delta Corporation made an S election on January 1 of the current year. Delta had been a C corporation since its inception before 1986. The corporation has the following operating results during the current year:

Ordinary income	$200,000
Long-term capital gains	130,000

The adjusted basis and FMV of capital assets held on January 1 and sold during the current year were $200,000 and $320,000, respectively, as of the January 1 beginning of the S election period.

a. Is Delta Corporation subject to the built-in gains tax under Sec. 1374? Explain.
b. What is the amount of corporate tax liability on the built-in gain (if applicable)?
c. How would your answers to Parts a and b change if Delta Corporation instead made its S election on January 31, 1986?

COMPREHENSIVE PROBLEM

I17-60 Charles is a 50% partner in CD Partnership, a calendar-year partnership. For 2001, Charles received a Schedule K-1 that reported his share of partnership items as follows:

Partnership ordinary income	$100,000
Tax-exempt income	1,000
Dividend income	3,000
Short-term capital loss	10,000
Sec. 1231 loss	12,000
Charitable contributions	2,000
Cash distribution	60,000

In addition, Charles and his wife, Charlene, had the following items relating to activities outside the partnership:

Charlene's salary	$90,000
Long-term capital gain	49,000
Interest income from corporate bonds	5,000
Mortgage interest expense	12,000
State income taxes	8,000
State sales taxes	5,000
Property taxes on home	3,000
Charitable contributions	5,500
Withholding on Charlene's salary	27,000
Estimated tax payments	20,000

Charles and Charlene have two dependent children, ages 7 and 9, and file a joint tax return. Required: Calculate the following items for Charles and Charlene:
a. Adjusted gross income (AGI)
b. Taxable income
c. Tax liability
d. Taxes due or refund

TAX FORM/RETURN PREPARATION PROBLEMS

I17-61 The XYZ Partnership reports the following items during 2000:

Sales	$240,000
Cost of goods sold	100,000
Dividends	10,000
Interest income on certificate of deposit held as an investment	6,000
Tax-exempt interest	12,000
Salaries to employees	20,000
Federal employment taxes	2,500
Guaranteed payments to partners	30,000
Net long-term capital gain	15,000*
Net short-term capital gain	5,000
Repairs	3,000
MACRS depreciation	8,000
Sec. 1231 losses	15,000

Charitable contributions	2,000
Amortization of organizational expenditures	1,000
Research and experimentation credit	3,000
Partner withdrawals	8,000

*Eligible to be taxed at a 20% tax rate.

Calculate ordinary income (or loss) by completing page 1 of Form 1065 and the Schedule K (Partners' Shares of Income, Credits, Deductions, etc.). Leave spaces blank on Form 1065 if information is not provided.

I17-62 Eagle Corporation, an S corporation, reports the following items during 2000:

Sales	$240,000
Cost of goods sold	100,000
Dividends	10,000
Interest income on certificate of deposit held as an investment	6,000
Tax-exempt interest income	12,000
Employees salaries	20,000
Federal employment taxes	2,500
Officers salaries	30,000
Net long-term capital gain	15,000*
Net short-term capital gain	5,000
Repairs	3,000
MACRS depreciation	8,000
Sec. 1231 losses	15,000
Charitable contributions	2,000
Amortization of organizational expenditures	1,000
Research and experimentation credit	3,000
Distributions to shareholders	9,000

*Eligible to be taxed at 20% rate.

Calculate ordinary income (or loss) by completing page 1 of Form 1120S and Schedule K (Shareholders' Shares of Income, Credits, Deductions, etc.). Leave spaces blank on Form 1120S if information is not provided.

CASE STUDY PROBLEMS

I17-63 Peggy, Phil, and Ralph each have unincorporated accounting practices, and they wish to pool their resources and operate as a single business entity. Peggy owns a building that has appreciated in value since she purchased it eight years ago. They intend to use this building for their office. Other than the building, they own office equipment, computer equipment and furniture, none of which is worth more than book value. They all have substantial outstanding accounts receivable with a zero basis because each individual uses the cash method of accounting. Each individual has substantial amounts of portfolio income (i.e., dividends and interest). Under the plan, accounts payable with a zero basis from the unincorporated accounting practices would be transferred to the new entity.

Each accountant has two or three employees each. They all agree that it is important to provide benefits to their employees, such as group health insurance, group term life insurance, and a retirement plan of some kind. Additionally, they wish to have their staff participate in the profits of the company and have some form of equity interest in the company.

Peggy, Phil, and Ralph use different computerized accounting and billing systems. They also have different documentation requirements for their client files. The computerized accounting records, billing records, and client files will all have to be consolidated from three systems to one system. The conversion will take place over a period of time. For this reason, they anticipate losses for the first tax year.

Peggy, Phil, and Ralph have agreed that they want to operate as a flow-through entity because they wish to avoid double taxation, and they want to use the losses from the first year immediately. They have come to you for advice. Write a client memo comparing the pros and cons of operating the accounting practice as a partnership and an S corporation.

I17-64 Dan is the partial owner of an S corporation that currently has 75 shareholders. In March of the current year, Dan sold some of his S corporation stock to each of his two adult children. In August, Dan redeemed the stock he sold because he is in the midst of a divorce and was fearful of the consequences associated with giving voting rights of his business to his children. Dan informs you, his tax consultant, of the stock sale and subsequent redemption. You explain to Dan that by selling the stock he created 77 shareholders between the months of March and August and that the S election had been terminated on the day preceding the date on which the corporation first had more than 75 shareholders. Dan tells you that he sees no reason to inform the IRS of the termination because he bought back the stock within the same tax year and the IRS probably would not discover the event. What are your responsibilities as a CPA under the SRTP rules as mandated by the AICPA concerning the S election termination? (See the *Statements on Responsibilities in Tax Practice* section in Chapter I15 and Appendix E for a discussion of these issues.) What advice can you offer Dan concerning reinstatement of the S election under the rules for inadvertent terminations?

TAX RESEARCH PROBLEMS

I17-65 Sandee is an employee of the Beach Group, an organization active in the Florida real estate industry. Sandee performs the task of finding real estate property on Miami Beach and subsequently organizing partnerships to acquire and finance the property. Sandee was particularly interested in one building in the Art Deco district that was to be purchased and renovated. She gathered interested investors who formed the Deco Partnership, consisting of two general partners and several limited partners. In exchange for her services in organizing the partnership, Sandee received a 3% limited partnership interest only in the profits of the Deco Partnership. As part of the agreement, the profits interest was transferable only at the discretion of the general partners. Based on the uncertainty in the South Florida real estate industry at the time, the partners could not estimate whether profits or losses would be generated when the renovation was completed in three years. Based on these facts, will Sandee's receipt of the limited partnership interest be a taxable event?

A partial list of research sources is

- Sec. 721
- Reg. Sec. 1.721-1(a)
- *William G. Campbell v. CIR*, 68 AFTR 2d 91-5425, 91-2 USTC ¶50,420 (8th Cir., 1991)
- *Sol Diamond v. CIR*, 33 AFTR 2d 74-852, 74-1 USTC ¶9306 (7th Cir., 1974)
- Rev. Proc. 93-27, 1993-2 C.B. 343

I17-66 Chuck, Cindy, and Clay are the three equal owners of Able Corporation common stock. Able was incorporated in the current year. Able elects to be taxed as an S corporation starting in its initial year. Chuck, Cindy, and Clay each contributed $10,000 cash to Able in exchange for their common stock. Able borrows $60,000 from a bank, and Chuck, Cindy, and Clay personally guaranteed the loan. In the current year, Able suffers a $90,000 ordinary loss. How much of the loss will be deductible by Chuck, Cindy, and Clay? (Assume that the at-risk and passive activity loss limitation rules do not apply.)

A partial list of research sources is

- Sec. 1366(d)(1)
- *Estate of Daniel Leavitt v. CIR*, 63 AFTR 2d 89-1437, 89-1 USTC ¶9332 (4th Cir., 1989)
- *Edward M. Selfe v. U.S.*, 57 AFTR 2d 86-464, 86-1 USTC ¶9115 (11th Cir., 1986)
- *Dennis E. Bolding v. U.S.*, 80 AFTR 2d 97-5481, 97-2 USTC ¶50,553 (7th Cir., 1997).

CHAPTER 18

TAXES AND INVESTMENT PLANNING

LEARNING OBJECTIVES
After studying this chapter, you should be able to

1. Apply the investment models to various investment alternatives
2. Use the investment models to make entity choices
3. Use the investment models to make current salary versus deferred compensation decisions
4. Understand the role of implicit taxes in investment decisions

CHAPTER OUTLINE

Investment Models...18-2
Other Applications of Investment Models...18-15
Implicit Taxes and Clienteles...18-26

This chapter has been derived from a book written by Myron S. Scholes and Mark A. Wolfson and takes what has become known as the Scholes-Wolfson approach to investment strategy.[1] Consequently, the chapter differs significantly from other chapters in this text. First, the chapter does not present details of tax law. Instead, it introduces a conceptual framework for understanding how taxes affect basic investment decisions. Second, the chapter develops and illustrates models for determining the after-tax outcomes of various investment alternatives. Although these models may look strange at first, they become familiar and manageable after some study and practice. Third, the chapter extends the models' application to the flow-through versus C corporation choice and the current salary versus deferred compensation decision. Fourth, the chapter introduces the role of implicit taxes as well as explicit taxes in investment decisions. As demonstrated later, the before-tax rate of return of a tax-favored asset will be reduced by market forces as investors increase their demand for these investments. This reduced rate of return is an implicit tax that investors need to consider when making their decisions.

INVESTMENT MODELS

OBJECTIVE 1

Apply the investment models to various investment alternatives

The investment models described in this chapter fall into four categories depending on how investment earnings are taxed. We refer to these models as:

▶ The Current Model—Investment earnings are taxed currently.
▶ The Deferred Model—Investment earnings are taxed at the end of the investment period.
▶ The Exempt Model—Investment earnings are exempt from explicit taxation.
▶ The Pension Model—The initial investment is deductible or excludable from gross income, and investment earnings are taxed at the end of the investment period.

These models in their basic form reflect the following assumptions:

▶ The investment's before-tax rate of return is constant over the investment period.
▶ The investor's marginal tax rate is constant over the investment period.
▶ Investment earnings are reinvested at the same rate of return as earned by the original investment.
▶ The investor knows future rates of returns and tax rates with certainty.
▶ The investor incurs no transaction costs.

KEY POINT

Future values are necessary to compare all amounts at the same point in time. This comparable time frame is critical in evaluating alternative investment opportunities.

The models can be modified, however, to accommodate changes to these assumptions. For example, we later show how to adapt the Current Model for changing tax rates (see Example I18-5).

THE CURRENT MODE

The Current Model gives the future value of an investment having the following characteristics:

▶ Only after-tax dollars are invested.
▶ The earnings on the investment are taxed annually (currently); thus, the reinvested earnings grow at the after-tax rate of return.

Common examples of investments taxed this way are savings accounts, money market funds, and taxable bonds, if the investor reinvests the after-tax earnings annually.

INVESTMENT WITH NO TAXATION. Before developing the Current Model, however, we first illustrate how an investment grows when compounded annually in a no-tax situation, and we introduce the notions of before-tax dollars and the before-tax rate of

---

[1] Myron S. Scholes, Mark A. Wolfson, Merle Erickson, Edward L. Maydew, and Terry Shevlin, *Taxes and Business Strategy: A Planning Approach*, Second Edition (Upper Saddle River, NJ: Prentice Hall, 2002).

EXAMPLE I18-1

Carla, an individual investor, lives in a land of no taxation and earns $1,000 of salary. She invests this amount in a bond that pays interest at 10% per year and holds the bond for three years, reinvesting the interest annually at the same 10% return. The following schedule details the investment's cash flow over the three years:

(1) Year	(2) Cumulative Investment at Beginning of Year	(3) Interest Income[a]	(4) Cumulative Investment at End of Year[b]
1	$1,000	$100	$1,100
2	1,100	110	1,210
3	1,210	121	1,331

[a] Column 2 × 10%
[b] Column 2 + Column 3

Thus, at the end of three years, the $1,000 original investment accumulates to $1,331.

The three-year accumulation determined in Example I18-1 also can be calculated as follows: $1,000 (1.1)^3 = $1,331, which is $1,000 compounded at 10% for three years. Thus, the general form of the compounding formula is:

$$\text{Accumulation} = \text{BT\$} (1 + R)^n$$

In this formula, BT$ stands for before-tax dollars invested. For instance, in Example I18-1, Carla invested the entire $1,000 because her salary was not reduced by taxes. Also in the formula, R is the before-tax rate of return (BTROR). Again, this return is a before-tax percentage because, as in Example I18-1, the interest on the investment is not taxed. Consequently, all the interest can be reinvested; nothing is siphoned away as taxes. Finally, n equals the number of years the investor holds the investment or, in other words, n represents the investment horizon. Thus, the formula gives the future value (accumulation) of before-tax dollars invested for n years while earning a BTROR equal to R.

THE CURRENT MODEL. Now assume our investor is subject to taxation at marginal tax rate t. In this case, any earned income, such as salary, will be subject to taxes, leaving only after-tax dollars available for investment.

EXAMPLE I18-2

ADDITIONAL COMMENT

In this chapter, we primarily use only federal tax rates. However, in real life situations, all taxes must be considered.

Assume the same facts as Example I18-1 except Carla's $1,000 salary is subject to tax, and her marginal tax rate is 40%. That is, t = 40% or 0.4. (For simplicity in this chapter, we use 40% instead of 39.6% as the top tax rate.) In this case, Carla has only $600 to invest. This amount is computed as follows:

Salary before taxes	$1,000
Minus: Taxes ($1,000 × 0.4)	(400)
After-tax dollars available to invest	$ 600

The $600 amount determined in Example I18-2 also can be calculated as follows:

After-tax dollars = $1,000 − ($1,000 × 0.4)
          = $1,000 (1 − 0.4) (Factoring out the $1,000 salary)
          = $1,000 × 0.6 = $600

In general, then, the relationship between before-tax dollars (BT$) and after-tax dollars (AT$) can be expressed as follows:

$$\text{AT\$} = \text{BT\$} (1 - t)$$

Now assume that the interest our investor earns also is taxed at her marginal tax rate. The following example shows the impact on the investor's after-tax cash flows.

EXAMPLE I18-3 ▶ Carla (from the two previous examples) again earns $1,000 of salary, but because of taxation at 40%, she has only $600 to invest, as shown in Example I18-2. She invests the $600 in a bond for three years that yields 10% interest per year before taxes. However, in this case, the interest income also is taxed at 40%. The following schedule details the investment's cash flow over the three years:

(1) Year	(2) Cumulative Investment at Beginning of Year	(3) Before-Tax Interest Income[a]	(4) Tax on Interest[b]	(5) After-Tax Interest Income[c]	(6) Cumulative Investment at End of Year[d]
1	$600.00	$60.00	$24.00	$36.00	$636.00
2	636.00	63.60	25.44	38.16	674.16
3	674.16	67.42	26.97	40.45	714.61

[a] Column 2 × 10%
[b] Column 3 × 40%
[c] Column 3 − Column 4
[d] Column 2 + Column 5

◀

In Example I18-3, after-tax interest in Column 5 for Year 1 also can be calculated as follows:

After-tax interest = $600 (0.1) − $600 (0.1) (0.4)
= $600 (0.1) (1 − 0.4)   (Factoring out the $600 after-tax salary and the 10% before-tax rate of return)
= $600 (0.1) (0.6)
= $600 (.06) = $36

Thus, although the BTROR is 10%, the after-tax rate of return (ATROR) is only 6%. In general, the relationship between the BTROR and the ATROR can be expressed as follows:

$$r = R(1 - t)$$

As before, R equals the BTROR, and t equals the investor's marginal tax rate. The new variable, r, equals the ATROR, which is easy to remember because taxes reduce big R to little r.

With knowledge of this ATROR, the three-year accumulation in Example I18-3 also can be calculated as follows: After-tax accumulation (ATA) = $600 (1.06)³ = $714.61, which is $600 compounded at 6% for three years. Thus, the general form of the after-tax compounding formula is:

The Current Model:
$$ATA = AT\$ (1 + r)^n \text{ or}$$
$$ATA = AT\$ [1 + R(1 - t)]^n$$

Note that, because of current taxation, investments conforming to the Current Model provide no deferral advantages because all earnings are taxed currently. As demonstrated later in this chapter, the other three models reflect certain tax advantages.

EXAMPLE I18-4 ▶ At the beginning of Year 1, Harry invests $5,000 (AT$) in a money market fund that pays a 5% annual return before taxes. Harry's marginal tax rate is 28%, and he allows all after-tax earnings to remain in the money market fund. That is, he withdraws only enough cash to pay taxes on the fund's annual earnings. The following table shows Harry's after-tax accumulation for various investment horizons. In this table, note that Harry's ATROR equals 3.6%, which is 5% (1 − 0.28). Thus, the Current Model appears as $5,000 [1 + 0.05 (1 − 0.28)]^n$ or $5,000 (1.036)^n$.

Investment Horizon (n)	Computation	After-Tax Accumulation
5 years	$5,000 (1.036)^5$	$ 5,967.18
10 years	$5,000 (1.036)^{10}$	$ 7,121.44
20 years	$5,000 (1.036)^{20}$	$10,142.97

Changes to Assumptions. As stated earlier, the Current Model (as well as other models) assumes that R and t are constant over the investment period. However, the model can be modified to accommodate changes to these assumptions. This modification is accomplished by breaking the model into separate components, as demonstrated in the next example.

EXAMPLE I18-5 ▶ At the beginning of Year 1, Dan invests $5,000 (AT$) in a money market fund that pays a 5% annual return before taxes. He plans to leave the after-tax earnings in the fund for 15 years. Dan expects his marginal tax rate to be 28% over the next five years but expects his tax rate to be 36% for the subsequent ten years. Thus, his ATROR for the first five years equals 3.6%, which is 5% (1 − 0.28). For the remaining ten years, his ATROR equals 3.2%, which is 5% (1 − 0.36). Dan's after-tax accumulation (ATA) after 15 years is calculated as follows:

$$ATA = \$5,000 \, (1.036)^5 \, (1.032)^{10} = \$8,176.47.$$

Note that the first part of this calculation, $\$5,000 \, (1.036)^5 = \$5,967.18$, gives the accumulation after the five years during which Dan's tax rate is 28%. This accumulation then continues to grow at the 3.2% ATROR for the remaining ten years as follows: $\$5,967.18 \, (1.032)^{10} = \$8,176.47$. ◀

THE DEFERRED MODEL

KEY POINT
Deferral is beneficial because the tax dollars not used currently to pay tax can be reinvested to help generate additional earnings.

The Deferred Model gives the future value of an investment having the following characteristics:

▶ Only after-tax dollars are invested (as with the Current Model).

▶ The earnings on the investment are not taxed annually; thus, they grow at the BTROR.

▶ The accumulated earnings are taxed at the end of the investment horizon when the investor cashes out of the investment; thus, taxation of these earnings is deferred.

The traditional nondeductible IRA described in Chapter I9 is a classic example of the Deferred Model. Recall that, if the taxpayer or the taxpayer's spouse is covered by an employer-sponsored qualified retirement plan and the taxpayer's AGI exceeds a specified amount,[2] the taxpayer may not deduct contributions to a traditional IRA. Moreover, if the taxpayer's AGI exceeds another threshold,[3] the taxpayer may not contribute to a Roth IRA. Nevertheless, a taxpayer precluded from making *deductible* contributions to a traditional IRA or contributions to a Roth IRA still may make *nondeductible* contributions up to $2,000 per year to a traditional IRA. These nondeductible contributions are after-tax dollars.

EXAMPLE I18-6 ▶ Marsha is in the 36% tax bracket and is ineligible to make deductible or Roth IRA contributions. Nevertheless, she wishes to contribute $2,000 to a traditional nondeductible IRA. She wants to know how much taxable salary she must earn to have $2,000 left for the contribution. Recall that AT$ = BT$ (1 − t). Rearranging these terms gives BT$ = AT$ / (1 − t). In words, we can "gross up" after-tax dollars by dividing after-tax dollars by one minus the tax rate. Accordingly, the before-tax dollars necessary to yield $2,000 after taxes equals $3,125, which is $2,000 / (1 − 0.36). Thus, Marsha must earn $3,125 of salary before taxes. The tax on this amount equals $1,125, which is $3,125 × 0.36, leaving $2,000 available for contribution to the IRA. ◀

---

[2] In 2001 for a taxpayer covered by an employer plan, this AGI amount is $63,000 for married filing jointly and $43,000 for other taxpayers except those married filing separately. If the taxpayer is not covered by an employer plan but his or her spouse is covered, the AGI amount is $160,000.

[3] The AGI amount is $160,000 for married filing jointly and $110,000 for other taxpayers except those married filing separately.

EXAMPLE I18-7 ▶ Suppose Marsha makes the $2,000 contribution to a traditional nondeductible IRA in the current year and makes no subsequent contributions. Suppose further that investments in the IRA yield 12% per year before taxes and that Marsha allows her investment to accumulate in the IRA for 15 years. At the end of 15 years, she withdraws all amounts from the IRA, at which time her marginal tax rate is 36%. The following calculation demonstrates one way to determine Marsha's after-tax accumulation in the IRA:

(1) Before-tax accumulation in the IRA [$2,000 (1.12)^{15}]	$10,947.13
(2) Minus: Original contribution	(2,000.00)
(3) Accumulated earnings before taxes	$ 8,947.13
(4) Times: Tax rate	0.36
(5) Tax on accumulated earnings	$ 3,220.97
(6) After-tax accumulation (Line 1 − Line 5)	$ 7,726.16 ◀

The calculation in Example I18-7 also can be formulated as follows:

$$ATA = \$2,000\,(1.12)^{15} - [\$2,000\,(1.12)^{15} - \$2,000] \times .036$$

The first term, $\$2,000\,(1.12)^{15}$, gives the total before-tax accumulation; the subtraction in brackets gives the accumulated before-tax earnings; and the multiplication by 36% gives the tax on the accumulated earnings. Subtracting these taxes from the first term gives the total after-tax accumulation. Factoring out the $2,000 investment yields the following expression:

$$ATA = \$2,000\,\{(1.12)^{15} - [(1.12)^{15} - 1] \times .036\}$$

Substituting our general symbols into this expression yields the following model, the component parts of which are shown in Figure I18-1:

$$ATA = AT\$\,\{(1 + R)^n - [(1 + R)^n - 1] \times t_n\}$$

The subscript n on the tax rate emphasizes that the rate in Year n applies rather than the rate in the investment year or any intervening year. To make the model easier to use computationally, we can simplify this model algebraically with the following three steps. Multiplying through by t_n yields:

$$ATA = AT\$\,\{(1 + R)^n - [t_n\,(1 + R)^n - t_n]\}$$

FIGURE I18-1 ▶ Deferred Model before Algebraic Simplification

Carrying the first minus sign through yields:

$$ATA = AT\$ [(1 + R)^n - t_n (1 + R)^n + t_n]$$

Factoring out $(1 + R)^n$ yields:

The Deferred Model:
$$ATA = AT\$ [(1 + R)^n (1 - t_n) + t_n]$$

We call this model the Deferred Model because the tax on investment earnings is deferred until the investor cashes out of the investment. This characteristic causes the Deferred Model investment to outperform the Current Model investment given equal BTRORs and constant tax rates.

EXAMPLE I18-8 ▶ Phillip can invest $1,000 (AT$) directly in a taxable bond outside an IRA, or he can contribute the $1,000 to a traditional nondeductible IRA and invest in the same bond through the IRA vehicle. In either case, the bond yields an annual 10% BTROR. Phillip's marginal tax rate is 36%, and he expects it to remain so for the entire investment horizon. The two alternatives give the following after-tax accumulations after 20 years:

Bond outside the IRA (Current Model):

$$\$1{,}000 [1 + 0.1 (1 - 0.36)]^{20} = \$1{,}000 (1.064)^{20} = \$3{,}458.06$$

Bond inside the IRA (Deferred Model):

$$\$1{,}000 \{(1.1)^{20} (1 - 0.36) + 0.36\} = \$4{,}665.60$$

The Deferred Model investment outperforms the Current Model investment because, within the IRA, the interest on the bond grows at the BTROR (10%), with taxation deferred until Year 20. ◀

ANNUALIZED ATROR. As we explained earlier, the ATROR in the Current Model is $r = R(1 - t)$. That is, an investment that fits the Current Model yields this ATROR annually. The annual ATROR is a useful number for comparison to annual ATRORs of other models. However, the annual ATROR of other models, such as the Deferred Model, is not always obvious. Therefore, to determine this comparable number, we compute a variable called the annualized ATROR. The annualized ATROR is the rate of return that would cause a Current Model investment to yield the same accumulation per after-tax dollar invested as does the model under consideration.

For example, we derive the annualized ATROR for the Deferred Model as follows:

$$(1 + r_{ann})^n = [(1 + R)^n (1 - t_n) + t_n]$$

Here, the left-hand side of the equation is the Current Model investment compounding at the annualized ATROR, which we symbolize as r_{ann}. The right-hand side is the Deferred Model with one after-tax dollar invested. Taking the nth root of each side yields:

$$(1 + r_{ann}) = [(1 + R)^n (1 - t_n) + t_n]^{1/n}$$

Subtracting 1 from each side yields:

$$r_{ann} = [(1 + R)^n (1 - t_n) + t_n]^{1/n} - 1$$

The general form for this relationship, which can be used for any model, is:

Annualized ATROR:
$$r_{ann} = [\text{Accumulation per AT\$ invested}]^{1/n} - 1$$

EXAMPLE I18-9 ▶ Consider the same facts as in Example I18-8. The annualized ATROR for the investment outside the IRA is 6.4%. No additional computation is necessary because the model already is in the Current Model form. The accumulation per AT$ invested inside the IRA (the Deferred Model) can be determined two ways. First, divide the total accumulation ($4,665.60) by the $1,000 (AT$) invested, which yields 4.6656. Alternatively, compute the accumulation per AT$ as follows: $[(1.1)^{20} (1 - 0.36) + 0.36] = 4.6656$. The annualized ATROR, then, is computed as follows: $r_{ann} = (4.6656)^{1/20} - 1 = .080054$ or 8.0054%. Thus, on an annualized basis, a 20-year investment outside the IRA (the Current Model) yields 6.4% after taxes, while a 20-year investment inside the IRA (the Deferred Model) yields 8.0054% after taxes. To check this result, simply put the 8.0054% annualized ATROR in the Current Model to see that it yields the same result as did the Deferred Model.

$$\text{ATA} = \$1,000 (1.080054)^{20} = \$1,000 (4.6656) = \$4,665.60$$ ◀

CAPITAL ASSETS. The Deferred Model also describes the after-tax growth of a capital asset. For example, suppose a stock grows annually at rate R and does not pay dividends, that is, the stock is strictly a growth stock. In n years, the stock will be worth $(1 + R)^n$. If the investor then sells the stock for its fair market value (FMV), the investor pays tax on the capital gain. Consequently, the tax on the gain is deferred until the investor sells the asset, which reflects the realization principle of taxation. Moreover, the capital gain may be taxed at a preferential tax rate, for example, the 20% maximum rate on long-term capital gains. Thus, when applied to capital assets, the Deferred Model provides two tax advantages: deferral and a preferential tax rate.

When Figure I18-1 is applied to this situation, the before-tax accumulation represents the selling price at the FMV, and the before-tax earnings represent the capital gain.

EXAMPLE I18-10 ▶ Brian purchases stock for $5,000. The stock appreciates (grows) at an 8% rate before taxes. Brian sells the stock ten years later for $10,794.62, which is $5,000 $(1.08)^{10}$. At the time of sale, his regular tax rate is 40%, but his long-term capital gains tax rate is 20%. One way to calculate Brian's after-tax proceeds is as follows:

(1) Selling price [$5,000 $(1.08)^{10}$]	$10,794.62
(2) Minus: Original investment (basis)	(5,000.00)
(3) Long-term capital gain	$ 5,794.62
(4) Times: long-term capital gains tax rate	0.2
(5) Tax on capital gain	$ 1,158.92
(6) After-tax proceeds (Line 1 − Line 5)	$ 9,635.70

Alternatively, the after-tax proceeds can be determined quickly with the Deferred Model as follows:

$$\text{ATA} = \$5,000 \,[(1.08)^{10} (1 - 0.2) + 0.2] = \$9,635.70$$ ◀

COMPARING CURRENT AND DEFERRED MODELS. As mentioned earlier, a Deferred Model investment always outperforms a Current Model investment if BTRORs are constant over time and equal across models and if tax rates also are constant and equal. However, when these conditions are not present, the models must be compared to determine which is preferable. One way to make this comparison is to set up a spreadsheet of the various alternatives.

EXAMPLE I18-11 ▶ As in Example I18-8, assume that Phillip can invest $1,000 (AT$) in a taxable bond either outside or inside a traditional nondeductible IRA. The bond yields 10% per year before taxes, and Phillip's marginal tax rate is 36%. Assume also that Phillip will be younger than 59½ when he withdraws the funds from the IRA. As described in Chapter I9, a taxpayer who withdraws amounts from a traditional IRA before reaching age 59½ generally must pay a 10% penalty tax on the taxable portion of the withdrawal. This penalty, in effect, increases the applicable tax rate in the Deferred Model. Thus, the following models apply (the Deferred Model with no penalty is repeated for comparison):

Bond outside the IRA (Current Model):

$$\$1,000 \,[1 + 0.1 (1 - 0.36)]^n = \$1,000 (1.064)^n$$

ADDITIONAL COMMENT

For traditional IRAs, minimum withdrawals must begin when a taxpayer reaches age 70½. Otherwise, the taxpayer faces a 50% penalty on the difference between the minimum required distribution and the actual distribution.

Bond inside the IRA (Deferred Model)—No penalty:

$$\$1{,}000\,[(1.1)^n\,(1 - 0.36) + 0.36]$$

Bond inside the IRA (Deferred Model)—With penalty:

$$\$1{,}000\,[(1.1)^n\,(1 - 0.46) + 0.46]$$

Notice that the 10% penalty increases the effective tax rate to 46%. Given the 10% penalty, which investment is better, the Current Model or the Deferred Model? The answer depends on the length of the investment horizon. Table I18-1 schedules the after-tax accumulations and related annualized ATRORs for various investment horizons (n) from one to 20 years.

Before considering the penalty situation, observe the no penalty case. For all values of n above one, the Deferred Model investment produces a greater after-tax accumulation than does the Current Model investment (compare Columns 2 and 3). This result also is apparent in the annualized ATRORs. For all values of n above one, the Deferred Model investment produces an annualized ATROR greater than 6.4% (compare Columns 5 and 6). Moreover, the greater n, the greater the annualized ATROR from the Deferred Model investment. This result occurs because tax deferral increases as the investment horizon lengthens. Thus, the longer the deferral, the better the annualized ATROR produced by the Deferred Model investment.

Now compare the Current Model to the Deferred Model with the 10% penalty. For investment horizons up to nine years, the Current Model investment outperforms the Deferred Model investment, while for horizons greater than nine years, the Deferred Model investment beats the Current Model investment (compare Columns 2 and 4). This result can be seen more easily with the annualized ATRORs, where beginning in Year 10, the annualized ATRORs for the

▼ TABLE I18-1
Comparison of Current and Deferred Models

	After-Tax Accumulations			Annualized ATRORs[d]		
(1) n	(2) Current Model[a]	(3) Deferred Model No Penalty[b]	(4) Deferred Model With Penalty[c]	(5) Current Model	(6) Deferred Model No Penalty	(7) Deferred Model With Penalty
1	$1,064	$1,064	$1,054	6.4%	6.400%	5.400%
2	1,132	1,134	1,113	6.4	6.508	5.518
3	1,205	1,212	1,179	6.4	6.614	5.635
4	1,282	1,297	1,251	6.4	6.718	5.750
5	1,364	1,391	1,330	6.4	6.819	5.864
6	1,451	1,494	1,417	6.4	6.917	5.977
7	1,544	1,607	1,512	6.4	7.013	6.087
8	1,643	1,732	1,618	6.4	7.106	6.196
9	1,748	1,869	1,733	6.4	7.197	6.302
10	1,860	2,020	1,861	6.4	7.284	6.406
11	1,979	2,186	2,001	6.4	7.369	6.507
12	2,105	2,369	2,155	6.4	7.450	6.606
13	2,240	2,569	2,324	6.4	7.529	6.703
14	2,383	2,790	2,511	6.4	7.605	6.796
15	2,536	3,033	2,716	6.4	7.679	6.887
16	2,698	3,301	2,941	6.4	7.749	6.975
17	2,871	3,595	3,189	6.4	7.817	7.061
18	3,055	3,918	3,462	6.4	7.882	7.143
19	3,250	4,274	3,763	6.4	7.945	7.223
20	3,458	4,666	4,093	6.4	8.005	7.300

[a] $1,000 (1.064)^n$
[b] $\$1{,}000\,[(1.1)^n\,(1 - 0.36) + 0.36]$
[c] $\$1{,}000\,[(1.1)^n\,(1 - 0.46) + 0.46]$
[d] $[(\text{ATA per AT\$})^{1/n} - 1] \times 100$

Deferred Model investment exceed 6.4% (compare Columns 5 and 7). The Current Model investment is better for short horizons because the applicable tax rate is 36% rather than 46% (rate + penalty). However, after nine years, the deferral benefit of the Deferred Model investment overcomes the penalty's detrimental effect. Thus, if an investor has a long enough investment horizon, a traditional nondeductible IRA subject to the 10% penalty may be the preferred method of accumulating savings, assuming the investor is ineligible for the Roth IRA. ◀

THE EXEMPT MODEL

The Exempt Model gives the future value of an investment having the following characteristics:

▶ Only after-tax dollars are invested (as with the Current and Deferred Models).

▶ Earnings on the investment are exempt from explicit taxation (unlike the Current and Deferred Models).

In fact, the Exempt Model is a special case of either the Current Model or the Deferred Model with the tax rate equal to zero. Consequently, the investment grows at the BTROR and appears as follows:

$$\text{The Exempt Model:} \\ ATA = AT\$ \, (1 + R)^n$$

REAL WORLD EXAMPLE

In 1997, individual taxpayers earned $48.5 billion of interest from tax-exempt investments.

State and local government obligations, such as municipal bonds, are classic examples of the Exempt Model. Under Sec. 103, interest on these instruments is excluded from gross income.

EXAMPLE I18-12 ▶ Carmen invests $10,000 (AT$) in tax-exempt municipal bonds, which yield 5% per year. She reinvests the interest and holds the bonds for ten years. Thus, the investment accumulates to $16,288.95, which is $10,000 $(1.05)^{10}$. ◀

Another example of the Exempt Model is the Roth IRA (see Chapter I9). Like the traditional nondeductible IRA, it does not allow a deduction for contributions. However, upon withdrawals, the accumulated earnings are not taxed. We will say more about the Roth IRA after developing the Pension Model.

STOP & THINK

Question: Does the Exempt Model imply that no taxation occures in the tax system for investments of this type?

Solution: No. Taxation occurs because the taxpayer invests after-tax dollars, which means the invested amount comes from some taxable source. If no taxation occurred at all, the model would appear as Accumulation = BT$ $(1 + R)^n$, which is the situation described on page I18-3 just after Example I18-1.

THE PENSION MODEL

The Pension Model gives the future value of an investment in a qualified retirement plan having the following characteristics:

▶ Before-tax dollars are invested (unlike the previous three models).

▶ The annual earnings on the investment grow at the BTROR (as with the Deferred and Exempt Models).

▶ The entire accumulation, not just the earnings, is taxed at the end of the investment horizon when the investor cashes out of the plan.

Thus, the Pension Model provides two levels of tax deferral. First, salary or earned income contributed to the plan escapes taxation when contributed but is taxed later upon withdrawal. Second, earnings on the underlying investment are not taxed while in the plan but also are taxed later upon withdrawal. This double deferral contrasts with the Deferral Model, in which only the taxes on investment earnings are deferred.

Deductible IRAs and H.R. 10 plans described in Chapter I9 are classic examples of the Pension Model. The taxpayer deducts the IRA or H.R. 10 contribution from gross income, the underlying investments grow at before-tax rates of return, and the taxpayer later includes any withdrawals in gross income.

EXAMPLE I18-13 ▶ Frank, whose marginal tax rate is 40%, earns $1,000 of salary and wishes to contribute this amount to a deductible IRA (Pension Model). He may do so because he can deduct the $1,000 contribution from gross income, leaving the entire $1,000 available for contribution. If, instead, Frank contributes to a traditional nondeductible IRA (Deferred Model) or a Roth IRA (Exempt Model), he can contribute only $600 because he must pay $400 of taxes on the $1,000 salary. Thus, Frank can contribute $1,000 before-tax dollars to a deductible IRA as contrasted with $600 after-tax dollars to a traditional nondeductible IRA or a Roth IRA. ◀

Other examples of the Pension Model include cash or deferred arrangements, commonly known as Sec. 401(k) plans, and tax-deferred annuities, sometimes referred to as Sec. 403(b) plans. Both of these type plans operate through a salary reduction agreement whereby the employee elects to have a specified amount of his or her salary contributed to the plan. The amount of salary contributed to the plan is excluded from the employee's gross income. However, annual contributions are limited to $10,500 (in 2001), with this limitation adjusted each year for inflation.[4] As with IRA and H.R. 10 plans, the underlying investments in Sec. 401(k) and Sec. 403(b) plans grow at before-tax rates of return, and the employee later includes any withdrawals in gross income. Withdrawals before the employee reaches age 59½, however, are subject to a 10% penalty in addition to the tax. Although most employers can offer Sec. 401(k) plans, only educational institutions and certain tax-exempt organizations may provide Sec. 403(b) plans.

Employer-sponsored qualified retirement plans also fit the Pension Model. In this case, the employer makes a deductible contribution on the employee's behalf, and the employee excludes the contribution from gross income. Upon retirement, the employee's retirement payments are fully taxed.

EXAMPLE I18-14 ▶ Frank in Example I18-13 makes the $1,000 contribution to a deductible IRA. The investment in the IRA will earn 10% per year before taxes, and Frank will withdraw all accumulated amounts from the IRA after 20 years. He expects his tax rate to be 28% at that time, and he will not be subject to the 10% penalty for early withdrawals. The following calculation demonstrates one way to determine Frank's after-tax accumulation in the IRA:

Before-tax accumulation in the IRA [$1,000 (1.1)^{20}]	$6,727.50
Minus: Tax on withdrawn accumulation ($6,727.50 × 0.28)	(1,883.70)
Accumulated earnings after taxes	$4,843.80 ◀

The calculation in Example I18-14 also can be formulated as follows:

$$ATA = \$1,000 \,(1.1)^{20} - [\$1,000 \,(1.1)^{20}] \times 0.28$$

Factoring out the before-tax accumulation of $1,000 (1.1)^{20} yields the following expression:

$$ATA = \$1,000 \,(1.1)^{20} \,(1 - 0.28)$$

Substituting our general symbols into this expression yields:

The Pension Model:
$$ATA = BT\$ \,(1 + R)^n \,(1 - t_n) \text{ or}$$
$$ATA = AT\$ \left[\frac{1}{(1 - t_o)} (1 + R)^n (1 - t_n) \right]$$

---

[4] Section 402(g) imposes this dollar limitation. Percentage of compensation limitations also apply to contributions to Sec. 401(k) and Sec. 403(b) plans, but these limitations are complex and beyond the scope of this chapter. See Chapter I9 and Secs. 403(b) and 415(c).

Recall that BT\$ = AT\$ / (1 − t). That is, before-tax dollars equal after-tax dollars grossed up by one minus the tax rate. Thus, the second form of the Pension Model is equivalent to the first form. The second form, however, has the same format as the other three models: AT\$ times a future value formula. This format allows the investor to compare all four models without considering a specific level of investment because each model in this format is stated in terms of the after-tax accumulation per AT\$ invested. In these models, t_o is the tax rate in Year 0, and t_n is the tax rate in Year n.

EXAMPLE I18-15 ▶ Given four options listed below, Beth wants to know the after-tax accumulation and annualized ATROR of each.

- Current Model: R = 10%, t = 28%, n = 5
- Deferred Model: R = 9%, t_n = 28%, n = 5
- Exempt Model: R = 8%, n = 5
- Pension Model: R = 10%, t_o = 28%, t_n = 36%, n = 5

The results of the four options are as follows:

Model	Computation	After-Tax Accumulation	Annualized ATROR
Current	$[1 + 0.1(1 - 0.28)]^5$	1.4157	7.20%
Deferred	$(1.09)^5 (1 - 0.28) + 0.28$	1.3878	6.77%
Exempt	$(1.08)^5$	1.4693	8.00%
Pension	$[1 / (1 - 0.28)] (1.1)^5 (1 - 0.36)$	1.4316	7.44% ◀

COMPARING EXEMPT AND PENSION MODELS. With equal BTRORs, constant tax rates (i.e., $t_o = t_n$), and no limitation on contributions, the Exempt and Pension Models are equivalent because the $1 / (1 - t_o)$ and $(1 - t_n)$ terms cancel out leaving the Pension Model (second form) to appear as AT\$ $(1 + R)^n$. However, if t_o and t_n differ, this equivalency disappears. Thus, the following relationships hold:

- If $t_o = t_n$, ATA per Exempt Model = ATA per Pension Model.
- If $t_o > t_n$, ATA per Exempt Model < ATA per Pension Model.
- If $t_o < t_n$, ATA per Exempt Model > ATA per Pension Model.

EXAMPLE I18-16 ▶ Consider the following situations:

- R = 10%, t_o = 28%, t_n = 28%, n = 10
- R = 10%, t_o = 40%, t_n = 28%, n = 10
- R = 10%, t_o = 28%, t_n = 40%, n = 10

The after-tax accumulations (ATAs) for the three situations are as follows:

Situation	Exempt Model	Pension Model
t_o = 28%, t_n = 28%	$(1.1)^{10} = 2.5937$	$[1 / (1 - 0.28)] (1.1)^{10} (1 - 0.28) = 2.5937$
t_o = 40%, t_n = 28%	$(1.1)^{10} = 2.5937$	$[1 / (1 - 0.40)] (1.1)^{10} (1 - 0.28) = 3.1125$
t_o = 28%, t_n = 40%	$(1.1)^{10} = 2.5937$	$[1 / (1 - 0.28)] (1.1)^{10} (1 - 0.40) = 2.1615$ ◀

DEDUCTIBLE IRA VERSUS ROTH IRA. The Exempt and Pension models can be used to compare investment in a traditional deductible IRA versus a Roth IRA. If the amount of before-tax dollars available for investment does not exceed the $2,000 limitation, the comparative results are similar to those in Example I18-16.

EXAMPLE I18-17 ▶ Marcy has $2,000 of salary before taxes available for contribution to either a traditional deductible IRA or a Roth IRA. The underlying investments will earn a 10% BTROR. After ten years, Marcy plans to withdraw the entire accumulation without penalty. If her marginal tax rate is 28% in the contribution year, she can contribute either $2,000 (BT\$) to the deductible IRA or $1,440 (AT\$) to the Roth IRA. If her marginal tax rate upon withdrawal is 28%, she will have the following after tax accumulations under each alternative:

Roth IRA [$1,440 (1.1)^{10}$]	$3,735.00
Deductible IRA [$2,000 (1.1)^{10} (1 − 0.28)$]	$3,735.00

Thus, with constant tax rates, the two alternatives yield the same after-tax accumulation.

If Marcy's current tax rate is 40%, and her later tax rate is 28%, the two alternatives yield the following after-tax accumulations:

Roth IRA [$1,200 (1.1)^{10}]	$3,112.00
Deductible IRA [$2,000 (1.1)^{10} (1 − 0.28)]	$3,735.00

Thus, with decreasing tax rates, the deductible IRA yields the better result.

Finally, if Marcy's current tax rate is 28%, and her later tax rate is 40%, the two alternatives yield the following after-tax accumulations:

Deductible IRA [$2,000 (1.1)^{10}] (1 − 0.4]	$3,112.00
Roth IRA [$1,440 (1.1)^{10}]	$3,735.00

Thus, with increasing tax rates, the Roth IRA yields the better result. ◀

In Example I18-17, the before-tax dollars available for contribution did not exceed the $2,000 limitation on IRA contributions. However, suppose the taxpayer wishes to compare a $2,000 contribution to a deductible IRA with a $2,000 contribution to a Roth IRA. In this case, the two contributions are not equivalent because the contribution to the deductible IRA is made with before-tax dollars while that to the Roth IRA is made with after-tax dollars. To have $2,000 after-tax dollars available for a Roth IRA contribution, the taxpayer must have $2,000/(1-t_o)$ before-tax dollars available for investment. If the taxpayer has this amount available and contributes $2,000 to a deductible IRA, the taxpayer will have some available funds left over for investment outside the deductible IRA.[5]

EXAMPLE I18-18 ▶ Mark wants to contribute $2,000 to either a deductible IRA or a Roth IRA. His current marginal tax rate is 28%. To contribute $2,000 (AT$) to a Roth IRA, his before-tax dollars available for investment must be $2,777.78, which is computed as BT$ = $2,000/(1 − 0.28). On the other hand, if he contributes $2,000 (BT$) to a deductible IRA, he has $777.78 remaining. This $777.78 is subject to tax so that, after taxes at 28%, Mark will have $560 (AT$) remaining for investment outside the IRA.

A convenient short-cut method to determine the amount remaining for outside investment is to multiply the $2,000 deduction by the tax rate to arrive at the tax savings from the traditional IRA deduction. Specifically, the $2,000 deduction will generate $560 of tax savings for outside investment, computed as $2,000 × 0.28 = $560. ◀

Given the previous discussion, the deductible IRA versus Roth IRA decision can be framed as follows:

Roth IRA	$2,000 (1 + R)^n
Versus	
Deductible IRA	$2,000 (1 + R)^n (1 − t_n$)
Plus	
Outside Investment	$2,000 (t_o$) [1 + R (1 − t)]^n

In this framework, $2,000 (t_o$) is the tax savings from the traditional IRA deduction, which is invested in an investment conforming to the Current Model. If the taxpayer's outside investment conforms to the Deferred Model or some other model, the alternative model can be substituted for the Current Model in this decision framework.

EXAMPLE I18-19 ▶ Helen wishes to invest $2,000 in either a deductible IRA or a Roth IRA. The underlying investments will earn a 10% BTROR. After ten years, Helen plans to withdraw the entire accumulation without penalty. Her marginal tax rate is 28% in the contribution year, and she expects her marginal tax rate upon withdrawal to be 28%. If she contributes to the deductible IRA, she will invest the tax savings in an investment yielding a 10% BTROR and which is currently taxable at 28%. The alternative investments yield the following results:

---

[5] For a detailed analysis of the Roth IRA decision, see K. E. Anderson and D. P. Murphy, "Framework for the Roth IRA Decision," *Journal of the American Society of CLU & ChFC*, March 1998, pp. 2-13.

Roth IRA [$2,000 (1.1)^{10}$]	$5,187.48
Deductible IRA [$2,000 (1.1)^{10} (1 - 0.28)$]	$3,734.99
Plus: Outside investment [$2,000 (0.28) (1.072)^{10}$]	1,122.37
Total	$4,857.36

With constant tax rates, the Roth IRA produces the better result because, with the deductible IRA, part of the investment goes to an outside investment taxed less favorably than the IRA. Note also that, because the $2,000 limitation is after-tax dollars for the Roth IRA but before-tax dollars for the deductible IRA, constant tax rates no longer produce equivalent results.

Suppose instead that Helen expects her tax rate to be 15% when she withdraws the IRA accumulation. In this case, the alternative investments yield the following results:

Roth IRA [$2,000 (1.1)^{10}$]	$5,187.48
Deductible IRA [$2,000 (1.1)^{10} (1 - 0.15)$]	$4,409.36
Plus: Outside investment [$2,000 (0.28) (1.072)^{10}$]	1,122.37
Total	$5,531.73

Thus, with a reduced tax rate in the withdrawal year, the deductible IRA (plus the outside investment) yields the better result. ◀

MULTIPERIOD STRATEGIES

All previous examples assumed a single amount invested for a specified time period. However, suppose an investor wants to invest a certain amount each year over several years. In this case, the investor may optimize his or her after-tax accumulation by investing in one type of investment in early years and another type investment in late years.

EXAMPLE I18-20 ▶ For the next 15 years, Jack wishes to invest $10,000 (AT$) at the beginning of each year into either nondividend paying stock that increases in value at 8.3% per year before taxes or a taxable bond that yields 10% per year before taxes. Jack's regular tax rate is 31%, but he pays only 20% on long-term capital gains. Jack wants to know which asset to invest in for each of the 15 years. The following models apply to this situation:

Stock (Deferred Model):

$$\$10,000 [(1.083)^n (1 - 0.2) + 0.2]$$

Taxable bond (Current Model):

$$\$10,000 [1 + 0.1 (1 - 0.31)]^n = \$10,000 (1.069)^n$$

Table I18-2 schedules the alternatives for each year. The stock produces the larger after-tax accumulations for investments made in Years 1 through 9. For Years 10 through 15, however, the taxable bonds outperform the stock. Consequently, Jack should invest in stock for each of the first nine years and hold the stock for the rest of the 15-year investment horizon. For the remaining six years, he should invest in taxable bonds. This switching strategy maximizes the total after-tax accumulation compared to investing in either stock or bonds for the entire 15-year period (compare Column 4 and 5 totals to Column 6 total).

The stock outperforms the taxable bonds for the first nine years even though the taxable bonds yield a higher BTROR than does the stock. This result occurs because the deferral benefit outweighs the lower BTROR for long investment horizons. ◀

SUMMARY AND COMPARISON OF BASIC INVESTMENT MODELS

Topic Review I18-1 summarizes the models along with simple examples. In the examples, each model assumes an investment earning 10% before taxes and assumes a constant 28% tax rate. With these assumptions, the Exempt and Pension Models outperform the Current and Deferred Models, and the Deferred Model outperforms the Current Model.

▼ TABLE I18-2
Multiperiod Investments

(1) Year	(2) n	(3) Amount Invested	(4) Stock[a] (Deferred Model)	(5) Taxable Bond[b] (Current Model)	(6) Greater of Column 4 or 5
1	15	$10,000	$ 28,456	$ 27,206	$ 28,456
2	14	10,000	26,428	25,450	26,428
3	13	10,000	24,556	23,807	24,556
4	12	10,000	22,827	22,271	22,827
5	11	10,000	21,231	20,833	21,231
6	10	10,000	19,757	19,488	19,757
7	9	10,000	18,396	18,231	18,396
8	8	10,000	17,140	17,054	17,140
9	7	10,000	15,979	15,953	15,979
10	6	10,000	14,908	14,923	14,923
11	5	10,000	13,919	13,960	13,960
12	4	10,000	13,005	13,059	13,059
13	3	10,000	12,162	12,216	12,216
14	2	10,000	11,383	11,428	11,428
15	1	10,000	10,664	10,690	10,690
Total ATA with no switching			$270,812	$266,569	
Total ATA with switching strategy					$271,047

[a] $10,000 [(1.083)^n (1 - 0.2) + 0.2]$
[b] $10,000 (1.069)^n$

OTHER APPLICATIONS OF INVESTMENT MODELS

In the previous section of this chapter, we developed four investment models and applied them to currently taxable investments, capital gains assets, tax-exempt bonds, and retirement plans. In this section, we present two additional applications: (1) the flow-through entity versus the C corporation form of business operations and (2) current salary versus deferred compensation.

OBJECTIVE 2

Use the investment models to make entity choices

FLOW-THROUGH ENTITY VERSUS C CORPORATION

Chapter I16 described how the government taxes C corporations and their shareholders, and Chapter I17 introduced the tax consequences of operating as a flow-through entity. Flow-through entities include partnerships, limited liability companies (LLCs), limited liability partnerships (LLPs), and S corporations. A flow-through entity's primary characteristic is that income escapes taxation at the entity level and flows through to be taxed at the ownership level. Corporate income, on the other hand, is taxed once at the entity level and again at the owner level. Taxation at the owner level occurs when the corporation distributes its earnings, when the shareholder sells his or her stock, or when the corporation liquidates.

In this section, we will show that the Current Model describes a flow-through entity and that a variation of the Deferred Model describes a C corporation. These models can be used to decide which form of business is best from a tax perspective. At first, one might think the flow-through entity is the better form because it avoids double taxation. But, in fact, the better alternative depends on a combination of factors, specifically, rates of returns, the corporate tax rate, the owner's tax rate, and the entity's expected life span (investment horizon).

ADDITIONAL COMMENT

Remember from earlier chapters that, as the income and deductions flow through to the owners of partnerships and S corporations, they retain their character. For example, ordinary income at the entity level is ordinary income to the owner; capital gains at the entity level flow through as capital gains.

Topic Review I18-1

Summary of Investment Models

Investment Model	Initial Income	Investment Earnings or Capital Gain	Examples[a]	ATA	ATA/AT$	R_{ANN}
Current: $AT\$ [1 + R(1-t)]^n$ — or — $AT\$ (1+r)^n$	Taxed currently	Taxed annually	$\$720 (1.072)^5$	$\$1,019.31$	1.4157[b]	7.20%
Deferred: $AT\$ [(1+R)^n (1-t_n) + t_n]$	Taxed currently	Tax deferred	$\$720 [(1.1)^5 (0.72) + 0.28]$	$\$1,036.49$	1.4396[c]	7.56%
Exempt: $AT\$ (1+R)^n$	Taxed currently	Tax exempt	$\$720 (1.1)^5$	$\$1,159.57$	1.6105[d]	10.00%
Pension: $BT\$ (1+R)^n (1-t_n)$ — or — $AT\$ \left[\dfrac{1}{(1-t_o)} (1+R)^n (1-t_n)\right]$	Tax deferred	Tax deferred	$\$1,000 (1.1)^5 (0.72)$ — or — $\$720 (1/0.72)(1.1)^5 (0.72)$	$\$1,159.57$	1.6105[e]	10.00%

Definitions of Variables:
ATA = After-tax accumulation (future value of an investment)
BT$ = Before-tax dollars
AT$ = After-tax dollars
R = Before-tax rate of return (BTROR)
r = After-tax rate of return (ATROR)
r_{ann} = Annualized ATROR
n = Investment horizon
t = Marginal tax rate, generally and for Current Model
t_o = Marginal tax rate in the year of investment (Year 0) for Pension Model
t_n = Marginal tax rate at the end of the investment horizon (Year n) for Deferred and Pension Models

[a] Initial before-tax income (BT$) = $1,000; AT$ = $1,000 (0.72) = $720; R = 10%; t = t_o = t_n = 28%; n = 5
[b] Also: $(1.072)^5 = 1.4157$
[c] Also: $(1.1)^5 (0.72) + 0.28 = 1.4396$
[d] Also: $(1.1)^5 = 1.6105$
[e] Note that the $1,159.57 after-tax accumulation is divided by $720, not $1,000, because $720 is the after-tax dollar equivalent of $1,000 before taxes. Also: $(1/0.72)(1.1)^5 (0.72) = 1.6105$

THE FLOW-THROUGH MODEL. To keep matters simple, we assume an S corporation with only one shareholder. The one-owner assumption allows us to focus on the entity decision without worrying about distributive shares and differential individual tax rates among owners. The model also applies to an S corporation, a partnership, an LLC, or an LLP with more than one owner. In addition, the model applies to a sole proprietorship because that form of business also entails one level of taxation.

EXAMPLE I18-21 ▶ Assume the following facts. Rebecca forms an S corporation by contributing $10,000 to the corporation in exchange for all the corporation's stock. The S corporation invests in assets that produce a 10% BTROR per year. At the end of each year, the S corporation distributes cash to Rebecca equal to the taxes she must pay on the S corporation's flow-through earnings. The corporation reinvests the remaining earnings in its business. Rebecca's tax rate is 40%. Immediately after the end of the second year, the S corporation liquidates, selling the assets and distributing the cash proceeds to Rebecca. Because the corporation reinvested its retained earnings, the basis of the assets on the sale date equals their FMV. Thus, the sale produces no realized gain at the entity level. The following schedule shows the results of these transactions at the entity and owner levels:

	Year 1	Year 2
Entity level:		
Investment at beginning of year	$10,000	$10,600
Plus: Earnings on investment (10% × investment)	1,000	1,060
Minus: Distribution to shareholder (40% × earnings)	(400)	(424)
Investment at end of year	$10,600	$11,236

Owner level:

Stock basis at beginning of year	$10,000	$10,600
Plus: Increase due to flow-through income	1,000	1,060
Minus: Decrease due to distribution	(400)	(424)
Stock basis at end of year	$10,600	$11,236

Upon liquidation, the S corporation sells the assets and distributes the $11,236 to Rebecca. Because Rebecca's stock basis equals $11,236, she recognizes no additional gain on the liquidation. Thus, after two years, she ends up with $11,236 on a $10,000 original investment. ◄

In Example I18-21, the S corporation was able to reinvest only its earnings after paying the shareholder's tax. Thus, the investment grew at a 6% ATROR, which is 10% (1 − 0.4). Consequently, the shareholder's after-tax accumulation also can be calculated as follows: ATA = $10,000 (1.06)² = $11,236. From the owner's viewpoint, then, the flow-through entity resembles the Current Model. In general terms, the owner's after-tax accumulation can be expressed as:

> The Flow-Through Model:
> $$\text{ATA} = \text{Contribution} [1 + R_f (1 - t_p)]^n$$

In this model, R_f equals the flow-through entity's BTROR, t_p is the owner's marginal tax rate (p is for personal), and n is the investment horizon. Although Example I18-21 assumes a liquidating distribution at the end of the investment, the same result would have occurred had the owner sold her ownership interest (stock in this case) to another party.

THE C CORPORATION MODEL. Again, to keep matters simple, we assume a C corporation with only one shareholder, and we further assume that the corporation retains all earnings after paying corporate level taxes. That is, the corporation pays no dividends. The model could be modified to reflect annual dividend payments, but such a model becomes extremely complicated and is beyond the scope of this chapter.[6]

EXAMPLE I18-22 ▶ Assume the same facts as in Example I18-21 except that Rebecca forms a C corporation instead of an S corporation. In this case, the corporation makes no annual distributions to Rebecca. Instead, the corporation pays its own taxes at a 35% rate and reinvests the after-tax retained earnings. Thus, the shareholder has no owner-level taxes until the corporation liquidates. Rebecca's ordinary tax rate remains 40%, but her capital gains tax rate is 20%. As in Example I18-21, the sale prior to liquidation produces no realized gain at the entity level. The following schedule shows the results of these transactions at the entity and owner levels:

	Year 1	Year 2
Entity level:		
Investment at beginning of year	$10,000	$10,650
Plus: Earnings on investment (10% × investment)	1,000	1,065
Minus: Corporate taxes (35% × earnings)	(350)	(373)
Investment at end of year	$10,650	$11,342
Owner level:		
Stock basis	$10,000	$10,000
(1) Liquidation proceeds		$11,342
(2) Minus: Stock basis		(10,000)
(3) Capital gain on liquidation		$ 1,342
(4) Times: Long-term capital gains tax rate		0.2
(5) Tax on capital gain		$ 268
(6) After-tax proceeds (Line 1 − Line 5)		$11,074

---

[6] See Scholes, Wolfson, Erickson, Maydew, and Shevlin, Chapter 4, footnote 8 for this expanded model.

Because the corporation is a C corporation, Rebecca makes no adjustments to her stock basis, which remains at $10,000. Consequently, she recognizes a capital gain upon liquidation, and after two years she ends up with $11,074 on a $10,000 original investment. ◀

In Example I18-22, the C corporation was able to reinvest only its after-tax earnings. Thus, at the corporate level, the investment grew at a 6.5% ATROR, which is 10% (1 − 0.35). Consequently, the corporate-level accumulation before distribution to the shareholders can be calculated as follows: $10,000 [1 + 0.1 (1 − 0.35)]^2 = $10,000 (1.065)^2 = $11,342. In general terms, this expression is: Contribution $[1 + R_c (1 − t_c)]^n$, or Contribution $[1 + r_c]^n$. This formulation is a variation of the Current Model, where R_c is the corporation's BTROR, r_c is the corporation's ATROR, and t_c is the corporation's marginal tax rate.

Upon liquidation, the shareholder receives the corporate-level accumulation and pays tax at rate t_p on the difference between the distribution and her stock basis. Thus, the shareholder's after-tax accumulation in Example I18-22 can be formulated as follows:

$$\text{ATA} = \$10,000\ (1.065)^2 - [\$10,000\ (1.065)^2 - \$10,000] \times 0.2$$

The first term, $10,000 (1.065)^2$, gives the corporate-level after-tax accumulation; the subtraction in brackets gives the shareholder's liquidation gain before shareholder-level taxes; and the multiplication by 20% gives the tax on the liquidation gain. Subtracting this tax from the first term gives the shareholder's total after-tax accumulation on the investment in the C corporation. Factoring out the $10,000 contribution yields the following expression:

$$\text{ATA} = \$10,000\ \{(1.065)^2 - [(1.065)^2 - 1] \times 0.2\}$$

Substituting our general symbols into this expression yields the following model, which is a variation of the Deferred Model shown earlier in Figure I18-1:

$$\text{ATA} = \text{Contribution}\ \{(1 + r_c)^n - [(1 + r_c)^n - 1] \times t_p\}$$

As done earlier with the Deferred Model, we can simplify this model algebraically to obtain:

The C Corporation Model:
$$\text{ATA} = \text{Contribution}\ [(1 + r_c)^n (1 - t_p) + t_p]\ \text{or}$$
$$\text{ATA} = \text{Contribution}\ \{[1 + R_c (1 - t_c)]^n (1 - t_p) + t_p\}$$

In the first form of this model, the corporation's ATROR (r_c) plays the same role as the BTROR plays in the Deferred Model developed earlier in this chapter. More specifically, in terms used in Example I18-10, r_c is the appreciation (growth) rate of the shareholder's stock investment, assuming the stock value reflects increases in the corporation's after-tax retained earnings. Thus, the corporation's ATROR functions as the shareholder's BTROR on his or her stock investment. The second form of the C Corporation Model emphasizes that the corporate-level accumulation (the Current Model) is embedded in the shareholder's after-tax accumulation model (the Deferred Model).

COMPARING THE FLOW-THROUGH AND C CORPORATION MODELS. Given these two models, an owner can compare whether operating as a flow-through entity or a C corporation provides the better result.

EXAMPLE I18-23 ▶ Assume the following facts. Mark forms Wolfson Corporation by contributing $5 million in exchange for the corporation's stock. The corporation expects to earn 18% per year before-taxes on this investment. The corporate tax rate is 34%, and Mark's individual tax rate on ordinary income is 40%. Because Wolfson stock qualifies as small business stock under Sec. 1202, any gain recognized on disposition of the stock after a five-year holding period qualifies for a 50% exclusion. The maximum capital gain rate on the included gain is 28% rather than 20%. Thus, Mark's effective rate on the *entire* capital gain is 20% if he holds the stock for five years or less and is 14% if he holds the stock for more than five years (that is, 28% of half the gain is equivalent to 14% of the entire gain). Wolfson can operate either as an S corporation or a C corporation. If the corporation elects S corporation status, each year it will distribute exactly enough cash for Mark to pay taxes on any flow-through income, and it will reinvest the remaining earnings in the business. If the corporation operates as a C corporation, it will make no annual distributions, reinvesting all after-tax earnings in the business. In either case, the corporation will liquidate at the end of the investment horizon. Mark wants to know how long he must operate the corporation to make the C corporation form better than the S corporation form. Table I18-3 gives Mark's after-tax accumulation for each alternative.

According to Table I18-3, if Mark decides to operate the corporation for ten years or less, the corporation should make the S corporation election. However, if he plans to operate for more than ten years, the corporation should remain a C corporation. ◄

STOP & THINK

Question: Assume that a flow-through entity and a C corporation earn the same BTROR, that is, $R_f = R_c$. Given the following comparisons of the corporate tax rate (t_c) and the owner's tax rate (t_p), can you tell from just looking at the two models which entity form is better from a tax perspective?

Comparison 1: $t_c = t_p$
Comparison 2: $t_c > t_p$
Comparison 3: $t_c < t_p$

Solution: In Comparisons 1 and 2, the flow-through entity is always better than the C corporation (given $R_f = R_c$). In Comparison 3, however, the answer is not obvious. Consider the two models:

Flow-through: $[1 + R_f (1 - t_p)]^n$
C corporation: $[1 + R_c (1 - t_c)]^n (1 - t_p) + t_p$

Notice that, if $R_f = R_c$ and $t_c = t_p$, the bracketed terms in the two models will be equal, which means the flow-through entity accumulation equals the corporate-level accumulation. The C corporation, however, entails additional taxation at the shareholder level, which is represented by the terms following the bracketed term. This additional tax makes the C corporation worse than the flow-through entity. If $t_c > t_p$, the bracketed term in the

▼ TABLE I18-3
S Corporation versus C Corporation

Years of Operation (n)	S Corporation[a]	C Corporation[b]
1	$ 5,540,000	$ 5,475,200
2	6,138,320	6,006,854
3	6,801,259	6,601,668
4	7,535,794	7,267,146
5	8,349,660	8,011,683
6	9,251,424	9,133,021
7	10,250,577	10,134,864
8	11,357,640	11,255,726
9	12,584,265	12,509,746
10	13,943,365	13,912,744
11	15,449,249	15,482,418
12	17,117,768	17,238,570

[a] For all n, ATA = $5,000,000 $[1 + 0.18 (1 - 0.4)]^n$
[b] For n = 1 through 5, ATA = $5,000,000 $\{[1 + 0.18 (1 - 0.34)]^n (1 - 0.2) + 0.2\}$
For n > 5, ATA = $5,000,000 $\{[1 + 0.18 (1 - 0.34)]^n (1 - 0.14) + 0.14\}$

C corporation model accumulates to a lesser amount than does the flow-through model, and the shareholder-level tax just makes matters worse. Thus, the flow-through entity again is the preferred form. Finally, if $t_c < t_p$, the bracketed term in the C corporation model accumulates to a greater amount than does the flow-through model, but the shareholder level tax lessens the overall benefit. However, whether the overall effect causes the C corporation to be better than the flow-through entity depends on how much t_p exceeds t_c and on how long the investment horizon (n) is. Thus, the answer is not obvious.

SUMMARY. The Flow-Through Model is an application of the Current Model, where taxation occurs only at the owner level. The C Corporation Model is a variation of the Deferred Model, where taxation occurs at both the entity and the owner levels. These models can help the planner decide whether the flow-through entity or the C corporation is the better alternative from a tax perspective. Topic Review I18-2 summarizes these models.[7]

OBJECTIVE 3

Use the investment models to make current salary versus deferred compensation decisions

CURRENT SALARY VERSUS DEFERRED COMPENSATION

Chapter I9 introduced the characteristics of a nonqualified deferred compensation plan. This arrangement differs from current salary in that the employer's deduction and the employee's inclusion in gross income occur later than with current salary. The key question, then, is whether an employee should choose current salary or deferred compensation. The decision model developed in this section helps answer this question. Because both the employer and the employee are affected by the timing of compensation, the decision model must incorporate these dual effects. Specifically, the model includes the current and future tax rates of the employer and employee as well as the employer's and employee's ATRORs.

REAL WORLD EXAMPLE

For a deferred compensation agreement to be effective, the parties must agree to the compensation before the services are performed. Sugar Ray Robinson was successful in deferring into subsequent years proceeds earned in his boxing match with Carmen Bassilio in 1957. Sugar Ray lost the crown but beat the IRS. *Ray S. Robinson*, 44 T.C. 20 (1965).

THE EMPLOYEE'S POINT OF VIEW. The employee can choose between current salary in Year 0 or deferred compensation in Year n. If the employee chooses current salary, the employee immediately pays taxes on the salary and invests the after-tax amount at his or her ATROR.[8] If, instead, the employee receives deferred compensation, the employee pays taxes on this compensation in Year n, leaving an after-tax amount of deferred compensation. These two alternatives are comparable because both are stated in terms of future values.

EXAMPLE I18-24

Bruce works for Xeron Corporation and is considering receiving either $10,000 of current salary or $25,000 of deferred compensation in ten years. His current tax rate is 40%, but he expects his tax rate to be 28% ten years from now. Bruce can invest any after-tax current salary at a 10% ATROR. If Bruce receives current salary and invests the after-tax amount, his investment will accumulate as follows:

$$\$10,000\,(1 - 0.4)\,(1.1)^{10} = \$15,562$$

Bruce's after-tax salary is $6,000, which grows to $15,562 in ten years if invested at a 10% ATROR. Thus, this calculation, which is an application of the Current Model, gives the future value of Bruce's after-tax current salary. Alternatively, if Bruce receives deferred compensation, his after-tax deferred compensation is calculated as follows:

$$\$25,000\,(1 - 0.28) = \$18,000$$

---

[7] For an interesting analysis of the flow-through versus C corporation decision, see D. S. Hulse and T. R. Pope, "The Effect of Income Taxes on the Preference of Organizational Forms for Small Businesses in the United States," *Journal of Small Business Management*, January 1996, pp. 24-35. The article demonstrates the tradeoffs of the two organizational forms using indifference curves based on BTRORs, the investment horizon (n), and tax rates.

[8] The employee also could spend the current salary. However, this current consumption is equivalent to the future consumption available if the employee invests and spends later. In this case, the investment assumption gives the future value of current consumption. Thus, whether the employee actually spends or invests, the investment assumption provides the future value of that decision.

Topic Review I18-2

Flow-Through and C Corporation Models

Flow-Through Model:
ATA = Contribution $[1 + R_f (1 - t_p)]^n$

C Corporation Model:
ATA = Contribution $[(1 + r_c)^n (1 - t_p) + t_p]$

or

ATA = Contribution $\{[1 + R_c (1 - t_c)]^n (1 - t_p) + t_p\}$

Definitions of Variables:
R_f = Flow-through entity's BTROR
R_c = C corporation's BTROR
t_p = Owner's marginal tax rate
t_c = C corporation's marginal tax rate
r_c = C corporation's ATROR
n = Investment horizon

In this case, Bruce prefers the deferred compensation alternative because he will have $18,000 in ten years instead of $15,562 under the current salary alternative. ◀

Using general terms, we can state the employee's current salary and deferred compensation alternatives as follows:

$$CSI = BT\$ \,(1 - t_{po})(1 + r_p)^n$$
$$DCI = BT\$ \,(D_n)(1 - t_{pn})$$

In these formulas, CSI stands for current salary income and is the employee's after-tax future value of current salary; DCI stands for deferred compensation income and is the employee's after-tax future value of deferred compensation; and BT$ stands for before-tax current salary. In the second formula, D_n is the amount of deferred compensation received in lieu of $1 currently. Accordingly, BT$ × D_n gives total deferred compensation before taxes. For example, in Example I18-24, BT$ = $10,000, and BT$ × D_n = $25,000. Thus, D_n = 2.50. In other words, Bruce could choose between $1 of current salary or $2.50 of deferred compensation, before taxes. The factor, BT$, converts these per dollar amounts to total dollars of current salary or deferred compensation. The other variables in the formulas are defined as follows:

▶ t_{po} = The employee's marginal tax rate in Year 0
▶ t_{pn} = The employee's marginal tax rate in Year n
▶ r_p = The employee's ATROR
▶ n = The number of years until the employee receives the deferred compensation

The employee prefers deferred compensation if DCI exceeds CSI. From the previous formulas, this relationship can be expressed as follows:

$$DCI > CSI \text{ or}$$
$$BT\$ \,(D_n)(1 - t_{pn}) > BT\$ \,(1 - t_{po})(1 + r_p)^n$$

Solving the second expression for D_n yields:

$$D_n > \frac{(1 - t_{po})(1 + r_p)^n}{(1 - t_{pn})}$$

The level of D_n that exactly equals the right-hand side of this expression makes the employee indifferent to receiving current salary or deferred compensation. That is, at the indifference level of D_n, the employee's current salary income (CSI) equals the employee's deferred compensation income (DCI). Levels of D_n above the indifference level make deferred compensation more beneficial than current salary to the employee.

EXAMPLE I18-25 ▶ Assume the same facts as in Example I18-24. Bruce prefers deferred compensation rather than $1 of current salary if D_n exceeds 2.1615, calculated as follows:

$$D_n > \frac{(1 - 0.4)(1.1)^{10}}{(1 - 0.28)} = 2.1615$$

Therefore, $D_n = 2.1615$ is Bruce's indifference level, as shown by the following calculation for $1 of current salary:

$$\text{CSI} = \$1(1 - 0.4)(1.1)^{10} = \$1.5562$$
$$\text{DCI} = \$1(2.1615)(1 - 0.28) = \$1.5562$$

Given a choice between $10,000 of current salary (BT$) and deferred compensation, Bruce will prefer deferred compensation to current salary if the deferred compensation exceeds $21,615, which is $10,000 × 2.1615. ◀

REAL WORLD EXAMPLE

Many contracts of professional athletes are structured using deferred compensation arrangements. The current value of the contract usually is publicized in nominal dollars. For example, a NBA player recently signed a contract for $5 million per year for 15 years and was reported as a $75 million contract. This approach ignores the time value of money.

THE EMPLOYER'S POINT OF VIEW. The issue from the employer's point of view is whether the employer is willing to pay deferred compensation in lieu of current salary. If the employer pays current salary, the employer takes a business deduction and obtains an immediate tax benefit. The current salary net of the tax benefit is the employer's after-tax salary expense. This after-tax amount must be projected to Year n to be comparable to the alternative deferred compensation expense. We compound the after-tax salary expense at the employer's ATROR because, if the employer does not pay the salary, the employer will have the after-tax amount available for investment in its business. This investment, in turn, grows at the employer's ATROR. Thus, compounding determines the future value of the employer's after-tax salary expense. If instead of paying salary the employer pays deferred compensation, the employer deducts the deferred compensation expense in Year n. The deferred compensation net of the Year n tax benefit is the employer's after-tax deferred compensation expense.

EXAMPLE I18-26 ▶ Again consider the facts in Example I18-24, that is, $10,000 of current salary versus $25,000 of deferred compensation in ten years. In addition, the employer's current tax rate is 34%, but the employer expects its tax rate to be 25% ten years from now. The employer's ATROR is 10%. If the employer pays current salary, its after-tax salary expense projected to Year n is calculated as follows:

$$\$10,000(1 - 0.34)(1.1)^{10} = \$17,119$$

Alternatively, the after-tax deferred compensation expense is calculated as follows:

$$\$25,000(1 - 0.25) = \$18,750$$

In this case, the employer's after-tax deferred compensation expense ($18,750) exceeds its after-tax salary expense ($17,119). Consequently, the employer is unwilling to pay Bruce the $25,000 of deferred compensation even though Bruce prefers that alternative. ◀

Using general terms, we can state the employer's current salary and deferred compensation alternatives as follows:

$$\text{CSE} = \text{BT\$}(1 - t_{co})(1 + r_c)^n$$
$$\text{DCE} = \text{BT\$}(D_n)(1 - t_{cn})$$

In these formulas, CSE stands for current salary expense and is the employer's after-tax salary expense projected to Year n; DCE stands for deferred compensation expense and is the employer's after-tax deferred compensation expense in Year n; and BT$ stands for before-tax current salary. As before, D_n equals the amount of deferred compensation paid in lieu of $1 currently. Accordingly, BT$ $\times$ D_n gives total deferred compensation before taxes. The other variables in the formulas are defined as follows:

- t_{co} = The employer's marginal tax rate in Year 0
- t_{cn} = The employer's marginal tax rate in Year n
- r_c = The employer's ATROR
- n = The number of years until the employer pays the deferred compensation

The employer will pay deferred compensation only if DCE does not exceed CSE. From the previous formulas, this relationship can be expressed as follows:

$$\text{DCE} \leq \text{CSE or}$$

$$\text{BT\$ } (D_n)(1 - t_{cn}) \leq \text{BT\$ } (1 - t_{co})(1 + r_c)^n$$

Solving the second expression for D_n yields:

$$D_n \leq \frac{(1 - t_{co})(1 + r_c)^n}{(1 - t_{cn})}$$

The level of D_n that exactly equals the right-hand side of this expression makes the employer indifferent to paying current salary or deferred compensation. That is, at the indifference level of D_n, the employer's current salary expense (CSE) equals the employer's deferred compensation expense (DCE). Levels of D_n below the indifference level make deferred compensation more beneficial than current salary to the employer.

EXAMPLE I18-27 ▶ Assume the same facts as in Example I18-26. Compared to $1 of current salary, the employer will pay deferred compensation only if D_n does not exceed 2.2825, calculated as follows:

$$D_n \leq \frac{(1 - 0.34)(1.1)^{10}}{(1 - 0.25)} = 2.2825$$

Therefore, D_n = 2.2825 is the employer's indifference level, as shown by the following calculation for $1 of current salary:

$$\text{CSE} = \$1 (1 - 0.34)(1.1)^{10} = \$1.7119$$
$$\text{DCE} = \$1 (2.2825)(1 - 0.25) = \$1.7119$$

Given a choice between $10,000 of current salary (BT$) and deferred compensation, the employer will pay deferred compensation instead of current salary only if deferred compensation does not exceed $22,825, which is $10,000 $\times$ 2.2825. ◀

COMPARING THE EMPLOYEE'S AND EMPLOYER'S VIEWS. Knowledge of the employee's and employer's acceptable levels of D_n gives the two parties the necessary tools to decide whether deferred compensation is preferable to current salary. Specifically, the employee and employer can apply the following decision rules:

- If the employee's indifference level of D_n exceeds the employer's indifference level of D_n, the employee must accept current salary because the employer will not pay the employee's required deferred compensation.
- If the employee's indifference level of D_n is less than the employer's indifference level of D_n, the employer can pay deferred compensation up to its indifference level.

Figure I18-2 shows these decision rules graphically. In both graphs, the shaded portion of the lines indicates the employee's and employer's acceptable levels of D_n. In the top graph, these areas are separated, leaving the middle part of the line empty. This empty region indicates the employee and employer cannot agree on a mutually acceptable level of D_n. In the bottom graph, however, the employee's and employer's acceptable levels of D_n overlap in the middle part of the line. Thus, both parties can accept any level of D_n in this region.

FIGURE I18-2 ▶ Comparing the Employee's and Employer's Views

EXAMPLE I18-28 ▶ Marsha and Todd are employed by Omega Corporation. They want to compare deferred compensation two years from now (n = 2) to $10,000 of current salary. Assume the following tax rates and rates of return:

	Year 0	Year n	ATROR
Marsha	$t_{po} = 0.28$	$t_{pn} = 0.15$	$r_p = 0.10$
Todd	$t_{po} = 0.40$	$t_{pn} = 0.15$	$r_p = 0.10$
Omega Corporation	$t_{co} = 0.39$	$t_{cn} = 0.25$	$r_c = 0.10$

The indifference level of D_n for each party is as follows:

Marsha: $$D_n = \frac{(1 - 0.28)(1.1)^2}{(1 - 0.15)} = 1.0249$$

Todd: $$D_n = \frac{(1 - 0.4)(1.1)^2}{(1 - 0.15)} = 0.8541$$

Omega Corporation: $$D_n = \frac{(1 - 0.39)(1.1)^2}{(1 - 0.25)} = 0.9841$$

Compared to $10,000 of current salary, Omega Corporation will pay no more than $9,841 of deferred compensation. Consequently, Marsha must settle for $10,000 of current salary because she requires more than $10,249 of deferred compensation to make that alternative preferable. This amount exceeds what Omega Corporation is willing to pay as deferred compensation.

Todd, on the other hand, can benefit from a deferred compensation arrangement. He requires deferred compensation exceeding $8,541, and Omega Corporation is willing to pay up to $9,841 of deferred compensation. ◀

We can provide additional insight into the salary versus deferred compensation decision by carrying Example I18-28 a bit further. If Omega Corporation pays Todd $9,841 of deferred compensation, Omega Corporation incurs the same after-tax expense it would have incurred had it paid $10,000 of current salary. Thus, Omega Corporation remains indifferent, and Todd obtains the full benefit of the deferred compensation arrangement. This outcome can be seen with the following income and expense amounts:

Todd: CSI = $10,000 (1 − 0.4) (1.1)² = $7,260
DCI = $10,000 (0.9841) (1 − 0.15) = $8,365

Omega Corporation: CSE = $10,000 (1 − 0.39) (1.1)² = $7,381
DCE = $10,000 (0.9841) (1 − 0.25) = $7,381

Because Omega Corporation pays its indifference level of D_n, its current salary and deferred compensation expenses are equal. Under the deferred compensation arrangement, however, Todd ends up with $8,365 rather than $7,260.

Suppose instead that Omega Corporation pays deferred compensation that makes Todd indifferent. In this case, Todd obtains the same amount of after-tax income as under the salary option, and Omega Corporation obtains the full benefit of the deferred compensation arrangement. This outcome can be seen with the following income and expense amounts:

Todd: CSI = $10,000 (1 − 0.4) (1.1)² = $7,260
DCI = $10,000 (0.8541) (1 − 0.15) = $7,260

Omega Corporation: CSE = $10,000 (1 − 0.39) (1.1)² = $7,381
DCE = $10,000 (0.8541) (1 − 0.25) = $6,406

Because Omega Corporation pays Todd's indifference level of D_n, Todd's current salary and deferred compensation income are equal. Under the deferred compensation arrangement, however, Omega Corporation's deferred compensation expense ($6,406) is less than the alternative current salary expense ($7,381).

In each case, one party was made indifferent while the other party benefited from the deferred compensation alternative. However, Omega Corporation also could pay deferred compensation somewhere between the two indifference levels of D_n. The shaded middle region in the bottom graph of Figure I18-2 depicts this range. For example, suppose Omega Corporation chose $D_n = 0.92$. The following outcomes would occur:

Todd: CSI = $10,000 (1 − 0.4) (1.1)² = $7,260
DCI = $10,000 (0.92) (1 − 0.15) = $7,820

Omega Corporation: CSE = $10,000 (1 − 0.39) (1.1)² = $7,381
DCE = $10,000 (0.92) (1 − 0.25) = $6,900

In this case, Todd's deferred compensation income is $7,820 rather than $7,260 of current salary income. In addition, Omega Corporation's deferred compensation expense is $6,900 rather than the $7,381 current salary expense. Thus, both parties are better off with the deferred compensation arrangement than with current salary. However, neither party is as well off had the other party remained indifferent. In short, they share the benefit.

The preceding analysis incorporated tax rates and ATRORs in the decision model for current salary versus deferred compensation. The outcomes in the examples, however, depended only on the differential tax rates across taxpayers and over time because the ATRORs of the employer and employees were the same. In other situations, the employer's ATROR may differ from that of the employees, further influencing the results.

STOP & THINK

Question: What nontax factors might affect the current salary versus deferred compensation decision, possibly overriding the tax factors?

Solution: In addition to tax factors, the parties must consider their cash-flow requirements. If the employee needs cash now, he or she may be unwilling to defer income despite a better result from the decision model. Similarly, an employer short on current cash may prefer deferred compensation even though the decision model suggests current salary as the better alternative. Deferred compensation also carries some risk. Under nonqualified deferred compensation plans, the employee becomes a general creditor of the employer.

Consequently, if the employer runs into financial difficulties later, the employer may not be able to pay the deferred compensation. The employee, therefore, may decide for the safe alternative, current salary, regardless of the decision model outcome. Finally, deferred compensation may lock the employee into continued employment unless the deferred compensation contract makes adequate provision for the employee's severance.

SUMMARY. The decision model developed in this section provides an analytic tool for employees and employers to plan current salary versus deferred compensation arrangements. The model takes into account the tax and ATROR attributes of both parties to the transaction. This approach prevents one party benefiting at the disadvantage of the other and therefore leads to the best overall solution. Topic Review I18-3 summarizes the decision model.

IMPLICIT TAXES AND CLIENTELES

OBJECTIVE 4

Understand the role of implicit taxes in investment decisions

Several of the investment vehicles we modeled earlier have certain tax benefits compared to other investments. For example, interest earned on tax-exempt investments, such as state and local bonds, is excluded from gross income. The Exempt Model reflects this tax benefit. As another example, assets that generate long-term capital gains also are tax favored. The taxation of the capital gain is deferred until realization, and then the realized gain may be subject to a preferential tax rate, specifically, the 20% maximum tax rate on

Topic Review I18-3

Current Salary Versus Deferred Compensation

EMPLOYEE'S POINT OF VIEW

$CSI = BT\$ (1 - t_{po})(1 + r_p)^n$
$DCI = BT\$ (D_n)(1 - t_{pn})$

$$D_n = \frac{(1 - t_{po})(1 + r_p)^n}{(1 - t_{pn})}$$

EMPLOYER'S POINT OF VIEW

$CSE = BT\$ (1 - t_{co})(1 + r_c)^n$
$DCE = BT\$ (D_n)(1 - t_{cn})$

$$D_n = \frac{(1 - t_{co})(1 + r_c)^n}{(1 - t_{cn})}$$

Decision rules:
▶ If the employee's indifference level of D_n exceeds the employer's indifference level of D_n, the employee must accept current salary because the employer will not pay the employee's required deferred compensation.
▶ If the employee's indifference level of D_n is less than the employer's indifference level of D_n, the employer can pay deferred compensation up to its indifference level.

Definitions of Variables:
 CSI = Current salary income; employee's after-tax future value of before-tax current salary
 DCI = Deferred compensation income; employee's after-tax future value of deferred compensation
 CSE = Current salary expense; employer's after-tax salary expense projected to Year n
 DCE = Deferred compensation expense; employer's after-tax deferred compensation expense in Year n
 $BT\$$ = Before-tax current salary
 D_n = Amount of deferred compensation paid in lieu of $1 of current salary
 t_{po} = Employee's marginal tax rate in Year 0
 t_{pn} = Employee's marginal tax rate in Year n
 r_p = Employee's ATROR
 t_{co} = Employer's marginal tax rate in Year 0
 t_{cn} = Employer's marginal tax rate in Year n
 r_c = Employer's ATROR
 n = Number of years until the deferred compensation is paid

long-term capital gains. The Deferred Model, when applied to capital gain assets, reflects this preferential taxation. For the sake of simplicity, however, this section focuses on tax-exempt bonds to introduce the concept of implicit taxes and clientele effects.

IMPLICIT TAXES. Consider what happens in the marketplace for tax-favored assets. Given a choice between a fully-taxable investment and a tax-favored investment, investors will prefer the tax-favored investment, assuming the two investments are equally risky. This preference manifests itself as an increased demand for the tax-favored investment, thereby driving up the asset's price. The increased price, in turn, causes the asset's BTROR to decrease. For example, the BTROR on a bond with an unlimited life (a perpetuity) is as follows:

$$\text{BTROR} = \frac{\text{Annual cash flow}}{\text{Bond's price}}$$

If the bond's price increases, the BTROR must decrease.

The difference between the BTRORs of the fully-taxable and tax-favored investments is an implicit tax, which can be expressed as follows:

$$\text{IT} = R_b - R_e$$

In this formula, IT stands for implicit tax, R_b is the BTROR on a fully-taxable benchmark investment, and R_e is the BTROR on a tax-favored investment having the same risk level as the benchmark. (Later in this chapter, we will show the problem with comparing investments of unequal risk.) Dividing the implicit tax by the benchmark BTROR (R_b) converts the implicit tax (IT) to an implicit tax *rate* (t_I), expressed as follows:

$$t_I = \frac{R_b - R_e}{R_b}$$

EXAMPLE I18-29 ▶ Maria invests $1,000 in a taxable bond that yields a 10% BTROR and another $1,000 in a tax-exempt bond that yields a 7.2% BTROR (i.e., R_b = 10%, and R_e = 7.2%). Maria's marginal tax rate is 28% (i.e., t = 28%). The two investments yield the following earnings each year:

	Taxable Bond	*Tax-Exempt Bond*
Before-tax interest	$100	$72
Minus: Tax on interest	(28)	0
After-tax interest	$ 72	$72

Although the tax-exempt bond is free from explicit taxation, it reflects a 2.8% implicit tax, which is $R_b - R_e$ = 10% − 7.2% = 2.8%. Here, we express the implicit tax as a 2.8% reduction in the BTROR. Stated in dollars, the implicit tax is $1,000 × 0.028 = $28. Thus, Maria incurs a $28 explicit tax on the taxable bond and a $28 implicit tax on the tax-exempt bond. Maria's implicit tax *rate* on the tax-exempt bond is 28%, calculated as follows:

$$t_I = \frac{R_b - R_e}{R_b} = \frac{10\% - 7.2\%}{10\%} = 0.28 \text{ or } 28\%$$

Thus, Maria incurs a 28% explicit tax *rate* on the taxable bond and a 28% implicit tax *rate* on the tax-exempt bond.

Maria's ATROR on each bond is 7.2%. For the taxable bond, the ATROR is calculated as follows: $r_b = R_b (1 - t) = 10\% (1 - 0.28) = 7.2\%$. For the tax-exempt bond, the ATROR is the same as the BTROR. ◀

EQUILIBRIUM CONDITION AND CLIENTELES. The degree to which R_e falls in relation to R_b depends on the marginal investor's tax rate. By definition, marginal investors are indifferent between fully-taxable and tax-favored investments. As marginal investors compete for a tax-favored investment, supply and demand forces drive up its price (and reduce its BTROR) to the point where the ATRORs of the fully-taxable and tax-favored investments are equal. That is, in equilibrium for marginal investors, the ATRORs for investments meet the following condition: $r_b = r_e$. For example, in Example I18-29,

ADDITIONAL COMMENT

Tax return filings show that high income taxpayers invest in tax-exempt bonds more than do lower income taxpayers. For those returns reporting tax-exempt interest in 1997, taxpayers with AGI over $200,000 averaged 5 times more tax-exempt interest than did taxpayers with AGI between $30,000 and $50,000.

Maria is a marginal investor because $r_b = r_e = 7.2\%$. Thus, Maria is indifferent between the two investments. (Note that, for tax-exempt bonds, $r_e = R_e$.)

In Example I18-29, Maria incurred a 28% tax rate on each investment, explicit on the fully-taxable bond and implicit on the tax-exempt bond. Thus, Maria did not realize a tax benefit on the tax-exempt bond. In fact, the term "tax-exempt" is a misnomer when implicit taxes are considered. The issuer of the tax-exempt bond, however, received a tax subsidy in the form of a reduced interest rate. Therefore, the transaction works as though Maria paid a tax while the bond issuer received a subsidy.

This result leads to the following question: Can any investor benefit from tax-exempt bonds? In a flat-rate tax system where only one tax rate prevails, the answer is no because all investors are marginal investors. In a progressive tax rate system, however, the answer is yes for an investor whose marginal tax rate exceeds that of the marginal investor. In this situation, investors form natural clienteles for the alternative investments.

EXAMPLE I18-30 ▶ Assume the same facts as in Example I18-29, where Maria is the indifferent marginal investor. Consider two other investors, Silvia and Bob. Silvia's tax rate is 40%, and Bob's tax rate is 15%. If Silvia invested in a fully-taxable bond, her ATROR would be as follows: $r_b = 10\% (1 - 0.4) = 6\%$. Consequently, Silvia will prefer the tax-exempt bond that yields a 7.2% ATROR (which also equals its BTROR). Silvia's high tax rate puts her in the clientele for tax-exempt bonds. By investing in the tax-exempt bond, Silvia converts her 40% explicit tax rate into a 28% implicit tax rate, thereby giving her the higher ATROR.

If Bob invests in the fully-taxable bond, his ATROR will be as follows: $r_b = 10\% (1 - 0.15) = 8.5\%$. Thus, Bob prefers the fully-taxable bond because he obtains an 8.5% ATROR rather than 7.2% from the tax-exempt bond. Bob's low tax rate puts him in the clientele for taxable bonds. If he mistakenly invests in the tax-exempt bond, he will convert a 15% explicit tax rate into a 28% implicit tax rate. Therefore, he should avoid the tax-exempt bond. ◀

Example I18-30 highlights a key planning concept. Investors must consider the ATRORs of investments in making their investment decisions. Doing so will ensure that all tax effects are accounted for, including implicit as well as explicit taxes.

RISKY ASSETS. A key requirement for calculating the implicit tax rate on a tax-favored investment is that the risk level be the same as the benchmark investment. The BTROR of a risky asset has two components, the riskless return and a risk premium. This relationship can be formulated as follows:

$$\tilde{R} = R + P$$

In this formula, $\tilde{R}$ is the risky return, R is the riskless return, and P is the risk premium. Investors who invest in risky assets require this premium as an incentive to make the investment. If the benchmark investment is a fully-taxable, riskless bond, the tax-favored investment's BTROR must be adjusted to remove this risk premium to obtain an accurate measure of the implicit tax rate.

EXAMPLE I18-31 ▶ A tax-exempt bond issued by Troubled City is highly risky and therefore yields a 12% BTROR, which is composed of a 6.9% riskless return and a 5.1% risk premium. A riskless benchmark investment yields a 10% BTROR. Computing the implicit tax rate with the 12% return yields the following incorrect (and negative) implicit tax rate:

$$t_I = \frac{R_b - \tilde{R}_e}{R_b} = \frac{10\% - 12\%}{10\%} = -0.2 \text{ or } -20\%$$

The correct implicit tax rate is calculated with the risk-adjusted return as follows:

$$t_I = \frac{R_b - R_e}{R_b} = \frac{10\% - 6.9\%}{10\%} = 0.31 \text{ or } 31\%$$

◀

SUMMARY. Market forces drive down the BTRORs of tax-favored assets. This reduced return is an implicit tax. Thus, potential tax benefits to a marginal investor are competed away, thereby providing an implicit subsidy to the asset's issuer or seller. Investors whose tax rate exceeds that of the marginal investor, however, still can reap some benefit through the clientele effect. Topic Review I18-4 summarizes the implicit tax rate formula.

Topic Review I18-4

Implicit Taxes

Implicit tax:
$$IT = R_b - R_e$$

Implicit tax rate:
$$t_I = \frac{R_b - R_e}{R_b}$$

Equilibrium condition for marginal investor:
$$r_b = r_e.$$

Definitions of Variables:
IT = Implicit tax
t_I = Implicit tax rate
R_b = BTROR on a fully-taxable benchmark investment
R_e = Risk-adjusted BTROR on a tax-favored investment
r_b = ATROR on a fully-taxable benchmark investment
r_e = Risk-adjusted ATROR on a tax-favored investment

Problem Materials

DISCUSSION QUESTIONS

I18-1 What is the primary distinguishing feature that causes the Current Model, Deferred Model, and Pension Model to differ?

I18-2 What is an annualized ATROR, and why is it useful?

I18-3 Why might an investment in a capital asset be preferable to an investment that is fully taxed currently even though the capital asset's BTROR is less than that of the fully-taxable investment?

I18-4 Suppose a taxpayer is trying to decide between saving outside an IRA or saving through a traditional IRA. If the taxpayer needs the savings before reaching age 59½, should he or she necessarily avoid the IRA because of the 10% early withdrawal penalty? Why or why not? If the taxpayer must make a withdrawal before age 59½, which IRA might be better, the traditional IRA or the Roth IRA?

I18-5 How does the length of the investment horizon affect the annualized ATROR of an investment conforming to the Deferred Model?

I18-6 Under what conditions are the Exempt Model and Pension Model equivalent? Under what conditions would one model perform better than the other? How does the $2,000 limitation on deductible and Roth IRA contributions affect the comparison of these two vehicles?

I18-7 What characteristics of a C corporation cause the shareholder's stock investment to conform to the Deferred Model?

I18-8 How does the tax treatment of deferred compensation differ from the tax treatment of current salary?

I18-9 What is the variable, D_n, and why is it important to the current salary versus deferred compensation decision?

I18-10 Why might the employee and/or employer prefer salary over deferred compensation even in cases where deferred compensation provides the better tax results?

I18-11 Why might an investment conforming to the Exempt Model have a lower BTROR than would an equivalent-risk investment conforming to the Current Model?

I18-12 What is an implicit tax, and how does it arise?

I18-13 What forces cause ATRORs of various investments to be equal for marginal investors?

I18-14 What is a clientele effect, and what conditions are necessary for it to occur?

I18-15 An article that appeared in the September 30, 1993 issue of *The Wall Street Journal* (p. A18) made the following statement:

> At the highest federal tax rates . . . dividends and interest from private sector investments are taxed at 39.6%, capital gains at 28% [now 20%], while interest from state and local debt instruments isn't taxed at all.

What problem do you see with the author's statement?

I18-16 Why would a flat-rate tax system eliminate clientele effects?

I18-17 Why might the BTROR on a tax-favored investment be higher than the BTROR on a fully-taxable investment even though implicit tax theory says that it should be lower?

I18-18 We have discussed implicit taxes using tax-exempt bonds as an example, and we have mentioned capital gains assets as another case where implicit taxes might occur. Give one or two other specific tax provisions that might cause implicit taxes to arise. In so doing, explain:
- How the implicit tax is manifested (e.g., increased prices, reduced returns, increased costs, etc.).
- Who "pays" the implicit tax.
- Who "receives" the implicit subsidy.

PROBLEMS

I18-19 *Tax-Exempt Bond.* Laura, who is in the 40% tax bracket, notices that tax-exempt municipal bonds are yielding a 7% return. What before-tax rate of return on a fully-taxable bond must Laura obtain to make her prefer the taxable bond over the tax-exempt bond?

I18-20 *After-Tax Rates of Return.* Suppose a bond is taxable for both federal and state purposes. Let R_b = the BTROR on the bond, t_{fed} = the federal tax rate, and t_{st} = the state tax rate. Determine the ATROR (i.e., after federal and state taxes) if:
a. The state tax is *not* deductible for either federal or state purposes.
b. The state tax *is* deductible for federal but not for state purposes.
After algebraic simplification, each answer should take the form: R_b (   ), with the rest of the answer inside the parentheses.

I18-21 *Investment Models.* David can make a single investment in one of three alternatives. The first investment conforms to the Current Model, the second investment conforms to the Deferred Model, and the third investment conforms to the Pension Model. The investment horizon is seven years, and the BTROR for each alternative is 10%. David will incur no penalties upon withdrawal.
a. Assuming David's tax rate will be 15% for all seven years, what is the accumulation and annualized ATROR for each investment. Which alternative should David choose?
b. Assuming David's tax rate will be 15% for the first six years but will be 28% in the seventh year, what is the accumulation and annualized ATROR for each investment. Which alternative should David choose?

I18-22 *Investment Models.* Mark is considering investing in either a tax-exempt municipal bond that yields 7% or a nondeductible IRA that contains investments that yield 10% before taxes. (Mark is ineligible to contribute to a Roth IRA.) Mark's current tax rate is 40%, and he plans to make a single investment now with a 15-year investment horizon.
a. Using after-tax accumulations and annualized ATRORs, show that the nondeductible IRA outperforms the municipal bonds assuming Mark's tax rate remains at 40%. Assume no additional penalty upon withdrawal from the IRA.
b. How high would Mark's tax rate have to rise in Year n to make the municipal bond more attractive than the nondeductible IRA. Assume the 7% and 10% BTRORs remain constant over time.

I18-23 *Investment Models and IRAs.* Brenda has $2,000 of before-tax dollars available for a one-time investment. She is in the 28% bracket and expects to remain in this bracket indefinitely. She can invest directly in a taxable bond yielding 8% before taxes, or she can open an IRA and invest in the bond within the IRA. She knows that she will need the accumulated funds before she reaches age 59½. Thus, if she invests in an IRA, she will incur a 10% penalty on taxable amounts withdrawn from the IRA. Note: The two parts to this problem are best solved using a spreadsheet.
a. If she invests in an IRA that allows immediate deduction of contributed amounts (i.e., a traditional deductible IRA), how many years must she wait before the IRA is a better vehicle than direct investment in the bond outside the IRA?

b. How many years must she wait if she invests in a Roth IRA? Reminder: Withdrawals from a Roth IRA first come from contributions and are a tax-free return of capital. However, if Brenda withdraws the *entire* accumulation before she attains age 59½, the accumulated earnings will be fully taxable and also subject to the 10% early withdrawal penalty. Hence, in this situation, the Roth IRA operates exactly like a traditional nondeductible IRA (the Deferred Model instead of the Exempt Model).

I18-24 *Investment Planning.* Martha, who is in the 40% tax bracket, has $40,000 of before-tax income with which she wants to make a one-time investment. She wants to put $20,000 of this income in a deductible H.R. 10 plan, and she wants to invest any remaining after-tax income outside the H.R. 10 plan. Two investments are available: (1) a taxable bond yielding a 10% BTROR and (2) a nondividend paying stock that appreciates at a 10% annual rate before taxes. She is considering two alternatives:
1. Have the H.R 10 plan invest in the stock, and Martha will invest in the bond outside the H.R. 10 plan.
2. Have the H.R 10 plan invest in the bond, and Martha will invest in the stock outside the H.R 10 plan.

The investment horizon is ten years with tax rates constant over this period. Capital gains upon sale of stock outside the H.R 10 plan are taxed at 20%. However, if the stock is placed in the H.R 10 plan, the H.R 10 plan will sell the stock after ten years and distribute the proceeds to Martha, triggering ordinary income recognition to Martha. Assume no early withdrawal penalties on H.R 10 plan distributions. Determine the total after-tax accumulation of Alternative 1 and of Alternative 2. Which of the two alternatives should Martha choose?

I18-25 *Roth IRA versus Deductible IRA.* Harry wants to contribute either $2,000 (BT$) to a traditional deductible IRA or $2,000 (AT$) to a Roth IRA. His current tax rate is 28% for ordinary income and 20% for capital gains. He expects his IRA investment to earn a 12% BTROR, and he plans to withdraw the IRA accumulation in 25 years, at which time he will be over age 59½. If he contributes to a deductible IRA, he will invest the tax savings from the deduction in a nondividend paying stock that he expects to grow at a 12% BTROR. Harry will sell the stock at the same time he withdraws the IRA accumulation.
a. Compare the two alternatives assuming that, at the time of withdrawal, Harry's tax rate will be 28% for ordinary income and 20% for capital gains.
b. Compare the two alternatives assuming that, at the time of withdrawal, Harry's tax rate will be 15% for ordinary income and 10% for capital gains.

I18-26 *Multiperiod Investment Strategy.* Given the following facts and assumptions, determine what investment strategy Karen should follow to maximize accumulations and how much she will have accumulated at the *beginning* of Year 10 (including her last paycheck).
- Karen's ordinary tax rate is 31%, and her long-term capital gains tax rate is 20%. These rates will remain constant over her investment horizon.
- Karen earns $20,000 per year, which she receives on the first day of each year.
- Karen saves all her income after paying income taxes on her earnings. Taxes are payable immediately upon receiving her paycheck.
- At the beginning of each year, Karen can invest her savings in any of three vehicles:
  1. A money market fund yielding 6% per year before taxes,
  2. A traditional deductible IRA that yields 6% per year before taxes, and/or
  3. Capital assets that grow at 5.1% per year before taxes.
- IRA contributions are limited to $2,000 per year and are deductible up to that amount.
- At the beginning of Year 10, Karen saves no more income. Instead, she withdraws any IRA and/or money market accumulations and sells her capital assets for their accumulated FMV before taxes. She also receives a $20,000 paycheck at the beginning of Year 10.
- IRA accumulations are taxable immediately upon withdrawal with no additional penalty.
- Ignore itemized deductions, standard deductions, exemptions, etc.

I18-27 *Proprietorship versus C Corporation.* Myron has $10,000 to invest in a business. He can either (1) operate as a sole proprietor or (2) form a regular C corporation by contributing the $10,000 in exchange for corporate stock. In either case, the $10,000 will be invested in business assets and will earn a 10% BTROR for the first five years and an 18% BTROR for years six through 15. All after-tax earnings will be reinvested in the business. If Myron uses the corporate form, the corporation will liquidate at the end of the investment horizon. Myron's personal tax rate is 40%; the corporate tax rate is 25%; and the maximum tax rate on capital gains for individuals is 20% (assume no 50% exclusion). Determine whether Myron should operate as a sole proprietor or form a C corporation if the investment horizon is 15 years. Show the after-tax accumulation for each alternative.

I18-28 *S Corporation versus C Corporation.* Consider the following facts:

$$R_f = R_c = 18\%$$
$$t_c = 34\%$$
$$t_p = 40\% \text{ for ordinary income}$$
$$ = 20\% \text{ for capital gains other than Sec. 1202 gains}$$
$$ = 14\% \text{ for Sec. 1202 gains (i.e., } 28\% \times 0.5)$$
$$n = 4, 12, \text{ or } 25 \text{ year}$$

Other information:
- The corporation is formed with a $10,000 contribution.
- First assume that Sec. 1202 does not apply.
- Then assume that Sec. 1202 does apply for stock held more than five years.

Compare after-tax accumulations for each investment horizon and for each assumption regarding Sec. 1202. See format below. Should the corporation make the S election for any of these investment horizons?

	Years (n)		
	4	12	25
S corporation			
C corporation (no Sec. 1202)			
C corporation (with Sec. 1202)			

I18-29 *S Corporation versus C corporation.* Prior to 1993 Tax Act changes to tax rates, S corporations were very popular. Using the data below, compare S corporation status to C corporation status before and after the 1993 Tax Act.

Variable	Pre-1993 Act	Post-1993 Act	Description of Variables
R	12%	12%	BTROR to S or C corporation
t_p	31%	40%	Shareholder's ordinary tax rate
t_c	34%	34%	C corporation tax rate
t_g	28%	14%*	Capital gains tax rate
n	30	30	Investment horizon

The C corporation pays no dividends, and the S corporation distributes annually only enough for the shareholder to pay current taxes. *Note: The 14% rate reflects the 28% maximum rate on Sec. 1202 capital gains in conjunction with the 50% exclusion on certain small business investments held more than five years.

a. What is the shareholder's 30-year accumulation for a $1 investment under Pre-1993 law for S and C corporation status? Which is better?

b. What is the shareholder's 30-year accumulation for a $1 investment under Post-1993 law for S and C corporation status? Which is better?

I18-30 *Current Salary versus Deferred Compensation.* Consider Marsha and Todd from Example I18-28 in the text. Suppose these employees worked for Learned University, a tax-exempt organization, instead of a taxable corporation. The university's BTROR equals its ATROR, i.e., $R_c = r_c = 0.10$. Would the university be willing to pay deferred compensation to either employee? If so, how much? That is, what is the university's indifference level of D_n?

I18-31 *Current Salary versus Deferred Compensation.* Consider the following facts:

Variables	Case 1	Case 2	Case 3
BT$	$10,000	$10,000	$10,000
t_{po}	.28	.28	.40
t_{pn}	.40	.40	.28
r_p	.10	.10	.10
t_{co}	.35	.35	.35
t_{cn}	.35	.35	.25
r_c	.15	.20	.10
n	3	3	3

a. Complete the following table for each case:

	Case 1	Case 2	Case 3
Employer's D_n			
Employee's D_n			
Decision (CS or DC?)			
CSI			
DCI (employer indiff.)			
CSE			
DCE (employer indiff.)			
CSI			
DCI (employee indiff.)			
CSE			
DCE (employee indiff.)			

b. Suppose in Case 3 from Part a that the employer and employee negotiate a D_n of 1.12. Compute CSI, DCI, CSE, and DCE with this D_n to show that each party to the deferred compensation contract shares in the tax benefit.

I18-32 *Current Salary versus Deferred Compensation.* Sandy will earn a $100,000 bonus that can be split between current and deferred compensation in any of the following ways:

Current (BT$)*	Deferred (BT$)*
$100,000	$ -0-
80,000	20,000
60,000	40,000
40,000	60,000
20,000	80,000
-0-	100,000

* The numbers in the above lists are BT$ as in the text formulas. Thus, the numbers in the second column are not BT$ × D_n.

Assume that Sandy is subject to the following progressive tax rate schedule in the current and future years:

Income Range	Marginal Tax Rate	Computation of Tax
$ 0–$20,000	30.0%	0.30 × TI
20,001– 40,000	32.5	$ 6,000 + 0.325 (TI − $20,000)
40,001– 60,000	35.0	$12,500 + 0.35 (TI − $40,000)
60,001– 80,000	37.5	$19,500 + 0.375 (TI − $60,000)
Over $80,000	40.0	$27,000 + 0.4 (TI − $80,000)

- Corporate tax rates are as follows: $t_{co} = .35$, $t_{cn} = .34$.
- Rates of return are as follows: $r_c = .08$; $r_p = .07$.
- The length of deferral is five years, i.e., n = 5.

a. What is the best way for Sandy to split the $100,000 bonus given a level of D_n that makes the corporation indifferent?
b. Now assume the bonus allocations are not restricted to $20,000 increments. What is the optimal allocation of the current and deferred bonus given the level of D_n that makes the employer indifferent?

I18-33   *Implicit Tax Rates and Clientele Effects.* Terry's marginal tax rate is 28%. He can invest in a taxable bond yielding 7.5% before taxes. What is the implicit tax rate on a tax-exempt bond of equivalent risk that yields 6%?
a. Which bond should Terry invest in? Why?
b. How would your answer to Part a change if Terry's statutory marginal tax rate were 15%?

I18-34   *Implicit Tax Rates and Clientele Effects.* Consider three taxpayers who are in the following tax brackets:

Alice	28%
Brad	36%
Camille	40%

The BTROR on a benchmark investment is 10% (i.e., $R_b = 10\%$). Compute the equilibrium BTROR and the implicit tax rate on a tax-exempt bond under each of the following three alternative assumptions.
a. Alice is the marginal investor.
b. Brad is the marginal investor.
c. Camille is the marginal investor.
d. Which taxpayer (Alice, Brad, or Camille) would Camille like to see be the marginal investor? Why?

2000 TAX TABLES AND RATE SCHEDULES

2000 Tax Table

T-2 Individuals ▼ 2000 Tax Tables and Rate Schedules

Use if your taxable income is less than $100,000.
If $100,000 or more, use the Tax Rate Schedules.

Example. Mr. and Mrs. Brown are filing a joint return. Their taxable income on line 39 of Form 1040 is $25,300. First, they find the $25,300–25,350 income line. Next, they find the column for married filing jointly and read down the column. The amount shown where the income line and filing status column meet is $3,799. This is the tax amount they should enter on line 40 of their Form 1040.

Sample Table

At least	But less than	Single	Married filing jointly*	Married filing separately	Head of a household
			Your tax is—		
25,200	25,250	3,784	3,784	4,213	3,784
25,250	25,300	3,791	3,791	4,227	3,791
25,300	25,350	3,799	(3,799)	4,241	3,799
25,350	25,400	3,806	3,806	4,255	3,806

If line 39 (taxable income) is— At least	But less than	Single	Married filing jointly*	Married filing separately	Head of a household
			Your tax is—		
0	5	0	0	0	0
5	15	2	2	2	2
15	25	3	3	3	3
25	50	6	6	6	6
50	75	9	9	9	9
75	100	13	13	13	13
100	125	17	17	17	17
125	150	21	21	21	21
150	175	24	24	24	24
175	200	28	28	28	28
200	225	32	32	32	32
225	250	36	36	36	36
250	275	39	39	39	39
275	300	43	43	43	43
300	325	47	47	47	47
325	350	51	51	51	51
350	375	54	54	54	54
375	400	58	58	58	58
400	425	62	62	62	62
425	450	66	66	66	66
450	475	69	69	69	69
475	500	73	73	73	73
500	525	77	77	77	77
525	550	81	81	81	81
550	575	84	84	84	84
575	600	88	88	88	88
600	625	92	92	92	92
625	650	96	96	96	96
650	675	99	99	99	99
675	700	103	103	103	103
700	725	107	107	107	107
725	750	111	111	111	111
750	775	114	114	114	114
775	800	118	118	118	118
800	825	122	122	122	122
825	850	126	126	126	126
850	875	129	129	129	129
875	900	133	133	133	133
900	925	137	137	137	137
925	950	141	141	141	141
950	975	144	144	144	144
975	1,000	148	148	148	148

1,000

At least	But less than	Single	Married filing jointly*	Married filing separately	Head of a household
1,000	1,025	152	152	152	152
1,025	1,050	156	156	156	156
1,050	1,075	159	159	159	159
1,075	1,100	163	163	163	163
1,100	1,125	167	167	167	167
1,125	1,150	171	171	171	171
1,150	1,175	174	174	174	174
1,175	1,200	178	178	178	178
1,200	1,225	182	182	182	182
1,225	1,250	186	186	186	186
1,250	1,275	189	189	189	189
1,275	1,300	193	193	193	193
1,300	1,325	197	197	197	197
1,325	1,350	201	201	201	201
1,350	1,375	204	204	204	204
1,375	1,400	208	208	208	208
1,400	1,425	212	212	212	212
1,425	1,450	216	216	216	216
1,450	1,475	219	219	219	219
1,475	1,500	223	223	223	223
1,500	1,525	227	227	227	227
1,525	1,550	231	231	231	231
1,550	1,575	234	234	234	234
1,575	1,600	238	238	238	238
1,600	1,625	242	242	242	242
1,625	1,650	246	246	246	246
1,650	1,675	249	249	249	249
1,675	1,700	253	253	253	253
1,700	1,725	257	257	257	257
1,725	1,750	261	261	261	261
1,750	1,775	264	264	264	264
1,775	1,800	268	268	268	268
1,800	1,825	272	272	272	272
1,825	1,850	276	276	276	276
1,850	1,875	279	279	279	279
1,875	1,900	283	283	283	283
1,900	1,925	287	287	287	287
1,925	1,950	291	291	291	291
1,950	1,975	294	294	294	294
1,975	2,000	298	298	298	298

2,000

At least	But less than	Single	Married filing jointly*	Married filing separately	Head of a household
2,000	2,025	302	302	302	302
2,025	2,050	306	306	306	306
2,050	2,075	309	309	309	309
2,075	2,100	313	313	313	313
2,100	2,125	317	317	317	317
2,125	2,150	321	321	321	321
2,150	2,175	324	324	324	324
2,175	2,200	328	328	328	328
2,200	2,225	332	332	332	332
2,225	2,250	336	336	336	336
2,250	2,275	339	339	339	339
2,275	2,300	343	343	343	343
2,300	2,325	347	347	347	347
2,325	2,350	351	351	351	351
2,350	2,375	354	354	354	354
2,375	2,400	358	358	358	358
2,400	2,425	362	362	362	362
2,425	2,450	366	366	366	366
2,450	2,475	369	369	369	369
2,475	2,500	373	373	373	373
2,500	2,525	377	377	377	377
2,525	2,550	381	381	381	381
2,550	2,575	384	384	384	384
2,575	2,600	388	388	388	388
2,600	2,625	392	392	392	392
2,625	2,650	396	396	396	396
2,650	2,675	399	399	399	399
2,675	2,700	403	403	403	403
2,700	2,725	407	407	407	407
2,725	2,750	411	411	411	411
2,750	2,775	414	414	414	414
2,775	2,800	418	418	418	418
2,800	2,825	422	422	422	422
2,825	2,850	426	426	426	426
2,850	2,875	429	429	429	429
2,875	2,900	433	433	433	433
2,900	2,925	437	437	437	437
2,925	2,950	441	441	441	441
2,950	2,975	444	444	444	444
2,975	3,000	448	448	448	448

3,000

At least	But less than	Single	Married filing jointly*	Married filing separately	Head of a household
3,000	3,050	454	454	454	454
3,050	3,100	461	461	461	461
3,100	3,150	469	469	469	469
3,150	3,200	476	476	476	476
3,200	3,250	484	484	484	484
3,250	3,300	491	491	491	491
3,300	3,350	499	499	499	499
3,350	3,400	506	506	506	506
3,400	3,450	514	514	514	514
3,450	3,500	521	521	521	521
3,500	3,550	529	529	529	529
3,550	3,600	536	536	536	536
3,600	3,650	544	544	544	544
3,650	3,700	551	551	551	551
3,700	3,750	559	559	559	559
3,750	3,800	566	566	566	566
3,800	3,850	574	574	574	574
3,850	3,900	581	581	581	581
3,900	3,950	589	589	589	589
3,950	4,000	596	596	596	596

4,000

At least	But less than	Single	Married filing jointly*	Married filing separately	Head of a household
4,000	4,050	604	604	604	604
4,050	4,100	611	611	611	611
4,100	4,150	619	619	619	619
4,150	4,200	626	626	626	626
4,200	4,250	634	634	634	634
4,250	4,300	641	641	641	641
4,300	4,350	649	649	649	649
4,350	4,400	656	656	656	656
4,400	4,450	664	664	664	664
4,450	4,500	671	671	671	671
4,500	4,550	679	679	679	679
4,550	4,600	686	686	686	686
4,600	4,650	694	694	694	694
4,650	4,700	701	701	701	701
4,700	4,750	709	709	709	709
4,750	4,800	716	716	716	716
4,800	4,850	724	724	724	724
4,850	4,900	731	731	731	731
4,900	4,950	739	739	739	739
4,950	5,000	746	746	746	746

(Continued on next page)

* This column must also be used by a qualifying widow(er).

2000 Tax Table—Continued

If line 39 (taxable income) is— At least	But less than	Single	Married filing jointly*	Married filing separately	Head of a household	If line 39 (taxable income) is— At least	But less than	Single	Married filing jointly*	Married filing separately	Head of a household	If line 39 (taxable income) is— At least	But less than	Single	Married filing jointly*	Married filing separately	Head of a household
		Your tax is—						Your tax is—						Your tax is—			
5,000						**8,000**						**11,000**					
5,000	5,050	754	754	754	754	8,000	8,050	1,204	1,204	1,204	1,204	11,000	11,050	1,654	1,654	1,654	1,654
5,050	5,100	761	761	761	761	8,050	8,100	1,211	1,211	1,211	1,211	11,050	11,100	1,661	1,661	1,661	1,661
5,100	5,150	769	769	769	769	8,100	8,150	1,219	1,219	1,219	1,219	11,100	11,150	1,669	1,669	1,669	1,669
5,150	5,200	776	776	776	776	8,150	8,200	1,226	1,226	1,226	1,226	11,150	11,200	1,676	1,676	1,676	1,676
5,200	5,250	784	784	784	784	8,200	8,250	1,234	1,234	1,234	1,234	11,200	11,250	1,684	1,684	1,684	1,684
5,250	5,300	791	791	791	791	8,250	8,300	1,241	1,241	1,241	1,241	11,250	11,300	1,691	1,691	1,691	1,691
5,300	5,350	799	799	799	799	8,300	8,350	1,249	1,249	1,249	1,249	11,300	11,350	1,699	1,699	1,699	1,699
5,350	5,400	806	806	806	806	8,350	8,400	1,256	1,256	1,256	1,256	11,350	11,400	1,706	1,706	1,706	1,706
5,400	5,450	814	814	814	814	8,400	8,450	1,264	1,264	1,264	1,264	11,400	11,450	1,714	1,714	1,714	1,714
5,450	5,500	821	821	821	821	8,450	8,500	1,271	1,271	1,271	1,271	11,450	11,500	1,721	1,721	1,721	1,721
5,500	5,550	829	829	829	829	8,500	8,550	1,279	1,279	1,279	1,279	11,500	11,550	1,729	1,729	1,729	1,729
5,550	5,600	836	836	836	836	8,550	8,600	1,286	1,286	1,286	1,286	11,550	11,600	1,736	1,736	1,736	1,736
5,600	5,650	844	844	844	844	8,600	8,650	1,294	1,294	1,294	1,294	11,600	11,650	1,744	1,744	1,744	1,744
5,650	5,700	851	851	851	851	8,650	8,700	1,301	1,301	1,301	1,301	11,650	11,700	1,751	1,751	1,751	1,751
5,700	5,750	859	859	859	859	8,700	8,750	1,309	1,309	1,309	1,309	11,700	11,750	1,759	1,759	1,759	1,759
5,750	5,800	866	866	866	866	8,750	8,800	1,316	1,316	1,316	1,316	11,750	11,800	1,766	1,766	1,766	1,766
5,800	5,850	874	874	874	874	8,800	8,850	1,324	1,324	1,324	1,324	11,800	11,850	1,774	1,774	1,774	1,774
5,850	5,900	881	881	881	881	8,850	8,900	1,331	1,331	1,331	1,331	11,850	11,900	1,781	1,781	1,781	1,781
5,900	5,950	889	889	889	889	8,900	8,950	1,339	1,339	1,339	1,339	11,900	11,950	1,789	1,789	1,789	1,789
5,950	6,000	896	896	896	896	8,950	9,000	1,346	1,346	1,346	1,346	11,950	12,000	1,796	1,796	1,796	1,796
6,000						**9,000**						**12,000**					
6,000	6,050	904	904	904	904	9,000	9,050	1,354	1,354	1,354	1,354	12,000	12,050	1,804	1,804	1,804	1,804
6,050	6,100	911	911	911	911	9,050	9,100	1,361	1,361	1,361	1,361	12,050	12,100	1,811	1,811	1,811	1,811
6,100	6,150	919	919	919	919	9,100	9,150	1,369	1,369	1,369	1,369	12,100	12,150	1,819	1,819	1,819	1,819
6,150	6,200	926	926	926	926	9,150	9,200	1,376	1,376	1,376	1,376	12,150	12,200	1,826	1,826	1,826	1,826
6,200	6,250	934	934	934	934	9,200	9,250	1,384	1,384	1,384	1,384	12,200	12,250	1,834	1,834	1,834	1,834
6,250	6,300	941	941	941	941	9,250	9,300	1,391	1,391	1,391	1,391	12,250	12,300	1,841	1,841	1,841	1,841
6,300	6,350	949	949	949	949	9,300	9,350	1,399	1,399	1,399	1,399	12,300	12,350	1,849	1,849	1,849	1,849
6,350	6,400	956	956	956	956	9,350	9,400	1,406	1,406	1,406	1,406	12,350	12,400	1,856	1,856	1,856	1,856
6,400	6,450	964	964	964	964	9,400	9,450	1,414	1,414	1,414	1,414	12,400	12,450	1,864	1,864	1,864	1,864
6,450	6,500	971	971	971	971	9,450	9,500	1,421	1,421	1,421	1,421	12,450	12,500	1,871	1,871	1,871	1,871
6,500	6,550	979	979	979	979	9,500	9,550	1,429	1,429	1,429	1,429	12,500	12,550	1,879	1,879	1,879	1,879
6,550	6,600	986	986	986	986	9,550	9,600	1,436	1,436	1,436	1,436	12,550	12,600	1,886	1,886	1,886	1,886
6,600	6,650	994	994	994	994	9,600	9,650	1,444	1,444	1,444	1,444	12,600	12,650	1,894	1,894	1,894	1,894
6,650	6,700	1,001	1,001	1,001	1,001	9,650	9,700	1,451	1,451	1,451	1,451	12,650	12,700	1,901	1,901	1,901	1,901
6,700	6,750	1,009	1,009	1,009	1,009	9,700	9,750	1,459	1,459	1,459	1,459	12,700	12,750	1,909	1,909	1,909	1,909
6,750	6,800	1,016	1,016	1,016	1,016	9,750	9,800	1,466	1,466	1,466	1,466	12,750	12,800	1,916	1,916	1,916	1,916
6,800	6,850	1,024	1,024	1,024	1,024	9,800	9,850	1,474	1,474	1,474	1,474	12,800	12,850	1,924	1,924	1,924	1,924
6,850	6,900	1,031	1,031	1,031	1,031	9,850	9,900	1,481	1,481	1,481	1,481	12,850	12,900	1,931	1,931	1,931	1,931
6,900	6,950	1,039	1,039	1,039	1,039	9,900	9,950	1,489	1,489	1,489	1,489	12,900	12,950	1,939	1,939	1,939	1,939
6,950	7,000	1,046	1,046	1,046	1,046	9,950	10,000	1,496	1,496	1,496	1,496	12,950	13,000	1,946	1,946	1,946	1,946
7,000						**10,000**						**13,000**					
7,000	7,050	1,054	1,054	1,054	1,054	10,000	10,050	1,504	1,504	1,504	1,504	13,000	13,050	1,954	1,954	1,954	1,954
7,050	7,100	1,061	1,061	1,061	1,061	10,050	10,100	1,511	1,511	1,511	1,511	13,050	13,100	1,961	1,961	1,961	1,961
7,100	7,150	1,069	1,069	1,069	1,069	10,100	10,150	1,519	1,519	1,519	1,519	13,100	13,150	1,969	1,969	1,969	1,969
7,150	7,200	1,076	1,076	1,076	1,076	10,150	10,200	1,526	1,526	1,526	1,526	13,150	13,200	1,976	1,976	1,976	1,976
7,200	7,250	1,084	1,084	1,084	1,084	10,200	10,250	1,534	1,534	1,534	1,534	13,200	13,250	1,984	1,984	1,984	1,984
7,250	7,300	1,091	1,091	1,091	1,091	10,250	10,300	1,541	1,541	1,541	1,541	13,250	13,300	1,991	1,991	1,991	1,991
7,300	7,350	1,099	1,099	1,099	1,099	10,300	10,350	1,549	1,549	1,549	1,549	13,300	13,350	1,999	1,999	1,999	1,999
7,350	7,400	1,106	1,106	1,106	1,106	10,350	10,400	1,556	1,556	1,556	1,556	13,350	13,400	2,006	2,006	2,006	2,006
7,400	7,450	1,114	1,114	1,114	1,114	10,400	10,450	1,564	1,564	1,564	1,564	13,400	13,450	2,014	2,014	2,014	2,014
7,450	7,500	1,121	1,121	1,121	1,121	10,450	10,500	1,571	1,571	1,571	1,571	13,450	13,500	2,021	2,021	2,021	2,021
7,500	7,550	1,129	1,129	1,129	1,129	10,500	10,550	1,579	1,579	1,579	1,579	13,500	13,550	2,029	2,029	2,029	2,029
7,550	7,600	1,136	1,136	1,136	1,136	10,550	10,600	1,586	1,586	1,586	1,586	13,550	13,600	2,036	2,036	2,036	2,036
7,600	7,650	1,144	1,144	1,144	1,144	10,600	10,650	1,594	1,594	1,594	1,594	13,600	13,650	2,044	2,044	2,044	2,044
7,650	7,700	1,151	1,151	1,151	1,151	10,650	10,700	1,601	1,601	1,601	1,601	13,650	13,700	2,051	2,051	2,051	2,051
7,700	7,750	1,159	1,159	1,159	1,159	10,700	10,750	1,609	1,609	1,609	1,609	13,700	13,750	2,059	2,059	2,059	2,059
7,750	7,800	1,166	1,166	1,166	1,166	10,750	10,800	1,616	1,616	1,616	1,616	13,750	13,800	2,066	2,066	2,066	2,066
7,800	7,850	1,174	1,174	1,174	1,174	10,800	10,850	1,624	1,624	1,624	1,624	13,800	13,850	2,074	2,074	2,074	2,074
7,850	7,900	1,181	1,181	1,181	1,181	10,850	10,900	1,631	1,631	1,631	1,631	13,850	13,900	2,081	2,081	2,081	2,081
7,900	7,950	1,189	1,189	1,189	1,189	10,900	10,950	1,639	1,639	1,639	1,639	13,900	13,950	2,089	2,089	2,089	2,089
7,950	8,000	1,196	1,196	1,196	1,196	10,950	11,000	1,646	1,646	1,646	1,646	13,950	14,000	2,096	2,096	2,096	2,096

* This column must also be used by a qualifying widow(er).

(Continued on next page)

T-4 Individuals ▼ 2000 Tax Tables and Rate Schedules

2000 Tax Table—Continued

If line 39 (taxable income) is—		And you are—				If line 39 (taxable income) is—		And you are—				If line 39 (taxable income) is—		And you are—			
At least	But less than	Single	Married filing jointly *	Married filing sepa- rately	Head of a house- hold	At least	But less than	Single	Married filing jointly *	Married filing sepa- rately	Head of a house- hold	At least	But less than	Single	Married filing jointly *	Married filing sepa- rately	Head of a house- hold
		Your tax is—						Your tax is—						Your tax is—			

14,000

14,000	14,050	2,104	2,104	2,104	2,104
14,050	14,100	2,111	2,111	2,111	2,111
14,100	14,150	2,119	2,119	2,119	2,119
14,150	14,200	2,126	2,126	2,126	2,126
14,200	14,250	2,134	2,134	2,134	2,134
14,250	14,300	2,141	2,141	2,141	2,141
14,300	14,350	2,149	2,149	2,149	2,149
14,350	14,400	2,156	2,156	2,156	2,156
14,400	14,450	2,164	2,164	2,164	2,164
14,450	14,500	2,171	2,171	2,171	2,171
14,500	14,550	2,179	2,179	2,179	2,179
14,550	14,600	2,186	2,186	2,186	2,186
14,600	14,650	2,194	2,194	2,194	2,194
14,650	14,700	2,201	2,201	2,201	2,201
14,700	14,750	2,209	2,209	2,209	2,209
14,750	14,800	2,216	2,216	2,216	2,216
14,800	14,850	2,224	2,224	2,224	2,224
14,850	14,900	2,231	2,231	2,231	2,231
14,900	14,950	2,239	2,239	2,239	2,239
14,950	15,000	2,246	2,246	2,246	2,246

15,000

15,000	15,050	2,254	2,254	2,254	2,254
15,050	15,100	2,261	2,261	2,261	2,261
15,100	15,150	2,269	2,269	2,269	2,269
15,150	15,200	2,276	2,276	2,276	2,276
15,200	15,250	2,284	2,284	2,284	2,284
15,250	15,300	2,291	2,291	2,291	2,291
15,300	15,350	2,299	2,299	2,299	2,299
15,350	15,400	2,306	2,306	2,306	2,306
15,400	15,450	2,314	2,314	2,314	2,314
15,450	15,500	2,321	2,321	2,321	2,321
15,500	15,550	2,329	2,329	2,329	2,329
15,550	15,600	2,336	2,336	2,336	2,336
15,600	15,650	2,344	2,344	2,344	2,344
15,650	15,700	2,351	2,351	2,351	2,351
15,700	15,750	2,359	2,359	2,359	2,359
15,750	15,800	2,366	2,366	2,366	2,366
15,800	15,850	2,374	2,374	2,374	2,374
15,850	15,900	2,381	2,381	2,381	2,381
15,900	15,950	2,389	2,389	2,389	2,389
15,950	16,000	2,396	2,396	2,396	2,396

16,000

16,000	16,050	2,404	2,404	2,404	2,404
16,050	16,100	2,411	2,411	2,411	2,411
16,100	16,150	2,419	2,419	2,419	2,419
16,150	16,200	2,426	2,426	2,426	2,426
16,200	16,250	2,434	2,434	2,434	2,434
16,250	16,300	2,441	2,441	2,441	2,441
16,300	16,350	2,449	2,449	2,449	2,449
16,350	16,400	2,456	2,456	2,456	2,456
16,400	16,450	2,464	2,464	2,464	2,464
16,450	16,500	2,471	2,471	2,471	2,471
16,500	16,550	2,479	2,479	2,479	2,479
16,550	16,600	2,486	2,486	2,486	2,486
16,600	16,650	2,494	2,494	2,494	2,494
16,650	16,700	2,501	2,501	2,501	2,501
16,700	16,750	2,509	2,509	2,509	2,509
16,750	16,800	2,516	2,516	2,516	2,516
16,800	16,850	2,524	2,524	2,524	2,524
16,850	16,900	2,531	2,531	2,531	2,531
16,900	16,950	2,539	2,539	2,539	2,539
16,950	17,000	2,546	2,546	2,546	2,546

17,000

17,000	17,050	2,554	2,554	2,554	2,554
17,050	17,100	2,561	2,561	2,561	2,561
17,100	17,150	2,569	2,569	2,569	2,569
17,150	17,200	2,576	2,576	2,576	2,576
17,200	17,250	2,584	2,584	2,584	2,584
17,250	17,300	2,591	2,591	2,591	2,591
17,300	17,350	2,599	2,599	2,599	2,599
17,350	17,400	2,606	2,606	2,606	2,606
17,400	17,450	2,614	2,614	2,614	2,614
17,450	17,500	2,621	2,621	2,621	2,621
17,500	17,550	2,629	2,629	2,629	2,629
17,550	17,600	2,636	2,636	2,636	2,636
17,600	17,650	2,644	2,644	2,644	2,644
17,650	17,700	2,651	2,651	2,651	2,651
17,700	17,750	2,659	2,659	2,659	2,659
17,750	17,800	2,666	2,666	2,666	2,666
17,800	17,850	2,674	2,674	2,674	2,674
17,850	17,900	2,681	2,681	2,681	2,681
17,900	17,950	2,689	2,689	2,689	2,689
17,950	18,000	2,696	2,696	2,696	2,696

18,000

18,000	18,050	2,704	2,704	2,704	2,704
18,050	18,100	2,711	2,711	2,711	2,711
18,100	18,150	2,719	2,719	2,719	2,719
18,150	18,200	2,726	2,726	2,726	2,726
18,200	18,250	2,734	2,734	2,734	2,734
18,250	18,300	2,741	2,741	2,741	2,741
18,300	18,350	2,749	2,749	2,749	2,749
18,350	18,400	2,756	2,756	2,756	2,756
18,400	18,450	2,764	2,764	2,764	2,764
18,450	18,500	2,771	2,771	2,771	2,771
18,500	18,550	2,779	2,779	2,779	2,779
18,550	18,600	2,786	2,786	2,786	2,786
18,600	18,650	2,794	2,794	2,794	2,794
18,650	18,700	2,801	2,801	2,801	2,801
18,700	18,750	2,809	2,809	2,809	2,809
18,750	18,800	2,816	2,816	2,816	2,816
18,800	18,850	2,824	2,824	2,824	2,824
18,850	18,900	2,831	2,831	2,831	2,831
18,900	18,950	2,839	2,839	2,839	2,839
18,950	19,000	2,846	2,846	2,846	2,846

19,000

19,000	19,050	2,854	2,854	2,854	2,854
19,050	19,100	2,861	2,861	2,861	2,861
19,100	19,150	2,869	2,869	2,869	2,869
19,150	19,200	2,876	2,876	2,876	2,876
19,200	19,250	2,884	2,884	2,884	2,884
19,250	19,300	2,891	2,891	2,891	2,891
19,300	19,350	2,899	2,899	2,899	2,899
19,350	19,400	2,906	2,906	2,906	2,906
19,400	19,450	2,914	2,914	2,914	2,914
19,450	19,500	2,921	2,921	2,921	2,921
19,500	19,550	2,929	2,929	2,929	2,929
19,550	19,600	2,936	2,936	2,936	2,936
19,600	19,650	2,944	2,944	2,944	2,944
19,650	19,700	2,951	2,951	2,951	2,951
19,700	19,750	2,959	2,959	2,959	2,959
19,750	19,800	2,966	2,966	2,966	2,966
19,800	19,850	2,974	2,974	2,974	2,974
19,850	19,900	2,981	2,981	2,981	2,981
19,900	19,950	2,989	2,989	2,989	2,989
19,950	20,000	2,996	2,996	2,996	2,996

20,000

20,000	20,050	3,004	3,004	3,004	3,004
20,050	20,100	3,011	3,011	3,011	3,011
20,100	20,150	3,019	3,019	3,019	3,019
20,150	20,200	3,026	3,026	3,026	3,026
20,200	20,250	3,034	3,034	3,034	3,034
20,250	20,300	3,041	3,041	3,041	3,041
20,300	20,350	3,049	3,049	3,049	3,049
20,350	20,400	3,056	3,056	3,056	3,056
20,400	20,450	3,064	3,064	3,064	3,064
20,450	20,500	3,071	3,071	3,071	3,071
20,500	20,550	3,079	3,079	3,079	3,079
20,550	20,600	3,086	3,086	3,086	3,086
20,600	20,650	3,094	3,094	3,094	3,094
20,650	20,700	3,101	3,101	3,101	3,101
20,700	20,750	3,109	3,109	3,109	3,109
20,750	20,800	3,116	3,116	3,116	3,116
20,800	20,850	3,124	3,124	3,124	3,124
20,850	20,900	3,131	3,131	3,131	3,131
20,900	20,950	3,139	3,139	3,139	3,139
20,950	21,000	3,146	3,146	3,146	3,146

21,000

21,000	21,050	3,154	3,154	3,154	3,154
21,050	21,100	3,161	3,161	3,161	3,161
21,100	21,150	3,169	3,169	3,169	3,169
21,150	21,200	3,176	3,176	3,176	3,176
21,200	21,250	3,184	3,184	3,184	3,184
21,250	21,300	3,191	3,191	3,191	3,191
21,300	21,350	3,199	3,199	3,199	3,199
21,350	21,400	3,206	3,206	3,206	3,206
21,400	21,450	3,214	3,214	3,214	3,214
21,450	21,500	3,221	3,221	3,221	3,221
21,500	21,550	3,229	3,229	3,229	3,229
21,550	21,600	3,236	3,236	3,236	3,236
21,600	21,650	3,244	3,244	3,244	3,244
21,650	21,700	3,251	3,251	3,251	3,251
21,700	21,750	3,259	3,259	3,259	3,259
21,750	21,800	3,266	3,266	3,266	3,266
21,800	21,850	3,274	3,274	3,274	3,274
21,850	21,900	3,281	3,281	3,281	3,281
21,900	21,950	3,289	3,289	3,289	3,289
21,950	22,000	3,296	3,296	3,303	3,296

22,000

22,000	22,050	3,304	3,304	3,317	3,304
22,050	22,100	3,311	3,311	3,331	3,311
22,100	22,150	3,319	3,319	3,345	3,319
22,150	22,200	3,326	3,326	3,359	3,326
22,200	22,250	3,334	3,334	3,373	3,334
22,250	22,300	3,341	3,341	3,387	3,341
22,300	22,350	3,349	3,349	3,401	3,349
22,350	22,400	3,356	3,356	3,415	3,356
22,400	22,450	3,364	3,364	3,429	3,364
22,450	22,500	3,371	3,371	3,443	3,371
22,500	22,550	3,379	3,379	3,457	3,379
22,550	22,600	3,386	3,386	3,471	3,386
22,600	22,650	3,394	3,394	3,485	3,394
22,650	22,700	3,401	3,401	3,499	3,401
22,700	22,750	3,409	3,409	3,513	3,409
22,750	22,800	3,416	3,416	3,527	3,416
22,800	22,850	3,424	3,424	3,541	3,424
22,850	22,900	3,431	3,431	3,555	3,431
22,900	22,950	3,439	3,439	3,569	3,439
22,950	23,000	3,446	3,446	3,583	3,446

* This column must also be used by a qualifying widow(er).

(Continued on next page)

2000 Tax Table—Continued

If line 39 (taxable income) is— At least	But less than	And you are— Single	Married filing jointly *	Married filing separately	Head of a household
		Your tax is—			

23,000

At least	But less than	Single	Married filing jointly	Married filing separately	Head of household
23,000	23,050	3,454	3,454	3,597	3,454
23,050	23,100	3,461	3,461	3,611	3,461
23,100	23,150	3,469	3,469	3,625	3,469
23,150	23,200	3,476	3,476	3,639	3,476
23,200	23,250	3,484	3,484	3,653	3,484
23,250	23,300	3,491	3,491	3,667	3,491
23,300	23,350	3,499	3,499	3,681	3,499
23,350	23,400	3,506	3,506	3,695	3,506
23,400	23,450	3,514	3,514	3,709	3,514
23,450	23,500	3,521	3,521	3,723	3,521
23,500	23,550	3,529	3,529	3,737	3,529
23,550	23,600	3,536	3,536	3,751	3,536
23,600	23,650	3,544	3,544	3,765	3,544
23,650	23,700	3,551	3,551	3,779	3,551
23,700	23,750	3,559	3,559	3,793	3,559
23,750	23,800	3,566	3,566	3,807	3,566
23,800	23,850	3,574	3,574	3,821	3,574
23,850	23,900	3,581	3,581	3,835	3,581
23,900	23,950	3,589	3,589	3,849	3,589
23,950	24,000	3,596	3,596	3,863	3,596

24,000

At least	But less than	Single	Married filing jointly	Married filing separately	Head of household
24,000	24,050	3,604	3,604	3,877	3,604
24,050	24,100	3,611	3,611	3,891	3,611
24,100	24,150	3,619	3,619	3,905	3,619
24,150	24,200	3,626	3,626	3,919	3,626
24,200	24,250	3,634	3,634	3,933	3,634
24,250	24,300	3,641	3,641	3,947	3,641
24,300	24,350	3,649	3,649	3,961	3,649
24,350	24,400	3,656	3,656	3,975	3,656
24,400	24,450	3,664	3,664	3,989	3,664
24,450	24,500	3,671	3,671	4,003	3,671
24,500	24,550	3,679	3,679	4,017	3,679
24,550	24,600	3,686	3,686	4,031	3,686
24,600	24,650	3,694	3,694	4,045	3,694
24,650	24,700	3,701	3,701	4,059	3,701
24,700	24,750	3,709	3,709	4,073	3,709
24,750	24,800	3,716	3,716	4,087	3,716
24,800	24,850	3,724	3,724	4,101	3,724
24,850	24,900	3,731	3,731	4,115	3,731
24,900	24,950	3,739	3,739	4,129	3,739
24,950	25,000	3,746	3,746	4,143	3,746

25,000

At least	But less than	Single	Married filing jointly	Married filing separately	Head of household
25,000	25,050	3,754	3,754	4,157	3,754
25,050	25,100	3,761	3,761	4,171	3,761
25,100	25,150	3,769	3,769	4,185	3,769
25,150	25,200	3,776	3,776	4,199	3,776
25,200	25,250	3,784	3,784	4,213	3,784
25,250	25,300	3,791	3,791	4,227	3,791
25,300	25,350	3,799	3,799	4,241	3,799
25,350	25,400	3,806	3,806	4,255	3,806
25,400	25,450	3,814	3,814	4,269	3,814
25,450	25,500	3,821	3,821	4,283	3,821
25,500	25,550	3,829	3,829	4,297	3,829
25,550	25,600	3,836	3,836	4,311	3,836
25,600	25,650	3,844	3,844	4,325	3,844
25,650	25,700	3,851	3,851	4,339	3,851
25,700	25,750	3,859	3,859	4,353	3,859
25,750	25,800	3,866	3,866	4,367	3,866
25,800	25,850	3,874	3,874	4,381	3,874
25,850	25,900	3,881	3,881	4,395	3,881
25,900	25,950	3,889	3,889	4,409	3,889
25,950	26,000	3,896	3,896	4,423	3,896

26,000

At least	But less than	Single	Married filing jointly	Married filing separately	Head of household
26,000	26,050	3,904	3,904	4,437	3,904
26,050	26,100	3,911	3,911	4,451	3,911
26,100	26,150	3,919	3,919	4,465	3,919
26,150	26,200	3,926	3,926	4,479	3,926
26,200	26,250	3,934	3,934	4,493	3,934
26,250	26,300	3,945	3,941	4,507	3,941
26,300	26,350	3,959	3,949	4,521	3,949
26,350	26,400	3,973	3,956	4,535	3,956
26,400	26,450	3,987	3,964	4,549	3,964
26,450	26,500	4,001	3,971	4,563	3,971
26,500	26,550	4,015	3,979	4,577	3,979
26,550	26,600	4,029	3,986	4,591	3,986
26,600	26,650	4,043	3,994	4,605	3,994
26,650	26,700	4,057	4,001	4,619	4,001
26,700	26,750	4,071	4,009	4,633	4,009
26,750	26,800	4,085	4,016	4,647	4,016
26,800	26,850	4,099	4,024	4,661	4,024
26,850	26,900	4,113	4,031	4,675	4,031
26,900	26,950	4,127	4,039	4,689	4,039
26,950	27,000	4,141	4,046	4,703	4,046

27,000

At least	But less than	Single	Married filing jointly	Married filing separately	Head of household
27,000	27,050	4,155	4,054	4,717	4,054
27,050	27,100	4,169	4,061	4,731	4,061
27,100	27,150	4,183	4,069	4,745	4,069
27,150	27,200	4,197	4,076	4,759	4,076
27,200	27,250	4,211	4,084	4,773	4,084
27,250	27,300	4,225	4,091	4,787	4,091
27,300	27,350	4,239	4,099	4,801	4,099
27,350	27,400	4,253	4,106	4,815	4,106
27,400	27,450	4,267	4,114	4,829	4,114
27,450	27,500	4,281	4,121	4,843	4,121
27,500	27,550	4,295	4,129	4,857	4,129
27,550	27,600	4,309	4,136	4,871	4,136
27,600	27,650	4,323	4,144	4,885	4,144
27,650	27,700	4,337	4,151	4,899	4,151
27,700	27,750	4,351	4,159	4,913	4,159
27,750	27,800	4,365	4,166	4,927	4,166
27,800	27,850	4,379	4,174	4,941	4,174
27,850	27,900	4,393	4,181	4,955	4,181
27,900	27,950	4,407	4,189	4,969	4,189
27,950	28,000	4,421	4,196	4,983	4,196

28,000

At least	But less than	Single	Married filing jointly	Married filing separately	Head of household
28,000	28,050	4,435	4,204	4,997	4,204
28,050	28,100	4,449	4,211	5,011	4,211
28,100	28,150	4,463	4,219	5,025	4,219
28,150	28,200	4,477	4,226	5,039	4,226
28,200	28,250	4,491	4,234	5,053	4,234
28,250	28,300	4,505	4,241	5,067	4,241
28,300	28,350	4,519	4,249	5,081	4,249
28,350	28,400	4,533	4,256	5,095	4,256
28,400	28,450	4,547	4,264	5,109	4,264
28,450	28,500	4,561	4,271	5,123	4,271
28,500	28,550	4,575	4,279	5,137	4,279
28,550	28,600	4,589	4,286	5,151	4,286
28,600	28,650	4,603	4,294	5,165	4,294
28,650	28,700	4,617	4,301	5,179	4,301
28,700	28,750	4,631	4,309	5,193	4,309
28,750	28,800	4,645	4,316	5,207	4,316
28,800	28,850	4,659	4,324	5,221	4,324
28,850	28,900	4,673	4,331	5,235	4,331
28,900	28,950	4,687	4,339	5,249	4,339
28,950	29,000	4,701	4,346	5,263	4,346

29,000

At least	But less than	Single	Married filing jointly	Married filing separately	Head of household
29,000	29,050	4,715	4,354	5,277	4,354
29,050	29,100	4,729	4,361	5,291	4,361
29,100	29,150	4,743	4,369	5,305	4,369
29,150	29,200	4,757	4,376	5,319	4,376
29,200	29,250	4,771	4,384	5,333	4,384
29,250	29,300	4,785	4,391	5,347	4,391
29,300	29,350	4,799	4,399	5,361	4,399
29,350	29,400	4,813	4,406	5,375	4,406
29,400	29,450	4,827	4,414	5,389	4,414
29,450	29,500	4,841	4,421	5,403	4,421
29,500	29,550	4,855	4,429	5,417	4,429
29,550	29,600	4,869	4,436	5,431	4,436
29,600	29,650	4,883	4,444	5,445	4,444
29,650	29,700	4,897	4,451	5,459	4,451
29,700	29,750	4,911	4,459	5,473	4,459
29,750	29,800	4,925	4,466	5,487	4,466
29,800	29,850	4,939	4,474	5,501	4,474
29,850	29,900	4,953	4,481	5,515	4,481
29,900	29,950	4,967	4,489	5,529	4,489
29,950	30,000	4,981	4,496	5,543	4,496

30,000

At least	But less than	Single	Married filing jointly	Married filing separately	Head of household
30,000	30,050	4,995	4,504	5,557	4,504
30,050	30,100	5,009	4,511	5,571	4,511
30,100	30,150	5,023	4,519	5,585	4,519
30,150	30,200	5,037	4,526	5,599	4,526
30,200	30,250	5,051	4,534	5,613	4,534
30,250	30,300	5,065	4,541	5,627	4,541
30,300	30,350	5,079	4,549	5,641	4,549
30,350	30,400	5,093	4,556	5,655	4,556
30,400	30,450	5,107	4,564	5,669	4,564
30,450	30,500	5,121	4,571	5,683	4,571
30,500	30,550	5,135	4,579	5,697	4,579
30,550	30,600	5,149	4,586	5,711	4,586
30,600	30,650	5,163	4,594	5,725	4,594
30,650	30,700	5,177	4,601	5,739	4,601
30,700	30,750	5,191	4,609	5,753	4,609
30,750	30,800	5,205	4,616	5,767	4,616
30,800	30,850	5,219	4,624	5,781	4,624
30,850	30,900	5,233	4,631	5,795	4,631
30,900	30,950	5,247	4,639	5,809	4,639
30,950	31,000	5,261	4,646	5,823	4,646

31,000

At least	But less than	Single	Married filing jointly	Married filing separately	Head of household
31,000	31,050	5,275	4,654	5,837	4,654
31,050	31,100	5,289	4,661	5,851	4,661
31,100	31,150	5,303	4,669	5,865	4,669
31,150	31,200	5,317	4,676	5,879	4,676
31,200	31,250	5,331	4,684	5,893	4,684
31,250	31,300	5,345	4,691	5,907	4,691
31,300	31,350	5,359	4,699	5,921	4,699
31,350	31,400	5,373	4,706	5,935	4,706
31,400	31,450	5,387	4,714	5,949	4,714
31,450	31,500	5,401	4,721	5,963	4,721
31,500	31,550	5,415	4,729	5,977	4,729
31,550	31,600	5,429	4,736	5,991	4,736
31,600	31,650	5,443	4,744	6,005	4,744
31,650	31,700	5,457	4,751	6,019	4,751
31,700	31,750	5,471	4,759	6,033	4,759
31,750	31,800	5,485	4,766	6,047	4,766
31,800	31,850	5,499	4,774	6,061	4,774
31,850	31,900	5,513	4,781	6,075	4,781
31,900	31,950	5,527	4,789	6,089	4,789
31,950	32,000	5,541	4,796	6,103	4,796

* This column must also be used by a qualifying widow(er).

(Continued on next page)

T-6 Individuals ▼ 2000 Tax Tables and Rate Schedules

2000 Tax Table—Continued

If line 39 (taxable income) is—		And you are—				If line 39 (taxable income) is—		And you are—				If line 39 (taxable income) is—		And you are—			
At least	But less than	Single	Married filing jointly *	Married filing sepa-rately	Head of a house-hold	At least	But less than	Single	Married filing jointly *	Married filing sepa-rately	Head of a house-hold	At least	But less than	Single	Married filing jointly *	Married filing sepa-rately	Head of a house-hold
			Your tax is—						Your tax is—						Your tax is—		
32,000						**35,000**						**38,000**					
32,000	32,050	5,555	4,804	6,117	4,804	35,000	35,050	6,395	5,254	6,957	5,254	38,000	38,050	7,235	5,704	7,797	6,078
32,050	32,100	5,569	4,811	6,131	4,811	35,050	35,100	6,409	5,261	6,971	5,261	38,050	38,100	7,249	5,711	7,811	6,092
32,100	32,150	5,583	4,819	6,145	4,819	35,100	35,150	6,423	5,269	6,985	5,269	38,100	38,150	7,263	5,719	7,825	6,106
32,150	32,200	5,597	4,826	6,159	4,826	35,150	35,200	6,437	5,276	6,999	5,280	38,150	38,200	7,277	5,726	7,839	6,120
32,200	32,250	5,611	4,834	6,173	4,834	35,200	35,250	6,451	5,284	7,013	5,294	38,200	38,250	7,291	5,734	7,853	6,134
32,250	32,300	5,625	4,841	6,187	4,841	35,250	35,300	6,465	5,291	7,027	5,308	38,250	38,300	7,305	5,741	7,867	6,148
32,300	32,350	5,639	4,849	6,201	4,849	35,300	35,350	6,479	5,299	7,041	5,322	38,300	38,350	7,319	5,749	7,881	6,162
32,350	32,400	5,653	4,856	6,215	4,856	35,350	35,400	6,493	5,306	7,055	5,336	38,350	38,400	7,333	5,756	7,895	6,176
32,400	32,450	5,667	4,864	6,229	4,864	35,400	35,450	6,507	5,314	7,069	5,350	38,400	38,450	7,347	5,764	7,909	6,190
32,450	32,500	5,681	4,871	6,243	4,871	35,450	35,500	6,521	5,321	7,083	5,364	38,450	38,500	7,361	5,771	7,923	6,204
32,500	32,550	5,695	4,879	6,257	4,879	35,500	35,550	6,535	5,329	7,097	5,378	38,500	38,550	7,375	5,779	7,937	6,218
32,550	32,600	5,709	4,886	6,271	4,886	35,550	35,600	6,549	5,336	7,111	5,392	38,550	38,600	7,389	5,786	7,951	6,232
32,600	32,650	5,723	4,894	6,285	4,894	35,600	35,650	6,563	5,344	7,125	5,406	38,600	38,650	7,403	5,794	7,965	6,246
32,650	32,700	5,737	4,901	6,299	4,901	35,650	35,700	6,577	5,351	7,139	5,420	38,650	38,700	7,417	5,801	7,979	6,260
32,700	32,750	5,751	4,909	6,313	4,909	35,700	35,750	6,591	5,359	7,153	5,434	38,700	38,750	7,431	5,809	7,993	6,274
32,750	32,800	5,765	4,916	6,327	4,916	35,750	35,800	6,605	5,366	7,167	5,448	38,750	38,800	7,445	5,816	8,007	6,288
32,800	32,850	5,779	4,924	6,341	4,924	35,800	35,850	6,619	5,374	7,181	5,462	38,800	38,850	7,459	5,824	8,021	6,302
32,850	32,900	5,793	4,931	6,355	4,931	35,850	35,900	6,633	5,381	7,195	5,476	38,850	38,900	7,473	5,831	8,035	6,316
32,900	32,950	5,807	4,939	6,369	4,939	35,900	35,950	6,647	5,389	7,209	5,490	38,900	38,950	7,487	5,839	8,049	6,330
32,950	33,000	5,821	4,946	6,383	4,946	35,950	36,000	6,661	5,396	7,223	5,504	38,950	39,000	7,501	5,846	8,063	6,344
33,000						**36,000**						**39,000**					
33,000	33,050	5,835	4,954	6,397	4,954	36,000	36,050	6,675	5,404	7,237	5,518	39,000	39,050	7,515	5,854	8,077	6,358
33,050	33,100	5,849	4,961	6,411	4,961	36,050	36,100	6,689	5,411	7,251	5,532	39,050	39,100	7,529	5,861	8,091	6,372
33,100	33,150	5,863	4,969	6,425	4,969	36,100	36,150	6,703	5,419	7,265	5,546	39,100	39,150	7,543	5,869	8,105	6,386
33,150	33,200	5,877	4,976	6,439	4,976	36,150	36,200	6,717	5,426	7,279	5,560	39,150	39,200	7,557	5,876	8,119	6,400
33,200	33,250	5,891	4,984	6,453	4,984	36,200	36,250	6,731	5,434	7,293	5,574	39,200	39,250	7,571	5,884	8,133	6,414
33,250	33,300	5,905	4,991	6,467	4,991	36,250	36,300	6,745	5,441	7,307	5,588	39,250	39,300	7,585	5,891	8,147	6,428
33,300	33,350	5,919	4,999	6,481	4,999	36,300	36,350	6,759	5,449	7,321	5,602	39,300	39,350	7,599	5,899	8,161	6,442
33,350	33,400	5,933	5,006	6,495	5,006	36,350	36,400	6,773	5,456	7,335	5,616	39,350	39,400	7,613	5,906	8,175	6,456
33,400	33,450	5,947	5,014	6,509	5,014	36,400	36,450	6,787	5,464	7,349	5,630	39,400	39,450	7,627	5,914	8,189	6,470
33,450	33,500	5,961	5,021	6,523	5,021	36,450	36,500	6,801	5,471	7,363	5,644	39,450	39,500	7,641	5,921	8,203	6,484
33,500	33,550	5,975	5,029	6,537	5,029	36,500	36,550	6,815	5,479	7,377	5,658	39,500	39,550	7,655	5,929	8,217	6,498
33,550	33,600	5,989	5,036	6,551	5,036	36,550	36,600	6,829	5,486	7,391	5,672	39,550	39,600	7,669	5,936	8,231	6,512
33,600	33,650	6,003	5,044	6,565	5,044	36,600	36,650	6,843	5,494	7,405	5,686	39,600	39,650	7,683	5,944	8,245	6,526
33,650	33,700	6,017	5,051	6,579	5,051	36,650	36,700	6,857	5,501	7,419	5,700	39,650	39,700	7,697	5,951	8,259	6,540
33,700	33,750	6,031	5,059	6,593	5,059	36,700	36,750	6,871	5,509	7,433	5,714	39,700	39,750	7,711	5,959	8,273	6,554
33,750	33,800	6,045	5,066	6,607	5,066	36,750	36,800	6,885	5,516	7,447	5,728	39,750	39,800	7,725	5,966	8,287	6,568
33,800	33,850	6,059	5,074	6,621	5,074	36,800	36,850	6,899	5,524	7,461	5,742	39,800	39,850	7,739	5,974	8,301	6,582
33,850	33,900	6,073	5,081	6,635	5,081	36,850	36,900	6,913	5,531	7,475	5,756	39,850	39,900	7,753	5,981	8,315	6,596
33,900	33,950	6,087	5,089	6,649	5,089	36,900	36,950	6,927	5,539	7,489	5,770	39,900	39,950	7,767	5,989	8,329	6,610
33,950	34,000	6,101	5,096	6,663	5,096	36,950	37,000	6,941	5,546	7,503	5,784	39,950	40,000	7,781	5,996	8,343	6,624
34,000						**37,000**						**40,000**					
34,000	34,050	6,115	5,104	6,677	5,104	37,000	37,050	6,955	5,554	7,517	5,798	40,000	40,050	7,795	6,004	8,357	6,638
34,050	34,100	6,129	5,111	6,691	5,111	37,050	37,100	6,969	5,561	7,531	5,812	40,050	40,100	7,809	6,011	8,371	6,652
34,100	34,150	6,143	5,119	6,705	5,119	37,100	37,150	6,983	5,569	7,545	5,826	40,100	40,150	7,823	6,019	8,385	6,666
34,150	34,200	6,157	5,126	6,719	5,126	37,150	37,200	6,997	5,576	7,559	5,840	40,150	40,200	7,837	6,026	8,399	6,680
34,200	34,250	6,171	5,134	6,733	5,134	37,200	37,250	7,011	5,584	7,573	5,854	40,200	40,250	7,851	6,034	8,413	6,694
34,250	34,300	6,185	5,141	6,747	5,141	37,250	37,300	7,025	5,591	7,587	5,868	40,250	40,300	7,865	6,041	8,427	6,708
34,300	34,350	6,199	5,149	6,761	5,149	37,300	37,350	7,039	5,599	7,601	5,882	40,300	40,350	7,879	6,049	8,441	6,722
34,350	34,400	6,213	5,156	6,775	5,156	37,350	37,400	7,053	5,606	7,615	5,896	40,350	40,400	7,893	6,056	8,455	6,736
34,400	34,450	6,227	5,164	6,789	5,164	37,400	37,450	7,067	5,614	7,629	5,910	40,400	40,450	7,907	6,064	8,469	6,750
34,450	34,500	6,241	5,171	6,803	5,171	37,450	37,500	7,081	5,621	7,643	5,924	40,450	40,500	7,921	6,071	8,483	6,764
34,500	34,550	6,255	5,179	6,817	5,179	37,500	37,550	7,095	5,629	7,657	5,938	40,500	40,550	7,935	6,079	8,497	6,778
34,550	34,600	6,269	5,186	6,831	5,186	37,550	37,600	7,109	5,636	7,671	5,952	40,550	40,600	7,949	6,086	8,511	6,792
34,600	34,650	6,283	5,194	6,845	5,194	37,600	37,650	7,123	5,644	7,685	5,966	40,600	40,650	7,963	6,094	8,525	6,806
34,650	34,700	6,297	5,201	6,859	5,201	37,650	37,700	7,137	5,651	7,699	5,980	40,650	40,700	7,977	6,101	8,539	6,820
34,700	34,750	6,311	5,209	6,873	5,209	37,700	37,750	7,151	5,659	7,713	5,994	40,700	40,750	7,991	6,109	8,553	6,834
34,750	34,800	6,325	5,216	6,887	5,216	37,750	37,800	7,165	5,666	7,727	6,008	40,750	40,800	8,005	6,116	8,567	6,848
34,800	34,850	6,339	5,224	6,901	5,224	37,800	37,850	7,179	5,674	7,741	6,022	40,800	40,850	8,019	6,124	8,581	6,862
34,850	34,900	6,353	5,231	6,915	5,231	37,850	37,900	7,193	5,681	7,755	6,036	40,850	40,900	8,033	6,131	8,595	6,876
34,900	34,950	6,367	5,239	6,929	5,239	37,900	37,950	7,207	5,689	7,769	6,050	40,900	40,950	8,047	6,139	8,609	6,890
34,950	35,000	6,381	5,246	6,943	5,246	37,950	38,000	7,221	5,696	7,783	6,064	40,950	41,000	8,061	6,146	8,623	6,904

* This column must also be used by a qualifying widow(er).

(Continued on next page)

2000 Tax Table—Continued

If line 39 (taxable income) is—		And you are—				If line 39 (taxable income) is—		And you are—				If line 39 (taxable income) is—		And you are—			
At least	But less than	Single	Married filing jointly *	Married filing separately	Head of a household	At least	But less than	Single	Married filing jointly *	Married filing separately	Head of a household	At least	But less than	Single	Married filing jointly *	Married filing separately	Head of a household
		Your tax is—						Your tax is—						Your tax is—			

41,000

41,000	41,050	8,075	6,154	8,637	6,918
41,050	41,100	8,089	6,161	8,651	6,932
41,100	41,150	8,103	6,169	8,665	6,946
41,150	41,200	8,117	6,176	8,679	6,960
41,200	41,250	8,131	6,184	8,693	6,974
41,250	41,300	8,145	6,191	8,707	6,988
41,300	41,350	8,159	6,199	8,721	7,002
41,350	41,400	8,173	6,206	8,735	7,016
41,400	41,450	8,187	6,214	8,749	7,030
41,450	41,500	8,201	6,221	8,763	7,044
41,500	41,550	8,215	6,229	8,777	7,058
41,550	41,600	8,229	6,236	8,791	7,072
41,600	41,650	8,243	6,244	8,805	7,086
41,650	41,700	8,257	6,251	8,819	7,100
41,700	41,750	8,271	6,259	8,833	7,114
41,750	41,800	8,285	6,266	8,847	7,128
41,800	41,850	8,299	6,274	8,861	7,142
41,850	41,900	8,313	6,281	8,875	7,156
41,900	41,950	8,327	6,289	8,889	7,170
41,950	42,000	8,341	6,296	8,903	7,184

42,000

42,000	42,050	8,355	6,304	8,917	7,198
42,050	42,100	8,369	6,311	8,931	7,212
42,100	42,150	8,383	6,319	8,945	7,226
42,150	42,200	8,397	6,326	8,959	7,240
42,200	42,250	8,411	6,334	8,973	7,254
42,250	42,300	8,425	6,341	8,987	7,268
42,300	42,350	8,439	6,349	9,001	7,282
42,350	42,400	8,453	6,356	9,015	7,296
42,400	42,450	8,467	6,364	9,029	7,310
42,450	42,500	8,481	6,371	9,043	7,324
42,500	42,550	8,495	6,379	9,057	7,338
42,550	42,600	8,509	6,386	9,071	7,352
42,600	42,650	8,523	6,394	9,085	7,366
42,650	42,700	8,537	6,401	9,099	7,380
42,700	42,750	8,551	6,409	9,113	7,394
42,750	42,800	8,565	6,416	9,127	7,408
42,800	42,850	8,579	6,424	9,141	7,422
42,850	42,900	8,593	6,431	9,155	7,436
42,900	42,950	8,607	6,439	9,169	7,450
42,950	43,000	8,621	6,446	9,183	7,464

43,000

43,000	43,050	8,635	6,454	9,197	7,478
43,050	43,100	8,649	6,461	9,211	7,492
43,100	43,150	8,663	6,469	9,225	7,506
43,150	43,200	8,677	6,476	9,239	7,520
43,200	43,250	8,691	6,484	9,253	7,534
43,250	43,300	8,705	6,491	9,267	7,548
43,300	43,350	8,719	6,499	9,281	7,562
43,350	43,400	8,733	6,506	9,295	7,576
43,400	43,450	8,747	6,514	9,309	7,590
43,450	43,500	8,761	6,521	9,323	7,604
43,500	43,550	8,775	6,529	9,337	7,618
43,550	43,600	8,789	6,536	9,351	7,632
43,600	43,650	8,803	6,544	9,365	7,646
43,650	43,700	8,817	6,551	9,379	7,660
43,700	43,750	8,831	6,559	9,393	7,674
43,750	43,800	8,845	6,566	9,407	7,688
43,800	43,850	8,859	6,574	9,421	7,702
43,850	43,900	8,873	6,585	9,435	7,716
43,900	43,950	8,887	6,599	9,449	7,730
43,950	44,000	8,901	6,613	9,463	7,744

44,000

44,000	44,050	8,915	6,627	9,477	7,758
44,050	44,100	8,929	6,641	9,491	7,772
44,100	44,150	8,943	6,655	9,505	7,786
44,150	44,200	8,957	6,669	9,519	7,800
44,200	44,250	8,971	6,683	9,533	7,814
44,250	44,300	8,985	6,697	9,547	7,828
44,300	44,350	8,999	6,711	9,561	7,842
44,350	44,400	9,013	6,725	9,575	7,856
44,400	44,450	9,027	6,739	9,589	7,870
44,450	44,500	9,041	6,753	9,603	7,884
44,500	44,550	9,055	6,767	9,617	7,898
44,550	44,600	9,069	6,781	9,631	7,912
44,600	44,650	9,083	6,795	9,645	7,926
44,650	44,700	9,097	6,809	9,659	7,940
44,700	44,750	9,111	6,823	9,673	7,954
44,750	44,800	9,125	6,837	9,687	7,968
44,800	44,850	9,139	6,851	9,701	7,982
44,850	44,900	9,153	6,865	9,715	7,996
44,900	44,950	9,167	6,879	9,729	8,010
44,950	45,000	9,181	6,893	9,743	8,024

45,000

45,000	45,050	9,195	6,907	9,757	8,038
45,050	45,100	9,209	6,921	9,771	8,052
45,100	45,150	9,223	6,935	9,785	8,066
45,150	45,200	9,237	6,949	9,799	8,080
45,200	45,250	9,251	6,963	9,813	8,094
45,250	45,300	9,265	6,977	9,827	8,108
45,300	45,350	9,279	6,991	9,841	8,122
45,350	45,400	9,293	7,005	9,855	8,136
45,400	45,450	9,307	7,019	9,869	8,150
45,450	45,500	9,321	7,033	9,883	8,164
45,500	45,550	9,335	7,047	9,897	8,178
45,550	45,600	9,349	7,061	9,911	8,192
45,600	45,650	9,363	7,075	9,925	8,206
45,650	45,700	9,377	7,089	9,939	8,220
45,700	45,750	9,391	7,103	9,953	8,234
45,750	45,800	9,405	7,117	9,967	8,248
45,800	45,850	9,419	7,131	9,981	8,262
45,850	45,900	9,433	7,145	9,995	8,276
45,900	45,950	9,447	7,159	10,009	8,290
45,950	46,000	9,461	7,173	10,023	8,304

46,000

46,000	46,050	9,475	7,187	10,037	8,318
46,050	46,100	9,489	7,201	10,051	8,332
46,100	46,150	9,503	7,215	10,065	8,346
46,150	46,200	9,517	7,229	10,079	8,360
46,200	46,250	9,531	7,243	10,093	8,374
46,250	46,300	9,545	7,257	10,107	8,388
46,300	46,350	9,559	7,271	10,121	8,402
46,350	46,400	9,573	7,285	10,135	8,416
46,400	46,450	9,587	7,299	10,149	8,430
46,450	46,500	9,601	7,313	10,163	8,444
46,500	46,550	9,615	7,327	10,177	8,458
46,550	46,600	9,629	7,341	10,191	8,472
46,600	46,650	9,643	7,355	10,205	8,486
46,650	46,700	9,657	7,369	10,219	8,500
46,700	46,750	9,671	7,383	10,233	8,514
46,750	46,800	9,685	7,397	10,247	8,528
46,800	46,850	9,699	7,411	10,261	8,542
46,850	46,900	9,713	7,425	10,275	8,556
46,900	46,950	9,727	7,439	10,289	8,570
46,950	47,000	9,741	7,453	10,303	8,584

47,000

47,000	47,050	9,755	7,467	10,317	8,598
47,050	47,100	9,769	7,481	10,331	8,612
47,100	47,150	9,783	7,495	10,345	8,626
47,150	47,200	9,797	7,509	10,359	8,640
47,200	47,250	9,811	7,523	10,373	8,654
47,250	47,300	9,825	7,537	10,387	8,668
47,300	47,350	9,839	7,551	10,401	8,682
47,350	47,400	9,853	7,565	10,415	8,696
47,400	47,450	9,867	7,579	10,429	8,710
47,450	47,500	9,881	7,593	10,443	8,724
47,500	47,550	9,895	7,607	10,457	8,738
47,550	47,600	9,909	7,621	10,471	8,752
47,600	47,650	9,923	7,635	10,485	8,766
47,650	47,700	9,937	7,649	10,499	8,780
47,700	47,750	9,951	7,663	10,513	8,794
47,750	47,800	9,965	7,677	10,527	8,808
47,800	47,850	9,979	7,691	10,541	8,822
47,850	47,900	9,993	7,705	10,555	8,836
47,900	47,950	10,007	7,719	10,569	8,850
47,950	48,000	10,021	7,733	10,583	8,864

48,000

48,000	48,050	10,035	7,747	10,597	8,878
48,050	48,100	10,049	7,761	10,611	8,892
48,100	48,150	10,063	7,775	10,625	8,906
48,150	48,200	10,077	7,789	10,639	8,920
48,200	48,250	10,091	7,803	10,653	8,934
48,250	48,300	10,105	7,817	10,667	8,948
48,300	48,350	10,119	7,831	10,681	8,962
48,350	48,400	10,133	7,845	10,695	8,976
48,400	48,450	10,147	7,859	10,709	8,990
48,450	48,500	10,161	7,873	10,723	9,004
48,500	48,550	10,175	7,887	10,737	9,018
48,550	48,600	10,189	7,901	10,751	9,032
48,600	48,650	10,203	7,915	10,765	9,046
48,650	48,700	10,217	7,929	10,779	9,060
48,700	48,750	10,231	7,943	10,793	9,074
48,750	48,800	10,245	7,957	10,807	9,088
48,800	48,850	10,259	7,971	10,821	9,102
48,850	48,900	10,273	7,985	10,835	9,116
48,900	48,950	10,287	7,999	10,849	9,130
48,950	49,000	10,301	8,013	10,863	9,144

49,000

49,000	49,050	10,315	8,027	10,877	9,158
49,050	49,100	10,329	8,041	10,891	9,172
49,100	49,150	10,343	8,055	10,905	9,186
49,150	49,200	10,357	8,069	10,919	9,200
49,200	49,250	10,371	8,083	10,933	9,214
49,250	49,300	10,385	8,097	10,947	9,228
49,300	49,350	10,399	8,111	10,961	9,242
49,350	49,400	10,413	8,125	10,975	9,256
49,400	49,450	10,427	8,139	10,989	9,270
49,450	49,500	10,441	8,153	11,003	9,284
49,500	49,550	10,455	8,167	11,017	9,298
49,550	49,600	10,469	8,181	11,031	9,312
49,600	49,650	10,483	8,195	11,045	9,326
49,650	49,700	10,497	8,209	11,059	9,340
49,700	49,750	10,511	8,223	11,073	9,354
49,750	49,800	10,525	8,237	11,087	9,368
49,800	49,850	10,539	8,251	11,101	9,382
49,850	49,900	10,553	8,265	11,115	9,396
49,900	49,950	10,567	8,279	11,129	9,410
49,950	50,000	10,581	8,293	11,143	9,424

* This column must also be used by a qualifying widow(er).

(Continued on next page)

T-8 Individuals ▼ 2000 Tax Tables and Rate Schedules

2000 Tax Table—Continued

If line 39 (taxable income) is—		And you are—				If line 39 (taxable income) is—		And you are—				If line 39 (taxable income) is—		And you are—			
At least	But less than	Single	Married filing jointly *	Married filing separately	Head of a household	At least	But less than	Single	Married filing jointly *	Married filing separately	Head of a household	At least	But less than	Single	Married filing jointly *	Married filing separately	Head of a household
		Your tax is—						Your tax is—						Your tax is—			

50,000

50,000	50,050	10,595	8,307	11,157	9,438
50,050	50,100	10,609	8,321	11,171	9,452
50,100	50,150	10,623	8,335	11,185	9,466
50,150	50,200	10,637	8,349	11,199	9,480
50,200	50,250	10,651	8,363	11,213	9,494
50,250	50,300	10,665	8,377	11,227	9,508
50,300	50,350	10,679	8,391	11,241	9,522
50,350	50,400	10,693	8,405	11,255	9,536
50,400	50,450	10,707	8,419	11,269	9,550
50,450	50,500	10,721	8,433	11,283	9,564
50,500	50,550	10,735	8,447	11,297	9,578
50,550	50,600	10,749	8,461	11,311	9,592
50,600	50,650	10,763	8,475	11,325	9,606
50,650	50,700	10,777	8,489	11,339	9,620
50,700	50,750	10,791	8,503	11,353	9,634
50,750	50,800	10,805	8,517	11,367	9,648
50,800	50,850	10,819	8,531	11,381	9,662
50,850	50,900	10,833	8,545	11,395	9,676
50,900	50,950	10,847	8,559	11,409	9,690
50,950	51,000	10,861	8,573	11,423	9,704

51,000

51,000	51,050	10,875	8,587	11,437	9,718
51,050	51,100	10,889	8,601	11,451	9,732
51,100	51,150	10,903	8,615	11,465	9,746
51,150	51,200	10,917	8,629	11,479	9,760
51,200	51,250	10,931	8,643	11,493	9,774
51,250	51,300	10,945	8,657	11,507	9,788
51,300	51,350	10,959	8,671	11,521	9,802
51,350	51,400	10,973	8,685	11,535	9,816
51,400	51,450	10,987	8,699	11,549	9,830
51,450	51,500	11,001	8,713	11,563	9,844
51,500	51,550	11,015	8,727	11,577	9,858
51,550	51,600	11,029	8,741	11,591	9,872
51,600	51,650	11,043	8,755	11,605	9,886
51,650	51,700	11,057	8,769	11,619	9,900
51,700	51,750	11,071	8,783	11,633	9,914
51,750	51,800	11,085	8,797	11,647	9,928
51,800	51,850	11,099	8,811	11,661	9,942
51,850	51,900	11,113	8,825	11,675	9,956
51,900	51,950	11,127	8,839	11,689	9,970
51,950	52,000	11,141	8,853	11,703	9,984

52,000

52,000	52,050	11,155	8,867	11,717	9,998
52,050	52,100	11,169	8,881	11,731	10,012
52,100	52,150	11,183	8,895	11,745	10,026
52,150	52,200	11,197	8,909	11,759	10,040
52,200	52,250	11,211	8,923	11,773	10,054
52,250	52,300	11,225	8,937	11,787	10,068
52,300	52,350	11,239	8,951	11,801	10,082
52,350	52,400	11,253	8,965	11,815	10,096
52,400	52,450	11,267	8,979	11,829	10,110
52,450	52,500	11,281	8,993	11,843	10,124
52,500	52,550	11,295	9,007	11,857	10,138
52,550	52,600	11,309	9,021	11,871	10,152
52,600	52,650	11,323	9,035	11,885	10,166
52,650	52,700	11,337	9,049	11,899	10,180
52,700	52,750	11,351	9,063	11,913	10,194
52,750	52,800	11,365	9,077	11,927	10,208
52,800	52,850	11,379	9,091	11,941	10,222
52,850	52,900	11,393	9,105	11,955	10,236
52,900	52,950	11,407	9,119	11,969	10,250
52,950	53,000	11,421	9,133	11,983	10,264

53,000

53,000	53,050	11,435	9,147	11,998	10,278
53,050	53,100	11,449	9,161	12,014	10,292
53,100	53,150	11,463	9,175	12,029	10,306
53,150	53,200	11,477	9,189	12,045	10,320
53,200	53,250	11,491	9,203	12,060	10,334
53,250	53,300	11,505	9,217	12,076	10,348
53,300	53,350	11,519	9,231	12,091	10,362
53,350	53,400	11,533	9,245	12,107	10,376
53,400	53,450	11,547	9,259	12,122	10,390
53,450	53,500	11,561	9,273	12,138	10,404
53,500	53,550	11,575	9,287	12,153	10,418
53,550	53,600	11,589	9,301	12,169	10,432
53,600	53,650	11,603	9,315	12,184	10,446
53,650	53,700	11,617	9,329	12,200	10,460
53,700	53,750	11,631	9,343	12,215	10,474
53,750	53,800	11,645	9,357	12,231	10,488
53,800	53,850	11,659	9,371	12,246	10,502
53,850	53,900	11,673	9,385	12,262	10,516
53,900	53,950	11,687	9,399	12,277	10,530
53,950	54,000	11,701	9,413	12,293	10,544

54,000

54,000	54,050	11,715	9,427	12,308	10,558
54,050	54,100	11,729	9,441	12,324	10,572
54,100	54,150	11,743	9,455	12,339	10,586
54,150	54,200	11,757	9,469	12,355	10,600
54,200	54,250	11,771	9,483	12,370	10,614
54,250	54,300	11,785	9,497	12,386	10,628
54,300	54,350	11,799	9,511	12,401	10,642
54,350	54,400	11,813	9,525	12,417	10,656
54,400	54,450	11,827	9,539	12,432	10,670
54,450	54,500	11,841	9,553	12,448	10,684
54,500	54,550	11,855	9,567	12,463	10,698
54,550	54,600	11,869	9,581	12,479	10,712
54,600	54,650	11,883	9,595	12,494	10,726
54,650	54,700	11,897	9,609	12,510	10,740
54,700	54,750	11,911	9,623	12,525	10,754
54,750	54,800	11,925	9,637	12,541	10,768
54,800	54,850	11,939	9,651	12,556	10,782
54,850	54,900	11,953	9,665	12,572	10,796
54,900	54,950	11,967	9,679	12,587	10,810
54,950	55,000	11,981	9,693	12,603	10,824

55,000

55,000	55,050	11,995	9,707	12,618	10,838
55,050	55,100	12,009	9,721	12,634	10,852
55,100	55,150	12,023	9,735	12,649	10,866
55,150	55,200	12,037	9,749	12,665	10,880
55,200	55,250	12,051	9,763	12,680	10,894
55,250	55,300	12,065	9,777	12,696	10,908
55,300	55,350	12,079	9,791	12,711	10,922
55,350	55,400	12,093	9,805	12,727	10,936
55,400	55,450	12,107	9,819	12,742	10,950
55,450	55,500	12,121	9,833	12,758	10,964
55,500	55,550	12,135	9,847	12,773	10,978
55,550	55,600	12,149	9,861	12,789	10,992
55,600	55,650	12,163	9,875	12,804	11,006
55,650	55,700	12,177	9,889	12,820	11,020
55,700	55,750	12,191	9,903	12,835	11,034
55,750	55,800	12,205	9,917	12,851	11,048
55,800	55,850	12,219	9,931	12,866	11,062
55,850	55,900	12,233	9,945	12,882	11,076
55,900	55,950	12,247	9,959	12,897	11,090
55,950	56,000	12,261	9,973	12,913	11,104

56,000

56,000	56,050	12,275	9,987	12,928	11,118
56,050	56,100	12,289	10,001	12,944	11,132
56,100	56,150	12,303	10,015	12,959	11,146
56,150	56,200	12,317	10,029	12,975	11,160
56,200	56,250	12,331	10,043	12,990	11,174
56,250	56,300	12,345	10,057	13,006	11,188
56,300	56,350	12,359	10,071	13,021	11,202
56,350	56,400	12,373	10,085	13,037	11,216
56,400	56,450	12,387	10,099	13,052	11,230
56,450	56,500	12,401	10,113	13,068	11,244
56,500	56,550	12,415	10,127	13,083	11,258
56,550	56,600	12,429	10,141	13,099	11,272
56,600	56,650	12,443	10,155	13,114	11,286
56,650	56,700	12,457	10,169	13,130	11,300
56,700	56,750	12,471	10,183	13,145	11,314
56,750	56,800	12,485	10,197	13,161	11,328
56,800	56,850	12,499	10,211	13,176	11,342
56,850	56,900	12,513	10,225	13,192	11,356
56,900	56,950	12,527	10,239	13,207	11,370
56,950	57,000	12,541	10,253	13,223	11,384

57,000

57,000	57,050	12,555	10,267	13,238	11,398
57,050	57,100	12,569	10,281	13,254	11,412
57,100	57,150	12,583	10,295	13,269	11,426
57,150	57,200	12,597	10,309	13,285	11,440
57,200	57,250	12,611	10,323	13,300	11,454
57,250	57,300	12,625	10,337	13,316	11,468
57,300	57,350	12,639	10,351	13,331	11,482
57,350	57,400	12,653	10,365	13,347	11,496
57,400	57,450	12,667	10,379	13,362	11,510
57,450	57,500	12,681	10,393	13,378	11,524
57,500	57,550	12,695	10,407	13,393	11,538
57,550	57,600	12,709	10,421	13,409	11,552
57,600	57,650	12,723	10,435	13,424	11,566
57,650	57,700	12,737	10,449	13,440	11,580
57,700	57,750	12,751	10,463	13,455	11,594
57,750	57,800	12,765	10,477	13,471	11,608
57,800	57,850	12,779	10,491	13,486	11,622
57,850	57,900	12,793	10,505	13,502	11,636
57,900	57,950	12,807	10,519	13,517	11,650
57,950	58,000	12,821	10,533	13,533	11,664

58,000

58,000	58,050	12,835	10,547	13,548	11,678
58,050	58,100	12,849	10,561	13,564	11,692
58,100	58,150	12,863	10,575	13,579	11,706
58,150	58,200	12,877	10,589	13,595	11,720
58,200	58,250	12,891	10,603	13,610	11,734
58,250	58,300	12,905	10,617	13,626	11,748
58,300	58,350	12,919	10,631	13,641	11,762
58,350	58,400	12,933	10,645	13,657	11,776
58,400	58,450	12,947	10,659	13,672	11,790
58,450	58,500	12,961	10,673	13,688	11,804
58,500	58,550	12,975	10,687	13,703	11,818
58,550	58,600	12,989	10,701	13,719	11,832
58,600	58,650	13,003	10,715	13,734	11,846
58,650	58,700	13,017	10,729	13,750	11,860
58,700	58,750	13,031	10,743	13,765	11,874
58,750	58,800	13,045	10,757	13,781	11,888
58,800	58,850	13,059	10,771	13,796	11,902
58,850	58,900	13,073	10,785	13,812	11,916
58,900	58,950	13,087	10,799	13,827	11,930
58,950	59,000	13,101	10,813	13,843	11,944

* This column must also be used by a qualifying widow(er).

(Continued on next page)

2000 Tax Table—Continued

If line 39 (taxable income) is—		And you are—				If line 39 (taxable income) is—		And you are—				If line 39 (taxable income) is—		And you are—			
At least	But less than	Single	Married filing jointly *	Married filing separately	Head of a household	At least	But less than	Single	Married filing jointly *	Married filing separately	Head of a household	At least	But less than	Single	Married filing jointly *	Married filing separately	Head of a household
		Your tax is—						Your tax is—						Your tax is—			

59,000

59,000	59,050	13,115	10,827	13,858	11,958
59,050	59,100	13,129	10,841	13,874	11,972
59,100	59,150	13,143	10,855	13,889	11,986
59,150	59,200	13,157	10,869	13,905	12,000
59,200	59,250	13,171	10,883	13,920	12,014
59,250	59,300	13,185	10,897	13,936	12,028
59,300	59,350	13,199	10,911	13,951	12,042
59,350	59,400	13,213	10,925	13,967	12,056
59,400	59,450	13,227	10,939	13,982	12,070
59,450	59,500	13,241	10,953	13,998	12,084
59,500	59,550	13,255	10,967	14,013	12,098
59,550	59,600	13,269	10,981	14,029	12,112
59,600	59,650	13,283	10,995	14,044	12,126
59,650	59,700	13,297	11,009	14,060	12,140
59,700	59,750	13,311	11,023	14,075	12,154
59,750	59,800	13,325	11,037	14,091	12,168
59,800	59,850	13,339	11,051	14,106	12,182
59,850	59,900	13,353	11,065	14,122	12,196
59,900	59,950	13,367	11,079	14,137	12,210
59,950	60,000	13,381	11,093	14,153	12,224

60,000

60,000	60,050	13,395	11,107	14,168	12,238
60,050	60,100	13,409	11,121	14,184	12,252
60,100	60,150	13,423	11,135	14,199	12,266
60,150	60,200	13,437	11,149	14,215	12,280
60,200	60,250	13,451	11,163	14,230	12,294
60,250	60,300	13,465	11,177	14,246	12,308
60,300	60,350	13,479	11,191	14,261	12,322
60,350	60,400	13,493	11,205	14,277	12,336
60,400	60,450	13,507	11,219	14,292	12,350
60,450	60,500	13,521	11,233	14,308	12,364
60,500	60,550	13,535	11,247	14,323	12,378
60,550	60,600	13,549	11,261	14,339	12,392
60,600	60,650	13,563	11,275	14,354	12,406
60,650	60,700	13,577	11,289	14,370	12,420
60,700	60,750	13,591	11,303	14,385	12,434
60,750	60,800	13,605	11,317	14,401	12,448
60,800	60,850	13,619	11,331	14,416	12,462
60,850	60,900	13,633	11,345	14,432	12,476
60,900	60,950	13,647	11,359	14,447	12,490
60,950	61,000	13,661	11,373	14,463	12,504

61,000

61,000	61,050	13,675	11,387	14,478	12,518
61,050	61,100	13,689	11,401	14,494	12,532
61,100	61,150	13,703	11,415	14,509	12,546
61,150	61,200	13,717	11,429	14,525	12,560
61,200	61,250	13,731	11,443	14,540	12,574
61,250	61,300	13,745	11,457	14,556	12,588
61,300	61,350	13,759	11,471	14,571	12,602
61,350	61,400	13,773	11,485	14,587	12,616
61,400	61,450	13,787	11,499	14,602	12,630
61,450	61,500	13,801	11,513	14,618	12,644
61,500	61,550	13,815	11,527	14,633	12,658
61,550	61,600	13,829	11,541	14,649	12,672
61,600	61,650	13,843	11,555	14,664	12,686
61,650	61,700	13,857	11,569	14,680	12,700
61,700	61,750	13,871	11,583	14,695	12,714
61,750	61,800	13,885	11,597	14,711	12,728
61,800	61,850	13,899	11,611	14,726	12,742
61,850	61,900	13,913	11,625	14,742	12,756
61,900	61,950	13,927	11,639	14,757	12,770
61,950	62,000	13,941	11,653	14,773	12,784

62,000

62,000	62,050	13,955	11,667	14,788	12,798
62,050	62,100	13,969	11,681	14,804	12,812
62,100	62,150	13,983	11,695	14,819	12,826
62,150	62,200	13,997	11,709	14,835	12,840
62,200	62,250	14,011	11,723	14,850	12,854
62,250	62,300	14,025	11,737	14,866	12,868
62,300	62,350	14,039	11,751	14,881	12,882
62,350	62,400	14,053	11,765	14,897	12,896
62,400	62,450	14,067	11,779	14,912	12,910
62,450	62,500	14,081	11,793	14,928	12,924
62,500	62,550	14,095	11,807	14,943	12,938
62,550	62,600	14,109	11,821	14,959	12,952
62,600	62,650	14,123	11,835	14,974	12,966
62,650	62,700	14,137	11,849	14,990	12,980
62,700	62,750	14,151	11,863	15,005	12,994
62,750	62,800	14,165	11,877	15,021	13,008
62,800	62,850	14,179	11,891	15,036	13,022
62,850	62,900	14,193	11,905	15,052	13,036
62,900	62,950	14,207	11,919	15,067	13,050
62,950	63,000	14,221	11,933	15,083	13,064

63,000

63,000	63,050	14,235	11,947	15,098	13,078
63,050	63,100	14,249	11,961	15,114	13,092
63,100	63,150	14,263	11,975	15,129	13,106
63,150	63,200	14,277	11,989	15,145	13,120
63,200	63,250	14,291	12,003	15,160	13,134
63,250	63,300	14,305	12,017	15,176	13,148
63,300	63,350	14,319	12,031	15,191	13,162
63,350	63,400	14,333	12,045	15,207	13,176
63,400	63,450	14,347	12,059	15,222	13,190
63,450	63,500	14,361	12,073	15,238	13,204
63,500	63,550	14,375	12,087	15,253	13,218
63,550	63,600	14,389	12,101	15,269	13,232
63,600	63,650	14,405	12,115	15,284	13,246
63,650	63,700	14,420	12,129	15,300	13,260
63,700	63,750	14,436	12,143	15,315	13,274
63,750	63,800	14,451	12,157	15,331	13,288
63,800	63,850	14,467	12,171	15,346	13,302
63,850	63,900	14,482	12,185	15,362	13,316
63,900	63,950	14,498	12,199	15,377	13,330
63,950	64,000	14,513	12,213	15,393	13,344

64,000

64,000	64,050	14,529	12,227	15,408	13,358
64,050	64,100	14,544	12,241	15,424	13,372
64,100	64,150	14,560	12,255	15,439	13,386
64,150	64,200	14,575	12,269	15,455	13,400
64,200	64,250	14,591	12,283	15,470	13,414
64,250	64,300	14,606	12,297	15,486	13,428
64,300	64,350	14,622	12,311	15,501	13,442
64,350	64,400	14,637	12,325	15,517	13,456
64,400	64,450	14,653	12,339	15,532	13,470
64,450	64,500	14,668	12,353	15,548	13,484
64,500	64,550	14,684	12,367	15,563	13,498
64,550	64,600	14,699	12,381	15,579	13,512
64,600	64,650	14,715	12,395	15,594	13,526
64,650	64,700	14,730	12,409	15,610	13,540
64,700	64,750	14,746	12,423	15,625	13,554
64,750	64,800	14,761	12,437	15,641	13,568
64,800	64,850	14,777	12,451	15,656	13,582
64,850	64,900	14,792	12,465	15,672	13,596
64,900	64,950	14,808	12,479	15,687	13,610
64,950	65,000	14,823	12,493	15,703	13,624

65,000

65,000	65,050	14,839	12,507	15,718	13,638
65,050	65,100	14,854	12,521	15,734	13,652
65,100	65,150	14,870	12,535	15,749	13,666
65,150	65,200	14,885	12,549	15,765	13,680
65,200	65,250	14,901	12,563	15,780	13,694
65,250	65,300	14,916	12,577	15,796	13,708
65,300	65,350	14,932	12,591	15,811	13,722
65,350	65,400	14,947	12,605	15,827	13,736
65,400	65,450	14,963	12,619	15,842	13,750
65,450	65,500	14,978	12,633	15,858	13,764
65,500	65,550	14,994	12,647	15,873	13,778
65,550	65,600	15,009	12,661	15,889	13,792
65,600	65,650	15,025	12,675	15,904	13,806
65,650	65,700	15,040	12,689	15,920	13,820
65,700	65,750	15,056	12,703	15,935	13,834
65,750	65,800	15,071	12,717	15,951	13,848
65,800	65,850	15,087	12,731	15,966	13,862
65,850	65,900	15,102	12,745	15,982	13,876
65,900	65,950	15,118	12,759	15,997	13,890
65,950	66,000	15,133	12,773	16,013	13,904

66,000

66,000	66,050	15,149	12,787	16,028	13,918
66,050	66,100	15,164	12,801	16,044	13,932
66,100	66,150	15,180	12,815	16,059	13,946
66,150	66,200	15,195	12,829	16,075	13,960
66,200	66,250	15,211	12,843	16,090	13,974
66,250	66,300	15,226	12,857	16,106	13,988
66,300	66,350	15,242	12,871	16,121	14,002
66,350	66,400	15,257	12,885	16,137	14,016
66,400	66,450	15,273	12,899	16,152	14,030
66,450	66,500	15,288	12,913	16,168	14,044
66,500	66,550	15,304	12,927	16,183	14,058
66,550	66,600	15,319	12,941	16,199	14,072
66,600	66,650	15,335	12,955	16,214	14,086
66,650	66,700	15,350	12,969	16,230	14,100
66,700	66,750	15,366	12,983	16,245	14,114
66,750	66,800	15,381	12,997	16,261	14,128
66,800	66,850	15,397	13,011	16,276	14,142
66,850	66,900	15,412	13,025	16,292	14,156
66,900	66,950	15,428	13,039	16,307	14,170
66,950	67,000	15,443	13,053	16,323	14,184

67,000

67,000	67,050	15,459	13,067	16,338	14,198
67,050	67,100	15,474	13,081	16,354	14,212
67,100	67,150	15,490	13,095	16,369	14,226
67,150	67,200	15,505	13,109	16,385	14,240
67,200	67,250	15,521	13,123	16,400	14,254
67,250	67,300	15,536	13,137	16,416	14,268
67,300	67,350	15,552	13,151	16,431	14,282
67,350	67,400	15,567	13,165	16,447	14,296
67,400	67,450	15,583	13,179	16,462	14,310
67,450	67,500	15,598	13,193	16,478	14,324
67,500	67,550	15,614	13,207	16,493	14,338
67,550	67,600	15,629	13,221	16,509	14,352
67,600	67,650	15,645	13,235	16,524	14,366
67,650	67,700	15,660	13,249	16,540	14,380
67,700	67,750	15,676	13,263	16,555	14,394
67,750	67,800	15,691	13,277	16,571	14,408
67,800	67,850	15,707	13,291	16,586	14,422
67,850	67,900	15,722	13,305	16,602	14,436
67,900	67,950	15,738	13,319	16,617	14,450
67,950	68,000	15,753	13,333	16,633	14,464

* This column must also be used by a qualifying widow(er).

(Continued on next page)

T-10 Individuals ▼ 2000 Tax Tables and Rate Schedules

2000 Tax Table—Continued

If line 39 (taxable income) is— At least / But less than	Single	Married filing jointly*	Married filing separately	Head of a household	If line 39 (taxable income) is— At least / But less than	Single	Married filing jointly*	Married filing separately	Head of a household	If line 39 (taxable income) is— At least / But less than	Single	Married filing jointly*	Married filing separately	Head of a household
68,000					**71,000**					**74,000**				
68,000 68,050	15,769	13,347	16,648	14,478	71,000 71,050	16,699	14,187	17,578	15,318	74,000 74,050	17,629	15,027	18,508	16,158
68,050 68,100	15,784	13,361	16,664	14,492	71,050 71,100	16,714	14,201	17,594	15,332	74,050 74,100	17,644	15,041	18,524	16,172
68,100 68,150	15,800	13,375	16,679	14,506	71,100 71,150	16,730	14,215	17,609	15,346	74,100 74,150	17,660	15,055	18,539	16,186
68,150 68,200	15,815	13,389	16,695	14,520	71,150 71,200	16,745	14,229	17,625	15,360	74,150 74,200	17,675	15,069	18,555	16,200
68,200 68,250	15,831	13,403	16,710	14,534	71,200 71,250	16,761	14,243	17,640	15,374	74,200 74,250	17,691	15,083	18,570	16,214
68,250 68,300	15,846	13,417	16,726	14,548	71,250 71,300	16,776	14,257	17,656	15,388	74,250 74,300	17,706	15,097	18,586	16,228
68,300 68,350	15,862	13,431	16,741	14,562	71,300 71,350	16,792	14,271	17,671	15,402	74,300 74,350	17,722	15,111	18,601	16,242
68,350 68,400	15,877	13,445	16,757	14,576	71,350 71,400	16,807	14,285	17,687	15,416	74,350 74,400	17,737	15,125	18,617	16,256
68,400 68,450	15,893	13,459	16,772	14,590	71,400 71,450	16,823	14,299	17,702	15,430	74,400 74,450	17,753	15,139	18,632	16,270
68,450 68,500	15,908	13,473	16,788	14,604	71,450 71,500	16,838	14,313	17,718	15,444	74,450 74,500	17,768	15,153	18,648	16,284
68,500 68,550	15,924	13,487	16,803	14,618	71,500 71,550	16,854	14,327	17,733	15,458	74,500 74,550	17,784	15,167	18,663	16,298
68,550 68,600	15,939	13,501	16,819	14,632	71,550 71,600	16,869	14,341	17,749	15,472	74,550 74,600	17,799	15,181	18,679	16,312
68,600 68,650	15,955	13,515	16,834	14,646	71,600 71,650	16,885	14,355	17,764	15,486	74,600 74,650	17,815	15,195	18,694	16,326
68,650 68,700	15,970	13,529	16,850	14,660	71,650 71,700	16,900	14,369	17,780	15,500	74,650 74,700	17,830	15,209	18,710	16,340
68,700 68,750	15,986	13,543	16,865	14,674	71,700 71,750	16,916	14,383	17,795	15,514	74,700 74,750	17,846	15,223	18,725	16,354
68,750 68,800	16,001	13,557	16,881	14,688	71,750 71,800	16,931	14,397	17,811	15,528	74,750 74,800	17,861	15,237	18,741	16,368
68,800 68,850	16,017	13,571	16,896	14,702	71,800 71,850	16,947	14,411	17,826	15,542	74,800 74,850	17,877	15,251	18,756	16,382
68,850 68,900	16,032	13,585	16,912	14,716	71,850 71,900	16,962	14,425	17,842	15,556	74,850 74,900	17,892	15,265	18,772	16,396
68,900 68,950	16,048	13,599	16,927	14,730	71,900 71,950	16,978	14,439	17,857	15,570	74,900 74,950	17,908	15,279	18,787	16,410
68,950 69,000	16,063	13,613	16,943	14,744	71,950 72,000	16,993	14,453	17,873	15,584	74,950 75,000	17,923	15,293	18,803	16,424
69,000					**72,000**					**75,000**				
69,000 69,050	16,079	13,627	16,958	14,758	72,000 72,050	17,009	14,467	17,888	15,598	75,000 75,050	17,939	15,307	18,818	16,438
69,050 69,100	16,094	13,641	16,974	14,772	72,050 72,100	17,024	14,481	17,904	15,612	75,050 75,100	17,954	15,321	18,834	16,452
69,100 69,150	16,110	13,655	16,989	14,786	72,100 72,150	17,040	14,495	17,919	15,626	75,100 75,150	17,970	15,335	18,849	16,466
69,150 69,200	16,125	13,669	17,005	14,800	72,150 72,200	17,055	14,509	17,935	15,640	75,150 75,200	17,985	15,349	18,865	16,480
69,200 69,250	16,141	13,683	17,020	14,814	72,200 72,250	17,071	14,523	17,950	15,654	75,200 75,250	18,001	15,363	18,880	16,494
69,250 69,300	16,156	13,697	17,036	14,828	72,250 72,300	17,086	14,537	17,966	15,668	75,250 75,300	18,016	15,377	18,896	16,508
69,300 69,350	16,172	13,711	17,051	14,842	72,300 72,350	17,102	14,551	17,981	15,682	75,300 75,350	18,032	15,391	18,911	16,522
69,350 69,400	16,187	13,725	17,067	14,856	72,350 72,400	17,117	14,565	17,997	15,696	75,350 75,400	18,047	15,405	18,927	16,536
69,400 69,450	16,203	13,739	17,082	14,870	72,400 72,450	17,133	14,579	18,012	15,710	75,400 75,450	18,063	15,419	18,942	16,550
69,450 69,500	16,218	13,753	17,098	14,884	72,450 72,500	17,148	14,593	18,028	15,724	75,450 75,500	18,078	15,433	18,958	16,564
69,500 69,550	16,234	13,767	17,113	14,898	72,500 72,550	17,164	14,607	18,043	15,738	75,500 75,550	18,094	15,447	18,973	16,578
69,550 69,600	16,249	13,781	17,129	14,912	72,550 72,600	17,179	14,621	18,059	15,752	75,550 75,600	18,109	15,461	18,989	16,592
69,600 69,650	16,265	13,795	17,144	14,926	72,600 72,650	17,195	14,635	18,074	15,766	75,600 75,650	18,125	15,475	19,004	16,606
69,650 69,700	16,280	13,809	17,160	14,940	72,650 72,700	17,210	14,649	18,090	15,780	75,650 75,700	18,140	15,489	19,020	16,620
69,700 69,750	16,296	13,823	17,175	14,954	72,700 72,750	17,226	14,663	18,105	15,794	75,700 75,750	18,156	15,503	19,035	16,634
69,750 69,800	16,311	13,837	17,191	14,968	72,750 72,800	17,241	14,677	18,121	15,808	75,750 75,800	18,171	15,517	19,051	16,648
69,800 69,850	16,327	13,851	17,206	14,982	72,800 72,850	17,257	14,691	18,136	15,822	75,800 75,850	18,187	15,531	19,066	16,662
69,850 69,900	16,342	13,865	17,222	14,996	72,850 72,900	17,272	14,705	18,152	15,836	75,850 75,900	18,202	15,545	19,082	16,676
69,900 69,950	16,358	13,879	17,237	15,010	72,900 72,950	17,288	14,719	18,167	15,850	75,900 75,950	18,218	15,559	19,097	16,690
69,950 70,000	16,373	13,893	17,253	15,024	72,950 73,000	17,303	14,733	18,183	15,864	75,950 76,000	18,233	15,573	19,113	16,704
70,000					**73,000**					**76,000**				
70,000 70,050	16,389	13,907	17,268	15,038	73,000 73,050	17,319	14,747	18,198	15,878	76,000 76,050	18,249	15,587	19,128	16,718
70,050 70,100	16,404	13,921	17,284	15,052	73,050 73,100	17,334	14,761	18,214	15,892	76,050 76,100	18,264	15,601	19,144	16,732
70,100 70,150	16,420	13,935	17,299	15,066	73,100 73,150	17,350	14,775	18,229	15,906	76,100 76,150	18,280	15,615	19,159	16,746
70,150 70,200	16,435	13,949	17,315	15,080	73,150 73,200	17,365	14,789	18,245	15,920	76,150 76,200	18,295	15,629	19,175	16,760
70,200 70,250	16,451	13,963	17,330	15,094	73,200 73,250	17,381	14,803	18,260	15,934	76,200 76,250	18,311	15,643	19,190	16,774
70,250 70,300	16,466	13,977	17,346	15,108	73,250 73,300	17,396	14,817	18,276	15,948	76,250 76,300	18,326	15,657	19,206	16,788
70,300 70,350	16,482	13,991	17,361	15,122	73,300 73,350	17,412	14,831	18,291	15,962	76,300 76,350	18,342	15,671	19,221	16,802
70,350 70,400	16,497	14,005	17,377	15,136	73,350 73,400	17,427	14,845	18,307	15,976	76,350 76,400	18,357	15,685	19,237	16,816
70,400 70,450	16,513	14,019	17,392	15,150	73,400 73,450	17,443	14,859	18,322	15,990	76,400 76,450	18,373	15,699	19,252	16,830
70,450 70,500	16,528	14,033	17,408	15,164	73,450 73,500	17,458	14,873	18,338	16,004	76,450 76,500	18,388	15,713	19,268	16,844
70,500 70,550	16,544	14,047	17,423	15,178	73,500 73,550	17,474	14,887	18,353	16,018	76,500 76,550	18,404	15,727	19,283	16,858
70,550 70,600	16,559	14,061	17,439	15,192	73,550 73,600	17,489	14,901	18,369	16,032	76,550 76,600	18,419	15,741	19,299	16,872
70,600 70,650	16,575	14,075	17,454	15,206	73,600 73,650	17,505	14,915	18,384	16,046	76,600 76,650	18,435	15,755	19,314	16,886
70,650 70,700	16,590	14,089	17,470	15,220	73,650 73,700	17,520	14,929	18,400	16,060	76,650 76,700	18,450	15,769	19,330	16,900
70,700 70,750	16,606	14,103	17,485	15,234	73,700 73,750	17,536	14,943	18,415	16,074	76,700 76,750	18,466	15,783	19,345	16,914
70,750 70,800	16,621	14,117	17,501	15,248	73,750 73,800	17,551	14,957	18,431	16,088	76,750 76,800	18,481	15,797	19,361	16,928
70,800 70,850	16,637	14,131	17,516	15,262	73,800 73,850	17,567	14,971	18,446	16,102	76,800 76,850	18,497	15,811	19,376	16,942
70,850 70,900	16,652	14,145	17,532	15,276	73,850 73,900	17,582	14,985	18,462	16,116	76,850 76,900	18,512	15,825	19,392	16,956
70,900 70,950	16,668	14,159	17,547	15,290	73,900 73,950	17,598	14,999	18,477	16,130	76,900 76,950	18,528	15,839	19,407	16,970
70,950 71,000	16,683	14,173	17,563	15,304	73,950 74,000	17,613	15,013	18,493	16,144	76,950 77,000	18,543	15,853	19,423	16,984

* This column must also be used by a qualifying widow(er).

(Continued on next page)

2000 Tax Table—Continued

If line 39 (taxable income) is—		And you are—				If line 39 (taxable income) is—		And you are—				If line 39 (taxable income) is—		And you are—			
At least	But less than	Single	Married filing jointly *	Married filing separately	Head of a house-hold	At least	But less than	Single	Married filing jointly *	Married filing separately	Head of a house-hold	At least	But less than	Single	Married filing jointly *	Married filing separately	Head of a house-hold
		Your tax is—						Your tax is—						Your tax is—			

77,000

77,000	77,050	18,559	15,867	19,438	16,998
77,050	77,100	18,574	15,881	19,454	17,012
77,100	77,150	18,590	15,895	19,469	17,026
77,150	77,200	18,605	15,909	19,485	17,040
77,200	77,250	18,621	15,923	19,500	17,054
77,250	77,300	18,636	15,937	19,516	17,068
77,300	77,350	18,652	15,951	19,531	17,082
77,350	77,400	18,667	15,965	19,547	17,096
77,400	77,450	18,683	15,979	19,562	17,110
77,450	77,500	18,698	15,993	19,578	17,124
77,500	77,550	18,714	16,007	19,593	17,138
77,550	77,600	18,729	16,021	19,609	17,152
77,600	77,650	18,745	16,035	19,624	17,166
77,650	77,700	18,760	16,049	19,640	17,180
77,700	77,750	18,776	16,063	19,655	17,194
77,750	77,800	18,791	16,077	19,671	17,208
77,800	77,850	18,807	16,091	19,686	17,222
77,850	77,900	18,822	16,105	19,702	17,236
77,900	77,950	18,838	16,119	19,717	17,250
77,950	78,000	18,853	16,133	19,733	17,264

78,000

78,000	78,050	18,869	16,147	19,748	17,278
78,050	78,100	18,884	16,161	19,764	17,292
78,100	78,150	18,900	16,175	19,779	17,306
78,150	78,200	18,915	16,189	19,795	17,320
78,200	78,250	18,931	16,203	19,810	17,334
78,250	78,300	18,946	16,217	19,826	17,348
78,300	78,350	18,962	16,231	19,841	17,362
78,350	78,400	18,977	16,245	19,857	17,376
78,400	78,450	18,993	16,259	19,872	17,390
78,450	78,500	19,008	16,273	19,888	17,404
78,500	78,550	19,024	16,287	19,903	17,418
78,550	78,600	19,039	16,301	19,919	17,432
78,600	78,650	19,055	16,315	19,934	17,446
78,650	78,700	19,070	16,329	19,950	17,460
78,700	78,750	19,086	16,343	19,965	17,474
78,750	78,800	19,101	16,357	19,981	17,488
78,800	78,850	19,117	16,371	19,996	17,502
78,850	78,900	19,132	16,385	20,012	17,516
78,900	78,950	19,148	16,399	20,027	17,530
78,950	79,000	19,163	16,413	20,043	17,544

79,000

79,000	79,050	19,179	16,427	20,058	17,558
79,050	79,100	19,194	16,441	20,074	17,572
79,100	79,150	19,210	16,455	20,089	17,586
79,150	79,200	19,225	16,469	20,105	17,600
79,200	79,250	19,241	16,483	20,120	17,614
79,250	79,300	19,256	16,497	20,136	17,628
79,300	79,350	19,272	16,511	20,151	17,642
79,350	79,400	19,287	16,525	20,167	17,656
79,400	79,450	19,303	16,539	20,182	17,670
79,450	79,500	19,318	16,553	20,198	17,684
79,500	79,550	19,334	16,567	20,213	17,698
79,550	79,600	19,349	16,581	20,229	17,712
79,600	79,650	19,365	16,595	20,244	17,726
79,650	79,700	19,380	16,609	20,260	17,740
79,700	79,750	19,396	16,623	20,275	17,754
79,750	79,800	19,411	16,637	20,291	17,768
79,800	79,850	19,427	16,651	20,306	17,782
79,850	79,900	19,442	16,665	20,322	17,796
79,900	79,950	19,458	16,679	20,337	17,810
79,950	80,000	19,473	16,693	20,353	17,824

80,000

80,000	80,050	19,489	16,707	20,368	17,838
80,050	80,100	19,504	16,721	20,384	17,852
80,100	80,150	19,520	16,735	20,399	17,866
80,150	80,200	19,535	16,749	20,415	17,880
80,200	80,250	19,551	16,763	20,430	17,894
80,250	80,300	19,566	16,777	20,446	17,908
80,300	80,350	19,582	16,791	20,461	17,922
80,350	80,400	19,597	16,805	20,477	17,936
80,400	80,450	19,613	16,819	20,492	17,950
80,450	80,500	19,628	16,833	20,508	17,964
80,500	80,550	19,644	16,847	20,523	17,978
80,550	80,600	19,659	16,861	20,539	17,992
80,600	80,650	19,675	16,875	20,554	18,006
80,650	80,700	19,690	16,889	20,570	18,020
80,700	80,750	19,706	16,903	20,585	18,034
80,750	80,800	19,721	16,917	20,603	18,048
80,800	80,850	19,737	16,931	20,621	18,062
80,850	80,900	19,752	16,945	20,639	18,076
80,900	80,950	19,768	16,959	20,657	18,090
80,950	81,000	19,783	16,973	20,675	18,104

81,000

81,000	81,050	19,799	16,987	20,693	18,118
81,050	81,100	19,814	17,001	20,711	18,132
81,100	81,150	19,830	17,015	20,729	18,146
81,150	81,200	19,845	17,029	20,747	18,160
81,200	81,250	19,861	17,043	20,765	18,174
81,250	81,300	19,876	17,057	20,783	18,188
81,300	81,350	19,892	17,071	20,801	18,202
81,350	81,400	19,907	17,085	20,819	18,216
81,400	81,450	19,923	17,099	20,837	18,230
81,450	81,500	19,938	17,113	20,855	18,244
81,500	81,550	19,954	17,127	20,873	18,258
81,550	81,600	19,969	17,141	20,891	18,272
81,600	81,650	19,985	17,155	20,909	18,286
81,650	81,700	20,000	17,169	20,927	18,300
81,700	81,750	20,016	17,183	20,945	18,314
81,750	81,800	20,031	17,197	20,963	18,328
81,800	81,850	20,047	17,211	20,981	18,342
81,850	81,900	20,062	17,225	20,999	18,356
81,900	81,950	20,078	17,239	21,017	18,370
81,950	82,000	20,093	17,253	21,035	18,384

82,000

82,000	82,050	20,109	17,267	21,053	18,398
82,050	82,100	20,124	17,281	21,071	18,412
82,100	82,150	20,140	17,295	21,089	18,426
82,150	82,200	20,155	17,309	21,107	18,440
82,200	82,250	20,171	17,323	21,125	18,454
82,250	82,300	20,186	17,337	21,143	18,468
82,300	82,350	20,202	17,351	21,161	18,482
82,350	82,400	20,217	17,365	21,179	18,496
82,400	82,450	20,233	17,379	21,197	18,510
82,450	82,500	20,248	17,393	21,215	18,524
82,500	82,550	20,264	17,407	21,233	18,538
82,550	82,600	20,279	17,421	21,251	18,552
82,600	82,650	20,295	17,435	21,269	18,566
82,650	82,700	20,310	17,449	21,287	18,580
82,700	82,750	20,326	17,463	21,305	18,594
82,750	82,800	20,341	17,477	21,323	18,608
82,800	82,850	20,357	17,491	21,341	18,622
82,850	82,900	20,372	17,505	21,359	18,636
82,900	82,950	20,388	17,519	21,377	18,650
82,950	83,000	20,403	17,533	21,395	18,664

83,000

83,000	83,050	20,419	17,547	21,413	18,678
83,050	83,100	20,434	17,561	21,431	18,692
83,100	83,150	20,450	17,575	21,449	18,706
83,150	83,200	20,465	17,589	21,467	18,720
83,200	83,250	20,481	17,603	21,485	18,734
83,250	83,300	20,496	17,617	21,503	18,748
83,300	83,350	20,512	17,631	21,521	18,762
83,350	83,400	20,527	17,645	21,539	18,776
83,400	83,450	20,543	17,659	21,557	18,790
83,450	83,500	20,558	17,673	21,575	18,804
83,500	83,550	20,574	17,687	21,593	18,818
83,550	83,600	20,589	17,701	21,611	18,832
83,600	83,650	20,605	17,715	21,629	18,846
83,650	83,700	20,620	17,729	21,647	18,860
83,700	83,750	20,636	17,743	21,665	18,874
83,750	83,800	20,651	17,757	21,683	18,888
83,800	83,850	20,667	17,771	21,701	18,902
83,850	83,900	20,682	17,785	21,719	18,916
83,900	83,950	20,698	17,799	21,737	18,930
83,950	84,000	20,713	17,813	21,755	18,944

84,000

84,000	84,050	20,729	17,827	21,773	18,958
84,050	84,100	20,744	17,841	21,791	18,972
84,100	84,150	20,760	17,855	21,809	18,986
84,150	84,200	20,775	17,869	21,827	19,000
84,200	84,250	20,791	17,883	21,845	19,014
84,250	84,300	20,806	17,897	21,863	19,028
84,300	84,350	20,822	17,911	21,881	19,042
84,350	84,400	20,837	17,925	21,899	19,056
84,400	84,450	20,853	17,939	21,917	19,070
84,450	84,500	20,868	17,953	21,935	19,084
84,500	84,550	20,884	17,967	21,953	19,098
84,550	84,600	20,899	17,981	21,971	19,112
84,600	84,650	20,915	17,995	21,989	19,126
84,650	84,700	20,930	18,009	22,007	19,140
84,700	84,750	20,946	18,023	22,025	19,154
84,750	84,800	20,961	18,037	22,043	19,168
84,800	84,850	20,977	18,051	22,061	19,182
84,850	84,900	20,992	18,065	22,079	19,196
84,900	84,950	21,008	18,079	22,097	19,210
84,950	85,000	21,023	18,093	22,115	19,224

85,000

85,000	85,050	21,039	18,107	22,133	19,238
85,050	85,100	21,054	18,121	22,151	19,252
85,100	85,150	21,070	18,135	22,169	19,266
85,150	85,200	21,085	18,149	22,187	19,280
85,200	85,250	21,101	18,163	22,205	19,294
85,250	85,300	21,116	18,177	22,223	19,308
85,300	85,350	21,132	18,191	22,241	19,322
85,350	85,400	21,147	18,205	22,259	19,336
85,400	85,450	21,163	18,219	22,277	19,350
85,450	85,500	21,178	18,233	22,295	19,364
85,500	85,550	21,194	18,247	22,313	19,378
85,550	85,600	21,209	18,261	22,331	19,392
85,600	85,650	21,225	18,275	22,349	19,406
85,650	85,700	21,240	18,289	22,367	19,420
85,700	85,750	21,256	18,303	22,385	19,434
85,750	85,800	21,271	18,317	22,403	19,448
85,800	85,850	21,287	18,331	22,421	19,462
85,850	85,900	21,302	18,345	22,439	19,476
85,900	85,950	21,318	18,359	22,457	19,490
85,950	86,000	21,333	18,373	22,475	19,504

* This column must also be used by a qualifying widow(er).

(Continued on next page)

T-12 Individuals ▼ 2000 Tax Tables and Rate Schedules

2000 Tax Table—Continued

If line 39 (taxable income) is—		And you are—				If line 39 (taxable income) is—		And you are—				If line 39 (taxable income) is—		And you are—			
At least	But less than	Single	Married filing jointly *	Married filing separately	Head of a house-hold	At least	But less than	Single	Married filing jointly *	Married filing separately	Head of a house-hold	At least	But less than	Single	Married filing jointly *	Married filing separately	Head of a house-hold
		Your tax is—						Your tax is—						Your tax is—			
86,000						**89,000**						**92,000**					
86,000	86,050	21,349	18,387	22,493	19,518	89,000	89,050	22,279	19,227	23,573	20,358	92,000	92,050	23,209	20,067	24,653	21,234
86,050	86,100	21,364	18,401	22,511	19,532	89,050	89,100	22,294	19,241	23,591	20,372	92,050	92,100	23,224	20,081	24,671	21,250
86,100	86,150	21,380	18,415	22,529	19,546	89,100	89,150	22,310	19,255	23,609	20,386	92,100	92,150	23,240	20,095	24,689	21,265
86,150	86,200	21,395	18,429	22,547	19,560	89,150	89,200	22,325	19,269	23,627	20,400	92,150	92,200	23,255	20,109	24,707	21,281
86,200	86,250	21,411	18,443	22,565	19,574	89,200	89,250	22,341	19,283	23,645	20,414	92,200	92,250	23,271	20,123	24,725	21,296
86,250	86,300	21,426	18,457	22,583	19,588	89,250	89,300	22,356	19,297	23,663	20,428	92,250	92,300	23,286	20,137	24,743	21,312
86,300	86,350	21,442	18,471	22,601	19,602	89,300	89,350	22,372	19,311	23,681	20,442	92,300	92,350	23,302	20,151	24,761	21,327
86,350	86,400	21,457	18,485	22,619	19,616	89,350	89,400	22,387	19,325	23,699	20,456	92,350	92,400	23,317	20,165	24,779	21,343
86,400	86,450	21,473	18,499	22,637	19,630	89,400	89,450	22,403	19,339	23,717	20,470	92,400	92,450	23,333	20,179	24,797	21,358
86,450	86,500	21,488	18,513	22,655	19,644	89,450	89,500	22,418	19,353	23,735	20,484	92,450	92,500	23,348	20,193	24,815	21,374
86,500	86,550	21,504	18,527	22,673	19,658	89,500	89,550	22,434	19,367	23,753	20,498	92,500	92,550	23,364	20,207	24,833	21,389
86,550	86,600	21,519	18,541	22,691	19,672	89,550	89,600	22,449	19,381	23,771	20,512	92,550	92,600	23,379	20,221	24,851	21,405
86,600	86,650	21,535	18,555	22,709	19,686	89,600	89,650	22,465	19,395	23,789	20,526	92,600	92,650	23,395	20,235	24,869	21,420
86,650	86,700	21,550	18,569	22,727	19,700	89,650	89,700	22,480	19,409	23,807	20,540	92,650	92,700	23,410	20,249	24,887	21,436
86,700	86,750	21,566	18,583	22,745	19,714	89,700	89,750	22,496	19,423	23,825	20,554	92,700	92,750	23,426	20,263	24,905	21,451
86,750	86,800	21,581	18,597	22,763	19,728	89,750	89,800	22,511	19,437	23,843	20,568	92,750	92,800	23,441	20,277	24,923	21,467
86,800	86,850	21,597	18,611	22,781	19,742	89,800	89,850	22,527	19,451	23,861	20,582	92,800	92,850	23,457	20,291	24,941	21,482
86,850	86,900	21,612	18,625	22,799	19,756	89,850	89,900	22,542	19,465	23,879	20,596	92,850	92,900	23,472	20,305	24,959	21,498
86,900	86,950	21,628	18,639	22,817	19,770	89,900	89,950	22,558	19,479	23,897	20,610	92,900	92,950	23,488	20,319	24,977	21,513
86,950	87,000	21,643	18,653	22,835	19,784	89,950	90,000	22,573	19,493	23,915	20,624	92,950	93,000	23,503	20,333	24,995	21,529
87,000						**90,000**						**93,000**					
87,000	87,050	21,659	18,667	22,853	19,798	90,000	90,050	22,589	19,507	23,933	20,638	93,000	93,050	23,519	20,347	25,013	21,544
87,050	87,100	21,674	18,681	22,871	19,812	90,050	90,100	22,604	19,521	23,951	20,652	93,050	93,100	23,534	20,361	25,031	21,560
87,100	87,150	21,690	18,695	22,889	19,826	90,100	90,150	22,620	19,535	23,969	20,666	93,100	93,150	23,550	20,375	25,049	21,575
87,150	87,200	21,705	18,709	22,907	19,840	90,150	90,200	22,635	19,549	23,987	20,680	93,150	93,200	23,565	20,389	25,067	21,591
87,200	87,250	21,721	18,723	22,925	19,854	90,200	90,250	22,651	19,563	24,005	20,694	93,200	93,250	23,581	20,403	25,085	21,606
87,250	87,300	21,736	18,737	22,943	19,868	90,250	90,300	22,666	19,577	24,023	20,708	93,250	93,300	23,596	20,417	25,103	21,622
87,300	87,350	21,752	18,751	22,961	19,882	90,300	90,350	22,682	19,591	24,041	20,722	93,300	93,350	23,612	20,431	25,121	21,637
87,350	87,400	21,767	18,765	22,979	19,896	90,350	90,400	22,697	19,605	24,059	20,736	93,350	93,400	23,627	20,445	25,139	21,653
87,400	87,450	21,783	18,779	22,997	19,910	90,400	90,450	22,713	19,619	24,077	20,750	93,400	93,450	23,643	20,459	25,157	21,668
87,450	87,500	21,798	18,793	23,015	19,924	90,450	90,500	22,728	19,633	24,095	20,764	93,450	93,500	23,658	20,473	25,175	21,684
87,500	87,550	21,814	18,807	23,033	19,938	90,500	90,550	22,744	19,647	24,113	20,778	93,500	93,550	23,674	20,487	25,193	21,699
87,550	87,600	21,829	18,821	23,051	19,952	90,550	90,600	22,759	19,661	24,131	20,792	93,550	93,600	23,689	20,501	25,211	21,715
87,600	87,650	21,845	18,835	23,069	19,966	90,600	90,650	22,775	19,675	24,149	20,806	93,600	93,650	23,705	20,515	25,229	21,730
87,650	87,700	21,860	18,849	23,087	19,980	90,650	90,700	22,790	19,689	24,167	20,820	93,650	93,700	23,720	20,529	25,247	21,746
87,700	87,750	21,876	18,863	23,105	19,994	90,700	90,750	22,806	19,703	24,185	20,834	93,700	93,750	23,736	20,543	25,265	21,761
87,750	87,800	21,891	18,877	23,123	20,008	90,750	90,800	22,821	19,717	24,203	20,848	93,750	93,800	23,751	20,557	25,283	21,777
87,800	87,850	21,907	18,891	23,141	20,022	90,800	90,850	22,837	19,731	24,221	20,862	93,800	93,850	23,767	20,571	25,301	21,792
87,850	87,900	21,922	18,905	23,159	20,036	90,850	90,900	22,852	19,745	24,239	20,878	93,850	93,900	23,782	20,585	25,319	21,808
87,900	87,950	21,938	18,919	23,177	20,050	90,900	90,950	22,868	19,759	24,257	20,893	93,900	93,950	23,798	20,599	25,337	21,823
87,950	88,000	21,953	18,933	23,195	20,064	90,950	91,000	22,883	19,773	24,275	20,909	93,950	94,000	23,813	20,613	25,355	21,839
88,000						**91,000**						**94,000**					
88,000	88,050	21,969	18,947	23,213	20,078	91,000	91,050	22,899	19,787	24,293	20,924	94,000	94,050	23,829	20,627	25,373	21,854
88,050	88,100	21,984	18,961	23,231	20,092	91,050	91,100	22,914	19,801	24,311	20,940	94,050	94,100	23,844	20,641	25,391	21,870
88,100	88,150	22,000	18,975	23,249	20,106	91,100	91,150	22,930	19,815	24,329	20,955	94,100	94,150	23,860	20,655	25,409	21,885
88,150	88,200	22,015	18,989	23,267	20,120	91,150	91,200	22,945	19,829	24,347	20,971	94,150	94,200	23,875	20,669	25,427	21,901
88,200	88,250	22,031	19,003	23,285	20,134	91,200	91,250	22,961	19,843	24,365	20,986	94,200	94,250	23,891	20,683	25,445	21,916
88,250	88,300	22,046	19,017	23,303	20,148	91,250	91,300	22,976	19,857	24,383	21,002	94,250	94,300	23,906	20,697	25,463	21,932
88,300	88,350	22,062	19,031	23,321	20,162	91,300	91,350	22,992	19,871	24,401	21,017	94,300	94,350	23,922	20,711	25,481	21,947
88,350	88,400	22,077	19,045	23,339	20,176	91,350	91,400	23,007	19,885	24,419	21,033	94,350	94,400	23,937	20,725	25,499	21,963
88,400	88,450	22,093	19,059	23,357	20,190	91,400	91,450	23,023	19,899	24,437	21,048	94,400	94,450	23,953	20,739	25,517	21,978
88,450	88,500	22,108	19,073	23,375	20,204	91,450	91,500	23,038	19,913	24,455	21,064	94,450	94,500	23,968	20,753	25,535	21,994
88,500	88,550	22,124	19,087	23,393	20,218	91,500	91,550	23,054	19,927	24,473	21,079	94,500	94,550	23,984	20,767	25,553	22,009
88,550	88,600	22,139	19,101	23,411	20,232	91,550	91,600	23,069	19,941	24,491	21,095	94,550	94,600	23,999	20,781	25,571	22,025
88,600	88,650	22,155	19,115	23,429	20,246	91,600	91,650	23,085	19,955	24,509	21,110	94,600	94,650	24,015	20,795	25,589	22,040
88,650	88,700	22,170	19,129	23,447	20,260	91,650	91,700	23,100	19,969	24,527	21,126	94,650	94,700	24,030	20,809	25,607	22,056
88,700	88,750	22,186	19,143	23,465	20,274	91,700	91,750	23,116	19,983	24,545	21,141	94,700	94,750	24,046	20,823	25,625	22,071
88,750	88,800	22,201	19,157	23,483	20,288	91,750	91,800	23,131	19,997	24,563	21,157	94,750	94,800	24,061	20,837	25,643	22,087
88,800	88,850	22,217	19,171	23,501	20,302	91,800	91,850	23,147	20,011	24,581	21,172	94,800	94,850	24,077	20,851	25,661	22,102
88,850	88,900	22,232	19,185	23,519	20,316	91,850	91,900	23,162	20,025	24,599	21,188	94,850	94,900	24,092	20,865	25,679	22,118
88,900	88,950	22,248	19,199	23,537	20,330	91,900	91,950	23,178	20,039	24,617	21,203	94,900	94,950	24,108	20,879	25,697	22,133
88,950	89,000	22,263	19,213	23,555	20,344	91,950	92,000	23,193	20,053	24,635	21,219	94,950	95,000	24,123	20,893	25,715	22,149

* This column must also be used by a qualifying widow(er).

(Continued on next page)

2000 Tax Table—Continued

If line 39 (taxable income) is—		And you are—				If line 39 (taxable income) is—		And you are—			
At least	But less than	Single	Married filing jointly *	Married filing separately	Head of a household	At least	But less than	Single	Married filing jointly *	Married filing separately	Head of a household
		Your tax is—						Your tax is—			

95,000

At least	But less than	Single	MFJ	MFS	HoH
95,000	95,050	24,139	20,907	25,733	22,164
95,050	95,100	24,154	20,921	25,751	22,180
95,100	95,150	24,170	20,935	25,769	22,195
95,150	95,200	24,185	20,949	25,787	22,211
95,200	95,250	24,201	20,963	25,805	22,226
95,250	95,300	24,216	20,977	25,823	22,242
95,300	95,350	24,232	20,991	25,841	22,257
95,350	95,400	24,247	21,005	25,859	22,273
95,400	95,450	24,263	21,019	25,877	22,288
95,450	95,500	24,278	21,033	25,895	22,304
95,500	95,550	24,294	21,047	25,913	22,319
95,550	95,600	24,309	21,061	25,931	22,335
95,600	95,650	24,325	21,075	25,949	22,350
95,650	95,700	24,340	21,089	25,967	22,366
95,700	95,750	24,356	21,103	25,985	22,381
95,750	95,800	24,371	21,117	26,003	22,397
95,800	95,850	24,387	21,131	26,021	22,412
95,850	95,900	24,402	21,145	26,039	22,428
95,900	95,950	24,418	21,159	26,057	22,443
95,950	96,000	24,433	21,173	26,075	22,459

96,000

At least	But less than	Single	MFJ	MFS	HoH
96,000	96,050	24,449	21,187	26,093	22,474
96,050	96,100	24,464	21,201	26,111	22,490
96,100	96,150	24,480	21,215	26,129	22,505
96,150	96,200	24,495	21,229	26,147	22,521
96,200	96,250	24,511	21,243	26,165	22,536
96,250	96,300	24,526	21,257	26,183	22,552
96,300	96,350	24,542	21,271	26,201	22,567
96,350	96,400	24,557	21,285	26,219	22,583
96,400	96,450	24,573	21,299	26,237	22,598
96,450	96,500	24,588	21,313	26,255	22,614
96,500	96,550	24,604	21,327	26,273	22,629
96,550	96,600	24,619	21,341	26,291	22,645
96,600	96,650	24,635	21,355	26,309	22,660
96,650	96,700	24,650	21,369	26,327	22,676
96,700	96,750	24,666	21,383	26,345	22,691
96,750	96,800	24,681	21,397	26,363	22,707
96,800	96,850	24,697	21,411	26,381	22,722
96,850	96,900	24,712	21,425	26,399	22,738
96,900	96,950	24,728	21,439	26,417	22,753
96,950	97,000	24,743	21,453	26,435	22,769

97,000

At least	But less than	Single	MFJ	MFS	HoH
97,000	97,050	24,759	21,467	26,453	22,784
97,050	97,100	24,774	21,481	26,471	22,800
97,100	97,150	24,790	21,495	26,489	22,815
97,150	97,200	24,805	21,509	26,507	22,831
97,200	97,250	24,821	21,523	26,525	22,846
97,250	97,300	24,836	21,537	26,543	22,862
97,300	97,350	24,852	21,551	26,561	22,877
97,350	97,400	24,867	21,565	26,579	22,893
97,400	97,450	24,883	21,579	26,597	22,908
97,450	97,500	24,898	21,593	26,615	22,924
97,500	97,550	24,914	21,607	26,633	22,939
97,550	97,600	24,929	21,621	26,651	22,955
97,600	97,650	24,945	21,635	26,669	22,970
97,650	97,700	24,960	21,649	26,687	22,986
97,700	97,750	24,976	21,663	26,705	23,001
97,750	97,800	24,991	21,677	26,723	23,017
97,800	97,850	25,007	21,691	26,741	23,032
97,850	97,900	25,022	21,705	26,759	23,048
97,900	97,950	25,038	21,719	26,777	23,063
97,950	98,000	25,053	21,733	26,795	23,079

98,000

At least	But less than	Single	MFJ	MFS	HoH
98,000	98,050	25,069	21,747	26,813	23,094
98,050	98,100	25,084	21,761	26,831	23,110
98,100	98,150	25,100	21,775	26,849	23,125
98,150	98,200	25,115	21,789	26,867	23,141
98,200	98,250	25,131	21,803	26,885	23,156
98,250	98,300	25,146	21,817	26,903	23,172
98,300	98,350	25,162	21,831	26,921	23,187
98,350	98,400	25,177	21,845	26,939	23,203
98,400	98,450	25,193	21,859	26,957	23,218
98,450	98,500	25,208	21,873	26,975	23,234
98,500	98,550	25,224	21,887	26,993	23,249
98,550	98,600	25,239	21,901	27,011	23,265
98,600	98,650	25,255	21,915	27,029	23,280
98,650	98,700	25,270	21,929	27,047	23,296
98,700	98,750	25,286	21,943	27,065	23,311
98,750	98,800	25,301	21,957	27,083	23,327
98,800	98,850	25,317	21,971	27,101	23,342
98,850	98,900	25,332	21,985	27,119	23,358
98,900	98,950	25,348	21,999	27,137	23,373
98,950	99,000	25,363	22,013	27,155	23,389

99,000

At least	But less than	Single	MFJ	MFS	HoH
99,000	99,050	25,379	22,027	27,173	23,404
99,050	99,100	25,394	22,041	27,191	23,420
99,100	99,150	25,410	22,055	27,209	23,435
99,150	99,200	25,425	22,069	27,227	23,451
99,200	99,250	25,441	22,083	27,245	23,466
99,250	99,300	25,456	22,097	27,263	23,482
99,300	99,350	25,472	22,111	27,281	23,497
99,350	99,400	25,487	22,125	27,299	23,513
99,400	99,450	25,503	22,139	27,317	23,528
99,450	99,500	25,518	22,153	27,335	23,544
99,500	99,550	25,534	22,167	27,353	23,559
99,550	99,600	25,549	22,181	27,371	23,575
99,600	99,650	25,565	22,195	27,389	23,590
99,650	99,700	25,580	22,209	27,407	23,606
99,700	99,750	25,596	22,223	27,425	23,621
99,750	99,800	25,611	22,237	27,443	23,637
99,800	99,850	25,627	22,251	27,461	23,652
99,850	99,900	25,642	22,265	27,479	23,668
99,900	99,950	25,658	22,279	27,497	23,683
99,950	100,000	25,673	22,293	27,515	23,699

$100,000 or over — use the Tax Rate Schedules on page T14

* This column must also be used by a qualifying widow(er).

2000 Tax Rate Schedules

Caution: Use **only** if your taxable income (Form 1040, line 39) is $100,000 or more. If less, use the **Tax Table**. Even though you cannot use the Tax Rate Schedules below if your taxable income is less than $100,000, all levels of taxable income are shown so taxpayers can see the tax rate that applies to each level.

Schedule X—Use if your filing status is Single

If the amount on Form 1040, line 39, is: Over—	But not over—	Enter on Form 1040, line 40		of the amount over—
$0	$26,250		15%	$0
26,250	63,550	$3,937.50 +	28%	26,250
63,550	132,600	14,381.50 +	31%	63,550
132,600	288,350	35,787.00 +	36%	132,600
288,350	----	91,857.00 +	39.6%	288,350

Schedule Y-1—Use if your filing status is Married filing jointly or Qualifying widow(er)

If the amount on Form 1040, line 39, is: Over—	But not over—	Enter on Form 1040, line 40		of the amount over—
$0	$43,850		15%	$0
43,850	105,950	$6,577.50 +	28%	43,850
105,950	161,450	23,965.50 +	31%	105,950
161,450	288,350	41,170.50 +	36%	161,450
288,350	----	86,854.50 +	39.6%	288,350

Schedule Y-2—Use if your filing status is Married filing separately

If the amount on Form 1040, line 39, is: Over—	But not over—	Enter on Form 1040, line 40		of the amount over—
$0	$21,925		15%	$0
21,925	52,975	$3,288.75 +	28%	21,925
52,975	80,725	11,982.75 +	31%	52,975
80,725	144,175	20,585.25 +	36%	80,725
144,175	----	43,427.25 +	39.6%	144,175

Schedule Z—Use if your filing status is Head of household

If the amount on Form 1040, line 39, is: Over—	But not over—	Enter on Form 1040, line 40		of the amount over—
$0	$35,150		15%	$0
35,150	90,800	$5,272.50 +	28%	35,150
90,800	147,050	20,854.50 +	31%	90,800
147,050	288,350	38,292.00 +	36%	147,050
288,350	----	89,160.00 +	39.6%	288,350

SINGLE Persons—MONTHLY Payroll Period
(For Wages Paid in 2001)

If the wages are—		And the number of withholding allowances claimed is—										
At least	But less than	0	1	2	3	4	5	6	7	8	9	10
		The amount of income tax to be withheld is—										
$0	$220	0	0	0	0	0	0	0	0	0	0	0
220	230	1	0	0	0	0	0	0	0	0	0	0
230	240	2	0	0	0	0	0	0	0	0	0	0
240	250	4	0	0	0	0	0	0	0	0	0	0
250	260	5	0	0	0	0	0	0	0	0	0	0
260	270	7	0	0	0	0	0	0	0	0	0	0
270	280	8	0	0	0	0	0	0	0	0	0	0
280	290	10	0	0	0	0	0	0	0	0	0	0
290	300	11	0	0	0	0	0	0	0	0	0	0
300	320	13	0	0	0	0	0	0	0	0	0	0
320	340	16	0	0	0	0	0	0	0	0	0	0
340	360	19	0	0	0	0	0	0	0	0	0	0
360	380	22	0	0	0	0	0	0	0	0	0	0
380	400	25	0	0	0	0	0	0	0	0	0	0
400	420	28	0	0	0	0	0	0	0	0	0	0
420	440	31	0	0	0	0	0	0	0	0	0	0
440	460	34	0	0	0	0	0	0	0	0	0	0
460	480	37	1	0	0	0	0	0	0	0	0	0
480	500	40	4	0	0	0	0	0	0	0	0	0
500	520	43	7	0	0	0	0	0	0	0	0	0
520	540	46	10	0	0	0	0	0	0	0	0	0
540	560	49	13	0	0	0	0	0	0	0	0	0
560	580	52	16	0	0	0	0	0	0	0	0	0
580	600	55	19	0	0	0	0	0	0	0	0	0
600	640	60	24	0	0	0	0	0	0	0	0	0
640	680	66	30	0	0	0	0	0	0	0	0	0
680	720	72	36	0	0	0	0	0	0	0	0	0
720	760	78	42	5	0	0	0	0	0	0	0	0
760	800	84	48	11	0	0	0	0	0	0	0	0
800	840	90	54	17	0	0	0	0	0	0	0	0
840	880	96	60	23	0	0	0	0	0	0	0	0
880	920	102	66	29	0	0	0	0	0	0	0	0
920	960	108	72	35	0	0	0	0	0	0	0	0
960	1,000	114	78	41	5	0	0	0	0	0	0	0
1,000	1,040	120	84	47	11	0	0	0	0	0	0	0
1,040	1,080	126	90	53	17	0	0	0	0	0	0	0
1,080	1,120	132	96	59	23	0	0	0	0	0	0	0
1,120	1,160	138	102	65	29	0	0	0	0	0	0	0
1,160	1,200	144	108	71	35	0	0	0	0	0	0	0
1,200	1,240	150	114	77	41	5	0	0	0	0	0	0
1,240	1,280	156	120	83	47	11	0	0	0	0	0	0
1,280	1,320	162	126	89	53	17	0	0	0	0	0	0
1,320	1,360	168	132	95	59	23	0	0	0	0	0	0
1,360	1,400	174	138	101	65	29	0	0	0	0	0	0
1,400	1,440	180	144	107	71	35	0	0	0	0	0	0
1,440	1,480	186	150	113	77	41	5	0	0	0	0	0
1,480	1,520	192	156	119	83	47	11	0	0	0	0	0
1,520	1,560	198	162	125	89	53	17	0	0	0	0	0
1,560	1,600	204	168	131	95	59	23	0	0	0	0	0
1,600	1,640	210	174	137	101	65	29	0	0	0	0	0
1,640	1,680	216	180	143	107	71	35	0	0	0	0	0
1,680	1,720	222	186	149	113	77	41	4	0	0	0	0
1,720	1,760	228	192	155	119	83	47	10	0	0	0	0
1,760	1,800	234	198	161	125	89	53	16	0	0	0	0
1,800	1,840	240	204	167	131	95	59	22	0	0	0	0
1,840	1,880	246	210	173	137	101	65	28	0	0	0	0
1,880	1,920	252	216	179	143	107	71	34	0	0	0	0
1,920	1,960	258	222	185	149	113	77	40	4	0	0	0
1,960	2,000	264	228	191	155	119	83	46	10	0	0	0
2,000	2,040	270	234	197	161	125	89	52	16	0	0	0
2,040	2,080	276	240	203	167	131	95	58	22	0	0	0
2,080	2,120	282	246	209	173	137	101	64	28	0	0	0
2,120	2,160	288	252	215	179	143	107	70	34	0	0	0
2,160	2,200	294	258	221	185	149	113	76	40	4	0	0
2,200	2,240	300	264	227	191	155	119	82	46	10	0	0
2,240	2,280	306	270	233	197	161	125	88	52	16	0	0
2,280	2,320	312	276	239	203	167	131	94	58	22	0	0
2,320	2,360	318	282	245	209	173	137	100	64	28	0	0
2,360	2,400	324	288	251	215	179	143	106	70	34	0	0
2,400	2,440	334	294	257	221	185	149	112	76	40	4	0

T-16 Individuals ▼ 2000 Tax Tables and Rate Schedules

MARRIED Persons—MONTHLY Payroll Period
(For Wages Paid in 2001)

If the wages are—		And the number of withholding allowances claimed is—										
At least	But less than	0	1	2	3	4	5	6	7	8	9	10
		The amount of income tax to be withheld is—										
$0	$540	0	0	0	0	0	0	0	0	0	0	0
540	560	2	0	0	0	0	0	0	0	0	0	0
560	580	5	0	0	0	0	0	0	0	0	0	0
580	600	8	0	0	0	0	0	0	0	0	0	0
600	640	12	0	0	0	0	0	0	0	0	0	0
640	680	18	0	0	0	0	0	0	0	0	0	0
680	720	24	0	0	0	0	0	0	0	0	0	0
720	760	30	0	0	0	0	0	0	0	0	0	0
760	800	36	0	0	0	0	0	0	0	0	0	0
800	840	42	6	0	0	0	0	0	0	0	0	0
840	880	48	12	0	0	0	0	0	0	0	0	0
880	920	54	18	0	0	0	0	0	0	0	0	0
920	960	60	24	0	0	0	0	0	0	0	0	0
960	1,000	66	30	0	0	0	0	0	0	0	0	0
1,000	1,040	72	36	0	0	0	0	0	0	0	0	0
1,040	1,080	78	42	6	0	0	0	0	0	0	0	0
1,080	1,120	84	48	12	0	0	0	0	0	0	0	0
1,120	1,160	90	54	18	0	0	0	0	0	0	0	0
1,160	1,200	96	60	24	0	0	0	0	0	0	0	0
1,200	1,240	102	66	30	0	0	0	0	0	0	0	0
1,240	1,280	108	72	36	0	0	0	0	0	0	0	0
1,280	1,320	114	78	42	6	0	0	0	0	0	0	0
1,320	1,360	120	84	48	12	0	0	0	0	0	0	0
1,360	1,400	126	90	54	18	0	0	0	0	0	0	0
1,400	1,440	132	96	60	24	0	0	0	0	0	0	0
1,440	1,480	138	102	66	30	0	0	0	0	0	0	0
1,480	1,520	144	108	72	36	0	0	0	0	0	0	0
1,520	1,560	150	114	78	42	5	0	0	0	0	0	0
1,560	1,600	156	120	84	48	11	0	0	0	0	0	0
1,600	1,640	162	126	90	54	17	0	0	0	0	0	0
1,640	1,680	168	132	96	60	23	0	0	0	0	0	0
1,680	1,720	174	138	102	66	29	0	0	0	0	0	0
1,720	1,760	180	144	108	72	35	0	0	0	0	0	0
1,760	1,800	186	150	114	78	41	5	0	0	0	0	0
1,800	1,840	192	156	120	84	47	11	0	0	0	0	0
1,840	1,880	198	162	126	90	53	17	0	0	0	0	0
1,880	1,920	204	168	132	96	59	23	0	0	0	0	0
1,920	1,960	210	174	138	102	65	29	0	0	0	0	0
1,960	2,000	216	180	144	108	71	35	0	0	0	0	0
2,000	2,040	222	186	150	114	77	41	5	0	0	0	0
2,040	2,080	228	192	156	120	83	47	11	0	0	0	0
2,080	2,120	234	198	162	126	89	53	17	0	0	0	0
2,120	2,160	240	204	168	132	95	59	23	0	0	0	0
2,160	2,200	246	210	174	138	101	65	29	0	0	0	0
2,200	2,240	252	216	180	144	107	71	35	0	0	0	0
2,240	2,280	258	222	186	150	113	77	41	5	0	0	0
2,280	2,320	264	228	192	156	119	83	47	11	0	0	0
2,320	2,360	270	234	198	162	125	89	53	17	0	0	0
2,360	2,400	276	240	204	168	131	95	59	23	0	0	0
2,400	2,440	282	246	210	174	137	101	65	29	0	0	0
2,440	2,480	288	252	216	180	143	107	71	35	0	0	0
2,480	2,520	294	258	222	186	149	113	77	41	4	0	0
2,520	2,560	300	264	228	192	155	119	83	47	10	0	0
2,560	2,600	306	270	234	198	161	125	89	53	16	0	0
2,600	2,640	312	276	240	204	167	131	95	59	22	0	0
2,640	2,680	318	282	246	210	173	137	101	65	28	0	0
2,680	2,720	324	288	252	216	179	143	107	71	34	0	0
2,720	2,760	330	294	258	222	185	149	113	77	40	4	0
2,760	2,800	336	300	264	228	191	155	119	83	46	10	0
2,800	2,840	342	306	270	234	197	161	125	89	52	16	0
2,840	2,880	348	312	276	240	203	167	131	95	58	22	0
2,880	2,920	354	318	282	246	209	173	137	101	64	28	0
2,920	2,960	360	324	288	252	215	179	143	107	70	34	0
2,960	3,000	366	330	294	258	221	185	149	113	76	40	4
3,000	3,040	372	336	300	264	227	191	155	119	82	46	10
3,040	3,080	378	342	306	270	233	197	161	125	88	52	16
3,080	3,120	384	348	312	276	239	203	167	131	94	58	22
3,120	3,160	390	354	318	282	245	209	173	137	100	64	28
3,160	3,200	396	360	324	288	251	215	179	143	106	70	34
3,200	3,240	402	366	330	294	257	221	185	149	112	76	40

APPENDIX A

TAX RESEARCH WORKING PAPER FILE

INDEX TO TAX RESEARCH FILE*

Item	Page Reference
Determine the Facts	A-2
Identify the Issues	A-2
Locate Applicable Authorities	A-2
Evaluate Authorities	A-4
Analyze the Facts in Terms of Applicable Law	A-4
Communicate Conclusions and Recommendations to Others	A-5
Memorandum-to-the-File	A-6
Client Letter	A-7

*Most accounting firms maintain a **client file** for each of their clients. Typically, this file contains copies of client letters, memoranda-to-the-file, relevant primary and secondary authorities, and billing information. In our case, the client file for Mercy Hospital would include copies of the following: (1) the September 12 letter to Elizabeth Feghali, (2) the September 9 memorandum-to-the-file, (3) IRC Sec. 119, (4) Reg. Sec. 1.119-1, (5) the *Kowalski* opinion, (6) the *Standard Federal Tax Reporter* annotation, and (7) pertinent billing information.

A-1

TAX RESEARCH FILE

As mentioned in Chapter C1 the tax research process entails six steps.

1. Determine the facts
2. Identify the issues
3. Locate applicable authorities
4. Evaluate these authorities
5. Analyze the facts
6. Communicate conclusions and recommendations to others.

Let us walk through each of these steps.

Determine the Facts Assume that we have determined the facts to be as follows:

> *Mercy Hospital maintains a cafeteria on its premises. In addition, it rents space to MacDougal's, a privately owned sandwich shop. The cafeteria closes at 8:00 p.m. MacDougal's is open 24 hours. Mercy provides meal vouchers to each of its 240 medical employees to enable them to remain on call in case of emergency. The vouchers are redeemable either at the cafeteria or at MacDougal's. Although the employees are not required to remain on or near the premises during meal hours, they generally do. Elizabeth Fegali, Mercy's Chief Administrator, has approached you with the following question: Is the value of a meal voucher includible in the employees' gross income?*

At this juncture, be sure you understand the facts before proceeding further. Remember, researching the wrong facts could produce the wrong results.

Identify the Issues Identifying the issues presupposes a minimum level of proficiency in tax accounting. This proficiency will come with time, effort, and perseverence. The central issue raised by the facts is the taxability of the meal vouchers. A resolution of this issue will hinge on the resolution of other issues raised in the course of the research.

Locate Applicable Authorities For some students, this step is the most difficult in the research process. It raises the perplexing question, "Where do I begin to look?" The answer depends on the tax resources at one's disposal, as well as one's research preferences. Four rules of thumb apply:

1. *Adopt an approach with which you are comfortable, and that you are confident will produce reliable results.*
2. *Always consult the IRC and other primary authorities.*
3. *Be as thorough as possible, taking into consideration time and billing constraints.*
4. *Make sure that the authorities you consult are current.*

One approach is to conduct a topical search. Begin by consulting the index to the Internal Revenue Code (IRC). Then read the relevant IRC section(s). If the language of the IRC is vague or ambiguous, turn to the Treasury Regulations. Read the relevant regulation section that elaborates or expounds on the IRC provision. If the language of the regulation is confusing or unclear, go to a commercial tax service. Read the relevant tax service paragraphs that explain or analyze the statutory and regulatory provisions. For references to other authorities, browse through the footnotes and annotations of the service. Then, consult these authorities directly. Finally, check the currency of the authorities consulted, with the aid of a citator or status (finding) list.

If a pertinent court decision or IRS ruling has been called to your attention, consult this authority directly. Alternatively, browse through the status (finding) list of a tax service for references to tax service paragraphs that discuss this authority. Better still, consult a citator or status list for references to court opinions or rulings that cite the authority. If you subscribe to a computerized tax service, conduct a keyword, citation, contents, or topical search. (For a discussion of these types of searches, see the computerized research supplement available for download at *www.prenhall.com/phtax*.) Then, hyperlink to the authorities cited within the text of the documents retrieved. So numerous are the approaches to tax research that one is virtually free to pick and choose. All that is required of the researcher is a basic level of skill and some imagination.

Let us adopt a topical approach to the issue of the meal vouchers. If we consult an index to the IRC, we are likely to find the heading "Meals and Lodging." Below this heading are likely to be several subheadings, some pertaining to deductions, others to exclusions. Because the voucher issue pertains to exclusions, let us peruse the latter subheadings. Most of these subheadings refer to IRC Sec. 119. If we look up this section, we will see the following passage:

Sec. 119. Meals or lodging furnished for the convenience of the employer.

(a) **Meals and lodging furnished to employee, his spouse, and his dependents, pursuant to employment.**
There shall be excluded from gross income of an employee the value of any meals or lodging furnished to him . . . by, or on behalf of his employer for the convenience of the employer, but only if—

(1) in the case of meals, the meals are furnished on the business premises of the employer . . .

(b) Special rules. For purposes of subsection (a)—
(4) **Meals furnished to employees on business premises where meals of most employees are otherwise excludable.** All meals furnished on the business premises of an employer to such employer's employees shall be treated as furnished for the convenience of the employer if . . . more than half of the employees to whom such meals are furnished on such premises are furnished such meals for the convenience of the employer.

Section 119 appears to be applicable. It deals with meals furnished to an employee on the business premises of the employer. Our case deals with meal vouchers furnished to employees for redemption at employer-maintained and employer-rented-out facilities. But here, additional issues arise. For purposes of Sec. 119, are meal vouchers the same as "meals"? (Do not assume they are.) Are employer-maintained and employer-rented-out facilities the same as "the business premises of the employer"? (Again, do not assume they are.) And what does the IRC mean by "for the convenience of the employer"? Because the IRC offers no guidance in this respect, let us turn to the Treasury Regulations.

The applicable regulation is Reg. Sec. 1.119-1. How do we know this? Because Treasury Regulation section numbers track the IRC section numbers. Regulation Sec. 1.119-1 is the only regulation under IRC Sec. 119. If we browse through this regulation, we will find the following provision:

(a) Meals . . .
(2) **Meals furnished without a charge**
(i) Meals furnished by an employer without charge to the employee will be regarded as furnished for the convenience of the employer if such meals are furnished for a substantial noncompensatory business reason of the employer . . .
(ii) (a) Meals will be regarded as furnished for a substantial noncompensatory business reason of the employer when the meals are furnished to the employee during his working hours to have the employee available for emergency call during his meal period . . .
(c) Business premises of the employer.
(1) In general. For purposes of this section, the term "business premises of the employer" generally means the place of employment of the employee . . .

Based on a reading of this provision, we might conclude that the hospital meals are furnished "for the convenience of the employer." Why? Because they are furnished for a "substantial noncompensatory business reason of the employer," namely, to have the employees available for emergency call during their meal periods. They also are furnished during the employees' working hours. Moreover, under IRC Sec. 119(b)(4), if more than half the employees satisfy the "for the convenience of the employer" test, all employees will be regarded as satisfying the test. But are the meals furnished on "the business premises of the employer"? Under the regulation, the answer would depend. If the meals are furnished in the hospital cafeteria, they may be furnished on "the business premises of the employer." The hospital is the place of employment of the medical employees. The cafeteria is part of the hospital. On the other hand, if the meals are furnished at MacDougal's, they probably are not furnished on "the business premises of the employer." MacDougals's is not the place of employment of the medical employees. Nor is it a part of the hospital. Thus, Reg. Sec. 1.119-1 is enlightening with respect to two statutory terms: "for the convenience of the employer" and "the business premises of the employer." However, it is obscure with respect to the third term, "meals." Because of this obscurity, let us turn to a tax service.

Although the index to CCH's *Standard Federal Tax Reporter* does not list "meal vouchers," it does list "cash allowances in lieu of meals" as a subtopic under Meals and Lodging. Are meal vouchers the same as cash meal allowances?—perhaps so; let us see. Next to the heading "cash allowances in lieu of meals" is a reference to CCH ¶7222.59. If we look up this reference, we will find the following annotation:

¶7222.59 Meal allowances.—Cash meal allowances received by an employee (state trooper) from his employee were not excludible from income. R.J. Kowalski, SCt., 77-2 USTC ¶9748, 434 US 77.[1]

Here we discover that, in the *Kowalski* case, the U.S. Supreme Court decided that cash meal allowances received by an employee were excludible from the employee's income. Is the *Kowalski* case similar to our case? It might be. Let us find out. If we turn to paragraph 9748 of the second 1977 volume of *United States Tax Cases*, we will find the text of the *Kowalski* opinion. A synopsis of this opinion is present below.

In the mid-1970s, the State of New Jersey provided cash meal allowances to its state troopers. The state did not require the troopers to use the allowances exclusively for meals. Nor did it require them to consume their meals on its business premises. One trooper, Robert J. Kowalski, failed to report a portion of his allowance on his tax return. The IRS assessed a deficiency, and Kowalski took the IRS to court. In court, Kowalski argued that the meal allowances were excludible, because they were furnished "for the convenience of the employer." The IRS contended that the allowances were taxable because they amounted to compensation. The Supreme Court took up the case and sided with the IRS. The Court held that the IRC Sec. 119 income exclusion does not apply to cash payments; it applies only to meals in kind.[2]

For the sake of illustration, let us assume that IRC Sec. 119, Reg. Sec. 1.119-1, and the *Kowalski* case are the *only* authorities "on point." How should we evaluate them?

Evaluate Authorities IRC Sec. 119 is the key authority applicable to our case. It supplies the operative rule for resolving the issue of the meal vouchers. It is vague, however, with respect to three terms: "meals," "business premises of the employer," and "for the convenience of the employer." The principal judicial authority is the *Kowalski* case. It provides an official interpretation of the term "meals." Because the U.S. Supreme Court decided *Kowalski*, the case should be assigned considerable weight. The relevant administrative authority is Reg. Sec. 1.119-1. It expounds on the terms "business premises of the employer" and "for the convenience of the employer." Because neither the IRC nor *Kowalski* explain these terms, Reg. Sec. 1.119-1 should be accorded great weight. But what if *Kowalski* had conflicted with Reg. Sec. 1.119-1? Which should be considered more authoritative? As a general rule, high court decisions "trump" the Treasury Regulations (and all IRS pronouncements for that matter). The more recent the decision, the greater its precedential weight. Had there been no Supreme Court decision and a division of appellate authority, equal weight should have been assigned to each of the appellate court decisions.

Analyze the Facts in Terms of Applicable Law Analyzing the facts in terms of applicable law involves applying the abstractions of the law to the concreteness of the facts. It entails expressing the generalities of the law in terms of the specifics of the facts. In this process, every legal condition must be satisfied for the result prescribed by the general rule to

---

[1] The researcher also might read the main *Standard Federal Tax Reporter* paragraph that discusses meals and lodging furnished by the employer (CCH ¶7222.01). Within this paragraph are likely to be references to other primary authorities.

[2] At this juncture, the researcher should consult a citator to determine whether *Kowalski* is still "good law," and to locate other authorities that cite *Kowalski*.

ensue. Thus, in our case, the conditions of furnishing "meals," "on the business premises of the employer," and "for the convenience of the employer" must be satisfied for the value of the "meals" to be excluded from the employee's income.

When analyzing the facts in terms of case law, the researcher should always draw an *analogy* between case facts and client facts. Likewise, he or she should always draw a *distinction* between case facts and client facts. Remember, under the rule of precedent, a court deciding the client's case will be bound by the precedent of cases involving *similar* facts and issues. By the same token, it will *not* be bound by the precedent of cases involving *dissimilar* facts and issues.

The most useful vehicle for analyzing client facts is the memorandum-to-the-file (see page A-6). The purpose of this document is threefold: first, it assists the researcher in recalling transactions long transpired; second, it apprises colleagues and supervisors of the nature of one's research; third, it provides "substantial authority" for the tax treatment of a particular item. Let us analyze the facts of our case by way of a memorandum-to-the-file. Notice the format of this document; it generally tracks the steps in the research process itself.

Communicate Conclusions and Recommendations to Others For three practical reasons, research results always should be communicated to the client *in writing*. First, a written communication can be made after extensive revisions. An oral communication cannot. Second, in a written communication, the researcher can delve into the intricacies of tax law. Often, in an oral communication, he or she cannot. Third, a written communication reinforces an oral understanding. Alternatively, it brings to light an oral misunderstanding.

The written communication usually takes the form of a client letter (see page A-7). The purpose of this letter is two-fold: first, it apprises the client of the results of one's research; second, it recommends to the client a course of action based on these results. A sample client letter is presented below. Notice the organization of this document; it is similar to that of the memorandum-to-the-file.

Memorandum-to-the-File

Date: December 9, 19X1
From: Rosina Havacek
Re: The taxability of meal vouchers furnished by Mercy Hospital to its medical staff.

Facts
[*State only the facts that are relevant to the Issue(s) and necessary for the Analysis.*] Our client, Mercy Hospital ("Mercy"), provides meal vouchers to its medical employees to enable them to remain on emergency call. The vouchers are redeemable at Mercy's onsite cafeteria and at MacDougal's, a privately owned sandwich shop. MacDougal's rents business space from the hospital. Although Mercy does not require its employees to remain on or near it premises during their meal hours, the employees generally do. Elizabeth Fegali, Mercy's Chief Administrator, has asked us to research whether the value of the meal vouchers is taxable to the employees.

Issues
[*Identify the issue(s) raised by the Facts. Be specific.*] The taxability of the meal vouchers depends on three issues: first, whether the meals are furnished "for the convenience of the employer"; second, whether they are furnished "on the business premises of the employer"; and third, whether the vouchers are equivalent to cash.

Applicable Law
[*Discuss those legal principles that both strengthen and weaken the client's case. Because the primary authority for tax law is the IRC, begin with the IRC.*] IRC Sec. 119 provides that the value of meals is excludible from an employee's income if the meals are furnished for the convenience of, and on the business premises of the employer. [*Discuss how administrative and/or judicial authorities expound on statutory terms.*] Under Reg. Sec. 1.119-1, a meal is furnished "for the convenience of the employer" if it is furnished for a "substantial noncompensatory business reason." A "substantial noncompensatory business reason" includes the need to have the employee available for emergency calls during his or her meal period. Under IRC Sec. 119(b)(4), if more than half the employees satisfy the "for the convenience of hte employer" test, all employees will be regarded as satisfying the test. Regulation Sec. 1.119-1 defines "business premises of the employer" as the place of employment of the employee.

[*When discussing court cases, present case facts in such a way as to enable the reader to draw an analogy with client facts.*] A Supreme Court case, *Kowalski v. CIR*, 434 U.S. 77, 77-2 USTC ¶9748, discusses what constitutes "meals" for purposes of IRC Sec. 119. In *Kowalski*, the State of New Jersey furnished cash meal allowances to its state troopers to enable them to eat while on duty. It did not require the troopers to use the allowances exclusively for meals. Nor did it require them to consume their meals on its business premises. One trooper, R.J. Kowalski, excluded the value of his allowances from his income. The IRS disputed this treatment, and Kowalski took the IRS to Court. In Court, Kowalski argued that the allowances were excludible because they were furnished "for the convenience of the employer." The IRS contended that the allowances were taxable because they amounted to compensation. The U.S. Supreme Court took up the case and decided for the IRS. The Court held that the IRC Sec. 119 income exclusion does not apply to payments in cash.

Analysis
[*The Analysis should (a) apply Applicable Law to the Facts and (b) address the Issue(s). In this section, every proposition should be supported by either authority, logic, or plausible assumptions.*]

Issue 1: The meals provided by Mercy seem to be furnished "for the convenience of the employer." They are furnished to have employees available for emergency call during their meal breaks. This is a "substantial noncompensatory reason" within the meaning of Reg. Sec. 1.119-1.

Issue 2: Although the hospital cafeteria appears to be the "business premises of the employer," MacDougal's does not appear to be. The hospital is the place of employment of the medical employees. MacDougal's is not.

Issue 3: [*In applying case law to the Facts, indicate how case facts are similar to/dissimilar from client facts. If the analysis does not support a "yes-no" answer, do not give one.*] Based on the foregoing authorities, it is unclear whether the vouchers are equivalent to cash. On the one hand, they are redeemable only in meals. Thus, they resemble meals-in-kind. On the other hand, they are redeemable at more than one institution. Thus, they resemble cash. Nor is it clear whether a court deciding this case would reach the same conclusion as the Supreme Court did in *Kowalski*. In the latter case, the State of New Jersey provided its meal allowances in the form of cash. It did not require its employees to use the allowances exclusively for meals. Nor did it require them to consume their meals on its business premises. In our case, Mercy provides its meal allowances in the form of vouchers. Thus, it indirectly requires its employees to use the allowances exclusively for meals. On the other hand, it does not require them to consume their meals on its business premises.

Conclusion
[*The conclusion should (a) logically flow from the Analysis, and (b) address the Issue(s).*] Although it appears that the meals acquired by voucher in the hospital cafeteria are furnished "for the convenience of the employer" and "on the business premises of the employer," it is unclear whether the vouchers are equivalent to cash. If they *are* equivalent to cash, *or* if they are redeemed at MacDougal's, their value is likely to be taxable to the employees. On the other hand, if they are not equivalent to cash, *and* they are redeemed only in the hospital cafeteria, their value is likely to be excludible.

Professional Accounting Associates
2701 First City Plaza
Suite 905
Dallas, Texas 75019

December 12, 19X1

Elizabeth Fegali, Chief Administrator
Mercy Hospital
22650 West Haven Drive
Arlington, Texas 75527

Dear Ms. Fegali:

[*Introduction. Set a cordial tone.*] It was great to see you at last Thursday's football game. If not for that last minute fumble, the Longhorns might have taken the Big 12 Conference championship!

[*Issue/Purpose.*] In our meeting of December 6, you asked us to research whether the value of the meal vouchers that Mercy provides to its medical employees is taxable to the employees. [*Short Answer.*] I regret to inform you that if the vouchers are redeemed at MacDougal's, their value is likely to be taxable to the employees. On the other hand, if the vouchers are redeemed in the hospital cafeteria, their value is likely to be excludible from the employee's income. [*The remainder of the letter should elaborate, support, and qualify this answer.*]

[*Steps Taken in Deriving Conclusion.*] In reaching this conclusion, we consulted relevant provisions of the Internal Revenue Code ("IRC"), applicable Treasury Regulations under the IRC, and a pertinent Supreme Court case. In addition, we reviewed the documents on employee benefits that you submitted to us at our earlier meeting.

[*Facts. State only the facts that are relevant to the Issue and necessary for the Analysis.*] The facts as we understand them are as follows: Mercy provides meal vouchers to its medical employees to enable them to eat while on emergency call. The vouchers are redeemable either in the hospital cafeteria or at MacDougal's. MacDougal's is a privately owned institution that rents business space from the hospital. Although Mercy's employees are not required to remain on or near the premises during their meal hours, they generally do.

Applicable Law. State, do not interpret.] Under the IRC, the value of meals is excludible from an employee's income if two conditions are met: first, the meals are furnished "for the convenience of the employer" and second, they are provided "on the business premises of the employer." Although the IRC does not explain what is meant by "for the convenience of the employer," "business premises of the employer," and "meals," other authorities do. Specifically, the Treasury Regulations define "business premises of the employer" to be the place of employment of the employees. The regulations state that providing meals during work hours to have an employee available for emergency calls is "for the convenience of the employer." Moreover, under the IRC, if more than half the employees satisfy the "for the convenience of the employer" test, all the employees will be regarded as satisfying the test. The Supreme Court has interpreted "meals" to mean food-in-kind. The Court has held that cash allowances do not qualify as "meals."

[*Analysis. Express the generalities of Applicable Law in terms of the specifics of the Facts.*] Clearly, the meals furnished by Mercy are "for the convenience of the employer." They are furnished during the employees' work hours to have the employees available for emergency call. Although the meals provided in the hospital cafeteria appear to be furnished "on the business premises of the employer," the meals provided at MacDougal's do not appear to be. The hospital is the place of employment of the medical employees. MacDougal's is not. What is unclear is whether the meal vouchers are equivalent to food-in-kind. On the one hand, they are redeemable at more than one institution and thus resemble cash allowances. On the other hand, they are redeemable only in meals and thus resemble food-in-kind.

[*Conclusion/Recommendation.*] Because of this lack of clarity, we suggest that you modify your employee benefits plan to allow for the provision of meals-in-kind exclusively in the hospital cafeteria. In this way, you will dispel any doubt that Mercy is furnishing "meals," "for the convenience of the employer," "on the premises of the employer."

[*Closing/Follow Up.*] Please call me at 475-2020 if you have any questions concerning this conclusion. May I suggest that we meet next week to discuss the possibility of revising your employee benefits plan.

Very truly yours,
Professional Accounting Associates

By: Rosina Havacek, Junior Associate

APPENDIX B

TAX FORMS

Form #	Form Title	Page No.
1040	U.S. Individual Income Tax Return	I2-8
1040	Schedule A—Itemized Deductions	I7-35
1040	Schedule B—Interest and Dividend Income	I3-31
1040	Schedule C—Profit or Loss from Business	I10-25
1040	Schedule D—Capital Gains and Losses	I5-34
1040	Schedule E—Supplemental Income and Loss	B-2
1040	Schedule F—Profit or Loss From Farming	B-4
1040	Schedule SE—Social Security Self-Employment Tax	B-6
1065	Facts for General Partnership	B-8
1116	Computation of Foreign Tax Credit	B-9
1120	Facts for C Corporation	B-11
1120S	Facts for S Corporation	B-13
2106	Employee Business Expenses	I9-45
2120	Multiple Support Declaration	I2-15
2210	Underpayment of Estimated Tax by Individuals, Estates, and Trusts	B-15
2441	Child and Dependent Care Expenses	B-18
3903	Moving Expenses	B-20
4562	Depreciation and Amortization	I10-23
4684	Casualties and Thefts	I13-28
4797	Sales of Business Property	I13-26
6251	Alternative Minimum Tax—Individuals	B-22
6252	Installment Sale Income	I11-29
8283	Noncash Charitable Contributions	B-24
8582	Passive Activity Loss Limitations	B-26
8615	Tax For Children Under Age 14 Who Have Investment Income of More Than $1,400	B-29

Note: Because of the availability of tax forms from many sources, only a limited number of forms are reprinted in this textbook. All federal forms are available from the Internal Revenue Service, either in paper form or from the IRS Web site, http://www.irs.ustreas.gov

SCHEDULE E
(Form 1040)

Department of the Treasury
Internal Revenue Service (99)

Supplemental Income and Loss
(From rental real estate, royalties, partnerships, S corporations, estates, trusts, REMICs, etc.)
▶ Attach to Form 1040 or Form 1041. ▶ See Instructions for Schedule E (Form 1040).

OMB No. 1545-0074

2000

Attachment Sequence No. **13**

Name(s) shown on return | Your social security number

Part I Income or Loss From Rental Real Estate and Royalties **Note.** Report income and expenses from your business of renting personal property on **Schedule C** or **C-EZ** (see page E-1). Report farm rental income or loss from **Form 4835** on page 2, line 39.

1 Show the kind and location of each **rental real estate property:**
   A _____
   B _____
   C _____

2 For each rental real estate property listed on line 1, did you or your family use it during the tax year for personal purposes for more than the greater of:
   • 14 days **or**
   • 10% of the total days rented at fair rental value?
   (See page E-1.)

	Yes	No
A		
B		
C		

		Properties			Totals
Income:		A	B	C	(Add columns A, B, and C.)
3 Rents received	3				3
4 Royalties received	4				4
Expenses:					
5 Advertising	5				
6 Auto and travel (see page E-2)	6				
7 Cleaning and maintenance	7				
8 Commissions	8				
9 Insurance	9				
10 Legal and other professional fees	10				
11 Management fees	11				
12 Mortgage interest paid to banks, etc. (see page E-2)	12				12
13 Other interest	13				
14 Repairs	14				
15 Supplies	15				
16 Taxes	16				
17 Utilities	17				
18 Other (list) ▶ _____	18				
19 Add lines 5 through 18	19				19
20 Depreciation expense or depletion (see page E-3)	20				20
21 Total expenses. Add lines 19 and 20	21				
22 Income or (loss) from rental real estate or royalty properties. Subtract line 21 from line 3 (rents) or line 4 (royalties). If the result is a (loss), see page E-3 to find out if you must file **Form 6198**	22				
23 Deductible rental real estate loss. **Caution.** Your rental real estate loss on line 22 may be limited. See page E-3 to find out if you must file **Form 8582**. Real estate professionals must complete line 42 on page 2	23 (	) (	) (	)	
24 **Income.** Add positive amounts shown on line 22. **Do not** include any losses					24
25 **Losses.** Add royalty losses from line 22 and rental real estate losses from line 23. Enter total losses here					25 ( )
26 Total rental real estate and royalty income or (loss). Combine lines 24 and 25. Enter the result here. If Parts II, III, IV, and line 39 on page 2 do not apply to you, also enter this amount on Form 1040, line 17. Otherwise, include this amount in the total on line 40 on page 2					26

Schedule E (Form 1040) 2000   Attachment Sequence No. **13**   Page **2**

Name(s) shown on return. Do not enter name and social security number if shown on other side. | **Your social security number**

Note. If you report amounts from farming or fishing on Schedule E, you must enter your gross income from those activities on line 41 below. Real estate professionals must complete line 42 below.

Part II — Income or Loss From Partnerships and S Corporations
Note. If you report a loss from an at-risk activity, you **must** check either column **(e)** or **(f)** on line 27 to describe your investment in the activity. See page E-5. If you check column **(f)**, you must attach **Form 6198**.

27	(a) Name	(b) Enter P for partnership; S for S corporation	(c) Check if foreign partnership	(d) Employer identification number	Investment At Risk? (e) All is at risk	(f) Some is not at risk
A						
B						
C						
D						
E						

	Passive Income and Loss		Nonpassive Income and Loss		
	(g) Passive loss allowed (attach Form 8582 if required)	(h) Passive income from Schedule K-1	(i) Nonpassive loss from Schedule K-1	(j) Section 179 expense deduction from Form 4562	(k) Nonpassive income from Schedule K-1
A					
B					
C					
D					
E					

28a Totals
 b Totals

29 Add columns (h) and (k) of line 28a **29**
30 Add columns (g), (i), and (j) of line 28b . . . . **30** ( )
31 Total partnership and S corporation income or (loss). Combine lines 29 and 30. Enter the result here and include in the total on line 40 below **31**

Part III — Income or Loss From Estates and Trusts

32	(a) Name	(b) Employer identification number
A		
B		

	Passive Income and Loss		Nonpassive Income and Loss	
	(c) Passive deduction or loss allowed (attach Form 8582 if required)	(d) Passive income from Schedule K-1	(e) Deduction or loss from Schedule K-1	(f) Other income from Schedule K-1
A				
B				

33a Totals
 b Totals

34 Add columns (d) and (f) of line 33a **34**
35 Add columns (c) and (e) of line 33b . . . . **35** ( )
36 Total estate and trust income or (loss). Combine lines 34 and 35. Enter the result here and include in the total on line 40 below **36**

Part IV — Income or Loss From Real Estate Mortgage Investment Conduits (REMICs)—Residual Holder

37	(a) Name	(b) Employer identification number	(c) Excess inclusion from Schedules Q, line 2c (see page E-6)	(d) Taxable income (net loss) from Schedules Q, line 1b	(e) Income from Schedules Q, line 3b

38 Combine columns (d) and (e) only. Enter the result here and include in the total on line 40 below **38**

Part V — Summary

39 Net farm rental income or (loss) from **Form 4835**. Also, complete line 41 below . . . **39**
40 **Total** income or (loss). Combine lines 26, 31, 36, 38, and 39. Enter the result here and on Form 1040, line 17 ▶ **40**

41 **Reconciliation of Farming and Fishing Income.** Enter your **gross** farming and fishing income reported on Form 4835, line 7; Schedule K-1 (Form 1065), line 15b; Schedule K-1 (Form 1120S), line 23; and Schedule K-1 (Form 1041), line 14 (see page E-6) . . . **41**

42 **Reconciliation for Real Estate Professionals.** If you were a real estate professional (see page E-4), enter the net income or (loss) you reported anywhere on Form 1040 from all rental real estate activities in which you materially participated under the passive activity loss rules . . **42**

Schedule E (Form 1040) 2000

B-4 Individuals ▼ **Appendix B**

SCHEDULE F (Form 1040) Department of the Treasury Internal Revenue Service (99)	**Profit or Loss From Farming** ▶ Attach to Form 1040, Form 1041, Form 1065, or Form 1065-B. ▶ See Instructions for Schedule F (Form 1040).	OMB No. 1545-0074 **2000** Attachment Sequence No. **14**

Name of proprietor | Social security number (SSN)

A Principal product. Describe in one or two words your principal crop or activity for the current tax year. | **B** Enter code from Part IV ▶

C Accounting method: (1) ☐ Cash (2) ☐ Accrual | **D** Employer ID number (EIN), if any

E Did you "materially participate" in the operation of this business during 2000? If "No," see page F-2 for limit on passive losses. ☐ Yes ☐ No

Part I Farm Income—Cash Method. Complete Parts I and II (Accrual method taxpayers complete Parts II and III, and line 11 of Part I.)
Do not include sales of livestock held for draft, breeding, sport, or dairy purposes; report these sales on Form 4797.

1	Sales of livestock and other items you bought for resale		1	
2	Cost or other basis of livestock and other items reported on line 1		2	
3	Subtract line 2 from line 1			3
4	Sales of livestock, produce, grains, and other products you raised			4
5a	Total cooperative distributions (Form(s) 1099-PATR)	5a	5b Taxable amount	5b
6a	Agricultural program payments (see page F-2)	6a	6b Taxable amount	6b
7	Commodity Credit Corporation (CCC) loans (see page F-3):			
a	CCC loans reported under election			7a
b	CCC loans forfeited	7b	7c Taxable amount	7c
8	Crop insurance proceeds and certain disaster payments (see page F-3):			
a	Amount received in 2000	8a	8b Taxable amount	8b
c	If election to defer to 2001 is attached, check here ▶ ☐		8d Amount deferred from 1999	8d
9	Custom hire (machine work) income			9
10	Other income, including Federal and state gasoline or fuel tax credit or refund (see page F-3)			10
11	**Gross income.** Add amounts in the right column for lines 3 through 10. If accrual method taxpayer, enter the amount from page 2, line 51 ▶			11

Part II Farm Expenses—Cash and Accrual Method. Do not include personal or living expenses such as taxes, insurance, repairs, etc., on your home.

12	Car and truck expenses (see page F-4—also attach **Form 4562**)	12		25	Pension and profit-sharing plans	25	
13	Chemicals	13		26	Rent or lease (see page F-5):		
14	Conservation expenses (see page F-4)	14		a	Vehicles, machinery, and equipment	26a	
15	Custom hire (machine work)	15		b	Other (land, animals, etc.)	26b	
16	Depreciation and section 179 expense deduction not claimed elsewhere (see page F-4)	16		27	Repairs and maintenance	27	
				28	Seeds and plants purchased	28	
				29	Storage and warehousing	29	
17	Employee benefit programs other than on line 25	17		30	Supplies purchased	30	
				31	Taxes	31	
18	Feed purchased	18		32	Utilities	32	
19	Fertilizers and lime	19		33	Veterinary, breeding, and medicine	33	
20	Freight and trucking	20		34	Other expenses (specify):		
21	Gasoline, fuel, and oil	21		a		34a	
22	Insurance (other than health)	22		b		34b	
23	Interest:			c		34c	
a	Mortgage (paid to banks, etc.)	23a		d		34d	
b	Other	23b		e		34e	
24	Labor hired (less employment credits)	24		f		34f	

35	**Total expenses.** Add lines 12 through 34f ▶	35	
36	**Net farm profit or (loss).** Subtract line 35 from line 11. If a profit, enter on **Form 1040, line 18,** and also on **Schedule SE, line 1.** If a loss, you **must** go on to line 37 (estates, trusts, and partnerships, see page F-6)	36	
37	If you have a loss, you **must** check the box that describes your investment in this activity (see page F-6). • If you checked 37a, enter the loss on **Form 1040, line 18,** and also on **Schedule SE, line 1.** • If you checked 37b, you **must** attach **Form 6198.**	37a ☐ All investment is at risk. 37b ☐ Some investment is not at risk.	

For Paperwork Reduction Act Notice, see Form 1040 instructions. | Cat. No. 11346H | Schedule F (Form 1040) 2000

Schedule F (Form 1040) 2000

Part III — Farm Income—Accrual Method (see page F-6)

Do not include sales of livestock held for draft, breeding, sport, or dairy purposes; report these sales on Form 4797 and do not include this livestock on line 46 below.

38	Sales of livestock, produce, grains, and other products during the year	38
39a	Total cooperative distributions (Form(s) 1099-PATR)	39a
	39b Taxable amount	39b
40a	Agricultural program payments	40a
	40b Taxable amount	40b
41	Commodity Credit Corporation (CCC) loans:	
a	CCC loans reported under election	41a
b	CCC loans forfeited	41b
	41c Taxable amount	41c
42	Crop insurance proceeds	42
43	Custom hire (machine work) income	43
44	Other income, including Federal and state gasoline or fuel tax credit or refund	44
45	Add amounts in the right column for lines 38 through 44	45
46	Inventory of livestock, produce, grains, and other products at beginning of the year	46
47	Cost of livestock, produce, grains, and other products purchased during the year	47
48	Add lines 46 and 47	48
49	Inventory of livestock, produce, grains, and other products at end of year	49
50	Cost of livestock, produce, grains, and other products sold. Subtract line 49 from line 48*	50
51	Gross income. Subtract line 50 from line 45. Enter the result here and on page 1, line 11 ▶	51

*If you use the unit-livestock-price method or the farm-price method of valuing inventory and the amount on line 49 is larger than the amount on line 48, subtract line 48 from line 49. Enter the result on line 50. Add lines 45 and 50. Enter the total on line 51.

Part IV — Principal Agricultural Activity Codes

Caution. File **Schedule C** (Form 1040), Profit or Loss From Business, or **Schedule C-EZ** (Form 1040), Net Profit From Business, instead of Schedule F if:

- Your principal source of income is from providing agricultural services such as soil preparation, veterinary, farm labor, horticultural, or management for a fee or on a contract basis or
- You are engaged in the business of breeding, raising, and caring for dogs, cats, or other pet animals.

These codes for the Principal Agricultural Activity classify farms by the type of activity they are engaged in to facilitate the administration of the Internal Revenue Code. These six-digit codes are based on the North American Industry Classification System (NAICS).

Select one of the following codes and enter the six-digit number on page 1, line B.

Crop Production

111100	Oilseed and grain farming
111210	Vegetable and melon farming
111300	Fruit and tree nut farming
111400	Greenhouse, nursery, and floriculture production
111900	Other crop farming

Animal Production

112111	Beef cattle ranching and farming
112112	Cattle feedlots
112120	Dairy cattle and milk production
112210	Hog and pig farming
112300	Poultry and egg production
112400	Sheep and goat farming
112510	Animal aquaculture
112900	Other animal production

Forestry and Logging

113000	Forestry and logging (including forest nurseries and timber tracts)

Schedule F (Form 1040) 2000

SCHEDULE SE	Self-Employment Tax	OMB No. 1545-0074
(Form 1040)	▶ See Instructions for Schedule SE (Form 1040).	2000
Department of the Treasury Internal Revenue Service (99)	▶ Attach to Form 1040.	Attachment Sequence No. 17

Name of person with **self-employment** income (as shown on Form 1040)	Social security number of person with **self-employment** income ▶

Who Must File Schedule SE
You must file Schedule SE if:
- You had net earnings from self-employment from **other than** church employee income (line 4 of Short Schedule SE or line 4c of Long Schedule SE) of $400 or more **or**
- You had church employee income of $108.28 or more. Income from services you performed as a minister or a member of a religious order **is not** church employee income. See page SE-1.

Note. Even if you had a loss or a small amount of income from self-employment, it may be to your benefit to file Schedule SE and use either "optional method" in Part II of Long Schedule SE. See page SE-3.

Exception. If your only self-employment income was from earnings as a minister, member of a religious order, or Christian Science practitioner **and** you filed Form 4361 and received IRS approval not to be taxed on those earnings, **do not** file Schedule SE. Instead, write "Exempt–Form 4361" on Form 1040, line 52.

May I Use Short Schedule SE or Must I Use Long Schedule SE?

Did You Receive Wages or Tips in 2000?

- **No** → Are you a minister, member of a religious order, or Christian Science practitioner who received IRS approval **not** to be taxed on earnings from these sources, **but** you owe self-employment tax on other earnings?
  - **Yes** → You Must Use Long Schedule SE on the Back
  - **No** → Are you using one of the optional methods to figure your net earnings (see page SE-3)?
    - **Yes** → You Must Use Long Schedule SE on the Back
    - **No** → Did you receive church employee income reported on Form W-2 of $108.28 or more?
      - **Yes** → You Must Use Long Schedule SE on the Back
      - **No** → You May Use Short Schedule SE Below

- **Yes** → Was the total of your wages and tips subject to social security or railroad retirement tax **plus** your net earnings from self-employment more than $76,200?
  - **Yes** → You Must Use Long Schedule SE on the Back
  - **No** → Did you receive tips subject to social security or Medicare tax that you **did not** report to your employer?
    - **Yes** → You Must Use Long Schedule SE on the Back
    - **No** → You May Use Short Schedule SE Below

Section A—Short Schedule SE. Caution: *Read above to see if you can use Short Schedule SE.*

1	Net farm profit or (loss) from Schedule F, line 36, and farm partnerships, Schedule K-1 (Form 1065), line 15a	1
2	Net profit or (loss) from Schedule C, line 31; Schedule C-EZ, line 3; Schedule K-1 (Form 1065), line 15a (other than farming); and Schedule K-1 (Form 1065-B), box 9. Ministers and members of religious orders, see page SE-1 for amounts to report on this line. See page SE-2 for other income to report	2
3	Combine lines 1 and 2	3
4	**Net earnings from self-employment.** Multiply line 3 by 92.35% (.9235). If less than $400, **do not** file this schedule; you do not owe self-employment tax ▶	4
5	**Self-employment tax.** If the amount on line 4 is: • $76,200 or less, multiply line 4 by 15.3% (.153). Enter the result here and on **Form 1040, line 52.** • More than $76,200, multiply line 4 by 2.9% (.029). Then, add $9,448.80 to the result. Enter the total here and on **Form 1040, line 52.**	5
6	**Deduction for one-half of self-employment tax.** Multiply line 5 by 50% (.5). Enter the result here and on **Form 1040, line 27**	6

For Paperwork Reduction Act Notice, see Form 1040 instructions.   Cat. No. 11358Z   Schedule SE (Form 1040) 2000

Tax Forms ▼ **Individuals B-7**

Schedule SE (Form 1040) 2000 — Attachment Sequence No. **17** — Page **2**

Name of person with **self-employment** income (as shown on Form 1040) | Social security number of person with **self-employment** income ▶

Section B—Long Schedule SE

Part I Self-Employment Tax

Note. If your only income subject to self-employment tax is **church employee income,** skip lines 1 through 4b. Enter -0- on line 4c and go to line 5a. Income from services you performed as a minister or a member of a religious order **is not** church employee income. See page SE-1.

A If you are a minister, member of a religious order, or Christian Science practitioner **and** you filed Form 4361, but you had $400 or more of **other** net earnings from self-employment, check here and continue with Part I . . . ▶ ☐

1	Net farm profit or (loss) from Schedule F, line 36, and farm partnerships, Schedule K-1 (Form 1065), line 15a. **Note.** Skip this line if you use the farm optional method. See page SE-3	1	
2	Net profit or (loss) from Schedule C, line 31; Schedule C-EZ, line 3; Schedule K-1 (Form 1065), line 15a (other than farming); and Schedule K-1 (Form 1065-B), box 9. Ministers and members of religious orders, see page SE-1 for amounts to report on this line. See page SE-2 for other income to report. **Note.** Skip this line if you use the nonfarm optional method. See page SE-3	2	
3	Combine lines 1 and 2	3	
4a	If line 3 is more than zero, multiply line 3 by 92.35% (.9235). Otherwise, enter amount from line 3	4a	
b	If you elect one or both of the optional methods, enter the total of lines 15 and 17 here	4b	
c	Combine lines 4a and 4b. If less than $400, **do not** file this schedule; you do not owe self-employment tax. **Exception.** If less than $400 and you had **church employee income,** enter -0- and continue ▶	4c	
5a	Enter your **church employee income** from Form W-2. **Caution:** See page SE-1 for definition of church employee income . . 5a		
b	Multiply line 5a by 92.35% (.9235). If less than $100, enter -0-	5b	
6	**Net earnings from self-employment.** Add lines 4c and 5b	6	
7	Maximum amount of combined wages and self-employment earnings subject to social security tax or the 6.2% portion of the 7.65% railroad retirement (tier 1) tax for 2000	7	76,200 00
8a	Total social security wages and tips (total of boxes 3 and 7 on Form(s) W-2) and railroad retirement (tier 1) compensation . . 8a		
b	Unreported tips subject to social security tax (from Form 4137, line 9) 8b		
c	Add lines 8a and 8b	8c	
9	Subtract line 8c from line 7. If zero or less, enter -0- here and on line 10 and go to line 11 ▶	9	
10	Multiply the **smaller** of line 6 or line 9 by 12.4% (.124)	10	
11	Multiply line 6 by 2.9% (.029)	11	
12	**Self-employment tax.** Add lines 10 and 11. Enter here and on **Form 1040, line 52**	12	
13	**Deduction for one-half of self-employment tax.** Multiply line 12 by 50% (.5). Enter the result here and on **Form 1040, line 27** . . 13		

Part II Optional Methods To Figure Net Earnings (See page SE-3.)

Farm Optional Method. You may use this method **only** if:
- Your gross farm income[1] was not more than $2,400 **or**
- Your net farm profits[2] were less than $1,733.

14	Maximum income for optional methods	14	1,600 00
15	Enter the **smaller** of: two-thirds (²⁄₃) of gross farm income[1] (not less than zero) or $1,600. Also include this amount on line 4b above	15	

Nonfarm Optional Method. You may use this method **only** if:
- Your net nonfarm profits[3] were less than $1,733 and also less than 72.189% of your gross nonfarm income[4] **and**
- You had net earnings from self-employment of at least $400 in 2 of the prior 3 years.

Caution: *You may use this method no more than five times.*

16	Subtract line 15 from line 14	16	
17	Enter the **smaller** of: two-thirds (²⁄₃) of gross nonfarm income[4] (not less than zero) **or** the amount on line 16. Also include this amount on line 4b above	17	

[1] From Sch. F, line 11, and Sch. K-1 (Form 1065), line 15b.
[2] From Sch. F, line 36, and Sch. K-1 (Form 1065), line 15a.
[3] From Sch. C, line 31; Sch. C-EZ, line 3; Sch. K-1 (Form 1065), line 15a; and Sch. K-1 (Form 1065-B), box 9.
[4] From Sch. C, line 7; Sch. C-EZ, line 1; Sch. K-1 (Form 1065), line 15c; and Sch. K-1 (Form 1065-B), box 9.

Schedule SE (Form 1040) 2000

Facts for General Partnership (Form 1065)

The same basic facts presented for the Andrew Lawrence proprietorship are used for the partnership except for the following:

1. Johns and Lawrence is instead a general partnership. Andrew Lawrence and Stephen Johns are both general partners and have equal capital and profits interests. The partnership was created on June 1, 1994. Johns and Lawrence each exchanged their $100,000 of property for a 50% interest in capital and a 50% interest in profits.

2. The book income for Johns and Lawrence is presented in the attached worksheet, which reconciles book income and partnership taxable income.

3. The $18,000 salaries paid to each partner are stipulated in the partnership agreement and are treated as guaranteed payments.

4. The partnership pays federal and state employment taxes on the wages paid to employees other than the partners Johns and Lawrence. The employment tax expense is $52,000 × 0.16 = $8,320. The guaranteed payments made to Johns and Lawrence are treated as self-employment income by the two partners.

5. The partnership paid no estimated federal income taxes.

6. The $28,212 in withdrawals were paid equally to the two partners.

7. Other deductions include:

Travel	$ 4,000
Meals and entertainment	8,000
Minus: 50% disallowance	(4,000)
Office expenses	16,000
Transportation	10,400
General and administrative	3,000
Advertising	13,000
Miscellaneous*	850
Total	$51,250

    *$150 of the miscellaneous expenses are related to the production of the dividend income and are separately stated.

8. Reconciliation of net income for the C corporation and the partnership occurs as follows:

Net income for C corporation	$63,412
Plus: Federal income taxes	14,000
Employment tax adjustment ($14,480 − $8,320)	6,160
Net income for partnership	$83,572

9. Total paid-in capital and accumulated profits were divided equally between the two partners in accordance with the actual contributions and allocation of partnership profits in the partnership agreement. Actual business operations may provide for an unequal allocation.

10. The balance sheet for Johns and Lawrence is presented on page 4 of Form 1065.

Note: Form 1065 can be downloaded (in Adobe Acrobat) on the text Web site at www.prenhall.com/phtax.

Tax Forms ▼ **Individuals B-9**

Form **1116**
Department of the Treasury
Internal Revenue Service (99)

Foreign Tax Credit
(Individual, Estate, Trust, or Nonresident Alien Individual)
▶ Attach to Form 1040, 1040NR, 1041, or 990-T.
▶ See separate instructions.

OMB No. 1545-0121

2000

Attachment
Sequence No. **19**

Name | Identifying number as shown on page 1 of your tax return

Use a separate Form 1116 for each category of income listed below. See **Categories of Income** on page 3 of the instructions. Check only one box on each Form 1116. Report all amounts in U.S. dollars except where specified in Part II below.

- **a** ☐ Passive income
- **b** ☐ High withholding tax interest
- **c** ☐ Financial services income
- **d** ☐ Shipping income
- **e** ☐ Dividends from a DISC or former DISC
- **f** ☐ Certain distributions from a foreign sales corporation (FSC) or former FSC
- **g** ☐ Lump-sum distributions
- **h** ☐ Section 901(j) income
- **i** ☐ Certain income re-sourced by treaty
- **j** ☐ General limitation income

k Resident of (name of country) ▶

Note: *If you paid taxes to only one foreign country or U.S. possession, use column A in Part I and line A in Part II. If you paid taxes to **more than one** foreign country or U.S. possession, use a separate column and line for each country or possession.*

Part I — Taxable Income or Loss From Sources Outside the United States (for Category Checked Above)

	Foreign Country or U.S. Possession — A	B	C	Total (Add cols. A, B, and C.)
I Enter the name of the foreign country or U.S. possession ▶				
1 Gross income from sources within country shown above and of the type checked above. See page 7 of the instructions:				**1**
Deductions and losses (Caution: See pages 8 and 9 of the instructions):				
2 Expenses **definitely related** to the income on line 1 (attach statement)				
3 Pro rata share of other deductions **not definitely related:**				
a Certain itemized deductions or standard deduction. See instructions				
b Other deductions (attach statement)				
c Add lines 3a and 3b				
d Gross foreign source income. See instructions				
e Gross income from all sources. See instructions				
f Divide line 3d by line 3e. See instructions				
g Multiply line 3c by line 3f				
4 Pro rata share of interest expense. See instructions:				
a Home mortgage interest (use worksheet on page 9 of the instructions)				
b Other interest expense				
5 Losses from foreign sources				
6 Add lines 2, 3g, 4a, 4b, and 5				**6**
7 Subtract line 6 from line 1. Enter the result here and on line 14, page 2 ▶				**7**

Part II — Foreign Taxes Paid or Accrued (See page 9 of the instructions.)

Country	Credit is claimed for taxes (you must check one) **(m)** ☐ Paid **(n)** ☐ Accrued	Foreign taxes paid or accrued
		In foreign currency				In U.S. dollars			
	(o) Date paid or accrued	Taxes withheld at source on:			**(s)** Other foreign taxes paid or accrued	Taxes withheld at source on:			**(w)** Other foreign taxes paid or accrued	**(x)** Total foreign taxes paid or accrued (add cols. (t) through (w))
		(p) Dividends	**(q)** Rents and royalties	**(r)** Interest		**(t)** Dividends	**(u)** Rents and royalties	**(v)** Interest		
A										
B										
C										

8 Add lines A through C, column (x). Enter the total here and on line 9, page 2 ▶ **8**

For Paperwork Reduction Act Notice, see page 12 of the instructions. Cat. No. 11440U Form **1116** (2000)

Form 1116 (2000) Page 2

Part III Figuring the Credit

9. Enter the amount from line 8. These are your total foreign taxes paid or accrued for the category of income checked above Part I ... **9**

10. Carryback or carryover (attach detailed computation) ... **10**

11. Add lines 9 and 10 ... **11**

12. Reduction in foreign taxes. See page 10 of the instructions ... **12**

13. Subtract line 12 from line 11. This is the total amount of foreign taxes available for credit ... **13**

14. Enter the amount from line 7. This is your taxable income or (loss) from sources outside the United States (before adjustments) for the category of income checked above Part I. See page 10 of the instructions ... **14**

15. Adjustments to line 14. See page 10 of the instructions ... **15**

16. Combine the amounts on lines 14 and 15. This is your net foreign source taxable income. (If the result is zero or less, you have no foreign tax credit for the category of income you checked above Part I. Skip lines 17 through 21. However, if you are filing more than one Form 1116, you must complete line 19.) ... **16**

17. **Individuals:** Enter the amount from Form 1040, line 37. If you are a nonresident alien, enter the amount from Form 1040NR, line 36.
    Estates and trusts: Enter your taxable income without the deduction for your exemption ... **17**
    Caution: If you figured your tax using the special rates on capital gains, see page 12 of the instructions.

18. Divide line 16 by line 17. If line 16 is more than line 17, enter "1" ... **18**

19. **Individuals:** Enter the amount from Form 1040, line 40. If you are a nonresident alien, enter the amount from Form 1040NR, line 39.
    Estates and trusts: Enter the total of Form 1041, Schedule G, lines 1a and 1b, or the total of Form 990-T, lines 36 and 37 ... **19**

20. Multiply line 19 by line 18 (maximum amount of credit) ... **20**

21. Enter the **smaller** of line 13 or line 20. If this is the only Form 1116 you are filing, skip lines 22 through 30 and enter this amount on line 31. Otherwise, complete the appropriate line in Part IV. See page 12 of the instructions ▶ **21**

Part IV Summary of Credits From Separate Parts III (See page 12 of the instructions.)

22. Credit for taxes on passive income ... **22**

23. Credit for taxes on high withholding tax interest ... **23**

24. Credit for taxes on financial services income ... **24**

25. Credit for taxes on shipping income ... **25**

26. Credit for taxes on dividends from a DISC or former DISC and certain distributions from a FSC or former FSC ... **26**

27. Credit for taxes on lump-sum distributions ... **27**

28. Credit for taxes on certain income re-sourced by treaty ... **28**

29. Credit for taxes on general limitation income ... **29**

30. Add lines 22 through 29 ... **30**

31. Enter the **smaller** of line 19 or line 30 ... **31**

32. Reduction of credit for international boycott operations. See instructions for line 12 on page 10 ... **32**

33. Subtract line 32 from line 31. This is your **foreign tax credit.** Enter here and on Form 1040, line 43; Form 1040NR, line 42; Form 1041, Schedule G, line 2a; or Form 990-T, line 40a ▶ **33**

Form **1116** (2000)

FACTS FOR C CORPORATION (FORM 1120)

The same basic facts presented for the Andrew Lawrence proprietorship are used for the C corporation except for the following:

1. Andrew Lawrence and Stephen Johns are the two 50% shareholders of Johns and Lawrence, Inc., a furniture manufacturer (Business Code 337000). Johns and Lawrence is located at 1234 University Ave., Gainesville, FL 32611. Its employer identification number is 76-3456789. The following information has been gathered about the 2000 corporate tax return:

   Compensation of Officers

Name	S.S. No.	Share	Title	Compensation
Stephen Johns	386-05-9174	1,000	President	$18,000
Andrew Lawrence	297-63-2110	1,000	V.P.	18,000
Total		2,000		$36,000

   All salaries owed to the shareholders were paid in 1999. None of the interest or rentals is paid to the shareholders.

2. The book income for the corporation is presented in the attached worksheet, which reconciles the corporation's book income and its taxable income.

3. The company was incorporated on June 1, 1994. Each of the two officers hold one-half the stock, which they acquired on that date for a total cash and property contribution of $200,000. No change in the stockholdings has occurred since incorporation. Johns and Lawrence each devote 100% of their time to the business. No expense allowances are provided. Properly substantiated expenses, however, are reimbursed. Both officers are U.S. citizens. Johns and Lawrence is not a member of a controlled group.

4. Addresses for the officers are: Andrew Lawrence, 436 N.W. 24th Ave., Gainesville, FL 32607; Stephen Johns, 1250 N.E. 12th Ave., Gainesville, FL 32601.

5. The corporation paid estimated taxes of $14,000 for tax year 2000.

6. Other deductions include:

Travel	$ 4,000
Meals and entertainment	8,000
Minus: 50% disallowance	(4,000)
Office expenses	16,000
Transportation	10,400
General and administrative	3,000
Miscellaneous	1,000
Total	$38,400

7. The charitable contributions deduction limitation is $7,694 (see footnote b in Reconciliation worksheet on next page). A carryover of $4,306 ($12,000 − $7,694) to 2001 and the four succeeding tax years is available.

8. The $28,212 of withdrawals made by the two owners are dividends coming from the corporation's earnings and profits. They are reported as gross income on the shareholders' individual tax returns.

   Note: Form 1120 can be downloaded (in Adobe Acrobat) on the text Web site at www.prenhall.com/phtax.

B-12 Individuals ▼ Appendix B

9. The beginning-of-the-year balance sheets for all entity forms are the same, which permits a direct comparison of the 2000 tax differences. Actually, the corporation would have reported tax differences in all prior years (1994 through 1999), which would have been included in the January 1, 2000 balance sheet. If these differences were so included, the direct comparisons would be much more difficult.

Johns and Lawrence, Inc. (C Corporation) Book Income to Taxable Income Reconciliation For Year Ending December 31, 2000

Account Name	Book Income Debit	Book Income Credit	Adjustments Debit	Adjustments Credit	Taxable Income Debit	Taxable Income Credit
Sales		869,658				869,658
Sales returns & allowances	29,242				29,242	
Cost of sales	540,204				540,204	
Dividends		1,000				1,000
Tax-exempt interest		18,000	18,000			0
Gain on stock sale		4,500				4,500
Worthless stock loss	2,100				2,100	
Officers' salaries	36,000				36,000	
Other salaries	52,000				52,000	
Rentals	36,000				36,000	
Bad debts	4,000				4,000	
Interest:						
Working capital loans	8,000				8,000	
Purchase tax-exempt bonds	2,000			2,000	0	
Employment taxes	14,480				14,480	
Taxes	1,520				1,520	
Repairs	4,800				4,800	
Depreciation(a)	12,000		476		12,476	
Charitable contributions(b)	12,000			4,306	7,694	
Travel	4,000				4,000	
Meals and entertainment(c)	8,000			4,000	4,000	
Office expenses	16,000				16,000	
Advertising	13,000				13,000	
Transportation expense	10,400				10,400	
General and administrative	3,000				3,000	
Pension plans	2,000				2,000	
Employee benefit programs	4,000				4,000	
Miscellaneous	1,000				1,000	
Federal income taxes	14,000			14,000	0	
Taxable income before spec. deds.			18,476	24,306	69,242	
Div. rec. ded. (10%-owned)(d)			700		700	
NOL deduction					0	
Net profit/Taxable income	63,412		5,130		68,542	
Total	893,158	893,158	24,306	24,306	875,158	875,158

(a) MACRS depreciation is $12,476 − $12,000 = $476
(b) Charitable contribution deduction limitation:

Gross income	$843,816
Minus: Deductions other than char. cont. & DRD	(766,880)
Charitable contribution base	$ 76,936
Times: 10%	× 0.10
Charitable contribution deduction	$ 7,694

(c) $8,000 × 0.50 disallowance rate = $4,000 disallowed expenses
(d) Dividends-received deduction: $1,000 × 0.70 = $700.

Facts for S Corporation (Form 1120S)

The same basic facts presented for the Andrew Lawrence proprietorship are used for the S corporation except for the following:

1. Johns and Lawrence, Inc. made an S corporation election on June 13, 1994. The election was effective for its initial tax year.

2. The book income for Johns and Lawrence is presented in the attached worksheet, which reconciles book income and S corporation taxable income.

3. The $18,000 salaries paid to each employee are subject to the same employment tax requirements as when paid by the C corporation. The total employment taxes ($14,480) are the same as for the C corporation.

4. The S corporation paid no estimated federal income taxes.

5. The $28,212 distribution was paid equally to the two shareholders. It is not included in the shareholder's gross income but instead reduces the basis for their stock.

6. Other deductions include:

Travel	$ 4,000
Meals and entertainment	8,000
Minus: 50% disallowance	(4,000)
Office expenses	16,000
Transportation	10,400
General and administrative	3,000
Miscellaneous*	850
Total	$38,250

    *$150 of the miscellaneous expenses are related to the production of the dividend income and are separately stated.

7. Reconciliation of net income for the C corporation and the S corporation occurs as follows:

Net income for C corporation	$63,412
Plus: Federal income taxes	14,000
Net income for S corporation	$77,412

    The S corporation return can be tied back to the partnership return. The only difference between the two returns is that the S corporation pays an additional $6,160 in employment taxes with respect to the shareholder-employee salaries, as compared to the partnership's guaranteed payments. This dollar difference is reflected in the net income numbers, the ordinary income numbers, capital account balances, and total asset amounts.

8. The balance sheet for Johns and Lawrence is presented on page 4 of Form 1120S.

    Note: Form 1120S can be downloaded (in Adobe Acrobat) on the text Web site at www.prenhall.com/phtax.

Johns and Lawrence, Inc. (S Corporation) Reconciliation of Book and Taxable Income For Year Ending December 31, 2000

Account Name	Book Income Debit	Book Income Credit	Adjustments Debit	Adjustments Credit	Taxable Income Debit	Taxable Income Credit	Form 1120S Schedule K Ordinary Income	Form 1120S Schedule K Separately Stated Items
Sales		869,658				869,658	869,658	
Sales returns & allowances	29,242				29,242		(29,242)	
Cost of sales	540,204				540,204		(540,204)	
Dividends		1,000				1,000		1,000
Tax-exempt interest		18,000	18,000			0		18,000
Gain on stock sale		4,500				4,500		4,500
Worthless stock loss	2,100				2,100			(2,100)
Officers salaries(a)	36,000				36,000		(36,000)	
Other salaries	52,000				52,000		(52,000)	
Rentals	36,000				36,000		(36,000)	
Bad debts	4,000				4,000		(4,000)	
Interest:								
Working capital loans	8,000				8,000		(8,000)	
Purchase tax-exempt bonds	2,000			2,000	0			(2,000)
Employment taxes	14,480				14,480		(14,480)	
Taxes	1,520				1,520		(1,520)	
Repairs	4,800				4,800		(4,800)	
Depreciation(b)	12,000		476		12,476		(12,476)	
Charitable contributions	12,000				12,000			(12,000)
Travel	4,000				4,000		(4,000)	
Meals and entertainment(c)	8,000			4,000	4,000		(4,000)	
Meals and ent. nondeductible								(4,000)
Office expenses	16,000				16,000		(16,000)	
Advertising	13,000				13,000		(13,000)	
Transportation expense	10,400				10,400		(10,400)	
General and administrative	3,000				3,000		(3,000)	
Pension plans(d)	2,000				2,000		(2,000)	
Employee benefit programs(e)	4,000				4,000		(4,000)	
Miscellaneous	1,000				1,000		(850)	(150)
Net profit/Taxable income	77,412			12,476	64,936			
Total	893,158	893,158	18,476	18,476	875,158	875,158	73,686	

(a) Salaries for the S corporation's shareholder-employees are deductible by the S corporation and are subject to the same employee taxes imposed on nonshareholder-employees.
(b) MACRS is depreciation is $12,476 − $12,000 = $476
(c) 50% of the meals and entertainment expense is not deductible for tax purposes but must be separately stated on the Schedules K and K-1.
(d) The pension plan expense is the same for book and tax purposes for this corporation. No pension expenses relate to pensions for the shareholder-employees.
(e) The employee benefit expense is the same for book and tax purposes for this corporation. None relates to shareholder-employee benefits.

Tax Forms ▼ Individuals B-15

Form **2210**
Department of the Treasury
Internal Revenue Service

**Underpayment of
Estimated Tax by Individuals, Estates, and Trusts**
▶ See separate instructions.
▶ Attach to Form 1040, 1040A, 1040NR, 1040NR-EZ, or 1041.

OMB No. 1545-0140

2000

Attachment Sequence No. **06**

Name(s) shown on tax return | Identifying number

Note: *In most cases, you **do not** need to file Form 2210. The IRS will figure any penalty you owe and send you a bill. File Form 2210 **only** if one or more boxes in Part I apply to you. If you do not need to file Form 2210, you still may use it to figure your penalty. Enter the amount from Part III, line 21, or Part IV, line 35, on the penalty line of your return, but **do not** attach Form 2210.*

Part I — Reasons for Filing
If 1a, 1b, or 1c below applies to you, you may be able to lower or eliminate your penalty. But you **must** check the boxes that apply and file Form 2210 with your tax return. If 1d below applies to you, check that box and file Form 2210 with your tax return.

1 Check whichever boxes apply (if none apply, see the **Note** above):

a ☐ You request a **waiver.** In certain circumstances, the IRS will waive all or part of the penalty. See **Waiver of Penalty** on page 1 of the instructions.

b ☐ You use the **annualized income installment method.** If your income varied during the year, this method may reduce the amount of one or more required installments. See page 5 of the instructions.

c ☐ You had Federal income tax withheld from wages and, for estimated tax purposes, you treat the withheld tax as paid on the dates it was actually withheld, instead of in equal amounts on the payment due dates. See the instructions for line 23 on page 3.

d ☐ Your required annual payment (line 14 below) is based on your 1999 tax and you filed or are filing a joint return for either 1999 or 2000 but not for both years.

Part II — Required Annual Payment

2 Enter your 2000 tax after credits (see page 2 of the instructions) 2
3 Other taxes (see page 2 of the instructions) 3
4 Add lines 2 and 3 4
5 Earned income credit 5
6 Additional child tax credit 6
7 Credit for Federal tax paid on fuels 7
8 Add lines 5, 6, and 7 8
9 Current year tax. Subtract line 8 from line 4 9
10 Multiply line 9 by 90% (.90) 10
11 Withholding taxes. **Do not** include any estimated tax payments on this line (see page 3 of the instructions) 11
12 Subtract line 11 from line 9. If less than $1,000, stop here; **do not** complete or file this form. You do not owe the penalty 12
13 Enter the tax shown on your 1999 tax return (108.6% of that amount if the adjusted gross income shown on that return is more than $150,000, or, if married filing separately for 2000, more than $75,000). **Caution:** *See page 3 of the instructions* 13
14 **Required annual payment.** Enter the **smaller** of line 10 or line 13 14
   Note: *If line 11 is equal to or more than line 14, stop here; you do not owe the penalty.* **Do not** *file Form 2210 unless you checked box 1d above.*

Part III — Short Method
(Caution: *See page 3 of the instructions to find out if you can use the short method. If you checked box **1b** or **1c** in Part I, skip this part and go to Part IV.*)

15 Enter the amount, if any, from line 11 above 15
16 Enter the total amount, if any, of estimated tax payments you made 16
17 Add lines 15 and 16 17
18 **Total underpayment for year.** Subtract line 17 from line 14. If zero or less, stop here; you do not owe the penalty. **Do not** file Form 2210 unless you checked box 1d above 18
19 Multiply line 18 by .05976 19
20 • If the amount on line 18 was paid **on or after** 4/15/01, enter -0-.
   • If the amount on line 18 was paid **before** 4/15/01, make the following computation to find the amount to enter on line 20.

   Amount on line 18 × Number of days paid before 4/15/01 × .00025 20

21 **Penalty.** Subtract line 20 from line 19. Enter the result here and on Form 1040, line 70; Form 1040A, line 45; Form 1040NR, line 69; Form 1040NR-EZ, line 27; or Form 1041, line 26 ▶ 21

For Paperwork Reduction Act Notice, see page 1 of separate instructions.   Cat. No. 11744P   Form **2210** (2000)

Form 2210 (2000) Page **2**

Part IV Regular Method (See page 3 of the instructions if you are filing Form 1040NR or 1040NR-EZ.)

Section A—Figure Your Underpayment

			Payment Due Dates			
			(a) 4/15/00	(b) 6/15/00	(c) 9/15/00	(d) 1/15/01
22	**Required installments.** If box 1b applies, enter the amounts from Schedule AI, line 26. Otherwise, enter 25% (.25) of line 14, Form 2210, in each column	22				
23	Estimated tax paid and tax withheld (see page 3 of the instructions). For column (a) only, also enter the amount from line 23 on line 27. If line 23 is equal to or more than line 22 for all payment periods, stop here; you do not owe the penalty. **Do not** file Form 2210 unless you checked a box in Part I	23				
	Complete lines 24 through 30 of one column before going to the next column.					
24	Enter amount, if any, from line 30 of previous column	24				
25	Add lines 23 and 24	25				
26	Add amounts on lines 28 and 29 of the previous column	26				
27	Subtract line 26 from line 25. If zero or less, enter -0-. For column (a) only, enter the amount from line 23	27				
28	If the amount on line 27 is zero, subtract line 25 from line 26. Otherwise, enter -0-	28				
29	**Underpayment.** If line 22 is equal to or more than line 27, subtract line 27 from line 22. Then go to line 24 of next column. Otherwise, go to line 30 ▶	29				
30	**Overpayment.** If line 27 is more than line 22, subtract line 22 from line 27. Then go to line 24 of next column	30				

Section B—Figure the Penalty (Complete lines 31 through 34 of one column before going to the next column.)

				4/15/00	6/15/00	9/15/00	
Rate Period 1	31	April 16, 2000—December 31, 2000 Number of days **from** the date shown above line 31 **to** the date the amount on line 29 was paid **or** 12/31/00, whichever is earlier	31	Days:	Days:	Days:	
	32	Underpayment on line 29 (see page 4 of the instructions) × (Number of days on line 31 / 366) × .09 ▶	32	$	$	$	
		January 1, 2001—April 15, 2001		12/31/00	12/31/00	12/31/00	1/15/01
Rate Period 2	33	Number of days **from** the date shown above line 33 **to** the date the amount on line 29 was paid **or** 4/15/01, whichever is earlier	33	Days:	Days:	Days:	Days:
	34	Underpayment on line 29 (see page 5 of the instructions) × (Number of days on line 33 / 365) × .09 ▶	34	$	$	$	$
35	**Penalty.** Add all amounts on lines 32 and 34 in all columns. Enter the total here and on Form 1040, line 70; Form 1040A, line 45; Form 1040NR, line 69; Form 1040NR-EZ, line 27; or Form 1041, line 26 ▶					35	$

Form **2210** (2000)

Tax Forms ▼ Individuals B-17

Form 2210 (2000) Page **3**

Schedule AI—Annualized Income Installment Method (See pages 5 and 6 of the instructions.)

Estates and trusts, **do not** use the period ending dates shown to the right. Instead, use the following: 2/29/00, 4/30/00, 7/31/00, and 11/30/00.

		(a) 1/1/00–3/31/00	(b) 1/1/00–5/31/00	(c) 1/1/00–8/31/00	(d) 1/1/00–12/31/00

Part I — Annualized Income Installments

Line	Description	(a)	(b)	(c)	(d)
1	Enter your adjusted gross income for each period (see instructions). (Estates and trusts, enter your taxable income without your exemption for each period.)				
2	Annualization amounts. (Estates and trusts, see instructions.)	4	2.4	1.5	1
3	Annualized income. Multiply line 1 by line 2				
4	Enter your itemized deductions for the period shown in each column. If you do not itemize, enter -0- and skip to line 7. (Estates and trusts, enter -0-, skip to line 9, and enter the amount from line 3 on line 9.)				
5	Annualization amounts	4	2.4	1.5	1
6	Multiply line 4 by line 5 (see instructions if line 3 is more than $64,475)				
7	In each column, enter the full amount of your standard deduction from Form 1040, line 36, or Form 1040A, line 22 (Form 1040NR or 1040NR-EZ filers, enter -0-. **Exception:** Indian students and business apprentices, enter standard deduction from Form 1040NR, line 35 or Form 1040NR-EZ, line 11.)				
8	Enter the **larger** of line 6 or line 7				
9	Subtract line 8 from line 3				
10	In each column, multiply $2,800 by the total number of exemptions claimed (see instructions if line 3 is more than $96,700). (Estates and trusts and Form 1040NR or 1040NR-EZ filers, enter the exemption amount shown on your tax return.)				
11	Subtract line 10 from line 9				
12	Figure your tax on the amount on line 11 (see instructions)				
13	Form 1040 filers only, complete Part II and enter your self-employment tax from line 35 below				
14	Enter other taxes for each payment period (see instructions)				
15	Total tax. Add lines 12, 13, and 14				
16	For each period, enter the same type of credits as allowed on Form 2210, lines 2, 5, 6, and 7 (see instructions)				
17	Subtract line 16 from line 15. If zero or less, enter -0-				
18	Applicable percentage	22.5%	45%	67.5%	90%
19	Multiply line 17 by line 18				

Caution: *Complete lines 20–26 of one column before going to the next column.*

Line	Description	(a)	(b)	(c)	(d)
20	Add the amounts in all previous columns of line 26				
21	Subtract line 20 from line 19. If zero or less, enter -0-				
22	Enter 25% (.25) of line 14 on page 1 of Form 2210 in each column				
23	Enter amount from line 25 of the previous column of this schedule				
24	Add lines 22 and 23 and enter the total				
25	Subtract line 21 from line 24. If zero or less, enter -0-				
26	Enter the **smaller** of line 21 or line 24 here and on Form 2210, line 22 ▶				

Part II — Annualized Self-Employment Tax

Line	Description	(a)	(b)	(c)	(d)
27	Net earnings from self-employment for the period (see instructions)				
28	Prorated social security tax limit	$19,050	$31,750	$50,800	$76,200
29	Enter actual wages for the period subject to social security tax or the 6.2% portion of the 7.65% railroad retirement (tier 1) tax				
30	Subtract line 29 from line 28. If zero or less, enter -0-				
31	Annualization amounts	0.496	0.2976	0.186	0.124
32	Multiply line 31 by the **smaller** of line 27 or line 30				
33	Annualization amounts	0.116	0.0696	0.0435	0.029
34	Multiply line 27 by line 33				
35	Add lines 32 and 34. Enter the result here and on line 13 above ▶				

Form **2210** (2000)

Form **2441**	**Child and Dependent Care Expenses**	OMB No. 1545-0068
Department of the Treasury Internal Revenue Service (99)	▶ Attach to Form 1040. ▶ See separate instructions.	**2000** Attachment Sequence No. **21**

Name(s) shown on Form 1040   Your social security number

Before you begin: You need to understand the following terms. See **Definitions** on page 1 of the instructions.

- Dependent Care Benefits   • Qualifying Person(s)   • Qualified Expenses   • Earned Income

Part I   **Persons or Organizations Who Provided the Care**—You **must** complete this part.
(If you need more space, use the bottom of page 2.)

1	(a) Care provider's name	(b) Address (number, street, apt. no., city, state, and ZIP code)	(c) Identifying number (SSN or EIN)	(d) Amount paid (see instructions)

Did you receive **dependent care benefits?**   No ⟶ Complete only Part II below.
   Yes ⟶ Complete Part III on the back next.

Caution: *If the care was provided in your home, you may owe employment taxes. See the instructions for Form 1040, line 56.*

Part II   **Credit for Child and Dependent Care Expenses**

2   Information about your **qualifying person(s)**. If you have more than two qualifying persons, see the instructions.

(a) Qualifying person's name		(b) Qualifying person's social security number	(c) **Qualified expenses** you incurred and paid in 2000 for the person listed in column (a)
First	Last		

3   Add the amounts in column (c) of line 2. **Do not** enter more than $2,400 for one qualifying person or $4,800 for two or more persons. If you completed Part III, enter the amount from line 24   **3**

4   Enter YOUR **earned income**   **4**

5   If married filing a joint return, enter YOUR SPOUSE'S earned income (if your spouse was a student or was disabled, see the instructions); **all others,** enter the amount from line 4   **5**

6   Enter the **smallest** of line 3, 4, or 5   **6**

7   Enter the amount from Form 1040, line 34   **7**

8   Enter on line 8 the decimal amount shown below that applies to the amount on line 7

If line 7 is—		Decimal amount is	If line 7 is—		Decimal amount is
Over	But not over		Over	But not over	
$0	10,000	.30	$20,000	22,000	.24
10,000	12,000	.29	22,000	24,000	.23
12,000	14,000	.28	24,000	26,000	.22
14,000	16,000	.27	26,000	28,000	.21
16,000	18,000	.26	28,000	No limit	.20
18,000	20,000	.25			

8   × .

9   Multiply **line 6** by the decimal amount on line 8. Enter the result here and on Form 1040, line 44. But if this amount is more than the amount on Form 1040, line 42, minus any amount on line 43, **or** you paid 1999 expenses in 2000, see the instructions for the amount to enter on line 44   **9**

For Paperwork Reduction Act Notice, see page 3 of the instructions.   Cat. No. 11862M   Form **2441** (2000)

Form 2441 (2000) Page **2**

Part III Dependent Care Benefits

10 Enter the total amount of **dependent care benefits** you received for 2000. This amount should be shown in box 10 of your W-2 form(s). **Do not** include amounts that were reported to you as wages in box 1 of Form(s) W-2 . . . . **10**

11 Enter the amount forfeited, if any. See the instructions **11**

12 Subtract line 11 from line 10 . . . . **12**

13 Enter the total amount of **qualified expenses** incurred in 2000 for the care of the **qualifying person(s)** **13**

14 Enter the **smaller** of line 12 or 13 . . . . **14**

15 Enter YOUR **earned income** **15**

16 If married filing a joint return, enter YOUR SPOUSE'S earned income (if your spouse was a student or was disabled, see the instructions for line 5); if married filing a separate return, see the instructions for the amount to enter; **all others,** enter the amount from line 15 . . **16**

17 Enter the **smallest** of line 14, 15, or 16 . . . . . **17**

18 **Excluded benefits.** Enter here the **smaller** of the following:
   - The amount from line 17 or
   - $5,000 ($2,500 if married filing a separate return and you were required to enter your spouse's earned income on line 16). **18**

19 **Taxable benefits.** Subtract line 18 from line 12. Also, include this amount on Form 1040, line 7. On the dotted line next to line 7, enter "DCB" **19**

To claim the child and dependent care credit, complete lines 20–24 below.

20 Enter $2,400 ($4,800 if two or more qualifying persons) **20**

21 Enter the amount from line 18 . . . . **21**

22 Subtract line 21 from line 20. If zero or less, **stop.** You cannot take the credit. **Exception.** If you paid 1999 expenses in 2000, see the instructions for line 9 . . . **22**

23 Complete line 2 on the front of this form. **Do not** include in column (c) any benefits shown on line 18 above. Then, add the amounts in column (c) and enter the total here . . **23**

24 Enter the **smaller** of line 22 or 23. Also, enter this amount on line 3 on the front of this form and complete lines 4–9 . . . . **24**

Form **2441** (2000)

B-20 Individuals ▼ Appendix B

Form **3903**
(Rev. October 1998)
Department of the Treasury
Internal Revenue Service

Moving Expenses

▶ Attach to Form 1040.

OMB No. 1545-0062

Attachment Sequence No. **62**

Name(s) shown on Form 1040

Your social security number

Before you begin, see the **Distance Test** and **Time Test** in the instructions to make sure you can take this deduction. If you are a member of the armed forces, see the instructions to find out how to complete this form.

1 Enter the amount you paid for transportation and storage of household goods and personal effects (see instructions) ... **1**

2 Enter the amount you paid for travel and lodging expenses in moving from your old home to your new home. **Do not** include meals (see instructions) ... **2**

3 Add lines 1 and 2 ... **3**

4 Enter the total amount your employer paid you for the expenses listed on lines 1 and 2 that is **not** included in the wages box (box 1) of your W-2 form. This amount should be identified with code **P** in box 13 of your W-2 form ... **4**

Is line 3 more than line 4?

Yes. Go to line 5.

No. You **cannot** deduct your moving expenses. If line 3 is less than line 4, subtract line 3 from line 4 and include the result on the "Wages, salaries, tips, etc." line of Form 1040.

5 Subtract line 4 from line 3. Enter the result here and on the "Moving expenses" line of Form 1040. This is your **moving expense deduction** ... **5**

General Instructions

A Change To Note

Beginning in 1998, include on lines 1 and 2 of Form 3903 **only** the amounts you actually paid for the expenses listed. Include on those lines the total amount you paid even if your employer reimbursed you for the expenses. Use line 4 to report amounts your employer paid directly to you for the expenses listed on lines 1 and 2 if they are **not** reported to you as wages on Form W-2.

Do not include on Form 3903 any amount your employer paid to a third party (such as a moving or storage company). Also, do not include the value of any services your employer provided in kind.

Purpose of Form

Use Form 3903 to figure your moving expense deduction if:
• You moved to a new principal place of work (workplace) within the United States or its possessions, OR
• You moved to a new workplace outside the United States or its possessions and you are a U.S. citizen or resident alien.

If you qualify to deduct expenses for more than one move, use a separate Form 3903 for each move.

For more details, see **Pub. 521,** Moving Expenses.

Who May Deduct Moving Expenses

If you moved to a different home because of a change in job location, you may be able to deduct your moving expenses. You may be able to take the deduction whether you are self-employed or an employee. But you must meet certain tests explained next.

Distance Test

Your new principal workplace must be at least 50 miles farther from your old home than your old workplace was. For example, if your old workplace was 3 miles from your old home, your new workplace must be at least 53 miles from that home. If you did not have an old workplace, your new workplace must be at least 50 miles from your old home. The distance between the two points is the shortest of the more commonly traveled routes between them.

TIP: If you are not sure if you meet the distance test, use the worksheet on this page.

Time Test

If you are an employee, you must work full time in the general area of your new workplace for at least 39 weeks during the 12 months right after you move. If you are self-employed, you must work full time in the general area of your new workplace for at least 39 weeks during the first 12 months and a total of at least 78 weeks during the 24 months right after you move.

What If You Do Not Meet the Time Test Before Your Return Is Due? If you expect to meet the time test, you may deduct

Distance Test Worksheet (keep a copy for your records)

1. Enter the number of miles from your **old home** to your **new workplace** ... 1. _____ miles
2. Enter the number of miles from your **old home** to your **old workplace** ... 2. _____ miles
3. Subtract line 2 from line 1. If zero or less, enter -0- ... 3. _____ miles

Is line 3 at least 50 miles?
Yes. You meet this test.
No. You do not meet this test. You **cannot** deduct your moving expenses. **Do not** complete Form 3903.

For Paperwork Reduction Act Notice, see back of form.   Cat. No. 12490K   Form **3903** (Rev. 10-98) your moving expenses in the year you move. But if you do not meet the time test, you must either:

1. Amend your tax return for the year you claimed the deduction (use **Form 1040X,** Amended U.S. Individual Income Tax Return, to do this), **or**

2. For the year you cannot meet the time test, report as income the amount of your moving expense deduction that reduced your income tax for the year you moved. For more details, see **Time Test** in Pub. 521.

If you do not deduct your moving expenses in the year you move and you later meet the time test, you may take the deduction by filing an amended return for the year you moved. To do this, use Form 1040X.

Example. You are an employee who moved to a new workplace in September 1998. Because you expect to meet the 39-week test by the end of 1999, you deduct your moving expenses on your 1998 return. If you do not meet the time test in 1999 and none of the exceptions to the time test (see below) apply, you must either amend your 1998 tax return to figure your tax without the moving expense deduction **or** report as income on your 1999 tax return the portion of your moving expense deduction that reduced your 1998 income tax.

Exceptions to the Time Test. The time test does not have to be met if any of the following apply:

- Your job ends because of disability.
- You are transferred for your employer's benefit.
- You are laid off or discharged for a reason other than willful misconduct.
- You meet the requirements (explained later) for retirees or survivors living outside the United States.
- You are filing this form for a decedent.

Members of the Armed Forces

If you are in the armed forces, you do not have to meet the **distance and time tests** if the move is due to a permanent change of station. A permanent change of station includes a move in connection with and within 1 year of retirement or other termination of active duty.

How To Complete the Form

Do not include on lines 1 and 2 any expenses for moving services that were provided by the government. If you and your spouse and dependents are moved to or from different locations, treat the moves as a single move.

On line 4, enter the total reimbursements and allowances you received from the government in connection with the expenses you claimed on lines 1 and 2. **Do not** include the value of moving services provided by the government. Complete line 5 if applicable.

Retirees or Survivors Living Outside the United States

If you are a retiree or survivor who moved to a home in the United States or its possessions and you meet the following requirements, you are treated as if you moved to a new workplace located in the United States. You are subject to the distance test.

Retirees

You may deduct moving expenses for a move to a new home in the United States when you actually retire if both your old principal workplace and your old home were outside the United States.

Survivors

You may deduct moving expenses for a move to a home in the United States if you are the spouse or dependent of a person whose principal workplace at the time of death was outside the United States. In addition, the expenses must be for a move **(1)** that begins within 6 months after the decedent's death, and **(2)** from a former home outside the United States that you lived in with the decedent at the time of death.

Reimbursements

You may choose to deduct moving expenses in the year you are reimbursed by your employer, even though you paid the expenses in a different year. However, special rules apply. See **How To Report** in Pub. 521.

Filers of Form 2555

If you file **Form 2555,** Foreign Earned Income, to exclude any of your income or housing costs, report the full amount of your deductible moving expenses on Form 3903 and on Form 1040. Report the part of your moving expenses that is not allowed because it is allocable to the excluded income on the appropriate line of Form 2555. For details on how to figure the part allocable to the excluded income, see **Pub. 54,** Tax Guide for U.S. Citizens and Resident Aliens Abroad.

Specific Instructions

You may deduct the following expenses you paid to move your family and dependent household members. Do not deduct expenses for employees such as a maid, nanny, or nurse.

Caution: See *A Change To Note* on page 1 before you complete lines 1 and 2.

Line 1

Moves Within or to the United States or its Possessions. Enter the amount you paid to pack, crate, and move your household goods and personal effects. You may also include the amount you paid to store and insure household goods and personal effects within any period of 30 days in a row after the items were moved from your old home and before they were delivered to your new home.

Moves Outside the United States or its Possessions. Enter the amount you paid to pack, crate, move, store, and insure your household goods and personal effects. Also, include the amount you paid to move your possessions to and from storage and to store them for all or part of the time the new workplace continues to be your principal workplace.

TIP: *You do not have to complete this form if you moved in an earlier year, you are claiming only storage fees during your absence from the United States, and any amount your employer paid for the storage fees is included in the wages box of your W-2 form. Instead, enter the storage fees on the "Moving expenses" line of Form 1040, and write "Storage" next to the amount.*

Line 2

Enter the amount you paid to travel from your old home to your new home. This includes transportation and lodging on the way. Include costs for the day you arrive. Although not all the members of your household have to travel together or at the same time, you may only include expenses for one trip per person.

If you use your own car(s), you may figure the expenses by using either:

- Actual out-of-pocket expenses for gas and oil, or
- Mileage at the rate of 10 cents a mile.

You may add parking fees and tolls to the amount claimed under either method. Keep records to verify your expenses.

Paperwork Reduction Act Notice. We ask for the information on this form to carry out the Internal Revenue laws of the United States. You are required to give us the information. We need it to ensure that you are complying with these laws and to allow us to figure and collect the right amount of tax.

You are not required to provide the information requested on a form that is subject to the Paperwork Reduction Act unless the form displays a valid OMB control number. Books or records relating to a form or its instructions must be retained as long as their contents may become material in the administration of any Internal Revenue law. Generally, tax returns and return information are confidential, as required by Internal Revenue Code section 6103.

The time needed to complete and file this form will vary depending on individual circumstances. The estimated average time is: **Recordkeeping,** 33 min.; **Learning about the law or the form,** 9 min.; **Preparing the form,** 13 min.; and **Copying, assembling, and sending the form to the IRS,** 14 min.

If you have comments concerning the accuracy of these time estimates or suggestions for making this form simpler, we would be happy to hear from you. See the Instructions for Form 1040.

B-22 Individuals ▼ Appendix B

Form **6251**	**Alternative Minimum Tax—Individuals**	OMB No. 1545-0227
Department of the Treasury Internal Revenue Service	► See separate instructions. ► Attach to Form 1040 or Form 1040NR.	**2000** Attachment Sequence No. **32**

Name(s) shown on Form 1040 | Your social security number

Part I — Adjustments and Preferences

1. If you itemized deductions on Schedule A (Form 1040), go to line 2. Otherwise, enter your standard deduction from Form 1040, line 36, here and go to line 6 .... **1**
2. Medical and dental. Enter the smaller of Schedule A (Form 1040), line 4 **or** 2½% of Form 1040, line 34 **2**
3. Taxes. Enter the amount from Schedule A (Form 1040), line 9 .... **3**
4. Certain interest on a home mortgage **not** used to buy, build, or improve your home **4**
5. Miscellaneous itemized deductions. Enter the amount from Schedule A (Form 1040) line 26 .... **5**
6. Refund of taxes. Enter any tax refund from Form 1040, line 10 or line 21 .... **6** ( )
7. Investment interest. Enter difference between regular tax and AMT deduction **7**
8. Post-1986 depreciation. Enter difference between regular tax and AMT depreciation **8**
9. Adjusted gain or loss. Enter difference between AMT and regular tax gain or loss **9**
10. Incentive stock options. Enter excess of AMT income over regular tax income **10**
11. Passive activities. Enter difference between AMT and regular tax income or loss **11**
12. Beneficiaries of estates and trusts. Enter the amount from Schedule K-1 (Form 1041), line 9 .... **12**
13. Tax-exempt interest from private activity bonds issued after 8/7/86 .... **13**
14. Other. Enter the amount, if any, for each item below and enter the total on line 14.
    - **a** Circulation expenditures
    - **b** Depletion
    - **c** Depreciation (pre-1987)
    - **d** Installment sales
    - **e** Intangible drilling costs
    - **f** Large partnerships
    - **g** Long-term contracts
    - **h** Loss limitations
    - **i** Mining costs
    - **j** Patron's adjustment
    - **k** Pollution control facilities
    - **l** Research and experimental
    - **m** Section 1202 exclusion
    - **n** Tax shelter farm activities
    - **o** Related adjustments **14**
15. Total Adjustments and Preferences. Combine lines 1 through 14 .... ► **15**

Part II — Alternative Minimum Taxable Income

16. Enter the amount from **Form 1040, line 37**. If less than zero, enter as a (loss) .... ► **16**
17. Net operating loss deduction, if any, from Form 1040, line 21. Enter as a positive amount **17**
18. If Form 1040, line 34, is over $128,950 (over $64,475 if married filing separately), and you itemized deductions, enter the amount, if any, from line 9 of the worksheet for Schedule A (Form 1040), line 28 .... **18** ( )
19. Combine lines 15 through 18 .... ► **19**
20. Alternative tax net operating loss deduction. See page 6 of the instructions **20**
21. **Alternative Minimum Taxable Income.** Subtract line 20 from line 19. (If married filing separately and line 21 is more than $165,000, see page 7 of the instructions.) .... ► **21**

Part III — Exemption Amount and Alternative Minimum Tax

22. **Exemption Amount.** (If this form is for a child under age 14, see page 7 of the instructions.)

IF your filing status is . . .	AND line 21 is not over . . .	THEN enter on line 22 . . .	
Single or head of household	$112,500	$33,750	
Married filing jointly or qualifying widow(er)	150,000	45,000	**22**
Married filing separately	75,000	22,500	

    If line 21 is **over** the amount shown above for your filing status, see page 7 of the instructions.
23. Subtract line 22 from line 21. If zero or less, enter -0- here and on lines 26 and 28 and stop here ► **23**
24. If you reported capital gain distributions directly on Form 1040, line 13, **or** you completed Schedule D (Form 1040) and have an amount on line 25 or line 27 (or would have had an amount on either line if you had completed Part IV) (as refigured for the AMT, if necessary), go to Part IV of Form 6251 to figure line 24. **All others:** If line 23 is $175,000 or less ($87,500 or less if married filing separately), multiply line 23 by 26% (.26). Otherwise, multiply line 23 by 28% (.28) and subtract $3,500 ($1,750 if married filing separately) from the result **24**
25. Alternative minimum tax foreign tax credit. See page 7 of the instructions **25**
26. Tentative minimum tax. Subtract line 25 from line 24 .... ► **26**
27. Enter your tax from Form 1040, line 40 (minus any tax from Form 4972 and any foreign tax credit from Form 1040, line 43) **27**
28. **Alternative Minimum Tax.** Subtract line 27 from line 26. If zero or less, enter -0-. Enter here and on Form 1040, line 41 .... ► **28**

For Paperwork Reduction Act Notice, see page 8 of the instructions. Cat. No. 13600G Form **6251** (2000)

Form 6251 (2000) Page **2**

Part IV — Line 24 Computation Using Maximum Capital Gains Rates

Caution: *If you **did not** complete Part IV of Schedule D (Form 1040), see page 8 of the instructions before you complete this part.*

29 Enter the amount from Form 6251, line 23 .... **29**

30 Enter the amount from Schedule D (Form 1040), line 27 (as refigured for the AMT, if necessary). See page 8 of the instructions **30**

31 Enter the amount from Schedule D (Form 1040), line 25 (as refigured for the AMT, if necessary). See page 8 of the instructions **31**

32 Add lines 30 and 31 .... **32**

33 Enter the amount from Schedule D (Form 1040), line 22 (as refigured for the AMT, if necessary). See page 8 of the instructions **33**

34 Enter the **smaller** of line 32 or line 33 .... **34**

35 Subtract line 34 from line 29. If zero or less, enter -0- ▶ **35**

36 If line 35 is $175,000 or less ($87,500 or less if married filing separately), multiply line 35 by 26% (.26). Otherwise, multiply line 35 by 28% (.28) and subtract $3,500 ($1,750 if married filing separately) from the result **36**

37 Enter the amount from Schedule D (Form 1040), line 36 (as figured for the regular tax). See page 8 of the instructions **37**

38 Enter the **smallest** of line 29, line 30, or line 37 ▶ **38**

39 Multiply line 38 by 10% (.10) **39**

40 Enter the **smaller** of line 29 or line 30 .... **40**

41 Enter the amount from line 38 .... **41**

42 Subtract line 41 from line 40 ▶ **42**

43 Multiply line 42 by 20% (.20) **43**

Note: *If line 31 is zero or blank, skip lines 44 through 47 and go to line 48.*

44 Enter the amount from line 29 .... **44**

45 Add lines 35, 38, and 42 .... **45**

46 Subtract line 45 from line 44 .... **46**

47 Multiply line 46 by 25% (.25) **47**

48 Add lines 36, 39, 43, and 47 .... **48**

49 If line 29 is $175,000 or less ($87,500 or less if married filing separately), multiply line 29 by 26% (.26). Otherwise, multiply line 29 by 28% (.28) and subtract $3,500 ($1,750 if married filing separately) from the result **49**

50 Enter the **smaller** of line 48 or line 49 here and on line 24 .... **50**

Form **6251** (2000)

B-24 Individuals ▼ Appendix B

Form **8283**
(Rev. October 1998)
Department of the Treasury
Internal Revenue Service

Noncash Charitable Contributions
▶ Attach to your tax return if you claimed a total deduction of over $500 for all contributed property.
▶ See separate instructions.

OMB No. 1545-0908
Attachment Sequence No. **55**

Name(s) shown on your income tax return | Identifying number

Note: *Figure the amount of your contribution deduction before completing this form. See your tax return instructions.*

Section A—List in this section **only** items (or groups of similar items) for which you claimed a deduction of $5,000 or less. Also, list certain publicly traded securities even if the deduction is over $5,000 (see instructions).

Part I Information on Donated Property—If you need more space, attach a statement.

1 | (a) Name and address of the donee organization | (b) Description of donated property

A
B
C
D
E

Note: *If the amount you claimed as a deduction for an item is $500 or less, you do not have to complete columns (d), (e), and (f).*

	(c) Date of the contribution	(d) Date acquired by donor (mo., yr.)	(e) How acquired by donor	(f) Donor's cost or adjusted basis	(g) Fair market value	(h) Method used to determine the fair market value
A						
B						
C						
D						
E						

Part II Other Information—Complete line 2 if you gave less than an entire interest in property listed in Part I. Complete line 3 if conditions were attached to a contribution listed in Part I.

2 If, during the year, you contributed less than the entire interest in the property, complete lines a–e.
 a Enter the letter from Part I that identifies the property ▶ _____ . If Part II applies to more than one property, attach a separate statement.
 b Total amount claimed as a deduction for the property listed in Part I: (1) For this tax year ▶ _____ .
  (2) For any prior tax years ▶ _____ .
 c Name and address of each organization to which any such contribution was made in a prior year (complete only if different from the donee organization above):
  Name of charitable organization (donee)

  Address (number, street, and room or suite no.)

  City or town, state, and ZIP code

 d For tangible property, enter the place where the property is located or kept ▶ _____
 e Name of any person, other than the donee organization, having actual possession of the property ▶ _____

3 If conditions were attached to any contribution listed in Part I, answer questions a – c and attach the required statement (see instructions).

		Yes	No
a	Is there a restriction, either temporary or permanent, on the donee's right to use or dispose of the donated property?		
b	Did you give to anyone (other than the donee organization or another organization participating with the donee organization in cooperative fundraising) the right to the income from the donated property or to the possession of the property, including the right to vote donated securities, to acquire the property by purchase or otherwise, or to designate the person having such income, possession, or right to acquire?		
c	Is there a restriction limiting the donated property for a particular use?		

For Paperwork Reduction Act Notice, see page 4 of separate instructions. Cat. No. 62299J Form **8283** (Rev. 10-98)

Form 8283 (Rev. 10-98) Page **2**

Name(s) shown on your income tax return | Identifying number

Section B—Appraisal Summary—List in this section only items (or groups of similar items) for which you claimed a deduction of more than $5,000 per item or group. **Exception.** Report contributions of certain publicly traded securities only in Section A.

If you donated art, you may have to attach the complete appraisal. See the **Note** in Part I below.

Part I — Information on Donated Property—To be completed by the taxpayer and/or appraiser.

4 Check type of property:
- ☐ Art* (contribution of $20,000 or more)
- ☐ Art* (contribution of less than $20,000)
- ☐ Real Estate
- ☐ Coin Collections
- ☐ Gems/Jewelry
- ☐ Books
- ☐ Stamp Collections
- ☐ Other

*Art includes paintings, sculptures, watercolors, prints, drawings, ceramics, antique furniture, decorative arts, textiles, carpets, silver, rare manuscripts, historical memorabilia, and other similar objects.

Note: *If your total art contribution deduction was $20,000 or more, you must attach a complete copy of the signed appraisal. See instructions.*

5	(a) Description of donated property (if you need more space, attach a separate statement)	(b) If tangible property was donated, give a brief summary of the overall physical condition at the time of the gift	(c) Appraised fair market value
A			
B			
C			
D			

	(d) Date acquired by donor (mo., yr.)	(e) How acquired by donor	(f) Donor's cost or adjusted basis	(g) For bargain sales, enter amount received	(h) Amount claimed as a deduction	(i) Average trading price of securities
A						
B						
C						
D						

(columns h, i under "See instructions")

Part II — Taxpayer (Donor) Statement—List each item included in Part I above that the appraisal identifies as having a value of $500 or less. See instructions.

I declare that the following item(s) included in Part I above has to the best of my knowledge and belief an appraised value of not more than $500 (per item). Enter identifying letter from Part I and describe the specific item. See instructions. ▶ _____

Signature of taxpayer (donor) ▶   Date ▶

Part III — Declaration of Appraiser

I declare that I am not the donor, the donee, a party to the transaction in which the donor acquired the property, employed by, or related to any of the foregoing persons, or married to any person who is related to any of the foregoing persons. And, if regularly used by the donor, donee, or party to the transaction, I performed the majority of my appraisals during my tax year for other persons.

Also, I declare that I hold myself out to the public as an appraiser or perform appraisals on a regular basis; and that because of my qualifications as described in the appraisal, I am qualified to make appraisals of the type of property being valued. I certify that the appraisal fees were not based on a percentage of the appraised property value. Furthermore, I understand that a false or fraudulent overstatement of the property value as described in the qualified appraisal or this appraisal summary may subject me to the penalty under section 6701(a) (aiding and abetting the understatement of tax liability). I affirm that I have not been barred from presenting evidence or testimony by the Director of Practice.

Sign Here

Signature ▶   Title ▶   Date of appraisal ▶

Business address (including room or suite no.) | Identifying number

City or town, state, and ZIP code

Part IV — Donee Acknowledgment—To be completed by the charitable organization.

This charitable organization acknowledges that it is a qualified organization under section 170(c) and that it received the donated property as described in Section B, Part I, above on ▶ _____ (Date)

Furthermore, this organization affirms that in the event it sells, exchanges, or otherwise disposes of the property described in Section B, Part I (or any portion thereof) within 2 years after the date of receipt, it will file **Form 8282**, Donee Information Return, with the IRS and give the donor a copy of that form. This acknowledgment does not represent agreement with the claimed fair market value.

Does the organization intend to use the property for an unrelated use? ▶ ☐ Yes ☐ No

Name of charitable organization (donee) | Employer identification number

Address (number, street, and room or suite no.) | City or town, state, and ZIP code

Authorized signature | Title | Date

B-26 Individuals ▼ Appendix B

Form **8582**	**Passive Activity Loss Limitations**	OMB No. 1545-1008
Department of the Treasury Internal Revenue Service	▶ See separate instructions. ▶ Attach to Form 1040 or Form 1041.	**2000** Attachment Sequence No. **88**
Name(s) shown on return		Identifying number

Part I — 2000 Passive Activity Loss
Caution: *See the instructions for Worksheets 1 and 2 on page 8 before completing Part I.*

Rental Real Estate Activities With Active Participation (For the definition of active participation see **Active Participation in a Rental Real Estate Activity** on page 4 of the instructions.)

- **1a** Activities with net income (enter the amount from Worksheet 1, column (a)) **1a**
- **b** Activities with net loss (enter the amount from Worksheet 1, column (b)) .... **1b** ( )
- **c** Prior years unallowed losses (enter the amount from Worksheet 1, column (c)) .... **1c** ( )
- **d** Combine lines 1a, 1b, and 1c **1d**

All Other Passive Activities

- **2a** Activities with net income (enter the amount from Worksheet 2, column (a)) **2a**
- **b** Activities with net loss (enter the amount from Worksheet 2, column (b)) .... **2b** ( )
- **c** Prior years unallowed losses (enter the amount from Worksheet 2, column (c)) .... **2c** ( )
- **d** Combine lines 2a, 2b, and 2c **2d**

3 Combine lines 1d and 2d. If the result is net income or zero, all losses are allowed, including any prior year unallowed losses entered on line 1c or 2c. **Do not** complete Form 8582. Report the losses on the forms and schedules normally used.
If this line and line 1d are losses, go to Part II. Otherwise, enter -0- on line 9 and go to line 10 .... **3**

Part II — Special Allowance for Rental Real Estate With Active Participation
Note: *Enter all numbers in Part II as positive amounts. See page 8 for examples.*

Note: *If your filing status is married filing separately and you lived with your spouse at any time during the year, **do not** complete Part II. Instead, enter -0- on line 9 and go to line 10.*

- **4** Enter the **smaller** of the loss on line 1d or the loss on line 3 .... **4**
- **5** Enter $150,000. If married filing separately, see page 8 .... **5**
- **6** Enter modified adjusted gross income, but not less than zero (see page 8) **6**

  Note: *If line 6 is greater than or equal to line 5, skip lines 7 and 8, enter -0- on line 9, and go to line 10. Otherwise, go to line 7.*

- **7** Subtract line 6 from line 5 .... **7**
- **8** Multiply line 7 by 50% (.5). **Do not** enter more than $25,000. If married filing separately, see page 9 .... **8**
- **9** Enter the **smaller** of line 4 or line 8 .... **9**

Part III — Total Losses Allowed

- **10** Add the income, if any, on lines 1a and 2a and enter the total **10**
- **11** Total losses allowed from all passive activities for 2000. Add lines 9 and 10. See page 11 to find out how to report the losses on your tax return **11**

For Paperwork Reduction Act Notice, see page 12 of the instructions.   Cat. No. 63704F   Form **8582** (2000)

Form 8582 (2000)
Page **2**

Caution: *The worksheets are not required to be filed with your tax return and may be detached before filing Form 8582. Keep a copy of the worksheets for your records.*

Worksheet 1—For Form 8582, Lines 1a, 1b, and 1c (See page 8.)

Name of activity	Current year		Prior years	Overall gain or loss	
	(a) Net income (line 1a)	(b) Net loss (line 1b)	(c) Unallowed loss (line 1c)	(d) Gain	(e) Loss
Total. Enter on Form 8582, lines 1a, 1b, and 1c ▶					

Worksheet 2—For Form 8582, Lines 2a, 2b, and 2c (See page 8.)

Name of activity	Current year		Prior years	Overall gain or loss	
	(a) Net income (line 2a)	(b) Net loss (line 2b)	(c) Unallowed loss (line 2c)	(d) Gain	(e) Loss
Total. Enter on Form 8582, lines 2a, 2b, and 2c ▶					

Worksheet 3—Use this worksheet if an amount is shown on Form 8582, line 9 (See page 9.)

Name of activity	Form or schedule to be reported on	(a) Loss	(b) Ratio	(c) Special allowance	(d) Subtract column (c) from column (a)
Total ▶			1.00		

Worksheet 4—Allocation of Unallowed Losses (See page 9.)

Name of activity	Form or schedule to be reported on	(a) Loss	(b) Ratio	(c) Unallowed loss
Total ▶			1.00	

Worksheet 5—Allowed Losses (See page 9.)

Name of activity	Form or schedule to be reported on	(a) Loss	(b) Unallowed loss	(c) Allowed loss
Total ▶				

Form **8582** (2000)

Form 8582 (2000) Page **3**

Worksheet 6—Activities With Losses Reported on Two or More Different Forms or Schedules (See page 10.)

Name of Activity:	(a)	(b)	(c) Ratio	(d) Unallowed loss	(e) Allowed loss
Form or Schedule To Be Reported on: _____					
1a Net loss plus prior year unallowed loss from form or schedule ▶					
b Net income from form or schedule ▶					
c Subtract line 1b from line 1a. If zero or less, enter -0- ▶					
Form or Schedule To Be Reported on: _____					
1a Net loss plus prior year unallowed loss from form or schedule ▶					
b Net income from form or schedule ▶					
c Subtract line 1b from line 1a. If zero or less, enter -0- ▶					
Form or Schedule To Be Reported on: _____					
1a Net loss plus prior year unallowed loss from form or schedule ▶					
b Net income from form or schedule ▶					
c Subtract line 1b from line 1a. If zero or less, enter -0- ▶					
Total ▶			1.00		

Form **8582** (2000)

Tax Forms ▼ Individuals B-29

Form **8615**
Department of the Treasury
Internal Revenue Service (99)

**Tax for Children Under Age 14
Who Have Investment Income of More Than $1,400**
▶ Attach only to the child's Form 1040, Form 1040A, or Form 1040NR.
▶ See separate instructions.

OMB No. 1545-0998

2000

Attachment Sequence No. **33**

Child's name shown on return | Child's social security number

Before you begin: If the child, the parent, or any of the parent's other children under age 14 received capital gains (including capital gain distributions) or farm income, see **Pub. 929,** Tax Rules for Children and Dependents. It explains how to figure the child's tax using the **Capital Gain Tax Worksheet** in the Form 1040 or Form 1040A instructions or **Schedule D** or **J** (Form 1040).

A Parent's name (first, initial, and last). **Caution:** See instructions before completing. | **B** Parent's social security number

C Parent's filing status (check one):
☐ Single ☐ Married filing jointly ☐ Married filing separately ☐ Head of household ☐ Qualifying widow(er)

Part I — Child's Net Investment Income

1. Enter the child's investment income, such as taxable interest, ordinary dividends, and capital gain distributions. See instructions. If this amount is $1,400 or less, **stop;** do not file this form ... **1**
2. If the child **did not** itemize deductions on **Schedule A** (Form 1040 or Form 1040NR), enter $1,400. If the child **did** itemize deductions, see instructions ... **2**
3. Subtract line 2 from line 1. If the result is zero or less, **stop;** do not complete the rest of this form but **do** attach it to the child's return ... **3**
4. Enter the child's **taxable income** from Form 1040, line 39; Form 1040A, line 25; or Form 1040NR, line 38 ... **4**
5. Enter the **smaller** of line 3 or line 4 ... **5**

Part II — Tentative Tax Based on the Tax Rate of the Parent Listed on Line A

6. Enter the parent's **taxable income** from Form 1040, line 39; Form 1040A, line 25; Form 1040EZ, line 6; TeleFile Tax Record, line K; Form 1040NR, line 38; or Form 1040NR-EZ, line 14. If less than zero, enter -0- ... **6**

   Note: *If the total of lines 4 and 6 above is not more than $43,850, lines 7 through 16 may not have to be completed. For details, see the instructions for line 6.*

7. Enter the total net investment income, if any, from Forms 8615, line 5, of **all other** children of the parent identified above. **Do not** include the amount from line 5 above ... **7**
8. Add lines 5, 6, and 7 ... **8**
9. Enter the tax on line 8 based on the **parent's** filing status. See instructions. If the **Capital Gain Tax Worksheet** or **Schedule D** or **J** (Form 1040) is used to figure the tax, check here ▶ ☐ ... **9**
10. Enter the parent's tax from Form 1040, line 40; Form 1040A, line 26, minus any alternative minimum tax; Form 1040EZ, line 10; TeleFile Tax Record, line K; Form 1040NR, line 39; or Form 1040NR-EZ, line 15. If any tax is from **Form 4972** or **8814,** see instructions. If the **Capital Gain Tax Worksheet** or **Schedule D** or **J** (Form 1040) was used to figure the tax, check here ▶ ☐ ... **10**
11. Subtract line 10 from line 9 and enter the result. If line 7 is blank, also enter this amount on line 13 and go to **Part III** ... **11**
12a. Add lines 5 and 7 ... **12a**
  b. Divide line 5 by line 12a. Enter the result as a decimal (rounded to at least three places) ... **12b** × .
13. Multiply line 11 by line 12b ... **13**

Part III — Child's Tax—If lines 4 and 5 above are the same, enter -0- on line 15 and go to line 16.

14. Subtract line 5 from line 4 ... **14**
15. Enter the tax on line 14 based on the **child's** filing status. See instructions. If the **Capital Gain Tax Worksheet** or **Schedule D** or **J** (Form 1040) is used to figure the tax, check here ▶ ☐ ... **15**
16. Add lines 13 and 15 ... **16**
17. Enter the tax on line 4 based on the **child's** filing status. See instructions. If the **Capital Gain Tax Worksheet** or **Schedule D** or **J** (Form 1040) is used to figure the tax, check here ▶ ☐ ... **17**
18. Enter the **larger** of line 16 or line 17 here and on Form 1040, line 40; Form 1040A, line 26; or Form 1040NR, line 39 ... **18**

For Paperwork Reduction Act Notice, see page 2 of the instructions. Cat. No. 64113U Form **8615** (2000)

APPENDIX C

MACRS AND ACRS TABLES

ACRS, MACRS and ADS Depreciation Methods Summary

System	Characteristics	Depreciation Method MACRS	ADS	Table No.[a] MACRS	ADS
MACRS & ADS	Personal Property:				
	1. Accounting Convention	Half-year or mid-quarter	Half-year or mid-quarter[b]		
	2. Life and Method				
	a. 3-year, 5-year, 7-year, 10-year	200% DB or elect straight-line	150% DB or elect straight-line	1, 2, 3, 4, 5	10, 11[c]
	b. 15-year, 20-year	150% DB or elect straight-line	150% DB or elect straight-line[d]	1, 2, 3, 4, 5	
	3. Luxury Automobile Limitations			6	
	Real Property:				
	1. Accounting Convention	Mid-month	Mid-month		
	2. Life and Method				
	a. Residential rental property	27.5 years, straight-line	40 years straight-line	7	12
	b. Nonresidential real property	39 years, straight-line[e]	40 years straight-line	9	12

	Characteristics	ACRS		Table No.[a] ACRS	
ACRS	Personal Property[f]				
	1. Accounting Convention	Half-year			
	2. Life and Method				
	a. 3-year, 5-year, 10-year, 15-year	150% DB or elect straight-line[g]			
	Real Property				
	1. Accounting Convention	First of month or Mid-month[h]			
	2. Life				
	a. 15-year property	Placed in service after 12/31/80 and before 3/16/84		16	
	b. 18-year property	Placed in service after 3/15/84 and before 5/9/85		14, 15	
	c. 19-year property	Placed in service after 5/8/85 and before 1/1/87		13	
	3. Method				
	a. All but low-income housing	175% DB or elect straight-line			
	b. Low-income housing property	200% DB or elect straight-line			

[a] All depreciation tables in this appendix are based upon tables contained in Rev. Proc. 87-57, as amended.
[b] General and ADS tables are available for property lives from 2.5-50.0 years using the straight-line method. These tables are contained in Rev. Proc. 87-57 and are only partially reproduced here.
[c] The mid-quarter tables are available in Rev. Proc. 87-57, but are not reproduced here.
[d] Special recovery periods are assigned certain MACRS properties under the alternative depreciation system.
[e] A 31.5-year recovery period applied to nonresidential real property placed in service under the MACRS rules prior to May 13, 1993. (See Table 8)
[f] The ACRS tables for personal property are not reproduced here.
[g] Special recovery periods are required or able to be elected for personalty and realty for which a straight-line ACRS election is made. These recovery periods can be as long as 45 years.
[h] The first-of-the-month convention is used with 15-year property and 18-year real property placed in service before June 23, 1984. The mid-month convention is used with 18-year real property placed in service after June 22, 1984 and 19-year real property.

▼ TABLE 1

General Depreciation System—MACRS
Personal Property Placed in Service after 12/31/86
Applicable Convention: Half-year
Applicable Depreciation Method: 200 or 150 Percent Declining Balance Switching to Straight Line

If the Recover Year Is:	3-Year	5-Year	7-Year	10-Year	15-Year	20-Year
	The Depreciation Rate Is:					
1	33.33	20.00	14.29	10.00	5.00	3.750
2	44.45	32.00	24.49	18.00	9.50	7.219
3	14.81	19.20	17.49	14.40	8.55	6.677
4	7.41	11.52	12.49	11.52	7.70	6.177
5		11.52	8.93	9.22	6.93	5.713
6		5.76	8.92	7.37	6.23	5.285
7			8.93	6.55	5.90	4.888
8			4.46	6.55	5.90	4.522
9				6.56	5.91	4.462
10				6.55	5.90	4.461
11				3.28	5.91	4.462
12					5.90	4.461
13					5.91	4.462
14					5.90	4.461
15					5.91	4.462
16					2.95	4.461
17						4.462
18						4.461
19						4.462
20						4.461
21						2.231

TABLE 2

General Depreciation System—MACRS
Personal Property Placed in Service after 12/31/86
Applicable Convention: Mid-quarter (Property Placed in Service in First Quarter)
Applicable Depreciation Method: 200 or 150 Percent Declining Balance Switching to Straight Line

If the Recovery Year Is:	And the Recovery Period Is: 3-Year	5-Year	7-Year	10-Year	15-Year	20-Year
	The Depreciation Rate Is:					
1	58.33	35.00	25.00	17.50	8.75	6.563
2	27.78	26.00	21.43	16.50	9.13	7.000
3	12.35	15.60	15.31	13.20	8.21	6.482
4	1.54	11.01	10.93	10.56	7.39	5.996
5		11.01	8.75	8.45	6.65	5.546
6		1.38	8.74	6.76	5.99	5.130
7			8.75	6.55	5.90	4.746
8			1.09	6.55	5.91	4.459
9				6.56	5.90	4.459
10				6.55	5.91	4.459
11				0.82	5.90	4.459
12					5.91	4.460
13					5.90	4.459
14					5.91	4.460
15					5.90	4.459
16					0.74	4.460
17						4.459
18						4.460
19						4.459
20						4.460
21						0.557

TABLE 3

General Depreciation System—MACRS
Personal Property Placed in Service after 12/31/86
Applicable Convention: Mid-quarter (Property Placed in Service in Second Quarter)
Applicable Depreciation Method: 200 or 150 Percent Declining Balance Switching to Straight Line

If the Recovery Year Is:	3-Year	5-Year	7-Year	10-Year	15-Year	20-Year
	The Depreciation Rate Is:					
1	41.67	25.00	17.85	12.50	6.25	4.688
2	38.89	30.00	23.47	17.50	9.38	7.148
3	14.14	18.00	16.76	14.00	8.44	6.612
4	5.30	11.37	11.97	11.20	7.59	6.116
5		11.37	8.87	8.96	6.83	5.658
6		4.26	8.87	7.17	6.15	5.233
7			8.87	6.55	5.91	4.841
8			3.33	6.55	5.90	4.478
9				6.56	5.91	4.463
10				6.55	5.90	4.463
11				2.46	5.91	4.463
12					5.90	4.463
13					5.91	4.463
14					5.90	4.463
15					5.91	4.462
16					2.21	4.463
17						4.462
18						4.463
19						4.462
20						4.463
21						1.673

TABLE 4

General Depreciation System—MACRS
Personal Property Placed in Service after 12/31/86
Applicable Convention: Mid-quarter (Property Placed in Service in Third Quarter)
Applicable Depreciation Method: 200 or 150 Percent Declining Balance Switching to Straight Line

If the Recovery Year Is:	And the Recovery Period Is: 3-Year	5-Year	7-Year	10-Year	15-Year	20-Year
	The Depreciation Rate Is:					
1	25.00	15.00	10.71	7.50	3.75	2.813
2	50.00	34.00	25.51	18.50	9.63	7.289
3	16.67	20.40	18.22	14.80	8.66	6.742
4	8.33	12.24	13.02	11.84	7.80	6.237
5		11.30	9.30	9.47	7.02	5.769
6		7.06	8.85	7.58	6.31	5.336
7			8.86	6.55	5.90	4.936
8			5.53	6.55	5.90	4.566
9				6.56	5.91	4.460
10				6.55	5.90	4.460
11				4.10	5.91	4.460
12					5.90	4.460
13					5.91	4.461
14					5.90	4.460
15					5.91	4.461
16					3.69	4.460
17						4.461
18						4.460
19						4.461
20						4.460
21						2.788

TABLE 5

General Depreciation System—MACRS
Personal Property Placed in Service after 12/31/86
Applicable Convention: Mid-quarter (Property Placed in Service in Fourth Quarter)
Applicable Depreciation Method: 200 or 150 Percent Declining Balance Switching to Straight Line

If the Recovery Year Is:	And the Recovery Period Is: 3-Year	5-Year	7-Year	10-Year	15-Year	20-Year
	The Depreciation Rate Is:					
1	8.33	5.00	3.57	2.50	1.25	0.938
2	61.11	38.00	27.55	19.50	9.88	7.430
3	20.37	22.80	19.68	15.60	8.89	6.872
4	10.19	13.68	14.06	12.48	8.00	6.357
5		10.94	10.04	9.98	7.20	5.880
6		9.58	8.73	7.99	6.48	5.439
7			8.73	6.55	5.90	5.031
8			7.64	6.55	5.90	4.654
9				6.56	5.90	4.458
10				6.55	5.91	4.458
11				5.74	5.90	4.458
12					5.91	4.458
13					5.90	4.458
14					5.91	4.458
15					5.90	4.458
16					5.17	4.458
17						4.458
18						4.459
19						4.458
20						4.459
21						3.901

TABLE 6

Luxury Automobile Limitations

	Year Automobile is Placed in Service[a]:						
	2001	2000	1999	1998	1997	1996	1995
Year 1	3,060	3,060	3,060	3,160	3,160	3,060	3,060
Year 2	4,900	4,900	5,000	5,000	5,000	4,900	4,900
Year 3	2,950	2,950	2,950	2,950	3,050	2,950	2,950
Year 4 and Each Succeeding Year	1,775	1,775	1,775	1,775	1,775	1,775	1,775

[a] For years prior to 1995, see Revenue Procedure for appropriate year.

TABLE 7
General Depreciation System—MACRS
Residential Rental Real Property Placed in Service after 12/31/86
Applicable Recovery Period: 27.5 Years
Applicable Convention: Mid-month
Applicable Depreciation Method: Straight Line

If the Recovery Year Is:	\multicolumn{12}{c}{And the Month in the First Recovery Year the Property Is Placed in Service Is:}												
	1	2	3	4	5	6	7	8	9	10	11	12
	\multicolumn{12}{l}{The Depreciation Rate Is:}												
1	3.485	3.182	2.879	2.576	2.273	1.970	1.667	1.364	1.061	0.758	0.455	0.152
2	3.636	3.636	3.636	3.636	3.636	3.636	3.636	3.636	3.636	3.636	3.636	3.636
3	3.636	3.636	3.636	3.636	3.636	3.636	3.636	3.636	3.636	3.636	3.636	3.636
4	3.636	3.636	3.636	3.636	3.636	3.636	3.636	3.636	3.636	3.636	3.636	3.636
5	3.636	3.636	3.636	3.636	3.636	3.636	3.636	3.636	3.636	3.636	3.636	3.636
6	3.636	3.636	3.636	3.636	3.636	3.636	3.636	3.636	3.636	3.636	3.636	3.636
7	3.636	3.636	3.636	3.636	3.636	3.636	3.636	3.636	3.636	3.636	3.636	3.636
8	3.636	3.636	3.636	3.636	3.636	3.636	3.636	3.636	3.636	3.636	3.636	3.636
9	3.636	3.636	3.636	3.636	3.636	3.636	3.636	3.636	3.636	3.636	3.636	3.636
10	3.637	3.637	3.637	3.637	3.637	3.637	3.636	3.636	3.636	3.636	3.636	3.636
11	3.636	3.636	3.636	3.636	3.636	3.636	3.637	3.637	3.637	3.637	3.637	3.637
12	3.637	3.637	3.637	3.637	3.637	3.637	3.636	3.636	3.636	3.636	3.636	3.636
13	3.636	3.636	3.636	3.636	3.636	3.636	3.637	3.637	3.637	3.637	3.637	3.637
14	3.637	3.637	3.637	3.637	3.637	3.637	3.636	3.636	3.636	3.636	3.636	3.636
15	3.636	3.636	3.636	3.636	3.636	3.636	3.637	3.637	3.637	3.637	3.637	3.637
16	3.637	3.637	3.637	3.637	3.637	3.637	3.636	3.636	3.636	3.636	3.636	3.636
17	3.636	3.636	3.636	3.636	3.636	3.636	3.637	3.637	3.637	3.637	3.637	3.637
18	3.637	3.637	3.637	3.637	3.637	3.637	3.636	3.636	3.636	3.636	3.636	3.636
19	3.636	3.636	3.636	3.636	3.636	3.636	3.637	3.637	3.637	3.637	3.637	3.637
20	3.637	3.637	3.637	3.637	3.637	3.637	3.636	3.636	3.636	3.636	3.636	3.636
21	3.636	3.636	3.636	3.636	3.636	3.636	3.637	3.637	3.637	3.637	3.637	3.637
22	3.637	3.637	3.637	3.637	3.637	3.637	3.636	3.636	3.636	3.636	3.636	3.636
23	3.636	3.636	3.636	3.636	3.636	3.636	3.637	3.637	3.637	3.637	3.637	3.637
24	3.637	3.637	3.637	3.637	3.637	3.637	3.636	3.636	3.636	3.636	3.636	3.636
25	3.636	3.636	3.636	3.636	3.636	3.636	3.637	3.637	3.637	3.637	3.637	3.637
26	3.637	3.637	3.637	3.637	3.637	3.637	3.636	3.636	3.636	3.636	3.636	3.636
27	3.636	3.636	3.636	3.636	3.636	3.636	3.637	3.637	3.637	3.637	3.637	3.637
28	1.970	2.273	2.576	2.879	3.182	3.485	3.636	3.636	3.636	3.636	3.636	3.636
29	0.000	0.000	0.000	0.000	0.000	0.000	0.152	0.455	0.758	1.061	1.364	1.667

TABLE 8

General Depreciation System—MACRS
Nonresidential Rental Real Property Placed in Service after 12/31/86 and before 5/13/93
Applicable Recovery Period: 31.5 Years
Applicable Convention: Mid-month
Applicable Depreciation Method: Straight Line

If the Recovery Year Is:	\multicolumn{12}{c}{And the Month in the First Recovery Year the Property Is Placed in Service Is:}
	1	2	3	4	5	6	7	8	9	10	11	12
	\multicolumn{12}{l}{The Depreciation Rate Is:}
1	3.042	2.778	2.513	2.249	1.984	1.720	1.455	1.190	0.926	0.661	0.397	0.132
2	3.175	3.175	3.175	3.175	3.175	3.175	3.175	3.175	3.175	3.175	3.175	3.175
3	3.175	3.175	3.175	3.175	3.175	3.175	3.175	3.175	3.175	3.175	3.175	3.175
4	3.175	3.175	3.175	3.175	3.175	3.175	3.175	3.175	3.175	3.175	3.175	3.175
5	3.175	3.175	3.175	3.175	3.175	3.175	3.175	3.175	3.175	3.175	3.175	3.175
6	3.175	3.175	3.175	3.175	3.175	3.175	3.175	3.175	3.175	3.175	3.175	3.175
7	3.175	3.175	3.175	3.175	3.175	3.175	3.175	3.175	3.175	3.175	3.175	3.175
8	3.175	3.174	3.175	3.174	3.175	3.174	3.175	3.175	3.175	3.175	3.175	3.175
9	3.174	3.175	3.174	3.175	3.174	3.175	3.174	3.175	3.174	3.175	3.174	3.175
10	3.175	3.174	3.175	3.174	3.175	3.174	3.175	3.174	3.175	3.174	3.175	3.174
11	3.174	3.175	3.174	3.175	3.174	3.175	3.174	3.175	3.174	3.175	3.174	3.175
12	3.175	3.174	3.175	3.174	3.175	3.174	3.175	3.174	3.175	3.174	3.175	3.174
13	3.174	3.175	3.174	3.175	3.174	3.175	3.174	3.175	3.174	3.175	3.174	3.175
14	3.175	3.174	3.175	3.174	3.175	3.174	3.175	3.174	3.175	3.174	3.175	3.174
15	3.174	3.175	3.174	3.175	3.174	3.175	3.174	3.175	3.174	3.175	3.174	3.175
16	3.175	3.174	3.175	3.174	3.175	3.174	3.175	3.174	3.175	3.174	3.175	3.174
17	3.174	3.175	3.174	3.175	3.174	3.175	3.174	3.175	3.174	3.175	3.174	3.175
18	3.175	3.174	3.175	3.174	3.175	3.174	3.175	3.174	3.175	3.174	3.175	3.174
19	3.174	3.175	3.174	3.175	3.174	3.175	3.174	3.175	3.174	3.175	3.174	3.175
20	3.175	3.174	3.175	3.174	3.175	3.174	3.175	3.174	3.175	3.174	3.175	3.174
21	3.174	3.175	3.174	3.175	3.174	3.175	3.174	3.175	3.174	3.175	3.174	3.175
22	3.175	3.174	3.175	3.174	3.175	3.174	3.175	3.174	3.175	3.174	3.175	3.174
23	3.174	3.175	3.174	3.175	3.174	3.175	3.174	3.175	3.174	3.175	3.174	3.175
24	3.175	3.174	3.175	3.174	3.175	3.174	3.175	3.174	3.175	3.174	3.175	3.174
25	3.174	3.175	3.174	3.175	3.174	3.175	3.174	3.175	3.174	3.175	3.174	3.175
26	3.175	3.174	3.175	3.174	3.175	3.174	3.175	3.174	3.175	3.174	3.175	3.174
27	3.174	3.175	3.174	3.175	3.174	3.175	3.174	3.175	3.174	3.175	3.174	3.175
28	3.175	3.174	3.175	3.174	3.175	3.174	3.175	3.174	3.175	3.174	3.175	3.174
29	3.174	3.175	3.174	3.175	3.174	3.175	3.174	3.175	3.174	3.175	3.174	3.175
30	3.175	3.174	3.175	3.174	3.175	3.174	3.175	3.174	3.175	3.174	3.175	3.174
31	3.174	3.175	3.174	3.175	3.174	3.175	3.174	3.175	3.174	3.175	3.174	3.175
32	1.720	1.984	2.249	2.513	2.778	3.042	3.175	3.174	3.175	3.174	3.175	3.174
33	0.000	0.000	0.000	0.000	0.000	0.000	0.132	0.397	0.661	0.926	1.190	1.455

TABLE 9

General Depreciation System—MACRS
Nonresidential Rental Real Property Placed in Service after 5/12/93
Applicable Recovery Period: 39 years
Applicable Depreciation Method: Straight Line

If the Recovery Year Is:	And the Month in the First Recovery Year the Property Is Placed in Service Is:											
	1	2	3	4	5	6	7	8	9	10	11	12
	The Depreciation Rate Is:											
1	2.461	2.247	2.033	1.819	1.605	1.391	1.177	0.963	0.749	0.535	0.321	0.107
2-39	2.564	2.564	2.564	2.564	2.564	2.564	2.564	2.564	2.564	2.564	2.564	2.564
40	0.107	0.321	0.535	0.749	0.963	1.177	1.391	1.605	1.819	2.033	2.247	2.461

TABLE 10

Alternative Depreciation System—MACRS (Partial Table)
Property Placed in Service after 12/31/86
Applicable Convention: Half-year
Applicable Depreciation Method: 150 Percent Declining Balance Switching to Straight Line

If the Recovery Year Is:	And the Recovery Period Is:					
	3	4	5	7	10	12
	The Depreciation Rate Is:					
1	25.00	18.75	15.00	10.71	7.50	6.25
2	37.50	30.47	25.50	19.13	13.88	11.72
3	25.00	20.31	17.85	15.03	11.79	10.25
4	12.50	20.31	16.66	12.25	10.02	8.97
5		10.16	16.66	12.25	8.74	7.85
6			8.33	12.25	8.74	7.33
7				12.25	8.74	7.33
8				6.13	8.74	7.33
9					8.74	7.33
10					8.74	7.33
11					4.37	7.32
12						7.33
13						3.66

▼ TABLE 11

Alternative Depreciation System—MACRS (Partial Table)
Property Placed in Service after 12/31/86
Applicable Convention: Half-year
Applicable Depreciation Method: Straight Line

If the Recovery Year Is:	And the Recovery Period Is:					
	3	4	5	7	10	12
	The Depreciation Rate Is:					
1	16.67	12.50	10.00	7.14	5.00	4.17
2	33.33	25.00	20.00	14.29	10.00	8.33
3	33.33	25.00	20.00	14.29	10.00	8.33
4	16.67	25.00	20.00	14.28	10.00	8.33
5		12.50	20.00	14.29	10.00	8.33
6			10.00	14.28	10.00	8.33
7				14.29	10.00	8.34
8				7.14	10.00	8.33
9					10.00	8.34
10					10.00	8.33
11					5.00	8.34
12						8.33
13						4.17

▼ TABLE 12

Alternative Depreciation System—MACRS
Real Property Placed into Service after 12/31/86
Applicable Recovery Period: 40 years
Applicable Convention: Mid-month
Applicable Depreciation Method: Straight Line

If the Recovery Year Is:	And the Month in the First Recovery Year the Property Is Placed in Service Is:											
	1	2	3	4	5	6	7	8	9	10	11	12
	The Depreciation Rate Is:											
1	2.396	2.188	1.979	1.771	1.563	1.354	1.146	0.938	0.729	0.521	0.313	0.104
2 to 40	2.500	2.500	2.500	2.500	2.500	2.500	2.500	2.500	2.500	2.500	2.500	2.500
41	0.104	0.312	0.521	0.729	0.937	1.146	1.354	1.562	1.771	1.979	2.187	2.396

TABLE 13
Depreciation System—ACRS
19-Year Real Property (19-Year 175% Declining Balance)
Mid-Month Convention
Property Placed in Service after 5/8/85 and before 1/1/87

If the Recovery Year Is:	\multicolumn{12}{c}{And the Month in the First Recovery Year the Property Is Placed in Service Is:}
	1	2	3	4	5	6	7	8	9	10	11	12
	\multicolumn{12}{l}{The Depreciation Rate Is:}
1	8.8	8.1	7.3	6.5	5.8	5.0	4.2	3.5	2.7	1.9	1.1	0.4
2	8.4	8.5	8.5	8.6	8.7	8.8	8.8	8.9	9.0	9.0	9.1	9.2
3	7.6	7.7	7.7	7.8	7.9	7.9	8.0	8.1	8.1	8.2	8.3	8.3
4	6.9	7.0	7.0	7.1	7.1	7.2	7.3	7.3	7.4	7.4	7.5	7.6
5	6.3	6.3	6.4	6.4	6.5	6.5	6.6	6.6	6.7	6.8	6.8	6.9
6	5.7	5.7	5.8	5.9	5.9	5.9	6.0	6.0	6.1	6.1	6.2	6.2
7	5.2	5.2	5.3	5.3	5.3	5.4	5.4	5.5	5.5	5.6	5.6	5.6
8	4.7	4.7	4.8	4.8	4.8	4.9	4.9	5.0	5.0	5.1	5.1	5.1
9	4.2	4.3	4.3	4.4	4.4	4.5	4.5	4.5	4.5	4.6	4.6	4.7
10	4.2	4.2	4.2	4.2	4.2	4.2	4.2	4.2	4.2	4.2	4.2	4.2
11	4.2	4.2	4.2	4.2	4.2	4.2	4.2	4.2	4.2	4.2	4.2	4.2
12	4.2	4.2	4.2	4.2	4.2	4.2	4.2	4.2	4.2	4.2	4.2	4.2
13	4.2	4.2	4.2	4.2	4.2	4.2	4.2	4.2	4.2	4.2	4.2	4.2
14	4.2	4.2	4.2	4.2	4.2	4.2	4.2	4.2	4.2	4.2	4.2	4.2
15	4.2	4.2	4.2	4.2	4.2	4.2	4.2	4.2	4.2	4.2	4.2	4.2
16	4.2	4.2	4.2	4.2	4.2	4.2	4.2	4.2	4.2	4.2	4.2	4.2
17	4.2	4.2	4.2	4.2	4.2	4.2	4.2	4.2	4.2	4.2	4.2	4.2
18	4.2	4.2	4.2	4.2	4.2	4.2	4.2	4.2	4.2	4.2	4.2	4.2
19	4.2	4.2	4.2	4.2	4.2	4.2	4.2	4.2	4.2	4.2	4.2	4.2
20	0.2	0.5	0.9	1.2	1.6	1.9	2.3	2.6	3.0	3.3	3.7	4.0

▼ TABLE 14

Depreciation System—ACRS
18-Year Real Property (18-Year 175% Declining Balance)
Mid-Month Convention
Property Placed in Service after 6/22/84 and before 5/9/85

If the Recovery Year Is:	\multicolumn{12}{c}{And the Month in the First Recovery Year the Property Is Placed in Service Is:}
	1	2	3	4	5	6	7	8	9	10	11	12
	\multicolumn{12}{l}{The Applicable Percentage Is:}
1	9	9	8	7	6	5	4	4	3	2	1	0.4
2	9	9	9	9	9	9	9	9	9	10	10	10.0
3	8	8	8	8	8	8	8	8	9	9	9	9.0
4	7	7	7	7	7	8	8	8	8	8	8	8.0
5	7	7	7	7	7	7	7	7	7	7	7	7.0
6	6	6	6	6	6	6	6	6	6	6	6	6.0
7	5	5	5	5	6	6	6	6	6	6	6	6.0
8	5	5	5	5	5	5	5	5	5	5	5	5.0
9	5	5	5	5	5	5	5	5	5	5	5	5.0
10	5	5	5	5	5	5	5	5	5	5	5	5.0
11	5	5	5	5	5	5	5	5	5	5	5	5.0
12	5	5	5	5	5	5	5	5	5	5	5	5.0
13	4	4	4	5	4	4	5	4	4	4	5	5.0
14	4	4	4	4	4	4	4	4	4	4	4	4.0
15	4	4	4	4	4	4	4	4	4	4	4	4.0
16	4	4	4	4	4	4	4	4	4	4	4	4.0
17	4	4	4	4	4	4	4	4	4	4	4	4.0
18	4	3	4	4	4	4	4	4	4	4	4	4.0
19		1	1	1	2	2	2	3	3	3	3	3.6

TABLE 15
Depreciation System—ACRS
18-Year Real Property (18-Year 175% Declining Balance)
Full-Month Convention
Property Placed in Service after 3/15/84 and before 6/23/84

If the Recovery Year Is:	And the Month in the First Recovery Year the Property Is Placed in Service Is:											
	1	2	3	4	5	6	7	8	9	10	11	12
	The Applicable Percentage Is:											
1	10	9	8	7	6	6	5	4	3	2	2	1
2	9	9	9	9	9	9	9	9	9	10	10	10
3	8	8	8	8	8	8	8	8	9	9	9	9
4	7	7	7	7	7	7	8	8	8	8	8	8
5	6	7	7	7	7	7	7	7	7	7	7	7
6	6	6	6	6	6	6	6	6	6	6	6	6
7	5	5	5	5	6	6	6	6	6	6	6	6
8	5	5	5	5	5	5	5	5	5	5	5	5
9	5	5	5	5	5	5	5	5	5	5	5	5
10	5	5	5	5	5	5	5	5	5	5	5	5
11	5	5	5	5	5	5	5	5	5	5	5	5
12	5	5	5	5	5	5	5	5	5	5	5	5
13	4	4	4	5	5	4	4	5	4	4	4	4
14	4	4	4	4	4	4	4	4	4	4	4	4
15	4	4	4	4	4	4	4	4	4	4	4	4
16	4	4	4	4	4	4	4	4	4	4	4	4
17	4	4	4	4	4	4	4	4	4	4	4	4
18	4	4	4	4	4	4	4	4	4	4	4	4
19		1	1	1	2	2	2	3	3	3	4	

▼ TABLE 16

Depreciation System—ACRS
Full Month Convention
1. All 15-Year Real Estate (Except Low-Income Housing)
Property Placed in Service after 12/31/80 and before 3/16/84

If the Recovery Year Is:	And the Month in the First Year the Property Is Placed in Service Is:											
	1	2	3	4	5	6	7	8	9	10	11	12
	The Applicable Percentage Is:											
1	12	11	10	9	8	7	6	5	4	3	2	1
2	10	10	11	11	11	11	11	11	11	11	11	12
3	9	9	9	9	10	10	10	10	10	10	10	10
4	8	8	8	8	8	8	9	9	9	9	9	9
5	7	7	7	7	7	7	8	8	8	8	8	8
6	6	6	6	6	7	7	7	7	7	7	7	7
7	6	6	6	6	6	6	6	6	6	6	6	6
8	6	6	6	6	6	6	5	6	6	6	6	6
9	6	6	6	6	5	5	5	5	6	6	6	6
10	5	6	5	6	5	5	5	5	5	6	6	5
11	5	5	5	5	5	5	5	5	5	5	5	5
12	5	5	5	5	5	5	5	5	5	5	5	5
13	5	5	5	5	5	5	5	5	5	5	5	5
14	5	5	5	5	5	5	5	5	5	5	5	5
15	5	5	5	5	5	5	5	5	5	5	5	5
16	—	—	1	1	2	2	3	3	4	4	4	5

2. Low-Income Housing
Property Placed in Service after 12/31/80 and before 5/9/85[a]

If the Recovery Year Is:	And the Month in the First Year the Property Is Placed in Service Is:											
	1	2	3	4	5	6	7	8	9	10	11	12
	The Applicable Percentage Is:											
1	13	12	11	10	9	8	7	6	4	3	2	1
2	12	12	12	12	12	12	12	13	13	13	13	13
3	10	10	10	10	11	11	11	11	11	11	11	11
4	9	9	9	9	9	9	9	9	10	10	10	10
5	8	8	8	8	8	8	8	8	8	8	8	8
6	7	7	7	7	7	7	7	7	7	7	7	7
7	6	6	6	6	6	6	6	6	6	6	6	6
8	5	5	5	5	5	5	5	5	5	5	6	6
9	5	5	5	5	5	5	5	5	5	5	5	5
10	5	5	5	5	5	5	5	5	5	5	5	5
11	4	5	5	5	5	5	5	5	5	5	5	5
12	4	4	4	5	4	5	5	5	5	5	5	5
13	4	4	4	4	4	4	5	4	5	5	5	5
14	4	4	4	4	4	4	4	4	4	5	4	4
15	4	4	4	4	4	4	4	4	4	4	4	4
16	—	—	1	1	2	2	2	3	3	3	4	4

[a] For the period after 5/8/85, see special IRS tables (not reproduced here).

TABLE 17
Lease Inclusion Dollar Amounts for Automobiles (Partial Table)
(Other Than for Electronic Automobiles)
With A Lease Term Beginning in Calendar Year 2000[a]

Fair Market Value of Automobiles Over	Not Over	1st	2nd	3rd	4th	5th and Later
$15,500	15,800	3	6	9	10	12
15,800	16,100	5	12	17	20	23
16,100	16,400	8	17	25	30	34
16,400	16,700	10	23	33	40	45
16,700	17,000	13	28	42	49	57
17,000	17,500	16	36	52	62	72
17,500	18,000	20	45	66	78	91
18,000	18,500	25	54	79	95	109
18,500	19,000	29	63	93	111	128
19,000	19,500	33	72	107	127	147
19,500	20,000	37	81	121	143	166
20,000	20,500	41	91	133	160	185
20,500	21,000	45	100	147	176	204
21,000	21,500	50	109	160	193	222
21,500	22,000	54	118	174	209	241
22,000	23,000	60	132	194	234	269
23,000	24,000	68	150	222	266	306
24,000	25,000	77	168	249	298	345
25,000	26,000	85	187	276	331	381
26,000	27,000	93	205	303	364	419
27,000	28,000	102	223	330	396	457
28,000	29,000	110	241	358	429	494
29,000	30,000	119	259	385	461	532
30,000	31,000	127	278	412	493	570
31,000	32,000	135	296	439	527	607
32,000	33,000	144	314	467	558	645
33,000	34,000	152	333	493	591	683
34,000	35,000	160	351	521	623	720
35,000	36,000	169	369	548	656	757
36,000	37,000	177	388	574	689	795
37,000	38,000	185	406	602	721	833
38,000	39,000	194	424	629	754	870
39,000	40,000	202	443	656	786	908
40,000	41,000	210	461	683	819	946
41,000	42,000	219	479	710	852	983
42,000	43,000	227	497	738	884	1,021
43,000	44,000	235	516	765	916	1,058
44,000	45,000	244	534	792	949	1,095
45,000	46,000	252	552	819	982	1,133
46,000	47,000	260	571	846	1,014	1,171
47,000	48,000	269	589	873	1,047	1,208
48,000	49,000	277	607	901	1,079	1,246
49,000	50,000	285	626	927	1,112	1,284
50,000	51,000	294	644	954	1,145	1,321
51,000	52,000	302	662	982	1,177	1,359
52,000	53,000	311	680	1,009	1,210	1,396
53,000	54,000	319	699	1,036	1,242	1,433
54,000	55,000	327	717	1,063	1,275	1,471

[a] Per *Rev. Proc.* 2000-18, I.R.B. 2000-9, 722. The table for 2001 had not been released at the date of the printing.

▼ TABLE 17 (continued)

Fair Market Value of Automobiles		Tax Year During Lease				
Over	Not Over	1st	2nd	3rd	4th	5th and Later
$55,000	56,000	336	735	1,090	1,308	1,508
56,000	57,000	344	754	1,117	1,340	1,546
57,000	58,000	352	772	1,145	1,372	1,584
58,000	59,000	361	790	1,172	1,405	1,621
59,000	60,000	369	808	1,199	1,438	1,659

[a]Per *Rev. Proc.* 2000-18, I.R.B. 2000-9, 722. The table for 2001 had not been released at the date of the printing.

APPENDIX D

GLOSSARY

Ability to pay A concept in taxation that holds that taxpayers be taxed according to their ability to pay such taxes, that is, taxpayers that have sufficient financial resources should pay the tax. This concept is an integral part of vertical equity.

Accelerated Cost Recovery System (ACRS) Established by ERTA in 1981, the ACRS provides an accelerated depreciation and shorter cost-recovery period for real and personal property. The Tax Reform Act of 1986 changed the previously allowed depreciation tables and assigned recovery periods that approach the asset's true economic life. The current depreciation system is referred to as MACRS.

Accounting method The method of determining the taxable year in which income and expenses are reported for tax purposes. Generally, the same method must be used for tax purposes as is used for keeping books and records. The accounting treatment used for any item of income or expense and of specific items (e.g., installment sales and contracts) is included in this term. See also each specific accounting method.

Accounting period The period of time, usually 12 months, used by taxpayers to compute their taxable income. Taxpayers who do not keep records must use a calendar year. Taxpayers who do keep books and records may choose between a calendar year or a fiscal year. The accounting period election is made on the taxpayer's first filed return and cannot be changed without IRS consent. The accounting period may be less than 12 months if it is the taxpayer's first or final return or if the taxpayer is changing accounting periods. Certain restrictions upon the use of a fiscal year apply to partnerships, S corporations, and personal service corporations.

Accountable plan A type of employee reimbursement plan that meets two tests, (1) substantiation, and (2) return of excess reimbursement. Under an accountable plan, reimbursements are excluded from the employee's gross income and the expenses are not deductible by the employee.

Accrual method of accounting Accounting method under which income is reported and expenses are deducted when (1) all events have occurred that fix the taxpayer's right to receive the income and (2) the amount of the item can be determined with reasonable accuracy. Taxpayers with inventories to report must use this method to report sales and purchases.

Accumulated earnings tax This penalty tax is intended to discourage companies from retaining excessive amounts of earnings if the funds are invested in earnings that are unrelated to the business's needs. The current tax rate is 39.6%.

Acquiescence policy IRS policy of announcing whether it agrees or disagrees with a regular Tax Court decision. Such statements are not issued for every case.

ACRS See Accelerated Cost Recovery System.

Active income Income that is produced by the taxpayer's involvement or participation—wages, salaries, and other business income—is considered active income. It is the opposite of passive income.

Additional depreciation The excess of the actual amount of accelerated depreciation (or cost-recovery deductions under ACRS) over the amount of depreciation that would be deductible under the straight-line method. Such depreciation applies to Section 1250 depreciable real property acquired prior to 1987.

Adjusted current earnings An AMT adjustment item for corporations used to compute the Alternative Minimum Tax. The term is a concept based on the traditional earnings and profits definition found in Sec. 312.

Adjusted gross income (AGI) A measure of taxable income that falls between gross income and taxable income. It is the income amount that is used as the basis for calculating the floor or the ceiling for numerous other tax computations.

Adjusted sales price The amount realized from the sale of a residence less any fixing-up expenses.

AGI See Adjusted gross income.

Alimony Payments made pursuant to divorce or separation or written agreement between spouses subject to conditions specified in the tax law. Alimony payments (as contrasted to property settlements) are deductible for AGI by the payor and are included in the gross income of the recipient.

All events test Rule holding that an accrual basis taxpayer must report an item of income (1) when all events have occurred that fix the taxpayer's right to receive the item of income and (2) when the amount of the item can be determined with reasonable accuracy. This test is not satisfied until economic performance has taken place.

Alternative minimum tax (AMT) Applies to individuals, corporations, and estates and trusts only if the tentative minimum tax (TMT) exceeds the taxpayer's regular tax liability. Most taxpayers are not subject to this tax.

Amount realized The amount realized equals the sum of money plus the fair market value of all other property received from the sale or other disposition of the property less any selling expenses (e.g., commissions, advertising, deed preparation costs, and legal expenses) incurred in connection with the sale.

AMT See Alternative Minimum Tax.

Annual accounting period See Accounting period.

Annuity A series of regular payments that will continue for either a fixed period of time or until the death of the recipient. Pensions are usually paid in this way.

Applicable federal rate The rate determined monthly by the federal government which is based on the rate paid by the government on borrowed funds. The rate varies with the term of the loan. Thus, short-term loans are for a period of under three years, mid-term loans are for over three years and under nine years, and long-term loans are for over nine years.

Asset depreciation range (ADR) system of depreciation Depreciation method allowed for property placed in service before January 1, 1981. This method prescribed useful lives for various classes of assets.

Average tax rate The taxpayer's total tax liability divided by the amount of his taxable income.

Backup withholding A modified withholding system intended to prevent abusive noncompliance situations.

Bad debt Bona fide debt that is uncollectible because it is worthless. Such debts are further characterized as "business bad debts,"

D-1

which give rise to an ordinary deduction, and "nonbusiness bad debts," which are treated as a short-term capital loss. A determination of whether a debt is worthless is made by reference to all the pertinent evidence (e.g., the debtor's general financial condition and whether the debt is secured by collateral). Such debts are deductible subject to certain requirements.

Bona fide debt A debt that (1) arises from a valid and enforceable obligation to pay a fixed or determinable sum of money and (2) results in a debtor-creditor relationship.

Boot Cash and nonlike-kind property given to complete an exchange of like-kind property where the property exchanged is not of equal vale. Gain on the exchange is limited to the amount of boot received.

Brother-sister controlled group This type of corporation exists if (1) five or fewer individuals, estates, or trusts own at least 80% of the stock of each corporation and (2) there is common ownership of at least 50% of the total value of all classes of the stock. Each shareholder must own an interest in each corporation.

Business bad debt See Bad debt.

Cafeteria plan Employer-financed plan that offers employees the option of choosing cash or statutory nontaxable fringe benefits (other than scholarships, fellowships, and Sec. 132 benefits such as discounts on merchandise). Such plans may not discriminate in favor of highly compensated individuals or their dependents or spouses.

Capital addition See Capital expenditure.

Capital asset This category of assets includes all assets except inventory, notes and accounts receivable, and depreciable property or land used in a trade or business (e.g., property, plant, and machinery).

Capital expenditure An expenditure that adds to the value of, substantially prolongs the useful life of, or adapts the property to a new or different use qualifies as a capital expenditure.

Capital gain Gain realized on the sale or exchange of a capital asset.

Capital gain dividend A distribution by a regulated investment company (i.e., a mutual fund) of capital gains realized from the sale of investments in the fund. Such dividends also include undistributed capital gains allocated to the shareholders.

Capital gain property Property that is contributed to a public charity upon which a long-term capital gain would be recognized if that property was sold at its fair market value.

Capital loss Loss realized on the sale or exchange of a capital asset.

Capital recovery A capital recovery amount is a deduction for depreciation or cost recovery. It is a factor in the determination of a property's adjusted basis.

Cash method of accounting Accounting method that requires the taxpayer to report income for the taxable year in which payments are actually or constructively received. Expenses are reported in the year they are paid. Most individuals and service businesses (i.e., businesses without inventories) use this method. Small businesses with inventories that have gross receipts of less than $1 million may also use the cash method.

Cash receipts and disbursements method of accounting See Cash method of accounting.

Casualty loss Loss that arises from an identifiable event that was sudden, unexpected, or unusual (e.g., fire, storm, shipwreck, other casualty, or theft). Within certain limitations individuals may deduct such losses from AGI. Business casualty losses are deductible for AGI.

C Corporation Form of business entity that is taxed as a separate tax-paying entity. Its income is subject to an initial tax at the corporate level. Its shareholders are subject to a second tax when dividends are paid from the corporation's earnings and profits. Under certain conditions, S corporation status may be elected for tax purposes. C corporations are sometimes referred to as "regular corporations."

CD See Certificate of deposit.

Charitable contribution deduction Contributions of money or property made to qualified organizations (i.e., public charities and private nonoperating foundations) may be deducted from AGI. The amount of the deduction depends upon (1) the type of charity receiving the contribution, (2) the type of property contributed, and (3) other limitations mandated by the tax law. See also Unrelated use property.

Closed-fact situation Situation or transaction that has already occurred.

Closely held C corporation For purposes of the at risk rules, a closely held C corporation is defined as a corporation where more than 50% of the stock is owned by five or fewer individuals at any time during the last half of the corporation's taxable year. These individuals may or may not be members of the same family.

Community income In any of the eight community property states, such income consists of the income from the personal efforts, investments, etc. of either spouse. Community income belongs equally to both spouses.

Compensation Payment for personal services. Salaries, wages, fees, commissions, tips, bonuses, and specialized forms of compensation such as director's fees and jury's fees fall into this category. However, certain fringe benefits and some foreign-earned income are not taxed.

Completed contract method of accounting Accounting method for long-term contracts undertaken by smaller companies. Income from the contract is reported in the taxable year in which the contract is completed. The completed contract method is limited to construction contracts undertaken by smaller companies.

Constant interest rate method Used to amortize the original issue discount ratably over the life of the bond, this method determines the amount of interest income by multiplying the interest yield to maturity by the adjusted issue price.

Constructive dividend Distribution that is intended to result in a deduction to the corporation. For example, excessive salary payments to shareholde-employees may be recharacterized as nondeductible dividends to the corporation to the extent that such amounts are not reasonable. The excess amount may be treated as dividend income to the shareholder-employees rather than as compensation provided that certain conditions are met.

Constructive receipt doctrine Rule holding that cash method taxpayers cannot turn their backs on the receipt of income if the funds are unqualifiedly made available.

Constructive stock ownership Shares that are indirectly or deemed to be owned by another shareholder due to related party situations.

Contributory pension plan A qualified pension plan to which employees make voluntary contributions.

Controlled group A controlled group is two or more separately incorporated businesses owned by the same individuals or entities. Such groups may consist of parent-subsidiary corporations, brother-sister corporations, or a combination of both (combined group).

Cost The amount paid for property in cash or the fair market value of the property given in exchange. The costs of acquiring the property and preparing it for use are included in the cost of the property.

Cost depletion method Calculation of the depletion of an asset (e.g., oil and gas properties) under which the asset's adjusted basis is divided by the estimated recoverable units to arrive at a per-unit depletion. This amount is then multiplied by the number of units sold to determine the cost depletion. This method may be alternated with the percentage depletion method as long as the calculation takes that into account.

Current year's exclusion The amount of the annuity payment that is excluded from gross income. This amount is determined by multiplying the exclusion ratio by the amount received during the year.

Customs duties A federal excise tax on imported goods.

Deductions for AGI Expenses one would see on an income statement prepared for financial accounting purposes, for example, compensation paid to employees, repairs to business property, and depreciation expenses. Certain nonbusiness deductions (e.g., alimony payments, moving expenses, and deductible payments to an individual retirement account (IRA) are also deductible for AGI.

Deductions from AGI Generally, deductions are allowed for certain personal expenses such as medical deductions and charitable contributions which are referred to as itemized deductions. Alternatively, individuals may deduct the standard deduction. Personal and dependency deductions are also deductions from AGI.

Deferred compensation Methods of compensating employees based upon their current service where the benefits are deferred until future periods (e.g., a pension plan).

Defined benefit pension plan Qualified pension plan which establishes a contribution formula based upon actuarial techniques that are intended to fund a fixed retirement benefit amount. Thus, the amount that will be available at the time of retirement is determined when the contributions are made.

Defined contribution pension plan Qualified pension plan under which a separate account is maintained for each participant and fixed amounts are contributed based upon a specific percentage-of-compensation formula. The retirement benefits are based on the value of the participant's account at the time of retirement. Defined contribution plans for self-employed individuals are referred to as *H.R. 10 plans*.

Dependent care assistance program Employer-financed programs that provide care for an employee's children or other dependents. An employee may exclude up to $5,000 from gross income although the ceiling amount (i.e., $2,400 or $4,800) on the child care credit is reduced by the amount of assistance that is excluded from gross income.

DIF See Discriminate Function System.

Discriminate Function System (DIF) System used by the IRS to select individual returns for audit. This system is intended to identify those tax returns which are most likely to contain errors.

Dividends-received deduction The deduction on dividends received by corporate shareholders that attempts to mitigate the triple taxation that would occur if one corporation paid dividends to a corporate shareholder who, in turn, distributed such amounts to its individual shareholders. Certain restrictions and limitations apply to this deduction.

E&P See Earnings and profits

Earnings and profits (E&P) A measure of the corporation's ability to pay a dividend from its current and accumulated earnings without an impairment of capital.

Economic performance test Economic performance occurs when the property or services to be provided are actually delivered.

Education expense Subject to certain limitations and restrictions, education expenses are deductible if they are incurred (1) to improve or maintain the individual's existing skills or (2) to meet requirements that are requisite to continued employment or meet the requirements of state law.

Effective tax rate The taxpayer's total tax liability divided by his total economic income.

Electronic Filing The method of filing a tax return with the IRS by electronic means instead of paper forms.

Employee achievement award Award given under circumstances that does not create a likelihood that it is really disguised compensation. It must be in the form of tangible personal property (other than cash) and be valued at no more than $400.

Employee stock ownership plan (ESOP) A qualified stock bonus plan or combined stock bonus plan and money purchase pension plan. ESOP's are funded by contributions of the employer's stock which are held for the employees' benefit.

Employment taxes Social security (FICA) and federal and state unemployment compensation taxes.

Entertainment expense Entertainment expenses (e.g., business meals) that are either directly related to or associated with the active conduct of a trade or business are deductible within certain limitations and restrictions. Directly related expenses are those that (1) derive a business benefit other than goodwill and (2) are incurred in a clear business setting. Expenses that are associated with the business are those that show a clear business purpose (e.g., obtaining new business) and occur on the same day the business is discussed.

ESOP See Employee stock ownership plan.

Estate tax Part of the federal unified transfer tax system, this tax is based upon the total property transfers an individual makes during his lifetime and at death.

Excess depreciation See Additional depreciation.

Exchange A transaction in which one receives a reciprocal transfer of property rather than cash and/or a cash equivalent.

Excise taxes Federal tax on alcohol, gasoline, telephone usage, oil and gas production, etc. State and local governments may impose similar taxes on goods and services.

Exclusion Any item of income that the tax law says is not taxable.

Exclusion ratio The portion of the annuity payment that is excluded from taxation. This amount equals the investment in the contract (its cost) divided by the expected return from the annuity.

Expected return The amount which a taxpayer can expect to receive from an annuity. It is determined by multiplying the amount of the annuity's annual payment by the expected return multiple.

Expected return multiple The number of years that the annuity is expected to continue. This amount may be a stated term or for the remainder of the taxpayer's life.

Fair market value (FMV) This amount is the price at which property would change hands between a willing buyer and a willing seller where neither party is under any compulsion to buy or sell.

Federal estate tax See estate tax.

Federal Insurance Contributions Act See FICA.

Federal Unemployment Tax Act See FUTA.

FICA Tax withheld through the payment of payroll taxes, FICA is intended to finance social security benefits for individuals who are not self-employed. Employees and employers contribute matching amounts until a federally-set annual earnings ceiling is reached. At that time, no further contributions need be made for that year. No ceiling exists for the hospital insurance (HI) portion of the tax. Self-employed individuals are subject to self-employment tax and currently receive a *for* AGI income tax deduction equal to 50% of their self-employment tax payments.

Field audit procedure Audit procedure generally used by the IRS for corporations or individuals engaged in a trade or business and conducted at either the taxpayer's place of business or his tax advisor's office. Generally, several items on the tax return are examined.

FIFO method of inventory valuation This flow of cost method assumes that the first goods purchased will be the first goods sold. Thus, the ending inventory consists of the last goods purchased.

Fiscal year An annual accounting period that ends on the last day of any month other than December. A fiscal year may be elected by taxpayers that keep books and records, such as businesses.

Fixing-up expenses Expenses incurred to assist in the sale of a residence (e.g., normal repairs and painting costs). Capital expenditures do not qualify as fixing-up expenses.

Flat tax See Proportional tax.

Foreign-earned income An individual's earnings from personal services rendered in a foreign country.

Foreign tax credit Tax credit given to mitigate the possibility of double taxation faced by U.S. taxpayers earning foreign income.

Former passive activity An activity that was formerly considered passive, but which is not considered to be passive with respect to the taxpayer for the current year.

Franchise tax State tax levy sometimes based upon a weighted average formula consisting of net worth, income, and sales.

Functional-use test A test used to determine whether property is considered similar or related in service or use for purposes of involuntary conversions of property under Sec. 1033. The functional-use test requires that the replacement property be functionally the same as the converted property.

FUTA Federal and state unemployment compensation tax.

GAAP See Generally accepted accounting principles.

Gain realized See Realized gain.

General business credit Special credit category consisting of tax credits commonly available to businesses. The more significant credit items are (1) the investment tax credit, (2) the work opportunity credit, (3) the research credit, (4) the low-income housing credit, (5) the empowerment zone employment credit, (6) the disabled access credit.

Generally accepted accounting principles (GAAP) The accounting principles that govern the preparation of financial reports to shareholders. GAAP does not apply to the tax treatment unless the method clearly reflects income. It is used only when the regulations do not specify the treatment of an item or when the regulations provide more than one alternative accounting method.

Gift tax A tax that is imposed upon the donor for transfers that are not supported by full and adequate consideration. A $10,000 annual exclusion is allowed per donee.

Goodwill The excess of the purchase price of a business over the fair market value of all identifiable assets acquired.

Gross income All income received in cash, property, or services, from whatever source derived and from which the taxpayer derives a direct economic benefit.

Gross tax For income tax purposes, the amount determined by multiplying taxable income by the appropriate tax rate(s). The gross tax may also be found in the appropriate tax table for the taxpayer's filing status.

Half year convention An assumption with respect to depreciation that assumes that all asset acquisitions and dispositions are made at the midpoint of the tax year.

Holding period The length of time an asset is held before it is disposed of. This period is used to determine whether the gain or loss is long- or short-term.

Horizontal equity A concept in taxation that refers to the notion that similarly-situated taxpayers should be treated equally under the tax law.

H.R. 10 Plan Special retirement plan rules applicable to self-employed individuals. Such plans are often referred to as "Keogh plans."

Hybrid method of accounting Accounting method that combines the cash and accrual methods. Under this method, taxpayers can report sales and purchases under the accrual method and other income and expense items under the cash method. See also the cash method of accounting and the accrual method of accounting.

IDCs See Intangible drilling and development costs.

Incrementalism A concept in taxation that described how the tax law has been changed or modified over the years. Under incrementalism, the tax law is changed or an incremental basis rather than a complete revision basis.

Imputed interest rule This rule reallocates the payments received in an installment sale between interest (fully taxable) and principal (only gain is taxable). To avoid this, the stated interest rate must equal at least 100% of the applicable federal rate as determined monthly according to the rate paid by the government on borrowed funds.

Incentive stock option plan (ISO) Stock option plan that allows executives to receive a proprietary interest in the corporation. The option to participate in this type of plan must be exercised according to certain requirements and must follow certain procedures.

Income The economic concept of income measures the amount an individual can consume during a period and remain as well off at the end of the period as at the beginning. The accounting concept of income is a measure of the income that is realized in a transaction. The tax concept of income is close to the accounting concept. It includes both taxable and nontaxable income from any source. However, it does not include a return of capital.

Indeterminate market value If the market value of the property in question cannot be determined by the usual methods, the "open transaction" doctrine may be applied and the tax consequences may be deferred until the transaction is closed. Alternatively, the property may be valued by using the fair market value of the property that is given in the exchange (e.g., the value of the services rendered).

Individual retirement account (IRA) Contribution for AGI that is deductible if (1) neither the taxpayer nor his spouse are active participants in an employer-sponsored retirement plan or (2) certain income limitations are met. Taxpayers who do not meet these requirements may make nondeductible IRA contributions.

Information Release An administrative pronouncement concerning an issue the IRS thinks the general public will be interested in. Such releases are issued in lay terms.

Innocent spouse rule Rule that exempts a spouse from penalty of from liability for the tax if such spouse had no knowledge of nor reason to know about an item of community income.

Installment sale Any disposition of property which involves receiving at least one payment after the close of the taxable year in which the sale occurs.

Installment sale method of accounting Taxpayers may use this method of accounting to reduce the tax burden from gains on the sale of property paid for in installments. Under this method, payment of the tax is deferred until the sale proceeds are collected. This method is not applicable to sales of publicly traded property or to losses.

Intangible drilling and development costs (IDCs) Expenditures made by an operator for wages, fuel, repairs, hauling supplies, and so forth, incident to and necessary for the preparation and drilling of oil and gas wells.

Intangible property Property that does not have physical substance, such as goodwill, patents, stocks and bonds, etc.

Interest The cost charged by a lender for the use of money. For example, finance charges, loan discounts, premiums, loan origination fees, and points paid by a buyer to obtain a mortgage loan are all interest expenses. The deductibility of the expense depends upon the purpose for which the indebtedness was incurred.

Internal Revenue Code The primary legislative source and authority for tax research, planning, and compliance activities.

Internal Revenue Service (IRS) The branch of the Treasury Department that is responsible for administering the federal tax law.

Interpretative Regulations Treasury Regulations that serve to broadly interpret the provisions of the Internal Revenue Code.

Inter vivos gifts Gifts made during the donor's life-time.

Investment expenses All deductions other than interest that are directly connected with the production of investment income.

Investment income Gross income from property held for investment and any net gain attributable to the disposition of such property. See also Net investment income.

Investment interest Interest expense on indebtedness incurred to purchase or carry property held for investment (e.g., income from interest, dividends, annuities, and royalties). Interest expenses incurred from passive activities are not subject to the investment interest limitations and interest incurred to purchase or carry tax-exempt securities is not deductible. Interest incurred from passive activities is subject to the passive activity loss limitation rules.

Involuntary conversion Such a conversion occurs when property is compulsorily converted into money or other property due to theft, seizure, requisition, condemnation, or partial or complete destruction. For example, an involuntary conversion occurs when the government exercises its right of eminent domain.

IRA See Individual retirement account.
IRC See Internal Revenue Code.
IRR See Internal rate of return.
IRS See Internal Revenue Service.
ISO See Incentive stock option.

Itemized deductions Also known as "deductions from AGI," these personal expenditures are allowable for such items as medical expenses, state and local taxes, charitable contributions, unreimbursed employee business expenses, interest on a personal residence, and casualty and theft losses. There are specific requirements for and limitations on the deductibility of each of these items. In addition, only those taxpayers whose total itemized deductions exceed the standard deduction amount can itemize their deductions. In general, for 2001, the total itemized deductions for an individual is reduced by 3% of AGI in excess of $132,950 ($128,950 in 2000), $66,475 ($64,475 in 2000) for married individuals filing a separate return).

Joint income Income from jointly-held property.

Judicial decisions Decisions of a court of law.

Keogh plan Retirement plan for self-employed individuals. This type of plan is also known as an "H.R. 10 plan."

LCM See Lower of cost or market method of inventory valuation.

Legislative Regulations Treasury Regulations issued at the mandate of the Internal Revenue Code. Legislative regulations have a higher degree of authority than interpretative regulations.

Letter Ruling Letter rulings originate from the IRS at the taxpayer's request. They describe how the IRS will treat a proposed transaction. It is only binding on the person requesting the ruling providing the taxpayer completes the transaction as proposed in the ruling. Those of general interest are published as Revenue Rulings.

LIFO method of inventory valuation This method assumes a last-in, first out flow of cost. It results in the lowest taxable income during periods of inflation because it shows the lowest inventory value. Price indexes are used for the valuation. The information in these indexes is grouped into groups (pools) of similar items. See also Simplified LIFO method.

Like class Classes of assets defined by the Regulations that are considered to be property of a like kind for purposes of Sec. 1031. Like class property is tangible personal property that is in the same General Asset Class or the Same Product Class as other property.

Like-kind exchange A direct exchange of like-kind property. The transferred property and the received property must be held for productive use either (1) in a trade or business or (2) as an investment. Nonrecognition of gain or loss is mandatory. Certain like-kind exchanges between related parties are restricted if either party disposes of the property within two years of the exchange.

Like-kind property Property with a similar nature and character. This term does not refer to either the grade or quality of the property.

Limited liability company (LLC) A corporation that is generally taxed under the partnership rules. Although similar to an S corporation, there is no limit to (1) the number of shareholders, (2) the number of classes of stock, or (3) the types of investments in related entities.

Limited liability partnerships (LLP) LLPs are taxes as partnerships but enjoy limited liability under state partnership laws (i.e., individual partners are liable for their own acts and acts of persons under their direction and control but not for negligence or misconduct by other partners).

Liquidating distribution A distribution that liquidates a partner's entire partnership interest due to retirement, death, or other business reason. Such distributions result in a capital gain or loss to the partner whose interest is liquidated. In a corporate liquidation, the liquidating corporation generally recognizes gains and losses on the distribution of the properties and its shareholders recognize capital gain or loss on the surrender of their stock.

Long-term capital gain (LTCG) Gain realized on the sale or exchange of a capital asset held longer than one year.

Long-term capital loss (LTCL) Loss realized on the sale or exchange of a capital asset held longer than one year.

Long-term contracts Building, manufacturing, installation, and construction contracts that are not completed in the same taxable year in which they are entered into. Service contracts do not qualify as long-term contracts. See also Completed contract method of accounting.

Look-back interest Interest that is assessed on any additional tax that would have been paid if the actual total cost of the contract was used to calculate the tax rather than the estimated cost. Thus, it is applicable to any contract of portion of a contract that is accounted for under either the hybrid or percentage of completion method of accounting.

Lower of cost or market method (LCM) of inventory valuation The valuation method is available to all taxpayers other than those using LIFO valuation. It is applied to each separate item in the inventory.

Marginal tax rate The tax that is applied to an incremental amount of taxable income that is added to the tax base. This rate can be used to measure the tax effect of a proposed transaction. Currently, the highest marginal tax rate for individuals is 39.6%.

Market value This term refers to replacement cost under the lower of cost or market inventory method. That is, it is the price at which the taxpayer can replace the goods in question. See also Fair market value.

Material participation The level of participation by a taxpayer in an activity that determines whether the activity is either passibe or active. If a taxpayer does not meet the material participation requirements, the activity is treated as a passive activity.

Medical expense deduction Unreimbursed medical expenses incurred for medical procedures or treatments that are (1) legal in the locality in which they are performed and (2) incurred for the purpose of alleviating a physical or mental defect or illness that affects the body's structure or function are deductible from AGI. Out-of-pocket travel costs incurred while en route to a medical facility, certain capital expenditures affecting the sick person, premiums for medical insurance, and in-patient hospital care are also deductible. Certain restrictions and limitations apply to this deduction.

Memorandum decision Decision issued by the Tax Court. They deal with factual variations on matters which were decided in earlier cases.

Method of accounting See Accounting method.

Miscellaneous itemized deductions Certain unreimbursed employee expenses (e.g., required uniforms, travel, entertainment, and so on) fall into this category. Miscellaneous itemized deductions also include certain investment expenses, appraisal fees for charitable contributions and fees for tax return preparation. The nature of the deduction depends on whether the taxpayer is an employee or a self-employed individual.

Modified percentage of completion method A variation of the regular percentage of completion method where an election may be made to defer reporting profit from a long-term contract until at least 10% of the estimated total cost has been incurred.

Moving expense Expenses incurred in relation to employment-related job transfers.

Necessary expense Expense that is deductible because it is appropriate and helpful in the taxpayer's business. Such expenses must also qualify as ordinary.

Net investment income The excess of the taxpayer's investment income over his investment expenses. See also Investment income.

Net operating loss (NOL) A net operating loss occurs when business expenses exceed business income for any taxable year. Such losses may be carried back two years or carried forward 20 years to a year in which the taxpayer has taxable income. Loss must be carried back first and must be deducted from years in chronological order.

Net Present Value (NPV) Method used by investment analysts to determine the anticipated return on an investment. This method uses a fixed discount rate to compute the net present value of future cash flows.

NOL See Net operating loss.

Net unearned income The amount of unearned income of a child under age 14 that is taxed at the child's parent's top marginal tax rate.

Nonaccountable plan A type of employee reimbursement plan that does not meet either of the two tests for an accountable plan (see accountable plan). Under a nonaccountable plan, reimbursements are included in the employee's gross income and the expenses are deductible by the employee, subject to the 2% of AGI floor.

Nonbusiness bad debt See Bad debt.

Noncontributory pension plan Only the employer makes contributions to this type of pension plan.

Nonliquidating distribution Distribution that reduces but does not eliminate, a partner's partnership interest. Such distributions are generally treated as tax-free returns of capital.

Nonqualified deferred compensation plan Type of plan used by employer to provide incentives or supplementary retirement benefits for executives. Such plans are not subject to the nondiscrimination and vesting rules.

Nonqualified stock option Stock option that does not meet the requirements for an incentive stock option.

Nonrefundable credit Allowances, such as the dependent child care credit, that have been created for various social, economic, and political reasons. The tax credits in this category do not result from payments made to the government in advance. Thus, they can be deducted from the tax, but they are not payable to the taxpayer in situations where the credit exceeds the tax.

NPV See Net Present Value

Office audit procedure IRS audit of a specific item on an individual's tax return. An office audit takes place at the IRS branch office.

Open-fact situation A situation that has not yet occurred. That is, one for which the facts and events are still controllable and can be planned for.

Ordinary expense An expense that is deductible because it is reasonable in amount and bears a reasonable and proximate relationship to the income-producing activity or property.

Ordinary income property For purposes of the charitable contribution deduction, any property that would result in the recognition of ordinary income if the property were sold. Such property includes inventory, works of art or manuscripts created by the taxpayer, capital assets that have been held for one year or less, and Section 1231 property that results in ordinary income due to depreciation recapture.

Organizational expenditures The amortizable legal, accounting, filing, and other fees incidental to organizing a partnership or a corporation.

Parent-subsidiary controlled group To qualify, a common parent must own at least 80% of the stock of at least one subsidiary corporation and at least 80% of each other component member of the controlled group must be owned by other members of the controlled group.

Partnership Syndicate, group pool, joint venture, or other unincorporateed organization which carries on a business or financial operation or venture.

Partnership interest The capital and/or profits interest in a partnership received in exchange for a contribution of properties or services (e.g., money or business equipment). The nature of a partnership interest is similar to that of corporate stock.

Passive activity To define what constitutes a passive activity for the purpose of applying the passive loss rules, it is necessary to (1) identify what constitutes an activity and (2) determine whether the taxpayer has materially participated in the activity. Temp. Reg. Sec. 1.469-4T contains detailed rules for making these determinations.

Passive income Income from an activity that does not require the taxpayer's material involvement or participation. Thus, income from tax shelters and rental activities fall into the category.

Passive loss Loss generated from a passive activity. Such losses are computed separately. They may be used to offset income from other passive activities, but may not be used to offset either active or portfolio income.

Percentage depletion method Depletion method for assets such as oil and gas that is equal to a specified percentage times the gross income from the property but which may not exceed 100% of the taxable income before depletion is deducted. Lease bonuses, advance royalties, and other amounts payable without regard to production may not be included in the calcualtion. This method is only available to small oil and gas producers and royalty owners and for certain mineral properties.

Percentage of completion method of accounting Accounting method generally used for long-term contracts under which income is reported in proportion to the amount of work that has been completed in a given year.

Personal exemption A deduction in an amount mandated by Congress. The amount for 2000 is $2,900 ($2,800 for 2000) and is adjusted for increases in the cost of living. An additional exemption is allowed for each individual who is a dependent. Personal and dependency exemptions are phased out for high income taxpayers.

Personal holding company (PHC) A closely held corporation (1) that is owned by a five or fewer shareholders who own more than 50% of the corporation's outstanding stock at any time during the last half of its taxable year and (2) whose PHC income equals at least 60% of the corporation's adjusted gross income for the tax year. Certain corporations (e.g., S corporations) are exempt from this definition.

Personal holding company tax This tax is equal to 39.6% of the undistributed personal holding company income. It is intended to prevent closely held companies from converting an operating company into a nonoperating investment company.

Personal interest All interest other than active business interest, investment interest, interest incurred in a passive activity, qualified residence interest, and interest incurred when paying the estate tax on an installment basis. Personal interest is currently treated as a nondeductible personal expenditure. See also Interest.

Personal property Property that is other than real property, such as equipment.

Personal service corporation (PSC) A regular C corporation whose principal activity is the performance of personal services that are substantially performed by owner-employees who own more than 10% of the value of the corporation's stock.

PHC See Personal holding company.

Portfolio income Dividends, interest, annuities, and royalties not derived in the ordinary course of business. Gains and losses on property that produces portfolio income are included in such income.

Primary cite The highest level official reporter which reports a particular case is called the primary cite.

Principal partner A partner owning 5% or more of the partnership profits and capital interests.

Principal residence The residence that the taxpayer occupies most of the time.

Private activity bond Obligation issued by a state of local government to finance non-governmental activities (e.g., a sports arena).

Private Letter Ruling See Letter Ruling

Production of income An activity of the taxpayer that is generally related to investment activities or matters connected with the determination of any tax. Deductions related to production of income activities are usually *from AGI*, although is some instances they may be *for AGI*, such as expenses connected with rental property.

Profit-sharing plan A qualified defined benefit plan which may be established in lieu of or in addition to a qualified pension plan. Contributions to a profit-sharing plan are usually based upon profits. Incidental benefits may or may not be included. In addition, the plan must meet certain requirements concerning determination of the amount and timing of the employer's contribution, how the employee wants to receive the employer's contribution, vesting, and forfeitures.

Progressive rate Tax that increases as the taxpayer's taxable income increases. The U.S. income tax is an example of a progressive tax.

Property settlement The division of property between spouses upon their separation or divorce.

Property tax Federal, state, or local tax levied on real and/or personal property (e.g., securities, a personal automobile).

Proportional tax A method of taxation under which the tax rate is the same for all taxpayers regardless of their income. State and local sales taxes are examples of this form of tax.

Proposed Regulations Issued following changes in the tax law. May or may not be amended after hearings are conducted and comments received. Proposed regulations are not binding on taxpayers.

PSC See Personal service corporation.

Qualified pension plan Pension plan that includes (1) systematic and definite payments made to a pension trust based upon actuarial methods and (2) usually provides for incidental benefits such as disability, or medical insurance benefits.

Qualified plan award Employee achievement awards given under a written plan or program that does not discriminate in favor of highly compensated employees. Such awards must be in the form of tangible personal property other than cash and be worth no more than $1,600.

Qualified residence interest Interest on an indebtedness which is secured by the taxpayer's qualified residence when it is paid or accrued. A taxpayer may have two qualified residences: a principal residence and a residence that he has personally used more than the greater of 14 days or 10% of the rental days during the year.

Readily ascertainable fair market value The fair market value of nonqualified stock options can be readily ascertained where the option is traded on an established options exchange.

Real property Property that is land or any structure permanently attached to the land, such as buildings.

Realized gain or loss The gain or loss computed by taking the amount realized from a sale of property and subtracting the property's adjusted basis.

Recapture provision A provision requiring recapture of earlier alimony payments as ordinary income by the payor if the payments decline sharply in either the second or third year.

Recovery of basis doctrine Rule that allows taxpayers to recover the basis of an asset without being taxed. Such amounts are considered a return of capital.

Refundable credit See Tax credit.

Regressive tax A form of taxation under which the tax rate decreases as the tax base (e.g., income) increases.

Regular corporation See C corporation.

Regular decision Tax Court decision that is issued on a particular issue for the first time.

Regulation See Treasury Regulation

Replacement property Property that is acquired to replace converted property in order to retain nonrecognition of gain status. Such property must generally be functionally the same as the converted property. For example, a business machine must be replaced with a similar business machine. There are exceptions to this rule: The taxpayer-use test applies to the involuntary conversion of rental property owned by an investor; condemnations of real property held for business or investment use may be replaced by like-kind property.

Residential rental property Property from which at least 80% of the gross rental income is rental from dwelling units. Residential units include manufactured homes that are used for rental purposes, but not hotels, motels, or other establishments for transient use.

Restricted property plan Such plans are used to attract and retain key executives by giving them an ownership interest in the corporation. The income recognition rules contained in Sec. 83 govern this type of plan.

Revenue Amounts received by the taxpayer from any source. It includes both taxable and nontaxable amounts and items that are a return of capital. Although closely related to income or gross income, differences between these items do exist.

Revenue Procedure Issued by the national office of the IRS, Revenue Procedures reflect the IRS' position on compliance relating to tax preparation issues. Revenue Procedures, which are published in the Cumulative Bulletin, have less weight than Treasury Regulations.

Revenue Ruling Issued by the national office of the IRS, Revenue Rulings reflect the IRS's interpretation of a narrow tax issue. Revenue Rulings, which are published in the Cumulative Bulletin, have less weight than the Treasury Regulations.

Royalties Ordinary income arising from amounts paid for the right to use property that belongs to another and is transferred for valuable consideration (e.g., a patent right where substantially all rights are transferred).

Sale A transaction where one receives cash and/or the equivalent of cash, including the assumption of debt, in exchange for an asset.

Sales tax State or local tax on purchases. Generally, food items and medicines are exempt from such tax.

S corporation Small business corporations may elect S corporation status if they meet the 35-shareholer limitation, the type of shareholder restrictions, and the one class of stock restriction. Taxation of such corporations parallels the tax rules that apply to partnerships.

Secondary cite Citation to secondary source (i.e., unofficial reporter).

Section 401(k) plan Type of plan that is often used to supplement a company's regular qualified pension and profit-sharing plan. Such plans, which generally contain a salary reduction feature, permit the employer to receive either cash or an equivalent contribution to the company's profit-sharing plan. The amount of the contribution is limited.

Section 1231 property Real or depreciable property that is (1) held for more than one year and (2) used in a trade or business. Certain property, such as inventory, U.S. government publications, copyrights, literary, musical, or artistic compositions, and letters, are excluded from this definition.

Section 1245 property Certain property subject to depreciation and, in some cases, amortization. Depreciable personal property such as equipment is Section 1245 property. However, most real property is not.

Section 1250 property Any real property that (1) is not Section 1245 property and (2) is subject to a depreciation allowance.

Security A long-term debt obligation. Long-term is generally defined as 10 years or more.

Separate property All property that is owned before marriage and any gifts or inheritances acquired after marriage are separate property. This distinction depends on the state of residence. However, it is possible even in community property states.

Severance damages Compensation for a decline in the value of the property remaining after part of the taxpayer's property is condemned. The IRS considers such damages analogous to the proceeds from property insurance.

Shifting income The process of transferring income from one family member to another. Methods for shifting income include gifts of stock or bonds to family members who are in lower tax brackets.

Short sale An investment activity where an investor sells a security at its current price and purchases the same security at a future date. A short sale is generally used when the price of a security is expected to decline.

Short-term capital gain (STCG) Gain realized on the sale or exchange of a capital asset held for one year or less.

Short-term capital loss (STCL) Loss realized on the sale or exchange of a capital asset held for one year or less.

Simplified LIFO method This method of inventory valuation allows taxpayers to use a single LIFO pool rather than multiple pools. See also LIFO method.

Small cases procedure When $10,000 or less is in question for a particular year, the taxpayer may opt to have the case heard by a special commissioner rather than the regular Tax Court. The decision of the commissioner cannot be appealed.

Social security benefits These benefits include (1) the basic monthly retirement and disability benefits paid under social security and (2) tier-one railroad retirement benefits.

Sole proprietorship Form of business entity owned by an individual who reports all items of income, expense, on his individual return on Schedule C.

Specific write-off method of accounting Method of accounting used for bad debts. Under this method, the taxpayer deducts each bad debt individually as it becomes worthless. This is the only allowable accounting method for bad debts arising after 1986.

Splitting income The process of creating additional taxable entities, especially corporations, in order to reduce an individual's effective tax rate.

Standard deduction A floor amount set by Congress to simplify the tax computation. It is used by taxpayers who do not have enough deductions to itemize. The amount of the deduction varies according to the taxpayer's filing status, age, and vision. Taxpayers who use this standard deduction are not required to keep records. See Chapter I2.

State corporate income tax See Franchise tax.

Statements on Responsibilities in Tax Practice (SRTP) Ethical guidelines of the AICPA-Federal Tax Division for CPAs to promote high standards of tax practice.

Statute of Limitations A period of time as provided by law in which a taxpayer's return may not be changed either by the IRS or the taxpayer. The Statute of Limitations is generally three years from the later of the date the tax return is filed or its due date. There is no Statute of Limitations for a fraudulent return.

Stock bonus plan A special type of defined benefit plan under which the employer's stock is contributed to a trust. The stock is then allocated and distributed to the participants. See also Employee stock ownership plan.

Stock dividend A dividend paid in the form of stock in the corporation issuing the dividend.

Stock option plan This category includes incentive stock options and nonqualified Stock option arrangements. Such plans are used to attract and retain key employees.

Substance-over-form doctrine Judicial weighing of a transaction's economic substance more heavily than its legal form.

Surviving spouse A special filing status available to widows and widowers who file a joint return for the year his or her spouse dies and for the following two years. The surviving spouse may not have remarried, must be a U.S. citizen or resident, have qualified to file a joint return for the year, and must have at least one dependent child living at home during the year.

Syndication fees The nonamortizable fees (e.g., brokerage and registration fees) incurred to promote and market partnership interests. Such fees are generally associated with tax-sheltered limited partnership interests.

Tangible property Property that has physical substance, such as land, buildings, natural resources, equipment, etc.

Tax A mandatory assessment levied under the authority of a political entity for the purpose of raising revenue to be used for public or governmental purposes. Such taxes may be levied by the federal, state, or local government.

Taxable income For individuals, taxable income is adjusted gross income reduced by deductions from adjusted gross income.

Tax base The amount to which the tax rate is applied to determine the tax due. For income tax purposes, the tax base is taxable income.

Tax benefit rule Recovery of an amount in a subsequent year that produced a tax benefit in a prior year and is thus taxable to the recipient.

Tax credit Amount that can be deducted from the gross tax to arrive at the net tax due or refund due. Prepaid amounts, that is, amounts paid to the government during the year, are tax credits. Such prepaid amounts are often referred to as "refundable credits."

Tax Deferred Bonds Bonds on which the interest is not subject to current taxation but is deferred to a future period of time, such as Series EE U.S. Savings Bonds.

Tax Exempt Bonds Bonds on which the interest is completely exempt from federal income taxation, such as state and municipal bonds

Tax law The tax law is comprised of the Internal Revenue Code, administrative and judicial interpretations, and the committee reports issued by the Congressional committees involved in the legislative process.

Taxpayer Compliance Measurement Program (TCMP) A stratified random sample used to select tax returns for audit. The program is intended to test the extent to which taxpayers are in compliance with the law.

Taxpayer-use test A test used to determine whether property is considered similar or related in service or use for purposes of involuntary conversions of property. This test is used by owner-investors (as opposed to owner-users) of property.

Tax research Search for the best possible solution to a problem involving either a proposed or completed transaction.

Tax shelter Passive activity which may lack economic substance other than creating tax deductions and credits that enable taxpayers to reduce or eliminate the income tax liability from their regular business activities. Section 469 restricts the current use of deductions and credits arising from passive activities.

Tax year See Accounting period.

TCMP See Taxpayer Compliance Measurement Program.

Technical Advice Memorandum Such memoranda are administrative interpretations issued in the form of letter ruling. Taxpayers may request them if they need guidance about the tax treatment of complicated technical matters which are being audited.

Temporary Regulations Temporary Regulations are Treasury Regulations that are issued to provide guidance for taxpayers pending the issuance of the final regulations. They are binding upon taxpayers. Temporary Regulations are also required to be issued as proposed regulations and must expire within three years.

Testamentary gift Transfer of property made at the death of the donor (i.e., bequests, devises, and inheritances).

Theft loss Loss of business, investment, or personal-use property due to crimes such as, but not limited to, larceny, embezzlement, robbery, extortion, blackmail, or kidnapping for ransom. Such losses are deductible from AGI, subject to certain limitations.

Total economic income The amount of the taxpayer's income, including exclusions and deductions from the tax base (e.g., tax-exempt bonds), is categorized as total economic income.

Trade or business A business activity of the taxpayer in which deductions are allowed as *for AGI* deductions.

Transportation expense The deductibility of this type of expense depends upon whether it is trade- or business-related, whether it is related to the production of income, whether the expense is employment related and therefore subject to the 2% nondeductible floor for miscellaneous itemized deductions. Commuting expenses are nondeductible. See also Travel expense.

Travel expense Such expenses include transportation, meals, and lodging incurred in the pursuit of a trade, business, or employment-related activity. There are limitations and restrictions on the deductibility of these expenses. See also Transportation expense.

Treasury bill Short-term (i.e., 90-day) obligation that is issued by the government at a discount from the maturity amount. The difference between the issue price and the maturity amount represents the interest income.

Treasury Regulation The principal administrative source of the federal tax law, these Regulations reflect the Treasury and the IRS's interpretation of the Internal Revenue Code. They may be either legislative or interpretative and they may be issued in either proposed, temporary, or final form.

Unfunded deferred compensation plan This type of plan is used for highly-compensated employees who wish to defer the recognition of income until future periods. Funding is generally accomplished through an escrow account for the employee's benefit.

Uniform Capitalization rules (UNICAP) The requirements under the tax law for determining inventory cost. Under UNICAP certain indirect overhead costs are required to be included in inventory for tax purposes which are generally not included for financial accounting.

Unrelated use property Capital gain property which is also tangible personal property and which is contributed to a public charity for a use that is unrelated to the charity's function. The contribution deduction (from AGI) for such property is equal to the property's fair market value minus the capital gain that would be recognized if the property was sold at that value.

Unreported decision District Court decisions that are not officially reported in the Federal Supplement. Such decisions may be reported in secondary reporters that report only tax-related cases.

U.S. Treasury Bill See Treasury bill.

Vertical equity A concept in taxation that provides that the incidence of taxation should be borne by taxpayers who have the ability to pay the tax. Taxpayers who are not similarly-situated should be treated differently under the tax law.

Wash sale A wash sale results when the taxpayer (1) sells stock or securities and (2) purchases substantially identical stock or securities within the 61-day period extending from 30 days before the date of sale to 30 days after the date of sale.

Wealth transfer tax A tax imposed upon the value of property transferred during one's lifetime (i.e., a gift tax) or upon the death of the transferor (i.e., an esate tax). The tax is imposed upon the transferor of property or upon the estate.

Writ of certiorari A petition to the U.S. Supreme court to request that the Court agree to hear a case. A writ of certiorari is requested by the party (IRS or taxpayer) that lost at the Court of Appeals level.

Zero coupon bond Bond that is issued at a cost that is substantially less than the current market rate because no interest payments are made. The original issue discount (OID) must be amortized over the term of the bond by investors using the constant rate method. Such bonds offer cash-flow advantages to corporate issuers since no cash outlay for interest is required until the bonds mature.

APPENDIX E

AICPA STATEMENTS ON STANDARDS FOR TAX SERVICES NOS. 1–8 (AUGUST 2000)

PREFACE

1. Practice standards are the hallmark of calling one's self a professional. Members should fulfill their responsibilities as professionals by instituting and maintaining standards against which their professional performance can be measured. Compliance with professional standards of tax practice also confirms the public's awareness of the professionalism that is associated with CPAs as well as the AICPA.

2. This publication sets forth ethical tax practice standards for members of the AICPA: Statements on Standards for Tax Services (SSTSs or Statements). Although other standards of tax practice exist, most notably Treasury Department Circular No. 230 and penalty provisions of the Internal Revenue Code (IRC), those standards are limited in that (1) Circular No. 230 does not provide the depth of guidance contained in these Statements, (2) the IRC penalty provisions apply only to income-tax return preparation, and (3) both Circular No. 230 and the penalty provisions apply only to federal tax practice.

3. The SSTSs have been written in as simple and objective a manner as possible. However, by their nature, ethical standards provide for an appropriate range of behavior that recognizes the need for interpretations to meet a broad range of personal and professional situations. The SSTSs recognize this need by, in some sections, providing relatively subjective rules and by leaving certain terms undefined. These terms and concepts are generally rooted in tax concepts, and therefore should be readily understood by tax practitioners. It is, therefore, recognized that the enforcement of these rules, as part of the AICPA's Code of Professional Conduct Rule 201, General Standards, and Rule 202, Compliance With Standards, will be undertaken with flexibility in mind and handled on a case-by-case basis. Members are expected to comply with them.

HISTORY

4. The SSTSs have their origin in the Statements on Responsibilities in Tax Practice (SRTPs), which provided a body of advisory opinions on good tax practice. The guidelines as originally set forth in the SRTPs had come to play a much more important role than most members realized. The courts, Internal Revenue Service, state accountancy boards, and other professional organizations recognized and relied on the SRTPs as the appropriate articulation of professional conduct in a CPA's tax practice. The SRTPs, in and of themselves, had become de facto enforceable standards of professional practice, because state disciplinary organizations and malpractice cases in effect regularly held CPAs accountable for failure to follow the SRTPs when their professional practice conduct failed to meet the prescribed guidelines of conduct.

5. The AICPA's Tax Executive Committee concluded that appropriate action entailed issuance of tax practice standards that would become a part of the Institute's Code of Professional Conduct. At its July 1999 meeting, the AICPA Board of Directors approved support of the executive committee's initiative and placed the matter on the agenda of the October 1999 meeting of the Institute's governing Council. On October 19, 1999, Council approved designating the Tax Executive Committee as a standard-setting body, thus authorizing that committee to promulgate standards of tax practice. These SSTSs, largely mirroring the SRTPs, are the result.

6. The SRTPs were originally issued between 1964 and 1977. The first nine SRTPs and the Introduction were codified in 1976; the tenth SRTP was issued in 1977. The original SRTPs concerning the CPA's responsibility to sign the return (SRTPs No. 1, *Signature of Preparers,* and No. 2, *Signature of Reviewer: Assumption of Preparer's Responsibility*) were withdrawn in 1982 after Treasury Department regulations were issued adopt-

Copyright © 2000 by the American Institute of Certified Public Accountants, Inc.
Reprinted with permission.

ing substantially the same standards for all tax return preparers. The sixth and seventh SRTPs, concerning the responsibility of a CPA who becomes aware of an error, were revised in 1991. The first Interpretation of the SRTPs, Interpretation 1-1, "Realistic Possibility Standard," was approved in December 1990. The SSTSs and Interpretation supersede and replace the SRTPs and their Interpretation 1-1 effective October 31, 2000. Although the number and names of the SSTSs, and the substance of the rules contained in each of them, remain the same as in the SRTPs, the language has been edited to both clarify and reflect the enforceable nature of the SSTSs. In addition, because the applicability of these standards is not limited to federal income-tax practice, the language has been changed to mirror the broader scope.

ONGOING PROCESS

7. The following Statements on Standards for Tax Services and Interpretation 1-1 to Statement No. 1, "Realistic Possibility Standard," reflect the AICPA's standards of tax practice and delineate members' responsibilities to taxpayers, the public, the government, and the profession. The Statements are intended to be part of an ongoing process that may require changes to and interpretations of current SSTSs in recognition of the accelerating rate of change in tax laws and the continued importance of tax practice to members.

8. The Tax Executive Committee promulgates SSTSs. Even though the 1999-2000 Tax Executive Committee approved this version, acknowledgement is also due to the many members whose efforts over the years went into the development of the original statements.

STATEMENT ON STANDARDS FOR TAX SERVICES NO. 1, TAX RETURN POSITIONS

INTRODUCTION

1. This Statement sets forth the applicable standards for members when recommending tax return positions and preparing or signing tax returns (including amended returns, claims for refund, and information returns) filed with any taxing authority. For purposes of these standards, a *tax return position* is (a) a position reflected on the tax return as to which the taxpayer has been specifically advised by a member or (b) a position about which a member has knowledge of all material facts and, on the basis of those facts, has concluded whether the position is appropriate. For purposes of these standards, a *taxpayer* is a client, a member's employer, or any other third-party recipient of tax services.

STATEMENT

2. The following standards apply to a member when providing professional services that involve tax return positions:

  a. A member should not recommend that a tax return position be taken with respect to any item unless the member has a good-faith belief that the position has a realistic possibility of being sustained administratively or judicially on its merits if challenged.
  b. A member should not prepare or sign a return that the member is aware takes a position that the member may not recommend under the standard expressed in paragraph 2a.
  c. Notwithstanding paragraph 2a, a member may recommend a tax return position that the member concludes is not frivolous as long as the member advises the taxpayer to appropriately disclose. Notwithstanding paragraph 2b, the member may prepare or sign a return that reflects a position that the member concludes is not frivolous as long as the position is appropriately disclosed.
  d. When recommending tax return positions and when preparing or signing a return on which a tax return position is taken, a member should, when relevant, advise the taxpayer regarding potential penalty consequences of such tax return position and the opportunity, if any, to avoid such penalties through disclosure.

3. A member should not recommend a tax return position or prepare or sign a return reflecting a position that the member knows—

  a. Exploits the audit selection process of a taxing authority.
  b. Serves as a mere arguing position advanced solely to obtain leverage in the bargaining process of settlement negotiation with a taxing authority.

4. When recommending a tax return position, a member has both the right and responsibility to be an advocate for the taxpayer with respect to any position satisfying the aforementioned standards.

EXPLANATION

5. Our self-assessment tax system can function effectively only if taxpayers file tax returns that are true, correct, and complete. A tax return is primarily a taxpayer's representation of facts, and the taxpayer has the final responsibility for positions taken on the return.

6. In addition to a duty to the taxpayer, a member has a duty to the tax system. However, it is well established that the taxpayer has no obligation to pay more taxes than are legally owed, and a member has a duty to the taxpayer to assist in achieving that result. The standards contained in paragraphs 2, 3, and 4 recognize the members' responsibilities to both taxpayers and to the tax system.

7. In order to meet the standards contained in paragraph 2, a member should in good faith believe that the tax return position is warranted in existing law or can be supported by a good-faith argument for an extension, modification, or reversal of existing law. For example, in reaching such a conclusion, a member may consider a well-reasoned construction of the applicable statute, well-reasoned articles or treatises, or pronouncements issued by the applicable taxing authority, regardless of whether such sources would be treated as *authority* under Internal Revenue

Code section 6662 and the regulations thereunder. A position would not fail to meet these standards merely because it is later abandoned for practical or procedural considerations during an administrative hearing or in the litigation process.

8. If a member has a good-faith belief that more than one tax return position meets the standards set forth in paragraph 2, a member's advice concerning alternative acceptable positions may include a discussion of the likelihood that each such position might or might not cause the taxpayer's tax return to be examined and whether the position would be challenged in an examination. In such circumstances, such advice is not a violation of paragraph 3a.

9. In some cases, a member may conclude that a tax return position is not warranted under the standard set forth in paragraph 2a. A taxpayer may, however, still wish to take such a position. Under such circumstances, the taxpayer should have the opportunity to take such a position, and the member may prepare and sign the return provided the position is appropriately disclosed on the return or claim for refund and the position is not frivolous. A frivolous position is one that is knowingly advanced in bad faith and is patently improper.

10. A member's determination of whether information is appropriately disclosed by the taxpayer should be based on the facts and circumstances of the particular case and the authorities regarding disclosure in the applicable taxing jurisdiction. If a member recommending a position, but not engaged to prepare or sign the related tax return, advises the taxpayer concerning appropriate disclosure of the position, then the member shall be deemed to meet these standards.

11. If particular facts and circumstances lead a member to believe that a taxpayer penalty might be asserted, the member should so advise the taxpayer and should discuss with the taxpayer the opportunity to avoid such penalty by disclosing the position on the tax return. Although a member should advise the taxpayer with respect to disclosure, it is the taxpayer's responsibility to decide whether and how to disclose.

12. For purposes of this Statement, preparation of a tax return includes giving advice on events that have occurred at the time the advice is given if the advice is directly relevant to determining the existence, character, or amount of a schedule, entry, or other portion of a tax return.

INTERPRETATION NO. 1-1, "REALISTIC POSSIBILITY STANDARD" OF STATEMENT ON STANDARDS FOR TAX SERVICES NO. 1, TAX RETURN POSITIONS

BACKGROUND

1. Statement on Standards for Tax Services (SSTS) No. 1, *Tax Return Positions*, contains the standards a member should follow in recommending tax return positions and in preparing or signing tax returns. In general, a member should have a good-faith belief that the tax return position being recommended has a realistic possibility of being sustained administratively or judicially on its merits, if challenged. The standard contained in SSTS No. 1, paragraph 2a, is referred to here as the realistic possibility standard. If a member concludes that a tax return position does not meet the realistic possibility standard:

   a. The member may still recommend the position to the taxpayer if the position is not frivolous, and the member recommends appropriate disclosure of the position; or
   b. The member may still prepare or sign a tax return containing the position, if the position is not frivolous, and the position is appropriately disclosed.

2. A *frivolous position* is one that is knowingly advanced in bad faith and is patently improper (see SSTS No. 1, paragraph 9). A member's determination of whether information is appropriately disclosed on a tax return or claim for refund is based on the facts and circumstances of the particular case and the authorities regarding disclosure in the applicable jurisdiction (see SSTS No. 1, paragraph 10).

3. If a member believes there is a possibility that a tax return position might result in penalties being asserted against a taxpayer, the member should so advise the taxpayer and should discuss with the taxpayer the opportunity, if any, of avoiding such penalties through disclosure (see SSTS No. 1, paragraph 11). Such advice may be given orally.

GENERAL INTERPRETATION

4. To meet the realistic possibility standard, a member should have a good-faith belief that the position is warranted by existing law or can be supported by a good-faith argument for an extension, modification, or reversal of the existing law through the administrative or judicial process. Such a belief should be based on reasonable interpretations of the tax law. A member should not take into account the likelihood of audit or detection when determining whether this standard has been met (see SSTS No. 1, paragraphs 3a and 8).

5. The realistic possibility standard is less stringent than the substantial authority standard and the more likely than not standard that apply under the Internal Revenue Code (IRC) to substantial understatements of liability by taxpayers. The realistic possibility standard is stricter than the reasonable basis standard that is in the IRC.

6. In determining whether a tax return position meets the realistic possibility standard, a member may rely on authorities in addition to those evaluated when determining whether substantial authority exists under IRC section 6662. Accordingly, a member may rely on well-reasoned treatises, articles in recognized professional tax publications, and other reference tools and sources of tax analyses commonly used by tax advisers and preparers of returns.

7. In determining whether a realistic possibility exists, a member should do all of the following:

- Establish relevant background facts
- Distill the appropriate questions from those facts
- Search for authoritative answers to those questions

- Resolve the questions by weighing the authorities uncovered by that search
- Arrive at a conclusion supported by the authorities

8. A member should consider the weight of each authority to conclude whether a position meets the realistic possibility standard. In determining the weight of an authority, a member should consider its persuasiveness, relevance, and source. Thus, the type of authority is a significant factor. Other important factors include whether the facts stated by the authority are distinguishable from those of the taxpayer and whether the authority contains an analysis of the issue or merely states a conclusion.

9. The realistic possibility standard may be met despite the absence of certain types of authority. For example, a member may conclude that the realistic possibility standard has been met when the position is supported only by a well-reasoned construction of the applicable statutory provision.

10. In determining whether the realistic possibility standard has been met, the extent of research required is left to the professional judgment of the member with respect to all the facts and circumstances known to the member. A member may conclude that more than one position meets the realistic possibility standard.

SPECIFIC ILLUSTRATIONS

11. The following illustrations deal with general fact patterns. Accordingly, the application of the guidance discussed in the General Interpretation section to variations in such general facts or to particular facts or circumstances may lead to different conclusions. In each illustration there is no authority other than that indicated.

12. *Illustration 1.* A taxpayer has engaged in a transaction that is adversely affected by a new statutory provision. Prior law supports a position favorable to the taxpayer. The taxpayer believes, and the member concurs, that the new statute is inequitable as applied to the taxpayer's situation. The statute is constitutional, clearly drafted, and unambiguous. The legislative history discussing the new statute contains general comments that do not specifically address the taxpayer's situation.

13. *Conclusion.* The member should recommend the return position supported by the new statute. A position contrary to a constitutional, clear, and unambiguous statute would ordinarily be considered a frivolous position.

14. *Illustration 2.* The facts are the same as in illustration 1 except that the legislative history discussing the new statute specifically addresses the taxpayer's situation and supports a position favorable to the taxpayer.

15. *Conclusion.* In a case where the statute is clearly and unambiguously against the taxpayer's position but a contrary position exists based on legislative history specifically addressing the taxpayer's situation, a return position based either on the statutory language or on the legislative history satisfies the realistic possibility standard.

16. *Illustration 3.* The facts are the same as in illustration 1 except that the legislative history can be interpreted to provide some evidence or authority in support of the taxpayer's position; however, the legislative history does not specifically address the situation.

17. *Conclusion.* In a case where the statute is clear and unambiguous, a contrary position based on an interpretation of the legislative history that does not explicitly address the taxpayer's situation does not meet the realistic possibility standard. However, because the legislative history provides some support or evidence for the taxpayer's position, such a return position is not frivolous. A member may recommend the position to the taxpayer if the member also recommends appropriate disclosure.

18. *Illustration 4.* A taxpayer is faced with an issue involving the interpretation of a new statute. Following its passage, the statute was widely recognized to contain a drafting error, and a technical correction proposal has been introduced. The taxing authority issues a pronouncement indicating how it will administer the provision. The pronouncement interprets the statute in accordance with the proposed technical correction.

19. *Conclusion.* Return positions based on either the existing statutory language or the taxing authority pronouncement satisfy the realistic possibility standard.

20. *Illustration 5.* The facts are the same as in illustration 4 except that no taxing authority pronouncement has been issued.

21. *Conclusion.* In the absence of a taxing authority pronouncement interpreting the statute in accordance with the technical correction, only a return position based on the existing statutory language will meet the realistic possibility standard. A return position based on the proposed technical correction may be recommended if it is appropriately disclosed, since it is not frivolous.

22. *Illustration 6.* A taxpayer is seeking advice from a member regarding a recently amended statute. The member has reviewed the statute, the legislative history that specifically addresses the issue, and a recently published notice issued by the taxing authority. The member has concluded in good faith that, based on the statute and the legislative history, the taxing authority's position as stated in the notice does not reflect legislative intent.

23. *Conclusion.* The member may recommend the position supported by the statute and the legislative history because it meets the realistic possibility standard.

24. *Illustration 7.* The facts are the same as in illustration 6 except that the taxing authority pronouncement is a temporary regulation.

25. *Conclusion.* In determining whether the position meets the realistic possibility standard, a member should determine the weight to be given the regulation by analyzing factors such as whether the regulation is legislative or interpretative, or if it is inconsistent with the statute. If a member concludes that the position does not meet the realistic possibility standard, because it is not frivolous, the position may nevertheless be recommended if the member also recommends appropriate disclosure.

26. *Illustration 8.* A tax form published by a taxing authority is incorrect, but completion of the form as published provides a benefit to the taxpayer. The member knows that the taxing authority has published an announcement acknowledging the error.

27. *Conclusion.* In these circumstances, a return position in accordance with the published form is a frivolous position.

28. *Illustration 9.* A taxpayer wants to take a position that a member has concluded is frivolous. The taxpayer maintains that even if the taxing authority examines the return, the issue will not be raised.

29. *Conclusion.* The member should not consider the likelihood of audit or detection when determining whether the realistic possibility standard has been met. The member should not prepare or sign a return that contains a frivolous position even if it is disclosed.

30. *Illustration 10.* A statute is passed requiring the capitalization of certain expenditures. The taxpayer believes, and the member concurs, that to comply fully, the taxpayer will need to acquire new computer hardware and software and implement a number of new accounting procedures. The taxpayer and member agree that the costs of full compliance will be significantly greater than the resulting increase in tax due under the new provision. Because of these cost considerations, the taxpayer makes no effort to comply. The taxpayer wants the member to prepare and sign a return on which the new requirement is simply ignored.

31. *Conclusion.* The return position desired by the taxpayer is frivolous, and the member should neither prepare nor sign the return.

32. *Illustration 11.* The facts are the same as in illustration 10 except that a taxpayer has made a good-faith effort to comply with the law by calculating an estimate of expenditures to be capitalized under the new provision.

33. *Conclusion.* In this situation, the realistic possibility standard has been met. When using estimates in the preparation of a return, a member should refer to SSTS No. 4, *Use of Estimates.*

34. *Illustration 12.* On a given issue, a member has located and weighed two authorities concerning the treatment of a particular expenditure. A taxing authority has issued an administrative ruling that required the expenditure to be capitalized and amortized over several years. On the other hand, a court opinion permitted the current deduction of the expenditure. The member has concluded that these are the relevant authorities, considered the source of both authorities, and concluded that both are persuasive and relevant.

35. *Conclusion.* The realistic possibility standard is met by either position.

36. *Illustration 13.* A tax statute is silent on the treatment of an item under the statute. However, the legislative history explaining the statute directs the taxing authority to issue regulations that will require a specific treatment of the item. No regulations have been issued at the time the member must recommend a position on the tax treatment of the item.

37. *Conclusion.* The member may recommend the position supported by the legislative history because it meets the realistic possibility standard.

38. *Illustration 14.* A taxpayer wants to take a position that a member concludes meets the realistic possibility standard based on an assumption regarding an underlying nontax legal issue. The member recommends that the taxpayer seek advice from its legal counsel, and the taxpayer's attorney gives an opinion on the nontax legal issue.

39. *Conclusion.* A member may in general rely on a legal opinion on a nontax legal issue. A member should, however, use professional judgment when relying on a legal opinion. If, on its face, the opinion of the taxpayer's attorney appears to be unreasonable, unsubstantiated, or unwarranted, a member should consult his or her attorney before relying on the opinion.

40. *Illustration 15.* A taxpayer has obtained from its attorney an opinion on the tax treatment of an item and requests that a member rely on the opinion.

41. *Conclusion.* The authorities on which a member may rely include well-reasoned sources of tax analysis. If a member is satisfied about the source, relevance, and persuasiveness of the legal opinion, a member may rely on that opinion when determining whether the realistic possibility standard has been met.

STATEMENT ON STANDARDS FOR TAX SERVICES NO. 2, ANSWERS TO QUESTIONS ON RETURNS

INTRODUCTION

1. This Statement sets forth the applicable standards for members when signing the preparer's declaration on a tax return if one or more questions on the return have not been answered. The term *questions* includes requests for information on the return, in the instructions, or in the regulations, whether or not stated in the form of a question.

STATEMENT

2. A member should make a reasonable effort to obtain from the taxpayer the information necessary to provide appropriate answers to all questions on a tax return before signing as preparer.

EXPLANATION

3. It is recognized that the questions on tax returns are not of uniform importance, and often they are not applicable to the particular taxpayer. Nevertheless, there are at least two reasons why a member should be satisfied that a reasonable effort has been made to obtain information to provide appropriate answers to the questions on the return that are applicable to a taxpayer.

   a. A question may be of importance in determining taxable income or loss, or the tax liability shown on the return, in which circumstance an omission may detract from the quality of the return.

   b. A member often must sign a preparer's declaration stating that the return is true, correct, and complete.

4. Reasonable grounds may exist for omitting an answer to a question applicable to a taxpayer. For example, reasonable grounds may include the following:

a. The information is not readily available and the answer is not significant in terms of taxable income or loss, or the tax liability shown on the return.
  b. Genuine uncertainty exists regarding the meaning of the question in relation to the particular return.
  c. The answer to the question is voluminous; in such cases, a statement should be made on the return that the data will be supplied upon examination.

5. A member should not omit an answer merely because it might prove disadvantageous to a taxpayer.

6. If reasonable grounds exist for omission of an answer to an applicable question, a taxpayer is not required to provide on the return an explanation of the reason for the omission. In this connection, a member should consider whether the omission of an answer to a question may cause the return to be deemed incomplete.

STATEMENT ON STANDARDS FOR TAX SERVICES NO. 3, CERTAIN PROCEDURAL ASPECTS OF PREPARING RETURNS

INTRODUCTION

1. This Statement sets forth the applicable standards for members concerning the obligation to examine or verify certain supporting data or to consider information related to another taxpayer when preparing a taxpayer's tax return.

STATEMENT

2. In preparing or signing a return, a member may in good faith rely, without verification, on information furnished by the taxpayer or by third parties. However, a member should not ignore the implications of information furnished and should make reasonable inquiries if the information furnished appears to be incorrect, incomplete, or inconsistent either on its face or on the basis of other facts known to a member. Further, a member should refer to the taxpayer's returns for one or more prior years whenever feasible.

3. If the tax law or regulations impose a condition with respect to deductibility or other tax treatment of an item, such as taxpayer maintenance of books and records or substantiating documentation to support the reported deduction or tax treatment, a member should make appropriate inquiries to determine to the member's satisfaction whether such condition has been met.

4. When preparing a tax return, a member should consider information actually known to that member from the tax return of another taxpayer if the information is relevant to that tax return and its consideration is necessary to properly prepare that tax return. In using such information, a member should consider any limitations imposed by any law or rule relating to confidentiality.

EXPLANATION

5. The preparer's declaration on a tax return often states that the information contained therein is true, correct, and complete to the best of the preparer's knowledge and belief based on all information known by the preparer. This type of reference should be understood to include information furnished by the taxpayer or by third parties to a member in connection with the preparation of the return.

6. The preparer's declaration does not require a member to examine or verify supporting data. However, a distinction should be made between (a) the need either to determine by inquiry that a specifically required condition, such as maintaining books and records or substantiating documentation, has been satisfied or to obtain information when the material furnished appears to be incorrect or incomplete and (b) the need for a member to examine underlying information. In fulfilling his or her obligation to exercise due diligence in preparing a return, a member may rely on information furnished by the taxpayer unless it appears to be incorrect, incomplete, or inconsistent. Although a member has certain responsibilities in exercising due diligence in preparing a return, the taxpayer has the ultimate responsibility for the contents of the return. Thus, if the taxpayer presents unsupported data in the form of lists of tax information, such as dividends and interest received, charitable contributions, and medical expenses, such information may be used in the preparation of a tax return without verification unless it appears to be incorrect, incomplete, or inconsistent either on its face or on the basis of other facts known to a member.

7. Even though there is no requirement to examine underlying documentation, a member should encourage the taxpayer to provide supporting data where appropriate. For example, a member should encourage the taxpayer to submit underlying documents for use in tax return preparation to permit full consideration of income and deductions arising from security transactions and from pass-through entities, such as estates, trusts, partnerships, and S corporations.

8. The source of information provided to a member by a taxpayer for use in preparing the return is often a pass-through entity, such as a limited partnership, in which the taxpayer has an interest but is not involved in management. A member may accept the information provided by the pass-through entity without further inquiry unless there is reason to believe it is incorrect, incomplete, or inconsistent, either on its face or on the basis of other facts known to the member. In some instances, it may be appropriate for a member to advise the taxpayer to ascertain the nature and amount of possible exposure to tax deficiencies, interest, and penalties, by contact with management of the pass-through entity.

9. A member should make use of a taxpayer's returns for one or more prior years in preparing the current return whenever feasible. Reference to prior returns and discussion of prior-year tax determinations with the taxpayer should provide information to determine the taxpayer's general tax status, avoid the omission or duplication of items, and afford a basis for the treatment of similar or related transactions. As with the examination

of information supplied for the current year's return, the extent of comparison of the details of income and deduction between years depends on the particular circumstances.

STATEMENT ON STANDARDS FOR TAX SERVICES NO. 4, USE OF ESTIMATES

INTRODUCTION

1. This Statement sets forth the applicable standards for members when using the taxpayer's estimates in the preparation of a tax return. A member may advise on estimates used in the preparation of a tax return, but the taxpayer has the responsibility to provide the estimated data. Appraisals or valuations are not considered estimates for purposes of this Statement.

STATEMENT

2. Unless prohibited by statute or by rule, a member may use the taxpayer's estimates in the preparation of a tax return if it is not practical to obtain exact data and if the member determines that the estimates are reasonable based on the facts and circumstances known to the member. If the taxpayer's estimates are used, they should be presented in a manner that does not imply greater accuracy than exists.

EXPLANATION

3. Accounting requires the exercise of professional judgment and, in many instances, the use of approximations based on judgment. The application of such accounting judgments, as long as not in conflict with methods set forth by a taxing authority, is acceptable. These judgments are not estimates within the purview of this Statement. For example, a federal income tax regulation provides that if all other conditions for accrual are met, the exact amount of income or expense need not be known or ascertained at year end if the amount can be determined with reasonable accuracy.

4. When the taxpayer's records do not accurately reflect information related to small expenditures, accuracy in recording some data may be difficult to achieve. Therefore, the use of estimates by a taxpayer in determining the amount to be deducted for such items may be appropriate.

5. When records are missing or precise information about a transaction is not available at the time the return must be filed, a member may prepare a tax return using a taxpayer's estimates of the missing data.

6. Estimated amounts should not be presented in a manner that provides a misleading impression about the degree of factual accuracy.

7. Specific disclosure that an estimate is used for an item in the return is not generally required; however, such disclosure should be made in unusual circumstances where nondisclosure might mislead the taxing authority regarding the degree of accuracy of the return as a whole. Some examples of unusual circumstances include the following:

   a. A taxpayer has died or is ill at the time the return must be filed.
   b. A taxpayer has not received a Schedule K-1 for a pass-through entity at the time the tax return is to be filed.
   c. There is litigation pending (for example, a bankruptcy proceeding) that bears on the return.
   d. Fire or computer failure has destroyed the relevant records.

STATEMENT ON STANDARDS FOR TAX SERVICES NO. 5, DEPARTURE FROM A POSITION PREVIOUSLY CONCLUDED IN AN ADMINISTRATIVE PROCEEDING OR COURT DECISION

INTRODUCTION

1. This Statement sets forth the applicable standards for members in recommending a tax return position that departs from the position determined in an administrative proceeding or in a court decision with respect to the taxpayer's prior return.

2. For purposes of this Statement, *administrative proceeding* also includes an examination by a taxing authority or an appeals conference relating to a return or a claim for refund.

3. For purposes of this Statement, *court decision* means a decision by any court having jurisdiction over tax matters.

STATEMENT

4. The tax return position with respect to an item as determined in an administrative proceeding or court decision does not restrict a member from recommending a different tax position in a later year's return, unless the taxpayer is bound to a specified treatment in the later year, such as by a formal closing agreement. Therefore, as provided in Statement on Standards for Tax Services (SSTS) No. 1, *Tax Return Positions,* the member may recommend a tax return position or prepare or sign a tax return that departs from the treatment of an item as concluded in an administrative proceeding or court decision with respect to a prior return of the taxpayer.

EXPLANATION

5. If an administrative proceeding or court decision has resulted in a determination concerning a specific tax treatment of an item in a prior year's return, a member will usually recommend this

same tax treatment in subsequent years. However, departures from consistent treatment may be justified under such circumstances as the following:
  a. Taxing authorities tend to act consistently in the disposition of an item that was the subject of a prior administrative proceeding but generally are not bound to do so. Similarly, a taxpayer is not bound to follow the tax treatment of an item as consented to in an earlier administrative proceeding.
  b. The determination in the administrative proceeding or the court's decision may have been caused by a lack of documentation. Supporting data for the later year may be appropriate.
  c. A taxpayer may have yielded in the administrative proceeding for settlement purposes or not appealed the court decision, even though the position met the standards in SSTS No. 1.
  d. Court decisions, rulings, or other authorities that are more favorable to a taxpayer's current position may have developed since the prior administrative proceeding was concluded or the prior court decision was rendered.

6. The consent in an earlier administrative proceeding and the existence of an unfavorable court decision are factors that the member should consider in evaluating whether the standards in SSTS No. 1 are met.

STATEMENT ON STANDARDS FOR TAX SERVICES NO. 6, KNOWLEDGE OF ERROR: RETURN PREPARATION

INTRODUCTION

1. This Statement sets forth the applicable standards for a member who becomes aware of an error in a taxpayer's previously filed tax return or of a taxpayer's failure to file a required tax return. As used herein, the term error includes any position, omission, or method of accounting that, at the time the return is filed, fails to meet the standards set out in Statement on Standards for Tax Services (SSTS) No. 1, *Tax Return Positions*. The term *error* also includes a position taken on a prior year's return that no longer meets these standards due to legislation, judicial decisions, or administrative pronouncements having retroactive effect. However, an error does not include an item that has an insignificant effect on the taxpayer's tax liability.

2. This Statement applies whether or not the member prepared or signed the return that contains the error.

STATEMENT

3. A member should inform the taxpayer promptly upon becoming aware of an error in a previously filed return or upon becoming aware of a taxpayer's failure to file a required return. A member should recommend the corrective measures to be taken. Such recommendation may be given orally. The member is not obligated to inform the taxing authority, and a member may not do so without the taxpayer's permission, except when required by law.

4. If a member is requested to prepare the current year's return and the taxpayer has not taken appropriate action to correct an error in a prior year's return, the member should consider whether to withdraw from preparing the return and whether to continue a professional or employment relationship with the taxpayer. If the member does prepare such current year's return, the member should take reasonable steps to ensure that the error is not repeated.

EXPLANATION

5. While performing services for a taxpayer, a member may become aware of an error in a previously filed return or may become aware that the taxpayer failed to file a required return. The member should advise the taxpayer of the error and the measures to be taken. Such recommendation may be given orally. If the member believes that the taxpayer could be charged with fraud or other criminal misconduct, the taxpayer should be advised to consult legal counsel before taking any action.

6. It is the taxpayer's responsibility to decide whether to correct the error. If the taxpayer does not correct an error, a member should consider whether to continue a professional or employment relationship with the taxpayer. While recognizing that the taxpayer may not be required by statute to correct an error by filing an amended return, a member should consider whether a taxpayer's decision not to file an amended return may predict future behavior that might require termination of the relationship. The potential for violating Code of Professional Conduct rule 301 (relating to the member's confidential client relationship), the tax law and regulations, or laws on privileged communications, and other considerations may create a conflict between the member's interests and those of the taxpayer. Therefore, a member should consider consulting with his or her own legal counsel before deciding upon recommendations to the taxpayer and whether to continue a professional or employment relationship with the taxpayer.

7. If a member decides to continue a professional or employment relationship with the taxpayer and is requested to prepare a tax return for a year subsequent to that in which the error occurred, the member should take reasonable steps to ensure that the error is not repeated. If the subsequent year's tax return cannot be prepared without perpetuating the error, the member should consider withdrawal from the return preparation. If a member learns that the taxpayer is using an erroneous method of accounting and it is past the due date to request permission to change to a method meeting the standards of SSTS No. 1, the member may sign a tax return for the current year, providing the tax return includes appropriate disclosure of the use of the erroneous method.

8. Whether an error has no more than an insignificant effect on the taxpayer's tax liability is left to the professional judgment of the member based on all the facts and circumstances known to the member. In judging whether an erroneous method of

accounting has more than an insignificant effect, a member should consider the method's cumulative effect and its effect on the current year's tax return.

9. If a member becomes aware of the error while performing services for a taxpayer that do not involve tax return preparation, the member's responsibility is to advise the taxpayer of the existence of the error and to recommend that the error be discussed with the taxpayer's tax return preparer. Such recommendation may be given orally.

STATEMENT ON STANDARDS FOR TAX SERVICES NO. 7, KNOWLEDGE OF ERROR: ADMINISTRATIVE PROCEEDINGS

INTRODUCTION

1. This Statement sets forth the applicable standards for a member who becomes aware of an error in a return that is the subject of an administrative proceeding, such as an examination by a taxing authority or an appeals conference. The term *administrative proceeding* does not include a criminal proceeding. As used herein, the term *error* includes any position, omission, or method of accounting that, at the time the return is filed, fails to meet the standards set out in Statement on Standards for Tax Services (SSTS) No. 1, *Tax Return Positions*. The term *error* also includes a position taken on a prior year's return that no longer meets these standards due to legislation, judicial decisions, or administrative pronouncements having retroactive effect. However, an error does not include an item that has an insignificant effect on the taxpayer's tax liability.

2. This Statement applies whether or not the member prepared or signed the return that contains the error. Special considerations may apply when a member has been engaged by legal counsel to provide assistance in a matter relating to the counsel's client.

STATEMENT

3. If a member is representing a taxpayer in an administrative proceeding with respect to a return that contains an error of which the member is aware, the member should inform the taxpayer promptly upon becoming aware of the error. The member should recommend the corrective measures to be taken. Such recommendation may be given orally. A member is neither obligated to inform the taxing authority nor allowed to do so without the taxpayer's permission, except where required by law.

4. A member should request the taxpayer's agreement to disclose the error to the taxing authority. Lacking such agreement, the member should consider whether to withdraw from representing the taxpayer in the administrative proceeding and whether to continue a professional or employment relationship with the taxpayer.

EXPLANATION

5. When the member is engaged to represent the taxpayer before a taxing authority in an administrative proceeding with respect to a return containing an error of which the member is aware, the member should advise the taxpayer to disclose the error to the taxing authority. Such recommendation may be given orally. If the member believes that the taxpayer could be charged with fraud or other criminal misconduct, the taxpayer should be advised to consult legal counsel before taking any action.

6. It is the taxpayer's responsibility to decide whether to correct the error. If the taxpayer does not correct an error, a member should consider whether to withdraw from representing the taxpayer in the administrative proceeding and whether to continue a professional or employment relationship with the taxpayer. While recognizing that the taxpayer may not be required by statute to correct an error by filing an amended return, a member should consider whether a taxpayer's decision not to file an amended return may predict future behavior that might require termination of the relationship. Moreover, a member should consider consulting with his or her own legal counsel before deciding on recommendations to the taxpayer and whether to continue a professional or employment relationship with the taxpayer. The potential for violating Code of Professional Conduct rule 301 (relating to the member's confidential client relationship), the tax law and regulations, laws on privileged communications, potential adverse impact on a taxpayer of a member's withdrawal, and other considerations may create a conflict between the member's interests and those of the taxpayer.

7. Once disclosure is agreed on, it should not be delayed to such a degree that the taxpayer or member might be considered to have failed to act in good faith or to have, in effect, provided misleading information. In any event, disclosure should be made before the conclusion of the administrative proceeding.

8. Whether an error has an insignificant effect on the taxpayer's tax liability is left to the professional judgment of the member based on all the facts and circumstances known to the member. In judging whether an erroneous method of accounting has more than an insignificant effect, a member should consider the method's cumulative effect and its effect on the return that is the subject of the administrative proceeding.

STATEMENT ON STANDARDS FOR TAX SERVICES NO. 8, FORM AND CONTENT OF ADVICE TO TAXPAYERS

INTRODUCTION

1. This Statement sets forth the applicable standards for members concerning certain aspects of providing advice to a taxpayer and considers the circumstances in which a member has a responsibility to communicate with a taxpayer when subsequent

developments affect advice previously provided. The Statement does not, however, cover a member's responsibilities when the expectation is that the advice rendered is likely to be relied on by parties other than the taxpayer.

STATEMENT

2. A member should use judgment to ensure that tax advice provided to a taxpayer reflects professional competence and appropriately serves the taxpayer's needs. A member is not required to follow a standard format or guidelines in communicating written or oral advice to a taxpayer.

3. A member should assume that tax advice provided to a taxpayer will affect the manner in which the matters or transactions considered would be reported on the taxpayer's tax returns. Thus, for all tax advice given to a taxpayer, a member should follow the standards in Statement on Standards for Tax Services (SSTS) No. 1, *Tax Return Positions*.

4. A member has no obligation to communicate with a taxpayer when subsequent developments affect advice previously provided with respect to significant matters, except while assisting a taxpayer in implementing procedures or plans associated with the advice provided or when a member undertakes this obligation by specific agreement.

EXPLANATION

5. Tax advice is recognized as a valuable service provided by members. The form of advice may be oral or written and the subject matter may range from routine to complex. Because the range of advice is so extensive and because advice should meet the specific needs of a taxpayer, neither a standard format nor guidelines for communicating or documenting advice to the taxpayer can be established to cover all situations.

6. Although oral advice may serve a taxpayer's needs appropriately in routine matters or in well-defined areas, written communications are recommended in important, unusual, or complicated transactions. The member may use professional judgment about whether, subsequently, to document oral advice in writing.

7. In deciding on the form of advice provided to a taxpayer, a member should exercise professional judgment and should consider such factors as the following:
  a. The importance of the transaction and amounts involved
  b. The specific or general nature of the taxpayer's inquiry
  c. The time available for development and submission of the advice
  d. The technical complications presented
  e. The existence of authorities and precedents
  f. The tax sophistication of the taxpayer
  g. The need to seek other professional advice

8. A member may assist a taxpayer in implementing procedures or plans associated with the advice offered. When providing such assistance, the member should review and revise such advice as warranted by new developments and factors affecting the transaction.

9. Sometimes a member is requested to provide tax advice but does not assist in implementing the plans adopted. Although such developments as legislative or administrative changes or future judicial interpretations may affect the advice previously provided, a member cannot be expected to communicate subsequent developments that affect such advice unless the member undertakes this obligation by specific agreement with the taxpayer.

10. Taxpayers should be informed that advice reflects professional judgment based on an existing situation and that subsequent developments could affect previous professional advice. Members may use precautionary language to the effect that their advice is based on facts as stated and authorities that are subject to change.

11. In providing tax advice, a member should be cognizant of applicable confidentiality privileges.

These Statements on Standards for Tax Services and Interpretation were unanimously adopted by the assenting votes of the twenty voting members of the twenty-one-member Tax Executive Committee.

Tax Executive Committee (1999–2000)

David A. Lifson, *Chair*	Jeffrey A. Porter
Pamela J. Pecarich, *Vice Chair*	Thomas J. Purcell, III
Ward M. Bukofsky	Jeffrey L. Raymon
Joseph Cammarata	Frederick H. Rothman
Stephen R. Corrick	Barry D. Roy
Anna C. Fowler	Jane T. Rubin
Jill Gansler	Douglas P. Stives
Diane P. Herndon	Philip J. Wiesner
Ronald S. Katch	Claude R. Wilson, Jr.
Allan I. Kruger	Robert A. Zarzar
Susan W. Martin	

SRTP Enforceability Task Force

J. Edward Swails, *Chair*	Michael E. Mares
Alan R. Einhorn	Dan L. Mendelson
John C. Gardner	Daniel A. Noakes
Ronald S. Katch	William C. Potter

AICPA Staff

Gerald W. Padwe	Edward S. Karl
Vice President	*Director*
Taxation	*Taxation*

The AICPA gratefully acknowledges the contributions of William A. Tate, Jean L. Rothbarth, and Leonard Podolin, former chairs of the Responsibilities in Tax Practice Committee; A. M. (Tony) Komlyn and Wilber Van Scoik, former members of the Committee; and Carol B. Ferguson, AICPA Technical Manager.

Note: Statements on Standards for Tax Services are issued by the Tax Executive Committee, the senior technical body of the Institute designated to promulgate standards of tax practice. Rules 201 and 202 of the Institute's Code of Professional Conduct require compliance with these standards.

APPENDIX F

INDEX OF CODE SECTIONS

1, 2-2*n*, 15-9 (Figure 15-??), 15-25
1(g)(7), 2-24*n*
1(h), 5-16*n*–5-17, 17-30
1(h)(2), 5-28*n*
1(h)(3), 7-15*n*
1(h)(4), 5-17*n*
1.1036-1(a), 12-5*n*
1.1377-1(a), 17-25
1.280A-2, 9-25*n*
2(a), 2-20*n*
2(b), 2-20*n*
2(c), 2-22*n*
11(b)(1), 16-8*n*
11(b)(2), 16-10*n*
21, 7-33, 14-10 (Table 14-1), 14-11*n*
21(b)(1), 14-11*n*
21(c), 14-12*n*
21(d)(2), 14-12*n*
21(e)(1), 14-11*n*
21(e)(6), 14-11*n*
22, 14-10 (Table 14-1)
22(c)(2), 14-12*n*
23, 14-10 (Table 14-1), 14-13*n*
24, 2-17, 14-10 (Table 14-1), 14-10*n*
24(c), 14-10*n*
25, 14-10 (Table 14-1)
25A, 14-10 (Table 14-1), 14-14*n*
25A(b), 14-14*n*
25A(c), 14-14*n*
25A(e)(2), 9-40*n*
26, 14-10*n*, 14-16
27, 14-10 (Table 14-1)
29, 14-10 (Table 14-1)
30, 14-10 (Table 14-1)
31, 14-10 (Table 14-1)
32, 14-10 (Table 14-1)
32(b)(1), 14-22*n*
32(c), 14-22*n*
32(c)(1)(A), 14-22*n*
38, 14-19–14-20
38(c), 14-18*n*, 14-21*n*
41, 14-10 (Table 14-1), 14-18
41(c)(2), 14-18*n*
41(c)(3), 14-18*n*
42, 13-15*n*, 14-10 (Table 14-1)
44, 14-10 (Table 14-1), 14-18*n*
47, 14-10 (Table 14-1), 14-19*n*
47(a)(1), 14-19*n*
47(a)(2), 14-19*n*

47(c)(1)(A), 14-19*n*
48, 14-10 (Table 14-1)
48(a)(2), 14-19*n*
50(c)(1), 14-19*n*
51, 14-10 (Table 14-1), 14-20*n*, 14-21
51A, 14-10 (Table 14-1), 14-20*n*
53, 14-6, 14-6*n*
55, 16-10*n*
55(a), 14-16
55(b)(1), 14-2*n*
55(d)(3), 14-3*n*
56(b)(2), 14-5*n*
56(b)(2)(D), 14-5*n*
57, 14-3, 14-3*n*, 16-11*n*
57(a)(1), 10-18*n*
57(a)(7), 14-4*n*
58, 16-10*n*
61, 3-22
61(a), 2-3*n*, 3-2, 3-12, 3-22, 4-2
61(a)(3), 5-2*n*
61(a)(12), 4-19
62, 6-3, 6-3*n*
62(a)(2), 9-2
62(a)(3), 5-2*n*
62(a)(15), 9-19*n*
63, 2-4*n*
63(c)(6), 2-11*n*
66(b), 3-7*n*
66(c), 3-7*n*
67, 9-3–9-4
67(c)(2), 7-28
68, 9-4*n*
68-232, 10-34
72, 9-29, 9-29*n*, 9-30, 9-38, 14-25*n*
72(e), 3-21*n*
72(e)(2), 4-6*n*
72(q), 4-6*n*
72(t), 9-38*n*
74, 3-22*n*, 4-4*n*, 4-7*n*, 4-12
74(b), 4-4
74(c), 4-12*n*, 4-30
79, 4-4, 17-28
79(a), 4-10*n*
82, 9-20, 9-20*n*
83, 9-31, 9-31*n*
83(b), 9-32*n*, 9-32–9-33
86, 3-14*n*, 3-23, 4-4
101, 4-4, 4-8, 4-8*n*
101(a), 4-5*n*

101(a)(2), 4-5*n*
102, 4-2, 4-4, 4-30
103, 4-4
103(a)(1), 3-13*n*
104, 4-4, 17-29
104(a), 4-8
104(a)(1), 4-9
104(a)(2), 3-25
104(a)(3), 4-8
105, 4-4, 17-29
105(a), 4-9*n*
105(h)(5), 4-10*n*
106, 4-4, 4-10, 7-6*n*, 17-29
108, 4-4, 4-19
108(f)(2), 4-19
109, 3-38, 4-30
111, 3-26*n*
117, 4-2, 4-4, 4-7*n*, 4-23, 9-21, 14-14
117(d), 4-30
119, 4-14, 17-29
121, 3-13*n*, 4-4, 12-2, 12-16–12-22, 12-25
121(a), 12-16*n*, 12-18*n*
121(b), 12-16
121(c), 12-19*n*
121(d)(2), 12-19*n*
121(d)(3), 12-19*n*
121(d)(5)(A), 12-20*n*
121(d)(5)(B), 12-20*n*
121(d)(6), 12-22*n*
121(d)(7), 12-33
121(d)(8), 12-20*n*
121(f), 12-22*n*
123, 4-30
124, 4-4
125, 4-4, 4-16*n*, 17-29
127, 4-16, 9-21, 9-21 (Table 9-3), 9-21*n*, 14-14, 17-29
129, 4-4, 4-23, 4-16*n*, 14-11–14-12, 14-12*n*, 17-29
132, 4-4, 4-9, 4-12–4-14, 4-23, 9-20, 16-7, 17-29
132(b), 4-13
132(c), 4-13, 4-30
132(d), 4-13
132(e), 4-13–4-14
132(f), 4-13
132(j)(4), 4-13
132(g), 9-20*n*
135, 3-28
135(c), 3-14*n*
135(c)(2)(B), 3-14*n*

146(d), 3-14*n*
148, 3-14*n*
149(b), 3-14*n*
151(b), 2-12*n*
151(d), 2-17*n*
152, 2-12*n*, 2-38, 7-2*n*
152(a), 15-5*n*
152(b)(5), 2-16*n*
152(c), 2-14*n*
152(d), 2-13*n*
152(e), 2-14*n*, 2-22*n*, 7-2
162, 1-26, 4-12, 4-12*n*, 6-2, 6-5, 6-8, 6-47, 7-9, 8-13, 9-2, 9-12, 10-16–10-17, 15-6, 16-3, 17-29
162(a), 9-6*n*
162(a)(1), 3-17*n*
162(a)(2), 9-60
162(c)(1), 6-12
162(c)(3), 6-13
162(e), 6-14
162(g), 6-13*n*
162(l), 4-10*n*, 6-3*n*
162(l)(1), 17-29*n*
162(l)(5), 17-29*n*
162(m), 6-9, 16-7*n*
163, 7-19
163(b), 11-22
163(d)(4), 11-25
163(d)(4)(B), 7-15*n*
163(d)(4)(C), 7-15*n*
163(h), 7-16*n*
163(h)(4)(C), 7-16*n*
164, 7-9–7-11
164(a), 5-5*n*
164(a)(3), 14-16*n*
164(c)(1), 7-11*n*
164(f), 1-11*n*, 6-3*n*, 7-11*n*, 9-36, 10-10*n*, 10-22, 14-7*n*
165, 8-3, 8-19, 8-23*n*, 8-25*n*, 15-11
165(d), 3-23*n*
165(g), 8-4, 15-11
165(g)(1), 5-22
165(g)(2), 5-22*n*, 8-3*n*
165(g)(3), 5-22*n*, 8-4*n*
165(h)(2)(A)(i), 15-9 (Figure 15-2)
165(h)(2)(A)(ii), 15-9 (Figure 15-2)
165(i), 8-23*n*
165(l), 8-29*n*
166, 8-25*n*

F-1

F-2 Individuals ▼ Appendix F

166(d)(1)(B), 5-15n
167, 5-13, 10-2
167(a), 10-2n
167(j)(2)(B), 10-8n
168, 10-2, 14-19
168(b)(3)(A), 13-14n
168(c)(1), 10-7n
168(d)(3), 10-5n
168(d)(3)(B), 10-5n
168(e)(1), 10-5n
168(e)(2)(A), 10-8n
168(f), 10-5n
168(g), 10-8n
169, 6-10, 10-13, 13-10n
169(a), 13-10n
170, 7-21, 7-36, 15-6, 16-6n
170(b)(1)(E), 7-22n
170(e), 7-24n, 16-7
170(e)(1)(A), 13-18n, 13-23n
170(e)(6), 7-24n
170(f)(3), 7-22n
170(f)(8), 7-34n
170(g), 7-21n
172, 8-29, 8-33, 16-6n
172(b)(1)(C), 8-33n
172(d)(2), 8-31n
172(d)(4)(C), 8-31n
172(f), 8-33n, 16-6n
174, 6-10n, 6-17, 10-13, 10-16n, 10-16–10-17, 11-7n, 14-18
175, 6-10n
175(a), 13-21n
179, 6-5, 6-11, 6-17, 9-11, 10-6, 10-6n, 10-9n, 10-9–10-10, 10-11n, 10-12, 10-14, 10-22, 10-29, 13-10, 13-10n, 13-21, 17-17
179(a), 13-21n
179(b)(1), 13-21n
179(b)(3), 10-10n
179(d)(10), 10-10n, 13-21n
180, 6-10n
183, 6-29–6-30, 6-32, 9-25n
183(d), 6-29, 6-29n
185, 13-10n
188, 13-10n
190, 6-10n, 13-10n
193, 6-10n, 13-10n
194, 13-10n
194(a), 13-10n
195, 6-15, 10-13, 10-16
197, 10-13–10-16, 10-13n, 10-21, 13-9
197(a), 5-27n, 10-13n
197(f)(1), 10-15n
197(f)(7), 10-15n
212, 2-4n, 6-2, 6-5, 6-7–6-8, 7-9, 7-28, 8-10n, 9-8–9-10, 9-12
212(1), 9-6n
213, 6-9, 7-3, 7-44
213(c), 7-6n
213(d), 7-6n
213(d)(10), 4-10n
217, 9-18, 9-19n, 9-20
217(d)(2), 9-44n
217(d)(3), 9-44n

219, 3-14n
219(g), 9-37n
224(a), 15-22 (Table 15-2)
243, 16-5n
246, 16-5n
248, 6-10, 10-13
259, 4-7
262, 2-4n
263, 6-10
263(c), 6-10n, 10-19n, 13-21n
263A, 5-5, 6-11, 11-11
263A(b)(2)(B), 11-11n
263A(f), 5-5n
263A(f)(1)(B), 5-5n
263A(f)(4)(B), 5-5n
265, 6-11, 6-17
266, 6-11, 6-17
267, 6-25–6-28, 6-28n, 7-20, 10-10, 15-6, 17-12, 17-12n
267(a), 12-8n
267(a)(2), 6-28n
267(b), 7-20n, 8-9n
267(c)(4), 7-18n, 15-5
267(e), 6-28n, 7-20n
268, 13-6n
269A(b), 6-28n
269A(b)(1), 8-13n
274, 4-5, 4-12n, 6-17, 9-8, 9-12–9-14
274(a)(3), 9-15n
274(b), 4-30
274(b)(1), 9-15n
274(c), 9-8n
274(d), 6-16n, 9-43, 9-43n, 15-36
274(h), 9-8n
274(j), 4-12n, 9-15n
274(k), 9-13n
274(l)(2), 9-16n
274(m)(3), 9-8n
274(n), 9-12
276(a), 6-14n
280A, 6-31n, 6-31–6-34, 6-34 (Figure 6-4), 7-31, 15-5, 15-25
280A(c)(1), 9-23n
280A(c)(5), 9-25n
280A(c)(5)(B), 6-32n
280A(d)(1), 6-31n, 7-18, 7-18n
280A(d)(2), 6-31n, 7-18n
280A(d)(2)(B), 6-31n
280A(d)(2)(C), 6-31n
280A(e)(1), 6-32n
280E, 6-14, 6-17, 8-3, 10-13
280F, 10-11n
280F(a)(2), 10-11n
280F(b)(3), 10-11n
280F(b)(4), 10-11n
280F(d)(3), 10-11n
280F(d)(4), 10-22
280H(k), 11-4n
291, 13-14n, 13-16–13-17
291(a), 13-12n, 13-24n
291(a)(1), 13-16n
302, 3-17n
302(b)(1), 16-29–16-31
302(b)(2), 16-30

302(b)(3), 15-8, 16-30, 16-48
302(b)(4), 16-31
302(c)(2), 16-48
302(c)(2)(A), 15-8
302(c)(2)(C)(i), 15-8
302(b)(4), 16-31n
302(c)(2), 16-30n
302(e), 16-31n
303, 16-31, 16-31n
304, 306, 341, or 1254, 17-30
305(b), 16-28n
306, 15-8
307(a), 5-11n
307(b)(1), 5-11n
311(a), 16-27n
311(b), 16-20n, 16-28n, 17-28n
311(b)(2), 16-28n
312, 16-11n, 16-25, 16-25n
316, 16-26
316(a), 3-16n
318, 6-28n, 8-13n, 16-29n, 17-28
318(a)(1), 15-8
331, 16-34
331(a)(1), 16-32n
332, 16-33–16-34
334(a), 16-32n
334(b)(1), 16-33n
336, 16-31n, 17-30
336(b), 16-28n
337, 16-33
351, 11-20, 13-23, 15-8, 16-20–16-24, 16-32–16-33, 16-39, 17-4, 17-6, 17-25
351(b), 16-20n
351(d), 16-20n
351(f), 16-20n
357(a), 16-22
357(b), 16-22n
357(c), 16-23n
357(c)(3), 16-23n
358(a), 16-21n
362(a), 16-22n
368(a)(1)(B), 15-6
368(c), 16-20n
381, 16-33n
385, 16-24
401(a), 9-28
401(a)(17), 9-36n
401(d), 9-36n
401(k), 9-27–9-30, 9-28n, 9-59
401-416, 9-27n
402(e), 9-30n
402(g), 18-11n
402(h)(2), 9-41n
403(b), 18-11n
404, 8-13n
404(a)(3)(A), 9-30n
404(l), 9-36n
408(k), 9-41n
408(p), 9-41n
408A, 9-38n
409(a), 9-28n
411(a), 9-29n
414(q), 9-28n
415(b)(1), 9-30n
415(c), 9-30n, 18-11n

415(c)(1), 9-36n
422, 9-32n–9-33n
441(a), 11-27
441(b), 15-22 (Table 15-??)
441(f), 11-3n
441(g), 11-2n
441(i)(2), 6-28n
442, 11-4n
443(b)(2), 11-6n
444, 11-4, 17-19n
446, 11-36
446(b), 6-18
446(e), 11-27
446, 11-7n
448, 6-20, 16-42
448(a), 11-8n
448(a)(2), 17-19n
448(b), 11-8n, 17-19n
448(c), 11-8n
448(c)(2), 16-13
448(c)(3), 16-13
451, 11-7n
452, 3-28
453, 11-7n, 11-18
453(b)(2), 11-18n
453(e), 11-21
453(i)(1), 13-19n
453(i)(1)(B), 13-20n
453(i)(2), 13-20n
453(k), 11-18n
453A(b)(2)(B), 11-21n
453A(c), 11-21n
453A(d), 11-20n
453B(a), 11-20n
460(a), 11-16n
460(b)(3), 11-17n
460(e), 11-16n
461(c), 6-21, 7-11
461(g), 6-19n, 7-19n
461(h), 6-20n, 6-21, 11-9n
465, 17-11n, 17-26n
465(a)(1)(B), 8-12n
465(c)(7), 8-13n
469, 3-14n, 7-14, 8-7, 17-11n, 17-26n
469(c)(1), 8-10n
469(c)(2), 8-10n
469(c)(6), 8-10n
469(e)(1), 8-8n
469(g), 8-8n
469(g)(2), 8-9n
469(h)(4), 8-13n
469(i)(1), 8-15n
469(j)(1), 8-12n
469(j)(2), 8-13n
469(j)(8), 8-10n
469(k)(2), 8-13n
471, 11-36
471(b), 11-14n
472(c), 11-12n
472(d), 11-30n
472(f), 11-13n
474(c), 11-13n
475, 5-14n
475(b), 5-14n
481, 11-27n
481(a), 11-26, 11-27n
481(b)(1), 11-27n

481(b)(2), 11-27n
481(c), 11-27n
483, 11-22
483(d), 11-22n
501(c)(3), 3-13, 7-24, 7-27
530, 9-40n, 14-14
531, 16-13n, 16-17
532(c), 16-14n
537, 16-13n
541, 16-15n, 16-17
542(a)(2), 8-12n
547, 16-15n, 16-16n
561, 16-14n, 16-16n
563, 16-14n
611, 17-10n
611(a), 10-18n
612, 10-18n
613(a), 10-18n
613A(c), 10-18n
616, 6-10n
617(d), 17-15
631, 13-5
631(a), 13-5n
631(c), 13-6n
631A(d)(1), 10-19n
678, 17-20n
691(c), 7-9n
704, 17-9
704(d), 17-11
704(e), 17-32n
705, 17-10
706, 17-18
706(d)(1), 17-9n
707, 17-12n
707(b), 8-9n, 17-12
707(b)(1), 6-28
709, 17-7n
721, 17-4–17-6, 17-8, 17-13, 17-46
721(b), 17-4n
722, 17-4
723, 17-6
731, 17-5, 17-8, 17-13n
741, 17-15
751, 17-13n–17-14n, 17-15
752, 17-5, 17-8
754, 17-15, 17-32–17-33
761(a), 17-2n
772(a), 17-17
773(a)(3), 17-17
773(a)(4), 17-17
773(b)(2), 17-17
773(b)(3), 17-17
775, 17-16
775(b), 17-16
852(b), 3-16n
902, 14-17n
904, 14-17n
911, 3-14n, 14-13n, 14-16n
911(a), 14-31n
911(b)(1)(B), 4-18n
911(b)(2), 4-17n
911(d), 4-18n
911(d)(2)(B), 4-18n
911(e)(2), 4-18n
911, 2-18, 4-4
931, 2-18
931, 3-14n

933, 2-18, 3-14n
1001, 8-2n, 15-6
1001(a), 4-3n, 5-2n
1012, 12-15n
1014(a), 5-8n–5-9n, 13-25n
1014(b)(6), 5-9n
1015(a), 5-6n
1015(d)(2), 5-7n
1015(d)(6), 5-7n
1031, 5-29, 12-2, 12-4, 12-9–12-10, 13-19
1031(a), 12-2, 12-2n, 12-5n
1031(a)(2), 12-4n
1031(a)(3)(A), 12-6n
1031(a)(3)(B), 12-6n
1031(b), 12-2n, 12-6n
1031(c), 12-6n
1031(d), 12-7n
1031(e), 12-4n
1031(f)(1)(C), 12-8n
1031(f)(2), 12-8n
1031(f)(3), 12-8n
1033, 12-2, 12-10–12-14, 12-16, 12-20, 13-19, 13-19n
1033(a), 12-13n
1033(a)(1), 12-10n
1033(a)(2), 12-12n
1033(a)(2)(A), 12-12n–12-13n, 12-15n
1033(a)(2)(A)(ii), 12-15n
1033(a)(2)(B), 12-15n
1033(a)(2)(B)(ii), 12-15n
1033(b), 12-13n
1033(d), 12-12n
1033(e), 12-12n
1033(f), 12-13n
1033(g)(1), 12-14n
1033(g)(2), 12-15n
1033(g)(4), 12-15n
1033(h)(1)(A), 12-21n
1034, 12-17, 12-18n, 12-32
1034(e), 12-17n
1034(b)(1), 15-27
1036, 12-5
1038, 11-20n
1060, 10-21
1091, 6-22, 6-24
1091(a), 6-23n
1201, 5-20n
1202, 1-14n, 5-17n, 5-17–5-19, 5-21, 5-28, 8-31n, 14-4, 17-15
1202(a), 4-20n
1202(b)(1), 4-20n
1202(d), 4-20n
1202(e), 4-20n
1211(a), 16-4n
1211(b), 5-18n
1212(a), 5-20n, 16-4n
1212(b), 5-18n
1221, 2-26, 5-12, 5-14, 5-44, 8-5n, 13-5
1221(2), 13-5n
1222, 5-21, 5-28n
1222(11), 5-16n
1223, 9-32n, 12-10n
1223(1), 5-28n–5-29n, 12-9n
1223(1)(A), 12-12n

1223(2), 17-6n
1223(5), 5-29n
1223(11), 5-29n
1231, 5-13, 5-29, 6-5n, 7-23, 7-23n, 8-3, 8-5, 8-7, 8-22, 8-24, 10-15–10-16, 11-19, 12-9, 13-1–13-20, 13-22–13-25, 13-29, 13-35, 15-8, 16-3, 16-35, 16-40, 17-6–17-7, 17-8 (Table 17-1), 17-12–17-13, 17-15, 17-17, 17-24–17-25, 17-41
1231(a)(1), 13-2n–13-3n
1231(a)(2), 13-2n–13-3n
1231(a)(3)(A), 13-6n
1231(a)(4)(B), 13-6n
1231(a)(4)(C), 13-7n
1231(b)(1), 13-5n
1231(b)(2), 13-6n
1231(b)(3), 13-6n
1231(b)(4), 13-6n
1231(c)(1), 13-3n
1231(c)(3), 13-2n
1231(c)(4), 13-2n
1234(a), 5-25n
1234(b), 5-21n
1235, 5-25–5-26
1235(a), 5-26n
1236, 5-14
1237, 5-15
1237(b)(3), 5-15n
1239, 13-22–13-23
1239(a), 13-22n
1239(b)(2), 13-23n
1239(c), 13-22n
1241, 5-27n
1244, 1-14n, 5-14, 8-4–8-5, 8-5n, 8-7, 16-32n, 16-33–16-34
1244(a), 5-14n
1244(b), 5-14n
1244(c)(2), 8-6n
1244(d)(1)(B), 16-48
1245, 7-23, 10-15–10-16, 11-18, 13-1–13-2, 13-5, 13-7–13-11, 13-9n–13-10n, 13-14–13-20, 13-22–13-25, 13-35, 17-8 (Table 17-1), 17-15
1245(a)(2)(C), 10-15n, 13-10n
1245(a)(3), 13-9n
1245(a)(3)(B)(i), 13-9n
1245(a)(3)(C), 13-10n
1245(a)(5), 13-10n, 13-14n
1245(a)(5)(C), 13-14n
1245(b)(1), 13-17n
1245(b)(2), 13-18n
1245(b)(3), 16-20n
1245(b)(4), 13-19n
1245(d), 13-17n
1250, 5-17, 5-19, 13-1–13-2, 13-4, 13-7–13-8, 13-10–13-20, 13-22, 13-24–13-25, 13-33, 13-35, 17-8 (Table 17-1), 17-15, 17-30
1250(a)(1)(B)(i), 13-15n

1250(a)(1)(B)(ii), 13-15n
1250(a)(1)(B)(iii), 13-15n
1250(a)(1)(B)(iv), 13-15n
1250(a)(1)(B)(v), 13-13n–13-14n
1250(a)(2)(B)(iii), 13-13n
1250(a)(2)(B)(v), 13-14n
1250(a)(3), 13-11n
1250(b)(1), 13-11n
1250(c), 13-11n
1250(d)(1), 13-17n
1250(d)(2), 13-18n
1250(d)(3), 16-20n
1250(d)(4), 13-19n
1250(i), 13-17n
1252, 13-21, 13-25, 17-15
1252(a)(1), 13-21n, 13-23n
1252(a)(3), 13-21n
1253, 5-26n, 5-26–5-27
1253(a), 5-26n
1253(b)(2), 5-27n
1253(e), 5-26n
1254, 13-25, 17-15
1254(a)(1), 13-21n
1255, 13-25
1271, 5-22n
1271(a)(2), 5-22n
1272(a)(3), 5-23n
1273(a)(1), 5-22n
1273(a)(3), 5-23n
1274, 11-22–11-23
1274(c)(4), 11-23n
1274A, 11-23
1274A(c), 11-24n
1276(a)(1), 5-24n
1276(b)(1), 5-24n
1276(b)(2), 5-24n
1278, 17-15
1278(a)(2)(C), 5-24n
1283, 17-15
1301, 3-10n
1341, 3-26n
1361, 17-19n
1361(b)(3), 17-20n
1362, 17-21n
1363, 17-24n
1366(a)(1), 17-26n
1366(d)(1), 17-26n, 17-46
1366(d)(1)(A), 17-26n
1366(e), 17-32n
1367, 17-25n
1367(a)(2), 17-26n
1368(b), 17-28n
1371(a)(1), 17-3n
1372(a), 17-29
1374, 17-29n, 17-30
1375(a), 17-30n
1377(a)(2), 17-22n, 17-25n
1378(a), 11-2n
1378(b), 17-28n
1396, 14-10 (Table 14-1), 14-21n
1402(a)(12), 1-11n
1501, 15-10n
1502, 15-10
1504, 17-20
1504(a)(2), 16-33n
1504(a)(8), 17-20n

F-4 Individuals ▼ Appendix F

1561, 16-17*n*
1563(a)(1), 16-18*n*
1563(a)(2), 16-18*n*
1563(a)(3), 16-19*n*
2032(a), 5-8*n*
2503(b), 1-8*n*, 5-7*n*, 5-31*n*
2512(b), 1-8*n*
2523(a), 1-8*n*
2601, 7-9*n*
3301, 1-11*n*
3302, 1-11*n*
3401, 4-23*n*
3402(f)(1)(E), 14-26*n*
3403, 14-24*n*
3405, 14-25*n*
3405(a)(4), 14-25*n*
3405(c), 14-25*n*
3406, 14-25*n*

4973(b), 9-38*n*
4975(e)(7), 9-28*n*
6012(a)(1), 2-29*n*
6012(c), 2-29*n*
6013, 2-19*n*
6013(d)(3), 2-28*n*
6013(g), 2-19*n*
6014, 14-32*n*
6015(b), 2-28*n*
6017, 14-7*n*
6018(a), 5-8*n*
6045(a), 5-36*n*
6045(c), 5-36*n*
6045(e)(4), 7-36*n*
6072(a), 2-30*n*
6110, 15-13
6115, 7-34*n*
6501(a), 1-22*n*

6501(b)(1), 1-22*n*
6501(c), 1-22*n*
6501(e), 1-22*n*
6511(a), 1-22*n*
6511(d)(1), 8-34*n*
6611(e), 1-22*n*, 14-30*n*
6621(a), 1-22*n*
6651(a)(1), 1-22*n*
6651(a)(2), 1-23*n*
6651(c)(1), 1-23*n*
6651(f), 1-22*n*
6654, 1-23*n*, 14-24*n*, 14-28*n*
6655(d), 16-36*n*
6655(e), 16-36*n*
6662, 1-23*n*, 15-37
6663, 1-23*n*
6672, 4-23*n*, 14-42
6674, 4-23*n*

6682, 14-25*n*
6682(a), 14-26*n*
6694, 15-35
6695(g), 14-33*n*
6721, 4-23*n*
7463, 15-17*n*
7491, 15-7
7503, 2-30*n*
7519, 17-19*n*
7519(b), 11-4*n*
7701, 15-8
7701(a)(2), 17-2*n*
7701(b), 2-16*n*
7704(c), 8-13*n*
7805, 15-10

APPENDIX G

INDEX OF TREASURY REGULATIONS

Final Regulations
1.2-2(d), 2-21n
1.44A-2(b)(3)(B)(ii), 14-12n
1.61-7, 3-13n
1.61-14(a), 3-23n
1.62-2(c), 9-16n
1.72-9, 3-20
1.74-1, 3-22n
1.79-3(d)(2), 4-11
1.83-7, 9-32n
1.102-1, 4-4n
1.109-1, 3-15n, 3-38
1.117-6(d)(5), 4-30
1.119-1(c)(1), 4-14n
1.123-1, 4-30
1.132-6(e)(1), 4-30
1.152-1(a)(2)(i), 2-13n
1.152-2, 2-38
1.152-2(d), 2-16n
1.162-2(a), 9-60
1.162-2(b)(1), 9-7n
1.162-4, 6-10n
1.162-5, 9-21n
1.162-27, 16-7n
1.163-10T(p)(3)(ii), 7-18
1.164-3(c), 7-10n
1.164-4, 7-11n
1.165-1(d)(2)(i), 8-22n
1.165-2, 5-21n
1.165-5, 15-11
1.165-5(i), 15-11
1.165-7(a)(2), 8-19n
1.165-7(a)(3), 8-18n
1.165-7(b)(2), 8-20n
1.165-7(b)(2)(ii), 8-20n
1.165-7(b)(3), 8-20n
1.165-8(d), 8-19n
1.165-9(a), 12-16n
1.165-9(b)(2), 5-9n
1.165-11(e), 8-35n
1.166-1(c), 8-24n
1.166-2, 8-26n
1.166-5(b)(2), 8-27n
1.167(a)-3, 10-13n
1.167(a)-8, 5-21n
1.167(a)-8(a)(4), 8-3n
1.167(g)-1, 5-9n, 10-4n
1.167(j)-3(b)(1)(i), 13-13n
1.168(d)-1(b)(3), 10-5n
1.170A-1(c)(2), 7-22
1.170A-13, 7-34n

1.170A-13(c), 7-33n
1.170A-4(b)(1), 7-23n
1.170A-4(d), 7-23n
1.170A-7(a)(1), 7-22n
1.172-3, 8-30n
1.172-5(a)(3)(ii), 8-34n
1.174-2(a)(2), 10-16n
1.174-3(b)(1), 10-22n
1.179-1(e), 10-10n, 13-21n
1.179-2(c)(5)(iv), 10-10n
1.183-1(b), 6-30n
1.183-2(b), 6-28
1.197-2(b)(1), 10-14n
1.213-1(a)(1), 7-6n
1.213-1(e)(1)(ii), 7-3n
1.213-1(e)(1)(iii), 7-5n, 7-44
1.217-2(b)(3), 9-19n
1.262-1b)(4), 12-16n
1.263(a)-2(h), 6-10n
1.267(c)-1(b), 6-26n
1.268-1, 13-6n
1.274-2(f)(2)(i)(b), 9-14n
1.274-4, 9-8n
1.302-4, 16-48
1.305-4, 3-16n
1.316-2(b), 16-27n
1.346-1(a), 16-31n
1.441-1(b)(4), 11-2n
1.441-2(c)(2), 11-5n
1.442-1(b)(2), 11-5n
1.442-1(c), 11-5n
1.442-1(e), 11-5n
1.443-1(a)(2), 11-5n
1.443-1(b)(2), 11-6n
1.446-1(a)(1), 11-7n
1.446-1(c)(1)(i), 11-8n
1.446-1(c)(1)(ii), 3-11n
1.446-1(c)(2)(i), 3-8n
1.446-1(e)(1), 11-26n
1.446-1(e)(2)(ii)(b), 11-26n
1.446-1(e)(3), 11-36
1.451-1(a), 3-11n, 11-9n
1.451-2(a), 9-31n
1.451-2(b), 3-10n
1.451-3(a)(1), 11-15n
1.451-3(b), 11-15n
1.451-5, 3-11n, 3-28
1.453-1(d)(3)(iii), 11-21n
1.454-1(a)(4), Ex. (1), 3-28n
1.461-1(a)(1), 11-8n
1.461-1(a)(2), 6-20n

1.461-1(c), 15-22 (Table 15-2)
1.461-4(d)(4)(i), 6-22
1.461-4(d)(6)(ii), 6-22
1.461-2(a)(1), 6-20n
1.469-4, 8-10n
1.469-4(g), 8-9
1.471-1, 11-8n
1.471-2, 11-36
1.471-2(a), 11-36
1.471-2(b), 11-14n
1.471-2(c), 11-11n, 11-14n
1.471-3(d), 11-36
1.471-4, 11-36
1.471-11(d)(3), 11-12n
1.472-2(c), 11-30n
1.472-2(e), 11-13n
1.472-3(a), 11-26n, 11-30n
1.611-1(b)(1), 13-6n
1.612-4(a), 13-21n
1.612-4(d), 10-21n
1.631-1, 13-5n
1.631-1(d)(4), 13-6n
1.631-3(a)(1), 13-6n
1.631-3(a)(2), 13-6n
1.631-3(b)(4), 13-6n
1.671-2(e), 15-22 (Table 15-2)
1.706-1(c)(2), 17-10n
1.706-1T, 11-2n
1.721-1(a), 17-4n, 17-46
1.721-1(b)(1), 17-4n
1.722-1, 17-5n
1.723-1, 17-6n
1.754-1(b), 17-32n
1.1001-1(c)(1), 5-3n
1.1001-2, 8-2n
1.1002-1(d), 5-21n
1.1012-1(c)(1), 5-6n
1.1012-1(e), 5-6n
1.1019-1, 3-15n
1.1031(a)-1(a)(1)(ii), 12-5n
1.1031(a)-1(b), 12-3n
1.1031(a)-2, 12-3n
1.1031(a)-2(b), 12-3n
1.1031(a)-2(b)(3), 12-4n
1.1031(a)-2(b)(7), 12-4n
1.1031(a)-2(c)(1), 12-4n
1.1031(b)-1(c), 12-7n
1.1031(d)-1(c), 12-8n
1.1033(a)-1, 12-11n
1.1033(a)-2(c), 12-15n
1.1033(a)-2(c)(2), 12-23n

G-1

1.1033(a)-2(c)(4), 12-15n
1.1034-1(a)(3)(ii), 12-22n
1.1034-1(b)(4), 12-17n
1.1034-1(b)(4)(i), 12-17n
1.1034-1(b)(5), 12-17n
1.1034-1(c)(3), 12-18n
1.1034-1(c)(4), 12-17n
1.1034-1(c)(3), 12-32
1.1212-1(b), 5-18n
1.1223-1(a), 12-9n-12-10
1.1223-1(a), 17-6n
1.1223-1(b), 5-28n
1.1223-1(e), 5-29n
1.1231-1(c)(5), 13-6n
1.1231-1(f), 13-6n
1.1234-1(b), 5-21n
1.1235-2, 5-44
1.1235-2(b), 5-26n
1.1244(c)-1(b), 16-48
1.1244(d)-2(a), 16-48

1.1245-2(a)(4), 13-17n, 13-19n
1.1245-2(c)(4), 13-19n
1.1245-4(d)(1), 13-19n
1.1245-6(a), 13-17n
1.1245-6(f), 13-22n
1.1250-1(c)(1), 13-17n
1.1250-2(d), 13-17n
1.1250-3(d), 13-19n
1.1361-1(l), 17-21n
1.1502-75(c), 16-19n
1.6013-1(a), 2-29n
1.6050H-1(f)(3), 7-18n
1.6081-4(a)(1), 2-30n
1.6081-4(a)(2), 2-30n
31.3401(a)(10)-1(a), 14-24n
31.3401(a)-1(a)(2), 14-24n
31.3401(a)-1(b)(9), 4-23n
31.3401(c)-1(b), 9-3n
31.3402(f)(2)-1, 14-26n
31.3402(g)-1(a), 14-25n

301.7701-1, 16-2n, 17-3n, 17-19n
301.7701-2, 16-2n, 17-3n, 17-19n
301.7701-3, 16-2n, 17-3n, 17-19n
301.7701-4, 17-3n
Proposed Regulations
1.671-2(e), 15-22 (Table 15-2)
Temporary Regulations
1.62-1T(e), 15-22 (Table 15-2)
1.163-8T, 7-12n
1.163-8T(c), 7-13n
1.163-8T(c)(4)(ii), 7-13n
1.163-8T(c)(4)(iv), 7-13n
1.170A-13(f), 7-34n
1.469-1(e)(3)(iii), 8-10n
1.469-5T(a), 8-11n
1.469-5T(c), 8-11n
1.469-5T(d), 8-12n
15A.453-1(c), 11-21n
15A.453-1(d)(2)(ii)(A), 11-21n

APPENDIX H

INDEX OF GOVERNMENT PROMULGATIONS

Announcements
98-1, 15-13, **15-22** (Table 15-2)
Information Releases
86-70, 15-13
Letter Rulings
8004111, 7-3n
8227010, 8-18n
8511075, 15-13
8544001, 8-18n
8752010, 7-16n
8906031, 7-16n
8919009, 7-4n
9237014, 9-8n
9526020, 4-7n
Notices
88-74, 7-16n, 15-22 (Table 15-2)
89-28, 8-29n
89-56, 7-33n
90-25, 7-33n
93-4, 7-36n
98-1, 15-13
News Releases
83-93, 7-20n
Revnue Procedures
71-21, 11-15n
72-18, 6-12n
74-33, 11-4n
77-28, 15-22 (Table 15-2)
84-58, 15-14n
87-15, 6-20n, 7-18n
87-32, 11-4n
87-56, 10-5n, 10-8, 12-3
87-57, 10-6
92-3, 12-18n
92-12A, 7-17n
93-27, 17-46
94-27, 6-19n–6-20n, 7-17n–7-18n
97-19, 15-12
97-37, 15-22 (Table 15-??)
99-49, 11-26n, 16-3n
2000-18, 10-13n
2000-22, 6-20n, 16-3, 16-3n, 17-8–17-9
2000-39, 9-18n
2000-48, 9-11n
2001-10, 16-3n
2001-13, 7-5n
Revenue Rulings
53-271, 12-13n
54-97, 5-33n
54-567, 2-16n
55-327, 8-18n
56-60, 5-8n
56-602, 6-24n
57-102, 4-2n
57-246, 14-8n
57-344, 2-13n
57-418, 6-16 (Figure 6-1)
57-599, 8-18n
58-67, 2-13n
58-234, 5-24n–5-25n
58-256, 11-5n
58-419, 2-13n
58-601, 11-28n
59-58, 4-30
59-102, 12-11n
60-31, 9-31n
60-329, 8-18n
61-119, 12-5n
62-197, 8-3n
62-210, 7-3n
63-91, 7-4n
63-144, 4-15, 4-15n
63-221, 12-11n
64-31, 12-18n
64-162, 17-27n
64-222, 2-13n
64-237, 12-14n
65-34, 2-16n
65-185, 11-19
65-261, 5-44
65-307, 2-13n
66-216, 7-6n
68-20, 4-7n
68-37, 12-13n
68-537, 17-27n
68-591, 9-22n
68-662, 7-29n
69-88, 8-18n
69-240, 12-13n
69-292, 9-23n
69-498, 8-3n
69-654, 12-11n
70-104, 16-31
70-598, 5-28n
71-21, 3-11, 3-28
71-41, 12-15
71-137, 12-2
71-468, 2-13n
71-475, 6-11
72-112, 8-19n
72-224, 3-6n
72-225, 6-24n
72-312, 3-6n
72-593, 7-4n
73-35, 12-13n
73-136, 7-12n
73-156, 2-38
74-7, 12-4n
74-78, 9-22n
74-144, 15-22 (Table 15-2)
74-187, 7-12n
75-168, 9-6n, 9-60
75-170, 9-7n
75-302, 7-7n, 7-31n
75-303, 7-6, 7-7n, 7-31n
75-502, 16-29n–16-30n
75-432, 9-60
75-538, 13-38
76-226, 9-3n
76-255, 2-29n
76-319, 12-14
76-364, 16-29n–16-30n
76-541, 12-32
77-77, 4-2
77-298, 12-22n
77-282, 2-13, 2-13n
78-39, 7-7n, 11-8n
78-146, 12-18n
79-174, 8-18n–8-19n
79-175, 7-6n
79-417, 11-26
80-45, 7-24
80-265, 15-12
81-180, 12-11n
82-26, 12-22n
82-74, 12-11n
82-149, 6-13n
82-166, 12-4n
82-204, 5-44
83-39, 12-23n
83-49, 12-13n
84-15, 17-7n
84-113, 9-6n
87-22, 6-20n, 7-18n
87-41, 9-3
87-106, 7-5n
87-138, 15-13
89-46, 3-29n
89-51, 7-22n
91-26, 17-29n
92-29, 6-6n, 7-29n
93-72, 7-6, 7-31n
93-86, 9-6, 9-6n, 15-6 (Figure 15-6)
94-47, 9-10n
97-9, 7-3n
97-37, 11-27n
98-1, 15-12
99-7, 9-6n, 9-10n
2000-22, 3-8n, 11-7n, 17-8n
2001-10, 11-7n, 17-8n
Technical Advice Memoranda
9801001, 15-13
Treasury Decisions
7224, 15-11
8756, 15-22 (Table 15-2)

APPENDIX I

INDEX OF COURT CASES

Acme Construction Co., Inc., 6-36n
Amax Coal Co., Michael O. Campbell v., 14-26
American Liberty Pipe Line Co. v. CIR, 11-36
Andrew, Giffin A., 8-25
Apkin, Philip, 3-28n
Arkansas Best Corporation v. CIR, 5-14, 5-14n
Arrowsmith, F. Donald Exr., v. CIR, 3-25n
Asjes, Jr., Everet,, 12-14
Astone, Anthony, 13-19
Ayers, Gary, 3-23n
Azar Nut Co. v. CIR, 5-44
Balistrieri, Joseph P., 12-11n
Barbetti, Desio, 2-38
Bart, Stuart, 8-27n
Belloff, Paul F., 15-18, 15-22 (Table 15-2)
Berger, Ernest H., 6-36n
Berry, Henry W., 8-18n
Berry, James E., v. Wiseman, 7-5
Bertolini, Raymond, Trucking Co. v. CIR, 6-12
Biscayne Bay Islands Co., 5-10
Black Limited, E. E., v. Alsup, 11-16n
Blood Enterprises, Inc., George, 3-17n
Bolding, Dennis E., v. U.S., 17-46
Bolton, Dorance D., v. CIR, 6-32n
Bonaire Development Co. v. CIR, 6-19n, 11-8n
Bonner v. City of Prichard, 15-20n
Boston Fish Market Corporation, 4-30
Bradley, M. A., Estate of, CIR v., 6-18n
Brumber, Loren S., 2-13n
Bufferd, Sheldon B. v. CIR, 15-23n-15-24
Burgess, Newton A., 7-20n
Burns, Howard F., v. U.S., 8-18n
Byrum, Marian A., U.S. v., 15-21n
Calhoun, Q.A., v. U.S., 11-3n
Campbell, William G., v. CIR, 17-46
Carlson, Ernest W., v. U.S., 14-42
Carpenter, William H., 8-19n
Cartwright, Douglas B., Executor, U.S. v., 15-10n
Central Illinois Public Service Co. v. CIR, 15-24n
Cesarini, Ermenegildo, v. U.S., 3-23n
Chaitlen, Morrie, 11-36
CIR v. American Liberty Pipe Line Co., 11-36
CIR v. Thor Power Tool Co., 11-36
Click, D. H., 12-33

Cohan, George M., v. CIR, 6-16n, 6-16–6-17
Commerford, Patrick, U.S. v., 3-23n
Cooney, James J., 3-10n
Coors, Adolph, Co., 4-14
Cordner, Warren C., v. U.S., 16-27
Corn Products Refining Co. v. CIR, 5-13n, 5-13–5-14
Correll, v. U.S., 9-7n, 9-60
Correll, O. Homer, U.S. v., 15-10n
Costello, Edward J., 3-26
Court Holding Co., CIR v., 1-30
Cramer, Virginia M., 8-22
Crane, Beulah B., v. CIR, 5-3n, 8-2n
Creative Solutions, Inc. v. U.S., 12-11n
Cumberland Public Service Co., U.S. v., 1-30
Cunningham, Grace H., CIR v., 3-38
Davis, Harold, v. U.S., 7-21n
Davis, Kenneth C., 9-22n
Davis, Maclin P., U.S. v., 15-21, 15-22 (Table 15-2), 16-30n
Dawson, Henry B., 5-9
Dayton Hudson Corp. v. CIR, 11-14n
Dean, J. Simpson, 15-18
DeMarco, Frank, 14-19
Demeter, Ann K., 12-18n
Diamond, Sol, v. CIR, 17-46
Diaz, Alfonso, 15-29
Diaz, Frank, 15-29
Diaz, Leonarda C., 15-28, 15-31
Dibblee, Isabel, 15-30 (Figure 15-6)
Disney, Roy O., U.S. v., 9-8
Drazen, Michael, 11-7
Duarte, Henry D., 15-22 (Table 15-2)
Duberstein, Mose, CIR v., 4-16n
DuPont, Pierre S., Deputy v., 6-6n
DuPont, Pierre S., Deputy v., 7-12n
Durden, Ray, 8-18n
Eboli, Saverio, 6-19
Eckell, Vincent W., 9-8
Ehret-Day Co., 11-16n
Eisner v. Myrtle H. Macomber, 3-6n, 3-16n, 3-33, 4-2
Fairmont Homes, Inc., 6-8
Farina, Antonino, v. McMahon, 3-23n
Farrelly-Walsh, Inc., 5-27n
Fausner, Donald W., v. CIR, 9-9
Fehlhaber, Robert v. CIR, 15-23n
Feldman, Richard L., 14-24
First National Bank of Gainesville, Trustee, 11-26

Flamingo Resort, Inc. v. U.S., 3-11
Flower, Harriet C., v. U.S., 2-13n
Flower, Harry M., 5-44
Flushingside Realty & Construction Co., 12-12n
Ford, Achille F., v. U.S., 5-33n
Forest City Chevrolet, 12-11n
Fox Chevrolet, Inc., 11-13
France, Rose C., v. CIR, 7-3n
Frank, Morton, 6-16 (Figure 6-1)
Franklin, H. C., CIR v., 7-20n
Fuchs, Frank, Estate of, v. CIR, 8-3n
German, Jr., Harry, 15-28
Gerstell, Robert S., 8-44
Golconda Mining Corp. v. CIR, 16-14n
Goldin, H.J., v. Baker, 3-24
Goldman, Estelle, 5-44
Golsen, Jack E., 15-21n
Gould v. Gould, 3-17n
Graham, Bette C., v. U.S., 13-22
Green, Charles T., v. CIR, 15-24n
Greene, Leonard, v. U.S., 15-20, 15-22 (Table 15-2)
Griswold, Donald G., 16-35
Guito, Ralph M., Jr. v. U.S., 14-24n
Gurvey, Gary, v. U.S., 5-27
Haberkorn, Ronald R., 6-31n
Hagaman v. Com., 3-17
Hallmark Cards, Inc. v U.S., 4-30
Hanlin, Marie, Executrix v. CIR, 6-24n
Harrah's Club v. U.S., 10-2
Harris, J. Wade, 13-19
Heininger, S. B., CIR v., 6-8n
Hezel, William J., 6-5
Higgins, Eugene v. CIR, 6-6n
Hollman, Emanuel, 2-38
Holt, Bill D., 8-3
Hooper, H. M., 5-28n
Horst, Helvering v., 3-30
Hort, Walter M., v. CIR, 5-27n
Howard, Jack R., 9-16
Humphreys, Murray, v. CIR, 3-23n
Hunt, C. L., 8-25n
Hunter Mfg. Co., 5-22
Huntsman, James R., v. CIR, 6-20n, 7-18n
Hutchinson, Charles L., 8-27n
Indopco, Inc., v. CIR, 6-10n
James, Eugene C., v. U.S., 3-23n
Janss, Peter F., 9-7
Jeanese, Inc. v. U.S., 15-10n
Johnson, Richard E., v. Bingler, 4-7n
Jones Co., Warren, 15-18

I-1

Justus & Parker Co., 11-36
Kahler, Charles F., 3-10*n*., 6-18*n*
Keenan, W. J. Jr., v. Bowers, 8-19*n*
Keller, Stephen A., v. CIR, 6-19*n*
Kelley, Daniel M. v. CIR, 15-23*n*
Kentucky & Indiana Terminal Railroad Co. v. U.S., 4-19
Kowalski, Robert J., CIR v., 4-14*n*
Kuh, Johannes L., 15-28
Lang Chevrolet Co., The, 3-17*n*
Leavitt, Estate of Daniel, v. CIR, 17-46
Ledbetter, Billie J., v. CIR, 8-2
Lerew, P.A., 7-44
Lessinger, Sol, v. CIR, 16-48
Levin, Samuel B., v. U.S., 6-6*n*
Lewis, Nat, 9-6
Liang, Walter K., v. CIR, 6-6*n*
Liddle, Brian P., 6-10*n*
Liddle v. Comr., 10-34
Limericks, Inc. v. CIR, 3-17*n*
Lindeman, Jack B., 4-14*n*
London Shoe Co. v. CIR., 4-6*n*
Loughlin, John O., v. U.S., 6-31*n*
Lucas v. Earl, 3-30
Lynch, William M., v. CIR, 16-48
Marinello Associates, Inc., Marco S., 12-13
Markarian, Frank, v. CIR, 2-13*n*
Marshman, Homer H., CIR v., 5-3*n*
Matheson, Chester, 8-35*n*
McDaniel, David, 8-18*n*
McDonald v. CIR, 15-10*n*
McKenna, James P., 3-23*n*
McKinney, Edith G., v. CIR, 6-32*n*
McKinney, Edith G., 15-18
McShain, John, 12-23*n*
McWilliams, John P., 6-24*n*
Meersman, J. P., v. U.S., 8-18*n*
Melat, George R., 2-13*n*
Menz, Norman W., 7-20*n*
Miller, John F., 2-13*n*
Miller, William R., 8-18*n*
Mizl, Daniel E., 7-3*n*
Monteleone, Michele, 8-44
Morris, Homer P., 4-3*n*
Morrison, James H., 7-23
Moss, John A., Estate of, 15-18
Mountain Fuel Supply Co. v. U.S., 11-27
Morgenstern, Joseph, 3-17*n*
Muncie, Curtis H., 8-19
Newark Morning Ledger Co. v. U.S., 10-14

Notter, George K., 8-19*n*
Nowland, Robert L., v. CIR, 4-3*n*
O'Connell, Emmett J., v. U.S., 8-18*n*
Ohio River Collieries, 11-9
Oppenheim's Inc. v. Kavanagh, 3-25*n*
Orr, J. Thomas, 15-28
Orr, William P., 16-23
Oswald, Vincent E., 6-36*n*
Pahl, J. G., 6-36*n*
Parker, James Edward, 2-13*n*
Patterson, v. Williams, 9-60
Peacock, Cassius L. III, 2-16*n*
Peterson & Pegau Baking Co., 3-17*n*
Picknally, Robert J., 9-22*n*
Plastics Universal Corp., 6-36*n*
Polacsek, R.A., 7-44
Pollock v. FarmersU Loan & Trust Co., 1-2*n*
Powers, William J., 8-3*n*
Poyner, Ernest L., v. CIR, 4-16*n*
Price, William K. III, 2-13*n*
Purvis, Ralph E., v. CIR, 6-6*n*
Quinn, Frank D. Exec., v. CIR, 11-9*n*
R. N. Smith v. U.S., 9-3*n*
Raphan, Benjamin, v. U.S., 15-19
Reeves, Richard A., 3-23
Ring, Vincent P., 7-4
Robbins, J.H., 7-44
Robinson, Willie C., 8-18*n*
Rose, Robert M., v. CIR, 7-7*n*, 7-31*n*
Rothenberg, George, 17-33
Ruddick Corp. v. U.S., 15-22 (Table 15-2)
Schiff, Renate, v. U.S., 14-24*n*
Schira, Mathias, v. CIR, 3-23*n*
Schlude, Mark E., v. CIR, 3-11
Schneider and Co., Charles, v. CIR, 6-36*n*
Schwerm, Gerald, 15-28
Selfe, Edward M., v. U.S., 17-46
Shaffer, Stephen R., 8-18*n*
Sharp, Jeffrey G. v. U.S., 15-20, 15-22 (Table 15-2)
Shauna C. Clinger, 10-34
Simon v. Comr., 10-34
Simon, Richard L., 6-10*n*
Sirbo Holdings Inc. v. CIR, 4-30
Smithgall, Charles A. v. U.S., 8-18*n*
Soffron, George N. v. CIR, 5-44
South Texas Lumber Co., CIR v., 15-10*n*
Stacey, Howard, 8-18*n*
Standard Fruit Product Co., 6-10*n*
Stein, Frank, 6-24*n*
Stewart, Spencer D., v. CIR, 12-12*n*

Stiegler, Rene A. Jr., 12-19*n*
Stolk, William C., v. CIR, 12-18*n*
Stone, Tracy Co., Flint v., 1-2*n*
Stuart, James P., 7-29
Sullivan, Manley S., U.S. v., 2-3*n*, 3-22*n*–3-23*n*
Sullivan, Neil, et al., CIR v., 6-14*n*
Sunstein, Cass, 3-23*n*
Super Food Services, Inc. v. U.S., 10-21
Sutter, Richard A., 4-15*n*
Tellier, Walter F., CIR v., 6-7*n*-6-8
Thoene, John J., 7-3*n*
Thompson-King-Tate, Inc. v. U.S., 11-16*n*
Thompson, Margie J., v. U.S., 15-19, 15-22 (Table 15-2)
Thompson, William, A., Jr., 6-47
Thor Power Tool Co. v. CIR, 11-11, 11-11*n*, 11-14, 11-36
Timberlake, J. E., v. CIR, 3-17*n*
Tomburello, Louis R., 4-5
Toner, Linda M., 15-28
Trent, John M., v. CIR, 8-27*n*
Tso, Raymond H., 7-3
Tsouprake, Ted E., v. U.S., 14-24*n*
Tucker, Marvin D., 2-13*n*
Tyler, Jean C., v. Tomlinson, 8-25*n*
U.S. v. ———, *See* opposing party
Vila, U.S. v., 8-22
Vogel Fertilizer Co., U.S. v., 15-10*n*
Vogel Fertilizer Co. v. U.S., 15-21*n*
Wagensen, F.S., 12-33
Wal-Mart Stores Inc. v. CIR, 11-14*n*
Wassenaar, Paul R., 15-28
Weiler, Jeffry L., 9-22*n*
Weiner, L., 3-23*n*
Welch, Thomas H., v. Helvering, 6-7*n*–6-8*n*, 6-47
Wells Lumber Co., J.W., Trust A., 15-18
White, John P., 8-18*n*
White, Layard M., 6-17*n*
Whiting, Lauren, 8-18*n*
Wilcox, Laird, CIR v., 3-23*n*
Williams, H.O., v. U.S., 11-36
Williams v. Patterson, 9-7*n*
Wisconsin Cheeseman, Inc. v. U.S., 6-12*n*
Wohlfeld, Nathan, 11-16*n*
Young, Minnie K., v. CIR, 5-22*n*
Zaninovich, Martin J., v. CIR, 6-19*n*, 11-8*n*
Zarin, David, v. CIR, 4-19*n*

APPENDIX J

SUBJECT INDEX

Abandoned spouse, *2-22*
Abandonment, of principal residence, *12-18–12-19*
Accelerated cost-recovery system (ACRS)
 alternative depreciation system, *10-8*
 listed property, *10-10–10-13*
 luxury automobiles, limitations on, *10-11–10-13*
 real property, classification/recovery rates for, *10-7–10-8*
 restrictions, *10-10–10-13*
 straight-line method, use of, *10-8*
 See also Modified ACRS
Accelerated death benefits, *4-6*
ACCESS legal data base, *1-25–1-26*
Accountable plan, *9-16*
Accounting methods
 accrual method, *3-11, 11-9–11-10*
 calendar-year requirement, *11-28*
 cash receipts and disbursements method, *3-8–3-10, 11-7–11-9*
 change in, *11-26–11-28*
  amount of change, *11-26–11-28*
  reporting amount of change, *11-27–11-28*
  voluntary changes, *11-27*
 definition of, *11-2*
 hybrid method, *3-11, 11-10*
 imputed interest, *11-22–11-25*
  accrual of interest, *11-23–11-24*
  applicable federal rate, *11-23*
  gift, shareholder and other loans, *11-24–11-25*
 installment sales, *11-28*
 inventories, *11-11–11-14, 11-28*
 special accounting methods, *11-15–11-22*
  deferred payment sales, *11-21*
  installment sales method, *11-17–11-21*
  long-term contracts, *11-15–11-17*
 See also specific methods
Accounting periods, *11-2–11-7, 11-28*
 52- to 53-week year, *11-3*
 calendar-year requirement, *11-3–11-4*
 See also specific methods
 changes in, *11-4–11-5*
  Form 1128, Application for Change in Accounting Period, *11-5*
 fiscal year, *11-2*
 periods of less than 12 months, returns for, *11-5*
 tax-planning considerations, *11-28*
Accrual method of accounting, *3-11, 6-20, 11-9–11-10*
 all-events test, *6-20–6-21, 11-9*
 deductible expenses, *6-20–6-22*
 economic performance test, *6-21, 11-9–11-10*,
 prepaid income, *3-11*
Accumulated earnings and profits, *16-25–16-27, 17-28*
Accumulated earnings tax, *16-14–16-15*
Acquiescence policy, U.S. Tax Court, *15-17*
Acquired property
 cost of, *5-5–5-6*
  capitalization of interest, *5-5–5-6*
  identification problems, *5-6*
  uniform capitalization rules, *5-5*
 received as gift, *5-6–5-7*
  gifts after 1921, *5-6–5-7*
  gifts after 1976, *5-7*
 received from decedent, *5-8–5-9*
  basis of property, *5-8–5-9*
  community property, *5-9*
 See also Property transactions
Acquisition indebtedness, *7-16–7-17*
Active trade/business, interest expense, *7-13*
Adjusted basis of property
 See also Basis
Adjusted current earnings, *16-11*
Adjusted gross income (AGI)
 deductions for, *2-4–2-5*
 deductions from, *2-4, 2-7–2-17*
  dependency exemptions, *2-12–2-17*
  itemized deductions, *2-7–2-10*
  personal exemptions, *2-12*
  standard deduction, *2-10–2-12*
 definition of, *2-4*
 state income taxes and, *1-7–1-8*
 See also Gross income
Adjusted ordinary gross income, *16-15*
Administrative appeal procedures, *1-23*
Administrative convenience, income, *3-3–3-4*
Administrative exclusion, definition of, *4-2*
Administrative interpretations, of tax law, *1-19*
 Treasury Regulations, *1-19*
 information releases, *1-19*
 letter rulings, *1-19*
 revenue procedures, *1-19*
 revenue rulings, *1-19*
 technical advice memoranda, *1-19*
Administrative interpretations, *15-11–15-13*
 announcements, *15-13*
 citations of, *15-11*
 information releases, *15-1*
 letter rulings, *15-12–15-13*
 notices, *15-13*
 revenue procedures, *15-12*
 revenue rulings, *15-11–15-12*
 technical advice memoranda, *15-13*
Adoption credit, *14-13–14-14*
Adoption expenses, *4-6–4-7*
Advance payments, annuities, *3-21*
Affiliated corporations, sale/exchange of securities in, *5-22*
Alimony
 as gross income, *3-17–3-19*
 definition of, *3-17–3-18*
 recapture provisions, *3-18–3-19*
 significance as income, *3-27*
All-events test, *6-20–6-21, 11-9*
Allocation of basis
 basket purchase, *5-10*
 common costs, *5-10*
 nontaxable stock dividends received, *5-10–5-11*
 nontaxable stock rights received, *5-11–5-12*
 See also Basis
Allocation of expenses
 residential property, *6-32–6-34*
 transportation expenses, *9-12*
Allocation of joint income, *3-6–3-7*
Alternative minimum tax (AMT), *14-2–14-7, 16-10–16-11*
 adjusted current earnings, *16-11*
 adjustments, *14-4–14-5, 16-11*
 alternative minimum taxable income, *14-2–14-3, 16-10–16-11*
 avoidance of, *14-29*
 computation aspects, *14-2–14-3, 16-10–16-11*
 filing procedures, *14-32*
 itemized deduction limitation, *14-4–14-5*
 minimum tax credit, *14-5–14-7, 16-11*
 tax preference items, *14-3–14-4, 16-11*

J-1

Alternative minimum tax (AMT), (*continued*)
   taxpayers subject to, *14-2, 16-10–16-11*
American Federal Tax Reports (AFTR) (Research Institute of America), *15-19*
Amortization
   Form 4562, *10-22*
   Sec. 197 intangibles, *10-13–10-17*
   of intangible assets, *10-13*
   reporting of, *10-22*
Announcements, tax law, *15-13*
Annuities
   advance payments, *3-21*
   as gross income, *3-19–3-21*
   current year exclusion, *3-19*
   exclusion ratio, *3-19*
   expected return, *3-19*
Appeals Court procedures, *15-20*
Appreciated property
   avoiding income tax on decedent's, *5-32*
   donation of, *7-32–7-33*
Asset depreciation range (ADR) system, *10-8*
Assets
   business-use assets, *10-10–10-11*
   capital assets, *2-26, 5-12–5-15, 5-30–5-31*
   intangible assets, amortization of, *10-13–10-17*
   partnership assets, basis of, *17-6*
   See also specific types of assets
   personal-use assets, *10-10*
   See also specific types of assets
Assignment, of income, *3-6*
"Associated with" entertainment expenditure, *9-13–9-14*
Athletic facilities, *4-12–4-13*
Audits
   field audit, *1-21*
   office audit, *1-21*
Automobile expenses
   actual expenses, *9-10–9-12*
   standard mileage rate method of deduction, *9-10–9-12*
   See also Transportation expenses; Travel expenses
Average tax rate, *1-6*
Awards
   court awards, *3-24–3-25*
   employee achievement awards, *4-12–4-13*
   employee length of service awards, *9-15*
   meritorious achievement awards, *4-7*
   See also Gifts
Away-from-tax-home requirement, travel expenses, *9-6*

Backup withholding, definition of, *14-25*
Bad debts
   bona-fide debtor-creditor relationship, *8-24–8-25*
      related-party transactions, *8-24–8-25*
   business bad debts, *8-28*

discharge of indebtedness, *3-21, 4-18–4-20*
employee loans, *8-27*
nonbusiness bad debts, *8-26–8-28*
recovery of, *8-28*
tax-planning considerations, *8-34*
worthlessness of debt, *8-26*
See also Business bad debts; Discharge of indebtedness; Nonbusiness bad debts
Basis
   allocation of, *5-10–5-12*
      basket purchase, *5-10*
      nontaxable stock dividends rights received, *5-10–5-12*
   bad debts, *8-25–8-26*
   documentation of, *5-33*
   of acquired property, from decedent, *5-8–5-9*
   of partnership assets, *17-6*
   of partnership interest, *17-9–17-10*
   of stock, wash sales, *6-22–6-25*
   property converted from personal use to business use, *5-9–5-10*
   property transactions, *5-5–5-12*
   S corporation stock, *17-25–17-26*
Basket purchase, *5-10*
Boot
   involuntary conversions, *12-10–12-16*
   like-kind exchanges, *12-2–12-10*
Bribes, as expense contrary to public policy, *6-12–6-13*
Brother - sister controlled groups, *16-18*
Business bad debts
   reserve method, *8-28*
   specific write-off method, *8-28*
   See also Bad debts; Discharge of indebtedness; Nonbusiness bad debts
Business energy credit, *14-19–14-20*
Business expenses, *6-4–6-16*
   business or investment requirement, *6-5*
   criteria for deductions, *6-4–6-16*
      activity engaged in for profit, *6-5–6-30*
      business investigation expenses, *6-15*
      capitalization versus expense deduction, *6-10–6-11*
      employee expenses, *9-2–9-4*
      expenses contrary to public policy, *6-12–6-14*
      expenses related to exempt income, *6-11–6-12*
      lobbying expenses, *6-14–6-15*
      necessary expense, *6-8*
      ordinary expense, *6-7–6-8*
      political contributions, *6-14–6-15*
      reasonable expense, *6-8–6-9*
   deductions/losses, *6-4–6-16*
   reporting employee expenses, *9-43*
Business income, as gross income, *3-13*
Business, definition of, *6-5–6-6*

C corporations
   accrual method of accounting and, *3-11*

calculation of tax liability, *16-8–16-10*
   tax formula, *2-24–2-25*
   See also Closely held C corporations; Corporations; S corporations
CCH Tax Court Memorandum Decisions, *15-18*
CD-ROM tax services, *1-26*
Cafeteria plans, as gross income exclusion, *4-16*
Calendar year
   requirement, *11-28*
   C corporations, *11-28*
   partnerships, *11-2, 11-28, 17-18–17-19, 17-36*
   S corporations, *11-2, 11-28, 17-28, 17-36*
   See also Tax year
Capital assets
   dealers in securities, *5-14*
   definition of, *2-26, 5-12–5-15*
   holding period, *5-28–5-29*
      nontaxable exchange, *5-29*
      property received as gift, *5-28–5-29*
      property received from decedent, *5-29*
      receipt of nontaxable stock dividends/stock rights, *5-29*
   nonbusiness bad debt, *5-15*
   real property subdivided for sale, *5-15*
   sale/exchange, *5-21–5-27*
      franchises, *5-26–5-27*
      lease cancellation payments, *5-27*
      options, *5-24–5-25*
      patents, *5-25–5-26*
      retirement of debt instruments, *5-22–5-24*
      trademarks, *5-26–5-27*
      worthless securities, *5-22*
   securities dealers, *5-14*
   See also Assets
Capital expenditures, definition of, *6-10–6-11*
Capital gain dividends, *3-16*
Capital gains/losses
   as inflation adjustment, *5-30–5-31*
   C corporations, *16-3–16-4*
   determination of, *5-2–5-5*
      realized gain or loss, *5-2–5-4*
      recognized gain or loss, *5-4–5-5*
   investment model, *18-8*
   net gains/losses, tax treatment of, *2-26*
   netting process, *5-16–5-19*
   noncorporate taxpayers, *5-16–5-20*
   property transactions, *5-1–5-36*
      basis considerations, *5-5–5-12*
      corporate taxpayer tax treatment, *5-20–5-21*
      documentation of basis, *5-33*
      holding period, *5-28–5-29*
      noncorporate taxpayer tax treatment, *5-16–5-20*
      sale/exchange, *5-21–5-27*
   recognition, *5-2–5-3*
   reporting on Schedule, D, *5-33–5-36*
   tax treatment after 1990, *5-19–5-20*
Capital losses, *5-18–5-20*
   corporate taxpayers, *5-20–5-21*
Capital recoveries, *5-4*

Capitalization
    of deduction items, *6-11*
    of interest, *5-5–5-6*
    of legal fees, *6-6–6-7*
    requirements for cash-method taxpayers, *11-8–11-9*
    versus expense deduction, *6-10–6-11*
        election to deduct currently, *6-10–6-11*
        general capitalization requirements, *6-10*
Carrybacks/carryovers
    net operating losses, *8-33*
        election to forgo carryback period, *8-33*
    of foreign tax credits, *14-17*
    passive losses, *8-8–8-9*
    recomputation of taxable income in carryover year, *8-33–8-34*
Cash receipts and disbursements method of accounting, *3-8–3-10, 6-18–6-20, 11-7–11-9, 17-19*
    capitalization requirements, *11-8–11-9*
    constructive receipt, *3-9–3-10*
    deductible expenses, *6-18–6-20*
        prepaid expenses, *6-19*
        prepaid interest, *6-19–6-20*
    exceptions, *3-10*
    recovery of previously deducted expenses, *3-25–3-26*
    tax benefit rule, *3-26*
Casualty losses, *8-17–8-23*
    as itemized deduction, *7-28*
    casualty defined, *8-17–8-19*
    deductible amount of, *8-19–8-20*
    disaster area election, *8-23, 8-35*
    exclusion of gain, *8-21–8-22, 12-10–12-16*
    reporting on Form 4684, *13-28–13-29*
    substantiation of loss, *8-34*
Certified public accountants (CPAs)
    "good faith" belief requirement, *15-35–15-37*
    knowledge of errors, *15-36–15-37*
    positions on tax returns, *15-35–15-37*
    procedural aspects of return preparation, *15-35*
    proper behavior of, *15-34–15-37*
    responsibilities, *15-34–15-37*
Charitable contributions, *7-21–7-26*
    C corporations, *16-35, 16-6–16-8*
    alternative minimum tax, *14-4*
    amount of deduction, *7-21–7-26*
    appreciated property, *7-32–7-33*
    athletic events, *7-25*
    capital gain property, *7-22–7-23*
        electing to reduce contribution, *7-32*
        to private nonoperating foundation, *7-22–7-23*
    carryovers, application of, *7-25*
    corporations
        donation of inventory, *7-24*
        limitation, *7-26*
        pledges made by accrual-basis corporation, *7-26*
    deduction limitations, *7-24*
        20% limitation, *7-25*

30% limitation, *7-25*
overall 50% limitation, *7-24*
ordinary income property, *7-23–7-24*
qualifying organizations, *7-21–7-22*
reporting of, *7-33–7-36*
services, *7-24*
to private nonoperating foundation, *7-22–7-23*
Child and dependent care credit, *14-11–14-12, 14-31*
    computation, *14-12*
    dependent care assistance, *14-12*
    employment-related expenses, *14-11–14-12*
Children
    as dependent with unearned income, *2-22–2-24*
    dependency exemptions for, *2-12–2-17*
    minor children, income of, *3-8*
Circuit court of appeals, precedential value of decisions, *15-20–15-21*
Citations
    administrative interpretations, *15-11–15-13*
    Internal Revenue Code, *15-8*
    judicial decisions, *15-14–15-24*
    Treasury Regulations, *15-8–15-11*
Citators, *15-28–15-33*
    Commerce Clearing House citator, *15-28–15-29*
    Research Institute of America Citator, 2nd Series, *15-31–15-33*
Citizenship test, for dependency exemptions, *2-16*
Claim of right doctrine, *3-26–3-27*
Client letter, *15-38*
Client-oriented tax research, *15-2–15-3*
    closed-fact situations, *15-2*
    open-fact situations, *15-2–15-3*
Clienteles, *18-27–18-29*
Closed-fact situations, client-oriented tax research and, *15-2*
Closed-fact situations, tax research, *15-19*
Closely held C corporations
    personal holding company, *16-15–16-16*
    See also C corporations
Closely held corporations
    C corporations, *8-12–8-13*
    material participation by, *8-13*
    personal service corporation, *8-13*
    See also C corporations
Club dues, *9-15*
Coal, Sec. 1231 and, *13-6*
Commerce Clearing House citator, *15-28–15-29*
    excerpt from, *15-30–15-31*
Commissioner of Internal Revenue, *1-20*
Community income, definition of, *3-6–3-7*
Community property, received from decedent, *5-9*
Compensation
    deduction limit, publicly-held corporations, *16-7–16-8, 6-8–6-9*
    deferred compensation, *3-29, 9-26–9-41*

employee compensation, as gross income, *3-12–3-13*
nonqualified deferred compensation plans, *9-31–9-32*
nontaxable compensation, employers' provision of, *9-42*
unreasonable compensation, *6-35–6-36*
See also specific types of compensation
Complete liquidation, *16-31–16-33*
Completed contract method, *11-16*
Computer applications
    CD-ROM tax services, *1-26*
    tax planning, *1-25*
    tax research, *1-25–1-26*
    tax return preparation, *1-25*
Computers, as tax research tool, *15-34*
Condemnations, Sec. 1231 gains/losses resulting from, *13-6–13-7*
Conference Committee, tax law and, *15-7–15-8*
Conformity with financial accounting, gross income, *17-7*
Conservation expenditures, Sec. 1252 recapture, *13-21*
Consolidated tax returns, *16-19*
Constructive dividends
    gross income, *3-16–3-17, 16-35*
Constructive receipt, *3-9–3-10*
Constructive stock ownership, corporations, *16-29*
Controlled groups, tax for, *16-16–16-19*
Controlled subsidiary corporations, liquidation of, *16-33*
Copyright, as asset, *5-13*
"Corn Products" doctrine, *5-13–5-14*
Corporations
    accumulated earnings tax, *16-14–16-15*
    alternative minimum tax, *16-10–16-11*
    capital gains/losses, *5-20–5-21, 16-3–16-4*
        corporate capital loss limitations, *16-4*
    capitalization of, *16-23–16-25*
        thin capitalization exception, *16-23–16-25*
    charitable contributions, *7-24, 16-6–16-8, 16-35*
    compared to individuals, *16-3*
    compared to other forms of business organization, *17-34–17-36*
    constructive stock ownership, *16-29*
    corporate formation, *16-20–16-25*
        Sec. 351 nonrecognition requirements, *16-20–16-21*
        basis considerations, *16-21–16-22*
        liabilities, treatment of, *16-22–16-23*
    debt versus equity, *16-23–16-25*
    distributions in complete liquidation, *16-31–16-33*
        liquidation of controlled subsidiary, *16-33*
        tax consequences to liquidated corporation, *16-31–16-32*

Corporations (continued)
   tax consequences to shareholders, 16-32
   dividends-received deduction, 16-5–16-6, 16-35
   earnings and profits (E&P), 16-25–16-27
     current versus accumulated E&P, 16-26–16-27
   filing requirements, 16-36
   net operating losses, 16-6
   personal holding company tax, 16-15–16-16
   property distributions, 16-27–16-28
     tax consequences to distributing corporation, 16-27–16-28
     tax consequences to shareholders, 16-27
   Schedule M reconciliation, 16-36–16-37
   stock redemptions, 16-28–16-31
     "not essentially equivalent to a dividend" defined, 16-31
     complete termination of shareholder's interest, 16-30–16-31
     substantially disproportionate redemption, 16-29–16-30
   tax computation, 16-8–16-19
   tax formula/rates, 1-5, 1-7, 2-24–2-25
   tax rates, 1-4–1-7, 2-25
   See also C corporations; Personal service corporations (PSCs); S corporations
Court system, overview of, 15-14
Covenant not to compete
   definition of, 10-15
   reporting requirements, 10-22
Credits
   accumulated earnings credit, 16-14–16-15
   business energy credits, 14-19–14-20
   child and dependent care credit, 14-11–14-12, 14-31
   disabled access credit, 14-18–14-19
   earned income credit, 14-22
   Empowerment zone employment credit, 14-21
   foreign tax credit, 14-16–14-17, 4-17
   general business credit, 14-9–14-10
   minimum tax credit, 14-5
   nonrefundable credits, 2-5–2-6, 14-18–14-20, 14-9
   partnerships, allocation to partners, 17-9–17-10
   personal tax credits, 14-11–14-13
     child and dependent care credit, 14-11–14-12
     credit for the elderly, 14-12–14-13
     earned income credit, 14-22
   rehabilitation expenditures, credit for, 14-19
   research activities, credit for, 14-18
   work opportunity credit, 14-20
   See also specific types of credit
Cumulative Bulletin (C.B.), 15-12, 15-17
Current investment model, 18-2, 18-2–18-5

Customs duties, 1-11
De minimis fringe benefits, 4-12, 4-13, 9-13n
Death benefits, employees, as gross income exclusion, 4-15
Debt
   retirement of debt instruments, 5-22–5-24
   taxpayer's basis in, 8-25–8-26
   worthlessness of, 8-26
   See also Bad debts; Business bad debts; Nonbusiness bad debts
Deduction equivalent, definition of, 8-16
Deductions for adjusted gross income, definition of, 2-4–2-5
Deductions from adjusted gross income, definition of, 2-4
Deductions
   AGI classification, 6-3–6-4
   criteria for deductions, 6-4–6-16
   expenses, 6-18–6-22
     accrual method of accounting, 6-20–6-22
     cash method of accounting, 6-18–6-20
     proper substantiation requirement, 6-16–6-18, 6-36–6-37
   special disallowance rules, 6-22–6-35
     hobby losses, 6-28–6-31, 6-35, 6-37
     home office expenses, 6-34–6-35
     related-party transactions, 6-25–6-28
     wash sales, 6-22–6-25
   See also Itemized deductions; Losses
Deferred compensation, 18-20–18-26
   avoiding constructive receipt, 3-29
   individual retirement accounts (IRAs), 9-36–9-41
   nonqualified plans, 9-31–9-32, 18-20
   qualified plans, 9-27–9-29
     pension plans, 9-27
     profit-sharing plans, 9-28
     qualification requirements for, 9-28–9-29
   self-employed individuals, 9-35–9-36
   stock option plans, 9-32–9-34
     incentive stock option plans, 9-33–9-34
     nonqualified stock option plans, 9-34
   tax treatment, 9-29–9-30
     employee retirement payments, 9-29–9-30
     employer contribution limitations, 9-30
   versus current salary, 18-20–18-26
   See also Individual retirement accounts (IRAs); Sec. 401(k) plans; qualified pension plans; nonqualified deferred compensation plans
Deferred gain
   corporate formation, 16-20–16-23
   involuntary conversions, 12-10–12-16
   like-kind exchange, 12-2–12-10
   partnership formation, 17-4

   sale of principal residence, 12-16–12-21
Deferred investment model, 18-2, 18-5–18-10
Deferred payment sales, 11-21
Defined benefit pension plan, 9-27
Defined contribution pension plan, 9-27
Demolition of property, losses from, 8-4
Dependency exemptions, 2-5, 2-12–2-17
   citizenship test, 2-16
   definition of, 2-5
   gross income test, 2-15
   joint return test, 2-16
   phase-out of, 2-17
   qualification as dependent, 2-12–2-17
   relationship test, 2-16
   support test, 2-13–2-15
Dependent care assistance programs, employees, as gross income exclusion, 14-12, 4-16
Depletion, 10-17–10-19
   intangible drilling and development costs (IDCs), treatment of, 10-19
   methods, 10-17–10-19
     cost depletion method, 10-18
     percentage depletion method, 10-18–10-19
   reporting of, 10-22
Depreciation
   accelerated cost-recovery system (ACRS)
     restrictions, 10-10–10-13
   asset depreciation range (ADR) system, 10-8
   Form 4562, 10-22
   modified ACRS (MACRS) rules, 10-2
     alternative depreciation system, 10-8
     conventions, 10-5–10-7
     real property, 10-7–10-8
     restrictions, 10-10–10-13
   reporting of, 10-22
   Sec. 179 expensing election, 10-9–10-10
   See also Accelerated cost-recovery system (ACRS); Modified ACRS system; and Sec. 179
"Directly related" entertainment expenses, 9-13
Disabled access credit, 14-18–14-19
Disaster losses, 8-23
Discharge of indebtedness
   gross income exclusion and, 4-18–4-20
   income from, as gross income, 3-21
Discounted notes, timing of interest deduction, 7-20
Discriminant Function (DIF) program, 1-21
Discrimination awards, 4-8
Distributions
   C corporations, 16-27–16-33
     dividends, 16-27
     liquidating, 16-31–16-33
     stock redemptions, 16-28–16-31
   S corporations, 17-28
   partnerships, 17-13–17-14
     liquidating distributions, 17-13

nonliquidating distributions, 17-13–17-14
District directors, IRS, 1-20
Dividends-received deduction
  general rules, 16-35
Dividends
  as gross income, 3-16–3-17
  capital gain dividends, 3-16
  gross income, 16-27
  liquidating, 16-31–16-33
  reporting, Form 5452, 16-37
  S corporations, 17-28
  stock dividends, 3-16
  stock redemptions, 16-28–16-31
Donations
  See also Charitable contributions
Due dates
  for filing corporate tax return, 16-36
  for filing individual income tax return, 2-30
  for filing partnership tax return, 17-36
Dues, club, 9-15

Earned income credit, 14-22
Earnings and profits (E&P), 16-25–16-27
  current versus accumulated E&P, 16-26–16-27
  reporting of, Form 5452, 16-37
Economic income, 1-6
Economic performance test, 6-21–6-22, 11-9–11-10
Education expenses
  employees, 9-20–9-23
    general requirements for deduction, 9-21–9-23
Educational assistance plan, 4-16
Educational travel deductions, 9-8
Effective tax rate, 1-6
Elderly, tax credit for the, 14-12–14-13
Employee achievement awards, 4-12–4-13
Employee compensation
  as gross income exclusion, 4-9–4-17
    cafeteria plans, 4-16
    dependent care, 4-16
    employee awards, 4-12–4-14
    employer-paid insurance, 4-9
    interest-free loans, 4-17
    meals/entertainment, 4-14–4-15
    meals/lodging, 4-14
    Sec. 132 benefits, 4-12–4-13
  as gross income, 3-12–3-13
Employee death benefits, 4-15–4-16
Employee expenses
  accountable plan, 9-16
  classification of, 9-2–9-4
    unreimbursed employee expense limitations, 9-3–9-4
  education expenses, 9-20–9-23
  entertainment expenses, 9-12–9-16
    business gifts, 9-15–9-16
    business meals, 9-14–9-15
    classification of expenses, 9-13–9-14
    entertainment facilities, 9-15
  moving expenses, 9-18–9-20, 9-41–9-42
    direct moving expenses, 9-19–9-20
    distance requirement, 9-19
    employee reimbursements, 9-20, 9-42
    employment duration, 9-19, 9-41–9-42
    expense classification, 9-19
    indirect moving expenses, 9-20
    reimbursement treatment, 9-20, 9-42
  office in home, 9-23–9-47, 9-47
    general requirements for deduction, 9-23
    gross income limitations, 9-25
    reporting of, Form 8829, 6-37, 9-47
  transportation expenses, 9-9–9-12
    automobile expenses, 9-10–9-12
    definition of, 9-9–9-10
  travel expenses, 9-4–9-8
    away-from-tax-home requirement, 9-6
    business versus pleasure, 9-7–9-8
    deductibility of, 9-4–9-5
    definition of, 9-5
    foreign travel, 9-8
  See also Unreimbursed employee expenses
Employee fringe benefits, tax planning, 4-21–4-22
Employee stock ownership plans (ESOPs), 9-28
Employer identification numbers (EINs), 2-31
Employer-employee relationship, definition of, 9-2–9-3
Employment taxes, 1-11, 14-29, 14-7–14-27
Empowerment zones employment credit, 14-21
Endowment policies, income from, as gross income, 3-21
Entertainment expenses, 9-12–9-16
  business gifts, 9-15–9-16
  business meals, 9-14–9-15
    partial disallowance for, 9-12–9-13
  entertainment ticket limitations, 9-16
  partial disallowance for, 9-12–9-13
    "associated with" entertainment expenditure, 9-13–9-14
    "directly related" entertainment expenses, 9-13
  substantiation of, 9-43
Equilibrium condition, investment, 18-27–18-29
Estate planning, selecting property to transfer at death, 5-32
Estate Planning, 15-25
Estate tax, 1-9–1-10
Estimated taxes
  C corporations, 16-36
  individuals
    required estimated tax payments, 14-28
    withholding and, 14-32
Exchange
  definition of, 5-21
  See also Sales/exchanges of property
Excise taxes, 1-11

Exclusion ratio, annuities, 3-19
Exclusions
  from gross income, 2-3, 4-1–4-23
    awards for meritorious achievement, 4-7
    employee fringe benefits, 4-9–4-17
    foreign-earned income exclusion, 4-17–4-18
    gifts, 4-4–4-5
    income from discharge of indebtedness, 4-18–4-20
    inheritances, 4-4–4-5
    injury/sickness payments, 4-8–4-9
    life insurance proceeds, 4-5–4-6
    sale of residence, 4-20, 12-19–12-21
    scholarships/fellowships, 4-7
    selling price of property, 4-3
    unrealized income, 4-2–4-3
Exempt income, expenses related to, 6-11–6-12
Exempt investment model, 18-10
Exemptions
  dependency exemptions, 2-5, 2-12–2-17
  personal exemptions, 2-12
Expected return, annuities, 3-19
Expenses
  accrual method of accounting, deductible expenses, 6-20–6-22
  allocation of
    residential property, 6-32–6-33
    transportation expenses, 9-9–9-12
  automobile expenses, 9-10–9-12
  business investigation expenses, 6-15
  cash receipts and disbursements method of accounting, deductible expenses, 6-18–6-20
  contrary to public policy, 6-12–6-14
    bribes, 6-12–6-13
    fines, 6-13
    illegal activity expenses, 6-14
    kickbacks, 6-12–6-13
    legal fees, 6-6–6-7
    penalties, 6-13
  disallowed expenses, 6-14–6-15
    business investigation expenses, 6-15
    lobbying expenses, 6-14–6-15
    political contributions, 6-14–6-15
    pre-operating/start-up costs, 6-15
  employee expenses, 9-1–9-26
  entertainment expenses, 9-12–9-16
  home office expenses, 6-34–6-35, 9-23–9-25
  interest expenses, 7-12–7-21
  investment expenses, 6-4–6-16
  medical expenses, 7-2–7-8
  moving expenses, 9-18–9-20
  taxpayer responsibility for, 6-16–6-18
  transportation expenses, 9-9–9-12
  travel expenses, 9-4–9-8
  unreimbursed employee expenses, limitations on, 9-3–9-4

Failure-to-file penalty, 1-22
Failure-to-pay penalty, 1-22

Fair market value (FMV)
  definition of, *5-3, 11-14*
Farming
  Sec. 1231 and, *13-5–13-6*
    livestock, *13-6*
    timber, *13-5–13-6*
    unharvested crops/land, *13-6*
  Sec. 1252 recapture, *13-21*
  conservation expenditures, *13-21*
Federal Claims Reporter, 15-20
Federal Court System, *1-19, 15-14–15-25*
  Appeals court procedures, *15-20*
  District court procedures, *15-19*
  Overview of court system, *15-14*
  Precedential value of various decisions, *15-21–15-24*
  Supreme Court, appeals to, *15-21*
  Tax Court procedures, *15-14–15-18*
    IRS acquiescence policy, *15-17*
    Small cases procedures, *15-17*
Federal Insurance Contributions Act (FICA), *1-11, 1-3, 14-7–14-24, 14-29*
Federal Reporter, Second Series, 15-19n
Federal Reporter, Third Series, 15-20
Federal Supplement (F. Supp.), *15-19*
Federal Tax Coordinator 2d (Research Institute of America), *15-26–15-27*
Federal tax revenue, breakdown of, *1-4*
Federal Taxation: Research, Planning, and Procedures (Norwood et al.), *1-24n*
Fellowships, exclusion from gross income, *4-7*
Field audit, *1-21*
Filing requirements
  C corporations, *16-36–16-37*
  individuals, *2-29–2-31, 14-32*
  partnerships, *17-32–17-33*
  S corporations, *17-33*
Filing status, standard deduction and, *2-10–2-12*
Final regulations, *15-9*
Finance Committee, U.S. Senate, tax law and, *15-7*
Finance charges, deductibility of, *7-12*
Financial accounting, conformity with, *17-7*
Financial planning, *1-24–1-25*
Fines
  as expense contrary to public policy, *6-13*
Fiscal year
  election, *11-2–11-7*
Flat tax, *1-5*
Flexible spending accounts, *4-16*
Foreign tax credit, *4-17, 14-16–14-17*
Foreign travel, deduction of expenses, *9-8*
Foreign-earned income
  definition of, *4-18*
  exclusion, *4-17–4-18*
Form 1040A, *2-30–2-31, 14-32–14-33*
Form 1040EZ, *2-30, 14-32–14-33*
Form 1040X, *8-35, 9-44*
Form 1040, *2-2, 2-30, 2-8–2-9, 3-29–3-32, 3-30, 5-33, 6-36, 7-36, 8-36, 9-44, 13-29*
  Schedule A, *3-29, 3-30, 6-36, 7-33–7-36, 9-43, 13-29,*

Schedule B, *3-29, 3-30, 3-32*
Schedule C-EZ, *9-47*
Schedule C, *3-30, 6-36, 7-36, 9-47, 10-22*
Schedule D, *3-30, 5-33, 8-36, 11-30, 13-25*
Schedule EIC, *14-33*
Schedule E, *3-29, 3-30, 6-36, 7-36, 10-22*
Schedule F, *3-30*
Schedule R, *14-32*
Schedule SE, *14-8*
Form 1045, *8-35–8-36*
Form 1065, *17-32–17-33*
  Schedule K-1, *17-33*
  Schedule K, *17-33*
Form 1099-B, *2-31, 5-36*
Form 1099-DIV, *2-31*
Form 1099-G, *2-31*
Form 1099-INT, *2-31*
Form 1099-MISC, *2-31*
Form 1099-R, *2-31*
Form 1116, *14-33*
Form 1120S, *17-33*
  Schedule K-1, *17-33–17-34*
  Schedule K, *17-33*
Form 1120, *16-36*
  Schedule D, *16-36*
Form 1128, *11-5*
Form 1139, *8-35*
Form 2106, *3-30, 6-36n, 9-43–9-44, 10-22*
Form 2119, *12-24*
Form 2120, *2-15*
Form 2210, *14-28*
Form 2441, *14-32*
Form 3468, *14-32*
Form 3800, *14-32*
Form 3903, *3-30, 6-36n, 9-43*
Form 4562, *10-22, 9-47*
Form 4626, *14-32, 16-36*
Form 4684, *13-25–13-29*
Form 4782, *9-44*
Form 4797, *3-30, 11-30, 13-25–13-27, 13-29*
Form 4868, *2-30*
Form 5213, *6-37*
Form 5452, *16-37*
Form 6251, *14-32*
Form 6252, *11-29–11-30*
Form 7004, *16-36*
Form 706, *5-33*
Form 8283, *7-33, 7-36*
Form 8829, *6-37, 9-47*
Form W-2, *2-31, 4-22–4-23, 9-43, 14-32*
Form W-4P, *14-25*
Form W-4, *14-26, 14-30*
Form W-5, *14-33*
Forum shopping, precedential value of decisions and, *15-23–15-24*
Franchise tax, *1-7–1-8*
Franchises, sale/exchange of, *5-26–5-27*
Fraud
  penalty for, *1-23*
Fringe benefits
  discrimination, *4-10*

partnerships, treatment of, *17-28–17-29*
S corporations, treatment of, *17-28–17-29*
See also Employee compensation
General business credit
  claiming the credit, *14-32*
  definition of, *14-9*
  limitation on, *14-9–14-10*
  nonrefundable credits, *2-5–2-6, 14-23*
Generally accepted accounting principles (GAAP), *11-11–11-12, 17-7*
Gift tax, *1-8–1-9*
  effect on basis, *5-7*
  general concepts/rules, *1-8–1-9*
  marital deduction, *1-8*
Gifts
  acquired property, *5-6–5-7*
  business gifts, *9-15–9-16*
  exclusion from gross income, *4-4–4-5*
  holding period, *5-28–5-29*
  imputed interest, *11-24–11-25*
    gift loans, *11-24–11-25*
  inter vivos gifts, *4-4*
  of property subject to recapture, *13-17*
  selection of property to transfer as, *5-31–5-32*
  testamentary gifts, *4-4*
  to employees, as gross income exclusion, *4-12*
"Good faith" belief requirement, certified public accountants (CPAs), *15-35–15-37*
Goodwill
  Sec. 197 intangibles, amortization of, *10-13–10-17*
Gray areas, tax research, *15-4*
Gross income test, for dependency exemptions, *2-15*
Gross income
  Sec. 61(a) definition, *3-2*
  alimony, *3-17–3-19*
  annuities, *3-19–3-21*
  awards, *3-22–3-23*
  business income, *3-13*
  compensation, *3-12–3-13*
  constructive dividends, *3-16–3-17*
  court awards, *3-24–3-25*
  definition of, *2-3*
  discharge of indebtedness, income from, *3-21*
  dividends, *3-16–3-17*
  endowment contracts, income from, *3-21*
  exclusions, *4-1–4-23*
  filing levels, *2-29–2-30*
  gains realized from property, *3-13*
  gambling winnings, *3-22–3-23*
  illegal income, *3-23*
  inclusions, *3-1–3-29*
    economic/accounting concepts of income, *3-2–3-3*
    tax concept of income, *3-3–3-6*
    to whom income is taxable, *3-6–3-8*
    when income is taxable, *3-8–3-11*

income passed through to taxpayer, 3-22
insurance proceeds, 3-24–3-25
interest, 3-13–3-15
    Series EE savings bonds exclusion, 3-14–3-15
    tax-exempt interest, 3-13–3-14
life insurance, income from, 3-21
pensions, 3-19–3-21
prizes, 3-22–3-23
property settlements, 3-17–3-18
recovery of previously deducted expenses, 3-25–3-26
    tax benefit rule, 3-26
rents, 3-15
    improvements by lessees, 3-15
royalties, 3-15
social security benefits, 3-23–3-24
treasure finds, 3-22–3-23
unemployment compensation, 3-23
when taxable, 3-9
See also Adjusted gross income (AGI)
Group term life insurance exclusion, 4-9
Guarantor, bad debts, 8-25

Head-of-household, 2-20–2-21
    abandoned spouse as, 2-22
Health insurance benefits, as gross income exclusion, 4-8–4-9
Hobby losses, 6-28–6-31, 6-35, 6-37
    deductible expenses, 6-30
    order of deductions, 6-30–6-31
Holding period
    capital assets, 5-28–5-29
    property transactions, 5-28–5-29
Home equity indebtedness, 7-17
Home office expenses
    general requirements for deduction, 9-23
    gross income limitations, 9-25
    reporting of, 6-37, 9-47
    See also Self-employed individuals
House trailers, as principal residence, 12-18
House-hunting trips, as indirect moving expense, 9-20
Houseboats, as principal residence, 12-18
H.R. 10 plans, 9-35–9-36
Hybrid method of accounting, 3-11, 11-10

Illegal activity expenses, nondeductibility of, 6-14
Illegal income, taxability of, 3-23
Illegal kickbacks, 6-12–6-13
Implicit taxes, 18-26–18-27
Imputed interest, 7-20, 11-22–11-25
    accrual of interest, 11-23–11-24
    applicable federal rate, 11-23
    gift, shareholder and other loans, 11-24–11-25
Incentive stock option (ISO) plans, 9-33–9-34
Income shifting, 3-27
    S corporations, 17-31–17-32
    to family members, 2-27
Income splitting
    between tax entities, 2-27
Income tax formula, 1-7

Income
    accounting concept of, 3-2–3-3
    allocation between married persons, 3-6–3-7
    assignment of, 3-6
    definition of, 2-3, 3-4–3-6
    economic concepts, 3-2
    economic income, 1-6
    of minor children, 3-8
    prepaid income, 3-11
    reporting of, 3-30
    tax concept of, 3-3–3-6
        administrative convenience, 3-3–3-4
        wherewithal-to-pay concept, 3-4
Independent contractor status, versus employee status, 9-3
Individual income tax
    capital gains and losses, treatment of, 2-26, 5-16–5-20
    determination of, 2-2–2-24
    due dates for filing returns, 2-30
    filing joint or separate returns, 2-28–2-29
    forms, 2-30–2-31
    formula, 2-2–2-7
    gross tax determination, 2-18–2-24
    rate structures, 1-4–1-7
        progressive tax rate, 1-4
        proportional tax rate, 1-5
        shifting income to family members, 2-27
    who must file, 2-29–2-30
Individual retirement accounts (IRAs), 9-36–9-41
    deductible contributions, 9-36–9-41
    investment model, 18-11–18-12
    nondeductible contributions, 9-38, 18-5–18-8
    tax advantages, 9-38
    tax rules, 9-38–9-41
Information releases, tax law, 15-13
Information releases, 1-19
Inheritances, exclusion from gross income, 4-4–4-5
Injury payments, as gross income exclusion, 4-8–4-9
Innocent spouse provision, 2-28–2-29
Insolvent financial institutions, deposits in, 8-28–8-29
Installment obligations, disposition of, 11-19–11-20
Installment sales, 11-17–11-21
    installment sale defined, 11-18
    recapture, 13-19–13-20
    related-party sales, 11-21
    reporting on Form 6252, 11-30–11-29
    repossession, 11-20
Insurance
    casualty losses, failure to file claim, 8-22
    employer-paid insurance, 4-9
    health insurance benefits, as gross income exclusion, 4-8–4-9
    life insurance, 4-5–4-6
        exclusion from gross income, 4-5–4-6

income from, 3-24–3-25
proceeds, 4-5–4-6
losses, 8-22–8-23
medical insurance, 7-6–7-8
tax treatment of, 4-10
Intangible assets
    amortization of, 10-13–10-17
    research expenditures, 10-16–10-17
    Sec. 197 intangibles, 10-13
Intangible drilling costs (IDCs), 10-19
    capitalization versus expense election, 10-20–10-21
    definition of, 10-17
    recapture provisions, 13-21–13-22
    tax preference item, 14-3–14-4
    treatment of, 10-19
Interest
    as gross income, 3-13–3-15
        Series EE savings bonds exclusion, 3-14–3-15, 3-28–3-29
        tax-exempt interest, 3-13–3-14
    as itemized deduction, 7-12–7-21
    capitalization of, 5-5–5-6
    definition of, 7-12
    imputed interest, 11-22–11-25
    interest expense
        acquisition indebtedness, 7-16–7-17
        active trade/business, 7-13
        classification of, 7-12–7-18
        incurred to generate tax-exempt income, 7-14
        investment interest, 7-14–7-15
        passive activity, 7-14
        personal, 7-16
        qualified residence interest, 7-16
    late payment of taxes, 1-22
    timing of interest deduction, 7-19–7-20
        discounted notes, 7-20
        interest paid with loan proceeds, 7-19–7-20
        prepaid interest, 7-19
Internal Revenue Bulletin (I.R.B.), 15-17
Internal Revenue Code, 1-18, 1-3, 15-8
    as source of tax law, 1-18–1-19
    general language of, 1-18
    history of, 15-8
    organizational scheme, 15-8
    tax law and, 15-8
Internal Revenue Service
    audits, 1-21
        selecting returns for, 1-21
    Discriminant Function (DIF) system, 1-21
    enforcement procedures, 1-21
    organization of, 1-20
    Taxpayer Compliance Measurement Program (TCMP), 15-19
Interpretations, tax law, 15-7
Interpretative regulations, 1-19, 15-10
Inventories, 11-11–11-14
    accounting methods, 11-11–11-14
    donation of, 7-24
Inventories (continued)
    generally accepted accounting principles (GAAP), 11-11–11-12
    inventory cost
        determination of, 11-11–11-14

"first-in, first-out" method (FIFO), *11-12*
"last-in, first-out" method (LIFO), *11-12–11-14*
lower of cost or market (LCM) method, *11-14*
mark-to-market method, *5-14*
uniform capitalization rules, *11-11–11-12*
valuation methods, *11-11–11-14*
Investment expenses, *6-4–6-16*
    deduction criteria, *6-4–6-16*
        activity engaged in for profit, *6-5–6-30*
        business/expense requirement, *6-5–6-30*
        expenses related to exempt income, *6-11–6-12*
        lobbying expenses, *6-14–6-15*
        necessary expense, *6-8*
        ordinary expense, *6-7–6-8*
        reasonable expense, *6-8–6-9*
        trade/business versus investment classification, *6-5–6-6*
Investment interest
    interest expense, *7-14–7-15, 7-31–7-32*
    net investment income, *7-14–7-15*
Investment models, *18-2–18-14*
    C corporation model, *18-17–18-20*
    flow through model, *18-16–18-17*
    multiperiod strategies, *18-14*
Investment tax credit (ITC), *14-19–14-20*
Investments
    fixed-income investments
        tax-exempt securities, tax preference item, *14-3–14-4*
Involuntary conversions, *12-10–12-16*
    condemnation, threat of, *12-11*
    definition of, *12-11–12-12*
    into boot, *12-12–12-13*
    into similar property, tax treatment of gain, *12-13*
    involuntary defined, *12-11–12-12*
    principal residence, *12-20–12-21*
    recapture, *13-19*
    replacement property, *12-13–12-14*
        functional use test, *12-14*
        replacement with like-kind property, *12-14*
        taxpayer-use test, *12-14*
    reporting of, *12-23*
    time requirements, for replacement, *12-15–12-16*
IRS Service centers, location of, *1-20*
IRS collection costs, *1-13–1-14*
IRS Letter Rulings (CCH), *15-13*
IRS rulings, *1-19*
Itemized deductions
    casualty/theft losses, *7-28*
    charitable contributions, *7-21–7-26*
        carryovers, *7-25*
        deduction limitations, *7-25*
        election to reduce amount of charitable contribution, *7-32*
        property contributions, *7-32–7-33*
        qualifying organizations, *7-21–7-22*
        reporting of, *7-33–7-36*
        special rules for corporations, *7-26*
        type of property contributed, *7-22–7-24*
    definition of, *2-4–2-5*
    interest, *7-12–7-21*
        definition of, *7-12*
        incurred to generate tax-exempt income, *7-14*
        interest expense classifications, *7-12–7-18*
        timing of deduction, *7-19–7-20*
    list of, *2-7*
    medical expenses, *7-2–7-8*
        amount/timing of deduction, *7-6–7-8*
        qualified expenses, *7-3–7-6, 7-30–7-31*
        qualified individuals, *7-2–7-3*
        reporting of, *7-33*
    miscellaneous deductions, *7-28–7-29*
        employment-related expenses, *7-28*
        expenses to produce income, *7-28*
        tax return preparation fees, *7-28–7-29*
    reduction for high-income taxpayers, *7-29*
    taxes, *7-9–7-11*
        deductible taxes, *7-9*
        definition, *7-9*
        reporting of, *7-36*
    See also specific deductions

Joint returns
    filing of, *2-28*
    innocent spouse provision, *2-28–2-29*
    surviving spouse and, *2-20*
    versus separate returns, *2-21*
    who may file, *2-19*
Journal of Corporate Taxation, The, *15-25*
Journal of Partnership Taxation, The, *15-25*
Journal of Real Estate Taxation, The, *15-25*
Journal of Taxation, The, *15-25*
Judicial decisions
    importance of facts, *15-5–15-6*
    tax law, *1-19*
        Circuit Court of Appeals, *15-20*
        Supreme Court, *15-21*
        U.S. Court of Federal Claims, *15-19–15-20*
        U.S. district courts, *15-19*
        U.S. Tax Court, *15-14–15-18*
        court system, overview of, *15-14*
        precedential value of decisions, *15-21–15-24*
Judicial doctrines, *1-19*
Judicial exclusions, definition of, *4-2*
Judicial interpretations, of tax law, *1-19*
    Federal Court System, *1-19*
Judicial interpretations, tax law, *15-14–15-24*
    citations, *15-11*
        primary cite, *15-19*
        secondary cite, *15-19*
    Federal court system, *15-14*
    precedential value, *15-21–15-24*

Keogh plans, *9-35–9-36*
Key employees, employer-paid insurance, *4-9*
Kickbacks, *6-12–6-13*
Kiddie tax, *2-22–2-24*

Law of Federal Income Taxation (Clark, Boardman, & Callaghan), *15-27*
Lease cancellation payments, *5-27*
Legal fees, as nondeductible expense, *6-6–6-7*
Legislative process, steps in, *1-18–1-20, 15-7–15-8*
Legislative reenactment doctrine, *15-10*
Legislative regulations, *1-19, 15-10*
Letter rulings, *1-19*
    tax law, *15-12–15-13*
LEXIS data base, *1-25–1-26*
Life insurance, *4-5–4-6*
    exclusion from gross income, *4-5–4-6*
        dividends, *4-6*
        surrender of policy before death, *4-6*
    income from, as gross income, *3-24–3-25*
LIFO method, *6-18, 11-12–11-14*
    simplified LIFO method, *11-13*
Like-kind exchanges, *12-2–12-10*
    basis of property received, *12-7–12-8*
    boot
        holding period, *12-10*
        property transfers involving liabilities, *12-7*
        receipt of, *12-6–12-7*
    definition of, *12-2–12-5*
    recapture, *13-19*
    related-party transactions, *12-8–12-9*
    three-party exchanges, *12-5–12-6*
Limited liability company (LLC), *17-4*
Limited liability partnership (LLP), *17-3–17-4*
Limited partnerships
    passive activity, *8-12*
Liquidating distributions
    corporations, *16-31–16-33*
    partnerships, *17-13*
Livestock, Sec. 1231 and, *13-6*
Loans
    compensation loans, *11-24*
    gift loans, *11-24*
    shareholder loans, *11-24*
    tax avoidance loans, *11-24*
Lobbying expenses, *6-14–6-15*
Locked-in effect, *6-27–6-28*
Long-term capital gains and losses (LTCG and LTCL), *2-26, 5-16–5-20*
Long-term care expenses, *7-5*
Long-term contracts, *11-15–11-17*
    completed contract method, *11-16*
    definition of, *11-15*
    look-back interest, *11-17*
    percentage of completion method, *11-16*
Losses
    casualty/theft losses, *8-17–8-23*
        casualty defined, *8-17–8-19*
        deductible amount of, *8-19–8-20*
        disaster area election, *8-35*

documentation of losses, *8-34*
limitations on personal-use property, *8-20*
netting casualty gains/losses on personal-use property, *8-21*
theft defined, *8-19*
when losses are deductible, *8-22–8-23*
classification of
disallowance possibilities, *8-6*
on tax return, *8-4*
ordinary versus capital loss, *8-5–8-6*
corporations, utilization of NOLs, *16-35*
disaster losses, *8-23*
hobby losses, *6-28–6-31, 6-34–6-35, 6-37*
insurance/other reimbursements, *8-22–8-23*
net operating losses, *8-29–8-34*
carryback/carryover periods, *8-33*
computation of, *8-30–8-33*
election to forgo carryback, *8-33*
recomputation of taxable income in carryover year, *8-33–8-34*
reporting the NOL, *8-35–8-36*
partnerships, allocation to partners, *17-9–17-10*
passive losses, *8-7–8-16*
carryovers, *8-8–8-9*
computation of, *8-7–8-10*
credits, *8-10*
passive activity defined, *8-10–8-12*
publicly traded partnerships, *8-13–8-14*
real estate trades or businesses, *8-14–8-16*
rental real estate, *8-14–8-16*
taxpayers subject to passive loss rules, *8-12–8-13*
rental real estate, *8-14–8-16*
active participation, *8-15*
limitation on deduction of loss, *8-15–8-16*
S corporations, allocation to shareholders, *17-26–17-27*
transactions that may result in, *8-2–8-4*
abandoned property, *8-3*
confiscated property, *8-3*
demolition of property, *8-4*
expropriated property, *8-3*
sale/exchange of property, *8-2–8-3*
seized property, *8-3*
worthless securities, *8-36, 8-3–8-4*
See also Bad debts; Capital gains/losses; specific types of losses
Lower of cost or market method, inventories, *11-14*
Low-income housing, *13-15*
Luxury automobiles, accelerated cost recovery system (ACRS and MACRS) and, limitations on, *10-11–10-13*
leased luxury automobiles, *10-13*
Luxury water travel, deductions for, *9-8*

Marginal tax rate, *1-4*
Market discount bonds, *5-23–5-24*
Market value, definition of, *5-3, 11-14*
Mark-to-market method, *5-14*
Married individuals
allocation of income between, *3-6–3-7*
joint returns, *2-19*
separate returns, *2-21*
Material participation
in active trade/business, *7-13, 8-11–8-12*
passive activity rules, *8-11–8-12*
by closely held corporations, *8-13*
by limited partnership, *8-12*
by personal service corporations (PSCs), *8-13*
Meals/lodging
as gross income exclusion, *4-14*
business meal disallowance, *9-14–9-15*
Medical expenses, *7-2–7-8*
amount/timing of deduction, *7-6–7-8*
limitation on amount deductible, *7-7*
medical insurance reimbursements, *7-7–7-8*
timing of payment, *7-6–7-7*
deductions vs. dependent care credit, *7-33*
qualified expenses, *7-3–7-6*
capital expenditures for medical care, *7-5–7-6*
cost of living in institutions, *7-6*
deductible medical services, *7-3–7-4*
long-term care expenses, *7-5*
medical insurance premiums, *7-6*
transportation, *7-4*
qualified individuals, *7-2–7-3*
working with AGI floor, *7-30–7-31*
Medical insurance
premiums, *7-6*
reimbursements, *7-7–7-8*
Medicare, tax rate, *9-3*
Meetings, travel deductions, *9-8*
Memorandum decisions, U.S. Tax Court, *15-18*
Minimum tax credit
corporations, *16-11*
individuals, *14-5–14-7*
Minimum vesting requirements, qualified pension plans, *9-29*
Minor children, income of, *3-8*
Modified ACRS (MACRS) System, *10-2*
alternative depreciation system, *10-8, 10-20*
listed property, *10-11*
luxury automobiles, limitations on, *10-11–10-13*
personal property
midquarter convention, *10-5–10-6*
year of disposition, *10-7*
real property,
classification/recovery rates for, *10-7–10-8*
residential rental property, *10-7–10-8*
restrictions, *10-10–10-12*
business-use assets, *10-10–10-11*

personal-use assets, *10-10*
recapture of excess cost-recovery deductions, *10-11*
straight-line method under, *10-8*
Moving expenses, *9-18–9-20, 9-41–9-42*
direct moving expenses, *9-19–9-20*
distance requirement, *9-19*
employer reimbursements, *9-20, 9-42*
employment duration, *9-19*
expense classification, *9-19*
indirect moving expenses, *9-20*
reporting of, *9-44*
Multiple support agreements, for medical expenses, *7-31*
Mutual funds, *3-16*

National Office, IRS, *1-20*
Natural resources
Sec. 1231 and, *13-5–13-6*
coal/domestic iron ore, *13-6*
livestock, *13-6*
timber, *13-5–13-6*
Necessary expense, *6-8*
Negligence penalty, *1-23*
Net capital gain, *5-16*
long-term, *5-16*
preferential treatment for, *5-19–5-20, 5-2, 5-30–5-31*
short-term, *5-16*
Net gains/losses, treatment of, *2-26, 5-16–5-20*
Net investment income, *7-14–7-15*
Net operating losses, *8-29–8-34*
carryback/carryover periods, *8-33*
election to forgo carryback period, *8-33*
loss carryovers from two or more years, *8-33*
computation of, *8-30–8-33*
corporations, *16-6*
definition of, *8-29*
obtaining the refund, *8-35–8-36*
S corporations, utilization of, *17-30–17-31*
Nonaccountable plans, *9-16, 9-17*
Nonbusiness bad debts
definition of, *8-26–8-27*
nonaccountable plan, *9-17*
partial worthlessness, *8-27–8-28*
tax treatment, *8-27*
See also Bad debts; Business bad debts
Noncontributory pension plan, *9-27*
Noncorporate taxpayers
capital gains/losses tax treatment, *5-16–5-20*
Noncustodial parents, dependency exemptions and, *2-14–2-15*
Nonliquidating distributions
corporations, *16-27–16-28*
partnerships, *17-13–17-14*
S corporations, *17-28*
Nonqualified deferred compensation plans, *9-31*
restricted property plans, *9-31–9-32*
unfunded deferred compensation plans, *9-31*
Nonqualified stock option plans, *9-34*

taxation of, *9-34*
Nonrefundable credits, definition of, *2-5–2-6*
Nonresident aliens, head-of-household status and, *2-20–2-21*
Nonresidential real estate
 Sec. 1250 recapture provisions, *13-14–13-15*
Nontaxable exchanges
 holding period, *5-28–5-29*
 of property, *12-1–12-24*
  involuntary conversions, *12-10–12-16*
  like-kind exchanges, *12-2–12-10*
  sale of principal residence, *12-16–12-21*
  reporting nontaxable exchanges, *12-23–12-24*
Nontaxable stock dividends received, *5-10–5-11*
Nontaxable stock rights received, *5-11–5-12*

Objectives of tax law, *1-14–1-15*
Office audit, *1-21*
Oil and gas property, working interest in, *8-12*
Open-fact situations, tax research, *15-2–15-3*
Options
 incentive stock option (ISO) plans, *9-33–9-34*
 nonqualified stock options, *9-34*
 sale/exchange of, *5-24–5-25*
 See also Call options, nonqualified stock option plans and stock option plans
Oral conclusions, tax research, *15-5*
Ordinary expense, *6-7–6-8*
Ordinary income property
 as charitable contribution, *7-23–7-24*
 donation of inventory by corporation, *7-24*
 definition of, *7-23*
Ordinary loss
 definition of, *5-22*
 versus capital loss, *8-5–8-6*
Original issue discount, *5-23*

Parent-subsidiary controlled groups, *16-18–16-19*
Partnerships
 allocation to partners, *17-9–17-10*
 basis adjustments for operating items, *17-10*
 basis of partnership assets, *17-6*
 basis of partnership interest, *17-4*
 capital contributions followed by distribution to partner, *17-12–17-13*
 cash method restrictions, *17-19*
 credits, allocation to partners, *17-9–17-10*
 deductions, allocation to partners, *17-9–17-10*
 distributions, *17-13–17-14*
  liquidating distributions, *17-13*
  nonliquidating distributions, *17-13–17-14*
 elections, *17-33*
 filing requirements, *17-32–17-33*
 financial accounting considerations, *17-7*
 Form 1065, *17-32–17-33*
 formation of, *17-4–17-7*
 fringe benefits, *17-28–17-29*
 guaranteed payments, *17-13*
 income, allocation to partners, *17-9–17-10*
 limited liability company (LLC), *17-3–17-4*
 limited liability partnership (LLP), *17-4*
 limited partnership interest, sale of, *17-14–17-15*
 losses
  allocation to partners, *17-9–17-10*
  limitations on, *17-11*
 operating items, basis adjustments for, *17-10*
 operations, *17-7*
 optional basis adjustments
  election under Sec. 754, *17-32*
 organizational expenses, *17-7*
 partnership interest
  holding period for, *17-6*
  sale of, *17-14–17-15*
 passive losses, limitations on, *17-11*
 required payments and fiscal years, *11-3–11-4*
 Sec. 751 ordinary income treatment, *17-15*
 special allocations, *17-9*
 syndication fees, *17-7*
 tax attributes, *17-34–17-36*
 tax year, *11-2, 11-28, 17-18–17-19, 17-36*
 transactions between partner and partnership, *17-12–17-13*
 See also Limited partnerships; Oil and gas limited partnerships
Passive activity
 definition of, *8-10–8-12*
 interest expense, *7-14*
 limited partnerships, *8-12*
 material participation, *8-11–8-12*
 working interest in oil and gas property, *8-12*
Passive losses, *8-7–8-16*
 carryovers
  from former passive activities, *8-9*
  taxable disposition of interest, *8-8–8-9*
 credits, *8-10*
 identification of an activity, *8-10–8-11*
 partnerships, limitations on, *17-11*
 passive activity defined, *8-10–8-12*
 passive income and, *8-8–8-10*
 publicly traded partnerships, *8-13–8-14*
 real estate trades or businesses, *8-14–8-16*
 rental real estate, *8-14–8-16*
 S corporations, *17-27*
 taxpayers subject to, *8-12–8-13*

Patents, sale/exchange of, *5-25–5-26*
Payment of taxes, *14-24–14-29, 16-36*
 corporations, *16-36*
 estimated tax payments, *14-27–14-28, 16-36*
 withholding, *14-24–14-27*
  withholding allowances/methods, *14-26*
Penalties
 as nondeductible expense, *6-13*
 summary, *1-22–1-23*
Pension investment model, *18-10–18-12*
Pension plans, *9-27–9-28*
 contributory pension plan, *9-27*
 defined benefit pension plan, *9-27*
 defined contribution pension plan, *9-27*
 non-contributory pension plan, *9-27*
 qualification of, *9-47*
 types of, *9-27–9-28*
Pensions
 advance payments, *3-21*
 as gross income, *3-19–3-21*
 determining nontaxable portion of, *3-19–3-21*
 paid as annuities, *3-19–3-21*
Percentage depletion method, *10-18–10-19*
Percentage of completion method, *11-16*
Personal exemption, *2-12–2-17*
 definition of, *2-5*
 phase-out of, *2-17*
Personal injury award, *4-8–4-9*
Personal interest, definition of, *7-16*
Personal property taxes, as itemized deduction, *7-10*
Personal service corporations (PSCs), *8-13*
 material participation by, *8-13*
 tax calculation, *16-10*
 tax year, *11-2–11-7*
Personal tax credits, *14-11–14-13*
 child and dependent care credit, *14-11–14-12*
 earned income credit, *14-22*
 reporting of, *14-32–14-33*
 tax credit for the elderly, *14-12–14-13*
Personal-use property
 conversions to business use, *10-4*
 limitations on, *8-20*
 netting casualty gains/losses on, *8-21*
 rental value, as nonincome item, *4-3*
 self-help and use of, personal use property, *4-22*
Points, as interest, *6-20, 7-12–7-18*
Policy-oriented research, *15-2*
Precedential value of decisions, *15-21–15-24*
 Circuit Court of Appeals, *15-23*
 forum shopping, *15-23–15-24*
 Tax Court, *15-21*
 U.S. Court of Federal Claims, *15-23*
 U.S. District Court, *15-23*
Prepaid expenses, cash method of accounting, *6-19*
Prepaid income
 accrual method of accounting and, *3-11*
 tax planning and, *3-27–3-28*

Prepaid interest
  cash method of accounting, 6-19–6-20
  timing of interest deduction, 7-19
Prepayments, as tax credits, 2-5–2-6
Previously deducted expenses
  recovery of, 3-25–3-26
  tax benefit rule, 3-26
Primary cites, 15-19
Principal residence, sale of, 12-16–12-21
  deferred gain, 12-16–12-21
  excluded gain, 12-16–12-21
  identifying principal residence, 12-22
  involuntary conversion, 12-20–12-21
  more than one residence in two-year period, 12-19
  principal residence defined, 12-18–12-19, 12-22
    property converted to business use, 12-22
    property rented prior to sale, 12-18–12-19
  realized gain, determination of, 12-17
  reporting of, 12-23–12-24
Private activity bonds, 14-4
Private letter ruling, 15-12–15-13
Private nonoperating foundations
  contributions to, 7-22–7-23
  20% limitation on capital gain property, 7-25
Prizes, as gross income, 3-22–3-23
Profit-sharing plans, 9-28
  distinguishing features, 9-28
  qualification of, 9-47
Progressive tax rate, 1-4
Property distributions
  C corporations, 16-27–16-28
    tax consequences to distributing corporation, 16-27–16-28
    tax consequences to shareholders, 16-27
  Partnerships, 17-13–17-14
  S corporations, 17-28
Property settlements, as gross income, 3-17–3-18
Property taxes, 1-11
Property transactions
  capital gains/losses, 5-1–5-36
    basis considerations, 5-5–5-12
    capital asset defined, 5-12–5-15
    corporate taxpayer tax treatment, 5-20–5-21
    determination of, 5-2–5-5
    holding period, 5-28–5-29
    noncorporate taxpayer tax treatment, 5-16–5-20
    reporting, 5-33–5-36
    sale/exchange, 5-21–5-27
  nontaxable exchanges, 12-1–12-24
    involuntary conversions, 12-10–12-16
    like-kind exchanges, 12-21, 12-2–12-10
    three-party exchanges, 12-5–12-6
    sale of principal residence, 12-16–12-21
  See also Recapture

Property transfers
  corporations, 16-20–16-23
    basis considerations, 16-21–16-22
    liabilities, treatment of, 16-22–16-23
    Sec. 351 nonrecognition requirements, 16-20–16-21
  like-kind exchanges, 12-2–12-10, 12-21
  recapture, 13-19
  partnerships, 17-4–17-7
    basis considerations, 17-4
    gain recognition, 17-4
    organization and syndication fees, 17-7
  selection of property to transfer at death, 5-32
  selection of property to transfer by gift, 5-31–5-32
Proportional tax rate, 1-5
Proposed regulations, 15-9
Publicly traded partnerships
  passive losses, 8-13–8-14
Published opinions, U.S. Tax Court, 15-17–15-18
Punitive damages, exclusion, 4-8

Qualified electric vehicle credit, 2-6
Qualified employee discounts, 4-12–4-13
Qualified pension plans, 9-27–9-28
  qualification requirements, 9-27
  tax treatment employees/employers, 9-29
    employee retirement payments, 9-29–9-30
    employer contribution limitations, 9-30
Qualified plan awards, 4-12–4-14
Qualified residence
  definition of, 7-18
  interest expense, 7-16–7-18
Qualified transportation fringes, 4-12–4-13

Real estate taxes, 1-11, 7-10–7-11
  apportionment of, 7-10–7-11
  as itemized deduction, 7-10–7-11
  real property assessments for local benefits, 7-11
Real estate trades or businesses, passive loss rules, 8-14–8-16
Real property
  assessments for local benefits, 7-11
  modified ACRS,
    classification/recovery rates for, 10-7–10-8
  subdivided for sale, 5-15
Realization, definition of, 3-2
Realized gain/loss, 5-2–5-4
  adjusted basis of property, 5-4
  amount realized, 5-3
  determination of, 5-2–5-5
  fair market value (FMV), 5-3
  recovery of basis doctrine, 5-4
Recapture
  alimony, gross income, 3-17–3-19
  avoiding depreciation recapture provisions, 13-23–13-25

  nonresidential real property, 13-24
  residential rental property, 13-24
  transferring property at death, 13-25
  charitable contributions, 13-18
  corporations, 13-16
  gifts of property subject to, 13-17
  installment sales, 13-19–13-20
  involuntary conversions, 13-19
  like-kind exchanges, 13-19
  of excess cost-recovery deductions, 10-11
  property transfers subject to at death, 13-18
  Sec. 1245 provisions, 13-8–13-11
  Sec. 1250 provisions, 13-11–13-16
Recognized gain/loss, determination of, 5-4–5-5
Recovery of basis doctrine, 5-4
Recovery of capital principle, 4-3
Refundable credits, definition of, 2-5–2-6
Regressive tax rate, 1-5
Regular decision, U.S. Tax Court, 15-14–15-17
Regular tax liability
  corporations, 16-8–16-10
  individuals, 14-2–14-3
Rehabilitation expenditures
  credit for, 14-19
Reimbursement
  automobile expenses, 9-12
  insurance, 8-22–8-23
  moving expenses, 9-20
    expense classification and, 9-19
Related party transactions
  definition of, 13-22–13-23
Related-party tranaction rules
  sales or exchanges, 11-21
Related-party transaction rules, 6-25–6-28
  definition of, 6-26–6-27
  disallowed losses, 6-27–6-28
  expense transactions, 6-28
Relationship test
  for dependency exemptions, 2-16
Rental real estate
  passive losses, 8-14–8-16
  principal residence, 12-18–12-19
  real property trades or businesses, 8-14–8-16
Rents
  as gross income, 3-15
Replacement property
  involuntary conversions, 12-13–12-14
    functional use test, 12-14
    replacement with like-kind property, 12-14
    taxpayer-use test, 12-14
  principal residence, 12-16–12-19
Repossession of property, 11-20
Research Institute of America citator, 15-31–15-33
  abbreviations used in, 15-31–15-32
  excerpt from, 15-30–15-31
  information included in, 15-31
Research expenditures, 10-16–10-17, 10-22, 14-18
  computation of, 10-16–10-17
  credit for, 14-18

Research expenditures (*continued*)
  deduction/amortization, *10-16–10-17*
Research
  client-oriented research, *15-2*
  closed-fact situations, *15-2*
  definition, *15-2*
  open fact situations, *15-2–15-3*
  steps in research process, *15-3–15-5*
  tax planning research, *15-3*
Reserve method, business bad debts and, *8-28*
Residence, exclusion for sale, *4-20*
Residential rental property
  allocation of expenses, *6-32–6-33*
  definition of, *6-31–6-32*
  Sec. 1250 recapture provisions, *13-11–13-16*
  used for both personal/rental purposes, *6-31–6-33*
Restricted property plans, *9-31–9-32*
  elections, *9-32*
Retirement payments, *9-29–9-30*
Returns, due dates for filing, *2-30, 16-36, 17-32–17-34*
Revenue Act of 1913, *1-3*
Revenue Act of 1938, Sec. 1231 and, *13-2*
Revenue Act of 1939, *1-3*
Revenue procedures, *1-19, 15-12*
Revenue rulings, *1-19, 15-11–15-12*
Revenue sources, *1-3*
Review of Taxation of Individuals, The, *15-25*
Royalties
  as gross income, *3-15*
  defined, *3-15*
Rulings
  letter rulings
    tax law, *15-11–15-13*
  revenue rulings, *15-11–15-12*

S corporations
  basis adjustments to stock, *17-25–17-26*
  corporate tax on built-in gains, *17-29–17-30*
  election requirements, *17-21*
  filing requirements, *17-33*
  fringe benefits, treatment of, *17-28–17-29*
  income shifting among family members, *17-31–17-32*
  losses, utilization of, *17-30–17-31*
    passive loss limitations, *17-27*
  operations, *17-23–17-25*
  qualification requirements, *17-19–17-21*
    corporate restrictions, *17-20–17-21*
    one class of stock restriction, *17-21*
    shareholder restrictions, *17-20*
    thirty-five shareholder limitation, *17-20*
  restoration of debt basis, *17-27*
  shareholder taxation, *17-26–17-27*
    cash/property distributions, *17-28*
    limitations on loss deductions, *17-26–17-27*

single class of stock requirement, *17-21*
tax attributes, *17-34–17-36*
  restrictions, *17-28*
tax year, *11-28, 11-2–11-7*
  required payments, *11-3–11-4*
taxation of, *17-19–17-30*
termination of election, *17-22–17-23*
  general effective date, *17-22*
  inadvertent termination, *17-22–17-23*
  involuntary revocations, *17-22–17-23*
  specified termination date, *17-22*
See also C corporations; Corporations
Salary reduction plans, *4-16*
Salary, dependency exemption gross income test and, *2-15*
Sales taxes, *1-11*
  exempt items, *1-11*
Sales/exchanges of property
  capital assets, *5-21–5-27*
  See also Capital Assets
Scholarships
  definition of, *4-7*
  dependency exemption gross income test and, *2-15*
  exclusion from gross income, *4-7*
Scholes, Myron and Mark Wolfson, *1-24, 18-2, 18-2n*
Sec. 102, gifts and, *4-4*
Sec. 104(a), payments for injury/sickness, *4-8–4-9*
Sec. 1221, properties not regarded as capital assets, *5-12–5-13*
Sec. 1231 property, *13-1–13-29*
  history of, *13-2*
  involuntary conversions, *13-6–13-7*
  property, *13-5–13-6*
    definition of, *13-5*
    relationship to capital assets, *13-5*
  reporting gains/losses on Form 4797, *13-25–13-29*
  tax treatment overview, *13-3–13-4*
  tax treatment procedure, *13-7–13-8*
    net gains, *13-3*
    net losses, *13-3–13-4*
Sec. 1237, subdividing real estate, *5-15*
Sec. 1239
  depreciable property, gain on sale between related parties, *13-22–13-23*
Sec. 1244, stock
  losses, *8-4, 8-5–8-6*
Sec. 1245
  property subject to, *13-9–13-11*
  purpose of, *13-9–13-11*
  recapture provisions, *13-8–13-11*
Sec. 1250
  purpose of, *13-11*
  recapture provisions, *13-11–13-16*
    low-income housing, *13-15*
    nonresidential real estate, *13-14–13-15*
    residential rental property, *13-12–13-13*
Sec. 1250 property defined, *13-11–13-12*

Sec. 1252, conservation/land clearing expenditures, *13-21*
Sec. 1253, transfer of franchise/trademark/trade name, *5-26–5-27*
Sec. 1254, oil and gas expenditures, *13-21*
Sec. 132
  employee fringe benefits, *4-12–4-13*
Sec. 179, *10-9–10-10*
  employee, conduct of trade or business, *10-10n*
  expensing election, *10-9–10-10*
  recapture provisions, *13-21*
  self-employed individuals, *10-10n*
Sec. 197 intangibles, *10-13–10-17*
Sec. 332, liquidation of controlled subsidiary, *16-33*
Sec. 351, nonrecognition requirements, *16-20–16-21*
Sec. 61, gross income, *3-12–3-27*
Sec. 721, nonrecognition rules, partnerships, *17-4*
Sec. 751, ordinary income treatment, *17-15*
Sec. 754, optional basis adjustments, election, *17-32*
Secondary cites, *15-19*
Securities
  like-kind exchanges, *12-5*
  See also Shareholders; Worthless securities
Securities dealers, *5-14*
Seized property, losses from, *8-3*
Self-employed individuals
  deferred compensation, *9-35–9-36*
  defined contribution H.R. 10 plan, *9-35–9-36*
  Keogh plans, *9-35–9-36*
  medical insurance plans, *7-6*
  Sec. 179 expensing election, *10-10n*
  See also Home office expenses; Individual retirement accounts (IRAs)
Self-employment tax, *14-7–14-9, 7-11*
  purpose of, *14-7*
  self-employment income defined, *14-8*
Seminar travel deductions, *9-8*
Separate maintenance, *3-17–3-19*
Separate property, definition of, *3-7*
Separate returns
  filing of, *2-28*
  joint returns versus, *2-21*
Series EE savings bonds
  accrued interest exclusion, *3-14–3-15*
  reporting interest income, *3-28–3-29*
Severance damages, *12-13*
Sex discrimination settlement, exclusion, *4-8*
Shareholders, C corporations
  complete liquidations, *16-32, 16-33*
  dividend distributions, *16-27, 16-35, 16-37, 3-16–3-17*
  Stock redemptions, *16-28–16-31*
Shareholders loans, *11-24*
Shareholders, S corporations
  cash/property distributions, *17-28*
  fringe benefits, *17-28–17-29*

limitations on loss deductions, 17-26–17-27
restrictions, 17-27
taxation, 17-26–17-27
Short-term capital gains and losses (STCG and STCL), 2-26, 5-16–5-18
Sickness payments, as gross income exclusion, 4-8–4-9
SIMPLE retirement plans, 9-41
Simplification of tax law, attempts at, 2-27
Simplified employee pensions, 9-41
Single class of stock requirement, S corporations, 17-21
Single taxpayers, 2-21
Small business stock, exclusion, 4-20
Small cases procedures, U.S. Tax Court, 15-17
Smith, Adam, 1-12
Social objectives, tax law, 1-15
Social security benefits, 3-23–3-24
dependency exemption gross income test and, 2-15
dependency exemption support test and, 2-13
filing status, 3-23–3-24
Social security (FICA) taxes, 1-11, 1-3, 14-29, 14-7–14-9
Sources of tax law, 1-18–1-19
Special accounting methods
deferred payment sales, 11-21
installment sales method, 11-17–11-21
long-term contracts, 11-15–11-17
See also Accounting methods
Specific write-off method, bad debts, 8-28
Standard deduction, 2-10–2-12, 2-4–2-5
Standard Federal Tax Reporter (CCH), 15-26, 15-28–15-29
Start-up costs, definition of, 6-15
State income taxes, 1-7–1-8
as itemized deduction, 7-10
Statements on Responsibilities in Tax Practice (SRTP), 15-34–15-37
Statute of limitations, 1-22
Statutory regulations, 15-10
Stock bonus plans, 9-28
Stock dividends, 3-16
allocation of basis, 5-10–5-11
holding period, 5-29
Stock option plans, 9-32–9-34
incentive stock option (ISO) plans, 9-33–9-34
employee requirements, 9-33–9-34
nonqualified stock option plans, 9-34
Stock redemptions, 16-28–16-31
as dividends or capital gains, 16-29–16-31
complete termination of shareholder's interest, 16-30–16-31
Stock rights, 5-11–5-12
Straight-line method (SL)
use under Modified ACRS, 10-8
Substantiation requirements, deduction, 6-16–6-18, 6-37
Support test
for dependency exemptions, 2-13–2-15
Supreme Court
tax law decisions, 15-14–15-24
Supreme Court Reporter (S.Ct.), 15-21

Surviving spouse
definition of, 2-20
joint returns and, 2-20
Sutter rule, 4-14–4-15
Syndication expenditures, partnerships, 17-7

Targeted jobs credit, 14-20
Tax Adviser, The, 15-25
Tax benefit rule, 3-26
Tax Court Memorandum Decision (Research Institute of America), 15-18
Tax Court of the United States Reports, 15-17–15-18
Tax law
Internal Revenue Code, 15-8
administration of, 1-20–1-23
administrative appeal procedures, 1-23
audits, selection of returns for, 1-21
enforcement procedures, 1-21
penalties, 1-22–1-23
statute of limitations, 1-22
administrative interpretations, 15-11–15-13
announcements, 15-13
information releases, 15-13
letter rulings, 15-12–15-13
notices, 15-13
revenue procedures, 15-12
revenue rulings, 15-11–15-12
technical advice memoranda, 15-13
definition of, 15-1–15-2, 15-7
enactment of, 1-18–1-20
judicial decisions, 15-14–15-24
circuit court of appeals, 15-20
court system, overview of, 15-14
precedential value of decisions, 15-21–15-24
Supreme Court, 15-21
U.S. Court of Federal Claims, 15-19–15-20
U.S. district courts, 15-19
U.S. Tax Court, 15-14–15-18
judicial interpretations, 1-19
legislative process, 15-7–15-8
objectives of, 1-14–1-15
economic objectives, 1-14
encouragement of certain activities and industries, 1-14–1-15
social objectives, 1-15
sources of, 1-18–1-19, 15-7–15-25
administrative interpretations, 1-19
Internal Revenue Code, 1-18–1-19
Treasury Regulations, 1-19
Treasury Department regulations, 15-8–15-11
authoritative weight, 15-10
citations, 15-11
final regulations, 15-9
interpretative regulations, 15-10
proposed regulations, 15-9
statutory regulations, 15-10
temporary regulations, 15-9
Tax Law Review, 15-25
Tax Management Portfolios (Bureau of National Affairs), 15-27–15-28
Tax Notes, 15-25

Tax periodicals, 15-24–15-25
Tax planning
accounting methods, 11-28
accounting periods, 11-28
alternative minimum Tax, 14-29
bad debts, 8-34
cash flow, 14-30
casualty losses, 8-34
charitable contributions, 7-32–7-33, 16-35
child and dependent care credit, 14-31
computer applications, 1-25–1-26
corporations, 16-33–16-35
dividend policy, 16-35
dividends-received deduction, 16-35
employee compensation, 4-21–4-22
employee expenses, 9-41–9-42
foreign earned income exclusion, 14-30–14-31
foreign tax credits, 14-30–14-31
general business tax credits, 14-30
gross income exclusions, 4-21–4-22
gross income inclusions, 3-27–3-29
hobby losses, 6-35
income shifting among family matters, 17-31–17-32
individual income tax, 2-27–2-29
installment sales method, 11-28
interest expense deduction, 7-31–7-32
itemized deductions, 7-30–7-33
like-kind exchanges, 12-21
losses, 8-34–8-35
medical expenses, 7-30–7-31
moving expenses, 9-41–9-42
net operating losses, 8-34–8-35, 17-30–17-31
nontaxable compensation, 9-42
nontaxable exchanges, 12-21–12-22
principal residence, sale of, 12-22
property transactions, capital gains/losses, 5-31–5-32
Selection of property to transfer at time of death, 5-32
Selection of property to transfer by gift, 5-31–5-32
S corporations, 17-30–17-32
self-help income, 4-22
timing of deductions, 6-36
underpayment penalty, 14-29–14-30
unreasonable compensation, 6-35–6-36
utilization of losses, 16-35
Tax practice
components of, 1-23–1-24
tax compliance/procedure, 1-23
tax planning, 1-24
tax research, 1-23–1-24
computer applications, 1-25–1-26
tax research applications, 1-25–1-26
tax return preparation, 1-25
tax-planning applications, 1-25
statements on responsibilities in, 15-34–15-37
Tax preference items
corporate alternative minimum tax, 16-10–16-11

Tax preference items (continued)
   individual alternative minimum tax, 14-3–14-4
Tax rate structures
   average tax rate, 1-6
   corporate income tax rate, 1-5
   effective tax rate, 1-6
   individual income tax rates, 1-4–1-5
     progressive tax rate, 1-4
     proportional tax rate, 1-5
     regressive tax rate, 1-5
   marginal tax rate, 1-5
Tax rates
   corporate, 16-8
   definition of, 1-4–1-5, 2-5
   self-employment tax, 14-7–14-9
Tax Reform Act of 1986
   preferential treatment for capital gain income and, 5-2
Tax Reform Proposals: Compliance and Tax Administration (U.S. Congress), 1-12–1-14
Tax research, 15-1–15-38
   citators, 15-28–15-33
     Commerce Clearing House Citator (CCH citator), 15-28–15-29
     RIA Citator, 2nd Series, 15-31–15-33
   client-oriented tax research, 15-2
   computers as research tool, 15-34
   definition of, 15-2
   end product of, 15-2
   gray areas, 15-4
   overview of, 15-2–15-3
   policy-oriented tax research, 15-2
   sample work papers and client letter, 15-38
   steps in process, 15-3–15-5
   tax advisors' conclusions, 15-5
   tax periodicals, 15-24–15-25
   tax services, 15-25–15-29
   tax treaties, 15-24
Tax services
   CCH's Federal Tax Service, 15-28
   Federal Tax Coordinator 2d, 15-26–15-34
   Law of Federal Income Taxation, 15-27
   research of tax questions, 15-25
   Standard Federal Tax Reporter (CCH service), 15-26
   Tax Management Portfolios, 15-27–15-28
   United States Tax Reporter, 15-25–15-26
Tax system structure
   criteria for, 1-12–1-14
Tax treaties, 15-24
Tax year, 11-2–11-7, 11-28, 17-18–17-19, 17-28, 17-36
   C corporations, 11-2, 11-28, 17-28, 17-36
   partnerships, 11-2, 11-28, 17-18–17-19, 17-36
   personal service corporations (PSCs), 11-2, 17-28, 17-36
   S corporations, 11-2, 11-28, 17-28, 17-36

Tax-deferred bonds, 3-28
Tax-exempt obligations, 3-28
   accrual of original issue discount, 5-23
   interest income, 3-28
     dependency exemption gross income test and, 2-15
     interest expense incurred to generate, 7-14
     tax preference item, 14-3–14-4
   private activity bonds, 14-4
Taxable bonds, 3-28
Taxable income
   corporations, 16-8
   individuals, 2-5
Taxable interest, dependency exemption gross income test and, 2-15
Taxation
   administration of, 1-20–1-23
   determination of, 2-1–2-31
   enactment of tax law, 1-18–1-20
   objectives of, 1-14–1-15
   See also Individual income tax
   tax rate structures, 1-4–1-7
     criteria for, 1-12–1-14
   taxes, types of, 1-7–1-11
   U.S. history, 1-2
     early periods, 1-2
     revenue acts, 1-3
     revenue sources, 1-3
Taxes
   deductible taxes, 7-9
   definition of, 7-9
   general sales tax, 7-11
   local income taxes, 7-10
   nondeductible taxes, 7-9–7-10
   payment of, 14-24–14-29
   personal property taxes, 7-10
   real estate taxes, 7-10–7-11
     apportionment of taxes, 7-10–7-11
     real property assessments for local benefits, 7-11
   reporting itemized deduction, 7-36
   state income taxes, 7-10
   types of, 1-7–1-11
     customs duties, 1-11
     employment taxes, 1-11
     federal excise taxes, 1-11
     franchise tax, 1-7–1-8
     property taxes, 1-11
     sales taxes, 1-11
     state income taxes, 1-7–1-8
     unemployment taxes, 1-11
     wealth transfer taxes, 1-8–1-10
Taxes—the Tax Magazine, 15-25
Taxpayer Compliance Measurement Program (TCMP), 15-25–15-29
Taxpayer identification numbers, 2-31
TC Memorandum Decisions (RIA), 15-18
Technical advice memoranda, 1-19
   tax law, 15-13
Temporary living expenses, as indirect moving expense, 9-20
Temporary regulations, 15-9
Testamentary gifts, 4-4
The Individual Income Tax (Goode), 1-3n
The Wealth of Nations (Smith), 1-12n
Theft losses
   as itemized deduction, 7-28

   deductible amount of, 8-19–8-20
   documentation of loss, 8-34
   identifiable event, 8-17–8-18
   measuring losses, 8-19–8-20
   reporting on Form 4684, 13-29–13-28
Three-party exchanges, of property, 12-5–12-6
Tickets, entertainment, limitations on, 9-16
Timber, Sec. 1231 and, 13-5–13-6
Trade, definition of, 6-5–6-6
Trademarks, sale/exchange of, 5-26–5-27
Transportation expenses, 9-9–9-12
   automobile expenses, 9-10–9-12
   deductibility of, 9-9
   definition of, 9-9–9-10
   reimbursed expenses, 9-12
   to medical facility, 7-4
Travel expenses, 9-4–9-8
   business versus pleasure, 9-7–9-8
   deductibility of, 9-4–9-5
   definition of, 9-5
   foreign travel, 9-8
   limitations, 9-8
   production or collection of income, 9-4–9-6
   qualification requirements, 9-6
   substantiation of, 6-16–6-18, 9-43
Treasure finds, as gross income, 3-22–3-23
Treasury Regulations, 1-19, 15-8–15-11
   authoritative weight, 15-10
   citations, 15-11
   forms of, 15-8–15-11
   interpretative regulations, 1-19, 15-10
   legislative regulations, 1-19
   statutory regulations, 15-10
Treble damages, as expenditure contrary to public policy, 6-13

Underpayment penalty
   avoidance of, 14-29–14-30
   estimated taxes, 14-28
Unearned income, dependents with, 2-22–2-24
Unemployment compensation, 3-23
Unemployment taxes, 1-11
Unfunded deferred compensation plans, 9-31
Unharvested crops/land, Sec. 1231 and, 13-6
Uniform capitalization rules, cost of acquired property and, 5-5, 11-11–11-12,
United States Board of Tax Appeals Reports, 15-23
United States Reports, Lawyers' Edition (L. Ed.), 15-21
United States Supreme Court Reports (U.S.), 15-21
United States Tax Reporter (Research Institute of America), 15-25–15-26
Unmarried individuals, surviving spouse/head-of-household status, 2-20–2-21
Unrealized income, as nonincome item, 4-2–4-3
Unreasonable compensation, tax-planning considerations, 6-35–6-36

Unreimbursed employee expenses
  deductibility, 9-3–9-4
    2% nondeductible floor, 9-3–9-4
    exceptions to floor, 9-4
    limitations on, 9-3–9-4
U.S. Circuit Court of Appeals, 15-20
  precedential value of decisions, 15-23
  primary cites, 15-19
  secondary cites, 15-19
  2% nondeductible floor, 9-3–9-4
U.S. Court of Federal Claims, 15-19–15-20
  precedential value of decisions, 15-23
  primary cites, 15-19
  secondary cites, 15-19
U.S. Tax Cases (USTC), 15-19
U.S. Tax Court, 15-14–15-18
  acquiescence policy, 15-17
  history of, 15-14
  language of, 15-17
  memo decisions, 15-18
  precedential value of decisions, 15-21
  published opinions and citations, 15-17–15-18
  regular decisions, 15-14–15-17
  small cases procedures, 15-17
U.S. district courts, 15-19
  precedential value of decisions, 15-23
  primary cites, 15-19
  secondary cites, 15-19
  unreported decisions, 15-19

Vacation home rental, 6-31–6-33
Voluntary changes, in accounting methods, 11-27

Wage reduction plans, 4-16
Wash sales, 6-22–6-25
  basis of stock, 6-24–6-25
  deduction of losses on, 6-22–6-25
  substantially identical stock/securities, 6-24
Ways and Means Committee, U.S. House of Representatives, tax law and, 15-7–15-8
Wealth transfer taxes
  estate tax, 1-9–1-10
  gift tax, 1-8–1-9
  See also Estate tax; Gift tax
Welfare benefits, dependency exemption support test and, 2-13
WESTLAW legal data base, 15-34
Wherewithal-to-pay concept, 3-4
Widow/widower, as surviving spouse, 2-20
Withholding, 4-22–4-23, 14-24–14-27, 14-32
  allowances/methods, 14-26
  backup withholding, 14-25
  failure to withhold, 4-23
  federal income tax withheld computation, 14-27
Wolfson, Mark and Myron Scholes, 18-2, 18-2n
Work opportunity credit, 14-20
Working condition benefits, 4-12–4-13
Worthless securities
  losses from, 8-3–8-4
  reporting losses from, 8-36
  sale/exchange of, 5-22
Writ of certiorari, 15-14
Written conclusions, tax research, 15-5

2001 TAX RATE SCHEDULES

ESTATES AND TRUSTS

If Taxable Income Is:		The Tax Is:	
Over—	But Not Over—		Of the Amount Over—
$0	$1,800	15%	$0
1,800	4,250	$270.00 + 28%	1,800
4,250	6,500	956.00 + 31%	4,250
6,500	8,900	1,653.50 + 36%	6,500
8,900		2,517.50 + 39.6%	8,900

CORPORATIONS

If Taxable Income Is:		The Tax Is:	
Over—	But Not Over—		Of the Amount Over—
$ 0	$ 50,000	15%	$ 0
50,000	75,000	$ 7,500 + 25%	50,000
75,000	100,000	13,750 + 34%	75,000
100,000	335,000	22,250 + 39%	100,000
335,000	10,000,000	113,900 + 34%	335,000
10,000,000	15,000,000	3,400,000 + 35%	10,000,000
15,000,000	18,333,333	5,150,000 + 38%	15,000,000
18,333,333		6,416,667 + 35%	18,333,333

UNIFIED CREDIT AMOUNT FOR ESTATE AND GIFT TAX

Year of Gift/Year of Death	Amount of Credit	Exemption Equivalent
January through June, 1977	$ 6,000	$ 30,000
July through December, 1977	30,000	120,666
1978	34,000	134,000
1979	38,000	147,333
1980	42,500	161,563
1981	47,000	175,625
1982	62,800	225,000
1983	79,300	275,000
1984	96,300	325,000
1985	121,800	400,000
1986	155,800	500,000
1987 through 1997	192,800	600,000
1998	202,050	625,000
1999	211,300	650,000
2000	220,550	675,000
2001	220,550	675,000
2002	229,800	700,000
2003	229,800	700,000
2004	287,300	850,000
2005	326,300	950,000
2006 and later years	345,800	1,000,000